A+ Guide to Managing and Maintaining Your PC

SEVENTH EDITION

Jean Andrews, Ph.D.

COURSE TECHNOLOGY
CENGAGE Learning

Australia • Canada • Mexico • Singapore • Spain • United Kingdom • United States

COURSE TECHNOLOGY
CENGAGE Learning™

A+ Guide to Managing and Maintaining Your PC, Seventh Edition
Jean Andrews

Vice President, Career and
Professional Editorial: Dave Garza

Executive Editor: Stephen Helba

Acquisitions Editor: Nick Lombardi

Managing Editor: Marah Bellegarde

Senior Product Manager: Michelle Ruelos Cannistraci

Developmental Editor: Jill Batistick

Editorial Assistant: Sarah Pickering

Vice President, Career and
Professional Marketing: Jennifer McAvey

Marketing Director: Deborah S. Yarnell

Senior Marketing Manager: Erin Coffin

Marketing Coordinator: Shanna Gibbs

Production Director: Carolyn Miller

Production Manager: Andrew Crouth

Content Project Manager: Jessica McNavich

Art Director: Jack Pendleton

Cover photo or illustration: Shutterstock

Manufacturing Coordinator: Denise Powers

Copyeditor: Katherine A. Orrino

Proofreader: Christine Clark

Compositor: Integra

For product information and technology assistance, contact us at
Cengage Learning Customer & Sales Support, 1-800-354-9706

For permission to use material from this text or product,
submit all requests online at **cengage.com/permissions**
Further permissions questions can be emailed to
permissionrequest@cengage.com

Library of Congress Control Number: 2009939179

ISBN-13: 978-1-435-49778-8

ISBN-10: 1-435-49778-3

Course Technology
20 Channel Center Street
Boston, MA 02210
USA

Some of the product names and company names used in this book have been used for identification purposes only and may be trademarks or registered trademarks of their respective manufacturers and sellers.

Microsoft and the Office logo are either registered trademarks or trademarks of Microsoft Corporation in the United States and/or other countries. Course Technology, a part of Cengage Learning, is an independent entity from the Microsoft Corporation, and not affiliated with Microsoft in any manner.

Any fictional data related to persons or companies or URLs used throughout this book is intended for instructional purposes only. At the time this book was printed, any such data was fictional and not belonging to any real persons or companies.

Course Technology and the Course Technology logo are registered trademarks used under license.

Course Technology, a part of Cengage Learning, reserves the right to revise this publication and make changes from time to time in its content without notice.

The programs in this book are for instructional purposes only. They have been tested with care, but are not guaranteed for any particular intent beyond educational purposes. The author and the publisher do not offer any warranties or representations, nor do they accept any liabilities with respect to the programs.

Cengage Learning is a leading provider of customized learning solutions with office locations around the globe, including Singapore, the United Kingdom, Australia, Mexico, Brazil, and Japan. Locate your local office at: **international.cengage.com/region**

Cengage Learning products are represented in Canada by Nelson Education, Ltd.

For your lifelong learning solutions, visit **course.cengage.com**

Visit our corporate website at **cengage.com**.

Printed in the United States of America
2 3 4 5 6 7 12 11 10

Table of Contents

APPENDIX A

APPENDIX B

CD Resource Contents:

Video Clips
CertBlaster Exam Preparation Software
PC Repair FAQs
eGlossary
Troubleshooting Flowcharts
Sample Reports
CompTIA A+ 2009 Mapping Grids
Appendices:
    ASCII Character and Set and Ansi.sys
    Behind the Scenes with DEBUG
    Calculating Drive Capacity on Older
      Drives
    Electricity and Multimeters
    FAT Details
    How an OS Uses System Resources
    Installations Using Legacy BIOS
    Introducing Linux
    Introducing the Mac OS
    Supporting SCSI and Legacy Devices
    Supporting Windows 9X/ME
    The Hexadecimal Number System and Memory
      Addressing
    Windows 9x Me Commands and Startup Disk

CompTIA A+ 220–701 Essentials Exam, 2009 Edition
Examination Objectives Mapped to Chapters

DOMAIN 1.0 HARDWARE

1.1 Categorize storage devices and backup media

OBJECTIVES	CHAPTERS	PAGE NUMBERS
◢ FDD	8	344–347
◢ HDD	8	330–331
• Solid state vs. magnetic	8	330–331
◢ Optical drives	10	480–489
• CD/DVD/RW/Blu-Ray	10	480–489
◢ Removable storage	10	489–497
• Tape drive	10	489–497
• Solid state (e.g. thumb drive, flash, SD cards, USB)	10	489–497
• External CD-RW and hard drive	10	489–497
• Hot swappable devices and non-hot swappable devices	10	489–497

1.2 Explain motherboard components, types and features

OBJECTIVES	CHAPTERS	PAGE NUMBERS
◢ Form Factor	4	112–122
	5	176–180
• ATX/BTX	4	112–122
	5	176–180
• micro ATX	4	112–122
	5	176–180
• NLX	4	112–122
	5	176–180
◢ I/O interfaces	5	184–196
	9	396–407
• Sound	5	194–196
	10	474–476
• Video	5	184–193
	9	407–425
• USB 1.1 and 2.0	5	186
	9	396–407
• Serial	5	184–196
	9	396–407
• IEEE 1394/Firewire	5	194–196
	9	396–407
• Parallel	5	194–196
	9	396–407
• NIC	5	194–196
	17	861–863
• Modem	5	194–196
• PS/2	9	396–397, 426–430
◢ Memory slots		
• RIMM	7	298–307
• DIMM	7	298–307
• SODIMM	7	298–307
• SIMM	7	298–307

1.3   Classify power supplies types and characteristics

1.4   Explain the purpose and characteristics of CPUs and their features

1.5   Explain cooling methods and devices

1.6   Compare and contrast memory types, characteristics and their purpose

1.7   Distinguish between the different display devices and their characteristics

1.8   Install and configure peripherals and input devices

DOMAIN 2.0 TROUBLESHOOTING, REPAIR AND MAINTENANCE

2.1 Given a scenario, explain the troubleshooting theory

OBJECTIVES	CHAPTERS	PAGE NUMBERS
◢ Identify the problem	11	534–544
• Question user and identify	3	92–93
user changes to computer	11	534–537
and perform backups before making changes		
◢ Establish a theory of probable cause (question the obvious)	11	534–544
◢ Test the theory to determine cause	11	534–544
• Once theory is confirmed determine next steps to resolve problem	11	534–544
• If theory is not confirmed re-establish new theory or escalate	11	534–544
◢ Establish a plan of action to resolve the problem and implement the solution	11	534–544
◢ Verify full system functionality and if applicable implement preventative measures	11	534–544
◢ Document findings, actions and outcomes	3	101
	11	534–544

2.2 Given a scenario, explain and interpret common hardware and operating system symptoms and their causes

OBJECTIVES	CHAPTERS	PAGE NUMBERS
◢ OS related symptoms	15	746–765
• Bluescreen	15	746–765
• System lock-up	15	746–765
• Input/output device	15	746–765
• Application install	12	585–589
• Start or load	15	765–802
• Windows specific printing problems	22	1186–1189
▪ Print spool stalled	22	1186–1189
▪ Incorrect/incompatible driver	22	1186–1189
◢ Hardware related symptoms		
• Excessive heat	4	134–135
	15	764–765
• Noise	4	134–135
	15	764–765
• Odors	4	134–135
	15	764–765
• Status light indicators	17	861–863
• Alerts	15	746–765
	17	861–863
• Visible damage (e.g. cable, plastic)	4	134–135
	15	764–765
◢ Use documentation and resources	11	534–544
• User/installation manuals	11	534–544
	15	764–765
• Internet/web based	11	534–544
	15	764–765
• Training materials	11	534–544
	15	764–765

2.3 Given a scenario, determine the troubleshooting methods and tools for printers

OBJECTIVES	CHAPTERS	PAGE NUMBERS
◢ Manage print jobs	22	1186–1189
◢ Print spooler	22	1186–1189
◢ Printer properties and settings	22	1186–1189
◢ Print a test page	22	1186–1189

2.4 Given a scenario, explain and interpret common laptop issues and determine the appropriate basic troubleshooting method

OBJECTIVES	CHAPTERS	PAGE NUMBERS
◢ Issues	21	1094–1028
• Power conditions	21	1114–1118
• Video	21	1124–1128
• Keyboard	21	1124–1128
• Pointer	21	1124–1128
• Stylus	21	1124–1128
• Wireless card issues	21	1110–1114
◢ Methods	21	1094–1028
• Verify power (e.g. LEDs, swap AC adapter)	21	1114–1118
• Remove unneeded peripherals	21	1114–1118
• Plug in external monitor	21	1124–1128
• Toggle Fn keys or hardware switches	21	1124–1128
• Check LCD cutoff switch	21	1124–1128
• Verify backlight functionality and pixilation	21	1124–1128
• Check switch for built-in WIFI antennas or external antennas	21	1110–1114

2.5 Given a scenario, integrate common preventative maintenance techniques

OBJECTIVES	CHAPTERS	PAGE NUMBERS
◢ Physical inspection	11	526–527, 534–544
◢ Updates	11	531–534
• Driver	15	746–765
• Firmware	5	196–201
• OS	12	582–584
	13	604–619
• Security	19	1031–1032
◢ Scheduling preventative maintenance	11	531–534
• Defrag	13	604–619
• Scandisk	13	604–619
• Check disk	13	604–619
• Startup programs	13	604–619
◢ Use of appropriate repair tools and cleaning materials	11	524–527, 531–534
• Compressed air	11	531–534
• Lint free cloth	11	531–534
• Computer vacuum and compressors	11	531–534
◢ Power devices		
• Appropriate source such as power strip, surge protector or UPS	4	139–143
	11	531–534
◢ Ensuring proper environment	11	524–527, 531–534
◢ Backup procedures	11	531–534
	13	620–642

3.4   Explain the basics of boot sequences, methods and startup utilities

DOMAIN 4.0 NETWORKING

4.1   Summarize the basics of networking fundamentals, including technologies, devices and protocols

DOMAIN 5.0 SECURITY

DOMAIN 6.0 OPERATIONAL PROCEDURE

6.1 Outline the purpose of appropriate safety and environmental procedures and given a scenario apply them

6.2 Given a scenario, demonstrate the appropriate use of communication skills and professionalism in the workplace

CompTIA A+ 220-702 Practical Application Exam, 2009 Edition
Examination Objectives Mapped to Chapters

DOMAIN 1.0 HARDWARE

1.1 **Given a scenario, install, configure and maintain personal computer components**

OBJECTIVES	CHAPTERS	PAGE NUMBERS
◢ Storage devices		
• HDD	8	347–372
▪ SATA	8	347–372
▪ PATA	8	347–372
▪ Solid state	8	347–372
• FDD	8	372–374
• Optical drives	10	502–512
▪ CD/DVD/RW/Blu-Ray	10	502–512
• Removable	10	502–512
• External	10	502–512
◢ Motherboards	5	210–231
• Jumper settings	5	210–231
• CMOS battery	5	210–231
• Advanced BIOS settings	5	210–231
• Bus speeds	5	210–231
• Chipsets	5	210–231
• Firmware updates	5	210–231
• Socket types	5	210–231
• Expansion slots	5	210–231
• Memory slots	5	210–231
• Front panel connectors	5	210–231
• I/O ports	9	435–458
▪ Sound, video, USB 1.1, USB 2.0, serial, IEEE 1394/Firewire, parallel, NIC, modem, PS/2)	9	435–458
◢ Power supplies	4	161–166
• Wattages and capacity	4	161–166
• Connector types and quantity	4	161–166
• Output voltage	4	161–166
◢ Processors	6	256–274
• Socket types	6	256–274
• Speed	6	256–274
• Number of cores	6	256–274
• Power consumption	6	256–274
• Cache	6	256–274
• Front side bus	6	256–274
• 32bit vs. 64bit	6	256–274
◢ Memory	7	307–320
◢ Adapter cards	9	445–458
• Graphics cards	9	445–458
• Sound cards	9	445–458
• Storage controllers	9	445–458
▪ RAID cards (RAID array – levels 0,1,5)	8	347–372
	9	445–458
▪ eSATA cards	9	445–458

1.2   **Given a scenario, detect problems, troubleshoot and repair/replace personal computer components**

1.3   Given a scenario, install, configure, detect problems, troubleshoot and repair/replace laptop components

1.4   Given a scenario, select and use the following tools

1.5   Given a scenario, detect and resolve common printer issues

OBJECTIVES	CHAPTERS	PAGE NUMBERS
◢ Symptoms		
• Paper jams	22	1191–1218
• Blank paper	22	1191–1218
• Error codes	22	1191–1218
• Out of memory error	22	1191–1218
• Lines and smearing	22	1191–1218
• Garbage printout	22	1191–1218
• Ghosted image	22	1191–1218
• No connectivity	22	1191–1218
◢ Issue resolution		
• Replace fuser	22	1191–1218
• Replace drum	22	1191–1218
• Clear paper jam	22	1191–1218
• Power cycle	22	1191–1218
• Install maintenance kit (reset page count)	22	1191–1218
• Set IP on printer	22	1191–1218
• Clean printer	22	1191–1218

DOMAIN 2.0 OPERATING SYSTEMS - UNLESS OTHERWISE NOTED, OPERATING SYSTEMS REFERRED TO WITHIN INCLUDE MICROSOFT WINDOWS 2000, WINDOWS XP PROFESSIONAL, XP HOME, XP MEDIACENTER, WINDOWS VISTA HOME, HOME PREMIUM, BUSINESS AND ULTIMATE

2.1   Select the appropriate commands and options to troubleshoot and resolve problems

OBJECTIVES	CHAPTERS	PAGE NUMBERS
◢ MSCONFIG	14	726–728
◢ DIR	13	644–646
◢ CHKDSK (/f /r)	13	651–652
◢ EDIT	13	653
◢ COPY (/a /v /y)	13	647–648
◢ XCOPY	13	648
◢ FORMAT	13	653–654
◢ IPCONFIG (/all /release /renew)	18	958–962, 974–977
◢ PING (-t –l)	18	958–962, 974–977
◢ MD/CD/RD	13	649–651
◢ NET	18	958–962, 974–977
◢ TRACERT	18	958–962, 974–977
◢ NSLOOKUP	18	958–962, 974–977
◢ [command name] /?	13	646
◢ SFC	16	812–816

2.2   Differentiate between Windows Operating System directory structures (Windows 2000, XP and Vista)

OBJECTIVES	CHAPTERS	PAGE NUMBERS
◢ User file locations	13	642–644
◢ System file locations	13	642–644
◢ Fonts	13	642–644
◢ Temporary files	13	642–644
◢ Program files	13	642–644
◢ Offline files and folders	13	642–644

2.3 Given a scenario, select and use system utilities/tools and evaluate the results

2.4 Evaluate and resolve common issues

DOMAIN 3.0 NETWORKING

3.1   **Troubleshoot client-side connectivity issues using appropriate tools**

3.2 **Install and configure a small office home office (SOHO) network**

DOMAIN 4.0 SECURITY

4.1 **Given a scenario, prevent, troubleshoot and remove viruses and malware**

4.2 **Implement security and troubleshoot common issues**

Introduction CompTIA A+

A+ Guide to Managing and Maintaining Your PC, Seventh Edition, Comprehensive was written to be the very best tool on the market today to prepare you to support personal computers. Updated to include the most current technologies with a new chapter on securing your PC and small network and new content on supporting Windows Vista, this book takes you from the just-a-user level to the I-can-fix-this level for PC hardware and software matters. This book achieves its goals with an unusually effective combination of tools that powerfully reinforce both concepts and hands-on, real-world experiences. It also provides thorough preparation for the new 2009 CompTIA A+ Certification exams. Competency in using a computer is a pre-requisite to using this book. No background knowledge of electronics is assumed. An appropriate pre-requisite course for this book would be a general course in microcomputer applications.

This book includes:

- ◢ **Comprehensive review and practice end-of-chapter material,** including a chapter summary, key terms, review questions that focus on A+ content, critical thinking questions, hands-on projects, and real-world problems to solve.
- ◢ **Step-by-step instructions** on installation, maintenance, optimization of system performance, and troubleshooting.
- ◢ **Video clips** featuring Jean Andrews illustrating key points from the text to aid your understanding of the material.
- ◢ **A wide array of photos, drawings, and screen shots** support the text, displaying in detail the exact hardware and software features you will need to understand to manage and maintain your PC.
- ◢ **Several in-depth, hands-on projects** at the end of each chapter designed to make certain that you not only understand the material, but also execute procedures and make decisions on your own.

In addition, the carefully structured, clearly written text is accompanied by graphics that provide the visual input essential to learning. For instructors using the book in a classroom, a special CD-ROM is available that includes an Instructor's Manual, an Online Testing system, and a PowerPoint presentation.

Coverage is balanced—while focusing on new hardware and software, the text also covers the real work of PC repair, where some older technology remains in widespread use and still needs support. For example, the book covers solid state hard drives, multi-core processors, DDR3 memory, and PCI Express expansion slot technologies, but also addresses using AGP expansion slots, dial-up networking, and impact printers because many individuals and businesses still use these older technologies. Also included is thorough coverage of operating system and applications support. At the writing of this book, Windows Vista and Windows XP are the current Microsoft operating systems used on desktop and laptop computers. Five chapters are devoted to supporting Vista and XP systems, which also include light coverage of Windows 2000. To reign in the physical size and weight of the book, most of the content on less significant and older technologies has been placed on the CD that accompanies the book. There you will find content on Linux, Mac OS, Windows 9x/Me, DOS, SCSI, the hexadecimal number system, electricity, multimeters, and legacy motherboards, hard drives, and processors.

This book provides thorough preparation for CompTIA's A+ 2009 Certification examinations and maps completely to these new exam objectives. This certification credential's popularity among employers is growing exponentially, and obtaining certification increases your ability to gain employment and improve your salary. To get more information on A+ certification and its sponsoring organization, the Computing Technology Industry Association, see their Web site at *www.comptia.org*.

The book is structured to make it easy for you to approach the content using your preferred organization. You use one of three organizations: (1) Comprehensive, (2) A+ Essentials followed by A+ Practical Application, (3) Hardware and Software. Figure 1 gives you an easy-to-follow map for all three approaches.

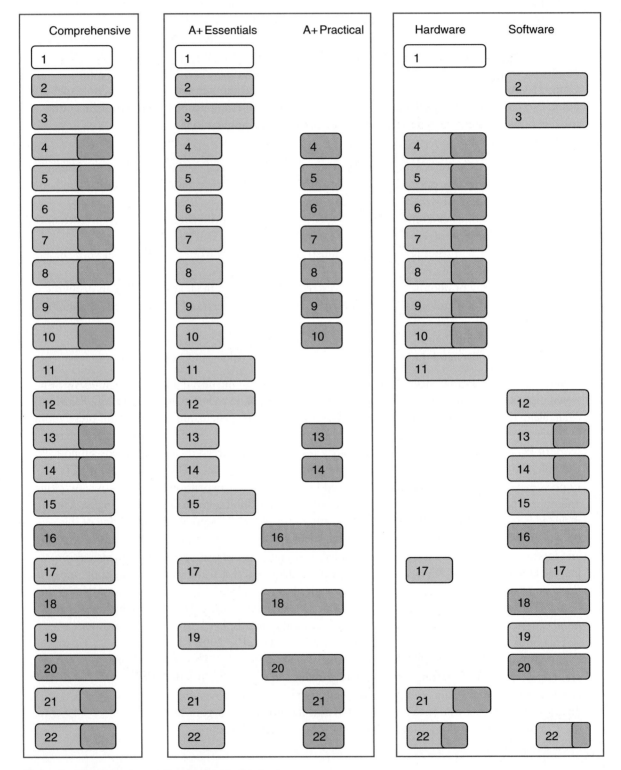

Figure 1 Three ways to use the chapters in this book
Courtesy: Course Technology/Cengage Learning

Notice from the diagram that some chapters cover only A+ Essentials content and others cover only A+ Practical Application content. Other chapters that include both A+ Essentials and A+ Practical Application content put the A+ Essentials in the first part of the chapter and the A+ Practical Application in the second part.

FEATURES

To ensure a successful learning experience, this book includes the following pedagogical features:

- ◢ **Learning Objectives:** Every chapter opens with a list of learning objectives that sets the stage for you to absorb the lessons of the text.
- ◢ **Emphasis on people skills:** Chapter 3 focuses on how to work with people in a technical world, which is a key to career success as well as an important part of the A+ certification exams. The skills learned in Chapter 3 are applied throughout the book with many projects that reinforce these skills.
- ◢ **Comprehensive Step-by-Step Troubleshooting Guidance:** Troubleshooting guidelines are included in almost every chapter. In addition, Chapter 11 gives insights into general approaches to troubleshooting that help apply the specifics detailed in each chapter for different hardware and software problems.
- ◢ **Step-by-Step Procedures:** The book is chock-full of step-by-step procedures covering subjects from hardware installation and maintenance to optimizing system performance.
- ◢ **Art Program:** Numerous detailed photographs, three-dimensional art, and screenshots support the text, displaying hardware and software features exactly as you will see them in your work.
- ◢ **CompTIA A+ Table of Contents:** This table of contents gives the page that provides the primary content for each certification objective on the A+ 2009 exams. This is a valuable tool for quick reference.
- ◢ **Applying Concepts:** These sections offer practical applications for the material being discussed. Whether outlining a task, developing a scenario, or providing pointers, the Applying Concepts sections give you a chance to apply what you've learned to a typical PC problem.

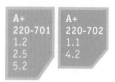

Notes: Note icons highlight additional helpful information related to the subject being discussed.

A+ Icons: All of the content that relates to CompTIA's 2009 A+ 220-701 Essentials and A+ 220-702 Practical Application Certification exams, whether it's a page or a sentence, is highlighted with an A+ icon. The icon notes the exam name and the objective number. This unique feature highlights the relevant content at a glance, so you can pay extra attention to the material.

A+ Tabs: Each chapter page is designated with a green A+ Essentials tab or a blue A+ Practical Application tab, allowing the reader to easily identify which exam is relevant to the content on each page.

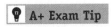 **A+ Exam Tip Boxes:** These boxes highlight additional insights and tips to remember if you are planning to take the CompTIA A+ Exams.

 **Caution Icons:** These icons highlight critical safety information. Follow these instructions carefully to protect the PC and its data and to ensure your own safety.

 Video Clips: Short video passages reinforce concepts and techniques discussed in the text, and offer insight into the life of a PC repair technician.

End-of-Chapter Material: Each chapter closes with the following features, which reinforce the material covered in the chapter and provide real-world, hands-on testing:

Chapter Summary: This bulleted list of concise statements summarizes all major points of the chapter.

Key Terms: The content of each chapter is further reinforced by an end-of-chapter key-term list. The definitions of all terms are included at the end of the book in a full-length glossary.

Review Questions: You can test your understanding of each chapter with a comprehensive set of review questions. The "Reviewing the Basics" questions check your understanding of fundamental concepts focused on A+ content, while the "Thinking Critically" questions help you synthesize and apply what you've learned and also focus on A+ content.

Hands-On Projects: You get to test your real-world understanding with hands-on projects involving a full range of software and hardware problems. Each hands-on activity in this book is preceded by the Hands-On icon and a description of the exercise that follows.

Real Problems, Real Solution: Each comprehensive problem allows you to find out if you can apply what you've learned in the chapter to a real-life situation.

CD Resource: The CD placed in the book includes video clips which features Jean Andrews illustrating key concepts in the text and providing advice on the real world of PC repair. Also included is less significant and older content that still might be important in some PC repair situations. Content includes: The Hexademical Number System and Memory Addressing, Supporting Windows 9x/Me, Windows 9x/Me Commands and Startup Disk, Introducing the MacOS, Introducing Linux, Electricity and Multimeters, Facts about Legacy Motherboards, How an OS Uses System Resources, Facts about Legacy Processors, All About SCSI, Behind the Scenes with DEBUG, FAT Details, and Selecting and Installing Hard Drives using Legacy Motherboards. Other helpful tools on the CD include Frequently Asked Questions, Sample Reports, Troubleshooting Flowcharts, and an electronic Glossary. CertBlaster Test Preparation Questions from dtiPublishing are included so students will have plenty of opportunity to practice, drill and rehearse for the exam once they have worked through this book. The unlock code for the A+ CertBlaster questions for CompTIA's A+ Essentials Exam (Exam#220-701) is: c_701 (case sensitive). The unlock code for CompTIA's A+ Practical Application Exam (Exam#220-702) is c_702 (case sensitive).

Web Site: For additional content and updates to this book and information about our complete line of CompTIA A+ and PC Repair topics, please visit our Web site at *www.cengage.com/pcrepair.*

WHAT'S NEW IN THE SEVENTH EDITION

Here's a summary of what's new in the Seventh Edition:

- Maps fully to CompTIA's 2009 A+ Exams.
- The content in each chapter is presented in two ways. A chapter either focuses completely on A+ 220-701 Essentials or A+ 220-702 Practical Application or it contains a combination of content from both exams. The combination chapters are split: the first part covers Essentials and the second part covers Practical Applications. This organization makes it easy for instructors to split the book into Essentials and Practical Application courses, if they choose to do so. However, instructors should realize that A+ Essentials represents about 70% of the content while A+ Practical Application represents about 30%.
- More focus on A+, with non-A+ content moved to the back-of-book CD or eliminated.
- New chapter devoted to PC Maintenance and Troubleshooting Strategies.
- In the previous edition, there were 4 chapters on Windows 2000/XP and 2 chapters on Windows 9x/ME. In this edition, there are 5 chapters on Windows Vista and XP with light coverage of Windows 2000. These chapters are organized by function (such as installing, maintaining, optimizing and fixing) rather than by individual operating systems. Content covering older operating systems has been moved to the CD.
- New content added (all new content was also new to the A+ 2009 exams).
  - Windows Vista is added. Operating systems covered are now Windows Vista and XP with light coverage of Windows 2000. Vista startup and recovery environment are covered in detail.
  - More emphasis on security with two chapters devoted to Security Essentials and Security Practices and includes increased content on dealing with an infected system.
  - Alternate OS installation methods
  - How to set up and use Remote Assistance
  - One chapter totally focuses on people skills with increased content. This chapter is moved earlier in the book to promote these skills and to apply them throughout the book.
  - Increased content on troubleshooting networking connections
  - Solid state hard drives
  - DDR3 memory and triple channeling
  - How to implement hardware and software RAID, and dynamic drives
  - Connecting a PC to a cellular network
  - Increased use of flowcharts when troubleshooting
  - Steps to install AMD processors and dual video cards
  - More coverage of 64-bit OS and systems
  - Power management
  - Disassemble laptop and replace internal components including processor, motherboard, CMOS battery, fans, and speakers
- In an effort to reduce the size of the book, appendices have been reduced to a minimum and extra content is put on the CD that accompanies the book.
- Mapping to A+ objectives is cleaner and easier to follow.
- Review questions focus on A+ type questions.

ANATOMY OF A PC REPAIR CHAPTER

This section is a visual explanation of the components that make up a PC Repair chapter. The figures identify some of our traditional instructional elements as well as the enhancements and new features we have included for the seventh edition.

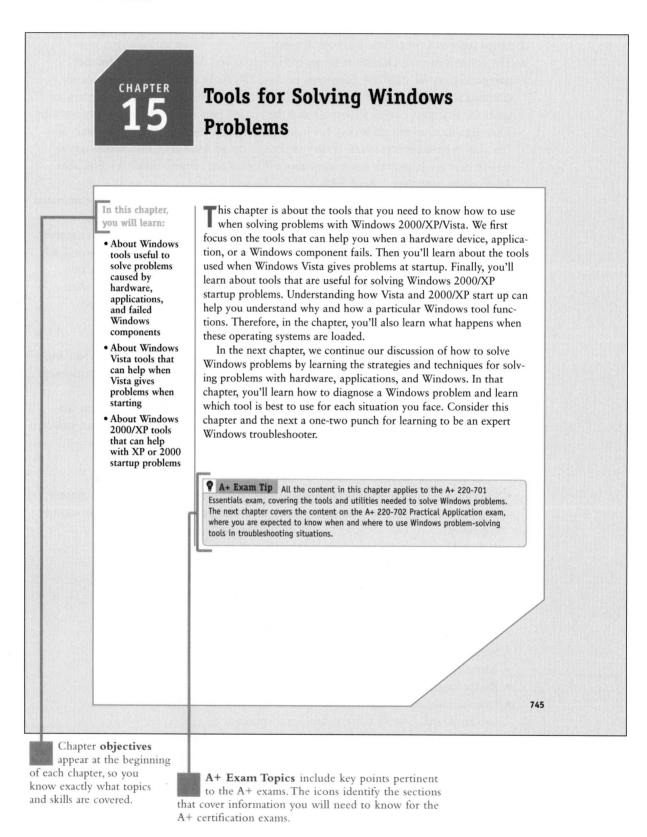

CHAPTER 15

Tools for Solving Windows Problems

In this chapter, you will learn:

- About Windows tools useful to solve problems caused by hardware, applications, and failed Windows components
- About Windows Vista tools that can help when Vista gives problems when starting
- About Windows 2000/XP tools that can help with XP or 2000 startup problems

This chapter is about the tools that you need to know how to use when solving problems with Windows 2000/XP/Vista. We first focus on the tools that can help you when a hardware device, application, or a Windows component fails. Then you'll learn about the tools used when Windows Vista gives problems at startup. Finally, you'll learn about tools that are useful for solving Windows 2000/XP startup problems. Understanding how Vista and 2000/XP start up can help you understand why and how a particular Windows tool functions. Therefore, in the chapter, you'll also learn what happens when these operating systems are loaded.

In the next chapter, we continue our discussion of how to solve Windows problems by learning the strategies and techniques for solving problems with hardware, applications, and Windows. In that chapter, you'll learn how to diagnose a Windows problem and learn which tool is best to use for each situation you face. Consider this chapter and the next a one-two punch for learning to be an expert Windows troubleshooter.

A+ Exam Tip All the content in this chapter applies to the A+ 220-701 Essentials exam, covering the tools and utilities needed to solve Windows problems. The next chapter covers the content on the A+ 220-702 Practical Application exam, where you are expected to know when and where to use Windows problem-solving tools in troubleshooting situations.

745

Chapter **objectives** appear at the beginning of each chapter, so you know exactly what topics and skills are covered.

A+ Exam Topics include key points pertinent to the A+ exams. The icons identify the sections that cover information you will need to know for the A+ certification exams.

Cautions identify critical safety information.

A+
220-702
1.2

⚡ **Caution**   Never replace a damaged motherboard with a good one without first testing or replacing the power supply. You don't want to subject another good board to possible damage.

A+
220-702
1.2
1.1

REPLACING THE POWER SUPPLY

📷 **Video**
Replacing a Power Supply

The easiest way to fix a power supply you suspect is faulty is to replace it. When selecting a replacement power supply, be sure the new power supply uses the correct form factor that provides the correct output voltages, is adequately rated for power in watts, and has all the power connectors needed by your system. To determine if the power supply really is the problem, turn off the PC, open the computer case, and set the new power supply on top of the old one. Disconnect the old power supply's cords and plug the PC devices into the new power supply. Turn on the PC and verify that the new power supply solves your problem before installing it.

💡 **A+ Exam Tip**   The A+ IT 220-702 Practical Application exam expects you to know how to select and install a power supply. Know it must match wattage requirements and have the correct connector types and number of connectors to meet the demands of the system.

⚡ **Caution**   Remember from earlier in the chapter that you need to consider the monitor and the power supply to be "black boxes." Never remove the cover or put your hands inside this equipment unless you know about the hazards of charged capacitors and have been trained to deal with them. Both the power supply and the monitor can hold a dangerous level of electricity even after you turn them off and disconnect them from a power source. The power supply and monitor contain enough power to give you a strong shock even when they are unplugged.

Follow these steps to replace a power supply:

1. Turn off the power to the computer, unplug the computer, and press the power button to drain the system of power.

2. Remove the power cable.

3. Remove the computer case cover.

4. Inside the case, disconnect all power cords from the power supply to other devices.

5. Determine which components must be removed before the power supply can be safely removed from the case. You might need to remove the hard drive, several cards, or the CD or DVD drive. In some cases, you may even need to remove the motherboard.

6. Remove all the components necessary to get to the power supply. Remember to protect the components from static electricity as you work.

7. Unscrew the screws on the back of the computer case that hold the power supply to the case.

8. Look on the bottom or back of the case for slots that hold the power supply in position. Often the power supply must be shifted in one direction to free it from the slots.

9. Remove the power supply.

10. Place the new power supply in position, sliding it into the slots the old power supply used.

Video icons indicate content shown with video on the accompanying CD. Videos illustrate key concepts.

A+
220-702
1.1
1.2

2. Push down on the lever and gently push it away from the socket to lift it. Lift the socket load plate (see Figure 6-35). If a protective cover is in place over the socket, remove it and save it to use later if there is not a processor in the socket.

Figure 6-35 Lift the socket load plate
Courtesy: Course Technology/Cengage Learning

3. Orient the processor so that the notches on the two edges of the processor line up with the two notches on the socket (see Figure 6-36). Gently place the processor in the socket. Socket 775 doesn't have those delicate pins that Socket 1366 has, but you still need to be careful to not touch the top of the socket or the bottom of the processor as you work.

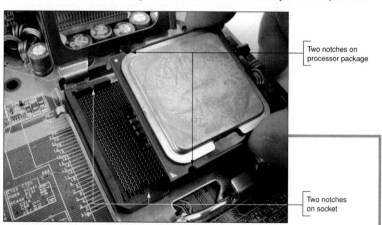

Two notches on processor package

Two notches on socket

Figure 6-36 Place the processor in the socket orienting the notches on two sides
Courtesy: Course Technology/Cengage Learning

4. Close the socket cover. Push down on the lever and gently return it to its locked position (see Figure 6-37).

5. If thermal compound is not already applied to the bottom of the cooler, put thermal compound either on the bottom of the cooler or top of the processor (not both).

Detailed **pictures** show actual computer and hardware components

KVM switches can support 2 to 16 computers or even more and can cost less than $30 to several hundred dollars. Be careful when selecting a KVM switch, so that the switch will support the keyboard, mice, and monitor you want to use. For example, some KVM switches only support ball mice (the type that has a ball that rolls on the bottom of the mouse) and not optical mice (the type that uses a light beam to sense movement). Many KVM switches only support PS/2 mice and keyboards and will not work with the USB variety. Also, less expensive KVM switches do not support keyboard and mice with extra features such as a keyboard zoom bar or Internet Explorer Favorites buttons. The monitor most likely can only use a 15-pin VGA port although a VGA to DVI adapter might work.

The switch does not require that you install device drivers to use it. Just plug in mouse, keyboard, and monitor cables from each computer to the device. Also plug in the one monitor, mouse, and keyboard to the device. Figure 9-52 shows the hardware configuration for the KVM switch in Figure 9-51. Switch between computers by using a hot key on the keyboard or buttons on the top of the KVM switch.

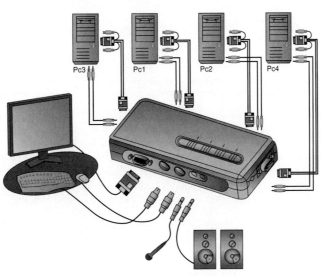

Figure 9-52 Hardware configuration for a four-port KVM switch that also supports audio
Courtesy: Course Technology/Cengage Learning

💡 **A+ Exam Tip** Content for the A+ 220-701 Essentials exam ends here, and content on the A+ 220-702 Practical Application exam begins.

INSTALLING AND CONFIGURING I/O DEVICES AND PORTS

You have just seen how to install several input devices. In this part of the chapter, we take hardware installations to the next level and learn how to configure and use ports on the motherboard and how to install expansion cards.

When installing hardware devices under Windows XP, you need to be logged onto the system with a user account that has the highest level of privileges to change the system. This type of account is called an administrative account. In Windows Vista, it is not necessary to

xxxvii

Notes indicate additional content that might be of interest or information about how best to study the material presented.

Notes Some motherboards provide extra ports that can be installed in faceplate openings off the back of the case. For example, Figure 9-62 shows a module that has a game port and two USB ports. To install the module, remove a faceplate and install the module in its place. Then connect the cables from the module to the appropriate connectors on the motherboard.

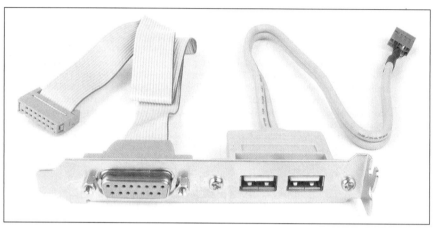

Figure 9-62 This connector provides two USB ports and one game port
Courtesy: Course Technology/Cengage Learning

APPLYING CONCEPTS

For motherboards that provide FireWire ports, the board might come with an internal connector for an internal FireWire hard drive. This connector can also be used for a module that provides additional FireWire ports off the back of the PC case. Figure 9-63 shows a motherboard with the pinouts of the FireWire connector labeled. The module is also shown in the figure. To install this module, remove a faceplate and install the module in its place. Then connect the cable to the motherboard connector.

P4P800 IEEE-1394 connector

TPA0− GND TPB0− +12V GND

1

TPA0+ GND TPB0+ +12V GND

Figure 9-63 This motherboard has a 10-pin FireWire header that can be used for an internal FireWire hard drive or to provide an extra external FireWire port
Courtesy: Course Technology/Cengage Learning

Applying Concepts sections provide practical advice or pointers by illustrating basic principles, identifying common problems, providing steps to practice skills and encouraging creating solutions.

Key Terms are defined as they are introduced and listed at the
end of each chapter. Definitions can be found in the Glossary
and on the accompanying CD.

>> KEY TERMS

For explanations of key terms, see the Glossary near the end of the book.

Accelerated Graphics Port (AGP)	I/O shield	sector
active partition	jumper	SLI (Scalable Link Interface)
audio/modem riser (AMR)	land grid array (LGA)	soft boot
boot loader	Master Boot Record (MBR)	South Bridge
boot record	North Bridge	spacers
booting	Ntldr	staggered pin grid array (SPGA)
BootMgr	on-board ports	standoffs
CMOS battery	partition table	startup password
cold boot	PCI (Peripheral Component	track
communication and networking	Interconnect)	user password
riser (CNR)	PCI Express (PCIe)	wait state
CrossFire	pin grid array (PGA)	warm boot
dual inline package (DIP) switch	power-on password	zero insertion force (ZIF) sockets
front panel header	program file	
hard boot	riser card	

>> REVIEWING THE BASICS

1. What are five main categories of form factors used for motherboards?

2. How many pins does the Intel Socket B have? What is another name for this socket?

3. How many pins does the AMD socket AM2 have?

4. Which is a better performing Intel chipset, the X58 or the P45?

5. Which part of the chipset connects directly to the processor, the North Bridge or the South Bridge?

6. What are the names of the two technologies used to install multiple video cards in the same system?

7. What are the two different voltages that a PCI slot can provide?

8. How does the throughput of PCI Express Version 1.1 compare to PCIe Version 1? How does PCIe Version 2 compare to Version 1?

9. What is the maximum wattage that a PCIe Version 2.0 expansion card can draw?

10. What new type of power connector on the motherboard was introduced with PCIe Version 1.0? How much power does this connector provide?

11. What new type of power connector was introduced with PCIe Version 2.0? How much power does this connector provide?

12. If you are installing an expansion card into a case that does not have enough clearance above the motherboard for the card, what device can you use to solve the problem?

13. What is the purpose of an AGP slot?

14. Which is faster, a PCI Express x16 bus or the latest AGP bus?

15. What is the purpose of a CNR slot?

16. What is the likely color of the PS/2 mouse port on the rear of a computer?

17. What is one reason to flash BIOS?

18. What is the easiest way to obtain the latest software to upgrade BIOS?

Reviewing the Basics sections
check understanding of fundamental
concepts.

Thinking Critically sections require you to analyze and apply what you've learned.

>> THINKING CRITICALLY

1. You install a hard drive and then turn on the PC for the first time. You access BIOS setup and see that the drive is not recognized. Which of the following do you do next?

   a. Turn off the PC, open the case, and verify that memory modules on the motherboard have not become loose.

   b. Turn off the PC, open the case, and verify that the data cable and power cable are connected correctly and jumpers on the drive are set correctly.

   c. Verify that BIOS autodetection is enabled.

   d. Reboot the PC and enter BIOS setup again to see if it now recognizes the drive.

2. Most motherboards that use SATA connectors have at least one PATA connector on the board. What is the most important reason this PATA connector is present?

   a. The hard drive used for booting the OS must use a PATA connector.

   b. The IDE controller will not work without at least one PATA connector.

   c. The board can accommodate older hard drives using the PATA connector.

   d. The PATA connector can be used for EIDE drives such as a CD or DVD drive.

>> HANDS-ON PROJECTS

PROJECT 8-1:   Examining the BIOS Setting for a Hard Drive

From the BIOS setup information on your computer, write down or print all the BIOS settings that apply to your hard drive. Explain each setting that you can. What is the size of the installed drive?

PROJECT 8-2:   Selecting a Replacement Hard Drive

Suppose the 640-GB Western Digital hard drive installed in the RAID array and shown in Figure 8-49 has failed. Search the Internet and find a replacement drive as close to this drive as possible. Print three Web pages showing the sizes, features, and prices of three possible replacements. Which drive would you recommend as the replacement drive and why?

>> REAL PROBLEMS, REAL SOLUTIONS

REAL PROBLEM 8-1: Data Recovery Problem

Your friend has a Windows XP desktop system that contains important data. He frantically calls you to say that when he turns on the computer, the lights on the front panel light up and he can hear the fan spin for a moment and then all goes dead. His most urgent problem is the data on his hard drive, which is not backed up. The data is located in several folders on the drive. What is the quickest and easiest way to solve the most urgent problem, recovering the data? List the major steps in that process.

Hands-On Projects provide practical exercises for each chapter so that you can practice the skills as they are learned.

Real Problems, Real Solutions allow you to apply what you've learned in the chapter to a real-life situation with these comprehensive problems.

INSTRUCTOR RESOURCES

The following supplemental materials are available when this book is used in a classroom setting. All of the supplements available with this book are provided to the instructor on a single CD-ROM (ISBN: 1435487397).

Electronic Instructor's Manual: The Instructor's Manual that accompanies this textbook includes additional instructional material to assist in class preparation, including suggestions for classroom activities, discussion topics, and additional projects.

Solutions: Answers to the end-of-chapter material are provided. These include the answers to the Review Questions and to the Hands-On Projects (when applicable).

ExamView®: This textbook is accompanied by ExamView, a powerful testing software package that allows instructors to create and administer printed, computer (LAN-based), and Internet exams. ExamView includes hundreds of questions that correspond to the topics covered in this text, enabling students to generate detailed study guides that include page references for further review. The computer-based and Internet testing components allow students to take exams at their computers, and also save the instructor time by grading each exam automatically.

PowerPoint Presentations: This book comes with Microsoft PowerPoint slides for each chapter. These are included as a teaching aid for classroom presentation, to make available to students on the network for chapter review, or to be printed for classroom distribution. Instructors, please feel at liberty to add your own slides for additional topics you introduce to the class.

Figure Files: All of the figures in the book are reproduced on the Instructor Resource CD, in bit-mapped format. Similar to the PowerPoint presentations, these are included as a teaching aid for classroom presentation, to make available to students for review, or to be printed for classroom distribution.

A+ Essentials and Practical Application Syllabus: To help prepare for class, a sample syllabus for the Essentials/Practical Applications courses is provided.

ACKNOWLEDGMENTS

Thank you to the wonderful people at Cengage Course Technology who continue to provide support, warm encouragement, patience, and guidance: Nick Lombardi, Michelle Ruelos Cannistraci, and Jessica McNavich. You've truly helped make this seventh edition fun! Thank you, Jill Batistick, Developmental Editor, for your careful attention to detail and your genuine friendship, and to Karen Annett, our excellent copy editor. Thank you, Nicole Ashton for your careful attention to the technical accuracy of the book. Thank you Abigail Reip for your research efforts. Thank you to Jill West who was here with me taking many photographs in the wee hours of the morning.

Thank you to all the people who took the time to voluntarily send encouragement and suggestions for improvements to the previous editions. Your input and help is very much appreciated. Thank you, Robert J. Maldavir, instructor at the Old Dominion Job Corps Center in Monroe, VA, for voluntarily sending many useful and detailed suggestions concerning the sixth edition. The reviewers of this edition all provided invaluable insights and showed a genuine interest in the book's success. Thank you to:

Nathan Catlin, East Ascension High School, Gonzales, LA

Michael Cotterman, Marion Technical College, Marion, OH

Leo Diede, Arapahoe Community College, Littleton, CA
Chas Feller, Pittsburgh Technical, Pittsburgh, PA
Gary Kearns, Forsyth Tech, Winston-Salem, NC
William Shurbert, NHTI Concord Community College, Concord, NH
Joyce Thompson, Lehigh Carbon Community College, Schnecksville, PA
Todd Verge, Nova Scotia Community College, Halifax, Nova Scotia
Jonathan Weissman, Finger Lakes Community College, Canandaigua, NY

When planning this edition, Course Technology sent out a survey to A+ and PC Repair instructors for your input to help us shape the edition. Over 150 instructors responded, for which I am grateful. I spent much time pouring over your answers to our questions, your comments, and suggestions. In addition, thank you to the following people who participated in advisory calls as the revision was just beginning: Michael Avolese – Virginia College of Huntsville, Patrick Brown – Barbara Jones High School, Leo Diede – Arapahoe Community College, C. Thomas Gilbert – Monroe Community College, Scott Horan – Jefferson County Public Schools, Debra Jarrell – Highland Springs Technical Center, Leah Noonan – Lehigh Carbon Community College, Beth Smith – Heald University, and Todd Verge – Nova Scotia Community College. You'll find many of your ideas fleshed out in the pages of this book. Thank you so much for your help!

To the instructors and learners who use this book, I invite and encourage you to send suggestions or corrections for future editions. Please write to me at jean.andrews@cengage.com. I never ignore a good idea! And to instructors, if you have ideas for how to make a class in PC Repair or A+ Preparation a success, please share your ideas with other instructors! You can access my social media pages where you can interact with me and other instructors by clicking the links found on www.cengage.com/pcrepair.

This book is dedicated to the covenant of God with man on earth.

Jean Andrews, Ph.D.

ABOUT THE AUTHOR

Jean Andrews has more than 30 years of experience in the computer industry, including more than 13 years in the college classroom. She has worked in a variety of businesses and corporations designing, writing, and supporting application software; managing a PC repair help desk; and troubleshooting wide area networks. She has written numerous books on software, hardware, and the Internet, including the bestselling A+ Guide to Hardware: Managing, Maintaining and Troubleshooting, Fifth Edition and A+ Guide to Software: Managing, Maintaining and Troubleshooting, Fifth Edition. She lives in Atlanta, Georgia.

READ THIS BEFORE YOU BEGIN

The following hardware, software, and other equipment are needed to do the Hands-on Projects in each chapter:

- You need a working PC that can be taken apart and reassembled. Use a Pentium or higher computer.
- Troubleshooting skills can better be practiced with an assortment of nonworking expansion cards that can be used to simulate problems.
- Windows Vista or XP is needed for all chapters. Except for a few instances, Windows Vista Ultimate or Business editions or Windows XP Professional is needed for Chapters 13-20.

◢ Equipment required to work on hardware includes a grounding mat and grounding strap and flat-head and Phillips-head screwdrivers. In addition, a power supply tester, cable tester, and can of compressed air are useful.

◢ Before undertaking any of the lab exercises, starting with Chapter 4, please review the safety guidelines in the next section.

Follow these instructions carefully for your own safety.

PROTECT YOURSELF, YOUR HARDWARE, AND YOUR SOFTWARE

When you work on a computer, it is possible to harm both the computer and yourself. The most common accident that happens when attempting to fix a computer problem is erasing software or data. Experimenting without knowing what you are doing can cause damage. To prevent these sorts of accidents, as well as the physically dangerous ones, take a few safety precautions. The text below describes the potential sources of damage and danger and how to protect against them.

POWER TO THE COMPUTER

To protect both yourself and the equipment when working inside a computer, turn off the power, unplug the computer, press the power button to drain residual power, and always use a grounding bracelet as described in Chapter 4. Consider the monitor and the power supply to be "black boxes." Never remove the cover or put your hands inside this equipment unless you know about the hazards of charged capacitors. Both the power supply and the monitor can hold a dangerous level of electricity even after they are turned off and disconnected from a power source.

PROTECT AGAINST ESD

To protect the computer against electrostatic discharge (ESD), commonly known as static electricity, always ground yourself before touching electronic components, including the hard drive, motherboard, expansion cards, processors, and memory modules. Ground yourself and the computer parts, using one or more of the following static control devices or methods:

◢ **Ground bracelet or static strap:** A ground bracelet is a strap you wear around your wrist. To protect components against ESD, the other end is attached to a grounded conductor such as the computer case or a ground mat.

◢ **Ground mats:** Ground mats can come equipped with a cord to plug into a wall outlet to provide a grounded surface on which to work. Remember, if you lift the component off the mat, it is no longer grounded and is susceptible to ESD.

◢ **Static shielding bags:** New components come shipped in static shielding bags. Save the bags to store other devices that are not currently installed in a PC.

The best solution to protect against ESD is to use a ground bracelet together with a ground mat. Consider a ground bracelet to be essential equipment when working on a computer. However, if you find yourself in a situation without one, touch the computer case before you touch a component. When passing a chip to another person, touch the other person first so that ESD is discharged between you and the other person before you pass the chip. Leave components inside their protective bags until ready to use. Work on hard floors, not carpet, or use antistatic spray on the carpets. Generally, don't work on a computer if you or the computer have just come inside from the cold.

For today's computers, always unplug the power cord before working inside a computer. Even though the power switch is turned off, know that power is still getting to the system when the computer is plugged in. After you've unplugged the power, press the power button to drain the system of power. Then and only then is it safe to open the case without concern for damaging a component. And don't forget to use that ground bracelet.

There is an exception to the ground-yourself rule. Inside a monitor case, laser printer, or power supply, there is substantial danger posed by the electricity stored in capacitors. When working inside these devices, you *don't* want to be grounded, as you would provide a conduit for the voltage to discharge through your body. In this situation, be careful *not* to ground yourself.

When handling motherboards and expansion cards, don't touch the chips on the boards. Don't stack boards on top of each other, which could accidentally dislodge a chip. Hold cards by the edges, but don't touch the edge connections on the card.

Don't touch a chip with a magnetized screwdriver. When using a multimeter to measure electricity, be careful not to touch a chip with the probes. When changing DIP switches, don't use a graphite pencil, because graphite conducts electricity; a very small screwdriver works very well.

After you unpack a new device or software that has been wrapped in cellophane, remove the cellophane from the work area quickly. Don't allow anyone who is not properly grounded to touch components. Do not store expansion cards within one foot of a monitor, because the monitor can discharge as much as 29,000 volts of ESD onto the screen.

Hold an expansion card by the edges. Don't touch any of the soldered components on a card. If you need to put an electronic device down, place it on a grounded mat, inside a static shielding bag, or on a flat, hard surface. Keep components away from your hair and clothing.

PROTECT HARD DRIVES AND DISKS

Always turn off a computer before moving it, to protect the hard drive, which might be spinning. Never jar a computer while the hard disk is running. Avoid placing a PC on the floor, where the user can accidentally kick it. To keep a computer well ventilated and cool, don't place it on thick carpet.

Follow the usual precautions to protect CD, DVD, and Blu-ray discs. Keep optical discs away from heat, direct sunlight, and extreme cold, and protect them from scratches. Treat discs with care and they'll generally last for years.

COMPTIA AUTHORIZED CURRICULUM PROGRAM

The logo of the CompTIA Authorized Curriculum Program and the status of this or other training material as "Authorized" under the CompTIA Authorized Curriculum Program signifies that, in CompTIA's opinion, such training material covers the content of the CompTIA's related certification exam. CompTIA has not reviewed or approved the accuracy of the contents of this training material and specifically disclaims any warranties of merchantability or fitness for a particular purpose. CompTIA makes no guarantee concerning the success of persons using any such "Authorized" or other training material in order to prepare for any CompTIA certification exam.

The contents of this training material were created for the CompTIA A+ 2009 certification exams.

STATE OF THE INFORMATION TECHNOLOGY (IT) FIELD

Most organizations today depend on computers and information technology to improve business processes, productivity, and efficiency. Opportunities to become global organizations and reach customers, businesses, and suppliers are a direct result of the widespread use of the Internet. Changing technology further changes how companies do business. This fundamental change in business practices has increased the need for skilled and certified IT workers across industries. This transformation has moved many IT workers out of traditional IT businesses and into various IT-dependent industries such as banking, government, insurance, and healthcare.

Note the following from the U.S. Department of Labor:

- "The computer systems design and related services industry is expected to experience rapid growth, adding 489,000 jobs between 2006 and 2016.
- Professional and related workers will enjoy the best job prospects, reflecting continuing demand for higher level skills needed to keep up with changes in technology."

Further, approximately nine million individuals are self-employed in this country. The members of this group who are computer specialists will need to keep their skills sharp as they navigate an ever-changing employment and technological landscape.

In any industry, the workforce is important to continuously drive business. Having correctly skilled workers in IT is a struggle with the ever-changing technologies. With such a quick product life cycle, IT workers must strive to keep up with these changes to continue to bring value to their employer.

CERTIFICATIONS

Different levels of education are required for the many jobs in the IT industry. Additionally, the level of education and type of training required varies from employer to employer, but the need for qualified technicians remains constant. As technology changes and advances in the industry continue to rapidly evolve, many employers consistently look for employees that possess the skills necessary to implement these new technologies. Traditional degrees and diplomas do not identify the skills that a job applicant has. With the growth of the IT industry, companies increasingly rely on technical certifications to identify the skills a particular job applicant possesses. Technical certifications are a way for employers to ensure the quality and skill qualifications of their computer professionals, and they can offer job seekers a competitive edge. According to Thomas Regional Industrial Market Trends, one of the 15 trends that will transform the workplace over the next decade is a severe labor and skill shortage, specifically in technical fields, which are struggling to locate skilled and educated workers.

There are two types of certifications, vendor neutral and vendor specific. Vendor neutral certifications are those that test for the skills and knowledge required in specific industry job roles and do not subscribe to a specific vendor's technology solution. Vendor neutral certifications include all of the Computing Technology Industry Association's (CompTIA) certifications, Project Management Institute's certifications, and Security Certified Program certifications. Vendor specific certifications validate the skills and knowledge necessary to be successful by utilizing a specific vendor's technology solution. Some examples of vendor specific certifications include those offered by Microsoft, IBM, Novell, and Cisco.

As employers struggle to fill open IT positions with qualified candidates, certifications are a means of validating the skill sets necessary to be successful within an organization.

In most careers, salary and compensation are determined by experience and education, but in IT, the number and type of certifications an employee earns also factors into salary and wage increases.

Certifications provide job applicants with more than just a competitive edge over their non-certified counterparts who apply for the same IT positions. Some institutions of higher education grant college credit to students who successfully pass certification exams, moving them further along in their degree programs. Certifications also give individuals who are interested in careers in the military the ability to move into higher positions more quickly. And many advanced certification programs accept, and sometimes require, entry-level certifications as part of their exams. For example, Cisco and Microsoft accept some CompTIA certifications as prerequisites for their certification programs.

CAREER PLANNING

Finding a career that fits a person's personality, skill set, and lifestyle is challenging and fulfilling, but can often be difficult. What are the steps individuals should take to find that dream career? Is IT interesting to you? Chances are that if you are reading this book, this question has been answered. What about IT do you like? The world of work in the IT industry is vast. Some questions to ask include the following: Are you a person who likes to work alone, or do you like to work in a group? Do you like speaking directly with customers or do you prefer to stay behind the scenes? Is your lifestyle conducive to a lot of travel, or do you need to stay in one location? All of these factors influence your decision when faced with choosing the right job. Inventory assessments are a good first step to learning more about your interests, work values, and abilities. There are a variety of Web sites that offer assistance with career planning and assessments.

The Computing Technology Industry Association (CompTIA) hosts an informational Web site called the TechCareer Compass™ (TCC) that defines careers in the IT industry. The TCC is located at *tcc.comptia.org*. This Web site was created by the industry and outlines many industry jobs. Each defined job includes a job description, alternate job titles, critical work functions, activities and performance indicators, and skills and knowledge required by the job. In other words, it shows exactly what the job entails so that you can find one that best fits your interests and abilities. Additionally, the TCC maps over 250 technical certifications to the skills required by each specific job, allowing you to research and plan your certification training. The Web site also includes a resource section, which is updated regularly with articles and links to other career Web sites. The TechCareer Compass is the one-stop location for IT career information.

In addition to CompTIA's TechCareer Compass, there are many other Web sites that cover components of IT careers and career planning. Many of these sites can also be found in the TCC Career Development section. In particular, you might want to give some time to *http://www.act.org/discover/*.

CITATION

Bureau of Labor Statistics, U.S. Department of Labor. *Career Guide to Industries, Computer Systems Design and Related Services.* On the Internet at http://stats.bls.gov/oco/cg/cgs033.htm (visited September 23, 2009).

Bureau of Labor Statistics, U.S. Department of Labor. *Labor Force Statistics from the Current Population Survey, Series Id: LNU02032192.* On the Internet at http://data.bls.gov/PDQ/servlet/SurveyOutputServlet (visited September 23, 2009).

WHAT'S NEW WITH COMPTIA A+ CERTIFICATION

In the spring of 2009, CompTIA *(www.comptia.org)* published the objectives for the 2009 CompTIA A+ Certification exams. These exams went live in August, 2009. However, you can still become CompTIA A+ certified by passing the older 2006 exams that are to remain available until February 2010. There are four 2006 exams. Everyone must pass the CompTIA A+ 220-601 Essentials exam. You must also pass one of three advanced exams, which are named the CompTIA A+ 220-602 exam, the CompTIA A+ 220-603 exam, and the CompTIA A+ 220-604 exam.

The A+ 2009 exams include only two exams, and you must pass both to become A+ certified. The two exams are the A+ 220-701 Essentials exam and the A+ 220-702 Practical Application exam.

Here is a breakdown of the domain content covered on the two A+ 2009 exams:

Domain Content	CompTIA A+ Essentials	CompTIA A+ Practical Application
Hardware	27%	38%
Troubleshooting, Repair, and Maintenance	20%	
Operating System and Software	20%	34%
Networking	15%	15%
Security	8%	13%
Operational Procedures	10%	

HOW TO BECOME COMPTIA CERTIFIED

This training material can help you prepare for and pass a related CompTIA certification exam or exams. In order to achieve CompTIA certification, you must register for and pass a CompTIA certification exam or exams. In order to become CompTIA certified, you must:

1. Select a certification exam provider. For more information please visit the following Web site: http://www.comptia.org/certifications/testprep/testingcenters.aspx

2. Register for and schedule a time to take the CompTIA certification exam(s) at a convenient location.

3. Read and agree to the Candidate Agreement, which will be presented at the time of the exam(s). The text of the Candidate Agreement can be found at the following Web site: http://www.comptia.org/certifications/testprep/policies/agreement.aspx

4. Take and pass the CompTIA certification exam(s).

For more information about CompTIA's certifications, such as their industry acceptance, benefits, or program news, please visit http://www.comptia.org/certifications.aspx

CompTIA is a non-profit information technology (IT) trade association. CompTIA's certifications are designed by subject matter experts from across the IT industry. Each CompTIA certification is vendor-neutral, covers multiple technologies, and requires demonstration of skills and knowledge widely sought after by the IT industry.

To contact CompTIA with any questions or comments, call + 1 630 678 8300 or send an email to *questions@comptia.org.*

Introducing Hardware

In this chapter, you will learn:

- That a computer requires both hardware and software to work
- About the many different hardware components inside of and connected to a computer

Like millions of other computer users, you have probably used your desktop or notebook computer to play games, update your blog, write papers, or build spreadsheets. You can use all these applications without understanding exactly what goes on inside your computer case or notebook. But if you are curious to learn more about personal computers, and if you want to graduate from simply being the end user of your computer to becoming the master of your machine, then this book is for you. It is written for anyone who wants to understand what is happening inside the machine, in order to install new hardware and software, diagnose and solve both hardware and software problems, and make purchasing decisions and then install new hardware and operating systems. The only assumption made here is that you are a computer user—that is, you can turn on your machine, load a software package, and use that software to accomplish a task. No experience in electronics is assumed.

In addition, this book prepares you to pass the A+ Essentials 220-701 exam and the A+ Practical Application 220-702 exam required by CompTIA (*www.comptia.org*) for A+ Certification.

HARDWARE NEEDS SOFTWARE TO WORK

In the world of computers, the term hardware refers to the computer's physical components, such as the monitor, keyboard, motherboard, and hard drive. The term software refers to the set of instructions that directs the hardware to accomplish a task. To perform a computing task, software uses hardware for four basic functions: input, processing, storage, and output (see Figure 1-1). Also, hardware components must communicate both data and instructions among themselves, which requires an electrical system to provide power, because these components are electrical. In this chapter, we introduce the hardware components of a computer system and how they work. In Chapter 2, we introduce operating systems and how they work.

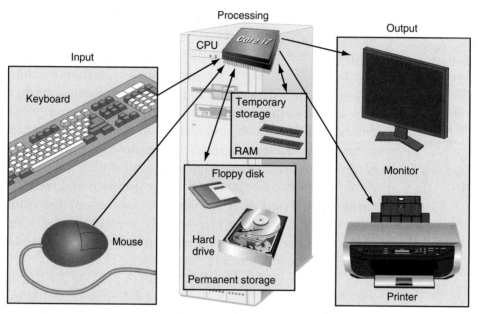

Figure 1-1 Computer activity consists of input, processing, storage, and output
Courtesy: Course Technology/Cengage Learning

A computer user must interact with a computer in a way that both the user and the software understand, such as with entries made by way of a keyboard or a mouse (see Figure 1-2). However, software must convert that instruction into a form that hardware can "understand." As incredible as it might sound, every communication between hardware and software, or between software and other software, is reduced to a simple yes or no, which is represented inside the computer by two simple states: on and off.

It was not always so. For almost half a century, people attempted to invent an electronic computational device that could store all 10 digits in our decimal number system and even some of our alphabet. Scientists were attempting to store a charge in a vacuum tube, which is similar to a light bulb. The charge would later be "read" to determine what had been stored there. Each digit in our number system, zero through nine, was stored with increasing degrees of charge, similar to a light bulb varying in power from off to dim all the way up to bright. However, the degree of "dimness" or "brightness" was difficult to measure, and it would change because the voltage in the equipment could not be accurately regulated. For example, an eight would be stored with a partially bright charge, but later it would be read as a seven or nine as the voltage on the vacuum tube fluctuated slightly.

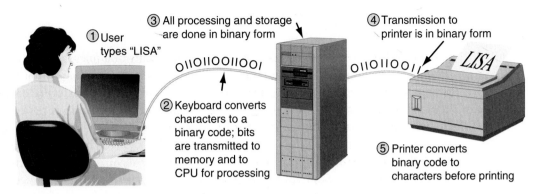

Figure 1-2 All communication, storage, and processing of data inside a computer are in binary form until
presented as output to the user
Courtesy: Course Technology/Cengage Learning

Then, in the 1940s, John Atanasoff came up with the brilliant idea to store and read only
two values, on and off. Either there was a charge or there was not a charge, and this was easy
to write and read, just as it's easy to determine if a light bulb is on or off. This technology of
storing and reading only two states is called binary, and the number system that only uses two
digits, 0 and 1, is called the binary number system. A 1 or 0 in this system is called a bit, or
binary digit. Because of the way the number system is organized, grouping is often done in
groups of eight bits, each of which is called a byte. (Guess what four bits are called? A nibble!)

> **Notes** To learn more about binary and computer terminology related to the binary and hexadecimal
> number system, look on the CD that accompanies this book for the content "The Hexadecimal Number
> System and Memory Addressing."

In a computer, all counting and calculations use the binary number system. Counting in
binary goes like this: 0, 1, 10, 11, 100, 101, and so forth. For example, in binary code the
number 25 is 0001 1001 (see Figure 1-3). When text is stored in a computer, every letter or
other character is first converted to a code using only zeros and ones. The most common coding method for text is ASCII (American Standard Code for Information Interchange). For
example, the uppercase letter A in ASCII code is 0100 0001 (see Figure 1-3).

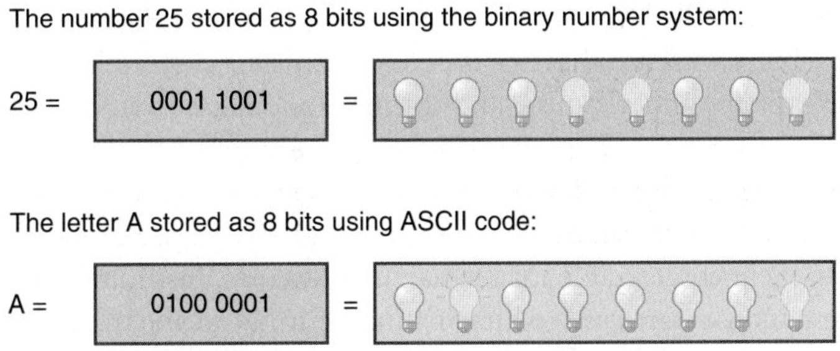

The number 25 stored as 8 bits using the binary number system:

25 =   [0001 1001]   =   💡💡💡💡💡💡💡💡

The letter A stored as 8 bits using ASCII code:

A =   [0100 0001]   =   💡💡💡💡💡💡💡💡

Figure 1-3 All letters and numbers are stored in a computer as a series of bits, each represented
in the computer as on or off
Courtesy: Course Technology/Cengage Learning

> **💡 A+ Exam Tip** The A+ 220-701 Essentials exam expects you to know all the key terms in this chapter.
> Pay careful attention to all these terms. In later chapters, notice the mapping lines in the margins of the
> chapters that mark the in-depth content for each A+ exam objective. As you read this chapter, consider it
> your introduction to the hardware content on the A+ 220-701 Essentials exam.

PC HARDWARE COMPONENTS

In this section, we cover the major hardware components of a microcomputer system used for input, output, processing, storage, electrical supply, and communication. Most input and output devices are outside the computer case. Most processing and storage components are contained inside the case. The most important component in the case is the central processing unit (CPU), also called the processor or microprocessor. As its name implies, this device is central to all processing done by the computer. Data received by input devices is read by the CPU, and output from the CPU is written to output devices. The CPU writes data and instructions in storage devices and performs calculations and other data processing. Whether inside or outside the case, and regardless of the function the device performs, each hardware input, output, or storage device requires these elements to operate:

▲ *A method for the CPU to communicate with the device.* The device must send data to and/or receive data from the CPU. The CPU might need to control the device by passing instructions to it, or the device might need to request service from the CPU.

▲ *Software to instruct and control the device.* A device is useless without software to control it. The software must know how to communicate with the device at the detailed level of that specific device, and the CPU must have access to this software in order to interact with the device. Each device responds to a specific set of instructions based on the device's functions. The software must have an instruction for each possible action you expect the device to accomplish.

▲ *Electricity to power the device.* Electronic devices require electricity to operate. Devices can receive power from the power supply inside the computer case, or they can have their own power supplied by a power cable connected to an electrical outlet.

In the next few pages, we take a sightseeing tour of computer hardware, first looking outside and then inside the case. I've tried to keep the terminology and concepts to a minimum in these sections, because in future chapters, everything is covered in much more detail.

HARDWARE USED FOR INPUT AND OUTPUT

Most input/output devices are outside the computer case. These devices communicate with components inside the computer case through a wireless connection or through cables attached to the case at a connection called a port. Most computer ports are located on the back of the case (see Figure 1-4), but some cases have ports on the front for easy access. The most popular input devices are a keyboard and a mouse, and the most popular output devices are a monitor and a printer.

The keyboard is the primary input device of a computer (see Figure 1-5). The keyboards that are standard today are called enhanced keyboards and hold 104 keys. Ergonomic keyboards are curved to make them more comfortable for the hands and wrists. In addition, some keyboards come equipped with a mouse port used to attach a mouse to the keyboard, although it is more common for the mouse port to be on the computer case. Electricity to run the keyboard comes from inside the computer case and is provided by wires in the keyboard cable.

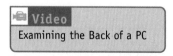

A mouse is a pointing device used to move a pointer on the screen and to make selections. The bottom of a mouse has a rotating ball or an optical sensor that tracks movement and controls the location of the pointer. The one, two, or three buttons on the top of the mouse serve different purposes for different software. For example, Windows Vista uses the left mouse button to execute a command and the right mouse button to display a shortcut menu of commands related to the item.

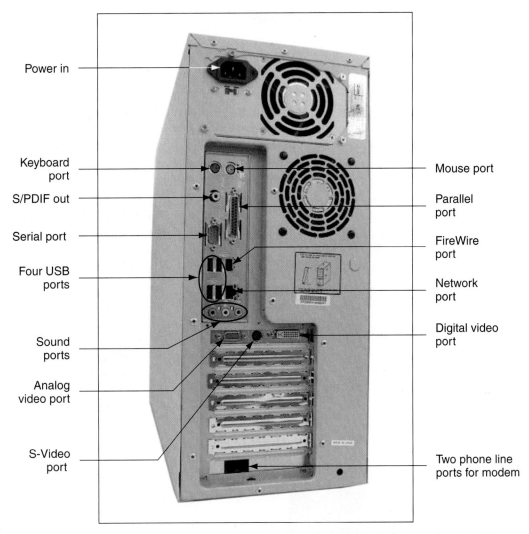

Power in

Keyboard port

S/PDIF out

Serial port

Four USB ports

Sound ports

Analog video port

S-Video port

Mouse port

Parallel port

FireWire port

Network port

Digital video port

Two phone line ports for modem

Figure 1-4 Input/output devices connect to the computer case by ports usually found on the back of the case
Courtesy: Course Technology/Cengage Learning

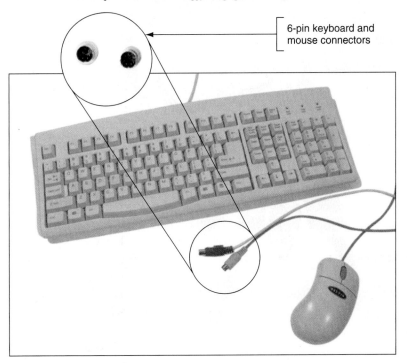

6-pin keyboard and mouse connectors

Figure 1-5 The keyboard and the mouse are the two most popular input devices
Courtesy: Course Technology/Cengage Learning

The monitor and the printer are the two most popular output devices (see Figure 1-6). The monitor is the visual device that displays the primary output of the computer. Hardware manufacturers typically rate a monitor according to the diagonal size of its screen (in inches) and by the monitor's resolution, which is a function of the number of dots on the screen used for display.

A very important output device is the printer, which produces output on paper, often called hard copy. The most popular printers available today are ink-jet, laser, thermal, and impact printers. The monitor and the printer need separate power supplies. Their electrical power cords connect to electrical outlets.

Figure 1-6 showed the most common connectors used for a monitor and a printer: a 15-pin analog video connector and a universal serial bus (USB) connector. In addition, a digital monitor can use a digital video connector and an older printer can use a 25-pin parallel connector (see Figure 1-7).

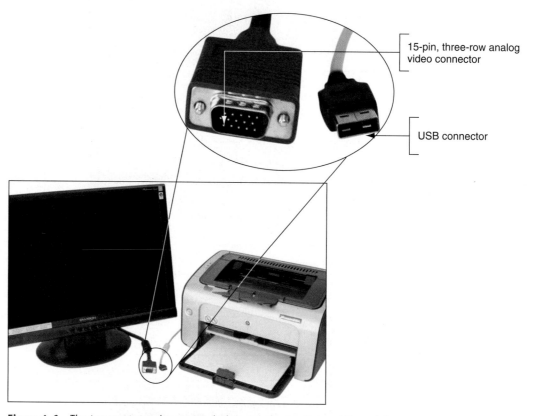

Figure 1-6 The two most popular output devices are the monitor and the printer
Courtesy: Course Technology/Cengage Learning

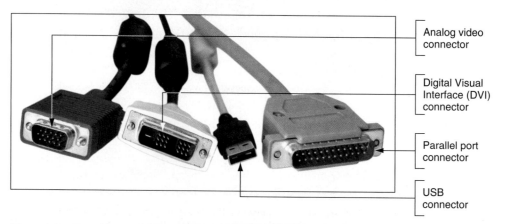

Figure 1-7 Two video connectors and two connectors used by a printer
Courtesy: Course Technology/Cengage Learning

HARDWARE INSIDE THE COMPUTER CASE

Most storage and all processing of data and instructions are done inside the computer case, so before we look at components used for storage and processing, let's look at what you see when you first open the computer case. Most computers contain these devices inside the case (see Figure 1-8):

- ◢ A motherboard containing the CPU, memory, and other components
- ◢ A hard drive and optical drive (CD or DVD) used for permanent storage
- ◢ A power supply with power cords supplying electricity to all devices inside the case
- ◢ Adapter cards used by the CPU to communicate with devices inside and outside the case
- ◢ Cables connecting devices to adapter cards and the motherboard

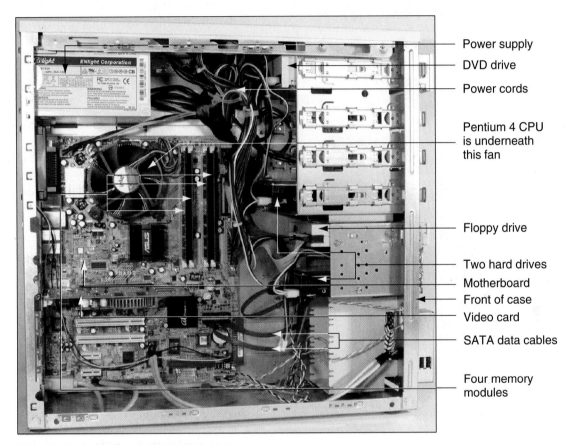

Figure 1-8   Inside the computer case
Courtesy: Course Technology/Cengage Learning

Some of the first things you'll notice when you look inside a computer case are adapter cards. An adapter card is a circuit board that holds microchips, or integrated circuits (ICs), and the circuitry that connects these chips. Adapter cards, also called expansion cards or simply cards, are installed in long narrow expansion slots on the motherboard. All adapter cards contain microchips, which are most often manufactured using CMOS (complementary metal-oxide semiconductor) technology. The other major components inside the case look like small boxes and include the power supply, hard drive, CD drive, and possibly a floppy drive.

There are two types of cables inside the case: data cables, which connect devices to one another, and power cables or power cords, which supply power. If the cable is flat, it most likely is a data cable. However, to know for sure what type of cable you're dealing with, trace the cable from its source to its destination.

THE MOTHERBOARD

The largest and most important circuit board in the computer is the motherboard, also called the main board, the system board, or the techie jargon term, the mobo (see Figure 1-9). The motherboard contains a socket to hold the CPU; the CPU is the component in which most processing takes place. The motherboard is the most complicated piece of equipment inside the case, and Chapter 5 covers it in detail. Because all devices must communicate with the CPU installed on the motherboard, all devices in a computer are either installed directly on the motherboard, directly linked to it by a cable connected to a port on the motherboard, or indirectly linked to it by expansion cards. A device that is not installed directly on the motherboard is called a peripheral device.

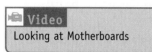
Video
Looking at Motherboards

Some ports on the motherboard stick outside the case to accommodate external devices such as a keyboard, and some ports provide a connection for a device, such as a CD drive, inside the case.

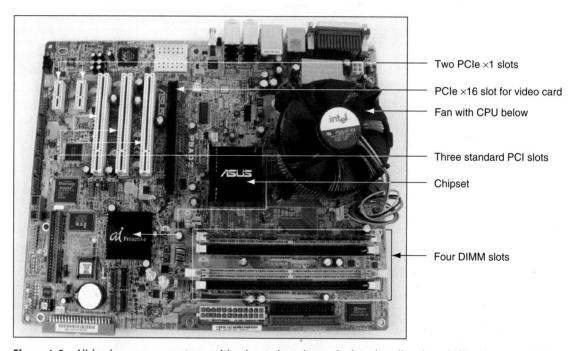

Two PCIe ×1 slots

PCIe ×16 slot for video card

Fan with CPU below

Three standard PCI slots

Chipset

Four DIMM slots

Figure 1-9 All hardware components are either located on the motherboard or directly or indirectly connected to it because they must all communicate with the CPU
Courtesy: Course Technology/Cengage Learning

Listed next are the major components found on all motherboards (some of them are labeled in Figure 1-9). In the sections that follow, we discuss these components in detail. Here are the components used primarily for processing:

◢ Processor or CPU (central processing unit), the computer's most important chip
◢ Chipset that supports the processor by controlling many motherboard activities

The component used for temporary storage is:

◢ RAM (random access memory), which holds data and instructions as they are processed

Components that allow the processor to communicate with other devices are as follows:

◢ Traces, or wires, on the motherboard used for communication
◢ Expansion slots to connect expansion cards to the motherboard
◢ The system clock that keeps communication in sync
◢ Connections for data cables to devices inside the case
◢ Ports for devices outside the case

The electrical system consists of:

▲ Power supply connections that provide electricity to the motherboard and expansion cards

Every motherboard has programming and setup data stored on it:

▲ Flash ROM, a memory chip used to permanently store instructions that control basic hardware functions (explained in more detail later in the chapter)
▲ CMOS RAM and CMOS setup chip that holds configuration data

Figure 1-10 shows the ports coming directly off a motherboard to the outside of the case: a keyboard port, a mouse port, a parallel port, two S/PDIF sound ports (for optical or coaxial cable), a FireWire port, a network port, four USB ports, six sound ports, and a wireless network antenna port. A **parallel port** transmits data in parallel and is most often used by an older printer. An **S/PDIF (Sony-Philips Digital Interface) sound port** connects to an external home theater audio system, providing digital output and the best signal quality. A FireWire port (also called an IEEE 1394 port, pronounced "I-triple-E 1394 port") is used for high-speed multimedia devices such as digital camcorders. A **universal serial bus (USB) port** can be used by many different input/output devices, such as keyboards, printers, scanners, and digital cameras. In addition to these ports, some older motherboards provide a **serial port** that transmits data serially (one bit following the next); it is often used for an external modem or scanner. A serial port looks like a parallel port, but is not as wide. You will learn more about ports in Chapter 9.

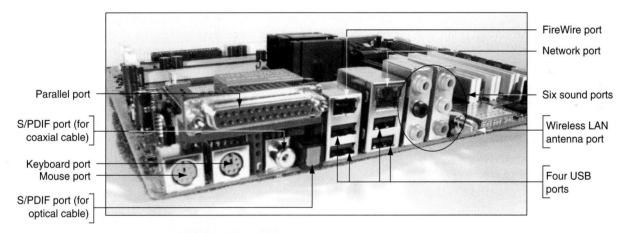

Figure 1-10 A motherboard provides ports for common I/O devices
Courtesy: Course Technology/Cengage Learning

THE PROCESSOR AND THE CHIPSET

The processor or CPU is the chip inside the computer that performs most of the actual data processing (see Figure 1-11). The processor could not do its job without the assistance of the **chipset**, a group of microchips on the motherboard that control the flow of data and instructions to and from the processor. The chipset is responsible for the careful timing and coordination of activities. The chipset is an integrated component of the motherboard and is contained in two packages embedded on the motherboard, which you saw in Figure 1-9.

In this book, we discuss various types of computers, but we focus on the most common personal computers (PCs); PCs often are referred to as IBM-compatible. These are built around microprocessors manufactured by Intel Corporation and AMD. The Macintosh family of computers, manufactured by Apple Computer, Inc., was formerly built around a family of microprocessors, the PowerPC microprocessors, built by Motorola and IBM. Currently, Apple computers are built using Intel processors. You will learn more about processors in Chapter 6.

Figure 1-11 The processor is hidden underneath the fan and the heat sink, which keep it cool
Courtesy: Course Technology/Cengage Learning

STORAGE DEVICES

In Figure 1-1, you saw two kinds of storage: temporary and permanent. The processor uses temporary storage, called primary storage or memory, to temporarily hold both data and instructions while it is processing them. However, when data and instructions are not being used, they must be kept in permanent storage, sometimes called secondary storage, such as a hard drive, CD, DVD, or USB drive. Primary storage is much faster to access than permanent storage. Figure 1-12 shows an analogy to help you understand the concept of primary and secondary storage.

In our analogy, suppose you must do some research at the library. You go to the stacks, pull out several books, carry them over to a study table, and sit down with your notepad

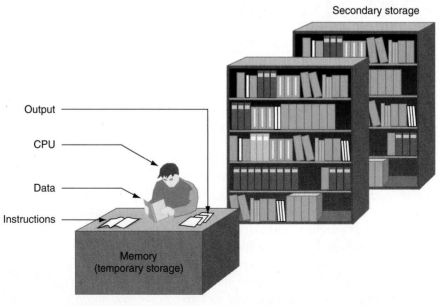

Figure 1-12 Memory is a temporary place to hold instructions and data while the CPU processes both
Courtesy: Course Technology/Cengage Learning

and pencil to take notes and do some calculations. When you're done, you leave with your notepad full of information and calculations, but you don't take the books with you. In this example, the stacks are permanent storage, and the books (data and instructions) are permanently kept there. The table is temporary storage, a place for you to keep data and instructions as you work with them. The notepad is your output from all that work, and you are the CPU, doing the work of reading the books and writing down information.

You kept a book on the table until you knew you were finished with it. As you worked, it would not make sense to go back and forth with a book, returning and retrieving it to and from the stacks. Similarly, the CPU uses primary storage, or memory, to temporarily hold data and instructions as long as it needs them for processing. Memory (your table) gives fast but temporary access, while secondary storage (the stacks) gives slow but permanent access.

PRIMARY STORAGE

Primary storage is provided by devices called memory or RAM (random access memory) located on the motherboard and on some adapter cards. RAM chips are embedded on a small board that plugs into the motherboard (see Figure 1-13). These small RAM boards are called memory modules, and the most common type of module is the DIMM (dual inline memory module). There are several variations of DIMMs, and generally you must match the module size and type to that which the motherboard supports. Also, video cards contain their own memory chips embedded on the card; these chips are called video memory.

DIMM

Three empty DIMM slots

Figure 1-13 A DIMM holds RAM and is mounted directly on a motherboard
Courtesy: Course Technology/Cengage Learning

Whatever information is stored in RAM is lost when the computer is turned off, because RAM chips need a continuous supply of electrical power to hold data or software stored in them. This kind of memory is called volatile because it is temporary in nature. By contrast, another kind of memory called non-volatile memory, holds its data permanently, even when the power is turned off. Non-volatile memory is used in flash drives, memory cards, and some types of hard drives.

APPLYING | CONCEPTS

Using Windows Vista, you can see what type of CPU you have and how much memory you have installed. Click **Start**, right-click **Computer**, and then select **Properties** on the shortcut menu. The System window appears (see Figure 1-14). You can also see which version of Windows you are using. Using Windows XP, click **Start**, right-click **My Computer**, select **Properties** on the shortcut menu, and click the **General** tab.

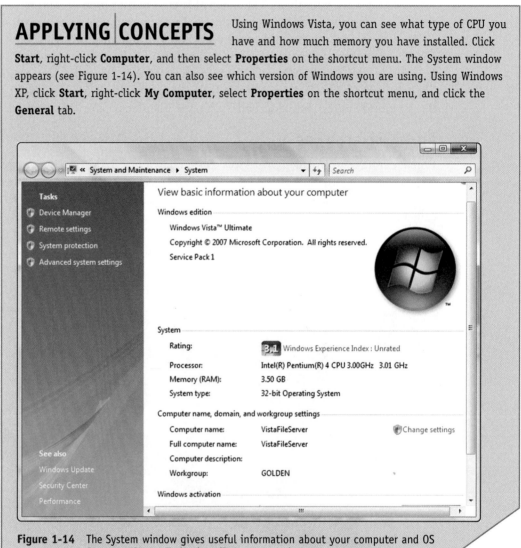

Figure 1-14 The System window gives useful information about your computer and OS
Courtesy: Course Technology/Cengage Learning

SECONDARY STORAGE

As you remember, RAM installed on the motherboard is called primary storage. Primary storage temporarily holds both data and instructions as the CPU processes them. These data and instructions are also permanently stored on devices, such as DVDs, CDs, hard drives, and USB drives, in locations that are remote from the CPU. Data and instructions cannot be processed by the CPU from this remote storage (called secondary storage), but must first be copied into primary storage (RAM) for processing. The most important difference between primary and secondary storage is that secondary storage is permanent. When you turn off your computer, the information in secondary storage remains intact. Secondary storage devices are often grouped in these three categories: hard drives, optical drives, and removable storage.

> **Notes** Don't forget that primary storage, or RAM, is temporary; as soon as you turn off the computer, any information there is lost. That's why you should always save your work frequently into secondary storage.

Hard Drives

The main secondary storage device of a computer is the hard drive, also called a hard disk drive (HDD). Most hard drives consist of a sealed case containing platters or disks that rotate at a high speed (see Figure 1-15). As the platters rotate, an arm with a sensitive read/write head reaches across the platters, both writing new data to them and reading existing data from them. The data is written as magnetic spots on the surface of each platter. These magnetic hard drives use an internal technology called Integrated Drive Electronics (IDE).

Figure 1-15 Hard drive with sealed cover removed
Courtesy: Seagate Technologies LLC

A newer technology for hard drives uses non-volatile flash memory chips, rather than using moving mechanical disks, to hold the data. These flash memory chips are similar to those used in USB flash drives. Any device that has no moving parts is called solid state (solid parts versus moving parts). Therefore, a drive made with flash memory is called a solid state drive (SSD), solid state disk (SSD), or solid state device (SSD). (Unfortunately, the acronym can have either definition.). Figure 1-16 shows four SSD drives. The two larger drives are used in desktop computers, and the two smaller drives are used in laptops. Because SSD drives have no moving parts, they are much faster, more rugged, consume less power, last longer, and are considerably more expensive than magnetic drives. SSD drives are used in industries that require extreme durability, such as the military, and are making their way into the retail markets as the prices go lower.

Regardless of the internal technology used, the interface between an internal hard drive and the motherboard is likely to conform to an ATA (AT Attachment) standard, as published by the American National Standards Institute (ANSI, see *www.ansi.org*). The two major ATA standards for a drive interface are serial ATA (SATA), the newer and faster

Figure 1-16 Four SSD drives
Courtesy: Course Technology/Cengage Learning

standard, and parallel ATA (PATA), the older and slower standard. Hard drives, CD drives, DVD drives, Zip drives, and tape drives, among other devices, can use these interfaces.

Figure 1-17 shows an internal SATA drive interface. SATA cables are flat and thin; one end connects to the device and the other end to the motherboard connector. The external SATA (eSATA) standard allows for a port on the computer case to connect an external eSATA hard drive or other device. Motherboards usually offer from two to eight SATA and eSATA connectors. A motherboard that uses SATA might also have a parallel ATA connector for older devices. External drives, including hard drives, optical drives, and other drives, might use a USB connection, a FireWire connection (which is faster than USB), or an eSATA connection (which is faster than FireWire).

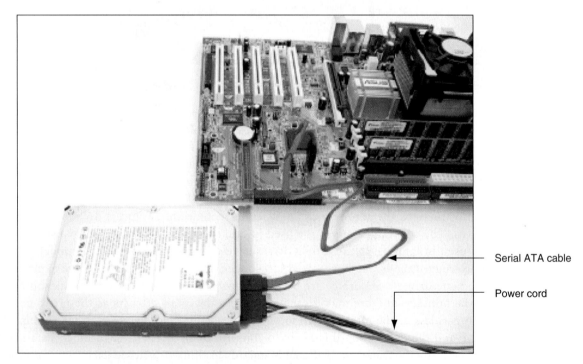

Serial ATA cable

Power cord

Figure 1-17 A hard drive subsystem using the serial ATA data cable
Courtesy: Course Technology/Cengage Learning

Parallel ATA, sometimes called the EIDE (Enhanced IDE) standard or the IDE standard, is slower than SATA and allows for only two connectors on a motherboard for two data cables (see Figure 1-18). Each IDE ribbon cable has a connection at the other end for an IDE device and a connection in the middle of the cable for a second IDE device. Using this interface, a motherboard can accommodate up to four IDE devices in one system. A typical system has one hard drive connected to one IDE connector and a CD drive connected to the other (see Figure 1-19). Figure 1-20 shows the inside of a computer case with three PATA devices. The CD-ROM drive and the Zip drive share an IDE cable, and the hard drive uses the other cable. Both cables connect to the motherboard at the two IDE connections.

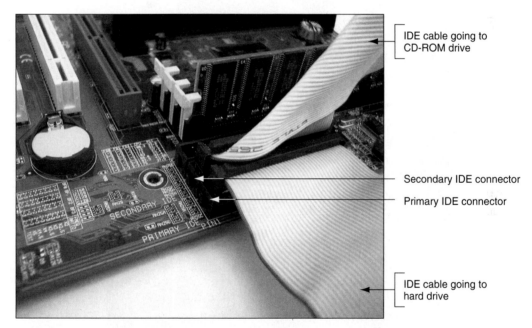

IDE cable going to CD-ROM drive

Secondary IDE connector

Primary IDE connector

IDE cable going to hard drive

Figure 1-18 Using a parallel ATA interface, a motherboard has two IDE connectors, each of which can accommodate two devices; a hard drive usually connects to the motherboard using the primary IDE connector
Courtesy: Course Technology/Cengage Learning

Notes Confusion with industry standards can result when different manufacturers call one standard by different names. This inconsistency happens all too often with computer parts. The industry uses the terms ATA, IDE, and EIDE almost interchangeably even though technically they have different meanings. Used correctly, "ATA" refers to drive interface standards as published by ANSI. Used correctly, "IDE" refers to the technology used internally by a hard drive, and "EIDE" is commonly used by manufacturers to refer to the parallel ATA interface that CD drives, DVD drives, Zip drives, tape drives, and IDE hard drives use to connect to a motherboard. The term "IDE" is more commonly used, when in fact "EIDE" is actually the more accurate name for the interface standards. In this book, to be consistent with manufacturer documentation, we loosely use the term "IDE" to indicate IDE, EIDE, and parallel ATA. For instance, look closely at Figure 1-18 where the motherboard connectors are labeled Primary IDE and Secondary IDE; technically they really should be labeled Primary EIDE and Secondary EIDE.

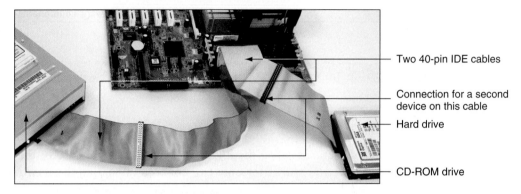

Two 40-pin IDE cables

Connection for a second device on this cable

Hard drive

CD-ROM drive

Figure 1-19 Two IDE devices connected to a motherboard using both IDE connections and two cables
Courtesy: Course Technology/Cengage Learning

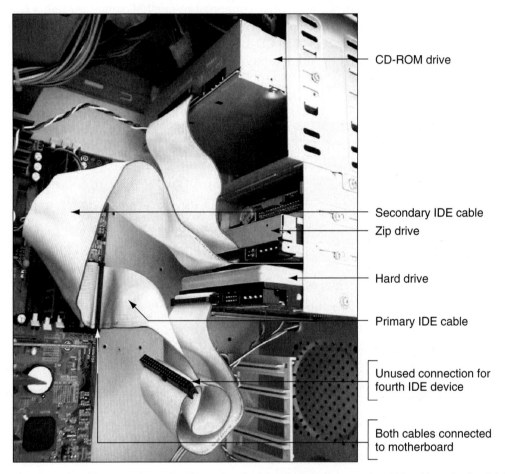

CD-ROM drive

Secondary IDE cable

Zip drive

Hard drive

Primary IDE cable

Unused connection for fourth IDE device

Both cables connected to motherboard

Figure 1-20 This system has a CD-ROM and a Zip drive sharing the secondary IDE cable and a hard drive using the primary IDE cable
Courtesy: Course Technology/Cengage Learning

Video
Identifying Drives

A hard drive receives its power from the power supply by way of a power cord (see Figure 1-21). Looking back at Figure 1-20, you can see the power connections to the right of the cable connections on each drive (the power cords are disconnected to make it easier to see the data cable connections). Chapter 8 covers how a hard drive works and how to install one.

Optical Drives

An optical drive is considered standard equipment on most computer systems today because most software is distributed on CDs or DVDs. Popular choices for optical drives are CD

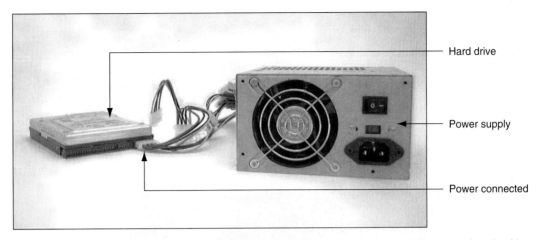

Figure 1-21 A hard drive receives power from the power supply by way of a power cord connected to the drive
Courtesy: Course Technology/Cengage Learning

drives, DVD drives, and Blu-ray Disc (BD) drives. If the drive can burn (write to) a disc as well as read a disc, RW is included in its name. For example, a CD-RW drive can both read and write to CDs. If the drive can only read a disc, it might have ROM (read-only memory) in its name, such as a DVD-ROM drive. (Don't let the use of the word memory confuse you; optical drives don't hold memory.) Figure 1-22 shows the rear of a CD drive with the IDE data cable and power cord connected. Chapter 10 discusses different CD, DVD, and Blu-ray Disc technologies and drives and the discs they can use.

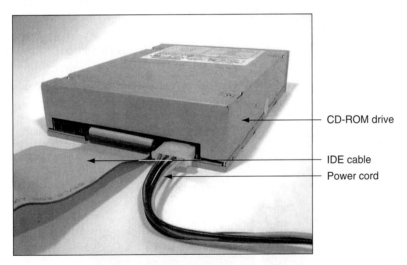

Figure 1-22 This CD drive is an EIDE device and connects to the motherboard by way of an IDE data cable
Courtesy: Course Technology/Cengage Learning

USB Flash Drives and Memory Cards

Two popular removable storage devices are USB flash drives (also called thumb drives) and memory cards commonly used with digital cameras. Both types of devices use non-volatile flash memory chips. USB flash drives (see Figure 1-23) are compact, easy to use, and currently hold up to 64 GB of data. Several types of memory cards are on the market. One example is the SD card shown in Figure 1-24, partially inserted into an SD card slot on a laptop. Notice the open and empty SD card slot in the digital camera sitting nearby. SD cards that follow the first SD card standard can hold up to 4 GB of data, but later SD card standards can accommodate much more data.

Figure 1-23   This flash drive, called the JumpDrive by Lexar, snaps into a USB port
Courtesy: Course Technology/Cengage Learning

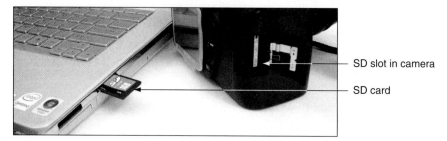

SD slot in camera

SD card

Figure 1-24   Most laptops have a memory card slot that can accommodate an SD card
Courtesy: Course Technology/Cengage Learning

Floppy Disk Drives

An older secondary storage device sometimes found inside the case is a floppy drive, also called a floppy disk drive (FDD), that can hold 3.5-inch disks containing up to 1.44 MB of data. Most motherboards provide a connection for a floppy drive cable (see Figure 1-25). The floppy drive cable can accommodate one or two drives (see Figure 1-26). The drive at the end of the cable is drive A. If another drive were connected to the middle of the cable, it would be drive B in a computer system. Electricity to a floppy drive is provided by a power cord from the power supply that connects to a power port at the back of the drive.

> 💡 **A+ Exam Tip**   The A+ 220-701 Essentials exam expects you to know these terms: HDD, FDD, CD, DVD, RW, and Blu-ray.

Floppy drive connector

Secondary IDE connector

Primary IDE connector

Figure 1-25   A motherboard usually provides a connection for a floppy drive cable
Courtesy: Course Technology/Cengage Learning

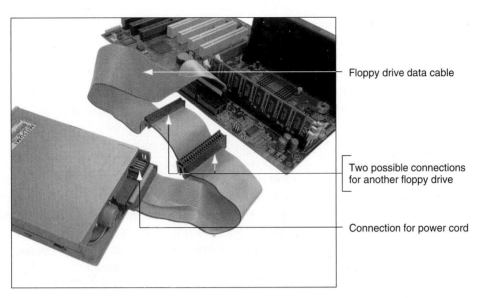

Figure 1-26 One floppy drive connection on a motherboard can support one or two floppy drives
Courtesy: Course Technology/Cengage Learning

Floppy drives are not as necessary as they once were because the industry is moving toward storage media, such as CDs, DVDs, and USB devices that can hold more data. For years, every PC and notebook computer had a floppy drive, but many newer notebook computers don't, and manufacturers often offer floppy drives on desktop systems as add-on options only.

MOTHERBOARD COMPONENTS USED FOR COMMUNICATION AMONG DEVICES

When you look carefully at a motherboard, you see many fine lines on both the top and the bottom of the board's surface (see Figure 1-27). These lines, sometimes called traces, are circuits or paths that enable data, instructions, and power to move from component to component on the board. This system of pathways used for communication and the protocol and methods used for transmission are collectively called the bus. (A protocol is a set of rules

Figure 1-27 On the bottom of the motherboard, you can see bus lines terminating at the CPU socket
Courtesy: Course Technology/Cengage Learning

and standards that any two entities use for communication.) The parts of the bus that we are most familiar with are the lines of the bus that are used for data; these lines are called the data bus.

Binary data is put on a line of a bus by placing voltage on that line. We can visualize that bits are "traveling" down the bus in parallel, but in reality, the voltage placed on each line is not "traveling"; rather, it is all over the line. When one component at one end of the line wants to write data to another component, the two components get in sync for the write operation. Then, the first component places voltage on several lines of the bus, and the other component immediately reads the voltage on these lines.

The CPU or other devices interpret the voltage, or lack of voltage, on each line on the bus as binary digits (0s or 1s). Some buses have data paths that are 8, 16, 32, 64, or 128 bits wide. For example, a bus that has eight wires, or lines, to transmit data is called an 8-bit bus. Figure 1-28 shows an 8-bit bus between the CPU and memory that is transmitting the letter A (binary 0100 0001). All bits of a byte are placed on their lines of the bus at the same time. Remember there are only two states inside a computer: off and on, which represent zero and one. On a bus, these two states are no voltage for a zero and voltage for a one. So, the bus in Figure 1-28 has voltage on two lines and no voltage on the other six lines in order to pass the letter A on the bus. This bus is only 8 bits wide, but most buses today are much wider: 16, 32, 64, 128, or 256 bits wide. Also, a bus might use a ninth bit for error checking. Adding a check bit for each byte allows the component reading the data to verify that it is the same data written to the bus.

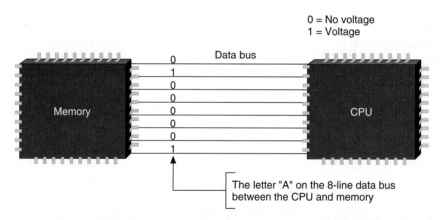

Figure 1-28 A data bus has traces or lines that carry voltage interpreted by the CPU and other devices as bits
Courtesy: Course Technology/Cengage Learning

The width of a data bus is called the data path size. A motherboard can have more than one bus, each using a different protocol, speed, data path size, and so on. The main bus on the motherboard that communicates with the CPU, memory, and the chipset goes by several names: system bus, front side bus (FSB), memory bus, host bus, local bus, or external bus. In our discussions, we'll use the term system bus or memory bus because they are more descriptive, but know that motherboard ads typically use the term front side bus. The data portion of most system buses on today's motherboards is 128 bits wide with or without additional lines for error checking.

One of the most interesting lines, or circuits, on a bus is the system clock or system timer, which is dedicated to timing the activities of the chips on the motherboard. A quartz crystal on the motherboard (see Figure 1-29), similar to that found in watches, generates the oscillation that produces the continuous pulses of the system clock. Traces carry these pulses over the motherboard to chips and expansion slots to ensure that all activities are synchronized.

Motherboard crystal generates the system clock

Figure 1-29 The system clock is a pulsating electrical signal sent out by this component that works much like a crystal in a wristwatch (one line, or circuit, on the motherboard bus is dedicated to carrying this pulse)
Courtesy: Course Technology/Cengage Learning

Remember that everything in a computer is binary, and this includes the activities themselves. Instead of continuously working to perform commands or move data, the CPU, bus, and other devices work in a binary fashion—do something, stop, do something, stop, and so forth. Each device works on a clock cycle or beat of the clock. Some devices, such as the CPU, do two or more operations on one beat of the clock, and others do one operation for each beat. Some devices might even do something on every other beat, but all work according to beats or cycles. You can think of this as similar to children jumping rope. The system clock (child turning the rope) provides the beats or cycles, while devices (children jumping) work in a binary fashion (jump, don't jump). In the analogy, some children jump two or more times for each rope pass.

How fast does the clock beat? The beats, called the **clock speed**, are measured in **hertz (Hz)**, which is one cycle per second; **megahertz (MHz)**, which is one million cycles per second; and **gigahertz (GHz)**, which is one billion cycles per second. Common ratings for motherboard buses today are 2600 MHz, 2000 MHz, 1600 MHz, 1333 MHz, 1066 MHz, 800 MHz, 533 MHz, or 400 MHz, although you might still see some motherboards around rated at 200 MHz, 133 MHz, or slower. In other words, data or instructions can be put on a 1600 MHz system bus at the rate of 1600 million every second. A CPU operates from 166 MHz to almost 4 GHz. The CPU can put data or instructions on its internal bus at a much higher rate than does the motherboard. Although we often refer to the speed of the CPU and the motherboard bus, talking about the frequency of these devices is more accurate, because the term "speed" implies a continuous flow, while the term "frequency" implies a digital or binary flow: on and off, on and off.

> **Notes** Motherboard buses are most often measured in frequencies such as 2600 MHz, but sometimes you see a motherboard bus measured in performance such as the nForce 730a motherboard by EVGA built to support an AMD processor including the Phenom X4 Quad Core processor (see *www.evga.com* and *www.amd.com*). This motherboard bus is rated at 5200 MT/s. One MT/s is one megatransfer per second or one million bytes per second transferred over the bus.

The lines of a bus, including data, instruction, and power lines, often extend to the expansion slots (see Figure 1-30). The size and shape of an expansion slot depend on the kind of bus it uses. Therefore, one way to determine the kind of bus you have is to examine the expansion slots on the motherboard.

Pins on connector edge of expansion card

PCI slot

Bus lines

Figure 1-30 The lines of a bus terminate at an expansion slot where they connect to pins that connect to lines on the expansion card inserted in the slot
Courtesy: Course Technology/Cengage Learning

PCI slots

AGP slot for video card

CPU with fan on top

Chipset

Four slots for RAM

Drive connectors

Power supply connection

CMOS battery

Figure 1-31 The one AGP slot used for a video card is set farther from the edge of the board than the PCI slots
Courtesy: Course Technology/Cengage Learning

Figure 1-31 shows an older motherboard with two types of expansion slots. Looking back at Figure 1-9, you can see a newer motherboard that uses a newer type of expansion slot. The types of slots shown on both boards include the following:

▲ PCI (Peripheral Component Interconnect) expansion slot used for input/output devices

▲ PCI Express (PCIe) slots that come in several lengths and are used by high-speed input/output devices

▲ AGP (Accelerated Graphics Port) expansion slot used for a video card

Notice in Figures 1-9 and 1-31 the white PCI slots are used on both the older and newer boards. A motherboard will have at least one slot intended for use by a video card. The older board uses an AGP slot for that purpose, and the newer board uses a long PCIe x16 slot for video. PCIe currently comes in four different slot sizes; the longest size (PCIe x16) and the shortest size (PCIe x1) are shown in Figure 1-9.

With a little practice, you can identify expansion slots by their length, by the position of the breaks in the slots, and by the distance from the edge of the motherboard to a slot's position.

In Chapter 5, you'll learn that each expansion slot communicates with the CPU by way of its own bus. There can be a PCI Express bus or an AGP bus and a PCI bus, each running at different speeds and providing different features to accommodate the expansion cards that use these different slots. But all these buses connect to the main bus or system bus, which connects to the CPU.

EXPANSION CARDS

Expansion cards are mounted in expansion slots on the motherboard (see Figure 1-32). Figure 1-33 shows the motherboard and expansion cards installed inside a computer case. By studying this figure carefully, you can see the video card installed in the PCIe x16 slot and a modem card and wireless network card installed in two PCI slots. The other three PCI slots are not used. (Notice the fan on the video card to help keep it cool.) Figure 1-33 also shows the ports these cards provide at the rear of the PC case.

Modem card

PCI slot

Motherboard
Phone line ports

Figure 1-32 This adapter card is a modem card and is mounted in a PCI slot on the motherboard
Courtesy: Course Technology/Cengage Learning

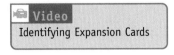

You can see a full view of a video card in Figure 1-34. These cards all enable the CPU to connect to an external device or, in the case of a modem card or network card, to a phone line or network. The video card, also called a graphics card, provides one or more ports for a monitor. The network card provides a port for a network cable to connect the PC to a network, and the modem card provides ports for phone lines. The technology

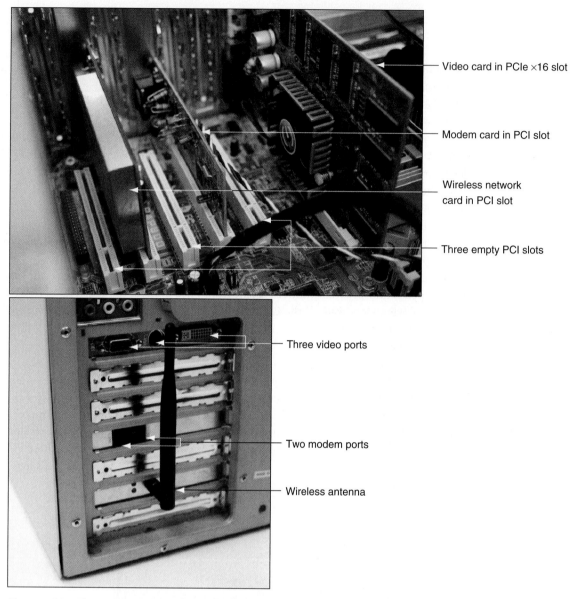

Video card in PCIe ×16 slot

Modem card in PCI slot

Wireless network card in PCI slot

Three empty PCI slots

Three video ports

Two modem ports

Wireless antenna

Figure 1-33 Three cards installed on a motherboard, providing ports for several devices
Courtesy: Course Technology/Cengage Learning

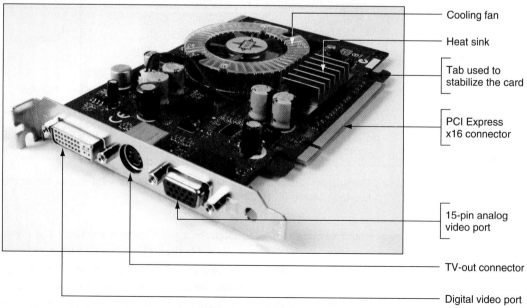

Cooling fan

Heat sink

Tab used to stabilize the card

PCI Express x16 connector

15-pin analog video port

TV-out connector

Digital video port

Figure 1-34 The easiest way to identify this video card is to look at the ports on the end of the card
Courtesy: Course Technology/Cengage Learning

to access these devices is embedded on the card itself, and the card also has the technology to communicate with the slot it is in, the motherboard, and the CPU.

The easiest way to determine the function of a particular expansion card (short of seeing its name written on the card, which doesn't happen very often) is to look at the end of the card that fits against the back of the computer case. A network card, for example, has a port designed to fit the network cable. A modem card has one, or usually two, telephone jacks as its ports. You'll get lots of practice in this book identifying ports on expansion cards. However, as you examine the ports on the back of your PC, remember that sometimes the motherboard provides ports of its own.

THE ELECTRICAL SYSTEM

The most important component of the computer's electrical system is the power supply, which is usually near the rear of the case (see Figure 1-35). This power supply does not actually generate electricity but converts and reduces it to a voltage that the computer can handle. A power supply receives 110–120 volts of AC power from a wall outlet and converts it to a much lower DC voltage. Older power supplies had power cables that provided either 5 or 12 volts DC. Newer power supplies provide 3.3, 5, and 12 volts DC. In addition to providing power for the computer, the power supply runs a fan directly from the electrical output voltage to help cool the inside of the computer case. Temperatures over 185 degrees Fahrenheit (85 degrees Celsius) can cause components to fail. When a computer is running, this and other fans inside the case and the spinning of the hard drive are the primary noisemakers.

Figure 1-35 Power supply with connections
Courtesy: Course Technology/Cengage Learning

A motherboard has one primary connection to receive power from the power supply (see Figure 1-36). This power is used by the motherboard, the CPU, and other components that receive their power from ports and expansion slots coming off the motherboard. In addition, there might be other power connectors on the motherboard to power a small fan that cools the CPU, to power the CPU itself, or to provide additional power to expansion cards.

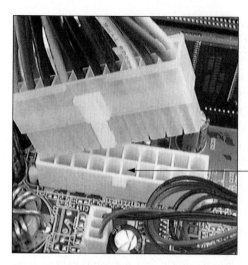

P1 power connector
on a motherboard

Figure 1-36   The motherboard receives its power from the power supply by way of a 20 or 24-pin connector
called the P1 connector
Courtesy: Course Technology/Cengage Learning

INSTRUCTIONS STORED ON THE MOTHERBOARD AND OTHER BOARDS

Some very basic instructions are stored on the motherboard—just enough to start the computer, use some simple hardware devices such as a monitor and keyboard, and search for an operating system stored on a storage device such as a hard drive or CD. These data and instructions are stored on special ROM (read-only memory) chips on the board and are called the BIOS (basic input/output system). Some adapter cards, such as a video card, also have ROM BIOS chips. In the case of ROM chips, the distinction between hardware and software becomes vague. Most of the time, it's easy to distinguish between hardware and software. For example, a USB flash drive is hardware, but a file on the drive containing a set of instructions is software. This software file, sometimes called a program, might be stored on the drive today, but you can erase that file tomorrow and write a new one to the drive. In this case, it is clear that a flash drive is a permanent physical entity, whereas the program is not. Sometimes, however, hardware and software are not so easy to distinguish. For instance, a ROM chip on an adapter card inside your computer has software instructions permanently etched into it during fabrication. This software is actually a part of the hardware and is not easily changed. In this case, hardware and software are closely tied together, and it's difficult to separate the two, either physically or logically. Software embedded into hardware is often referred to as firmware because of its hybrid nature. Figure 1-37 shows an embedded firmware chip on a motherboard that contains the ROM BIOS programs.

The motherboard ROM BIOS serves three purposes: The BIOS that is sometimes used to manage simple devices is called system BIOS, the BIOS that is used to start the computer is called startup BIOS, and the BIOS that is used to change some settings on the motherboard is called BIOS setup or CMOS setup.

These motherboard settings are stored in a small amount of RAM located on the firmware chip and are called CMOS RAM or just CMOS. Settings stored in CMOS RAM include such things as the current date and time, which hard drives are present, and how the parallel port is configured. When the computer is first turned on, it looks to settings in CMOS RAM to find out what hardware it should expect to find. CMOS RAM is volatile memory. When the computer is turned off, CMOS RAM is powered by a trickle of electricity from a small battery located on the motherboard or computer case, usually close to the

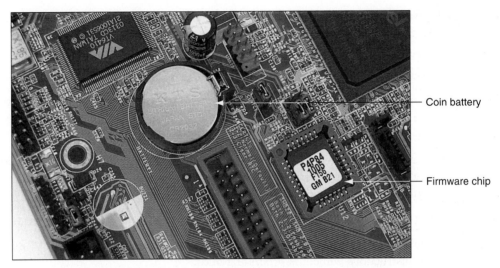

Figure 1-37 This firmware chip contains flash ROM and CMOS RAM; CMOS RAM is powered by the coin battery located near the chip
Courtesy: Course Technology/Cengage Learning

firmware chip (refer back to Figure 1-37). This battery power is necessary so that the motherboard configuration is not lost when the PC is turned off.

Motherboard manufacturers often publish updates for the ROM BIOS on their motherboards; if a board is giving you problems or you want to use a new feature just released, you might want to upgrade the BIOS. In the past, this meant buying new ROM chips and exchanging them on the motherboard. However, ROM chips on motherboards today are made of non-volatile memory and can be reprogrammed. Called **flash ROM**, the software stored on these chips can be overwritten by new software that remains on the chip until it is overwritten. (You will learn how to do this in Chapter 5; the process is called flashing ROM.)

>> CHAPTER SUMMARY

- ◢ A computer requires both hardware and software to work.

- ◢ The four basic functions of the microcomputer are input, output, processing, and storage of data.

- ◢ Data and instructions are stored in a computer in binary form, which uses only two states for data—on and off, or 1 and 0—which are called bits. Eight bits equal one byte.

- ◢ The four most popular input/output devices are the mouse, keyboard, printer, and monitor.

- ◢ The most important component inside the computer case is the motherboard, also called the main board or system board. It holds the most important microchip inside the case, the central processing unit (CPU), a microprocessor or processor. The motherboard also gives access to other circuit boards and peripheral devices. All communications between the CPU and other devices must pass through the motherboard.

◢ Most microchips are manufactured using CMOS (complementary metal-oxide semiconductor) technology.

◢ Each hardware device needs a method to communicate with the CPU, software to control it, and electricity to power it.

◢ Devices outside the computer case connect to the motherboard through ports on the case. Common ports are network, FireWire, sound, serial, parallel, USB, keyboard, and mouse ports.

◢ An adapter card inserted in an expansion slot on the motherboard can provide an interface between the motherboard and a peripheral device, or can itself be a peripheral. (An example is a network card.)

◢ The chipset on a motherboard controls most activities on the motherboard.

◢ Primary storage, called memory or RAM, is temporary storage the CPU uses to hold data and instructions while it is processing both.

◢ Most RAM sold today is stored on memory chips embedded on memory modules, which are called DIMMs.

◢ Secondary storage is slower than primary storage, but it is permanent storage. Some examples of secondary storage devices are hard drives, CD drives, DVD drives, Blu-ray drives, flash drives, memory cards, Zip drives, and floppy drives.

◢ Most older hard drives, CD drives, and DVD drives use the parallel ATA (PATA) interface standard, also called the EIDE (Enhanced Integrated Drive Electronics) standard, which can accommodate up to four EIDE or IDE devices on one system. Newer drives use the serial ATA (SATA) interface standard.

◢ The system clock is used to synchronize activity on the motherboard. The clock sends continuous pulses over the bus that different components use to control the pace of activity.

◢ A motherboard can have several buses, including the system bus, the PCI Express bus, the PCI bus, and the older AGP bus.

◢ The frequency of activity on a motherboard is measured in megahertz (MHz), or one million cycles per second. The processor operates at a much higher frequency than other components in the system, and its activity is often measured in gigahertz (GHz), or one billion cycles per second.

◢ The power supply inside the computer case supplies electricity to components both inside and outside the case. Some components external to the case get power from their own electrical cables.

◢ A ROM BIOS or firmware microchip is a hybrid of hardware and software containing programming embedded into the chip.

◢ ROM BIOS on a motherboard holds the basic software needed to start a PC and begin the process of loading an operating system. Most ROM chips are flash ROM, meaning that these programs can be updated without exchanging the chip.

◢ The BIOS setup program is part of ROM BIOS stored on the firmware chip. This program is used to change motherboard settings or configuration information. When power to the PC is turned off, a battery on the motherboard supplies power to CMOS RAM that holds these settings.

>> KEY TERMS

For explanations of key terms, see the Glossary near the end of the book.

adapter card
binary number system
BIOS (basic input/output system)
BIOS setup bit
bus
byte
cards
central processing unit (CPU)
chipset
clock speed
CMOS (complementary metal-oxide semiconductor)
CMOS RAM
CMOS setup
data bus
data path size
DIMM (dual inline memory module)
expansion cards
expansion slots
firmware
flash ROM
floppy disk drive (FDD)
floppy drive

front side bus (FSB)
gigahertz (GHz)
graphics card
hard copy
hard disk drive (HDD)
hard drive
hardware
hertz (Hz)
host bus
keyboard
magnetic hard drive
main board
megahertz (MHz)
memory
microprocessor
monitor
motherboard
mouse
non-volatile memory
parallel ATA (PATA)
parallel port
peripheral device
port
power supply

primary storage
printer
processor
program
protocol
RAM (random access memory)
ROM (read-only memory)
S/PDIF (Sony-Philips Digital Interface) sound port
secondary storage
serial ATA (SATA)
serial port
software
solid state drive (SSD)
startup BIOS
system BIOS
system board
system bus
system clock
traces
universal serial bus (USB) port
video card
video memory
volatile

>> REVIEWING THE BASICS

1. Why is all data stored in a computer in binary form?

2. What are the four primary functions of hardware?

3. What are the two main input devices and two main output devices?

4. What three things do electronic hardware devices need in order to function?

5. How many bits are in a byte?

6. What is the purpose of an expansion slot on a motherboard?

7. Which component on the motherboard is used primarily for processing?

8. Name the two main CPU manufacturers.

9. Order the following ports according to speed, placing the fastest port first: FireWire, eSATA, USB.

10. What are two other names for the system bus?

11. What type of output does an S/PDIF port provide?

12. Why is an SSD hard drive more reliable under rugged conditions than an IDE hard drive?

13. How is the best way to determine if a cable inside a computer is a data cable or a power cable?

14. List three types of ports that are often found coming directly off the motherboard to be used by external devices.

15. What is the purpose of the S/PDIF port?

16. What is the most common type of memory module?

17. What is the difference between volatile and non-volatile memory?

18. Of the two types of storage in a system, which type is generally faster and holds data and instructions while the data is being processed? Which type of storage is generally slower, but more permanent?

19. What technology standard provides for up to four devices on a system, including the hard drive as one of those devices? What are two common industry names loosely used to describe this standard?

20. What is a measurement of frequency of a system bus and CPU? Which is faster, the system bus or the CPU?

21. Name three types of buses that are likely to be on a motherboard today.

22. A power supply receives 120 volts of _____ power from a wall outlet and converts it to 3.3, 5, and 12 volts of _____ power.

23. ROM BIOS or firmware chips that can be upgraded without replacing the chips are called _____.

24. BIOS setup allows a technician to change configuration settings on a motherboard stored in _____.

25. Name three examples of secondary storage devices.

26. A hertz is _____ cycle per second; a megahertz is _____ cycles per second, and a gigahertz is _____ cycles per second.

27. An AGP slot is normally used for a(n) _____ expansion card.

28. How many sizes of PCI Express slots are currently manufactured for personal computers?

29. Name the three purposes the motherboard ROM BIOS serves.

30. From where does CMOS RAM receive its power when the computer is not turned on?

>> THINKING CRITICALLY

1. When selecting secondary storage devices for a new desktop PC, which is more important, a CD drive or a floppy drive? Why?

2. Based on what you have learned in this chapter, when working on a Microsoft Word document, why is it important to save your work often? Explain your answer using the two terms primary storage and secondary storage.

3. Most buses are 16, 32, 64, or 128 bits wide. Why do you think these bus widths are multiples of eight?

4. You purchase a new computer system that does not have a modem port, and then you decide that you want to use a dial-up connection to the Internet. What is the least expensive way to obtain a modem port?
   a. Trade in the computer for another computer that has a modem port
   b. Purchase a second computer with a modem port

1

c. Purchase a modem card and install it in your system

d. Purchase an external modem that connects to your PC by way of a USB port

5. In this chapter, a light bulb is used to demonstrate the binary concept used for computer storage and communication. Give another example in everyday life to explain this binary concept. Get creative.

6. If the CMOS battery inside your computer system died, when you first turn on your system, will you expect the system to boot up normally to the operating system level? What information do you think the system would not have available for a successful boot?

7. Which device is a solid state device, a CD drive or a memory module? Why?

>> HANDS-ON PROJECTS

PROJECT 1-1: Identifying Ports on Your Computer

Look at the back of your home or lab computer and make a diagram showing the ports. Label all the ports in the diagram and note which ones are used and which ones are not used.

PROJECT 1-2: Researching Motherboards Using the Internet

The Internet is an incredibly rich source of information about computer hardware and software. Answer these questions about a motherboard, using the Internet as your source:

1. ASUS is a major manufacturer of motherboards. Go to the Asus Web site at *www.asus.com* and print a Web page advertising a motherboard for a desktop computer.

2. What is the frequency of the system bus? What is the system bus called?

3. List the expansion slots contained on the motherboard. What processors does this board support?

4. Go to Google.com and search on "motherboard review." List three Web sites that review motherboards. Search these three sites. Which ones review the ASUS motherboard you selected in Step 1? What is one statement that one review makes about this motherboard?

PROJECT 1-3: Identifying Motherboard Components

Look on the CD that accompanies this book for the diagram, "A Motherboard Diagram with Labels Missing," which is also shown in Figure 1-38, and print the diagram. Label as many of the components on the diagram as you can, using the photographs in Figures 1-9 and 1-31, and other photographs in the chapter. This exercise is very important to help you recognize motherboard components in motherboard documentation.

> 🔦 **A+ Exam Tip** The A+ 220-701 Essentials exam expects you to be able to recognize components on a motherboard diagram similar to the one in Figure 1-38.

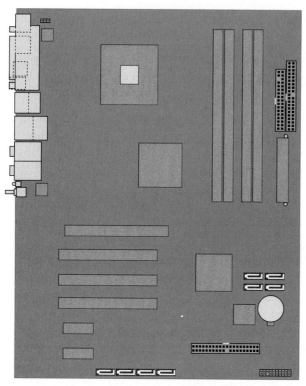

Figure 1-38   A motherboard diagram with labels missing
Courtesy: Course Technology/Cengage Learning

PROJECT 1-4:   Examining Your Computer

What type of CPU does your computer have, and how much memory is installed? To answer these questions, using Windows Vista, click **Start**, right-click **Computer**, and select **Properties** on the shortcut menu. The System window opens. (Using Windows XP, click **Start**, right-click **My Computer**, select **Properties** on the shortcut menu, and click the **General** tab.) The CPU information is listed in this window. Print a screen shot of this window. One quick and easy way to get a hard copy of a screen is to use Paint. Follow these directions to print the screen:

1. Press the **PrintScrn** (print screen) key. This puts the screen capture on your Windows Clipboard.

> **Notes**   You can capture just the active window, instead of the entire screen, by pressing Alt+PrintScrn instead of PrintScrn.

2. Open Paint. Click **Start, All Programs, Accessories, Paint.**

3. Click **Edit, Paste** to put the contents of the Clipboard into Paint. If necessary, click **Yes** to the dialog box that pops up to confirm the paste.

4. To print the page, click **File, Print**, select a printer in the Print dialog box, and click **Print**.

PROJECT 1-5:   Learning to Think in Binary and Hex

Look on the CD that accompanies this book for the content "The Hexadecimal Number System and Memory Addressing" and "ASCII Character Set and Ansi.sys" to answer these questions:

1. What is the ASCII code in binary and in decimal for a lowercase z?
2. What is the ASCII code in binary and in decimal for a period?
3. Write the binary numbers from 1 to 20.
4. What is the largest decimal number that can be stored using 8 bits, or 1 byte?
5. Write the hex numbers from 1 to 20.
6. Convert 43 to binary. Convert 43 to hex.
7. What is 1101 1001 in decimal? In hex?

>> REAL PROBLEMS, REAL SOLUTIONS

REAL PROBLEM 1-1: Reading a Technical Ad for a Computer System

Computer ads can sometimes be difficult to read, especially those targeting tech-savvy computer buyers. Figure 1-39 shows an advertisement published by GIM Computer Corp (*www.gimcomputers.com*), a computer parts store that assembles systems from parts and sells them as a single unit price with a one-year warranty on all parts. Answer the following questions about this ad for their high-end games computer:

1. What is the system bus called? What is the system bus frequency?
2. What is the frequency for the processor?
3. What is the brand of the processor?
4. How much RAM is installed?
5. What type of expansion slot is used for the video card?
6. What type of interface does the hard drive use?
7. How much data can the hard drive store?
8. What is the brand of the motherboard?
9. What type of optical drive is installed?
10. List the terms in the ad that you do not understand (many are not covered in this chapter) and save this list. In future chapters, you will learn the meanings of all these terms.

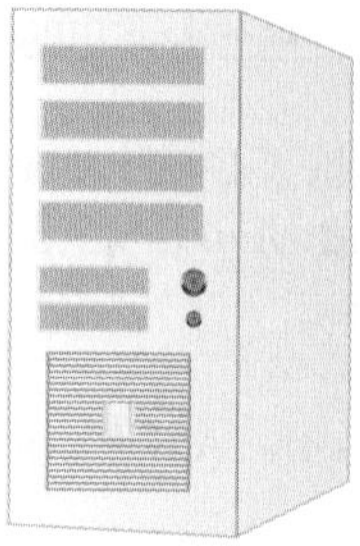

GIM Intel Gamer's Dream System

Model

Brand	General Intelligence Machines
Model	GIM Intel Gamer's Dream System

Tech Spec

Motherboard	ASUS P6T Deluxe
Processor	Intel Core i7 920 2.66Ghz Quad Core, 8MB Cache, 1066FSB
Memory	Crucial 6GB DDR3 1600Mhz (3z2GB)
Primary Hard Drive	Raid 0, 2 pcs of Seagate 1TB 32M Buffer SATA2 3G 7200rpm Hard Drive
Secondary Hard Drive	
Case	Lian-Li PC60 Aluminum Mid Tower Case w/ Nspire extreme 750 Watt PSU
Video	niVidia GTX280 1GB PCI-Express Video Card
Audio	Onboard Sound
LAN	Onboard Gigagit NIC
Optical Drive	LG GGW-H20L Blue Ray Burner

Warranty

Parts	1 year limited
Labor	3 year limited

Figure 1-39 GIM Computer sells preassembled systems to tech-savvy customers
Courtesy: Course Technology/Cengage Learning

CHAPTER 2

Introducing Operating Systems

In Chapter 1, you were introduced to the different hardware devices. In this chapter, you'll learn about the different operating systems, how they are designed and work, and what they do. You'll learn about the different components of an OS and see how an OS provides the interface that users and applications need to command and use hardware devices. You'll learn to use several Windows tools and utilities that are useful to examine a system, change desktop settings, and view and manage some hardware devices.

As you work through this chapter, you'll learn that computer systems contain both hardware and software and that it's important for you as a computer technician to understand how they work together. Although the physical hardware is the visible part of a computer system, the software is the intelligence of the system that makes it possible for hardware components to work.

OPERATING SYSTEMS PAST AND PRESENT

An operating system (OS) is software that controls a computer. It manages hardware, runs applications, provides an interface for users, and stores, retrieves, and manipulates files. In general, you can think of an operating system as the middleman between applications and hardware, between the user and hardware, and between the user and applications (see Figure 2-1).

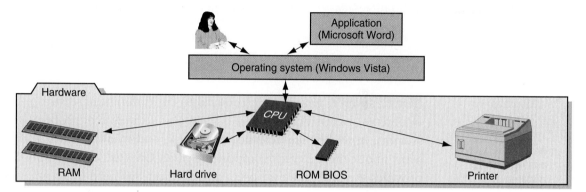

Figure 2-1 Users and applications depend on the OS to relate to all applications and hardware components
Courtesy: Course Technology/Cengage Learning

Several applications might be installed on a computer to meet various user needs, but a computer really needs only one operating system. As a PC support technician, you should be aware of the older and current operating systems and how these operating systems have evolved.

DOS (DISK OPERATING SYSTEM)

In 1986, MS-DOS (also known as DOS) was introduced and quickly became the most popular OS among IBM computers and IBM-compatible computers using the Intel 8086 processors. Figure 2-2 shows a computer screen using the DOS operating system. In those days, all computer screens used text and no graphics. DOS is outdated as a viable option for a desktop computer operating system today. However, you might occasionally encounter a diagnostic utility used to fix the most stubborn hardware or software problem that is booted from a floppy disk or CD that uses the DOS operating system.

```
C:\>DIR \GAME

 Volume in drive C has no label
 Volume Serial Number is 0F52-09FC
 Directory of C:\GAME

 .              <DIR>       02-18-93     4:50a
 ..             <DIR>       02-18-93     4:50a
 CHESS          <DIR>       02-18-93     4:50a
 NUKE           <DIR>       02-18-93     4:51a
 PENTE          <DIR>       02-18-93     4:52a
 NETRIS         <DIR>       02-18-93     4:54a
 BEYOND         <DIR>       02-18-93     4:54a
         7 file(s)              0 bytes
                        9273344 bytes free

 C:\>
```

Figure 2-2 DOS provides a command-line prompt to receive user commands
Courtesy: Course Technology/Cengage Learning

DOS WITH WINDOWS 3.X

Early versions of Windows, including Windows 3.1 and Windows 3.11 (collectively referred to as Windows 3.x) used DOS as the operating system. Windows 3.x had to use DOS because Windows 3.x didn't perform OS functions, but simply served as a user-friendly intermediate program between DOS, applications, and the user (see Figure 2-3). Windows 3.x offered a graphical user interface, the Windows desktop, the windows concept, and the ability to keep more than one application open at the same time. A **graphical user interface** (GUI; pronounced "GOO-ee") is an interface that uses graphics as compared to a command-driven interface. A **desktop** is the initial screen that is displayed when an OS has a GUI interface loaded. All these concepts are still with us today.

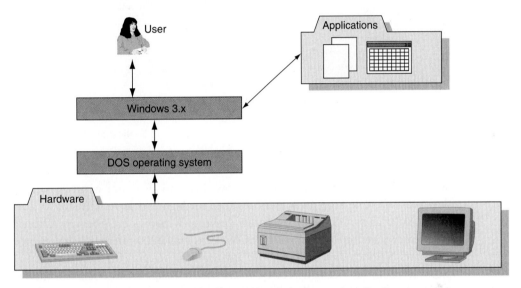

Figure 2-3 Windows 3.x was layered between DOS and the user and applications to provide a graphics interface for the user and a multitasking environment for applications
Courtesy: Course Technology/Cengage Learning

WINDOWS 9X/ME

Windows 95, Windows 98, and Windows Me, collectively called Windows 9x/Me, used some DOS programs as part of the underlying OS (called a DOS core), and therefore had some DOS characteristics. However, these were true operating systems that provided a user-friendly interface shown in Figure 2-4. Because of the DOS core, technicians sometimes used a DOS startup disk to troubleshoot Windows 9x. To learn more about Windows 9x/Me, see the content "Supporting Windows 9x/Me" and the content "Windows 9x/Me Commands and Startup Disk" on the CD that accompanies this book.

WINDOWS NT

Windows NT (New Technology) came in two versions: Windows NT Workstation and Windows NT Server. The workstation version was used on high-end corporate or engineering desktop computers, and the server version was used to control a network. Windows NT corrected many problems with Windows 9x/Me because it completely rewrote the OS core, totally eliminating the DOS core, and introduced many new problems of its own that were later solved by Windows 2000 and Windows XP.

Windows NT was the first Windows OS that did all its processing using 32 bits at a time as compared to DOS, which processed 16 bits at a time and Windows 9x/Me, which used a combination of 16-bit and 32-bit processing.

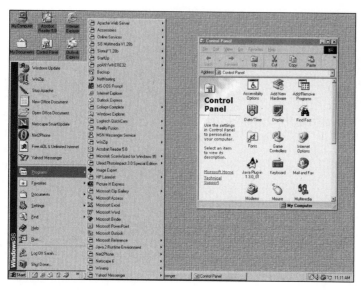

Figure 2-4   Windows 98 SE desktop
Courtesy: Course Technology/Cengage Learning

WINDOWS 2000

Windows 2000 was an upgrade of Windows NT, and also came in several versions, some designed for the desktop and others designed for high-end servers. Windows 2000 Professional was popular as an OS for the corporate desktop. Windows 2000 Server, Advanced Server, and Datacenter Server are network server OSs. Windows 2000 offered several improvements over Windows NT, including a more stable environment, support for Plug and Play, Device Manager, Recovery Console, Active Directory, better network support, and features specifically targeting notebook computers. The Windows 2000 Professional desktop is shown in Figure 2-5.

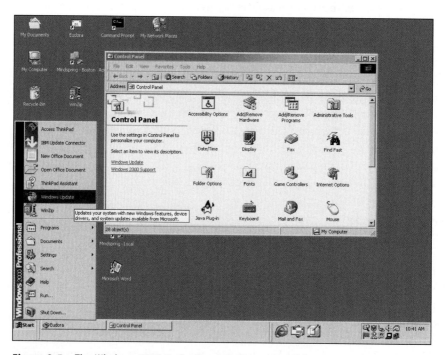

Figure 2-5   The Windows 2000 Professional desktop
Courtesy: Course Technology/Cengage Learning

Microsoft didn't target Windows 2000 to the home computer and game computer market because Windows 9x/Me was still serving those markets. Also, Microsoft did not make a commitment for Windows 2000 to be backward-compatible with older software and hardware. Therefore, many hardware devices and applications that worked under Windows 9x/Me did not work under Windows 2000.

Windows 2000 is considered a dying OS, although as a PC support technician you still need to know how to support it because it is still in use. However, you cannot buy a new license for it, and Microsoft no longer supports it.

> **A+ Tip** The only operating systems covered on the A+ exams are Windows 2000, Windows XP, and Windows Vista.

WINDOWS XP

Windows XP is an upgrade of Windows 2000 and attempts to integrate Windows 9x/Me and 2000, while providing added support for multimedia and networking technologies. The two main versions are Windows XP Home Edition and Windows XP Professional, though other less significant editions include Windows XP Media Center Edition, Windows XP Tablet PC Edition, and Windows XP Professional x64 Edition.

The Windows XP desktop (see Figure 2-6) has a different look from the desktops for earlier Windows. Windows XP is the first Windows OS to allow multiple users to log on simultaneously to the OS, each with their own applications open. Windows Messenger and Windows Media Player are inherent parts of Windows XP. And XP includes several new security features, including Windows Firewall.

Although Windows XP was first released with some bugs, the second service pack (Service Pack 2) resolved most of these problems. A service pack is a major update or fix to an OS occasionally released by Microsoft. Minor updates or fixes that are released more frequently are called patches. Windows XP has undergone three service packs, making it an extremely

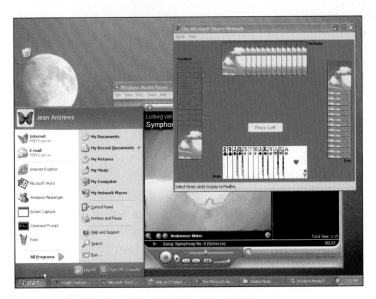

Figure 2-6 The Windows XP desktop and Start menu
Courtesy: Course Technology/Cengage Learning

stable OS, and is popular in both the home and corporate markets. Because it does not require as much hardware resources as Windows Vista and most compatibility issues and bugs have been resolved, many people and corporations still prefer it over Windows Vista. Because of consumers' demands, Microsoft has been forced to extend support for XP long past their initial timeframe. Currently, manufacturers can still purchase a license for a new PC (called an **original equipment manufacturer (OEM) license**). However, these OEM licenses are about to become available only for low-end PCs that cannot support Windows Vista. Microsoft still publishes services packs and patches for XP.

WINDOWS VISTA

Windows Vista, an upgrade to Windows XP, is the latest Windows desktop operating system by Microsoft. Vista has a new 3D user interface called the **Aero user interface**, which is not available for all versions of Vista and requires 1 GB of RAM and a video card or on-board video that supports the DirectX 9 graphics standard and has at least 128 MB of graphics memory. The Windows Vista desktop and Start menu are shown in Figure 2-7. Notice the Windows XP Start button has been replaced by the Vista sphere with a Windows flag.

Figure 2-7   Windows Vista desktop and Start menu
Courtesy: Course Technology/Cengage Learning

Vista was better tested than XP was before its release, therefore Vista did not present as many initial problems as did XP. However, the greatest complaints against Vista are the lack of compatibility with older hardware and software (called legacy hardware and software), the large amount of computer resources that Vista requires, and its slow performance. The first problem is partly caused by hardware manufacturers not providing Vista drivers for their devices that were originally sold with XP drivers. The second problem means that many low-end desktop and laptop computers can't run Vista. And the slow performance of Vista is partly due to the many unnecessary features (fluff) it offers; these features weigh heavy on system resources.

Vista comes in five versions: Windows Vista Home Basic, Home Premium, Business, Enterprise, and Ultimate. (Vista Starter is a sixth version available only to developing nations.) Also, Vista comes in 32-bit versions and 64-bit versions; an explanation of the differences between these versions is covered later in the chapter.

WINDOWS 7

With many frustrations over Windows Vista still not resolved, some consumers have dubbed Windows 7 "the ultimate Vista fix." Windows 7 is the next generation of Microsoft operating systems, and was due to be released not long after the printing of this book. Now that technicians have taken a first look at Windows 7 and have compared it to Vista, it appears that Windows 7 will perform better, be more compatible with legacy hardware and software, and provide a leaner and simpler user interface.

It is expected that Windows 7 will run on netbooks that currently run only on Windows XP or Linux. A **netbook** is a low-end inexpensive laptop with a small 9- or 10-inch screen and no optical drive. Netbooks are generally used for Web browsing, e-mail, and word processing by users on the go.

MAC OS

Currently, the Mac OS, which has its roots in the UNIX OS, is available only on Macintosh computers from the Apple Corporation (*www.apple.com*). The Mac and the Mac OS were first introduced in 1984. The latest OS is Mac OS X (ten), which has had several releases. The latest release is called Mac OS X Leopard. Figure 2-8 shows the Mac OS X Leopard desktop with a browser open.

Figure 2-8 The Mac OS X Leopard desktop and browser window
Courtesy: Course Technology/Cengage Learning

At one time, all Macintosh computers were built using PowerPC processors by IBM or Motorola. Macs now use Intel processors, which make it possible for Windows to run on a Mac. Boot Camp software by Apple can be used to install Windows on a Mac computer as a dual boot with Mac OS X. (A dual boot makes it possible to boot a computer into one of two installed OSs.) Also, an application called VMWare Fusion can be installed on a Mac; the application creates a virtual machine on the Mac. (A virtual machine (VM) is an environment created by software that works as though it is a standalone computer system. A VM is a logical computer within a physical computer. Software testers often use multiple VMs on a single PC to test software under different OSs.) Windows is then installed on this virtual machine, making it possible to run both Mac OS X and Windows at the same time without having to reboot the system. Applications written for Windows can then be installed in the virtual machine environment. You will learn to use a virtual machine in a project at the end of Chapter 12.

Because it is stable and easy to use, the Mac OS has been popular in educational environments, from elementary school through the university level. It also provides excellent support for graphics and multimedia applications and is popular in the graphics and musical markets. Currently, about 10 percent of personal computers sold today are Macs. In the past, a Mac was more expensive than a comparable Windows computer and applications for the Mac were limited. But now costs are about the same and tons of Mac applications exist, many of them free. Macs are beginning to gain ground in both the corporate and home markets because Macs are stable and fun to use, costs are down, and software is more available.

> **Notes** You can learn more about the Mac OS by reading the content "Introducing the Mac OS," which you can find on the CD that accompanies this book.

LINUX

Linux is a variation of UNIX that was created by Linus Torvalds when he was a student at the University of Helsinki in Finland. Versions of this OS are available for free, and all the underlying programming instructions (called source code) are also freely distributed. Like UNIX, Linux is distributed by several different companies, whose versions of Linux are sometimes called distributions. Popular distributions of Linux include SuSE (*www.novell.com/linux/suse*), RedHat (*www.redhat.com*), TurboLinux (*www.turbolinux.com*), Slackware Linux (*www.slackware.com*), and Ubuntu (*www.ubuntu.com*).

> **A+ Exam Tip** The A+ exams do not cover Linux, the Mac OS, or server operating systems.

Network services such as a Web server or e-mail server often are provided by a computer running the Linux operating system. Linux is well suited to support various types of server applications. Because Linux is extremely reliable and does not require a lot of computing power, it is sometimes used as a desktop OS. It is not as popular for this purpose because it is not easy to install or use and fewer Linux applications exist, as compared to those written for Windows or the Mac OS. Linux is also used on netbooks because it requires less system resources than Windows. (A technician would say it has a small footprint.) Recently, Linux has gained popularity as an embedded operating system on mobile devices such as smart phones. Linux is an excellent training tool for learning UNIX.

A shell is the portion of an OS that relates to the user and to applications. The first Linux and UNIX shells consisted of commands entered at a command prompt. Two popular command-line shells for UNIX and Linux are the older Bourne shell and the newer Bourne-Again shell (BASH). But many users prefer a Windows-style GUI desktop. These GUI shells are built using a technology called X Windows. The most popular GUI shells are GNOME, KDE, and Xfce. A typical Linux desktop is shown in Figure 2-9.

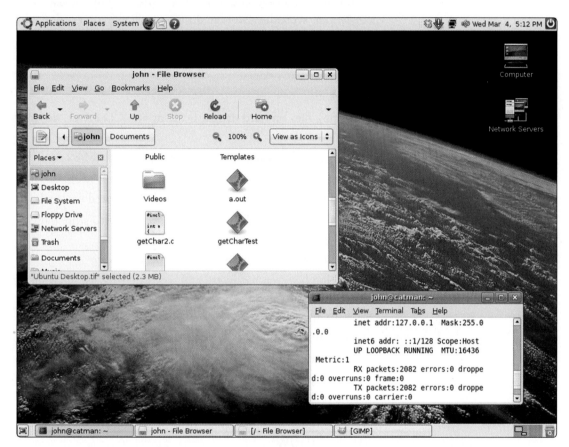

Figure 2-9 A desktop using the Ubuntu distribution of Linux
Courtesy: Course Technology/Cengage Learning

> **Notes** You can find out more about Linux by reading the content "Introducing Linux" on the CD that accompanies this book or by visiting the Web site, *www.linux.org*.

Now that you know a little about operating systems in general, let's turn our attention to learning about the Windows 2000/XP/Vista operating system.

HOW WINDOWS 2000/XP/VISTA WORKS

Windows 2000, XP, and Vista are three evolutions of the same basic operating system. Therefore, they have many things in common. In this part of the chapter, we'll look under the hood of these OSs to see how they are built, what are the main components, and how the OS interfaces with users, applications, data, and hardware. We begin our discussion by looking at the four main functions of any OS, and then we'll look at how Windows accomplishes these four functions.

WHAT AN OPERATING SYSTEM DOES

Although there are important differences among them, all operating systems share the following four main functions:

▲ *Function 1.* Provide a user interface

- Performing housekeeping procedures requested by the user, often concerning secondary storage devices, such as reorganizing a hard drive, deleting files, copying files, and changing the system date
- Providing a way for the user to manage the desktop, hardware, applications, and data

▲ *Function 2.* Manage files

- Managing files on hard drives, DVD drives, CD drives, floppy drives, and other drives
- Creating, storing, retrieving, deleting, and moving files

▲ *Function 3.* Manage hardware

- Managing the BIOS (programs permanently stored on hardware devices)
- Managing memory, which is a temporary place to store data and instructions as they are being processed
- Diagnosing problems with software and hardware
- Interfacing between hardware and software (that is, interpreting application software needs to the hardware and interpreting hardware needs to application software)

▲ *Function 4.* Manage applications

- Installing and uninstalling applications
- Running applications and managing the interface to the hardware on behalf of an application

COMPONENTS OF WINDOWS

Every operating system has three main internal components: the shell, the kernel, and configuration data. Recall that a shell is the portion of an OS that relates to the user and to applications; the kernel is responsible for interacting with hardware. Configuration data is information the OS keeps about hardware, applications, data, and users. As a support technician, you don't need to understand all of how they work, but it does help to know some basic concepts. Figure 2-10 shows how the shell and kernel relate to users, applications, and hardware. Use the diagram as a reference for this discussion of how the components of Windows work.

THE WINDOWS SHELL

The shell provides a way for the user to do such things as select music to burn to a CD, install an application, or change the wallpaper on the Windows desktop. The shell does this using various interface tools such as Windows Explorer, the Control Panel, or My Computer, which can have command, menu, or icon-driven interfaces for the user. For applications, the shell provides commands and procedures that applications can call on to do such things as print a spreadsheet, read from a database, or display a photograph on-screen.

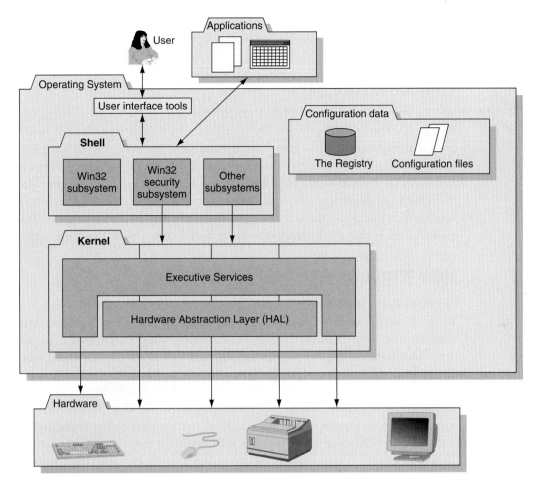

Figure 2-10 Inside an operating system, different components perform various functions
Courtesy: Course Technology/Cengage Learning

The shell is made up of several subsystems that all operate in **user mode**, which means these subsystems have only limited access to system information and can access hardware only through other OS services. One of these subsystems, the Win32 security subsystem, provides logon to the system and other security functions, including privileges for file access. All applications relate to Windows by way of the Win32 subsystem.

THE WINDOWS KERNEL

The kernel, or core, of the OS is responsible for interacting with hardware. It has more power to communicate with hardware devices than the shell has, and operates in **kernel mode**. Therefore, applications operating under the OS cannot get to hardware devices without the shell passing those requests to the kernel. This module approach that says, "You do your job and I'll do mine, and we won't mess with each other's work," provides for a more stable system. If you think of an OS as a restaurant, the shell is like the hosts and waiters that serve customers, and the kernel is like the chefs and kitchen staff. Hosts and waiters are responsible for customer interaction but aren't allowed in the kitchen where the food is prepared.

The kernel has two main components. The **HAL (hardware abstraction layer)** is the layer closest to the hardware and the **executive services** interface between the subsystems in user mode and the HAL. Executive services components manage hardware resources by way of the HAL and device drivers. When Windows is first installed, it builds the

HAL based on the type of CPU installed. The HAL cannot be moved from one computer to another, which is one reason you cannot copy a Windows installation from one computer to another.

CONFIGURATION DATA

An operating system needs a place to keep hardware and software configuration information, user preferences, and application settings. This information is used when the OS is first loaded and when needed by hardware, applications, and users. Windows uses a database called the Registry for most of this information. In addition, Windows keeps some data in text files called initialization files, which often have an .ini or .inf file extension. For example, an application might store in a text file or in the Registry the settings preferred by the last user, such as background color, font, and text size. When the application is launched, the first thing it does is read the Registry or text file and then loads the user's preferred settings.

HOW WINDOWS MANAGES APPLICATIONS

When an application is first installed, its program files are normally stored on the hard drive. When the application is launched, the program is copied from the hard drive into memory and there it is called a process. A **process** is a program that is running, together with the system resources assigned to it. System resources might include other programs it has started and memory addresses to hold its data. When the process makes a request for resources to be used, this request is made to the Win32 subsystem and is called a thread. A thread is a single task, such as the task of printing a file, that the process requests from the kernel. Figure 2-11 shows two threads in action, which is called multithreading. Sometimes a process is called an instance, such as when you say to a user, "Open two instances of Internet Explorer." Technically, you are saying to open two Internet Explorer processes.

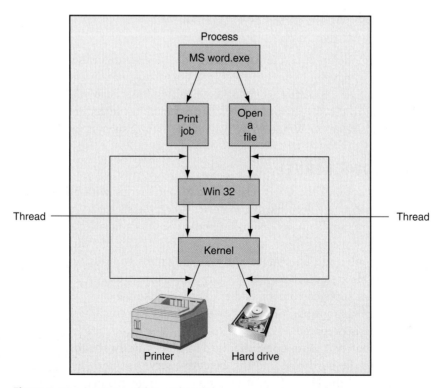

Figure 2-11 A process with two threads
Courtesy: Course Technology/Cengage Learning

HOW WINDOWS MANAGES HARDWARE

The kernel uses device drivers to communicate with a hardware device. Device drivers are small programs stored on the hard drive that tell the computer how to communicate with a specific hardware device such as a printer, network card, or modem. These drivers are installed on the hard drive when the OS is first installed, or when new hardware is added to the system.

The OS provides some device drivers, and the manufacturer of the hardware device provides others. You also need to know that when a computer is first turned on, it uses some devices such as the keyboard, monitor, and hard drive before the OS starts up. In this situation, the system BIOS provides the instructions to the CPU to communicate with these devices. Recall from Chapter 1 that the system BIOS uses settings stored in the CMOS RAM chip on the motherboard to know how to start the system.

Later during the boot process, the OS is started, and it then uses device drivers to communicate with these same devices, although there still might be limited use of the system BIOS. Figure 2-12 shows that the kernel communicates with hardware by way of its own drivers, manufacturer drivers, or system BIOS.

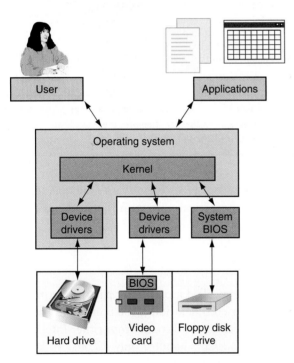

Figure 2-12 An OS relates to hardware by way of device drivers and possibly system BIOS
Courtesy: Course Technology/Cengage Learning

A device driver is written to work for a specific OS, such as Windows XP or Windows Vista. Therefore, when you upgrade a computer from Windows XP to Windows Vista, it is necessary to obtain Vista drivers for each installed device. Manufacturers usually publish the latest device drivers on their Web sites.

When you purchase a printer, DVD drive, Zip drive, digital camera, scanner, or other hardware device, bundled with the device might be a CD that contains the device drivers (see Figure 2-13). Sometimes, the device also comes bundled with a user manual and applications software that interfaces with the device. You use the operating system to install the device drivers so it will have the necessary software to control the device. You will learn how to install devices and their drivers in Chapter 9.

Figure 2-13   A device such as this video card comes packaged with its device drivers stored on a CD; alternately, you can use device drivers built into the OS
Courtesy: Course Technology/Cengage Learning

Notes Device drivers come from a number of sources. Some come with and are part of the operating system, some come with hardware devices when they are purchased, and some are provided for downloading over the Internet from a device manufacturer's Web site.

So now you have been introduced to four types of software: the operating system, applications, device drivers, and BIOS. Every software program is considered to be one of these four types of software.

HOW MANY BITS AT A TIME?

A+
220-701
3.1

The CPU (Central Processing Unit), also called a processor, partly determines which operating system can be installed. One major consideration is the number of bits a CPU processes at a time. All desktop and laptop processors sold today from either Intel or AMD can process 64 bits at a time, but older processors handled only 32 bits. To know which type of operating system to install, you need to be aware of three categories of processors currently used on desktop and laptop computers:

- *32-bit processors*. These are known as x86 processors because Intel used the number 86 in the model number of these earlier processors. These processors must use a 32-bit operating system.
- *Processors that use underlying 32-bit processing with 64-bit instructions*. These hybrid processors are known as x86-64bit processors. AMD was the first to produce one (the Athlon 64) and called the technology AMD64. Intel followed with a version of its Pentium 4 processors and called the technology Extended Memory 64 Technology (EM64T). Because of their hybrid nature, these processors can handle a 32-bit OS or a 64-bit OS. All desktop or laptop processors made after 2007 are of this type.
- *64-bit processors*. Intel makes several 64-bit processors for workstations or servers that use fully implemented 64-bit processing, including the Itanium and Xeon processors.

Intel calls the technology IA64, but they are also called x64 processors. They are not compatible with 32-bit processing and require a 64-bit operating system.

Windows 2000 is a 32-bit OS. Windows XP Professional x64 Edition is a 64-bit OS, and all other Windows XP editions are 32-bit operating systems. Vista Home Basic, Home Premium, Business, Enterprise, and Ultimate editions all come in either 32-bit or 64-bit versions. When you purchase of the retail version of the Ultimate Edition, the 32-bit DVD and 64-bit DVD are included in the package. For the other Vista editions, you must request the 64-bit DVD from Microsoft after you have purchased the retail version of the OS. The OEM version of each Vista OS can be purchased in 32-bit or 64-bit code.

Most modern desktop and laptop processors today can handle either a 32-bit or 64-bit OS, which are sometimes referred to as an x86 or x64 OS. Keep these discussion points in mind when deciding which to install:

▲ *Point 1.* 64-bit processing is faster than 32-bit processing because the CPU is handling more bits at once. However, a 64-bit OS requires more resources than a 32-bit OS.

▲ *Point 2.* A 64-bit OS requires that device drivers operating in kernel mode be 64-bit drivers. These 64-bit drivers must be available from the device manufacturer.

▲ *Point 3.* An application is compiled to process 64 bits or 32 bits. A 64-bit OS can run either 64-bit applications or 32-bit applications, but 64-bit applications are faster. Also, 64-bit applications cannot run on a 32-bit OS.

▲ *Point 4.* A 32-bit OS can only address up to 4 GB of memory. More than that might be installed on the motherboard, but the OS cannot use it because it does not have enough memory addresses to assign to the physical memory. A 64-bit OS theoretically can address up to 1 terabyte (TB) of memory, although in practice, most motherboards can only hold from 12 to 16 GB of memory. (A terabyte is roughly 1000 GB or 1 trillion bytes).

▲ *Point 5.* If you open many applications at the same time and have high computing needs and enough hard drive space and memory, you can benefit from 64-bit computing. To get the most out of it, the processor, motherboard, operating system, drivers, and applications must all be 64 bit, and you should have installed the maximum amount of memory the motherboard supports.

Often a manufacturer will install a 32-bit OS on a computer that could support a 64-bit OS. In Vista, to find out what type of processor and OS is installed, click **Start**, right-click **Computer**, and select **Properties** from the shortcut menu. Figure 2-14 shows the results for one laptop. It shows a 32-bit operating system installed with a Core2 Duo CPU. This CPU could have handled a 64-bit OS.

Here's one more important tip you need to know about 64-bit computing. When Microsoft publishes a patch or update for Windows on its Web site, some patches are designated for specific processors, and error messages use terminology that might be confusing if you don't understand the terms. Follow these guidelines when reading error messages or documentation on the Microsoft site:

▲ The term x86 refers to 32-bit processors and to 32-bit operating systems. For example, you need to download a patch from Microsoft to fix a Vista problem you are having with USB devices. The article on the Microsoft Web site that applies to your problem says to download the patch if you are using a Windows Vista, x86-based version. Take that to mean you can use this patch if you are using a 32-bit version of Vista.

▲ The term x86-64 refers to a 64-bit OS or to 32-bit processors that process 64-bit instructions such as the Intel Core2 Duo or 64-bit AMD processors (AMD64 refers specifically to these AMD processors). For example, a Windows error message might be, "You are attempting to load an x86-64 operating system." Take that to mean you

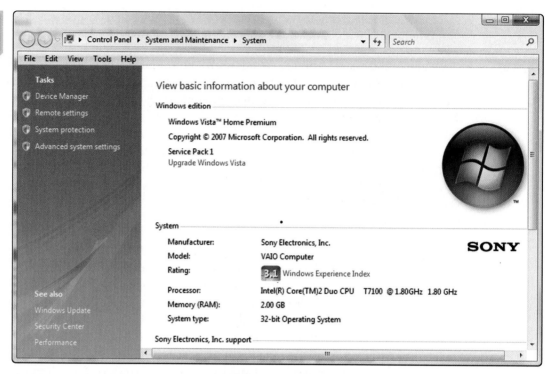

Figure 2-14   A 32-bit version of Vista is installed with a 64-bit processor
Courtesy: Course Technology/Cengage Learning

are attempting to load a 64-bit OS onto a computer that has a hybrid 32-bit/64-bit processor installed, such as the Athlon 64 or Intel Core2 Duo.

◢ The term IA64 refers specifically to 64-bit Intel processors such as the Xeon or Itanium. For example, you are selecting a utility to download from the Microsoft Web site. One choice for the utility specifies an IA64 platform. Only select this choice if you have installed an Itanium or Xeon processor. (By the way, a techie uses the word platform to mean the hardware and software on which other software is running. In this context, the operating system's platform is the processor.)

◢ The term x64 refers to 64-bit operating systems. For example, Microsoft offers two versions of Vista Home Premium: the x86 version and the x64 version.

> 💡 **A+ Tip**   The A+ 220-701 Essentials exam expects you to know the difference between Windows XP and Windows Vista 32-bit and 64-bit versions. You are also expected to be familiar with the terms 32-bit, 64-bit, x86, and x64.

Now that you have a general idea of how Windows manages applications, hardware, users, and their data, let's look at some of the tools for using Windows.

USING WINDOWS 2000/XP/VISTA

Every PC support technician needs to be a power user of Windows. You need to know how the Windows desktop is organized and how it works. You also need to know how to use Windows utilities such as My Computer, Windows Explorer, the Control Panel, System Information, and the Command Prompt window. All these tools are covered in this part of the chapter. In other chapters, you'll learn to use more Windows tools.

A+
220-701
3.1
3.2

2

A+ 220-701

THE WINDOWS VISTA DESKTOP

The Windows desktop is the primary tool provided by the Windows shell. In this section, you will learn about the features of the desktop, including the Start menu, taskbar, and Vista sidebar. You will also learn how to manage shortcuts and icons on the desktop. We'll use Vista as our primary OS for learning and then discuss what is different about the Windows XP and 2000 desktops.

THE START MENU

The Vista Start menu is shown in Figure 2-15. Notice in the figure that the username for the person currently logged on is shown at the top right of the Start menu.

Figure 2-15   The Vista desktop and Start menu
Courtesy: Course Technology/Cengage Learning

Applications at the top left of the Start menu are said to be "pinned" to the menu—in other words, permanently listed there until you change them in a Start menu setting. Applications that are used often are listed below the pinned applications and can change from time to time. The programs in the white column on the left side of the Start menu are user-oriented applications. Entries in the black column on the right side of the menu give access to user files and OS utilities.

THE VISTA SIDEBAR AND GADGETS

The Windows Sidebar and gadgets for the Vista desktop are new with Windows Vista. If the sidebar is not installed, you can use the Control Panel to install it. Click **Start** and click **Control Panel**. In the Control Panel window, click **Appearances and Personalization** and then click

Windows Sidebar Properties. From the properties box, you can choose to start the sidebar each time Windows starts, decide where on the desktop the sidebar appears, and remove the gadgets currently in the sidebar. To add new gadgets, click the + sign at the top left of the sidebar. A window of gadgets appears (see Figure 2-16). Drag a gadget from this window to the sidebar.

Figure 2-16 Windows Sidebar can be customized with installed and downloaded gadgets
Courtesy: Course Technology/Cengage Learning

HOW TO LAUNCH AN APPLICATION

Let's open a few applications and then see how the Windows desktop can be used to manage these open applications. Four options to open an application are:

▲ *Use the Start menu.* Click the **Start** button, select **All Programs**, and then select the program from the list of installed software.
▲ *Use the Search box.* Click the **Start** button, and then enter the name of the program file or command in the Start Search box (see Figure 2-17). In Windows 2000/XP, use the Run dialog box. Incidentally, the Vista search box can also find data files and folders and will search text within document files.
▲ *Use Windows Explorer or the Computer window.* Execute a program or launch an application file by double-clicking the filename in Windows Explorer or the Computer window.

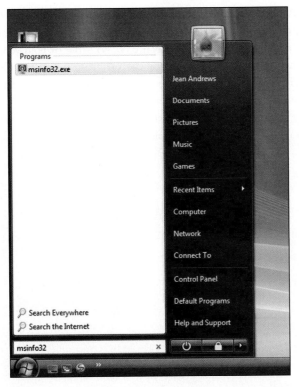

Figure 2-17 Use the Vista Search box to launch a program
Courtesy: Course Technology/Cengage Learning

(In Windows XP, the Computer window is called My Computer.) To use the Computer window, click **Start, Computer.** The Computer window shown in Figure 2-18 appears. Double-click the drive on which the program file is stored. In our example, we double-clicked **Local Disk (C:).** Then drive down to the program file on the drive. Double-click the program file to launch it.

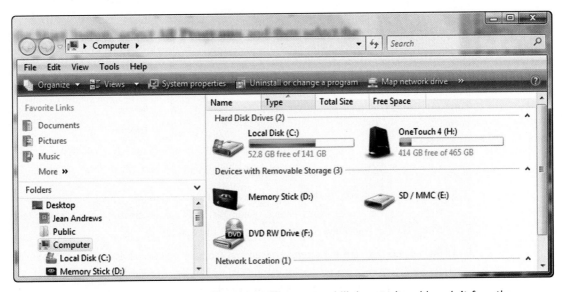

Figure 2-18 If you know the location of a program file, you can drill down to it and launch it from the Computer window
Courtesy: Course Technology/Cengage Learning

A+
220-701
3.1
3.2

◢ *Use a shortcut icon.* A quick way to open an application you use often is to place a shortcut icon to the program on the desktop. A shortcut icon is a clickable item on the desktop that points to a program you can execute, or to a file or folder. One way to create a shortcut for a program is to right-click the program file in the Computer or Windows Explorer window and select Create Shortcut from the menu that appears.

APPLYING CONCEPTS

Follow these steps to launch three instances of Microsoft Paint:

1. From the Start menu, launch the Paint program, which is in the Accessories folder.

2. The program file is mspaint.exe. Use the Search box to launch the program.

3. The program file is normally located at C:\Windows\System32. Use the Computer window to drill down to and launch the program.

To create and use a shortcut to the Microsoft Paint program, follow these steps:

1. In the Computer window, drill down to the mspaint.exe file in the C:\Windows\System32 folder.

2. Right-click it and select **Create Shortcut** (see Figure 2-19).

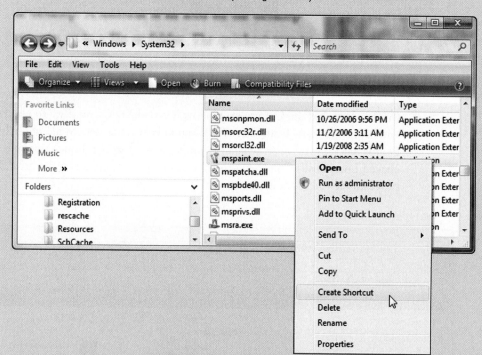

Figure 2-19 Create a shortcut
Courtesy: Course Technology/Cengage Learning

3. If a dialog box appears saying, "Windows cannot create a shortcut here. Do you want the shortcut to be placed on the desktop instead?" click **Yes**. (If Windows creates a shortcut in the folder where the file is located, drag the shortcut to the desktop.)

4. On the desktop, to see the properties of the shortcut, right-click it and select **Properties**. Figure 2-20 shows the properties of the Microsoft Paint shortcut icon, which points to the program in the E:\Windows\System32 folder.

5. Use the shortcut to launch Microsoft Paint.

A+
220-701
3.1
3.2

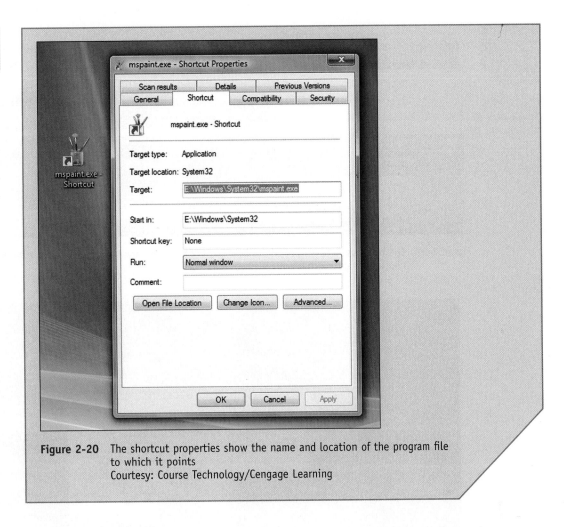

Figure 2-20 The shortcut properties show the name and location of the program file to which it points
Courtesy: Course Technology/Cengage Learning

If you're following along at your computer while reading this chapter, you might want to leave the instances of Microsoft Paint open so you can practice managing open applications in the sections that follow.

A+
220-701
3.2

THE TASKBAR AND NOTIFICATION AREA (SYSTEM TRAY)

The **taskbar** is normally located at the bottom of the Windows desktop, displaying information about open programs and providing quick access to others (see Figure 2-21). Items displayed in the taskbar can be programs running or not running. An open application displays its title in the taskbar (see Figure 2-21). If you are using the Aero interface, when you hover over the title, a thumbnail of the open application appears. Quick Launch icons on the left are displayed in the taskbar so you can quickly find and launch them. Click the double right arrow to the right of the Quick Launch area to reveal more icons.

> **Notes** To get a flip view of applications, press **Alt+Tab**, and to minimize all applications, click **Show the Desktop** in the Quick Launch area. If you are using the Aero interface, in the Quick Launch area, click the **Switch between windows** icon to see the flip 3D view of open applications (see Figure 2-22). Alternately, you can press **Win+Tab** (the Windows key and the Tab key). Then use the Tab key to move from one open application to another.

The **notification area**, also called the **system tray** or **systray**, is usually on the right side of the taskbar and displays open services. A **service** is a program that runs in the background to

A+
220-701
3.2

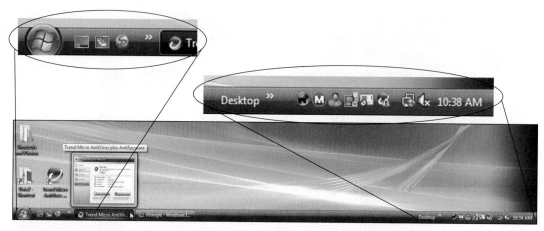

Figure 2-21 The Windows Vista taskbar with a thumbnail of one open application
Courtesy: Course Technology/Cengage Learning

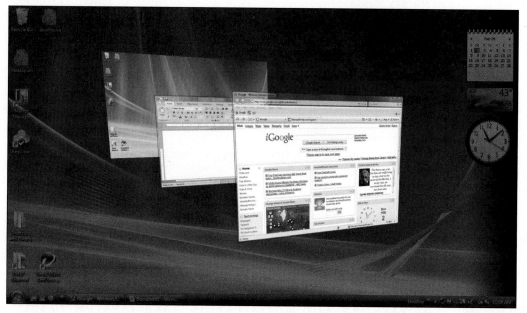

Figure 2-22 Press Win+Tab to view open applications in a flip 3D view when using the Vista Aero interface
Courtesy: Course Technology/Cengage Learning

support or serve Windows or an application. The services in the notification area include the volume control and network connectivity. Windows automatically hides these icons. To display them, click the left arrow on the right side of the taskbar. If you have a sluggish Windows system, one thing you can do is look at all the running services in the notification tray and try to disable the services that are taking up system resources. How to do that is covered in later chapters.

Notes Microsoft insists that using the term system tray or systray for the notification area is wrong, although in some Microsoft documentation, you'll find these terms used.

To control the Start menu, taskbar, notification area, and open applications, right-click the taskbar and use the shortcut menu. Using it, you can turn the Quick Launch display on or off, add items to the taskbar, control the way open windows appear on the desktop, and, if you unlock the taskbar, you can move it to other places on the screen. When you choose

A+
220-701
3.2

Properties from this shortcut menu, the Taskbar and Start Menu Properties dialog box appears (see Figure 2-23). Using it, you can further control the Start menu and the taskbar.

Figure 2-23   Use the Taskbar and Start Menu Properties window to control what appears in the Start menu and taskbar
Courtesy: Course Technology/Cengage Learning

💡 **A+ Exam Tip**   The A+ 220-701 Essentials exam expects you to know how to configure and use the Start Menu, taskbar, and notification area, also called the systray.

PERSONALIZE THE WINDOWS DESKTOP

You can also personalize the desktop. To use the Personalization window, right-click anywhere on the desktop, and choose **Personalize** from the shortcut menu (see Figure 2-24). Using this window, you can personalize the way Windows appears, including the desktop, sounds, mouse action, color themes, and display settings. As a support technician, you are often called on to solve problems with display settings. When and how to change these settings are covered in Chapter 9.

DEFAULT PROGRAMS AND FILE ASSOCIATIONS

A+
220-701
3.3

The Default Programs entry in the right column of the Start menu accesses the Default Program window to change default programs associated with certain file extensions and activities. For example, look at the top left of the Start menu column in Figure 2-15, and you can see that the current default browser is Internet Explorer and the default e-mail software is Windows Mail. You can use the Default Programs window to change these applications to another browser or e-mail software. You can also use this window to change the way audio CDs, DVD movies, games, pictures, video files, and audio files are handled and to change the default program associated with a certain file extension. A file extension is one or more characters following the last period in a filename, such as .exe, .txt, or .avi. The file extension indicates how the file is organized or formatted, the type content in the file, and what program uses the file. For example, the .avi file extension is a video file that is normally played by Windows Media Player.

A+
220-701
3.3

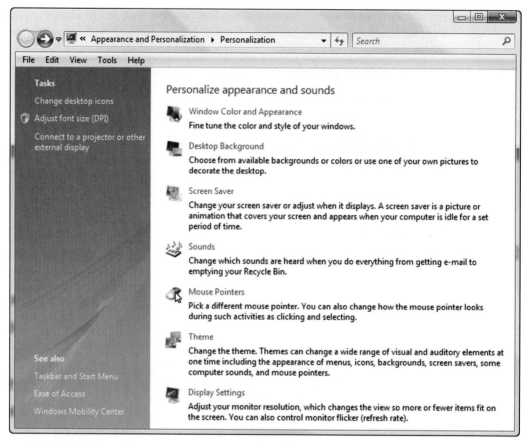

Figure 2-24 Use the Personalization window to change the appearance of Windows
Courtesy: Course Technology/Cengage Learning

Follow these steps to use the Default Programs window to change the program associated with a file extension:

1. Click **Start** and then click **Default Programs**. The Default Programs window opens (see Figure 2-25).

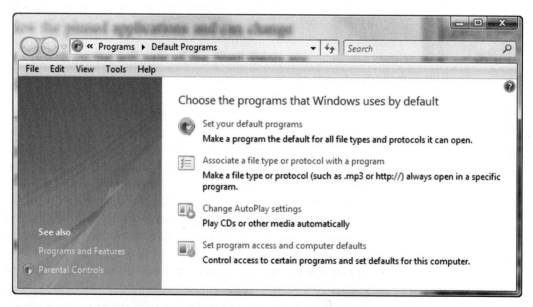

Figure 2-25 The Default Programs window is used to change file associations
Courtesy: Course Technology/Cengage Learning

A+
220-701
3.3

2. Click **Associate a file type or protocol with a program**. The list of current associations appears.

3. Select the file extension you want to change and click **Change program**. The Open With dialog box appears (see Figure 2-26).

4. The box displays installed programs that can handle .avi files. Make your selection and click **OK** and then click **Close**. Close the Default Programs window.

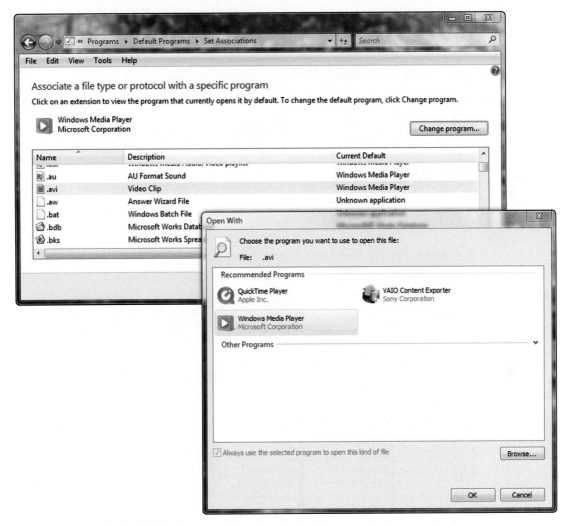

Figure 2-26 Select the default program to play an .avi video file
Courtesy: Course Technology/Cengage Learning

A+
220-701
3.1
3.2

DIFFERENCES IN THE WINDOWS XP/2000 DESKTOP AND THE VISTA DESKTOP

Comparing the Windows XP desktop shown in Figure 2-27 to the Vista desktop, you can see many similarities. When you point to **All Programs** in Figure 2-27, the list of currently installed software appears. Figure 2-28 shows the default entries that appear when you point to **Accessories** and then **System Tools**. You can use these tools to back up data, clean up a hard drive, schedule tasks, restore Windows settings, and do various other things when solving problems with Windows. In Vista, the System Tools group includes all the XP tools plus a new one: Internet Explorer (No Add-ons). This tool makes it possible to open Internet Explorer in its bare-bones state with no add-ons running; this state is useful when troubleshooting. Windows 2000 menus are organized similar to those of Windows XP.

A+
220-701
3.1
3.2

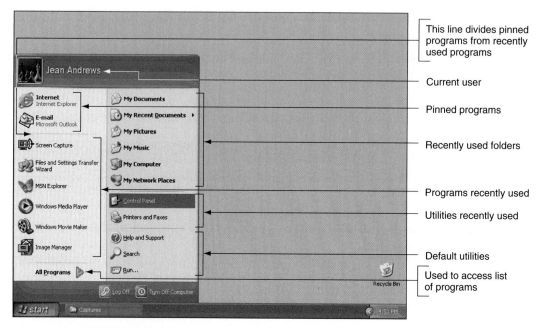

Figure 2-27 The Windows XP desktop and Start menu
Courtesy: Course Technology/Cengage Learning

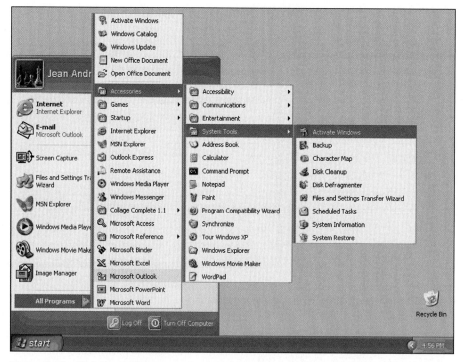

Figure 2-28 Click Start, All Programs to view the list of currently installed software
Courtesy: Course Technology/Cengage Learning

You can control the Start menu and taskbar in Windows XP/2000 in a similar way as in Vista. However, Windows XP/2000 uses the Display Properties window rather than the Personalization window of Vista to control the appearance of Windows. You access the window the same way as the Personalization window of Vista: Right-click the desktop and select Properties from the shortcut menu (see Figure 2-29). The left side of Figure 2-29 shows the Desktop tab of the Display Properties window for Windows XP.

A+
220-701
3.1
3.2

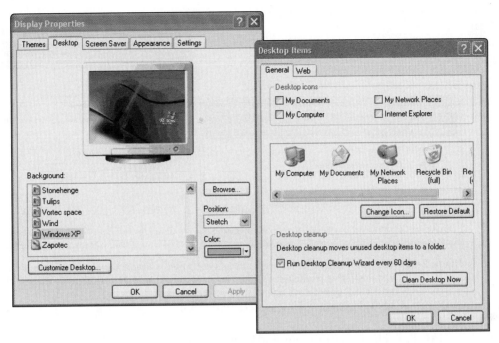

Figure 2-29 Windows XP Display Properties window lets you change settings for your desktop
Courtesy: Course Technology/Cengage Learning

The right side of Figure 2-29 shows the dialog box that appears when you click Customize Desktop. You can accomplish about the same things using the Vista Personalization window and the XP Display Properties window, but they are organized differently. For Windows 2000, the Taskbar and Start Menu Properties window and the Display Properties window are organized slightly differently than for Windows XP, but both work about the same as in XP.

When you first install Windows XP, only the Recycle Bin shows on the desktop by default. You can add other shortcuts by using the Display Properties window. In the window, click the **Desktop tab and then** click **Customize Desktop** to display the Desktop Items window, which is shown in Figure 2-29. You can check My Documents, My Computer, My Network Places, and Internet Explorer to add these icons to the desktop. Also notice on this window the option to have Windows clean up your desktop by moving any shortcuts that you have not used in the last 60 days to a separate folder.

VISTA USER ACCOUNT CONTROL BOX

A+
220-701
3.1

A new security feature introduced with Windows Vista is the User Account Control (UAC) dialog box, shown in Figure 2-30. This box appears each time a user attempts to perform an action that can be done only with administrative privileges. In Vista, there are two types of user accounts: An administrator account and a standard account. An administrator account has more privileges than a standard account and is used by those responsible for maintaining and securing the system. When the UAC box appears, if a user is logged on as an administrator, all she has to do is click Continue to close the box and move on, as shown in Figure 2-30(a). If the user account does not have administrative privileges, the user has the opportunity to enter a password of an administrative account to continue, as shown in Figure 2-30(b).

The purposes of the UAC box are: (1) to prevent malicious background tasks from doing harm when the administrator is logged on, and (2) to make it easier for an administrator to log in using a less powerful user account for normal desktop activities, but still be able to perform administrative tasks while logged in as a regular user. It is possible to disable the

(a)

(b)

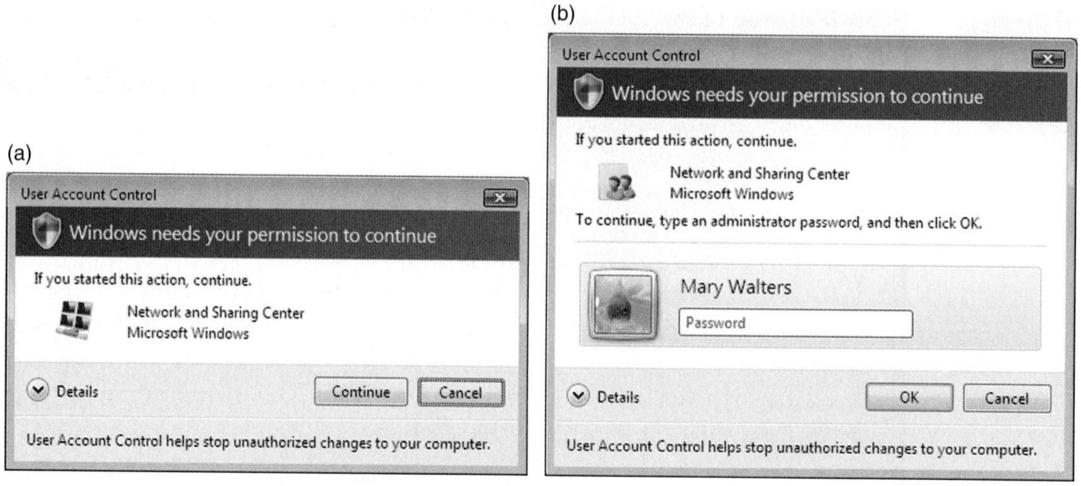

Figure 2-30 The User Account Control box appears each time a user attempts to perform an action requiring administrative privileges: (a) the current account has administrative privileges; (b) the current account does not have administrative privileges
Courtesy: Course Technology/Cengage Learning

UAC box, but for security purposes, that is not recommended. For example, suppose someone is logged on as an administrator with the UAC box turned off and clicks a malicious link on a Web site. Malware can download and install itself without the user's knowledge and might get admin privileges on the computer. If he's logged on as a standard user and the UAC box is turned off, the malware might still install without the user's knowledge but with lesser privileges. The UAC box stands as a gatekeeper to malware installing behind your back because someone has to click the UAC box before the installation can proceed.

It's interesting to know the color codes that the UAC box uses to help you decide if software being installed is safe:

- ◢ If the top of the UAC box is red, Vista does not trust this program one bit and is not happy with you installing it. In fact, it refuses to allow the installation to continue.
- ◢ If the top of the UAC box is yellow (see Figure 2-31), Vista doesn't know or trust the publisher. It will allow you to continue, but with a serious warning.

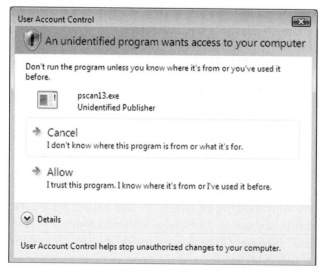

Figure 2-31 This UAC box using a yellow bar indicates the program has not been approved by Microsoft
Courtesy: Course Technology/Cengage Learning

▲ If the top of the UAC box is green, Vista is happy to accept one of its own Windows components to be installed.

▲ If the top of the UAC box is gray, the program has signed in with Microsoft and Vista is happy to install it.

WINDOWS EXPLORER AND THE COMPUTER WINDOW

The two most useful tools to explore files and folders on your computer are Windows Explorer and the Vista Computer window. (Windows 2000/XP calls the Computer window the My Computer window.) With Windows Vista and Windows XP, these windows are really the same tools with different names. Under Windows 2000, there are slight differences between the My Computer window and Windows Explorer. Because all the windows work about the same way, in this part of the chapter we'll cover them for all three operating systems together.

To access the Computer or My Computer window, use one of these methods:

▲ For Windows Vista, click **Start** and click **Computer**.

▲ For Windows XP, click **Start** and click **My Computer**.

▲ For Windows 2000, double-click **My Computer** on the desktop.

Earlier in the chapter, you saw the Vista Computer window in Figure 2-18. Figure 2-32 shows the Windows XP My Computer window, which looks the same as the Windows 2000 My Computer window.

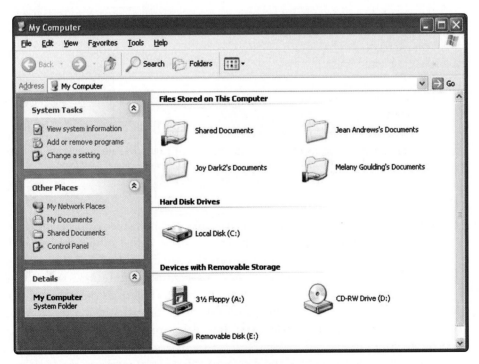

Figure 2-32 Use Windows XP My Computer to manage system resources
Courtesy: Course Technology/Cengage Learning

Regardless of the OS, Windows Explorer is easily opened in these two ways:

▲ Right-click **Computer** or **My Computer** and select **Explore** from the menu.

▲ Right-click **Start** and select **Explore** from the menu.

A+
220-701
3.2
3.3

A+
220-701
3.3

Let's now turn our attention to how to use the Computer, My Computer, and Explorer windows in all three OSs to manage files and folders and other system resources.

FILES AND DIRECTORIES

Every OS manages a hard drive, optical drive, floppy disk, or USB drive by using directories (also called folders), subdirectories, and files. The drive is organized with a single **root directory** at the top of the top-down hierarchical structure of subdirectories, as shown in Figure 2-33. The exception to this rule is a hard drive because it can be divided into partitions that can have more than one **volume** such as drive C and drive D on the same physical hard drive. For a volume, such as drive C, the root directory is written as C:\. Each volume has its own root directory and hierarchical structure of subdirectories.

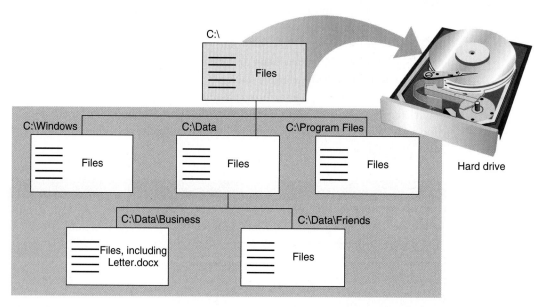

Figure 2-33 Storage devices such as a USB drive, CD, or hard drive, are organized into directories and subdirectories that contain files
Courtesy: Course Technology/Cengage Learning

As shown in Figure 2-33, the root directory can hold files or other directories, which can have names such as C:\Data. These directories, called **subdirectories**, **child directories**, or **folders**, can, in turn, have other directories listed in them. Any directory can have files and other subdirectories listed in it; for example, Figure 2-33 shows C:\Data\Business\Letter.docx. In this path to the file, the C: identifies the volume. If a directory is on a floppy disk, then either A: or B: identifies it. If a directory is on a volume on a hard drive or on a CD, USB drive, or DVD, a letter such as C:, D:, or F: identifies it.

When you refer to a drive and directories that are pointing to the location of a file, as in C:\Data\Business\Letter.docx, the drive and directories are called the **path** to the file (see Figure 2-34). As you learned earlier in the chapter, when naming a file, the first part of the name before the period is called the **filename** (Letter), and the part after the period is called the file extension (docx), which has one or more characters to identify the type file. The .docx file extension identifies the file type as a Microsoft Word 2007 document file.

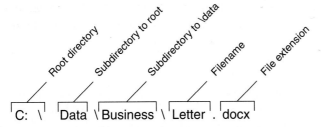

Figure 2-34 The complete path to a file includes the volume letter, directories, filename, and file extension; the colon, backslashes, and period are required to separate items in the path
Courtesy: Course Technology/Cengage Learning

NAVIGATE THE DIRECTORY STRUCTURE

When working with the Windows Explorer or Computer window, these tips can make your work easier:

- ▲ *Tip 1.* Drill down to subfolders inside folders by double-clicking the folder to cause files and subdirectories (also called subfolders) to appear in the right pane. When you click the white arrow to the left of a folder in Vista or click the plus sign to the left of a folder in 2000/XP, its subfolders appear underneath it in the left pane.
- ▲ *Tip 2.* To control what information appears about files and subfolders in the right pane, right-click the heading bar in the pane (see Figure 2-35). Check items you want to appear as columns in the right pane.
- ▲ *Tip 3.* Often-used folders are listed at the top of the left pane in the Favorite Links area. Click an entry there to display its contents.
- ▲ *Tip 4.* For Vista, to find a folder or file, use the Search box in the upper-right corner of the window.
- ▲ *Tip 5.* For Vista, use the forward and back arrows in the upper-left corner to move forward and backward to previous views.

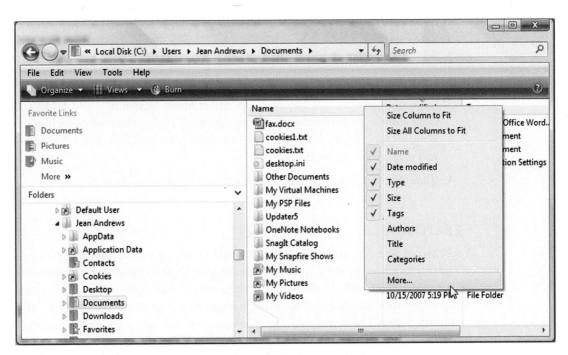

Figure 2-35 Right-click the column heading to select columns to display
Courtesy: Course Technology/Cengage Learning

A+
220-701
3.3

As a PC support technician, you need to understand where Windows puts important user files and folders. Here's the default layout, although later in the book you will learn how to change these locations:

◢ In Windows Vista, user data and settings are stored in a user folder and its subfolders. The folder name is the user account name and the folder is created under the *%SystemDrive%*\Users folder, for example, C:\Users\Jean Andrews.

◢ In Windows 2000/XP, the user folder is also named after the user account name. The folder is created under the *%SystemDrive%*\Documents and Settings folder, for example, C:\Documents and Settings\Jean Andrews. The subfolders under the user folder are organized differently under Windows 2000/XP than under Windows Vista.

> **Notes** In Microsoft documentation, the *%SystemDrive%* folder means the volume on which Windows is installed. Most often, this drive is C:, although in a dual boot environment, one OS might be installed on C: and another on a different drive. For example, Windows XP can be installed on C: and Windows Vista installed on E:. You will learn how to set up these dual boot installations in Chapter 12.

CHANGING FOLDER OPTIONS

You can also view and change options assigned to folders; these options control how users view the files in the folder and what they can do with these files.

Windows identifies file types primarily by the file extension. In Windows Explorer and the Computer window, Windows has an annoying habit of hiding the extensions of certain files. By default, Windows hides the file extension of a file if it knows which application to use to open or execute the file. For example, just after installation, it hides .exe, .com, .sys, and .txt file extensions, but does not hide .doc, .ppt, or .xls file extensions until the software to open these files has been installed. Also, Windows really doesn't want you to see its own system files, and it hides these files from view until you force it to show them.

To view hidden files and file extensions, do the following:

1. Select the folder where system files are located.

2. Click **Tools** and then click **Folder Options**. The Folder Options window opens.

3. Click the **View** tab (see Figure 2-36). Select **Show hidden files and folders**. Uncheck **Hide extensions for known file types**. Uncheck **Hide protected operating system files**. Windows complains it doesn't want to show you these files. Click **Yes** to confirm that you really want to see them.

4. Click **Apply**. Click **OK** to close the Folder Options window.

CREATE A FILE

You can create a file using a particular application, or you can create a file using Windows Explorer or the Computer window. In Explorer and the Computer window, to create a file, right-click in the unused white area in the right pane of the window and select **New** from the shortcut menu. (Alternately, in the menu bar, you can click File and then click New.) The menu lists applications you can use to create the file in the current folder (see Figure 2-37). Click the application and the file is created. You can then rename the filename. However, to keep the proper file association, don't change the file extension.

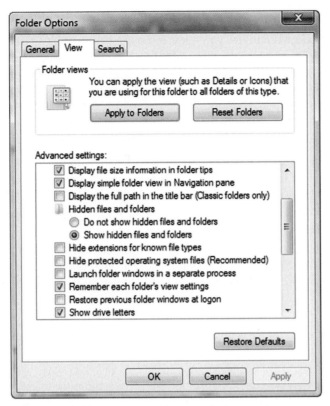

Figure 2-36 Use the Folder Options window to display hidden system files
Courtesy: Course Technology/Cengage Learning

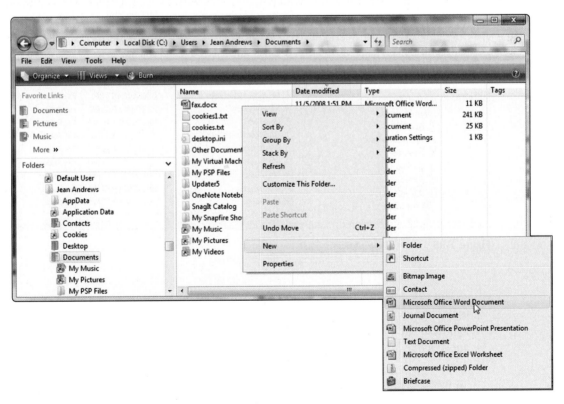

Figure 2-37 Create a new file using Windows Explorer
Courtesy: Course Technology/Cengage Learning

A+
220-701
3.3

CREATE A FOLDER

To create a folder, first select the folder you want to be the parent folder. (Remember that a parent folder is the folder that contains the child folder.) Right-click in the white area of the right pane and select **New** from the shortcut menu (or click File, New in the menu bar). The menu in Figure 2-37 appears. Notice in the menu that for Vista, you have three choices for folder types. These choices are explained here:

- ◢ Folder creates a regular folder.
- ◢ Compressed (zipped) Folder creates a compressed folder with a .zip extension. Any file or folder that you put in this folder will be compressed to a smaller size than normal. A compressed folder is often used to compress files to a smaller size so they can more easily be sent by e-mail. When you remove a file or folder from a compressed folder, the file or folder is uncompressed back to its original size.
- ◢ Briefcase creates a Briefcase folder, which is a folder that can be used to sync up files in this folder with its corresponding Briefcase folder on another computer. (Windows offers two ways to sync files: Briefcase and Offline Files, both of which are covered in Chapter 17.)

Make your selection and the folder is created and highlighted so that you can rename it (see Figure 2-38).

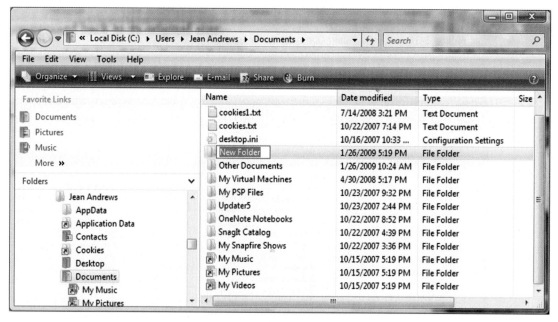

Figure 2-38 Edit the new folder's name
Courtesy: Course Technology/Cengage Learning

You can create folders within folders within folders, but there is a limitation as to the maximum depth of folders under folders; how deep you can nest folders depends on the length of the folder names themselves. In Chapter 13, you will learn that you can also create and rename a folder using commands from a command prompt.

💡 **A+ Exam Tip** The A+ 220-701 Essentials exam expects you to know how to create folders, navigate the directory structure, create files, and change file attributes.

It's also interesting to know that the Windows desktop is itself a folder. The Desktop of the currently logged in user is always listed as the first entry at the top of the Folders list in the Explorer or Computer window. However, the Desktop folder is located at *%SystemDrive%* Users*username*\Desktop for Windows Vista. For example, if the user, Anne, wants to create a folder named Presentations on the Vista desktop, she can right-click anywhere on the desktop and select New, Folder from the shortcut menu. The folder is created and she can then rename it Presentations. The folder appears on the desktop each time she logs onto the system. The actual location of this folder is at C:\Users\Anne\Desktop\Presentations.

COPY OR DELETE FILES OR FOLDERS

To copy a file or folder, right-click it and select Copy from the shortcut menu. Then click in the white area of the folder where the copied item is to go and select Paste from the shortcut menu. You can also drag and drop the item to its new location. If the location is on the same drive as the original location, the file or folder will be automatically deleted from its original location. If you don't want it deleted, hold down the Ctrl key while you drag and drop.

To delete a file or folder using Explorer, right-click the file or folder and select **Delete** from the shortcut menu. A confirmation dialog box asks if you are sure you want to delete the item. If you click **Yes**, you send the file or folder and all its contents, including subfolders, to the Recycle Bin. You can also hold down the Shift or Ctrl key as you click to select multiple items to delete, copy, or move at the same time.

> **Notes** Appendix B lists handy keystrokes to save you time when working with Windows.

Emptying the Recycle Bin will free up your disk space. Files and folders sent to the Recycle Bin are not *really* deleted until you empty the bin. To do that, right-click the **bin** and select **Empty Recycle Bin** from the shortcut menu. In Chapter 13, you will learn that you can also copy and delete files and folders using commands from a command prompt.

CHANGE FILE ATTRIBUTES

Using Explorer or the Computer window, you can view and change the properties assigned to a file; these properties are called the file attributes. Using these attributes, you can do such things as hide a file, make it a read-only file, or flag a file to be backed up. From Explorer or the Computer window, right-click a file and select **Properties** from the shortcut menu. The Properties window shown on the left side of Figure 2-39 opens.

From the Properties window, you can change the read-only, hidden, archive, and indexing attributes of the file. (Indexing is used only in Windows Vista.) To make the file a read-only file or to hide the file so that it does not appear in the directory list, check the appropriate box and click **Apply**. The archive attribute is used to determine if a file has changed since the last backup. To change its value, click **Advanced** in the Properties window (see the right side of Figure 2-39). Make your change and click **OK**.

Also notice in the Advanced Attributes box in Figure 2-39 the option to Index this file for faster searching. An index is a list of items that is used to speed up a search, and Vista is the first Windows OS to use indexing for its searches. By default, it includes in the index only common user data files and folders that are normally searched for. Program files and Windows files are not included by default. Using the Advanced Attributes box, you can include or exclude the file or folder from the index. Incidentally, to change the type of files that Vista indexes, in the left pane of Control Panel, click **Change how Windows searches.**

A+
220-701
3.3

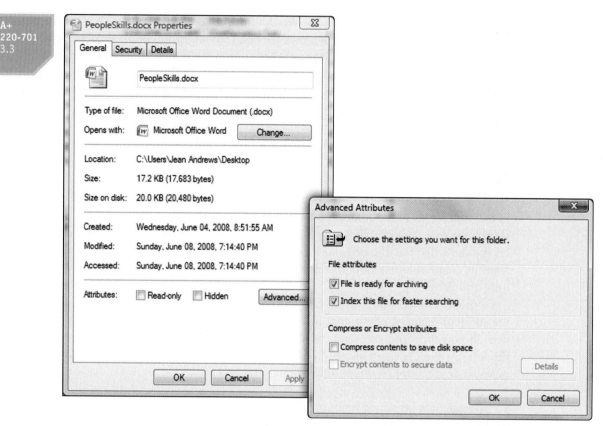

Figure 2-39 Properties of a file in Windows
Courtesy: Course Technology/Cengage Learning

A+
220-701
3.2

THE CONTROL PANEL

The Control Panel is a window containing several small utility programs called applets that are used to manage hardware, software, users, and the system. For Windows Vista and XP, to access the Control Panel, click **Start** and then click **Control Panel**. For Windows 2000, to open Control Panel, click **Start, Settings,** and **Control Panel**.

Figure 2-40 shows the Windows Vista Control Panel, and Figure 2-41 shows the Windows XP Control Panel in Category View. Select a category to see the applets in that category, or click **Switch to Classic View** to see the applets when you first open Control Panel as they are displayed in earlier versions of Windows.

Besides accessing the several applets in Control Panel from the Control Panel window, each applet can be accessed directly. You will learn how to do this as you learn to use these applets later in the book. For all the applets, if you know the name of the applet program file, you can launch the applet by using the Vista Start dialog box (called the Run dialog box in Windows 2000/XP). For example, to open the Mouse Properties applet, type **Main.cpl** in the Start box, and then press **Enter**. An applet has a .cpl file extension.

> 💡 **A+ Exam Tip** The A+ 220-701 Essentials exam expects you to be familiar with the Control Panel and its applets.

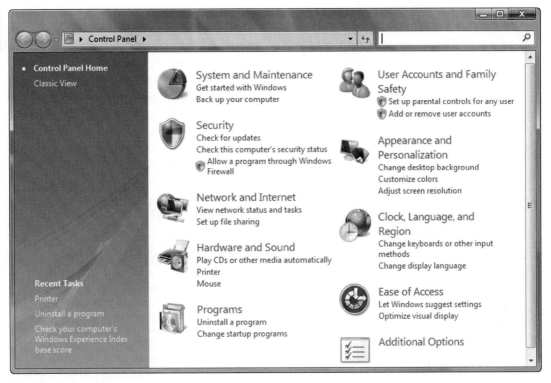

Figure 2-40 The Windows Vista Control Panel is organized by category, although you can easily switch to Classic View
Courtesy: Course Technology/Cengage Learning

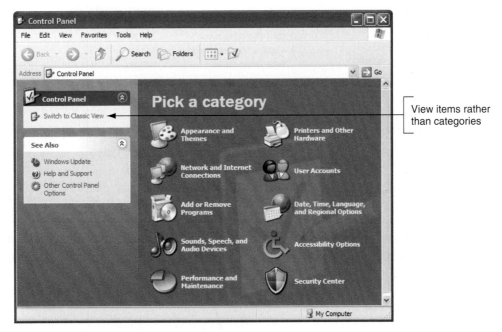

View items rather than categories

Figure 2-41 The Windows XP Control Panel
Courtesy: Course Technology/Cengage Learning

A+
220-701
3.2

SYSTEM INFORMATION UTILITY

The System Information utility (see Figure 2-42) gives a wealth of information about installed hardware and software, the current system configuration, and currently running programs. For example, you can use it to find out what processor or BIOS version is installed on the motherboard, how much RAM is installed, the directory where the OS is installed, the size of the hard drive, the names of currently running drivers, and much more. The System Information window is a composite of information available from several other windows and is especially useful when talking with a technical support person on the phone because it provides a broad technical view of information about the system.

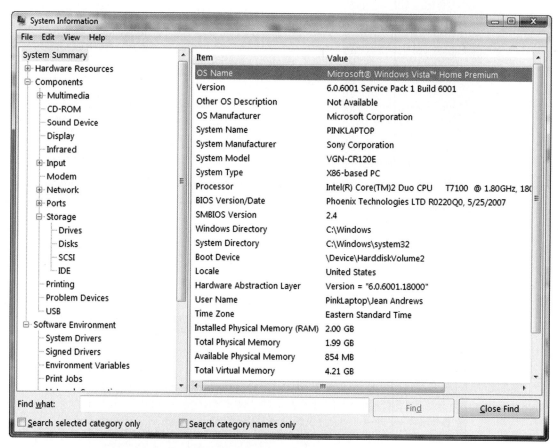

Figure 2-42   Use the Windows System Information utility to examine your system
Courtesy: Course Technology/Cengage Learning

To run System Information in Windows Vista, click **Start**, and enter **Msinfo32.exe** in the Start box and press **Enter**. The System Information window opens. For Windows 2000/XP, click **Start**, click **Run**, enter **Msinfo32.exe** in the Run dialog box, and press **Enter**.

System Information can be useful when strange error messages appear during startup. Use it to get a list of drivers that loaded successfully. If you have saved the System Information report when the system was starting successfully, comparing the two reports can help identify the problem device.

> 💡 **A+ Exam Tip**   The A+ 220-701 Essentials exam expects you to be familiar with and know how to use the Windows 2000/XP/Vista desktop, Computer, My Computer, Windows Explorer, Control Panel, System Information, and the Command Prompt windows. All these tools are discussed in this section. If the utility can be accessed by more than one method, you are expected to know all of the methods.

COMMAND PROMPT WINDOW

As you have already seen in this chapter, individual commands can be entered in the Vista Search box or the Windows 2000/XP Run box. However, you can also open a command prompt window and use it to enter multiple commands to perform a variety of tasks. To open the window, in the Vista Start box or the Windows 2000/XP Run box, enter **cmd.exe** and press **Enter**. Alternately, you can click **Start, All Programs, Accessories,** and **Command Prompt**. The Vista Command Prompt window is shown in Figure 2-43.

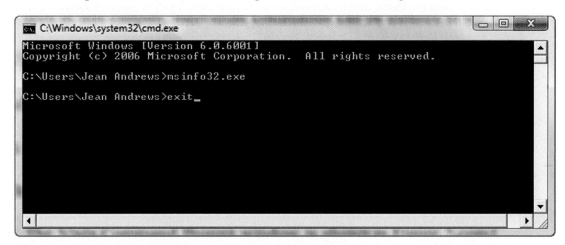

Figure 2-43   Use the Exit command to close the Command Prompt window
Courtesy: Course Technology/Cengage Learning

When you're working in the window, to clear the text in the window, type **cls** and press **Enter**. To close the window, type **exit** and press **Enter**, as shown in the figure. Alternately, you can click the X close window icon in the upper-right corner of the window. Throughout this book, you will learn many commands that work from this window, and you can also launch a program from this window. For example, when you enter the **msinfo32.exe** program name, the System Information window is launched.

Windows Vista has two levels of command prompt windows: a standard window and an elevated window. The standard window is shown in Figure 2-43. Notice in the figure that the default directory is the currently logged on user's folder. Commands that require administrative privileges will not work from this standard command prompt window. To get an elevated command prompt window, click **Start, All Programs, Accessories,** and right-click **Command Prompt**. Then select **Run as administrator** from the shortcut window and respond to the UAC box. The resulting command prompt window is shown in Figure 2-44. Notice the word

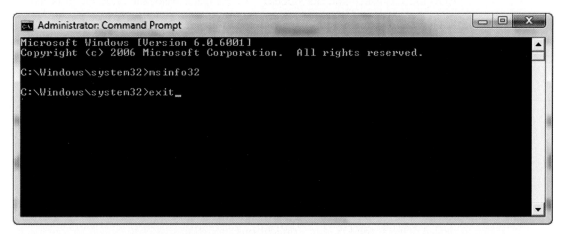

Figure 2-44   An elevated command prompt window
Courtesy: Course Technology/Cengage Learning

Administrator in the title bar, which indicates the elevated window, and the default directory, which is the *%systemdrive%\Windows\system32* folder.

>> CHAPTER SUMMARY

▲ Operating systems that have been or are being used for desktop computers include DOS, Windows 9x/Me, Windows NT/2000/XP/Vista, UNIX, a version of UNIX called Linux, and the Mac OS. Windows 7 is the next Microsoft operating system.

▲ A dual boot makes it possible to boot a computer from one of two installed operating systems.

▲ A virtual machine is software that creates one or more logical computers on a physical computer.

▲ An operating system manages hardware, runs applications, provides an interface for users, and stores, retrieves, and manipulates files.

▲ Every OS is composed of two main internal components: a shell portion to interact with users and applications and a kernel portion to interact with hardware. In addition, an OS needs a place to store configuration information, which is normally stored in a database such as the Windows Registry, or in text files, called initialization files.

▲ An application is launched as a Windows process which can then create multiple threads to the OS requesting tasks to be done.

▲ An OS manages hardware by way of device drivers or by using system BIOS (firmware). Sometimes, device drivers are considered part of the OS.

▲ Current processors can process 32 bits or 64 bits at a time. Most processors used with desktop or laptop systems are hybrid processors: They use a 32-bit core and can work using either a 32-bit instruction set or a 64-bit instruction set.

▲ Operating systems process either 32 bits or 64 bits. Microsoft calls 32-bit operating systems x86-based OSs. The term x64 applies to 64-bit OSs.

▲ 64-bit operating systems require 64-bit drivers.

▲ Each edition of Vista comes in 32-bit and 64-bit versions. Windows XP Professional comes in a 64-bit version.

▲ The Vista desktop differs from the Windows 2000/XP desktop in that Vista offers the Aero user interface and the sidebar with gadgets. Also, the Start menu is reorganized.

▲ Four ways to launch an application are to use the Start menu, the Search box (Windows 2000/XP Run box), Windows Explorer (similar to the Vista Computer or Windows 2000/XP My Computer window), or a shortcut icon.

▲ The right side of the taskbar is called the notification area, which some call the system tray.

▲ Windows uses the file extension to know which application to open to manage the file, which is called the file association.

▲ The Vista UAC box is used to protect the system against malware.

▲ Windows Explorer, the Vista Computer window, and the XP/2000 My Computer window are used to manage files and folders in secondary storage.

▲ System Information gives much information about the computer, including hardware, device drivers, the OS, and applications.

◢ Control Panel holds a group of applets to manage the system.

◢ Multiple commands can be issued from a Command Prompt window.

>> KEY TERMS

For explanations of key terms, see the Glossary near the end of the book.

administrator account	filename	service
Aero user interface	folders	service pack
backward-compatible	graphical user interface (GUI)	shell
Briefcase	HAL (hardware abstraction layer)	standard account
child directory	initialization files	subdirectory
command prompt window	kernel	system tray
Compressed (zipped) Folder	kernel mode	systray
desktop	netbook	taskbar
device driver	notification area	thread
distribution	operating system (OS)	User Account Control (UAC)
dual boot	original equipment manufacturer	dialog box
elevated command prompt	(OEM) license	user mode
window	patches	virtual machine (VM)
executive services	path	volume
file attribute	Registry	
file extension	root directory	

>> REVIEWING THE BASICS

1. Which Microsoft operating system was the first to use all 32-bit processing?

2. What are the hardware requirements to use the Vista Aero user interface?

3. What is the application mentioned in the chapter that creates a virtual machine on a computer?

4. List four major functions of an OS.

5. What is the next Microsoft operating system for desktop computers to be released in 2010?

6. The Windows shell operates in _____ mode and the kernel operates in _____ mode.

7. How many bits does an x86-based operating system process at one time?

8. What term does Intel use to describe a processor technology that uses all 64-bit processing?

9. What term does AMD use to describe the processor technology that uses a 64-bit instruction set with 32-bit internal core processing?

10. In question 9 above, what term does Intel use to describe the same technology?

11. Which Windows XP operating system is a 64-bit OS?

12. Which edition of Vista comes packaged with a 32-bit DVD as well as a 64-bit DVD?

13. What is the memory limitation for a 32-bit operating system?

14. On the Vista Start menu, where might you expect to be able to access user files?

15. How can you add the sidebar to the Vista desktop?

16. When is the Vista flip 3D view available to Vista?

17. What is the keyboard shortcut to the flip 3D view?

18. The taskbar notification area includes icons for currently running services. What is another term for this area?

19. What part of a filename does Windows use to know which application to open to manage the file?

20. When does a user need to enter a password into the UAC box in order to continue?

21. What extension is used to name a compressed folder?

22. What is the path and folder name to the desktop folder for the user Jane when Windows Vista is installed on drive C?

23. List five file attributes. Which attribute applies only to Vista?

24. How do you access the Properties box for a file to change an attribute?

25. What is the program name for the System Information utility?

>> THINKING CRITICALLY

1. If your printer is giving you trouble, what is the best way to obtain an update for the device driver?

2. What Windows tool can you use to know how much RAM is installed on your system?

3. Why is 16-bit Windows software considered to be legacy software?

4. Can you install Vista Ultimate 32-bit version or 64-bit version on an Intel Quad Core system manufactured in 2008?

5. Mary wants her x86-based version of Windows Vista Business edition to run faster. She has 4 GB of memory installed on the motherboard. She decides more memory will help. She installs an additional 2 GB of memory for a total of 6 GB, but does not see any performance improvement. What is the problem and what should you tell Mary?

   a. She should use Device Manager to install the memory in Vista. After it is installed, performance should improve. Tell Mary how to open Device Manager.

   b. A 32-bit OS cannot use more than 4 GB of memory. Tell Mary she has wasted her money.

   c. A 32-bit OS cannot use more than 4 GB of memory. Tell Mary to upgrade her system to the 64-bit version of Vista Business.

   d. A 32-bit OS cannot use more than 4 GB of memory. Explain to Mary the problem and discuss with her the possible solutions.

6. Jack needs to e-mail two documents to a friend but the files are so large his e-mail server bounced them back as undeliverable. What is your advice?

   a. Tell Jack to open the documents and break each of them into two documents and then e-mail the four documents separately.

   b. Tell Jack to put the two documents in a compressed folder and e-mail the folder.

   c. Tell Jack to put each document in a different compressed folder and e-mail each folder separately.

   d. Tell Jack to put the documents on a USB drive and snail mail the drive to his friend.

>> HANDS-ON PROJECTS

PROJECT 2-1:   Using the System Information Utility

Do the following to run the System Information utility and gather information about your system:

1. In the Vista Search box or the XP/2000 Run box, type **Msinfo32.exe** and press **Enter**. The System Information window opens.

2. Browse through the different levels of information in this window and answer the following questions:

   a. What OS and OS version are you using?

   b. What is your CPU speed?

   c. What is your BIOS manufacturer and version?

   d. How much video RAM is available to your video adapter card? Explain how you got this information.

   e. What is the name of the driver file that manages your parallel port? Your USB ports?

PROJECT 2-2:   Using a Freeware Diagnostic Utility

You can download many freeware diagnostic utilities from the Internet and use them to examine, troubleshoot, and benchmark a system. Do the following to download and use one utility to examine your system:

1. Go to the CNET Networks Web site at *www.download.com* and use the Web site search box to search for Fresh Diagnose. Download the utility, saving it to a folder on your hard drive named **Downloads**.

2. Double-click the file to execute the program and install the software. When given the opportunity, choose to create a shortcut to the software on your desktop.

3. Double-click the shortcut to run the Fresh Diagnose program.

4. Browse through the Fresh Diagnose menus and answer the same questions listed in Project 2-1 for the Windows 2000/XP/Vista System Information utility.

5. Compare the two utilities, Fresh Diagnose and System Information, by answering the following questions:

   a. Which utility is easier to use and why?

   b. Which utility gives more information about your system?

   c. What is one advantage that System Information has over Fresh Diagnose?

   d. What is one advantage that Fresh Diagnose has over System Information?

   e. Which utility do you prefer and why?

PROJECT 2-3: Using the Taskbar

Using a Windows 2000/XP/Vista computer, do the following and answer the following questions about the taskbar:

1. List the items in the Quick Launch area of the taskbar. What is the program name and path to each item?

2. List the items in the notification area (system tray) of the taskbar. Don't forget to list the items hidden in this area. Investigate and describe the purpose of each program.

3. Move the taskbar from the bottom of the screen to the left side. List the steps you took to do that.

4. If you are using a Vista computer, press **Win+Tab** and describe the results. Are you using the Vista Aero user interface?

PROJECT 2-4: Practicing Keystrokes

Refer to Appendix B, *Keystroke Shortcuts in Windows*, for help with this project. Disconnect your mouse and then practice using the keyboard in case you must troubleshoot a system when the mouse does not work. Do the following:

1. Open Explorer and display the files in the root directory of drive C. List the steps and keystrokes you used to do this.

2. Unhide all the files in this folder. From the Tools menu, select **Folder Options**, select the **View** tab, and then select **Show hidden files and folders**. Also uncheck **Hide extensions for known file types** and uncheck **Hide protected operating system files**. List the steps and keystrokes you used.

3. What is the exact size of the file Pagefile.sys in bytes, and the date and time the file was last modified?

PROJECT 2-5: Using Windows Explorer

Do the following to practice using Windows Explorer:

1. Open Windows Explorer.

2. Create a folder under the root directory of the hard drive called \Temp. List the steps you took.

3. Add a subfolder to \Temp called \MyFiles. List the steps you took.

4. Create a text file in the MyFiles folder named **Text1.txt**. List the steps you took.

5. Create a shortcut to that folder on the Windows desktop. List the steps you took.

6. Rename the file **Text2.txt**.

7. Double-click the shortcut on the desktop. What error did you get?

8. To clean up after yourself, delete the \Temp folder and the shortcut.

>> *REAL PROBLEMS, REAL SOLUTIONS*

REAL PROBLEM 2-1: Becoming a PC Support Technician

You've just been hired as a PC support technician in the IT department of your university. At the job interview, you were promised a two-week training period, but by noon on your first day on the job it dawns on you that "training period" means you gotta train yourself *really quick*! Listed below are some problems you encounter that day. How do you solve these problems and what Windows tools do you use?

1. A history professor calls you into his office and tells you he thinks the memory on his Vista computer needs upgrading. He wants you to tell him how much RAM is currently installed. What do you do?

2. A PE instructor discovers the history professor has Windows Vista on his desktop. She thinks she has Windows XP on her desktop and wants you to tell her exactly which OS she has installed. What do you do?

3. Your boss asks you to go down the hall to the Windows XP computer in the break room and find out the path and name of the device driver for the optical drive (CD drive or DVD drive) that is installed. What steps do you use? What is the path and name of the optical drive device driver on your Windows XP or Vista system?

4. The Office Administrator for Career Education uses MSWord often and wants you to place a shortcut on her desktop to launch this application. List the steps to do that.

5. A student in a computer lab is trying to answer a question in the lab about the Windows Vista sidebar. She needs to add a gadget to the sidebar to show the current temperature in Seattle. What steps do you give her to find the answer? Print the screen showing the gadget. List the steps you took to print the screen.

REAL PROBLEM 2-2: Becoming a PC Technician Researcher

Windows Help might provide useful information when you try to resolve a problem. To access Windows Help, click **Start**, and then click **Help and Support**. Also, the Microsoft Web site (*http://support.microsoft.com*) has lots of information on troubleshooting. Search for the device, an error message, a Windows utility, a symptom, a software application, an update version number, or keywords that lead you to articles about problems and solutions. You can also go to *www.microsoft.com* to browse for links on hardware and software compatibility. Other sources of help are user and installation manuals for applications and hardware devices, training materials, and the Web sites of application and device manufacturers. You can also use a search engine such as Google (*www.google.com*). Enter the error message, software application, symptom, or Windows utility in the search box to search the Web for answers, suggestions, and comments.

> **Notes** If you are serious about learning to provide professional support for Windows, each OS has a resource kit, including support software and a huge reference book containing inside information about the OS. Check out *Microsoft Windows Vista Resource Kit, Microsoft Windows XP Professional Resource Kit,* or *Microsoft Windows 2000 Professional Resource Kit.* All three are put out by Microsoft Press.

Beware, however, that you don't bump into a site that does more harm than good. Some sites are simply guessing, offering incomplete and possibly wrong solutions, and even offering a utility the site claims will solve your problem but really contains only pop-up ads or spyware. Use only reputable sites you can trust. You'll learn about several of these excellent sites in this book.

Answer the following questions using any of the resources mentioned previously:

1. You have just purchased Vista Home Premium edition, which comes on a 32-bit DVD. List the steps to buy the 64-bit DVD version of Vista Home Premium. What sources of information did you use?

2. Your Vista system is slow and you decide to turn off the Aero user interface to save on resources. List the steps to do that and the source of information you used.

3. You have upgraded your Windows XP system to Vista but now the network connection will not work. You realize you need to install Vista drivers for the network port that comes directly off your ASUS P4P800 motherboard. What is the name of the driver file you need to download and how did you find it?

4. Your friend has asked you if you know how to turn off the UAC box so it never appears on his Vista system. List the steps to do that and the source of information you used.

5. What was the first Intel processor to use the EM64T technology? What is your source of information?

Working with People in a Technical World

In the last two chapters, you were introduced to hardware and software. In this chapter, the focus is on relating to people and your career as a professional PC support technician. As a professional PC technician, you can manage your career by staying abreast of new technology, using every available resource to do your job well, and striving for top professional certifications. There was a time when most PC support jobs had to do with simply working with hardware and software, and the perception was that people skills were not that important. But times have changed and our vocation has become much more service oriented.

Knowing how to effectively work with people in a technical world is one of the most sought-after skills in today's service-oriented work environments. Just before writing this book, an employer told me, "It's not hard to find technically proficient people these days. But it's next to impossible to find people who know how to get along with others and can be counted on when managers are not looking over their shoulders." I could sense his frustration, but I also felt encouraged to know that good social skills and good work ethics can take you far in today's world. My advice to you is to take this chapter seriously. It's important to be technically proficient, but the skills learned in this chapter just might be the ones that make you stand out above the crowd to land that new job or promotion.

In this chapter, you'll learn about the job roles of a professional PC support technician, including the certifications and record keeping and informational tools you might use. Then we focus on interpersonal skills (people skills) needed by a technical support technician.

Notes If you meet someone who doesn't have a smile, give them yours.

JOB ROLES AND RESPONSIBILITIES

As a PC troubleshooter, you might have to solve a problem on your own PC or for someone else. As a PC technician, you might fulfill several different job roles:

Figure 3-1 Picture yourself here and think about your job role in this position
Courtesy: iStockphoto

▲ *PC support technician.* A PC support technician works on site, closely interacting with users, and is responsible for ongoing PC maintenance. Of the job roles in this list, a PC support technician is the only one responsible for the PC before trouble occurs. Therefore, you are able to prepare for a problem by performing routine preventive maintenance, keeping good records, and making backups (or teaching users how to do so). You might also be expected to provide desk-side support, helping computer users with all sorts of hardware and application concerns. Some job titles that fall into this category include enterprise technician, IT administrator, PC technician, support technician, PC support specialist, and desk-side support technician.

▲ *PC service technician.* A PC service technician goes to a customer site in response to a service call and, if possible, repairs the PC on site. PC service technicians are usually not responsible for ongoing PC maintenance but usually do interact with users. Other job titles might include field technician or field service technician.

▲ *Technical retail associate.* Those responsible for selling computers and related equipment are often expected to have technical knowledge about the products they sell. These salespeople work in somewhat of a consulting role and are expected to advise customers about the best technology to meet their needs, how to apply the technology, and maybe even how to configure entire networks and interconnected applications and equipment. Sometimes job roles involve only one stage of the sale. For instance, less technical people might make the initial contact with the customer and begin the sales process, and those who are more technically knowledgeable can act as technical sales consultants to complete the details of the sale.

▲ *Bench technician.* A bench technician works in a lab environment, might not interact with users of the PCs being repaired, and is not permanently responsible for them. Bench technicians probably don't work at the site where the PC is kept. They might be able to interview the user to get information about the problem, or they might simply receive a PC to repair without being able to talk to the user. A bench technician is sometimes called a depot technician.

◢ *Help-desk technician.* A help-desk technician provides telephone or online support. Help-desk technicians, who do not have physical access to the PC, are at the greatest disadvantage of the types of technicians listed. They can interact with users over the phone, by a chat session, or by remote control of the user's computer and must obviously use different tools and approaches than technicians who are at the PC. Other job titles in this category include remote support technician and call center technician.

Now let's turn our attention to the need to be certified, and then we'll look at the record-keeping and information tools needed by a technician.

Figure 3-2 PC support technicians might have limited contact with users
Courtesy: iStockphoto

CERTIFICATION AND PROFESSIONAL ORGANIZATIONS

Many people work as PC technicians without any formal classroom training or certification. However, by having certification or an advanced technical degree, you prove to yourself, your customers, and your employers that you are prepared to do the work and are committed to being educated in your chosen profession. Certification and advanced degrees serve as recognized proof of competence and achievement, improve your job opportunities, create a higher level of customer confidence, and often qualify you for promotions and other training or degrees.

The most significant certifying organization for PC technicians is the Computing Technology Industry Association (CompTIA, pronounced "comp-TEE-a"). CompTIA sponsors the A+ Certification Program, and manages the exams. The CompTIA home page for A+ Certification is *http://certification.comptia.org/a*, shown in Figure 3-3. Follow the *Download A+ Objectives* link on the page to get the list of objectives for the

Figure 3-3 CompTIA A+ Certification Web page
Courtesy: Course Technology/Cengage Learning

latest exams, which are currently the A+ 2009 exams. To become certified, you must pass the A+ 220-701 exam that covers content on hardware, operating systems, security, and soft skills (skills involving relationships with people). Passing the A+ 220-701 exam validates entry-level skills in any PC repair job. You must also pass the A+ 220-702 exam to get your A+ Certification.

A+ Certification has industry recognition, so it should be your first choice for certification as a PC technician. CompTIA has more than 13,000 members from every major company that manufactures, distributes, or publishes computer-related products and services. For more information about CompTIA and A+ Certification, see the CompTIA Web site at *www.comptia.org*.

Other certifications are more vendor specific. For example, Microsoft, Novell, and Cisco offer certifications to use and support their products. These are excellent choices for additional certifications when your career plan is to focus on these products.

In addition to becoming certified and seeking advanced degrees, the professional PC technician should also stay abreast of new technology. Helpful resources include on-the-job training, books, magazines, the Internet, trade shows, and interaction with colleagues, seminars, and workshops. One popular trade show is Interop by CMP Media (*www.interop.com*), where you can view the latest technology, hear industry leaders speak, and network with vast numbers of organizations and people. Using the Internet, a convenient and inexpensive way to keep up with the latest technologies is to subscribe to newsletters by e-mail. Two newsletters I read regularly are those published by PC World at *www.pcworld.com* and PCstats at *www.pcstats.com*.

RECORD-KEEPING AND INFORMATION TOOLS

If you work for a service organization, it will probably have most of the tools you need to do your job, including printed forms, online record keeping, procedures, and manuals. In some cases, help-desk support personnel might have software to help them do their jobs, such as programs that support the remote control of customers' PCs. Examples of this type of software are Control-F1 by Blueloop at *www.blueloop.net* and Windows XP/Vista Remote Assistance, which you will learn about in Chapter 18.

Other types of resources, records, and information tools that can help you support PCs are listed below:

◢ *Tool 1.* The specific software or hardware you support must be available to you to test, observe, and study and to use to re-create a customer's problem whenever possible.

◢ *Tool 2.* You need a copy of the same documentation the user sees, and should be familiar with that documentation.

◢ *Tool 3.* Hardware and software products generally have more technical documentation than just a user manual. A company should make this technical documentation available to you when you support its product. If you don't find it on hand, know that you are likely to find user manuals and technical support manuals as .PDF files that can be downloaded from the product manufacturers' Web sites.

◢ *Tool 4.* Online help targeted to field technicians and help-desk technicians is often available for a product. This online help will probably include a search engine that searches by topics, words, error messages, and the like.

◢ *Tool 5.* An expert system is software that is designed and written to help solve problems. It uses databases of known facts and rules to simulate human experts' reasoning and decision making. Expert systems for PC technicians work by posing questions about a problem to be answered by the technician or the customer. The response to each question triggers another question from the software, until the expert system arrives at a possible solution or solutions. Many expert systems are "intelligent," meaning the system will record your input and use it in subsequent sessions to select more questions to ask and approaches to try. Therefore, future troubleshooting sessions on this same type of problem tend to zero in more quickly toward a solution.

◢ *Tool 6.* Call tracking can be done electronically or on paper. Large organizations use an electronic call-tracking system that tracks: (1) the date, time, and length of help-desk or on-site calls; (2) causes of and solutions to problems already addressed; (3) who did what and when; and (4) how each call was officially resolved. When someone initiates a call for help, the technician starts the process by creating a ticket. The ticket is entered into the call-tracking system and stays open until the issue is resolved. People assigned to the ticket then document their progress under this ticket in the call-tracking system. As an open ticket ages, more attention and resources are assigned to it, and the ticket might be escalated to those higher up in the support chain until the problem is finally resolved and the ticket closed. Help-desk personnel and managers acknowledge and sometimes even celebrate those who consistently close the most tickets!

Now let's focus on our customers and what they expect from us beyond our technical knowledge.

> **A+ Exam Tip** The content in this chapter applies to the A+ 220-701 Essentials exam.

WHAT CUSTOMERS WANT: BEYOND TECHNICAL KNOW-HOW

A+
220-701
6.2

Probably the most significant indication that a PC technician is doing a good job is that customers are consistently satisfied. In your career as a support technician, commit to providing excellent service and to treating customers as you would want to be treated in a similar situation. One of the most important ways to achieve customer satisfaction is to do your best by being prepared, both technically and personally. Being prepared includes knowing what customers want, what they don't like, and what they expect from a PC technician.

Your customers can be "internal" (you both work for the same company, in which case you might consider the customer your colleague) or "external" (your customers come to you or your company for service). Customers can be highly technical or technically naive, represent a large company or simply own a home PC, be prompt or slow at paying their bills, want only the best (and be willing to pay for it) or be searching for bargain service, be friendly and easy to work with or demanding and condescending. In each situation, the key to success is always the same: Don't allow circumstances or personalities to affect your commitment to excellence and to treating the customer as you would want to be treated.

The following traits distinguish one competent technician from another in the eyes of the customer:

▲ *Trait 1. **A positive and helpful attitude.*** This helps establish good customer relationships. You communicate your attitude in your tone of voice, the words you choose, how you use eye contact, your facial expressions, how you dress, and in many other

APPLYING CONCEPTS Josie walked into a computer parts store and wandered over to the cleaning supplies looking for Ace monitor wipes. She saw another brand of wipes, but not the ones she wanted. Looking around for help, she noticed Mary stocking software on the shelves in the next aisle. She walked over to Mary and asked her if she could help her find Ace monitor wipes. Mary put down her box, walked over to the cleaning supply aisle without speaking, picked up a can of wipes and handed them to Josie, still without speaking a word. Josie explained she was looking for Ace wipes. Mary yells over three aisles to a coworker in the back room, "Hey, Billy! This lady says she wants Ace monitor wipes. We got any?" Billy comes from the back room and says, "No, we only carry those," pointing to the wipes in Mary's hand, and returns to the back room. Mary turns to Josie and says, "We only carry these," and puts the wipes back on the shelf. She turns to walk back to her aisle when Josie says to Mary, "Well, those Ace wipes are great wipes. You might want to consider carrying them." Mary says, "I'm only responsible for software." Josie leaves the store.

Discuss this situation in a small group of students and answer the following questions:

1. If you were Josie, how would you feel about the service in this store?
2. What would you have expected to happen that did not happen?
3. If you were Mary, how could you have provided better service?
4. If you were Billy, is there anything more you could have done to help?
5. If you were the store manager, what principles of good customer service would you want Billy and Mary to know that would have helped them in this situation?

subjective and subtle ways. Generally, your attitudes toward your customers stem from how you see people, how you see yourself, and how you see your job. Your attitude is a heart issue, not a head issue. To improve your attitude, you must do it from your heart. That's pretty subjective and cannot be defined with a set of rules, but it always begins with a decision to change. As you work with customers or users, make it a habit to not talk down to or patronize them. Don't make the customers or users feel inferior. People appreciate it when they feel your respect for them even when they have made a mistake or are not knowledgeable. If a problem is simple to solve, don't make the other person feel he or she has wasted your time. Your customer or user should always be made to feel that the problem is important to you.

▲ *Trait 2. **Listening without interrupting your customer.*** When you're working with or talking to a customer, focus on him or her. Don't assume you know what your customer is about to say. Let her say it, listen carefully, and don't interrupt. Make it your job to satisfy this person, not just your organization, your boss, your bank account, or the customer's boss.

▲ *Trait 3. **Proper and polite language.*** Speak politely and use language that won't confuse your customer. Avoid using slang or jargon (technical language that only technical

Figure 3-4 Learn to listen before you decide what a user needs or wants
Courtesy: iStockphoto

A+
220-701
6.2

people can understand). Avoid acronyms (initial letters that stand for words). For example, don't say to a nontechnical customer, "I need to ditch your KVM switch," when you could explain yourself better by saying to the customer, "I need to replace that little switch box on your desk that controls your keyboard, monitor, and mouse."

▲ *Trait 4. **Sensitivity to cultural differences**.* Cultural differences happen because we are from different countries and societies or because of physical handicaps. Culture can cause us to differ in how we define or judge good service. For example, culture can affect our degree of tolerance for uncertainty. Some cultures are willing to embrace uncertainty and others strive to avoid it. Those who tend to avoid uncertainty can easily get upset when the unexpected happens. For these people, you need to make special efforts to communicate early and often when things are not going as expected. For the physically challenged, especially the deaf or blind, communication can be more difficult. It's your responsibility in these situations to do whatever is necessary to find a way to communicate. And it's especially important to have an attitude of patience and tolerance which you will unconsciously express in your tone of voice, your choice of words, and your actions.

▲ *Trait 5. **Taking ownership of the problem**.* Taking ownership of the customer's problem means to accept the customer's problem as your own problem. Doing that builds trust and loyalty because the customer knows you can be counted on. Taking ownership of a problem also increases your value in the eyes of your coworkers and boss. People who don't take ownership of the problem at hand are likely to be viewed as lazy, uncommitted, and uncaring. One way to take ownership of a problem is to not engage your boss in unproductive discussions about a situation that he expects you to handle on your own.

▲ *Trait 6. **Dependability**.* Customers appreciate and respect those who do as they say. If you promise to be back at 10:00 the next morning, be back at 10:00 the next morning. If you cannot keep your appointment, never ignore your promise. Call, apologize, let the customer know what happened, and reschedule your appointment.

Figure 3-5 When talking with customers, make sure they understand what to expect from you
Courtesy: iStockphoto

APPLYING CONCEPTS

Jack had had a bad day on the phones at the networking help desk in Atlanta. An electrical outage coupled with a generator failure had caused servers in San Francisco to be down most of the day. The entire help-desk team had been fielding calls all day explaining to customers why they did not have service and about expected recovery times. The servers were finally online, but it was taking hours to get everything reset and functioning. No one had taken a break all afternoon, but the call queue was still running about 20 minutes behind. Todd, the boss, had asked the team to work late until the queue was empty. It was Jack's son's birthday and his family was all expecting Jack home on time. Jack moaned as he realized he might be late for Tyler's party. Everyone pushed hard to empty the queue. As Jack watched the last call leave the queue, he logged off, stood up, and reached for his coat.

And then the call came. Jack was tempted to ignore it, but decided it had to be answered. It was Lacy. Lacy was the executive secretary to the CEO and when Lacy calls, all priorities yield to Lacy and Lacy knows it. The CEO was having problems printing to the laser printer in his office. Would Jack please walk down to his office and fix the problem. Jack asks Lacy to check the simple things like, "Is the printer turned on? Is it plugged up?" Lacy gets huffy and says, "Of course, I've checked that. Now come right now. I need to go." Jack walks down to the CEO's office, takes one look at the printer and turns it on.

He turns to Lacy and says, "I suppose the on/off button was just too technical for you." Lacy glares at him in disbelief. Jack says, "I'll be leaving now." As he walks out, he begins to form a plan as to how he'll defend himself to his boss in the morning, knowing the inevitable call to Todd's office will come.

In a group of two or four students, role play Jack and Todd and discuss these questions:

1. Todd is informed the next morning of Jack's behavior. Todd calls Jack into his office. He likes Jack and wants him to be successful in the company. Jack is resistant and feels justified in what he did. As Todd, what do you think is important that Jack understand? How can you explain this to Jack so he can accept it? What would you advise Jack to do? In role play, one student plays the role of Jack and another the role of Todd.

2. Switch roles or switch team members and replay the roles.

3. What are three principles of relating to people that would be helpful for Jack to keep in mind?

▲ *Trait 7. Credibility.* Convey confidence to your customers. Don't allow yourself to appear confused or befuddled. Troubleshoot the problem in a systematic way that portrays confidence and credibility. Get the job done, and do it with excellence. Credible technicians also know when the job is beyond their expertise and when to ask for help.

▲ *Trait 8. Integrity and honesty.* Don't try to hide your mistakes from your customer or your boss. Everyone makes mistakes, but don't compound them by a lack of integrity. Accept responsibility and do what you can to correct the error.

▲ *Trait 9. Know the law with respect to your work.* For instance, observe the laws concerning the use of software. Don't use or install pirated software.

▲ *Trait 10. Looking and behaving professionally.* A professional at work knows to not allow his emotions to interfere with business relationships. If a customer is angry, allow the customer to vent, keeping your own professional distance (You do, however, have the right to expect a customer not to talk to you in an abusive way.) Dress appropriately for the environment. Take a shower each day, and brush your teeth after each meal. Use mouthwash. Iron your shirt. If you're not in good health, try as best you can to take care of the problem. Your appearance matters. And finally—don't use inappropriate language. It is *never* appropriate.

Figure 3-6 Allow an irate customer to vent and then speak calmly
Courtesy: iStockphoto

> **Notes** Your customers might never remember what you said or what you did, but they will always remember how you made them feel.

PLANNING FOR GOOD SERVICE

Customers want good service. And to provide good service, you need to have a good plan when servicing customers on the phone or online, on site, or in a shop. This section surveys the entire service situation, from the first contact with the customer to closing the call. We begin with the first contact you have with the customer.

> **A+ Exam Tip** The A+ 220-701 Essentials exam expects you to know that when servicing a customer, you should be on time, avoid distractions, set and meet expectations and timelines, communicate the status of the solution with the customer, and deal appropriately with customer confidential materials.

INITIAL CONTACT WITH A CUSTOMER

Your initial contact with a customer might be when the customer comes to you such as in a retail setting, when you go to the customer's site, when the customer calls you on the phone, or when the customer reaches you by chat or e-mail. In each situation, always follow the specific guidelines of your employer. Let's look at some general guidelines when you go to the customer's site and when the customer calls you on the phone.

BEGINNING A SITE VISIT PROFESSIONALLY

When a technician makes an on-site service call, customers expect him or her to have both technical and interpersonal skills. Prepare for a service call by reviewing information given you by whoever took the call. Know the problem you are going to address, the urgency of the situation, and what computer, software, and hardware needs servicing. Arrive with a complete set of equipment appropriate to the visit, which might include a tool kit, flashlight, multimeter, grounding strap and mat, and bootable CDs and DVDs.

When you arrive at the customer's site, greet the customer in a friendly manner and shake his or her hand. Use Mr. or Ms. and last names rather than first names when addressing the

Figure 3-7 A frustrated customer will appreciate your confidence and friendly attitude
Courtesy: iStockphoto

customer, unless you are certain the customer expects you to use first names. If the site is a residence, know that you should never stay at a site when only a minor is present. If a minor child answers the door, ask to speak with an adult and don't allow the adult to leave the house with only you and the child present.

After initial greetings, the first thing you should do is listen and ask questions. As you listen, it's fine to take notes, but don't start the visit by filling out your paperwork. Save the paperwork for later or have the essentials already filled out before you reach the site.

Figure 3-8 Begin each new relationship with a handshake
Courtesy: iStockphoto

A+
220-701
6.2

BEGINNING A PHONE CALL PROFESSIONALLY

When you answer the phone, identify yourself and your organization. (Follow the guidelines of your employer on what to say.) Then ask for and write down the name and phone number of the caller. Ask for spelling if necessary. If your help desk supports businesses, get the name of the business the caller represents.

Follow company policies to obtain other specific information you should take when answering an initial call. For example, your company might require that you obtain a licensing or warranty number to determine whether the customer is entitled to receive your support. Be familiar with your company's customer service policies. You might need to refer questions about warranties, licenses, documentation, or procedures to other support personnel or customer relations personnel. After you have obtained all the information you need to know that you are authorized to help the customer, open up the conversation for the caller to describe the problem.

> 💡 **Notes** If you spend many hours on the phone at a help desk, use a headset instead of a regular phone to reduce strain on your ears and neck. Investing in a high-quality headset will be worth the money.

Figure 3-9 Teaching a user how to fix her problem can prevent it from reoccurring
Courtesy: iStockphoto

A+
220-701
6.2
2.1

INTERVIEW THE CUSTOMER

Troubleshooting begins by interviewing the user. As you ask the user questions, take notes and keep asking questions until you thoroughly understand the problem. Have the customer reproduce the problem, and carefully note each step taken and its results. This process gives you clues about the problem and about the customer's technical proficiency, which helps you know how to communicate with the customer.

Here are some questions that can help you learn as much as you can about the problem and its root cause:

1. Please describe the problem. What error messages, unusual displays, or failures did you see? (Possible answer: I see this blue screen with a funny-looking message on it that makes no sense to me.)

2. When did the problem start? (Possible answer: When I first booted after loading this neat little screensaver I downloaded from the Web.)

3. What was the situation when the problem occurred? (Possible answers: I was trying to start up my PC. I was opening a document in MS Word. I was researching a project on the Internet.)

4. What programs or software were you using? (Possible answer: I was using Internet Explorer.)

5. Did you move your computer system recently? (Possible answer: Well, yes. Yesterday I moved the computer case across the room.)

6. Has there been a recent thunderstorm or electrical problem? (Possible answer: Yes, last night. Then when I tried to turn on my PC this morning, nothing happened.)

7. Have you made any hardware, software, or configuration changes? (Possible answer: No, but I think my sister might have.)

8. Has someone else used your computer recently? (Possible answer: Sure, my son uses it all the time.)

9. Is there some valuable data on your system that is not backed up that I should know about before I start working on the problem? (Possible answer: Yes! Yes! My term paper! It's not backed up! You gotta save that!)

10. Can you show me how to reproduce the problem? (Possible answers: Yes, let me show you what to do.)

After you have interviewed the user, ask him to listen while you repeat the problem to make sure you understand it correctly. If you don't understand what the customer is telling you, ask open-ended questions to try to narrow down the specifics of the problem. Re-create the circumstances that existed when the problem occurred in as much detail as you can. Make no assumptions. All users make simple mistakes and then overlook them. And before you begin work, be sure to ask the very important Question 9 listed above, "Does the system hold important data that is not backed up?" Then watch the user reproduce the problem. Or, if the user is not at the computer and you are at the computer, follow his directions to reproduce the problem yourself.

Use diplomacy and good manners when you work with a user to solve a problem. For example, if you suspect that the user dropped the PC, don't ask, "Did you drop the PC?" Put the question in a less accusatory manner: "Could the PC have been dropped?"

> 💡 **A+ Exam Tip** The A+ 220-701 Essentials exam expects you to be able to clarify customer statements by asking open-ended questions to narrow the scope of the problem and by restating the issue or question.

SET AND MEET CUSTOMER EXPECTATIONS

A professional technician knows that it is his responsibility to set and meet expectations with a customer. It's important to create an expectation of certainty with customers so that they are not left hanging and don't know what will happen next.

Part of setting expectations is to establish a timeline with your customer for the completion of a project. If you cannot solve the problem immediately, explain to the customer what needs to happen and the timeline that she should expect for a solution. Then keep the customer informed about the progress of the solution. For example, you can say to a customer, "I need to return to the office and research the cost of parts that need replacing. I'll call you tomorrow

A+
220-701
6.2

before 10:00 AM with an estimate." If later you find out you need more time, call the customer before 10:00 AM, explain your problem, and give her a new time to expect your call. This kind of service is very much appreciated by customers and, if you are consistent, you will quickly gain their confidence.

Another way to set expectations is to give the customer an opportunity to make decisions about repairs to the customer's equipment. When explaining to the customer what needs to be done to fix a problem, offer repair or replacement options if they apply. Don't make decisions for your customer. Explain the problem and what you must do to fix it, giving as many details as the customer wants. When a customer must make a choice, state the options in a way that does not unfairly favor the solution that makes the most money for you as the technician or for your company. For example, if you must replace a motherboard (a costly repair in parts and labor), explain to the customer the total cost of repairs and then help her decide if it is to her advantage to purchase a new system or repair this one.

Figure 3-10   Advise and then allow a customer to make purchasing decisions
Courtesy: iStockphoto

WORKING WITH A CUSTOMER ON SITE

As you work with a customer on site, avoid distractions as you work. Don't accept personal calls on your cell phone. Most organizations require that you answer calls from work, but keep the call to a minimum. Be aware that the customer might be listening, so be careful to not discuss problems with coworkers, the boss, or other situations that might put the company, its employees, or products in a bad light with the customer. If you absolutely must excuse yourself from the service call for personal reasons, explain to the customer the situation and return as soon as possible.

As you work, be as unobtrusive as possible. Consider yourself a guest in the customer's office or residence. Don't make a big mess. Keep your tools and papers out of the customer's way. Don't use the phone or sit in the customer's desk chair without permission. If the customer needs to work while you are present, do whatever is necessary to accommodate that.

A+
220-701
6.2

Protect the customer's confidential materials. Don't read these materials. For example, if you are working on the printer and discover a budget report in the out tray, quickly turn it over so you can't read it and hand it to the customer. If you notice a financial spreadsheet is displayed on the customer's computer screen, step away and suggest to the user he close the spreadsheet. If sensitive documents are lying on the customer's desk, you might let him know so he can put them in a safe place.

When working at a user's desk, follow these general guidelines:

1. Don't take over the mouse or keyboard from the user without permission.

2. Ask permission again before you use the printer or other equipment.

3. Don't use the phone without permission.

4. Don't pile your belongings and tools on top of the user's papers, books, and so forth.

5. Accept personal inconvenience to accommodate the user's urgent business needs. For example, if the user gets an important call while you are working, delay your work until the call is over.

6. Also, if the user is present, ask permission before you make a software or hardware change, even if the user has just given you permission to interact with the PC.

Figure 3-11 Consider yourself a guest at the customer's site
Courtesy: iStockphoto

In some PC support situations, it is appropriate to consider yourself a support to the user as well as to the PC. Your goals can include educating the user, as well as repairing the computer. If you want users to learn something from a problem they caused, explain how to fix the problem and walk them through the process if necessary. Don't fix the problem yourself unless they ask you to. It takes a little longer to train the user, but it is more productive in the end because the user learns more and is less likely to repeat the mistake.

A+
220-701
6.2

WORKING WITH A CUSTOMER ON THE PHONE

Phone support requires more interaction with customers than any other type of PC support. To understand the problem and also give clear instructions, you must be able to visualize what the customer sees at his or her PC. Patience is required if the customer must be told each key to press or command button to click. Help-desk support requires excellent communication skills, good phone manners, and lots of patience. As your help-desk skills improve, you will learn to think through the process as though you were sitting in front of the PC yourself. Drawing diagrams and taking notes as you talk can be very helpful.

If your call is accidentally disconnected, call back immediately. Don't eat or drink while on the phone. If you must put callers on hold, tell them how long it will be before you get back to them. Speak clearly and don't talk too fast. Don't complain about your job, your boss or coworkers, your company, or other companies or products to your customers. A little small talk is okay and is sometimes beneficial in easing a tense situation, but keep it upbeat and positive.

APPLYING CONCEPTS

Julie and James were good friends who worked together at the corporate help desk for internal customers. Staying on the phones all day can be tense and demanding and they had learned that good humor and occasional chit-chat can break up the day. Julie was on a long troubleshooting call and the call queue was getting backed up. James was answering one call after another trying to keep up. Julie says to her customer, "I have to check with another technician. I'll be right back," and puts the customer on hold. She turns to James and says, "You gonna go to that new movie on Saturday?" James puts his caller on hold and answers, "I sure want to. Wonder what times it's showing. Let me see." James and Julie browse through the movie listings and decide when to meet for the movie and where to eat later. About 10 minutes later, Julie and James return to their callers. Julie says to her caller, "Okay, I have the information I need. Let's continue."

In a small group, discuss this situation and answer the following questions:

1. If you were Julie's caller, how would you feel about being left on hold for 10 minutes in the middle of a long call?

2. What principles of customer service do you think Julie and James need to reconsider?

3. If you were Julie or James, how do you think you would handle this situation?

DEALING WITH DIFFICULT CUSTOMERS

Most customers are polite and appreciate your help. And, if you make it a habit to treat others as you want to be treated, you'll find that most of your customers will tend to treat you well, too. However, occasionally you'll have to deal with a difficult customer. In this part of the chapter, you'll learn how to work with customers who are not knowledgeable, who are overly confident, and who complain.

WHEN THE CUSTOMER IS NOT KNOWLEDGEABLE

A help-desk call is the most difficult situation to handle when a customer is not knowledgeable about how to use a computer. When on site, you can put a PC in good repair without depending on a customer to help you, but when you are trying to solve a problem over

Figure 3-12 Learn to be patient and friendly when helping users
Courtesy: iStockphoto

the phone, with a customer as your only eyes, ears, and hands, a computer-illiterate user can present a challenge. Here are some tips for handling this situation:

- *Tip 1*. Be specific with your instructions. For example, instead of saying, "Open Windows Explorer," say, "Using your mouse, right-click the Start button and select Explore from the menu."
- *Tip 2*. Don't ask the customer to do something that might destroy settings or files without first having the customer back them up carefully. If you think the customer can't handle your request, ask for some on-site help.
- *Tip 3*. Frequently ask the customer what is displayed on the screen to help you track the keystrokes and action.
- *Tip 4*. Follow along at your own PC. It's easier to direct the customer, keystroke by keystroke, if you are doing the same things.
- *Tip 5*. Give the customer plenty of opportunity to ask questions.
- *Tip 6*. Compliment the customer whenever you can to help the customer gain confidence.
- *Tip 7*. If you determine that the customer cannot help you solve the problem without a lot of coaching, you might need to tactfully request that the caller have someone with more experience call you. The customer will most likely breathe a sigh of relief and have someone take over the problem.

> **Notes** When solving computer problems in an organization other than your own, check with technical support within that organization instead of working only with the PC user. The user might not be aware of policies that have been set on the PC to prevent changes to the OS, hardware, or applications.

WHEN THE CUSTOMER IS OVERLY CONFIDENT

Sometimes customers are proud of their computer knowledge. Such customers might want to give advice, take charge of a call, withhold information they think you don't need to know, or execute commands at the computer without letting you know, so you don't have

A+
220-701
6.2

enough information to follow along. A situation like this must be handled with tact and respect for the customer. Here are a few tips:

▲ *Tip 1*. When you can, compliment the customer's knowledge, experience, or insight.

▲ *Tip 2*. Slow the conversation down. You can say, "Please slow down. You're moving too fast for me to follow. Help me catch up."

▲ *Tip 3*. Don't back off from using problem-solving skills. You must still have the customer check the simple things, but direct the conversation with tact. For example, you can say, "I know you've probably already gone over these simple things, but could we just do them again together?"

▲ *Tip 4*. Be careful not to accuse the customer of making a mistake.

▲ *Tip 5*. Even though the customer might be using technical jargon, keep to your policy of not doing so with this customer unless you're convinced he truly understands you.

> **♥ A+ Exam Tip** The A+ 220-701 Essentials exam expects you to know that it is important to not minimize a customer's problem and to not be judgmental toward a customer.

WHEN THE CUSTOMER COMPLAINS

When you are on site or on the phone, a customer might complain to you about your organization, products, or service or the service and product of another company. Consider the complaint to be helpful feedback that can lead to a better product or service and better customer relationships. Here are a few suggestions that can help you handle complaints and defuse customer anger:

▲ *Suggestion 1*. Be an active listener, and let customers know they are not being ignored. Look for the underlying problem. Don't take the complaint or the anger personally.

▲ *Suggestion 2*. Give the customer a little time to vent, and apologize when you can. Then start the conversation from the beginning, asking questions, taking notes, and solving problems. Unless you must have the information for problem solving, don't spend a lot of time finding out exactly whom the customer dealt with and what happened to upset the customer.

▲ *Suggestion 3*. Don't be defensive. It's better to leave the customer with the impression that you and your company are listening and willing to admit mistakes. No matter how much anger is expressed, resist the temptation to argue or become defensive.

▲ *Suggestion 4*. Know how your employer wants you to handle a situation where you are verbally abused. If this type of language is happening, you might say something like this in a very calm tone of voice: "I'm sorry, but my employer does not require me to accept this kind of talk."

▲ *Suggestion 5*. If the customer is complaining about a product or service that is not from your company, don't start off by saying, "That's not our problem." Instead, listen to the customer complain. Don't appear as though you don't care.

▲ *Suggestion 6*. If the complaint is against you or your product, identify the underlying problem if you can. Ask questions and take notes. Then pass these notes on to people in your organization who need to know.

▲ *Suggestion 7.* Sometimes simply making progress or reducing the problem to a manageable state reduces the customer's anxiety. As you are talking to a customer, summarize what you have both agreed on or observed so far in the conversation.

▲ *Suggestion 8.* Point out ways that you think communication could be improved. For example, you might say, "I'm sorry, but I'm having trouble understanding what you want. Could you please slow down, and let's take this one step at a time."

Figure 3-13 When a customer is upset, try to find a place of agreement
Courtesy: iStockphoto

APPLYING CONCEPTS

Andy was one of the most intelligent and knowledgeable support technicians in his group working for NetServe, Inc. He was about to be promoted to software engineer and today was his last day on the help desk. Sarah, a potential customer with little computer experiences, calls asking for help accessing the company Web site. Andy says, "The URL is www dot netserve dot com." Sarah responds, "What's a URL?" Andy's patience grows thin. He's thinking to himself, "Oh, help! Just two more hours and I'm off these darn phones." He answers Sarah in a tone of voice that says, hey, I really think you're an idiot! He says to her, "You know, lady! That address box at the top of your browser. Now enter www dot netserve dot com!" Sarah gets all flustered and intimidated and doesn't know what to say next. She really wants to know what is a browser, but instead she says, "Wait. I'll just ask someone in the office to help me," and hangs up the phone.

Discuss the situation with others in a small group and answer these questions:

1. If you were Andy's manager and overheard this call, how would you handle the situation?

2. What principles of working with customers does Andy need to keep in mind?

Two students sit back to back, one playing the role of Andy and the other playing the role of Sarah. Play out the entire conversation. Others in the group can offer suggestions and constructive criticism.

A+
220-701
6.2

THE CUSTOMER DECIDES WHEN THE WORK IS DONE

When you think you've solved the problem, allow the customer to decide when the service is finished to his or her satisfaction. For remote support, generally, the customer ends the call or chat session, not the technician. If you end the call too soon and the problem is not completely resolved, the customer can be frustrated, especially if it is difficult to contact you again.

For on-site work, after you have solved the problem, complete these tasks before you close the call:

1. If you changed anything on the PC after you booted it, reboot one more time to make sure you have not caused a problem with the boot.

2. Allow the customer enough time to be fully satisfied that all is working. Does the printer work? Print a test page. Does the network connection work? Can the customer log on to the network and access data on it?

3. If you backed up data before working on the problem and then restored the data from backups, ask the user to verify that the data is fully restored.

4. Review the service call with the customer. Summarize the instructions and explanations you have given during the call. This is an appropriate time to fill out your paperwork and explain to the customer what you have written. Then ask if she has any questions.

5. Explain preventive maintenance to the customer (such as deleting temporary files from the hard drive or cleaning the mouse). Most customers don't have preventive maintenance contracts for their PCs and appreciate the time you take to show them how they can take better care of their computers.

It's a good idea to follow up later with the customer and ask if he is still satisfied with your work and if he has any more questions. For example, you can say to the customer, "I'll call you on Monday to make sure everything is working and you're still satisfied with the work." And then on Monday make that call.

> 💡 **A+ Exam Tip**   The A+ 220-701 Essentials exam expects you to know to follow up with the customer at a later date to verify his or her satisfaction.

SOMETIMES YOU MUST ESCALATE A PROBLEM

You are not going to solve every computer problem you encounter. Knowing how to escalate a problem to those higher in the support chain is one of the first things you should learn on a new job. Know your company's policy for escalation. What documents do you fill out? Who gets them? How do you pass the problem on (e-mail, phone call, or an online entry in a database)? Do you remain the responsible "support" party, or does the person now addressing the problem become the new contact? Are you expected to keep in touch with the customer and the problem, or are you totally out of the picture?

For help-desk support, escalation is most likely done in the call-tracking system where you keep your call notes. It's very important to include detailed information in your notes so that the next person can pick up the call without having to waste time finding out information you already knew.

When you escalate, let the customer know. Tell the customer you are passing the problem on to someone who is more experienced or has access to more extensive resources. In most cases, the person who receives the escalation will immediately contact the customer and assume responsibility for the problem. However, in some situations you should follow through, at least to confirm that the new person and the customer have made contact.

A+
220-701
6.2

If you check back with the customer only to find out that the other support person has not called or followed through to the customer's satisfaction, don't lay blame or point fingers. Just do whatever you can to help within your company guidelines. Your call to the customer will go a long way toward helping the situation.

A+
220-701
6.2
2.1

THE JOB ISN'T FINISHED UNTIL THE PAPERWORK IS DONE

For onsite support, a customer expects documentation about your services. Include in the documentation sufficient details broken down by cost of individual parts, hours worked, and cost per hour. Give the documentation to the customer at the end of the service and keep a copy for yourself. For phone support, the documentation stays in house.

If your organization is using an electronic tracking system and you're providing phone support, most likely you're typing notes as the call happens. Be clear with your notes, especially if others must handle the problem. If you cannot solve the problem on this one call, the next time you talk with the customer, you'll be dependent on your notes to remember the details of the previous call. You'll also want to use the solution to help build your knowledge base about this type of problem. Make the notes detailed enough so that you can use them later when solving similar problems. Also, know that tracking-system notes are sometimes audited.

If you don't have an electronic tracking system, after the call, create a written or digital record to build your own knowledge base. Record the initial symptoms of the problem, the source of the problem you actually discovered, how you made that discovery, and how the problem was finally solved. File your documentation according to symptoms or according to solutions.

APPLYING CONCEPTS

Daniel had not been a good note taker in school and this lack of skill was affecting his work. His manager, Jonathon, had been watching Daniel's notes in the ticketing system at the help desk he worked on, and was not happy with what he saw. Jonathon had pointed out to Daniel more than once that his cryptic notes with sketchy information would one day cause major problems. On Monday morning, calls were hammering the help desk as a server had gone down over the weekend and many internal customers were not able to get to their data. Daniel escalated one call from a customer named Matt to a tier-two help desk. Later that day, Sandra, a tier-two technician, received the escalated ticket and to her dismay the phone number of the customer was missing. She called Daniel. "How am I to call this customer? You only have his first name and these notes about the problem don't even make sense!" Daniel apologized to Sandra, but the damage was done.

Two days later, an angry Matt calls the manager of the help desk to complain that his problem is still not solved. Jonathon listens to Matt vent and apologies for the problem his help desk has caused. It's a little embarrassing to Jonathon to have to ask Matt for his call-back information and to repeat the details of the problem. He gives the information to Sandra and the problem gets a quick resolution.

Discuss this situation in a small group and answer the following questions:

1. If you were Daniel, what could you do to improve note taking in the ticketing system?

2. After Sandra called, do you think Daniel should have told Jonathon about the problem? Why or why not?

3. If you were Jonathon, how would you handle the situation with Daniel?

Two students play the role of Daniel and Jonathon when Jonathon calls Daniel into his office to discuss the call he just received from Matt. The other students in the group can watch and make suggestions as to how to improve the conversation.

A+
220-701
6.2

WORKING WITH COWORKERS

Learn to be a professional when working with coworkers. A professional at work is someone who puts business matters above personal matters. In big bold letters I can say the key to that is to learn to not be offended when someone lets you down or does not please you. Remember, most people do the best they can considering the business and personal constraints they're up against. Getting offended leads to becoming bitter about others and about your job. Learn to keep negative opinions to yourself, and to expect the best of others. When a coworker starts to gossip, try to politely change the subject.

Practice good organizational skills. Clean your desk before you leave work each day. Put things away. Use a good filing system. If you don't know how to organize your things, ask someone in the office for advice. Organize your time by making to-do lists and sticking with them as best you can. It's amazing the positive impression good organization makes with coworkers and the boss.

Figure 3-14 Co-workers who act professionally are fun to work with
Courtesy: iStockphoto

Know your limitations and be willing to admit when you can't do something. For example, Larry's boss stops by his desk and asks him to accept one more project. Larry already is working many hours overtime just to keep up. He needs to politely say to his boss, "I can accept this new project only if you relieve me of these tasks."

Learn how to handle conflict at work. Few of us have enough social skills to be able to effectively confront a coworker about his faults. In almost every situation, when a coworker disappoints us, the appropriate response is to shake it off, to not gossip to other coworkers about the problem, and move on. If you can't do that, the next best thing is to go to your boss or the coworker's boss with the problem. Hopefully your boss has been trained in handling conflict and will take care of the problem. If you do find yourself in a situation where you want to help a coworker with his problem, go to the coworker with a good

A+
220-701
6.2

attitude and a sincere offer to help resolve the problem. And one more tip: Never give bad news or point out a fault by e-mail. Using e-mail, you are not able to communicate your tone of voice or read the facial expression of the other person. And, if miscommunication happens, you will not be able to immediately clear it up. Speak face to face, and if that is not possible, speak by telephone.

3

APPLYING | CONCEPTS

Ray was new at the corporate help desk that supported hospitals across the nation. He had only had a couple weeks of training before he was turned loose on the phones. He was a little nervous the first day he took calls without a mentor sitting beside him. His first call came from Fernanda, a radiology technician who was trying to log onto her computer system to start the day. When Fernanda entered her user account and passcode, an error message appeared saying her user account was not valid. She told Ray she had tried it several times on two different computers. Ray checked his database and found her account, which appeared to be in good order. He asked her to try it again. She did and got the same results. In his two weeks of training, this problem had never occurred. He told her, "I'm sorry, I don't know how to solve this problem." She said, "Okay, well, thank you anyway," and hung up. She immediately called the help desk number back and the call was answered by Jackie, who sits across the room from Ray. Fernanda said, "The other guy couldn't fix my problem. Can you help me?"

"What other guy?" Jackie asks. "I think his name was Ray." "Oh, him! He's new and he doesn't know much and besides that he should have asked for help. Tell me the problem." Jackie resets the account and the problem is solved.

In a group of three or more students, discuss and answer the following questions:

1. What mistake did Ray make? What should he have done or said?

2. What mistake did Jackie make? What should she have done or said?

3. What are three principles of relating to customers and coworkers that would be helpful for Ray and Jackie to keep in mind?

>> CHAPTER SUMMARY

◢ Five key job roles of a PC support technician include PC support technician, PC service technician, retail sales associate, bench technician, and help-desk technician.

◢ A+ Certification by CompTIA is the most significant and most recognized certification for PC repair technicians.

◢ Staying abreast of new technology can be done by attending trade shows, reading trade magazines, researching the Internet, subscribing to email newsletters, and attending seminars and workshops.

◢ Customers want more than just technical know-how. They want a positive and helpful attitude, respect, good communication, ownership of their problem, dependability, credibility, and professionalism.

>> KEY TERMS

A+ Certification	escalate	technical documentation
call tracking	expert system	ticket

>> REVIEWING THE BASICS

1. Name five job roles that can all be categorized as a PC technician.

2. Of the five jobs in Question 1, which one job might never include interacting with the PC's primary user?

3. Assume that you are a customer who wants to have a PC repaired. List five main characteristics that you would want to see in your PC repair person.

4. What is one thing you should do when you receive a phone call requesting on-site support, before you make an appointment?

5. You make an appointment to do an on-site repair, but you are detained and find out that you will be late. What is the best thing to do?

6. When you arrive for an on-site service call, how important is your greeting? What would be a good greeting to start off a good business relationship?

7. When making an on-site service call, what should you do before making any changes to software or before taking the case cover off a computer?

8. What should you do after finishing your PC repair?

9. What is a good strategy to follow if a conflict arises between you and your customer?

10. If you are about to make an on-site service call to a large financial organization, is it appropriate to show up in shorts and a T-shirt? Why or why not?

11. You have exhausted your knowledge of a problem and it still is not solved. Before you escalate it, what else can you do?

12. If you need to make a phone call while on a customer's site and your cell phone is not working, what do you do?

13. When someone calls your help desk, what is the first thing you should do?

14. List the items of information you would want to record at the beginning of a help-desk call.

15. What is one thing you can do to help a caller who needs phone support and is not a competent computer user?

16. Describe what you should do when a customer complains to you about a product or service that your company provides.

17. What are some things you can do to make your work at a help desk easier?

18. Why is it important to be a certified technician?

19. When applying for a position as a help-desk technician, you discover the job interview will happen by telephone. Why do you think the employer has chosen this method for the interview?

20. What organization offers A+ certification?

>> THINKING CRITICALLY

1. You own a small PC repair company and a customer comes to you with a PC that will not boot. After investigating, you discover the hard drive has crashed. What should you do first?

   a. Install a hard drive the same size and speed as the original.

b. Ask the customer's advice about the size drive to install, but select a drive the same speed as the original drive.

c. Ask the customer's advice about the size and speed of the new drive to install.

d. If the customer looks like he can afford it, install the largest and fastest drive the system can support.

2. You have repaired a broken LCD panel in a notebook computer. However, when you disassembled the notebook, you bent the hinge on the notebook lid so that it now does not latch solidly. When the customer receives the notebook, he notices the bent hinge and begins shouting at you. What do you do first? Second?

a. Explain to the customer you are sorry but you did the best you could.

b. Listen carefully to the customer and don't get defensive.

c. Ask the customer what he would like you to do to resolve the problem.

d. Tell the customer he is not allowed to speak to you like that.

>> HANDS-ON PROJECTS

PROJECT 3-1: Evaluating Your Own Interpersonal Skills with Customers and Coworkers

Assume that you are working as a PC support technician for a corporation. Your job requires you to give desk-side support to users, answer the phone at the help desk, and make an occasional on-site call at corporate branches. Answer the following questions:

1. In the role of desk-side support to users, what do you think is your strongest social skill that would help you succeed in this role?

2. What is likely to be your greatest interpersonal weakness that might present a challenge to you in this role?

3. What is one change you might consider making that will help you to improve on this weakness?

4. In the role of phone support at the help desk, what part of that job would you enjoy the most? What part would give you the greatest challenge?

5. When making on-site calls to corporate branches, what part of this job would you enjoy the most? What interpersonal skills, if any, would you need to develop so that you could do your best in this role?

PROJECT 3-2: The Johari Window Online Game

The Johari (pronounced "Joe-Harry" after the two men who created it) window reveals an interesting view of how we relate to others. Sometimes when we evaluate our own interpersonal skills, we overlook our greatest assets that others can see. This project is designed to help others reveal to you those assets. The house in Figure 3-15 represents who we are. Room 1 is what we know about ourselves that we allow others to see. Room 2 is what others see about us that we don't see ourselves (our blind spots). Room 3 is what we see about ourselves that we hide from others. And Room 4 contains traits in us that we don't know about and neither do others see—traits yet to be discovered.

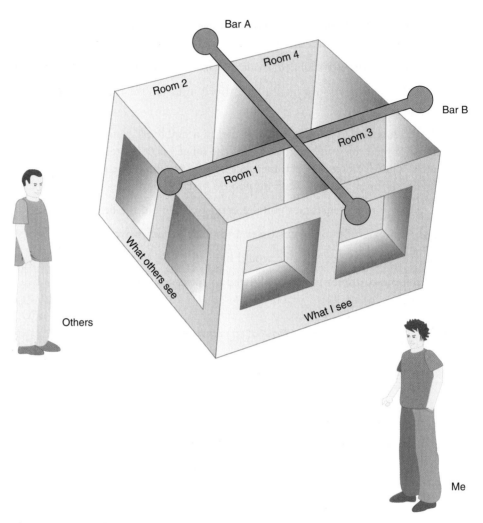

Figure 3-15 A Johari Window demonstrates the complexity of how we see ourselves and how
others see us
Courtesy: Course Technology/Cengage Learning

As we move Bar A to the right, we are making a conscious decision to reveal more about
ourselves to others, which is a technique successful salespeople often use to immediately
connect with their customers. The theory is that if you move Bar A to the right, not only
are you choosing to reveal what you normally would hide, but you are also moving the bar
so that more of Room 4 can be seen in Room 2. This means that others can see more
about you that you don't see. When we allow others to tell us something about ourselves,
we are moving Bar B away from us, which, in effect, allows us to see more of who we
really are. Therefore, to learn more about yourself, you can do two things: Reveal more of
yourself to others and allow others to tell you more about yourself. Try playing the
Interactive Johari Window game at *www.kevan.org/johari* by Kevan Davis. Then answer
the following questions:

1. What are the five or six descriptive words you used to describe yourself at the beginning
   of the game?

2. What are words others used to describe you?

3. How has input from your friends adjusted how you see yourself?

4. How might this adjustment affect the way you will relate to customers and coworkers on the job?

5. If you were to play the Interactive Johari Window game a second time, would you still use the same five or six descriptive words that you used the first time? If your answer is no, what new words would you use?

PROJECT 3-3: Handling Conflict at Work

Jenny works with a team of seven other professionals. Linda, a team member, is a very close personal friend of the boss. With the boss's approval, Linda took a sudden and unexpected two-week vacation to go on a cruise during the team's most difficult month of the year. One team member, Jason, had to work 16 days nonstop, without a day off during Linda's vacation. Other team members soon began complaining and resenting Linda for the unbearable workload that vacation caused them. A few weeks back from vacation, Linda began to notice that she was being excluded from informal luncheons and after-work gatherings. She confided in Jenny that she could not understand why everyone seemed to be mad at her. Jenny, not wanting to cause trouble, said nothing to Linda. In a group of four or five classmates, discuss the answers to the following questions:

1. If you were Jenny, what would you do?

2. What would you do if you were Linda?

3. What would you do if you were Jason?

4. What would you do if you were another team member?

5. If you were the boss and got wind of the resentment against Linda, what would you do?

PROJECT 3-4: Learning to Be a Good Communicator

Working with a partner, discuss ways to respond to the following statements made by a customer. Then decide on your best response.

1. My computer is all dark.

2. I got so mad at my laptop, I threw it to the floor. Now it won't start. I think it's still under warranty.

3. My dog chewed the mouse cord and now nothing works.

4. I heard you tell that other customer that your product stinks. I came here to buy one. Now what am I to do?

5. I don't see the "any" key. Where is it?

PROJECT 3-5: Interacting with the User

Rob, a PC service technician, has been called on site to repair a PC. He has not spoken directly with the user, Lisa, but he knows the floor of the building where she works and can look for her name on her cubicle. The following is a description of his actions. Create a table with two columns. List in one column the mistakes he made in the following description and in the next column the correct action he should have taken.

Rob's company promised that a service technician would come some time during the next business day after the call was received. Rob was given the name and address of the user and the problem, which was stated as "PC will not boot." Rob arrived the following day at about 10 AM. He found Lisa's cubicle, but she was not present. Because Lisa was not present, Rob decided not to disturb the papers all over her desk, so he laid his notebooks and tools on top of her work.

Rob tried to boot the PC, and it gave errors indicating a corrupted file system on the hard drive. He successfully booted from a CD and was able to access a directory list of drive C. The list was corrupted and jumbled and he realized most of the files were corrupted. Next, Rob used a recovery utility to try to recover the files and directories but was unable to do so. He began to suspect that a virus had caused the problem, so he ran a virus scan program that did not find the suspected virus.

He made a call to his technical support to ask for suggestions. Technical support suggested he try erasing everything on the hard drive to remove any possible viruses and then reinstall Windows. Rob cleaned everything off the hard drive and was on the phone with technical support, in the process of reloading Windows from the company's file server, when Lisa arrived.

Lisa took one look at her PC and gasped. She caught her breath and asked where her data was. Rob replied, "A virus destroyed your hard drive. I had to reformat."

Lisa tried to explain the importance of the destroyed data. Rob replied, "Guess you'll learn to make backups now." Lisa left to find her manager.

>> REAL PROBLEMS, REAL SOLUTIONS

REAL PROBLEM 3-1: Looking for a PC Support Job

Suppose you've finished your PC repair curriculum and have achieved A+ Certification. Now it's time to find a job. Research the online job sites and newspapers for PC support jobs in your area. Look for jobs that require A+ Certification and also look for PC support-related jobs that don't require certification. Don't forget to check out retail jobs selling computers and computer parts. Find at least three job ads. If you can't find ads in your immediate area, branch out into nearby cites. Make printouts or copies of the three job ads and answer these questions:

1. What source (newspaper, Web site, or other source) did you use to find the job?

2. What is the job title?

3. What are the qualifications of the job?

4. What is the salary?

5. What additional experience or certification do you need to qualify for the job?

6. If you were actually looking for a PC support-related job, which of the three jobs would be your first choice? Why?

REAL PROBLEM 3-2: Write Your Own Scenario for Developing Interpersonal Social Skills

In the chapter, you read several scenarios where technical support people failed to serve their customers well or failed to relate professionally with coworkers. Recall a similar situation where you observed poor service from a technician or salesperson. Write the scenario using fictitious names. Then write three questions to cause other students to think through what went wrong, what should have happened, and what are some principles of relating to customers or coworkers that could have helped if they had been applied. Present your scenario in class or with a student group for discussion.

Form Factors, Power Supplies, and Working Inside a Computer

This chapter focuses on the power supply, which provides power to all other components inside the computer case. Several types of power supplies are available. The form factor of the computer case and motherboard drive which type of power supply can be installed in a system. Therefore, we begin the chapter discussing the form factors of computer cases, motherboards, and power supplies. To troubleshoot problems with the power system of a PC, you need a basic understanding of electricity. You'll learn about the measurements of electricity and the form in which it comes to you as house current. The chapter then covers how to select a power supply and how to protect a computer system from damage caused by electrical problems. Next, we discuss how to take a computer apart and put it back together again. Finally, we talk about ways to detect and correct problems with the PC's electrical system, including how to change a defective power supply.

This chapter is the first in a group of chapters to learn how to service computer hardware. We begin with the electrical system because it's so important that you know how to protect yourself and the equipment against electrical dangers as you work. In later chapters, you'll want to apply the safety skills learned in this chapter. Other skills learned in this chapter, such as taking a computer apart and putting it back together, will be useful to know in future chapters in which you will exchange other computer parts besides the power supply.

FORM FACTORS USED BY COMPUTER CASES, MOTHERBOARDS, AND POWER SUPPLIES

A+
220-701
1.2

This chapter is all about a computer's electrical system and power supply, such as the one shown in Figure 4-1. However, because motherboards, power supplies, and computer cases are often sold together and must be compatible with each other, we begin by looking at these three components as an interconnecting system. When you put together a new system, or replace components in an existing system, the motherboard, power supply, and case must all be compatible. The standards that describe the size, shape, and major features of these components so that they work together are called form factors.

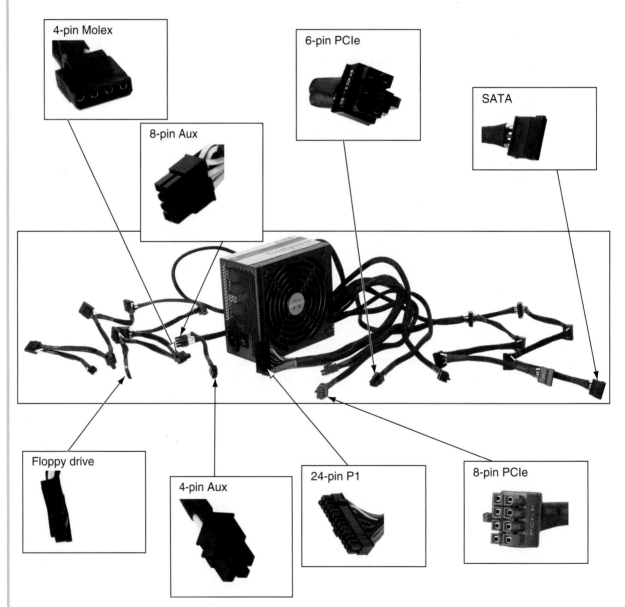

Figure 4-1 Computer power supply with connectors
Courtesy: Course Technology/Cengage Learning

When you are deciding which form factor to use, the motherboard drives the decision because it determines what the system can do. After you've decided to use a certain form factor for the motherboard, you must use the same form factor for the case and power supply. Using a matching form factor for the motherboard, power supply, and case assures you that:

- The motherboard fits in the case.
- The power supply cords to the motherboard provide the correct voltage, and the connectors match the connections on the board.
- The holes in the motherboard align with the holes in the case for anchoring the board to the case.
- Holes in the case align with ports coming off the motherboard.
- For some form factors, wires for switches and lights on the front of the case match up with connections on the motherboard.
- The holes in the power supply align with holes in the case for anchoring the power supply to the case.

TYPES OF FORM FACTORS

When selecting a computer case, motherboard, and power supply, choose a design that fits its intended use. For instance, you might find that you need a high-end tower system, a rack-mounted server, or a low-profile desktop. When you understand the intended use, you then can decide which form factor you will use.

The current and better-known form factors are listed in Table 4-1. These form factors are discussed next.

Form Factor	Motherboard Size	Description
ATX, full size	Up to 12" x 9.6"	Most popular form factor, which has had many revisions
MicroATX	Up to 9.6" x 9.6"	Smaller version of ATX
FlexATX	Up to 9" x 7.5"	Smaller version of MicroATX
BTX	Up to 12.8" wide	Has improvements over ATX and can have up to seven expansion slots
MicroBTX	Up to 10.4" wide	Has up to four expansion slots
PicoBTX	Up to 8" wide	None or one expansion slot
NLX	Up to 9" x 13.6"	Used in low-end systems with a riser card

Table 4-1 Form factors

> 💡 **A+ Exam Tip** The A+ 220-701 Essentials exam expects you to recognize and know the more important features of the ATX, BTX, Micro ATX, and NLX motherboards.

ATX FORM FACTOR

ATX (Advanced Technology Extended) is the most commonly used form factor today. It is an open, nonproprietary industry specification originally developed by Intel in 1995, and has undergone several revisions since then.

An ATX motherboard measures up to 12" x 9.6". The CPU and memory slots sit beside expansion slots so that full-length expansion cards don't bump into the CPU or memory modules (see Figure 4-2). The original ATX form factor had case fans blowing air into the case but early revisions to the form factor had fans blowing air out of the case. Blowing air out of the case does a better job of keeping the system cool.

The first ATX power supplies and motherboards used a single power connector called the **P1 connector** that had 20 pins

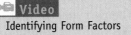

Video

Identifying Form Factors

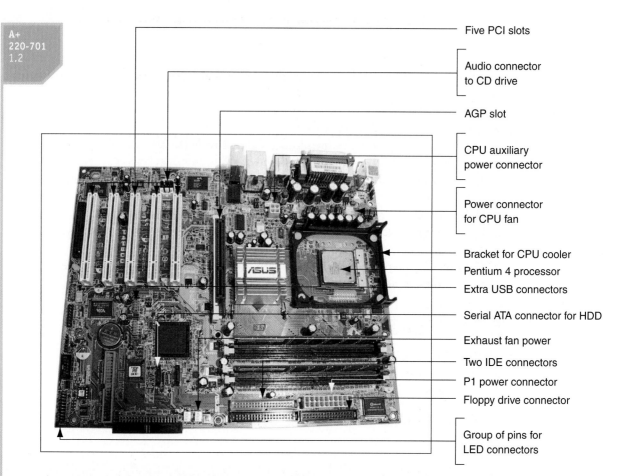

Five PCI slots

Audio connector
to CD drive

AGP slot

CPU auxiliary
power connector

Power connector
for CPU fan

Bracket for CPU cooler

Pentium 4 processor

Extra USB connectors

Serial ATA connector for HDD

Exhaust fan power

Two IDE connectors

P1 power connector

Floppy drive connector

Group of pins for
LED connectors

Figure 4-2 The CPU on an ATX motherboard sits opposite the expansion slots and does not block the room needed
for long expansion cards
Courtesy: Course Technology/Cengage Learning

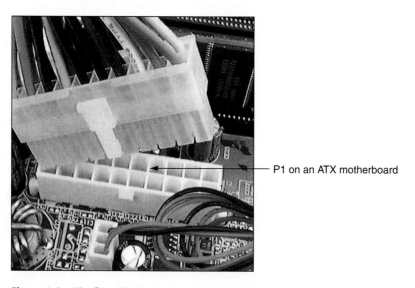

P1 on an ATX motherboard

Figure 4-3 The first ATX P1 power connector used 20 pins
Courtesy: Course Technology/Cengage Learning

(see Figure 4-3). These pins provided +3.3 volts, +5 volts, +12 volts, -12 volts, and an optional
and rarely used -5 volts. The electrical requirements for motherboards change over time as
new technologies make additional demands for power. When processors began to require more
power, the ATX Version 2.1 specifications added a 4-pin auxiliary connector near the processor socket to provide an additional 12 V of power (see Figure 4-4). A power supply that provides this 4-pin 12-volt power cord is called an **ATX12V power supply**. Later boards changed

Figure 4-4 The 4-pin 12-volt auxiliary power connector on a motherboard
Courtesy: Course Technology/Cengage Learning

the 4-pin 12-volt power connector to an 8-pin connector that provided more amps for the processor.

Later, when PCI Express slots were added to motherboards, more power was required and a new ATX specification (ATX Version 2.2) allowed for a 24-pin P1 connector, which is backward compatible with the 20-pin P1 connector. The extra 4 pins on the connector provide +12 volts, +5 volts, and +3.3 volts pins. Motherboards that support PCI Express and have the 24-pin P1 connector are sometimes called Enhanced ATX boards. Figure 4-5 shows a 20-pin P1 power cord from the power supply and a 24-pin P1 connector on a motherboard. Figure 4-6 shows the pinouts for the 24-pin power cord connector, which is color-coded to wires from the power supply. The 20-pin connector is missing the lower four pins in the photo and diagram.

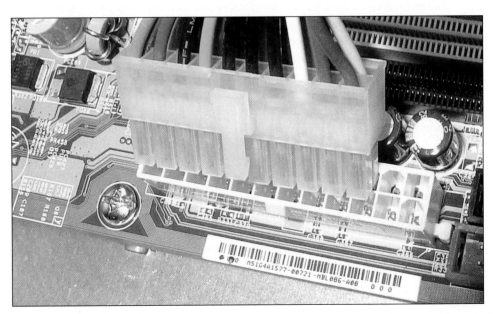

Figure 4-5 A 20-pin power cord ready to be plugged into a 24-pin P1 connector on an ATX motherboard
Courtesy: Course Technology/Cengage Learning

A+
220-701
1.2

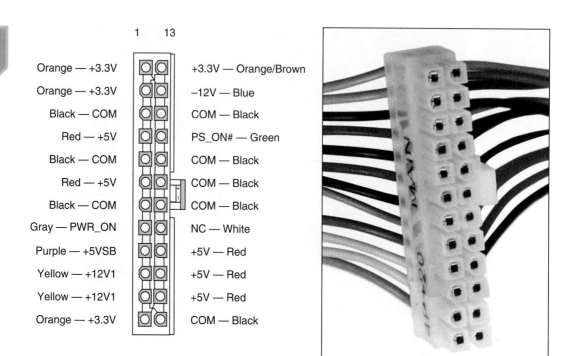

Figure 4-6 P1 24-pin power connector follows ATX Version 2.2 and higher standards
Courtesy: Course Technology/Cengage Learning

> **Notes** For more information about all the form factors discussed in this chapter, check out the form factor Web site sponsored by Intel at *www.formfactors.org*.

Another feature of an ATX motherboard is a **soft switch**, sometimes called the **soft power** feature. If an operating system supports the feature, it can turn off the power to a system after the shutdown procedure is done. In addition, BIOS setup can be configured to cause a keystroke or network activity to power up the system (wake on LAN). When a user presses the power switch on the front of the case while the computer is on, the OS goes through a normal shutdown procedure before powering off. There are several variations of ATX motherboards. A less popular one is the Mini-ATX, which is a smaller ATX motherboard (11.2" x 8.2") that can be used with ATX cases and power supplies. Another less popular one is the Extended ATX (eATX) motherboard that can be up to 12" x 13" in size; it is used in rack-mounted servers.

MICROATX FORM FACTOR

The MicroATX form factor is a major variation of ATX and addresses some technologies that have emerged since the original development of ATX. MicroATX reduces the total cost of a system by reducing the number of expansion slots on the motherboard, reducing the power supplied to the board, and allowing for a smaller case size. A MicroATX motherboard (see Figure 4-7) will fit into a case that follows the ATX 2.1 or higher standard. A variation of the MicroATX is the Mini-ITX. This form factor is smaller than the MicroATX and designed for small systems such as a home theatre system.

A+
220-701
1.2

4

A+ 220-701

Figure 4-7 This MicroATX motherboard by Biostar is designed to support an AMD processor
Courtesy: Course Technology/Cengage Learning

FLEXATX FORM FACTOR

FlexATX is a variation of MicroATX. It allows for maximum flexibility (giving it the name FlexATX), and therefore can be a good choice for custom systems. A FlexATX motherboard can be up to 9" x 7.5". The motherboard costs less, has fewer features, and is smaller than a MicroATX board. FlexATX is commonly used in slimline and all-in-one cases, but can fit into any FlexATX, MicroATX, or ATX case that follows the ATX 2.03 or higher standard.

BTX FORM FACTOR

The BTX (Balanced Technology Extended) form factor was designed by Intel in 2003 for flexibility and can be used by everything from large tower systems to those ultrasmall systems that sit under a monitor. BTX was designed to take full advantage of serial ATA, USB 2.0, and PCI Express technologies. The BTX form factor design focuses on reducing heat with better airflow and improved fans and coolers. It also gives better structural support for the motherboard than does ATX. BTX motherboards use a 24-pin power connector that has the same pinout arrangement as the ATX 24-pin P1 connector. The BTX form factor can also use one or more auxiliary power connectors for the processor, fans, and lighting inside the case (for really cool-looking systems). Because the 24-pin connectors are the same, a BTX motherboard can use an ATX power supply.

In the case configuration shown in Figure 4-8, notice how the processor is sitting immediately in front of the intake fan installed on the front of the case. This intake fan together with the exhaust fan on the rear of the case produce a strong wind tunnel effect over the processor, making it unnecessary to have a fan on top of the processor itself. Also notice in Figure 4-8 that memory modules and expansion cards fit into the slots parallel to airflow rather than blocking airflow as they sometimes do with ATX form factors. Airflow in a BTX system is also designed to flow underneath the BTX motherboard.

A+
220-701
1.2

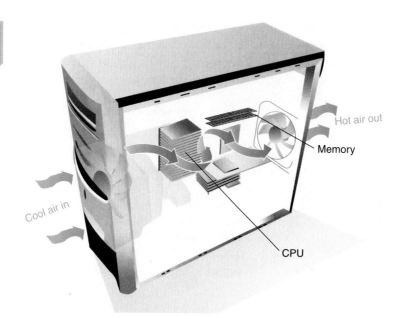

Figure 4-8   Improved airflow in a BTX case and motherboard makes it unnecessary
to have a fan on top of the processor
Courtesy: Course Technology/Cengage Learning

A BTX case by Gateway with a motherboard installed is shown in Figure 4-9. This BTX
case has fans on the front and rear to force air over the processor heat sink. Notice in the
figure the green encasement that directs airflow over the heat sink. Also notice the vents on
the front case panel to help with airflow.

Figure 4-9   A Gateway BTX system is designed for optimum airflow
Courtesy: Course Technology/Cengage Learning

A+
220-701
1.2

When the BTX form factor was first introduced, it was expected to replace ATX. However, BTX has not gained as much popularity with those who build custom systems as was first anticipated. Even though Dell and Gateway have both produced their own BTX brand name systems, it appears ATX will continue to be the most popular form factor.

NLX FORM FACTOR

The **NLX (New Low-profile Extended)** form factor for low-end personal computer motherboards was developed by Intel in 1998 to improve on an older and similar form factor, called the LPX form factor. In these systems, the motherboard has only one expansion slot, in which a **riser card** (also called a **bus riser, daughter card**, or daughter board), is mounted. Expansion cards are mounted on the riser card, and the card also contains connectors for the floppy and hard drives. The riser card on an NLX motherboard is on the edge of the board, which differs from the LPX motherboard that had the riser card near the center of the board. The NLX standard applies only to motherboards; NLX motherboards are designed to use ATX power supplies. An example of an NLX system is shown in Figure 4-10.

> **♀ A+ Exam Tip** The A+ 220-701 Essentials exam expects you to know the purpose of the riser card (also called a daughter board) used with the NLX form factor.

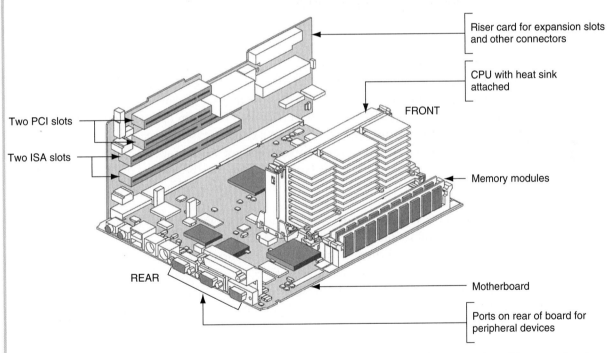

Figure 4-10 The NLX form factor uses a riser card that connects to the motherboard; the riser card provides expansion slots for the expansion cards
Courtesy: Course Technology/Cengage Learning

TYPES OF COMPUTER CASES

Several types and sizes of cases are on the market for each form factor. The computer case, sometimes called the chassis, houses the power supply, motherboard, expansion cards, and drives. The case has lights and switches on the front panel that can be used to control and monitor the PC. Generally, the larger the case, the larger the power supply and the more amps (current) it carries. These large cases allow for the extra space and power needed for a larger number of devices, such as multiple hard drives needed in a server.

A+
220-701
1.2

Computer cases come in different colors and have cool features, such as clear plastic panels so you can see lights inside. Ports that connect by cables to the motherboard might be mounted on the front, top, side, or rear of the case. When you select a case, be aware that the power supply is often included with the case and it's important to match the power supply to the electrical needs of the system. How to do that is coming up later in the chapter.

Cases for personal computers and notebooks fall into three major categories: desktop cases, tower cases, and notebook cases. Figure 4-11 shows examples of each of the three main tower cases, as well as two desktop cases.

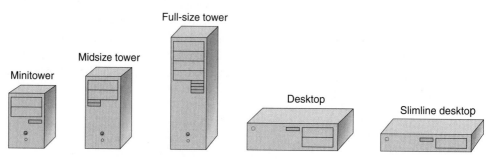

Figure 4-11   Tower and desktop cases
Courtesy: Course Technology/Cengage Learning

The following sections discuss each in turn.

DESKTOP CASES

The first personal computers used a desktop case that sat flat on a desktop doing double duty as a monitor stand. The motherboard sat on the bottom of a desktop case, and the power supply was near the back. If you have a desktop case designed to lie flat, don't place it on its end because the CD or DVD drive might not work properly. Desktop cases are built to accommodate all form factors for personal computers. Because of the space a desktop case takes, it has fallen out of favor in recent years and is being replaced by smaller and more space-efficient cases.

For low-end desktop systems, compact cases, sometimes called low-profile cases or slimline cases, follow the MicroATX, FlexATX, or NLX form factor. Likely to have fewer drive bays, they generally still provide for some expansion. Some cases lay flat and can be used as a monitor stand and others stand upright. You can see an upright slimline case in Figure 4-12. Slimline desktop cases are gaining in popularity for low-end personal computers because they come in nice colors and do double duty as a monitor stand.

TOWER CASES

A tower case sits upright on the floor or a desk and can be as high as two feet and has room for several drives. Often used for servers, this type of case is also good for PC users who anticipate upgrading, because tower cases provide maximum space for working inside a computer and moving components around.

The variations in tower cases are as follows:

▲ Midsize towers, also called midi-towers or mid-towers, are the most versatile and most popular. They are midrange in size and generally have around six expansion slots and four drive bays, providing moderate potential for expansion. They are used for ATX, MicroATX, Extended ATX, Mini-ATX, and BTX systems.

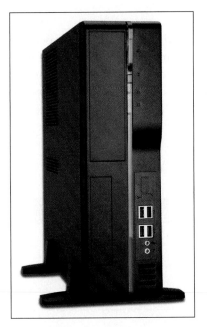

Figure 4-12 This slimline case by ENlight supports a MicroATX motherboard
Courtesy of ENlight Corp

- ▲ The minitower, also called a microtower, is the smallest type of tower case and does not provide room for expansion. They are popular for MicroATX and FlexATX systems.
- ▲ Full-size towers are used for high-end personal computers and servers. They are usually built to accommodate ATX, Mini-ATX, and BTX systems (see Figure 4-13).

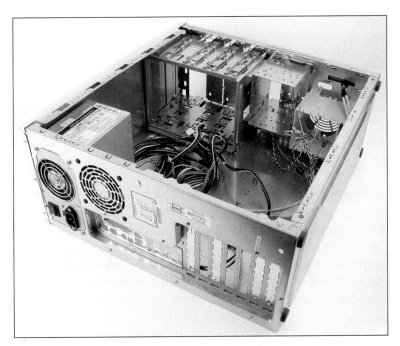

Figure 4-13 Full-size tower case for an ATX motherboard
Courtesy: Course Technology/Cengage Learning

NOTEBOOK CASES

Notebook cases are used for portable computers that have all the components of a desktop computer. The cost and power of notebook systems vary widely. As with other small systems, notebooks can present difficulties in expansion. The smallest notebook cases are called subnotebooks or netbooks. Notebook designs are often highly proprietary, but are generally designed to conserve space, allow portability, use less power, and produce less heat. The case fan in a notebook usually attaches to a thermometer and runs only when temperature needs to be lowered.

Table 4-2 lists a few case and power supply manufacturers.

Manufacturer	Web Site
Antec	www.antec.com
ASUS	www.asus.com
Cooler Master	www.coolermaster.com
ENlight Corporation	www.enlightcorp.com
Lian Li	www.lian-li.com
PC Power and Cooling	www.pcpowerandcooling.com
Rosewill	www.rosewill.com
Silverstone	www.silverstonetek.com
Sunus Suntek	www.suntekgroup.com
Thermaltake	www.thermaltakeusa.com
Zalman	www.zalman.com

Table 4-2 Manufacturers of cases and power supplies for personal computers

> **Notes** Resellers sometimes closely match the domain name of a manufacturer so that you might accidentally land on their site. For example, if you key in *www.lianli.com* (without the hyphen) you're taken to a reseller's site rather than the Lian Li site.

Toward our goal of learning about power supplies and the electrical current they provide, let's turn our attention to understanding how electricity is measured and about some of its properties.

MEASURES AND PROPERTIES OF ELECTRICITY

In our modern world, we take electricity for granted, and we miss it terribly when it's cut off. Nearly everyone depends on it, but few really understand it. But to become a successful PC technician (that is, you don't tend to encounter fried motherboards, smoking monitors, or frizzed hair), you need to understand electricity. In addition, you need to know how to use it, how it's measured, and how to protect computer equipment from its damaging power.

Let's start with the basics. To most people, volts, ohms, watts, and amps are vague terms that simply mean electricity. All these terms can be used to measure some characteristic of electricity, as listed in Table 4-3.

Unit	Definition	Computer Example
Volt (for example, 115 V)	A measure of electrical "pressure" differential. Volts are measured by finding the potential difference between the pressures on either side of an electrical device in a circuit. The symbol for volts is V.	An ATX or BTX power supply provides these separate voltages: +12 V, -12 V, +5 V, and +3.3 V. (-5 V is included in the specs for these power supplies but is almost never used.)
Amp or ampere (for example, 1.5 A)	A measure of electrical current. Amps are measured by placing an ammeter in the flow of current. The symbol for Amps is A.	A 17-inch monitor requires less than 4 A to operate. A small laser printer uses about 2 A. A CD-ROM drive uses about 1 A.
Ohm (for example, 20 Ω)	A measure of resistance to electricity. Devices are rated according to how much resistance they offer to electrical current. The ohm rating of a resistor or other electrical device is often written somewhere on the device. The symbol for ohm is Ω.	Current can flow in typical computer cables and wires with a resistance of near zero Ω (ohm).
Watt (for example, 20 W)	A measure of electrical power. Whereas volts and amps are measured to determine their value, watts are calculated by multiplying volts by amps. Watts measure the total electrical power needed to operate a device. The symbol for watts is W.	A computer power supply is rated at 200 to 800 W.

Table 4-3   Measures of electricity

> **Notes** To learn more about how volts, amps, ohms, and watts measure the four properties of electricity, see the content "Electricity and Multimeters" on the CD that accompanies this book.

Now let's look at how electricity gets from one place to another and how it is used in house circuits and computers.

AC AND DC

Electricity can be either AC, alternating current, or DC, direct current. Alternating current (AC) goes back and forth, or oscillates, rather than traveling in only one direction. House current in the United States is AC and oscillates 60 times in one second (60 hertz). Voltage in the system is constantly alternating from positive to negative, which causes the electricity to flow first in one direction and then in the other. Voltage alternates from +110 V to -110 V. AC is the most economical way to transmit electricity to our homes and workplaces. By decreasing current and increasing voltage, we can force alternating current to travel great distances. When alternating current reaches its destination, it is made more suitable for driving our electrical devices by decreasing voltage and increasing current.

Direct current (DC) travels in only one direction and is the type of current that most electronic devices require, including computers. A rectifier is a device that converts AC to DC, and an inverter is a device that converts DC to AC. A transformer is a device that changes the ratio of voltage to current. Large transformers reduce the high voltage on power lines coming to your neighborhood to a lower voltage before the current enters your home. The transformer does not change the amount of power in this closed system; if it decreases voltage, it increases current. The overall power stays constant, but the ratio of voltage to current changes is illustrated in Figure 4-14.

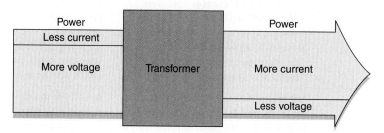

Figure 4-14   A transformer keeps power constant but changes the ratio of current to voltage
Courtesy: Course Technology/Cengage Learning

A computer power supply changes and conditions the house electrical current in several ways, functioning as both a transformer and a rectifier. It steps down the voltage from the 110-volt house current to 3.3, 5, and 12 volts, and changes incoming alternating current to direct current, which the computer and its peripherals require. The monitor, however, receives the full 110 volts of AC voltage, converting that current to DC.

Direct current flows in only one direction. Think of electrical current like a current of water that flows from a state of high pressure to a state of low pressure or rest. Electrical current flows from a high-pressure state (called hot) to a state of rest (called ground or neutral). For a PC, a line may be either +5 or -5 volts in one circuit, or +12 or -12 volts in another circuit. The positive or negative value is determined by how the circuit is oriented, either on one side of the power output or the other. Several circuits coming from the power supply accommodate different devices with different power requirements.

HOT, NEUTRAL, AND GROUND

When AC comes from the power source at the power station to your house, it travels on a hot line and completes the circuit from your house back to the power source on a neutral line, as shown in Figure 4-15.

When the two lines reach your house and enter an electrical device, such as a lamp, electricity flows through the device to complete the circuit between the hot line and the neutral line. The device contains resistors and other electrical components that control the flow of electricity between the hot and neutral lines. In a controlled environment, the hot source then seeks and finds a state of rest by returning to the power station on the neutral line.

A short circuit, or a short, occurs when uncontrolled electricity flows from the hot line to the neutral line or from the hot line to ground. Electricity naturally finds the easiest route to a state of rest. Normally that path is through some device that controls the current flow and then back through the neutral line. If an easier path (one with less resistance) is available, the electricity follows that path. This can cause a short, a sudden increase in flow that can also create a sudden increase in temperature—enough to start a fire and injure both people and equipment. Never put yourself in a position where you are the path of least resistance between the hot line and ground!

> **Notes**   A Class C fire extinguisher is used to put out fires fueled by electricity.

A fuse is a component included in a circuit and designed to prevent too much current from flowing through the circuit. A fuse is commonly a wire inside a protective case, which is rated in amps. If too much current begins to flow, the wire gets hot and eventually melts, breaking the circuit, as an open switch would, and stopping the current flow. Many devices have fuses, which can be easily replaced when damaged.

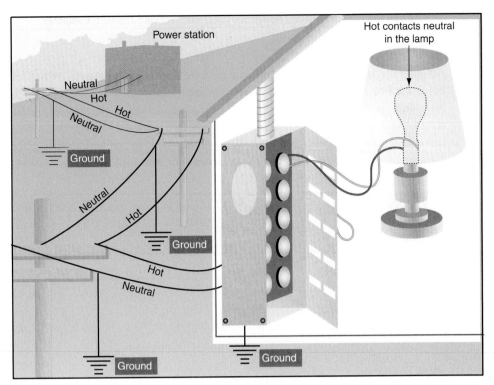

Figure 4-15 Normally, electricity flows from hot to neutral to make a closed circuit in the controlled environment of an electrical device such as a lamp
Courtesy: Course Technology/Cengage Learning

To prevent uncontrolled electricity from continuing to flow indefinitely, which can happen because of a short, the neutral line is grounded. Grounding a line means that the line is connected directly to the earth, so that, in the event of a short, the electricity flows into the earth and not back to the power station. Grounding serves as an escape route for out-of-control electricity. The earth is at no particular state of charge and so is always capable of accepting a flow of current.

> ⚡ **Caution** Beware of the different uses of black wire. In PCs and in DC circuits, black is used for ground, but in home wiring and in AC circuits, black is used for hot!

The neutral line to your house is grounded many times along its way (in fact, at each electrical pole) and is also grounded at the breaker box where the electricity enters your house. You can look at a three-prong plug and see the three lines: hot, neutral, and ground (see Figure 4-16).

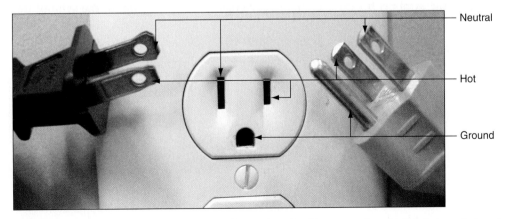

Figure 4-16 A polarized plug showing hot and neutral, and a three-prong plug showing hot, neutral, and ground
Courtesy: Course Technology/Cengage Learning

Generally, electricians use green or bare wire for the ground wire, white for neutral, and black for hot in home wiring for 110-volt circuits. In a 220-volt circuit, black and red are hot, white is neutral, and green or bare is ground. To verify that a wall outlet is wired correctly, use a simple receptacle tester, as shown in Figure 4-17. Even though you might have a three-prong outlet in your home, the ground plug might not be properly grounded. To know for sure, always test the outlet with a receptacle tester.

> **Notes** House AC voltage in the United States is about 110 V, but know that in other countries, this is not always the case. In many countries, the standard is 220 V. Outlet styles also vary from one country to the next.

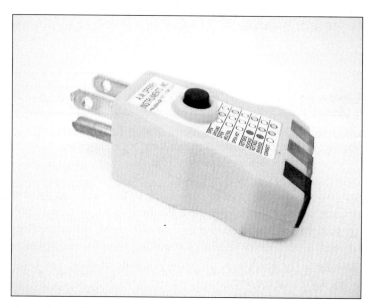

Figure 4-17 Use a receptacle tester to verify that hot, neutral, and ground are wired correctly
Courtesy: Course Technology/Cengage Learning

SOME COMMON ELECTRONIC COMPONENTS

It's important you understand what basic electronic components make up a PC and how they work. Basic electronic components in a PC include transistors, capacitors, diodes, and resistors (each of which we will discuss in detail in a moment). Figure 4-18 shows the symbols for these components. Also notice in the figure the symbol for ground.

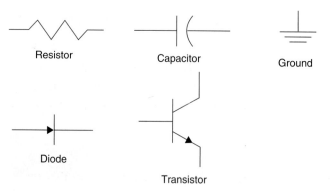

Figure 4-18 Symbols for some electronic components and for ground
Courtesy: Course Technology/Cengage Learning

To understand how these components are constructed, it helps to know that all the materials used to make the components fall into one of these three categories:

- ▲ *Conductors.* Material, such as gold or copper, that easily conducts electricity
- ▲ *Insulators.* Material, such as glass or ceramic, that resists the flow of electricity
- ▲ *Semiconductors.* Material, such as silicon, whose ability to conduct electricity, when a charge is applied, falls between that of a conductor and an insulator

> ⚡ **Caution** It's very important that PC components be properly grounded. Never connect a PC to an outlet or use an extension cord that doesn't have the third ground plug. The third line can prevent a short from causing extreme damage. In addition, the bond between the neutral and ground helps eliminate electrical noise (stray electrical signals) within the PC sometimes caused by other electrical equipment sitting very close to the computer.

TRANSISTOR

A transistor is an electronic device that can serve as a gate or switch for an electrical signal and can amplify the flow of electricity. Invented in 1947, the transistor is made of three layers of semiconductor material.

A charge (either positive or negative, depending on the transistor's design) placed on the center layer can cause the two outer layers of the transistor to complete a circuit to create an "on" state. An opposite charge placed on the center layer can make the reverse happen, causing the transistor to create an "off" state. Manipulating these charges to the transistor allows it to hold a logic state of either on or off. The on state represents binary 1 and the off state represents binary 0 when used to hold data in a computer.

When the transistor maintains this state, it requires almost no electrical power. Because the initial charge sent to the transistor is not as great as the resulting current that the transistor creates, a transistor sometimes is used as a small amplifier. For instance, transistors are used to amplify the tiny dots or pixels on an LCD monitor screen used to create a sharper image. The transistor is also used as the basic building block of an integrated circuit (IC), which is used to build a microchip.

CAPACITOR

A capacitor is an electronic device that can hold an electrical charge for a period of time and can smooth the uneven flow of electricity through a circuit. Capacitors inside a PC power supply create the even flow of current the PC needs. Capacitors maintain their charge long after current is no longer present, which is why the inside of a power supply can be dangerous even when it is unplugged. You can see many capacitors on motherboards, video cards, and other circuit boards (see Figure 4-19).

DIODE

A diode is a semiconductor device that allows electricity to flow in only one direction. (A transistor contains two diodes.) One to four diodes used in various configurations can be used to convert AC to DC. Singularly or collectively, depending on the configuration, these diodes are called a rectifier.

RESISTOR

A resistor is an electronic device that limits the amount of current that can flow through it. In a circuit, a resistor is used to protect a circuit from overload or to control the current. Resistors are color-coded to indicate the degree of resistance measured in ohms.

Crosshatch on top
of capacitor

Figure 4-19   Capacitors on a motherboard or other circuit board often have embedded crossed lines on top
Courtesy: Course Technology/Cengage Learning

SELECTING A POWER SUPPLY

A+
220-701
1.3

Now that you have a basic understanding of electricity, you're ready to take a closer look at the features of a power supply and how to select one. A **power supply**, also known as a **power supply unit (PSU)**, is a box inside a computer case (see Figure 4-20) that supplies power to the motherboard and other installed devices.

Recall that a power supply serves as both a rectifier and transformer to convert AC house current to DC and to step down voltage from 110 V or 220 V to 3.5, 5, and 12 V. Let's now turn our attention to the features of a power supply.

TYPES AND CHARACTERISTICS OF POWER SUPPLIES

As you select the right power supply for a system, you need to be aware of the following power supply features:

▲ *Feature 1.* The form factor of a power supply determines the size of the power supply and the placement of screw holes used to anchor the power supply to the case (see Figure 4-21).
▲ *Feature 2.* Consider the type and number of power cables and connectors the unit provides. Connector types are shown in Table 4-4. If a power supply doesn't have the

4

Figure 4-20 This case comes with a power supply, power cord, and bag of screws
Courtesy: Course Technology/Cengage Learning

connector you need, it is likely you can use an adapter to convert one connector to another. To find an adapter, search a good Web site such as Cables To Go (*www.cablestogo.com*) that sells computer parts and cables. For example, if your power supply does not have a 12 V 6-pin connector for your PCIe x16 video card, you can buy an inexpensive adapter to convert two Molex cables to this type of connector (see Figure 4-22).

▲ *Feature 3.* A power supply might have a **voltage selector switch** on the back. For example, the voltage selector switch on the power supply in Figure 4-21 can be set to 230 V or 115 V. When in the United States, set the switch to 115 V. Be sure to never change the switch setting until you first turn off and unplug the power supply.

A+
220-701
1.3

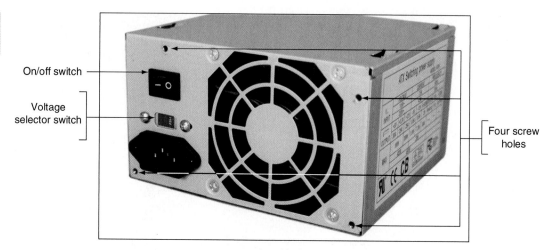

On/off switch

Voltage selector switch

Four screw holes

Figure 4-21   Holes in the rear of an ATX power supply match up with holes in the ATX case to anchor the power supply to the case
Courtesy: Course Technology/Cengage Learning

Connector	Description
	P1 20+4 pin connector is the main motherboard power connector
	P1 20+4 pin connector with four pins removed so the connector can fit into a 20-pin P1 motherboard connector
	4-pin 12 V auxiliary motherboard connector used for extra power to the processor
	8-pin 12 V auxiliary motherboard connector used for extra power to the processor, providing more power than the older 4-pin auxiliary connector
	Molex 4-pin connector is used for IDE drives

Table 4-4   Power supply connectors
Courtesy: Course Technology/Cengage Learning

4

A+ 220-701

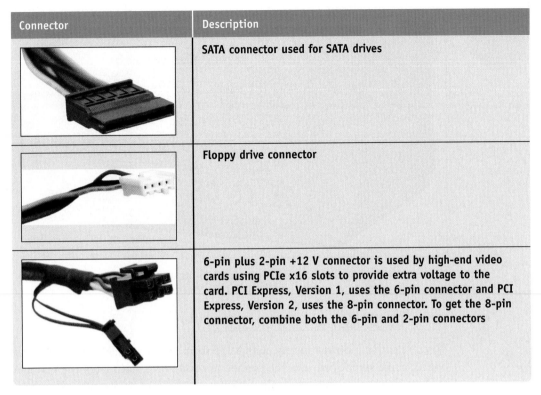

A+ 220-701 1.3	Connector	Description
		SATA connector used for SATA drives
		Floppy drive connector
		6-pin plus 2-pin +12 V connector is used by high-end video cards using PCIe x16 slots to provide extra voltage to the card. PCI Express, Version 1, uses the 6-pin connector and PCI Express, Version 2, uses the 8-pin connector. To get the 8-pin connector, combine both the 6-pin and 2-pin connectors

Table 4-4   Power supply connectors (continued)
Courtesy: Course Technology/Cengage Learning

Figure 4-22   This adapter converts two Molex cables to a single 12 V 6-pin PCIe connector
Courtesy: Course Technology/Cengage Learning

◢ *Feature 4*. Every power supply has a fan inside its case; some have two fans. The fan can be mounted on the back or top of the PSU. Fans range in size from 80mm to 120mm wide.

◢ *Feature 5*. A power supply might have an on/off switch that controls power to the system (refer back to Figure 4-21).

◢ *Feature 6*. A power supply has wattage ratings, which are the amounts of power it can supply. These wattage capacities are listed in the documentation and on the side of a power supply, as shown in Figure 4-23. When selecting a power supply, pay particular attention to the capacity for the +12 V rail. (A rail is the term used to describe each voltage line of the power supply.) The +12 V rail is the most used one, especially in high-end gaming systems. Sometimes you need to use a power supply with a higher-than-needed overall wattage in order to get enough wattage on this one rail.

◢ *Feature 7*. Consider the warranty of the power supply and the overall quality. Some come in bright colors, and cables might be of higher quality than others. The more expensive power supplies are quieter, last longer, and don't put off as much heat as less expensive ones. Also, expect a good power supply to protect the system against over voltage.

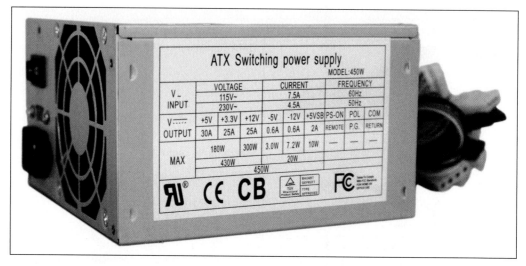

Figure 4-23   Look on the side of a power supply for its wattage ratings
Courtesy: Course Technology/Cengage Learning

HOW TO SELECT A POWER SUPPLY

When selecting a power supply, match the form factor to that used by the case and motherboard, make sure it provides the connectors you need, and match the wattage capacity to the requirements of the system. In addition, consider the warranty, price, and the additional features you learned about in the previous section.

When deciding what wattage capacity you need for the power supply, consider the total wattage requirements of all components inside the case as well as USB and FireWire devices that get their power from ports connected to the motherboard.

Keep these points in mind when selecting the correct wattage capacity for a power supply:

▲ *Point 1*. A power supply produces slightly higher wattage at room temperature than it does when the temperature inside the case has risen above room temperature (called operating temperature). Therefore, a power supply might have two ratings: one wattage rating for room temperature (called the peak rating) and another rating for continuous operation at operating temperature (sometimes called the actual rating). If a power supply has only one rating, assume that rating is the peak rating for room temperature. To calculate the rating for continuous operation, deduct about 10 to 15 percent off the peak rating. For example, the Silencer 610 power supply by PC Power and Cooling is rated at 610 W at operating temperature and continuous operation but has a peak rating of 670 W.

▲ *Point 2*. Video cards draw the most power in a system, and they draw from the +12 V output. So pay particular attention to this rating. For example, in Figure 4-23, you can see the +12 V output is 300 W. Notice in the figure the unit is rated at total peak load of 450 W.

▲ *Point 3*. Use a power supply that is rated about 30 percent higher than you expect the system will use. Power supplies that run at less than peak performance last longer and don't overheat. In addition, a power supply loses some of its capacity over time. Also, don't worry about a higher-rated power supply using too much electricity. Components only draw what they need. To know what size power supply you need, add up the wattage requirements of all components, and add 30 percent. Device technical documentation might give you the information you need. Table 4-5 lists appropriate wattage ratings for common devices with the 30 percent extra already added in.

▲ *Point 4*. The Web sites of some power supply and motherboard manufacturers have a wattage calculator where you can enter the components in your system and then the calculator will recommend the wattage you need for your power supply. You will see one example of a wattage calculator in Project 4-7 at the end of this chapter.

Devices	Approximate Wattage
Moderately priced motherboard, processor, RAM, keyboard, and mouse	100 watts
High-end motherboard, processor, RAM, keyboard, and mouse	100 to 150 watts
Fan	5 watts
IDE hard drive	25 watts
SATA or SCSI hard drive	35 watts
CD-RW drive	25 watts
DVD-RW or Blu-ray drive	35 watts
Tape drive	25 watts
Low-end AGP or PCI video card	40 watts
Moderately priced video card	100 watts
High-end PCIe x16 video card	150–300 watts
PCI card	20 watts
PCI e x16 card	100 watts
Liquid cooling system	50–150 watts

Table 4-5   To calculate power supply rating, add up total wattage

Here are the wattage needs of four typical systems:

- *Example 1.* A regular desktop system with a moderately priced motherboard using socket LGA775 for Intel processors or an AMD2 socket for AMD processors, one moderately priced video card, two SATA hard drives, a DVD-RW drive, and two fans needs a power supply rated at about 300 to 350 watts.

- *Example 2.* A desktop system used as a file server with a high-end motherboard, Intel or AMD processor, moderately priced video card, six SATA hard drives, DVD-RW drive, tape drive, PCI RAID card, and four fans needs a power supply rated at about 550 watts.

- *Example 3.* A gaming system with a high-end motherboard using socket LGA775 for Intel processors or an AMD2 socket for AMD processors, two high-end video cards, two SATA hard drives, a Blu-ray drive, and four fans needs a power supply rated at about 800 watts. (The two high-end video cards require about 275 watts each.)

- *Example 4.* If a liquid cooling system used by gamers for overclocking a system is installed in the gaming system described above, the power supply wattage rating should be increased to about 1000 watts. (Overclocking is running a processor, motherboard, or video card at a higher frequency than the manufacturer recommends and is not considered a best practice. It might also void the warranty of a component.)

▲ *Point 5.* Dell ATX power supplies and motherboards might not use the standard P1 pinouts for ATX, although the power connectors look the same. For this reason, never use a Dell power supply with a non-Dell motherboard, or a Dell motherboard with a non-Dell power supply, without first verifying that the power connector pinouts

A+
220-701
1.3

match; otherwise, you might destroy the power supply, the motherboard, or both. End PC Noise (*www.endpcnoise.com*) sells a pinout converter to convert the connector of a Dell power supply or motherboard to standard ATX. Also, PC Power and Cooling (*www.pcpowerandcooling.com*) makes power supplies modified to work with a Dell motherboard.

PROTECT YOURSELF AND THE EQUIPMENT AGAINST ELECTRICAL DANGERS

A+
220-701
6.1

In this part of the chapter, you'll learn about the physical dangers of supporting personal computers and how to protect yourself and others. Then you'll learn about what can happen to damage a computer or other equipment while you are working on it and what to do to prevent that damage. As you work with computers, to stay safe and protect the equipment, always make it a habit to apply all the safety precautions discussed here.

PROTECT YOURSELF AGAINST ELECTRICAL SHOCK AND BURNS

A+
220-701
6.1
2.2

To protect yourself against electrical shock, when working with any electrical device, including computers, printers, scanners, and network devices, disconnect the power if you notice a dangerous situation that might lead to electrical shock or fire. When you disconnect the power, do so by pulling on the plug at the AC outlet. To protect the power cord, don't pull on the cord itself. Also, don't just turn off the on/off switch on the device; you need to actually disconnect the power. Note that any of the following can indicate a potential danger:

- ◢ The power cord is frayed or otherwise damaged in any way.
- ◢ Water or other liquid is on the floor around the device or spilled on it.
- ◢ The device has been exposed to excess moisture.
- ◢ The device has been dropped or you notice physical damage.
- ◢ You smell a strong electronics odor.
- ◢ The power supply or fans are making a whining noise.
- ◢ You notice smoke coming from the computer case or the case feels unusually warm.

When working on the inside of computers, printers, and other electrical devices, remove your jewelry that might come in contact with components. Jewelry is made of metal and might conduct electricity if it touches a component.

Power supplies and CRT monitors (the old-fashioned monitors that have a large case with a picture tube) contain capacitors. A capacitor holds its charge even after the power is turned off and the device is unplugged. A ground is the easiest possible path for electricity to follow. If you are grounded and touch a charged capacitor, its charge can flow through you to the ground, which can shock you! Therefore, if you ever work inside one of these devices, be careful that you are not grounded. Later in the chapter, you will learn that being grounded while working on sensitive low-voltage electronic equipment such as a motherboard or processor is a good thing, and the best way to ground yourself is to wear an antistatic grounding bracelet connected to ground. However, when working on a CRT monitor, power supply, or laser printer, *don't* wear the antistatic bracelet because you don't want to be ground for these high-voltage devices. How to work inside a power supply or CRT monitor is not covered in this book and is not considered a skill needed by an A+ certified support technician. The power supply and monitor are both considered to be a **field replaceable unit (FRU)**. That means, as a support technician, you are expected to know how to replace one when it breaks, but not how to repair one.

> **Tip** Go to *www.youtube.com* and search on "discharge a CRT monitor" to see some interesting videos that demonstrate the charge inside a monitor long after the monitor is turned off and unplugged. As for proper procedures, I'm not endorsing all these videos; just watch for fun.

> **A+ Exam Tip** The A+ exams expect you to know about the dangers of high voltage when working inside a power supply, CRT monitor, or laser printer.

PROTECT THE EQUIPMENT AGAINST STATIC ELECTRICITY OR ESD

Suppose you come indoors on a cold day, pick up a comb, and touch your hair. Sparks fly! What happened? Static electricity caused the sparks. Electrostatic discharge (ESD), commonly known as static electricity, is an electrical charge at rest. When you came indoors, this charge built up on your hair and had no place to go. An ungrounded conductor (such as wire that is not touching another wire) or a nonconductive surface (such as your hair) holds a charge until the charge is released. When two objects with dissimilar electrical charges touch, electricity passes between them until the dissimilar charges become equal.

To see static charges equalizing, turn off the lights in a room, scuff your feet on the carpet, and touch another person. Occasionally, you can see and feel the charge in your fingers. If you can feel the charge, you discharged at least 1,500 volts of static electricity. If you hear the discharge, you released at least 6,000 volts. If you see the discharge, you released at least 8,000 volts of ESD. A charge of only 10 volts can damage electronic components! You can touch a chip on an expansion card or motherboard, damage the chip with ESD, and never feel, hear, or see the discharge.

ESD can cause two types of damage in an electronic component: catastrophic failure and upset failure. A catastrophic failure destroys the component beyond use. An upset failure damages the component so that it does not perform well, even though it may still function to some degree. Upset failures are more difficult to detect because they are not consistent and not easily observed. Both types of failures permanently affect the device.

> **Caution** A CRT monitor can also damage components with ESD. Don't place or store expansion cards on top of or next to a CRT monitor, which can discharge as much as 29,000 volts onto the screen.

To protect the computer against ESD, always ground yourself before touching electronic components, including the hard drive, motherboard, expansion cards, processors, and memory modules. You can ground yourself and the computer parts by using one or more of the following static control devices or methods:

▲ *Ground bracelet.* A ground bracelet, also called an antistatic wrist strap or ESD bracelet, is a strap you wear around your wrist. The strap has a cord attached with an alligator clip on the end. Attach the clip to the computer case you're working on, as shown in Figure 4-24. Any static electricity between you and the case is now discharged. Therefore, as you work inside the case, you will not damage the components with static electricity. The bracelet also contains a resistor that prevents electricity from harming you.

A+
220-701
6.1

Figure 4-24 A ground bracelet, which protects computer components from ESD, can clip to the side of the computer case and eliminate ESD between you and the case
Courtesy: Course Technology/Cengage Learning

▲ *Ground mats.* Ground mats dissipate ESD and are commonly used by bench technicians (also called depot technicians) who repair and assemble computers at their workbenches or in an assembly line. Ground mats have a connector in one corner that you can use to connect the mat to ground (see Figure 4-25). If you lift a component off the mat, it is no longer grounded and is susceptible to ESD, so it's important to use a ground bracelet with a ground mat.

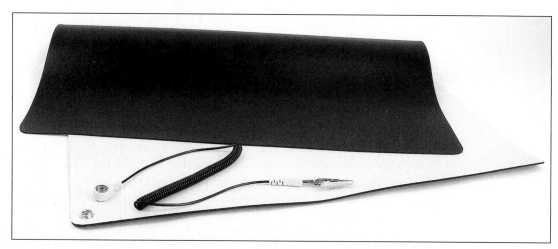

Figure 4-25 A ground mat dissipates ESD and should be connected to ground
Courtesy: Course Technology/Cengage Learning

▲ *Static shielding bags.* New components come shipped in static shielding bags, also called antistatic bags. These bags are a type of Faraday cage, named after Michael Faraday, who built the first cage in 1836. A Faraday cage is any device that protects against an electromagnetic field. Save the bags to store other devices that are not currently installed in a PC. As you work on a computer, know that a device is not protected from ESD if you place it on top of the bag; the protection is inside the bag (see Figure 4-26).

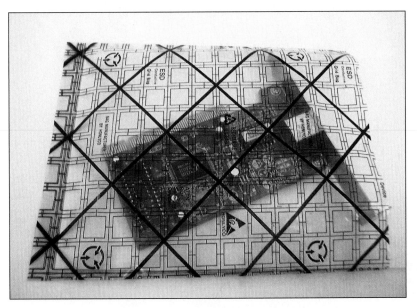

Figure 4-26 Static shielding bags help protect components from ESD
Courtesy: Course Technology/Cengage Learning

▲ *Antistatic gloves.* You can purchase antistatic gloves designed to prevent an ESD discharge between you and a device as you pick it up and handle it (see Figure 4-27). The gloves can be substituted for an antistatic bracelet, and are good for moving, packing, or unpacking sensitive equipment. However, they tend to get in the way when working inside computer cases.

The best way to guard against ESD is to use a ground bracelet together with a ground mat. Consider a ground bracelet essential equipment when working on a computer. However, if you are in a situation in which you must work without one, touch the computer case or the power supply before you touch a component. When passing a circuit board, memory module, or other sensitive component to another person, ground yourself and then touch the other person before you pass the component. Leave components inside their protective bags until you are ready to use them. Work on hard floors, not carpet, or use antistatic spray on the carpets. Generally, don't work on a computer if you or the computer have just come in from the cold, because there is more danger of ESD when the atmosphere is cold and dry.

With ATX and BTX cases, know that residual power is still on even when the power switch on the rear of the case is turned off. Some motherboards even have a small light inside the case to remind you of this fact and to warn you that power is still getting to the system. For this reason, when working on ATX and BTX systems, be certain to unplug the power cord and then press the power button to completely drain the power supply. Only then would it be safe to work inside the case.

Figure 4-27 Use antistatic gloves to prevent static discharge between you and the equipment you are handling
Courtesy: Course Technology/Cengage Learning

> 💡 **A+ Exam Tip** The A+ 220-701 Essentials exam emphasizes that you should know how to protect computer equipment as you work on it.

PROTECT AGAINST ELECTROMAGNETIC INTERFERENCE

Another phenomenon that can cause electrical problems with computers is electromagnetic interference (EMI). EMI is caused by the magnetic field produced as a side effect when electricity flows. EMI in the radio frequency range is called radio frequency interference (RFI). CRT monitors and the older CRT television sets contain electronic magnets that can emit EMI. Other devices that are known to emit EMI/RFI are PDAs, cell phones, cordless phones, microwave ovens, magnets, laser printers, power supplies, fluorescent lighting, AC adapters, bug zappers, and other electric and electronic devices.

EMI and RFI are reduced in these devices by using EMI/RFI shielding (a type of Faraday cage) inside the device. This shielding might be a second layer of housing inside the device housing, but is more commonly done with a chemical coating on the inside of the device housing. This chemical coating might be made of an acrylic compound, nickel, silver, or copper, and is sprayed or brushed onto the inside of the housing.

Many electronic devices are affected by EMI/RFI, including computers, CRT monitors, and data cables. If a CRT monitor flickers occasionally, try moving it to a new location, away from fluorescent lighting or a laser printer, or turn them off. If the problem goes away or lessens, suspect EMI/RFI. For laser printers, you can check with the manufacturer for instructions on how to verify that the RFI shield inside the printer is properly installed.

Data in data cables that cross an electromagnetic field or that run parallel with power cables can become corrupted by EMI/RFI, causing crosstalk. Crosstalk can be partially controlled by using data cables covered with a protective material; these cables are called shielded cables. One thing you can do to prevent crosstalk is to use only shielded data cables, especially when installing network cable. However, shielded cables are more

A+
220-701
6.1

expensive than unshielded cables. Also, you might need to reroute data cables so they are not running parallel to power cables or alongside fluorescent lighting.

> **Notes** PCs can emit EMI to other nearby PCs, which is one reason a computer needs to be inside a case. To help cut down on EMI between PCs, always install face plates in empty drive bays or slot covers over empty expansion slots.

If mysterious, intermittent errors persist on a PC, one thing to suspect is EMI/RFI. Try moving the PC to a new location. If the problem continues, try moving it to a location that uses an entirely different electric circuit. Move the PC away from any suspected device to eliminate it as a source. A simple way to detect EMI is to use an inexpensive AM radio.

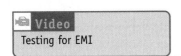
Video
Testing for EMI

Turn the tuning dial away from a station and all the way down into a low-frequency range. With the radio on, you can hear the static that EMI produces. Try putting the radio next to several electronic devices to detect the EMI they emit.

If EMI in the electrical circuits coming to the PC causes a significant problem, you can use a line conditioner to filter the electrical noise that causes the EMI. Line conditioners are discussed later in the chapter.

> **Notes** After you remove the source of EMI or RFI, the problem that the EMI or RFI is causing goes away. In contrast, the problems caused by ESD permanently damage a component.

SURGE PROTECTION AND BATTERY BACKUP

A+
220-701
6.1
2.5

The power supplies in most computers can operate over a wide range of electrical voltage inputs; however, operating the computer under these conditions for extended periods of time can shorten not only the power supply's life, but also the computer's. Also, electrical storms can end a computer's life quite suddenly. To prevent such things from happening, consider installing a device to filter AC input.

A wide range of devices that stand between the AC outlet and computer equipment are on the market and generally fall into these four categories:

- Power strips that provide additional outlets without providing any protection from changes in AC power
- Surge protectors which protect equipment against power spikes or surges
- Line conditions that condition or smooth out the highs and lows in power
- Uninterruptible power supplies (UPSs) that provide backup power when the AC fails

All these devices should have the UL (Underwriters Laboratory) logo, which says that the laboratory, a provider of product safety certification, has tested the device. The UL standard that applies to surge suppressors is UL 1449, first published in 1985 and revised in 1998. Let's look at the features and benefits of the last three items in the list: surge protectors, line conditioners, and UPSs.

SURGE PROTECTORS

A **surge protector**, also called a **surge suppressor**, protects equipment against sudden changes in power level, such as spikes from lightning strikes. The device, such as the ones shown in Figure 4-28, typically provides one or more power outlets, an on/off switch, and

Figure 4-28 Both surge suppressors alert you when protection is not working. The small surge suppressor is designed to travel with a laptop
Courtesy: Course Technology/Cengage Learning

a protection light that indicates the device is protecting equipment from overvoltage (also called transient voltage) on AC power lines and telephone lines. Surge suppressors can come as power strips, wall-mounted units that plug into AC outlets, or consoles designed to sit beneath the monitor on a desktop. Some provide RJ-11 telephone jacks to protect modems and fax machines from spikes. Be aware, too, that not all power strips are surge suppressors; some power strips only multiply the number of outlets without offering any protection from a power surge.

A surge suppressor might be a shunt type that absorbs the surge, a series type that blocks the surge from flowing, or a combination of the two. A suppressor is rated in joules, which is a measure of work or energy. One **joule** (pronounced "jewel") is the work or energy required to produce one watt of power in one second, and a suppressor is rated as to the amount of joules it can expend before it no longer can work to protect the circuit from the power surge. Suppressors are commonly rated from 250 joules to several thousand joules—the higher the better.

Some suppressors are also rated by **clamping voltage** (also called let-through voltage), which is the voltage point at which a suppressor begins to absorb or block voltage. Normally, house current is rated at 110 V, so you would think the clamping voltage should be close to this number, such as around 130 V. However, the clamping voltage value is best not set this low. House current regularly spikes past 200 V, and a PC power supply is designed to handle these types of quick spikes. If the surge suppressor kicks in to work on these spikes, not only is it unnecessary, but the suppressor is likely to wear out prematurely. A clamping voltage of 330 V or higher is appropriate.

The difference between a joule rating and a clamping voltage rating for a suppressor is that the clamping voltage rating determines at what point the suppressor begins to work and the joule rating has to do with how much work the suppressor can do.

The circuitry inside the suppressor that handles a surge can burn out if a surge is too high or lasts too long. In this case, most suppressors continue to work just like a normal extension cord, providing no surge protection. Because of this fact, it's important that a surge suppressor have a light indicator that says the suppressor part of the device is still working. Otherwise, you might not have protection and not even know it.

> **Notes** Whenever a power outage occurs, unless you have a reliable power conditioner installed at the breaker box in your house or building, unplug all power cords to the PC, printers, monitors, and the like. Sometimes when the power returns, sudden spikes are accompanied by another brief outage. You don't want to subject your equipment to these surges. When buying a surge suppressor, look for those that guarantee against damage from lightning and that reimburse for equipment destroyed while the surge suppressor is in use.

When shopping for a surge protector, look for these features:

- Joules rating (more than 600 joules) and the time it takes for the protection to start working (less than 2 nanoseconds is good)
- Warranty for connected equipment
- UL seal of approval
- A light that indicates the surge protection is working
- Let-through voltage rating
- Line noise filtering
- If you use a phone line for Internet access, look for a data line protector to protect the modem from spikes in the phone line.

When you plug in a surge protector, know that if the protector is not grounded using a three-prong outlet, the protector cannot do its job. One more thing to consider: You can purchase a whole-house surge protection system that is installed by an electrician at your breaker box. It's more expensive, but your entire house or office building is protected.

LINE CONDITIONERS

In addition to providing protection against spikes, line conditioners, also called power conditioners, regulate, or condition, the power, providing continuous voltage during brownouts. These voltage regulators can come as small desktop units. They provide a degree of protection against swells or spikes (temporary voltage surges) and raise the voltage when it drops during brownouts or sags (temporary voltage reductions). They also filter EMI/RFI interference from the electrical line. Power conditioners are measured by the load they support in watts, volt-amperes (VA), or kilovolt-amperes (kVA).

To determine the VA required to support your system, multiply the amperage of each component by 120 volts and then add up the VA for all components. For example, a 17-inch LCD monitor has "1.3 A" written on its back, which means 1.3 amps. Multiply that value by 120 volts, and you see that the monitor requires 156 VA or 156 watts. A Pentium PC with a 17-inch monitor requires about 500 VA or 500 watts of support. Figure 4-29 shows a line conditioner by Tripp Lite that is rated at 1800 watts.

Power conditioners are a good investment if the AC in your community suffers excessive spikes and brownouts. However, a device rated under 1kVA will probably provide corrections only for brownouts, not for spikes. Line conditioners, like surge suppressors, provide no protection against a total blackout (complete loss of power).

UNINTERRUPTIBLE POWER SUPPLY

Unlike a line conditioner, the uninterruptible power supply (UPS) provides backup power in the event that the AC fails completely. The UPS also provides some filtering of the AC. A UPS offers these benefits:

- Conditions the line to account for both brownouts and spikes
- Provides backup power during a blackout
- Protects against very high spikes that could damage equipment

A+
220-701
6.1
2.5

Figure 4-29   Line conditioner by Tripp Lite has six outlets and is rated to support up to 1800 watts of conditioned power
Courtesy of TrippLite

A UPS device that is suitably priced for personal computer systems is designed as a standby device (battery-powered circuit is used when AC input fails), an inline device (battery-powered circuit is used continually), or a line-interactive device (which combines features of the first two). Several variations of these three types of UPS devices are on the market at widely varying prices.

A common UPS device is a rather heavy box that plugs into an AC outlet and provides one or more outlets for the computer and the monitor (see Figure 4-30). It has an on/off switch, requires no maintenance, and is very simple to install. Use it to provide uninterruptible power to your desktop computer and monitor during a blackout. It's best not to connect it to nonessential devices such as a laser printer or scanner. Expect a UPS to provide power during a blackout long enough for you to save your work and shut down the system. Also know that a UPS is not as essential for a laptop computer as it is for a desktop because a laptop has a battery that can sustain it during a blackout.

The Smart UPS

When you look through ads of UPS devices, some of them are labeled as a smart UPS. A smart UPS (also called an intelligent UPS) can be controlled by software from a computer. For example, from the front panel of some UPSs you can check for a weak battery, but with a smart UPS, you can perform the same function from utility software installed on your computer. To accommodate this feature, a UPS has a USB connection to the PC and a microprocessor on board.

Some activities this utility software and a smart UPS can do include the following:

◢ Diagnose the UPS.
◢ Check for a weak battery.
◢ Monitor the quality of electricity received.
◢ Monitor the percentage of load the UPS is carrying during a blackout.
◢ Automatically schedule the weak-battery test or UPS diagnostic test.
◢ Send an alarm to workstations on a network to prepare for a shutdown.

Figure 4-30   Uninterruptible power supply (UPS)
Courtesy of American Power Conversion Corp.

⊿ Close down all servers protected by the UPS during a blackout.

⊿ Provide pager notification to a facilities manager if the power goes out.

⊿ After a shutdown, allow for startup from a remote location over the Internet.

What to Consider When Buying a UPS

The UPS rating is given in VA and watts, and the VA rating is generally about 60 percent higher than the watts rating. The VA rating is the theoretical rating that is calculated by multiplying volts by amps and then added up for all the equipment. The watts rating is the actual draw available to the equipment it protects. Make sure both ratings are adequate for your equipment. When matching a UPS to the needs of your equipment, add up total watts needed by your equipment and double it for the VA rating. Then check to make sure the wattage capacity of the UPS is about 25 to 30 percent higher than the total watts required.

You do not want to buy a UPS that runs at full capacity. This is especially important for an inline UPS because this type of UPS is constantly recharging the battery. If this battery charger is operating at full capacity, it is producing a lot of heat, which can reduce the battery's life.

You should also be aware of the degree of line conditioning that the UPS provides. Consider the warranty and service policies as well as the guarantee the UPS manufacturer gives for the equipment that the UPS protects. For example, one standby UPS by Tripp Lite that costs less than $100 claims to support up to 450 VA or 280 watts power requirements for up to 4 minutes during a complete power failure or 225 VA/140 watts for up to 15 minutes. The battery has an expected lifetime of three to six years. This smart UPS has a USB connector to a computer, and carries a guarantee on connected equipment of $100,000.

> ⚲ **A+ Exam Tip**   Content on the A+ 220-701 Essentials exam ends here and content on the A+ 220-702 Practical Application exam begins.

HOW TO WORK INSIDE A COMPUTER CASE

In this section, you'll learn how to take a computer apart and put it back together. This skill is needed in this and other chapters as you learn to replace computer parts inside the case and perhaps even build a system from scratch. We begin with looking at the tools a PC support technician needs to work inside a computer and then look at safety precautions you need to take to protect yourself and the equipment. Finally, you'll see the step-by-step procedures to take a PC apart and put it back together.

PC SUPPORT TECHNICIAN TOOLS

Several hardware and software tools can help you maintain a computer and diagnose and repair computer problems. The tools you choose depend on the amount of money you can spend and the level of PC support you expect to provide.

Essential tools for PC troubleshooting are listed here, and several of them are shown in Figure 4-31. You can purchase some of these tools in a PC toolkit, although most PC toolkits contain items you really can do without.

Figure 4-31   PC support technician tools
Courtesy: Course Technology/Cengage Learning

Here is a list of essential tools:

- ◢ Ground bracelet, ground mat, or ground gloves to use when working inside the computer case. How to use them is covered earlier in the chapter.
- ◢ Flathead screwdriver
- ◢ Phillips-head or crosshead screwdriver

▲ Torx screwdriver set, particularly size T15

▲ Tweezers, preferably insulated ones, for picking pieces of paper out of printers or dropped screws out of tight places

▲ Extractor, a spring-loaded device that looks like a hypodermic needle (When you push down on the top, three wire prongs come out that can be used to pick up a screw that has fallen into a place where hands and fingers can't reach.)

▲ Recovery CD or DVD for any OS you might work on (You might need several, depending on the OSs you support. You'll learn more about these in Chapter 12.)

The following tools might not be essential, but they are very convenient:

▲ Cans of compressed air, small portable compressor, or antistatic vacuum cleaner to clean dust from inside a computer case

▲ Cleaning solutions and pads such as contact cleaner, monitor wipes, and cleaning solutions for CDs, DVDs, tapes, and drives

▲ Multimeter to check cables and the power supply output

▲ Power supply tester

▲ Needle-nose pliers for removing jumpers and for holding objects (especially those pesky nuts on cable connectors) in place while you screw them in

▲ Cable ties to tie cables up and out of the way inside a computer case

▲ Flashlight to see inside the PC case

▲ AC outlet ground tester

▲ Network cable tester (you will learn to use this tool in Chapter 17)

▲ Loop-back plugs to test ports (you'll learn about these plugs in Chapter 9)

▲ Small cups or bags to help keep screws organized as you work

▲ Antistatic bags (a type of Faraday cage) to store unused parts

▲ Chip extractor to remove chips (to pry up the chip, a simple screwdriver is usually more effective, however)

▲ Pen and paper for taking notes

▲ POST diagnostic cards

▲ Utility software, virus-detection software, and diagnostic software on CD or floppy disk (you will learn to use several products in later chapters)

Keep your tools in a toolbox designated for PC troubleshooting. If you put disks and hardware tools in the same box, be sure to keep the disks inside a hard plastic case to protect them from scratches and dents. In addition, make sure the diagnostic and utility software you use is recommended for the hardware and software you are troubleshooting.

Now let's turn our attention to the details of several support technician tools, including diagnostic cards, power supply tester, and multimeter.

POST DIAGNOSTIC CARDS

Although not an essential tool, a POST diagnostic card can be of great help to discover and report computer errors and conflicts at POST. The POST (power-on self test) is a series of tests performed by the startup BIOS when you first turn on a computer. These tests determine if startup BIOS can communicate correctly with essential hardware components required for a successful boot. If you have a problem that prevents the PC from booting that you suspect is related to hardware, you can install the diagnostic card in an expansion slot on the motherboard and then attempt to boot. The card monitors the boot process and reports errors, usually as coded numbers on a small LED panel on the card. You then look up the number in the documentation that accompanies the card to get more information about the error and its source.

A+
220-702
1.4

Examples of these cards are listed below. Some manufacturers make cards for either desktop or laptop computers. The Post Code Master card is shown in Figure 4-32:

▲ PC POST Diagnostic Test Card by Elston System, Inc. (*www.elstonsystems.com*)
▲ PCI POST Diagnostic Test Card by StarTech.com (*www.startech.com*)
▲ Post Code Master by Microsystems Development, Inc. (*www.postcodemaster.com*)

Figure 4-32   Post Code Master diagnostic card by Microsystems Developments, Inc.
Courtesy: Course Technology/Cengage Learning

Before purchasing these or any other diagnostic tools or software, read the documentation about what they can and cannot do, and, if possible, read some product reviews. The Internet is a good source of information. Try using Google.com and searching on "PC diagnostic card reviews."

POWER SUPPLY TESTER

A power supply tester is used to measure the output of each connector coming from the power supply. You can test the power supply when it is outside or inside the case. Connect the motherboard P1 connector to the tester, plug up the power supply, and turn on the tester. An LCD panel reports the output of each lead (see Figure 4-33). The tester also has plugs for other cables, including the SATA cable, PCIe x16 cable, and Molex cable. In Figure 4-33, the +12 V line on the additional 4 pins of the P1 connector reads LL, which indicates low output.

MULTIMETER

A multimeter (see Figure 4-34) is a more general-purpose tool that can measure several characteristics of electricity in a variety of devices. Some multimeters can measure voltage, current, resistance, or continuity. (Continuity determines that two ends of a cable or fuse are connected without interruption.) Set to measure voltage, you can use it to measure output of each pin on a power supply connector. Set to measure continuity, a multimeter is useful to test fuses or to determine if a cable is good or to match pins on one end of a cable to pins

📹 Video
Using a Multimeter

on the other end. To learn how to use a multimeter to measure the voltage output of a power supply and determine if it is supplying correct voltages, see the content "Electricity and Multimeters" on the CD that accompanies this book.

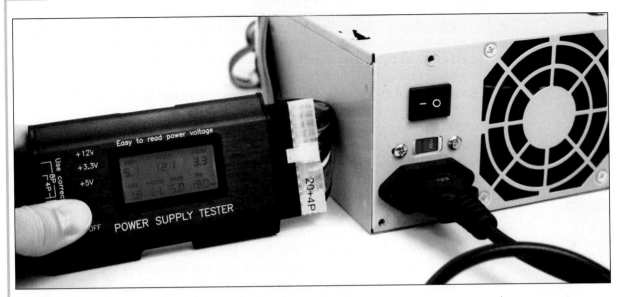

Figure 4-33 Use a power supply tester to test the output of each power connector on a power supply
Courtesy: Course Technology/Cengage Learning

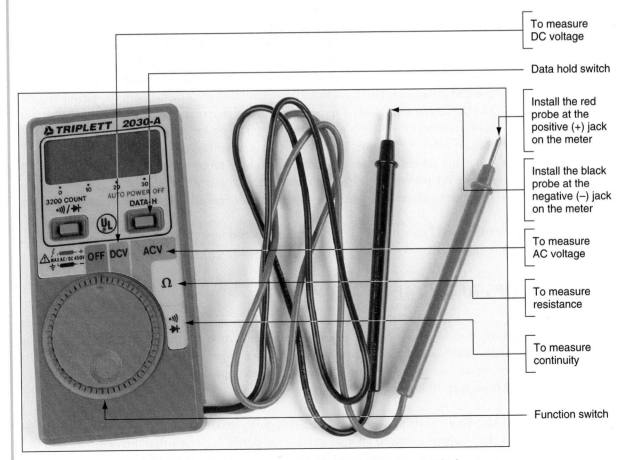

Figure 4-34 This digital multimeter can be set to measure voltage, resistance, or continuity
Courtesy: Course Technology/Cengage Learning

SAFETY PRECAUTIONS

Here are some important safety precautions that will help keep you and your equipment safe as you go through the process of taking it apart and putting it back together:

- ◢ Make notes as you work so that you can backtrack later if necessary. (When you're first learning to take a computer apart, it's really easy to forget where everything fits when it's time to put it back together. Also, in troubleshooting, you want to avoid repeating or overlooking things to try.)
- ◢ To stay organized and not lose small parts, keep screws and spacers orderly and in one place, such as a cup or tray.
- ◢ Don't stack boards on top of each other: You could accidentally dislodge a chip this way.
- ◢ When handling motherboards and expansion cards, don't touch the chips on the boards. Hold expansion cards by the edges. Don't touch any soldered components on a card, and don't touch the edge connectors unless it's absolutely necessary. All this helps prevent damage from static electricity.
- ◢ To protect the chip, don't touch it with a magnetized screwdriver.
- ◢ Don't use a graphite pencil to change DIP (dual inline package) switch settings, because graphite is a conductor of electricity, and the graphite can lodge in the switch. These on/off switches are used on older motherboards to configure the board.
- ◢ In a classroom environment, after you have reassembled everything, have your instructor check your work before you put the cover back on and power up.
- ◢ To protect both yourself and the equipment when working inside a computer, turn off the power, unplug the computer, and then press the power button to completely drain the power. Always use a ground bracelet.
- ◢ Never ever touch the inside of a computer that is turned on.
- ◢ Consider the monitor and the power supply to be "black boxes." Never remove the cover or put your hands inside this equipment unless you know about the hazards of charged capacitors, and have been trained to deal with them. Both the power supply and the monitor can hold a dangerous level of electricity even after you turn them off and disconnect them from a power source. The power supply and monitor contain enough power to kill you, even when they are unplugged.
- ◢ When unpacking hardware or software, to help protect against static electricity, remove the packing tape and cellophane from the work area as soon as possible.
- ◢ To protect against static electricity, keep components away from your hair and clothing.

Now that you know about PC technician tools and how to keep safe, let's look at the steps to take apart a computer.

STEPS TO TAKE APART A COMPUTER

A PC technician needs to be comfortable with taking apart a computer and putting it back together. In most situations, the essential tools you'll need for the job are a ground bracelet, a Phillips-head screwdriver, a flat-head screwdriver, paper, and pen. As you work inside a computer, be sure to use a ground bracelet, the safety precautions in the chapter, and the guidelines in the following list:

1. If you are starting with a working computer, make sure important data is first backed up. Copy the data to an external storage device such as a flash drive or external hard drive. How to perform good backups is covered in Chapter 13.

2. Power down the system, unplug it, and press the power button. Unplug the monitor, mouse, keyboard, and any other peripherals or cables attached and move them out of your way.

3. Put the computer on a table with plenty of room. Have a plastic bag or cup handy to hold screws. When you reassemble the PC, you will need to insert the same screws in the same holes. This is especially important with the hard drive, because screws that are too long can puncture the hard drive housing.

Video
Opening a Computer Case

4. Sometimes I think figuring out how to open a computer case is the most difficult part of disassembling. If you need help figuring it out, check the user manual or Web site of the case manufacturer. To remove the cover of your PC, do the following:

▲ Many newer cases require you to remove the faceplate on the front of the case first. Other cases require you to remove a side panel first, and really older cases require you to first remove the entire sides and top as a single unit. Study your case for the correct approach.

▲ Most cases have panels on each side of the case that can be removed. It is usually necessary to only remove the one panel to expose the top of the motherboard. To know which panel to remove, look at where the ports are on the rear of the case. For example, in Figure 4-35, the ports on this motherboard are on the left side of the case, indicating the bottom of the motherboard is on the left. Therefore, you will want to remove the right panel to expose the top of this

Motherboard is mounted to this side of the case

Figure 4-35 Decide which side panel to remove
Courtesy: Course Technology/Cengage Learning

A+ 220-702

4

A+
220-702
1.1

motherboard. Lay the case down to its left so the ports and the motherboard are sitting on the bottom. Later, depending on how drives are installed, it might become necessary to remove the bottom panel in order to remove the screws that hold the drives in place.

◢ Locate the screws that hold the side panel in place. Be careful not to unscrew any screws besides these. The other screws probably are holding the power supply, fan, and other components in place (see Figure 4-36).

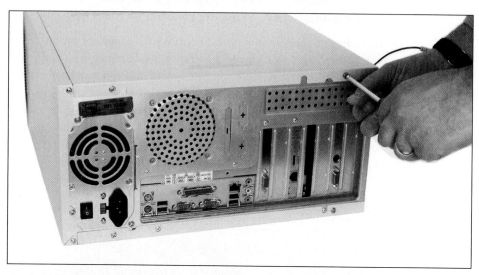

Figure 4-36 Locate the screws that hold the top cover in place
Courtesy: Course Technology/Cengage Learning

◢ After the screws are removed, slide the panel toward the rear, and then lift it off the case (see Figure 4-37).

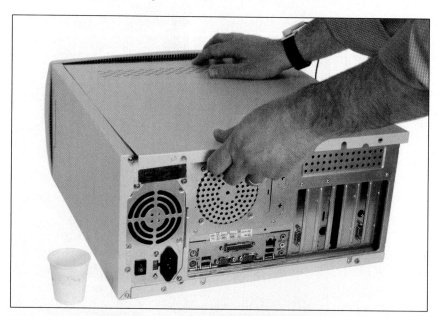

Figure 4-37 Slide the panel to the rear of the case
Courtesy: Course Technology/Cengage Learning

◢ Newer cases require you to pop the front panel off the case before removing the side panels. Look for a lever on the bottom of the panel and hinges at the top. Squeeze the lever to release the front panel and lift it off the case (see Figure 4-38).

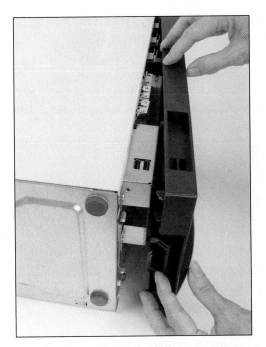

Figure 4-38 Newer cases require you to remove the front panel before removing
the side panel of a computer case
Courtesy: Course Technology/Cengage Learning

Then remove a single screw (see Figure 4-39) and slide the side panel to the front
and then off the case (see Figure 4-40). Also, know that some case panels don't use
screws; these side panels simply pop up and out with a little prying and pulling.

Figure 4-39 One screw holds the side panel in place
Courtesy: Course Technology/Cengage Learning

5. If you plan to remove several components, draw a diagram of all cable connections to
the motherboard, adapter cards, and drives. You might need the cable connection diagram to help you reassemble. Note where each cable begins and ends, and pay particular
attention to the small wires and connectors that connect the front of the case to the
motherboard. It's important to be careful about diagramming these because it is so easy

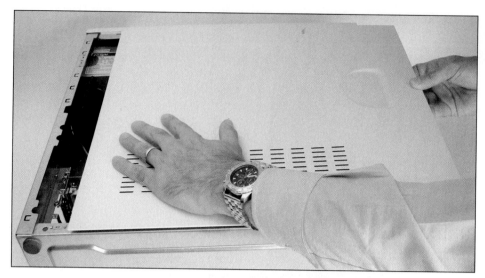

Figure 4-40   Slide the side panel to the front of the case and then lift it off the case
Courtesy: Course Technology/Cengage Learning

to connect them in the wrong position later when you reassemble. If you want, use a felt-tip marker to make a mark across components, to indicate a cable connection, board placement, motherboard orientation, speaker connection, brackets, and so on, so that you can simply line up the marks when you reassemble. This method, however, probably won't work for the front case wires because they are so small. For these, consider writing down the color of the wires and their position on the pins (see Figure 4-41).

Figure 4-41   Diagram the pin locations of the color-coded wires that connect to the front of the case
Courtesy: Course Technology/Cengage Learning

6. Drives are connected to the motherboard with ribbon cables or thinner serial ATA cables. Before removing any ribbon cables, look for a red color or stripe down one side of each cable. This edge color marks this side of the cable as pin 1. Look on the board or drive that the cable is attached to. You should see that pin 1 or pin 2 is clearly marked, as shown in Figure 4-42. However, some boards mark pin 34 or pin 40. For these boards, pin 1 is on the other side of the connector. Also know that some boards and drives don't mark the pins, but rather have a notch in the connector

Figure 4-42 Pin 1 for this IDE connection is clearly marked
Courtesy: Course Technology/Cengage Learning

so that a notched ribbon cable can only be inserted in one direction (see Figure 4-43).
Verify that the edge color is aligned with pin 1. Serial ATA cables can only connect to
serial ATA connectors in one direction (see Figure 4-44).

Figure 4-43 The notch on the side of this floppy drive connector allows the floppy drive cable to
connect in only one direction
Courtesy: Course Technology/Cengage Learning

7. A system might have up to three types of ribbon cables. A floppy drive cable has 34 pins
and a twist in the cable. IDE cables have 40 pins. A CD or DVD drive can use either a 40-
conductor IDE cable or a higher-quality 80-conductor IDE cable. Older hard drives use an
80-conductor IDE ribbon cable. (Newer drives use narrow SATA cables rather than ribbon cables.) See Figure 4-45 for a comparison of the three
ribbon cables. Remove the cables to all drives. Remove
the power supply cords from the drives. Notice as you
disconnect the power cord, the Molex connector is shaped
so it only connects in one direction (see Figure 4-46).

Video
Replacing an Expansion Card

A+
220-702
1.1

Figure 4-44 A serial ATA cable connects to a serial ATA connector in only one direction.
Use red connectors on the motherboard first
Courtesy: Course Technology/Cengage Learning

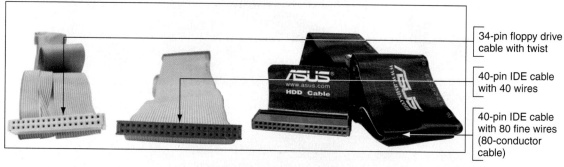

34-pin floppy drive
cable with twist

40-pin IDE cable
with 40 wires

40-pin IDE cable
with 80 fine wires
(80-conductor
cable)

Figure 4-45 A system might have up to three types of ribbon cables
Courtesy: Course Technology/Cengage Learning

8. Do the following to remove the expansion cards:

◢ Remove any wire or cable connected to the card.

◢ Remove the screw holding the card to the case (see Figure 4-47).

◢ Grasp the card with both hands and remove it by lifting straight up. If you have trouble removing it from the expansion slot, you can *very slightly* rock the card from end to end (*not* side to side). Rocking the card from side to side might spread the slot opening and weaken the connection.

◢ As you remove the card, don't put your fingers on the edge connectors or touch a chip, and don't stack the cards on top of one another. Lay each card aside on a flat surface.

> **Notes** Some video cards use a latch that helps to hold the card securely in the slot. To remove these cards, use one finger to hold the latch back from the slot, as shown in Figure 4-48, as you pull the card up and out of the slot.

9. Depending on the system, you might need to remove the motherboard next or remove the drives next. My choice is to first remove the motherboard. It and the processor are the most expensive and easily damaged parts in the system. I like to get them out of

Figure 4-46 Molex power connector to a drive orients in only one direction
Courtesy: Course Technology/Cengage Learning

Figure 4-47 Remove the screw holding an expansion card to the case
Courtesy: Course Technology/Cengage Learning

harm's way before working with the drives. However, in some cases, you must remove the drives or the power supply before you can get to the motherboard. Study your situation and decide which to do first. To remove the motherboard, do the following:

▲ Unplug the power supply lines to the motherboard. You'll find a main power line, and maybe one auxiliary power line from the power supply to the motherboard. There might also be an audio wire from the CD drive to the motherboard. Disconnect it from the motherboard.

A+
220-702
1.1

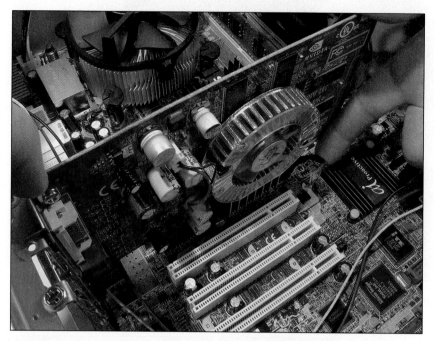

Figure 4-48 Hold the retention mechanism back as you remove a video card from its expansion slot
Courtesy: Course Technology/Cengage Learning

◢ The next step is to disconnect wires leading from the front of the computer case to the motherboard. If you don't have the motherboard manual handy, be very careful to diagram how these wires connect because they are never labeled well on a motherboard. Make a careful diagram and then disconnect the wires. Figure 4-49 shows five leads and the pins on the motherboard that receive these leads. The pins are color-coded and cryptically labeled on the board. You'll learn more about matching these wires to their connectors in Chapter 5.

◢ You're now ready to remove the screws that hold the motherboard to the case. For an older motherboard, instead of screws you'll see spacers that keep the board

Figure 4-49 Five leads from the front panel connect to two rows of pins on the motherboard
Courtesy: Course Technology/Cengage Learning

from resting directly on the bottom of the computer case. Carefully pop off these spacers and/or remove the screws (up to nine) that hold the board to the case (see Figure 4-50) and then remove the board. Set it aside in a safe place. Figure 4-51 shows a motherboard sitting to the side of these spacers. One spacer is in place and the other is lying beside its case holes. Also notice in the photo the two holes in the motherboard where screws are used to connect the board to the spacers.

▲ The motherboard should now be free and you can carefully remove it from the case, as shown in Figure 4-52.

Figure 4-50 Remove up to nine screws that hold the motherboard to the case
Courtesy: Course Technology/Cengage Learning

Figure 4-51 This motherboard connects to a case using screws and spacers that keep the board from touching the case
Courtesy: Course Technology/Cengage Learning

A+
220-702
1.1

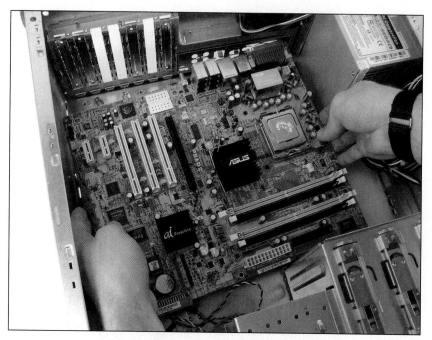

Figure 4-52 Remove the motherboard from the case
Courtesy: Course Technology/Cengage Learning

> ⚡ **Caution** Some processors have heavy cooling assemblies installed on top of them. For these systems, it is best to remove the cooler before you take the motherboard out of the case because the motherboard is not designed to support this heavy cooler when the motherboard is not securely seated in the case. How to remove the cooler is covered in Chapter 6.

10. To remove the power supply from the case, look for screws that attach the power supply to the computer case, as shown in Figure 4-53. Be careful not to remove any screws that hold the power supply housing together. You do not want to take the housing apart. After you have removed the screws, the power supply still might not be free. Sometimes, it is attached to the case on the underside by recessed slots. Turn the case over and look on the bottom for these slots. If they are present, determine in which direction you need to slide the power supply to free it from the case.

11. Remove each drive next, handling the drives with care. Here are some tips:

    ◢ Some drives have one or two screws on each side of the drive attaching the drive to the drive bay. After you remove the screws, the drive slides to the front or to the rear and then out of the case.

    ◢ Sometimes, there is a catch underneath the drive that you must lift up as you slide the drive forward.

    ◢ Some drive bays have a clipping mechanism to hold the drive in the bay. First release the clip and then pull the drive forward and out of the bay (see Figure 4-54). Handle the drives with care.

    ◢ Some cases have a removable bay for small drives (see Figure 4-55). These bays can hold narrow drives such as hard drives, floppy drives, and Zip drives. The bay is removed first and then the drives are removed from the bay. To remove the bay, first remove the screws or release the clip holding the bay in place and then slide the bay out of the case. The drives are usually installed in the bay with two screws on each side of each drive. Remove the screws and then the drives (see Figure 4-56).

Figure 4-53 Removing the power supply mounting screws
Courtesy: Course Technology/Cengage Learning

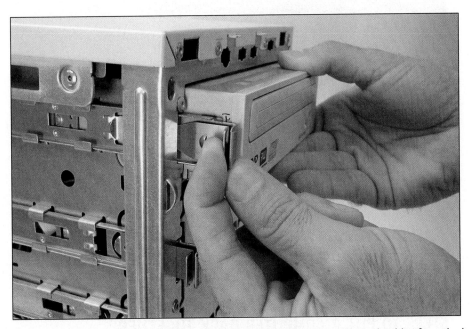

Figure 4-54 To remove this CD drive, first pull the clip forward to release the drive from the bay
Courtesy: Course Technology/Cengage Learning

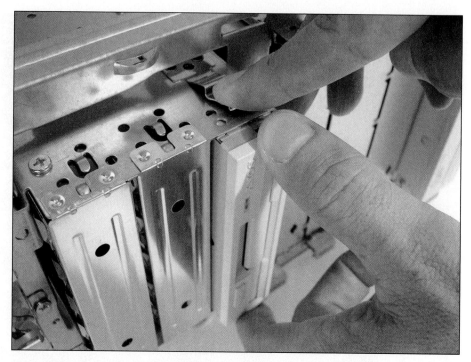

Figure 4-55 Push down on the clip and then slide the removable bay forward and out of the case
Courtesy: Course Technology/Cengage Learning

Figure 4-56 Drives in this removable bay are held in place with screws on each side of the bay
Courtesy: Course Technology/Cengage Learning

STEPS TO PUT A COMPUTER BACK TOGETHER

To reassemble a computer, reverse the process of disassembling. Do the following:

1. Install components in the case in this order: power supply, drives, motherboard, and cards. When installing drives, know that for some systems, it's easier to connect data

cables to the drives and then slide the drives into the bay. If the drive is anchored to the bay with screws, be careful to align the front of the drive flush with the front of the case before installing screws (see Figure 4-57).

Figure 4-57 Align the front of the drive flush with the case front and then anchor with a screw
Courtesy: Course Technology/Cengage Learning

2. Connect all data and power cables. Before you replace the cover, take a few minutes to double-check each connection to make sure it is correct and snug.

3. Plug in the keyboard, monitor, and mouse.

4. In a classroom environment, have the instructor check your work before you power up.

5. Turn on the power and check that the PC is working properly. If the PC does not work, most likely the problem is a loose connection. Just turn off the power and go back and check each cable connection and each expansion card. You probably have not solidly seated a card in the slot. After you have double-checked, try again.

TROUBLESHOOTING THE ELECTRICAL SYSTEM

Electrical problems can occur before or after the boot and can be consistent or intermittent. Many times PC repair technicians don't recognize the cause of a problem to be electrical because of the intermittent nature of some electrical problems. In these situations, the hard drive, memory, the OS, or even user error might be suspected as the source of the problem and then systematically eliminated before the electrical system is suspected. This section will help you to be aware of symptoms of electrical problems so that you can zero in on the source of an electrical problem as quickly as possible.

APPLYING CONCEPTS Your friend Sharon calls to ask for your help with a computer problem. Her system has been working fine for over a year, but now strange things are happening. Sometimes, the system powers down for no apparent reason while she is working and sometimes Windows locks up. As you read this section, look for clues as to what the problem might be. Also, as you read, think of questions to ask your friend that will help you.

Possible symptoms of a problem with the electrical system are:

▲ The PC appears "dead"—no lights, no spinning drive, or fan.

▲ The PC sometimes halts during booting. After several tries, it boots successfully.

▲ Error codes or beeps occur during booting, but they come and go.

▲ You smell burnt parts or odors. (Definitely not a good sign!)

▲ The PC powers down at unexpected times.

▲ The PC appears dead except you hear a whine coming from the power supply.

Without opening the computer case, the following list contains some questions you can ask and things you can do to solve a problem with the electrical system. The rule of thumb is "try the simple things first." Most PC problems have simple solutions.

▲ If you smell any burnt parts or odors, don't try to turn the system on. Identify the component that is fried and replace it.

▲ When you first plug up power to a system and hear a whine coming from the power supply, the power supply might be inadequate for the system or there might be a short. Don't press the power button to start up the system. Unplug the power cord so that the power supply will not be damaged. The next step is to open the case and search for a short. If you don't find a short, consider upgrading the power supply.

▲ Is the power cord plugged in? If it is plugged into a power strip or surge suppressor, is the device turned on and also plugged in?

▲ Is the power outlet controlled by a wall switch? If so, is the switch turned on?

▲ Are any cable connections loose?

▲ Is the circuit breaker blown? Is the house circuit overloaded?

▲ Are all switches on the system turned on? Computer? Monitor? Uninterruptible power supply?

▲ Is there a possibility the system has overheated? If so, wait awhile and try again. If the system comes on, but later turns itself off, you might need additional cooling fans inside the unit. Where and how to install them is covered in Chapter 6.

The next step is to open the computer case and then do the following:

▲ If the fan is not running, turn off the computer, unplug it, press the power button, open the case, and check the connections to the power supply. Are they secure? Are all cards securely seated?

▲ If you smell burnt parts, turn off the system and carefully search for the source of the problem. Look for shorts and frayed and burnt wires. Disassemble the parts until you find the one that is damaged.

As you read through the rest of this section on troubleshooting, you'll see other possible solutions to electrical problems during the boot such as loose internal connections.

PROBLEMS WITH EXTERNAL POWER

A brownout (reduced current) of the house current might cause symptoms of electrical power problems. If you suspect the house current could be low, check other devices that are using the same circuit. A copy machine, laser printer, or other heavy equipment might be drawing too much power. Remove the other devices from the same house circuit.

A line conditioner might solve the problem of intermittent errors caused by noise in the power line to the PC. Try installing a line conditioner to condition voltage to the PC.

A+
220-702
1.2

PROBLEMS WITH LOOSE INTERNAL CONNECTIONS

Loose connections inside the computer case can cause a system to appear dead or reboot itself. For most of the ATX and BTX power supplies, a wire runs from the power switch on the front of the case to the motherboard. This wire must be connected to the pins on the motherboard and the switch turned on before power comes up. Check that the wire is connected correctly to the motherboard. Figure 4-58 shows a wire, which is labeled "REMOTE SW," connected to pins on the motherboard labeled "PWR.SW." If you are not sure of the correct connection on the motherboard, see the motherboard documentation. While inside the case, check all power connections from the power supply to the motherboard and drives. Also, some cases require the case's front panel be in place before the power-on button will work.

Remote SW

Figure 4-58 For an ATX or BTX power supply, the remote switch wire must be connected to the motherboard before power will come on
Courtesy: Course Technology/Cengage Learning

Notes Remember from earlier in the chapter that strong magnetic or electrical interference can affect how a power system functions. Sometimes an old monitor emits too much static and EMI (electromagnetic interference) and brings a whole system down. When you troubleshoot power problems, remember to check for sources of electrical or magnetic interference such as an old monitor, fluorescent lighting, or an electric fan sitting near the computer case.

PROBLEMS THAT COME AND GO

If a system boots successfully to the Windows desktop, you still might have a power system problem. Some problems are intermittent; that is, they come and go. Here are some symptoms that might indicate an intermittent problem with the electrical system after the boot:

- The computer stops or hangs for no reason. Sometimes it might even reboot itself.
- Memory errors appear intermittently.
- Data is written incorrectly to the hard drive.
- The keyboard stops working at odd times.
- The motherboard fails or is damaged.
- The power supply overheats and becomes hot to the touch.
- The power supply fan becomes very noisy or stops.

Generally, intermittent problems (those that come and go) are more difficult to solve than a dead system. There can be many causes of intermittent problems, such as an inadequate power supply, overheating, and devices and components damaged by ESD. Each of these sources of intermittent problems is covered in this section.

PROBLEMS WITH AN INADEQUATE POWER SUPPLY

If you have just installed a new device such as a second hard drive or a DVD drive and are concerned that the power supply is not adequate, you might test it after you finish the installation.

Make all the devices in your system work at the same time. For instance, you can make two hard drives and the DVD drive work at the same time by copying files from one hard drive to the other while playing a movie on the DVD. If the new drive and the other drives each work independently, but data errors occur when all work at the same time, suspect a shortage of electrical power.

If you prefer a more technical approach, you can estimate how much total wattage your system needs by calculating the watts required for each device and adding them together. You learned how to match a power supply to the wattage requirements of the system earlier in the chapter.

A system with a standard power supply of about 250 watts that has multiple hard drives, multiple CD drives, and several expansion cards is most likely operating above the rated capacity of the power supply, which can cause the system to unexpectedly reboot or give intermittent, otherwise unexplained, errors. If the power supply is grossly inadequate, it will whine when you first plug up the power. Upgrade the power supply as needed to accommodate an overloaded power system.

PROBLEMS WITH A FAULTY POWER SUPPLY

If you suspect the power supply is faulty, you can test it using either a power supply tester (the easier method) or a multimeter (the more tedious method). However, know that a power supply that gives correct voltages when you measure it might still be the source of problems, because power problems can be intermittent. Also be aware that an ATX power supply monitors the range of voltages provided to the motherboard and halts the motherboard if voltages are inadequate. Therefore, if the power supply appears "dead," your best action is to replace it.

PROBLEMS WITH THE POWER SUPPLY FANS

An improperly working fan sometimes causes power supply problems. Usually just before a fan stops working, it hums or whines, especially when the PC is first turned on. If this has just happened, replace the fan if you are trained to service the power supply. If not, replace the entire power supply. If you replace the power supply or fan and the fan still does not work, assume the problem wasn't the fan. A short somewhere else in the system drawing too much power might cause the problem. Don't operate the PC if the fan does not work. Computers without cooling fans can quickly overheat and damage chips.

To troubleshoot a nonfunctional fan, which might be a symptom of another problem and not a problem of the fan itself, follow these steps:

1. Turn off the power and remove all power cord connections to all components except the motherboard. Turn the power back on. If the fan works, the problem is with one of the systems you disconnected, not with the power supply, the fan, or the motherboard.

2. Turn off the power and reconnect one card or drive at a time until you identify the device with the short.

3. If the fan does not work when all devices except the motherboard are disconnected, the problem is the motherboard or the power supply. Since the power supply is less expensive and easier to replace than the motherboard, try replacing it first.

PROBLEMS WITH OVERHEATING

If a computer powers down after it has been operating for a few minutes or a few hours, the problem might be caused by overheating. Leave the system turned off for about 30 minutes and then try again. If the computer works for a while and then stops again, check its internal temperature. You might need to install additional fans. How to check the internal temperature and solve overheating problems are covered in Chapter 6.

POWER PROBLEMS WITH THE MOTHERBOARD

The motherboard, like all other components inside the computer case, should be grounded to the chassis. Look for a metal screw that grounds the board to the computer case. However, a short might be the problem with the electrical system if some component on the board makes improper contact with the chassis. This short can seriously damage the motherboard. For some cases, check for missing standoffs (small plastic or metal spacers that hold the motherboard a short distance away from the chassis). A missing standoff most often causes these improper connections. Also check for extra standoffs not used by the motherboard that might be touching a wire on the bottom of the board and causing a short.

Shorts in the circuits on the motherboard might also cause problems. Look for damage on the bottom of the motherboard. These circuits are coated with plastic, and quite often damage is difficult to spot. Also look for burned-out capacitors that are spotted brown or corroded. You'll see examples of burned out capacitors in the next chapter.

APPLYING | CONCEPTS

Back to Sharon's computer problem. Here are some questions that will help you identify the source of the problem:

- Have you added new devices to your system? (These new devices might be drawing too much power from an overworked power supply.)
- Have you moved your computer recently? (It might be sitting beside a heat vent or electrical equipment.)
- Does the system power down or hang after you have been working for some time? (This symptom might have more than one cause, such as overheating or a power supply, processor, memory, or motherboard about to fail.)
- Has the computer case been opened recently? (Someone working inside the case might not have used a ground bracelet and components are now failing because of ESD damage.)
- Are case vents free so that air can flow? (The case might be close to a curtain covering the vents.)

Intermittent problems like the one Sharon described are often heat related. If the system only hangs but does not power off, the problem might be caused by faulty memory or bad software, but because it actually powers down, you can assume the problem is related to power or heat.

If Sharon tells you that the system powers down after she's been working for several hours, you can probably assume overheating. Check that first. If that's not the problem, the next thing to do is replace the power supply.

A+
220-702
1.2

⚡ Caution | Never replace a damaged motherboard with a good one without first testing or replacing the power supply. You don't want to subject another good board to possible damage.

A+
220-702
1.2
1.1

REPLACING THE POWER SUPPLY

📹 Video

Replacing a Power Supply

The easiest way to fix a power supply you suspect is faulty is to replace it. When selecting a replacement power supply, be sure the new power supply uses the correct form factor that provides the correct output voltages, is adequately rated for power in watts, and has all the power connectors needed by your system. To determine if the power supply really is the problem, turn off the PC, open the computer case, and set the new power supply on top of the old one. Disconnect the old power supply's cords and plug the PC devices into the new power supply. Turn on the PC and verify that the new power supply solves your problem before installing it.

💡 **A+ Exam Tip** The A+ IT 220-702 Practical Application exam expects you to know how to select and install a power supply. Know it must match wattage requirements and have the correct connector types and number of connectors to meet the demands of the system.

⚡ Caution | Remember from earlier in the chapter that you need to consider the monitor and the power supply to be "black boxes." Never remove the cover or put your hands inside this equipment unless you know about the hazards of charged capacitors and have been trained to deal with them. Both the power supply and the monitor can hold a dangerous level of electricity even after you turn them off and disconnect them from a power source. The power supply and monitor contain enough power to give you a strong shock even when they are unplugged.

Follow these steps to replace a power supply:

1. Turn off the power to the computer, unplug the computer, and press the power button to drain the system of power.

2. Remove the power cable.

3. Remove the computer case cover.

4. Inside the case, disconnect all power cords from the power supply to other devices.

5. Determine which components must be removed before the power supply can be safely removed from the case. You might need to remove the hard drive, several cards, or the CD or DVD drive. In some cases, you may even need to remove the motherboard.

6. Remove all the components necessary to get to the power supply. Remember to protect the components from static electricity as you work.

7. Unscrew the screws on the back of the computer case that hold the power supply to the case.

8. Look on the bottom or back of the case for slots that hold the power supply in position. Often the power supply must be shifted in one direction to free it from the slots.

9. Remove the power supply.

10. Place the new power supply in position, sliding it into the slots the old power supply used.

11. Replace the power supply screws.

12. Replace all other components and cables.

13. Replace the case cover and connect the power cord.

14. Turn on the PC and verify all is working.

4

>> CHAPTER SUMMARY

▲ A form factor is a set of specifications for the size and configuration of hardware components, such as cases, power supplies, and motherboards.

▲ The most common form factor today is ATX. Popular variations in ATX include MicroATX (a smaller version of ATX) and FlexATX (a smaller version of MicroATX).

▲ Other current form factors are BTX and NLX. NLX uses a riser card that plugs into the motherboard.

▲ Case types include desktop, low-profile or slimline desktops, minitower, mid-tower, full-size tower, and notebook. The most popular case type in use today is the mid-tower.

▲ Electrical voltage is a measure of the potential difference in an electrical system.

▲ Electrical current is measured in amps, and electrical resistance is measured in ohms.

▲ Wattage is a measure of electrical power. Wattage is calculated by multiplying volts by amps in a system.

▲ Microcomputers require direct current (DC), which is converted from alternating current (AC) by the PC's power supply inside the computer case.

▲ A PC power supply is actually a transformer and rectifier, rather than a supplier of power.

▲ Materials used to make electrical components include conductors, insulators, and semiconductors.

▲ A transistor is a gate or switch for an electrical signal, a capacitor holds an electrical charge, a diode allows electricity to flow in one direction, and a resistor limits electrical current.

▲ Important features of a power supply to consider when purchasing it are its form factor, number and type of connector types it provides, voltage selector switch, fan size and position, on/off switch, wattage capacity, and warranty.

▲ To decide on the wattage capacity of a power supply, add up the wattage requirements for all components in a system and then increase that total by about 30 percent.

▲ Power supplies and monitors are considered field replaceable units and you should not work inside one unless you are trained to do so.

▲ To protect a computer system against ESD, use a ground bracelet, ground mat, and static shielding bags.

▲ Protect a computer system against EMI or RFI by covering expansion slots (which also reduces dust inside the case and improves airflow), by not placing the system close to or on the same circuit as high-powered electrical equipment, and by using line conditioners.

▲ Devices that control the electricity to a computer include surge suppressors, line conditioners, and UPSs.

▲ A surge suppressor protects a computer against damaging spikes in electrical voltage.

◢ Line conditioners level the AC to reduce brownouts and spikes.

◢ A UPS provides enough power to perform an orderly shutdown during a blackout.

◢ There are two kinds of UPSs: the true UPS (called the inline UPS) and the standby UPS.

◢ The inline UPS is more expensive because it provides continuous power. The standby UPS must switch from one circuit to another when a blackout begins.

◢ Utility software at a remote computer or a computer connected to the UPS through a USB cable can control and manage a smart UPS.

◢ Data line protectors are small surge suppressors designed to protect modems from spikes on telephone lines.

◢ Tools necessary for a PC support technician include a ground bracelet, screwdrivers, tweezers, extractor, and recovery CDs.

◢ A POST diagnostic card is useful when troubleshooting startup errors caused by hardware.

◢ A power supply tester and multimeter can be used to measure the voltage output of power supplies. In addition, a multimeter can be used to test cables and fuses.

◢ A faulty power supply can cause memory errors, data errors, system hangs, or reboots; it can damage a motherboard or other components.

◢ When troubleshooting the electrical system, consider the problem might be caused by external power problems, loose connections, bad components drawing too much power, the power supply, the motherboard, or overheating.

>> KEY TERMS

For explanations of key terms, see the Glossary near the end of the book.

alternating current (AC)
amp
ampere
antistatic wrist strap
ATX
ATX12V power supply
brownouts
BTX (Balanced Technology Extended)
bus riser
capacitor
clamping voltage
compact cases
data line protector
daughter card
desktop case
diagnostic card
diode
DIP (dual inline package) switch
direct current (DC)
electromagnetic interference (EMI)
electrostatic discharge (ESD)

field replaceable unit (FRU)
FlexATX
form factor
ground bracelet
intelligent UPS
inverter
joule
line conditioners
low-profile cases
MicroATX
mid-tower
multimeter
NLX
notebook cases
overclocking
P1 connector
POST (power-on self test)
power conditioners
power supply
power supply tester
power supply unit (PSU)
radio frequency interference (RFI)

rectifier
resistor
riser card
sags
slimline cases
smart UPS
soft power
soft switch
spikes
static electricity
surge protector
surge suppressor
swells
tower case
transformer
transistor
uninterruptible power supply (UPS)
volt
voltage selector switch
watt

>> *REVIEWING THE BASICS*

1. How many pins does the P1 connector have that use the ATX Version 2.2 standard?

2. What are the maximum dimensions for a motherboard that uses the MicroATX form factor?

3. Which form factor is a smaller version of the MicroATX form factor?

4. Which form factor uses a riser card on the edge of the motherboard?

5. How many pins does the main power connector on a BTX motherboard have?

6. Which type of case form factor is best for keeping a system cool?

7. Which type of computer case is most popular for desktop systems?

8. What is the normal voltage of house electricity in the United States?

9. Hot wires in home wiring are normally colored _____ and ground wires in computers are normally colored _____ .

10. What is the difference between a transformer and a rectifier? Which are found in a PC power supply?

11. What are the five voltages that can be produced by an ATX or BTX power supply? Which voltage is seldom used?

12. What device uses the 12 V 6-pin power connector?

13. What device uses the 12 V 8-pin power connector?

14. What is the purpose of the 4-pin auxiliary connector on a motherboard?

15. What is the purpose of the 4-pin Molex connector?

16. How do you determine the wattage capacity needed by a power supply?

17. Which one component in a high-end gaming computer is likely to draw the most power?

18. Why is a power supply dangerous even after the power is disconnected?

19. Which tool of a PC support technician is the most important tool to protect the system against ESD?

20. Which permanently damages a computer component, damage caused by ESD or damage caused by EMI?

21. What is a simple way to detect EMI?

22. What is an unintended, high-current, closed connection between two points in a circuit called?

23. What device protects a system against lighting strikes but does not protect against sags and brownouts?

24. What device protects a system against blackouts?

25. What two measurements are used to rate the capacity of a UPS?

26. What unit of measure is used to describe the amount of work a surge suppressor can do before it stops protecting the circuit from an electrical surge?

27. Why is it important to have an indicator light on a surge suppressor?

28. What are the two main types of uninterruptible power supplies?

29. How does a smart UPS differ from one that is not smart?

30. What is the purpose of a POST diagnostic card?

31. When taking a computer apart, why is it important to not stack boards on top of each other?

32. When assembling a system, which do you install first, the drives or the motherboard?

33. List four computer symptoms that indicate a faulty power supply.

>> **THINKING CRITICALLY**

1. How much power is consumed by a load drawing 5 A with 120 V across it?

2. You suspect that a power supply is faulty, but you use a multimeter to measure its voltage output and find it to be acceptable. Why is it still possible that the power supply may be faulty?

3. Someone asks you for help with a computer that hangs at odd times. You turn it on and work for about 15 minutes, and then the computer freezes and powers down. What do you do first?

    a. Replace the surge protector.

    b. Replace the power supply.

    c. Wait about 30 minutes for the system to cool down and try again.

    d. Install an additional fan.

4. When working on a computer, which of the following best protects against ESD? Why?

    a. Always touch the computer case before touching a circuit board inside the case.

    b. Always wear a ground bracelet clipped to the side of the case.

    c. Always sit a computer on an antistatic mat when working on it.

5. What is a reasonable wattage capacity for a power supply to be used with a system that contains a DVD drive, three hard drives, and a high-end video card?

    a. 250 watts

    b. 1000 watts

    c. 700 watts

    d. 150 watts

>> **HANDS-ON PROJECTS**

PROJECT 4-1:   Taking a Lab Computer Apart and Putting It Back Together

Working with a partner and using a lab computer designated to be disassembled, take a computer apart. It is not necessary to remove the processor from the motherboard, but be very careful to properly support the motherboard and processor as you remove them from the case. Then reassemble the system. Don't replace the computer case panel until your instructor has inspected all cable connections. Then turn on the computer and verify all is working.

4

PROJECT 4-2:   Making Price and Value Comparisons

Using the two computer parts retail Web sites, Tiger Direct (*www.tigerdirect.com*) and Micro Electronics (*www.microcenter.com*), find out the following about products discussed in the chapter:

1. Compare the prices and ratings of two different surge suppressors. Print Web pages of your findings. How are the surge suppressors rated?

2. Compare the prices and ratings of two different UPS devices. Compare a smart UPS to one that does not interface with a PC, but otherwise has similar ratings.

3. Compare the prices and features of two different power supplies that are rated at 500 watts.

PROJECT 4-3:   Finding PC Power Supply Facts

Remove the cover from your home or lab PC, and answer the following questions:

1. How many watts are supplied by your power supply? (The number is usually printed on the label on the top of the power supply.)

2. How many cables are supplied by your power supply?

3. Where does each cable lead?

4. Does the back of the power supply have a switch that can be set for 230 volts (Europe) or 115 volts (U.S.)?

PROJECT 4-4:   Building a Circuit to Turn On a Light

1. From the following components, build a circuit to turn on a light:

   ◢ An AC light bulb or LED (*Note*: An LED has polarity—it must be connected with the negative and positive terminals in the correct positions.)

   ◢ A double-A battery (*Note*: A 9-volt battery can burn out some bulbs.)

   ◢ A switch (A knife switch or even a DIP switch will work.)

   ◢ Three pieces of wire to connect the light, the switch, and the battery

2. Add a second battery to the circuit, and record the results.

3. Add a resistor to the circuit, and record the results.

4. Place an extra wire in the middle of the circuit running from the battery to the switch (thus making a short), and record the results.

PROJECT 4-5:   Researching the Market for a UPS for Your Computer System

On a computer system that you can access, determine how much wattage output a UPS should have in the event of a total blackout, and estimate how long the UPS should sustain power. Research the market and report on the features and prices of a standby UPS and an inline UPS. Include the following information in your report:

▲ Wattage supported

▲ Length of time the power is sustained during total blackout

▲ Line-conditioning features

▲ AC backup present or not present for the inline UPS

▲ Surge suppressor present or not present

▲ Number of power outlets on the box, and other features

▲ Written guarantees

▲ Brand name, model, vendor, and price of the device

PROJECT 4-6: Detecting EMI

Use a small, inexpensive AM radio. Turn the dial to a low frequency, away from a station. Put the radio next to several electronic devices. List the devices in order, from the one producing the most static to the one producing the least static. Listen to the devices when they are idle and in use.

PROJECT 4-7: Calculating Wattage Capacity for Your System

Do the following to compare the wattage capacity of the power supply installed in your computer to the recommended value:

1. Using the free power supply wattage calculator at *www.antec.outervision.com/PSUEngine*, enter the information about your computer system. Print the resulting calculations.

2. What is the recommended wattage capacity for a power supply for your system?

3. Look on the printed label on the power supply currently installed in your computer. What is its wattage capacity?

4. If you had to replace the power supply in your system, what wattage capacity would you select?

PROJECT 4-8: Exploring Computer System Form Factors

You will need to open your computer case to answer these questions about your computer system:

▲ What type of case do you have?

▲ What are the dimensions of your motherboard in inches?

▲ What form factor does your motherboard use?

▲ How many pins does the main power connection on the motherboard have?

>> *REAL PROBLEMS, REAL SOLUTIONS*

REAL PROBLEM 4-1: Replacing a Power Supply

Suppose you turn on a system and everything is dead—no lights, nothing on the monitor screen, and no spinning fan or hard drive. You verify the power to the system works, all power connections and power cords are securely connected, and all pertinent switches are turned on. You can assume the power supply has gone bad. It's time to replace it. To prepare for this situation in a real work environment, exchange power supplies with another student in your lab who is using a computer that has a power supply rated at about the same wattage as yours. Then verify that your system starts up and works.

4

All About Motherboards

In the last chapter, you learned about form factors and power supplies. You also learned how to work inside a computer. In this chapter, we build on all that knowledge to learn about motherboards, which techies sometimes call the mobo. You'll learn about the many different features of a motherboard and how to match one up with other components in a system. The firmware on the motherboard controls the beginning of the boot, so we'll look at the details of that process. Then you'll learn how to support a motherboard and that includes installing, replacing, configuring, and maintaining it. A motherboard is considered a field replaceable unit, so it's important to know how to replace one, but the good news is you don't need to know how to repair one that is broken. Troubleshooting a motherboard works hand in hand with troubleshooting the processor, so we'll leave troubleshooting both until the end of Chapter 6, Supporting Processors.

MOTHERBOARD TYPES AND FEATURES

A+
220-701
1.2

A motherboard is the most complicated component in a computer. When you put together a computer from parts, generally you start with deciding on which processor and motherboard you will use. Everything else follows those decisions. Take a look at the details of Figure 5-1, which shows a motherboard designed with gamers in mind. If you were shopping for a motherboard for a gaming system, you'd have to compare many features among numerous boards. Generally, you'd need to pay attention to form factor, processor sockets, chipsets, buses and number of bus slots, and other connectors, slots, and ports. In this part of the chapter, we'll look at the details of each of these features so that in the future you'll be able to read a mobo ad with the knowledge of a pro. We'll also look at how configuration information is stored on a motherboard and the best strategies to use when selecting a motherboard.

Figure 5-1 Intel DX58SO motherboard is designed with the gamer in mind
Courtesy: Course Technology/Cengage Learning

> **Notes** If you are interested in learning about legacy motherboards and their features, see the content "Facts about Legacy Motherboards" on the CD that accompanies this book.

MOTHERBOARD FORM FACTORS

You learned about motherboard form factors in the last chapter, so we won't repeat that here. To summarize, recall that a motherboard form factor determines the size of the board and its features that make it compatible with power supplies, cases, processors, and expansion cards. The most popular motherboard form factors are ATX, MicroATX, FlexATX, BTX, and NLX, in that order. ATX motherboards have been around for a long time and have seen many improvements. Figure 5-1 shows an ATX motherboard and Figure 5-2 shows a MicroATX board. A BTX motherboard is shown in Figure 5-3. Each form factor has several sizes for motherboards which are listed in Table 4-1 in Chapter 4. In addition to these form factors, you might encounter the ITX form factor. It's smaller than a MicroATX and sometimes used in home theatre systems.

Socket AM2+

Four DDR2
DIMM slots

PCIe x16 slot

Two PCI slots

North Bridge

Figure 5-2 This MicroATX motherboard by Biostar has an AM2 socket that supports an AMD processor
Courtesy: Course Technology/Cengage Learning

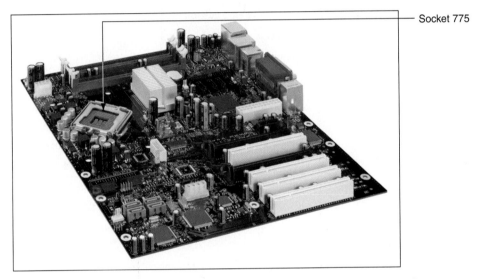

Socket 775

Figure 5-3 A BTX motherboard with an LGA 775 Land socket that supports an Intel processor
Courtesy of Intel Corporation

> 💡 **A+ Exam Tip** The A+ 220-701 Essentials exam expects you to know about the ATX, BTX, MicroATX, and NLX form factors.

PROCESSOR SOCKETS

Another important feature of a motherboard is the processor socket. This socket and the chipset determine which processors a board can support. A socket will hold either an Intel or AMD processor. Some older processors were installed on the motherboard in a long narrow slot, but all processors sold today use sockets. Table 5-1 lists the sockets currently used by Intel processors for desktop systems. The types of memory listed in the table that are used with these sockets are explained in detail in Chapter 7. Also know that Intel makes several Itanium and Xeon processors designed for servers. These server processors use different sockets than those listed in the table.

Intel Socket Names	Used by Processor Family	Description
LGA1366 or Socket B	Core i7	◢ 1366 pins that touch pads on the processor ◢ Works with DDR3 memory ◢ Expected to replace LGA771 and LGA775 sockets
LGA771 or Socket J	Core 2 Extreme	◢ 771 pins that touch pads on the processor ◢ Used on high-end workstations and low-end servers ◢ Works with DDR2 memory on boards that have two processor sockets
LGA775 or Socket T	Core 2 Extreme Core 2 Quad Core 2 Duo Pentium Dual-Core Pentium Extreme Edition Pentium D Pentium Pentium 4 Many Celeron processors	◢ 775 lands or pads ◢ Works with DDR3 and DDR2 memory ◢ Most popular Intel socket
Socket 478	Pentium 4 Celeron processors	◢ 478 holes for pins ◢ Uses a dense micro PGA (mPGA) ◢ No longer sold
Socket 423	Pentium 4	◢ 423 holes for pins ◢ 39 x 39 SPGA grid ◢ No longer sold

Table 5-1 Sockets for Intel processors used for desktop computers

Earlier Pentiums used a pin grid array (PGA) socket, with pins aligned in uniform rows around the socket. Later sockets used a staggered pin grid array (SPGA), with pins staggered over the socket to squeeze more pins into a small space. Small pins can easily be bent as the processor is installed in the socket. Later Intel sockets use a land grid array (LGA) that uses lands rather than pins. The first LGA socket is the LGA775 socket. It has 775 lands and is shown with the socket lever and top open in Figure 5-4. The lands look like tiny pads that the pins on the processor contact.

The latest Intel socket is the LGA1366 socket. It's called a land grid array socket, but the lands in the socket are actually more like pins that connect with lands on the bottom of the processor. Figure 5-5 shows an LGA1366 socket with the load plate and load lever lifted so that the socket is open and ready to receive the processor.

PGA, SPGA, and LGA sockets are all square or nearly square. So that even force is applied when inserting the processor in the socket, all current processor sockets have a lever on the side of the socket. These sockets are called zero insertion force (ZIF) sockets, and this lever is used to lift the processor up and out of the socket. Push the lever down and the processor moves into its pin or land connectors with equal force over the entire housing. With this method, you can easily

A+
220-701
1.2

remove and replace the processor if necessary. However, know that processors generally should not be removed or replaced repeatedly because this can damage the delicate pins or socket holes.

Table 5-2 lists the AMD sockets for desktop systems. AMD has chosen to use the PGA socket architecture for its desktop processors. (Some of AMD's server processors use Socket F, which is an LGA socket.) Figure 5-6 shows the AM2+ socket. The lever on the side of the socket is lifted, and an Athlon 64 processor is about to be inserted. If you look closely near the lower edge of the processor, you can see the small pins that will seat into the holes of the socket.

As you glance over Tables 5-1 and 5-2, you'll notice the same processor family listed under several different sockets. For example, the AMD Athlon family of processors offers many versions of the Athlon. Among these are the Athlon X2 Dual-Core, the Athlon Neo, and the Athlon 64 X2 Dual-Core. Because these various processors within the same processor family use different sockets, you must be careful when matching a processor to a motherboard. To be certain you have a good match, search the Intel (*www.intel.com*) or AMD (*www.amd.com*) Web site for the exact processor you are buying and make sure the socket it uses is the same as the socket on the motherboard you plan to use.

5

A+ 220-701

Plastic cover protects the socket when it's not in use

Figure 5-4 Socket LGA775 is the first Intel socket to use lands rather than pins
Courtesy: Course Technology/Cengage Learning

Load plate

Open socket

Load lever

Figure 5-5 Socket LGA1366 is the latest Intel socket used by desktop, workstation, and low-end server systems
Courtesy: Course Technology/Cengage Learning

AMD Socket	Used by Processor Family	Description
AM3 or AMD3	Phenom II	▲ 938 holes for pins (PGA) ▲ Works with DDR3 memory
AM2+ or AMD2+	Phenom II, Phenom, and Athlon	▲ 940 holes for pins (PGA) ▲ Works with DDR2 memory ▲ Faster than AMD2
AM2 or AMD2	Athlon and Sempron	▲ 940 holes for pins (PGA) ▲ Works with DDR2 memory
Socket 754	Athlon and Sempron	▲ 754 holes for pins (PGA) ▲ Works with DDR memory
Socket 940	Athlon	▲ 940 holes for pins (PGA) ▲ Works with DDR memory
Socket 939	Athlon and Sempron	▲ 939 holes for pins (PGA) ▲ Works with DDR memory ▲ No longer sold
Socket A	Athlon, Sempron, and Duron	▲ 462 holes for pins (PGA) ▲ Works with DDR memory ▲ Rarely sold today

Table 5-2 Sockets for AMD processors used for desktop computers

Also, look at the motherboard documentation for a list of processors that the motherboard supports. It is not likely to support every processor that uses its socket because the motherboard chipset is designed to only work with certain processors.

Figure 5-6 AMD Athlon 64 processor to be inserted into an AM2+ socket
Courtesy: Course Technology/Cengage Learning

> **♥ A+ Exam Tip** The A+ 220-701 Essentials exam expects you to be familiar with the desktop processor sockets in use today. You also need to know about notebook processor sockets, which are covered in Chapter 21.

THE CHIPSET

Recall from Chapter 1 that a chipset is a set of chips on the motherboard that collectively controls the memory, buses on the motherboard, and some peripherals. A few motherboard manufacturers, such as Intel and AMD, make their own chipsets. But other motherboard manufacturers use chipsets made by another manufacturer. The major chipset manufacturers are Intel (*www.intel.com*), AMD (*www.amd.com*), NVIDIA (*www.nvidia.com*), and SiS (*www.sis.com*), in that order.

Intel has produced far too many chipsets to list them here. To see a complete comparison chart of all Intel chipsets, start at the Intel link *http://compare.intel.com/PCC/intro.aspx*.

A few of the more popular chipsets are listed here:

- **High-performance chipsets.** The X58 chipset supports the Intel LGA1366 socket, the Core i7 processors, and PCI Express Version 2. It can also support either SLI or CrossFire technologies. (SLI and CrossFire are two competing technologies that allow for multiple video cards installed in one system.) The X58 chipset does not control memory because the memory controller is embedded in the Core i7 processor. The 975X Express chipset supports the Pentium Extreme Edition processor, multiple video cards, and up to 8 GB of memory.
- **Mainstream desktop chipsets.** The P45, P43, P35, G45, and G31 chipsets support Core 2 Quad and Core 2 Duo Intel processors. P45, P43, and G45 can support up to 16 GB of DDR3 or DDR2 memory. The P35 chipset supports up to 8 GB of DDR3 or DDR2 memory. It also supports the Core 2 Extreme processor. The G31 chipset supports up to 4 GB of DDR2 memory. The Q45 chipset uses DDR3 or DDR2 memory and supports the Core 2 Duo and Core 2 Quad processors. All these chipsets use socket LGA775.
- **Value desktops.** The 910GL, 845E, 845G, and 865G chipsets support the Pentium 4, Celeron, and Celeron D processors in low-end systems. The 910GL chipset uses the LGA775 socket. The 845E, 845G, and 865G chipsets use the 478PGA socket. All these chipsets use DDR memory.
- **Older value desktops.** The 845 and 845GL chipsets support the Pentium 4 or Celeron processors in a low-end system using the 478PGA socket. They support up to 2 GB of DDR memory.

Beginning with the Intel i800 series of chipsets, a hub is used to connect buses. All I/O buses (input/output buses) connect to a hub, which connects to the system bus. This hub is called the hub interface, and the architecture is called Accelerated Hub Architecture (see Figure 5-7). The fast end of the hub, which contains the graphics and memory controller, connects to the system bus and is called the hub's North Bridge. The slower end of the hub, called the South Bridge, contains the I/O controller hub. All I/O devices, except display and memory, connect to the hub by using the slower South Bridge. Notice in Figure 5-7 the primary PCI Express slot, the slot designated for the video card, has direct access to the North Bridge, but other PCI Express slots must access the processor by way of the slower South Bridge. On a motherboard, when you see two major chips for the chipset, one is controlling the North Bridge and the other is controlling the South Bridge (refer to Figure 5-1). Other chipset manufacturers besides Intel also use the North Bridge and South Bridge architecture for their chipsets.

The latest Intel chipset for desktop PCs is the X58 chipset, which is used by the motherboard in Figure 5-1. You can see a close-up of part of this board in Figure 5-8. The board comes with a fan that can be clipped to the top of the North Bridge to help keep the chipset

A+
220-701
1.2

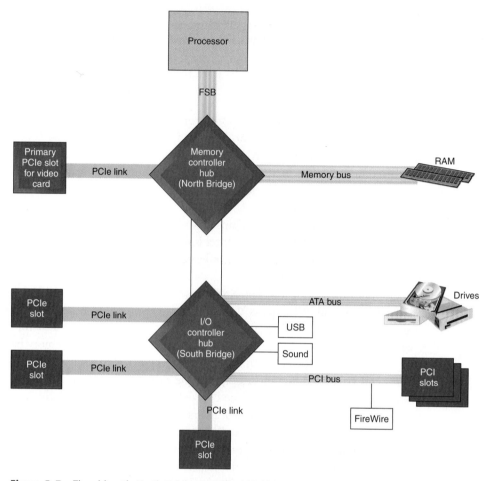

Figure 5-7   The chipset's North Bridge and South Bridge control access to the processor for all components
Courtesy: Course Technology/Cengage Learning

Figure 5-8   The X58 chipset uses heat sinks to stay cool
Courtesy: Course Technology/Cengage Learning

cool. With previous Intel chipsets, the memory controller was part of the North Bridge, but the Core i7 processor contains the memory controller within the processor housing. This new architecture for the Core i7 and the X58 chipset is shown in Figure 5-9. Notice that memory connects directly to the processor rather than to the North Bridge.

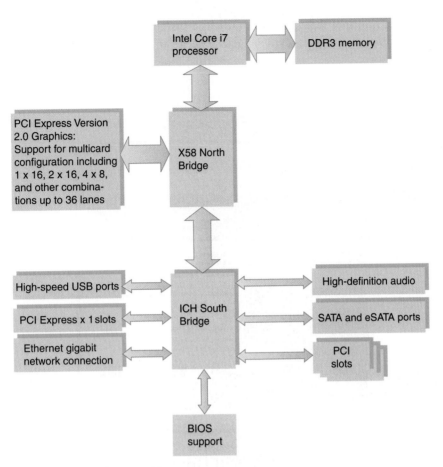

Figure 5-9 X58 chipset architecture
Courtesy: Course Technology/Cengage Learning

The X58 chipset works well for a gaming machine because it is designed to support multiple video cards. The motherboard shown in Figure 5-8 has two PCI Express x16 slots that work with either of two technologies to install multiple video cards in the same system. The two solutions are SLI (Scalable Link Interface) by NVIDIA and CrossFire by ATI Technologies. You will see how to set up a dual video card gaming PC in Chapter 9.

AMD purchased ATI Technologies, a maker of chipsets and graphics processors (called a graphics processor unit or GPU), in 2006, which increased AMD chipset and GPU offerings. Significant chipsets by AMD include the following:

- The AMD 7-series (AMD 790FX, 790X, 790GX, 780, and 770) chipsets are designed with the gamer, hobbyist, and multimedia enthusiast in mind. They focus on good graphics capabilities and support overclocking.
- The AMD 580X Crossfire chipset supports ATI CrossFire.
- The AMD 780V chipset is designed for business needs.
- The AMD 740G and 690 chipsets are designed for low-end, inexpensive systems.

NVIDIA makes graphics processors and chipsets. Because the company specializes in graphics, its nForce series of chipsets are great at supporting high-end graphics solutions popular with gamers. In the past, nForce chipsets were made to work only with AMD processors, but recently the nForce 700 series has been produced to work with the AMD Phenom processor as well as the Intel Core 2 processor. Recall that NVIDIA's method of connecting multiple video cards in the same system is called SLI. If you're planning a gaming computer with two video cards, check out a motherboard that supports SLI and uses the nForce chipset. In motherboard ads, look for the SLI and nForce logos, as shown in Figure 5-10.

Figure 5-10 SLI and nForce logos both by NVIDIA
Courtesy: Course Technology/Cengage Learning

Currently, Intel dominates the chipset market for several reasons: It knows more about its own Intel processors than other manufacturers do, and it produces the chipsets most compatible with the Intel family of processors. Intel's investment in research and development also led to the creation of the PCI bus, the universal serial bus (USB), the AGP bus for video cards, and the Accelerated Hub Architecture.

Chipsets generate heat, but not as much heat as a processor generates. Some chipsets today have a heat sink installed on top that is appropriate to keep the chipset cool. These heat sinks are considered part of the motherboard and you should never have to replace or install one. However, some motherboards, such as the Intel DX58SO board, have an optional small fan that you can install on top of the North Bridge chipset to help keep it cool.

BUSES AND EXPANSION SLOTS

As cities grow, so do their transportation systems. Small villages have only simple, two-lane roads, but large cities have one-way streets, four-lane roads, and major freeways, each with their own set of traffic laws, including minimum and maximum speeds, access methods, and protocols. As microcomputer systems have evolved, so too have their "transportation" systems. The earliest PC had only a single simple bus. Today's PCs have four or five buses, each with different speeds, access methods, and protocols. As you have seen in previous chapters, backward compatibility dictates that older buses be supported on a motherboard, even when faster, better buses exist. All this makes for a maze of buses on a motherboard.

Look on the bottom of the motherboard, and you see a maze of circuits that make up a bus. These embedded wires carry four kinds of cargo:

▲ *Electrical power.* Chips on the motherboard require power to function. These chips tap into a bus's power lines and draw what they need.

▲ *Control signals.* Some wires on a bus carry control signals that coordinate all the activity.

▲ *Memory addresses.* Components pass memory addresses to one another, telling each other where to access data or instructions. The number of wires that make up the memory address lines of the bus determines how many bits can be used for a memory address. The number of wires thus limits the amount of memory the bus can address.

▲ *Data.* Data passes over a bus in a group of wires, just as memory addresses do. The number of lines in the bus used to pass data determines how much data can be passed in parallel at one time. The number of lines depends on the type of processor and determines the number of bits in the data path. (Remember that a data path is the part of the bus on which the data is placed; it can be 8, 16, 32, 64, or more bits wide.)

Just as a city's road system improves to increase the speed and number of lanes of traffic, buses have evolved around similar issues, data path and speed. Cars on a freeway generally travel at a continuous speed, but traffic on a computer's processor or bus is digital (on and off), rather than analog (continuous). The system clock keeps the beat for components. If a component on the motherboard works by the beat, or clock cycle, then it is synchronized, or in sync, with the processor. For example, the back-side bus of the Pentium works at half the speed of the processor. This means that the processor does something on each clock cycle, but the back-side bus is doing something on every other clock cycle.

Some components don't attempt to keep in sync with the processor, even to work at one-half or one-third of clock cycles. These components work asynchronously with the processor. They might work at a rate determined by the system clock or by another crystal on or off the motherboard. Either way, the frequency is much slower than the processor's and not in sync with it. If the processor requests something from one of these devices and the device is not ready, the device issues a wait state, which is a command to the processor to wait for slower devices to catch up.

Table 5-3 lists the various buses used on motherboards today, in order of throughput speed from fastest to slowest. (Throughput is sometimes called bandwidth.) Looking at the second column of Table 5-3, you can see that a bus is called an expansion bus, local bus, local I/O bus, or local video bus. A bus that does not run in sync with the system clock is called an expansion bus and always connects to the slow end of the chipset, the South Bridge. Most buses today are local buses, meaning they run in sync with the system clock. If a local bus connects to the slower I/O controller hub or South Bridge of the chipset, it is called a local I/O bus. Because the video card needs to run at a faster rate than other expansion cards, this one slot always connects to the faster end of the chipset, the North Bridge. This video slot can be either an AGP slot or a PCI Express x16 slot, and the bus is called a local video bus.

The AGP buses were developed specifically for video cards, and the PCI buses are used for many types of cards, including video cards. We'll now look at the details of the PCI and AGP buses and the less significant AMR and CNR slots. The FireWire and USB buses are discussed in Chapter 9.

THE PCI BUSES

PCI (Peripheral Component Interconnect) buses have been improved several times; there are currently three major categories and within each category, several variations of PCI. In the following sections, we discuss each category in turn.

A+
220-701
1.2

Conventional PCI

The first PCI bus had a 32-bit data path, supplied 5 V of power to an expansion card, and operated at 33 MHz. It was the first bus that allowed expansion cards to run in sync with the CPU. PCI Version 2.x introduced the 64-bit, 3.3-V PCI slot, doubling data throughput of the bus. Because a card can be damaged if installed in the wrong voltage slot, a notch in a PCI slot distinguishes between a 5-V slot and a 3.3-V slot. A Universal PCI card can use either a 3.3-V or 5-V slot and contains both notches (see Figure 5-11). Conventional PCI now has four types of slots and six possible PCI card configurations to use these slots (see Figure 5-12).

Bus	Bus Type	Data Path in Bits	Address Lines	Bus Frequency	Throughput
System bus	Local	64	32 or 64	Up to 1600 MHz	Up to 3.2 GB/sec
PCI Express Version 2	Local video and local I/O	Serial with up to 32 lanes	Up to 32 lanes	2.5 GHz	Up to 500 MB/sec per lane in each direction
PCI Express Version 1.1	Local video and local I/O	Serial with up to 16 lanes	Up to 16 lanes	1.25 GHz	Up to 250 MB/sec per lane in each direction
PCI Express Version 1	Local video and local I/O	Serial with up to 16 lanes	Up to 16 lanes	1.25 GHz	Up to 250 MB/sec per lane in each direction
PCI-X	Local I/O	64	32	66, 133, 266, or 533 MHz	Up to 8.5 GB/sec
PCI	Local I/O	32 or 64	32 or 64	33, 66 MHz	133, 266, or 532 MB/sec
AGP 1x, 2x, 3x, 4x, 8x	Local video	32	NA	66, 75, 100 MHz	266 MB/sec to 2.1 GB/sec
FireWire 400 and 800	Local I/O or expansion	1	Serial	NA	Up to 3.2 Gbps (gigabits per second)
USB 1.1, 2.0, and 3.0	Expansion	1	Serial	3 MHz	12 or 480 Mbps (megabits per second) or 5.0 Gbps (gigabits per second)

Table 5-3 Buses listed by throughput

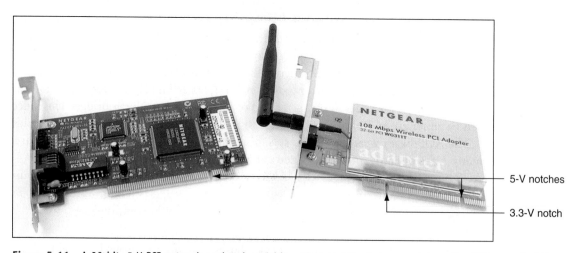

5-V notches

3.3-V notch

Figure 5-11 A 32-bit, 5-V PCI network card and a 32-bit, universal PCI wireless card show the difference in PCI notches set to distinguish voltages in a PCI slot
Courtesy: Course Technology/Cengage Learning

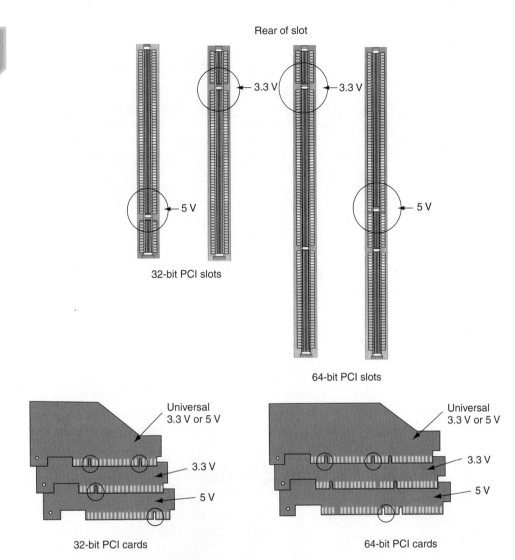

Figure 5-12 With PCI Version 2.x, there are four possible types of expansion slots and six differently configured PCI expansion cards to use these slots
Courtesy: Course Technology/Cengage Learning

PCI-X

The next evolution of PCI is PCI-X, which has had three major revisions; the latest is PCI-X 3.0. All PCI-X revisions are backward compatible with conventional PCI cards and slots, except 5-V PCI cards are no longer supported. PCI-X is focused on technologies that target the server market; therefore, it's unlikely you'll see PCI-X slots in desktop computers. Motherboards that use PCI-X tend to have several different PCI slots with some 32-bit or 64-bit slots running at different speeds. For example, Figure 5-13 shows a motherboard with three types of slots. The two long green slots are PCI-X; the three white slots are PCI, and the one offset lime green slot is AGP. The two PCI-X slots can use most 32-bit and 64-bit PCI or PCI-X cards. PCI-X is being replaced by PCI Express.

PCI Express

PCI Express (PCIe) uses an altogether different architectural design than conventional PCI and PCI-X; PCIe is not backward compatible with either. PCI Express will ultimately replace

A+
220-701
1.2

Figure 5-13   The two long green PCI-X slots can support PCI cards
Courtesy of Super Micro Computer Inc.

both these buses as well as the AGP bus, although it is expected PCI Express will coexist with conventional PCI for some time to come (see Figure 5-14). Whereas PCI uses a 32-bit or 64-bit parallel bus, PCI Express uses a serial bus, which is faster than a parallel bus because it transmits data in packets similar to how an Ethernet network, USB, and FireWire transmit data. A PCIe expansion slot can provide one or more of these serial lanes.

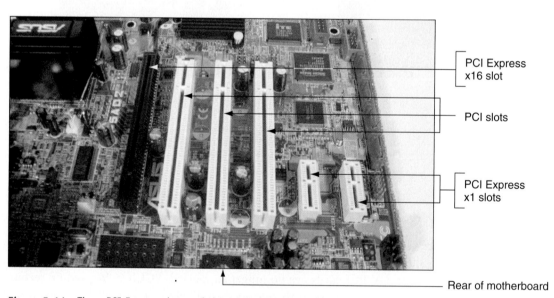

Figure 5-14   Three PCI Express slots and three PCI slots on a motherboard
Courtesy: Course Technology/Cengage Learning

Another difference in PCI Express is how it connects to the processor. Looking back at the right side of Figure 5-7, you can see that all conventional PCI slots connect to the processor by way of a single PCI bus, which connects to the I/O controller hub or South Bridge. With PCI Express, the left side of Figure 5-7 shows each PCI Express slot for a PCIe card has its own link or bus to the South Bridge, and one PCI Express slot has a direct link to the faster memory controller hub or North Bridge. This last PCI Express slot is intended to be used by a PCIe video card.

PCI Express currently comes in four different slot sizes called PCI Express x1 (pronounced "by one"), x4, x8, and x16. Figure 5-15 shows three of these slots. Notice in the photograph how the PCIe slots are not as tall and the pins closer together than the conventional PCI slot. A PCI Express x1 slot contains a single lane for data, which is actually four wires. One pair of wires is used to send data and the other pair receives data, one bit at a time. The x16 slot contains 16 lanes, each lane timed independently of other lanes. The more lanes you have, the more data gets transmitted in a given time. This is similar to the way lanes of traffic on a freeway work; the more lanes you have, the more traffic can flow. Therefore, a x16 slot is faster than a x4 slot, which is faster than a x1 slot. A shorter PCI Express card (such as a x1 card) can be installed in a longer PCI Express slot (such as a x4 slot).

Figure 5-15 Three types of PCIe slots and one conventional PCI slot
Courtesy: Course Technology/Cengage Learning

There has been one minor revision of PCIe (PCIe Version 1.1), and one major revision (PCIe Version 2). PCIe version 1.1 allowed for more wattage to PCIe cards. The original PCIe allowed for 150 W (75 W from pins on the expansion slot and 75 W from the 6-pin connector from the power supply). PCIe Version 1.1 increased the wattage to 225 watts by allowing two 6-pin connectors from the power supply to the card (75 W from the slot and 150 W from the two connectors).

PCIe Version 2 doubled the frequency of the PCIe bus, theoretically doubling the throughput. It also allows for up to 32 lanes on one slot. However, few cards are manufactured today that take full advantage of the increased throughput, and no cards or slots are yet made that have 32 lanes. The allowed wattage to one PCIe 2.0 card was increased to a total of 300 watts by using a new 8-pin power supply connector that provides 150 W (see Figure 5-16). The 300 watts to the card come from the slot (75 W), from the 8-pin connec-

Video
PCI Express and On-Board Wireless

tor (150 W), and an additional 75 W come from a second auxiliary connector on the motherboard. This second connector can be a 6-pin PCIe connector, a Molex-style connector, or a SATA-style connector. You'll see an example of these connectors later in the chapter.

According to the PCIe Version 2.0 specifications, all Version 2 motherboards and cards should be compatible with PCIe Version 1.0 and Version 1.1. However, in practice this might not be true. The x16, x8, x4, and x1 PCIe slots look the same for all versions, but PCIe Version 2 cards might not work in Version 1.0 or 1.1 slots. However, most likely a PCIe Version 1.1 or 1.0 card should work in a Version 2 slot. If you install a PCIe card of a different version in a

A+
220-701
1.2

8-pin connector

Figure 5-16 8-pin PCIe Version 2.0 power connector
Courtesy: Course Technology/Cengage Learning

PCIe slot and it does not work, contact the manufacturer and ask for a fix to the problem they created by not accurately following the PCIe standards. How do you know what version PCIe card or slot you have? You can't tell by looking at the card or slot, so you have to depend on finding the information in the documentation, user manual, or manufacturer Web site.

To get the full potential of PCIe Version 2.0, use PCIe Version 2 cards in Version 2 slots. If you install a PCIe Version 1.x card in a PCIe Version 2.0 slot, the slot runs at a slower speed to accommodate the card. If you install a PCIe Version 2.0 card in a PCIe Version 1.x slot, the card runs at the slower speed of the slot.

PCIe version 3.0 is expected to be published sometime in 2010; it will double the throughput of Version 2. However, after a standard is published, it takes some time for manufacturers to produce the new products. For more information on PCIe, see the PCI Special Interest Group site at *www.pcisig.com*.

PCI Riser Cards Used to Extend the Slots

Recall that an NLX motherboard uses a riser card that provides expansion slots for other cards. You can also use a riser card in other systems besides NLX to extend an expansion slot. For example, suppose you are installing a microATX motherboard into a low-profile or slimline case that does not give you enough room to install a PCI card standing up in an expansion slot. In this situation, a PCI riser card can solve the problem. The riser card installs in the slot and provides another slot that sits parallel to the motherboard. When you install the expansion card in this riser card slot, the card also sits parallel to the motherboard, taking up less space. These riser cards come for all types of PCI slots including PCIe, PCI-X, and conventional PCI (see Figure 5-17).

THE AGP BUSES

Motherboard video slots and video cards used the Accelerated Graphics Port (AGP) standards for many years, but AGP has mostly been replaced by PCI Express. Even though AGP is a dying technology, you still need to know how to support it. A motherboard will have a PCI Express x16 slot or an AGP slot, but not both.

AGP evolved over several years, and the different AGP standards can be confusing. AGP standards include three major releases (AGP 1.0, AGP 2.0, and AGP 3.0), one major change in the AGP slot length standard (AGP Pro), four different speeds (1x, 2x, 4x, and 8x) yielding four different throughputs, three different voltages (3.3 V, 1.5 V, and 0.8 V), and six different expansion slots (AGP 3.3 V, AGP 1.5 V, AGP Universal, AGP Pro 3.3 V, APG Pro 1.5 V, and AGP Pro Universal). To help you make sense of all this, Table 5-4 sorts it all out.

As you can see from Table 5-4, there are several different AGP slots and matching card connectors that apply to the different standards. When matching video cards to AGP slots, be

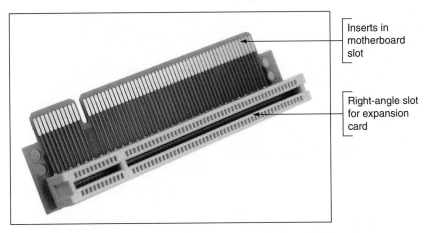

Inserts in
motherboard
slot

Right-angle slot
for expansion
card

Figure 5-17 PCI riser card provides a 3.3-V slot or 5-V slot depending on which direction the
card is inserted in the PCI slot
Courtesy: Course Technology/Cengage Learning

Standard	Speeds (Cycles Per Clock Beat)	Maximum Throughput	Voltage	Slots Supported
AGP 1.0	1x	266 MB/sec	3.3 V	Slot keyed to 3.3 V
AGP 2.0	1x, 2x, or 4x	533 MB/sec or 1.06 GB/sec	3.3 V or 1.5 V	Slot keyed to 1.5 V Slot keyed to 3.3 V Universal slot (for either 1.5-V or 3.3-V cards)
AGP Pro	Applies to all speeds	NA	3.3 V or 1.5 V	AGP Pro 3.3 V keyed AGP Pro 1.5 V keyed AGP Pro Universal (for either 1.5-V or 3.3-V cards)
AGP 3.0	4x or 8x	2.12 GB/sec	1.5 V and 0.8 V	Universal AGP 3.0 (4x/8x) slot Slot keyed to 1.5 V Slot keyed to AGP Pro 1.5 V

Table 5-4 AGP standards summarized

aware of these several variations. For instance, the first two slots in Figure 5-18 are used by
cards that follow the AGP 1.0 or AGP 2.0 standards. These slots have key positions so that
you cannot put an AGP 3.3-V card in an AGP 1.5-V slot or vice versa. The third slot is a
universal slot that can accommodate 3.3-V or 1.5-V cards. All three slots are 2.9 inches wide
and have 132 pins, although some pins are not used. Figure 5-19 shows a motherboard with
an older AGP 3.3-V slot. Notice how the keyed 3.3-V break in the slot is near the back side
of the motherboard where expansion cards are bracketed to the case.

Another AGP standard, called AGP Pro, has provisions for a longer slot. This 180-pin
slot has extensions on both ends that contain an additional 20 pins on one end and
28 pins on the other end, to provide extra voltage for a high-end AGP video card that
consumes more than 25 watts of power. These wider slots might be keyed to 3.3 V or

A+
220-701
1.2

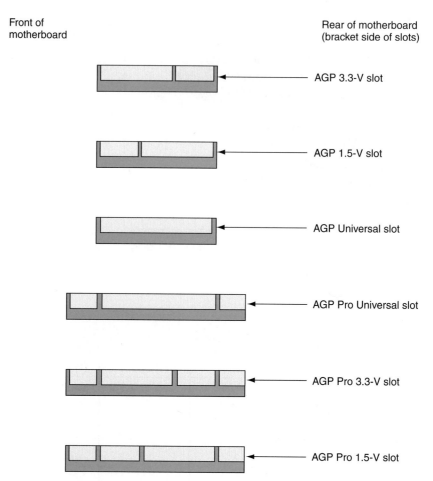

Figure 5-18   Six types of AGP slots
Courtesy: Course Technology/Cengage Learning

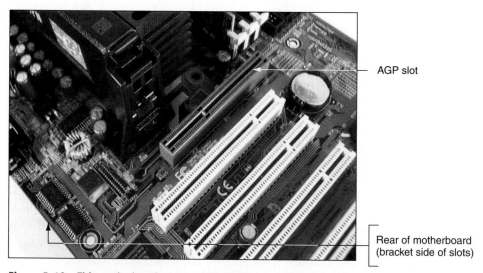

Figure 5-19   This motherboard uses an AGP 3.3-V slot, which accommodates an AGP 1.0 video card
Courtesy: Course Technology/Cengage Learning

1.5 V or might be a Universal Pro slot that can hold either 3.3-V or 1.5-V cards. Also, when using an AGP Pro video card, leave the PCI slot next to it empty to improve ventilation and prevent overheating.

A+
220-701
1.2

The last AGP standard, AGP 3.0, runs at 8x or 4x speeds. APG 3.0 cards can be installed in an AGP 1.5-V slot, but signals are put on the data bus using 0.8 V. It's best to install an AGP 3.0 card in a slot that is designed to support AGP 3.0 cards. However, if you install an AGP 3.0 card in an older AGP 1.5-V slot, the card might or might not work, but the card will not be damaged.

An AGP video card will be keyed to 1.5 V or 3.3 V or a universal AGP video card has both keys so that it can fit into either a 1.5-V keyed slot or a 3.3-V keyed slot. A universal AGP video card also fits into a universal AGP slot. If an AGP video card does not make use of the extra pins provided by the AGP Pro slot, it can still be inserted into the AGP Pro slot if it has a registration tab that fits into the end of the Pro slot near the center of the motherboard. In Chapter 9, you'll learn about AGP video cards.

> **Notes** If you're trying to buy an AGP video card to match a motherboard slot, you have to be really careful. When reading an AGP ad, it's hard to distinguish between AGP 3.3 V and AGP 3.0, but there's a big difference in these standards, and they are not interchangeable.

AMR AND CNR SLOTS

To reduce the total cost of a computer system, some older motherboards might have a small expansion slot, about the length of a PCI Express x1 slot. This small slot can be an audio/modem riser (AMR) slot or a communication and networking riser (CNR) slot (see Figure 5-20). These small slots accommodate small, inexpensive expansion cards called riser cards, such as a modem riser card, audio riser card, or network riser card. (These are not the same riser cards used in NLX systems or riser cards used to extend an expansion slot.) Part of a riser card's audio, modem, or networking logic is on the card, and part is on a controller on the motherboard. If you see an older motherboard and it has a short slot beside a PCI or AGP slot, suspect that it's a CNR or AMR slot. AMR and CNR slots are rarely used today and it's next to impossible to find the cards that fit them.

> **A+ Exam Tip** The A+ 220-701 Essentials exam expects you to be familiar with an AMR slot, CNR slot, and riser card, sometimes called a daughter board.

CNR slot

Figure 5-20 A CNR slot is smaller than a PCI slot but about the same height
Image copyright 2009, Slobodan Djajic. Used under license from Shutterstock.com

5

A+ 220-701

Even more rare is an ACR (Advanced Communications Riser) slot. It looks like a PCI slot, but it sits a little closer to the rear of the motherboard than does a PCI slot and the notch in the slot is in a different position than the notch in a PCI slot. ACR cards might be used for wireless or wired networking, FireWire, or modems.

ON-BOARD PORTS AND CONNECTORS

In addition to expansion slots, a motherboard might also have several on-board ports and internal connectors. Ports coming directly off the motherboard are called on-board ports or integrated components. Almost all motherboards have two or more USB ports and sound ports. Boards might also offer a network port, modem port, FireWire (IEEE 1394) port, video port, keyboard port, mouse port, parallel port, serial port, one or more eSATA ports (for external SATA hard drives), and a port for a wireless antenna. Figures 5-21, 22, and 23 show ports on three motherboards. Figure 5-21 shows an older motherboard. Figure 5-22 shows a current low-end motherboard, and Figure 5-23 shows a current high-end motherboard. We'll discuss how to use all these ports in Chapter 9.

When you purchase a motherboard, the package includes an I/O shield, which is the plate that you install in the computer case that provides holes for these I/O ports. The I/O shield is

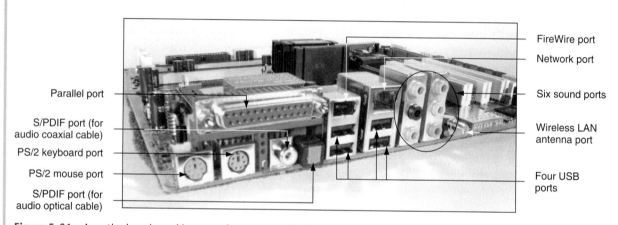

Figure 5-21 A motherboard provides ports for common I/O devices
Courtesy: Course Technology/Cengage Learning

Figure 5-22 Ports on a value Biostar motherboard
Courtesy: Course Technology/Cengage Learning

A+
220-701
1.2

the size designed for the case's form factor and the holes in the shield are positioned for the motherboard ports (see Figure 5-24). When you first install a motherboard, you might need to install the drivers that come on the CD bundled with the board before some of the motherboard ports will work. How to install the motherboard drivers is covered later in the chapter.

Some motherboards come with connector modules that provide additional ports off the rear of the case. For example, Figure 5-25 shows three modules that came bundled with one

Figure 5-23   Intel DX58SO motherboard on-board ports
Courtesy: Course Technology/Cengage Learning

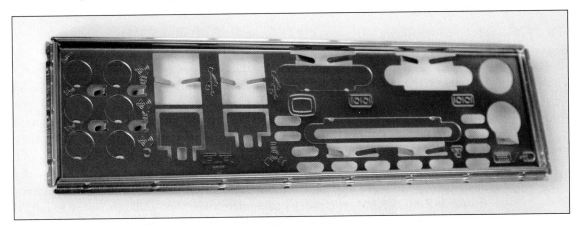

Figure 5-24   The I/O shield fits the motherboard ports to the computer case
Courtesy: Course Technology/Cengage Learning

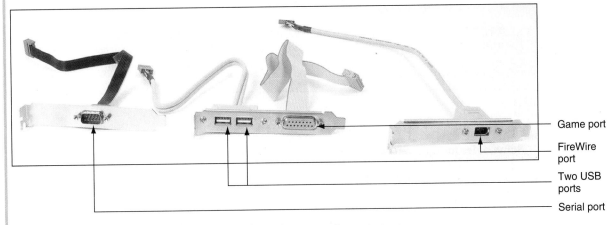

Figure 5-25   These modules provide additional ports off the rear of a computer case
Courtesy: Course Technology/Cengage Learning

5

A+ 220-701

A+
220-701
1.2

motherboard. To use the ports on a module, you connect its cable to a connector on the motherboard and install the module in a slot on the rear of the case intended for an expansion card.

A motherboard might have several internal connectors, including parallel ATA connectors (also called EIDE connectors), a floppy drive connector, serial ATA connectors, SCSI connectors, or a FireWire (IEEE 1394) connector. When you purchase a motherboard, look in the package for the motherboard manual either printed or on CD. It will show a diagram of the board with a description of each connector. For example, the connectors for the motherboard in Figure 5-26 are labeled as the manual describes them. If a connector is a group of pins sticking up on the board, the connector is called a header. You will learn to use most of these connectors in later chapters.

Figure 5-26 Internal connectors on a motherboard for drives and ports on the front of the case
Courtesy: Course Technology/Cengage Learning

A+
220-701
1.2
2.5
5.2

HARDWARE CONFIGURATION

Settings on the motherboard are used to enable or disable a connector or port, set the frequency of the CPU, system bus, or other buses, control security features, and control what happens when the PC first boots. In the past, configuring these and other motherboard settings was done in three different ways: DIP switches, jumpers, and CMOS RAM. Storing configuration information by physically setting DIP switches or jumpers on the motherboard or peripheral devices was extremely inconvenient, because it often required us to open the computer case to make a change. A more convenient method is to hold configuration information in CMOS RAM, and today's computers store almost all configuration data there. A program in BIOS, called BIOS setup or CMOS setup, can easily make changes to the setup values stored in CMOS RAM. Now let's see how all three methods work.

> **Notes** You don't have to replace an entire motherboard if one port fails. Most ports on a motherboard can be disabled through BIOS setup. On older motherboards, look for jumpers or DIP switches to disable a port. For newer boards, use BIOS setup to disable the port. Then use an expansion card for the port instead.

SETUP DATA STORED BY DIP SWITCHES

Some older motherboards and expansion cards store setup data using a dual inline package (DIP) switch, as shown in Figure 5-27. A DIP switch has an ON position and an OFF position. ON represents binary 1 and OFF represents binary 0. If you add or remove equipment, you can communicate that to the computer by changing a DIP switch setting. When you change a DIP switch setting, use a pointed instrument such as a ballpoint pen to push the switch. Don't use a graphite pencil because graphite conducts electricity. In addition, pieces of graphite dropped into the switch can damage it.

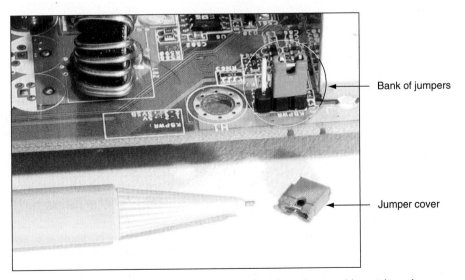

Figure 5-27 DIP switches used to store setup data on older motherboards
Courtesy: Course Technology/Cengage Learning

SETUP DATA STORED BY JUMPERS

Older motherboards can also retain setup or installation information in different settings of jumpers on the board. Jumpers are considered open or closed based on whether a jumper cover is present on two small posts or metal pins that stick up off the motherboard (see Figure 5-28). On these older boards, a group of jumpers might be used to tell the system at what speed the CPU is running, or to turn a power-saving feature on or off. Look at the jumper cover in Figure 5-29(b) that is "parked," meaning it is hanging on a single pin for safekeeping, but is not being used to turn a jumper setting on.

Most motherboards today allow you to set a supervisor password or user password to control access to the system. For example, you can set two passwords in BIOS setup: one to control access to BIOS setup (supervisor password) and the other to lock access to the computer (user password). If both passwords are forgotten, you cannot use the computer.

Bank of jumpers

Jumper cover

Figure 5-28 Setup information about the motherboard can be stored by setting a jumper on (closed) or off (open). A jumper is closed if the cover is in place, connecting the two pins that make up the jumper; a jumper is open if the cover is not in place
Courtesy: Course Technology/Cengage Learning

A+
220-701
1.2
2.5
5.2

a   b   c

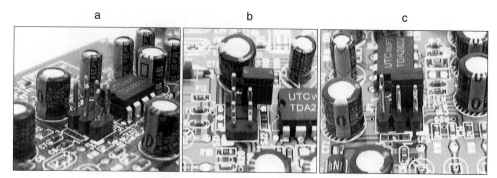

Figure 5-29 A 6-pin jumper group on a circuit board (a) has no jumpers set to on, (b) has a cover parked on one pin, and (c) is configured with one jumper setting turned on
Courtesy: Course Technology/Cengage Learning

However, jumpers can be set to clear both passwords. Also, BIOS firmware might need updating to solve a problem with the motherboard or to use a new motherboard feature. If updating BIOS fails, jumpers can be set to undo the update. How to set and clear passwords, update BIOS, and undo a failed BIOS update are covered later in the chapter.

SETUP DATA STORED IN CMOS RAM

Computers today store most configuration information in CMOS RAM, also called the real-time clock/non-volatile RAM (RTC/NVRAM) chip, which retains the data even when the computer is turned off. Motherboard manuals should contain a list of all BIOS settings (also called CMOS settings), an explanation of their meanings, and their recommended values. When you purchase a motherboard or a computer, be sure the manual is included as a printed booklet or on CD. If you don't have the manual, you can sometimes go to the motherboard manufacturer's Web site and download the information you need to understand the specific BIOS settings of your computer. Table 5-5 lists some BIOS settings. Several of these are discussed in future chapters. As you're reading the table, keep in mind that the categories for BIOS settings are not universal. Each BIOS manufacturer decides which screen holds a particular setting.

> **Notes** Even though a computer has many CMOS chips, the term "CMOS chip" has come to mean the one chip on the motherboard that holds the configuration or setup information. If you hear someone ask: "What does CMOS say?" or "Let's change CMOS," the person is talking about the configuration or setup information stored on this one CMOS chip.

Category	Setting	Description
Standard	**Date and time**	Sets the system date and time (called the CMOS setup real-time clock). Windows picks up these values when it starts up.
	Keyboard	Tells the system if the keyboard is installed or not; useful if the computer is used as a print or file server and you don't want someone changing settings.
	Hard disk type	Records the size and mapping of the drive or sets to automatically detect the HDD (discussed in Chapter 8).
	Language	Languages the BIOS setup screens use.

Table 5-5 BIOS settings and their purpose

Category	Setting	Description
	Floppy disk type	Sets the floppy disk type; choices are usually 3½-inch and 5¼-inch. If you must choose a size in MB or inches, the most likely choices are 1.44 MB (the maximum data size) and 3.5 inch (the physical size of the disk).
	System information	Reports installed processor and speed, BIOS version, installed RAM.
BIOS Features Menu	Quick boot	Enable/disable. Enable to cause POST to skip some tests and speed up booting. Disable this feature when installing or testing a motherboard to get a thorough POST.
	Above 1 MB memory test	Disables POST check of this memory to speed up booting; the OS checks this memory anyway.
	Memory parity error check	For older motherboards, enables parity checking to ensure that memory is correct.
	System boot sequence	Establishes the device the system turns to first to look for an OS. Possible devices are the hard drive (drive C), CD drive, DVD drive, USB device, floppy drive (drive A), or the network.
	External cache memory	Enables L2 cache. A frequent error in setup is to have cache, but not use it, because it's disabled here. Used on older motherboards that have on-board cache memory.
	Password checking option	Establishes a startup password. Use this only if you need to prevent someone from using your PC. Sometimes there are two passwords, each with different levels of security.
	System ROM Shadow F000, 64 K	Enabling shadow system ROM is recommended. Shadowing ROM is copying ROM programs into RAM. Programs are then executed from RAM, which is faster than executing programs from ROM.
	IDE multiblock mode or block mode	Enables a hard drive to read or write several sectors at a time; depends on the kind of hard drive you have.
	Plug and Play (PnP)	Enable/disable. Disable for Windows 2000/XP/Vista, which does all the PnP configuration. Enable for Windows 9x, which uses PnP data from BIOS.
Advanced Chipset Setup	Audio controller	Enable/disable.
	Network port	Enable/disable.
	Wireless network controller	Enable/disable.
	AGP capability	Switches between AGP 1x, AGP 2x, AGP 4x, and AGP 8x versions to accommodate different AGP video cards.
	AGP aperture size	Adjusts the amount of system memory AGP can address.
	AGP voltage	Sets AGP operating voltage according to video card requirements.
	VGA BIOS sequence	Determines the order in which PCI/AGP is initialized; important mainly with dual monitors on legacy systems.
	Processor serial number	Allows processor ID# to be switched off for privacy (Pentium III only).

Table 5-5 BIOS settings and their purpose (continued)

A+
220-701
1.2
2.5
5.2

Category	Setting	Description
	Serial port	Sets beginning I/O address and IRQ; sometimes you can enable/disable the port. (IRQs are discussed later in the chapter.)
	Parallel port mode	ECP or EPP (differences are discussed in Chapter 9).
	Infrared	Enable/disable (sometimes enabling infrared disables the second serial port, which uses the same resources).
	USB configuration	Enable/disable and sets to high speed or legacy speed.
	CPU configuration	Enable/disable Hyper Threading (covered in Chapter 6). Sets thermal control.
	PCI slots	Controls IRQ assignments to PCI slots.
	Speech reporter	Startup BIOS reports messages in speech.
	Overclocking	Enables/disables overclocking.
Power Management Menu	Suspend mode	Enable/disable suspending power when the system is inactive (discussed in Chapter 21).
	Power button	Controls what happens when power button is pressed.
	Video off	Sets which way video to the monitor will be suspended.
	HDD power down	Disables or enables the feature to shut down the hard drive after a period of inactivity.
	Wake on LAN	Allows your PC to be booted from another computer on the same network; it requires an ATX or BTX power supply that supports the feature.
	Wake on mouse	Allows you to power up your PC by clicking the mouse.
	Wake on RTC	Allows the PC to power up at a certain time of day.
	Wake on keyboard	Allows you to power up your PC by pressing a certain key combination.
Hard Drive Settings	IDE HDD autodetect	Detects HDDs installed on either IDE channel; allows you to specify Normal, Large, or LBA mode, but Autodetect is recommended.
	Serial ATA	Configure to IDE or RAID.
	SMART monitoring	Monitors the HDD for failure.
Hardware Device Settings	Processor operating speed	Sets the appropriate speed for your processor; used for throttling and overclocking.
	External clock	Sets the system bus speed.
	I/O voltage	Sets the appropriate I/O voltage for the processor.
	Core voltage	Sets the appropriate core voltage for the processor.
Boot Settings	Boot device priority, a.k.a. Boot sequence	Determines the sequence of devices the BIOS looks to for an OS to load. (Same as System boot sequence under the BIOS Features Menu)
	Boot settings	Quick boot skips tests made at startup by BIOS. (Same as Quick boot under the BIOS Features Menu) Enable/disable mouse support at startup. Controls what is displayed at startup.
		Enables/disables message at startup to press a certain key to enter BIOS setup.

Table 5-5 BIOS settings and their purpose (continued)

Category	Setting	Description
	Supervisor password	Enable/disable and set supervisor password to enter BIOS setup and make changes.
	User password	Enable/disable and set user password to access the system or to enter and view BIOS setup. (Same as Password checking option under the BIOS Features Menu)
	Boot sector virus protection	Gives a warning that the boot sector of the hard drive is being edited. When installing or upgrading an operating system, disable this protection so the OS install process can alter the boot sector without interruption. (How the boot sector works is discussed in Chapter 8.)
Exit Menu	Exit	Options are to exit and save changes, exit and discard changes, or discard changes and not exit.
	Load default settings	Return BIOS setup to factory default settings. Use this option if you suspect faulty changes have been made or the system has become unstable.

Note: The titles, locations, and inclusion or exclusion of BIOS categories and settings depend on the manufacturer, BIOS version, or both. For instance, Hardware Device Settings might be a group of settings sharing a category with other settings in one version of BIOS, whereas Hardware Device Settings might be its own category in another BIOS version.

Table 5-5 BIOS settings and their purpose (continued)

> **Notes** In documentation, a.k.a. stands for "also known as."

> **A+ Exam Tip** The A+ 220-701 Essentials exam expects you to know how the drive boot order is set and the type of boot devices you can use.

Battery Power to CMOS RAM

A small trickle of electricity from a nearby lithium coin-cell battery enables CMOS RAM to hold configuration data, even while the main power to the computer is off. If the CMOS battery is disconnected or fails, setup information is lost. An indication that the battery is getting weak is that the system date and time are incorrect after power has been disconnected to the PC. A coin-cell battery is shown in Figure 5-30.

> **A+ Exam Tip** The A+ 220-701 Essentials exam expects you to know about the CMOS battery.

HOW TO SELECT A MOTHERBOARD

Because the motherboard determines so many of your computer's features, selecting the motherboard is, in most cases, your most important decision when you purchase a computer or assemble one from parts. Depending on which applications and peripheral devices you plan to use with the computer, you can take one of three approaches to selecting a motherboard. The first approach is to select the board that provides the most room for expansion, so you can upgrade and exchange components and add devices easily. A second approach is to select the board that best suits the needs of the computer's current configuration, knowing that when you need to

Figure 5-30   The coin-cell battery powers CMOS RAM when the system is turned off
Courtesy: Course Technology/Cengage Learning

upgrade, you will likely switch to new technology and a new motherboard. The third approach is to select a motherboard that meets your present needs with moderate room for expansion.

Ask the following questions when selecting a motherboard:

1. What form factor does the motherboard use?

2. Does the motherboard support the number and type of processor you plan to use (for example, Socket LGA 775 for the Intel Pentium Dual Core processor up to 3.3GHz)?

3. What are the supported frequencies of the system bus (for example, 1066/800/ 533 MHz)?

4. What chipset does the board use?

5. What type of memory does the board support (DDR2 or DDR3), and how much memory can the board hold?

6. What type and how many expansion slots are on the board (for example, PCI, PCI Express 2.0, or AGP)?

7. What hard drive controllers and connectors are on the board (for example, IDE, serial ATA, RAID, and SCSI)?

8. What are the embedded devices on the board, and what internal slots or connections does the board have? (For example, the board might provide a network port, wireless antenna port, FireWire port, two or more USB ports, mouse port, and so forth.)

9. Does the board fit the case you plan to use?

10. What are the price and the warranty on the board?

11. How extensive and user-friendly is the documentation?

12. How much support does the manufacturer supply for the board?

Sometimes a motherboard contains an on-board component more commonly offered as a separate device. One example is support for video. The video port might be on the motherboard or might require a video card. The cost of a motherboard with an embedded component is usually less than the combined cost of a motherboard with no embedded component and an expansion card. If you plan to expand, be cautious about choosing a proprietary board that has many embedded components. Often such boards do not easily accept add-on devices from other manufacturers. For example, if you plan to add a more powerful video card, you might not want to choose a motherboard that contains an embedded video controller. Even though you can often disable the proprietary video controller in BIOS setup, there is little advantage to paying the extra money for it.

> **Tip** If you have an embedded component, make sure you can disable it so you can use another external component if needed. Components are disabled in BIOS setup.

Table 5-6 lists some manufacturers of motherboards and their Web addresses.

Manufacturer	Web Address
Abit	www.abit.com.tw
ASUS	www.asus.com
BIOSTAR Group	www.biostar.com.tw
Evga	www.evga.com
Foxconn	www.foxconn.com
Gigabyte Technology Co., Ltd.	www.giga-byte.com
Intel Corporation	www.intel.com
Micro-Star International (MSI)	www.msicomputer.com
Super Micro Computer, Inc.	www.supermicro.com
Tyan Computer Corporation	www.tyan.com

Table 5-6 Major manufacturers of motherboards

HOW STARTUP BIOS CONTROLS THE BOOT PROCESS

A+ 220-701 1.2 3.4

When you first turn on a PC, startup BIOS on the motherboard is in control until the operating system is loaded and takes over. In this part of the chapter, you'll learn what startup BIOS does to boot up the system, check and initialize critical hardware components, find an OS, begin the process of loading that OS, and then turn over control to the OS. The purpose of this part of the chapter is to help you understand how startup BIOS controls the boot. Later in the chapter, you'll learn how to use this knowledge to help you troubleshoot a failed boot before the operating system is loaded. Then, in Chapters 15 and 16, you will learn what happens when Windows Vista or Windows XP completes loading itself and initializes the system, and what to do when things go wrong with the OS startup.

> **A+ Exam Tip** The A+ 220-701 Essentials exam expects you to know how BIOS controls POST and the beginning of the boot.

A+
220-701
1.2
3.4

BOOTING A COMPUTER

The term booting comes from the phrase "lifting yourself up by your bootstraps" and refers to the computer bringing itself up to a working state without the user having to do anything but press the on button. This boot can be a "hard boot" or a "soft boot." A hard boot, or cold boot, involves turning on the power with the on/off switch. A soft boot, or warm boot, involves using the operating system to reboot. For Windows Vista, one way to soft boot is to click **Start**, click the right arrow, and click **Restart** (see Figure 5-31). For Windows XP, one way to soft boot is to click **Start**, click **Turn Off Computer**, and then click **Restart** (see Figure 5-32).

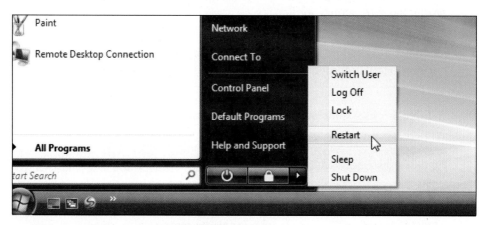

Figure 5-31   Windows Vista menu to perform a restart
Courtesy: Course Technology/Cengage Learning

Figure 5-32   Windows XP Turn off computer dialog box
Courtesy: Course Technology/Cengage Learning

CHOOSING BETWEEN A HARD BOOT AND A SOFT BOOT

A hard boot takes more time than a soft boot because in a soft boot, the initial steps of a hard boot don't happen. To save time in most circumstances, you should use the soft boot to restart. A hard boot initializes the processor and clears memory. If a soft boot doesn't work or you want to make certain you get a fresh start, use a hard boot. If you cannot boot from the operating system, look for power or reset buttons on the front or rear of the case. For example, one computer has three power switches: a power button and a reset button on the front of the case and a power switch on the rear of the case (see Figure 5-33). They work like this:

- The power button in front is a "soft" power button, causing a normal Windows shutdown and restart.
- The reset button initializes the CPU so that it restarts at the beginning of the BIOS startup program. The computer behaves as though the power were turned off and back on and then goes through the entire boot process.

▲ The switch on the rear of the case simply turns off the power abruptly and is a "hard" power button. If you use this switch, wait 30 seconds before you press the power button on the front of the case to boot the system. This method gives you the greatest assurance that memory will clear. However, if Windows is abruptly stopped, it might give an error message when you reboot.

How the front two buttons work can be controlled in BIOS setup. Know, however, that different cases offer different options.

Soft power button does a normal Windows shutdown

Hard power switch on rear of case

Hard power button abruptly reboots

Figure 5-33 This computer case has two power buttons on the front and one power switch on the rear of the case
Courtesy: Course Technology/Cengage Learning

THE STARTUP BIOS CONTROLS THE BEGINNING OF THE BOOT

The startup BIOS is programming contained on the firmware chip on the motherboard that is responsible for getting a system up and going, and finding an OS to load. A successful boot depends on the hardware, the BIOS, and the operating system all performing without errors. If errors occur, they might stall or lock up the boot. Errors are communicated as beeps, as text messages on-screen, or as recorded voice messages.

The functions performed during the boot can be divided into four parts, as shown in the following list. The first two items in the list are covered in detail in this section. (The last two steps depend on the OS being used and are covered in later chapters.)

1. *The startup BIOS runs the POST and assigns system resources.* Recall from Chapter 4 that the POST (power-on self test) is a series of tests performed by the startup BIOS to determine if it can communicate correctly with essential hardware components required for a successful boot. The startup BIOS surveys hardware resources and needs, and assigns system resources to meet those needs (see Figure 5-34). The startup BIOS begins the startup process by reading configuration information stored primarily in CMOS RAM, and then comparing that information to the hardware—the processor, video slot, PCI slots, hard drive, and so on. (Recall that CMOS RAM is a small amount of memory on the motherboard that holds information about installed hardware.)

2. *The startup BIOS program searches for and loads an OS.* Most often the OS is loaded from drive C: on the hard drive. The boot sequence information stored in CMOS RAM tells startup BIOS where to look for the OS. Most BIOSs support loading the OS from the hard drive, a floppy disk, a CD, a DVD, or a USB device. The BIOS turns to the specified device, reads the beginning files of the OS, copies them into memory, and then turns control over to the OS. This part of the loading process works the same for any operating system; only the OS files being loaded change.

A+
220-701
1.2
3.4

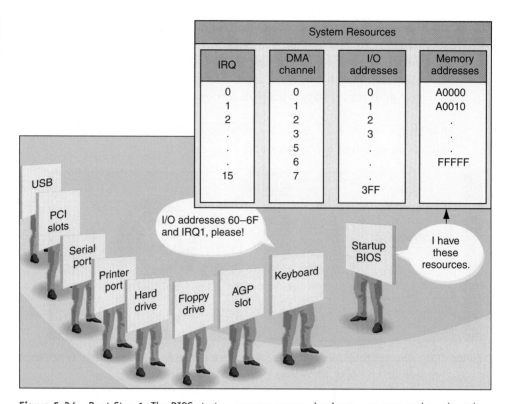

Figure 5-34 Boot Step 1: The BIOS startup program surveys hardware resources and needs and assigns system resources to satisfy those needs
Courtesy: Course Technology/Cengage Learning

3. *The OS configures the system and completes its own loading.* The OS checks some of the same settings and devices that startup BIOS checked, such as available memory and whether that memory is reliable. Then the OS loads the core components necessary to access the files and folders on the hard drive and to use memory, the expansion buses on the motherboard, and the cards installed in these expansion slots. The user is given a screen to log onto the system. The OS loads the software to control installed devices, such as the mouse, the video card, the DVD drive, or the scanner. These devices generally have device drivers stored on the hard drive. The Windows desktop is then loaded using preferences assigned to the currently logged in user.

4. *Application software is loaded and executed.* Sometimes an OS is configured to automatically launch application software as part of the boot. After this, the user is in control. When the user tells the OS to execute an application, the OS first must find the application software on the hard drive, CD, or other secondary storage device, copy the software into memory, and then turn control over to it. Finally, the user can command the application software, which makes requests to the OS, which, in turn, uses the system resources, system BIOS, and device drivers to interface with and control the hardware.

Notes The four system resources on a motherboard that the OS and processor use to interact with hardware are IRQ lines, I/O addresses, memory addresses, and DMA channels, all defined in Table 5-7. Older systems using DOS and Windows 9x/Me required a technician to make decisions about managing these resources when installing hardware devices, but newer systems generally manage these resources without our involvement. For an explanation of how each resource works, see the content, "How an OS uses system resources," on the CD that accompanies this book.

System Resource	Definition
IRQ numbers	A line of a motherboard bus that a hardware device or expansion slot can use to signal the CPU that the device needs attention. Some lines have a higher priority for attention than others. Each IRQ line is assigned a number (0 to 15) to identify it.
I/O addresses	Numbers assigned to hardware devices that software uses to send a command to a device. Each device "listens" for these numbers and responds to the ones assigned to it. I/O addresses are communicated on the address bus.
Memory addresses	Numbers assigned to physical memory located either in RAM or ROM chips. Software can access this memory by using these addresses. Memory addresses are communicated on the address bus.
DMA channels	A number designating a channel on which the device can pass data to memory without involving the CPU. Think of a DMA channel as a shortcut for data moving to and from the device and memory.

Table 5-7 System resources used by software and hardware

STEP 1: POST AND ASSIGNMENT OF SYSTEM RESOURCES

When you turn on the power to a PC, the processor begins the boot by initializing itself and then turning to startup BIOS for instructions. The startup BIOS first performs POST. The following list contains the key steps in this process:

1. When the power is first turned on, the system clock begins to generate clock pulses.

2. The processor begins working and initializes itself (resetting its internal values).

3. The processor turns to memory address FFFF0h, which is the memory address always assigned to the first instruction in the ROM BIOS startup program.

4. This instruction directs the processor to run POST.

5. POST first checks the BIOS program operating it and then tests CMOS RAM.

6. A test determines that there has been no battery failure.

7. Hardware interrupts are disabled. (This means that pressing a key on the keyboard or using another input device at this point does not affect anything.)

8. Tests are run on the processor, and it is initialized further.

9. A check determines if this is a cold boot. If so, the first 16 KB of RAM are tested.

10. Hardware devices installed on the computer are inventoried and compared to configuration information.

11. The video card is tested and configured. During POST, before the processor has checked the video system, beeps or speech communicate errors. Short and long beeps indicate an error; the coding for the beeps depends on the BIOS. After POST checks and verifies the video controller card (note that POST does not check to see if a monitor is present or working), POST can use video to display its progress.

12. POST checks RAM by writing and reading data. The monitor might display a running count of RAM during this phase.

13. Next, the keyboard is checked, and if you press and hold any keys at this point, an error occurs with some BIOSs. Secondary storage—including floppy disk drives and

A+
220-701
1.2
3.4

hard drives—ports, and other hardware devices are tested and configured. The hardware devices that POST finds are checked against the data stored in the CMOS chip, jumpers, and/or DIP switches to determine if they agree. IRQ, I/O addresses, and DMA assignments are made; the OS completes this process later. Some hardware devices have BIOSs of their own that request resources from startup BIOS, which attempts to assign these system resources as requested.

14. Some devices are set up to go into "sleep mode" to conserve electricity.

15. The DMA and interrupt controllers are checked.

16. BIOS setup is run if requested.

17. BIOS begins its search for an OS.

STEP 2: STARTUP BIOS FINDS AND LOADS THE OS

After POST and the first pass at assignment of resources are complete, the next step is to load an OS. The startup BIOS looks to CMOS RAM to find out which device is set to be the boot device. Most often the OS is loaded from drive C on the hard drive. The minimum information required on the hard drive to load an OS is shown in the following list. You can see some of these items labeled in Figure 5-35.

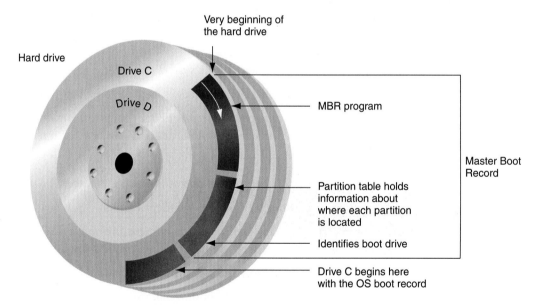

Figure 5-35   For a successful boot, a hard drive must contain a healthy Master Boot Record (MBR) and a healthy OS boot record
Courtesy: Course Technology/Cengage Learning

▲ Even though a hard drive is a circular affair, it must begin somewhere. A drive is laid out in a series of concentric circles called tracks. Each track is divided into segments called sectors, and each sector can hold 512 bytes of data. On the outermost track, one sector (512 bytes) is designated the "beginning" of the hard drive. This sector, called the Master Boot Record (MBR), contains two items. The first item is the master boot program, which is needed to locate the beginning of the OS on the drive. (A record and a sector are both 512-byte segments of a hard drive.)

▲ The second item in the MBR is a table, called the partition table, which contains a map to the partitions on the hard drive. This table tells BIOS how many partitions

A+
220-701
1.2
3.4

the drive has, where each partition begins and ends, and which partition is used for booting (called the **active partition**). A partition is sometimes called a volume. The first volume on the hard drive used to boot the OS is called drive C. Chapter 8 covers partitions in more detail.

◢ At the beginning of the boot drive (usually drive C) is the OS **boot record**. This 512-byte sector is physically the second sector on the hard drive right behind the MBR. This OS boot record contains a small program that points to a larger OS program file that is responsible for starting the OS load. (A **program file** contains a list of instructions stored in a file.) For Windows Vista, the OS boot record program points to **BootMgr**. For Windows XP, that program is **Ntldr**. Figure 5-36 shows the steps the BIOS follows to find this first OS program.

5

A+ 220-701

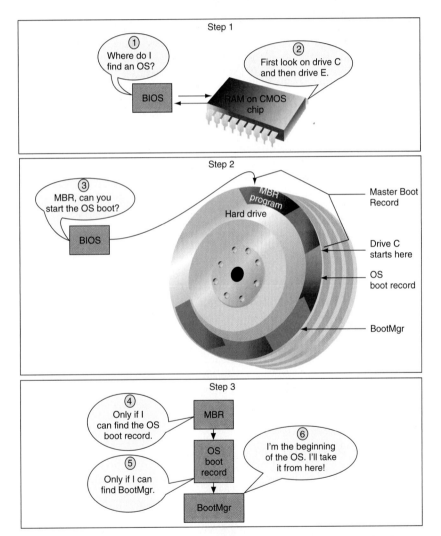

Figure 5-36 Numbered steps show how BIOS searches for and begins to load an operating system (in this example, Windows Vista is the OS)
Courtesy: Course Technology/Cengage Learning

Notes Program files can be a part of the OS or applications and have a .com, .sys, .bat, or .exe file extension. BootMgr and Ntldr are exceptions to that rule because they have no file extension.

◢ The first OS program (BootMgr or Ntldr) begins the process of loading the OS into memory. For Windows XP, Ntldr is responsible for loading the OS, and is, therefore, called the boot loader program. In Vista, BootMgr turns the job over to Winload.exe, which loads the OS. Therefore, for Vista, Winload.exe is the boot loader program. You will learn about the details of loading the OS in Chapters 15 and 16.

> **Notes** Future desktop and notebook systems are likely to use replacement technologies for both the BIOS firmware on the motherboard and the MBR method of organizing a hard drive. Even now, in Windows Vista, you can choose between two disk-partitioning systems: MBR and GPT. Using the MBR system, you can have up to four partitions on a hard drive, although one of them can have multiple volumes, which are called logical drives. The GPT (Globally Unique Identifier Partition Table) disk-partitioning system can support up to 128 partitions, and these partitions are more stable and can be larger than MBR partitions. To use the GPT system for your bootable hard drive, your computer motherboard must contain an EFI or UEFI chip rather than the traditional BIOS chip. For more information on the GPT method of organizing a hard drive, go to the *www.microsoft.com* site and search on GPT.
>
> EFI (Extensible Firmware Interface) and UEFI (Unified EFI) are two standards for the interface between firmware on the motherboard and the operating system. The standards replace the legacy BIOS standards and improve on processes for booting, handing over the boot to the OS, and loading device drivers and applications before the OS loads. For more information on either standard, see the UEFI consortium at *www.uefi.org*.

Let's now turn our attention to maintaining, installing, and configuring a motherboard.

> 📍 **A+ Exam Tip** Content on the A+ 220-701 Essentials exam ends here and content on the A+ 220-702 Practical Application exam begins.

MAINTAINING, INSTALLING, AND CONFIGURING A MOTHERBOARD

When supporting personal computers, you need to know how to maintain a motherboard. A motherboard is considered a field replaceable unit, so you also need to know how to replace one when it goes bad. After the new board is installed, you'll need to configure the board using BIOS setup. All these skills are covered in this part of the chapter.

> 📍 **A+ Exam Tip** The A+ 220-702 Practical Application exam expects you to know how to maintain a motherboard by updating drivers and firmware, setting BIOS jumpers, and replacing a CMOS battery.

MAINTAINING A MOTHERBOARD

The two chores you need to know how to do to maintain a motherboard are how to update the motherboard drivers and how to flash BIOS. You also need to know how to configure the BIOS jumpers on a motherboard to recover from a forgotten power-on password or failed BIOS update and how to replace a CMOS battery. All these tasks are covered next.

UPDATING MOTHERBOARD DRIVERS

A motherboard comes bundled with a CD that contains drivers for all the onboard components and documentation in PDF files. Most likely, Windows can use its own internal drivers for these components, but if you have trouble with an onboard component or want to use a feature that is not working, use the motherboard CD to install the manufacturer drivers into Windows.

The motherboard CD might also contain useful utilities, including one that you can install in Windows, to monitor the CPU temperature and alert you if overheating occurs. Figure 5-37 shows the main menu for one motherboard driver CD.

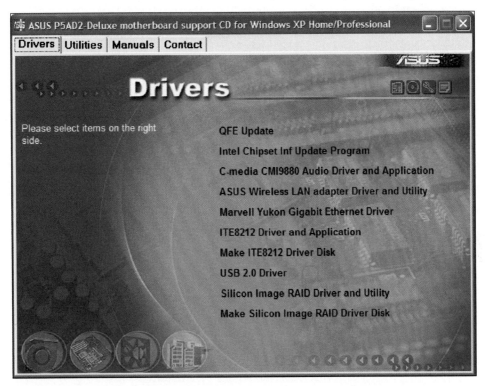

Figure 5-37 Main menu of motherboard drivers, utilities, and documentation CD
Courtesy: Course Technology/Cengage Learning

The motherboard manufacturer updates motherboard drivers from time to time. For an unstable motherboard, you can try downloading and installing updated chipset drivers and other drivers for onboard components. Figure 5-38 shows the download page for one Intel motherboard where you can download BIOS and drivers.

To download the right drivers, you need to first identify your motherboard brand and model number. Your documentation for the PC should contain that information. If you don't have that, open the case and look for the brand and model imprinted somewhere on the board (see Figure 5-39).

FLASHING ROM BIOS

Recall that ROM BIOS includes the BIOS setup program, the startup BIOS that manages the startup process, and the system BIOS that manages basic I/O functions of the system. All these programs are considered firmware and are stored on a chip on the motherboard, called the ROM BIOS chip or firmware chip. If a motherboard becomes unstable (such as when the system hangs at odd times), some functions are lost (such as a USB port stops working), or you want to incorporate some new feature or component on the board (such as when you upgrade the processor), you might need to upgrade the programming stored on the ROM BIOS chip. The process of upgrading or refreshing the ROM BIOS chip is called updating the BIOS, flashing BIOS, or flashing ROM. The BIOS updates are downloaded from the motherboard manufacturer's Web site. If you can't find an upgrade on this site, try the BIOS manufacturer Web site or a third-party site.

A+
220-702
1.1

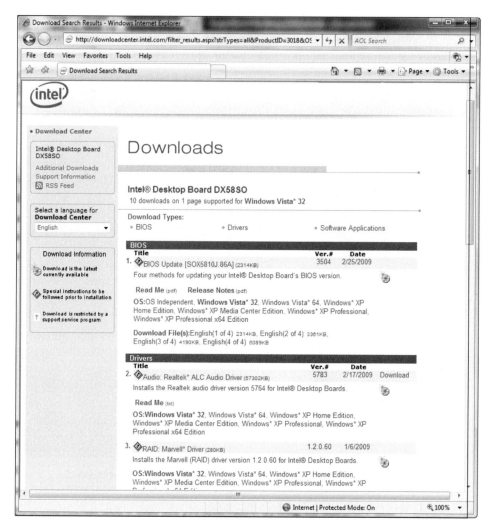

Figure 5-38   Download BIOS and driver updates from the motherboard Web site
Courtesy: Course Technology/Cengage Learning

Figure 5-39   The motherboard brand and model are imprinted somewhere on the board
Courtesy: Course Technology/Cengage Learning

The methods of installing the BIOS updates are listed here:

▲ *Express BIOS update.* Some motherboards allow for an express BIOS update, which is done from Windows. Download the update file to your hard drive. Close all open applications. Double-click the file, which runs the update program, and follow directions on-screen. The system will reboot to enable the update.

▲ *Update from a bootable floppy disk.* Most systems let you use a floppy disk if the update is small enough to fit on the disk and your system has a floppy drive. (Many PCs today don't have one.) Download the update file to your hard drive, copy it to the disk, and double-click the file. The program creates a bootable disk. Boot from the floppy, which will install the update. Remove the floppy and reboot the system.

▲ *Update from a bootable USB drive or bootable CD.* Creating a bootable USB drive or CD is more difficult than creating a bootable floppy disk. You first use a utility program to make a USB drive or CD bootable. Then you download and copy the BIOS update to the drive or CD. Make sure the boot sequence turns to the CD or USB drive before the hard drive to load the OS. Then boot from the device, follow directions on-screen, and remove the device. Reboot the system and the update is installed.

▲ *Recovery from a failed update.* If the BIOS update is interrupted or the update gives errors, you might be able to revert to the earlier version. To do this, generally, you download the recovery file from the Web site, and copy the file to a floppy disk, USB drive, or CD. Then set the jumper on the motherboard to recover from a failed update. Put the floppy disk, USB drive, or CD in the system and reboot. The BIOS automatically reads from the device and performs the recovery. (In most cases, it is not necessary that the floppy disk, USB drive, or CD is bootable.) After the recovery is completed, remove the media and power down the system. Reset the jumper to the normal setting and boot the system.

Your motherboard might use one or more of these methods. To know how to update the BIOS, read the motherboard documentation, as different motherboards use different methods. If you can't find the documentation, check the motherboard manufacturer's Web site. To find the right update, you'll need to identify your motherboard and also know the version of BIOS you are currently using. Do the following:

1. To identify the model of the motherboard, look on the motherboard for the brand and model imprinted on the board.

2. To identify the BIOS version, boot the system and enter the BIOS setup utility. The BIOS version number is displayed on the opening menu. Alternately, you can use the Msinfo32.exe utility in Windows to display the BIOS version.

When you download the update, the downloaded compressed file will most likely include detailed instructions. Or you might find the instructions on the Web site. Print the instructions, read them to make sure you understand everything, and then follow them carefully. If you are given the opportunity to save the current BIOS to another media before you perform the update, do so because you might need to backtrack later if the update gives problems.

> **Notes** After flashing BIOS, if the motherboard gives problems, you need to consider that the chipset drivers might also need updating. To update the chipset drivers, go to the Web site of the motherboard manufacturer and download the chipset driver files for the OS you are using. Then follow the manufacturer's instructions to perform the update.

A+
220-702
1.1

Makers of BIOS code are likely to change BIOS frequently, because providing the upgrade on the Internet is so easy for them. Generally, however, follow the principle that "if it's not broke, don't fix it;" update your BIOS only if you're having a problem with your motherboard or there's a new BIOS feature you want to use. Also, don't update the BIOS unless the update is a later version than the one installed. One last word of caution: it's very important the update not be interrupted while it is in progress. A failed update can make your motherboard totally unusable. Be sure you don't interrupt the update, and make sure there are no power interruptions. Using a UPS while updating BIOS is a good idea.

> **⚡ Caution** Be *very careful* that you upgrade BIOS with the correct upgrade and that you follow the manufacturer's instructions correctly. Upgrading with the wrong file could make your system BIOS useless. If you're not sure that you're using the correct upgrade, *don't guess*. Check with the technical support for your BIOS before moving forward. Before you call technical support, have the information that identifies your BIOS and motherboard available.

If you can't find an upgrade on your motherboard or BIOS manufacturer Web site, try the drivers and BIOS Upgrades Web site by eSupport.com, Inc. at *www.esupport.com*. Table 5-8 lists BIOS manufacturers. A list of motherboard manufacturers is given in Table 5-6 earlier in the chapter.

Company	URL
American Megatrends, Inc. (AMI)	*www.megatrends.com or www.ami.com*
Compaq and Hewlett-Packard	*www.hp.com*
Dell	*www.dell.com*
eSupport.com (drivers and BIOS upgrades)	*www.esupport.com*
Gateway	*www.gateway.com*
IBM	*www.ibm.com/support*
Phoenix Technologies (First BIOS, Phoenix, and Award)	*www.phoenix.com*
Wim's BIOS	*www.wimsbios.com*

Table 5-8 BIOS manufacturers

A+
220-702
1.1
4.2

USING THE BIOS JUMPERS ON THE MOTHERBOARD

Most motherboards today have a group of BIOS jumpers that can be used to recover from a failed BIOS update or forgotten power-on password. For example, Figure 5-40 shows a group of three jumpers on one board. (The tan jumper cap is positioned on the first two jumper pins on the left side of the group.) Figure 5-41 shows the motherboard documentation on how to use these jumpers. When jumpers 1 and 2 are closed, which they are in the figure, normal booting happens. When jumpers 2 and 3 are closed, passwords to BIOS setup can be cleared on the next boot. When no jumpers are closed, on the next boot, the BIOS will recover itself from a failed update. Once set for normal booting, the jumpers should be changed only if you are trying to recover when the power-up password is lost or flashing BIOS has failed. To know how to set jumpers, see the motherboard documentation.

BIOS
jumper
group

Figure 5-40 This group of three jumpers controls the BIOS configuration
Courtesy: Course Technology/Cengage Learning

Jumper Position	Mode	Description
1 · 3	Normal (default)	The current BIOS configuration is used for booting.
1 · 3	Configure	After POST, the BIOS displays a menu in CMOS setup that can be used to clear the user and supervisor power-on passwords.
1 · 3	Recovery	Recovery is used to recover from a failed BIOS update. Details can be found on the motherboard CD.

Figure 5-41 BIOS configuration jumper settings
Courtesy: Course Technology/Cengage Learning

REPLACE THE CMOS BATTERY

The CMOS battery on the motherboard is considered a field replaceable unit. The battery is designed to last for years and recharges when the motherboard has power. However, on rare occasions you might need to replace one if the system loses BIOS settings when it is unplugged. Make sure the replacement battery is an exact match to the original or is one the motherboard manufacturer recommends for the board. Power down the system, unplug it, press the power button to drain the power, and remove the case cover. Use your ground bracelet to protect the system against ESD. The old battery can be removed with a little prying using a flathead screwdriver. The new battery pops into place. For more specific direction, see the motherboard documentation.

Now let's turn our attention to installing or replacing a motherboard.

INSTALLING OR REPLACING A MOTHERBOARD

When you purchase a motherboard, the package comes with the board, I/O shield, documentation, drivers, and various screws, cables, and connectors (see Figure 5-42). When you replace a motherboard, you pretty much have to disassemble an entire computer, install the new motherboard, and reassemble the system, which you learned to do in Chapter 4. The following list is meant to be a general overview of the process and is not meant to include the details of all possible installation scenarios, which can vary according to the components and OS you are using.

Fan and mounting bracket for North Bridge cooling

Documentation and drivers

Decorative cover for North Bridge

SATA cables

I/O shield

Figure 5-42 A new motherboard package
Courtesy: Course Technology/Cengage Learning

The general process for replacing a motherboard is as follows:

💡 **A+ Exam Tip** The A+ 220-702 Practical Application exam expects you to know how to install and configure a motherboard.

1. *Verify that you have selected the right motherboard to install in the system.* The new motherboard should have the same form factor as the case, support the RAM modules and processor you want to install on it, and have other internal and external connectors you need for your system.

2. *Get familiar with the motherboard documentation, features, and settings.* Especially important are any connectors and jumpers on the motherboard. It's a great idea to read the motherboard manual from cover to cover. At the least, get familiar with what it has to offer and study the diagram in it that labels all the components on the board. Learn how each connector and jumper is used. You can also check the manufacturer Web site for answers to any questions you might have.

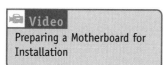

▶ Video

Preparing a Motherboard for Installation

3. *Remove components so you can reach the old motherboard.* Use a ground bracelet. Turn off the system and disconnect all cables and cords. Open the case cover and remove all internal cables and cords connected to the motherboard. Remove all expansion cards. To safely remove the old motherboard, you might have to remove drives. If the processor cooler is heavy and bulky, you might remove it from the old motherboard before you remove the motherboard from the case.

4. *Set any jumpers on the new motherboard.* This is much easier to do before you put the board in the case. Verify the BIOS startup jumper is set for normal startup.

5. *Install the motherboard.* Place the motherboard into the case and, using spacers or screws, securely fasten the board to the case. Because coolers are heavy, most processor instructions say to install the motherboard before installing the processor and cooler to better protect the board or processor from being damaged. On the other hand, some motherboard manufacturers say to install the processor and cooler and then install the motherboard. Follow the order given by the motherboard manufacturer.

6. *Install the processor and processor cooler.* The processor comes already installed on some motherboards, in which case you just need to install the cooler. How to install a processor and cooler is covered in Chapter 6.

7. *Install RAM into the appropriate slots on the motherboard.* How to install RAM is covered in Chapter 7.

8. *Attach cabling that goes from the case switches to the motherboard, and from the power supply and drives to the motherboard.* Pay attention to how cables are labeled and to any information in the documentation about where to attach them. Position and tie cables neatly together to make sure they don't obstruct the fans and the air flow.

9. *Install the video card on the motherboard.* This card should go into the AGP slot or the primary PCI Express x16 slot. If you plan to install multiple video cards, install only one now and check out how the system functions before installing the second one.

10. *Plug the computer into a power source, and attach the monitor and keyboard.* Note that you do not attach the mouse now, for the initial setup. Although the mouse generally does not cause problems during setup, initially install only the things you absolutely need.

11. *Boot the system and enter BIOS setup.* How to do this is coming up in the next section.

12. *Make sure settings are set to the default.* If the motherboard comes new from the manufacturer, it will already be at default settings. If you are salvaging a motherboard from another system, you might need to reset settings to the default. You will need to do the following while you are in BIOS setup:

   ◢ Check the time and date.
   ◢ Check the floppy drive type if you have one.
   ◢ Make sure abbreviated POST is disabled. While you're installing a motherboard, you generally want it to do as many tests as possible. After you know the system is working, you can choose to abbreviate POST.
   ◢ Set the boot order to the hard drive, and then a CD, if you will be booting the OS from the hard drive.
   ◢ Make sure "autodetect hard disk" is set so that the system automatically looks for drives.
   ◢ Leave everything else at their defaults unless you know that particular settings should be otherwise.
   ◢ Save and exit.

13. *Observe POST and verify that no errors occur.*

14. *Check for conflicts with system resources.* If Windows is already installed on the hard drive, boot to the Windows desktop. Use Device Manager to verify that the OS recognizes all devices and that no conflicts are reported.

15. *Install the motherboard drivers.* If your motherboard comes with a CD that contains some motherboard drivers, install them now. You will probably need Internet access, so that the setup process can download the latest drivers from the motherboard manufacturer's Web site. Reboot the system one more time, checking for errors.

16. *Install any other expansion cards and drivers.* Install each device and its drivers, one device at a time, rebooting and checking for conflicts after each installation.

17. *Verify that everything is operating properly, and make any final OS and BIOS adjustments, such as power management settings.*

A+
220-702
1.1

Notes Whenever you install or uninstall software or hardware, keep a notebook with details about the components you are working on, configuration settings, manufacturer specifications, and other relevant information. This helps if you need to backtrack later, and can also help you document and troubleshoot your computer system. Keep all hardware documentation for this system together with the notebook in an envelope in a safe place.

Here are the general steps for installing the motherboard in the case:

1. Install the I/O shield, which is a metal plate that comes with the motherboard and fits over the ports to create a well-fitting enclosure for them. A case might come with a standard I/O shield already in place (see Figure 5-43). But when you hold the motherboard up to that shield, you can see the ports on the board will not fit into the holes. Remove this I/O shield (for this particular case, you have to punch it out). The I/O shield that comes packaged with the board can then be installed (see Figure 5-44).

Figure 5-43 The computer case comes with an installed I/O shield but it does not match up with ports on the motherboard
Courtesy: Course Technology/Cengage Learning

2. Some cases have **standoffs**, also called **spacers**, which are round plastic or metal pegs that separate the motherboard from the case, so that components on the back of the motherboard do not touch the case. Make sure the locations of the standoffs match the screw holes on the motherboard (see Figure 5-45). If you need to remove a standoff to move it to a new slot, needle-nose pliers work well to unscrew or unplug the standoff. The case will have more holes than you need to support several types of

Figure 5-44 Install the I/O shield in the hole at the rear of the PC case
Courtesy: Course Technology/Cengage Learning

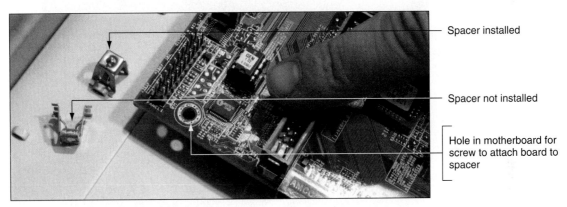

Spacer installed

Spacer not installed

Hole in motherboard for
screw to attach board to
spacer

Figure 5-45 The spacers line up with the holes on the motherboard and keep it from touching the case
Courtesy: Course Technology/Cengage Learning

motherboards. Other cases don't use the standoffs because the screw holes are elevated to keep the bottom of the motherboard from touching the case. For these cases, use screws to connect the motherboard to the case.

> ⚡ **Caution** As with any installation, remember the importance of using a ground strap (ground bracelet) to ground yourself when working inside a computer case to protect components against ESD.

3. Place the motherboard inside the case (see Figure 5-46), and use screws to attach it to the case. Figure 5-47 shows how you must align the screw holes on the motherboard with those in the case. There should be at least six screw sets, and there might be as many as nine. Use as many as there are holes in the motherboard. Figure 5-48 shows one screw being put in place.

4. Connect the power cords from the power supply to the motherboard. A system will always need the main P1 power connector and most likely will need the 4-pin

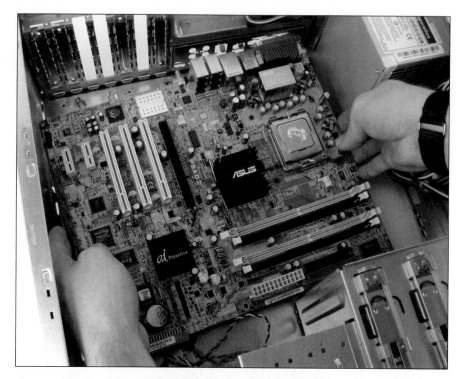

Figure 5-46 Place the motherboard in the case
Courtesy: Course Technology/Cengage Learning

Figure 5-47 Align screw holes in the case with those on the motherboard
Courtesy: Course Technology/Cengage Learning

auxiliary connector for the processor. Other power connectors might be needed depending on the devices you later install in the system. Here are the details:

◢ Connect the P1 power connection from the power supply to the motherboard (see Figure 5-49).

Figure 5-48 Use one screw in each screw hole on the motherboard
Courtesy: Course Technology/Cengage Learning

Figure 5-49 The 24-pin connector supplies power to the motherboard
Courtesy: Course Technology/Cengage Learning

▲ Connect the 4-pin auxiliary power cord coming from the power supply to the motherboard, as shown in Figure 5-50. This cord supplies the supplemental power required for the processor.

▲ A board might have a 6-pin or 8-pin PCIe power connector. You saw a photograph of an 8-pin connector earlier in the chapter in Figure 5-16. If the board has either connector, connect the 6-pin or 8-pin cord from the power supply to the connector.

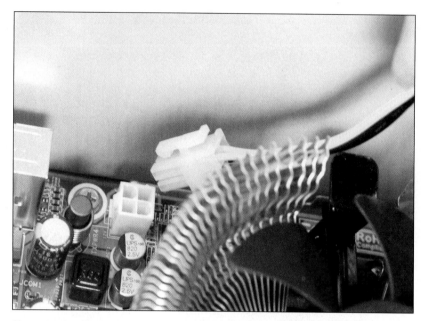

Figure 5-50   The auxiliary 4-pin power cord provides power to the processor
Courtesy: Course Technology/Cengage Learning

If your power supply doesn't have this connector, recall from Chapter 4 that you can purchase an adapter to convert two Molex connectors to a PCIe connector.

▲ Some boards designed to support multiple PCIe video cards will have additional power connectors on the board to power these wattage-hungry cards. For example, Figure 5-51(a) shows a 1 x 4 Molex-style connector on one board that provides auxiliary power to PCIe graphics cards. This same board offers a SATA-style connector, shown in Figure 5-51(b). The motherboard documentation says to use just one of these auxiliary power connectors to provide additional wattage for PCIe video cards.

▲ To power the case fan, connect the power cord from the fan to pins on the motherboard labeled Fan Header. Alternately, some case fans use a 4-pin Molex connector that connects to a power cable coming directly from the power supply.

▲ Later, after the CPU cooler is installed, you'll need to connect the power cord from that fan to the pins on the motherboard labeled CPU Fan Header.

5. Connect the wire leads from the front panel of the case to the motherboard. These are the wires for the switches, lights, and ports on the front of the computer. Because your

SATA-style power connector

Molex-style power connector

Figure 5-51   Auxiliary power connectors to support PCIe
Courtesy: Course Technology/Cengage Learning

case and your motherboard might not have been made by the same manufacturer, you need to pay close attention to the source of the wires to determine where they connect on the motherboard. For example, Figure 5-52 shows a computer case that has seven connectors from the front panel that connect to the motherboard. Figure 5-53 shows the corner of the motherboard that has the front panel header for lights and switches. If you look closely at this last photo, you can see labels on the board identifying the pins.

Figure 5-52 Seven connectors from the front panel connect to the motherboard
Courtesy: Course Technology/Cengage Learning

Figure 5-53 Front panel header uses color-coded pins
Courtesy: Course Technology/Cengage Learning

The five wires on the right side of Figure 5-52 from right to left are labeled as follows:

▲ *Power SW.* Controls power to the motherboard; must be connected for the PC to power up

A+
220-702
1.1

◢ *HDD LED.* Controls a light on the front panel that lights up when any IDE device is in use. (HDD stands for hard disk drive; LED stands for light-emitting diode; and an LED is a light on the front panel.)

◢ *Power LED+.* Positive LED used to indicate that power is on

◢ *Power LED-.* Negative LED used to indicate that power is on

◢ *Reset SW.* SwiFtch used to reboot the computer

To help orient the connector on the motherboard pins, look for a small triangle embedded on the connector that marks one of the outside wires as pin 1 (see Figure 5-54). Look for pin 1 to be labeled on the motherboard as a small 1 embedded to either the right or the left of the group of pins. Also, sometimes the documentation marks pin 1 as a square pin in the diagram, rather than round like the other pins. The diagram in Figure 5-55 shows what you can expect from motherboard documentation. Sometimes the motherboard documentation is not clear, but guessing is okay when connecting a wire to a front panel header connection. If it doesn't work, no harm is done. Figure 5-56 shows all front panel wires in place and the little speaker also connected to the front panel header pins.

6. Connect wires to ports on the front panel of the case. Depending on your motherboard and case, there might be cables to connect audio ports or USB ports on the front of

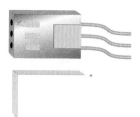

Figure 5-54 Look for the small triangle embedded on the wire lead connectors to orient the connector correctly to the motherboard connector pins
Courtesy: Course Technology/Cengage Learning

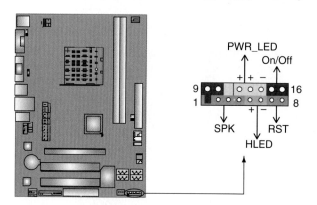

Pin	Assignment	Function	Pin	Assignment	Function
1	+5 V		9	N/A	N/A
2	N/A	Speaker	10	N/A	
3	N/A	connector	11	N/A	N/A
4	Speaker		12	Power LED (+)	
5	HDD LED (+)	Hard drive	13	Power LED (+)	Power LED
6	HDD LED (–)	LED	14	Power LED (–)	
7	Ground	Reset button	15	Power button	Power-on button
8	Reset control		16	Ground	

Figure 5-55 Documentation for front panel header connections
Courtesy: Course Technology/Cengage Learning

Speaker connected
to front panel
header

Figure 5-56 Front panel header with all connectors in place
Courtesy: Course Technology/Cengage Learning

the case to connectors on the motherboard. Audio and USB connectors are shown as the two left connectors in Figure 5-52. You can see these ports for audio and USB on the front of the case in Figure 5-57. Look in the motherboard documentation for the location of these connectors. The audio and USB connectors are labeled for one board in Figures 5-58(a) and (b).

Audio-out and
microphone ports

USB ports

Figure 5-57 Ports on the front of the computer case
Courtesy: Course Technology/Cengage Learning

After you install the motherboard and connect all cables and cords, next you install the video card and plug in the keyboard and monitor. Make one last check to verify all required power cords are connected correctly and the video card is seated solidly in its slot. You are now ready to turn on the system and observe POST occurs with no errors. After the Windows desktop loads, insert the CD that came bundled with the motherboard and execute any setup program on the CD. Follow the steps on-screen to install any drivers, which might include drivers for onboard devices and ports such as video, network, audio, USB, RAID, or the chipset.

Look back at the general list of steps to replace a motherboard at the beginning of this section for the list of things to check and do to complete the installation, and return the system to good working order.

A+
220-702
1.1

CONFIGURING THE MOTHERBOARD USING BIOS SETUP

The motherboard configuration stored in BIOS setup does not normally need to be changed except, for example, when there is a problem with hardware, a new floppy drive is installed, or a power-saving feature needs to be disabled or enabled. The BIOS setup can also hold one or two power-on passwords to help secure a system. Know that these passwords are not the same password that can be required by a Windows OS at startup. In this part of the chapter, you'll learn how to access and use the BIOS setup program. Earlier in the chapter, you saw listed most BIOS settings in Table 5-5.

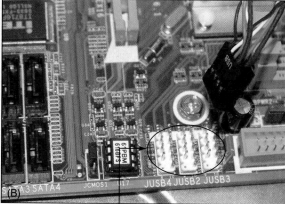

└─ Front audio header   └─ Three USB headers

Figure 5-58   Connectors for front panel ports
Courtesy: Course Technology/Cengage Learning

> 💡 **A+ Exam Tip**   The A+ 220-702 Practical Application exam expects you to know how to change advanced BIOS settings.

ACCESSING THE BIOS SETUP PROGRAM

You access the BIOS setup program by pressing a key or combination of keys during the boot process. The exact way to enter setup varies from one motherboard manufacturer to another. Table 5-9 lists the keystrokes needed to access BIOS setup for some common BIOS types.

BIOS	Key to Press During POST to Access Setup
AMI BIOS	Del
Award BIOS	Del
Older Phoenix BIOS	Ctrl+Alt+Esc or Ctrl+Alt+s
Newer Phoenix BIOS	F2 or F1
Dell computers using Phoenix BIOS	Ctrl+Alt+Enter
Compaq computers such as the ProLinea, Deskpro, Deskpro XL, Deskpro XE, or Presario	Press the F10 key while the cursor is in the upper-right corner of the screen, which happens just after the two beeps during booting.*

*For Compaq computers, the BIOS setup program is stored on the hard drive in a small, non-DOS partition of about 3 MB. If this partition becomes corrupted, you must run setup from a bootable CD or floppy disk that comes with the system. If you cannot run setup by pressing F10 at startup, suspect a damaged partition or a virus taking up space in memory.

Table 5-9   How to access BIOS setup

For the exact method you need to use to enter setup, see the documentation for your motherboard. A message such as the following usually appears on the screen near the beginning of the boot:

```
Press DEL to change Setup
```

or

```
Press F2 for Setup
```

When you press the appropriate key or keys, a setup screen appears with menus and Help features that are often very user-friendly. Although the exact menus depend on the maker and version of components you are working with, the sample screens that follow will help you become familiar with the general contents of BIOS setup screens. Figure 5-59 shows a main menu for setup. On this menu, you can change the system date and time, the keyboard language, and other system features.

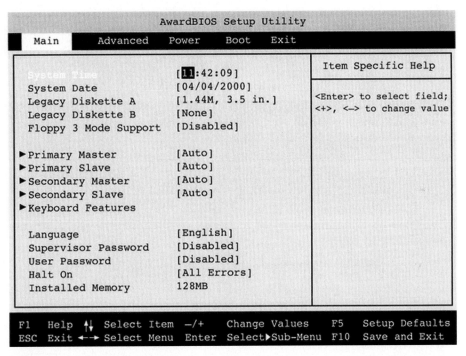

Figure 5-59 BIOS Setup Main menu
Courtesy: Course Technology/Cengage Learning

The power menu in BIOS setup allows you to configure automatic power-saving features for your system, such as suspend mode or a sleep state. Figure 5-60 shows a sample power menu. In most situations, it is best to allow the OS to manage power rather than use BIOS settings. You will learn more about power management in Chapter 21.

CHANGING THE BOOT SEQUENCE

Figures 5-61 and 62 show two examples of a boot menu in BIOS setup. Here, you can set the order in which the system tries to boot from certain devices (called the boot sequence). Most likely when you first install a hard drive or an operating system, you will want to have the BIOS attempt to first boot from a CD and, if no CD is present, turn to the hard drive. After the OS is installed, to prevent accidental boots from a CD or other media, change BIOS setup to boot first from the hard drive. You will learn more about this in Chapter 12.

A+
220-702
1.1

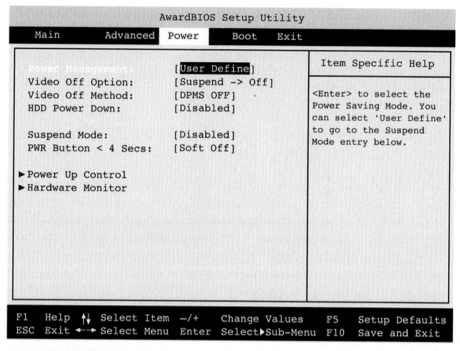

Figure 5-60   BIOS Setup Power menu
Courtesy: Course Technology/Cengage Learning

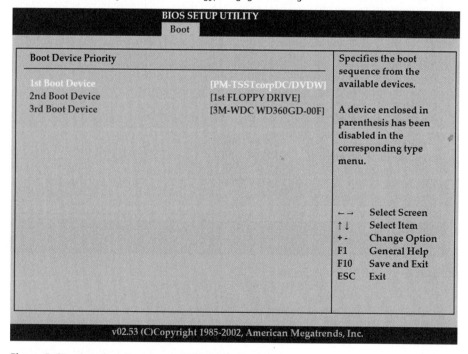

Figure 5-61   American Megatrends BIOS Setup Boot menu
Courtesy: Course Technology/Cengage Learning

A+
220-702
1.1
4.2

PASSWORD PROTECTION TO BIOS SETUP AND TO THE SYSTEM

Access to a computer can be controlled using a startup password, sometimes called a user password or power-on password. If the password has been enabled and set in BIOS setup, the startup BIOS asks for the password during the boot just before the BIOS begins searching for an OS. If the password is entered incorrectly, the boot process terminates. The password is stored in CMOS RAM and is changed by accessing the setup screen. (This password is not the same as the OS password.) Many computers also provide jumpers near the chip holding CMOS RAM; you saw

A+
220-702
1.1
4.2

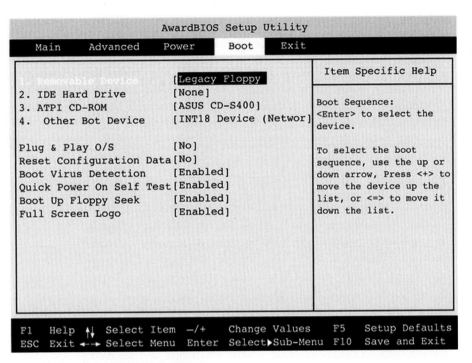

Figure 5-62 Award BIOS Setup Boot menu
Courtesy: Course Technology/Cengage Learning

how to use these jumpers earlier in the chapter. By using these jumpers, you can disable a forgotten password.

EXITING THE BIOS SETUP MENUS

A+
220-702
1.1

When you finish, an exit screen such as the one shown in Figure 5-63 gives you various options, such as saving or discarding changes and then exiting the program, restoring default settings, or saving changes and remaining in the program.

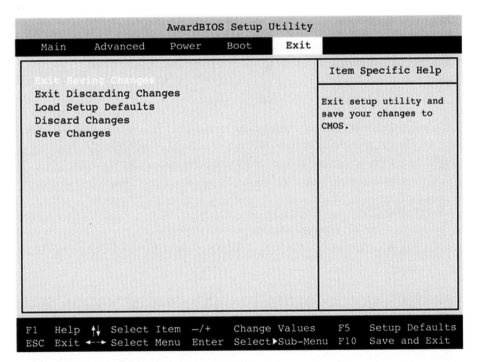

Figure 5-63 BIOS Setup Exit menu
Courtesy: Course Technology/Cengage Learning

A+
220-702
1.1

APPLYING CONCEPTS

Reboot your PC and look for the message on the first or second display screen that tells you how to enter BIOS setup. Press that key. What version of BIOS are you using? Explore the BIOS setup menus until you find the boot sequence. What is the order of storage media that startup BIOS uses to find an OS? What keystrokes do you use to change that order? Exit setup without making any changes. The system should reboot to the Windows desktop.

CHANGING BIOS SETUP FOR BRAND-NAME COMPUTERS

Many brand-name computer manufacturers, such as IBM, Dell, and Gateway, use their own custom-designed setup screens. These screens differ from the ones just shown. For example, Figure 5-64 shows the IBM BIOS Setup main menu for an IBM Thinkpad notebook computer. Under the Config option on the screen, you can configure the network port, serial port, parallel port, PCI bus, USB port, floppy drive, keyboard, display settings, power settings, power alarm, and memory settings.

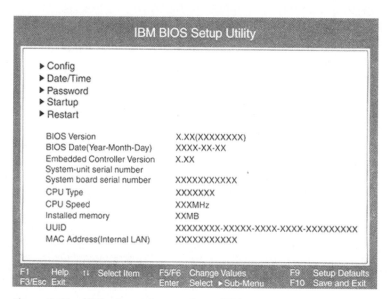

Figure 5-64   BIOS setup main menu for an IBM computer
Courtesy: Course Technology/Cengage Learning

Compare this BIOS setup main menu to the one shown in Figure 5-65 for a Gateway desktop computer. For all these different brand-name computers, what you can configure is similar, but the setup screens are likely to be organized differently.

> **A+ Exam Tip**   The A+ 220-702 Practical Application exam expects you to be able to configure a motherboard. You need to know how and when to use BIOS setup to make appropriate changes. And to help secure a computer, you need to know how to set startup passwords.

PROTECTING DOCUMENTATION AND CONFIGURATION SETTINGS

If the battery goes bad or is disconnected, you can lose the settings saved in CMOS RAM. If you are using default settings, reboot with a good battery and instruct setup to restore the default settings. Setup has to autodetect the hard drive present, and you need to set the date

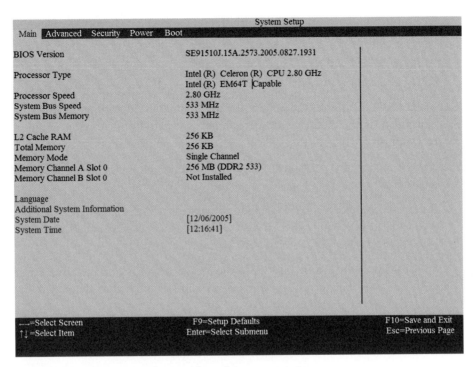

A+
220-702
1.1

Figure 5-65 BIOS setup main menu for a Gateway computer
Courtesy: Course Technology/Cengage Learning

and time, but you can easily recover from the problem. However, if you have customized some BIOS settings, you need to restore them. The most reliable way to restore settings is to keep a written record of all the changes you make to CMOS RAM. This is not that difficult to do since you're most likely only changing a few default settings. You can write them on a sticker and paste it to the side of the case or record the changes in the motherboard manual. You can't easily make screen shots or printouts of the BIOS setup screens, but you can use a digital camera to photograph these screens.

If you are responsible for the ongoing maintenance and care of a computer, you should consider keeping a written record of what you have done to maintain it. Use a small notebook or similar document to record BIOS settings that are not the default settings, hardware and software installed, network settings, and similar information. Keep the documentation well labeled in a safe place. If you have several computers to maintain, you might consider a filing system for each computer. For example, you can put all the documentation in a large brown envelope that is labeled to identify the PC. Another method is to carefully tape a cardboard folder to the inside top or side of the computer case and safely tuck the hardware documentation there. This works well if you are responsible for several computers spread over a wide area.

Regardless of the method you use, it's important that you keep your records up to date and stored with the hardware documentation in a safe place. Leaving it in the care of users who might not realize its value is probably not a good idea. The notebook and documentation will be invaluable as you solve future problems with this PC.

>> CHAPTER SUMMARY

◢ The motherboard is the most complicated of all components inside the computer. It contains the processor and accompanying chipset, real-time clock, ROM BIOS, CMOS configuration chip, RAM, system bus, expansion slots, jumpers, ports, and power supply connections. The motherboard you select determines both the capabilities and limitations of your system.

- ◢ The most popular motherboard form factors are ATX, MicroATX, FlexATX, BTX, and NLX, in that order.

- ◢ A motherboard will have one or more Intel sockets for an Intel processor or one or more AMD sockets for an AMD processor.

- ◢ Intel, AMD, NVIDIA, and SiS are the most popular chipset manufacturers. The chipset embedded on the motherboard determines what kind of processor and memory the board can support.

- ◢ Two or more video cards installed on a motherboard use NVIDIA SLI or ATI CrossFire technology.

- ◢ Buses used on motherboards include conventional PCI, PCI-X, PCI Express, and AGP. AGP is used solely for video cards. PCI Express has been revised three times and is expected to replace all the other bus types.

- ◢ Some components can be built in to the motherboard, in which case they are called on-board components. Other components can be attached to the system in some other way, such as on an expansion card.

- ◢ A bus is a path on the motherboard that carries electrical power, control signals, memory addresses, and data to different components on the board.

- ◢ The most common method of configuring components on a motherboard is BIOS setup. Some motherboards also use jumpers or DIP switches to contain configuration settings.

- ◢ Startup BIOS controls the beginning of the boot. It first checks critical hardware components in a process called POST (power on self test). It then looks to the boot device priority order stored in CMOS RAM to know which device will be used to load the OS.

- ◢ A hard drive has a Master Boot Record (MBR) at the beginning of the drive that contains the partition table, which contains a map to partitions on the drive.

- ◢ The next sector on the drive contains the OS boot record. The first file that the OS used to load the OS is BootMgr for Windows Vista and Ntldr for Windows XP.

- ◢ Motherboard drivers might need updating to fix a problem with a board component or to use a new feature provided by the motherboard manufacturer.

- ◢ Sometimes ROM BIOS programming stored on the firmware chip needs updating or refreshing. This process is called updating BIOS or flashing BIOS.

- ◢ When installing a motherboard, first study the motherboard and set jumpers and DIP switches on the board. Sometimes the processor and cooler are best installed before installing the motherboard in the case. When the cooling assembly is heavy and bulky, it is best to install it after the motherboard is securely seated in the case.

- ◢ ROM chips contain the programming code to manage POST and the system BIOS and to change BIOS settings. CMOS RAM holds configuration information.

- ◢ The BIOS setup program is used to change the settings in CMOS RAM.

>> KEY TERMS

For explanations of key terms, see the Glossary near the end of the book.

Accelerated Graphics Port (AGP)
active partition
audio/modem riser (AMR)
boot loader
boot record
booting
BootMgr
CMOS battery
cold boot
communication and networking
   riser (CNR)
CrossFire
dual inline package (DIP) switch
front panel header
hard boot

I/O shield
jumper
land grid array (LGA)
Master Boot Record (MBR)
North Bridge
Ntldr
on-board ports
partition table
PCI (Peripheral Component
   Interconnect)
PCI Express (PCIe)
pin grid array (PGA)
power-on password
program file
riser card

sector
SLI (Scalable Link Interface)
soft boot
South Bridge
spacers
staggered pin grid array (SPGA)
standoffs
startup password
track
user password
wait state
warm boot
zero insertion force (ZIF) sockets

5

>> REVIEWING THE BASICS

1. What are five main categories of form factors used for motherboards?

2. How many pins does the Intel Socket B have? What is another name for this socket?

3. How many pins does the AMD socket AM2 have?

4. Which is a better performing Intel chipset, the X58 or the P45?

5. Which part of the chipset connects directly to the processor, the North Bridge or the South Bridge?

6. What are the names of the two technologies used to install multiple video cards in the same system?

7. What are the two different voltages that a PCI slot can provide?

8. How does the throughput of PCI Express Version 1.1 compare to PCIe Version 1? How does PCIe Version 2 compare to Version 1?

9. What is the maximum wattage that a PCIe Version 2.0 expansion card can draw?

10. What new type of power connector on the motherboard was introduced with PCIe Version 1.0? How much power does this connector provide?

11. What new type of power connector was introduced with PCIe Version 2.0? How much power does this connector provide?

12. If you are installing an expansion card into a case that does not have enough clearance above the motherboard for the card, what device can you use to solve the problem?

13. What is the purpose of an AGP slot?

14. Which is faster, a PCI Express x16 bus or the latest AGP bus?

15. What is the purpose of a CNR slot?

16. What is the likely color of the PS/2 mouse port on the rear of a computer?

17. What is one reason to flash BIOS?

18. What is the easiest way to obtain the latest software to upgrade BIOS?

19. What can you do if the power-on password and the supervisor password to a system have been forgotten?

20. Where is the boot priority order for devices kept?

21. What is the difference between a hard boot and a soft boot?

22. How is CMOS RAM powered when the system is unplugged?

23. Describe how you can access the BIOS setup program.

24. If a USB port on the motherboard is failing, what is one task you can do that might fix the problem?

25. What might the purpose be for a SATA-style power connector on a motherboard?

>> THINKING CRITICALLY

1. Why does a motherboard sometimes support more than one system bus speed?

2. Why don't all buses on a motherboard operate at the same speed?

3. When you turn off the power to a computer at night, it loses the date, and you must reenter it each morning. What is the problem and how do you solve it?

4. Why do you think the trend is to store configuration information on a motherboard in CMOS RAM rather than by using jumpers or switches?

5. When troubleshooting a motherboard, you discover the network port no longer works. What is the best and least expensive solution to this problem?

   a. Replace the motherboard.

   b. Disable the network port and install a network card in an expansion slot.

   c. Use a wireless network device in a USB port to connect to a wireless network.

   d. Return the motherboard to the factory for repair.

6. A computer freezes at odd times. At first you suspect the power supply or overheating, but you have eliminated overheating and replaced the power supply without solving the problem. What do you do next?

   a. Replace the processor.

   b. Replace the motherboard.

   c. Reinstall Windows.

   d. Replace the memory modules.

   e. Flash BIOS.

>> HANDS-ON PROJECTS

PROJECT 5-1:   Examining the Motherboard in Detail

1. Look at the back of your computer. Without opening the case, list the ports that you believe come directly from the motherboard.

2. Remove the cover of the case, which you learned to do in Chapter 4. List the different expansion cards in the expansion slots. Was your guess correct about which ports come from the motherboard?

3. To expose the motherboard so you can identify its parts, remove all the expansion cards, as discussed in Chapter 4.

4. Draw a diagram of the motherboard and label these parts:

    ▲ Processor (Include the prominent label on the processor housing.)

    ▲ RAM (each DIMM slot)

    ▲ CMOS battery

    ▲ Expansion slots (Identify the slots as PCI, PCIe x1, PCIe x4, PCIe x16, and AGP.)

    ▲ Each port coming directly from the motherboard

    ▲ Power supply connections

    ▲ SATA or IDE drive connectors and floppy drive connector

5. Draw a rectangle on the diagram to represent each bank of jumpers on the board.

6. What is the brand and model of the motherboard?

7. Locate the manufacturer's Web site. If you can find the motherboard manual on the site, download it.

8. You can complete the following activity only if you have the documentation for the motherboard: Locate the jumper on the board that erases CMOS and/or the startup password, and label this jumper on your diagram. It is often found near the battery. Some boards might have more than one, and some have none.

9. Reassemble the computer, as you learned to do in Chapter 4.

PROJECT 5-2: Examining BIOS Settings

Access the BIOS setup program on your computer and answer the following questions:

1. What brand and version of BIOS are you using?

2. What is the frequency of your processor?

3. What is the boot sequence order of devices?

4. Do you have a floppy drive installed? If so, what type of drive?

5. Do you have a CD or DVD drive installed? What are the details of the installed drive?

6. What are the details of the installed hard drive?

7. Does the BIOS offer the option to set a supervisor or power-on password? What is the name of the screen where these passwords are set?

8. Does the BIOS offer the option to overclock the processor? If so, list the settings that apply to overclocking.

9. Can you disable the USB ports on the PC? If so, what is the name of the screen where this is done?

10. List the BIOS settings that control how power is managed on the computer.

PROJECT 5-3: Inserting and Removing Motherboards

Using old or defective expansion cards and motherboards, practice inserting and removing expansion cards and motherboards. In a lab or classroom setting, the instructor can provide extra cards and motherboards for exchange.

PROJECT 5-4: Understanding Hardware Documentation

Obtain the manual for the motherboard for your PC. (If you cannot find the manual, try downloading it from the motherboard manufacturer's Web site.) Answer these questions:

1. What processors does the board support?

2. What type of RAM does the board support?

3. What is the maximum RAM the board can hold?

4. If the board has a PCIe slot, what version of PCIe does the board use?

5. What chipset does the board use?

PROJECT 5-5: Using the Internet for Research

In this project, you will learn how useful the Internet can be for a PC support technician.

1. Using your own or a lab computer, pretend that the motherboard manual is not available and you need to replace a faulty processor. Identify the manufacturer and model of the motherboard by looking for the manufacturer name and model number stamped on the board. Research the Web site for that manufacturer. Print the list of processors the board can support.

2. Research the Web site for your motherboard and print the instructions for flashing BIOS.

3. Research the Abit Web site (*www.abit.com.tw*) and print a photograph of a motherboard that has a riser slot. Also print the photograph of the riser card that fits this slot. What is the function of the riser card?

PROJECT 5-6: Exchanging the CMOS Battery

To practice the steps for exchanging a CMOS battery, do the following:

1. Locate the CMOS battery on your computer's motherboard. What is written on top of the battery?

2. Using the Internet, find a replacement for this battery. Print the Web page showing the battery. How much does the new battery cost?

3. Enter BIOS setup on your computer. Write down any BIOS settings that are not default settings. You'll need these settings later when you reinstall the battery.

4. Turn off and unplug the PC, press the power button to drain the system of power, remove the battery, and boot the PC. What error messages appear? What is the system date and time?

5. Power down the PC, unplug it, press the power button to drain the power, replace the battery, and boot the PC. Return BIOS settings to the way you found them.

PROJECT 5-7: Labeling the Motherboard

Figure 5-66 shows a blank diagram of an ATX motherboard. Using what you learned in this chapter and in previous chapters, label as many components as you can. If you would like to print the diagram, look for "Figure 5-66" on the CD that accompanies this book.

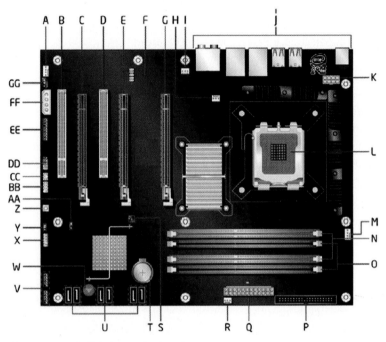

Figure 5-66 Label the motherboard
Courtesy of Intel Corporation

>> REAL PROBLEMS, REAL SOLUTIONS

REAL PROBLEM 5-1: Troubleshooting an Unstable Motherboard

Mary is responsible for all the PCs used by herself and her 10 coworkers in a small real estate firm. When a problem gets too complicated for her, she packs up the PC and sends it off to a local computer store for repair. For the last couple of weeks, Adriana's computer has been hanging at odd times. Last week, Mary reinstalled Windows XP, but the problem has not gone away, so now Mary suspects a hardware problem. The next thing she wants to do is reinstall the drivers for the motherboard. To practice this skill, locate the CD that came with your motherboard and explore what's on the CD. Then install all the drivers stored on the CD that pertain to your system, along with any updates to these drivers published on the motherboard manufacturer's Web site. Answer these questions:

1. What is the brand and model of the motherboard?

2. What chipset does this board use?

3. What troubleshooting utilities are found on the CD that came bundled with the board?

4. What manuals (most likely in PDF format) are found on the CD?

5. What drivers are stored on the CD?

6. Which of these drivers did you install on your system?

7. Which updates to drivers were you able to find on the Internet and use?

Assume you can't find the CD that came bundled with the board. Go to the Web site of the motherboard manufacturer and locate the support pages for this board. List all the utilities, documentation, and drivers for this board found on the Web site.

REAL PROBLEM 5-2: Selecting a Replacement Motherboard

When a motherboard fails, you can select and buy a new board to replace it. Suppose the motherboard used in Real Problem 5-1 has failed and you want to buy a replacement and keep your repair costs to a minimum. Try to find a replacement motherboard on the Internet that can use the same case, power supply, processor, memory, and expansion cards as your current system. If you cannot find a good match, what other components might have to be replaced (for example, the processor or memory)? What is the total cost of the replacement parts? Print Web pages showing what you need to purchase.

CHAPTER 6

Supporting Processors

In the last chapter, you learned all about motherboards. In this chapter, you'll learn about the most important component on the motherboard, which is the processor. You'll learn how a processor works, about the many different types and brands of processors and how to match a processor to the motherboard. Coolers must be used so that a processor will not overheat, so this chapter covers the various cooling systems used for processors.

The processor is considered a field replaceable unit (FRU), and so you'll learn how to install and upgrade a processor. Finally, you need to be prepared when things go wrong. Therefore, at the end of the chapter, you'll learn about things to try and strategies to use when problems arise with the processor and the motherboard and what to do when the system gives problems from overheating. Because the BIOS on the motherboard controls the boot process before an operating system is loaded, troubleshooting the boot is also included in the troubleshooting sections of this chapter.

TYPES AND CHARACTERISTICS OF PROCESSORS

A+
220-701
1.4

The processor installed on a motherboard is the primary component that determines the computing power of the system (see Figure 6-1). The two major manufacturers of processors are Intel (*www.intel.com*) and AMD (*www.amd.com*).

Figure 6-1 An AMD Athlon 64 X2 installed in socket AM2+ with cooler not yet installed
Courtesy: Course Technology/Cengage Learning

Processors are rated based on several features that affect performance and the motherboards that can support them. These features are listed here:

▲ *Feature 1*. The system bus speeds the processor supports. Current Intel processors work with system buses that run at 1600, 1333, 1066, or 800 MHz. Current AMD processors work with system buses that run at 1800, 1000, or 800 MHz.

▲ *Feature 2*. Processor core frequency is measured in gigahertz, such as 3.2 GHz.

▲ *Feature 3*. The motherboard socket and chipset the processor can use. Recall from Chapter 5 that current Intel sockets for desktop systems are the LGA1366, LGA771, LGA775, and 478 sockets. AMD's current desktop sockets are AM3, AM2+, AM2, 754, and 940 sockets.

▲ *Feature 4*. Multiprocessing ability, which is the ability of a system to do more than one thing at a time. This is accomplished by several means, including two processing units installed within a single processor (first used by Pentium processors), a motherboard using two processor sockets (supported, for example, by Xeon processors for servers), and multiple processors installed in the same processor housing (called dual-core, triple-core, quad-core, or octo-core processing).

◢ *Feature 5.* The amount of memory included with the processor, called a memory cache. Today's processors all have some memory on the processor chip (called a die). Memory on the processor die is called Level 1 cache (L1 cache). Memory in the processor package, but not on the processor die, is called Level 2 cache (L2 cache). Some processors use a third cache farther from the processor core, but still in the processor package, which is called Level 3 cache (L3 cache).

◢ *Feature 6.* The amount and type of memory (DDR, DDR2, or DDR3) installed on the motherboard that the processor can support. Recall from Chapter 5 that the chipset, processor, and type of memory must all be compatible on the motherboard.

◢ *Feature 7.* Computing technologies the processor can use. Probably the best-known technologies used by processors are Intel's Hyper-Threading and AMD's HyperTransport. Both allow each logical processor within the processor package to handle an individual thread in parallel with other threads being handled by other processors within the package. Later in the chapter, you'll learn about other processor technologies that improve performance and functionality.

◢ *Feature 8.* The voltage and power consumption of the processor. Today's processors have technologies that put the processor in a sleep state when they are inactive and reduce voltage requirements and CPU frequency depending on the demands placed on the processor. Intel calls this technology Enhanced Intel SpeedStep Technology (EIST) and AMD uses PowerNow!.

Let's now turn our attention to a discussion of how a processor works, including the processor features just listed. Then you'll learn about the families of Intel and AMD processors. If you want to know more about older processors, see the content "Facts about Legacy Processors" on the CD that accompanies this book.

HOW A PROCESSOR WORKS

A processor contains three basic components: an input/output (I/O) unit, a control unit, and one or more arithmetic logic units (ALUs), as shown in Figure 6-2. The I/O unit manages data and instructions entering and leaving the processor. The control unit manages all activities inside the processor itself. The ALU does all logical comparisons and calculations.

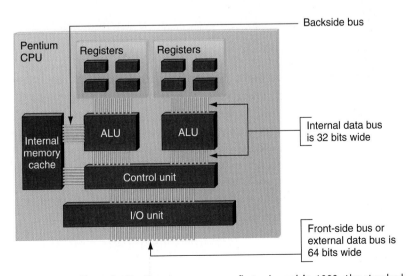

Figure 6-2 Since the Pentium processor was first released in 1993, the standard has been for a processor to have two arithmetic logic units so that it can process two instructions at once
Courtesy: Course Technology/Cengage Learning

Registers are small holding areas on the processor chip that work much as RAM does outside the processor. Registers hold counters, data, instructions, and addresses that the ALU is currently processing. In addition to registers, the processor has its own internal memory caches (L1, L2, and possibly L3) that hold data and instructions waiting to be processed by the ALU. Also notice in Figure 6-2 the external bus, where data, instructions, addresses, and control signals are sent into and out of the processor. The bus is said to be an external bus because it's external to the processor. The data portion of the external bus is 64 bits wide. This bus is sometimes called the front-side bus (FSB) because it connects to the front side of the processor that faces the outside world. Inside the processor housing, data, instructions, addresses, and control signals use the internal bus. The data portion of that bus, called the internal data bus, is 32 bits wide. In Figure 6-2, you can see this internal data bus connects to each of the ALUs. The portion of the internal bus that connects the processor to the internal memory cache is called the back-side bus (BSB). The processor's internal bus operates at a much higher frequency than the external bus (system bus).

Let's now look at the details of the several characteristics of processors, including processor speed, multiprocessing abilities, memory, and the technologies a processor can use.

PROCESSOR FREQUENCY OR SPEED

Processor frequency is the speed at which the processor operates internally. If the processor operates at 3.2 GHz internally but 800 MHz externally, the processor frequency is 3.2 GHz, and the system bus frequency is 800 MHz. In this case, the processor operates at four times the system bus frequency. This factor is called the multiplier. If you multiply the system bus frequency by the multiplier, you get the processor frequency:

$$\text{System bus frequency x multiplier} = \text{processor frequency}$$

Unless you're trying to overclock a system, you need not be concerned about these frequencies. Firmware on the motherboard automatically detects the processor speed and adjusts the system bus speed accordingly. Your only responsibility is to make sure you install a processor that runs at a speed the motherboard can support.

> **Notes** Processor frequencies or speeds are rated at the factory and included with the processor documentation. However, sometimes the actual speed of the processor might be slightly higher or lower than the advertised speed. One way to know the actual speed is to access BIOS setup, which reports the processor and system bus speeds.

Overclocking

For most motherboards and processors, you can override the default frequencies by changing a setting in BIOS setup. Running a motherboard or processor at a higher speed than the manufacturer suggests is called overclocking and is not recommended because the speed is not guaranteed to be stable. Also, know that running a processor at a higher-than-recommended speed can result in overheating, which can damage the processor. Dealing with overheating is a major concern when overclocking a system. And warranties for the motherboard or processor are sometimes voided when they are overclocked. All things considered, some folks still consider overclocking a great hobby and are willing to take the risk with their gaming computers. In a business environment, however, never overclock a computer.

Throttling

Most motherboards and processors offer some protection against overheating so that, if the system overheats, it will throttle down or shut down to prevent the processor from being damaged permanently. Another reason to throttle a CPU is to reduce power consumption when demands on the processor are low. Processor technologies that can throttle a CPU are PowerNow! by AMD and Enhanced Intel SpeedStep Technology (EIST) by Intel. You will learn about BIOS settings that affect power management later in the chapter.

MULTIPROCESSING, MULTIPLE PROCESSORS, AND MULTI-CORE PROCESSING

CPU designers have come up with several creative ways of doing more than one thing at a time to improve performance. Three methods are popular: multiprocessing, dual processors, and multi-core processing. Multiprocessing is accomplished when a processor contains more than one ALU. Older processors had only a single ALU. Pentiums, and those processors coming after them, have at least two ALUs. With two ALUs, processors can process two instructions at once and, therefore, are true multiprocessing processors.

A second method of improving performance is installing more than one processor on a motherboard, creating a **multiprocessor platform**. A motherboard must be designed to support more than one processor by providing more than one processor socket (see Figure 6-3).

Figure 6-3 This motherboard for a server has two processor sockets, which allow for a multiprocessor platform
Courtesy of Intel Corporation

The latest advancement in multiple processing is **multi-core processing**. Using this technology, the processor housing contains two or more cores that operate at the same frequency, but independently of each other. Each core is a logical processor which contains two ALUs; therefore, each core can process two instructions at once. A CPU using multi-core processing can have two cores (**dual core** supporting four instructions at once), three cores (**triple core** supporting six instructions at once), four cores (**quad core** supporting eight instructions at once), or eight cores (**octo core** supporting sixteen instructions at once). Figure 6-4 shows how quad-core processing can work if the processor uses an L3 cache and an internal memory controller. Each core within a processor has its own independent internal L1 and L2 caches. The L1 cache is on the die and the L2 cache is off the die. In addition, all the cores might share an L3 cache within the processor package.

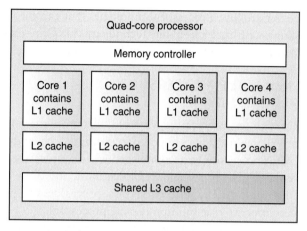

Figure 6-4   Quad-core processing with L1, L2, and L3 cache and the memory controller
within the processor housing
Courtesy: Course Technology/Cengage Learning

MEMORY CACHE AND THE MEMORY CONTROLLER

A memory cache, such as an L1, L2, or L3 cache, is RAM that holds data and instructions that
the memory controller anticipates the processor will need next. Using a cache improves performance because the controller does not have to make as many calls to RAM on the motherboard
to fetch data or instructions (see Figure 6-5). Performance also improves because RAM stored in
memory modules (DIMMs) on the motherboard is dynamic RAM or DRAM (pronounced
"D-Ram") and memory in a memory cache is static RAM or SRAM (pronounced "S-Ram").
Dynamic RAM loses data rapidly and must be refreshed often. SRAM does not need refreshing
and can hold its data as long as power is available. You might be asking why DIMMs are not
made of SRAM so they will work faster, too. The answer is that SRAM is much more expensive

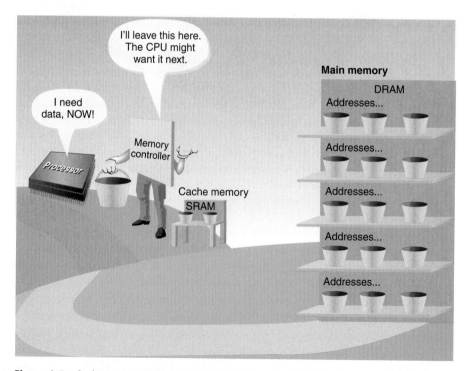

Figure 6-5   Cache memory (SRAM) is used to temporarily hold data in expectation of what
the processor will request next
Courtesy: Course Technology/Cengage Learning

than DRAM. To make DIMMs of SRAM would significantly increase the cost of a system. Therefore, a processor has a small memory cache and the bulk of memory is stored in DIMMs.

Notice in Figure 6-4 that a memory controller is included in the processor package. AMD was the first to put the memory controller inside the package, which it uses with all its current processors. Intel put the memory controller inside the package beginning with the Core i7 processors. Recall that prior to the memory controller being in the processor package, it was part of the North Bridge chipset. Data and instructions were transferred from DIMMs to the North Bridge and then to the processor. Putting the controller inside the processor package resulted in a significant increase in system performance. Incidentally, this trend of putting memory and its controller inside the processor package began several years ago when L2 and L3 caches were moved from the motherboard to the processor package.

> **Notes** When making purchasing decisions about processors, consider that the more L1, L2, and L3 caches the processor contains, generally the better the processor performs.

TECHNOLOGIES THE PROCESSOR CAN USE

Groups of instructions that accomplish fundamental operations, such as comparing or adding two numbers, are permanently built into the processor chip. These instructions are called **microcode** and the groups of instructions are collectively called the instruction set. Intel calls these instruction sets its instruction set architecture (ISA). As Intel or AMD produce processors using a new instruction set, for the system to take advantage of the technology, the operating system, application, and sometimes a hardware device (such as a graphics card or motherboard BIOS) must support it. A processor must support not only the latest instruction sets but all the old ones that an OS, application, or device might use. Here is a list of computing technologies you might expect to see a processor support:

1. **MMX (Multimedia Extensions)** was the first technology to support repetitive looping, whereby the processor receives an instruction and then applies it to a stream of data that follows. Prior to MMX, each data set had to be preceded by an instruction to process it. MMX helps with processing multimedia data, which includes a lot of repetition when managing audio and graphics data.

2. **SSE (Streaming SIMD Extension)** was an improvement over MMX. **SIMD** stands for "single instruction, multiple data." As with MMX, it allows the CPU to receive a single instruction and then execute it on multiple pieces of data. SSE also improves on 3D graphics.

3. **3DNow!** by AMD is a processor instruction set designed to improve performance with 3D graphics and other multimedia data.

4. **SSE2** has a larger instruction set than SSE, and **SSE3** improves on SSE2. **SSE4** increases the instruction set to improve 3D imaging for gaming and improve performance with data mining applications.

5. Recall from earlier in the chapter that Intel Hyper-Threading and AMD HyperTransport allow each processor within a processor package to handle its own individual thread in parallel with other threads being processed at the same time.

6. **PowerNow!** by AMD increases performance and lowers power requirements.

7. **Cool'n'Quiet** by AMD lowers power requirements and helps keep a system quiet.

8. **Enhanced Intel SpeedStep Technology (EIST)** by Intel steps down processor frequency when the processor is idle to conserve power and lower heat.

A+
220-701
1.4

9. **Execute Disable Bit** by Intel is a security feature that prevents software from executing or reproducing itself if it appears to be malicious.

10. Recall from Chapter 2 that a processor can use 32-bit instructions and operating systems or 64-bit instructions and operating systems. All desktop and notebook processors sold today are hybrid processors that can support either 32-bit or 64-bit computing. Recall that Intel calls this technology EM64T (Extended Memory 64 Technology); the processors are also known as x86-64bit processors.

💡 **A+ Exam Tip** The A+ 220-701 Essentials exam expects you to be familiar with the characteristics of processors. Know the purposes and characteristics of Hyper-Threading, dual-core, triple-core, and quad-core processing, overclocking, L1 and L2 caches, and 32-bit versus 64-bit processing.

INTEL PROCESSORS

Intel's current families of processors for the desktop include four major groups: the Core, the Pentium, the Celeron, and the Atom families. The processors in each family are listed in Table 6-1. Some significant retired processors are also listed.

Processor	Clock Speed	Front Side Bus	Description
Core Family			
Core i7 Extreme	3.20 GHz	6.4 GT/s	8 MB cache, quad-core, DDR3 memory, desktop
Core i7	2.66 to 2.93 GHz	4.8 GT/s	8 MB cache, quad-core, DDR3 memory, desktop
Core 2 Extreme	2.53 to 3.2 GHz	800 to 1600 MHz	4 to 12 MB cache, quad-core, dual-core, desktop, or mobile
Core 2 Quad	2.0 to 3.0 GHz	1066 to 1333 MHz	4 to 12 MB cache, quad-core, desktop, or mobile
Core 2 Duo	1.06 to 3.33 MHz	533 to 1333 MHz	2 to 6 MB cache, dual-core, desktop, or mobile
Core Duo	1.5 to 2.33 GHz	533 to 667 MHz	2 MB cache, dual-core, desktop, or mobile
Core 2 Solo	1.06 to 1.2 GHz	533 or 800 MHz	Single-core mobile
Core Solo	1.06 to 1.83 GHz	533 or 667 MHz	Single-core mobile
Pentium Family			
Pentium Extreme	3.20 to 3.73 GHz	800 or 1066 MHz	2 or 4 MB cache, dual-core for gaming
Pentium 4 Extreme	3.20 to 3.46 GHz	800 or 1066 MHz	2 MB cache, high performance
Pentium Dual-Core	1.6 to 2.6 GHz	800 MHz	1 or 2 MB cache, dual-core, mobile, and desktop
Pentium D	2.66 to 3.6 GHz	533 or 800 MHz	2 or 4 MB cache, dual-core, desktop
Pentium M	1.0 to 2.26 GHz	400 or 533 MHz	1 or 2 MB cache, mobile
Pentium	1.6 to 2.7 GHz	533 or 800 MHz	1 MB cache, dual-core, desktop, or mobile

Table 6-1 Current Intel processors

Processor	Clock Speed	Front Side Bus	Description
Pentium 4	2.8 to 3.8 GHz	800 MHz	256 K to 2 MB cache, single-core, desktop, or mobile
Mobile Pentium 4	2.8 to 3.46 GHz	533 MHz	512 K or 1 MB cache, single-core, mobile
Celeron Family			
Celeron	1.6 to 2.2 GHz	667 or 800 MHz	128 KB to 1 MB cache, for basic computing, desktop, and mobile
Celeron D	2.13 to 3.6 GHz	533 MHz	256 KB to 512 KB cache, some only 32-bit processing, desktop
Celeron M	900 MHz to 2.16 GHz	400 to 667 MHz	128 KB to 1 MB cache, some only 32-bit processing, mobile
Atom Family			
Atom	800 MHz to 1.86 GHz	400 or 533 MHz	512 K or 1 MB cache, single-core, low-end desktop, or mobile

Table 6-1 Current Intel processors (continued)

The Intel Core i7 processor is shown in Figure 6-6. You can purchase a processor with or without the cooler. When it's purchased with a cooler, it's called a boxed processor. The cooler is also shown in the photo. If you purchase the cooler separately, make sure it fits the socket you are using.

Figure 6-6 The Intel Core i7 processor (processor number i7-920) with boxed cooler
Courtesy: Course Technology/Cengage Learning

Each processor listed in Table 6-1 represents several processors that vary in performance and functionality. To help identify a processor, Intel uses a processor number. For example, the two Core i7 processors currently sold are identified as i7-940 and i7-920. The Core 2 Quad processors all use a five-character value that begins with "Q." This consistency doesn't work with the other Core, Pentium, or Celeron processors. However, you can count on the processor number along with the processor family name to uniquely identify the processor, making it easier to compare processor benefits and features when making purchasing decisions.

Every Intel processor also has a specification number called an sSpec number printed somewhere on the processor. If you can find and read the number (sometimes difficult), you can use the Intel Processor Spec Finder site (*processorfinder.intel.com*) to identify the exact processor. For example, suppose you read SLAPB on the processor. Figure 6-7 shows the results of searching the Intel site for this processor information. If you're trying to replace a processor with an exact match, using the sSpec number is the way to go.

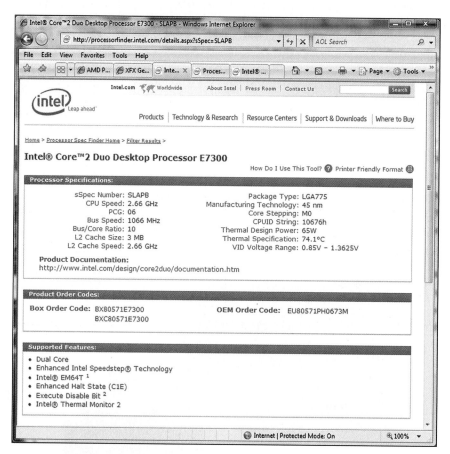

Figure 6-7   Processor Spec Finder using the Intel Web site
Courtesy: Course Technology/Cengage Learning

Some of the Intel mobile processors are packaged in the Centrino processor technology. Using the Centrino technology, the Intel processor, chipset, and wireless network adapter are all interconnected as a unit, which improves laptop performance. Core 2 Quad, Core 2 Duo, Core Solo, Pentium M, Pentium Dual-Core, and Celeron mobile processors have been packaged as a Centrino processor. You also need to be aware of the Intel Atom processor, which is Intel's smallest processor and is used in low-cost PCs, laptops, and netbooks.

AMD PROCESSORS

Processors by Advanced Micro Devices, Inc., or AMD (*www.amd.com*), are popular in the game and hobbyist markets, and are generally less expensive than comparable Intel processors. Recall that AMD processors use different sockets than do Intel processors, so the motherboard must be designed for one manufacturer's processor or the other, but not both. Many motherboard manufacturers offer two comparable motherboards—one for an Intel processor and one for an AMD processor.

The current AMD processor families are the Phenom, Athlon, Sempron, Turion Mobile, Athlon for Notebook, and Sempron for Notebook. Table 6-2 lists the current AMD processors for desktops and laptops. Figure 6-8 shows an Athlon 64 X2 Dual-Core processor.

Processor	Core Speed	Description
Phenom Family		
Phenom II X3	2.6 to 2.8 GHz	7 to 9 MB cache
Phenom II X4	2.5 to 3.0 GHz	5 to 7 MB cache
Phenom X4 Quad-Core	2.1 to 2.6 GHz	8 MB cache
Phenom X3 Triple-Core	1.9 to 2.5 GHz	3 MB cache
Athlon Family		
Athlon 64	1.8 to 2.8 GHz	2 MB cache
Athlon 64 X2 Dual-Core	1.9 to 3.1 GHz	2 MB cache, business computing
Athlon FX	2.2 to 3.0 GHz	1 to 2 MB cache, for extreme gaming
Sempron Family		
Sempron	1.6 to 2.3 GHz	1 MB cache, basic computing
Mobile Processors		
Turion X2 Ultra Dual-Core	2.1 to 2.4 GHz	2 MB cache, for thin and light notebooks
Turion X2 Dual-Core	1.9 to 2.2 GHz	1 MB cache
Athlon 64 X2	1.6 GHz	1 MB cache, for high-performance notebooks
Athlon Neo	1.6 GHz	512 MB cache, for ultra-thin notebooks
Sempron	1.0 or 1.5 GHz	256 MB cache, for basic notebooks

Table 6-2 Current AMD processors

Figure 6-8 The Athlon 64 X2 Dual-Core processor
Courtesy of AMD

We now turn our attention to methods and devices to keep the processor and the entire system cool.

COOLING METHODS AND DEVICES

A+
220-701
1.5

The processor produces heat, and, if it gets overheated, it can become damaged and unstable. If the entire system overheats, other sensitive electronic components can also be damaged. Devices that are used to keep a system cool include CPU fans, case fans, coolers, heat sinks, liquid cooling systems, and dust-preventing tools. Although the focus of this chapter is the processor, in this part of the chapter, we'll consider the methods and devices used to keep not only the processor cool, but the entire system cool.

COOLERS, FANS, AND HEAT SINKS

Because a processor generates so much heat, computer systems use a cooling assembly to keep temperatures below the Intel maximum limit of 185 degrees Fahrenheit/85 degrees Celsius. Good processor coolers maintain a temperature of 90–110 degrees F (32–43 degrees C). The cooler (see Figure 6-9) sits on top of the processor and consists of a fan and a heat sink, which are fins that draw heat away from the processor. The fan can then blow the heat away.

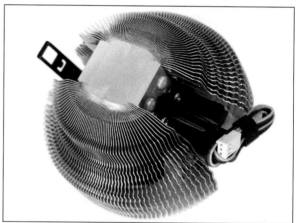

Figure 6-9 A cooler sits on top of a processor to help keep it cool
Courtesy: Course Technology/Cengage Learning

A cooler is made of aluminum, copper, or a combination of both. Copper is more expensive, but does a better job of conducting heat. For example, the Thermaltake (*www.thermaltake.com*) multisocket cooler shown in Figure 6-10 is made of copper and has an adjustable fan control.

The cooler is bracketed to the motherboard using a wire or plastic clip. A creamlike thermal compound is placed between the bottom of the cooler heatsink and the top of the processor. This compound eliminates air pockets, helping to draw heat off the processor. The thermal compound transmits heat better than air and makes an airtight connection between the fan and the processor. When processors and coolers are boxed together, the cooler heatsink might have thermal compound already stuck to the bottom (see Figure 6-11).

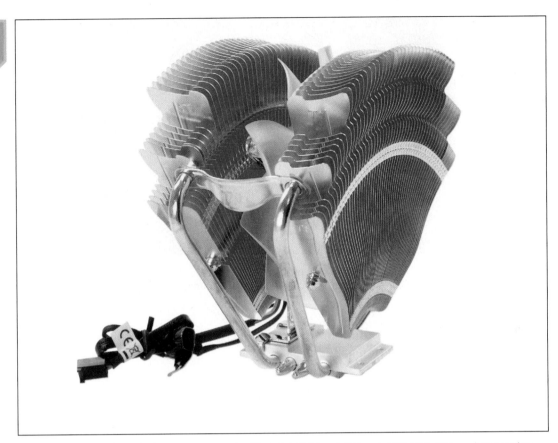

Figure 6-10 The Thermaltake V1 cooper cooler fits Intel 1366 and 775 and AMD AM2, 939, and 754 sockets
Courtesy: Course Technology/Cengage Learning

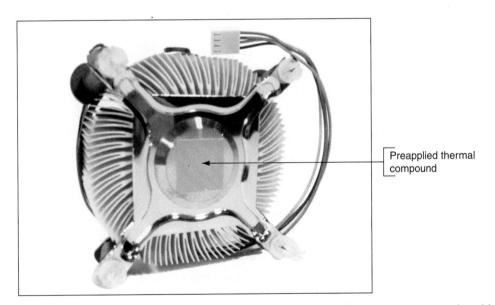

Preapplied thermal compound

Figure 6-11 Thermal compound is already stuck to the bottom of this cooler that was purchased boxed
with the processor
Courtesy: Course Technology/Cengage Learning

To get its power, the fan power cord connects to a 4-pin fan header on the motherboard
(see Figure 6-12). The fan connector will have three or four holes. A three-hole connector
can fit onto a 4-pin header; just ignore the last pin. A 4-pin header on the motherboard
supports pulse width modulation (PWM) that controls fan speed in order to reduce the

A+
220-701
1.5

Figure 6-12   A cooler fan gets its power from a 4-pin PWM header on the motherboard
Courtesy: Course Technology/Cengage Learning

overall noise in a system. If you use a fan power cord with three pins, know that the fan will always operate at the same speed.

CASE FANS AND OTHER FANS AND HEAT SINKS

To prevent overheating, you can also install additional case fans. Most cases have one or more positions on the case to hold a case fan to help draw air out of the case. Figure 6-13 shows holes on the rear of a case designed to hold a case fan.

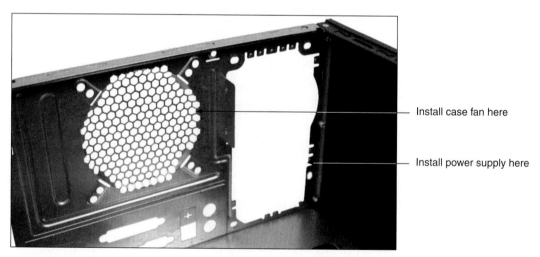

Figure 6-13   Install a case fan on the rear of this case to help keep the system cool
Courtesy: Course Technology/Cengage Learning

High-end systems can have as many as seven or eight fans mounted inside the computer case. Using the BTX form factor, fewer fans are required and the processor might only have a heat sink sitting on top of it. Ball-bearing case fans last longer than other kinds. Also, some fans are larger than others; generally, the larger the fan, the better it performs.

Processors and graphics cards are the two highest heat producers in a system. Some graphics cards come with a fan on the side of the card. You can also purchase heat sinks and fans to mount on a card to keep it cool. Another solution is to use a fan card mounted next to the graphics card. Figure 6-14 shows a PCI fan card. Be sure you select the fan card that fits the expansion slot you plan to use, and make sure there's enough clearance beside the graphics card for the fan card to fit.

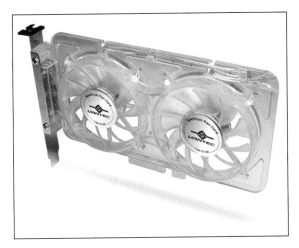

Figure 6-14 A PCI fan card by Vantec can be used next to a high-end graphics card to help keep it cool
Courtesy of Vantec Thermal Technologies

For additional cooling, consider a RAM cooler such as the one in Figure 6-15. It clips over a DDR, DDR2, or DDR3 module. The fan is powered by a 4-pin Molex connector to the power supply.

Figure 6-15 A RAM cooler keeps memory modules cool
Courtesy: Course Technology/Cengage Learning

When selecting any fan or cooler, take into consideration the added noise level and the ease of installation. Some coolers and fans can use a temperature sensor that controls the fan. Also consider the guarantee made by the cooler or fan manufacturer.

LIQUID COOLING SYSTEMS

In addition to using fans and heat sinks to keep a processor cool, there are more exotic options such as refrigeration, peltiers, and water coolers. These solutions are described in the following list. For the most part, they are used by hobbyists attempting to overclock to

A+
220-701
1.5

the max a processor in a gaming computer. These cooling systems might include a PCI card that has a power supply, temperature sensor, and processor to control the cooler.

▲ A peltier is a heat sink carrying an electrical charge that causes it to act as an electrical thermal transfer device. The peltier's top surface can be as hot as 500 degrees F while the bottom surface next to the processor can be as cool as 45 degrees. The major disadvantage of a peltier is that this drastic difference in temperature can cause condensation inside the case when the PC is turned off.

▲ Refrigeration can also be used to cool a processor. These units contain a small refrigerator compressor that sits inside the case and can reduce temperatures to below zero.

▲ The most popular method of cooling overclocked processors is a liquid cooling system. A small pump sits inside the computer case, and tubes move water or other liquid around components and then away from them to a place where fans can cool the liquid.

Some manufacturers of these types of cooling systems are AquaStealth (*www.aquastealth.com*), asetek (*www.vapochill.com*), Thermaltake (*www.thermaltake.com*), and FrozenCPU (*www.frozencpu.com*). Figure 6-16 shows one liquid cooling system where the liquid is cooled by fans sitting inside a large case. Sometimes, however, the liquid is pumped outside the case where it is cooled. Remember, overclocking is not a recommended best practice.

Figure 6-16   A liquid cooling system pumps liquid outside away from components where fans can then cool the liquid
Courtesy of Thermaltake (USA) Inc.

DEALING WITH DUST

Dust is not good for a PC because it insulates PC parts like a blanket, which can cause them to overheat. Dust inside fans can jam fans, and fans not working can cause a system to overheat (see Figure 6-17). Therefore, ridding the PC of dust is an important part of keeping a system cool and should be done as part of a regular preventive maintenance plan, at least twice a year. Some PC technicians don't like to use a vacuum inside a PC because

Figure 6-17   This dust-jammed fan caused a system to overheat
Courtesy: Course Technology/Cengage Learning

Preventive Maintenance

they're concerned that the vacuum might produce ESD. However, inside the PC case, it's safe to use a special antistatic vacuum designed to be used around sensitive equipment (see Figure 6-18). If you don't have one of these vacuums, you can use a can of compressed air to blow the dust out of the chassis, power supply, and fans. The dust will get all over everything; you can then use a regular vacuum to clean up the mess. Or, if you have a small portable compressor or blower, use it to blow air out of a computer case. Whenever you open a computer case, take a few minutes to rid the inside of dust. And while you're cleaning up dust, don't forget to blow or vacuum out the keyboard.

Figure 6-18   An antistatic vacuum designed to work inside sensitive electronic equipment such as computers and printers
Courtesy of Metropolitan Vacuum Cleaner

In the next part of the chapter, you'll learn the detailed steps to select and install a processor in each of the popular Intel and AMD sockets used by a desktop computer.

> **A+ Exam Tip** Content on the A+ 220-701 Essentials exam ends here and content on the A+ 220-702 Practical Application exam begins.

SELECTING AND INSTALLING A PROCESSOR

A+
220-702
1.1
1.2

A PC repair technician is sometimes called on to assemble a PC from parts, exchange a processor that is faulty, add a second processor to a dual-processor system, or upgrade an existing processor to improve performance. In each situation, it is necessary to know how to match a processor for the system in which it is installed. And then you need to know how to install the processor on the motherboard for each of the current Intel and AMD sockets used for desktop and laptop systems. In this part of the chapter, you'll learn about selecting and installing processors in desktops. In Chapter 21, you'll learn about selecting and installing processors in laptops.

SELECT A PROCESSOR TO MATCH SYSTEM NEEDS

When selecting a processor, the first requirement is to select one that the motherboard is designed to support. A motherboard can support several processors. Among the processors the board supports, you need to select the best one that meets the general requirements of the system and the user needs. To get the best performance, use the highest-performing processor the board supports. However, sometimes you need to sacrifice performance for cost. Follow these steps:

1. Read the motherboard documentation to find out what processors the motherboard supports, what socket the motherboard uses, and the frequencies the Front Side Bus can use. For example, suppose you are building a new system and you're buying a motherboard and processor from an online retail site. You have selected the Gigabyte G31M-ES2L motherboard, which is a microATX board that uses socket 775. The ad for the board lists the processors, memory, and bus frequencies the board supports. Be aware, however, that advertisements sometimes make errors. To be certain you have the right information, go to the motherboard manufacturer's Web site. The manufacturer documentation says the board supports dual-core and quad-core processors, including the Intel Core 2 Duo, Core 2 Extreme, Core 2 Quad, Pentium Dual Core, Pentium LGA775, and Celeron Dual Core. It lists the Front Side Bus frequencies as 800 MHz, 1066 MHz, 1333 MHz, and 1600 MHz (when overclocking), and says the board uses DDR2 memory. This is enough information about the board to select the processor.

2. Select a processor by comparing the processors that the board supports. Generally, you're looking for the best features at a price you are willing to pay. When you search the retail sites for each processor, pay attention to these processor characteristics:

   ▲ The socket the processor uses (for example, not all Pentium processors use socket 775)
   ▲ Speed or frequency of the processor (the higher the better)
   ▲ FSB speed (the higher the better so that the FSB runs as high as the motherboard supports without overclocking)
   ▲ The number of cores (quad, triple, dual, single; the more the better)
   ▲ Memory cache (the L2 cache is most likely the one advertised; the more the better)

A+
220-702
1.1
1.2

◢ Computing technologies (for example, SSE2, SSE3, and SSE4)

◢ Power consumption features such as EIST and PowerNow!

◢ 32-bit versus 64-bit (a very few low-end processors don't support this feature; look for it if you plan to use a 64-bit OS)

◢ Price (range can be drastic, such as less than $40 to more than $500)

3. Select the cooler assembly. If your processor doesn't come boxed with a cooler, select a cooler that fits the processor socket and gets good reviews. You'll also need some thermal compound if it is not included with the cooler.

6

A+ 220-702

APPLYING | CONCEPTS

Your friend, Alice, is working toward her A+ certification. She has decided the best way to get the experience she needs to sit for the exam is to build a system from scratch. She has purchased an ASUS motherboard and asked you for some help selecting the right processor. She tells you that the system will later be used for light business needs and she wants to install a processor that is moderate in price to fit her budget. She says she doesn't want to install the most expensive processor the motherboard can support, but neither does she want to sacrifice too much performance or power.

The documentation for the ASUS P5QL Pro motherboard board gives this information:

◢ The board uses socket 775 and DDR2 memory.

◢ The documentation says that it supports Intel Core 2 Extreme, Core 2 Quad, Core 2 Duo, Pentium Dual-Core, Celeron Dual-Core, and Celeron processors.

◢ The front side bus can run at 1333, 1066, or 800 MHz, although it can be overclocked to 1600 MHz.

Based on what Alice has told you, you decide to eliminate the most expensive processors (the Core 2 Extremes) and the least-performing processors (the Celerons). That decision narrows your choices down to the Core 2 Quad, Core 2 Duo, and Pentium Dual-Core. You glance at Table 6-1 shown earlier in the chapter and realize the Pentium Dual-Core only uses a front side bus of 800 MHz. You decide it would not be a good choice for this motherboard, because the motherboard would have to adjust its bus down to its slowest frequency. Running at 800 MHz would slow performance. So you decide to look for a not-too-pricey processor that supports a system bus frequency of 1333 or 1066 MHz. (Since Alice plans to use this system for business needs, you decide overclocking is too risky.) Searching some processor retail Web sites, you discover all the Core 2 Quads are too pricey for Alice's budget. You've now narrowed down the choice to a Core 2 Duo processor.

Searching the retail sites, you are able to find these three choices for Alice, which are listed from highest to lowest price:

◢ Core 2 Duo, processor number E8400, with 6 MB cache, 1333 MHz FSB, 3.0 GHz, boxed with cooler

◢ Core 2 Duo, processor number E6300, with 2 MB cache, 1066 MHz FSB, 1.86 GHz, boxed with cooler

◢ Core 2 Duo, processor number E7400, with 3 MB cache, 1066 MHz FSB, 2.8 GHz, boxed with cooler

The first processor is about $30 higher than the second, which is about $30 higher than the last processor listed. You give the list to Alice for her to decide among the three.

A+
220-702
1.1
1.2

INSTALL A PROCESSOR

Now let's look at the details of installing a processor in an Intel LGA1366, LGA775, 478, and AMD AM2+ socket.

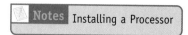

INSTALLING AN INTEL PROCESSOR IN SOCKET 1366

The Intel Core i7 Processor 920 we're installing in Socket 1366 is shown in Figure 6-19. The processor is sitting in its protective cover and the socket also has its cover in place. Because this cooler is so heavy, we need to install it after the motherboard is securely seated in the case.

> **A+ Exam Tip** The A+ 220-702 Practical Application exam expects you to know how to install a processor in current processor sockets.

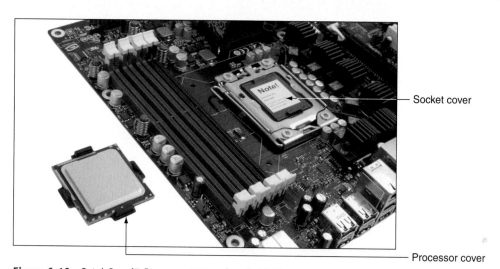

Socket cover

Processor cover

Figure 6-19 Intel Core i7 Processor 920 and socket LGA1366
Courtesy: Course Technology/Cengage Learning

When building a new system, if the motherboard is not already installed in the case, follow the directions of the motherboard manufacturer to install the motherboard and then the processor or to install the processor and then the motherboard. The order of installation varies among manufacturers. When replacing a processor in an existing system, power down the system, unplug the power cord, press the power button to drain the system of power, and open the case. Follow these steps to install the processor and cooler using socket 1366:

1. Read all directions carefully and follow them in order.

2. Use a ground bracelet to protect the processor, motherboard, and other components against ESD.

3. Open the socket by pushing down on the socket lever and gently pushing it away from the socket to lift the lever (see Figure 6-20).

4. Lift the socket load plate, as shown in Figure 6-21.

5. Remove the socket protective cover (see Figure 6-22). Keep this cover in a safe place. If you ever remove the processor, put the cover back in the socket to protect the socket. While the socket is exposed, be *very careful* to not touch the pins in the socket. These socket pins are delicate, so work slowly and take care.

Figure 6-20   Release the lever from the socket
Courtesy: Course Technology/Cengage Learning

Figure 6-21   Lift the socket load plate
Courtesy: Course Technology/Cengage Learning

Figure 6-22   Remove the socket protective cover
Courtesy: Course Technology/Cengage Learning

A+
220-702
1.1
1.2

6. Remove the protective cover from the processor (see Figure 6-23). While the processor contacts are exposed, take extreme care to not touch the bottom of the processor. Hold it only at its edges. Put the processor cover in a safe place and use it to protect the processor if you ever remove the processor from the socket.

Figure 6-23 Remove the protective cover from the processor
Courtesy: Course Technology/Cengage Learning

7. Hold the processor with your index finger and thumb and orient the processor so that the notches on the two edges of the processor line up with the two posts on the socket. You can see the notch and post on the right side of the processor and socket in Figure 6-24. Gently lower the processor straight down into the socket. Don't allow the processor to tilt, slide, or shift as you put it in the socket. To protect the pins, it needs to go straight down into the socket.

Right notch

Right post

Figure 6-24 Orient the processor over the socket so that the notches on each side of the processor match the posts on each side of the socket
Courtesy: Course Technology/Cengage Learning

8. Check carefully to make sure the processor is aligned correctly in the socket. Closing the socket without the pins aligned correctly can destroy the socket. Close the socket load plate (see Figure 6-25).

Figure 6-25 Close the socket load plate
Courtesy: Course Technology/Cengage Learning

9. Push down on the lever and gently return it to its locked position (see Figure 6-26).

Figure 6-26 Return the lever to its locked position
Courtesy: Course Technology/Cengage Learning

You are now ready to install the cooler. Before installing a cooler, read the directions carefully and make sure you understand them. Clips that hold the fan and heat sink to the processor frame or housing are sometimes difficult to install. The instructions might give you important tips. Follow these general steps:

1. The motherboard has four holes to anchor the cooler (see Figure 6-27). Examine the cooler posts that fit over these holes and the clips, screws, or wires that will hold the cooler firmly in place. Make sure you understand how this mechanism works.

2. If the cooler has thermal compound preapplied, remove the plastic from the compound. If the cooler does not have thermal compound applied, put a thin layer of compound on top of the processor or on the bottom of the cooler. Don't use too much—just enough to create a thin layer. If you use too much compound, it can slide off the housing and damage the processor or circuits on the motherboard.

3. Verify the locking pins are turned perpendicular to the heat sink, which is as far as they will go in a counterclockwise direction (see Figure 6-28).

Four holes
to install cooler

Figure 6-27   Four holes in the motherboard to connect the cooler to the board
Courtesy: Course Technology/Cengage Learning

Figure 6-28   Align the locking pins so they are perpendicular to the heat sink
Courtesy: Course Technology/Cengage Learning

4. Align the cooler over the processor so that all four posts fit into the four holes on the motherboard and the fan power cord can reach the fan header on the motherboard (see Figure 6-29).

Figure 6-29   Align the cooler over the four holes in the motherboard
Courtesy: Course Technology/Cengage Learning

5. Push down on each locking pin until you hear it pop into the hole (see Figure 6-30). To help keep the cooler balanced and in position, push down two opposite pins and then push the remaining two pins in place. Using a flathead screwdriver, turn the locking pin clockwise to secure it. (Later, if you need to remove the cooler, turn each locking pin counterclockwise to release it from the hole.)

Figure 6-30 Push down on a locking pin to lock it into position
Courtesy: Course Technology/Cengage Learning

6. Connect the power cord from the cooler fan to the motherboard power connector near the processor, as shown in Figure 6-31.

Figure 6-31 Connect the cooler fan power cord to the motherboard CPU fan header
Courtesy: Course Technology/Cengage Learning

After the processor and cooler are installed, make sure cables and cords don't obstruct airflow, especially airflow around the processor and video card. Use cable ties to tie cords and cables up and out of the way.

Make one last check to verify all power connectors are in place and other cords and cables connected to the motherboard are correctly done. You are now ready to plug back up

A+
220-702
1.1
1.2

the system, turn it on, and verify all is working. If the power comes on (you hear the fan spinning and see lights), but the system fails to work, most likely the processor is not seated solidly in the socket or some power cord has not yet been connected or is not solidly connected. Turn everything off and recheck your installation. If the system comes up and begins the boot process, but suddenly turns off before the boot is complete, most likely the processor is overheating because the cooler is not installed correctly. Turn everything off and verify the cooler is securely seated and connected.

After the system is up and running, you can check BIOS setup to verify that the system recognized the processor correctly. The setup screen for the Core i7 processor is shown in Figure 6-32. Look for items on the screen that manage processor features and make sure each is set correctly. For example, in Figure 6-32, items listed in blue can be changed. Verify the two blue items that apply to the processor; verify that all processor cores are active and Hyper-Threading Technology is enabled.

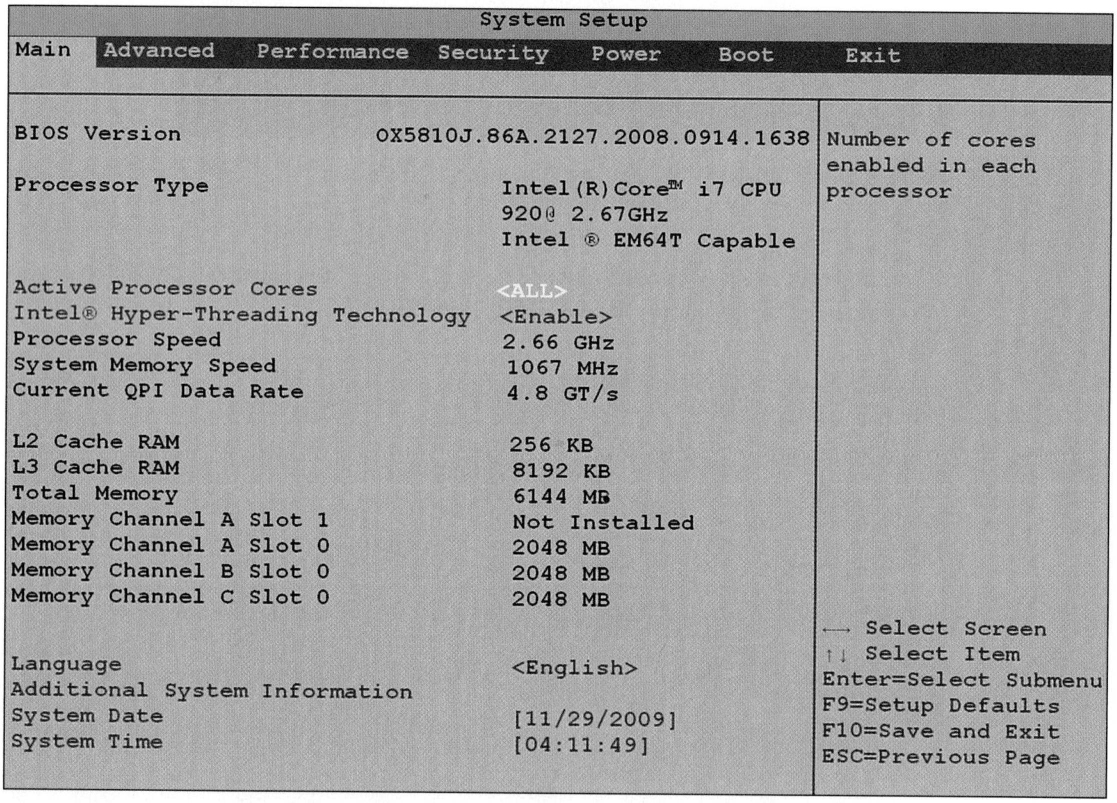

```
                            System Setup
 Main   Advanced   Performance  Security   Power     Boot      Exit


 BIOS Version              OX5810J.86A.2127.2008.0914.1638   Number of cores
                                                             enabled in each
 Processor Type            Intel(R)Core™ i7 CPU              processor
                           920@ 2.67GHz
                           Intel ® EM64T Capable

 Active Processor Cores    <ALL>
 Intel® Hyper-Threading Technology <Enable>
 Processor Speed           2.66 GHz
 System Memory Speed       1067 MHz
 Current QPI Data Rate     4.8 GT/s

 L2 Cache RAM              256 KB
 L3 Cache RAM              8192 KB
 Total Memory              6144 MB
 Memory Channel A Slot 1   Not Installed
 Memory Channel A Slot 0   2048 MB
 Memory Channel B Slot 0   2048 MB
 Memory Channel C Slot 0   2048 MB
                                                     ─→ Select Screen
                                                     ↑↓ Select Item
 Language                  <English>                 Enter=Select Submenu
 Additional System Information                       F9=Setup Defaults
 System Date               [11/29/2009]              F10=Save and Exit
 System Time               [04:11:49]                ESC=Previous Page
```

Figure 6-32 Verify the CPU is recognized correctly by BIOS setup
Courtesy: Course Technology/Cengage Learning

Also check in setup the CPU and motherboard temperatures to verify the CPU is not overheating. For one BIOS setup, this screen is under the Advanced menu, Hardware Monitoring window, as shown in Figure 6-33. Other troubleshooting tips for processors are covered at the end of the chapter.

INSTALLING AN INTEL PROCESSOR IN SOCKET 775

The Pentium 4 we're installing in Socket 775 is shown in Figure 6-34 along with the cooler and motherboard. In the photo, the socket is open and the protective cover removed. The processor is lying upside down in front of the cooler.

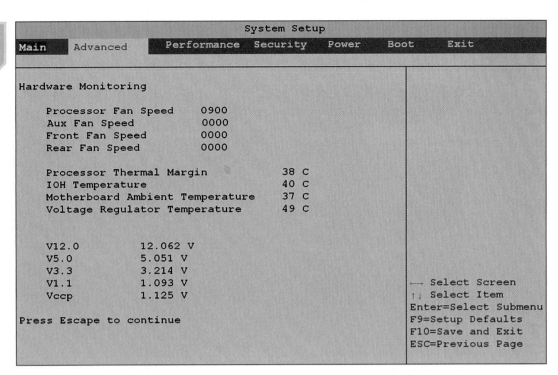

```
                              System Setup
Main    Advanced        Performance  Security   Power    Boot    Exit


Hardware Monitoring

      Processor Fan Speed      0900
      Aux Fan Speed            0000
      Front Fan Speed          0000
      Rear Fan Speed           0000

      Processor Thermal Margin         38 C
      IOH Temperature                  40 C
      Motherboard Ambient Temperature  37 C
      Voltage Regulator Temperature    49 C


      V12.0        12.062 V
      V5.0          5.051 V
      V3.3          3.214 V
      V1.1          1.093 V
      Vccp          1.125 V                      ↔ Select Screen
                                                 ↑↓ Select Item
Press Escape to continue                         Enter=Select Submenu
                                                 F9=Setup Defaults
                                                 F10=Save and Exit
                                                 ESC=Previous Page
```

Figure 6-33   The CPU and motherboard temperature are monitored by BIOS setup
Courtesy: Course Technology/Cengage Learning

Figure 6-34   A Pentium, cooler, and open socket 775
Courtesy: Course Technology/Cengage Learning

The installations of all processors and sockets in this part of the chapter are similar to that of installing a processor in Socket 1366, so we will not repeat many of those steps. Do the following to install a processor and cooler using socket 775:

1. Be careful to use a ground bracelet to protect components against ESD. Read all directions that came with the processor and cooler and make sure you understand everything.

A+
220-702
1.1
1.2

2. Push down on the lever and gently push it away from the socket to lift it. Lift the socket load plate (see Figure 6-35). If a protective cover is in place over the socket, remove it and save it to use later if there is not a processor in the socket.

Figure 6-35 Lift the socket load plate
Courtesy: Course Technology/Cengage Learning

3. Orient the processor so that the notches on the two edges of the processor line up with the two notches on the socket (see Figure 6-36). Gently place the processor in the socket. Socket 775 doesn't have those delicate pins that Socket 1366 has, but you still need to be careful to not touch the top of the socket or the bottom of the processor as you work.

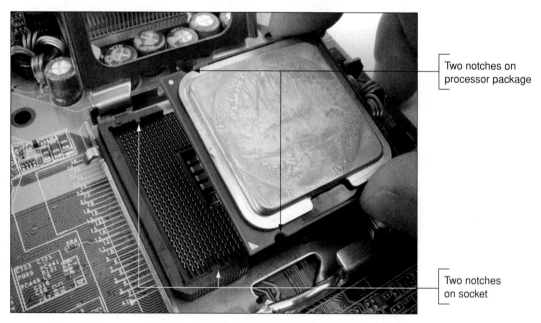

Two notches on processor package

Two notches on socket

Figure 6-36 Place the processor in the socket orienting the notches on two sides
Courtesy: Course Technology/Cengage Learning

4. Close the socket cover. Push down on the lever and gently return it to its locked position (see Figure 6-37).

5. If thermal compound is not already applied to the bottom of the cooler, put thermal compound either on the bottom of the cooler or top of the processor (not both).

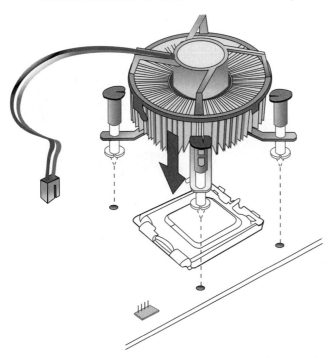

Figure 6-37   Force is applied to the processor when the lever is pushed into position
Courtesy: Course Technology/Cengage Learning

6. Figure 6-38 shows how the cooler is aligned over the processor so that all four spacers fit into the four holes on the motherboard and the fan power cord connects to the power connector on the motherboard. Place the cooler over the four holes and push down on each fastener until you hear it pop into the hole (see Figure 6-39). (Later, if you need to remove the cooler, use a flathead screwdriver to turn each fastener counterclockwise to release it from the hole.)

Figure 6-38   Four spacers on the cooler pop into each hole on the motherboard
Courtesy: Course Technology/Cengage Learning

7. Connect the power cord from the cooler fan to the motherboard 4-pin CPU fan header.

8. Double-check all power connections and make sure the cooler is firmly anchored. Plug in the system, turn it on, and verify all is working.

A+
220-702
1.1
1.2

Four holes for
cooler fasteners

Cooler power
connector

Figure 6-39   The cooler is installed on the motherboard using four holes in the motherboard
Courtesy: Course Technology/Cengage Learning

INSTALLING AN INTEL PROCESSOR IN SOCKET 478

Installing a processor in Socket 478 works about the same way as it does in Socket 775.
Follow these steps:

1. Use the lever to open the socket, open the load plate, carefully install the processor,
   and return the lever to its position. Figure 6-40 shows the processor installed. In the
   figure, notice the frame or retention mechanism used to hold the cooler in place. This

CPU

Frame to hold cooler

Socket 478

Figure 6-40   A Pentium installed in Socket 478
Courtesy: Course Technology/Cengage Learning

frame might come separately from the board or be preinstalled. If necessary, follow the directions that come with the motherboard to install the frame.

2. Put thermal compound on the processor or the bottom of the cooler.

3. Carefully examine the clip assembly that surrounds the fan and heat sink. Line up the clip assembly with the retention mechanism already installed on the motherboard, and press lightly on all four corners to attach it (see Figure 6-41).

Figure 6-41 Carefully push the cooler assembly clips into the retention mechanism on the motherboard until they snap into position
Courtesy: Course Technology/Cengage Learning

4. After the cooling assembly is in place, push down the two clip levers on top of the processor fan (see Figure 6-42). Different coolers use different types of clipping mechanisms, so follow the directions that come with the cooler. Sometimes the clipping mechanism is difficult to clip onto the processor, and the plastic levers and housing are flimsy, so work carefully.

Figure 6-42 The clip levers attach the cooling assembly to the retention mechanism around the processor
Courtesy: Course Technology/Cengage Learning

A+
220-702
1.1
1.2

5. Connect the power cord from the fan to the fan header on the motherboard next to the cooler (see Figure 6-43).

Figure 6-43 Connect the CPU fan power cord to the motherboard fan header
Courtesy: Course Technology/Cengage Learning

INSTALLING AN AMD PROCESSOR IN SOCKET AM2+

Follow these steps to install a processor in the AMD socket AM2 or AM2+:

1. Read all directions that come with the processor and cooler before you begin. Be sure to use a ground bracelet to protect against ESD.

2. Open the lever. If there's a protective cover over the socket, remove it. Be sure to save the cover in case you need it later to protect the socket if it does not have a processor installed.

3. Holding the processor very carefully so you don't touch the bottom, orient the four empty positions on the bottom with the four empty positions in the socket (see Figure 6-44). Carefully lower the processor into the socket. Don't allow it to tilt or

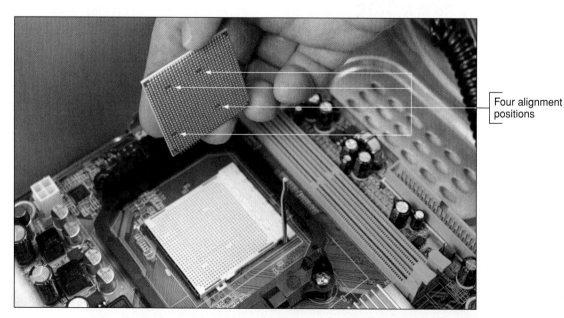

Four alignment positions

Figure 6-44 Orient the four empty positions on the bottom of the processor with those in the socket
Courtesy: Course Technology/Cengage Learning

slide as it goes into the socket. The pins on the bottom of the processor are very delicate, so take care as you work.

4. Check carefully to make sure the pins in the processor are sitting slightly into the holes. Make sure the pins are not offset from the holes. If you try to use the lever to put pressure on these pins and they are not aligned correctly, you can destroy the processor. You can actually feel the pins settle into place when you're lowering the processor into the socket correctly.

5. Press the lever down and gently into position (see Figure 6-45).

6. If thermal compound is not preapplied to the bottom of the cooler, put thermal compound on the processor or the bottom of the cooler. A toothpick works well to do the job (see Figure 6-46).

Figure 6-45 Lower the lever into place, which puts pressure on the processor
Courtesy: Course Technology/Cengage Learning

Figure 6-46 Apply a thin layer of thermal compound
Courtesy: Course Technology/Cengage Learning

7. The cooler in this assembly clips to the side of the black retention mechanism that is already installed on the motherboard (see Figure 6-47). Sit the cooler on top of the processor, aligning it inside the retention mechanism.

A+
220-702
1.1
1.2

Figure 6-47 Align the cooler over the retention mechanism
Courtesy: Course Technology/Cengage Learning

8. Clip into place the clipping mechanism on one side of the cooler. Then push down firmly on the clip on the opposite side of the cooler assembly; the clip will snap into place. Figure 6-48 shows the clip on one side in place for a system that has a yellow retention mechanism and a black cooler clip. Later, if you need to remove the cooler, use a Phillips screwdriver to remove the screws holding the retention mechanism in place. Then remove the retention mechanism along with the entire cooler assembly.

Cooler clip

Retention mechanism

Figure 6-48 The cooler clips onto the retention mechanism mounted to the motherboard
Courtesy: Course Technology/Cengage Learning

9. Connect the power cord from the fan to the 4-pin fan header on the motherboard next to the CPU.

Now let's see how to configure the power management settings in BIOS that apply to the processor.

BIOS POWER MANAGEMENT SETTINGS FOR THE PROCESSOR

After the processor is installed and you have verified other processor settings in BIOS setup, it's a good idea to check power management settings that pertain to the processor. These settings are designed to conserve power consumption for the system. The current set of standards that is used by BIOS, hardware, and the OS to manage power is Advanced Configuration and Power Interface (ACPI). Using this standard, there are four modes, S1 through S4, used to indicate different levels of power-saving functions. They are listed below from the least to the greatest energy-saving level:

- In S1 state, the hard drive and monitor are turned off and everything else runs normally. Some manufacturers call this mode the sleep mode or standby mode.
- In S2 state, the hard drive, monitor, and processor are turned off. This mode is also called standby or sleep mode.
- In S3 state, everything is shut down except RAM and enough of the system to respond to a wake-up call such as pressing the keyboard or moving the mouse. This mode is sometimes called sleep mode, suspend mode, standby mode, or suspend to RAM.
- S4 state is called hibernation. In hibernation, everything in RAM is copied to a file on the hard drive and then the system shuts down. Later, when a power button is pressed, the system does not have to go through the slow boot process, but can quickly read contents of the hibernation file and restore the system to exactly as it was before S4 state was enabled.

ACPI also defines CPU P states, which save power by lowering the CPU frequency and voltage. P0 has the highest frequency and higher P state values have lower frequencies. EIST and PowerNow! implement these P states if the technology is enabled in BIOS setup. The P states can also be controlled by Windows power management if EIST or PowerNow! is enabled in BIOS.

C states, also defined by ACPI, are used by the processor to stop its internal operations to conserve power. In C0 state, a processor can execute an instruction. Using C1 though C6 states, the processor shuts down various internal components (for example, the core clock, buffers, cache, and core voltage) to conserve power. The deeper the C state, the longer it takes for the processor to wake up. Mobile processors usually offer more C states than desktop processors. The feature must be enabled in BIOS.

Some ACPI power-management features can be controlled from Windows and others can be controlled from BIOS. In many situations, Windows and BIOS share the control of a power-management feature, which can often cause conflicts and confusion. The trend is to manage power using Windows. For example, hibernation settings can be controlled from Windows, but hibernation in BIOS must be enabled before it will work. You will learn how to control power from Windows in Chapter 21 for laptops.

To control power using the BIOS, go to BIOS setup and access the Power menu. Figure 6-49 shows the default settings for one processor. Notice in the figure that you can control ACPI S states, Enhanced Intel SpeedStep Technology (P states), and CPU C states, among other power features. For most situations, the default values are correct.

A+
220-702
1.1
1.2

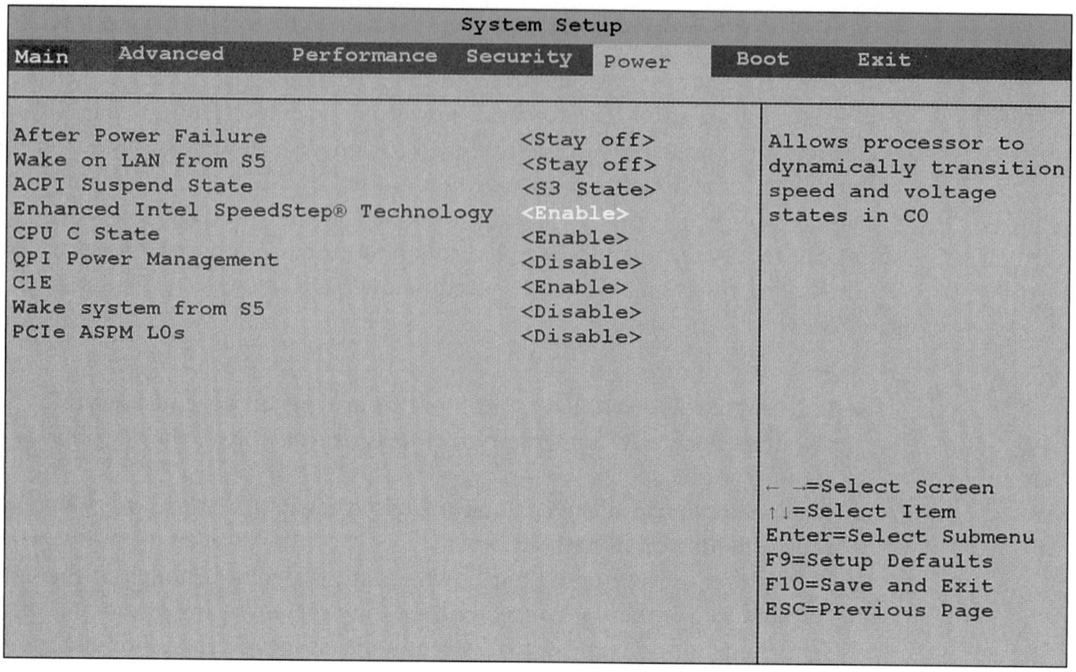

```
                              System Setup
 Main     Advanced     Performance   Security   Power     Boot      Exit

  After Power Failure                   <Stay off>        Allows processor to
  Wake on LAN from S5                   <Stay off>        dynamically transition
  ACPI Suspend State                    <S3 State>        speed and voltage
  Enhanced Intel SpeedStep® Technology  <Enable>          states in C0
  CPU C State                           <Enable>
  QPI Power Management                  <Disable>
  C1E                                   <Enable>
  Wake system from S5                   <Disable>
  PCIe ASPM L0s                         <Disable>




                                                          ←→=Select Screen
                                                          ↑↓=Select Item
                                                          Enter=Select Submenu
                                                          F9=Setup Defaults
                                                          F10=Save and Exit
                                                          ESC=Previous Page
```

Figure 6-49   BIOS settings that control power management
Courtesy: Course Technology/Cengage Learning

TROUBLESHOOTING THE MOTHERBOARD AND PROCESSOR

A+
220-702
1.2

Recall that items that can be exchanged without returning the motherboard to the factory are called field replaceable units (FRUs). On motherboards, FRU components are the processor, the processor cooler assembly, RAM, and the CMOS battery. Also, the motherboard itself is an FRU. As you troubleshoot the motherboard and discover that some component is not working, such as a network port, you might be able to disable that component in BIOS setup and install a card to take its place.

> 💡 **A+ Exam Tip**   The A+ 220-702 Practical Application exam expects you to know how to troubleshoot problems with motherboards and processors.

Remember that you can try substituting good hardware components for those you suspect are bad. Be cautious here. A friend once had a computer that would not boot. He replaced the hard drive, with no change. He replaced the motherboard next. The computer booted up with no problem; he was delighted, until it failed again. Later he discovered that a faulty power supply had damaged his original motherboard. When he traded the bad one for a good one, the new motherboard also got zapped! If you suspect problems with the power supply, check the voltage coming from the power supply before putting in a new motherboard! (Instructions on troubleshooting the power supply are in Chapter 4.)

> ⚡ **Caution**   Before opening the case of a brand name computer, such as a Gateway or Dell, consider the warranty. If the system is still under warranty, sometimes the warranty is voided if the case is opened. If the warranty prevents you from opening the case, you might need to return the system to a manufacturer service center for repairs.

In the following sections, we'll look at descriptions of some common problems and what to do about them when installations of the processor or motherboard fail and when problems with the processor or motherboard occur during normal operations. Overheating can sometimes cause a processor or motherboard to give problems. Therefore, we also discuss how to recognize a problem with overheating and what to do about it. And finally, because BIOS on the motherboard is responsible for booting up a system and finding an OS to load, troubleshooting problems before the OS is loaded is covered.

PROBLEMS WITH INSTALLATIONS

If you have just installed a new processor on a working motherboard and the system does not boot, do the following:

1. When troubleshooting an installation, it's easy to forget to check the simple things first. Are the system and monitor plugged in and turned on? Are the monitor, keyboard, and mouse connected to the system? Is the case front cover securely in place?

2. Is the installed processor one the motherboard supports? To be certain, double-check the processor to the motherboard documentation, making certain the board supports this particular processor. Match the processor to the motherboard, considering all the processor features discussed earlier in the chapter.

3. As you work inside the case, don't forget to use your ground bracelet. Open the case and check these things:

   ◢ Did you install thermal compound between the processor and the heat sink?
   ◢ Is the cooler securely fastened to the frame on the motherboard? If the cooler and thermal compound are not installed correctly, the CPU can overheat during the boot, causing BIOS to immediately power down the system.
   ◢ Is the power cable from the cooler fan connected to the correct fan header on the motherboard? Look in the motherboard documentation for the correct header.
   ◢ Did other components or connectors become dislodged during the installation? Check RAM modules, the P1 power connector, the 4-pin CPU auxiliary power connector, hard drive connectors, and auxiliary PCIe power connectors.

4. Remove the processor from its socket and look for bent or damaged pins or lands on the socket and processor.

5. Consider whether the case does not have enough cooling. Is a case fan installed and running at the rear of the case? Are cables and cords tied up out of the way of airflow?

6. Reinstall the processor and try the boot again.

7. Reinstall the old processor, flash BIOS, and then try the new processor again.

APPLYING | CONCEPTS

Lance is putting together a computer from parts for the first time. He has decided to keep costs low and is installing an AMD processor on a microATX motherboard, using all low-cost parts. He installed the hard drive, CD drive, and power supply in the computer case. Then he installed the motherboard in the case, followed by the processor, cooler, and memory. Before powering up the system, he checked all connections to make sure they were solid and read through the motherboard documentation to make sure he did not forget anything important. Next, he plugs in the monitor to the onboard video port and then plugs in the keyboard and power cord. He takes a deep breath and turns on the power switch on the back of the computer. Immediately, he hears a faint whine, but he's not sure what is

A+
220-702
1.2

making the noise. When he presses the power button on the front of the case, nothing happens. No fans, no lights. Here are the steps Lance takes to troubleshoot the problem:

1. He turns off the power switch and unplugs the power cord. He remembers to put on his ground bracelet and carefully checks all power connections. Everything looks okay.

2. He plugs in the system and presses the power button again. Still all he hears is the faint whine.

3. He presses the power button a second and third time. Suddenly a loud pop followed by smoke comes from the power supply, and the strong smell of electronics fills the room! Lance jumps back in dismay.

4. He removes a known-good power supply from another computer, disconnects the blown power supply, and connects the good one to the computer. When he turns on the power switch, he hears that same faint whine. Quickly he turns off the switch and unplugs the power cord. He does not want to lose another power supply!

5. Next, Lance calls technical support of the company that sold him the computer parts. A very helpful technician listens carefully to the details and tells Lance that the problem sounds like a short in the system. He explains that a power supply might whine if too much power is being drawn. As Lance hangs up the phone, he begins to think that the problem might be with the motherboard installation.

6. He removes the motherboard from the case, and the source of the problem is evident: he forgot to install spacers between the board and the case. The board was sitting directly on the bottom of the case, which had caused the short.

7. Lance installs the spacers and reinstalls the motherboard. Using the good power supply, he turns on the system. The whine is gone, but the system is dead.

8. Lance purchases a new power supply and motherboard, and this time, carefully uses spacers in every hole used by the motherboard screws. Figure 6-50 shows one installed spacer and one ready to be installed. The system comes up without a problem.

Figure 6-50   Spacers installed in case holes keep the motherboard from causing a short
Courtesy: Course Technology/Cengage Learning

In evaluating his experience with his first computer build, Lance declares the project a success. He was grateful he had decided to use low-cost parts for his first build. He learned much from the experience and will never, ever forget to use spacers. He told a friend, "I made a serious mistake, but I learned from it. I feel confident I know how to put a system together now, and I'm ready to tackle another build. When you make mistakes and get past them, your confidence level actually grows because you learn you can face a serious problem and solve it."

If you have just installed a new motherboard that is not working, check the following:

1. Are the system and monitor plugged in and turned on? Are the monitor, keyboard, and mouse connected to the system?

2. Have you installed the front cover on the case? Sometimes a system refuses to power up until this cover is in place.

3. Is there a power switch on the back of the case that is not turned on? Is the voltage switch on the power supply set to the correct value?

4. If the system can boot into Windows, install all motherboard drivers on the CD that came bundled with the board.

5. Open the computer case and check the following:

   ◢ Study the motherboard documentation and verify all connections are correct. Most likely this is the problem. Remember the Power Switch lead from the front of the case must be connected to the header on the motherboard. Check all connectors from the front of the case to the front panel header.
   ◢ Is the BIOS jumper group set for a normal boot?
   ◢ Are cards seated firmly in their slots? Is the screw in place that holds the card to the back of the case?
   ◢ Are DIMMs seated firmly in their slots? Remove the DIMMs and reseat them.
   ◢ Are all I/O cables from the front panel connected to the right connector on the motherboard? Check the USB cable and the audio cable.
   ◢ Verify the processor, thermal compound, and cooler are all installed correctly.
   ◢ Are standoffs or spacers in place? Verify that a standoff that is not being used by the motherboard is not under the motherboard and causing a short.

6. Check the motherboard Web site for other things you can check or try.

PROBLEMS WITH THE MOTHERBOARD OR PROCESSOR

Recall that if a power-on password has been forgotten, you can use the BIOS jumper group to reset the password. How to do that is covered in Chapter 5. See the motherboard documentation for any other jumper groups on the board that might need to be changed.

Also recall that the CMOS battery can fail. This failure can be reported by startup BIOS during the POST or you might notice the problem when CMOS RAM has lost its settings or the system date and time are wrong. If you need to replace the battery, be sure to use a replacement that fits the motherboard. Power down the system, unplug it, and press the power button to drain the system of power. Then pop out the battery using a flathead screwdriver. See the online documentation for the motherboard for more specific directions when exchanging the battery.

Symptoms that a motherboard or processor is failing can appear as:

◢ The system begins to boot but then powers down.
◢ An error message is displayed during the boot. Investigate this message.
◢ The system becomes unstable, hangs, or freezes at odd times. (This symptom can have multiple causes, including a failing power supply, RAM, hard drive, motherboard or processor, Windows errors, and overheating.)
◢ Intermittent Windows or hard drive errors occur. (You will learn how to diagnose Windows errors in Chapters 15 and 16. Hard drive errors are discussed in Chapter 8.)
◢ Components on the motherboard or devices connected to it don't work.

Remember the troubleshooting principle to check the simple things first. The motherboard and processor are expensive and time consuming to replace. Unless you're certain the problem is one of these two components, don't replace either until you first eliminate other components as the source of the problem. If the system is hanging or freezing at odd times, refusing to boot, or components on the motherboard are failing, before you trade out the motherboard or processor, do the following to eliminate other components:

1. The problem could be as simple as a power-saving feature that the user does not know how to use. Is the system in hibernation or sleep mode? Pressing any key usually causes operations to resume exactly where the user left off. Power-saving features are enabled and set in BIOS setup and in Windows. Check and correct any problems with these settings and explain to the user how to use them.

2. Suspect the problem is caused by an application or by Windows. How to troubleshoot application or Windows problems is covered in Chapter 15. The best tool Windows offers to check for potential hardware problems is Event Viewer, which is covered in Chapter 15.

3. Suspect the problem might be as simple as a power cord that needs replacing or that the power cord is not connected properly at each end.

4. Suspect the problem is caused by a failing hard drive. How to troubleshoot a failing drive is covered in Chapter 8.

5. Suspect the problem is caused by overheating. How to confirm the system is overheating and solve the problem are covered later in this chapter.

6. Suspect the problem is caused by a failing RAM module. How to test memory is covered in Chapter 15.

7. Suspect the problem is caused by a failing power supply. It's less expensive and easier to replace than the motherboard or processor, so eliminate it before you move on to the motherboard or processor. How to troubleshoot a failing power supply is covered in Chapter 4.

8. Reduce the system to essentials. Remove any unnecessary hardware, such as expansion cards, and then watch to see if the problem is solved.

If the problem with a hanging system persists, you can now assume the problem is with the processor or motherboard. Try the following:

1. Using a ground bracelet, open the computer case and verify all components and connectors are solid.

2. Check BIOS setup. Look on the Advanced BIOS settings screens. Have settings been tampered with? Is the system bus speed set incorrectly or is it overclocked? Try restoring default settings.

3. Disable any quick booting features in BIOS so that you get a thorough report of POST. Then look for errors reported on the screen during startup.

4. Flash BIOS to update the firmware on the board.

5. Look for physical damage on the motherboard. Look for frayed traces on the bottom of the board or brown or burnt capacitors on the board. (You'll see a photograph of burnt capacitors later in the chapter.)

6. Try using the CD that came with the motherboard, which most likely has diagnostic tests on it that might identify the problem with the motherboard.

7. Update all drivers of board components that are not working. For example, if the USB ports are not working, try updating the USB drivers with those downloaded from the motherboard manufacturer's Web site. This process can also update the chipset drivers.

8. If an onboard component isn't working but the motherboard is stable, go into BIOS setup and disable the component. Then install a replacement component using a port or expansion slot.

9. Search the support section of the Web sites of the motherboard and processor manufacturers for things to do and try. Then do a general search of the Web using a search engine such as *www.google.com*. Search on the error message, symptom, motherboard model, processor model, or other text related to the problem. Most likely, you'll find a forum where someone else has posted the same problem, and others have posted a solution.

10. Verify the installed processor is supported by the motherboard. Perhaps someone has installed the wrong processor.

11. Exchange the processor.

12. Exchange the motherboard, but before you do, measure the voltage output of the power supply or simply replace it, in case it is producing too much power and has damaged the board.

> ⚡ **Caution** Never replace a damaged motherboard with a good one without first testing or replacing the power supply. You don't want to subject another good board to possible damage.

PROBLEMS WITH OVERHEATING

Keeping a system cool is important; if the system overheats, components can be damaged. An overheated system can cause intermittent problems or cause the system to reboot or refuse to boot. In fact, the temperature inside the case should never exceed 100 degrees F (38 degrees C). The processor cooler assembly, heat sinks, and case fans are normally used to keep a system cool. Because fans are mechanical devices, they are more likely to fail than the electronic devices inside the case.

Processors can sense their operating temperatures and report that information to BIOS. You can view that information in BIOS setup. To protect the expensive processor and other components, you can also purchase a temperature sensor. The sensor plugs into a power connection coming from the power supply and mounts on the side of the case or in a drive bay. The sensor sounds an alarm when the inside of the case becomes too hot. To decide which temperature sensor to buy, use one recommended by the case manufacturer.

You can also purchase utility software that monitors and reports the temperature to Windows. If you use one of these products, make sure the software is approved by Intel or AMD for the processor you are using; some products give inaccurate results.

Here are some symptoms that a system is overheating:

- ▲ The system hangs or freezes at odd times or freezes just a few moments after the boot starts.
- ▲ A Windows error occurs during the boot, giving white text on a blue background screen (called a blue screen of death).
- ▲ You cannot hear a fan running or the fan makes a whining sound.
- ▲ You cannot feel air being pulled into or out of the case.

A+
220-702
1.1
1.2

Here are some simple things you can do to solve an overheating problem:

1. If the system refuses to boot or hangs after a period of activity, suspect overheating. Immediately after the system hangs, go into BIOS setup and find the CPU screen that reports the temperature. The temperature should not exceed 38 degrees C.

2. Use compressed air, a blower, or an antistatic vacuum to remove dust from the power supply, the vents over the entire computer, and the processor heat sink. Excessive dust insulates components and causes them to overheat.

3. Check airflow inside the case. Are all fans running? You might need to replace a fan. Is there an empty fan slot on the rear of the case? If so, install a case fan in the slot (see Figure 6-51). Orient the fan so that it blows air out of the case. The power cord to the fan can connect to a fan header on the motherboard or to a power connector coming directly from the power supply.

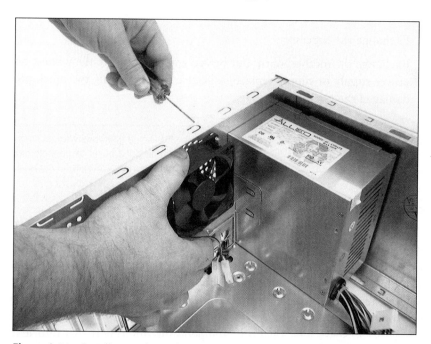

Figure 6-51   Install one exhaust fan on the rear of the case to help pull air through the case
Courtesy: Course Technology/Cengage Learning

4. If there are other fan slots on the side or front of the case, you can also install fans in these slots. However, don't install more fans than the case is designed to use.

5. Can the side of the case hold a chassis air guide that guides outside air to the processor? If it has a slot for the guide and the guide is missing, install one. However, don't install a guide that obstructs the CPU cooler. How to install an air guide is covered later in this section.

6. A case is generally designed for optimal airflow when slot openings on the front and rear of the case are covered and when the case cover is securely in place. To improve airflow, replace missing faceplates over empty drive bays and replace missing slot covers over empty expansion slots.

7. Are cables in the way of airflow? Use tie wraps to secure cables and cords so that they don't block airflow across the processor.

8. A case needs some room to breathe. Place it so there are at least a few inches of space on both sides and top of the case. If the case is sitting on carpet, put it on a

computer stand so that air can circulate under the case and also to reduce carpet dust inside the case. Many cases have a vent on the bottom front of the case and carpet can obstruct airflow into this vent (see Figure 6-52). Make sure drapes are not hanging too close to fan openings.

Figure 6-52 Keep a tower case off carpet to allow air to flow into the bottom air vent
Courtesy: Course Technology/Cengage Learning

9. Verify the cooler is connected properly to the processor. If it doesn't fit well, the system might not boot and certainly the processor will overheat. Has thermal compound been installed between the cooler and processor?

10. After you close the case, leave your system off for a few hours. When you power up the computer again, let it run for 10 minutes, go into BIOS setup, check the temperature readings, and reboot. Next, let your system run until it shuts down. Power it up again and check the temperature in setup again. A significant difference in this reading and the first one you took after running the computer for 10 minutes indicates an overheating problem.

11. Check BIOS setup to see if the processor is being overclocked. Overclocking can cause a system to overheat. Try restoring the processor and system bus frequencies to default values.

12. Have too many peripherals been installed inside the case? Is the case too small for all these peripherals? Larger tower cases are better designed for good airflow than smaller slimline cases. Also, when installing cards, try to leave an empty slot between each card for better airflow. The same goes for drives. Try not to install a group of drives in adjacent drive bays. For better airflow, leave empty bays between drives.

13. Flash BIOS to update the firmware on the board.

14. Thermal compound should last for years, but eventually it will harden and need replacing. If the system is several years old, replace the thermal compound.

> 💡 **A+ Exam Tip** The A+ 220-702 Practical Application exam expects you to recognize that a given symptom is possibly power or heat related.

If you try the above list of things to do and still have an overheating problem, it's time to move on to more drastic solutions. Consider the case design is not appropriate for good airflow,

A+
220-702
1.1
1.2

and the problem might be caused by poor air circulation inside the case. The power supply fan in ATX cases blows air out of the case, pulling outside air from the vents in the front of the case across the processor to help keep it cool. Another exhaust fan is usually installed on the back of the case to help the power supply fan pull air through the case. In addition, most processors require a cooler with a fan installed on top of the processor. Figure 6-53 shows a good arrangement of vents and fans for proper airflow and a poor arrangement.

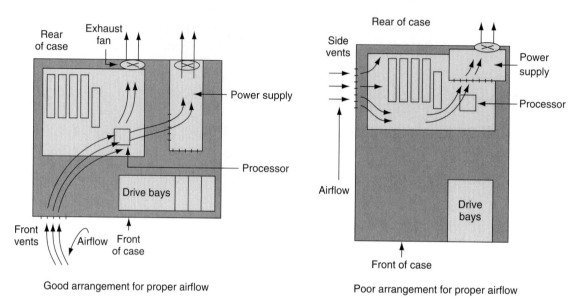

Good arrangement for proper airflow   Poor arrangement for proper airflow

Figure 6-53   Vents and fans need to be arranged for best airflow
Courtesy: Course Technology/Cengage Learning

For better ventilation, use a power supply that has vents on the bottom and front of the power supply. Note in Figure 6-54 airflow is coming into the bottom of the power supply because of these bottom vents. The power supply in Figure 6-51 has vents only on the front and not on the bottom. Compare that to the power supply in Figure 6-54, which has vents on both the front and bottom.

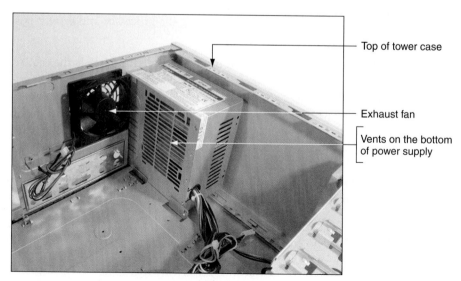

Figure 6-54   This power supply has vents on the bottom to provide better airflow inside the case
Courtesy: Course Technology/Cengage Learning

An intake fan on the front of the case might help pull air into the case. Intel recommends you use a front intake fan for high-end systems, but AMD says a front fan for ATX systems is not necessary. Check with the processor and case manufacturers for specific instructions as to the placement of fans and what type of fan and heat sink to use.

Intel and AMD both recommend a chassis air guide (CAG) as part of the case design. This air guide is a round air duct that helps to pull and direct fresh air from outside the case to the cooler and processor (see Figure 6-55). The guide should reach inside the case very close to the cooler, but not touch it. Intel recommends the clearance be no greater than 20 mm and no less than 12 mm. If the guide obstructs the cooler, you can remove the guide, but optimum airflow will not be achieved.

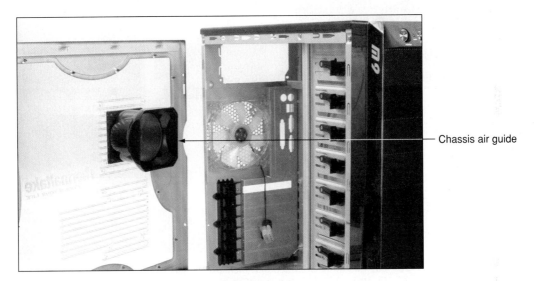

Chassis air guide

Figure 6-55 Use a chassis air guide to direct outside air over the cooler
Courtesy: Course Technology/Cengage Learning

Be careful when trying to solve an overheating problem. Excessive heat can damage the CPU and the motherboard. Never operate a system if the case fan, power-supply fan, or cooler fan is not working.

BOOT PROBLEMS BEFORE THE OPERATING SYSTEM LOADS

It's been a long day. You've worked late, and now you sit down in front of your home PC to have a little relaxing fun surfing the Web, chatting with friends in foreign places, and updating your blog. You turn on your PC, and this big problem smacks you in the face. You just want to cry. Been there? I have.

What do you do first? The first thing to remember is don't panic. Most PC problems are simple and can be simply solved, but you do need a game plan. That's what Figure 6-56 gives you. As we work our way through it, you're eliminating one major computer subsystem after another until you zero in on the problem. After you've discovered the problem, many times the solution is obvious.

Does the PC boot properly? If not, then ask, "Is the screen blank?" If it is blank and you cannot hear any spinning fans or drives and see no lights, then assume the problem has to do with the electrical system and begin troubleshooting there. Troubleshooting the electrical system is covered in Chapter 4. If the screen is blank and you heard a

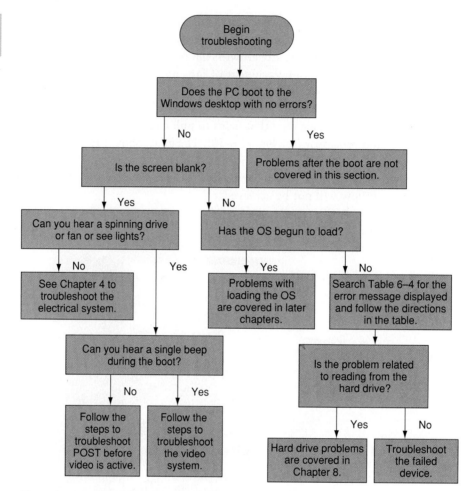

Figure 6-56   Use this flowchart when first facing a computer problem
Courtesy: Course Technology/Cengage Learning

single beep, then the BIOS has signaled that POST completed successfully. At this point, you can assume the problem must be with the video system, and you need to begin troubleshooting video. If you see an error message on-screen, but Windows has not started to load, then use the error message to help you identify the problem. We're now going to discuss troubleshooting POST before video is active, troubleshooting problems with video that prevent BIOS messages from displaying, and troubleshooting error messages during the boot before the OS loads.

TROUBLESHOOTING POST BEFORE VIDEO IS ACTIVE

Error messages on the screen indicate that video and the electrical system are working. If you observe that power is getting to the system (you see lights and hear fans or beeps) but the screen is blank, turn off the system and turn it back on and carefully listen to any beep codes or speech messages. Recall that, before BIOS checks video, POST reports any error messages as beep codes. When a PC boots, one beep indicates that all is well after POST. If you hear more than one beep, look up the beep code in the motherboard or BIOS documentation or on the Web sites of these manufacturers. Each BIOS manufacturer has its own beep codes, and Table 6-3 lists the more common meanings.

Beeps During POST	Description
One beep followed by three, four, or five beeps	Motherboard problems, possibly with DMA, BIOS setup chip, timer, or system bus. Most likely the motherboard will need replacing.
Two beeps	The POST numeric code is displayed on the monitor. See the list of numeric codes later in this section.
Two beeps followed by three, four, or five beeps	First 64 K of RAM has errors. The solution is to replace RAM, which is covered in Chapter 7.
Three beeps followed by three, four, or five beeps	Keyboard controller failed or video controller failed. Most likely these are embedded components on the motherboard.
Four beeps followed by two, three, or four beeps	Problem with serial or parallel ports or system timer, which probably means the motherboard must be replaced.
Continuous beeps	Problem with power supply. The power supply might need replacing; see Chapter 4. Sometimes a continuous beep can also mean something is holding down a key on the keyboard.
Siren sound	The processor has overheated.

Table 6-3 Beep Codes and Their Meanings

Here is a list of the Web sites for the most common BIOS manufacturers:

▲ American Megatrends, Inc. (AMI) BIOS: *www.ami.com*
▲ Award BIOS and Phoenix BIOS: *www.phoenix.com*
▲ Compaq or HP: *www.hp.com*
▲ Dell: *www.dell.com*
▲ IBM: *www.ibm.com/support*
▲ Gateway: *www.gateway.com*

Figure 6-57 shows the Web site for AMI with explanations of beep codes produced by its startup BIOS.

If no beeps are heard, even after you reboot a couple of times, do the following:

1. Suspect the electrical system or power supply is failing. Check Chapter 4 for things to do and try.

2. Suspect overheating. How to diagnose and solve this problem is covered earlier in the chapter.

3. Do you hear excessive noise such as a whining sound? Suspect a fan or hard drive is failing.

4. Do you smell an unusual odor? Suspect an electronic component is failing. Turn off and unplug the system. Don't turn it back on until you have identified and replaced the bad component.

5. Look for visible damage to cables, connectors, and other components. Check for melted plastic inside the case.

6. If the fan is running, you can assume power is getting to the system. Reseat RAM. Try installing a DIMM in a different slot. A POST code diagnostic card is a great help at this point. These cards are discussed in Chapter 4.

A+
220-702
2.4

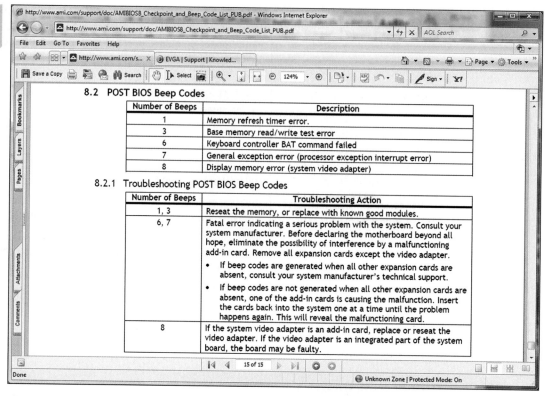

Figure 6-57 The BIOS manufacturer's Web site is a good source of information about beep codes
Courtesy: Course Technology/Cengage Learning

7. Sometimes a dead computer can be fixed by simply disassembling it and reseating cables, adapter cards, and DIMMs. Bad connections and corrosion are common problems.

8. Check the BIOS jumpers and BIOS settings. Have they been tampered with? Try restoring all settings to default values.

9. Look for physical damage on the motherboard. Look for frayed traces on the bottom of the board or brown or burnt capacitors on the board.

10. A dead or dying battery may cause problems. Sometimes, after a computer sits with no power connected for several weeks or months, a weak battery causes CMOS to forget its configuration.

11. Reduce the system to essentials. Remove any unnecessary hardware, such as expansion cards, and then try to boot again.

12. Exchange the processor.

13. Exchange the motherboard, but before you do, measure the voltage output of the power supply or simply replace it, in case it is producing too much power and has damaged the board.

TROUBLESHOOTING VIDEO

If you hear one beep during the boot and you see a blank screen, then BIOS has successfully completed POST, which includes a test of the video card. You can then assume the problem must be with the monitor or the monitor cable. Ask these questions and try these things:

1. Is the monitor electrical cable plugged in?

2. Is the monitor turned on? Try pushing the power button on the front of the monitor. It should turn yellow or green, indicating the monitor has power.

3. Is the monitor cable plugged into the video port at the back of the PC and the connector on the rear of the monitor?

4. Try a different monitor and a different monitor cable that you know are working.

More things to do and try concerning the video system are covered in Chapter 9.

TROUBLESHOOTING ERROR MESSAGES DURING THE BOOT

If video and the electrical systems are working, then most boot problems show up as an error message displayed on-screen. These error messages can have several sources:

- After video is active, a hardware device such as the keyboard, hard drive, or CD drive failed POST.
- After POST, when startup BIOS turned to the hard drive to find an OS, it could not read from the drive. Recall that it must be able to read the Master Boot Record containing the master boot program and partition table, the OS boot record, and the first OS boot program (BootMgr or Ntldr).
- After BootMgr or Ntldr is in control, it could not find the OS files it uses to load the OS.

Now let's look at some possible error messages listed in Table 6-4, along with their meanings. For other error messages, look in your motherboard or computer documentation or use a good search engine to search for the error message on the Internet.

If a specific component is giving an error message, update its drivers. If the component is embedded on the motherboard, download updated drivers from the motherboard manufacturer's Web site. If this update doesn't work, you can disable the onboard component in BIOS setup and install a replacement component using a port or by installing a card in an expansion slot.

If you're not sure which component is giving the problem, try using the CD that came with the motherboard. It might have diagnostic tests on it that might identify the problem with the motherboard. Also, a POST diagnostic card might give you a clue as to which component is giving a problem.

Notice in Table 6-4 that several problems pertain to BIOS not being able to read from the hard drive, and the suggested next step is to try booting from another media, which can be either a CD or DVD.

Each OS provides one or more methods and media to use if booting from the hard drive fails. Windows Vista uses a DVD or set of CDs for this purpose, and Windows XP uses a setup CD. In Chapters 15 and 16, you'll learn to use these CDs and DVDs for each OS.

Error Message	Meaning of the Error Message
PROCESSOR_THERMAL_TRIP_ERROR	The processor overheated and the system has restarted.
MULTI_BIT_ECC_ERROR SINGLE_BIT_ECC_ERROR	Memory failure; replace RAM.
CMOS_BATTERY_ERROR	The CMOS battery most likely needs replacing.
CMOS_CHECKSUM_ERROR	CMOS RAM has given an error. Try flashing BIOS.
MEMORY_SIZE_DECREASE_ERROR	A RAM module is not working; replace RAM.
INTRUDER_DETECTION_ERROR	An intrusion detection device installed on the motherboard has detected that the computer case was opened.
MEM_OPTIMAL_ERROR	The installed memory in each slot does not match for optimal performance. Chapter 7 explains how to correct the problem.
OVERCLOCKING FAILED. PLEASE ENTER SETUP TO RE-CONFIGURE YOUR SYSTEM.	Overclocking should be discontinued. However, this error might not be related to overclocking; it can occur when the power supply is failing.
Hard drive not found Fixed disk error	The BIOS cannot locate the hard drive. How to solve hard drive problems is covered in Chapter 8.
Invalid drive specification Inaccessible boot drive	The BIOS is unable to find a hard drive. Look for errors in BIOS setup.
No boot device available Invalid boot disk	The hard drive is not formatted, or the format is corrupted, and there is no CD in the CD drive. Examine the hard drive for errors, which you will learn to do in Chapter 8.
Missing NTLDR Missing BOOTMGR	The boot loading program for the OS could not be found. Examine the hard drive for errors. How to do that is covered in Chapters 15 and 16.
Missing operating system, error loading operating system	The MBR is unable to locate or read the OS boot sector on the active partition. Boot from an OS setup CD or DVD and examine the hard drive file system for corruption.
Device or service has failed to start An error message about a reference to a device or service in the registry	These errors occur late in the boot when the OS is loading services and device drivers. How to handle these errors is covered in Chapters 15 and 16.
Device or program in registry not found	Windows might be corrupted or a device driver might be missing or corrupted. See Chapters 15 and 16 for solutions.
While Windows Vista/XP is loading, an unknown error message on a blue background is displayed and the system halts	These errors are called stop errors or blue screen errors and are usually caused by viruses, errors in the file system, a corrupted hard drive, a corrupted system file, or a hardware problem. How to handle blue screen errors is covered in Chapters 15 and 16.

Table 6-4 Error Messages and Their Meanings

A+
220-702
2.4

APPLYING | CONCEPTS   Jessica complained to Wally, her PC support technician, that Windows was occasionally giving errors, data would get corrupted, or an application would not work as it should. At first, Wally suspected Jessica might need a little more training in how to open and close an application or save a file, but he discovered user error was not the problem. He tried reinstalling the application software Jessica most often used, and even reinstalled Windows, but the problems persisted.

> **Notes** Catastrophic errors (errors that cause the system to not boot or a device to not work) are much easier to resolve than intermittent errors (errors that come and go).

Then he began to suspect a hardware problem. Carefully examining the motherboard revealed the source of the problem: failing capacitors. Look carefully at Figure 6-58 and you can see five bad capacitors with bulging and discolored heads. (Know that sometimes a leaking capacitor can also show crusty corrosion at the base of the capacitor.) When Wally replaced the motherboard, the problems went away.

Bad capacitors

Figure 6-58 These five bad capacitors have bulging and discolored heads
Courtesy: Course Technology/Cengage Learning

>> CHAPTER SUMMARY

▲ The most important component on the motherboard is the processor, or central processing unit. The two major manufacturers of processors are Intel and AMD.

▲ Processors are rated by the speed of the system bus the processor can support, the processor's core speed, the socket and chipset the processor can use, multi-core rating, how much internal memory cache the processor has, and the computing technologies the processor can use.

◢ A processor's memory cache inside the processor housing can be an L1 cache (contained on the processor die), L2 cache (off the die), and L3 cache (farther from the core than L2 cache).

◢ The processor multiplier is the value the system bus speed is multiplied by to get the processor speed.

◢ Overclocking is running a system bus or processor at a faster frequency than the component is designed to support.

◢ The core of a processor has two arithmetic logic units (ALUs). Multi-core processors have two, three, or four cores (called dual core, triple core, and quad core). Each core can process two threads at once.

◢ A memory cache is made of static RAM chips. RAM stored on DIMMs installed on the motherboard is made of dynamic RAM. SRAM is faster than DRAM and is more expensive.

◢ A multi-core processor can have L1, L2, and L3 caches. The L3 cache is shared by all cores.

◢ The memory controller can be part of the North Bridge of the chipset or installed inside the processor package.

◢ Computing technologies a processor can use include MMX, SSE, SSE2, SSE3, SSE4, and 32-bit and 64-bit processing.

◢ The technology that allows a processor to handle multiple threads in parallel is called Hyper-Threading by Intel and HyperTransport by AMD.

◢ The current families of Intel processors for desktops and laptops are the Core, the Pentium, and the Celeron families. Several different processors are within each family.

◢ The current families of AMD processors for desktops and laptops are the Phenom, Athlon, Sempron, Turion Mobile, Athlon for Notebook, and Sempron for Notebook families. Several processors exist within each family.

◢ Devices that are used to keep a system cool include CPU fans, case fans, coolers, heat sinks, liquid cooling systems, and dust-preventing tools.

◢ A creamlike thermal compound is placed between the cooler and the processor to eliminate air pockets and to draw heat off the processor.

◢ A 4-pin CPU fan header on the motherboard supports pulse width modulation (PWM) that controls fan speed in order to reduce the overall noise in a system.

◢ Case fans help to draw air into and out of the case.

◢ Liquid cooling systems are sometimes used by hobbyists when overclocking a system.

◢ Dust can insulate components in the case and cause them to overheat. Use cans of compressed air, an antistatic vacuum, or blower to remove dust.

◢ When installing a processor, install the motherboard in the case first and then install the processor and cooler assembly.

▲ The symptom of the system becoming unstable, hanging, or freezing at odd times can have multiple causes, including a failing power supply, RAM, hard drive, motherboard or processor, Windows errors, and overheating.

▲ When troubleshooting, eliminate the simple and less expensive fixes first before you exchange a motherboard or processor.

▲ An overheating problem can be solved by replacing a faulty fan, adding a new fan, solving problems that obstruct airflow, replacing old thermal compound, reducing the number of components, or using a larger, better-designed case.

▲ Don't allow a system to run if all the fans are not working. Replace any faulty fans.

>> KEY TERMS

For explanations of key terms, see the Glossary near the end of the book.

3DNow!	heat sink	processor frequency
Advanced Configuration and Power Interface (ACPI)	Hyper-Threading	quad core
	HyperTransport	S1 state
back-side bus (BSB)	internal bus	S2 state
blue screen errors	Level 1 cache (L1 cache)	S3 state
C states	Level 2 cache (L2 cache)	S4 state
case fan	Level 3 cache (L3 cache)	SIMD
Centrino	liquid cooling system	SRAM
chassis air guide (CAG)	memory cache	SSE (Streaming SIMD Extension)
Cool'n'Quiet	microcode	SSE2
cooler	MMX (Multimedia Extensions)	SSE3
DRAM	multi-core processing	SSE4
dual core	multiplier	static RAM
dynamic RAM	multiprocessor platform	stop errors
Enhanced Intel SpeedStep Technology (EIST)	octo core	thermal compound
	overclocking	triple core
Execute Disable Bit	P states	
front-side bus (FSB)	PowerNow!	

>> REVIEWING THE BASICS

1. Who are the two major manufacturers of processors?

2. What are the four system bus frequencies used by current Intel processors?

3. What three sockets are currently used for Intel processors in motherboards for desktop systems?

4. What is the name of the memory cache that is on the same die as the processor?

5. What is the name of the memory cache that is closest to the processor die but is not housed on the die?

6. What is the name of the Intel technology that allows a processor to handle multiple threads at the same time?

7. How many threads can a quad-core processor handle at once?

8. What is the name of the memory cache that is shared by cores in a multi-core processor?

9. Which is faster, SRAM or DRAM? Why?

10. Which is the first computing technology used by a processor to support repetitive looping whereby a processor receives an instruction and then applies it to a stream of data that follows?

11. Which computing technology (SSE1, SSE2, SSE3, or SSE4) better supports data-mining applications?

12. Which Intel processor family is better performing, the Pentium family or the Core family?

13. Which AMD processor (Turion or Phenom) is designed for laptops?

14. What are the two major components of a processor cooler assembly?

15. How many pins does the CPU fan header on a motherboard have?

16. If the power connector from the CPU fan has only three pins, it can still connect to the 4-pin header, but what functionality is lost?

17. What is the major disadvantage of using a peltier heat sink?

18. Name three tools that can be used to rid the inside of the case from dust.

19. Why is it important to insert a processor straight down into a socket rather than sliding the processor in from the side or allowing it to tilt into the socket?

20. List three possible causes of a system hanging or freezing at odd times.

>> THINKING CRITICALLY

1. When overclocking a system, what two problems are most likely to occur?

   a. "Low memory" errors

   b. An unstable system that causes intermittent errors

   c. Loss of hard drive space used by the overclocking virtual memory file

   d. Overheating

2. When a new computing technology is invented by Intel or AMD, why must their processors still support the older and less efficient technologies?

3. You upgrade a faulty PCIe video card to a recently released higher-performing card. Now users complain to you that Windows Vista hangs a lot and gives errors. Which is the most likely source of the problem? Which is the least likely source?

   a. Overheating

   b. Windows does not support the new card.

   c. The drivers for the card need updating.

   d. Memory is faulty.

>> HANDS-ON PROJECTS

PROJECT 6-1:   Recognizing Processors

Using your home or lab computer, open the computer case and examine the processor and cooler assembly. Answer these questions:

1. What motherboard is installed?

2. What processor is installed?

3. What socket is the processor using?

4. Describe the cooler assembly. Does it contain a heat sink and fan?

PROJECT 6-2:   Researching a Processor Upgrade or Replacement

Assume the processor in Project 6-1 has gone bad. Do the following to find the best replacement for this processor:

1. Using the documentation for the motherboard, list the processors the board supports. (If you don't have the motherboard manual, use the motherboard documentation on the manufacturer's Web site.)

2. Find and print three Web pages showing the details and prices of the highest-performing, moderately performing, and lowest-performing processors the board supports.

3. Which processor would you recommend for this system? Explain your recommendation.

Now assume the Core i7 920 processor that you saw installed in the chapter has gone bad. The motherboard in which it is installed is the Intel DX58SO desktop board. The owner of the motherboard has requested that you keep the replacement cost as low as possible. What processor would you recommend for the replacement? Print a Web page showing the processor and its cost.

PROJECT 6-3:   Understanding Processor Configuration

Using your home or lab computer, use BIOS setup and Windows to answer these questions:

1. What is the processor frequency? How did you find your answer?

2. In BIOS setup, list the settings that apply to the processor and the current configuration of each setting.

PROJECT 6-4:   Understanding Dual-Processor Motherboards

Print the Web page of a picture of a motherboard that supports dual processors. Use one of these Web sites to find the picture:

▲ ASUS at *www.asus.com*

▲ Intel at *www.intel.com*

▲ Abit at *www.abit.com.tw*

Answer these questions about the motherboard:

1. What is the manufacturer and model number of the motherboard?

2. What is the frequency of the motherboard FSB?

3. What operating systems does the board support?

4. What processors does the board support?

PROJECT 6-5: Inserting and Removing a Processor

In this project, you remove and install a processor. As you work, be very careful to not bend pins on the processor or socket and protect the processor and motherboard against ESD. Do the following:

1. Verify the computer is working. Turn off the system, unplug it, press the power button, and open the computer case. Put on your ground bracelet. Remove the cooler assembly and processor.

2. You are now ready to reinstall the processor and cooler. But first have your instructor check the thermal compound. You might need to install a small amount of compound to account for compound lost when you removed the cooler.

3. Reinstall the processor and cooler. Power up the system and verify all is working.

PROJECT 6-6: Using the Internet for Research

Search the Web sites of Intel and AMD (*www.intel.com* and *www.amd.com*), and print information on the following:

◢ The most recent processor for a desktop offered by each company

◢ The most recent processor for a laptop offered by each company

>> REAL PROBLEMS, REAL SOLUTIONS

REAL PROBLEM 6-1: Troubleshooting a Hung System

A user complains to you that her system hangs for no known reason. After asking her a few questions, you identify these symptoms:

1. The system hangs after about 15–20 minutes of operation.

2. When the system hangs, it doesn't matter what application is open or how many applications are open.

3. When the system hangs, it appears as though power is turned off: there are no lights, spinning drives, or other evidence of power.

You suspect overheating might be the problem. To test your theory, you decide to do the following:

1. You want to verify that the user has not overclocked the system. How do you do that?

2. You decide to check for overheating by examining the temperature of the system immediately after the system is powered up and then again immediately after the system hangs. Describe the steps you take to do this.

3. After doing the first two steps, you decide overheating is the cause of the problem. What are four things you can do to fix the problem?

6

Upgrading Memory

In earlier chapters, we talked about several important hardware components, how they work, and how to support them. In this chapter, we look at another component, memory, and examine the different memory technologies and how to upgrade memory. Memory technologies have evolved over the years. When you support an assortment of desktop and notebook computers, you'll be amazed at all the different variations of memory modules used in newer computers and older computers still in use. A simple problem of replacing a bad memory module can become a complex research project if you don't have a good grasp of current and past memory technologies.

The first part of the chapter is devoted to studying all these technologies. Then we look at how to upgrade memory. Adding more memory to a system can sometimes greatly improve performance. Finally, you'll learn how to deal with problems with memory. In later chapters, you'll learn how to manage memory using Windows Vista and Windows XP.

MEMORY TECHNOLOGIES

A+
220-701
1.2
1.6

Recall that random access memory (RAM) temporarily holds data and instructions as the CPU processes them and that RAM is divided into two categories, DRAM (dynamic RAM) and SRAM (static RAM). In Chapter 6, you learned that static RAM (SRAM) is used for a memory cache and is contained within the processor housing. Static RAM is called that because it holds its data as long as the RAM has power. In this chapter, we focus on dynamic RAM (DRAM). Dynamic RAM loses its data rapidly, and the memory controller must refresh it several thousand times a second. However, when the power is turned off, both SRAM and DRAM lose all their data, and are therefore called volatile memory. All the RAM discussed in this chapter is dynamic RAM. DRAM is stored on memory modules, which are installed in memory slots on the motherboard (see Figure 7-1).

DDR2 DIMM

Three empty DIMM slots for additional RAM

Figure 7-1 RAM on motherboards today is stored on DIMMs
Courtesy: Course Technology/Cengage Learning

> 💡 **A+ Exam Tip** The A+ 220-701 Essentials exam expects you to know the purposes and characteristics of the following memory technologies: DRAM, SRAM, SDRAM, DDR, DDR2, DDR3, and Rambus.

Recall that a new motherboard sold today uses a memory module called a DIMM (dual inline memory module). Laptops use a smaller version of a DIMM called a SO-DIMM (small outline DIMM and pronounced "sew-dim"). MicroDIMMs are used on subnotebook computers and are smaller than SO-DIMMs. Occasionally you'll see an older motherboard that requires one of two older type modules. These two older types are a RIMM, which is designed by Rambus, Inc., and a SIMM (single inline memory module). The major differences among these modules are the width of the data path that each type of module accommodates and the way data moves from the system bus to the module. Table 7-1 shows some examples of memory modules.

A+
220-701
1.2
1.6

Description of Module	Example
240-pin DDR3 DIMM is currently the fastest memory. It can support triple or dual channels or be installed as a single DIMM. It has an offset notch farther from the center than a DDR2 DIMM.	
240-pin DDR2 DIMM can support dual channels or be installed as a single DIMM. Has one notch near the center of the edge connector.	
184-pin DDR DIMM can support dual channels or be installed as a single DIMM. Has one offset notch.	
168-pin SDRAM DIMM has two notches on the module. The positions of these notches depend on the memory features the DIMM uses.	
RIMM has 184 pins and two notches near the center of the edge connector.	
72-pin SIMM must be installed two modules to a bank of memory.	
30-pin SIMM must be installed four modules to a bank of memory.	

Table 7-1 Types of memory modules
Courtesy: Course Technology/Cengage Learning

In this chapter, you'll see tons of different technologies used by RAM and so many can get a little overwhelming. You need to know about them because each motherboard you might support requires a specific type of RAM. Figure 7-2 is designed to help you keep all these technologies straight. You might find it a useful roadmap as you study each technology in the chapter. And who keeps up with all these technologies? JEDEC (*www.jedec.org*) is the organization responsible for standards used by solid-state devices, including RAM technologies. The goal of each new RAM technology approved by JEDEC is to increase speed and performance without greatly increasing the cost.

When a new technology is introduced, it can take months or years before motherboard and memory manufacturers produce the related product. Also, even though an older RAM technology is no longer used by new motherboards, RAM manufacturers continue to produce the older RAM because older motherboards require these replacement modules.

7

A+ 220-701

A+
220-701
1.2
1.6

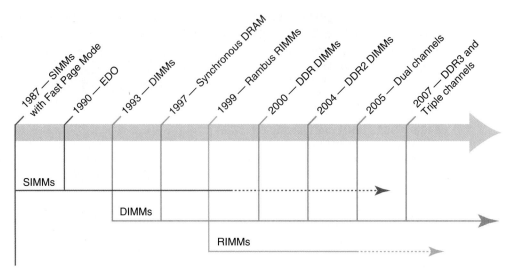

Figure 7-2   Timeline of memory technologies
Courtesy: Course Technology/Cengage Learning

> **Note**   For an interesting discussion on how RAM works, complete with animation, see the Web site by HowStuffWorks, Inc. at *www.howstuffworks.com/ram.htm*.

Looking at Figure 7-2, you can see that SIMMs and RIMMs are among these technologies now considered outdated. All new motherboards today use DIMMs. However, if you check some retail Web sites, you can see that SIMMs and RIMMs can still be purchased.

We'll now look at each of the three types of DIMM, RIMM, and SIMM modules, and wrap up the chapter section with a quick summary of the technologies. In Chapter 21, you'll learn about SO-DIMM modules.

DIMM TECHNOLOGIES

DIMMs use a 64-bit data path. (Some early DIMMs had a 128-bit data path, but they're now obsolete.) A DIMM (dual inline memory module) gets its name because it has independent pins on opposite sides of the module. (Older SIMMs have pins on both sides of the module, too, but with a SIMM, each pin pair is tied together into a single contact.)

SIMMs and the early DIMMs did not run in sync with the system clock because they were too slow to keep up. Their speeds are measured in nanoseconds (ns), which is how long it takes for the module to read or write data. The first DIMM to run synchronized with the system clock was **synchronous DRAM (SDRAM)**, which has two notches, and uses 168 pins. (Don't confuse SDRAM with SRAM. SRAM is static RAM used in processor memory caches, and SDRAM is dynamic RAM used on DIMMs.) Synchronized memory runs in step with the processor and system clock, and its speeds are measured just as processor and bus speeds are measured in MHz.

Double Data Rate SDRAM (DDR SDRAM, or **SDRAM II,** or simply **DDR)** is an improved version of SDRAM. DDR runs twice as fast as regular SDRAM, has one notch, and uses 184 pins. Instead of processing data for each beat of the system clock, as regular SDRAM does, it processes data when the beat rises and again when it falls, doubling the data rate of memory. If a motherboard runs at 200 MHz, DDR memory runs at 400 MHz. Two other improvements over DDR are DDR2 and DDR3. **DDR2** is faster and uses less power than DDR. **DDR3** is faster and uses less power than DDR2. Both DDR2 and DDR3 use 240 pins, although their

A+
220-701
1.2
1.6

notches are not in the same position. They are not compatible, and the different notch positions keep someone from installing a DDR2 or DDR3 DIMM in the wrong memory slot.

Factors that affect the capacity, features, and performance of DIMMs include how much RAM is on one DIMM, how chips are installed and addressed on the DIMMs, the number of channels they use, the speed, error-checking abilities, buffering, and access timing. All these factors are discussed next.

SINGLE-SIDED, DOUBLE-SIDED, SINGLE RANKED, AND DUAL RANKED

A DIMM can have memory chips installed on one side of the module (called single-sided) or both sides of the module (called double-sided). Most desktop and laptop processors address memory 64 bits at a time. A memory bank is the memory a processor addresses at one time and is 64 bits wide. Because DIMMs use a 64-bit data path, it takes only a single DIMM to provide one memory bank to the processor. This explains why DIMMs can always be installed as single DIMMs on a motherboard. However, some double-sided DIMMs provide more than one bank, which means the chips on the DIMM are grouped so that the memory controller addresses one group and then addresses another.

Double-sided DIMMs that provide two 64-bit banks are said to be dual ranked. Single-sided DIMMs are always single ranked, meaning they provide only one 64-bit bank. DIMMs that provide four banks are said to be quad ranked. These quad-ranked DIMMs are only used on servers. Some double-sided DIMMs are single ranked, meaning that all chips on both sides of the DIMM are addressed at every read or write. When the memory controller only addresses a portion of the chips on the module, the controller does not have to be as sophisticated or expensive as when it must address every chip on the module every time it accesses the module. Dual and quad ranks are a method of reducing the overall price of memory in a system, but at the expense of performance. Single-ranked DIMMs cost more but perform better because the controller accesses all chips at the same time. Terms can get confusing, so remember that double sided refers to the physical location of the chips on the DIMM, and dual ranked refers to how the memory on the DIMM is addressed.

SINGLE, DUAL, AND TRIPLE CHANNELS

Channels have to do with how many DIMM slots the memory controller can address at a time. Early DIMMs only used a single channel, which means the memory controller can only access one DIMM at a time. To improve overall memory performance, dual channels allow the memory controller to communicate with two DIMMs at the same time, effectively doubling the speed of memory access. A motherboard that supports triple channels can access three DIMMs at the same time. DDR, DDR2, and DDR3 DIMMs can use dual channels. DDR3 DIMMs can also use triple channels. For dual channels or triple channels to work, the motherboard and the DIMM must support the technology.

When setting up dual channeling, know that the pair of DIMMs in a channel must be equally matched in size, speed, and features, and it is recommended they come from the same manufacturer. A motherboard using dual channels was shown in Figure 7-1. The two yellow DIMM slots make up the first channel, and the two black slots make up the second channel. To use dual channeling in the yellow slots, matching DIMMs must be installed in these slots. To use dual channeling in the black slots, matching DIMMs must be installed in these two slots. However, the second pair of DIMMs does not have to match the first pair of DIMMs because the first channel runs independently of the second channel. If the two DIMM slots of a channel are not populated with matching pairs of DIMMs, the motherboard will revert to single channeling. You'll see an example of motherboard documentation using dual channeling later in the chapter.

A+
220-701
1.2
1.6

💡 **A+ Exam Tip** The A+ 220-701 Essentials exam expects you to be able to distinguish between single-channel and dual-channel memory installations and between single-sided and double-sided memory.

For a triple-channel installation, three DIMM slots must be populated with three matching DDR3 DIMMs (see Figure 7-3). The three DIMMs are installed in the three blue slots on the board. This motherboard has a fourth black DIMM slot. You can barely see this black slot behind the three filled slots in the photo. If the fourth slot is used, then triple channeling is disabled, which can slow down performance. If a matching pair of DIMMs is installed in the first two slots and another matching pair of DIMMs is installed in the third and fourth slots, then the memory controller will use dual channels. Dual channels are not as fast as triple channels, but certainly better than single channels.

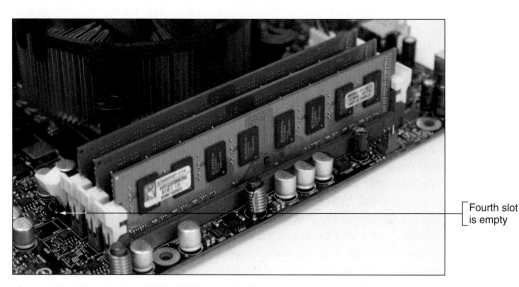

Fourth slot is empty

Figure 7-3 Three identical DDR3 DIMMs installed in a triple-channel configuration
Courtesy: Course Technology/Cengage Learning

DIMM SPEEDS

DIMM speeds are measured either in MHz (such as 800 MHz) or PC rating (such as PC6400). A PC rating is a measure of the total bandwidth of data moving between the module and the CPU. To understand PC ratings, let's take an example of a DDR DIMM module that runs at 800 MHz. The module has a 64-bit (8-byte) data path. Therefore, the transfer rate is 8 bytes multiplied by 800 MHz, which yields 6400 MB/second. This value equates to the PC rating of PC6400 for a DDR DIMM. A DDR2 PC rating is usually labeled PC2, and a DDR3 PC rating is labeled PC3.

Some current PC ratings for DDR3 memory are PC3-16000 (2000 MHz), PC3-14400 (1800 MHz), PC3-12800 (1600 MHz), and PC3-10600 (1333 MHz). A couple of current PC ratings for DDR2 memory are PC2-6400 (800 MHz) and PC2-5400 (667 MHz). DDR memory might be rated at PC6400 (800 MHz), PC4000 (500 MHz), PC3200 (400 MHz), or PC2700 (333 MHz). An older 168-pin SDRAM DIMM might run at PC100 or PC133.

ERROR CHECKING AND PARITY

DIMMs intended to be used in servers must be extremely reliable and use an error-checking technology called ECC (error-correcting code). Some SDRAM, DDR, DDR2, and DDR3 memory modules support ECC. A DIMM normally has an even number of chips on the module, but a DIMM that supports ECC has an odd number of chips on the module. The odd chip is the ECC chip. ECC compares bits written to the module to what is later read from the module, and it can detect and correct an error in a single bit of the byte. If there are errors in two bits of a byte, ECC can detect the error but cannot correct it. The data path width for DIMMs is normally 64 bits, but with ECC, the data path is 72 bits. The extra 8 bits are used for error checking. ECC memory costs more than non-ECC memory, but it is more reliable. For ECC to work, the motherboard and all installed modules must support it. Also, it's important to know that you cannot install a mix of ECC and non-ECC memory on the motherboard because this causes the system to not work.

Older SIMMs used an error-checking technology called parity. Using parity checking, a ninth bit is stored with every 8 bits in a byte. If memory is using odd parity, it makes the ninth or parity bit either a 1 or a 0, to make the number of ones in the nine bits odd. If it uses even parity, it makes the parity bit a 1 or a 0 to make the number of ones in the nine bits even.

> **A+ Exam Tip** The A+ 220-701 Essentials exam expects you to know that parity memory uses 9 bits (8 bits for data and 1 bit for parity). You also need to be familiar with ECC and non-ECC memory technologies.

Later, when the byte is read back, the memory controller checks the odd or even state. If the number of bits is not an odd number for odd parity or an even number for even parity, a parity error occurs. A parity error always causes the system to halt. On the screen, you see the error message "Parity Error 1" or "Parity Error 2" or a similar error message about parity. Parity Error 1 is a parity error on the motherboard; Parity Error 2 is a parity error on an expansion card.

> **Notes** RAM chips that have become undependable and cannot hold data reliably can cause errors. Sometimes this happens when chips overheat or power falters.

As with most other memory technologies discussed in this chapter, when buying memory to add to a motherboard, match the type of memory to the type the board supports. To see if your motherboard supports parity or ECC memory, look for the ability to enable or disable the feature in BIOS setup, or check the motherboard documentation.

SIZE AND DENSITY OF A DIMM

DIMMs can hold from 8 MB to 2 GB of RAM. The amount of RAM installed on one DIMM is called the DIMM size or the DIMM capacity. Sometimes the amount of RAM is expressed as a formula. For example, take a look at Figure 7-4. The first entry in the ad is for a 256 MB DDR2 DIMM. The formula for this DIMM is 32 MB x 64. The 64 is the data path width for the DIMM in bits. To get the size of the DIMM in bits, multiply 32 MB by 64, and then divide by 8 to convert to bytes. Doing this arithmetic is not necessary, however, because the size of the DIMM is already given as 256 MB. The importance of the formula is so you can see that the data path width is 64, as opposed to 72 for other DIMMs listed in the ad. The 64 indicates the DIMM is non-ECC, and the 72 for other DIMMs indicates ECC memory.

DDR2-533 / PC2-4200 DDR2				
Memory Module	Part Number	Our Price	Qty	Order
256MB, DDR2, PC2-4200 32Meg x 64, 240 Pin, DDR533, 1.8v, CL=4	81384	$14.99	1	Add to Cart
512MB, DDR2, PC2-4200 64Meg x 64, 240 Pin, DDR533, 1.8v, CL=4	81385	$19.99	1	Add to Cart
256MB, DDR2, PC2-4200, ECC 32Meg x 72, 240 Pin, DDR533, 2.5v, CL=4	81387	$24.99	1	Add to Cart
1GB, DDR2, PC2-4200 128Meg x 64, 240 Pin, DDR533, 1.8v, CL=4	81386	$24.99	1	Add to Cart
512MB, DDR2, PC2-4200, ECC 64Meg x 72, 240 Pin, DDR533, 2.5v, CL=4	81388	$29.99	1	Add to Cart

Figure 7-4 Memory ads for DDR2 DIMMs show DIMM density as a formula
Courtesy: Course Technology/Cengage Learning

Sometimes the density of a single chip is given in a memory ad expressed as x4, x8, or x16 (see Figure 7-5). The 4, 8, or 16 is the data path width for one chip on the DIMM. The most important consideration about the chip density is to not mix DIMMs with different chip data path widths on the same motherboard.

Memory upgrades from Kingston:

Part Number	Description	Price
KVR333D8R25/512	512MB 333MHz DDR ECC Registered CL2.5 DIMM Dual Rank, x8	Get Price
KVR333S4R25/512	512MB 333MHz DDR ECC Registered CL2.5 DIMM Single Rank, x4	Get Price
KVR333S8R25/512	512MB 333MHz DDR ECC Registered CL2.5 DIMM Single Rank, x8	Get Price
KVR333D8R25/1G	1GB 333MHz DDR ECC Registered CL2.5 DIMM Dual Rank, x8	Get Price
KVR333S4R25/1G	1GB 333MHz DDR ECC Registered CL2.5 DIMM Single Rank, x4	Get Price
KVR333D4R25/2G	2GB 333MHz DDR ECC Registered CL2.5 DIMM Dual Rank, x4	Get Price

To locate a distributor or reseller nearest you, click here.

Figure 7-5 In this memory ad, chip density is given at the end of each description
Courtesy: Course Technology/Cengage Learning

BUFFERED AND REGISTERED DIMMS

Buffers and registers hold data and amplify a signal just before the data is written to the module. Some DIMMs use buffers, some use registers, and some use neither. If a DIMM uses buffers, it's called a buffered DIMM. If it uses registers, it's called a registered DIMM. If a memory module doesn't support registers or buffers, it's referred to as an unbuffered DIMM. Looking at the ad in Figure 7-6, you can see a pair of DDR3 DIMMs. The ad says

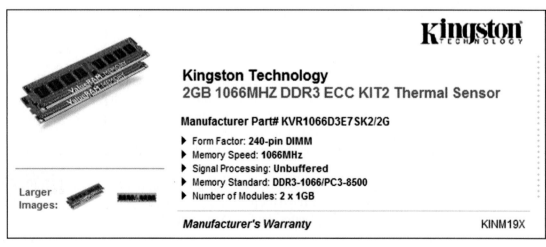

Kingston
TECHNOLOGY

Kingston Technology
2GB 1066MHZ DDR3 ECC KIT2 Thermal Sensor

Manufacturer Part# KVR1066D3E7SK2/2G

▶ Form Factor: **240-pin DIMM**
▶ Memory Speed: **1066MHz**
▶ Signal Processing: **Unbuffered**
▶ Memory Standard: **DDR3-1066/PC3-8500**
▶ Number of Modules: **2 x 1GB**

Larger Images:

Manufacturer's Warranty   KINM19X

Figure 7-6 A kit of two unbuffered DDR3 DIMMs by Kingston
Courtesy: Course Technology/Cengage Learning

A+
220-701
1.2
1.6

the DIMMs are unbuffered. A fully buffered DIMM (FB-DIMM) uses an advanced buffering technique that makes it possible for servers to support a large number of DIMMs.

Notches on SDRAM DIMMs are positioned to identify the technologies that the module supports. In Figure 7-7, the position of the notch on the left identifies the module as registered (RFU), buffered, or unbuffered memory. The notch on the right identifies the voltage used by the module. The position of each notch not only helps identify the type of module, but also prevents the wrong kind of module from being used on a motherboard.

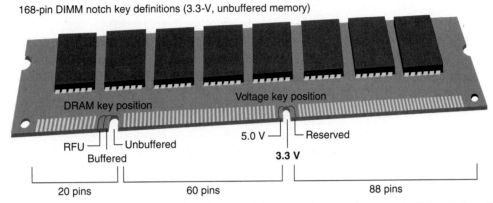

168-pin DIMM notch key definitions (3.3-V, unbuffered memory)

Figure 7-7 The positions of two notches on an SDRAM DIMM identify the type of DIMM and the voltage requirement and also prevent the wrong type from being installed on the motherboard
Courtesy: Course Technology/Cengage Learning

CAS LATENCY AND RAS LATENCY

Two other memory features are **CAS Latency** (CAS stands for "column access strobe") and **RAS Latency** (RAS stands for "row access strobe"), which are two ways of measuring access timing. Both features refer to the number of clock cycles it takes to write or read a column or row of data off a memory module. CAS Latency is used more than RAS Latency. Lower values are better than higher ones. For example, CL8 is a little faster than CL9.

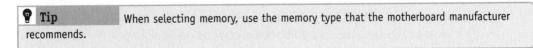

Notes In memory ads, CAS Latency is sometimes written as CL, and RAS Latency might be written as RL.

Ads for memory modules sometimes give the CAS Latency value within a series of timing numbers, such as 5-5-5-15. The first value is CAS Latency, which means the module is CL5. The second value is RAS Latency.

Tip When selecting memory, use the memory type that the motherboard manufacturer recommends.

RIMM TECHNOLOGIES

Direct Rambus DRAM (sometimes called **RDRAM** or **Direct RDRAM** or simply **Rambus**) is named after Rambus, Inc., the company that developed it. A Rambus memory module is called a **RIMM**. RIMMs are expensive and are now slower than current DIMMs. No new motherboards are built to use RIMMs, but you might be called on to support an old motherboard that uses them.

RIMMs that use a 16-bit data bus have two notches and 184 pins (see Figure 7-8). RIMMs that use a 32-bit data bus have a single notch and 232 pins. The 232-pin RIMMs

7

A+ 220-701

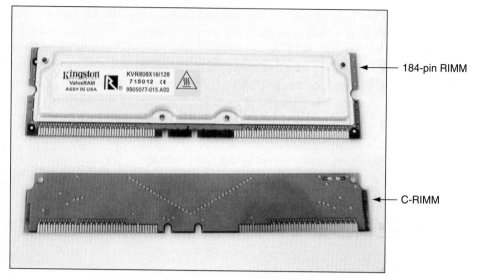

184-pin RIMM

C-RIMM

Figure 7-8 A RIMM or C-RIMM must be installed in every RIMM slot on the motherboard
Courtesy: Course Technology/Cengage Learning

can support dual channels. RIMMs can be ECC or non-ECC and vary in size and speed. Size can vary from 64 MB to 512 MB, and speed ratings are 800 MHz or 1066 MHz.

With RIMMs, each memory slot on the motherboard must be filled to maintain continuity throughout all slots. If a slot does not hold a RIMM, it must hold a placeholder module called a **C-RIMM (Continuity RIMM)** to ensure continuity throughout all slots. The C-RIMM contains no memory chips. A C-RIMM is shown in Figure 7-8.

SIMM TECHNOLOGIES

SIMMs are rated by speed, measured in nanoseconds (ns). Common SIMM speeds are 60, 70, or 80 ns. This speed is a measure of access time, which is the time it takes for the processor to access the data stored on a SIMM. The access time includes the time it takes for the processor to request the data, for the memory controller to locate the data on the SIMM and place the data on the memory bus, for the processor to read the data off the bus, and for the memory controller to refresh the memory chip on the SIMM. Note that an access time of 60 ns is faster than an access time of 70 ns. Therefore, the smaller the speed rating is, the faster the chip.

Two major categories of SIMMs are 72-pin SIMMs and 30-pin SIMMs. The 72-pin SIMMs use a data path of 32 bits. Because processors expect to address 64 bits of memory at a time (one memory bank), 72-pin SIMMs are installed in matching pairs. 30-pin SIMMs use a 16-bit address bus, and, therefore, must be installed in four matching modules per bank to accommodate a 64-bit address bus to the processor.

Hopefully, you'll never face having to support a *really* old motherboard that uses SIMMs. But just in case the need arises, be aware of these technologies used by SIMMs that must match up with what that old motherboard supports:

- ◢ **FPM (fast page memory)** can be used with 30-pin or 72-pin SIMMs or some really old 168-pin DIMMs.
- ◢ **EDO (extended data out)** improved on FPM and is used on 72-pin SIMMs or some 168-pin DIMMs.
- ◢ **Burst EDO (BEDO)** improved on EDO, but was rarely used. You might encounter it on some 72-pin SIMMs or 168-pin DIMMs.

MEMORY TECHNOLOGIES AND MEMORY PERFORMANCE

A+ 220-701 1.2 1.6

So now let's summarize the different memory technologies and consider how they affect overall memory performance. Factors to consider when looking at the overall performance of memory are listed below:

- ▲ *The total RAM installed.* The more memory there is, the faster the system. Generally use as much memory in a system as the motherboard and the OS can support and you can afford.
- ▲ *The memory technology used.* DDR3 is faster than DDR2. DDR2 is faster than DDR, and DDR is faster than SDRAM. When required by the motherboard, buffered or registered memory can improve performance. For all these technologies, use what the board supports.
- ▲ *The speed of memory in MHz, PC rating, or ns.* Use the fastest memory the motherboard supports. If you install modules of different speeds in the same system, the system will run at the slowest speed or might become unstable. Know that most computer ads today give speeds in MHz or PC rating, but some ads give both values.
- ▲ *ECC/parity or non-ECC/nonparity.* Non-ECC or nonparity is faster and less expensive, but might not be as reliable. Use what the board supports.
- ▲ *CL or RL rating.* The lower the better. Use what the board supports, although most boards don't specify a particular CL rating. The CL rating might be expressed as a series of timing numbers.
- ▲ *Single, dual, or triple channeling.* DIMMs that differ in capacity or speed can function on a motherboard in single channels as long as you use DIMMs that the board supports and match ECC and parity ratings. However, to improve performance, use dual or triple channeling if the board supports the feature. To use dual or triple channeling, install matching pairs or triplets of DIMMs from the same manufacturer in each group of channel slots. These matching modules for dual or triple channeling are sometimes sold as memory kits.

When selecting memory, you need to know one more fact about memory technologies. On a motherboard, the connectors inside the memory slots are made of tin or gold, as are the edge connectors on the memory modules. It used to be that all memory sockets were made of tin, but now most are made of gold. You should match tin leads to tin connectors and gold leads to gold connectors to prevent a chemical reaction between the two metals, which can cause corrosion. Corrosion can create intermittent memory errors and even make the PC unable to boot.

> 💡 **A+ Exam Tip** Content on the A+ 220-701 Essentials exam ends here and content on the A+ 220-702 Practical Application exam begins.

HOW TO UPGRADE MEMORY

A+ 220-702 1.1

To upgrade memory means to add more RAM to a computer. Adding more RAM might solve a problem with slow performance, applications refusing to load, or an unstable system. When Windows does not have adequate memory to perform an operation, it gives an "Insufficient memory" error or it slows down to a painful crawl.

When first purchased, many computers have empty slots on the motherboard, allowing you to add DIMMs to increase the amount of RAM. Sometimes a memory module goes bad and must be replaced.

When you add more memory to your computer, you need answers to these questions:

- ▲ How much RAM do I need and how much is currently installed?
- ▲ How many and what kind of memory modules are currently installed on my motherboard?

A+
220-702
1.1

▲ How many and what kind of modules can I fit on my motherboard?
▲ How do I select and purchase the right modules for my upgrade?
▲ How do I physically install the new modules?

All these questions are answered in the following sections.

HOW MUCH MEMORY DO I NEED AND HOW MUCH IS CURRENTLY INSTALLED?

With the demands today's software places on memory, the answer is probably, "All you can get." For Windows XP, a system needs at least 512 MB of RAM, and Windows Vista needs at least 2 GB for acceptable performance. However, both OSs can benefit from much more. The limit for a 32-bit OS is 4 GB installed RAM. Using more memory than 4 GB requires installing a 64-bit version of Windows.

APPLYING | CONCEPTS   HOW MUCH MEMORY IS CURRENTLY INSTALLED?

One way to determine how much memory is installed for Windows Vista or Windows XP is to use the System Information window. To use System Information, in the Vista Start Search box or the Windows XP Run box, type **Msinfo32** and press **Enter**. The System Information window shown in Figure 7-9 reports the total and available amounts of physical and virtual memory. The physical memory is installed RAM available to the operating system. Virtual memory is space on the hard drive that the OS can use as overflow memory. (You'll learn how to manage virtual memory in Chapter 13.) If the amounts of available physical and virtual memory are low and your system is sluggish, it's a good indication you need to upgrade memory.

Looking at Figure 7-9, you can see the OS reports 3.5 GB installed RAM. This particular system would not benefit much from installing additional RAM. The maximum RAM that a 32-bit OS can

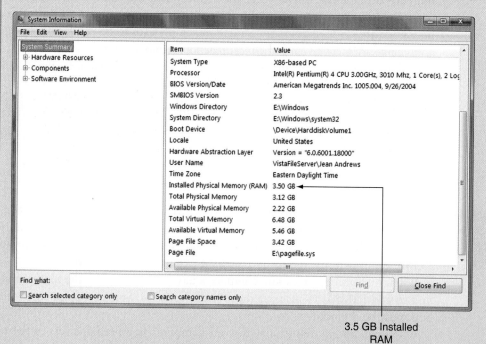

3.5 GB Installed
RAM

Figure 7-9   The System Information window reports total and available physical and virtual memory
Courtesy: Course Technology/Cengage Learning

address is 4 GB and some of that is used by the expansion slots on the motherboard and is not available to the OS. If the system really needs more memory, the OS would have to be upgraded to a 64-bit OS and then more RAM could be used.

HOW MANY AND WHAT KIND OF MEMORY MODULES ARE CURRENTLY INSTALLED?

The next step to upgrading memory is to determine what type of memory modules the motherboard is currently using, and how many memory slots are used. In this section, we also take into consideration the fact that you might be dealing with a motherboard that has no memory currently installed. If the board already has memory installed, you want to do your best to match the new modules with whatever is already installed. To learn what type and how many modules are already installed, do the following:

- ◢ Open the case and look at the memory slots. How many slots do you have? How many are filled? Remove each module from its slot and look on it for imprinted type, size, and speed. For example, a module might say "PC2-4200/512MB." The PC2 tells you the memory is DDR2, the 4200 is the PC rating and tells you the speed, and the 512 MB is the size. This is not enough information to know exactly what modules to purchase, but it's a start.

- ◢ Examine the module for the physical size and position of the notches. Compare the notch positions to those in Table 7-1 and Figure 7-7.

- ◢ Read your motherboard documentation. If the documentation is not clear (and some is not) or you don't have the documentation, look on the motherboard for the imprinted manufacturer and model (see Figure 7-10). With this information, you can search a good memory Web site such as Kingston (*www.kingston.com*) or Crucial (*www.crucial.com*), which can tell you what type modules this board supports.

- ◢ Look in the documentation to see if the board supports dual channels or triple channels. If it does, most likely the memory slots on the board will be color coded. For example, a dual channel board might have two yellow slots for Channel A and two blue slots for Channel B. If the board supports dual or triple channeling and modules are already installed, verify that matching DIMMs are installed in each channel.

- ◢ If you still have not identified the module type, you can take the motherboard and the old memory modules to a good computer parts store and they should be able to match it for you.

HOW MANY AND WHAT KIND OF MODULES CAN FIT ON MY MOTHERBOARD?

Now that you know what memory modules are already installed, you're ready to decide how much and what kind of modules you can add to the board. Keep in mind that if all memory slots are full, sometimes you can take out small-capacity modules and replace them with larger-capacity modules, but you can only use the type, size, and speed of modules that the board is designed to support. Also, if you must discard existing modules, the price of the upgrade increases.

Video
Selecting Memory

A+
220-702
1.1

Figure 7-10 Look for the manufacturer and model of a motherboard imprinted somewhere on the board
Courtesy: Course Technology/Cengage Learning

To know how much memory your motherboard can physically hold, read the documentation that comes with the board. Not all sizes of memory modules fit on any one computer. You need to use the right number of DIMMs, RIMMs, or SIMMs with the right amount of memory on each module to fit the memory banks on your motherboard. Next, let's look at what to consider when deciding how many and what kind of DIMMs, RIMMs, or SIMMs to add to a system.

DIMM MODULES

You can always install DIMMs as single modules, but you might not get the best performance by doing so. If the motherboard supports dual channeling, install matching DIMMs in each channel. A dual-channel board is likely to have four DIMM slots; two slots make up Channel A and two slots make up Channel B. Therefore, for best performance you would install a matching pair of DIMMs in Channel A and another matching DIMM pair in Channel B. But, if you install DIMMs in all four slots that don't match, the memory will still work, just not at top performance. A DDR3 board might support triple channeling. To get the best performance on this board, you need to install three matching DIMMs in the triple-channel slots. Now let's look at a few examples.

Motherboard Using DDR3 Triple-Channel DIMMs

The Intel motherboard shown earlier in Figure 7-3 has four DDR3 memory slots that can be configured for single, dual, or triple channeling. The four empty slots are shown in Figure 7-11. If triple channeling is used, three matching DIMMs are used in the three blue

A+
220-702
1.1

slots. If the fourth slot is populated, the board reverts to single channeling. For dual channeling, install two matching DIMMs in the two blue slots farthest from the processor and leave the other two slots empty. If only one DIMM is installed, it goes in the blue slot in the farthest position from the processor.

Figure 7-11 Four DDR3 slots on a motherboard
Courtesy: Course Technology/Cengage Learning

The motherboard documentation says that these types of DIMMs can be used:

- The DIMM voltage rating no higher than 1.6 V
- Non-ECC DDR3 memory
- Serial Presence Detect (SPD) memory only
- Gold-plated contacts
- 1333 MHz, 1066 MHz, or 800 MHz (best to match the system bus speed)
- Unbuffered, nonregistered single or double-sided DIMMs
- Up to 16 GB total installed RAM (less than 4 GB is recognized when using a 32-bit OS)

The third item in the list needs an explanation. Serial Presence Detect (SPD) is a DIMM technology that declares to system BIOS at startup the module's size, speed, voltage, and data path width. If the DIMM does not support SPD, the system might not boot or boot with errors. Today's memory always supports SPD.

Motherboard Using DDR DIMMs with Dual Channeling

Let's look at another example of a DIMM installation. The motherboard is the ASUS P4P800 shown in Chapter 6, Figure 6-41. The board allows you to use three different speeds of DDR DIMMs in one to four sockets on the board. The board supports dual channeling. Looking carefully at the photo in Figure 6-41, you can see two blue memory slots and two black slots. The two blue slots use one channel and the two black slots use a different channel. For dual channeling to work, matching DIMMs must be installed in the two blue sockets. If two DIMMs are installed in the two black sockets, they must match each other.

This board supports up to 4 GB of unbuffered 184-pin non-ECC memory running at PC3200, PC2700, or PC2100. The documentation says the system bus can run at 800 MHz, 533 MHz, or 400 MHz, depending on the speed of the processor installed. Therefore, the speed of the processor determines the system bus speed, which determines the speed of memory modules.

Figure 7-12 outlines the possible configurations of these DIMM modules, showing that you can install one, two, or four DIMMs and which sockets should hold these DIMMs. To take advantage of dual channeling on this motherboard, you must populate the sockets according to Figure 7-12, so that identical DIMM pairs are working together in DIMM_A1 and DIMM_B1 sockets (the blue sockets), and another pair can work together in DIMM_A2 and DIMM_B2 sockets (the black sockets).

Mode		Sockets			
		DIMM_A1	DIMM_A2	DIMM_B1	DIMM_B2
Single channel	(1)	Populated	—	—	—
	(2)	—	Populated	—	—
	(3)	—	—	Populated	—
	(4)	—	—	—	Populated
Dual channel*	(1)	Populated	—	Populated	—
	(2)	—	Populated	—	Populated
	(3)	Populated	Populated	Populated	Populated

*Use only identical DDR DIMM pairs

Figure 7-12 Motherboard documentation shows that one, two, or four DIMMs can be installed
Courtesy: Course Technology/Cengage Learning

This motherboard has two installed DDR DIMMs. The label on one of these DIMMs is shown in Figure 7-13. The important items on this label are the size (256 MB), the speed (400 MHz or 3200 PC rating), and the CAS Latency (CL3). With this information and knowledge about what the board can support, we are now ready to select and buy the memory for the upgrade. For example, if you decide to upgrade the system to 1 GB of memory, you would buy two DDR, 400 MHz, CL3 DIMMs that support dual channeling. For best results, you need to also match the manufacturer and buy Elixir memory.

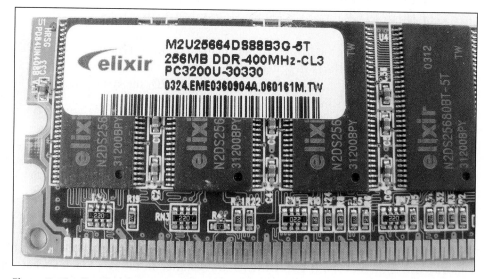

Figure 7-13 Use the label on this DIMM to identify its features
Courtesy: Course Technology/Cengage Learning

Pentium Motherboard Using DDR DIMMs

One Pentium motherboard uses 168-pin single-sided DIMM modules, and the documentation says to use unbuffered, 3.3-V, ECC, PC100 DIMM SDRAM modules. The PC100 means that the modules should be rated to work with a motherboard that runs at 100 MHz. You can choose to use ECC modules. If you choose not to, BIOS setup should show the feature disabled. Three DIMM slots are on the board, which the motherboard documentation calls sockets. Each socket holds one bank of memory. Figure 7-14 shows the possible combinations of DIMMs that can be installed in these sockets.

DIMM Location	168-Pin DIMM		Total Memory
Socket 1 (Rows 0 & 1)	SDRAM 8, 16, 32, 64, 128, 256 MB	×1	
Socket 2 (Rows 2 & 3)	SDRAM 8, 16, 32, 64, 128, 256 MB	×1	
Socket 3 (Rows 4 & 5)	SDRAM 8, 16, 32, 64, 128, 256 MB	×1	
	Total System Memory (Max 768 MB)	=	

Figure 7-14 This table is part of the motherboard documentation and is used to show possible DIMM sizes and calculate total memory on the motherboard
Courtesy: Course Technology/Cengage Learning

Motherboard Using DDR DIMMs, Single- or Double-Sided

This next example involves a motherboard that can use a combination of single-sided and double-sided DIMMs. The Intel CC820 motherboard has two DIMM slots that can use two single-sided DIMMs, two double-sided DIMMs, or one single-sided and one double-sided DIMM. In the last case, the single-sided DIMM must be in the first slot. Figure 7-15 shows part of the board's documentation explaining how these DIMMs can be installed.

Types of DIMMs to be installed	Slot 0	Slot 1
One DIMM	DIMM	Empty
Two DIMMs - Same size, same number of sides (both single-sided or both double-sided)	Either DIMM	Either DIMM
Two DIMMs - Different sizes	Larger DIMM	Smaller DIMM
Two DIMMs - Same size, one is single-sided and one is double-sided	Single-sided DIMM	Double-sided DIMM

Figure 7-15 The Intel CC820 motherboard can use a combination of single-side and double-sided DIMMs
Courtesy: Course Technology/Cengage Learning

Motherboard with Three Slots Using DDR DIMMs in Four Banks

This next example is a little more complicated and a bit odd, which is why it's included in our examples. The Abit ZM6 board has three DIMM slots, and the chipset can support up to four 64-bit banks. Using three slots to fill four banks is accomplished by installing a combination of single-sided and double-sided, dual-banked DIMMs. Figure 7-16 shows how this can be done, considering that a single-sided DIMM uses only one bank, but a double-sided DIMM uses two banks of the four available.

RIMM MODULES

Systems using RIMMs are no longer made, but you might be called on to support one. Recall that all RIMM slots must be filled with either RIMMs or C-RIMMs. When you upgrade, you replace one or more C-RIMMs with RIMMs. Match the new RIMMs with those already on the motherboard, following the recommendations of the motherboard documentation.

Bank 1	Bank 2	Bank 3	Bank 4	Slots used
Single-sided DIMM				1
Double-sided DIMM				1
Single-sided DIMM	Single-sided DIMM			2
Single-sided DIMM	Single-sided DIMM	Single-sided DIMM		3
Double-sided DIMM		Single-sided DIMM		2
Double-sided DIMM		Double-sided DIMM		2
Double-sided DIMM		Single-sided DIMM	Single-sided DIMM	3

Figure 7-16 How three DIMM slots can use four 64-bit memory banks supported by a motherboard chipset
Courtesy: Course Technology/Cengage Learning

Let's look at one example of a RIMM configuration. The current system has 256 MB installed RAM. The motherboard is an Intel D850MV board, which has four RIMM slots. The first two slots are populated with RIMMs and the second two slots hold C-RIMMs. The label on one of the RIMMs is shown in Figure 7-17. Before we interpret this rather cryptic label, however, let's examine the motherboard documentation concerning upgrading RAM.

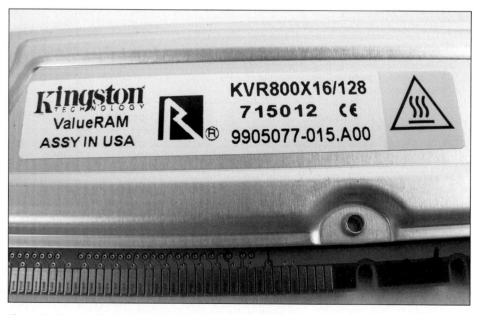

Figure 7-17 Use the label on this RIMM to identify its features
Courtesy: Course Technology/Cengage Learning

Table 7-2 shows the table found in the motherboard manual to be used to decide how to upgrade RAM. The column headings in the table are not as clear as they need to be, but I've included them as they are written in the motherboard documentation, so that you can learn to understand this kind of cryptic documentation. In the table, a chip on a RIMM module is called a component (sometimes it's also called a device). The first column tells us the amount of memory stored on one component (one chip). This value is

A+
220-702
1.1

Rambus Technology	Capacity with 4 DRAM Components per RIMM	Capacity with 6 DRAM Components per RIMM	Capacity with 8 DRAM Components per RIMM	Capacity with 12 DRAM Components per RIMM	Capacity with 16 DRAM Components per RIMM
128/144 MB	64 MB	96 MB	128 MB	192 MB	256 MB
256/288 MB	128 MB	192 MB	256 MB	384 MB	512 MB

Table 7-2 One motherboard's memory configurations using RIMMs

called the density of the RIMM, which is 128 MB (megabits) or 256 MB (megabits). If you multiply the density times the number of components on a RIMM, you get the total amount of memory on one RIMM. The remaining columns in the table list the number of components per RIMM supported by this board, which are 4, 6, 8, 12, or 16 components per RIMM.

Let's look at one sample calculation from the table. Look in the first row of the first column and read the value 128 MB. The second column shows the amount of memory for RIMMs with four components. To get that amount, multiply 128 MB by 4, which yields 512 MB (megabits). Divide that number by 8 to convert the value to megabytes, which gives 64 MB of RAM on this RIMM.

One last item in the table needs explaining. This board supports ECC or non-ECC memory, so that's why there are two values in the first column. For example, in the first row the density is stated as 128/144 MB. The second number, 144 MB, applies to the ECC version of a non-ECC 128-MB chip. In the second row, the 288-MB RIMM is the ECC version of the 256-MB RIMM. The extra bits are used for error correcting. A data path on a RIMM is 16 bits without ECC and 18 bits with ECC. The extra 2 bits are used for error correcting. For a 128-MB component, an additional 16 MB are required for error correcting.

This motherboard has two memory banks with two slots in each bank. The board requires that the RIMMs in a bank must match in size and density. As for speed, the board supports PC600 or PC800 RDRAM, which for a RIMM refers to the speeds of 600 MHz or 800 MHz. All RIMMs installed must run at the same speed. For ECC to work, all RIMMs installed must support ECC.

With this information in hand, let's look back at Figure 7-17 and interpret the label on this RIMM. The important information for us is "800X16/128." The value 128 is the size of the RIMM, 128 MB. The value 800 is the speed, 800 MHz. The value X16 tells us this RIMM is a non-ECC RIMM. (If it had been ECC compliant, the value would have been X18.)

Now we know exactly what kind of RIMM to buy for our upgrade. The RIMMs in the second bank don't have to match in size or density with the RIMMs in the first bank. To upgrade this system to 512 MB, we'll need to purchase two non-ECC, 800-MHz RIMMs that each contain 128 MB of RAM. It's also best to match the manufacturer and buy Kingston modules.

SIMM MODULES

Recall that to accommodate a 64-bit system bus data path, 72-pin SIMMs have a 32-bit data path and are installed in groups or banks of two. Most older motherboards that use these SIMMs have one to three banks that can be filled with two, four, or six SIMMs. The two SIMMs in each bank must match in size and speed. See the motherboard documentation for the sizes and type of SIMMs the board supports.

A+
220-702
1.1

Also recall that on even older motherboards, 30-pin SIMMs are installed in groups of four. SIMMs in each group or bank must be the same type and size. See the motherboard documentation for the exact combination of SIMMs in each bank that the board can support.

As you can see, the motherboard documentation is essential when selecting memory. If you can't find the motherboard manual, look on the motherboard manufacturer's Web site.

HOW DO I SELECT AND PURCHASE THE RIGHT MEMORY MODULES?

You're now ready to make the purchase. As you select your memory, you might find it difficult to find an exact match to DIMMs, RIMMs, or SIMMs already installed on the board. If necessary, here are some compromises you can make:

- Mixing unbuffered memory with buffered or registered memory won't work.
- When matching memory, for best results, also match the module manufacturer. But in a pinch, you can try using memory from two different manufacturers.
- If you mix memory speeds, know that all modules will perform at the slowest speed. (For SIMMs, always put the slower SIMMs in the first bank because the first bank drives the speed of all banks, and all banks must operate at the speed of the slowest SIMMs.)

Now let's look at how to select top-quality memory and how to use a Web site or other computer ad to search for the right memory.

BUYING HIGH-QUALITY MEMORY

Before you buy, you need to be aware that chips embedded on a memory module can be high-grade, low-grade, remanufactured, or used. Higher-quality memory modules have heat sinks installed to reduce heat and help the module last longer. Poor-quality memory chips can cause frequent errors in Windows, or cause the system to be unstable, so it pays to know the quality and type of memory you are buying.

Stamped on each chip of a RAM module is a chip ID that identifies the date the chip was manufactured. Look for the date in the YYWW format, where YY is the year the chip was made, and WW is the week of that year. For example, 0910 indicates a chip made in the tenth week of 2009. Date stamps on a chip that are older than one year indicate that the chip is probably used memory. If some chips are old, but some are new, the module is probably remanufactured. When buying memory modules, look for ones with dates on all chips that are relatively close together and less than one year old.

New chips have a protective coating that gives them a polished, reflective surface. If the chip's surface is dull or matted, or you can scratch off the markings with a fingernail or knife, suspect that the chip has been re-marked. Re-marked chips have been used, returned to the factory, marked again, and then resold. For best results, buy memory from a reputable source that sells only new components.

USING A WEB SITE TO RESEARCH YOUR PURCHASE

When purchasing memory from a Web site such as Crucial Technology's site (*www.crucial.com*) or Kingston Technology's site (*www.kingston.com*), look for a search utility that will match memory modules to your motherboard (see Figure 7-18). These utilities are easy to use and help you confirm you have made the right decisions about type, size, and speed to buy. They can also help if motherboard documentation is inadequate, and you're not exactly sure what memory to buy.

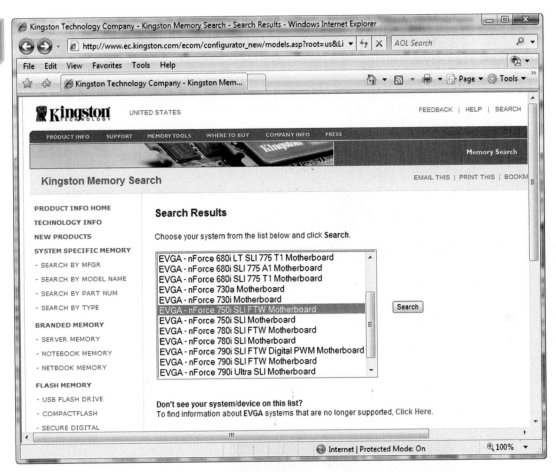

Figure 7-18 Web sites used to purchase memory, such as this Kingston site, often provide search utilities to help you select the right memory modules for your motherboard
Courtesy: Course Technology/Cengage Learning

Let's look at one example on the Crucial site where we know exactly what memory you need. Suppose we're looking for three DDR3, 1333 MHz, unbuffered, non-ECC, SPD, gold contact DIMMs. The system is running 64-bit Windows Vista Home Premium, so we decide to install 6 GB of RAM. Therefore, each DIMM should hold 2 GB. Figure 7-19 shows the Crucial Web site where the match was found. However, check prices on different sites so you know you've found the best buy.

HOW DO I INSTALL THE NEW MODULES?

When installing RAM modules, remember to protect the chips against static electricity, as you learned in Chapter 4. Follow these precautions:

- Always use a ground bracelet as you work.
- Turn off the power, unplug the power cord, press the power button, and remove the cover to the case.
- Handle memory modules with care.
- Don't touch the metal contacts on the memory module or on expansion cards.
- Don't stack cards or modules because you can loosen a chip.

A+
220-702
1.1

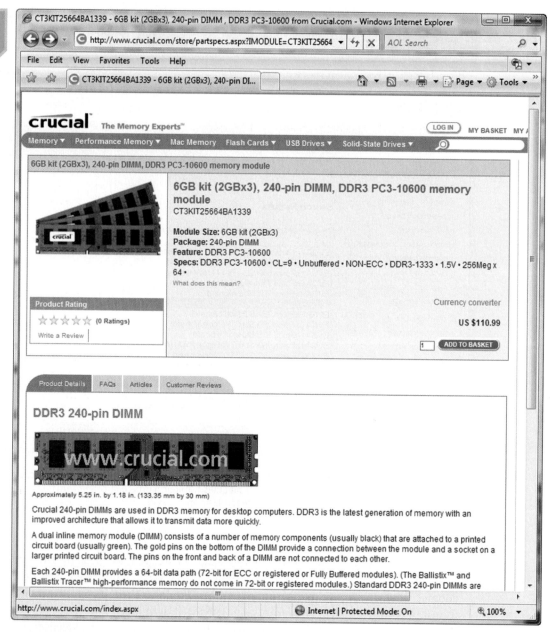

Figure 7-19 Selecting memory off the Crucial Web site
Courtesy: Course Technology/Cengage Learning

▲ Usually modules pop into place easily and are secured by spring catches on both ends. Make sure that you look for the notches on one side or in the middle of the module that orient the module in the slot.

Let's now look at the details of installing a DIMM, a RIMM, and a SIMM.

INSTALLING DIMMS

For DIMM modules, small clips latch into place on each side of the slot to hold the module in the slot, as shown in Figure 7-20. To install a DIMM, first pull the supporting arms on the sides of the slot outward. Look on the DIMM edge connector for the notches, which help you

Figure 7-20   Clips on each side of a slot hold a DIMM in place
Courtesy: Course Technology/Cengage Learning

orient the DIMM correctly over the slot, and insert the DIMM straight down into the slot.
When the DIMM is fully inserted, the supporting clips should pop back into place.
Figure 7-21 shows a DIMM being inserted into a slot on a motherboard.

Figure 7-21   Insert the DIMM into the slot by pressing down until the support clips lock into position
Courtesy: Course Technology/Cengage Learning

Most often, placing memory on the motherboard is all that is necessary for installation.
When the computer powers up, it counts the memory present without any further instruction
and senses the features that the modules support, such as ECC or buffering. For some really
old computers, you must tell BIOS setup the amount of memory present. Read the motherboard documentation to determine what yours requires. If the new memory is not recognized,
power down the system and reseat the module. Most likely it's not installed solidly in the slot.

A+
220-702
1.1

INSTALLING RIMMS

For RIMM modules, install the RIMMs beginning with bank 0, followed by bank 1. If a C-RIMM is already in the slot, remove the C-RIMM by pulling the supporting clips on the sides of the socket outward and pulling straight up on the C-RIMM. When installing the RIMM, notches on the edge of the RIMM module will help you orient it correctly in the socket. Insert the module straight down in the socket (see Figure 7-22). When it is fully inserted, the supporting clips should pop back into place.

RIMM supporting clips
in outward position

Figure 7-22 Install RIMM modules in banks beginning with bank 0
Courtesy: Course Technology/Cengage Learning

INSTALLING SIMMS

For most SIMMs, the module slides into the slot at an angle, as shown in Figure 7-23. (Check your documentation for any instructions specific to your modules.) As you install each SIMM, make sure each module is securely placed in its slot. Then turn on the PC and watch POST count the amount of memory during the boot process. If the memory count is not what you expect, power off the system, and then carefully remove and reseat each module. To remove a module, release the latches on both sides of the module and gently rotate it out of the socket at a 45-degree angle.

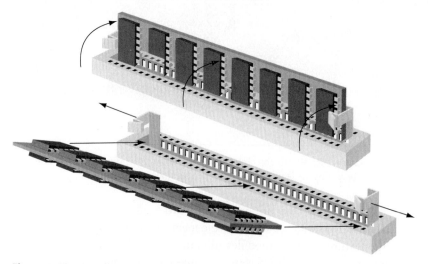

Figure 7-23 Installing a SIMM module
Courtesy: Course Technology/Cengage Learning

TROUBLESHOOTING MEMORY

A+
220-702
1.2

Issues with memory modules can cause a variety of problems, including boot failure; errors that cause the system to hang, freeze, or become unstable; and intermittent application errors. In Windows, memory errors can cause frequent General Protection Fault (GPF) errors. We now look at things that can go wrong with memory and what to do about them.

UPGRADE PROBLEMS

When upgrading memory, if the computer does not recognize new DIMMs, RIMMs, or SIMMs, or if memory error messages appear, do the following:

- Remove and reinstall the module. Make sure it sits in the socket at the same height as other modules, and clips on each side of the slot are in latched positions.
- Check that you have the right memory modules supported by your motherboard. Verify that BIOS setup recognizes the memory features correctly.
- Check that you have installed the right module size, as stated in the motherboard documentation. Verify each module that was already installed or newly installed.
- For dual or triple channeling, verify that modules match in size, CL, density, features, and brand.
- Can your OS support all the memory installed? A 32-bit OS can only address up to 4 GB of RAM, but about 512 MB of that is used by graphics cards. Therefore, the most RAM that Windows can report is about 3.5 GB.
- Remove the newly installed memory and check whether the error message disappears. Try the memory in different sockets. Try installing the new memory without the old installed. If the new memory works without the old, the problem is that the modules are not compatible.
- Clean the module edge connectors with a soft cloth or contact cleaner. Blow or vacuum dust from the memory sockets. Don't touch the edge connectors or the slot.
- Try flashing BIOS. Perhaps BIOS has problems with the new memory that a BIOS upgrade can solve.

RECURRING PROBLEMS

Recurring errors during normal operations can mean unreliable memory. If the system locks up, you regularly receive error messages about illegal operations, General Protection Faults occur during normal operation, and you have not just upgraded memory, do the following:

- Run a current version of antivirus software to check for viruses.
- In Windows Vista, use the Memory Diagnostics tool to test memory. Even if Vista is not installed, you can still run the tool by booting the system from the Vista setup DVD. How to use the tool is covered in Chapter 15.
- Run diagnostic software such as PC Technician (*www.windsortech.com*) to test memory.
- Are the memory modules properly seated? Remove and reinstall each one. For a DIMM module, try a different memory slot.

▲ Try swapping DIMMs. For example, if the system only recognizes 1 GB out of 2 GB of installed RAM, swap the two DIMM modules. Did the amount of recognized RAM change? You might be able to solve the problem just by reseating the modules.

▲ Replace memory modules one at a time. Look for matching DIMMs in another system that you can use to see if they solve the problem. If so, then purchase new DIMMs for this machine.

▲ Sometimes a problem can result from a bad socket or a broken trace (a fine-printed wire or circuit) on the motherboard. If so, you might have to replace the entire motherboard.

▲ The problem might be with the OS or applications. Download the latest patch for the software from the manufacturer's Web site. Make sure Windows has all the latest patches and service packs applied.

▲ If you have just installed new hardware, the hardware device might be causing an error, which the OS interprets as a memory error. Try uninstalling the new hardware.

▲ A Windows error that occurs randomly and generates an error message with "exception fault 0E at >>0137:BFF9z5d0" or similar text is probably a memory error. Test, reseat, or replace RAM.

▲ Excessive hard drive use and a sluggish system might indicate excessive paging. Check virtual memory settings, which you will learn to do in Chapter 13.

> **Notes** Other than the Vista Memory Diagnostics tool and PC Technician, you can use the Memtest86 utility to test installed memory modules. Check the site *www.memtest86.com* to download this program.

A sluggish system that occasionally gives "Insufficient memory" errors probably needs more RAM. Try the following:

▲ Scan the system for viruses and other malicious software. Clean up and defrag the hard drive (how to do this is covered in Chapter 13).

▲ Using the System Information window, find out how much RAM is installed, and compare that to the recommended amounts. Consider adding more RAM.

▲ Verify that virtual memory settings are optimized for your system. (Virtual memory is covered in Chapter 13.)

▲ Don't open too many applications at the same time. Look for running background services that are not necessary and using up valuable memory resources.

>> CHAPTER SUMMARY

▲ DRAM is stored on three kinds of modules: DIMM, SO-DIMM, RIMM, and SIMM modules.

▲ Types of DIMMs are DDR3 and DDR2 DIMMs that have 240 pins, DDR DIMMs with 184 pins, and SDRAM DIMMs with 168 pins. A RIMM has 184 pins, and SIMMs can have 72 or 30 pins. SIMMs and RIMMs are outdated technologies.

▲ DIMMs can have gold or tin edge connectors. Match the metal to the metal used in the memory slot.

▲ A DIMM can hold 8 MB to 2 GB of RAM. One chip on a DIMM can have a 4-bit, 8-bit, or 16-bit data path width.

7

▲ DIMMs can be single sided or double sided. Some double-sided DIMMs provide more than one memory bank and are called dual ranked or quad ranked. A memory bank has a 64-bit data path and is accessed by the processor independently of other banks.

▲ DIMMs can work together in dual channels or triple channels so that the memory controller can access more than one DIMM at a time to improve performance. In a channel, all DIMMs must match in size, speed, and features. DDR3 DIMMs can use dual or triple channeling, but DDR and DDR2 DIMMs can only use dual channels.

▲ DIMM and RIMM speeds are measured in MHz (for example, 1333 MHz) or PC rating (for example, PC3-10600). SIMM speeds are measured in ns (for example, 80 ns).

▲ The memory controller can check memory for errors and possibly correct those errors using ECC (error-correcting code). Using parity, an older technology, the controller could only recognize an error had occurred, but not correct it.

▲ Buffers and registers are used to hold data and amplify a data signal. A fully buffered DIMM (FB-DIMM) uses advanced buffering to make it possible for servers to support a large number of DIMMs.

▲ CAS Latency (CL) and RAS Latency (RL) measure access time to memory. The lower values are faster than the higher values.

▲ RIMMs require that every RIMM slot be populated. If a RIMM is not installed in the slot, install a placeholder module called a C-RIMM.

▲ SIMMs are installed in banks of four or two modules.

▲ When upgrading memory, use the type, size, and speed the motherboard supports and match new modules to those already installed. Features to match include buffered, registered, unbuffered, single-sided, double-sided, CL rating, tin or gold connectors, support for dual or triple channeling, ECC, non-ECC, parity, nonparity, speed in ns, MHz, or PC rating, DDR, DDR2, DDR3, and size in MB or GB. Using memory made by the same manufacturer is recommended.

▲ When buying memory, beware of remanufactured and re-marked memory chips, because they have been either refurbished or re-marked before resale.

▲ When troubleshooting Windows memory errors, know the problems might be caused by a virus, Windows corruption, application corruption, failing hardware device, memory modules not seated properly, or failing memory modules.

>> KEY TERMS

For explanations of key terms, see the Glossary near the end of the book.

Burst EDO (BEDO)
CAS Latency
C-RIMM (Continuity RIMM)
DDR
DDR2
DDR3
Direct Rambus DRAM
Direct RDRAM
Double Data Rate SDRAM
   (DDR SDRAM, SDRAM II,
   DDR)
double-sided

dual channels
dual ranked
ECC (error-correcting code)
EDO (extended data out)
FPM (fast page memory)
General Protection Fault (GPF)
memory bank
parity
parity error
Rambus
RAS Latency
RDRAM

re-marked chips
RIMM
SIMM (single inline memory
   module)
single channel
single ranked
single-sided
SO-DIMM (small outline
   DIMM)
synchronous DRAM (SDRAM)
triple channels

>> REVIEWING THE BASICS

1. How many pins are on a DDR3 DIMM? DDR2 DIMM?

2. How many pins are on a DDR DIMM? SDRAM DIMM?

3. How many notches does a DDR 3 DIMM have?

4. Which two metals might be used for the edge connectors of memory modules and memory in which slots they install?

5. What was the first type of DIMM that ran synchronized with the system clock?

6. What major improvement did DDR make over regular SDRAM?

7. When a DIMM has chips on both sides of the module, do the pins on one side of the module work independently or dependently to pins on the other side of the module?

8. What prevents a DDR DIMM from being installed in a DDR2 DIMM slot on a motherboard?

9. Which module, a DDR3 or DDR2 DIMM, uses lower voltage?

10. In a memory ad for DIMMs, you notice 64Meg x72 for one DIMM and 64Meg x64 for another DIMM. What does the 72 tell you about the first DIMM?

11. A DIMM that contains memory chips in two memory banks on the module is said to be ____.

12. Generally, which DIMM gives better performance, a single-ranked DIMM or a dual-ranked DIMM?

13. What type of DIMM supports triple channeling?

14. What is the speed rating in MHz for a DIMM that has a PC rating of PC2-6400? What type of DIMM is assigned a PC2 rating?

15. If two bits of a byte are in error when the byte is read from ECC memory, can ECC detect the error? Can it fix the error?

16. When parity memory detects an error, what happens?

17. How many notches are on an SDRAM DIMM?

18. Looking at an SDRAM DIMM, how can you know for certain the voltage needed by the module?

19. A DIMM memory ad displays 5-5-5-15. What is the CAS Latency value of this DIMM?

20. What is the most amount of RAM that can be used by a 32-bit installation of Windows XP Professional?

21. A motherboard uses dual channeling, but you have four DIMMs available that differ in size. The motherboard supports all four sizes. Can you install these DIMMs on the board? Will dual channeling be enabled?

22. What is the purpose of the memory technology called SPD?

23. You need to upgrade memory on a motherboard that uses RIMMs. You notice one RIMM and one C-RIMM module are already installed on the board. Which module should you replace?

24. What types of memory can be used on a 100-MHz motherboard?

25. How many 30-pin SIMMs are installed in one bank?

26. How many 72-pin SIMMs are installed in one bank?

27. Which is faster, CL3 memory or CL5 memory?

28. You are looking to purchase two DIMMs running at 400 MHz. You find DIMMs advertised at PC4000 and PC3200. Which do you purchase?

29. You need to find out how much RAM is installed in a system. What command do you enter in the Vista Start Search box or the XP Run dialog box to launch the System Information utility?

30. Although ECC memory costs more than non-ECC memory, why would you choose to use it?

>> THINKING CRITICALLY

1. You need to upgrade memory in a system but you don't have the motherboard documentation available. You open the case and notice that the board has four DIMM slots; three slots are colored yellow and one slot is black. What type of DIMM does the board likely use? How can you be sure?

2. If your motherboard supports DIMM memory, will RIMM memory still work on the board?

3. If your motherboard supports ECC SDRAM memory, can you substitute non-ECC SDRAM memory? If your motherboard supports buffered SDRAM memory, can you substitute unbuffered SDRAM modules?

4. You have just upgraded memory on a computer from 256 MB to 512 MB by adding one DIMM. When you first turn on the PC, the memory count shows only 256 MB. Which of the following is most likely the source of the problem? What can you do to fix it?

   a. Windows is giving an error because it likely became corrupted while the PC was disassembled.

   b. The new DIMM you installed is faulty.

   c. The new DIMM is not properly seated.

   d. The DIMM is installed in the wrong slot.

5. Your motherboard supports dual channeling, and you currently have two DIMMs installed in two slots used in Channel A on the board. You want to install an additional 512 MB of RAM. Will your system run faster if you install two 256 MB DIMMs or one 512 MB DIMM? Explain your answer.

>> HANDS-ON PROJECTS

PROJECT 7-1:   Help Desk Support

1. A friend calls while sitting at his computer and asks you to help him determine how much RAM he has on his motherboard. Step him through the process. List at least two ways to find the answer. He is using Windows XP.

2. Answer Question 1, but assume that your friend is using Windows Vista.

3. Your friend has discovered he has 128 MB of RAM installed in two slots on his motherboard that has four slots and supports dual channeling. The board runs at 667 MHz and uses DDR2

non-ECC DIMMs. Your friend can spend no more than $75 on the upgrade. How many and which modules do you suggest he buy? Print a Web page showing the modules for sale.

PROJECT 7-2: Explaining to a Customer Why He Needs a RAM Upgrade

Bernie, a retired high school coach, enjoys his computer but is not knowledgeable about hardware. He has come to Jack's small computer repair shop complaining that his PC is too slow and asking for a fix. Jack notices that Bernie's Windows XP system has only 128 MB of RAM installed and decides the best way to improve performance is to upgrade RAM. To Bernie, "RAM," "memory," "hard drive," "storage," and "capacity" all mean the same thing. In a group of four students, do the following to practice and evaluate communication skills:

1. As two students observe, two students play the roles of Bernie and Jack. Jack tries to explain to Bernie why he needs a RAM upgrade in terms Bernie can understand and agree to. Bernie needs convincing his money will be well spent. Bernie also seems to enjoy giving Jack a hard time.

2. The two observers can now evaluate Jack's communication skills. What did he do well? How can he improve?

3. Now the first two observers play the roles of Bernie and Jack and the other two students observe and evaluate.

PROJECT 7-3: Planning and Pricing Memory

You need the documentation for your motherboard for this project. If you don't have it, download it from the Web site of the motherboard manufacturer. Use this documentation and the motherboard to answer the following:

1. What is the maximum amount of memory the banks on your motherboard can accommodate?

2. What type of memory does the board support?

3. How many modules are installed, and how much memory does each hold?

4. Look at a retail Web site such as MicroCenter (*www.microcenter.com*) or Crucial Technology (*www.crucial.com*) to determine how much it will cost to fill the banks to full capacity. Don't forget to match the speed of the modules already installed, and plan to use only the size modules your computer can accommodate. How much will the upgrade cost?

PROJECT 7-4: Upgrading Memory

To practice installing additional memory in a computer in a classroom environment, remove the DIMMs, RIMMs, or SIMMs from one computer and place them in another computer. Boot the second computer and check that it counts the additional memory. When finished, return the borrowed modules to the original computer.

PROJECT 7-5: Memory Research Game

In a group of four players with Internet access and a fifth person who is the scorekeeper, play the Memory Research Game. The scorekeeper asks a question and then gives players one minute to find the best answer. Five points is awarded to the player who has the best answer at the end of each one-minute play. The scorekeeper can use these questions or make up his or her own. If you use these questions, mix up the order:

1. What is the fastest DDR DIMM sold today?

2. What is the lowest price for a 232-pin non-ECC Rambus RIMM?

3. What is the largest size DDR DIMM sold today?

4. What is the largest size fully buffered ECC 240-pin DDR2 DIMM sold today?

5. What is the lowest price for a 2 GB 240-pin ECC DDR3 DIMM?

PROJECT 7-6:   Troubleshooting Memory

Follow the rules outlined in Chapter 4 to protect the PC against ESD as you work. Remove the memory module in the first memory slot on a motherboard, and boot the PC. Did you get an error? Why or why not?

>> REAL PROBLEMS, REAL SOLUTIONS

REAL PROBLEM 7-1: Troubleshooting Memory

A friend has asked for your help in solving a problem with his desktop computer. The computer hangs at odd times and sometimes gives "Insufficient memory" errors. The Windows XP system has 512 MB of installed RAM, so you decide it really doesn't need a memory upgrade. You suspect one of the DIMM modules installed might be going bad. To test this theory, you download a memory-testing utility from the Internet to test the modules. Do the following:

1. Find and download a memory-testing utility. Use the utility to test the memory on your computer. What utility did you use? What were the results of the test?

2. If the test was successful, but the problem didn't go away, list the next five things you would suspect to be the source of the problem and describe what you would do to eliminate each possible source.

Supporting Hard Drives

The hard drive is the most important secondary storage device in a computer, and supporting hard drives is one of the more important tasks of a PC support technician. This chapter introduces the different kinds of hard drive technologies that have accounted for the continual upward increase in hard drive capacities and speeds over the past few years. The ways a computer interfaces with a hard drive have also changed several times over the years as both the computer and hard drives improve the technologies and techniques for communication. In this chapter, you will learn about past and present methods of communication between the computer and drive so that you can support both older and newer drives.

Floppy drives are becoming obsolete, but they have not completely disappeared. In this chapter, you'll learn just enough about them to know how to support this older technology. One benefit to studying floppy drives is that they are similar in design to hard drives and yet much easier to understand. Therefore, they can be a great aid in understanding how hard drives work. Finally, you'll learn how to install the different types of hard drives and what to do if you have problems with a hard drive.

INSIDE A HARD DRIVE

A+
220-701
1.1

A hard disk drive (HDD), most often called a hard drive, comes in two sizes for personal computers: the 2.5" size is used for laptop computers and the 3.5" size is used for desktops. In addition, a smaller 1.8" size (about the size of a credit card) hard drive is used in some low-end laptops and other equipment such as MP3 players.

All three sizes of hard drives use the same types of hardware technologies inside the drive: solid state or magnetic. In addition, some drives use a combination of both technologies. As a support technician, you need to understand a little about solid state and magnetic technologies, and you also need to know how data is organized inside a hard drive. Both topics are covered in this part of the chapter.

SOLID STATE, MAGNETIC, AND HYBRID DRIVES

Inside the drive housing, two types of technologies can be used: solid state and magnetic. A solid state drive (SSD), also called a solid state device (SSD), is called solid state because it has no moving parts. The drives are built using nonvolatile flash memory, which is similar to that used for USB flash drives. Recall from Chapter 1 that nonvolatile memory does not lose its data even after the power is turned off. Because the technology is expensive, solid state drives are currently 2.5" drives used only in laptop computers. However, by the time this book is in print, it is expected that solid state external hard drives and solid state drives for desktop computers will be available. Figure 8-1 shows two sizes of solid state drives (2.5" and 1.8") and what the inside of an SSD hard drive looks like. Solid state hard drives cost more and are more rugged than magnetic hard drives. Because they have no moving parts, they also last longer, use less power, and are more reliable.

1.8" solid-state drive

Inside an SSD drive

2.5" solid-state drive

Figure 8-1   Solid state drives by Toshiba
Courtesy of Toshiba America Electronic Components

A magnetic hard drive has one, two, or more platters, or disks, that stack together and spin in unison inside a sealed metal housing that contains firmware to control reading and writing data to the drive and to communicate with the motherboard. The top and bottom of each disk have a read/write head that moves across the disk surface as all the disks rotate on a spindle

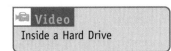

(see Figure 8-2). All the read/write heads are controlled by an actuator, which moves the read/write heads across the disk surfaces in unison. The disk surfaces are covered with a magnetic medium that can hold data as magnetized spots. Almost all hard drives sold today for desktop computers are magnetic hard drives.

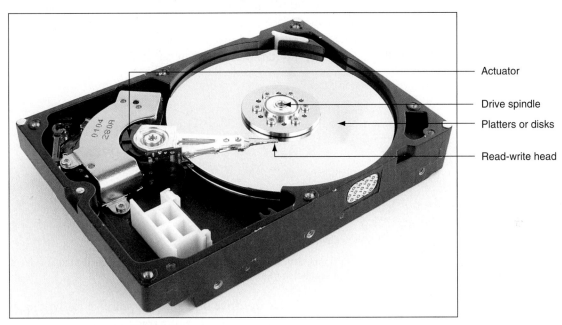

Actuator
Drive spindle
Platters or disks
Read-write head

Figure 8-2 Inside a hard drive
Courtesy: Course Technology/Cengage Learning

Figure 8-3 shows a close-up of the hard drive in Figure 8-2. You can see that this drive has two platters. Both sides of each platter are used to store data. Each side, or surface, of one hard drive platter is called a **head**. (Don't confuse this with the read/write mechanism that moves across a platter, which is called a read/write head.) Thus, the drive in Figure 8-3 has four heads because there are two platters, each having two heads.

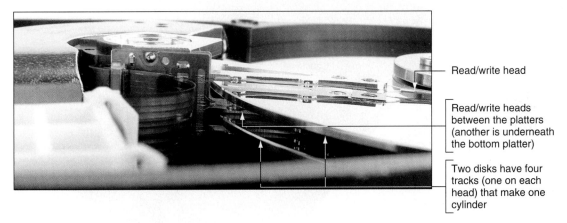

Read/write head

Read/write heads
between the platters
(another is underneath
the bottom platter)

Two disks have four
tracks (one on each
head) that make one
cylinder

Figure 8-3 A hard drive with two platters
Courtesy: Course Technology/Cengage Learning

Some hard drives are **hybrid hard drives**, using both technologies. For example, the 2.5" Seagate Momentus hybrid hard drive holds 80 GB of data and has a 256 MB flash component. Often-used data is stored on the faster flash component. Also, when data is first written to the drive, the data is written to the faster flash component and later moved to the slower magnetic component. For a hybrid drive to function, the operating system must support it. Windows Vista technology that supports a hybrid drive is called **ReadyDrive**.

8

A+ 220-701

HOW DATA IS ORGANIZED ON A HARD DRIVE

Each disk surface on a hard drive is divided into concentric circles, called tracks. Recall from Chapter 5 that each track is further divided into 512-byte segments called sectors (also called records). All the tracks that are the same distance from the center of the platters make up one cylinder. Track and sector markings (see Figure 8-4) are written to a hard drive before it leaves the factory in a process called low-level formatting. The total number of sectors on the drive determines the drive capacity. Today's drive capacities are usually measured in GB (gigabytes) or TB (terabytes, each of which is 1,024 gigabytes).

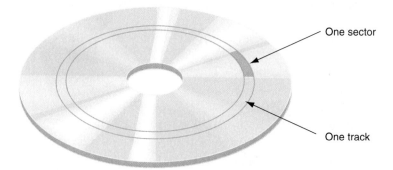

One sector

One track

Figure 8-4 A hard drive or floppy disk is divided into tracks and sectors; several sectors make one cluster
Courtesy: Course Technology/Cengage Learning

Firmware on a circuit board inside the drive housing is responsible for writing and reading data to these tracks and sectors and for keeping track of where everything is stored on the drive. Figure 8-5 shows the bottom side of a hard drive, which has this circuit board exposed. Some drives protect the board inside the drive housing. BIOS and the OS use a simple sequential numbering system called logical block addressing (LBA) to address all the sectors on the hard drive without regard to where these sectors are located.

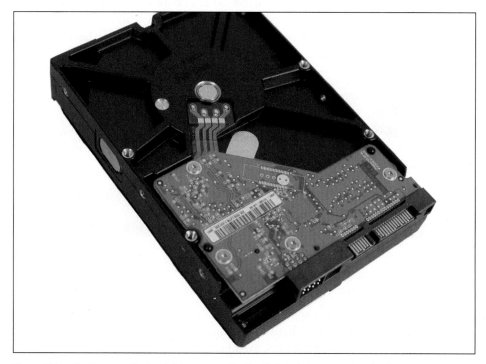

Figure 8-5 The bottom of a hard drive shows the circuit board that contains the firmware that controls the drive
Courtesy: Course Technology/Cengage Learning

When a hard drive is first installed in a system, Windows initializes the drive and identifies it as a basic disk. A basic disk is a single hard drive that works independently of other hard drives. The initializing process writes a Master Boot Record (MBR) to the drive. Recall from Chapter 5 that the MBR is the first sector at the beginning of a hard drive (512 bytes). It contains two items:

◢ The master boot program (446 bytes), which loads the OS boot program stored in the OS boot record. (This program begins the process of loading the OS.)

◢ The partition table, which contains the description, location, and size of each partition on the drive. For Windows-based systems, the MBR has space for four 16-byte entries that are used to define up to four partitions on the drive. For each partition, the 16 bytes are used to hold the beginning and ending location of the partition, the number of sectors in the partition, and whether or not the partition is bootable. The one bootable partition is called the active partition.

The next step is to create a partition on the drive in a process called high-level formatting or operating system formatting. During this process, you specify the size of the partition and what file system it will use. A partition can be a primary partition or an extended partition. A primary partition is also called a volume or a simple volume. The volume is assigned a drive letter (such as drive C: or drive D:) and is formatted using a file system. A file system is the overall structure an OS uses to name, store, and organize files on a drive. In a file system, a cluster is the smallest unit of space on a disk for storing a file and is made up of one or more sectors. A file system tracks how these clusters are used for each file stored on the disk. The active partition is always a primary partition.

One of the four partitions on a drive can be an extended partition (see Figure 8-6). An extended partition can be divided into one or more logical drives. Each logical drive is assigned a drive letter (such as drive G:) and is formatted using its own file system.

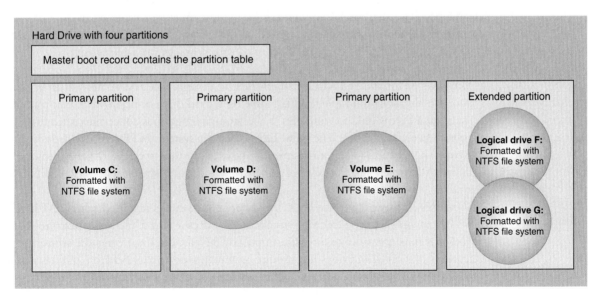

Figure 8-6 A hard drive with four partitions; the fourth partition is an extended partition
Courtesy: Course Technology/Cengage Learning

Primary and extended partitions can be created on a hard drive when the drive is first installed, when an OS is first installed, or after an existing partition becomes corrupted. When an OS is first installed, the installation process partitions and formats the drive, if necessary. After Windows is installed, you can use the Disk Management tool to view and manage partitions on a drive. For example, look at the Disk Management window shown in Figure 8-7. The system has two hard drives installed, labeled Disk 0 and Disk 1. Disk 0 has two primary partitions (drives C: and J:) with some space not yet allocated. Disk 1 has three primary partitions (drives E:, F:, and G:) and one extended partition. The one extended partition has been divided into two logical drives (drives H: and I:) and still has some free space left over. This example is not a very practical way to partition the drives in a system, but is done this way so you can see what is possible. Figure 8-8 shows Windows Explorer and the seven drives. How to use Disk Management is covered later in the chapter.

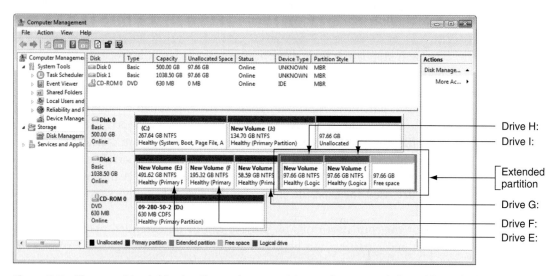

Figure 8-7   The second hard drive has three primary partitions and one extended partition, which contains two logical drives
Courtesy: Course Technology/Cengage Learning

Before a primary partition or volume can be used, it must be formatted using a file system. For the extended partition, each logical drive must be formatted with a file system. Depending on the situation, you can have up to three choices for a file system:

◢ Windows XP offers the FAT32 or the NTFS file system. The FAT32 file system is named after the file allocation table (FAT), a table on a hard drive or floppy disk that tracks how space on a disk is used to store files. It has storage limitations concerning hard drive size, volume size, and file size. The New Technology file system (NTFS) is designed to provide greater security and to support more storage capacity than the FAT32 file system.

◢ If Vista's Service Pack 1 is not yet installed, Windows Vista offers only the NTFS file system.

◢ Windows Vista with Service Pack 1 or later service packs installed offers FAT32, NTFS, and exFAT. The exFAT (extended FAT) uses a 64-bit file allocation table. It does not have the storage limitation that FAT32 has, does not offer the security features of NTFS, and does not require as much overhead as NTFS. exFAT is normally used in low-end systems with smaller hard drives where security is not a big concern. In most situations, your best choice is NTFS.

◢ In addition to FAT32 and NTFS, Windows XP will offer exFAT if Service Packs 2 and 3 are installed and you download and install an additional update from Microsoft.

Figure 8-8 Windows Explorer shows five volumes and two logical drives
Courtesy: Course Technology/Cengage Learning

Now that you have a general understanding of how hard drives work and how the OS organizes data on the drive, let's turn our attention to how the drive's firmware communicates with the motherboard.

HARD DRIVE INTERFACE STANDARDS

A+
220-701
1.2

Hard drives have different ways to interface with the computer. Some standards compete with others and each type of interface standard has evolved over time, which can make for a confusing mess of standards. To help keep them all straight, use Figure 8-9 as your guideline for the standards used by internal drives.

The three current methods used by internal hard drives are Parallel ATA (PATA), Serial ATA (SATA), and SCSI. External hard drives can connect to a computer by way of external SATA (eSATA), SCSI, FireWire, USB, or a variation of SCSI called Fibre Channel. Currently, the most popular solutions for external hard drives are USB and FireWire, which you will learn about in Chapter 9. All the other interface standards are discussed in this section. By far, the most popular standards for internal drives are the ATA standards, so we begin there.

> **Notes** In technical documentation, you might see a hard drive abbreviated as HDD (hard disk drive). However, this chapter uses the term "hard drive."

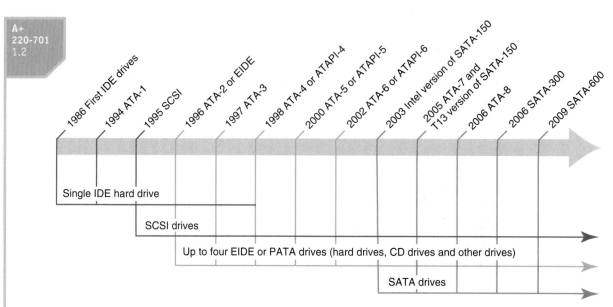

Figure 8-9 Timeline of interface standards used by internal drives
Courtesy: Course Technology/Cengage Learning

THE ATA INTERFACE STANDARDS

The ATA interface standards define how hard drives and other drives such as CD, DVD, tape, and Blu-ray drives interface with a computer system. The standards define data speeds and transfer methods between the drive controller, the BIOS, the chipset on the motherboard, and the OS. The standards also define the type of cables and connectors used by the drive and the motherboard or expansion cards.

The ATA interface standards are developed by Technical Committee T13 (*www.t13.org*) and published by **ANSI (American National Standards Institute,** *www.ansi.org*.) As these standards developed, different drive manufacturers called them different names, which can be confusing when reading documentation or advertisements.

The ATA standards can be categorized into two groups: PATA and SATA. PATA (pronounced "*pay*-ta") is the older and slower standard that has seen many changes. SATA (pronounced "*say*-ta") is the faster and newer standard, which, so far, has had only three revisions. SATA is slowly replacing PATA, but you need to know how to support both. In fact, many motherboards sold today will have a mix of SATA and PATA connectors on the same board.

The ATA standards have undergone several revisions, which are summarized in Table 8-1. All but the last two standards apply only to PATA except for S.M.A.R.T., which is supported by all SATA and PATA drives sold today. **S.M.A.R.T. (Self-Monitoring Analysis and Reporting Technology)** is a system BIOS feature that monitors hard drive performance, disk spin up time, temperature, distance between the head and the disk, and other mechanical activities of the drive in order to predict when the drive is likely to fail. If S.M.A.R.T. suspects a drive failure is about to happen, it displays a warning message. S.M.A.R.T. can be enabled and disabled in BIOS setup.

> **Notes** Remember from Chapter 7 that many memory standards exist because manufacturers and consortiums are always trying to come up with faster and more reliable technologies. The many ATA standards exist for the same reasons. It's unfortunate that you have to deal with so many technologies, but the old ones do stick around for many years after faster and better technologies are introduced.

Standard (Can Have More Than One Name)	Data Transfer Rate	Description
ATA* IDE/ATA	From 2.1 MB/sec to 8.3 MB/sec	The first T13 and ANSI standard for IDE hard drives. Limited to no more than 528 MB. Supports PIO modes 0-2.
ATA-2* ATAPI, Fast ATA, Parallel ATA (PATA), Enhanced IDE (EIDE)	Up to 16.6 MB/sec	Broke the 528-MB barrier. Allows up to four IDE devices; defines the EIDE standard. Supports PIO modes 3-4 and DMA modes 1-2.
ATA-3*	Up to 16.6 MB/sec (little speed increase)	Improved version of ATA-2 and introduced S.M.A.R.T.
ATA/ATAPI-4* Ultra ATA, Fast ATA-2, Ultra DMA Modes 0-2, DMA/33	Up to 33.3 MB/sec	Defined Ultra DMA modes 0-2 and an 80-conductor cable to improve signal integrity.
ATA/ATAPI-5* Ultra ATA/66, Ultra DMA/66	Up to 66.6 MB/sec	Defined Ultra DMA modes 3-4. To use these modes, an 80-conductor cable is required.
ATA/ATAPI-6* Ultra ATA/100, Ultra DMA/100	Up to 100 MB/sec	Requires the 80-conductor cable. Defined Ultra DMA mode 5 and supports drives larger than 137 GB.
ATA/ATAPI-7* Ultra ATA/133, Serial ATA (SATA), SAS STP	Parallel transfer speeds up to 133 MB/sec Serial transfer speeds up to 1.5 GB/sec	Can use the 80-conductor cable or serial ATA cable. Defines Ultra DMA mode 6, serial ATA (SATA), and Serial Attached SCSI (SAS) coexisting with SATA by using STP (SATA Tunneling Protocol).
ATA/ATAPI-8*	N/A	Defined hybrid drives and improvements to SATA.

*Name assigned by the T13 Committee

Table 8-1 Summary of ATA interface standards for storage devices

Let's now look first at the PATA standards and then we'll discuss the SATA standards.

PARALLEL ATA OR EIDE DRIVE STANDARDS

Parallel ATA, also called the EIDE (Enhanced IDE) standard or, more loosely, the IDE (Integrated Drive Electronics) standard, allows for one or two IDE connectors on a motherboard, each using a 40-pin data cable. These ribbon cables can accommodate one or two drives, as shown in Figure 8-10. All PATA standards since ATA-2 support this configuration. Using this standard, up to four parallel ATA devices can connect to a motherboard using two data cables.

Parallel ATA or EIDE applies to other drives besides hard drives, including CD drives, DVD drives, tape drives, and so forth. An EIDE drive such as a CD or DVD drive must follow the ATAPI (Advanced Technology Attachment Packet Interface) standard in order to connect to a system using an IDE connector. Therefore, if you see ATAPI mentioned in an ad for a CD drive, know that the text means the drive connects to the motherboard using an IDE connector.

A+
220-701
1.2

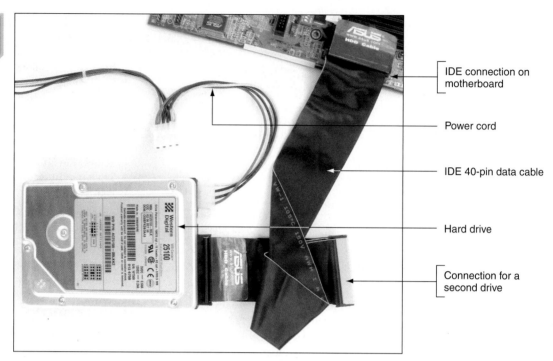

IDE connection on motherboard

Power cord

IDE 40-pin data cable

Hard drive

Connection for a second drive

Figure 8-10 A PC's hard drive subsystem using parallel ATA
Courtesy: Course Technology/Cengage Learning

> **Notes** Acronyms sometimes change over time. Years ago, technicians knew *IDE* to mean *Integrated Drive Electronics*. As the term began to apply to other devices than hard drives, we renamed the acronym to become **Integrated Device Electronics**.

Other technologies and changes mentioned in Table 8-1 that you need to be aware of are the two types of PATA data cables, DMA and PIO modes used by PATA, and Independent Device Timing. All these concerns are discussed next.

Two Types of PATA Ribbon Cables

Under parallel ATA, two types of ribbon cables are used. The older cable has 40 pins and 40 wires. The 80-conductor IDE cable has 40 pins and 80 wires. Forty wires are used for communication and data, and an additional 40 ground wires reduce crosstalk on the cable. For maximum performance, an 80-conductor IDE cable is required by ATA/66 and above. Figure 8-11 shows a comparison between the two parallel cables. The 80-conductor cable is

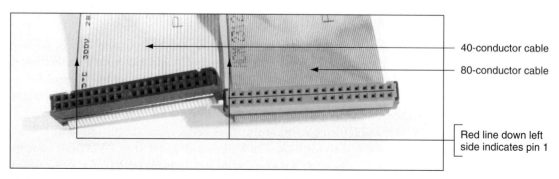

40-conductor cable

80-conductor cable

Red line down left side indicates pin 1

Figure 8-11 In comparing the 80-conductor cable to the 40-conductor cable, note they are about the same width, but the 80-conductor cable has many more and finer wires
Courtesy: Course Technology/Cengage Learning

color-coded with the blue connector always connected to the motherboard. The connectors on each cable otherwise look the same, and you can use an 80-conductor cable in place of a 40-conductor cable in a system.

The maximum recommended length of both cables is 18", although it is possible to purchase 24" cables. A ribbon cable usually comes bundled with a motherboard that has a PATA connector. Because ribbon cables can obstruct airflow inside a computer case, you can purchase a smaller round PATA cable that is less obstructive to the airflow inside the case.

DMA or PIO Transfer Modes

A hard drive uses one of two methods to transfer data between the hard drive and memory: DMA (direct memory access) transfer mode or PIO (Programmed Input/Output) transfer mode. DMA transfers data directly from the drive to memory without involving the CPU. PIO mode involves the CPU and is slower than DMA mode.

There are different modes for PIO and DMA, due to the fact that both standards have evolved over the years. There are five PIO modes used by hard drives, from the slowest (PIO mode 0) to the fastest (PIO mode 4), and seven DMA modes from the slowest (DMA mode 0) to the fastest (DMA mode 6). All motherboards today support Ultra DMA, which means that data is transferred twice for each clock beat, at the beginning and again at the end.

Most often, when installing a drive, the startup BIOS autodetects the drive and selects the fastest mode that the drive and the BIOS support. After installation, you can go into BIOS setup and see which DMA mode is being used.

Independent Device Timing

As you saw in Table 8-1, there are different hard drive standards, each running at different speeds. If two hard drives share the same parallel ATA cable but use different standards, both drives will run at the speed of the slower drive unless the motherboard chipset controlling the ATA connections supports a feature called Independent Device Timing. Most chipsets today support this feature and with it, the two drives can run at different speeds as long as the motherboard supports those speeds.

SERIAL ATA STANDARDS

A consortium of manufacturers, called the Serial ATA International Organization (SATA-IO; see *www.sata-io.org*) and led by Intel, developed the serial ATA (SATA) standards. These standards also have the oversight of the T13 Committee. SATA uses a serial data path rather than the traditional parallel data path. (Essentially, the difference between the two is that data is placed on a serial cable one bit following the next, but with parallel cabling, all data in a byte is placed on the cable at one time.) The three major revisions to SATA are summarized in Table 8-2.

Serial ATA interfaces are much faster than PATA interfaces and are used by all types of drives, including hard drives, CD, DVD, Blu-ray, and tape drives. A motherboard can have two, four, six, or more SATA connectors, which are much easier to configure and use than PATA connectors. SATA supports hot-swapping, also called hot-plugging. With hot-swapping, you can connect and disconnect a drive while the system is running.

A SATA drive connects to one internal SATA connector on the motherboard by way of a SATA data cable. An internal SATA data cable can be up to 1 meter in length, has 7 pins, and is much narrower compared to the 40-pin parallel IDE cable (see Figure 8-12). The thin cables don't hinder airflow inside a case as much as the wide parallel ATA cables do.

A+
220-701
1.2

SATA Standard	Data Transfer Rate	Comments
SATA Revision 1.x* SATA 1 Serial ATA-150 SATA/150 SATA-150	1.5 Gb/sec	First introduced with ATA/ATAPI-7
SATA Revision 2.x* SATA 2 Serial ATA-300 SATA/300 SATA-300	3 Gb/sec	Currently, the most popular SATA standard
SATA Revision 3.x* SATA 3 Serial ATA-600 SATA/600 SATA-600	6 Gb/sec	Currently used only by SSD hard drives for laptops

*Name assigned by the SATA-IO organization

Table 8-2 SATA Standards

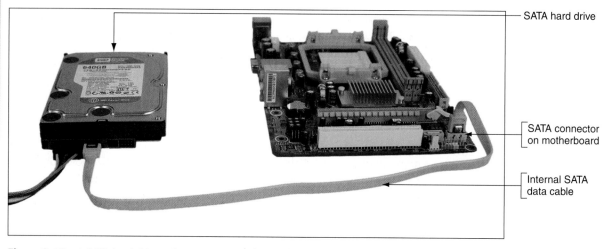

Figure 8-12 A SATA hard drive subsystem uses an internal SATA data cable
Courtesy: Course Technology/Cengage Learning

In addition to internal SATA connectors, the motherboard or an expansion card can provide external SATA (eSATA) ports for external drives (see Figure 8-13). **External SATA (eSATA)** is up to six times faster than USB or FireWire. External SATA drives use a special external shielded serial ATA cable up to 2 meters long.

When purchasing a SATA hard drive, keep in mind that the SATA standards for the drive and the motherboard need to match. If either the drive or the motherboard use a slower SATA standard than the other device, the system will run at the slower speed. Other hard drive characteristics to consider when selecting a drive are covered later in the chapter.

Figure 8-13   Two eSATA ports on a motherboard
Courtesy: Course Technology/Cengage Learning

SCSI TECHNOLOGY

Other than ATA, another interface standard for drives and other devices is SCSI, which is primarily used in servers. SCSI standards can be used by many internal and external devices, including hard drives, CD-ROM drives, DVD drives, printers, and scanners. **SCSI** (pronounced "scuzzy") stands for **Small Computer System Interface**, and is a standard for communication between a subsystem of peripheral devices and the system bus. The SCSI bus can support up to 7 or 15 devices, depending on the SCSI standard. SCSI devices tend to be faster, more expensive, and more difficult to install than similar ATA devices. Because they are more expensive and more difficult to install, they are mostly used in corporate settings and are seldom seen in the small office or used on home PCs.

THE SCSI SUBSYSTEM

If a motherboard does not have an embedded SCSI controller, the gateway from the SCSI bus to the system bus is the **SCSI host adapter card**, commonly called the **host adapter**. The host adapter is inserted into an expansion slot on the motherboard and is responsible for managing all devices on the SCSI bus. A host adapter can support both internal and external SCSI devices, using one connector on the card for a ribbon cable or round cable to connect to internal devices, and an external port that supports external devices (see Figure 8-14).

All the devices and the host adapter form a single daisy chain. In Figure 8-14, this daisy chain has two internal devices and two external devices, with the SCSI host adapter in the middle of the chain. An example of a host adapter card is shown in Figure 8-15. It fits into a PCI slot and provides two internal SCSI connectors and one external connector. Even though there are three connectors and all can be used at the same time, logically the host adapter manages all devices as a single SCSI chain and can support up to 15 devices.

> 💡 **A+ Exam Tip** The A+ 220-701 Essentials exam expects you to know that a motherboard might provide a SCSI controller and connector or that the SCSI host adapter can be a card installed in an expansion slot.

A+
220-701
1.2
1.9

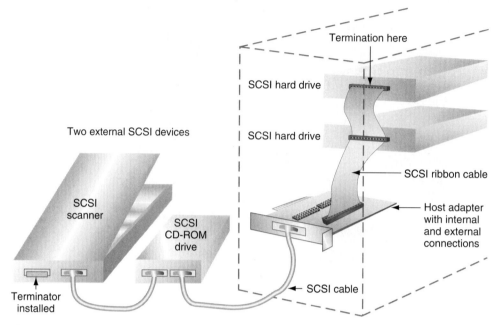

Figure 8-14   Using a SCSI bus, a SCSI host adapter card can support internal and external SCSI devices
Courtesy: Course Technology/Cengage Learning

Figure 8-15   PCI SCSI host adapter card by StarTech
Courtesy of StarTech.com

All devices go through the host adapter to communicate with the CPU or directly with each other without involving the CPU. Each device on the bus is assigned a number from 0 to 15 called the SCSI ID, by means of DIP switches, dials on the device, or software settings. The host adapter is assigned SCSI ID 7, which has the highest priority over all other devices. The priority order is 7, 6, 5, 4, 3, 2, 1, 0, 15, 14, 13, 12, 11, 10, 9, and 8. Cables connect the devices physically in a daisy chain, sometimes called a straight chain. The devices can be either internal or external, and the host adapter can be at either end of the chain or somewhere in the middle. The SCSI ID identifies the physical device, which can have several logical devices embedded in it. For example, a CD-ROM jukebox—a CD-ROM changer with trays for multiple CDs—might have seven trays. Each tray is considered a logical device and is assigned a Logical Unit Number (LUN) to identify it, such as 1 through 7 or 0 through 6. The ID and LUN are written as two numbers separated by a colon. For instance, if the SCSI ID is 5, the fourth tray in the jukebox is device 5:4.

To reduce the amount of electrical "noise," or interference, on a SCSI cable, each end of the SCSI chain has a terminating resistor. The terminating resistor can be a hardware device plugged into the last device on each end of the chain (see Figure 8-16), or the device can have firmware-controlled termination resistance, which makes installation simpler.

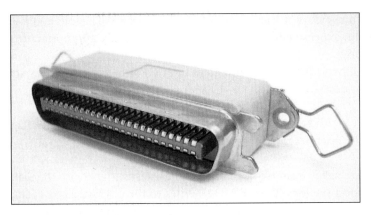

Figure 8-16 External SCSI terminator
Courtesy: Course Technology/Cengage Learning

VARIOUS SCSI STANDARDS

Just as with IDE/ATA standards, SCSI standards have improved over the years and use different names. SCSI standards are developed by the SCSI T10 Technical Committee (*www.t10.org*) and sent to ANSI, which publishes and maintains the official versions of the standards. The SCSI Trade Association (*www.scsita.org*) promotes SCSI devices and standards, and the T10 Technical Committee (*www.t10.org*) publishes information about SCSI. In addition to varying standards, SCSI also uses different types of cabling, connectors, and bus widths. Because there are so many variations with SCSI, when setting up a SCSI subsystem, it's important to pay careful attention to compatibility and make sure all devices, the host adapter, cables, and connectors can work together.

The three major versions of SCSI are SCSI-1, SCSI-2, and SCSI-3, commonly known as Regular SCSI, Fast SCSI, and Ultra SCSI. The latest SCSI standard, serial SCSI, also called serial attached SCSI (SAS), allows for more than 15 devices on a single SCSI chain, uses smaller, longer, round cables, and uses smaller hard drive form factors that can support larger capacities than earlier versions of SCSI. SAS can be compatible with SATA drives in the same system, and claims to be more reliable and better performing than SATA. For more information on SCSI, see the content "All About SCSI" on the CD that accompanies this book.

FIBRE CHANNEL

Fibre Channel is a type of SCSI technology, but in the industry, it is sometimes considered a rival of SCSI for high-end server solutions. Using Fibre Channel, you can connect up to 126 devices together on a single Fibre Channel bus. Fibre Channel is faster than other SCSI implementations, when more than five hard drives are strung together to provide massive secondary storage. However, Fibre Channel is too expensive and has too much overhead, except when used in high-end server solutions.

Now let's look at how multiple hard drives can work together in various RAID configurations.

RAID: HARD DRIVES WORKING TOGETHER

A technology that configures two or more hard drives to work together as an array of drives is called RAID (redundant array of inexpensive disks or redundant array of independent disks). Two reasons you might consider using RAID are:

▲ To improve fault tolerance, which is a computer's ability to respond to a fault or catastrophe, such as a hardware failure or power outage, so that data is not lost. If data is important enough to justify the cost, you can protect the data by continuously writing two copies of it, each to a different hard drive. This method is most often used on high-end, expensive file servers, but it is occasionally appropriate for a single-user workstation.

▲ To improve performance by writing data to two or more hard drives so that a single drive is not excessively used.

Several levels of RAID exist, but the three most commonly used are RAID 0, RAID 1, and RAID 5. Here is a brief description of each:

▲ RAID 0 uses space from two or more physical disks to increase the disk space available for a single volume. RAID 0 writes to the physical disks evenly across all disks so that no one disk receives all the activity, and therefore improves performance. Windows calls RAID 0 a striped volume. To understand that term, think of data striped—or written across—several hard drives.

▲ RAID 1 is a type of drive imaging. It duplicates data on one drive to another drive and is used for fault tolerance. (A drive image is a duplication of everything written to a hard drive.) Each drive has its own volume, and the two volumes are called mirrors. If one drive fails, the other continues to operate and data is not lost. A variation of mirroring is disk duplexing, which uses two hard drive controllers, one for each drive. If one controller fails, the other controller keeps on working, providing more assurance of fault tolerance than mirroring. Windows calls RAID 1 a mirrored volume.

▲ RAID 5 stripes data across three or more drives and uses parity checking, so that if one drive fails, the other drives can re-create the data stored on the failed drive. Data is not duplicated, and, therefore, RAID 5 makes better use of volume capacity. RAID 5 drives increase performance and provide fault tolerance. Windows calls these drives RAID-5 volumes.

> 💡 **A+ Exam Tip**   The A+ 220-701 Essentials exam expects you to be able to contrast RAID 0, RAID 1, and RAID 5.

Besides the three levels of RAID listed, another practice of tying two drives together in an array is called spanning. With spanning, two hard drives are configured as a single volume. Data is written to the first drive, and when it is full, the data continues to be written to the second drive. The advantage of spanning is that you can have a very large file that is larger than either drive. The disadvantages of spanning are that it does not provide fault tolerance, and that it does not improve performance. Sometimes spanning is called JBOD (Just a Bunch of Disks).

All RAID configurations can be accomplished at the hardware level or the operating system level. Configuring RAID at the hardware level is considered best practice because, if Windows gets corrupted, the hardware might still be able to protect the data. Also, hardware RAID is generally faster than operating system RAID. You will learn how to implement hardware RAID later in the chapter. Windows RAID is covered in Chapter 13.

ABOUT FLOPPY DRIVES

Even though a floppy disk drive (FDD) holds only 1.44 MB of data, these drives are still used in some computers today, and you need to know how to support them. Floppy drives can be especially useful when recovering from a failed BIOS update. Also, floppy disks are inexpensive and easy for transferring small amounts of data. In this part of the chapter, you'll learn about the hardware and file system used by floppy drives.

A+
220-701
1.1

FLOPPY DRIVE HARDWARE

Years ago, floppy drives came in two sizes to accommodate either a 5¼" or 3½" floppy disk. The 3½" disks were formatted as high density (1.44 MB), extra-high density (2.88 MB), and double density (720 K). The only floppy drives you see in use today are the 3½" high-density drives that hold 1.44 MB of data.

Figure 8-17 shows the floppy drive subsystem, which consists of the floppy drive, its ribbon cable, power cable, and connections. The ribbon data cable connects to a 34-pin floppy drive connector on the motherboard. Recall that most hard drives use the larger Molex connector as a power connector, but floppy drives use the smaller Berg connector. The Berg power connector has a small plastic latch that snaps in place when you connect it to the drive.

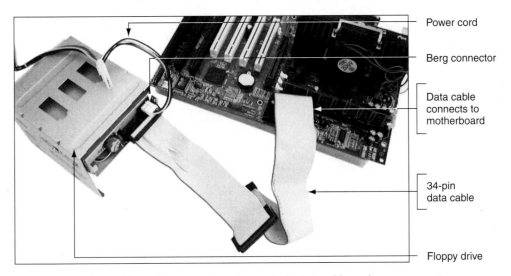

Figure 8-17 Floppy drive subsystem: floppy drive, 34-pin data cable, and power connector
Courtesy: Course Technology/Cengage Learning

Today's floppy drive cables have a connector at each end and accommodate a single drive, but older cables, like the one in Figure 8-17, have an extra connector or two in the middle of the cable for a second floppy drive. For these systems, you can install two floppy drives on the same cable, and the drives will be identified by BIOS as drive A and drive B. Figure 8-18 shows an older floppy drive cable. Notice in the figure the twist in the cable. The drive that has the twist between it and the controller is drive A. The drive that does not have the twist between it and the controller is drive B. Also notice in the figure the edge color down one side of the cable, which identifies the pin-1 side of the 34-pin connector.

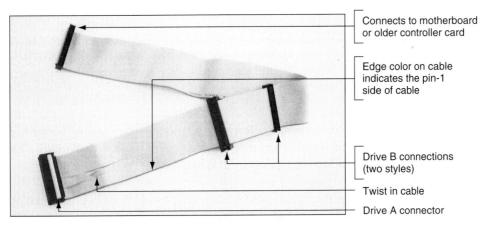

Figure 8-18 Twist in cable determines which drive is drive A
Courtesy: Course Technology/Cengage Learning

💡 **A+ Exam Tip** The A+ 220-701 Essentials exam expects you to be familiar with a floppy disk drive (FDD).

FLOPPY DRIVE FILE SYSTEM

Learning about the details of a floppy drive file system can help you understand how a hard drive is organized. The floppy drive file system is similar to that of a hard drive file system, yet it is simpler and easier to understand.

When floppy disks are first manufactured, the disks have nothing on them; they are blank sheets of magnetically coated plastic. During the formatting process, tracks and sectors to hold the data are written to the blank surface (see Figure 8-19).

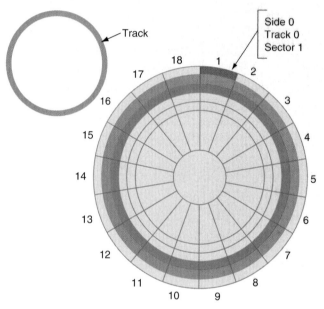

Figure 8-19 3½", high-density floppy disk showing tracks and sectors
Courtesy: Course Technology/Cengage Learning

There are 80 tracks, or circles, on the top side of the disk and 80 more tracks on the bottom. The tracks are numbered 0 through 79. Each track has 18 sectors, numbered 1 through 18 for a total of 1440 sectors on each side. Because each sector holds 512 bytes of data, a 3½", high-density floppy disk has 2880 x 512 = 1,474,560 bytes of data. Divide this number by 1024 to convert bytes to kilobytes and you will find out that the storage capacity of this disk is 1440 kilobytes. You can then divide 1440 by 1000 to convert kilobytes to megabytes, and the storage is 1.44 MB.

📝 **Notes** There is a discrepancy in the way the computer industry defines a megabyte. Sometimes 1 megabyte = 1,000 kilobytes; at other times, we use the relationship 1 megabyte = 1,024 kilobytes. Computers calculate in powers of 2, and 1,024 is 2 raised to the 10th power.

Most floppy disks come already formatted, but occasionally you will need to format one. Whether you use the format command at a command prompt or Windows Explorer to format a floppy disk, the following are created:

▲ *Tracks and sectors*. These tracks and sectors provide the structure to hold data on the disk.
▲ *The boot record*. The first sector on the disk, called the boot sector or boot record, contains the information about how the disk is organized and the file system used.

A+
220-701
1.1

▲ *Two copies of the file allocation table (FAT).* Under Windows, a hard drive can use either the NTFS or FAT32 file system, but a floppy drive is always formatted using the FAT12 file system. Using FAT12, each entry in the file allocation table (FAT) is 12 bits. Each FAT entry lists how each cluster (or file allocation unit) on the disk is currently used. Using FAT12, one sector equals one cluster, so every sector or cluster on the disk is accounted for in the FAT. A file is stored in one or more clusters that do not have to be contiguous on the disk.

▲ *The root directory.* The root directory contains a fixed number of rows to accommodate a predetermined number of files and subdirectories. A 3½", high-density floppy disk has 224 entries in the root directory. Some important items in a directory are a list of filenames and their extensions, the time and date of creation or last update of each file, and the file attributes. Attributes are on/off switches indicating the archive, system file, hidden file, and read-only file status of the file or directory.

The root directory and all subdirectories contain the same information about each file. Only the root directory has a limitation on the number of entries because it has a fixed length that it uses to store all filenames and folder names created in the root directory. Subdirectories can have as many entries as disk space allows. Because long filenames require more room in a directory than short filenames, assigning long filenames reduces the number of files that can be stored in the root directory.

> **Notes** For tech-hungry readers, you can use the DEBUG command to view the contents of the boot record or FAT. How to do that is covered in the "Behind the Scenes with DEBUG" content that you can find on the CD that accompanies this book. Also, to see a group of tables showing the contents of the floppy disk boot record, the root directory, and the meaning of each bit in the attribute byte, see the content on the CD titled "FAT Details."

Let's now turn our attention back to hard drives and focus on what you need to know when selecting one.

> **A+ Exam Tip** The content on the A+ 220-701 Essentials exam ends here and the content on the A+ 220-702 Practical Application exam begins.

HOW TO SELECT AND INSTALL HARD DRIVES AND FLOPPY DRIVES

A+
220-702
1.1

In this part of the chapter, you'll learn how to select a hard drive for your system. Then, you'll learn the details of installing a serial ATA drive and a parallel ATA drive in a system. Next, you'll learn how to deal with the problem of installing a hard drive in a bay that is too wide for it and also how to set up a RAID system. Lastly, you'll see how to install a floppy drive.

SELECTING A HARD DRIVE

When selecting a hard drive, keep in mind that there are many hard drive standards. To get the best performance from the system, the system BIOS on the motherboard or the firmware on the hard drive controller card must use the same standards used by the drive. If the motherboard

A+
220-702
1.1

or controller card does not use the same standards as the hard drive, they will probably revert to a slower standard that both can use, or the drive will not work at all. There's no point in buying an expensive hard drive with features that your system cannot support.

Therefore, when making purchasing decisions, you need to know what standards the motherboard or controller card uses. To find out, see the documentation for the board or the card. For the motherboard, you can look at BIOS setup screens to see which standards are mentioned. However, know that when installing a drive, you don't need to know which ATA standard a hard drive supports, because the startup BIOS uses autodetection. With autodetection, the BIOS detects the new drive and automatically selects the correct drive capacity and configuration, including the best possible standard supported by both the hard drive and the motherboard.

One more point is important to know: Legacy motherboards or hard drives might present complex situations. If you install a new drive that the startup BIOS of a legacy motherboard is not designed to support, the BIOS will either not recognize the drive at all or will detect the drive and report in BIOS setup that the drive has a smaller capacity than it actually does. The solution is to flash BIOS, replace the controller card, or replace the motherboard. For a full discussion of how to deal with legacy motherboards or drives, see the content "Selecting and Installing Hard Drives using Legacy Motherboards" on the CD that accompanies this book.

When purchasing a hard drive, consider the following factors that affect performance, use, and price:

- ◢ *The capacity of the drive.* Today's hard drives for desktop systems are in the range of 80 GB to more than 1.5 TB. The more gigabytes or terabytes, the higher the price.
- ◢ *The spindle speed.* Hard drives for desktop systems run at 5400, 7200, or 10,000 RPM (revolutions per minute). The most common is 7200 RPM. The higher the RPMs, the faster the drive.
- ◢ *The interface standard.* Use the standards your motherboard supports. For SATA, most likely that will be SATA-300. For a PATA IDE drive, most likely that will be Ultra ATA-100. For external drives, common standards are eSATA, FireWire 800 or 400, and Hi-Speed USB.
- ◢ *The cache or buffer size.* Buffers improve hard drive performance and can range in size from 2 MB to 32 MB. The more the better, though the cost goes up as the size increases.
- ◢ *The average seek time (time to fetch data).* Look for 13 to 8.5 ms (milliseconds). The lower the number, the higher the drive performance and cost.
- ◢ *Hybrid drive.* A hybrid drive costs more, but performs better than other comparable desktop drives. Solid state drives are currently only available for laptops.

When selecting a drive, consider the manufacturer warranty and be sure to match the drive to what your motherboard supports. Also, be sure to keep the receipt with the warranty statement. After you know what drive your system can support, you then can select a drive that is appropriate for the price range and intended use of your system. For example, Seagate has two lines of IDE hard drives: The Barracuda is less expensive and intended for the desktop market, and the Cheetah is more expensive and targets the server market. When purchasing a drive, you can compare price and features by searching retail sites or the Web sites of the drive manufacturers. Some of the more popular ones are listed in Table 8-3. The same manufacturers usually produce ATA drives and SCSI drives.

Now let's turn our attention to the step-by-step process of installing a Serial ATA drive.

STEPS TO INSTALL A SERIAL ATA DRIVE

A motherboard that has serial ATA connectors most likely has one or more PATA connectors, too. A PATA connector can be used for an optical drive or some other EIDE drive

Manufacturer	Web Site
Hitachi	*www.hitachigst.com*
Maxtor Corporation (currently owned by Seagate Technology)	*www.maxtor.com*
Samsung	*www.samsung.com*
Seagate Technology	*www.seagate.com*
Western Digital	*www.wdc.com*

Table 8-3   Hard drive manufacturers

including a hard drive. But SATA drives are faster than PATA drives, so it's best to use the PATA connector for other type drives than the hard drive.

> **💡 A+ Exam Tip**   The A+ 220-702 Practical Application exam expects you to know how to configure PATA and SATA devices in a system.

In Figure 8-20, you can see the back of two hard drives; one uses a serial ATA interface and the other uses a parallel ATA interface. Notice the parallel ATA drive has a bank of jumpers and a 4-pin power connector. These jumpers are used to determine master or slave settings on the IDE channel. Because a serial data cable accommodates only a single drive, there is no need for jumpers on the drive for master or slave settings. However, a serial ATA drive might have jumpers used to set features such as the ability to power up from standby mode. Most likely, if jumpers are present on a serial ATA drive, the factory has set them as they should be, and advises you not to change them.

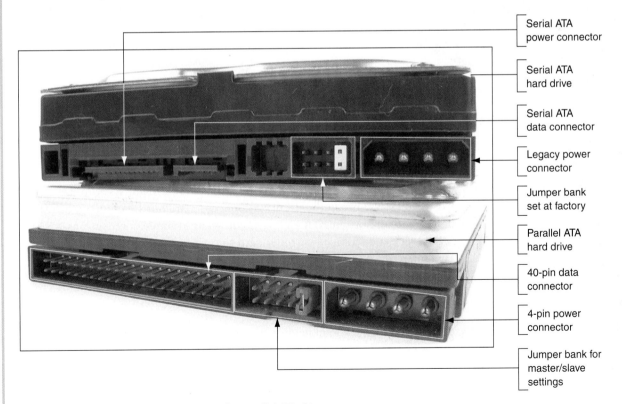

Serial ATA power connector
Serial ATA hard drive
Serial ATA data connector
Legacy power connector
Jumper bank set at factory
Parallel ATA hard drive
40-pin data connector
4-pin power connector
Jumper bank for master/slave settings

Figure 8-20   Rear of a serial ATA drive and a parallel ATA drive
Courtesy: Course Technology/Cengage Learning

A+
220-702
1.1

Some serial ATA drives have two power connectors, as does the one in Figure 8-20. Choose between the serial ATA power connector (which is the preferred connector) or the legacy 4-pin connector, but never install two power cords to the drive at the same time, because this could damage the drive.

If you have a PATA drive and a SATA connector on the motherboard, or you have a SATA drive and a PATA connector on the motherboard, you can purchase an adapter to make the hard drive connector fit your motherboard connector. Figure 8-21 shows two converters: one converts SATA drives to PATA motherboards and the other converts PATA drives to SATA motherboards. When you use a converter, know that the drive will run at the slower PATA speed.

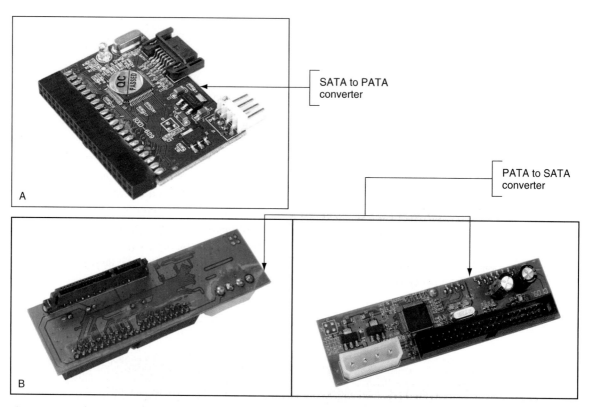

Figure 8-21   SATA to PATA and PATA to SATA converters
Courtesy: Course Technology/Cengage Learning

You can also purchase a SATA and/or PATA controller card that can provide internal PATA or SATA connectors and external eSATA connectors. You might want to use a controller card when (1) the motherboard drive connectors are not functioning; or (2) the motherboard does not support an ATA standard you want to implement (such as a SATA II drive). Figure 8-22 shows a storage controller card that offers one Ultra ATA-133/IDE connection, two internal SATA I connections, and one eSATA port.

Now let's look at the step-by-step process of installing a SATA drive.

STEP 1: PREPARE FOR THE INSTALLATION

Prepare for the installation by knowing your starting point, reading the documentation, and preparing your work area.

Know Your Starting Point

As with installing any other devices, before you begin installing your hard drive, make sure you know where your starting point is. Do this by answering these questions: How is your

Figure 8-22 EIDE and SATA storage controller card
Courtesy: Course Technology/Cengage Learning

system configured? Is everything working properly? Verify which of your system's devices are working before installing a new one. Later, if a device does not work, the information will help you isolate the problem. Keeping notes is a good idea whenever you install new hardware or software or make any other changes to your PC system. Write down what you know about the system that might be important later.

> **Notes** When installing hardware and software, don't install too many things at once. If something goes wrong, you won't know what's causing the problem. Install one device, start the system, and confirm that the new device is working before installing another.

As always, just in case you lose BIOS setup information in the process, write down any variations in setup from the default settings. Two good places to record BIOS settings are the notebook you keep about this computer and the manual for the motherboard.

Read Documentation

Before you take anything apart, carefully read all the documentation for the drive and controller card, as well as the part of your motherboard documentation that covers hard drive installation. Make sure that you can visualize all the steps in the installation. If you have any questions, keep researching until you locate the answer. You can also call technical support, or ask a knowledgeable friend for help. As you get your questions answered, you might discover that what you are installing will not work on your computer, but that is better than coping with hours of frustration and a disabled computer. You cannot always anticipate every problem, but at least you can know that you made your best effort to understand everything in advance. What you learn in thorough preparation pays off every time!

Prepare Your Work Area and Take Precautions

The next step is to prepare a large, well-lit place to work. Set out your tools, documentation, new hardware, and notebook. Remember the basic rules concerning static electricity, which you learned in Chapter 4. Be sure to protect against ESD by wearing a ground bracelet during the installation. You need to also avoid working on carpet in the winter when there's a lot of static electricity.

Some added precautions for working with a hard drive are as follows:

- Handle the drive carefully.
- Do not touch any exposed circuitry or chips.
- Prevent other people from touching exposed microchips on the drive.
- When you first take the drive out of the static-protective package, touch the package containing the drive to a screw holding an expansion card or cover, or to a metal part of the computer case, for at least two seconds. This drains the static electricity from the package and from your body.
- If you must set down the drive outside the static-protective package, place it component-side-up on a flat surface.
- Do not place the drive on the computer case cover or on a metal table.

If you're assembling a new system, it's best to install drives before you install the motherboard so that you will not accidentally bump sensitive motherboard components with the drives.

STEP 2: INSTALL THE DRIVE

So now you're ready to get started. Follow these steps to install the drive in the case:

1. Turn off the computer and unplug it. Press the power button to drain the power. Remove the computer case cover. Check that you have an available power cord from the power supply for the drive.

> **Notes** If there are not enough power cords from a power supply, you can purchase a Y connector that can add an additional power cord.

2. Decide which bay will hold the drive. To do that, examine the locations of the drive bays and the length of the data cables and power cords. Bays designed for hard drives do not have access to the outside of the case, unlike bays for optical drives and other drives in which disks are inserted. Also, some bays are wider than others to accommodate wide drives such as CD drives and DVD drives. Will the data cable reach the drives and the motherboard connector? If not, rearrange your plan for locating the drives in the bays, or purchase a custom-length data cable. Some bays are stationary, meaning the drive is installed inside the bay as it stays in the case. Other bays are removable; you remove the bay and install the drive in the bay, and then return the bay to the case.

3. For a stationary bay, slide the drive in the bay, and secure one side of the drive with one or two short screws (see Figure 8-23). It's best to use two screws so the drive will not move in the bay, but sometimes a bay only provides a place for a single screw on each side.

A+
220-702
1.1

Figure 8-23 Secure one side of the drive with one or two screws
Courtesy: Course Technology/Cengage Learning

⚡ Caution Be sure the screws are not too long. If they are, you can screw too far into the drive housing, which will damage the drive itself.

4. Carefully, without disturbing the drive, turn the case over and put one or two screws on the other side of the drive (see Figure 8-24).

— Hard drive

Figure 8-24 Secure the other side of the drive with one or two screws
Courtesy: Course Technology/Cengage Learning

📝 Notes Do not allow torque to stress the drive. In other words, don't force a drive into a space that is too small for it. Also, placing two screws in diagonal positions across the drive can place pressure diagonally on the drive.

5. Check the motherboard documentation to find out which serial ATA connectors on the board to use first. For example, four serial ATA connectors are shown in Figure 8-25. The documentation says to use the two red connectors (labeled SATA1 and SATA2 on the board) before you use the black connectors (labeled SATA3 and SATA4). Connect

A+
220-702
1.1

Figure 8-25   This motherboard has four serial ATA connectors
Courtesy: Course Technology/Cengage Learning

the serial ATA data cable to the hard drive and to the red SATA1 connector. For both the drive and the motherboard, you can only plug the cable into the connector in one direction.

6. Connect a SATA or 4-pin power connector from the power supply to the drive (see Figure 8-26).

Figure 8-26   Connect the SATA power cord to the drive
Courtesy: Course Technology/Cengage Learning

7. Check all your connections and power up the system.

8. To verify the drive was recognized correctly, enter BIOS setup and look for the drive. Figure 8-27 shows a BIOS setup screen on a system that has two SATA connectors and one PATA connector. A hard drive is installed on one SATA connector and a CD drive is installed on the PATA connector.

A+
220-702
1.1

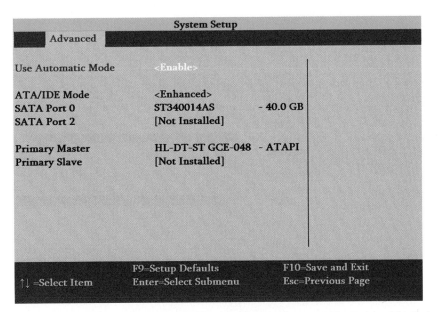

Figure 8-27 BIOS setup screen showing a SATA hard drive and PATA CD drive installed
Courtesy: Course Technology/Cengage Learning

8

A+ 220-702

Notes If the drive light on the front panel of the computer case does not work after you install a new drive, try reversing the LED wire on the motherboard pins.

A+
220-702
1.1
1.2
2.3

STEP 3: USE WINDOWS TO PARTITION AND FORMAT THE NEW DRIVE

If you are installing a new hard drive in a system that is to be used for a new Windows installation, after you have physically installed the drive, boot from the Windows setup CD or DVD, and follow the directions on the screen to install Windows on the new drive. The setup process partitions and formats the new drive before it begins the Windows installation. How to install Windows is covered in Chapter 12.

If you are installing a second hard drive in a system that already has Windows installed on the first hard drive, use Windows to partition and format the second drive. Follow these steps:

1. Boot the system to the Windows Vista desktop.

2. Click **Start**, right-click **Computer** (for Windows XP, right-click **My Computer**), and select **Manage** from the shortcut menu. Respond to the UAC box. In the Computer Management window, click **Disk Management**. The Disk Management window opens (see Figure 8-28).

3. In Figure 8-28, the new hard drive shows as Disk 1. Right-click **Disk 1** and select **Initialize Disk** from the shortcut menu, as shown in the figure.

4. On the next screen (see Figure 8-29), select **MBR (Master Boot Record)** and click **OK**. The drive will be initialized as a Basic Disk.

5. To format the drive, right-click the unallocated space on the drive and select **New Simple Volume** from the shortcut menu (see Figure 8-30). The New Simple Volume

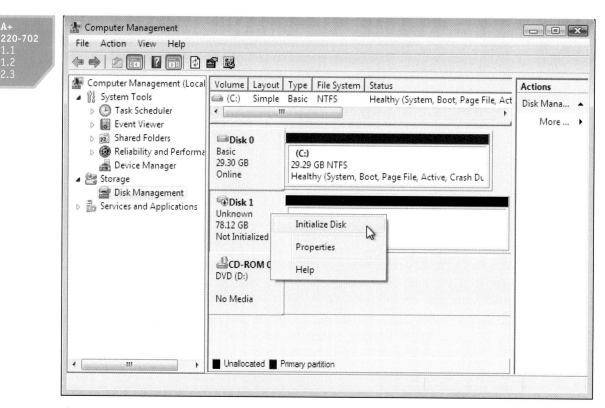

Figure 8-28   Use Disk Management to partition the new drive
Courtesy: Course Technology/Cengage Learning

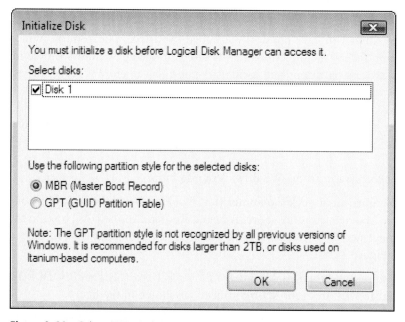

Figure 8-29   Select MBR as the partition style for the new drive
Courtesy: Course Technology/Cengage Learning

A+
220-702
1.1
1.2
2.3

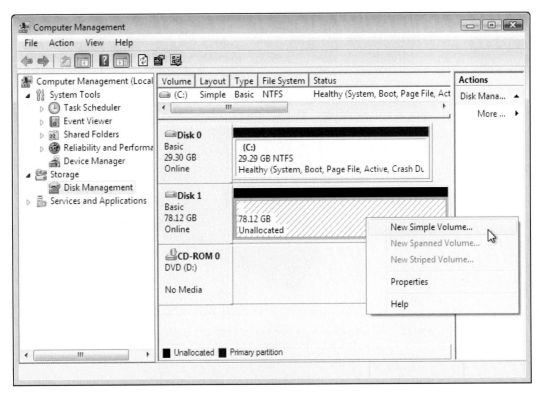

Figure 8-30 Simple volumes are created on basic disks
Courtesy: Course Technology/Cengage Learning

Wizard appears. Follow the wizard to choose a volume size, assign a drive letter to the volume, assign a volume name, and select the type of file system. Depending on which Windows OS you are using and the service packs installed, your choices for a file system will be NTFS, FAT32, or FAT (which is exFAT). For most situations, select NTFS, which is always available as a choice. The drive will format and then be ready to use. When you use Vista to create partitions, the first three partitions will be primary partitions and the fourth partition will be an extended partition. Windows XP allows you to decide which partition will be the extended partition.

> **Notes** Solid state drives are currently only used on laptops. However, by the time this book is in print, it is expected that SSD drives will be available for desktop computers. Some SSD drives come preformatted from the manufacturer using the NTFS file system. Other SSD drives require you to partition and format them the same way you format magnetic drives. SSD drives can use either a SATA or PATA connection in laptops. The installation of an SSD drive in a computer case works the same way as does a magnetic drive installation.

A+
220-702
1.1
1.2

INSTALLING A SATA DRIVE IN A REMOVABLE BAY

Now let's see how a drive installation goes when you are dealing with a removable bay. Figure 8-31 shows a computer case with a removable bay that has a fan at the front of the bay to help keep the drives cool. (The case manufacturer calls the bay a fan cage.) The bay is anchored to the case with three black locking devices. The third locking device from the bottom of the case is disconnected in the photo.

A+
220-702
1.1
1.2

Three locking pins
used to hold the
bay in the case

Figure 8-31 The removable bay has a fan in front and is anchored to the case with locking pins
Courtesy: Course Technology/Cengage Learning

Turn the handle on each locking device counterclockwise to remove it. Then slide the bay to the front and out of the case. Insert the hard drive in the bay, and use two screws on each side to anchor the drive in the bay (see Figure 8-32). Slide the bay back into the case, and reinstall the locking pins. The installation now goes the same way as when you are using a stationary bay.

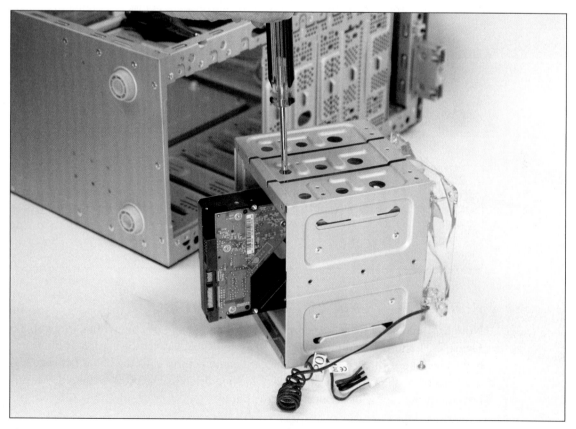

Figure 8-32 Install the hard drive in the bay using two screws on each side of the drive
Courtesy: Course Technology/Cengage Learning

A+
220-702
1.1
1.2

STEPS TO CONFIGURE AND INSTALL A PARALLEL ATA DRIVE

Following the PATA or EIDE standard, a motherboard can support up to four EIDE devices using either 80-conductor or 40-conductor cables. The motherboard offers two IDE connectors (see Figure 8-33). Each connector accommodates one IDE channel, and each channel can accommodate one or two IDE devices. One channel is called the primary channel, while the other channel is called the secondary channel. Each IDE connector uses one 40-pin cable. The cable has two connectors on it: one connector in the middle of the cable and one at the far end. An EIDE device can be a hard drive, DVD drive, CD drive, tape drive, or another type of drive. One device is configured to act as the master controlling the channel, and the other device on the channel is the slave. There are, therefore, four possible configurations for four EIDE devices in a system:

- ◢ Primary IDE channel, master device
- ◢ Primary IDE channel, slave device
- ◢ Secondary IDE channel, master device
- ◢ Secondary IDE channel, slave device

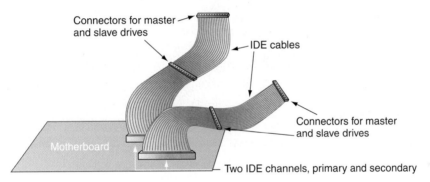

Figure 8-33   A motherboard supporting PATA has two IDE channels; each can support a master and slave drive using a single EIDE cable
Courtesy: Course Technology/Cengage Learning

The master or slave designations are made by setting jumpers or DIP switches on the devices, or by using a special cable-select data cable. Documentation can be tricky. Some hard drive documentation labels the master drive setting as the Drive 0 setting and the slave drive setting as the Drive 1 setting rather than using the terms master and slave. The connectors on a parallel ATA 80-conductor cable are color-coded (see Figure 8-34). Use the blue end to connect to the motherboard; use the black end to connect to the drive.

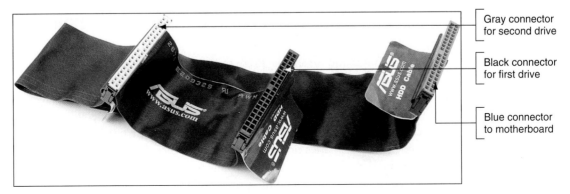

Figure 8-34   80-conductor cable connectors are color-coded
Courtesy: Course Technology/Cengage Learning

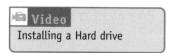

Video

Installing a Hard drive

If you only have one drive connected to the cable, put it on the black connector at the end of the cable, not the gray connector in the middle.

> **Notes** When installing a hard drive on the same channel with an ATAPI drive such as a CD drive, always make the hard drive the master and make the ATAPI drive the slave. An even better solution is to install the hard drive on the primary channel and the CD drive and any other drive on the secondary channel.

The motherboard might also be color-coded so that the primary channel connector is blue (see Figure 8-35) and the secondary channel connector is black. This color-coding is intended to ensure that the ATA/66/100/133 hard drive is installed on the primary IDE channel.

Figure 8-35   The primary IDE channel connector is often color-coded as blue
Courtesy: Course Technology/Cengage Learning

> 💡 **A+ Exam Tip**   The A+ 220-702 Practical Application exam expects you to know how to install a device such as a hard drive. Given a list of steps for the installation, you should be able to order the steps correctly or identify an error in a step.

As with installing SATA drives, know your starting point, read the documentation for the drive and the motherboard, prepare your work area, and be careful when handling the drive to protect it against ESD. Wear a ground bracelet as you work. Now let's look at the steps for installing a PATA drive.

STEP 1: OPEN THE CASE AND DECIDE HOW TO CONFIGURE THE DRIVES

Turn off the computer and unplug it. Press the power button to drain the power. Remove the computer case cover. Check that you have an available power cord from the power supply for the drive.

You must decide which IDE connector to use, and if another drive will share the same IDE data cable with your new drive. When possible, leave the hard drive as the single drive on one channel, so that it does not compete with another drive for access to the channel and possibly slow down performance. Use the primary channel before you use the secondary channel. Place the fastest devices on the primary channel, and the slower devices on the secondary channel. This pairing helps keep a slow device from pulling down a faster device.

As an example of this type of pairing, suppose you have a tape drive, CD drive, and two hard drives. Because the two hard drives are faster than the tape drive and CD drive, put the two hard drives on one channel and the tape drive and CD drive on the other.

> **Notes** If you have three or fewer devices, allow the fastest hard drive to be your boot device and the only device on the primary channel.

STEP 2: SET THE JUMPERS ON THE DRIVE

Often, diagrams of the jumper settings are printed on the top of the hard drive housing (see Figure 8-36). If they are not, see the documentation, or visit the Web site of the drive manufacturer. (Hands-On Project 8-4 gives you practice researching jumper settings.)

Table 8-4 lists the four choices for jumper settings, and Figure 8-37 shows a typical jumper arrangement for a drive that uses three of these settings. In Figures 8-36 and 8-37, note that a black square represents an empty pin and a black rectangle represents a pair of pins with a jumper in place. Know that your hard drive might not have the first configuration as an option, but it should have a way of indicating if the drive will be the master device. The factory default setting is usually correct for the drive to be the single drive on a system. Before you change any settings, write down the original ones. If things go wrong,

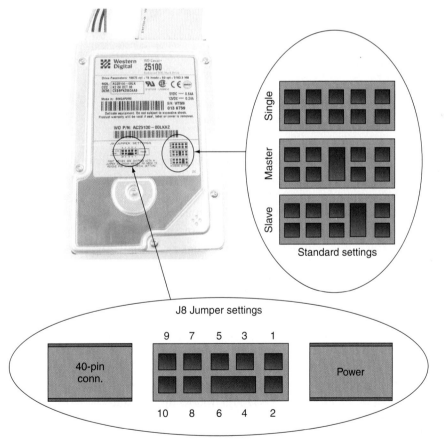

Figure 8-36   A PATA drive most likely will have diagrams of jumper settings for master and slave options printed on the drive housing
Courtesy: Course Technology/Cengage Learning

Configuration	Description
Single-drive configuration	This is the only hard drive on this EIDE channel. (This is the standard setting.)
Master-drive configuration	This is the first of two drives; it most likely is the boot device.
Slave-drive configuration	This is the second drive using this channel or data cable.
Cable-select configuration	The cable-select (CS or CSEL) data cable determines which of the two drives is the master and which is the slave.

Table 8-4   Jumper settings on a parallel ATA hard drive

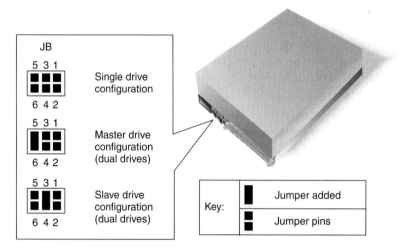

Figure 8-37   Jumper settings on a hard drive and their meanings
Courtesy: Course Technology/Cengage Learning

you can revert to the original settings and begin again. If a drive is the only drive on a channel, set it to single. For two drives on a controller, set one to master and the other to slave.

Some hard drives have a cable-select configuration option. If you choose this configuration, you must use a cable-select data cable. When using an 80-conductor cable-select cable, the drive nearest the motherboard is the master, and the drive farthest from the motherboard is the slave. You can recognize a cable-select cable by a small hole somewhere in the data cable or by labels (master or slave) on the connectors.

STEP 3: MOUNT THE DRIVE IN THE BAY

Now that you've set the jumpers, your next step is to look at the drive bay that you will use for the drive. The bay can be stationary or removable. You saw both types of bays earlier in the chapter. In the following steps, you will see how the hard drive is installed in a computer case that has three other drives: a DVD drive, a Zip drive, and a floppy drive. All three drives install in a removable bay. Do the following to install the hard drive in the bay:

1. Remove the bay from the case and insert the hard drive in the bay. You can line up the drive in the bay with the front of the computer case (see Figure 8-38) to see how drives will line up in the bay. Put the hard drive in the bay flush with the front of the bay so it will butt up against the computer case once the bay is in position (see Figure 8-39). Line up other drives in the bay so they are flush with the front of the computer case. In Figure 8-39, a floppy drive and Zip drive are already in the bay.

Figure 8-38 Line up the floppy drive in the removable bay so it's flush with the front of the case
Courtesy: Course Technology/Cengage Learning

Figure 8-39 Position the hard drive flush with the end of the bay
Courtesy: Course Technology/Cengage Learning

2. You must be able to securely mount the drive in the bay; the drive should not move when it is screwed down. Line up the drive and bay screw holes, and make sure everything will fit. After checking the position of the drive and determining how screws are placed, install four screws (two on each side) to mount the drive in the bay.

3. Decide whether to connect the data cable to the drive before or after you insert the bay inside the computer case, depending on how accessible the connections are. In this

A+
220-702
1.1
1.2

example, the data cables are connected to the drives first and then the bay is installed inside the computer case. In Figure 8-40, the data cables for all the drives in the bay are connected to the drives.

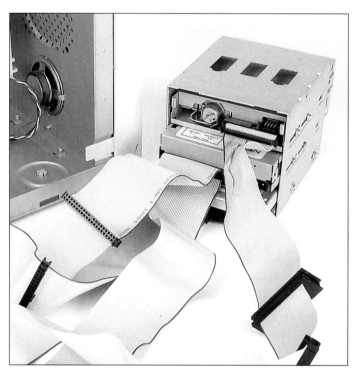

Figure 8-40   Connect the cables to all three drives
Courtesy: Course Technology/Cengage Learning

4. The next step is to place the bay back into position and secure the bay with the bay screw or screws (see Figure 8-41). Note that some bays are secured with clips. For example, for the bay shown in Figure 8-42, when you slide the bay into the case, you will hear the clipping mechanism pop into place when the bay is all the way in.

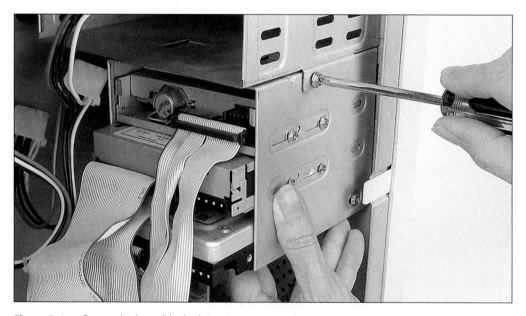

Figure 8-41   Secure the bay with the bay screw
Courtesy: Course Technology/Cengage Learning

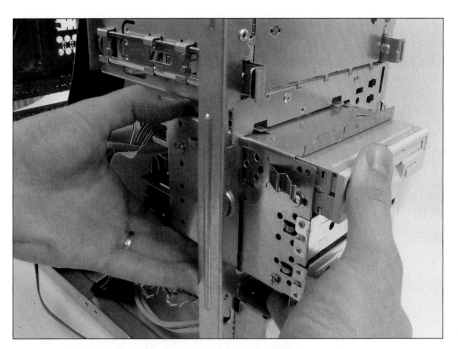

Figure 8-42 Slide the bay into the case as far as it will go
Courtesy: Course Technology/Cengage Learning

5. You can now install a power connection to each drive (Figure 8-43). In Figure 8-43, the floppy drive uses the small Berg power connection, and the other drives use the large Molex ones. It doesn't matter which of the power cords you use, because they all produce the same voltage. Also, the cord only goes into the connection one way.

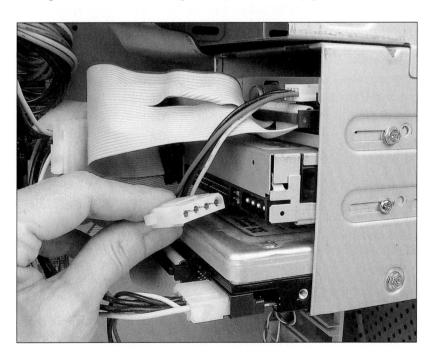

Figure 8-43 Connect a power cord to each drive
Courtesy: Course Technology/Cengage Learning

6. Next, connect the data cable to the IDE connector on the motherboard (see Figure 8-44). Make certain pin 1 and the edge color on the cable align correctly at both ends of the cable. Normally, pin 1 is closest to the power connection on the drive.

A+
220-702
1.1
1.2

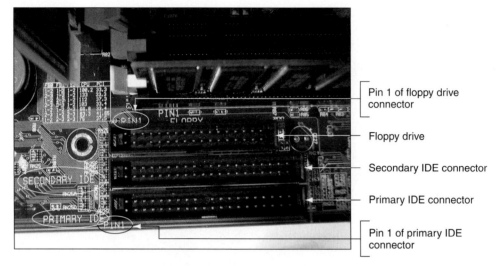

Pin 1 of floppy drive connector

Floppy drive

Secondary IDE connector

Primary IDE connector

Pin 1 of primary IDE connector

Figure 8-44   Floppy drive and two IDE connectors on the motherboard
Courtesy: Course Technology/Cengage Learning

7. When using a motherboard connection, if the wire connecting the motherboard to the hard drive light on the front of the case was not connected when the motherboard was installed, connect it now. If you reverse the polarity of the LED wire, the light will not work. Your motherboard manual should tell you the location of the LED wires on the motherboard.

8. Before you replace the case cover, plug in the monitor and turn on the computer. (On the other hand, some systems won't power up until the front panel is installed.) Verify that your system BIOS can find the drive before you replace the cover and that it recognizes the correct size of the drive. If you have problems, refer to the troubleshooting section at the end of this chapter.

After you confirm that your drive is recognized, the size of the drive is detected correctly, and supported features are set to be automatically detected, reboot the system. Then the next thing to do is to use an operating system to prepare the drive for first use.

INSTALLING A HARD DRIVE IN A WIDE BAY

If you are mounting a hard drive into a bay that is too large, a universal bay kit can help you securely fit the drive into the bay. These inexpensive kits should create a tailor-made fit. In Figure 8-45, you can see how the universal bay kit adapter works. The adapter spans the distance between the sides of the drive and the bay. Figure 8-46 shows the drive installed in a wide bay.

HOW TO IMPLEMENT HARDWARE RAID

RAID can be implemented by hardware (using a RAID controller on the motherboard or on a RAID controller card) or by the operating system. When RAID is implemented at the hardware level, the motherboard does the work and Windows is not aware of a hardware RAID implementation. If the motherboard does not have RAID connectors on the board, you can purchase a RAID adapter card (also called a RAID controller card) to provide the RAID hard drive connectors and to manage the RAID array. Some SCSI host adapter cards support RAID or you can use a RAID controller card

Side brackets connect to hard drive

Figure 8-45 Use the universal bay kit to make the drive fit the bay
Courtesy: Course Technology/Cengage Learning

Figure 8-46 Hard drive installed in a wide bay using a universal bay kit adapter
Courtesy: Course Technology/Cengage Learning

that provides IDE or serial ATA connectors. Figure 8-47 shows a RAID controller card by Sabrent that provides four SATA ports.

> **♀ A+ Exam Tip** The A+ 220-702 Practical Application exam expects you to be able to detect problems, troubleshoot, and replace a RAID controller card.

Figure 8-48 shows a motherboard that has two regular IDE connectors, two serial ATA connectors that can be configured for RAID, and two IDE RAID connectors. This board supports spanning, RAID 0, RAID 1, and a combination of RAID 0 and RAID 1 (called RAID 0+1). For another motherboard, six SATA connectors on the motherboard can be used as RAID connectors if RAID is enabled in BIOS setup.

A+
220-702
1.1
1.2

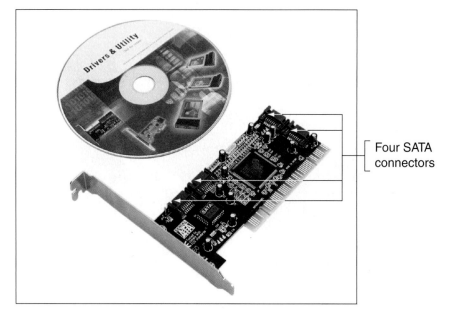

Figure 8-47   RAID controller card provides four SATA internal connectors
Courtesy: Course Technology/Cengage Learning

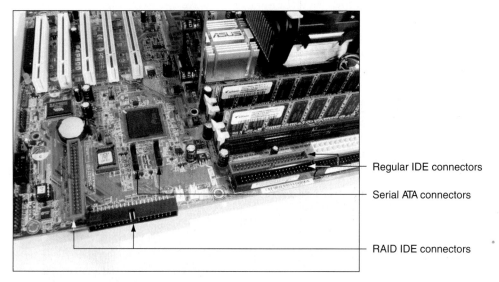

Figure 8-48   This motherboard supports RAID 0 and RAID 1
Courtesy: Course Technology/Cengage Learning

When installing a hardware RAID system, for best performance, all hard drives in an array should be identical in brand, size, speed, and other features. Also, if Windows is to be installed on a hard drive that is part of a RAID array, RAID must be implemented before Windows is installed. As with installing any hardware, first read the documentation that comes with the motherboard or RAID controller and follow those specific directions rather than the general guidelines given here. For one motherboard that has six SATA connectors that support RAID, here are the general directions to install the RAID array using three matching hard drives in a RAID 5 array:

1. Install the three SATA drives in the computer case and connect each drive to a SATA connector on the motherboard (see Figure 8-49). To help keep the drives cool, the drives are installed with an empty bay between each drive.

Figure 8-49 Install three matching hard drives in a system
Courtesy: Course Technology/Cengage Learning

2. Boot the system and enter BIOS setup. On the Advanced setup screen, verify the three drives are recognized. Select the option to configure SATA and then select RAID from the menu (see Figure 8-50).

3. Reboot the system and a message is displayed on-screen: "Press <Ctrl-I> to enter the RAID Configuration Utility." Press **Ctrl** and **I** to enter the utility (see Figure 8-51).

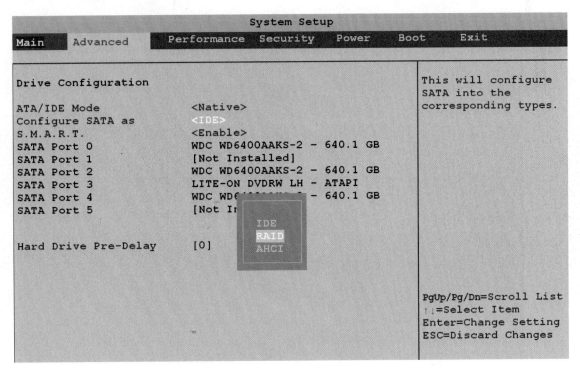

Figure 8-50 Configure SATA ports on the motherboard to enable RAID
Courtesy: Course Technology/Cengage Learning

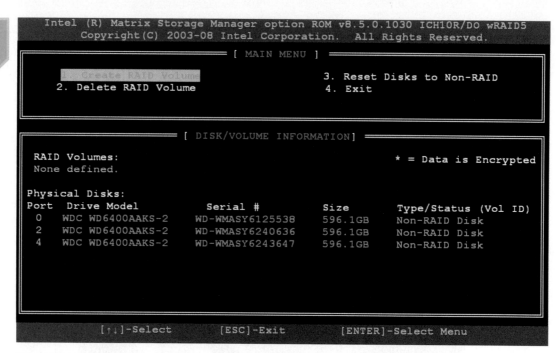

Figure 8-51 BIOS utility to configure a RAID array
Courtesy: Course Technology/Cengage Learning

Notice in the information area that the three drives are recognized and their current status is Non-RAID Disk.

4. Select option 1 to "**Create RAID Volume.**" On the next screen shown in Figure 8-52, enter a volume name (FileServer in our example).

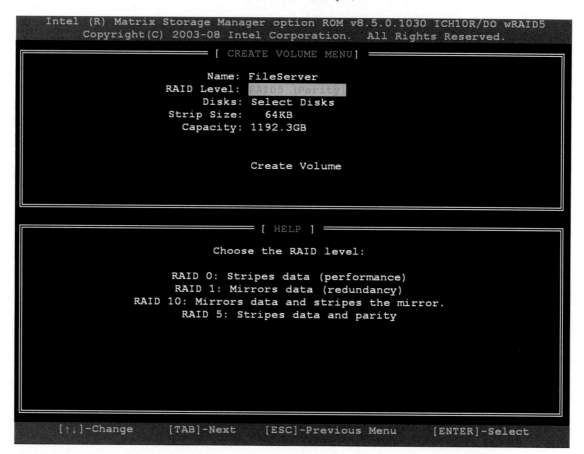

Figure 8-52 Make your choices for the RAID array
Courtesy: Course Technology/Cengage Learning

A+
220-702
1.1
1.2

5. Under RAID Level, select **RAID5 (Parity)**. Because we are using RAID 5, which requires three hard drives, the option to select the disks for the array is not available. All three disks will be used in the array.

6. Select the value for the Strip Size. (This is the amount of space devoted to one strip across the striped array. Choices are 32 KB, 64 KB, or 128 KB.)

7. Enter the size of the volume. The available size is shown in Figure 8-52 as 1192 GB, but you don't have to use all the available space. The space you don't use can later be configured as another array. (In this example, I entered 500 GB.)

8. Select **Create Volume** to complete the RAID configuration. A message appears warning you, that if you proceed, all data on all three hard drives will be lost. Type **Y** to continue. The array is created and the system reboots.

You are now ready to install Windows. Do the following:

1. Boot from the Windows setup CD or DVD.

2. For Windows XP, at the beginning of Windows setup, you are given the opportunity to press F6 to install a RAID or SCSI driver. Press **F6** and insert the RAID driver CD that came bundled with the motherboard. Windows Vista does not require the RAID drivers and the installation proceeds as normal. (The details of installing Windows XP and Vista are covered in Chapter 12.)

Figure 8-53 shows the Disk Management window for this system immediately after Vista was installed. Notice Vista recognizes one hard drive, which it partitioned and formatted during the installation process as drive C:. The drive C: size is 500 GB, which is the amount of space that was dedicated to the RAID array. As far as Vista knows, there is a single 500 GB hard drive. BIOS is managing the RAID array without Vista's awareness. If we install the RAID drivers that are found on the motherboard driver CD, then we can manage the RAID array from within Windows. Alternately, the RAID array can be managed from the BIOS utility by pressing Ctrl-I during the boot.

For file servers using RAID 5 that must work continuously and hold important data, it might be practical to use hardware that allows for hard drive hot-swapping, which means you can remove one hard drive and insert another without powering down the computer. However, hard drives that can be hot-swapped cost significantly more than regular hard drives. RAID hard drive arrays are sometimes used as part of a storage area network (SAN). A SAN is a network that has the primary purpose of providing large amounts of data storage.

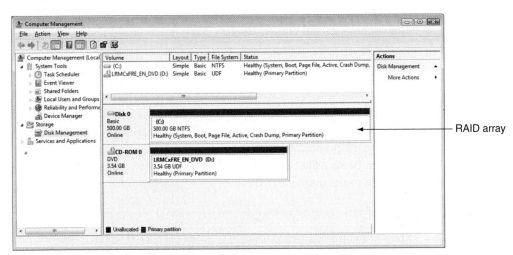

Figure 8-53 Vista Disk Management sees the RAID array as a single 500 GB hard drive
Courtesy: Course Technology/Cengage Learning

A+
220-702
1.1
1.2

STEPS TO INSTALL A FLOPPY DRIVE

Many computers today come with a hard drive and CD or DVD drive, but don't include a floppy drive, although the motherboard most likely has a 34-pin floppy drive connector. Most computer cases also have one or more empty bays for a 3½" floppy drive.

If you have no extra bay and want to add a floppy drive, you can attach an external drive that comes in its own case and has its own power supply. Most external drives today connect to the main system using a USB port, such as the one in Figure 8-54.

Figure 8-54   An external floppy drive uses a USB connection
Courtesy: Course Technology/Cengage Learning

Here are the steps to add or replace a floppy drive. Be sure to protect the computer against ESD as you work.

1. Turn off the computer, unplug the power cord, press the power button, and remove the cover.

2. Unplug the power cable to the old floppy drive. Steady the drive with one hand while you dislodge the power cable with the other hand. Unplug the data cable from the old drive.

3. Unscrew and dismount the drive. Some drives have one or two screws on each side that attach the drive to the drive bay. After you remove the screws, the drive usually slides to the front and out of the case. Sometimes, you must lift a catch underneath the drive as you slide the drive forward. Sometimes, the drive is installed into a removable bay. For this type of case, first unscrew the screws securing the bay (most likely these screws are on the front of the case) and remove the bay. Then unscrew and remove the drive from the bay.

4. Slide the new drive into the bay. Screw the drive down with the same screws used on the old drive. Make sure the drive is anchored so that it cannot slide forward or backward, or up or down, even if a user turns the case on its side.

5. If you are adding (not replacing) a floppy drive, connect the floppy drive data cable to the motherboard. Align the edge color of the ribbon cable with pin 1 on the motherboard connectors. Some connectors only allow you to insert the cable in one direction. Be sure the end of the cable with the twist connects to the drive and the other end to the motherboard.

> **Notes** If your power supply doesn't have the smaller Berg connector for the floppy drive, you can buy a Molex-to-Berg converter to accommodate the floppy drive power connector.

A+
220-702
1.1
1.2

6. Connect the data cable and power cord to the drive. Make sure that the data cable's colored edge is connected to the pin-1 side of the connection, as shown in Figure 8-55. With some newer floppy drives, pin 1 is marked as an arrow on the drive housing (see Figure 8-56).

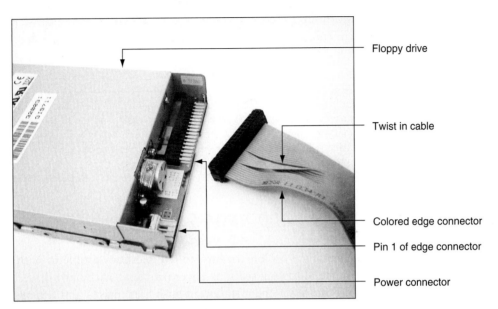

Floppy drive

Twist in cable

Colored edge connector

Pin 1 of edge connector

Power connector

Figure 8-55 Connect colored edge of cable to pin 1
Courtesy: Course Technology/Cengage Learning

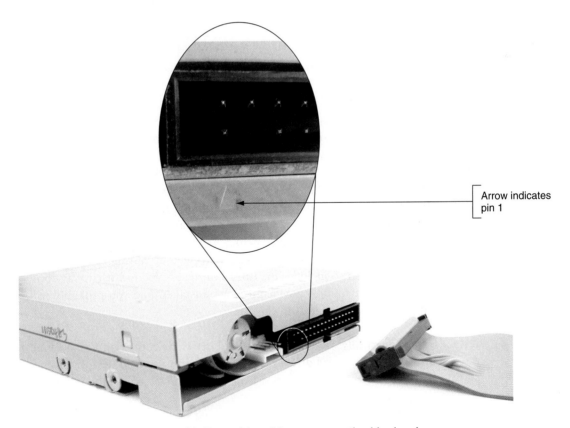

Arrow indicates pin 1

Figure 8-56 Pin 1 is marked on this floppy drive with an arrow on the drive housing
Courtesy: Course Technology/Cengage Learning

A+
220-702
1.1
1.2

Most connections on floppy drives are oriented the same way, so this one probably has the same orientation as the old drive. The power cable goes into the power connection in only one direction. Be careful not to offset the connection by one pin.

7. Replace the cover, turn on the computer, and enter BIOS setup to verify the drive is recognized with no errors. If you are adding (not replacing) a floppy drive, you must inform BIOS setup by accessing setup and changing the drive type. Boot to the Windows desktop and test the drive by formatting a disk or copying data to a disk.

> **Notes** Note that you can turn on the PC and test the drive before you replace the computer case cover. If the drive doesn't work, having the cover off makes it easier to turn off the computer, check connections, and try again. Just make certain that you don't touch anything inside the case while the computer is on. Leaving the computer on while you disconnect and reconnect a cable is very dangerous for the PC and will probably damage something—including you!

TROUBLESHOOTING HARD DRIVES

A+
220-702
1.2

In this part of the chapter, you'll learn how to troubleshoot problems with hard drives and floppy drives. The following sections cover problems with hard drive installations, and problems that occur after the installation with hard drives and floppy drives. Problems with booting the PC caused by hard drive hardware are also covered. How to deal with problems caused by a corrupted Windows installation is covered in Chapters 15 and 16.

PROBLEMS WITH HARD DRIVE INSTALLATIONS

Sometimes, trouble crops up during an installation. Keeping a cool head, thinking things through carefully a second, third, and fourth time, and using all available resources will most likely get you out of any mess.

Installing a hard drive is not difficult, unless you have an unusually complex situation. For example, your first hard drive installation should not involve the intricacies of installing a second SCSI drive in a system that has two SCSI host adapters. Nor should you install a

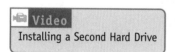
Video
Installing a Second Hard Drive

second drive in a system that uses an IDE connection for one drive on the motherboard and an adapter card in an expansion slot for the other drive. If a complicated installation is necessary and you have never installed a hard drive, ask for expert help.

The following list describes the errors that cropped up during a few hard drive installations; the list also includes the causes of the errors, and what was done about them. Everyone learns something new when making mistakes, and you probably will, too. You can then add your own experiences to this list.

◢ Shawn physically installed an IDE hard drive. He turned on the machine and accessed BIOS setup. The hard drive was not listed as an installed device. He checked and discovered that autodetection was not enabled. He enabled it and rebooted. Setup recognized the drive.

◢ When first turning on a previously working PC, John received the following error message: "Hard drive not found." He turned off the machine, checked all cables, and discovered that the data cable from the motherboard to the drive was loose. He reseated the cable and rebooted. POST found the drive.

▲ Lucia physically installed a new hard drive, replaced the cover on the computer case, and booted the PC with a Windows setup CD in the drive. POST beeped three times and stopped. Recall that diagnostics during POST are often communicated by beeps if the tests take place before POST has checked video and made it available to display the messages. Three beeps on most computers signal a memory error. Lucia turned off the computer and checked the memory modules on the motherboard. A module positioned at the edge of the motherboard next to the cover had been bumped as she replaced the cover. She reseated the module and booted again, this time with the cover still off. The error disappeared.

▲ Jason physically installed a new hard drive and turned on the computer. He received the following error: "No boot device available." He forgot to insert a Windows setup CD. He put the disc in the drive and rebooted the machine successfully.

▲ The hard drive did not physically fit into the bay. The screw holes did not line up. Juan got a bay kit, but it just didn't seem to work. He took a break, went to lunch, and came back to make a fresh start. Juan asked others to help view the brackets, holes, and screws from a fresh perspective. It didn't take long to discover that he had overlooked the correct position for the brackets in the bay.

▲ Maria set the jumpers on a PATA hard drive and physically installed the drive. She booted and received the following error message: "Hard drive not present." She rechecked all physical connections and found everything okay. After checking the jumper settings, she realized that she had set them as if this were the second drive of a two-drive system, when it was the only drive. She restored the jumpers to their original state. In this case, as in most cases, the jumpers were set at the factory to be correct when the drive is the only drive.

If BIOS setup does not recognize a newly installed hard drive, check the following:

▲ Has BIOS setup been correctly configured for autodetection?
▲ Are the jumpers on the drive set correctly?
▲ Have the power cord and data cable been properly connected? Verify that each is solidly connected at both ends.
▲ Check the Web site of the drive manufacturer for suggestions, if the above steps don't solve your problem. Look for diagnostic software that can be downloaded from the Web site and used to check the drive.

> **A+ Exam Tip** The A+ 220-702 Practical Application exam might give you a symptom and expect you to select a probable source of a problem from a list of sources. These examples of what can go wrong can help you connect problem sources to symptoms.

> **Caution** One last warning: When things are not going well, you can tense up and make mistakes more easily. Be certain to turn off the machine before doing anything inside! Not doing so can be a costly error. For example, a friend had been trying and retrying to boot for some time, and got frustrated and careless. He plugged the power cord into the drive without turning the PC off. The machine began to smoke and everything went dead. The next thing he learned was how to replace a power supply!

HOW TO APPROACH A HARD DRIVE PROBLEM AFTER THE INSTALLATION

After the hard drive is working, problems can arise later, such as corrupted data files, a corrupted Windows installation, or a hardware problem that causes the system to refuse to boot. In this section, you'll learn about some tools you can use to solve hard drive problems and how to approach the problem and prioritize what to do first. Then, in later sections, we'll look at some specific error messages and symptoms and how to deal with them.

START WITH THE END USER

When an end user brings a problem to you, begin the troubleshooting process by interviewing the user. When you interview the user, you might want to include these questions:

- Can you describe the problem and describe when it occurs?
- Was the computer recently moved?
- Was any new hardware or software recently installed?
- Was any software recently reconfigured or upgraded?
- Did someone else use your computer recently?
- Does the computer have a history of similar problems?
- Is there important data on the drive that is not backed up?
- Can you show me how to reproduce the problem?

After you gather this basic information, you can prioritize what to do and begin diagnosing and addressing the hard drive problems.

PRIORITIZE WHAT YOU HAVE LEARNED

If a hard drive is not functioning and data is not accessible, setting priorities helps focus your work. For most users, data is the first priority unless they have a recent backup. Software can also be a priority if it is not backed up. Reloading software from the original installation disks or CD can be time consuming, especially if the configuration is complex or software macros or scripts are on the drive and not backed up.

If a system won't boot from the hard drive, your first priority might be to recover data on the drive. Therefore, before you try to solve the hardware or Windows problem that prevents booting, consider removing the drive and installing it as a second drive in a working system. If the partition table on the problem drive is intact, you might be able to copy data from the drive to the primary drive in the working system. Then turn your attention to solving the original problem.

If you have good backups of both data and software, hardware might be your priority. It could be expensive to replace, but downtime can be costly, too. The point is, when trouble arises, determine your main priority and start by focusing on that.

BE AWARE OF AVAILABLE RESOURCES

Be aware of the resources available to help you resolve a problem:

- *User manuals* often list error messages and their meanings.
- *Installation manuals* most likely will have a troubleshooting section and list any diagnostic tools available.

▲ *The Internet* can also help you diagnose hardware and software problems. Go to the Web site of the product manufacturer, and search for the FAQs (frequently asked questions) list or a support forum. It's likely that others have encountered the same problem and posted the question and answer. If you search and cannot find your answer, you can post a new question. Use a search engine such as *www.google.com* to search for the error, the hardware device, the problem, the technology used, and other keywords that can help you find useful information. Many technicians enjoy sharing what they know online, and the Internet can be a rich source of all kinds of technical information and advice. Be careful, however. Not all technical advice is correct or well intentioned.

▲ *Training materials* can offer insights, explain concepts and tools, and give you a general direction as to how to approach a problem.

▲ *Telephone, chat, or e-mail technical support* from the hardware and software manufacturers can help you interpret an error message, or it can provide general support in diagnosing a problem. Most technical support is available during working hours by telephone. Check your documentation for telephone numbers. An experienced computer troubleshooter once said, "The people who solve computer problems do it by trying something and making phone calls, trying something else and making more phone calls, and so on, until the problem is solved."

▲ *PartitionMagic* by Symantec (*www.symantec.com*) lets you manage partitions on a hard drive for Windows XP. You can change the size of partitions and move partitions without losing data while you work. You can switch file systems without disturbing your data, and you can hide and show partitions to secure your data. For Vista, Disk Management performs many of the same functions.

▲ *SpinRite* by Gibson Research (*www.grc.com*) is hard drive utility software that has been around for years. Still a DOS application without a sophisticated GUI interface, SpinRite has been updated to adjust to new drive technologies. It supports NTFS, FAT32, and SCSI drives. It can be installed and run from any bootable device, including a CD, USB drive, or floppy disk, which means that it doesn't require much system overhead. Because it is written in a language closer to the binary code that the computer understands, it is more likely to detect underlying hard drive problems than software that uses Windows, which can stand as a masking layer between the software and the hard drive. SpinRite analyzes the entire hard drive surface, performing data recovery of corrupted files and file system information. Sometimes, SpinRite can recover data from a failing hard drive when other software fails.

▲ *GetDataBack* by Runtime Software (*www.runtime.org*) can recover data and program files even when Windows cannot recognize the drive. It can read NTFS and FAT32 file systems and can solve problems with a corrupted partition table, boot record, or root directory.

▲ *Hard drive manufacturer's diagnostic software* is available for download from the Web sites of many hard drive manufacturers. For example, you can download Data Lifeguard Diagnostic for DOS from the Western Digital Web site (*www.wdc.com*), burn the software to CD, and boot from the CD (see Figure 8-57). Using the software, you can do a quick test to check Western Digital drives for physical problems or an extended test to repair any correctable problems. You can also write zeros to every sector on the drive to get a fresh start with the drive. There's also a Windows version that can be used to test a second hard drive in your system. Another similar program is SeaTools by Seagate

A+
220-702
1.2

Figure 8-57 Download hard drive diagnostic software from the drive manufacturer's Web site
Courtesy: Course Technology/Cengage Learning

(see Figure 8-58) that can be downloaded and used to create a bootable CD or floppy that can be used to test and analyze most ATA and SCSI drives by Seagate and other manufacturers.

> **Notes** Always check compatibility between utility software and the operating system with which you plan to use it. One place you can check for compatibility is the service and support section of the software manufacturer's Web site.

> **Notes** Remember one last thing: After making a reasonable and diligent effort to resolve a problem, getting the problem fixed could become more important than resolving it yourself. There comes a time when you might need to turn the problem over to a more experienced technician.

> 💡 **A+ Exam Tip** The A+ 220-702 Practical Application exam expects you to know how to troubleshoot problems with SATA, PATA, and solid state hard drives and with floppy disk drives.

A+
220-702
1.2

Figure 8-58   Use SeaTools by Seagate to create a diagnostic CD or floppy to test and analyze hard drives
Courtesy: Course Technology/Cengage Learning

A+
220-702
1.2
2.3
2.4

BOOT PROBLEMS CAUSED BY HARD DRIVE HARDWARE

In this section, we look at different problems with the hard drive that present themselves during the boot. These problems can be caused by the hard drive subsystem, by the partition table or file system on the drive, or by files required for the OS to boot. When trying to solve a problem with the boot, you need to decide if the problem is caused by hardware or software. All the problems discussed in this section are caused by hardware. In Chapters 15 and 16, you'll learn how to deal with problems that cause errors when loading the operating system and problems with missing or corrupted data files. All these type errors are caused by software.

PROBLEMS AT POST

Recall from Chapter 5 that the BIOS performs the POST at the beginning of the boot to verify that essential hardware devices are working. Hardware problems usually show up at POST, unless there is physical damage to an area of the hard drive that is not accessed during POST. Hardware problems often make the hard

A+
220-702
1.2
2.3
2.4

drive totally inaccessible. If BIOS cannot find a hard drive at POST, it displays an error message similar to this:

```
Hard drive not found

Fixed disk error

Invalid boot disk

Inaccessible boot device

Inaccessible boot drive

Numeric error codes in the 1700s or 10400s
```

The reasons BIOS cannot access the drive can be caused by the drive, the data cable, the electrical system, the motherboard, the controller card (if one is present), or a loose connection. Here is a list of things to do and check:

1. If BIOS displays numeric error codes or cryptic messages during POST, check the Web site of the BIOS manufacturer for explanations of these codes or messages.

2. For a RAID array, use the BIOS utility to check the status of each disk in the array and to check for errors.

3. In BIOS setup, look for the ability to disable block mode. **Block mode** speeds up access time by allowing blocks of data to be read from the drive at one time. Disabling it will slow down drive performance but might solve the problem.

4. Remove and reattach all drive cables, Check for correct pin-1 orientation.

5. If you're using a RAID, eSATA, SATA, PATA, or SCSI controller card, remove and reseat it or place it in a different slot. Check the documentation for the card, looking for directions for troubleshooting.

6. Check the jumper settings on the drive.

7. Inspect the drive for damage, such as bent pins on the connection for the cable.

8. Determine if the hard drive is spinning by listening to it or lightly touching the metal drive (with power on).

9. Check the cable for frayed edges or other damage.

10. Check the installation manual for things you might have overlooked. Look for a section about system setup, and carefully follow all directions that apply.

11. Be sure the power cable and drive data cable connections are good.

12. Check BIOS setup for errors in the hard drive configuration. If you suspect an error, set CMOS to default settings, make sure autodetection is turned on, and reboot the system.

13. Try booting from another media such as the Windows setup CD. If you can boot using another media, you have proven that the problem is isolated to the hard drive subsystem. Windows recovery tools to use from the setup CD are covered in Chapters 15 and 16.

14. Check the drive manufacturer Web site for diagnostic software. Run the software to test the drive for errors.

15. If it is not convenient to create a boot CD with hard drive diagnostic software installed, you can move the drive to a working computer and install it as a second

drive in the system. Then you can use the diagnostic software installed on the primary hard drive to test the problem drive. While you have the drive installed in a working computer, be sure to find out if you can copy data from it to the good drive, so that you can recover any data not backed up. Note that for these temporary tests, you don't have to physically install the drive in the working system. Open the computer case. Carefully lay the drive on the case and connect a power cord and data cable (see Figure 8-59). Then turn on the PC. While you have the PC turned on, be *very careful* to not touch the drive or touch inside the case. Also, while a tower case is lying on its side like the one in Figure 8-59, don't use the CD or DVD drive.

Figure 8-59 Temporarily connect a faulty hard drive to another system to diagnose the problem and try to recover data
Courtesy: Course Technology/Cengage Learning

16. If the drive still does not boot, exchange the three field replaceable units—the data cable, the adapter card (optional), and the hard drive itself—for a hard drive subsystem. Do the following, in order:

   ◢ Reconnect or swap the drive data cable.
   ◢ Reseat or exchange the drive controller card, if one is present.
   ◢ Exchange the hard drive for a known good unit.

17. If the hard drive refuses to work but its light stays on even after the system has fully booted, the problem might be a faulty controller on the hard drive or motherboard. Try replacing the hard drive. Next, try an ATA controller card to substitute for the ATA connectors on the motherboard or replace the motherboard.

18. Sometimes older drives refuse to spin at POST. Drives that have trouble spinning often whine at startup for several months before they finally refuse to spin altogether. If your drive whines loudly when you first turn on the computer, never turn off the computer. One of the worst things you can do for a drive that is having difficulty starting up is to leave the computer turned off for an extended period of time. Some drives, like old cars, refuse to start if they are unused for a long time.

A+
220-702
1.2
2.3
2.4

📖 **Notes** You can purchase an inexpensive converter such as the one in Figure 8-60 to connect a failing PATA hard drive to a working computer using a USB port. The kit also comes with a converter for a notebook hard drive. (A PATA connector on a laptop is shorter than a desktop PATA connector.) Figure 8-61 shows a SATA to USB converter kit. The SATA connector can be used for desktop or laptop hard drives because a SATA connector is the same for both. These ATA to USB converters are really handy when troubleshooting problems with hard drives that refuse to boot.

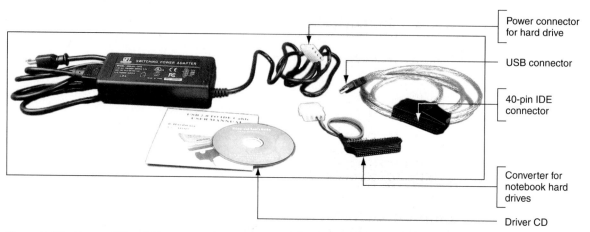

Power connector for hard drive

USB connector

40-pin IDE connector

Converter for notebook hard drives

Driver CD

Figure 8-60 Use an IDE to USB converter for diagnostic testing and to recover data from a failing PATA hard drive
Courtesy: Course Technology/Cengage Learning

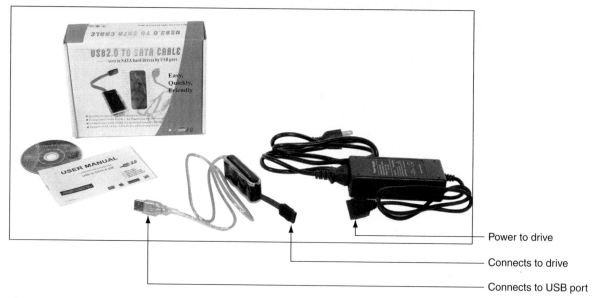

Power to drive

Connects to drive

Connects to USB port

Figure 8-61 Use a SATA to USB converter to recover data from a drive using a SATA connector
Courtesy: Course Technology/Cengage Learning

A bad power supply or a bad motherboard also might cause a disk boot failure. If the problem is solved by exchanging one of the field replaceable units listed, you still must reinstall the old unit to verify that the problem was not caused by a bad connection.

BUMPS ARE BAD!

The read/write heads at the ends of the read/write arms on a hard drive get extremely close to the platters, but do not actually touch them. This minute clearance between the heads and platters makes hard drives susceptible to destruction. Should a computer be bumped or moved while the hard drive is operating, a head can easily bump against the platter and scratch the surface. Such an accident causes a "hard drive crash," often making the hard drive unusable.

If the head mechanism is damaged, the drive and its data are probably total losses. If the first tracks that contain the partition table, boot record, MFT (for the NTFS file system), or root directory are damaged, the drive could be inaccessible, although the data might be unharmed.

Here's a trick that might work for a hard drive whose head mechanism is intact but whose first few tracks are damaged. First, find a working hard drive that has the same partition table information as the bad drive. Take the computer case off, place the good drive on top of the bad drive housing, and connect a spare power cord and the ATA data cable to the good drive. Leave a power cord connected to the bad drive. Boot from a bootable CD or floppy disk. No error message should show at POST. Access the good drive by entering C: at the command prompt. The C prompt should show on the monitor screen.

Without turning off the power, gently remove the data cable from the good drive and place it on the bad drive. Do not disturb the power cords on either drive or touch chips on the drive logic boards. Immediately copy the data you need from the bad drive to another media, using the Copy command. If the area of the drive where the data is stored, the FAT or MFT, and the directory are not damaged, this method should work.

Here's another trick for an older hard drive having trouble spinning when first turned on. Remove the drive from the case, hold it firmly in both hands, and give the drive a quick and sudden twist that forces the platters to turn inside the drive housing. Reinstall the drive. It might take several tries to get the drive spinning. After the drive is working, immediately make a backup and plan to replace the drive soon.

INVALID DRIVE OR DRIVE SPECIFICATION

If you get the error message "Invalid drive or drive specification," the system BIOS cannot read the partition table information. You'll need to boot from the Windows setup CD or DVD and check the partition table. How to do that is covered in Chapters 15 and 16.

BAD SECTOR ERRORS

Track and sector markings on a drive sometimes "fade" off the hard drive over time, which causes "bad sector" errors to crop up. These errors can also occur if an area of the drive has become damaged. Do not trust valuable data to a drive that has this kind of trouble. Plan to replace the drive soon. In the meantime, make frequent backups and leave the power on. You'll learn more about this and other software errors in later chapters.

SOLID STATE DRIVES

Recall that solid state drives have no moving parts, so you don't have to be concerned with bumping the drive while it is in use. They might come from the factory already partitioned and formatted using the NTFS file system, or you might have to format them yourself. If the drive gives errors, try using diagnostic software specific for this drive if it is available from the drive manufacturer. Also check the support section of the Web site for troubleshooting tips. SATA and PATA connections and BIOS settings for solid state drives look and work the same as for other drives.

TROUBLESHOOTING FLOPPY DRIVES AND DISKS

Table 8-5 lists errors that occur during and after the boot with the floppy drive or disks.

Problem or Error Message	What to Do About It
During the boot, numeric error messages in the 600 range or text error messages about the floppy drive appear on-screen.	◢ The floppy drive did not pass POST, which can be caused by problems with the drive, data cable, or motherboard. Check power and data cable connections. ◢ Try a different power cord. ◢ Check BIOS setup and reboot. ◢ Replace the drive.
Cannot read from a floppy disk	◢ The disk is not formatted. Try a different disk or try formatting this disk. ◢ The shuttle window on the floppy disk cannot open fully. ◢ The disk is inserted incorrectly. ◢ Something is lodged inside the disk's plastic housing. Check the shuttle window. ◢ Does the drive light come on? BIOS setup might be wrong, or the command you're using is wrong.
Non-system disk or disk error. Replace and strike any key when ready. No operating system found **Missing NTLDR** Invalid system disk Invalid boot disk	◢ You are trying to boot from a disk that is not bootable. Try a different disk or remove the disk and boot from the hard drive.
Not ready reading drive A:, Abort, Retry, Fail?	◢ The disk in drive A is not readable. Try formatting the disk.
General failure reading drive A:, Abort, Retry, Fail?	◢ The disk is badly corrupted or not yet formatted.
Track 0 bad, disk not usable	◢ The disk is bad or you are trying to format it using the wrong parameters on the Format command.
Write-protect error writing drive A:	◢ The disk is write-protected and the application is trying to write to it. Close the switch shown in Figure 8-62.
Bad sector or sector not found reading drive A, Abort, Retry, Ignore, Fail?	◢ Sector markings are corrupted or fading. Press I to ignore that sector and move on. Don't trust this disk with important data.

Table 8-5 Floppy drive and floppy disk errors that can occur during and after the boot

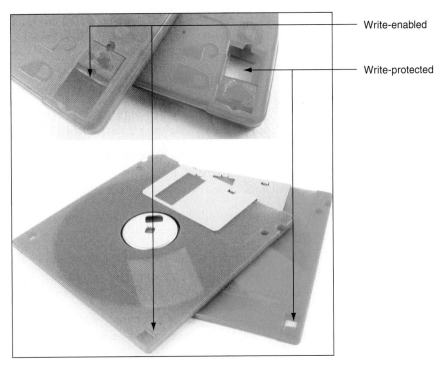

8

Figure 8-62 For you to write to a disk, the write-protect notch must be closed
Courtesy: Course Technology/Cengage Learning

>> CHAPTER SUMMARY

▲ A hard disk drive (HDD) comes in two sizes: 3.5" for desktop computers, and 2.5" for laptops.

▲ A hard drive can be a magnetic drive, a solid state drive, or a hybrid drive. A solid state drive is more expensive, faster, more reliable, and uses less power than a magnetic drive.

▲ A hard drive is low-level formatted at the factory where track and sector markings are written to the drive. Drive capacity is measured in GB or TB.

▲ When Windows prepares a drive as a basic disk, it installs a Master Boot Record (MBR) which contains a partition table and a master boot program.

▲ A primary partition is also called a volume, simple volume, or basic volume. An extended partition can have more than one logical drive.

▲ Two file systems used for hard drives are FAT32 (the older system) and NTFS (the newer system).

▲ Most hard drives use the ATA interface standards. The two main categories of ATA are parallel ATA and serial ATA. Serial ATA is easier to configure and better performing than PATA. External SATA ports are called eSATA ports.

▲ S.M.A.R.T. is a self-monitoring technology whereby the BIOS monitors the health of the hard drive and warns of an impending failure.

▲ ATAPI standards are used by optical drives and other drives that use the ATA interface on a motherboard or controller card.

▲ Several PATA standards are Fast ATA, Ultra ATA, Ultra ATA/66, Ultra ATA/100, and Ultra ATA/133.

▲ Three SATA standards provide data transfer rates of 1.5 Gb/sec, 3.0 Gb/sec, and 6.0 Gb/sec. Currently, the second standard is the most popular and is sometimes called SATA-300.

▲ SCSI is an interface standard for high-end hard drives used in servers.

▲ RAID technology uses an array of hard drives used to provide fault tolerance and/or improvement in performance.

▲ Today's floppy disks are 3½", high-density disks that hold 1.44 MB of data.

▲ When selecting a hard drive, consider the capacity of the drive, the spindle speed (for magnetic drives), the interface standard used, the cache or buffer size, and the average seek time. Also, solid state or hybrid drives are faster than magnetic drives.

▲ SATA drives require no configuration and are installed using a power cord and a single SATA data cable.

▲ PATA drives require you to set a jumper to determine if the drive will be the master or slave on a single cable. The PATA cable can accommodate two drives. A PATA motherboard has two PATA connectors for a total of four PATA drives in the system.

▲ After a hard drive is installed, verify it is recognized by BIOS and then use Windows to partition and format the drive. Solid state drives might be preformatted using the NTFS file system.

▲ Hardware RAID can be implemented by the motherboard or a RAID controller card. Software RAID is implemented by Vista or Windows XP. Best practice is to use hardware RAID rather than software RAID.

▲ After a floppy disk drive is installed, you must configure the drive in BIOS setup.

>> KEY TERMS

For explanations of key terms, see the Glossary near the end of the book.

80-conductor IDE cable
active partition
ANSI (American National
    Standards Institute)
ATAPI (Advanced
    Technology Attachment
    Packet Interface)
autodetection
basic disk
block mode
boot record
boot sector
cluster
DMA (direct memory access)
    transfer mode
drive image
EIDE (Enhanced IDE)
extended partition
external SATA (eSATA)
FAT12
fault tolerance
file allocation table (FAT)
file allocation unit
file system
floppy disk drive (FDD)

formatting
hard disk drive (HDD)
hard drive
head
high-level formatting
host adapter
hot-plugging
hot-swapping
hybrid hard drives
Integrated Device Electronics
Logical Unit Number (LUN)
logical drives
low-level formatting
magnetic hard drive
mirrored volume
New Technology file system
    (NTFS)
operating system formatting
parallel ATA
PIO (Programmed Input/Output)
    transfer mode
primary partition
RAID (redundant array of
    inexpensive disks or redundant
    array of independent disks)

RAID 0
RAID 1
RAID 5
RAID-5 volumes
read/write head
ReadyDrive
SCSI ID
SCSI host adapter card
serial ATA (SATA)
serial ATA cable
serial attached SCSI (SAS)
simple volume
S.M.A.R.T. (Self-Monitoring
    Analysis and Reporting
    Technology)
solid state device (SSD)
solid state drive (SSD)
spanning
striped volume
terminating resistor
volume

>> REVIEWING THE BASICS

1. What are the two common sizes for hard drives?

2. Why is a solid state drive referred to as solid state?

3. If a magnetic drive has four platters, how many heads does it have?

4. What is the name of the Vista technology that supports a hybrid drive?

5. When the OS addresses the sectors on a hard drive as one long list of sequential sectors, what is this technology called?

6. What are the main two components of the Master Boot Record on a hard drive?

7. What is the smallest unit of space on a hard drive that can be used to store a file?

8. What two file systems can Windows use to format a hard drive? Which system supports the most storage capacity?

9. Which ATA standard for hard drives first introduced S.M.A.R.T.?

10. Which ATA standard is the latest standard that made improvements to PATA?

11. A CD drive that uses a PATA connection must follow what standard?

12. How many pins does a PATA cable have? What is the maximum recommended length of a PATA cable?

13. What transfer mode can transmit data from a device to memory without involving the CPU?

14. What term describes the technology that allows you to exchange a hard drive without powering down the system?

15. Which RAID level mirrors one hard drive with a second drive so that the same data is written to both drives?

16. Which RAID level stripes data across multiple drives to improve performance and also provides fault tolerance?

17. How many pins does a floppy drive cable have?

18. Which file system does a floppy disk use?

19. What are three current ratings for spindle speed for a magnetic hard drive?

20. What Windows utility can be used to partition and format a hard drive?

21. What are the four possible configurations for a PATA drive installed in a system?

22. If a motherboard has one blue IDE connector and one black IDE connection, which do you use to install a single drive?

23. When implementing RAID on a motherboard, where do you enable the feature?

24. To write to a floppy disk, is it necessary for the write-protect notch to be open or closed?

25. What is the name of the Seagate utility that can be used to test a hard drive and diagnose a hard drive problem?

>> THINKING CRITICALLY

1. You install a hard drive and then turn on the PC for the first time. You access BIOS setup and see that the drive is not recognized. Which of the following do you do next?

   a. Turn off the PC, open the case, and verify that memory modules on the motherboard have not become loose.

   b. Turn off the PC, open the case, and verify that the data cable and power cable are connected correctly and jumpers on the drive are set correctly.

   c. Verify that BIOS autodetection is enabled.

   d. Reboot the PC and enter BIOS setup again to see if it now recognizes the drive.

2. Most motherboards that use SATA connectors have at least one PATA connector on the board. What is the most important reason this PATA connector is present?

   a. The hard drive used for booting the OS must use a PATA connector.

   b. The IDE controller will not work without at least one PATA connector.

   c. The board can accommodate older hard drives using the PATA connector.

   d. The PATA connector can be used for EIDE drives such as a CD or DVD drive.

3. You want to set up your desktop system to use a solid state drive, but the only solid state drives you can find are 2.5" drives intended for laptops. Which of the following do you do?

   a. Buy a laptop computer with a solid state drive.

   b. Buy a bay adapter that will allow you to install a 2.5" drive in a desktop case bay.

   c. Flash BIOS so that your system will support a laptop hard drive.

   d. Use a special SATA controller card that will support a laptop hard drive.

>> HANDS-ON PROJECTS

PROJECT 8-1:   Examining the BIOS Setting for a Hard Drive

From the BIOS setup information on your computer, write down or print all the BIOS settings that apply to your hard drive. Explain each setting that you can. What is the size of the installed drive?

PROJECT 8-2:   Selecting a Replacement Hard Drive

Suppose the 640-GB Western Digital hard drive installed in the RAID array and shown in Figure 8-49 has failed. Search the Internet and find a replacement drive as close to this drive as possible. Print three Web pages showing the sizes, features, and prices of three possible replacements. Which drive would you recommend as the replacement drive and why?

PROJECT 8-3:   Preparing for Hard Drive Hardware Problems

1. Boot your PC and make certain that it works properly. Turn off your computer, remove the computer case, and disconnect the data cable to your hard drive. Turn on the computer again. Write down the message that you get.

2. Turn off the computer and reconnect the data cable. Reboot and make sure the system is working again.

3. Turn off the computer and disconnect the power supply cord to the hard drive. Turn on the computer. Write down the error that you get.

4. Turn off the computer, reconnect the power supply, and reboot the system. Verify the system is working again.

PROJECT 8-4:   Researching with the Internet

Suppose a friend has asked you to install an old hard drive in his computer. The drive is the Maxtor Quantum Fireball Plus AS 20.5-GB hard drive. You want the drive to be the slave drive, and you know that you must change the current jumper settings. The four jumpers on the drive are labeled *DS*, *CS*, *PK*, and *Rsvd*. The description of the jumpers doesn't tell you how to set the jumpers so the drive is the slave. The documentation is not available. What do you do?

The best solution is to use the Internet to access the drive manufacturer's Web site for this information. In this case, the site is *www.maxtor.com*. Use this example or some other example given by your instructor to determine the correct settings for the jumpers.

PROJECT 8-5:   Researching Floppy Drives on the Internet

Use the Internet to answer the following questions:

▲ What is the price of an internal floppy drive?

▲ What kind of connections do external floppy disk drives use? What is the price of an external drive?

▲ Why do you think external drives cost more than internal drives? What are the advantages of external drives? Internal drives?

PROJECT 8-6:   Installing a Hard Drive

In a lab that has one hard drive per computer, you can practice installing a hard drive by removing a drive from one computer and installing it as a second drive in another computer. When you boot up the computer with two drives, verify that both drives are accessible in Windows Explorer. Then remove the second hard drive, and return it to its original computer. Verify that both computers and drives are working.

>> REAL PROBLEMS, REAL SOLUTIONS

REAL PROBLEM 8-1: Data Recovery Problem

Your friend has a Windows XP desktop system that contains important data. He frantically calls you to say that when he turns on the computer, the lights on the front panel light up and he can hear the fan spin for a moment and then all goes dead. His most urgent problem is the data on his hard drive, which is not backed up. The data is located in several folders on the drive. What is the quickest and easiest way to solve the most urgent problem, recovering the data? List the major steps in that process.

REAL PROBLEM 8-2: Salvaging Valuable Data on a Floppy Disk

On the job as a PC repair technician at a local university, a distraught student comes to you in a panic. Susan shows you the plastic housing of her floppy disk has been chipped and cracked so she can't insert it into a floppy disk drive. The problem is it holds her only copy of her term paper that is due tomorrow! She desperately needs your help.

You examine the floppy disk and confirm that, yes, the housing is completely destroyed. You ask her how that happened and she begins to turn red as she describes a very vindictive little brother. You begin to feel sorry for her and decide to take the time to help. You notice the disk inside the housing appears to be in good shape. Can you remove the disk from the floppy disk housing and carefully place it in a new housing so she can insert it in a floppy disk drive? Test your theory by removing a floppy disk that has data written to it from one housing, putting it into another housing, and then reading the data on the disk.

REAL PROBLEM 8-3: Using Hardware RAID

You work as a PC technician for a boss who believes you are really bright and can solve just about any problem he throws at you. Folks in the company have complained one time too many that the file server downtime is just killing them, so he asks you to solve this problem. He wants you to figure out what hardware is needed to implement hardware RAID for fault tolerance. Here are the first steps you take:

1. You check the file server's configuration and discover it has a single hard drive using a serial ATA connection with Windows Server 2003 installed. There are four empty bays in the computer case and four extra 4-pin power cords.

2. You discover the server's motherboard has an empty PCIe x4 slot. You think the slot might accommodate a RAID controller.

3. After doing a little searching on the Web, you find the Intel RAID Controller SASMF8I (*http://www.intel.com/products/server/raid-controllers/sasmf8i/sasmf8i-overview.htm*). You think it might work.

4. The next steps are to read the documentation about this controller, and then decide on which RAID configuration you should use and how many and what kind of hard drives you should buy.

Complete the investigation and do the following:

1. Decide what hardware you must purchase and print Web pages showing the products and their cost.

2. What levels of RAID does this controller support? Which RAID level is best to use? Print any important information in the RAID controller documentation that supports your decisions. If you prefer, you can recommend a different RAID controller.

3. What is the total hardware cost of implementing RAID? Estimate how much time you think it will take for you to install the devices and test the setup.

Installing and Supporting I/O Devices

This chapter is packed full of details about the many I/O devices a PC support technician must be familiar with and must know how to install and support. We begin with looking at the features and characteristics of several input and output devices, including motherboard ports, display devices, and expansion cards. Then you'll learn how to install common peripherals, input devices, expansion cards, dual monitors, and multiple video cards. Troubleshooting is always an important skill for technicians, and so we end the chapter with a discussion of what can go wrong with I/O devices and how to identify the source of the problem and fix it. This chapter builds the foundation for Chapter 10, in which you will learn about multimedia devices.

BASIC PRINCIPLES TO SUPPORT I/O DEVICES

A+
220-701
3.3

An I/O device can be either internal (installed inside the computer case) or external (installed outside the case). Internal devices can be expansion cards inserted in expansion slots on the motherboard, such as a network card, sound card, video capture card, and video card. External devices include keyboards, monitors, mice, printers, scanners, digital cameras, and flash drives. You can connect an external device to the system using ports coming off the motherboard (serial, parallel, USB, IEEE 1394, and so forth), or a port can be provided by an expansion card.

In this chapter, you will learn a ton of information about these many I/O devices. However, for all these different devices, some basic principles apply to supporting each one of them. These principles are applied in numerous places throughout this chapter and are summarized here so you can get a first look at them. Consider these fundamental principles and concepts used when supporting I/O devices:

▲ *Every I/O device is controlled by software.* When you install a new I/O device, such as a barcode reader, you must install both the device and the device drivers to control the device. These device drivers must be written for the OS you are using. Recall from earlier chapters that the exception to this principle is some simple devices, such as the keyboard, that are controlled by the system BIOS or device drivers embedded in the OS.

▲ *When it comes to installing or supporting a device, the manufacturer knows best.* In this chapter, you will learn a lot of principles and procedures for installing and supporting a device, but when you're on the job installing a device or fixing a broken one, read the manufacturer documentation and follow those guidelines first. For example, for most installations, you install the device before you install the device driver. However, for some devices, such as a digital camera and a wireless keyboard, you install the device driver first. Check the device documentation to know which to do first.

▲ *Some devices need application software to use the device.* For example, after you install a scanner and its device drivers, you might also need to install Adobe Photoshop to use the scanner.

▲ *Problems with a device can sometimes be solved by updating the device drivers or firmware.* Device manufacturers often release updates to device drivers. Update the drivers to solve problems with the device or to add new features. The firmware on the device might also need updating to solve a problem or add a new feature.

▲ *Learning about I/O devices is a moving target.* No matter how much information can be packed into this chapter, it won't be enough. I've done my best to make sure everything presented in this chapter is current, but I know that by the time this book is in print, some of the content will already be outdated. To stay abreast of all the latest technologies, an excellent source for information is the Internet. Use a good search engine to look up additional information about the I/O devices in this chapter and to learn about others. For the most reliable information about a device, see the manufacturer's Web site.

▲ *Devices and their device drivers are managed using Device Manager.* Device Manager is the primary Windows tool to manage hardware devices. When you first install a device, use Device Manager to verify that Windows recognizes the device with no errors. You can also use it to uninstall, enable, or disable a device and view any problems that Windows sees concerning the device. Device Manager is also the tool to use to update drivers for a

A+
220-701
3.3

device. Device drivers that Microsoft has certified to work with Windows are digitally signed by Microsoft. Digitally signed drivers are required for all 64-bit versions of Vista.

◢ *Some devices are expected to follow the Energy Star standards.* **Energy Star** systems and peripherals have the U.S. Green Star, indicating that they satisfy certain energy-conserving standards of the U.S. Environmental Protection Agency (EPA), sometimes called the Green Standards. Devices that can carry the Green Star include computers, monitors, printers, copiers, and fax machines.

> **Notes** Office equipment is among the fastest growing source of electricity consumption in industrialized nations. Much of this electricity is wasted because people often leave computers and other equipment on overnight. Because Energy Star devices go into sleep mode when they are not used, they create overall energy savings of about 50 percent.

> 💡 **A+ Exam Tip** The A+ 220-701 Essentials exam expects you to know how to find and download a device driver.

9

A+ 220-701

APPLYING CONCEPTS

Suppose you have just borrowed an HP Photosmart 7760 Deskjet printer from a friend, but you forgot to borrow the CD with the printer drivers on it. Instead of going back to your friend's apartment, you can go to the Hewlett-Packard Web site (*www.hp.com*), download the drivers to a folder on your PC, and install the driver under Windows. Figure 9-1 shows a Web page from the site listing downloadable drivers for ink-jet printers. Be sure to download the drivers for the version of Windows you are using.

Figure 9-1 Download the latest device drivers from a manufacturer's Web site
Courtesy: Course Technology/Cengage Learning

We now turn our attention to the types and characteristics of I/O devices and peripherals for a PC.

TYPES AND FEATURES OF I/O DEVICES

A+
220-701
1.2

In this part of the chapter, you'll learn about the I/O ports on a motherboard, display devices, including a monitor, projector, and video card, and other expansion cards. Later in the chapter, you'll learn how to install, configure, and troubleshoot these devices.

I/O PORTS ON THE MOTHERBOARD

Devices can plug into a port that comes directly off the motherboard, such as a USB, FireWire (IEEE 1394), sound, video, PS/2, network, serial, or parallel port. Or a port such as an eSATA, FireWire, USB, parallel, serial, video, or SCSI port can be provided by an expansion card. In this section, you'll learn about the details of the serial, parallel, USB, and FireWire ports that come directly off a motherboard.

Figure 9-2 shows the ports on the rear of a computer case; some of them are provided by the motherboard and others are provided by an expansion card. When deciding what type of port a new device should use, the speed of the port is often a tiebreaker. Table 9-1 shows the speeds of various ports, from fastest to slowest.

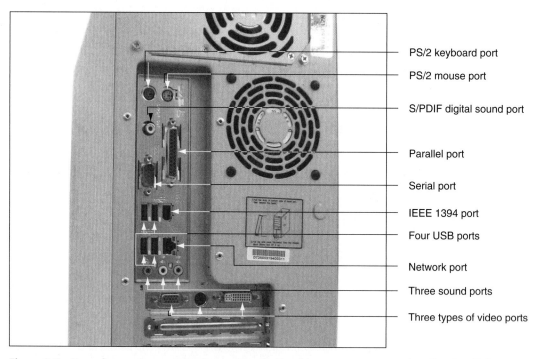

PS/2 keyboard port
PS/2 mouse port
S/PDIF digital sound port
Parallel port
Serial port
IEEE 1394 port
Four USB ports
Network port
Three sound ports
Three types of video ports

Figure 9-2   Rear of computer case showing ports; only the video ports are not coming directly off the motherboard
Courtesy: Course Technology/Cengage Learning

💡 **A+ Exam Tip**   The A+ 220-701 Essentials exam expects you to know about these motherboard I/O ports: Sound, video, USB 1.1 and 2.0, serial, IEEE 1394 (FireWire), parallel, and PS/2.

A+
220-701
1.2

Port Type	Maximum Speed
SuperSpeed USB 3.0	5.0 Gbps (gigabits per second)
eSATA-300 (eSATA Version 2)	3.0 Gbps
1394b (FireWire)*	1.2 Gbps or 800 Mbps (megabits per second)**
Hi-Speed USB 2.0	480 Mbps
1394a (FireWire)	400 Mbps
Original USB (USB 1.1)	12 Mbps or 1.5 Mbps
Parallel	1.5 Mbps
Serial	115.2 Kbps (kilobits per second)

*IEEE 1394b has been designed to run at 3.2 Gbps, but products using this speed are not yet manufactured.
**FireWire 800 is the industry name for 1394b running at 800 Mbps.

Table 9-1 Data transmission speeds for various port types

A+
220-701
1.2
3.3

USB PORTS

USB ports are fast becoming the most popular ports for slower I/O devices such as printers, mice, keyboards, scanners, joysticks, modems, digital cameras, fax machines, barcode readers, external floppy drives, external hard drives, and digital telephones. USB is much easier to configure and faster than regular serial or parallel ports and uses higher-quality cabling. In addition, power to the device can be drawn from the USB port so that a USB device might not need its own power source. Two or more USB ports are found on all motherboards (see Figure 9-3). Sometimes a case will have one or more USB ports on the front for easy access (see Figure 9-4). And some newer monitors might have a USB port provided by a USB cable plugged into a port on the back of the PC.

USB Version 1.1 (sometimes called Basic Speed USB or Original USB) allows for two speeds, 1.5 Mbps and 12 Mbps, and works well for slow I/O devices. USB Version 2.0 (sometimes called Hi-Speed USB or USB2) allows for up to 480 Mbps, which is 40 times

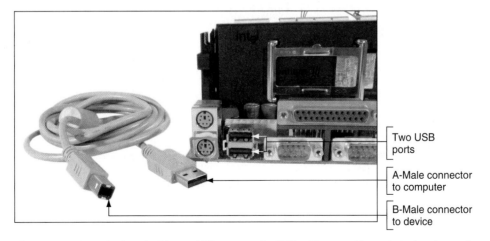

Two USB
ports

A-Male connector
to computer

B-Male connector
to device

Figure 9-3 A motherboard with two USB ports and a USB cable; note the rectangular shape of the connection as compared to the nearby serial and parallel D-shaped ports
Courtesy: Course Technology/Cengage Learning

A+
220-701
1.2
3.3

Figure 9-4   One or more USB ports on the front of a computer case make for easy access
Courtesy: Course Technology/Cengage Learning

⚡ **Caution**   Even though USB devices are hot-swappable, it's not always a good idea to plug or unplug a device while it is turned on. If you do so, especially when using a low-quality USB cable, you can fry the port or the device if wires in the USB connectors touch (creating a short) as you plug or unplug the connectors. Also, to protect the data on a USB storage device, double-click the **Safely Remove Hardware** icon in the notification area (see Figure 9-5) before removing the device. Select the device and click **Stop** (see Figure 9-6). It is then safe to remove the device.

Safely Remove
Hardware icon

Figure 9-5   Safely Remove Hardware icon in Windows Vista
Courtesy: Course Technology/Cengage Learning

Figure 9-6   Stop the device before removing it
Courtesy: Course Technology/Cengage Learning

faster than Original USB. Hi-Speed USB is backward compatible with slower USB devices. The latest USB standard is USB 3.0, which is called SuperSpeed USB and runs at 5.0 Gbps. SuperSpeed USB is about 10 times faster than Hi-Speed USB and roughly five times faster than FireWire 800. SuperSpeed USB devices are expected to be on the market sometime in 2010. The USB Implementers Forum, Inc. (*www.usb.org*), the organization responsible for developing USB, has adopted the symbols shown in Figure 9-7 to indicate if the product is certified by the organization as compliant with SuperSpeed, HiSpeed, or Original USB. Windows Vista supports Hi-Speed USB, and Windows XP supports it only if service packs are applied. Windows 7 is expected to support SuperSpeed USB.

Figure 9-7 SuperSpeed, Hi-Speed, and Original USB logos appear on products certified by the USB forum
Courtesy: Course Technology/Cengage Learning

As many as 127 USB devices can be daisy chained together using USB cables. In a daisy chain, one device provides a USB port for the next device. There can also be a stand-alone hub into which several devices can be plugged. Figure 9-8 shows an adapter that has two PS/2 connectors so that you can plug a PS/2 keyboard and mouse into the adapter and then use a single USB port for both devices.

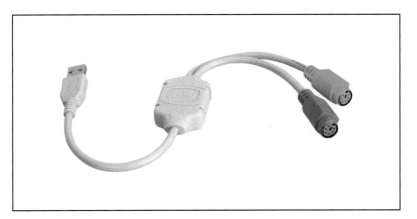

Figure 9-8 PS/2 to USB adapter allows a PS/2 keyboard and mouse to use a single USB port
Courtesy: Course Technology/Cengage Learning

A USB cable has four wires, two for power and two for communication. The two power wires (one is hot and the other is ground) allow the host controller to provide power to a device. The connector on the host computer or hub end is called the A-Male connector, and the connector on the device end of the cable is called the B-Male connector. The A-Male connector is flat and wide, and the B-Male connector is square. (Look back at Figure 9-3 to see both these connectors.) In addition, because some devices such as a digital camera are so small, USB standards allow for mini-A connectors and mini-B connectors. You can see one of these mini-B connectors in Figure 9-9 used with a digital camera. The A-Male connector of this USB cable is regular size to connect to a computer's USB port.

A+
220-701
1.2
3.3

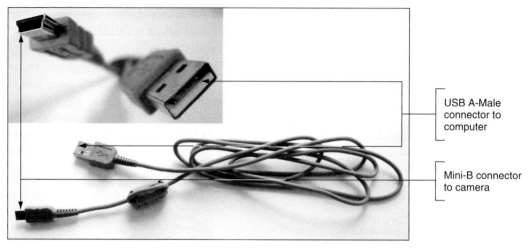

USB A-Male
connector to
computer

Mini-B connector
to camera

Figure 9-9 The digital camera USB cable uses a mini-B connector and a regular size A-Male connector
Courtesy: Course Technology/Cengage Learning

USB cables for Original USB can be up to 3 meters (9 feet, 10 inches) and Hi-Speed USB cables can be up to 5 meters (16 feet, 5 inches). If you need to put a USB device farther from the PC than the cable is long, you can use a USB hub in the middle to effectively double the distance.

A+
220-701
1.2

FIREWIRE (IEEE 1394) PORTS

FireWire and i.Link are common names for another peripheral bus officially named IEEE 1394 (or sometimes simply called 1394). FireWire is similar in design to USB, using serial transmission of data. FireWire devices are hot-pluggable and up to 63 FireWire devices can be daisy chained together.

Notes For interesting information about 1394, surf the 1394 Trade Association's Web site at *www.1394ta.org*.

The two standards for IEEE 1394 that apply to speed are IEEE 1394a and 1394b. 1394a supports speeds up to 400 Mbps and is sometimes called FireWire 400. 1394a allows for cable lengths up to 4.5 meters (15 feet) and for up to 16 cables daisy chained together. 1394a supports two types of connectors and cables: a 4-pin connector that does not provide voltage to a device and a 6-pin connector that does. Figure 9-10 shows a cable that plugs into a 6-pin FireWire port to provide a 4-pin connector for a FireWire device. Figure 9-11 shows an IEEE 1394a controller card that provides two external and one internal FireWire 400 6-pin connectors and one external FireWire 400 4-pin connector.

Tip IEEE 1394a ports with 6 pins are the most common FireWire ports on motherboards.

A+
220-701
1.2

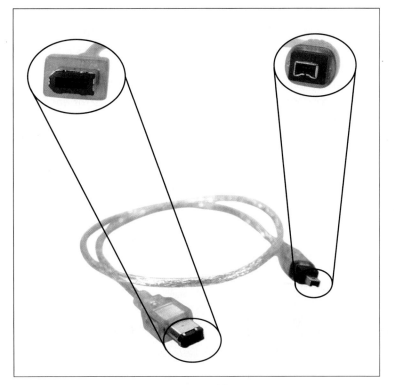

Figure 9-10 IEEE 1394a cable provides a smaller 4-pin and larger 6-pin connectors
Courtesy: Course Technology/Cengage Learning

9

A+ 220-701

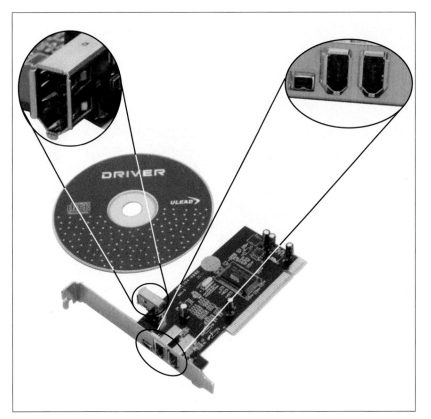

Figure 9-11 IEEE 1394a controller card provides internal and external FireWire 400 ports
Courtesy: Course Technology/Cengage Learning

A+
220-701
1.2

The newer standard, 1394b, supports speeds up to 3.2 Gbps, but current devices on the market are running at only 800 Mbps, which is why 1394b is also called FireWire 800. 1394b can use cables up to 100 meters (328 feet), and uses a 9-pin rectangular connector. You can use a 1394 cable that has a 9-pin connector at one end and 4-pin or 6-pin connector at the other end to connect a slower 1394a device to a faster 1394b computer port. However, know that when you mix standards for speed, the port and the device will run at the slower speed. Figure 9-12 shows a FireWire 800 adapter that provides three 1394 ports: two 1394b 9-pin ports and one 1394a 6-pin port. The power cable connected to the card plugs into a 4-pin power cable from the power supply to provide extra power to the card. The latest 1394 standard is 1394c, which allows FireWire 800 to use a standard network port and network cable. No devices are yet on the market that use this standard.

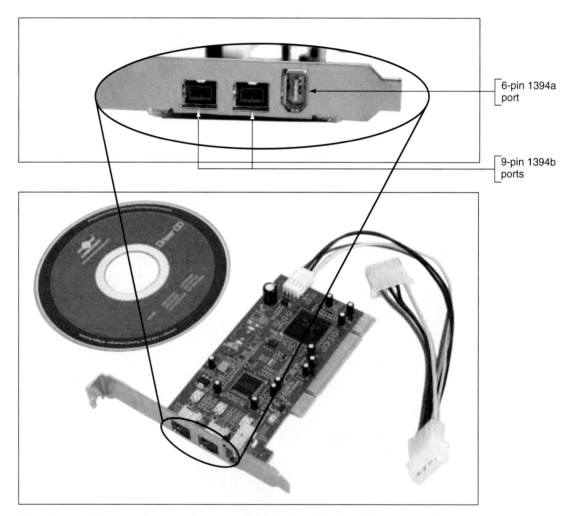

6-pin 1394a port

9-pin 1394b ports

Figure 9-12 This 1394 adapter card supports both 1394a and 1394b and uses a 32-bit PCI slot
Courtesy: Course Technology/Cengage Learning

Notes A variation of 1394 is **IEEE 1394.3**, which is designed for peer-to-peer data transmission. Using this standard, imaging devices such as scanners and digital cameras can send images and photos directly to printers without involving a computer.

IEEE 1394 uses isochronous data transfer, meaning that data is transferred continuously without breaks. This works well when transferring real-time data such as that received by television transmission. Because of the real-time data transfer and the fact that data can be transferred from one device to another without involving the CPU, IEEE 1394 is an ideal medium for data transfers between consumer electronics products, such as camcorders, digital video recorders (for example, TiVo), TVs, and digital cameras.

Figure 9-13 shows an example of how this data transfer might work. A person can record a home movie using a digital camcorder and download the data through a digital video recorder to a 1394-compliant external hard drive. The 1394-compliant digital recorder can connect to and send data to the hard drive without involving the PC. The PC can later read the data off the hard drive and use it as input to video-editing application software. A user can edit the data and design a professional video presentation complete with captioning and special effects. Furthermore, if the digital camcorder is also 1394-compliant, it can download the data directly to the PC by way of a 1394 port on the PC. The PC can then save the data to a regular internal hard drive.

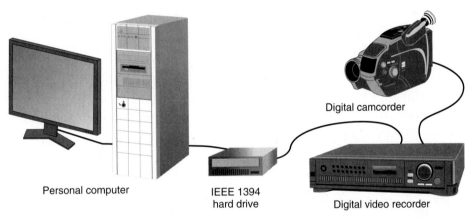

Digital camcorder

Personal computer   IEEE 1394
                           hard drive   Digital video recorder

Figure 9-13   IEEE 1394 can be used as the interface technology to connect consumer multimedia
equipment to a PC
Courtesy: Course Technology/Cengage Learning

SERIAL PORTS

Serial ports were originally intended for input and output devices such as a mouse or an external modem. Recall from Chapter 1 that a serial port transmits data in single bits, one bit following the next. You can identify these ports on the back of a PC case by (1) counting the pins and (2) determining whether the port is male or female. Serial ports have been mostly outdated by USB ports, and few new computers today have a serial port.

Figure 9-14 shows two serial ports, one parallel port, and one game port for comparison. (A game port is an outdated, legacy port used for joysticks.) Serial ports are sometimes called DB9 and DB25 connectors. DB stands for data bus and refers to the number of pins on the connector. The DB9 port is the most common. Serial ports are almost always male ports, and parallel ports are almost always female ports. A serial port is provided by the motherboard or might be provided by an adapter card called an I/O controller card. The controller card is likely to also provide a parallel port or game port. A serial port on the motherboard can be enabled and disabled in BIOS setup.

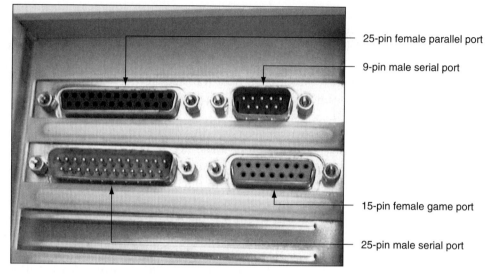

25-pin female parallel port

9-pin male serial port

15-pin female game port

25-pin male serial port

Figure 9-14 Serial, parallel, and game ports
Courtesy: Course Technology/Cengage Learning

Serials ports can go by more than one name. Because a serial port conforms to the interface standard called RS-232c (Reference Standard 232 revision c or Recommended Standard 232 revision c), it is sometimes called an RS-232 port. A serial port might also be called a COM1 (Communications port 1) or COM2 port. The controller logic on a motherboard that manages serial ports is called UART (Universal Asynchronous Receiver-Transmitter) or UART 16550, which leads us to sometimes call a serial port a UART port. By the way, the UART chip might also control an internal modem that uses resources normally assigned to the serial port.

PARALLEL PORTS

Parallel ports, commonly used by older printers, transmit data in parallel, eight bits at a time. Parallel ports that can handle communication in both directions are called bidirectional parallel ports. Today's printers and OSs expect the printer to be able to communicate with the OS such as when it needs to tell the OS that it is out of paper. These printers require bidirectional parallel ports.

Parallel ports fall into three categories: Standard Parallel Port (SPP), EPP (Enhanced Parallel Port), and ECP (Extended Capabilities Port). The standard parallel port is sometimes called a normal parallel port or a Centronics port, named after the 36-pin Centronics connection used by printers (see Figure 9-15). A standard port allows data to flow in only one direction and is the slowest of the three types of parallel ports. In contrast to a standard port, EPP and ECP are both bidirectional. ECP was designed to increase speed over EPP by using a DMA channel; therefore, when using ECP mode, you are using a DMA channel. Both EPP and ECP are covered under the IEEE 1284 specifications of the Institute of Electrical and Electronics Engineers (IEEE).

Most parallel cables are only 6 feet (1.8 meters) long, though no established standard sets maximum cable length. However, to ensure data integrity, you should avoid using a parallel cable longer than 15 feet (4.5 meters). (In fact, Hewlett-Packard recommends that cables be no longer than 10 feet, or 3 meters.) If the data is transmitted in parallel over a very long cable, the data integrity is sometimes lost. Although USB ports are replacing parallel ports, most computers still come with one parallel port.

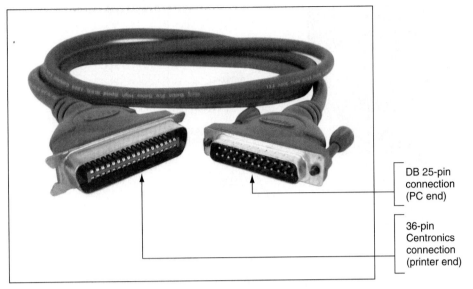

DB 25-pin
connection
(PC end)

36-pin
Centronics
connection
(printer end)

Figure 9-15 A parallel cable has a DB25 connection at the PC end of the cable and a 36-pin
Centronics connection at the printer end of the cable
Courtesy of Belkin Corporation

> **Notes** When using EPP or ECP printers and parallel ports, be sure to use a printer cable that is IEEE
> 1284–compliant. Older, noncompliant cables will not work properly with these printers. To find out if a
> cable is compliant, look for the label somewhere on the cable. Also, note that a printer using a parallel
> port can use a 36-pin Centronics connector, or some newer printers use the smaller 36-pin Micro-
> Centronics or Mini-Centronics connector.

INFRARED TRANSCEIVERS

An infrared transceiver, also called an IrDA (Infrared Data Association) transceiver or an
IR transceiver, provides an infrared port for wireless communication. Television remote
controls communicate with the TV or set top box using infrared transmission. On
desktop and notebook computers, infrared can be used by wireless keyboards, mice, cell
phones, PDAs, and printers. On notebooks, an infrared receiver is often used for
communication between the notebook and a PDA (such as a Pocket PC, Blackberry, or
smartphone) to transfer information. Also, an older PC might use an infrared device to
connect to a network.

> **A+ Exam Tip** The A+ 220-701 Essentials exam expects you to know how an infrared transceiver
> might be used on a notebook computer.

Figure 9-16 shows a remote control that can be used with multimedia applications
installed on a notebook computer. The remote communicates with the notebook by way
of an IR transceiver connected to a USB port. To use the remote, the device drivers that
came bundled with the device are installed and then the IR transceiver is connected to the
USB port.

A+
220-701
1.10

Figure 9-16 This remote control is an infrared device that uses an IR transceiver connected to a notebook by way of a USB port
Courtesy: Course Technology/Cengage Learning

Motherboards that support infrared are likely to have two IR header pins, the IR receiver and IR transmitter headers (see Figure 9-17). To use the IR headers, you need to enable infrared in BIOS setup, connect an infrared transceiver to the headers, and install the software in Windows that uses your infrared device. Later, if you have problems with infrared, be sure the infrared drivers that came bundled with the motherboard are installed. Also, try updating these drivers using those you download from the motherboard manufacturer Web site. Older motherboards that support IR transmissions might use the resources normally used by a serial port for IR. For these boards, if you enable infrared in BIOS setup, a serial port might be disabled.

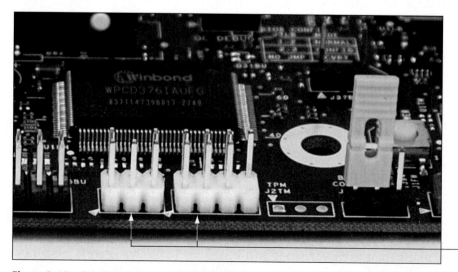

Pair of IR headers

Figure 9-17 Two IR headers on this motherboard are used to install an IR receiver and IR transmitter
Courtesy: Course Technology/Cengage Learning

Here's a warning and some advice: Finding an infrared transceiver that fits your motherboard IR headers might be difficult and expensive. If you need to use Infrared with a desktop system, the easiest and least expensive solution is to purchase a USB infrared transceiver for a few dollars and use it in a USB port on the board.

Infrared wireless is becoming obsolete because of the line-of-sight issue: There must be an unobstructed "view" between the infrared device and the receiver. Short-range radio technology such as Bluetooth is becoming the most popular way to connect a wireless I/O device to a nearby computer, because with radio waves there is no line-of-sight issue.

> **Notes** Infrared standards are defined by the Infrared Data Association (IrDA). Its Web site is *www.irda.org*.

DISPLAY DEVICES

The primary output device of a computer is the monitor. The two necessary components for video output are the monitor and the video card (also called the video controller, video adapter, and graphics adapter) or a video port on the motherboard. The two main categories of monitors are the CRT (cathode-ray tube) monitor (which takes up a lot of desk space and costs less) and the LCD (liquid crystal display) monitor (which frees your desk space, looks cool, and costs more). The older CRT technology was first used in television sets, and the newer LCD technology was first used in notebook PCs. LCD monitors are also called flat panel monitors for desktop computers.

Let's now briefly look at how CRT and LCD monitors work, and then we'll look at the different LCD and CRT technologies you need to consider when selecting a monitor. In this part of the chapter, you'll also learn about projectors, which are useful when display is needed for a larger group of people, and then we'll turn our attention to the technologies used with video cards. Later in the chapter, you'll learn how to install and troubleshoot monitors, projectors, and video cards.

HOW A CRT MONITOR WORKS

Many monitors use CRT technology, in which the filaments at the back of the cathode tube shoot a beam of electrons to the screen at the front of the tube, as illustrated in Figure 9-18. Plates on the top, bottom, and sides of the tube control the direction of the beam. The beam is directed by these plates to start at the top of the screen, move from left to right to make

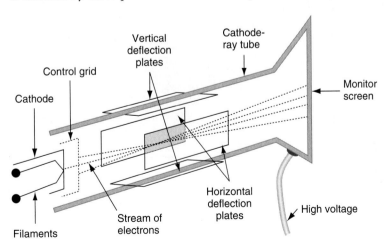

Figure 9-18 How a CRT monitor works
Courtesy: Course Technology/Cengage Learning

A+
220-701
1.2
1.7

one line, and then move down to the next line, again moving from left to right. As the beam moves vertically down the screen, it builds the image. By turning the beam on and off and selecting the correct color combination, the grid in front of the filaments controls what goes on the screen when the beam hits that portion of the line or a single dot on the screen. When hit, special phosphors on the back of the monitor screen light up and produce colors. The grid controls which one of three electron guns fires, each gun targeting a different color (red, green, or blue) positioned on the back of the screen. The three colors used are called the RGB (red, green, and blue) color space. These three dots, one for each color, are called a triad, and the distance between any two dots in the triad is called the dot pitch.

> **Notes** Television and CRT technology were invented by Phil Farnsworth. He got the idea in 1920 of an electron beam drawing a picture by moving across one line and back across the next while plowing a field at the age of 14.

With prices of LCD monitors dropping, CRT monitors are becoming obsolete. One reason to use a CRT monitor is for children. The surface of an LCD monitor can easily be damaged, but CRT monitor surfaces can handle children touching them. Also, some people feel that the display quality of CRT monitors is better than that of LCD monitors.

HOW AN LCD MONITOR WORKS

An LCD monitor produces an image using a liquid crystal material made of large, easily polarized molecules. Figure 9-19 shows the layers of the LCD panel that together create the image. At the center of the layers is the liquid crystal material. Next to it is the layer responsible for providing color to the image. These two layers are sandwiched between two grids of electrodes. One grid of electrodes is aligned in columns, and the other electrodes are aligned in rows. The two layers of electrodes make up the electrode matrix. Each intersection of a row electrode and a column electrode forms one pixel on the LCD panel. Software can manipulate each pixel by activating the electrodes that form it. The image is formed by scanning the column and row electrodes, much as the electronic beam scans a CRT monitor screen.

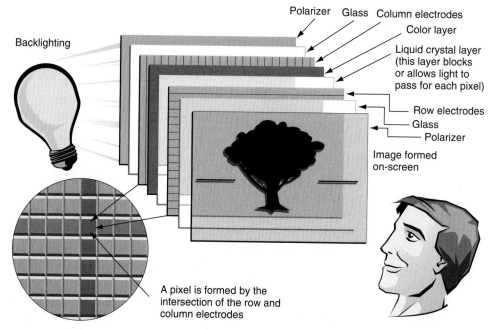

Figure 9-19   Layers of an LCD panel
Courtesy: Course Technology/Cengage Learning

A+
220-701
1.2
1.7

The polarizer layers outside the glass layers in Figure 9-19 are responsible for preventing light from passing through the pixels when the electrodes are not activated. When the electrodes are activated, light on the backside of the LCD panel can pass through one pixel on the screen, picking up color from the color layer as it passes through the pixel.

Many LCD monitors are built to receive either an analog signal or a digital signal from the video card and have two ports to accommodate either signal. If the signal is analog, it must be converted to digital before the monitor can process it. LCD monitors are designed to receive an analog signal so that a 15-pin analog video port on a computer can be used. Figure 9-20 shows the back of an LCD monitor.

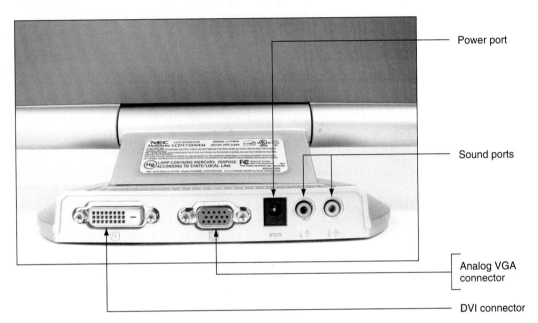

Figure 9-20 The rear of this LCD monitor shows digital and analog video ports to accommodate a video cable with either a 15-pin analog VGA connector or a digital DVI connector
Courtesy: Course Technology/Cengage Learning

LCD AND CRT TECHNOLOGIES

Table 9-2 summarizes the features and technologies that apply to LCD and CRT monitors. Several of the more important ones are discussed in the following subsections.

> **A+ Exam Tip** The A+ 220-701 Essentials exam expects you to know about these monitor settings: Refresh rate, resolution, degauss, and multiple monitors.

Refresh Rate and Response Time

The refresh rate is the number of times one screen or frame is built in one second. For CRT monitors, the Video Electronics Standards Association (VESA) set a minimum refresh rate standard of 70 Hz, or 70 complete vertical refreshes per second, as one requirement of Super VGA (SVGA) monitors. Many older VGA (Video Graphics Adapter) monitors are still in use, but all sold today meet the standards for SVGA. Slower refresh rates make the image appear to flicker, whereas faster refresh rates make the image appear solid and stable. For LCD monitors, the response time, also called the refresh rate, is the time it takes for an LCD monitor to build all the pixels for one screen or frame, and is measured in ms (milliseconds) or Hz. An LCD monitor with a response time of 16 ms yields about the same results as a CRT refresh rate of 60 Hz. LCD response times overall have been slightly less than CRT refresh rates.

9

A+ 220-701

Monitor Characteristic	CRT Monitor	LCD Monitor	Description
Screen size	X	X	Diagonal length of the screen surface. Values can range from 14 to 30 inches. (If you use an LCD television as a monitor, the size can go much higher.)
Refresh rate	X	X	The number of times a screen is built in one second. Common refresh rates are 60, 70, and 75 Hz. A monitor rated at 75 Hz can build 75 frames per second. (For comparison, a movie displays 24 frames per second.)
Interlaced	X		The electronic beam draws every other line with each pass, which lessens the overall effect of a lower refresh rate.
Response time		X	The time it takes for an LCD monitor to build one screen. The lower the better. A monitor with a 12-ms response time can build 83 frames per second, and a 16-ms monitor can build 63 frames per second.
Pixel pitch	X	X	A pixel is a spot or dot on the screen that can be addressed by software. The pixel pitch is the distance between adjacent pixels on the screen. An example of a pixel pitch is .283 mm. The smaller the number, the better.
Resolution	X	X	The number of spots or pixels on a screen that can be addressed by software. Values can range from 640 x 480 up to 1920 x 1200 for high-end monitors.
Native resolution		X	The number of pixels built into the LCD monitor.
Color quality	X	X	The number of bits used to store data about color for each pixel. Values are 8 bits, 16 bits, 24 bits, and 32 bits. Windows calls 24-bit and 32-bit color Truecolor.
Multiscan	X		CRT monitors that offer a variety of refresh rates so they can support several video cards.
Connectors	X	X	Options for connectors are VGA, DVI-I, DVI-D, and HDMI. These and other connectors used by video cards are discussed later in the chapter.
Contrast ratio	X	X	The contrast between true black and true white on the screen. The higher the contrast the better. 1000:1 is better than 700:1.
Viewing angle		X	The angle of view when an LCD monitor becomes difficult to see. A viewing angle of 170 degrees is better than 140 degrees.
Display type for CRT monitors	X		Flat screen monitors are high-end monitors that use a flat screen to help prevent glare.
Display type for LCD monitors		X	TFT (active matrix) is better than DSTN (passive matrix). TFT uses a transistor at each pixel to enhance the pixel.
Backlighting or brightness		X	For LCD monitors, some use better backlighting than others, which yields a brighter and clearer display. Brightness is measured in cd/m^2 (candela per square meter).
Other features		X	LCD monitors can also provide microphone input, speakers, USB ports, adjustable stands, and perhaps even a port for your iPod. Some monitors are also touch screen, so they can be used with a stylus as an input device.

Table 9-2 Important Features of a Monitor

⚡ Caution   If you spend many hours in front of a computer, you may strain your eyes. To protect your eyes from strain, look away from the monitor into the distance every few minutes. Use a good monitor with a high refresh rate or response time. The lower rates that cause monitor flicker can tire and damage your eyes. Because the refresh rates of CRT monitors are generally higher than the response times of LCD monitors, people who spend hours and hours in front of a monitor often prefer a CRT monitor. Also, when you first install a monitor, set the rate at the highest value the monitor can support.

Interlaced or Noninterlaced

Interlaced CRT monitors draw a screen by making two passes. On the first pass, the electronic beam strikes only the even lines, and on the second pass, the beam strikes only the odd lines. The result is that a monitor can have a slow refresh rate with a less noticeable overall effect than there would be if the beam hit all lines for each pass. A noninterlaced monitor (also called a progressive monitor) draws the entire screen in one pass. Interlaced monitors generally have slightly less flicker than noninterlaced monitors. Buy an interlaced monitor if you plan to spend long hours staring at the monitor. Your eyes will benefit.

Resolution

For CRT monitors, resolution is a measure of how many pixels on a CRT screen are addressable by software. Because resolution depends on software, the video controller card must support the resolution, and the software you are using must make use of the monitor's resolution capabilities. The minimum resolution for most monitors is 800 × 600 pixels, although many monitors offer a much-higher resolution.

Whereas a CRT monitor is designed to use several resolutions, an LCD monitor uses only one resolution, called the native resolution, which is the actual (and fixed) number of pixels built into the monitor. When you change display settings to use a different resolution than the monitor's native resolution, the LCD displayed area is reduced in size (creating a black area around the display) or video driver software builds each screen by mapping data using the chosen resolution onto the native resolution. This scaling process can slow down response time and/or cause an LCD monitor to appear fuzzy, which is why most serious gamers prefer CRT monitors to LCD monitors. For the sharpest images when using an LCD monitor, use the native resolution. If you do decide to use a different resolution than the native resolution, for the sharpest display, select a resolution that uses the same ratio of horizontal pixels to vertical pixels that the native resolution uses.

Most often, the native resolution is the highest resolution the monitor supports, but this is not always the case. To know for certain what is the native resolution, see the documentation that came with the monitor. Sometimes the monitor displays the native resolution on-screen when you attempt to set the resolution higher than the native resolution. The message displayed by the monitor recommends you use the native resolution.

The different resolution standards are as follows:

💡 **A+ Exam Tip**   The A+ 220-701 Essentials exam expects you to know about these resolutions used on LCD monitors: XGA, SXGA+, UXGA, and WUXGA. In addition, you need to be familiar with these terms: contrast ratio and native resolution.

- ◢ VGA (Video Graphics Array) supports up to 640 x 480, which is a 4:3 ratio between horizontal pixels and vertical pixels.
- ◢ SVGA (Super VGA) supports up to 800 x 600.
- ◢ XGA (eXtended Graphics Array) supports up to 1024 x 768.

A+
220-701
1.2
1.7

▲ SXGA (Super XGA) supports up to 1280 x 1024 and was first to use a 5:4 ratio between horizontal pixels and vertical pixels.

▲ SXGA+ is a variation of SXGA and uses a resolution of 1400 x 1050.

▲ WSXGA+ (Wide SXGA+) uses a resolution of 1680 x 1050.

▲ UXGA (Ultra XGA) supports up to 1600 x 1200.

▲ WUXGA (Wide UXGA) supports up to 1920 x 1200.

▲ QWXGA (Quad Wide XGA) supports up to 2048 x 1152 and is used by 23" monitors.

▲ WQXGA (Wide Quad XGA) supports up to 2560 x 1600 and is used by 30" monitors.

To convert the resolution to the number of pixels, multiply the horizontal pixels by vertical pixels. For example, SXGA supports up to 1280 x 1024 pixels or 1.3 million pixels.

CHANGING MONITOR SETTINGS

Settings that apply to the monitor can be managed by using the monitor buttons and Windows utilities. Using the monitor buttons, you can adjust the horizontal and vertical position of the screen on the monitor surface and change the brightness and contrast settings. For laptops, the brightness and contrast settings can be changed using function keys on the laptop. Also, some CRT monitors have a degauss button. Press the **degauss button** to eliminate accumulated or stray magnetic fields around the monitor, which can cause a CRT monitor to flicker or have wavy lines.

Monitor and video card settings can be changed by using Windows tools or by using the manufacturer's video card utility that was installed at the time the manufacturer's video card drivers were installed. If this utility is installed, you can access it by right-clicking the desktop and selecting the utility from the shortcut menu. For example, in Figure 9-21, the utility is named NVIDIA Control Panel. Manufacturer drivers for a video card are optional because Windows has its own embedded video drivers. However, for best performance of the card, always install the manufacturer drivers. You will learn how to do this later in the chapter.

To use Windows Vista to adjust resolution and refresh rate, follow these steps:

1. Right-click the Windows desktop and select **Personalize** from the shortcut menu (see Figure 9-21). The Personalization window opens. Click **Display Settings**. (Alternately, you can open the Control Panel and click **Adjust screen resolution**.) The Display Settings dialog box opens (see Figure 9-22).

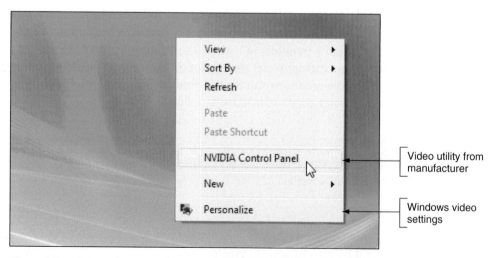

Figure 9-21 Two options are available on this system to adjust display settings
Courtesy: Course Technology/Cengage Learning

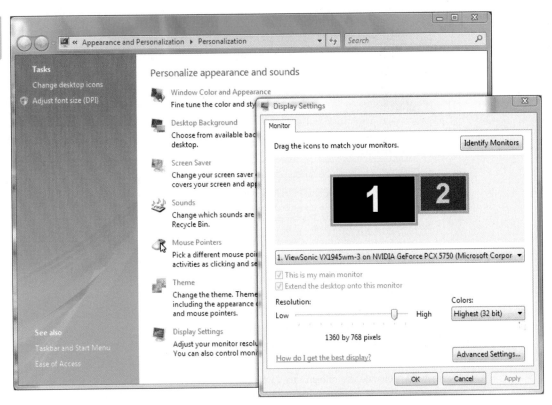

Figure 9-22 Use the Display Settings box to adjust screen resolution
Courtesy: Course Technology/Cengage Learning

2. Use the sliding bar to adjust the resolution. Then click **Apply**. The screen changes and the message "Do you want to keep these display settings?" appears. Click **Yes**.

3. To change the refresh rate, click **Advanced Settings**. The monitor property box opens. Click the **Monitor** tab. Select the largest refresh rate (see Figure 9-23) and click **Apply**. Respond **Yes** to the message, "Do you want to keep these display settings?" Click **OK** to close the properties box.

4. Click **OK** to close the Display Settings box.

Windows supports a standard group of resolutions and normally only lists the ones that a monitor can use. However, sometimes it does not list the monitor's native resolution, or the native resolution is not a standard resolution that Windows offers. If the native resolution is not listed in the Display Settings window, you can do the following:

◢ In the Display Settings window, click **Advanced Settings** (see Figure 9-24). The adapter and monitor properties box appears. Click **List All Modes**. In the List All Modes box, shown on the right of Figure 9-24, select the resolution you need and click **OK**. Click **Apply**.

◢ If the native resolution is not listed in the List All Modes box, you can build a customized resolution. The option might be available if a video utility was installed with the video adapter card and the utility includes this option. Right-click the desktop and look for the utility in the shortcut menu (refer back to Figure 9-21). Open the utility and look on the utility window for the option to create a

A+
220-701
1.2
1.7

Figure 9-23   Change the refresh rate to the highest setting
Courtesy: Course Technology/Cengage Learning

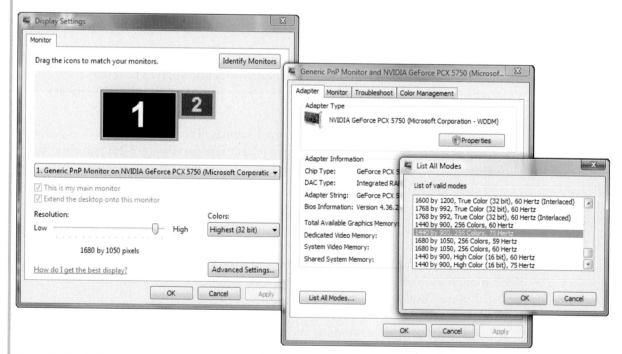

Figure 9-24   Add a new resolution to available resolutions
Courtesy: Course Technology/Cengage Learning

customized resolution. For example, Figure 9-25 shows one utility. To create a customized resolution, select **Manage custom resolution** in the left pane and click **Create** in the right pane. Then, in the Custom Resolutions dialog box, enter the horizontal pixels and vertical lines and click **Test**.

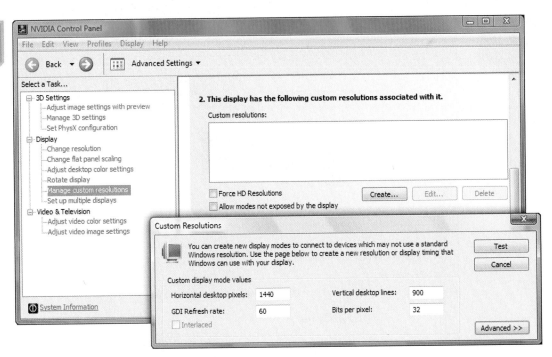

Figure 9-25 Create a customized resolution
Courtesy: Course Technology/Cengage Learning

APPLYING CONCEPTS — INSTALLING DUAL MONITORS

To increase the size of your Windows desktop, you can install more than one monitor for a single computer. To install dual monitors, you can use two video cards, one for each monitor, or you can use a video card that provides two video ports.

To install a second monitor in a dual-monitor setup using two video cards, follow these steps:

1. Verify that the original video card works properly, determine whether it is PCI Express or AGP, and decide whether it is to be the primary monitor.

2. Boot the PC and enter BIOS setup. If BIOS setup has the option to select the order that video cards are initialized, verify that the currently installed card is configured to initialize first. If it does not initialize first, then, when you install the second card, video might not work at all when you first boot with two cards.

3. Install a second video card in an empty PCI or PCI Express slot, and attach the second monitor.

4. Boot the system. Windows recognizes the new hardware and launches the Found New Hardware wizard. You can use the wizard to install the video card drivers or cancel the wizard and install them manually. To install the drivers manually, insert the CD that came with the card and launch the setup program on the CD.

5. Now you are ready to configure the new monitor. For Vista, right-click the desktop and select **Personalize** from the shortcut menu. Then click **Display Settings**. The Display Settings box appears (see Figure 9-26). For XP, right-click the desktop and select **Properties** from the shortcut menu. The Display Properties dialog box for Windows XP appears. Select the **Settings** tab.

A+
220-701
1.2

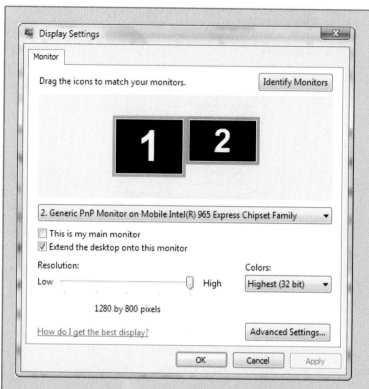

Figure 9-26 You must choose to activate a second monitor before it will be used by Windows Vista
Courtesy: Course Technology/Cengage Learning

6. Notice that there are two numbered boxes that represent your two monitors. When you click one of these boxes, the drop-down menu changes to show the selected monitor, and the screen resolution and the color quality display settings also follow the selected monitor. This lets you customize the settings for each monitor. If necessary, arrange the boxes so that they represent the physical arrangement of your monitors.

7. Adjust your resolution and the color quality settings according to your preferences. To cause Windows to extend your desktop onto the second monitor, check **Extend the desktop onto this monitor**. To save the settings, click **Apply**. The second monitor should initialize and show the extended desktop.

8. Close the Vista Display Settings or XP Display Properties dialog box. Open an application and verify that you can use the second monitor by dragging the application over to the second monitor's desktop.

After you add a second monitor to your system, you can move from one monitor to another simply by moving your mouse. Switching from one monitor to the other does not require any special keystroke or menu option.

Using Dual Monitors

Notes In Figure 9-26, if you arrange the two windows side by side, your extended desktop will extend left or right. If you arrange the two windows one on top of the other, your extended desktop will extend up and down.

PROJECTORS

A monitor gives excellent performance when only two or three people are viewing, but you may want to use a projector in addition to a monitor when larger groups of people are watching. Projectors are great in the classroom, for sales presentations, or for watching the Super Bowl with your friends. The prices of projectors have dropped significantly in the past few years, making them more of an option for business and pleasure. One portable projector, shown in Figure 9-27, has a native resolution of XGA 1024 x 768, and can connect to a desktop or notebook computer by way of a 15-pin video port or S-Video port.

Figure 9-27 Portable XGA projector by Panasonic
Courtesy of Panasonic

To use a projector, you'll need an extra video port. For desktop computers, you'll need to install a second video card or use a video card that has two video ports. Most notebook computers are designed to be used with projectors and provide the extra 15-pin video port or S-Video port. To use a projector, plug in the projector to the extra port and then turn it on. For a notebook computer, use a function key to activate the video port. For most notebooks, you can toggle the function key to: (1) use the LCD display and not use the port; (2) use both the LCD display and the port; or (3) use the port and don't use the LCD display. Also, when you first use the projector, it will show a mirrored image of exactly what you see on your LCD panel. If you want to make the projector an extension of the desktop, you can open the Vista Display Setting box or the XP Display Properties box, select the second monitor, and select **Extend the desktop onto this monitor.** The projector now works as a dual monitor.

> **Notes** Many of us use Microsoft PowerPoint for group presentations. If you configure your projector as a dual monitor, you can use PowerPoint to display a presentation to your audience on the projector at the same time you are using your LCD display to manage your computer. To do so for PowerPoint 2007, select the **Slide Show** tab, **Set Up** group. Then click **Set Up Slide Show.** In the Set Up Show box under Multiple monitors, check **Show Presenter View** and click **OK.**

VIDEO CARDS

Video cards (see Figure 9-28) are sometimes called graphic adapters, graphics cards, or display cards. Sometimes the video controller with a video port is integrated into the motherboard. If you are buying a motherboard with an integrated video controller, make sure that you can disable the controller on the motherboard if it gives you trouble. You can then install a video card and bypass the controller and port on the motherboard. Recall from

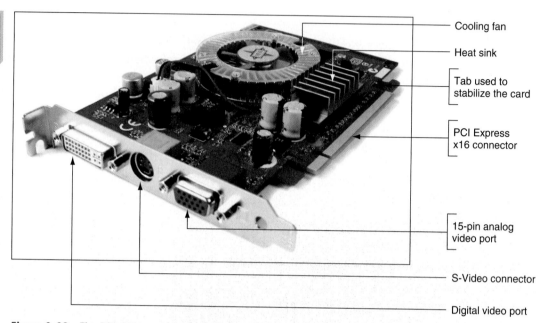

Figure 9-28   The PCX 5750 graphics card by MSI Computer Corporation uses the PCI Express x16 local bus
Courtesy of MSI Computer Corporation

Chapter 5 that a video card can use an AGP, PCI, or PCI Express slot on the motherboard. The fastest slot to use is a PCIe x16 slot.

Now let's look at the ports provided by video cards and other features to consider when selecting a video card.

Ports Provided by Video Cards

Video cards and display devices might use one or more of the following video ports:

◀ *15-pin VGA port*. This is the standard analog video method of passing three separate signals for red, green, and blue (RGB), which older video cards and CRT monitors use. The video card in Figure 9-29 has this 15-pin VGA port.

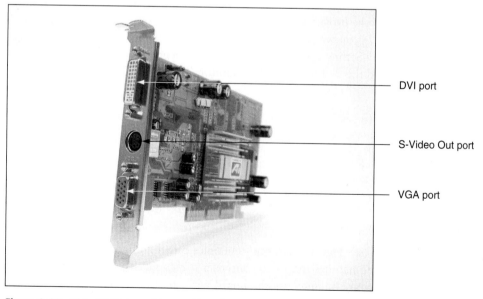

Figure 9-29   This ATI Radeon video card has three ports for video out: DVI, S-Video, and the regular VGA port
Courtesy of ATI Technologies, Inc.

A+
220-701
1.2
1.7
1.9

▲ *DVI (Digital Visual Interface)*. This method is the digital interface standard used by digital monitors such as a digital LCD monitor and digital TVs (HDTV). For a video card that only has a DVI port, you can purchase a VGA converter so you can connect a standard VGA video cable to use a regular analog monitor (see Figure 9-30). There are two types of DVI ports, which are shown in Figure 9-31. The DVI-I port supports both analog and digital signals and the DVI-D port works only with digital monitors. If a video card has a DVI port, most likely it will be the DVI-I port (the one with the four extra holes) so that you can use an adapter to convert the port to a VGA port.

Figure 9-30 Digital to analog video port converter using DVD-I connector with extra four pins
Courtesy: Course Technology/Cengage Learning

a   b

Figure 9-31 Two types of DVI ports: (a) DVI-D, (b) DVI-I
Courtesy: Course Technology/Cengage Learning

▲ *Composite out port*. Using this port, the red, green, and blue (RGB) are mixed together in the same signal. This is the method used by television, and can be used by a video card that is designed to send output to a TV. A composite out port is round and is the same size as the S-Video Out port shown in Figure 9-29, but has only a single pin in the center of the port. Composite video does not produce as sharp an image as RGB video or S-Video.

A+
220-701
1.2
1.7
1.9

▲ *S-Video (Super-Video) port.* An S-Video port sends two signals over the cable, one for color and the other for brightness, and is used by some high-end TVs and video equipment. It uses a 4-pin round port. The television and the video card must support this method and you must use an S-Video cable like the one shown in Figure 9-32. This standard is not as good as RGB for monitors, but is better than composite video when output to a television.

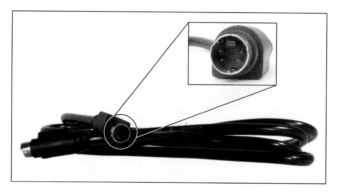

Figure 9-32 An S-Video cable used to connect a video card to an S-Video port on a television
Courtesy: Course Technology/Cengage Learning

▲ *HDMI port.* HDMI (High-Definition Multimedia Interface) is the latest digital audio and video interface standard. It is not widely available on video cards or motherboards, but is expected to ultimately replace DVI. HDMI is currently used on televisions and other home theater equipment. To connect a PC to this equipment that uses HDMI, you can purchase an HDMI to DVI cable such as the one shown in Figure 9-33.

Figure 9-33 An HDMI to DVI cable can be used to connect a PC that has a
DVI port to home theater equipment that uses an HDMI port
Courtesy of Belkin Corporation

💡 **A+ Exam Tip** The A+ 220-701 Essentials exam expects you to know about these video connector types: VGA, HDMI, S-Video, composite (RGB), DVI-D, and DVI-I connectors.

A+
220-701
1.2
1.7
1.9

Other Video Card Features

Video cards offer many different features that affect price and performance. Video cards have their own processor called a graphics processor unit (GPU) or video processor unit (VPU). These processors use graphics RAM installed on the card so that RAM on the motherboard is not tied up with video data. (If a motherboard offers a video port rather than using a video card, the GPU is part of the onboard video controller and RAM on the motherboard is used for video data.)

The more RAM installed on the card, the better the performance. Older video cards used older video memory technologies, including VRAM (video RAM), SGRAM (synchronous graphics RAM), WRAM (window RAM), MultiBank DRAM (MDRAM), 3-D RAM, Direct RDRAM (DRDRAM), and DDR. Most video cards used and sold today use DDR2, DDR3, Graphics DDR3 (GDDR3), or GDDR4 memory. Graphics DDR memory is faster than regular DDR memory and does a better job of storing 3-D images. Some video cards have as much as 2 GB of graphics memory.

A+
220-701
1.2
1.7
1.9
3.2

VIDEO MEMORY AND WINDOWS VISTA

Recall from Chapter 2 that most versions of Windows Vista offer the Aero user interface (also called Aero glass), which has a 3D appearance. For these versions of Vista to enable the interface, the onboard video or video card must support DirectX 9 or higher, have at least 128 MB of video memory, and use the Windows Display Driver Model (WDDM). The Windows Display Driver Model is a Windows component new to Windows Vista that manages graphics. DirectX is a Microsoft software development tool that software developers can use to write multimedia applications such as games, video-editing software, and computer-aided design software. Components of DirectX include DirectDraw, DirectMusic, DirectPlay, and Direct3D. The video firmware on the video card or motherboard chipset can interpret DirectX commands to build 3D images as presented to them by the WDDM. In addition, Vista relies on DirectX and the WDDM to produce the Aero user interface.

You can use the dxdiag.exe command to display information about hardware and diagnose problems with DirectX. To use the command in Vista, click Start, type dxdiag.exe in the Start Search box, and press Enter. The opening window appears in Figure 9-34. Click the Display tab to see information about the installed video card (see Figure 9-35).

The 128 MB or more of video memory can be the graphics memory embedded on the video card, system memory, or a combination of both. To see the video memory available to Vista, open the Display Settings dialog box and click Advanced Settings. The video properties box appears. Figure 9-36 shows two properties boxes for two systems. The box on the left is for a notebook computer and the one on the right is for a desktop computer that has a video card.

Here is an explanation of the four entries in the dialog box that concern video memory:

- Total Available Graphics Memory is total memory that may be available to the video subsystem.
- Dedicated Video Memory that is found on a video card. Since the notebook has no video card, the value is zero. The video card in the desktop system has 128 MB of graphics memory. Memory on the video card is dedicated to video because no other component has access to it.
- System Video Memory is system RAM dedicated to video. No other application or component can use it.
- Shared System Memory is system RAM that might be available to video if another application or component is not already using it.

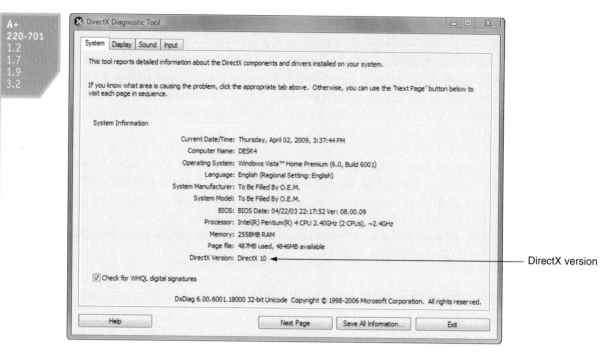

Figure 9-34   The DirectX Diagnostic tool reports information about DirectX components
Courtesy: Course Technology/Cengage Learning

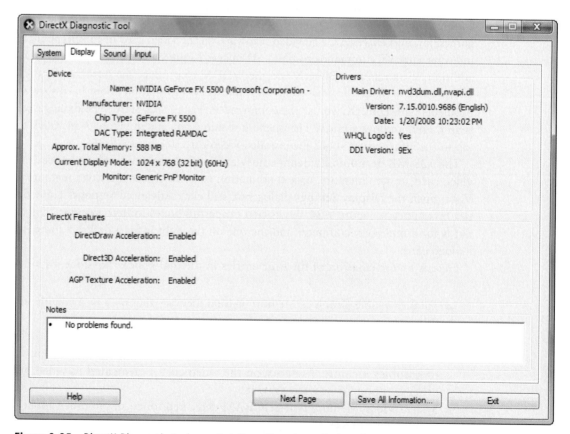

Figure 9-35   DirectX Diagnostic tool reports information about the installed video card and drivers
Courtesy: Course Technology/Cengage Learning

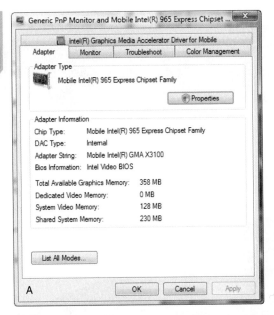
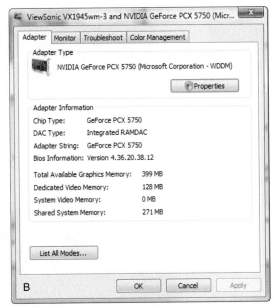

Figure 9-36 Memory allocated to video under Windows Vista (a) for a notebook computer and (b) for a desktop computer with video card
Courtesy: Course Technology/Cengage Learning

For Vista to enable the Aero user interface, at least 128 MB must be dedicated to video. In other words, Dedicated Video Memory and System Video Memory must add up to at least 128 MB. Because this is true for both the notebook and desktop computers, they both use the Aero user interface.

DUAL VIDEO CARDS

Recall from Chapter 5 that the serious game enthusiast who has a motherboard with two PCI Express x16 slots can use two video cards designed to work in tandem using one of two technologies: SLI by NVIDIA and CrossFire by ATI Technologies. Figure 9-37 shows a video card that supports SLI. Notice in the figure the connector on the card that can be used to connect this card to the second video card using an SLI bridge shown in Figure 9-38. You'll see an example of how to install dual SLI video cards later in the chapter.

> **Notes** Even though high-end graphics cards can have heat sinks and fans, they can still overheat. One possible solution is a slot fan such as the one shown in Figure 9-39 that mounts in any empty slot. Put it next to the video card to help keep it cool.

Figure 9-37   This video card is SLI compliant and can be installed with a second matching video card in a system
Courtesy: Course Technology/Cengage Learning

A+
220-701
1.7
1.9

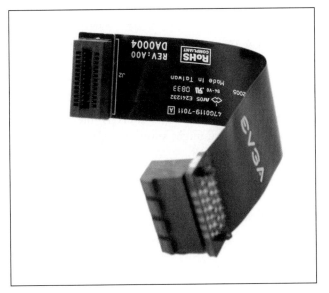

Figure 9-38 SLI bridge connects two SLI video cards
Courtesy: Course Technology/Cengage Learning

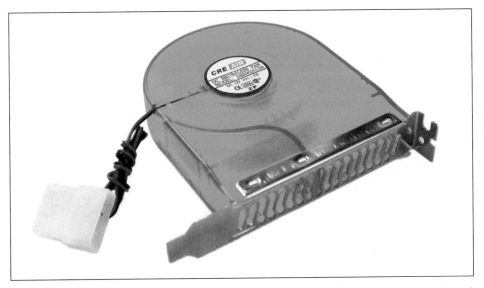

Figure 9-39 Mount this slot fan by Cables Unlimited next to the video card to help keep it cool
Courtesy: Course Technology/Cengage Learning

A+
220-701
1.9

EXPANSION CARDS

Listed below, in no particular order, are some common types of expansion cards, many of which you have already learned about in this and other chapters:

1. An I/O controller card can provide serial, parallel, USB, or game ports.

2. A storage controller card can provide SATA and PATA internal ports and eSATA external ports. In addition, the card might support RAID. You learned about SATA, PATA, eSATA, and RAID in Chapter 8.

3. A SCSI host controller card (also called a SCSI adapter) can provide internal and external SCSI ports. SCSI is covered in Chapter 8.

4. A FireWire controller card can provide one or more types of FireWire ports.

5. A sound card provides various sound ports used for input and output. Sound cards are covered in Chapter 10.

6. A video card can use a PCI, PCIe, or AGP slot.

7. A fan card installs in a slot and provides one or two fans used to cool cards in adjacent slots.

8. Network cards can provide network ports for a wired network or an antenna for a wireless network. You'll learn to use these cards in Chapter 18.

9. A modem card can be used to connect your computer to a phone line. You can then use that phone line to connect to the Internet. Modem connections to the Internet are covered in Chapters 17 and 18.

10. A TV tuner card can turn your computer into a television by providing a jack for you to plug up your TV cable. A capture card not only receives TV input but can capture that input into video and audio files. These cards are covered in more detail in Chapter 10.

When selecting an expansion card, consider all the features of the card, the bus slot the card uses, the operating system the card is compatible with, the hardware resources it requires (processor, RAM, and free hard drive space), and the application software that works with the card. You will learn how to install an expansion card later in the chapter.

INSTALLING INPUT DEVICES

A+
220-701
1.2
1.8

Installing input devices is easy to do and usually goes without a hitch. All devices need device drivers or BIOS to control them and to interface with the operating system. Simple input devices, such as the mouse and keyboard, can be controlled by the BIOS or have embedded device drivers built into the OS. For these devices, you don't have to install additional device drivers.

In this part of the chapter, you'll learn how to install a keyboard, mouse, touch screen, barcode reader, and fingerprint reader. These installations are similar, so learning to do one will help you do the next. And finally, you'll learn how to install a KVM (Keyboard, Video, and Mouse) switch that can be used to connect a single keyboard, mouse, and monitor to multiple computers.

HOW TO INSTALL A KEYBOARD AND MOUSE

Most often, installing a keyboard and mouse simply means plugging them in and turning on the PC. Keyboards and mice connect to a PC by one of four methods: a 5-pin round DIN connector (mostly outdated now), a 6-pin PS/2 connector (sometimes called a mini-DIN), a USB port, or

A+
220-701
1.2
1.8

a wireless connection. DIN and PS/2 connectors are shown in Figure 9-40. Adapters can be used to connect a PS/2 device into a USB connector or a USB device into a PS/2 connector.

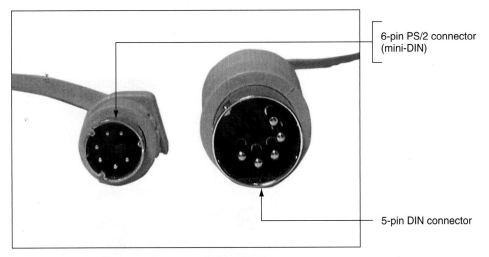

6-pin PS/2 connector
(mini-DIN)

5-pin DIN connector

Figure 9-40 Two PS/2 and DIN connectors used by keyboards and mice
Courtesy: Course Technology/Cengage Learning

> **Notes** Most computer cases have two PS/2 connectors: one for the mouse and the other for the keyboard. Physically, the mouse or keyboard connector fits into either port, but the mouse connector only works in the mouse port, and the keyboard connector only works in the keyboard port. This can make for a frustrating experience when setting up a computer. To help tell the two ports apart, know that a green PS/2 port is probably the mouse port and a purple port is most likely the keyboard port. Older motherboards did not color-code the mouse and keyboard ports, but you might find small icons imprinted beside the ports to help you distinguish one from the other.

A keyboard or mouse might use a wireless connection, such as the mouse shown in Figure 9-41. The wireless connection is made through a receiver that plugs into a USB port. To install the device, plug the receiver into a USB port and then use the mouse.

Figure 9-41 Wireless mouse and USB receiver
Courtesy: Course Technology/Cengage Learning

A+
220-701
1.2
1.8

Sometimes you'll need to install drivers with a keyboard and mouse that have special features. For example, the keyboard shown in Figure 9-42 has a zoom bar and buttons and the mouse has extra buttons. If you don't want to use these special features, you can plug the keyboard or mouse into a USB port and use it with no further installation. However, to use the special features, you have to first install the drivers on the CD that came bundled with the two devices.

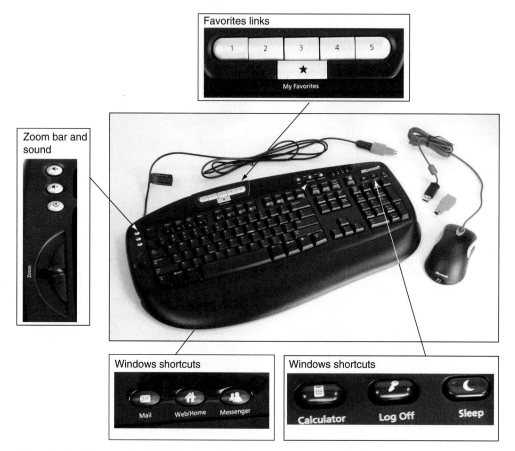

Figure 9-42 The mouse and keyboard require drivers to use the extra buttons and zoom bar
Courtesy: Course Technology/Cengage Learning

Do the following to install this keyboard and mouse:

1. Insert the CD in the CD drive and run the Setup.exe program on the CD. In Vista, respond to the UAC box.

2. On the installation screen, accept the end-user license agreement (EULA) and select the keyboard and mouse from a list the CD supports. The drivers then install.

3. After the drivers are installed, you must restart the computer. Then plug in the keyboard and mouse to USB ports.

4. Use the two utilities installed on the Windows desktop to configure the mouse and keyboard buttons (see Figure 9-43).

Most devices that have been installed in a system appear listed in Device Manager. And you can use Device Manager to uninstall, disable, or enable the device. However, USB devices are managed differently. To uninstall a USB device, in the Vista Control Panel, click **Uninstall a program** (see Figure 9-44). In the Programs and Features window (see Figure 9-45), select the device and click **Change**. Follow directions on-screen to uninstall the device.

A+
220-701
1.2
1.8

Figure 9-43 Utilities to configure the keyboard and mouse
Courtesy: Course Technology/Cengage Learning

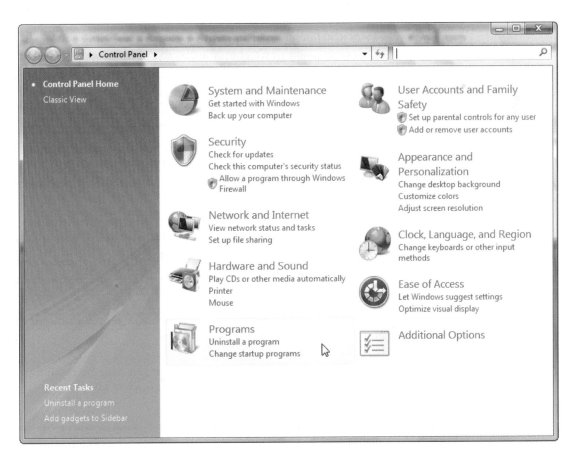

Figure 9-44 Use Control Panel to uninstall a USB device
Courtesy: Course Technology/Cengage Learning

9

A+ 220-701

A+
220-701
1.2
1.8

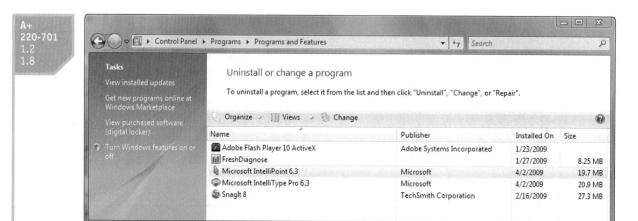

Figure 9-45 USB devices are listed as installed programs
Courtesy: Course Technology/Cengage Learning

A+
220-701
1.8

HOW TO INSTALL A TOUCH SCREEN

A touch screen is an input device that uses a monitor or LCD panel as the backdrop for input options. In other words, the touch screen is a grid that senses clicks and drags (similar to those created by a mouse) and sends these events to the computer by way of a USB or serial connection.

When someone is using a touch screen, the monitor displays user options and the user touches one of these options. The touch screen receives that touch in a way similar to how a mouse would receive a click. A touch screen can be embedded inside a monitor for a desktop system or an LCD panel in a notebook, or the touch screen can be installed on top of the monitor screen or LCD panel as an add-on device. As an add-on device, the touch screen has its own AC adapter to power it.

When installing a touch screen, follow the manufacturer's directions to connect the USB or serial cable and the power cable and install the touch screen device drivers and management software. Here are general directions to install a touch screen:

1. Run the setup.exe program on the CD that came bundled with the touch screen. The program will install the device drivers for the touch screen and software to manage the device. Restart your computer.

2. Run the management software to select how much of the monitor screen will be devoted to the touch screen or which monitor in a dual-monitor setup will use the touch screen.

3. Connect the USB or serial cable to the touch screen and the computer. The Windows Found New Hardware message appears. Follow directions on-screen to complete the Found New Hardware wizard.

4. Use the management software to calibrate the touch screen to account for the monitor's resolution.

Later, if the monitor resolution is changed, the touch screen must be recalibrated. The screen can be cleaned with a damp cloth using a mild solution of alcohol and water.

HOW TO INSTALL A BARCODE READER

A barcode reader is used to scan barcodes on products to maintain inventory or at the point of sale (POS). Barcode readers come in a variety of shapes, sizes, and features, including a pen wand (simplest and least expensive), slot scanners (to scan ID cards as they are slid

A+
220-701
1.8

through a slot), a CCD scanner (a charge-coupled device scanner is a gun-type scanner often used at checkout counters), an image scanner (includes a small video camera), and a laser scanner (most expensive and best type).

A barcode reader can interface with a PC using several methods. Some readers use a wireless connection, a serial port, a USB port, or a keyboard port. If the reader uses a keyboard port, most likely it has a splitter (called a keyboard wedge) on it for the keyboard to use, and data read by the barcode reader is input into the system as though it were typed using the keyboard. Figure 9-46 shows a barcode reader by Intermec that is a laser scanner and that uses Bluetooth to connect wirelessly to the PC.

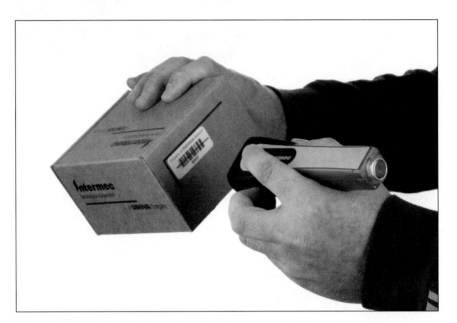

Figure 9-46   Handheld or hands-free barcode scanner by Intermec Technologies
Photograph courtesy of Intermec Technologies

When a barcode reader scans a barcode, it converts the code into numbers that are transferred to software on the computer. This software identifies two types of information from the numeric code: the company and the product. At point of sale, this information is then used to look up the price of the product in price tables accessed by the software.

To install a barcode reader, first install the device drivers and then plug in the device to the keyboard, USB, or serial port. For a Bluetooth connection, follow the barcode reader's documentation to use the Bluetooth management software on the PC to sync the reader to the PC.

HOW TO INSTALL A FINGERPRINT READER

A+
220-701
1.8
5.2

A biometric device is an input device that inputs biological data about a person, which can be input data to identify a person's fingerprints, handprints, face, voice, eye, and handwritten signature. For convenience, some people enjoy using a fingerprint reader to log onto their Windows desktop or a Web site rather than having to enter a password. These fingerprint readers are not to be considered as the only authentication to control access to sensitive data: for that, use a strong password, which you will learn about in Chapter 19.

Fingerprint readers can look like a mouse and use a wireless or USB connection, such as the one shown in Figure 9-47. Or they can be embedded on the side of a keyboard or

A+
220-701
1.8
5.2

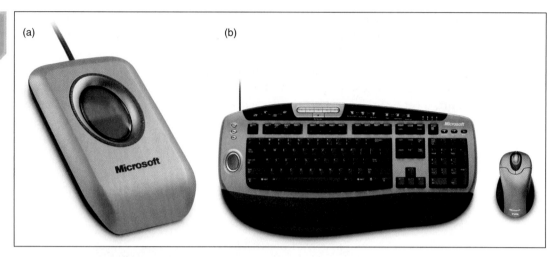

(a)   (b)

Figure 9-47 Fingerprint readers can (a) look like a mouse, but smaller, or (b) be embedded on a keyboard
Courtesy of Microsoft Corporation

on the side of a flash drive. For notebook computers, a reader might be embedded on the notebook or use a device fitted in a PC Card slot, or the notebook has a fingerprint reader embedded near the keyboard. To use some fingerprint readers, you press your finger on the oval input surface, and for other readers, you slide your finger across a bar that scans your fingerprint as it goes by.

> **Notes** For more information about biometric devices and how they can be used, see the Web site of the International Biometric Industry Association at *www.ibia.org.*

> **A+ Exam Tip** The A+ 220-701 Essentials exam expects you to know how to install and configure these input devices: mouse, keyboard, barcode reader, biometric devices, and touch screens. All these devices are covered in this part of the chapter.

Most fingerprint readers that are not embedded in other devices use a USB connection. For most USB devices, you install the software before you plug in the device. For example, to use the fingerprint reader by Microsoft, which is shown in Figure 9-47, do the following:

1. Insert the setup CD in the optical drive. The installation program on the CD launches. You must accept the license agreement. Figure 9-48 shows one window of the installation process where you are reminded that a fingerprint reader is not to be used when security is required.

2. During the installation process, you are told to plug in the reader so it can be enabled. Do so when you are prompted.

3. Next, the Fingerprint Registration Wizard launches so that you can record your fingerprint (called registering your fingerprint). Figure 9-49 shows one screen in the wizard where you select which finger it is you are about to record.

A+
220-701
1.8
5.2

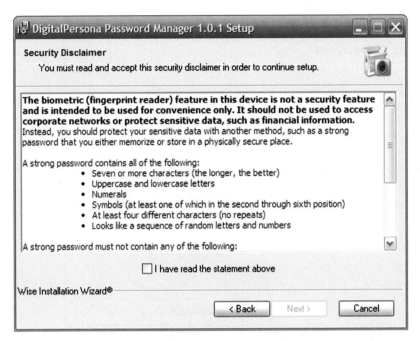

Figure 9-48 The setup program for this fingerprint reader warns to not rely on the reader to protect sensitive data
Courtesy: Course Technology/Cengage Learning

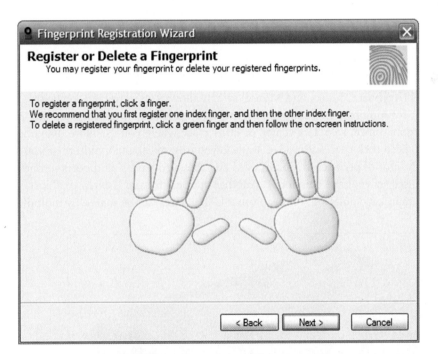

Figure 9-49 To register a fingerprint, select the finger you want to record
Courtesy: Course Technology/Cengage Learning

4. Then on the next screen, which is shown in Figure 9-50, press the reader four times to verify your fingerprint. You can then record more fingerprints or close the wizard.

5. To use your fingerprints in the place of passwords, when you are logging onto Windows or onto a Web site, press your finger to the fingerprint reader.

A+
220-701
1.8
5.2

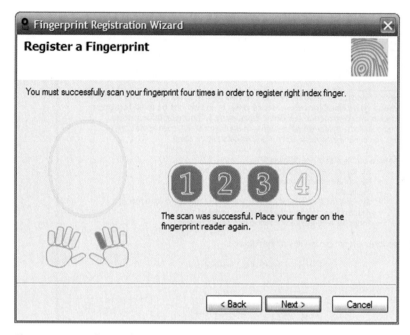

Figure 9-50   A fingerprint is registered after it is recorded four times
Courtesy: Course Technology/Cengage Learning

Fingerprint readers that are used a lot can get dirty and refuse to read. To clean a fingerprint reader, use the sticky side of duct tape or clear tape, or clean it with a mild solution of glass cleaner containing ammonia. Don't use an alcohol solution to clean fingerprint readers.

A+
220-701
1.8

HOW TO INSTALL A KVM SWITCH

A KVM (Keyboard, Video, and Mouse) switch allows you to use one keyboard, mouse, and monitor for multiple computers (see Figure 9-51). A KVM switch can be useful in a dorm room, server room, office, help desk center, or other place where you use more than one computer and want to keep desk space clear of multiple keyboards, mice, and monitors or you simply want to lower the cost of peripherals. Some KVM switches also have sound ports so one set of speakers can be used for multiple computers. Another optional feature is extra USB ports for other USB devices than keyboards and mice, so other USB devices can be shared by multiple computers.

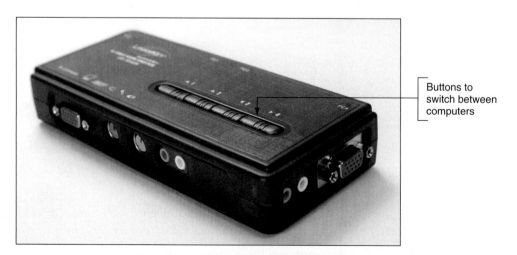

Buttons to switch between computers

Figure 9-51   This KVM switch supports up to four computers, uses PS/2 ports for the keyboard and mouse, and provides microphone and speaker ports for sound
Courtesy: Course Technology/Cengage Learning

KVM switches can support 2 to 16 computers or even more and can cost less than $30 to several hundred dollars. Be careful when selecting a KVM switch, so that the switch will support the keyboard, mice, and monitor you want to use. For example, some KVM switches only support ball mice (the type that has a ball that rolls on the bottom of the mouse) and not optical mice (the type that uses a light beam to sense movement). Many KVM switches only support PS/2 mice and keyboards and will not work with the USB variety. Also, less expensive KVM switches do not support keyboard and mice with extra features such as a keyboard zoom bar or Internet Explorer Favorites buttons. The monitor most likely can only use a 15-pin VGA port although a VGA to DVI adapter might work.

The switch does not require that you install device drivers to use it. Just plug in mouse, keyboard, and monitor cables from each computer to the device. Also plug in the one monitor, mouse, and keyboard to the device. Figure 9-52 shows the hardware configuration for the KVM switch in Figure 9-51. Switch between computers by using a hot key on the keyboard or buttons on the top of the KVM switch.

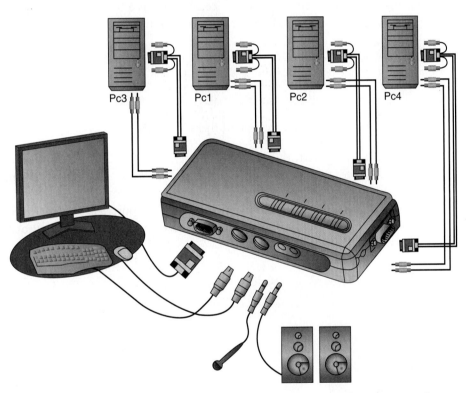

Figure 9-52 Hardware configuration for a four-port KVM switch that also supports audio
Courtesy: Course Technology/Cengage Learning

💡 **A+ Exam Tip** Content for the A+ 220-701 Essentials exam ends here, and content on the A+ 220-702 Practical Application exam begins.

INSTALLING AND CONFIGURING I/O DEVICES AND PORTS

You have just seen how to install several input devices. In this part of the chapter, we take hardware installations to the next level and learn how to configure and use ports on the motherboard and how to install expansion cards.

When installing hardware devices under Windows XP, you need to be logged onto the system with a user account that has the highest level of privileges to change the system. This type of account is called an administrative account. In Windows Vista, it is not necessary to

A+
220-702
1.1

be logged in with an administrative account because of the User Account Control (UAC) box. When the box appears, you can enter the password for an administrative account in the UAC box, and then Vista will allow you to proceed with the installation. You will learn more about administrative accounts and other less-privileged accounts in Chapter 19.

Other than USB devices, most hardware devices are monitored and managed using Device Manager. Therefore, we begin our discussion with learning to use Device Manager.

A+
220-702
1.1
2.3

USING DEVICE MANAGER

Device Manager (devmgmt.msc) is your primary Windows tool for managing hardware. It gives a graphical view of hardware devices configured under Windows and the resources and drivers they use. Using Device Manager, you can disable or enable a device, update its drivers, uninstall a device, and undo a driver update (called a driver rollback). For instance, when a device driver is being installed, Windows might inform you of a resource conflict, or the device simply might not work. You can use Device Manager as a useful fact-finding tool for resolving the problem. You can also use Device Manager to print a report of system configuration.

> **♀ A+ Exam Tip** The A+ 220-702 Practical Application exam expects you to know in what scenario it is appropriate to use Device Manager. You also need to know how to use the utility and how to evaluate its results.

To access Device Manager, use one of these methods:

▲ For Vista, click **Start**, right-click **Computer**, and then select **Properties** on the shortcut menu. The System window appears (see Figure 9-53). Click **Device Manager** and respond to the UAC box. The Device Manager window opens.

▲ For Windows XP, click **Start**, right-click **My Computer**, select **Properties** from the shortcut menu, and then select the **Hardware** tab from the System Properties window. Finally, click **Device Manager**.

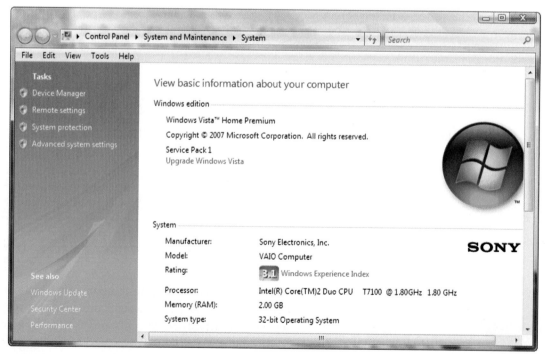

Figure 9-53   Windows Vista System window
Courtesy: Course Technology/Cengage Learning

▲ For Vista or XP, you can enter **Devmgmt.msc** in the Vista Start Search box or the XP Run box and press **Enter**. For Vista, respond to the UAC box.

Device Manager for Windows Vista is shown in Figure 9-54. Click a plus sign to expand the view of an item, and click a minus sign to collapse the view.

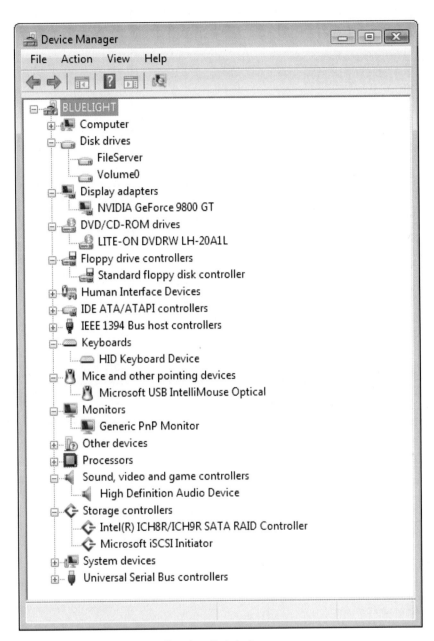

Figure 9-54 Device Manager lists installed devices
Courtesy: Course Technology/Cengage Learning

One thing you can do if you have a problem with an installed device is to use Device Manager to uninstall the device. Right-click the device and click **Uninstall** on the shortcut menu (see Figure 9-55). Then reboot and reinstall the device, looking for problems during the installation that point to the source of the problem. Sometimes reinstalling a device is all that is needed to solve the problem. Notice in Figure 9-55 that the device selected is a USB mouse. Sometimes USB devices are listed in Device Manager and sometimes they are not.

To find out more information about a device, right-click the device and select **Properties** on the shortcut menu. Figure 9-56 shows the properties box for the onboard audio controller. Many times, the source of a problem shows up in this window. Windows is reporting that the device cannot start and suggests how to search for a solution.

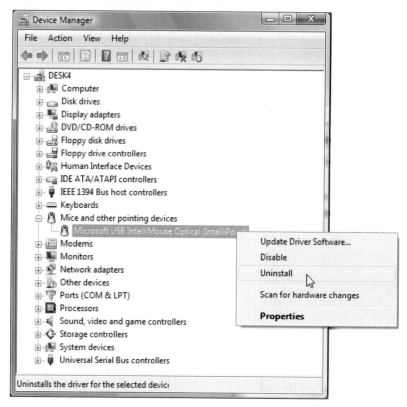

Figure 9-55 Use Device Manager to uninstall a device
Courtesy: Course Technology/Cengage Learning

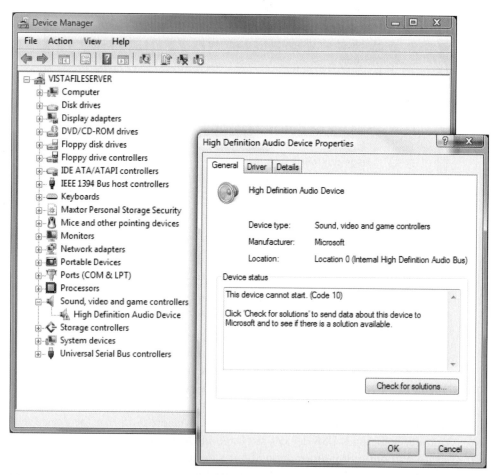

Figure 9-56 Windows reports an error with a device
Courtesy: Course Technology/Cengage Learning

A+
220-702
1.1
2.3

Another Properties box is shown in Figure 9-57; this one is for the network card. Notice the Diagnostics tab in the properties dialog box. If this tab is present, most likely you will find diagnostic software there that can be executed to test the device and report problems.

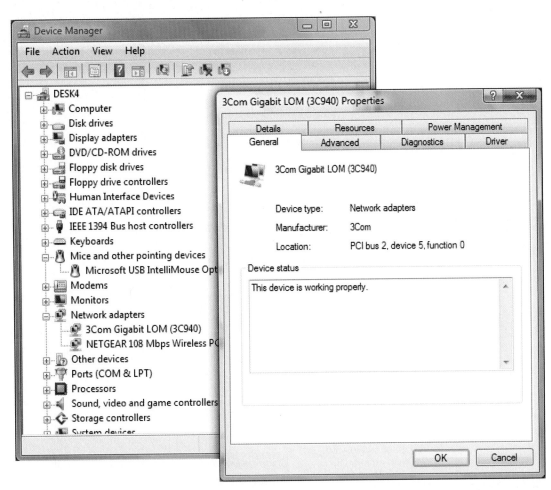

Figure 9-57 A device properties box in Device Manager can be used to report problems and test a device
Courtesy: Course Technology/Cengage Learning

Click the **Driver** tab (see Figure 9-58) to view details about the installed drivers, update the drivers, undo a driver update, disable, or enable a device. Notice in Figure 9-58 that the Driver tab shows the driver for the network card is not digitally signed. Compare this box to the Driver tab of a RAID controller properties box shown in Figure 9-59 where the driver is digitally signed.

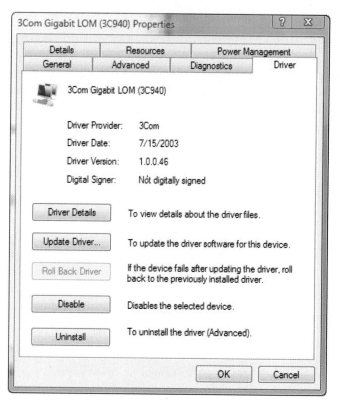

Figure 9-58 Manage the drivers for a device
Courtesy: Course Technology/Cengage Learning

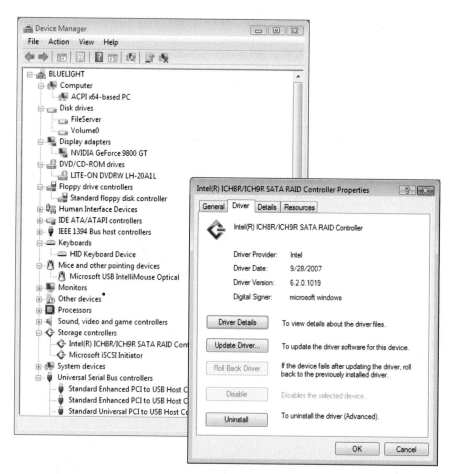

Figure 9-59 The driver for this installed RAID controller is digitally signed
Courtesy: Course Technology/Cengage Learning

Now let's look at how to manage the ports on the motherboard.

USING PORTS ON THE MOTHERBOARD

Ports on the motherboard include sound, video, USB 1.1, USB 2.0, serial, IEEE 1394, parallel, network, modem, and PS/2 ports. Recall that ports on the motherboard can be disabled or enabled in BIOS setup. If you're having a problem with a port, check BIOS setup to make sure the port is enabled. For example, Figure 9-60 shows a BIOS setup screen where you can enable and disable the audio ports, 1394 (FireWire) port, LAN (network) port, Wi-Fi (wireless) connector, serial port, parallel port, and game port. Know that, for ports and expansion slots, BIOS setup recognizes the port or slot, but not the device or expansion card using that slot. Any device that shows up in BIOS setup should also be listed in Device Manager. However, not all devices listed in Device Manager are listed in BIOS setup.

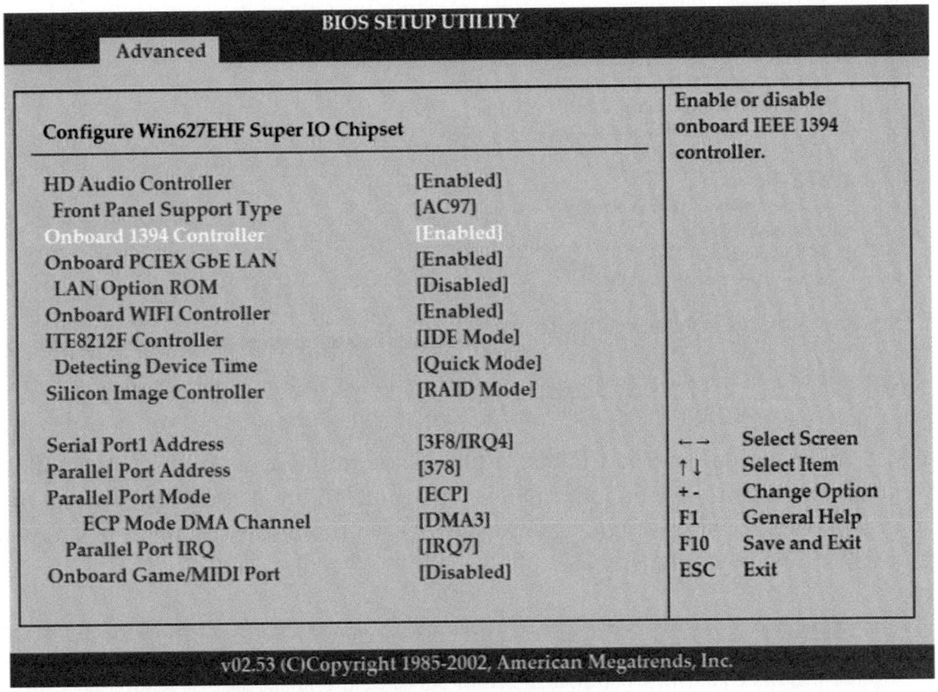

BIOS SETUP UTILITY

Advanced

Configure Win627EHF Super IO Chipset   Enable or disable onboard IEEE 1394 controller.

HD Audio Controller	[Enabled]
Front Panel Support Type	[AC97]
Onboard 1394 Controller	[Enabled]
Onboard PCIEX GbE LAN	[Enabled]
LAN Option ROM	[Disabled]
Onboard WIFI Controller	[Enabled]
ITE8212F Controller	[IDE Mode]
Detecting Device Time	[Quick Mode]
Silicon Image Controller	[RAID Mode]
Serial Port1 Address	[3F8/IRQ4]
Parallel Port Address	[378]
Parallel Port Mode	[ECP]
ECP Mode DMA Channel	[DMA3]
Parallel Port IRQ	[IRQ7]
Onboard Game/MIDI Port	[Disabled]

←→   Select Screen
↑↓   Select Item
+ -   Change Option
F1   General Help
F10   Save and Exit
ESC   Exit

v02.53 (C)Copyright 1985-2002, American Megatrends, Inc.

Figure 9-60   In BIOS setup, you can disable and enable motherboard ports and other components
Courtesy: Course Technology/Cengage Learning

When having a problem with a port, after you know the port is enabled in BIOS setup, turn to Device Manager to make sure it recognizes the port without an error. For example, in Figure 9-61, Device Manager reports no problems with the FireWire port or controller. If you are having problems with a motherboard port, don't forget to update the motherboard drivers that control the port.

Now let's look at the details of managing USB, FireWire, parallel, and serial ports.

USING USB AND FIREWIRE PORTS

Some USB and FireWire devices, such as a USB printer, require that you plug in the device before installing the drivers, and some devices require you to install the drivers before plugging in the device. For some devices, it doesn't matter which is installed first. Carefully read and follow the device documentation. For example, the documentation for one digital camera says that if you install the camera before installing the driver, the drivers will not install properly.

Before you begin the installation, make sure the drivers provided with the device are written for the OS you are using. For example, if you are about to install a USB scanner and the

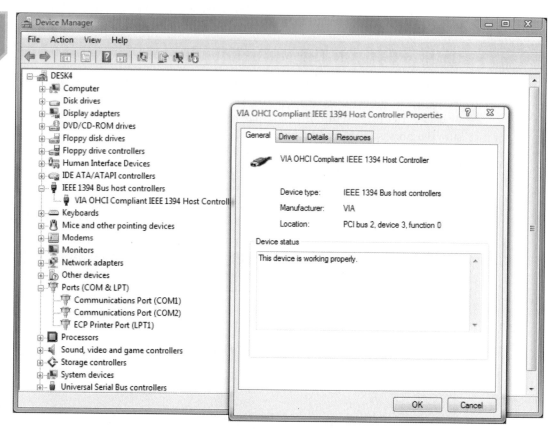

Figure 9-61 Device Manager reports no problems with the FireWire controller or port
Courtesy: Course Technology/Cengage Learning

documentation says the CD that is bundled with the scanner supports Windows 2000 and XP, know that these drivers will not work under Vista. Check the Web site of the scanner manufacturer to see if you can download Vista drivers. If you find them, download the driver file to your hard drive and double-click the file to install the Vista drivers.

> **Notes** Using BIOS setup, you can enable or disable USB or FireWire ports and sometimes the options are there to configure a USB port to use Hi-Speed USB, original USB, or both.

To use a USB or FireWire port with Windows, follow these steps:

1. Verify that Device Manager recognizes that a USB or IEEE 1394 controller is present and reports no errors with the port. If the controller is not installed or is not working, reinstall the motherboard drivers for the port.

2. Read the device documentation to decide if you install the drivers first or plug in the device first.

3. If you plug in the device first, plug it into the FireWire or USB port. The Found New Hardware wizard appears and steps you through the installation of drivers.

4. If you need to install the drivers first, follow the documentation instructions to run a setup program on CD. It might be necessary to restart the system after the installation. After the drivers are installed, plug the device into the port. The device should immediately be recognized by Windows.

5. Install the application software to use the device. For example, a FireWire camcorder is likely to come bundled with video-editing software. Run the software to use the device.

📝 **Notes** Some motherboards provide extra ports that can be installed in faceplate openings off the back of the case. For example, Figure 9-62 shows a module that has a game port and two USB ports. To install the module, remove a faceplate and install the module in its place. Then connect the cables from the module to the appropriate connectors on the motherboard.

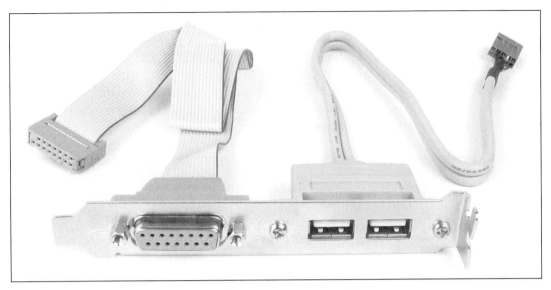

Figure 9-62 This connector provides two USB ports and one game port
Courtesy: Course Technology/Cengage Learning

APPLYING CONCEPTS

For motherboards that provide FireWire ports, the board might come with an internal connector for an internal FireWire hard drive. This connector can also be used for a module that provides additional FireWire ports off the back of the PC case. Figure 9-63 shows a motherboard with the pinouts of the FireWire connector labeled. The module is also shown in the figure. To install this module, remove a faceplate and install the module in its place. Then connect the cable to the motherboard connector.

P4P800 IEEE-1394 connector

TPA0−   GND   TPB0−   +12V   GND

1   TPA0+   GND   TPB0+   +12V   GND

Figure 9-63 This motherboard has a 10-pin FireWire header that can be used for an internal FireWire hard drive or to provide an extra external FireWire port
Courtesy: Course Technology/Cengage Learning

A+
220-702
1.1

CONFIGURING PARALLEL PORTS

Older motherboards required you to configure parallel and serial ports to use certain hardware and OS resources and to avoid conflicts. However, motherboards today are much easier to configure. For example, the BIOS setup on one system to configure the parallel port is shown in Figure 9-64. Unless you are having a problem with the port or suspect a conflict with other hardware, keep the default setting of ECP. Recall that ECP uses a DMA channel. Allow setup to keep DMA3 unless you suspect a conflict with another device trying to use DMA. You can also select an **IRQ (interrupt request) line** for the port. BIOS manages these request lines that are used by a device to hail the CPU asking for data to be processed, and you do not need to change this value.

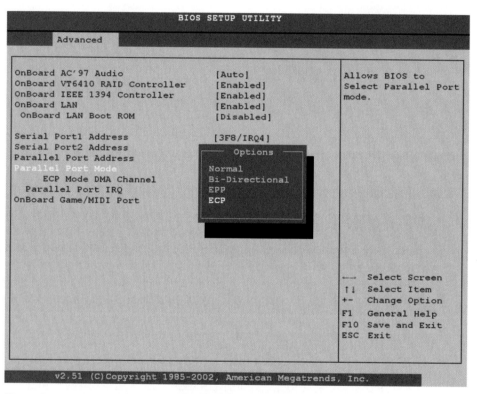

Figure 9-64   BIOS settings for a parallel port on one motherboard
Courtesy: Course Technology/Cengage Learning

> **Notes**   If you have trouble using a motherboard port, such as a serial, parallel, USB, or 1394 port, check BIOS setup to make sure the port is enabled. If you have problems with resource conflicts, try disabling ECP mode for the parallel port. EPP mode gives good results and does not tie up a DMA channel.

In Device Manager, a parallel port is known as LPT1: or LPT2:. The **LPT (Line Printer Terminal)** assignments refer to the system resources a parallel port will use to manage a print job. Check Device Manager for errors. In Figure 9-65, note the parallel port is listed as ECP Printer Port (LPT1).

CONFIGURING SERIAL PORTS

Looking back at Figure 9-64, you can see the two serial ports on this system can be configured to use certain resources. The first serial port is using 3F8/IRQ4 and the second serial port is using 2F8/IRQ3. The first values (3F8 and 2F8) indicate I/O addresses used by the ports,

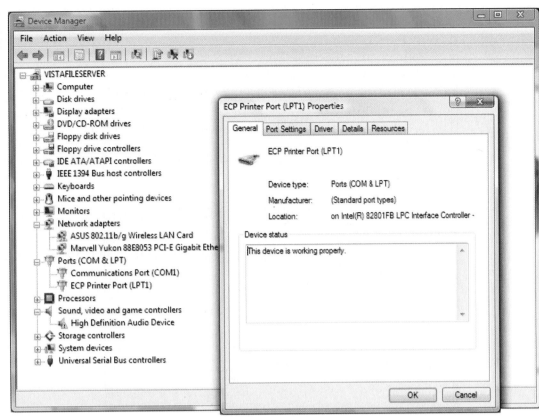

Figure 9-65 The parallel port in Device Manager is known as the LPT port
Courtesy: Course Technology/Cengage Learning

which are numbers the CPU uses to hail the port. The second values (IRQ4 and IRQ5) are lines the port uses to hail the CPU. For most situations, these default settings are appropriate and will never need changing. In Device Manager, the serial ports are known as COM ports. Settings for a serial port can be seen in the properties box for the port on the Port Settings tab (see Figure 9-66). These settings are used by modem cards that are installed in expansion slots on the system. The default values shown in Figure 9-66 are correct for modem settings and should not be changed.

INSTALLING AND CONFIGURING ADAPTER CARDS

In this part of the chapter, you will learn to install and configure adapter cards. These cards include a video card, sound card, storage controller card, I/O card, wired or wireless network card, or capture card. Regardless of the type of card you are installing, when preparing to install an adapter card, be sure to verify and do the following:

▲ *Verify the card fits an empty expansion slot.* Recall from Chapter 5 that there are several AGP, PCI, and PCI Express standards. Know that shorter PCIe cards can be installed in longer PCIe slots. Also, know that you can install a 32-bit PCI card into a longer 64-bit PCI slot. In these cases, the extended end of the long PCIe or PCI slot is unused. For AGP and PCI cards, you must match the notches on the card to the keys in the AGP or PCI slot so that the voltage requirements of the card will match the voltage provided by the slot. And one more tip: To help with air flow, try to leave an empty slot between cards. Especially try to leave an empty slot beside the video card, which puts off a lot of heat.

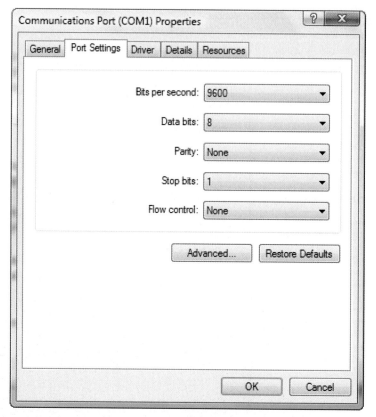

Figure 9-66 Port settings for a serial port as reported by Device Manager
Courtesy: Course Technology/Cengage Learning

▲ *Verify the device drivers for your OS are available.* Drivers written for one OS will not work with another. Check the card documentation and make sure you have the drivers for your OS. It might be possible to download drivers for your OS from the Web site of the card manufacturer.

▲ *Back up important data that is not already backed up.* How to perform backups is covered in Chapter 13.

▲ *Know your starting point.* Know what works and doesn't work on the system. Can you connect to the network and the Internet, print, and use other installed adapter cards without errors?

Here are the general directions to install an adapter card. They apply to any type card.

1. Read the documentation that came with the card. For most cards, you install the card first and then the drivers, but some adapter card installations might not work this way.

2. If you are installing a card to replace an onboard port, access BIOS setup and disable the port.

3. Wear a ground bracelet as you work to protect the card and the system against ESD.

4. Shut down the system, unplug power cords and cables, and press the power button to drain the power. Remove the computer case cover.

5. Locate the slot you plan to use and remove the faceplate cover from the slot if one is installed. Sometimes a faceplate punches or snaps out, and sometimes you have to remove a faceplate screw to remove the faceplate. Remove the screw in the top of the expansion slot. Save the screw; you'll need it later.

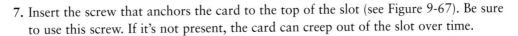

A+
220-702
1.1

6. Remove the card from its antistatic bag and insert it into the expansion slot. Be careful to push the card straight down into the slot, without rocking the card from side to side. Rocking it from side to side can widen the expansion slot, making it difficult to keep a good contact. If you have a problem getting the card into the slot, resist the temptation to push the front or rear of the card into the slot first. You should feel a slight snap as the card drops into the slot. Later, if you find out the card does not work, most likely it is not seated snuggly into the slot. Check that first and then, if possible, try a different slot.

7. Insert the screw that anchors the card to the top of the slot (see Figure 9-67). Be sure to use this screw. If it's not present, the card can creep out of the slot over time.

Figure 9-67 Secure the card to the case with a single screw
Courtesy: Course Technology/Cengage Learning

8. Replace the case cover, power cord, and other peripherals. (If you want, you can leave the case cover off until you've tested the card, in case it doesn't work and you need to reseat it.)

9. Start the system. When Windows starts, Windows Plug and Play should detect a new hardware device is present. The Found New Hardware wizard should launch and you can use it to complete the installation.

Now let's look at the specific details when installing a FireWire controller card, a video card, and a SATA controller card that supports RAID.

> 💡 **A+ Exam Tip** The A+ 220-702 Practical Application exam expects you to know how to install and configure these adapter cards: graphics card, RAID and eSATA storage controller card, and I/O controller cards that provide FireWire, USB, parallel, and serial ports. All these adapter card installations are covered in this part of the chapter.

A+
220-702
1.1

HOW TO INSTALL A FIREWIRE CONTROLLER CARD

The FireWire controller card shown earlier in the chapter in Figure 9-12 uses a PCI slot and has a power connector to provide extra power to the FireWire ports. Do the following to install the card:

1. Follow the general directions given earlier to install the card in a PCI slot.

2. Connect the power cord to the card and to a 4-pin power connector from the power supply.

3. Start Windows, which automatically detects the card and installs its own embedded Windows IEEE 1394 drivers. See Figure 9-68 for Vista and Figure 9-69 for XP.

Figure 9-68 Vista installs embedded Windows drivers
Courtesy: Course Technology/Cengage Learning

Figure 9-69 Windows XP finds the IEEE 1394 controller and installs drivers
Courtesy: Course Technology/Cengage Learning

4. To verify the installation, go to Device Manager and look for the new IEEE 1394 Host Controller installed and listed with no errors.

5. You can now plug up FireWire devices to the ports on the card.

If you later have problems with the card, you can use the driver CD to install the drivers that came with the device. For this device, the CD contains drivers for 32-bit and 64-bit Vista and XP. Locate the driver file on the CD for the OS you are using and double-click the file. Follow the directions on-screen to install the drivers.

HOW TO INSTALL A VIDEO CARD

Recall that Windows has embedded video drivers so that you can use video even if the manufacturer drivers are not installed. However, to get the best performance from the card and to be able to use all its features, always install the manufacturer drivers. Follow these steps to install a video card and its drivers:

1. If the video card is intended to replace an onboard video port, go into BIOS setup and disable the onboard video port.

2. Follow the general steps given earlier to install the video card in a PCI, AGP, or PCIe slot. AGP and PCIe slots use a retention mechanism in the slot to help stabilize a heavy

video card (see Figure 9-70). Check your motherboard documentation for specific instructions to insert the card in this type slot. You might have to use one finger to push the stabilizer to the side as you push the card into the slot. Alternately, the card might snap into the slot and then the retention mechanism snaps into position. Later, if you need to remove the card, use one finger to push the retention mechanism down or to the side and then remove the card. Figure 9-71 shows a PCIe video card installed in a PCIe x16 slot. Notice the fan and heat sink on the card to keep it cool.

Figure 9-70 A white retention mechanism on a PCIe x16 slot pops into place to help stabilize a heavy video card
Courtesy: Course Technology/Cengage Learning

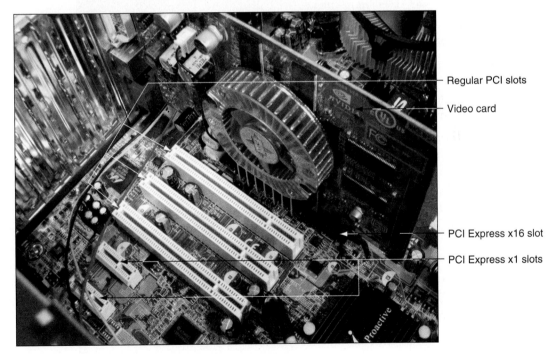

Regular PCI slots

Video card

PCI Express x16 slot

PCI Express x1 slots

Figure 9-71 A PCIe video card installed in a PCIe x16 slot
Courtesy: Course Technology/Cengage Learning

3. If the video card has a 6-pin or 8-pin PCIe power connector, connect a power cord from the power supply to the connector (see Figure 9-72). If the power supply does not have the right connector, you can buy an inexpensive adapter to convert a 4-pin Molex connector to a PCIe connector.

4. When Windows starts up, it will launch the Found New Hardware Wizard (see Figure 9-73). You can install the embedded generic Windows video drivers by allowing the wizard to complete. However, to get the best performance from the card, cancel the wizard (see Figure 9-74) so you can use the drivers that came with the card.

A+
220-702
1.1

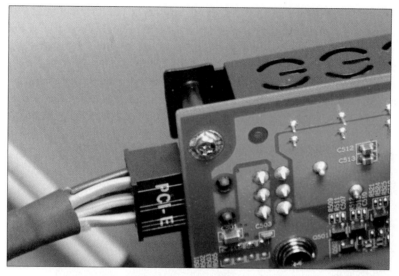

Figure 9-72 Connect a power cord to the PCIe power connector on the card
Courtesy: Course Technology/Cengage Learning

Figure 9-73 The Vista Found New Hardware Wizard attempts to install device drivers
Courtesy: Course Technology/Cengage Learning

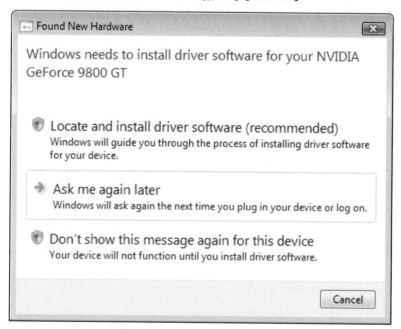

Figure 9-74 Cancel the automatic Windows installation
Courtesy: Course Technology/Cengage Learning

5. Insert the CD that came bundled with the card and launch the setup program on the CD. The card documentation will tell you the name of the program (examples are Setup.exe and Autorun.exe). Figure 9-75 shows the opening menu for one setup program. Click **Install Video Drivers** and follow the on-screen instructions to install the drivers.

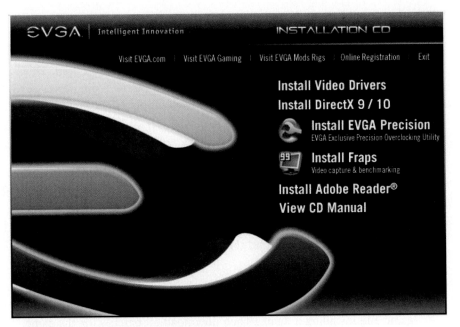

Figure 9-75 Opening menu to install video drivers
Courtesy: Course Technology/Cengage Learning

6. During the installation, Windows will ask you if you want to install the drivers. If the Microsoft Windows Hardware Quality Labs (WHQL) have certified the drivers, the Vista message will look like the one in Figure 9-76. (Later in the chapter, you will see a message indicating drivers are not certified by Microsoft.) Even though drivers have not been certified by Microsoft, it is safe to click **Install this driver software anyway** to continue with the installation.

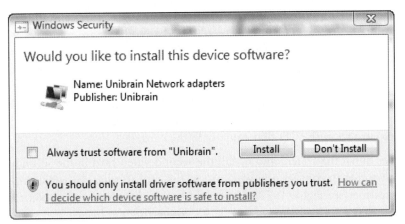

Figure 9-76 Windows recognizes the drivers and asks for your permission to install them
Courtesy: Course Technology/Cengage Learning

7. After the drivers are installed, use the Vista Display Settings or the XP Display Properties window to check the resolution and refresh rate for the monitor.

💡 **A+ Exam Tip** The A+ IT 220-702 Practical Application exam expects you to know how to install a video card.

When you install a video card, here is a list of things that can go wrong and what to do about them:

1. *When you first power up the system, you hear a whining sound.* This is caused by the card not getting enough power. Make sure a 6-pin or 8-pin power cord is connected to the card if it has this connector. The power supply might be inadequate.

2. *When you first start up the system, you see nothing but a black screen.* Most likely this is caused by the onboard video port not being disabled in BIOS setup. Disable the port.

3. *When you first start up the system, you hear a series of beeps.* BIOS cannot detect a video card. Make sure the card is securely seated. The video slot or video card might be bad.

4. *Error messages about video appear when Windows starts.* This can be caused by a conflict in onboard video and the video card. Try disabling onboard video in Device Manager.

5. *Games crash or lock up.* Try updating drivers for the motherboard, the video card, and the sound card. Also install the latest version of DirectX. Then try uninstalling the game and installing it again. Then download all patches for the game.

> **Notes** When you match a monitor to a video card, a good rule of thumb is to match a low-end video card to a low-end monitor, a midrange video card to a midrange monitor, and a high-end video card to a high-end monitor, to get the best performance from both devices. However, you can compare the different features of the video card to those of the monitor, such as the resolutions and the refresh rates supported.

Installing Two Video Cards

For extreme graphics performance, you can use SLI or CrossFire to install two or more video cards in a system. For two video cards, you'll need a motherboard with two PCIe x16 slots and two matching video cards. The board and cards must support SLI or CrossFire. Follow these steps to install the cards using SLI by NVIDIA (CrossFire installs about the same way):

1. Install the first video card in the first PCIe x16 slot (the slot closest to the processor). Boot up the system and make sure the display is working. Install the drivers for the video card from the CD that came with the card.

2. Power down the system and install the second video card in the second PCIe x16 slot. Don't forget to connect a power cord to the card if it has the 6-pin or 8-pin power connection (see Figure 9-77). You might be curious about the ribbon cable in the photo that runs over the two cards. It's connecting the front panel switches and lights to the front panel header. The cable is so short it barely reaches.

3. Leave the monitor cable connected to the first card. Reboot and install the drivers for the second video card. After this installation, Device Manager should report two video cards installed with no problems (see Figure 9-78).

4. To configure the video cards to work in tandem, open the video adapter utility. The easiest way to open the utility is to right-click the desktop and select **NVIDIA Control Panel** from the shortcut menu (refer back to Figure 9-21). For this particular utility, select **Manage 3D settings** in the left pane and select **Multiple display performance mode** in the right pane, as shown in Figure 9-79.

Figure 9-77 Two video cards installed in a system
Courtesy: Course Technology/Cengage Learning

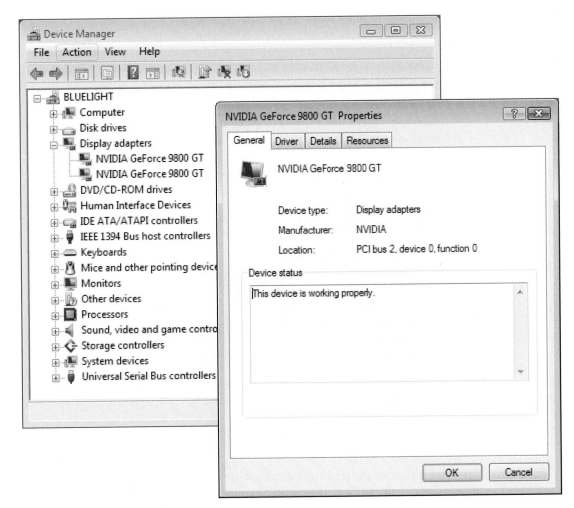

Figure 9-78 Two video cards are installed
Courtesy: Course Technology/Cengage Learning

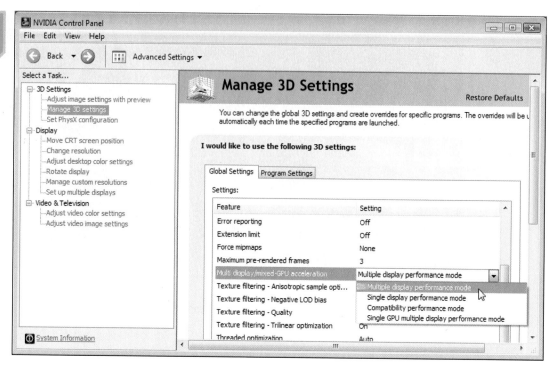

Figure 9-79   Configure the two video cards to work in tandem
Courtesy: Course Technology/Cengage Learning

5. Test the graphics to see if performance improves. If you believe performance should be better than it is, you can install an optional SLI bridge (see Figure 9-80). Connect each side of the SLI bridge to the gold connectors at the top of each SLI-ready video card. The SLI bridge improves performance because the cards can communicate by way of the bridge as well as by way of the PCIe slots.

Figure 9-80   SLI bridge is used to improve communication between two SLI video cards
Courtesy: Course Technology/Cengage Learning

HOW TO INSTALL A SATA, ESATA, AND RAID STORAGE CONTROLLER CARD

Installing and configuring a storage controller card that manages hard drives connected to ports on the card can be a little more complex than other adapter card installations. Not only do you have to install drivers to control the SATA and eSATA connectors on the card, but you might also have to install a utility program to manage a RAID array.

As with all installations, follow the manufacturer's specific instructions for installing and configuring the card. Here are some general guidelines to install and configure a storage controller card to be used by drives that are not holding the Windows installation:

1. Following instructions given earlier in the chapter, install the controller card in an empty expansion slot. Attach one or more drives to the card SATA connectors.

2. Boot the computer. The Found New Hardware wizard finds the card and displays the message shown in Figure 9-81.

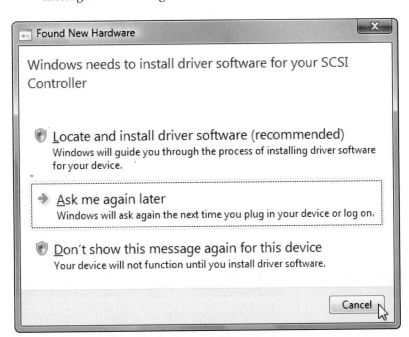

Figure 9-81 Vista wants to install drivers for the device it just found
Courtesy: Course Technology/Cengage Learning

3. For most installations, select **Locate and install driver software (recommended)**. However, if the controller card documentation says to cancel the Windows installation and use the Setup program on the driver CD instead, click **Cancel**.

4. If you are using the Windows installation method, Windows displays the message in Figure 9-82. Insert the card's driver CD and click **Next**. (Notice in Figure 9-81 that Vista believes it is installing a SCSI host adapter when, in fact, it is installing a SATA controller. The confusion will clear up after the installation.) If the controller card supports RAID, you might need to choose between non-RAID and RAID drivers.

5. If you are using the manufacturer installation routine, insert the driver CD and locate the Setup.exe program. Notice in Figure 9-83 ten folders on a CD listed on the right side of the screen. Each folder contains a Setup program and drivers for ten controller card models that this one CD supports. Look for your model number printed on the adapter card box. Double-click **Setup.exe** in your model's folder, respond to the UAC box, and follow the instructions on-screen to complete the installation.

6. During either the Windows installation or the manufacturer installation, if Windows detects the device drivers have not been certified by Microsoft, the warning message in Figure 9-84 appears. To continue the installation, click **Install the driver software anyway**.

7. After the installation, you will probably be prompted to restart the system. If so, do that now.

A+
220-702
1.1

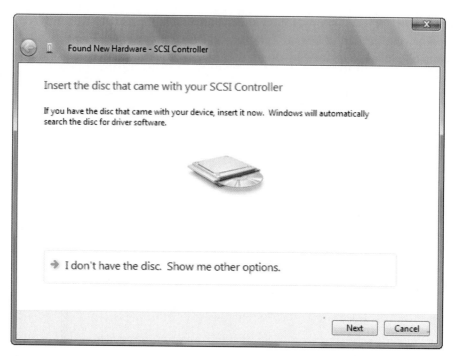

Figure 9-82   Insert the drive CD to continue the installation
Courtesy: Course Technology/Cengage Learning

Figure 9-83   Locate the correct folder containing the Setup program on CD
Courtesy: Course Technology/Cengage Learning

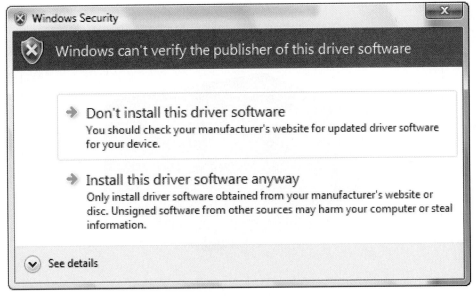

Figure 9-84 Windows warns drivers are not Microsoft certified
Courtesy: Course Technology/Cengage Learning

8. If you want to create a RAID array using the card, you might need to install a RAID utility to manage the array. The card documentation will tell you which folder on the CD contains the utility setup program. Find the setup program and double-click it to install the utility. You can then use it to create and monitor the RAID array. You will have to select the hard drives used in the array, the type of RAID (0, 1, or 5), and the amount of space on each drive devoted to the array (same for each drive). Chapter 8 gives more information about configuring RAID.

> **Notes** Suppose you have a hard drive that is intended to be installed inside a computer case and you want to install it outside the case as an external drive. If you have an available eSATA external port, you can use a protective **hard drive dock** that will house and protect a hard drive outside the computer case. These devices are hot-pluggable and sometimes called a toaster because that's what they look like (see Figure 9-85). Plug the toaster into a power outlet and pop your internal hard drive into the toaster. Use the toaster's SATA cable to connect the drive to an eSATA port on your system. But be cautious: some toasters are not reliable. Be sure to read several online reviews about a toaster before you buy one.

Sometimes the controller card will manage the hard drive on which Windows is installed. Here are three situations you might encounter and how to handle them:

▲ *New Windows installation.* For a fresh installation of Windows, you'll need to prepare a floppy disk that Windows setup will need while it is installing Vista or XP. On another computer, copy the RAID or non-RAID driver files from the card's driver CD to the disk. Read the card documentation to find out which folder on the CD contains these files. If your system does not have a floppy drive, most likely you can use a USB drive to hold the drivers.

Then begin the Windows installation by booting the computer from the Windows setup CD or DVD. On the first screen of the Windows installation, a message appears at the bottom of the screen to select load driver (for Windows Vista) or press F6 (for Windows XP) to install storage drivers. Click **load driver** or press **F6**, insert the floppy disk, and follow the instructions on-screen to install the drivers. The Windows installation then proceeds normally.

Figure 9-85   Use a hard drive dock to connect one or more internal hard drives to external ports
on your computer
Courtesy of StarTech.com

▲ *Existing Windows installation uses the controller card.* To move the Windows hard
drive from a motherboard connection to the storage controller card, first install the
card under Windows. Then power down the system and move the SATA cable from
the motherboard to the controller card. Restart the system.

▲ *Change the bootable hard drive to the controller card's drive.* Another situation is
when you already have a Windows bootable hard drive installed that is using a motherboard connection and you want to use a second hard drive connected to the
controller card as your boot device. For this situation, first install the controller card
with the new drive attached. Then boot into BIOS setup and look for the option to
Boot SCSI first. If BIOS setup has the option, enable it so that the system will boot to
the drive connected to the controller card.

APPLYING|CONCEPTS   Bill was hurriedly setting up a computer for a friend.
When he got to the modem, he installed it as he had
installed many modems in the past. He put the modem card in the PCI slot and turned on the PC
for Plug and Play to do its job. When the Found New Hardware Wizard launched, he installed the
drivers, but the modem wouldn't work. He tried again and again to reinstall the modem, but still
it didn't work. After four hours of trying to get the modem to work, he concluded the modem
was bad. Then it hit him to read the instructions that came with the modem. He opened
the booklet and in very large letters on the very first page it said, "The modem WILL NOT
WORK if you install the card first and the software second." Bill took the card out and
followed the instructions and within five minutes he was surfing the Net. Bill says that
from that day forward he *always* reads *all* instructions first and leaves his ego at the
door! And for all other impatient installers, know that most devices come with a
Quick Start guide.

TROUBLESHOOTING I/O DEVICES

Generally, when troubleshooting an I/O device, including adapter cards and devices plugged into motherboard ports, follow these steps:

1. For a new installation, suspect the device or drivers are not installed correctly, or the application software does not work. Start at the beginning of the installation and redo and recheck each step. Use Device Manager to uninstall the device. Then restart the system and install the drivers again, this time looking carefully for error messages.

2. For adapter cards, verify the card is securely seated in the slot. Try a different slot. Does the card need a power cord that is not connected to it?

3. For problems after an installation, ask the user what has just changed in the system. For example, if there has been a recent thunderstorm, the device might have been damaged by electricity. Maybe the user has just installed some software or changed Windows settings.

4. Analyze the situation and try to isolate the problem. For example, decide if the problem is most likely caused by hardware or software.

5. Check simple things first. Is the device getting power? Is it turned on? Is the data connection secure? Try rebooting the system to get a fresh start.

6. Exchange the device for a known good one or install the suspected device in a working system.

7. Sources that you can use to help you understand an error message or a symptom include the Internet (manufacturer Web site or a general search), device documentation, training materials, technical support from the device manufacturer (by chat, phone, forums, and blogs), and technical people in your organization.

8. After the problem is fixed, document the symptoms, the source of the problem, and the solution so you have that to take into the next troubleshooting situation.

Let's now look at specific instructions for troubleshooting I/O ports, a keyboard, a monitor and video card, and other adapter cards.

TROUBLESHOOTING MOTHERBOARD I/O PORTS

When you are having a problem with an I/O port on the motherboard, do the following:

1. Verify the problem is not with the device using the port. Try moving the device to another port on the same computer or move the device to another computer. If it works there, return it to this port. The problem might have been a bad connection.

2. Go into BIOS setup and verify the port is enabled.

3. Check Device Manager and verify Windows recognizes the port with no errors.

4. Uninstall and reinstall the drivers for the device using the port.

5. Update the motherboard drivers. You might be able to download drivers for this type port from the motherboard manufacturer Web site.

6. If you have a loop-back plug, use it to test the port. A **loop-back plug** is a tool used to test a serial, parallel, USB, network, or other port. To use one to test a port, you plug

A+
220-702
1.2
1.4

in the loop-back plug and then run the software that comes with the plug to test the port. Figure 9-86 shows loop-back plugs that come with CheckIt diagnostic software from SmithMicro Software (*www.smithmicro.com*).

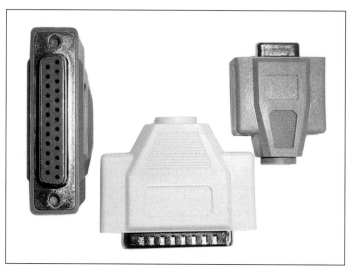

Figure 9-86   Loop-back plugs used to test serial and parallel ports
Courtesy of Smith Micro Software, Inc.

7. If the problem is still not solved, disable the port in BIOS setup and install an I/O controller card to provide the same type port.

TROUBLESHOOTING KEYBOARDS

A+
220-702
1.2

Keyboards can give problems if they are not kept clean. If dirt, food, or drink is allowed to build up, one or more keys might stick or not work properly. Chips inside the keyboard can fail, and the keyboard cable or port connector can go bad. Because of its low cost, when a keyboard doesn't work, the solution is most often to replace it. However, you can try a few simple things to repair one, as listed next:

1. If a few keys don't work, turn the keyboard upside down and bump it to dislodge debris and use compressed air to blow out debris.

2. If the keyboard does not work at all, check to see if the cable is plugged in. Maybe it's plugged into the mouse port by mistake. Next, swap it with a known good keyboard.

3. If a PS/2 keyboard does not work, try a USB keyboard. The PS/2 port might be bad. Know that some motherboards have a jumper that must be set for a PS/2 or USB keyboard. For other motherboards, the option to use a USB keyboard must be enabled in BIOS setup. And for still other motherboards, you can install a USB keyboard without changing any jumpers or BIOS settings.

> **Notes**   Older computers refused to boot unless a keyboard was present. However, newer computers allow you to boot without a keyboard, and you can then plug in the keyboard after the boot.

4. If coffee or sugary drinks are spilled on the keyboard, the best solution is to simply replace the keyboard. You can try to save the keyboard by thoroughly rinsing it in running water, perhaps from a bathroom shower. Make sure the keyboard dries thoroughly before you

use it. Let it dry for two days on its own, or fewer if you set it out in the sun or in front of a fan. In some situations, such as a factory setting where dust and dirt are everywhere, consider using a clear plastic keyboard cover.

TROUBLESHOOTING MONITORS AND VIDEO CARDS

For monitors as well as other devices, if you have problems, try doing the easy things first. For instance, try to make simple hardware and software adjustments. Many monitor problems are caused by poor cable connections or bad contrast/brightness adjustments.

> 💡 **Tip**   A user very much appreciates a PC support technician who takes a little extra time to clean a system being serviced. When servicing a monitor, take the time to clean the screen with a soft dry cloth or monitor wipe.

Typical monitor and video card problems and how to troubleshoot them are described next.

POWER LIGHT (LED) DOES NOT GO ON; NO PICTURE

For this problem, try the following:

- Is the monitor plugged in? Verify that the wall outlet works by plugging in a lamp, radio, or similar device. Is the monitor turned on? Look for a cutoff switch on the front and on the back. Some monitors have both.
- If the monitor power cord is plugged into a power strip or surge protector, verify that the power strip is turned on and working and that the monitor is also turned on.
- If the monitor power cord is plugged into the back of the computer, verify that the connection is tight and the computer is turned on.
- A blown fuse could be the problem. Some monitors have a fuse that is visible from the back of the monitor. It looks like a black knob that you can remove (no need to go inside the monitor cover). Remove the fuse and look for the broken wire indicating a bad fuse.
- The monitor might have a switch on the back for choosing between 110 volts and 220 volts. Check that the switch is in the right position.
- The problem might be with the video card. If you have just installed the card and the motherboard has onboard video, go into BIOS setup and disable the video port on the motherboard.
- Verify that the video cable is connected to the video port on the video card and not to a disabled onboard video port.

> ⚡ **Caution**   A monitor retains a charge even after the power cord is unplugged. If you are trained to open a monitor case to replace a fuse, unplug the monitor and wait at least 60 minutes before opening the case so that capacitors have completely discharged.

> 📝 **Notes**   When you turn on your PC, the first thing you see on the screen is the firmware on the video card identifying itself. You can use this information to search the Web, especially the manufacturer's Web site, for troubleshooting information about the card.

9

A+ 220-702

If none of these solutions solves the problem, the next step is to take the monitor to a service center.

POWER LED IS ON, NO PICTURE ON POWER-UP

For this problem, try the following:

- ▲ Check the contrast adjustment. If there's no change, leave it at a middle setting.
- ▲ Check the brightness or backlight adjustment. If there's no change, leave it at a middle setting.
- ▲ Make sure the cable is connected securely to the computer.
- ▲ If the monitor-to-computer cable detaches from the monitor, exchange it for a cable you know is good, or check the cable for continuity.
- ▲ If this solves the problem, reattach the old cable to verify that the problem was not simply a bad connection.
- ▲ Test a monitor you know is good on the computer you suspect to be bad. If you think the monitor is bad, make sure that it also fails to work on a good computer.
- ▲ If the monitor works while the system boots up, but the screen goes blank when Windows starts to load, the problem is more likely to be with Windows than with the monitor or video card. Try booting Windows in Safe Mode, which you will learn to do later in the chapter. Safe Mode allows the OS to select a generic display driver and low resolution. If this works, change the driver and resolution.
- ▲ Reseat the video card. For a PCI card, move the card to a different expansion slot. Clean the card's edge connectors, using a contact cleaner purchased from a computer supply store.
- ▲ If there are socketed chips on the video card, remove the card from the expansion slot and then use a screwdriver to press down firmly on each corner of each socketed chip on the card. Chips sometimes loosen because of temperature changes; this condition is called chip creep.
- ▲ Trade a good video card for the video card you suspect is bad. Test the video card you think is bad on a computer that works. Test a video card you know is good on the computer that you suspect is bad. Whenever possible, do both.
- ▲ Go into BIOS setup and disable the shadowing of video ROM.
- ▲ Test the RAM on the motherboard with diagnostic software.
- ▲ For a motherboard that is using an AGP or a PCI-Express video card, try using a PCI video card in a PCI slot.
- ▲ Trade the motherboard for one you know is good. Sometimes, though rarely, a peripheral chip on the motherboard can cause the problem.
- ▲ For notebook computers, is the LCD switch turned on? Function keys are sometimes used for this purpose.
- ▲ For notebook computers, try connecting a second monitor to the notebook and use the function key to toggle between the LCD panel and the second monitor. If the second monitor works, but the LCD panel does not work, the problem might be with the LCD panel hardware. How to solve problems with notebook computers is covered in Chapter 21.

POWER IS ON, BUT MONITOR DISPLAYS THE WRONG CHARACTERS

For this problem, try the following:

- ▲ Wrong characters are usually not the result of a bad monitor but of a problem with the video card. Trade the video card for one you know is good.
- ▲ Exchange the motherboard. Sometimes a bad ROM or RAM chip on the motherboard displays the wrong characters on the monitor.

A+
220-702
1.2

MONITOR FLICKERS, HAS WAVY LINES, OR BOTH

For this problem, try the following:

- Monitor flicker can be caused by poor cable connections. Check that the cable connections are snug.
- Does the monitor have a degauss button to eliminate accumulated or stray magnetic fields? If so, press it.
- Check if something in the office is causing a high amount of electrical noise (EMI). For example, you might be able to stop a flicker by moving the office fan to a different outlet. Bad fluorescent lights or large speakers can also produce interference. Two monitors placed very close together can also cause problems.
- If the refresh rate is below 60 Hz, a screen flicker might appear. Change the refresh rate to the highest value the monitor supports.
- For older monitors that do not support a high enough refresh rate, your only cure might be to purchase a new monitor. Before making a purchase, verify that the new monitor will solve the problem.

NO GRAPHICS DISPLAY OR THE SCREEN GOES BLANK WHEN LOADING CERTAIN PROGRAMS

For this problem, try the following:

- A special graphics or video accelerator card is not present or is defective.
- Video card drivers need updating. Use Device Manager to update the drivers.
- Updating Windows can sometimes solve video problems. How to update Windows is covered in Chapter 12.
- The video card does not support the resolution and/or color setting.
- There might not be enough video RAM. An older video card might have empty sockets on the card to hold additional video memory. See the card documentation to find out if additional video memory can be added.
- A virus is disrupting normal Windows operations. Scan the system for viruses using an updated version of antivirus software. How to solve problems with viruses is covered in Chapter 20.

SCREEN GOES BLANK 30 SECONDS OR ONE MINUTE AFTER THE KEYBOARD IS LEFT UNTOUCHED

A Green motherboard (one that follows energy-saving standards) used with an Energy Saver monitor can be configured to go into standby or sleep mode after a period of inactivity. This might be the case if the monitor resumes after you press a key or move the mouse. Video might be set to turn off display after a period set as short as 20 seconds to as long as one hour. The power LED normally changes from green to orange to indicate sleep mode. How to set sleep modes in Windows is covered in Chapter 21.

> **Notes** Problems might occur if the motherboard power-saving features are turning off the monitor, and Windows screen saver is also turning off the monitor. If the system hangs when you try to get the monitor going again, try disabling one or the other. If this doesn't work, disable both.

You might be able to change the doze features by entering BIOS setup and looking for an option such as Power Management. In addition, note that some monitors have a Power Save switch on the back. Make sure this is set as you want.

9

A+ 220-702

A+
220-702
1.2

The screen saver feature of Windows can also set the monitor to turn off after so many minutes of inactivity. For Vista, right-click the desktop and select **Personalize** from the shortcut menu. In the Personalization window, click **Screen Saver**. Set the minutes in the Screen Saver Settings box. For XP, the number of minutes is set in the Display Properties window. Open Control Panel, select **Display**, and then select **Screen Saver**.

POOR COLOR DISPLAY

For this problem, try the following:

▲ Read the monitor documentation to learn how to use the color-adjusting buttons to fine-tune the color.

▲ Exchange video cards.

▲ Your video card might allow you to install additional video RAM. See the card's documentation.

▲ Check if a fan, a large speaker (speakers have large magnets), or a nearby monitor could be causing interference.

▲ If a CRT monitor displays blue and green, but no red, then the red electron gun might be bad. Replace the monitor. Same for missing blue or green colors.

▲ Odd-colored blotches on the screen might indicate a device such as a speaker or fan is sitting too close to the monitor and emitting EMI. Move any suspected device away from the monitor.

PICTURE OUT OF FOCUS OR OUT OF ADJUSTMENT

For this problem, try the following:

▲ Change the resolution of an LCD monitor to its native resolution. If the highest resolution seems stretched or fuzzy, it is likely the video card or monitor manufacturer drivers have not been installed and this highest resolution is not the monitor's native resolution. Download the latest drivers for your OS from the video card manufacturer Web site and install them. Also install the latest drivers for your OS from the Web site of the monitor manufacturer.

▲ Using the display utility from the video card manufacturer, try different adjustments and settings to see if you can discover the best settings for your monitor. To access the utility, look for it listed in the shortcut menu when you right-click the Windows desktop.

▲ Check the adjustment knobs on the control panel on the outside of the monitor.

▲ Change the refresh rate. Sometimes this can make the picture appear more focused.

▲ You can also make adjustments inside the monitor that might solve the problem. If you have not been trained to work inside the monitor, take it to a service center.

Notes For LCD monitors and Windows XP, you can improve how fonts are displayed on the screen. On the Display Properties window, click the **Appearance** tab and then click **Effects**. The Effects dialog box appears (see Figure 9-87). Check **Use the following method to smooth edges of screen fonts**. Then, from the drop-down list, select **ClearType**. Click **OK** twice to close both windows.

A+
220-702
1.2

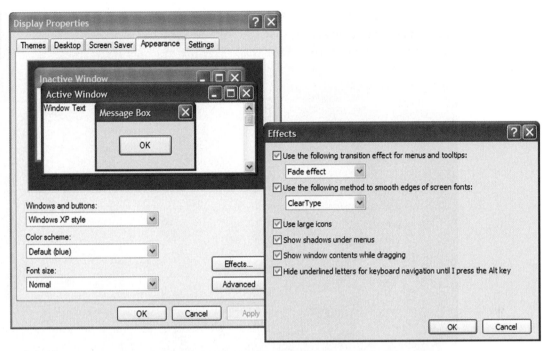

Figure 9-87 Use the Effects dialog box to improve displayed fonts using an LCD monitor
Courtesy: Course Technology/Cengage Learning

9

A+ 220-702

CRT MONITOR MAKES A CRACKLING SOUND

Dirt or dust inside the unit might be the cause. Someone at a computer monitor service center trained to work on the inside of the monitor can vacuum inside it. Recall from Chapter 4 that a monitor holds a dangerous charge of electricity, and you should not open one unless trained to do so.

> **Tip** For laptops, you can adjust the brightness of the display using function keys. See your notebook user manual to find out how.

DISPLAY SETTINGS MAKE THE SCREEN UNREADABLE

When the display settings don't work, you can easily return to standard VGA settings, which include a resolution of 640 x 480. Do the following:

- Reboot the system and press the **F8** key after the first beep. The Advanced Boot Options menu appears. Figure 9-88 shows the Vista menu; the XP menu is similar.
- Select **Safe Mode** to boot up with minimal configurations and standard VGA display mode. For Windows XP, you can also try **Enable VGA Mode** from the Advanced Options menu. And for Vista, you can try **Enable low-resolution video** (640 x 480).
- Use the Vista Display Settings box or the XP Display Properties box to correct the video settings.

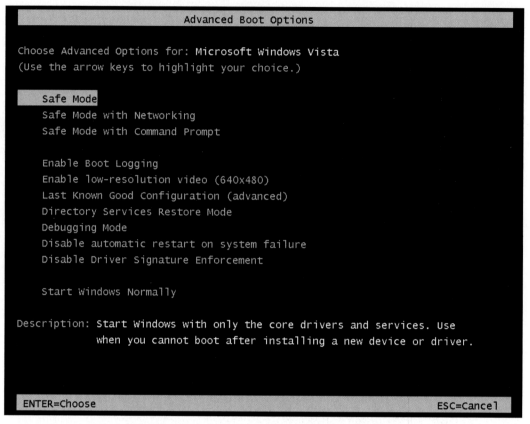

```
                        Advanced Boot Options


Choose Advanced Options for: Microsoft Windows Vista
(Use the arrow keys to highlight your choice.)


    Safe Mode
    Safe Mode with Networking
    Safe Mode with Command Prompt

    Enable Boot Logging
    Enable low-resolution video (640x480)
    Last Known Good Configuration (advanced)
    Directory Services Restore Mode
    Debugging Mode
    Disable automatic restart on system failure
    Disable Driver Signature Enforcement


    Start Windows Normally

Description: Start Windows with only the core drivers and services. Use
             when you cannot boot after installing a new device or driver.




ENTER=Choose                                              ESC=Cancel
```

Figure 9-88   Press F8 to see the Advanced Boot Options menu
Courtesy: Course Technology/Cengage Learning

> ⚡ **Caution**   A CRT monitor screen is made of leaded glass, and a monitor contains capacitors that can hold a charge even after the monitor is unplugged. Therefore, it's important to dispose of a monitor correctly. For capacitors to fully discharge, it is not safe to remove the cover of a monitor until it has remained unplugged for at least one hour. To know how to dispose of a monitor, check with local county or environment officials for laws and regulations that apply to your area.

TROUBLESHOOTING OTHER ADAPTER CARDS

For adapter cards other then the video card, follow these steps:

1. Make sure the device connected to the card is working. For example, if an external CD drive is using an eSATA port on a storage controller card, move the drive to another eSATA port. If the drive works on that port, return it to the controller card. Perhaps a bad connection was the problem.

2. Update the driver drivers for the card. Download the latest drivers from the manufacturer Web site. Also, use the process described in Chapter 12 to make sure all Windows updates are current.

3. Try uninstalling the card. Use Device Manager to uninstall the card drivers. An exception to this might be a storage controller card. Its drivers might need to be uninstalled by executing the Setup.exe program on the driver CD. For example, when you run this program for one card, the window in Figure 9-89 appears. Select **Remove** and click **Next** to uninstall the drivers.

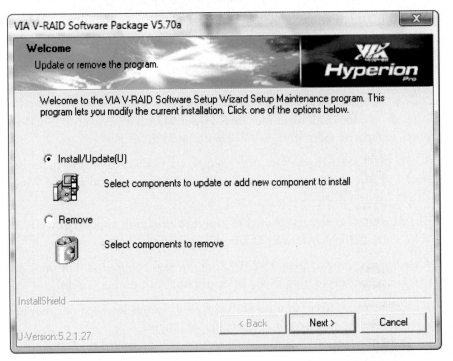

A+
220-702
1.2

9

Figure 9-89 Use the Setup program on CD to uninstall the adapter card drivers
Courtesy: Course Technology/Cengage Learning

4. Then reboot the system and install the drivers again. Watch for error messages during the installation.

5. Try reseating the card or moving it to a different slot.

6. Search for diagnostic software on the driver CD or on the manufacturer Web site.

7. Use technical resources available on the manufacturer Web site for things to do and try.

8. Search the Internet for error messages and problems and solutions with the card.

9. Try replacing the card with one you know is good.

>> CHAPTER SUMMARY

▲ Adding new devices to a computer requires installing hardware and software. Even if you know how to generally install an I/O device, always follow the specific instructions of the product manufacturer.

▲ Use Device Manager under Windows to manage hardware devices.

▲ I/O ports on a motherboard include eSATA, FireWire, USB, parallel, serial, and PS/2 ports.

▲ USB ports can run at SuperSpeed USB (up to 5.0 Gbps), Hi-Speed USB (480 Mbps), or Original USB (1.5 Mbps or 12 Mbps) with up to 127 USB devices daisy chained together.

▲ Two popular versions of FireWire are FireWire 800 (800 Mbps) and FireWire 400 (400 Mbps).

▲ Serial ports use a DB9 or DB25 connector.

⬛ Parallel ports can support EPP or ECP. ECP is faster and requires a DMA channel.

⬛ Technologies and features of CRT and LCD monitors include screen size, refresh rate, interlacing (for CRT), response time (for LCD), pixel pitch, resolution, native resolution (for LCD), color quality, multiscan (for CRT), contrast ratio, and viewing angle (for LCD). In addition, consider the type connectors that a monitor uses. Most common types are VGA and DVI.

⬛ Ports on a video card might include a 15-pin VGA port, one or more DVI-I or DVI-D ports, composite video port, S-Video port, and HDMI port.

⬛ To use the Aero user interface, Vista requires a video card or onboard video to have at least 128 MB of video RAM, support DirectX version 9, and use the Windows Display Driver Model (WDDM).

⬛ The dxdiag.exe command is used to report information about hardware, including the video card and which version of DirectX it is using.

⬛ A keyboard can use a DIN, PS/2, USB, or wireless connection. For most installations, all that is necessary is to plug in the keyboard and turn on the system.

⬛ A touch screen is likely to use a USB port. Software is installed to calibrate the touch screen to the monitor screen and receive data input.

⬛ Biometric input devices, such as a fingerprint reader, collect biological data and compare it to that recorded about the person to authenticate the person's access to a system.

⬛ A KVM switch lets you use one keyboard, monitor, and mouse with multiple computers.

⬛ Most likely an adapter card is physically installed in a system and when Windows starts up, it detects the card and then you install the drivers using the Windows wizard. However, always follow instructions from the device manufacturer when installing an adapter card because the order of installing the card and drivers might be different.

⬛ When installing Windows on a hard drive that is controlled by a storage controller adapter card, the card drivers must be installed during the Windows installation. You are given an opportunity at the beginning of the Windows installation to provide the drivers on floppy disk or perhaps a USB device.

>> KEY TERMS

For explanations of key terms, see the Glossary near the end of the book.

biometric device
chip creep
COM1 (Communications port 1)
CRT (cathode-ray tube)
degauss button
DVI-D
DVI-I
dxdiag.exe
ECP (Extended Capabilities Port)
Energy Star
EPP (Enhanced Parallel Port)
FireWire
flat panel monitors
hard drive dock
HDMI (High-Definition Multimedia Interface)
hub

i.Link
I/O controller card
IEEE 1284
IEEE 1394
IEEE 1394.3
infrared transceiver
interlaced
IR transceiver
IrDA (Infrared Data Association) transceiver
IRQ (Interrupt ReQuest) line
isochronous data transfer
KVM (Keyboard, Video, and Mouse) switch
LCD (Liquid Crystal Display) monitor
LPT (Line Printer Terminal)

native resolution
noninterlaced
refresh rate
resolution
RGB (red, green, and blue)
RS-232c (Reference Standard 232 revision c or Recommended Standard 232 revision c)
standard parallel port (SPP)
Super VGA (SVGA)
S-Video port
touch screen
UART (Universal Asynchronous Receiver-Transmitter)
VGA (Video Graphics Adapter)

>> REVIEWING THE BASICS

1. Which is faster, an eSATA port or a FireWire 800 port?

2. What is the speed for Hi-Speed USB?

3. How many times faster is a Hi-Speed USB port than an Original USB port running at 12 Mbps?

4. How many times faster is a FireWire 800 port than a FireWire 400 port?

5. Which USB port is square and which USB port is flat and wide?

6. Does Windows XP without any service packs applied support Hi-Speed USB?

7. How many pins does a FireWire 800 port have?

8. Which parallel port standard uses a DMA channel?

9. How many pins does the most common type of serial port have?

10. What type of wireless transmission requires a line-of-sight clearance?

11. Which is better for your eyes, a monitor that supports 75 Hz refresh rate or one that supports 60 Hz refresh rate?

12. For an LCD monitor, what is the best resolution to use?

13. Which type port gives the best output, a composite out port or an S-Video port?

14. What command do you use to find out what version of DirectX your video card is using?

15. Name three types of ports a keyboard might use.

16. What two types of ports might a touch screen use?

17. Which Windows utility is most likely the one to use when uninstalling an expansion card?

18. Would you expect all the devices listed in BIOS setup to also be listed in Device Manager? Would you expect all devices listed in Device Manager to also be listed in BIOS setup?

19. If ECP mode does not work on your parallel port, what should you do next?

20. Why is it best to leave a slot empty between two expansion cards?

21. What two technologies allow you to use more than one video card in a system?

22. If you are installing Windows on a hard drive that is managed by a RAID storage controller card, when and how do you install the RAID drivers?

23. If a monitor displays wrong characters, which device is likely to be the problem?

24. What is the display resolution for standard VGA settings?

25. What key do you press at startup to display the Vista Advanced Boot Options window?

>> THINKING CRITICALLY

1. If a PS/2 keyboard does not work on your system and yet you know the keyboard is good, what is the best solution?

    a. Disable the PS/2 port in BIOS setup and use a PS/2 splitter to install a keyboard and mouse using the PS/2 mouse port.

b. Install a USB keyboard on a USB port.

c. Exchange the PS/2 port on your motherboard.

d. Replace the motherboard.

2. You plug a new scanner into a USB port on your Windows XP system. When you first turn on the scanner, what should you expect to see?

a. A message displayed by the scanner software telling you to reboot your system.

b. You see the Found New Hardware Wizard launch.

c. Your system automatically reboots.

d. An error message from the USB controller.

3. You install the software bundled with your digital camera to download pictures from your camera to your system using a serial port. Next, you plug up the camera to the port using a serial cable and turn on your camera. You attempt to use the software to download pictures, but the software does not recognize the camera is present. What do you do next?

a. Return the camera and purchase one that uses a USB port for downloading.

b. Reinstall the bundled software.

c. Access BIOS setup and verify that the serial port is enabled.

d. Use Device Manager to verify that the OS recognizes the serial port.

e. Replace the serial cable.

4. You turn on your Windows Vista computer and see the system display POST messages. Then the screen turns blue with no text. Which of the following items could be the source of the problem?

a. The video card

b. The monitor

c. Windows

d. MS Word software installed on the system

>> HANDS-ON PROJECTS

PROJECT 9-1:   Installing a Device

Install a device on a computer. If you are working in a classroom environment, you can simulate an installation by moving a device from one computer to another. Devices that you might consider installing are a video card, Web camera, I/O controller card, CD drive, or fingerprint reader.

PROJECT 9-2:   Researching a Computer Ad

Pick a current Web site or magazine ad for a complete, working computer system, including computer, monitor, keyboard, and software, together with extra devices such as a mouse or printer. Research the details of the ad and write a two- to four-page report describing and explaining these details. This project provides a good opportunity to learn about the latest offerings on the market as well as current pricing.

PROJECT 9-3:   Comparing Two Computer Ads

Find two ads for computer systems containing the same processor. Compare the two ads. Include in your comparison the different features offered and the weaknesses and strengths of each system.

PROJECT 9-4:   Searching the Internet for a Video Driver

You are about to upgrade your PC from Windows XP to 32-bit Windows Vista. Before performing the upgrade, search the Internet for a new video driver for your Matrox G450x4 MMS graphics card. What is the name of the file you need to download from the Matrox Web site for the upgrade?

PROJECT 9-5:   Preparing for Windows Vista

Microsoft says that to get the best video experience from Windows Vista, your graphics card must qualify for the OS. Do the following to find out if your system qualifies:

1. Find out what graphics card is installed on your computer. What card is installed and how did you find out?

2. Search the Microsoft Web site (*www.windowsmarketplace.com*) for your card. If your card qualifies, print the Web page that shows your card qualifies for Vista.

3. If your card does not qualify, print the Web page of another video card that will work in your computer and that does qualify for Vista. How much does the upgrade card cost?

PROJECT 9-6:   Working with a Monitor

Do the following to practice changing monitor settings and troubleshooting monitor problems:

1. Using a Windows OS, list the steps to change the monitor resolution.

2. Using Windows Vista or Windows XP, practice changing the display settings, including the wallpaper, screen saver, and appearance. If you are not using your own computer, be sure to restore each setting after making changes.

3. Pretend you have made a mistake and selected a combination of foreground and background colors that makes reading the screen impossible. Solve the problem by booting Windows into Safe Mode. Correct the problem and then reboot.

4. Change the monitor resolution using the sliding bar in the Display Settings or Display Properties box. Make a change and then make the change permanent. You can go back and adjust it later if you want.

5. Work with a partner who is using a different computer. Unplug the monitor in the computer lab or classroom, loosen or disconnect the computer monitor cable, or turn the contrast and brightness all the way down, while your partner does something similar to the other PC. Trade PCs and troubleshoot the problems.

6. Wear a ground bracelet. Turn off the PC, press the power button, remove the case cover, and loosen the video card. Turn on the PC and write down the problem as a user would describe it. Turn off the PC, reseat the card, and verify that everything works.

7. Turn off your system. Insert into the system a defective video card provided by your instructor. Turn on the system. Describe the resulting problem in writing, as a user would.

>> REAL PROBLEMS, REAL SOLUTIONS

REAL PROBLEM 9-1: Helping with Upgrade Decisions

Upgrading an existing system can sometimes be a wise thing to do, but sometimes the upgrade costs more than the system is worth. Also, if existing components are old, they might not be compatible with components you want to use for the upgrade. A friend, Renata, asks your advice about several upgrades she is considering. Answer these questions:

1. Renata has a Windows XP PC that does not have a FireWire port. She wants to use a camcorder that has a FireWire 400 interface to a PC. How would she perform the upgrade and what is the cost? Print Web pages to support your answers.

2. Her computer has one USB port, but she wants to use her USB printer at the same time she uses her USB scanner. How can she do this and how much will it cost? Print Web pages to support your answers.

3. Renata also uses her Windows XP computer for gaming. The computer has an AGP 2.0 1.5-V video slot and three PCI slots. What is the fastest and best graphics card she can buy? How much does it cost? Print Web pages to support your answer.

4. What is the total cost of all the upgrades that Renata wants? Do you think it is wise for her to make these upgrades or purchase a new system? How would you explain your recommendation to her?

REAL PROBLEM 9-2: Using Input Director

Input Director is software that lets you use one keyboard and mouse to control two or more computers that are networked together. You can download the free software from *www.inputdirector.com*. To use the software, you need to know the host name of each computer that will share the keyboard and mouse. To find out the host name, right-click **Computer** (**My Computer** in Windows XP) and select **Properties**. The host name is listed in Vista as the Computer name and in XP as Full computer name.

Working with a partner, download and install Input Director and configure it so that you and your partner's computers are using the same keyboard and mouse.

Multimedia Devices
and Mass Storage

The ability to create output in a vast array of media—audio, video, and animation, as well as text and graphics—has turned PCs into multimedia machines. The multimedia computer has much to offer, from videoconferencing for executives to tools for teaching the alphabet to four-year-olds. This chapter examines multimedia devices, what they can do, how they work, and how to support them. You will also learn about storage devices such as CDs, DVDs, removable drives, tape drives, and external hard drives, including installation and troubleshooting.

MULTIMEDIA ADAPTER CARDS

A+
220-701
1.2
1.9

The goal of multimedia technology is to use sights, sounds, and animation to make computer output look as much like real life as possible. Remember that computers store data digitally and ultimately as a stream of only two numbers: 0 and 1. In contrast, sights and sounds have an infinite number of variations and are analog in nature. The challenge for multimedia technology is to bridge these two worlds.

In this section, you'll learn about sound cards and onboard sound and then we'll look at TV tuner cards and video capture cards.

SOUND CARDS AND ONBOARD SOUND

A sound card (an expansion card with sound ports) or onboard sound (sound ports embedded on a motherboard) can record sound, save it in a file on your hard drive, and play it back. Some sound cards and onboard sound give you the ability to mix and edit sound, and even to edit the sound using standard music score notation. Sound cards or motherboards with onboard sound have output ports for external speakers and input ports for a microphone, CD or DVD player, or other digital sound equipment. Figure 10-1 shows a sound card by Creative. This Sound Blaster X-Fi Titanium card uses a PCIe x1 slot and supports up to eight surround sound 7.1 speakers.

Figure 10-1   Sound Blaster X-Fi Titanium sound card by Creative uses a PCIe x1 slot
Courtesy of Creative Technology Ltd.

The number and type of sound ports on a motherboard or sound card depend on the sound standards the card or board supports. For good sound, you definitely need two or more external speakers and an amplifier. Most cards sold today support the audio compression methods also used by HDTV (high-definition TV). Popular methods include several variations and overlapping standards of Dolby TrueHD, Dolby Digital (also known as AC-3), and Dolby surround sound. TrueHD and Dolby Digital use and build on the surround sound technologies. Three popular variations of surround sound are 5.1, 7.1, and 9.1. The 9.1 surround standard can support up to 10 separate sound channels of sound information for up to 10 different speakers, each producing a different sound. These speakers are known as front left and right, front center, rear left and right, subwoofer, two additional rear speakers, and two additional front speakers mounted high above the main

A+
220-701
1.2
1.9

left and right front speakers. (Very few systems use all these speakers.) The 5.1 standard uses six speakers, while the 7.1 standard uses eight. Because each channel is digital, there is no background noise on the channel, and a sound engineer can place sound on any one of these speakers. The sound effects can be awesome!

> **A+ Exam Tip** The A+ 220-701 Essentials exam expects you to know about the functions of a sound card, TV tuner card, and capture card.

The motherboard shown in Figure 10-2 contains onboard sound. Device drivers and a user manual for sound come bundled with the motherboard on CD. The purposes of the eight sound ports are listed in Table 10-1 for 2-, 4-, 6-, and 8-channel sound. The two S/PDIF (Sony/Philips Digital Interconnect Format) ports are used to connect to external sound equipment such as a CD or DVD player. If you are using a single speaker or two speakers with a single sound cable, connect the cable to the green sound port on the motherboard, which is usually the middle port.

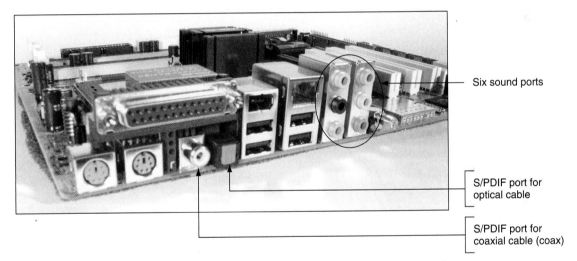

Six sound ports

S/PDIF port for optical cable

S/PDIF port for coaxial cable (coax)

Figure 10-2 This motherboard with onboard sound has eight sound ports
Courtesy: Course Technology/Cengage Learning

Port	2-Channel (Headset)	4-Channel	6-Channel	8-Channel
Light blue	Line in	Line in	Line in	Line in
Lime	Line out	Front speaker out	Front speaker out	Front speaker out
Pink	Mic in	Mic in	Mic in	Mic in
Gray	N/A	Rear speaker out	Rear speaker out	Rear speaker out
Black	N/A	N/A	N/A	Side speaker out
Yellow-orange	N/A	N/A	Center or subwoofer	Center or subwoofer
Gray half-oval	Optical S/PDIF out port connects an external audio output device using a fiber-optic S/PDIF cable			
Yellow	Coaxial S/PDIF out port connects an external audio output device using a coaxial S/PDIF cable			

Table 10-1 Sound ports on a motherboard

Also, sound cards might be Sound Blaster-compatible, meaning that they understand the commands sent to them that have been written for a Sound Blaster card, which is generally considered the de facto standard for PC sound cards. (A de facto standard is a standard generally accepted by the industry but not authorized by any official standards organization.) In addition, some cards have internal input connectors to connect to a CD or DVD drive or TV Tuner card so that analog or digital sound goes directly from the device to the sound card, bypassing the CPU. Sound can be recorded on a single channel (mono) or on two channels (stereo). After the sound is recorded and digitized, many sound cards convert and compress the digitized sound to MP3 format, which takes up less space on a hard drive or other media than raw digitized sound. MP3 sound files have an .mp3 file extension, and common file extensions for raw, uncompressed sound files are .wav and .aif. Table 10-2 lists some sound card manufacturers.

Manufacturer	Web Site
Creative Technology	www.creative.com and www.soundblaster.com
Diamond Multimedia	www.diamondmm.com
Guillemot Corporation	www.hercules.com
PPA	www.ppa-usa.com
Sabrent	www.sabrent.com
StarTech	www.startech.com
Turtle Beach	www.turtlebeach.com

Table 10-2   Sound card manufacturers

> **Notes** A good source for information about hardware devices (and software) is a site that offers product reviews and technical specifications and compares product prices and features. Check out these sites: CNET Networks (www.cnet.com), Price Watch (www.pricewatch.com), Tom's Hardware Guide (www.tomshardware.com), and Epinions, Inc. (www.epinions.com).

TV TUNER AND VIDEO CAPTURE CARDS

A TV tuner card can turn your computer into a television. A port on the card receives input from a TV cable and lets you view television on your computer monitor. If the TV signal is analog, the TV tuner card can convert it to digital. A video capture card lets you capture this video input and save it to a file on your hard drive. Some cards are a combination TV tuner card and video capture card, making it possible for you to receive television input and save that input to your hard drive. A high-end TV tuner/video capture card might also serve as your video card. Also, some motherboards and notebook computers have onboard TV tuners and TV captures, such as the notebook shown in Figure 10-3.

To use this notebook to watch TV and capture live TV, plug in a TV coaxial cable (also called "coax" for short) to the RF adapter that is included. Then plug the adapter into the

A+
220-701
1.9

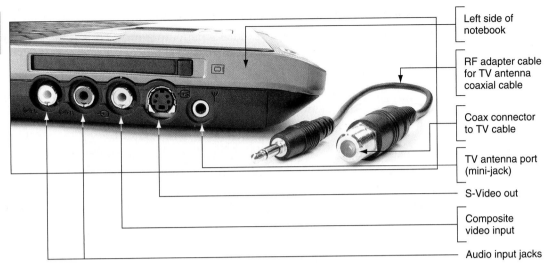

Left side of notebook

RF adapter cable for TV antenna coaxial cable

Coax connector to TV cable

TV antenna port (mini-jack)

S-Video out

Composite video input

Audio input jacks

Figure 10-3 This notebook computer has embedded TV tuner and video capture abilities
Courtesy: Course Technology/Cengage Learning

10

A+ 220-701

antenna mini-jack port on the laptop. Other ports labeled in Figure 10-3 can be used to capture input from a camcorder or VCR, or input data from other audio and video equipment that use these audio input and composite video ports. You can also use this notebook as your display for a game box. For example, you can connect the RCA cable shown in Figure 10-4 to the red, white, and yellow ports on the laptop and the other end of the cable to an Xbox.

Figure 10-4 Standard RCA cable harness connects to game box
Courtesy: Course Technology/Cengage Learning

Captured video can be saved as motion clips or stills, and then edited. With the right card and software, you can create your own video and animated CDs and DVDs. To help you select a video capture card, look for these features on the card:

A+
220-701
1.9

▲ Consider the input and output ports the card offers:

- A card might have video input/output ports such as an S-Video or composite-out video port (also might be called an RCA port).

- A FireWire input/output port can be used to receive data from a video camera and possibly output data back to the camera. Make sure the card has the input port your video camera uses.

- For live camera input such as that used by security cameras, a card might have multiple BNC connectors (round connectors used by coaxial cable) to receive simultaneous input from three or four security cameras.

- A capture card might have one or more audio input ports, which might be called RCA ports.

- If the card is also a video card, it will have a VGA analog port or a DVI port for a monitor.

- Because of the many ports a card might support, it might use a breakout box. The box provides multiple ports and connects to the card using a short cable.

▲ The type of slot the card uses. PCI Express is much faster than PCI.

▲ Data-processing abilities. The card might encode and compress data without involving the CPU. Look for output formats which might include DVD, CD, MPEG4, MPEG2, MPEG1, Windows Streaming Media, Real Networks Media, QuickTime, and AVI.

▲ Software bundled with the card which might include video-editing software such as Adobe Premiere (video editing), Impression DVD SE (DVD and CD authoring software), Photoshop LE (image editor), and SmartSound (add background music). Read reviews on each software program you think you might want to use.

▲ System requirements of the card, including operating system, processor, and memory.

▲ Ability to transfer data back to a digital camcorder.

For a TV tuner card, look for these features:

▲ Ability to do instant replay and program scheduling.

▲ Input ports for coaxial cable TV, TV antenna, video equipment, and game boxes.

▲ Ability to handle analog and digital (including HDTV) input signals.

▲ TV or VCR port for output.

▲ Remote control, so you can flip TV channels from across the room.

If a TV tuner card is also a capture card, most likely the capture component of the card offers only basic functionality. One example of a TV tuner and video capture card is the AVerTV Combo PCI-E card shown in Figure 10-5.

Also, an external device can be used as a TV tuner and to capture video and stills. For notebook computers, the device can use the PC Card slot, or it can use a USB port. One example is the WinTV-USB2 device by Hauppauge Computer Works shown in Figure 10-6. It connects to a USB 2.0 port and comes with a remote control to change channels, adjust volume, and record or play a video.

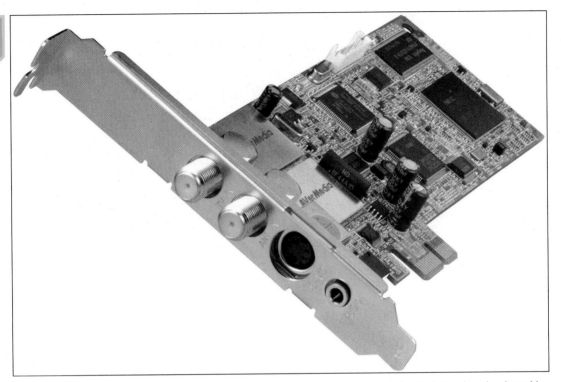

Figure 10-5 The AVerTV Combo PCI-E TV tuner and video capture card uses a PCIe x1 slot and works alongside a regular video card
Courtesy of AVerMedia Technologies, Inc. USA

Figure 10-6 The external WinTV-USB2 TV tuner and video capture device by Hauppauge Computer Works, Inc.
Courtesy of Hauppauge Computer Works, Inc.

A+
220-701
1.9

Table 10-3 lists some manufacturers of TV tuner and video capture cards.

Manufacturer	Web Site
ATI (now AMD)	*www.ati.com*
AVerMedia	*www.aver.com*
Creative Technology	*www.creative.com*
Hauppauge Computer Works	*www.hauppauge.com*
Matrox	*www.matrox.com*
Pinnacle Systems	*www.pinnaclesys.com*
Sabrent	*www.sabrent.com*

Table 10-3 Video capture and TV tuner card manufacturers

OPTICAL STORAGE TECHNOLOGY

A+
220-701
1.1

CDs and DVDs are popular storage media for multimedia data, and CDs are the most popular way of distributing software. Both DVD and CD technologies use patterns of tiny lands and pits on the surface of a disc to represent bits, which a laser beam can then read. This is why they are called optical storage technologies. CD (compact disc) drives use the CDFS (Compact Disc File System) or the UDF (Universal Disk Format) file system, while DVD (digital versatile disc or digital video disc) drives use the newer UDF file system. The latest optical storage technology is Blu-ray Disc (BD), which uses the UDF version 2.5 file system. HD DVD is an optical storage technology that, at one time, competed with Blu-ray, but is now obsolete.

Blu-ray drives are backward compatible with DVD and CD technologies. Depending on the drive features, a Blu-ray drive might be able to read and write to BDs, DVD, and CDs. DVD drives can handle both DVDs and CDs. A CD drive cannot handle DVDs or BDs. An internal optical drive can interface with the motherboard by way of a PATA or SATA connection. An external drive might use an eSATA, FireWire, SCSI, or USB port. Figure 10-7 shows an internal DVD drive and Figure 10-8 shows an external DVD drive.

Now let's look at how data is read and written to optical discs, how much data these discs can hold, and the different standards that CD, DVD, and Blue-ray drives might support.

HOW DATA IS READ AND WRITTEN TO OPTICAL DISCS

Data is written to optical discs by using a laser beam to burn or etch pits into the surface of the disc. Lands are smooth and level areas, and pits are recessed areas on the surface; each represents either a 1 or a 0, respectively. The bits are read by the drive with a laser beam that distinguishes between a pit and a land by the amount of deflection or scattering that occurs when the light beam hits the surface. Figure 10-9 shows the pits and lands and layers of a CD.

CDs and DVDs both use red laser beams, but the wavelength of the DVD laser beam is shorter than that of the CD laser beam. The shorter wavelength allows the beam to be more accurate. This accuracy means that more data can be stored on a DVD than on a CD. Blu-ray uses a blue laser beam, which is shorter than any red beam, allowing Blu-ray technology to store more data than a DVD.

A+
220-701
1.1

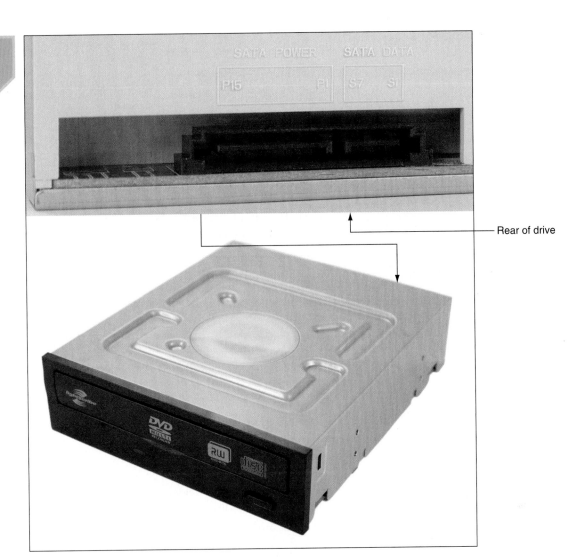

Rear of drive

Figure 10-7 This internal DVD drive uses a SATA connection
Courtesy: Course Technology/Cengage Learning

Figure 10-8 The PX-610U external DVD±RW drive by Plextor uses a USB 2.0 port
Courtesy of Plextor

10

A+ 220-701

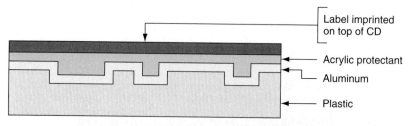

Figure 10-9 A CD is constructed of plastic, aluminum, and acrylic
Courtesy: Course Technology/Cengage Learning

Data is only written to one side of a CD, but can be written to one or both sides of a DVD or Blu-ray disc. Also, a DVD or Blu-ray disc can hold data in two layers on each side. This means these discs can hold a total of four layers on one disc (see Figure 10-10).

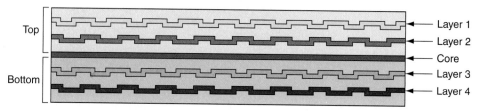

Figure 10-10 A DVD can hold data in double layers on both the top and bottom of the disc, yielding a maximum capacity of 17 GB
Courtesy: Course Technology/Cengage Learning

Data on an optical disc is laid out as one continuous spiral of sectors of equal length that hold equal amounts of data (see Figure 10-11). For a CD, if laid out in a straight line, this spiral would be 3.5 miles long. Hard drives spin at a constant rate, or revolutions per minute, but optical drives use variable speeds depending on the type of media being read. In order to read each sector on the spiral at a constant linear velocity (CLV), the disc spins faster when the read-write head is near the center of the disc. In addition, CDs playing audio data spin at the slowest rates compared to other media. To show video and motion without a choppy effect, however, the speed of the drives was increased to double speed, quad speed, and so on. CD drives with speeds at 52x and 56x (52 and 56 times the audio speed) are not uncommon now. When playing music CDs, these drives still drop to the slower rates.

Figure 10-11 The spiral layout of sectors on an optical disc surface
Courtesy: Course Technology/Cengage Learning

HOW MUCH DATA CAN BE STORED ON OPTICAL DISCS

Here's the breakdown of how much data can be held on CDs, DVDs, and BDs:
A CD can hold 700 MB of data. The different amounts of data that can be stored on a DVD depend on these factors:

- Single-sided, single-layer DVD can hold 4.7 GB
- Single-sided, dual-layer DVD can hold 8.5 GB

◢ Double-sided, single-layer DVD can hold 9.4 GB
◢ Double-sided, dual-layer DVD can hold 17 GB

The data that can be stored on a BD are:

◢ Double-sided, single-layer BD can hold 25 GB
◢ Double-sided, dual-layer BD can hold 50 GB

BDs that can have up to 20 layers are expected in the future. These BDs are expected to hold up to 500 GB.

> **Notes** The discrepancy in the computer industry between one billion bytes (1,000,000,000 bytes) and 1 GB (1,073,741,824 bytes) exists because 1 KB equals 1,024 bytes. Even though documentation might say that a DVD holds 17 GB, in fact it holds 17 billion bytes, which is only 15.90 GB.

STANDARDS SUPPORTED BY CD, DVD, AND BD DRIVES

Table 10-4 lists the three different CD standards that might be used by a CD drive. You can tell the difference between a CD and a CD-R or CD-RW disc by the color of the bottom of the disc. CD-R and CD-RW discs are blue, black, or some other color, and read-only CDs are silver. Read-only CDs are called CD-ROMs (Read-Only Memory), but keep in mind they are not considered a type of memory.

CD Standard	Description
CD-ROM	*CD-read-only memory.* A CD-ROM drive can read CDs. Newer CD-ROM drives can read any type of CD, including CD-R and CD-RW discs.
CD-R	*CD recordable.* A CD-R drive can record or write to a CD-R disc. A CD-R disc is sometimes called a write-once CD.
CD-RW	*CD rewriteable.* A CD-RW drive can write to a CD-RW or CD-R disc and also overwrite a CD-RW disc. CD-RW drives have made CD-R drives obsolete. Blank CD-RW discs cost more than blank CD-R discs. The CD-RW technology is sometimes called write-many technology.

Table 10-4 CD standards

Table 10-5 describes the DVD standards used for reading and writing. All have similar but not identical features, so compatibility of standards is an issue. Most DVD drives support several competing standards. When buying a DVD drive, look for the standards it supports and also look for its ability to burn CDs.

Table 10-6 lists the Blu-ray disc standards. It is expected that new BD standards will be released in the future.

CD-RW, DVD-RW, DVD+RW, and BD-RE discs can be written to and overwritten thousands of times and are considered a replacement for the older floppy disks. (USB drives are also replacing floppy disks as inexpensive and quick-and-easy removable storage devices.)

DVD Standard	Description
DVD-ROM	*DVD read-only memory.* A DVD-ROM drive can also read CDs or DVDs.
DVD-R	*DVD recordable, single layer.* A DVD-R holds about 4.7 GB of data and is a write-once disc.
DVD-R DL	*DVD recordable in dual layers.* Doubles storage to 8.5 GB of data on one surface.
DVD-RW	*DVD rewriteable.* Also known as an erasable, recordable device or a write-many device.
DVD-RW DL	*DVD rewriteable, dual layers.* Doubles storage capacity to 8.5 GB.
DVD+R	*DVD recordable* is similar to but faster than DVD-R. Holds about 4.7 GB of data.
DVD+R DL	*DVD recordable, dual layers.* Doubles storage to 8.5 GB of data on one surface.
DVD+RW	*DVD rewriteable.* Faster than DVD-RW.
DVD-RAM	*DVD Random Access Memory is rewriteable and erasable.* You can erase or rewrite certain sections of a DVD-RAM disc without disturbing other sections of the disc and the discs can handle many times over the number of rewrites (around 100,000 rewrites), compared to about a thousand rewrites for DVD-RW and DVD+RW discs. These features make DVD-RAM discs more popular for some applications than are DVD-RW or DVD+RW discs. DVD-RAM discs are popular media used in camcorders and set-top boxes.

Table 10-5 DVD standards

BD Standard	Description
BD-ROM	*BD read-only memory.* A BD-ROM drive can also read DVDs and some can read CDs.
BD-R	*BD recordable.* A BD-R drive might also write to DVDs or CDs.
BD-RE	*BD rewriteable.* A BD-RE drive might also write to DVDs or CDs.

Table 10-6 BD standards

FEATURES OF OPTICAL DRIVES

Optical drives can be external or internal drives. When selecting a CD, DVD, or BD drive, consider the interface it uses and the disc standards it supports. Also consider the read speed, write-once speeds, and the rewriteable speeds. For example, one Blu-ray burner supports 4x speed for BD-R writes, 2x speeds for BD-RE writes, 12x speeds for DVD+R writes, 8x speeds for DVD+RW writes, 32x speeds for CD-R writes, and 24x speeds for CD-RW writes.

> **Notes** Half-life (sometimes called life expectancy or shelf life) of a storage media is the time it takes for the strength of the medium to weaken by half. Magnetic media, including traditional hard drives and floppy disks, have a half-life of five to seven years, but writeable optical media such as CD-Rs have a half-life of 30 years.

One more feature that you might look for in an optical drive is the ability to burn labels on the top of a disc. Two competing technologies for this purpose are Labelflash and LightScribe. Using either technology, you flip a Labelflash or LightScribe CD or DVD upside down and insert it in the drive tray so that the drive can then burn a label on top of the disc. The drive and disc must support the technology for it to work, and the two technologies are not compatible. Figure 10-12 shows a LightScribe CD-R that was just labeled using LightScribe. Another way to print labels on a disc is to use special discs that have a white paperlike surface. Insert the disc into an ink-jet printer that will print the label. The printer has to be the type that will print on optical discs. It is not recommended that you glue paper labels on the top of discs because they can throw the disc off balance or clog up a drive if the labels come loose. You can use a permanent felt-tip marker to handwrite labels on a disc.

Figure 10-12 This disc label was written using a DVD burner that supports LightScribe
Courtesy: Course Technology/Cengage Learning

💡 **A+ Exam Tip** The A+ 220-701 Essentials exam expects you to know about the drive speeds and media types of CD, DVD, and BD drives.

APPLYING CONCEPTS Windows XP can burn a CD without any extra software installed. It's very simple; first select all files you want to burn on the CD. To do that, right-click a file and select **Send To** from the shortcut menu, or you can drag and drop the file onto the CD drive. Then select the CD drive (see Figure 10-13). After all files are selected, the next step is to burn the CD. Using My Computer, double-click the CD-RW drive. The files you have selected will appear in the right pane (see Figure 10-14). To burn the CD, click **Write these files to CD**. Windows Vista can burn CDs and DVDs without extra software and the steps are similar. Windows XP cannot burn DVDs unless you install third-party software.

A+
220-701
1.1

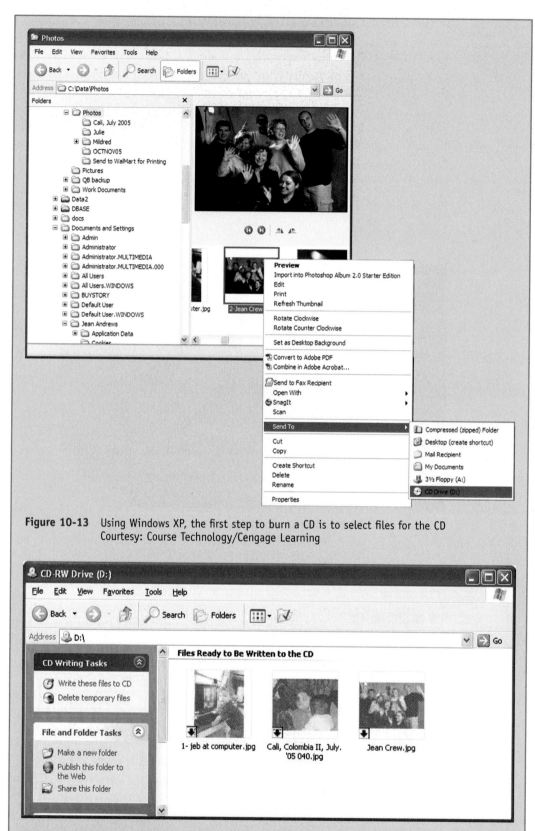

Figure 10-13 Using Windows XP, the first step to burn a CD is to select files for the CD
Courtesy: Course Technology/Cengage Learning

Figure 10-14 Files ready to be written to a CD
Courtesy: Course Technology/Cengage Learning

If you plan to burn a lot of CDs or want to create music or video CDs, you might want to use software designed for that purpose to make your job easier. Some CD-RW drives come bundled with burn software. One example is Nero by Nero Inc. (*www.nero.com*).

When purchasing a CD-R/RW drive, know that some CD-RW drives can also read a DVD. These drives are called combo drives, and are becoming popular as the prices of optical drives continue to drop.

CARING FOR OPTICAL DRIVES AND DISCS

Most problems with CD, DVD, and BD discs are caused by dust, fingerprints, scratches, surface defects, or random electrical noise. Also, an optical drive will not properly read or write a disc when the drive is standing vertically, such as when someone turns a desktop PC case on its side to save desk space or lays a tower case on its side.

Use these precautions when handling CDs, DVDs, or BDs:

- ◢ Hold the disc by the edge; do not touch the bright side of the disc where data is stored.
- ◢ To remove dust or fingerprints, use a clean, soft, dry cloth. Don't wipe the disc in a circular motion. Always wipe from the center of the disc out toward the edge.
- ◢ Don't paste paper on the surface of a disc. Don't paste any labels on the top of the disc, because this can imbalance the disc and cause the drive to vibrate. You can label the top of a disc that is not a dual-sided disc using a felt-tip pin. Don't label a DVD or BD if both sides hold data.
- ◢ Don't subject a disc to heat or leave it in direct sunlight.
- ◢ Don't make the center hole larger.
- ◢ Don't bend a disc.
- ◢ Don't drop a disc or subject it to shock.
- ◢ If a disc gets stuck in the drive, use the emergency eject hole to remove it. Turn off the power to the PC first. Then insert an instrument such as a straightened paper clip into the hole to eject the tray manually.
- ◢ When closing a CD, DVD, or BD tray, don't push on the tray. Press the close button on the front of the drive.
- ◢ Don't use cleaners, alcohol, and the like on a disc unless you use a cleaning solution specifically designed for optical discs like the cleaning kit in Figure 10-15. Using this kit, you can spray the cleaning solution on a disc and then wipe it off with the soft purple cloth. To fix a scratch on a disc, use the repair solution made of aluminum oxide. Apply a small amount to the scratch and gently rub it with the yellow cloth. Then clean the disc using the cleaning solution.

Optical drives and other removable storage technologies are interesting to study. For the tech-hungry reader, I suggest you check out the animated explanation at the Web site of HowStuffWorks, Inc. (*www.howstuffworks.com*). Search on "How Removable Storage Works." Table 10-7 lists manufacturers of optical drives.

Notes CDs, DVDs, and BDs are expected to hold their data for many years; however, you can prolong the life of a disc by protecting it from exposure to light.

A+
220-701
1.1

Figure 10-15   Use a cleaning solution and repair solution to clean and repair scratches
on optical discs
Courtesy: Course Technology/Cengage Learning

Manufacturer	Web Site
Creative Labs	www.creative.com
LG Electronics	www.lge.com
LITE-ON IT	www.liteonit.com
Panasonic	www.panasonic.com
Pioneer	www.pioneerelectronics.com
Plextor	www.plextor.com
Samsung	www.samsung.com
Sony Electronics	www.sonystyle.com

Table 10-7   Optical drive manufacturers

REMOVABLE STORAGE

Removable storage can be either an external or internal device. Examples of removable storage are solid-state devices such as a USB flash drive or flash memory card, an external hard drive, a tape drive, an older and outdated Zip drive or floppy drive, and optical discs. Using removable storage devices provides several advantages:

◢ Increases the overall storage capacity of a system
◢ Makes it easy to move large files from one computer to another

A+
220-701
1.1

- Serves as a convenient medium for making backups of hard drive data
- Makes it easy to secure important files (To keep important files secure, keep the removable device locked in a safe when it is not being used.)

Now let's look at three removable storage devices: solid-state devices, external hard drives, and tape drives.

SOLID-STATE STORAGE

A storage device that uses memory chips and no moving parts to store data instead of spinning disks (such as those used by hard drives and CD drives) is called a solid-state device (SSD), also called a solid-state drive. Examples of solid-state devices are USB flash drives, flash memory cards, and solid-state hard drives. You learned about solid-state hard drives in Chapter 8.

> 💡 **A+ Exam Tip** The A+ 220-701 Essentials exam expects you to know about USB drives and flash memory cards.

USB flash drives currently for sale range in size from 128 MB to 256 GB, and go by many names, including a flash pen drive, jump drive, thumb drive, and key drive. Several USB flash drives are shown in Figure 10-16. Both Windows Vista and Windows XP have embedded drivers to support flash drives. To use one, simply insert the device in a USB port. It then shows in Windows Explorer as a drive with an assigned letter. Most flash drives sold today use USB 2.0 speed.

Figure 10-16 USB flash drives come in a variety of styles and sizes
Courtesy: Course Technology/Cengage Learning

Before you remove the flash drive from the PC, double-click the **Safely Remove Hardware** icon in the notification area (see Figure 10-17). The Safely Remove Hardware box opens, also shown in Figure 10-17. Select the device to remove and click **Stop**. It is then safe to remove the device.

Several types of flash memory cards on the market today are shown and described in Table 10-8. These cards might be used in digital cameras, cell phones, MP3 players, handheld computers, digital camcorders, and other portable devices.

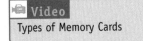
Video
Types of Memory Cards

A+
220-701
1.1

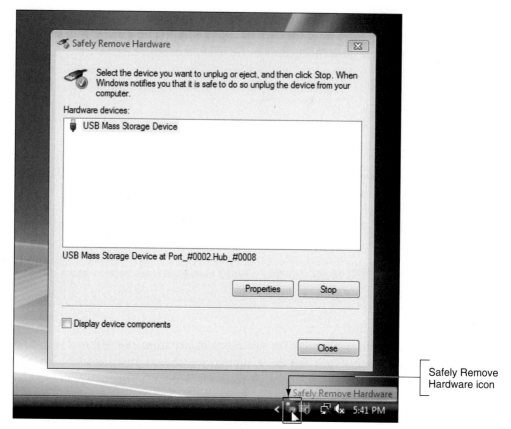

Figure 10-17 Safely Remove Hardware icon and dialog box
Courtesy: Course Technology/Cengage Learning

Flash Memory Device	Example
Current Flash Memory Devices	
Secure Digital HC (SDHC) cards follow SD 2.0 standards and hold from 4 GB to 32 GB. HC stands for high capacity.	
MicroSDHC card is currently the smallest and most popular type of card. It is about the size of a fingernail and is used in PDAs, cell phones, MP3 players, and digital cameras. You can buy adapters to make the card fit into SD, MicroSD, Memory Stick PRO Duo, or USB slots. Current sizes are up to 8 GB.	
MiniSDHC card is a smaller version of the SDHC card, but not as small as the MicroSDHC card. The cards hold up to 8 GB.	

Table 10-8 Flash memory devices

Flash Memory Device	Example
Secure Digital (SD) cards were the most popular flash memory cards for several years, and hold up to 4 GB of data.	
The *MiniSD* card is about half the size of SD cards, but uses the same interface standards. You can buy an adapter that lets you use a miniSD card in an SD slot.	
The Sony *Memory Stick PRO Duo* is about half the size of the Memory Stick PRO, but is faster and has a higher storage capacity (currently up to 2 GB). You can use an adapter to insert the Memory StickPRO Duo in a regular Memory Stick slot.	
Sony *Memory Stick Micro M2* is used in Sony Ericsson mobile phones and currently holds up to 4 GB. An adapter can be used so it will fit into Memory Stick PRO Duo slots.	
MicroSD is about half the size of a miniSD card and currently comes in sizes up to 16 GB. *TransFlash* cards look the same as microSD cards and they are interchangeable except that TransFlash cards don't offer the same functions in some devices.	
CompactFlash (CF) cards come in two types, Type I (CFI) and Type II (CFII). Type II cards are slightly thicker. CFI cards will fit a Type II slot, but CFII cards will not fit a Type I slot. The CF standard allows for sizes up to 137 GB, although current sizes range upto 32 GB. UDMA CompactFlash cards are faster than other CompactFlash cards. UDMA (Ultra Direct Memory Access) transfers data from the device to memory without involving the CPU.	
Older Flash Memory Devices	
MultiMedia Card (MMC) looks like an SD card, but the technology is different and they are not interchangeable. Generally, SD cards are faster than MMC cards.	
Reduced Size Multimedia Card (RS-MMC) is about half the size of a regular MultiMedia Card.	

Table 10-8 Flash memory devices (continued)

A+
220-701
1.1

Flash Memory Device	Example
A *Microdrive CF* uses the CompactFlash II form factor, but is actually a tiny hard drive, meaning the data is stored on a magnetic disk and is not a solid-state device.	
The *Memory Stick* is used in Sony cameras and camcorders. A later version, the *Memory Stick PRO*, improved on the slower transfer rate of the original Memory Stick.	
The *xD-Picture Card* has a compact design (about the size of a postage stamp), and currently holds up to 8 GB of data. You can use an adapter to insert this card into a PC Card slot on a notebook computer or a CF slot on a digital camera.	
SmartMedia is an outdated flash memory card that does not have a self-contained controller used by more current cards. Because the camera must manage the data on the card, use only the SmartMedia card recommended by the camera manufacturer.	

Table 10-8 Flash memory devices (continued)
Courtesy: Course Technology/Cengage Learning

Sometimes a flash memory card is bundled with one or more adapters so that a smaller card will fit a larger card slot. Figure 10-18 shows a MicroSDHC card that came packaged with four adapters, which are labeled in the figure. Figure 10-19 shows a Sony digital camera that has a Memory Stick PRO slot. An adapter allows a Memory Stick PRO Duo to use the slot. Figure 10-20 shows several flash memory cards together so you can get an idea of their relative sizes.

EXTERNAL HARD DRIVES

External hard drives are a great method of keeping backups of data stored on your hard drive. They can easily be moved from one computer to another and some are designed for travel. External hard drives can be magnetic or solid-state drives. The solid-state drives are much more durable, especially when traveling. They are also faster and cost more than magnetic drives. External hard drives use USB 2.0, FireWire, eSATA, or SCSI ports to connect to a computer. Figure 10-21 shows a Maxtor external hard drive that holds 500 GB and uses a USB connection.

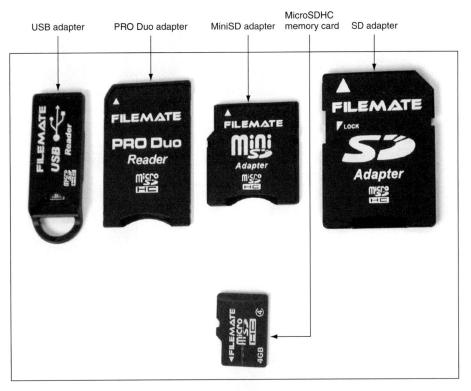

USB adapter PRO Duo adapter MiniSD adapter MicroSDHC memory card SD adapter

Figure 10-18 MicroSDHC card with four adapters
Courtesy: Course Technology/Cengage Learning

Figure 10-19 This Sony digital camera has a Memory Stick PRO slot that can accommodate a
Memory Stick PRO Duo with adapter; images upload by way of a USB cable
Courtesy: Course Technology/Cengage Learning

A+
220-701
1.1

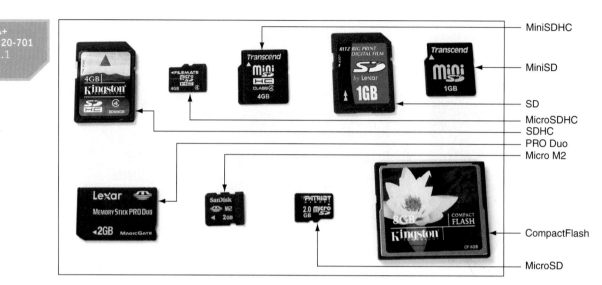

Figure 10-20 Flash memory cards
Courtesy: Course Technology/Cengage Learning

Figure 10-21 The OneTouch external hard drive holds 500 GB and uses a Hi-Speed USB connection
Courtesy: Course Technology/Cengage Learning

TAPE DRIVES

Tape drives (see Figure 10-22) are an inexpensive way of backing up an entire hard drive or portions of it. Tape drives are less expensive for backups than external hard drives, CDs, DVDs, or USB flash drives, which is why they are still popular for backups even though other methods are more convenient. Tapes currently have capacities of 20 GB to 1.3 TB compressed and come in several types and formats. Although tape drives don't require that you use special backup software to manage

A+
220-701
1.1

Figure 10-22 The LTO-4 HH tape drive by Quantum writes to LTO Ultrium 4 and LTO Ultrium 3 tapes and reads from LTO Ultrium 4, LTO Ultrium 3, and LTO Ultrium 2 tapes and comes with backup software
Courtesy of Quantum Corporation

10

A+ 220-701

them, you might want to invest in specialized backup software to make backups as efficient and effortless as possible. Many tape drives come with bundled software, and Windows offers a Backup utility that can use tape drives. Several of the more common standards and types of tapes and tape drives are described in this section.

> **A+ Exam Tip** The A+ 220-701 Essentials exam expects you to be able to categorize the different types of backup media, including tape drives, solid-state devices, external optical drives, and external hard drives.

The biggest disadvantage of using tape drives is that data is stored on tape by sequential access; to read data from anywhere on the tape, you must start at the beginning of the tape and read until you come to the sought-after data. Sequential access makes recovering files slow and inconvenient, which is why tapes are not used for general-purpose data storage.

Tape drives accommodate one of two kinds of tapes: full-sized data cartridges are 4 x 6 x ⅝ inches, and the smaller minicartridges, like the one in Figure 10-23, are 3¼ x 2½ x ⅗ inches. Minicartridges are more popular because their drives can fit into a standard 3-inch drive bay of a PC case.

Here is a list of some of the more common types of tape cartridges:

1. DDS-1, DDS-2, DDS-3, and DDS-4 are popular types. DDS-4 holds up to 20 GB native or 40 GB compressed data.

2. DAT72 (also called DDS-5) holds up to 36 GB native or 72 GB compressed data.

3. LTO Ultrium 2, LTO Ultrium 3, and LTO Ultrium 4 are sometimes referred to as LTO cartridges. LTO Ultrium 4 holds up to 800 GB native or 1.6 TB compressed data.

4. DLT IV or DLT-4 holds up to 40 GB native or 80 GB compressed data.

5. Super DLTtape II holds up to 300 GB native or 600 GB compressed data.

Write-protect switch

Figure 10-23   Minicartridge for a tape drive has a write-protect switch
Courtesy: Course Technology/Cengage Learning

6. Travan data types of cartridges vary from TR-1 through TR-7. The TR-7 holds 20 GB native and 40 GB compressed data.

7. AIT types have been around a long time and include AIT Turbo, AIT-1 through AIT-5, and S-AIT. S-AIT holds up to 1.3 TB compressed data.

8. SLR types include SLR1 through SLR140. SLR140 holds 70 GB native or 140 GB compressed data.

One popular tape standard is the LTO Ultrium 3. For example, the Maxell LTO Ultrium 3 data tape cartridge can hold 400 GB of data or 800 GB of compressed data (see Figure 10-24). It can be used by the LTO-4 HH tape drive by Quantum shown earlier in Figure 10-22.

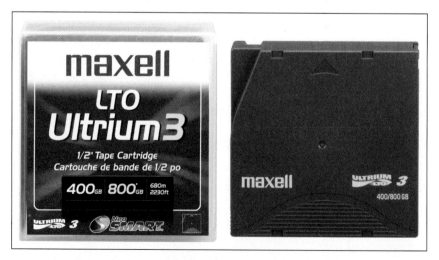

Figure 10-24   This Maxell LTO Ultrium 3 data tape cartridge can hold up to 800 GB of compressed data
Courtesy: Course Technology/Cengage Learning

When selecting a tape drive, consider how many and what type of cartridges the drive can use and how it interfaces with the computer. The drive might be able to read from more types of cartridges than it can write to. A tape drive can be external or internal. An external tape drive costs more but can be used by more than one computer. An internal tape drive can interface with a computer using a SCSI, PATA, or SATA connection. An external tape drive can connect to a computer using a USB, FireWire, SCSI, SAS, or eSATA port.

> **♀ Tip**   For an interesting photo gallery of tape media, see *www.BackupWorks.com*.

INSTALL AND CONFIGURE MULTIMEDIA PERIPHERALS

If you enjoy multimedia on a PC, you might have already downloaded pictures from your digital camera to your PC or installed a webcam to use with MSN Messenger or some other chat software. This part of the chapter shows you how to do these things and much more. The installations are usually very easy and straightforward. So let's look at how to install a digital camera, media reader and writer, Web camera, microphone, and MIDI device.

INSTALLING DIGITAL CAMERAS

Digital cameras can hold their images both in embedded memory that cannot be removed or exchanged, and in removable flash memory cards. Both these types of memory retain data without a battery. Here are two ways to transfer images from your camera to the PC:

▲ *Connect the camera to the PC using a cable.* Using embedded memory or flash memory cards, you can connect the camera to your computer using a cable. The cable might attach directly to the camera or connect to a cradle the camera sits in to recharge or upload images. The cable can use a USB, FireWire (IEEE 1394), serial, or parallel connection. Also, some cameras use an infrared or other wireless connection. To connect the camera to the PC, you might need to first install the software and then connect the camera or you might need to connect the camera and then install the software. Read the camera documentation to find out which order to use. After the camera and software are installed, the software displays a menu to download images from the camera.

▲ *Install the memory card in the PC.* If images are stored on a flash memory card installed in your camera, you can remove the card and then insert it in a flash memory card slot on your computer. Most laptop computers have one or more flash memory card slots (see Figure 10-25). If your computer doesn't have this slot, or the slot is not compatible with the type of card you are using, you have two choices:

• Perhaps you can purchase an adapter so that your smaller memory card will fit into a larger memory slot. Figure 10-18 shows examples of these adapters.

• You can use a media reader that provides a memory card slot to fit your card. How to install and use a media reader is covered later in the chapter.

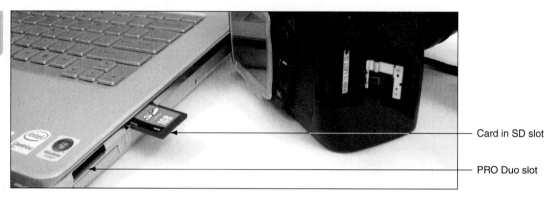

Card in SD slot

PRO Duo slot

Figure 10-25 This laptop has two flash memory card slots
Courtesy: Course Technology/Cengage Learning

When the memory card is recognized by Windows, it is assigned a drive letter and you can see it listed in Windows Explorer. Use Windows Explorer to copy, move, and delete files from the card.

> **Notes** It's interesting to know that TWAIN (Technology Without An Interesting Name) is a standard format used by scanners and digital cameras and other devices for transferring images.

> **A+ Tip** The A+ 220-701 Essentials exam expects you to know how to install the software bundled with your digital camera before attaching the camera to your PC.

After the images are on the PC, use the camera's image-editing software, or another program such as Adobe Photoshop, to view, touch up, crop, and print the picture. For Windows Vista, you can use Windows Photo Gallery, which is an embedded part of Vista. The picture file, which is usually in **JPEG (Joint Photographic Experts Group)** format, can then be imported into documents. JPEG is a common compression standard for storing photos. Most JPEG files have a .jpg file extension. In addition, a high-end camera might support the uncompressed TIFF format. **TIFF (tagged image file format)** files are larger than JPEG files, but retain more image information and give better results when printing photographs.

INSTALLING WEBCAMS AND MICROPHONES

A webcam (Web camera) is a video camera that is used to capture digital video that can be used to feed live video on the Internet. The camera usually connects to a computer by way of a USB, FireWire, composite video, or S-video port. Besides the larger Web cameras used to produce live video for webcam sites, you can buy an inexpensive Web camera, such as the one shown in Figure 10-26, to use for personal chat sessions and videoconferencing.

> **A+ Exam Tip** The A+ 220-701 Essentials exam expects you to know the purposes and characteristics of digital cameras, Web cameras, and microphones.

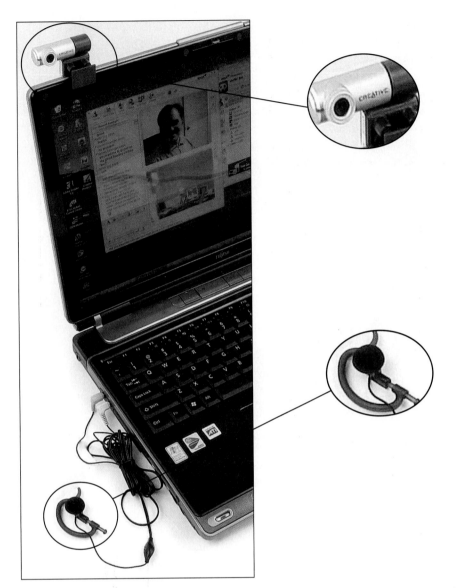

Figure 10-26 This personal Web camera clips to the top of your notebook and comes packaged with an ear clip headset that includes a microphone and speaker
Courtesy: Course Technology/Cengage Learning

First, use the setup CD to install the software and then plug in the webcam to a USB port. You can use the camera with or without the headset. If you want to include sound in your chat sessions, plug the two sound connectors into the speaker out and microphone in ports on your computer. These ports are embedded in notebook computers, as shown in Figure 10-26. For desktop computers, the ports are part of the sound card or they are onboard ports.

Next, use chat software such as Windows Live Messenger to create a live video session. For example, when you open Messenger, if you or your chat friend has a webcam installed, a small camera icon appears to the left of your photo (see Figure 10-27). Click it to invite your friend to view your webcam streaming video.

If you both have a speaker and microphone connected, you can also create a videoconferencing session with video and voice. To begin a video conversation with sound, on the menu at the top of the Messenger window, click **Call** and then select **Call computer**.

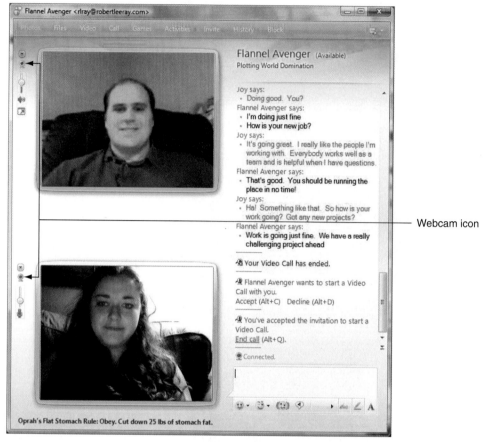

Figure 10-27 Windows Live Messenger session using a webcam
Courtesy: Course Technology/Cengage Learning

INSTALLING MIDI DEVICES

MIDI (musical instrument digital interface), pronounced "middy," is a set of standards that are used to represent music in digital form. Whereas MP3 is a method of storing a sound file in compressed format, MIDI is a method of digitally describing and storing every individual note played by each individual instrument used in making music. With MIDI files and MIDI software, you can choose to listen to only a single instrument being played, or change one note played by that instrument. MIDI can be used to creatively produce synthesized music, mute one instrument or voice, and edit a song with your own voice or instrument. MIDI standards are used to connect electronic music equipment, such as musical keyboards and mixers, or to connect this equipment to a PC for input and output. Most sound cards can play MIDI files, and most electronic instruments have MIDI ports. To mix and edit music using MIDI on your PC, you'll need MIDI editing software such as JAMMER Pro by SoundTrek (*www.soundtrek.com*).

A MIDI port is a 5-pin DIN port that looks like a keyboard port, only larger. Figure 10-28 shows MIDI ports on electronic drums. A MIDI port is either an input port or an output port, but not both. Normally, you would connect the MIDI output port to a mixer, but you can also use it to connect to a PC.

Here are ways to connect a musical instrument to a PC using the MIDI standards:

◢ *MIDI to MIDI:* A few sound cards provide MIDI ports. Use two MIDI cables to connect output jack to input jack and to connect input jack to output jack.

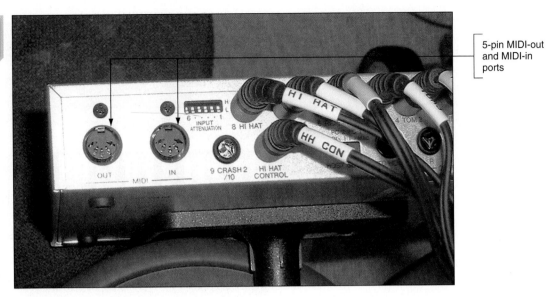

5-pin MIDI-out and MIDI-in ports

Figure 10-28 MIDI ports on an electronic drum set
Courtesy: Course Technology/Cengage Learning

▲ *MIDI to USB:* If your PC does not have MIDI ports, you can use a MIDI-to-USB cable like the one in Figure 10-29. The two MIDI connectors on the cable are for input and output.

▲ *USB to USB:* Newer instruments have a USB port to interface with a PC using MIDI data transmissions. For example, the keyboard shown in Figure 10-30 has a USB port and can output sound to a PC or receive standard MIDI files (SMF) to play.

▲ *USB to MIDI:* A USB port on an instrument can also connect to MIDI ports on a computer sound card.

> **A+ Exam Tip** The A+ 220-701 Essentials exam expects you to know how to install and configure MIDI devices.

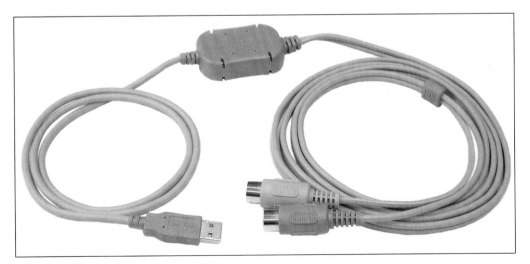

Figure 10-29 MIDI-to-USB cable lets you connect an electronic musical instrument to your PC
Courtesy: Course Technology/Cengage Learning

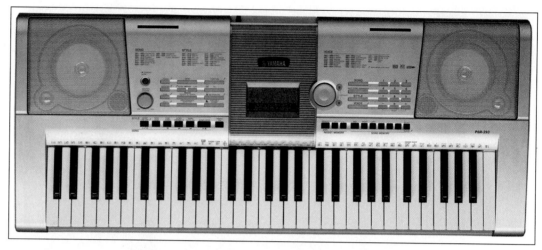

Figure 10-30 This keyboard by Yamaha has a USB port to be used as a MIDI interface
Courtesy: Course Technology/Cengage Learning

Before connecting the instrument to your PC, install the software that you intend to use to manage the music. Then, connect the instrument. The software is likely to have a menu where you select the type of instrument you have connected. You can then use the software to download music to your instrument or input digitized music from the instrument to the PC. Some software can receive the music you compose and play on your instrument and produce a musical score that you can then edit and play back on the PC. You can also download the edited music to this or another instrument.

> 💡 **A+ Exam Tip** Content on the A+220-701 Essentials exam ends here and content on the A+ 220-702 Practical Application exam begins.

INSTALL AND CONFIGURE MULTIMEDIA AND MASS STORAGE DEVICES

In this part of the chapter, you'll learn to install media readers, optical drives, capture cards, TV tuner cards, and external hard drives. Recall that Windows XP requires you be logged onto the system using an account with administrator privileges to install hardware or software. Windows Vista requires that you be logged in using an admin account, or you can provide the password for an admin account when the UAC box appears at the beginning of an installation.

INSTALLING A MEDIA READER

A media reader (also called a card reader or memory card reader/writer) provides slots for memory cards and can be an internal or external device. An external device such as the one in Figure 10-31 uses a USB port and has one or more memory card slots to accommodate several types of memory cards. Some external media readers also provide extra USB ports.

To use an external media reader, plug the device into a USB port. Most likely, the device will be recognized by Windows without installing drivers. If you get an error or the reader does not work, unplug the device and install software on the CD that came bundled with the device. Then try to use the media reader again.

Figure 10-31 This Hi-Speed USB card reader/writer by Targus can read CompactFlash I and II, MicroDrive, SDHC, SD, MMC, xD, Memory Stick, PRO Duo, and Mini SD cards
Courtesy: Course Technology/Cengage Learning

> 💡 **A+ Exam Tip** The A+ 220-702 Practical Application exam expects you to know how to install an external hard drive, capture card, and media reader.

Later, if you have a problem with an external reader, verify the data cable is seated securely in the USB port. Check Device Manager for errors. Try the reader in a different port. Next, try the reader on a different computer. If it works on another computer, return it to the original computer. Perhaps the problem was a loose connection.

You can also install an internal media reader such as the one shown in Figure 10-32. This device installs in a drive bay in a desktop computer. The cord on the back of the drive connects to a USB header on the motherboard. The USB interface also provides power to the device. The device provides multiple memory card slots and a USB port. It supports more than 50 types of memory cards, including multiple variations of CompactFlash, MicroDrive, SmartMedia, TransFlash, Memory Stick, SD, MMC, and RS MMC media. The media reader can be installed without drivers because Windows Vista or XP will recognize the technology and use embedded drivers. However, for best performance, install the drivers that came on the CD with the device.

A+
220-702
1.1

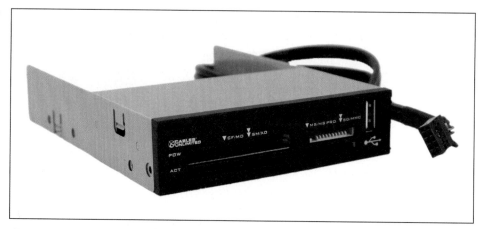

Figure 10-32   Internal media reader and writer uses an internal USB connection
Courtesy: Course Technology/Cengage Learning

INSTALLING AN OPTICAL DRIVE

Internal optical drives use a SCSI, PATA, or SATA interface. Figure 10-33 shows the rear of a PATA CD drive. Note the jumper bank that can be set to cable select, slave, or master.

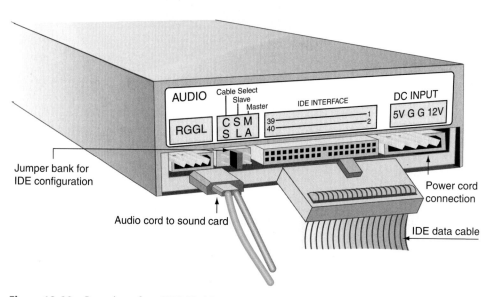

Figure 10-33   Rear view of an EIDE CD drive
Courtesy: Course Technology/Cengage Learning

Recall from Chapter 8, that for EIDE, there are four choices for drive installations: primary master, primary slave, secondary master, and secondary slave. If the drive will be the second drive installed on the cable, then set the drive to slave. If the drive is the only drive on the cable, choose master, because single is not a choice. The cable select setting is used if a special EIDE cable-select cable determines which drive is master or slave. If the optical drive shares an IDE channel with a hard drive, make the hard drive the master and the optical drive the slave.

> **💡 A+ Exam Tip**   The A+ 220-701 Essentials exam expects you to know how to install a CD, DVD, or Blu-ray drive.

A+
220-702
1.1

When given the choice of putting the optical drive on the same cable with a hard drive or on its own cable, choose to use its own cable. A CD drive that shares a cable with a hard drive can slow down the hard drive's performance. Older sys-

tems have two EIDE connections on the motherboard, probably labeled IDE1 and IDE2, so most likely you will be able to use IDE2 for the CD drive. Newer systems have more than one SATA connection and one PATA connection. Use SATA connections for all hard drives. The optical drive can use the one PATA connection or a SATA connection.

Also, optical drives might have a connection for an audio port so that sound from audio CDs can be sent directly to the audio controller. The DVD drive in Figure 10-34 has two connectors for audio. The 4-pin connector is used for analog sound and the 2-pin connector is used for digital sound. Most often you'll use the 4-pin analog connection to connect to a sound card or to the motherboard. The 2-pin connector is seldom used because Windows Vista and XP transfer digital sound from the drive to the sound card without the use of a direct cable connection.

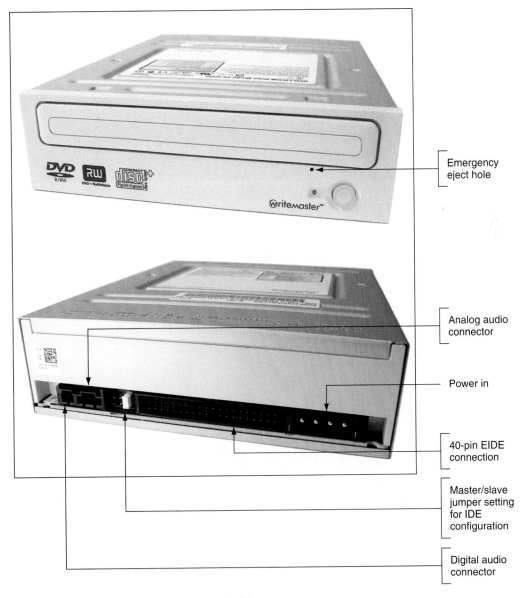

Figure 10-34 Front and rear of an EIDE DVD drive
Courtesy: Course Technology/Cengage Learning

10

A+ 220-702

A+
220-702
1.1

APPLYING | CONCEPTS

Follow these general steps to install an optical drive using a PATA or SATA connection:

1. A computer case has some wide bays for DVD, CD, or Blu-ray drives and some narrow ones for hard drives and floppy drives. Open the case and decide which large bay to use for the drive. If you use the top bay, the drive will be up and out of the way of other components inside the case.

2. For a PATA interface, set the jumper on the rear of the drive (see Figure 10-35).

Figure 10-35   Set the jumper of an EIDE optical drive
Courtesy: Course Technology/Cengage Learning

3. Older and less expensive cases use screws to secure the drive to the sides of the bay, and some bays have a clipping mechanism to secure the drive. For the case shown in Figure 10-36, you must first remove the front panel of the case. A clipping mechanism is then exposed. Next, using two fingers, squeeze the two clips on each side of the bay together to release them and pull them forward. You also need to remove the faceplate from the front of the bay.

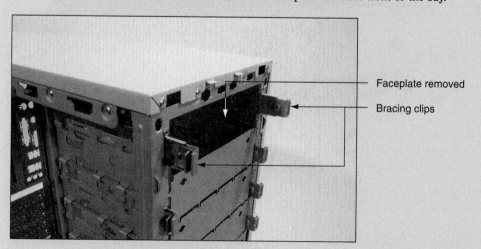

Faceplate removed

Bracing clips

Figure 10-36   To prepare a large bay for an optical drive, punch out the faceplate and pull the bracing clips forward
Courtesy: Course Technology/Cengage Learning

4. Slide the drive into the bay (see Figure 10-37). To see how far to push the drive into the bay, align it with the front of the case, as shown in Figure 10-38. For other cases, such as the one shown in Figure 10-39, the case front panel is not removed. For this case, you remove the case side panel and the faceplate for the drive bay. Then you slide the drive into the bay so it's flush with the front panel.

Figure 10-37   Slide the optical drive into the bay
Courtesy: Course Technology/Cengage Learning

Figure 10-38   To judge how far to insert the optical drive in the bay, align it with the
front of the case
Courtesy: Course Technology/Cengage Learning

A+
220-702
1.1

Figure 10-39   Slide the drive into the bay flush with the front panel
Courtesy: Course Technology/Cengage Learning

5. To secure the drive, push the clips back into position. For bays that use screws, put two screws on each side of the drive, tightening the screws so the drive can't shift, but avoiding overtightening them. Use the screws that come with the drive; screws that are too long can damage the drive. If necessary, buy a mounting kit to extend the sides of the drive so that it fits into the bay and attaches securely.

6. Connect a power cord to the drive.

7. For EIDE drives, connect the 40-pin cable to the IDE motherboard connector and the drive, being careful to follow the pin-1 rule: Match the edge color on the cable to pin 1 on both the adapter card and the drive. Generally, the colored edge is closest to the power connector. For SATA drives, connect a SATA cable to the drive and to a SATA connector on the motherboard. Figure 10-40 shows the rear of a SATA DVD drive. Notice the SATA power connector and the SATA data connector on the drive.

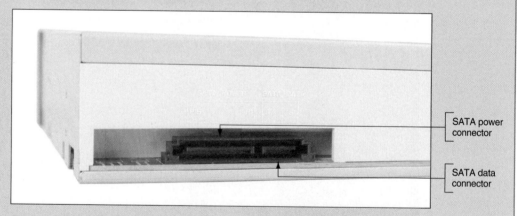

SATA power connector

SATA data connector

Figure 10-40   Rear of a SATA optical drive
Courtesy: Course Technology/Cengage Learning

8. If the drive has an audio connector, attach one end of the audio cord to the drive and the other end to the sound card or, for onboard sound, to the motherboard audio header. Figure 10-41 shows an audio cord connected to the motherboard. See your motherboard documentation for the location of this header.

Figure 10-41 The audio cable connected to the audio connector on the motherboard; the other end of the cable is connected to the optical drive
Courtesy: Course Technology/Cengage Learning

9. Check all connections and turn on the power. Press the eject button on the front of the drive. If it works, then you know power is getting to the drive. Put the case cover back on.

10. Turn on the PC. Windows launches the Found New Hardware Wizard. Windows Vista and XP support reading from CD and DVD drives using their own embedded drivers without add-on drivers. Therefore, after the Found New Hardware Wizard completes, Windows should recognize the drive.

11. The drive is now ready to use. Press the eject button to open the drive shelf, and place a CD or DVD in the drive. Now access the disc using Windows Explorer.

12. To use all the functions of the drive, install the drivers that come on the CD bundled with the drive. For example, these drivers might include the options to burn a DVD (Windows XP does not natively support this feature) or to use LightScribe to burn labels to discs.

> **Notes** If you have a problem reading a CD, verify that you placed the CD in the tray label-side-up.

> **Notes** An optical drive can be set so that when you insert a disc, software on the disc automatically executes, a feature called AutoPlay. To customize how Windows Vista handles a disc, in Control Panel, click **Play CDs or other media automatically.** The AutoPlay window opens (see Figure 10-42). Make your selections for a variety of situations. For Windows XP, in Windows Explorer or My Computer window, right-click the drive, and select **Properties** from the shortcut menu. The CD drive Properties dialog box opens; click the **AutoPlay** tab (see Figure 10-43).
> To prevent a CD, DVD, or BD from automatically playing when AutoPlay is enabled, hold down the Shift key when inserting a disc.

INSTALLING AN EXTERNAL HARD DRIVE

When you first plug up an external hard drive to your PC, Windows recognizes the drive and assigns it a drive letter. You can then view and use the drive using Windows

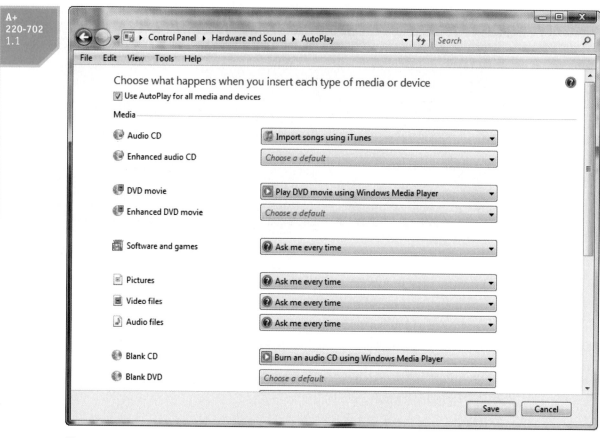

Figure 10-42   Options to control what happens when a disc is inserted
Courtesy: Course Technology/Cengage Learning

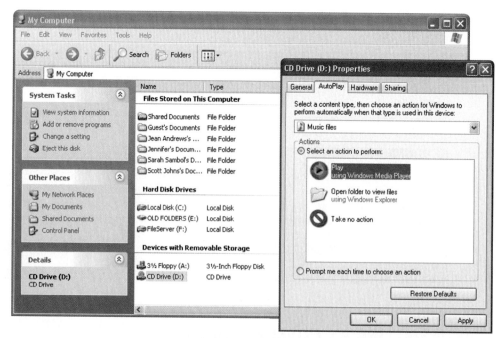

Figure 10-43   For Windows XP, use My Computer to tell the OS how to handle the AutoPlay feature
for your CD drive
Courtesy: Course Technology/Cengage Learning

Explorer. Most external drives also include a backup software program. You can install and use this program to set up a backup routine to back up data on your internal drive to the external drive. For example, the OneTouch drive shown earlier in the chapter in Figure 10-21 has a program in the root directory named Launch.exe. Use this program to install backup software under Windows. You can then execute the backup software from the Windows Start menu. Using the backup software, you can set up a scheduled backup routine. Figure 10-44 shows one window in the process where you select days and time to back up. In another window, you select folders to back up. Backups then happen routinely until you disable the function. At any time you want, you can also press a button on the front of the OneTouch drive which causes the software to immediately perform a backup. When you first set up the backup, it performs a full backup of all the folders you've specified. Later, it only backs up files that have changed so as to save space on the external drive. You will learn more about backups in Chapter 13.

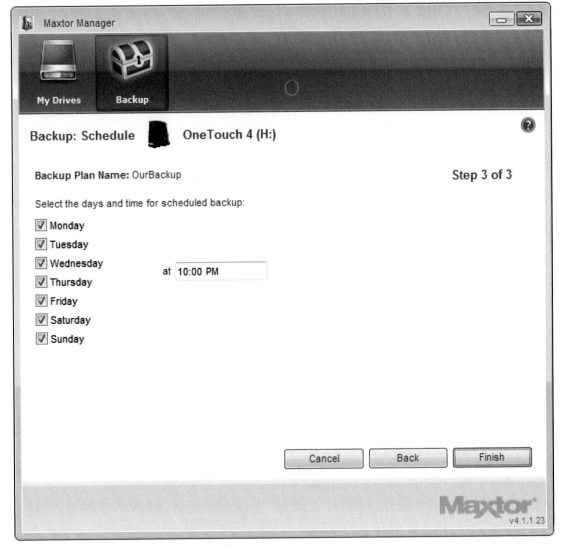

Figure 10-44   One window in the process of setting up a backup routine
Courtesy: Course Technology/Cengage Learning

A+
220-702
1.1

INSTALLING A CAPTURE CARD

A video capture card comes bundled with drivers and software to use the card. As with all installations, follow the specific directions of the device manufacturer. Here are some general guidelines as given by one capture card manufacturer:

1. Uninstall all previous device drivers for capture cards or software to use a capture card.

2. Install DirectX version 10 software that is bundled with the capture card.

3. Install the capture card in an empty slot on the motherboard. Specific instructions for how to install an adapter card can be found in Chapter 9. Don't forget to use your ground bracelet to protect the system against ESD.

4. Start up the PC. When the Found New Hardware Wizard launches, cancel it.

5. Insert the CD that contains the drivers and run the **Setup.exe** program on the CD. Follow instructions to install the drivers. The Setup program also installs an application to use the card.

6. Shut down the system and install the microphone and camera input cables.

7. Restart the system. The application software to configure the card launches. Stepping through each configuration screen, you will select the format that will be used for input files, where the input files will be stored, and how capturing will work.

8. Restart the system one more time. If continuous input is to be captured, the application will begin capturing after the restart. The application also has a control panel where you can view the input from each camera. You can open the control panel by using a shortcut the application installed on the desktop.

Read the user manual to find out how to use the software to control the video capture card. If the card is receiving input from multiple security cameras, each camera input is called a channel. You can control how the input from each channel is recorded or captured. For example, you might set one channel to record all input and set others to only record at a scheduled time or when motion has been detected.

TROUBLESHOOTING MULTIMEDIA DEVICES

A+
220-702
1.2

This section covers some troubleshooting guidelines for optical drives, other removable storage devices, and capture cards.

> 💡 **A+ Exam Tip** The A+ 220-702 Practical Application exam expects you to be a good PC troubleshooter and presents different troubleshooting scenarios for you to solve. This section is good preparation for that skill.

PROBLEMS WITH OPTICAL DRIVES

Use the following general guidelines when a CD, DVD, or Blu-ray drive installation causes problems. These guidelines are useful if your computer does not recognize the drive (for example, no drive D is listed in Windows Explorer):

◢ Check the data cable and power cord connections to the drive. For an EIDE drive, is the stripe on the data cable correctly aligned to pin 1? (Look for an arrow or small 1 printed on the drive. For a best guess, pin 1 is usually next to the power connector.)

- For an EIDE drive, is the correct master/slave jumper set? For example, if both the hard drive and the CD or DVD drive are hooked to the same ribbon cable, one must be set to master and the other to slave. If the CD or DVD drive is the only drive connected to the cable, then it should be set to single or master.
- For an EIDE drive, is the IDE connection on the motherboard disabled in BIOS setup? If so, enable it.
- Using Device Manager, verify that the drive and the IDE controller are recognized without errors and are enabled. Rarely, the drivers for the drive or controller might need updating. To update the IDE controller drivers, download the drivers from the motherboard manufacturer Web site. For the optical drive, install the drivers that came on CD with the drive.
- If you are using a SCSI drive, are the proper IDs set? Is the device terminated if it is the last device in the SCSI chain? Are the correct SCSI drivers installed?
- Download updates to Windows. Sometimes installing Windows patches can solve problems with hardware.
- Suspect a boot virus. This is a common problem. Download the latest updates to an antivirus program, and then scan the system for viruses.

PROBLEMS WHEN BURNING A CD, DVD, OR BD

When trying to burn a CD, DVD, or BD, sometimes Windows refuses to perform the burn or the burned disc is not readable. Here are some things that might go wrong and what to do about them:

- A CD can hold about 700 MB of data. Be sure your total file sizes don't exceed this amount. For other discs, make sure the type of disc can hold the total file sizes that you are trying to burn. Also verify that the disc is a recordable or rewriteable disc. For recordable discs, verify the disc has not already been used.
- The hard drive needs some temporary holding space for the write process. Make sure you have at least 1 GB of free space.
- If something interrupts the write process before the burning is done, you might end up with a bad disc. Disable any screen saver and close other programs before you begin.
- If several discs give you problems, try a different brand of discs.
- The burn process requires a constant flow of data to the disc. If you have a sluggish Windows system, a disc might not burn correctly. Try using a slower burn rate to adjust for a slow data transfer rate. To slow the burn rate in Vista, open Windows Media Player, click the down arrow under **Burn**, and select **More Options** from the drop-down menu. In the Options box that appears, click the Burn tab and then select the burn rate (see Figure 10-45). The rate applies to any burner you use on this computer. To slow the burn rate in XP, right-click the optical drive in Windows Explorer and select **Properties** from the shortcut menu. Click the **Recording** tab (see Figure 10-46). Choose a slower write speed from the drop-down menu. Notice in the Recording tab window you can also point to a drive different from drive C to hold temporary files for burning. Use this option if drive C is full, and another drive has more available space.

Notes If a disc gets stuck in the drive, use the emergency eject hole to remove it. Turn off the power to the PC first. Then insert an instrument such as a straightened paper clip into the hole to eject the tray manually.

10

A+ 220-702

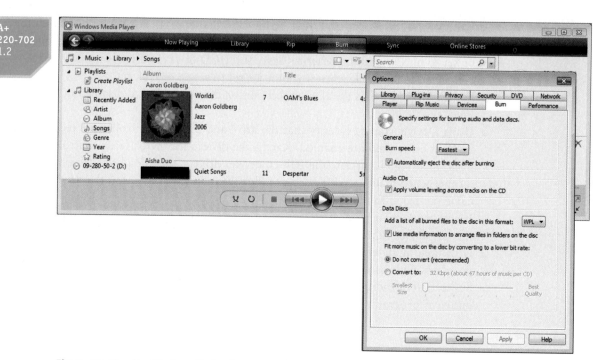

Figure 10-45 Use Windows Media Player to select the burn rate in Vista
Courtesy: Course Technology/Cengage Learning

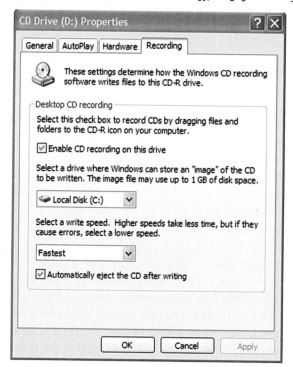

Figure 10-46 Slow down the CD-RW burn speed to account for a slow Windows XP system
Courtesy: Course Technology/Cengage Learning

PROBLEMS WITH REMOVABLE STORAGE DEVICES

When a removable storage device does not work, do the following:

▲ For an external hard drive, verify the data cable is solidly connected to the port. Open Device Manager and verify the port and drive are recognized correctly with no errors.

It is not normally necessary to install drivers for an external hard drive unless you want to use backup software installed on the drive.

▲ If Device Manager reports a problem with the port, try updating device drivers for the motherboard, which will include USB, FireWire, and eSATA drivers.

▲ Is the drive connected to a USB hub that needs power? Is the power cord connected to the hub?

▲ For a USB flash drive or external hard drive, try a different port. Try the device on another computer. If it works on another computer, return it to the original computer. Perhaps the problem was a loose connection.

PROBLEMS WITH CAPTURE CARDS

As with troubleshooting any adapter card, try the easy things first. Here are a few tips:

▲ Open Device Manager and verify it recognizes the card with no errors. Is the card enabled?

▲ Verify the peripherals (microphone, speakers, camera, video cable, or TV cable) are connected to the card and the peripherals are working.

▲ Verify the application software that uses the card is working. Does the software give errors? Try repairing the software using the utility that came bundled with the card. Most likely you can run the setup program on the CD to repair the software.

▲ Has the card ever worked? Read the documentation to make sure everything is installed correctly. Most installations for capture cards require a couple of restarts. Try restarting the system.

▲ Try uninstalling and reinstalling the card and software. Use Device Manager to uninstall the card device drivers. Use an uninstall routine to uninstall the application software. Then begin again and reinstall everything, being very careful to follow installation instructions.

▲ Try installing the card in Safe Mode. First uninstall the card and then boot the system into Safe Mode. To boot Windows into Safe Mode, press the F8 key during startup and select **Safe Mode with Networking** from the Windows Advanced Options Menu. Windows Safe Mode launches a bare-bones hardware and software configuration. Now install the card. Next, restart the system normally and watch for errors.

▲ Check the Web site of the card manufacturer for troubleshooting tips. The site might offer forums, blogs, and chat sessions with technical support.

>> CHAPTER SUMMARY

▲ Multimedia PCs and devices are designed to create and reproduce lifelike presentations of sight and sound.

▲ MP3 is a version of MPEG compression used for audio files.

▲ A TV tuner card turns your PC or notebook into a television. A video capture card allows you to capture input from a camcorder or directly from TV. Combo cards have both abilities.

▲ CDs, DVDs, and BDs are optical devices with data physically embedded into the surface of the disc. Laser beams are used to read data off the disc by measuring light reflection.

◢ CDs use the CDFS or UDF file systems. DVDs use the UDF file system, and BDs use the UDF version 2.5 file system.

◢ Optical discs can be recordable (such as a CD-R disc) or rewriteable (such as a DVD-RW disc).

◢ Optical discs can use laser-burned labels using LightScribe or Labelflash, or labels can be printed on the top surface of a disc using an ink-jet printer with this capability.

◢ Solid-state storage devices include USB flash drives, flash memory cards, and solid-state hard drives.

◢ Current types of flash memory cards include SDHC, MicroSDHC, MiniSDHC, SD, MiniSD, Memory Stick PRO Duo, Memory Stick Micro M2, MicroSD, CompactFlash I and II, and UDMA CompactFlash. Older types of flash memory cards include MMC, RS-MMC, Microdrive CF, Memory Stick, xD-Picture Card, and SmartMedia.

◢ External hard drives can use a USB, FireWire, eSATA, or SCSI port.

◢ Tape drives are an inexpensive way to back up an entire hard drive or portions of it. Tape drives are more convenient for backups than removable disks. The disadvantage of tape drives is that data can only be accessed sequentially.

◢ Two types of file formats used for images are JPEG and TIFF.

◢ MIDI is a set of standards used to represent music in digital form.

◢ Internal optical drives can have an EIDE, serial ATA, or SCSI interface, and external optical drives can use a USB port, 1394 port, or SCSI port.

>> KEY TERMS

For explanations of key terms, see the Glossary near the end of the book.

Blu-ray Disc (BD)
card reader
CD (compact disc)
CDFS (Compact Disc File System)
constant linear velocity (CLV)
data cartridge
DVD (digital versatile disc or digital video disc)
half-life

JPEG (Joint Photographic Experts Group)
lands
media reader
memory card reader/writer
MIDI (musical instrument digital interface)
minicartridge
MP3
pits

sequential access
surround sound
TIFF (tagged image file format)
TV tuner card
UDF (Universal Disk Format) file system
video capture card

>> REVIEWING THE BASICS

1. Which speaker port should you use when connecting a single speaker to a PC?

2. What type of compression format is popular for audio files?

3. What type of adapter card allows you to watch TV using your computer?

4. What type of file system is used by Blu-ray discs?

5. What two types of interfaces might be used by an internal DVD drive?

6. How much data can a CD hold?

7. How much data can a double-sided, double-layer DVD hold?

8. What color laser beam does a CD and DVD drive use?

9. What color laser beam does a Blu-ray drive use?

10. How much data can a double-sided, single-layer BD hold?

11. How much data can a double-sided, dual-layer BD hold?

12. Which costs more, a CD-R or a CD-RW disc?

13. Which type of flash memory card is currently the smallest type of card and the most popular?

14. What type of flash memory card looks the same and is interchangeable with a MicroSD card?

15. Which type of removable storage device can only access its data sequentially and not randomly?

16. Which type of image file format typically produces a larger file size, a JPEG file or a TIFF file?

17. What are the group of standards that represent music in digital form?

18. Why might a musical keyboard have two MIDI ports?

19. If you need your laptop to read an SD card but the laptop does not have a memory card slot, what device can you buy to read the card?

20. What Windows Vista utility is used to change the burn speed for CDs and DVDs?

>> THINKING CRITICALLY

1. You have just installed a new sound card and its drivers and connected the speakers and amplifier. You insert a music CD into the drive to test the drive. Windows Media Player launches and says it is playing the CD, but you don't hear music. What do you do first?

    a. Check the volume controls on the speaker amplifier.

    b. Check the connections of the amplifier and speakers to the card.

    c. Check Device Manager for errors with the sound card.

    d. Verify that the amplifier has power.

2. You have just upgraded your computer from Windows XP to Windows Vista. Now your system has no sound. What are the first two things you do?

    a. Check Device Manager to see if the sound card is recognized and has no errors.

    b. Reinstall Windows XP.

    c. Use Device Manager to uninstall the sound card.

    d. Identify your sound card by opening the case and looking on the card for manufacturer and model.

    e. Identify your sound card by finding the documentation and driver CD that came with the card.

    f. Download Windows XP drivers for the sound card from the sound card manufacturer's Web site.

3. You have just installed a new DVD drive and its drivers under Windows XP. The drive will read a CD but not a DVD. You decide to reload the device drivers. What is the first thing you do?

   a. Open the Control Panel and launch the Add New Hardware Wizard.

   b. Open Device Manager and choose Update Driver.

   c. Remove the data cable from the DVD drive so Windows will no longer recognize the drive and allow you to reinstall the drivers.

   d. Open Device Manager and uninstall the drive.

>> HANDS-ON PROJECTS

PROJECT 10-1: Practicing Troubleshooting Skills

1. A friend calls to say that he just purchased a new sound card and speakers to install in his PC. He wants some help from you over the phone. Your friend installed the sound card in an expansion slot and connected the audio wire to the sound card and the CD drive. List the steps you would guide him through to complete the installation.

2. Suppose that the audio wire connection in Step 1 does not fit the connection on the CD drive. You think that if the problem is a wrong fit, perhaps you can improvise to connect audio from the CD drive directly to the sound card. Your friend tells you that the CD drive has a port for a headphone connection and the sound card has a port for audio in. How might you improvise to provide this direct connection? Check your theory using the appropriate audio wire.

3. Work with a partner. Each of you should set up a problem with sound on a PC and have the other troubleshoot it. Suggestions for a problem to set up include:

   ◢ Speaker cables disconnected

   ◢ Speaker turned off

   ◢ Speaker cable plugged into the wrong jack

   ◢ Volume turned down all the way

   As you troubleshoot the problem, write down its initial symptoms as a user would describe them, and the steps you take toward the solution.

PROJECT 10-2: Using the Internet for Research

Make a presentation or write a paper about digital cameras. Cover what features to look for when buying one and how to compare quality from one camera to another. Use the following Web sites, as well as three other Web sites in your research:

◢ *www.imaging-resource.com*

◢ *www.pcphotoreview.com*

◢ *www.steves-digicams.com*

10

PROJECT 10-3: Compare Blank CD, DVD, and BD Prices

Fill in Table 10-9 to compare prices of various types of CDs, DVDs, and BDs. To print the table, look for Table 10-9 on the CD that accompanies this book.

Disc	Manufacturer	Capacity of a Disc	Cost of Packet and Number of Discs in One Packet	Cost Per Disc
CD-R				
CD-RW				
DVD-R				
DVD+R				
DVD-R DL				
DVD-RW				
DVD+RW				
DVD-R with LightScribe				
DVD-R with Labelflash				
DVD-R printable				
BD-R				
BD-R DL				
BD-RE				

Table 10-9 Compare optical disc capacities and prices

PROJECT 10-4: Find a Printer That Can Print Labels on CDs and DVDs

Search retail Web sites to find an ink-jet printer that is capable of printing color labels directly on the surface of a CD or DVD. Print the Web page showing the printer and its cost. Find a comparable ink-jet printer that does not offer the feature to print to optical discs. Print the Web page showing the printer and its cost. Based on your comparison, how much does the feature of printing to optical discs cost?

PROJECT 10-5: Exploring Multimedia on the Web

Do the following to investigate how to experience multimedia on the Web:

1. Go to the Adobe Web site (*www.adobe.com*) and download the latest version of Adobe Flash Player, software used to add animation, video, and sound to Web sites.

2. Using a search engine, find at least two Flash-enabled Web sites, and then use Flash to explore these sites.

3. Windows Media Player is software used to play music and video stored locally or online. Windows Vista has Windows Media Player embedded in the OS. If you are using Windows XP, go to the Microsoft Web site (*www.microsoft.com*) and download the latest version of Windows Media Player.

4. Use Media Player to play a music CD, a radio station on the Web, and a video clip on the Web.

5. Answer these questions:

   a. What are the two sites you found that use Adobe Flash?

   b. What music CD did you play?

   c. What radio station did you play? What was the station's Web site URL?

   d. What video clip did you play? At which Web site did you locate the clip?

>> REAL PROBLEMS, REAL SOLUTIONS

REAL PROBLEM 10-1: Search for Drivers

After you upgrade your Windows XP computer to Windows Vista, you discover that the onboard sound ports no longer work. You know that the sound ports did work before you started the upgrade. Therefore, you can conclude that the problem is related to software and not hardware. You begin your search on the Internet to find audio drivers that work under Windows Vista. Here are the steps you take:

1. You search the Web site of the motherboard manufacturer for the drivers. You find the drivers for Windows 2000/XP for your particular motherboard, but you don't find the Vista drivers.

2. The chipset is made by Intel, so you go to the Intel Web site (*www.intel.com*) and search for Vista drivers for the chipset. You find these drivers, download them, and install them, but sound still does not work. You conclude that the chipset drivers don't include audio.

3. You search the Internet for information about your motherboard and read on several PC support forums that others are having similar problems and have not been able to find Vista drivers. On one forum, you discover that the audio controller on your motherboard is made by C-Media (*www.c-media.com*), and the forum even gives the model number of the controller. You search the C-Media site, but still don't find the drivers.

4. You make one last effort to find the drivers by searching reliable Web sites that offer drivers and help with Windows. Some of these sites are listed in Table 10-10. Again, you find XP drivers for your onboard audio, but no Vista drivers. (As you search the Internet, don't download and run free driver-scanning software that offers to update your system automatically. Too often, this software is really spyware or adware.)

5. You conclude that the Vista drivers don't exist and decide to purchase a new sound card with Vista drivers for your system.

Do the following to find Vista drivers for the sound on your home or lab computer:

1. If your home or lab computer uses onboard sound, identify the motherboard manufacturer. If your computer uses a sound card, identify the sound card manufacturer. How did you identify the device?

Site	URL
Computing.NET	www.computing.net
The Driver Guide	www.driverguide.com
Drivezone by Barry Fanion	www.driverzone.com
HelpWithWindows.com	www.helpwithwindows.com
Hermanson, LLC	www.windrivers.com
Marco Volpe	www.mrdriver.com
Microsoft Support	support.microsoft.com technet.microsoft.com
PC Pitstop	www.pcpitstop.com
Windows User Group Network	www.wugnet.com

Table 10-10 Help with Windows troubleshooting and Windows drivers

2. Find one PC support forum where your sound card or motherboard audio is discussed. Print one question and answer on the forum. For help finding forums, try using Google.com and search on "PC hardware forums."

3. Find the Vista drivers for your sound device on the Internet. Print the Web page where you can download the Vista drivers. If you cannot find Vista drivers, describe the process you went through to conclude the drivers don't exist.

10

PC Maintenance and Troubleshooting Strategies

In the last several chapters, you have learned much about the hardware components of a system, including features and characteristics of the power supply, motherboard, processor, RAM, hard drive, I/O devices, and multimedia devices. You've learned how to select, install, and configure each device. And you've also learned steps you can take to troubleshoot problems with these devices. In this chapter, you can take a step back from all the details of supporting hardware devices and think about strategy. When supporting personal computers and their users, having a strategy in mind when faced with day-to-day tasks and challenges can make all the difference between feeling overwhelmed and feeling in charge. A strategy gives you direction, purpose, and a plan. This chapter is about having a plan so you know where you're going and you have a strategy to get there.

Staying safe and protecting equipment are essential to your strategy as a professional support technician. And the best support technicians are good at preventing a problem from happening in the first place, so in this chapter, you'll learn how to develop a preventive maintenance plan and use it. Finally in this chapter, you'll learn a strategy to solve any computer problems. You can apply this strategy to all the troubleshooting skills you've learned so far in this book. You can then build on this strategy in future troubleshooting situations to become an expert problem solver, confident that you can face any computer problem.

A+ Exam Tip This chapter has three major sections. All the sections cover objectives on the A+ 220–701 Essentials exam that apply to operational procedures, preventive maintenance techniques, and troubleshooting theory.

OPERATIONAL PROCEDURES WHEN SUPPORTING PERSONAL COMPUTERS

A+
220-701
6.1

In this part of the chapter, you'll learn about the physical dangers of supporting personal computers and how to protect yourself and others. Then you'll learn about what can happen to damage a computer or other equipment while you are working on it and what to do to prevent that damage. You'll also learn how to dispose of used equipment and move computer equipment. And finally, you'll learn about the software copyright law that you need to be aware of when installing and supporting software.

STAY SAFE AND KEEP OTHERS SAFE

Recall from Chapter 4 that you need to immediately unplug electrical equipment that has been damaged physically or exposed to water, moisture, or electrical shorts. In addition, some printer components such as the drum on a laser printer will get so hot they will burn you. Other dangers to watch out for are chemical burns, cables that can cause people to trip, and heavy equipment that can hurt your back. You also need to be careful when working with computer cases because some have sharp edges that can cut you.

Now let's look at safety precautions to take when using cleaning pads and solutions, managing cables that might be trip hazards, and lifting heavy objects.

PROPER USE OF CLEANING PADS AND SOLUTIONS

As a PC technician, you'll find yourself collecting different cleaning solutions and cleaning pads to clean a variety of devices, including the mouse and keyboard, CDs, DVDs, Blu-ray discs and their drives, tapes and tape drives, and CRT and LCD monitors. Figure 11-1

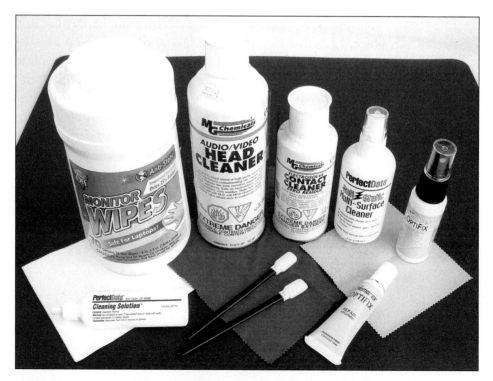

Figure 11-1 Cleaning solutions and pads
Courtesy: Course Technology/Cengage Learning

A+
220-701
6.1

shows a few of these products. The contact cleaner in the figure is used to clean the contacts on expansion cards, which might solve a problem with a faulty connection.

Most of these cleaning solutions contain flammable and poisonous materials. Take care when using them so that they don't get on your skin or in your eyes. To find out what to do if you are accidentally exposed to a dangerous solution, look on the instructions printed on the can or check out the material safety data sheet (see Figure 11-2). A Material Safety Data Sheet (MSDS) explains how to properly handle substances such as chemical solvents.

Figure 11-2 Each chemical you use should have available a material safety data sheet
Courtesy: Course Technology/Cengage Learning

An MSDS includes information such as physical data, toxicity, health effects, first aid, storage, shipping, disposal, and spill procedures. It comes packaged with the chemical, you can order one from the manufacturer, or you can find one on the Internet (see *www.ilpi.com/msds*).

If you have an accident with these or other dangerous products, your company or organization might require you to report the accident to your company and/or fill out an accident report. Check with your organization to find out how to handle reporting these types of incidents.

MANAGING CABLES

People can trip over cables or cords left on the floor, so be careful that cables are in a safe place. If you must run a cable across a path or where someone sits, use a cable or cord cover that can be nailed or screwed to the floor. Don't leave loose cables or cords in a traffic area where people can trip over them (called a trip hazard).

LIFTING HEAVY OBJECTS

Back injury, caused by lifting heavy objects, is one of the most common injuries that happen at work. Whenever possible, put heavy objects, such as a large laser printer, on a cart to

11

A+ 220-701

move them. If you do need to lift a heavy object, follow these guidelines to keep from injuring your back:

1. Looking at the object, decide which side of the object to face so that the load is the most balanced.

2. Stand close to the object with your feet apart.

3. Keeping your back straight, bend your knees and grip the load.

4. Lift with your legs, arms, and shoulders, and not with your back or stomach.

5. Keep the load close to your body and avoid twisting your body while you're holding it.

6. To put the object down, keep your back as straight as you can and lower the object by bending your knees.

Don't try to lift an object that is too heavy for you. Don't be afraid to ask for help.

PHYSICALLY PROTECT YOUR EQUIPMENT

There are some things you can do to physically protect your computer equipment. Here is my list of dos and don'ts (you can probably add your own tips to the list):

▲ *Don't move or jar your computer when it's turned on.* Before you move the computer case even an inch or so, power it down. Don't put the computer case under your desk where it might get bumped or kicked. Although modern hard drives are tougher than earlier models, it's still possible to crash a drive by banging into it while it's reading or writing data.

▲ *Don't smoke around your computer.* Tar from cigarettes can accumulate on fans, causing them to jam, which in turn will cause the system to overheat. For older hard drives that are not adequately sealed, smoke particles can get inside and crash a drive.

▲ *Don't leave the PC turned off for weeks or months at a time.* Once my daughter left her PC turned off for an entire summer. At the beginning of the new school term, the PC would not boot. We discovered that the boot record at the beginning of the hard drive had become corrupted. PCs, like old cars, can give you problems after long spans of inactivity.

▲ *Don't block air vents on the front and rear of the computer case or on the monitor.* Proper air circulation is essential to keeping a system cool. Also, for optimum air flow, put covers on expansion slot openings on the rear of the case and put faceplates over empty bays on the front of the case (see Figure 11-3). Don't set a tower case directly on thick carpet because the air vent on the bottom front of the case can be blocked.

▲ *Use keyboard covers in dirty environments.* You can purchase plastic keyboard covers to protect the keyboard in a dirty or extremely dusty environment.

▲ *High humidity can be dangerous for hard drives.* I once worked in a basement with PCs, and hard drives failed much too often. After we installed dehumidifiers, the hard drives became more reliable.

▲ *In BIOS setup, disable the ability to write to the boot sector of the hard drive.* This alone can keep boot viruses at bay. However, before you upgrade your OS, such as when you upgrade Windows XP to Windows Vista, be sure to enable writing to the boot sector, which the OS setup will want to do.

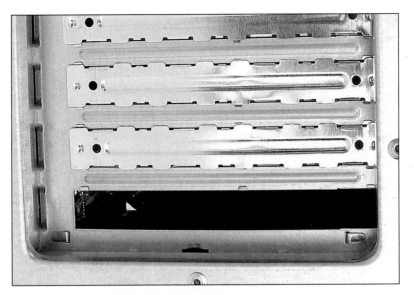

Figure 11-3 For optimum airflow, don't leave empty expansion slots and bays uncovered
Courtesy: Course Technology/Cengage Learning

▲ *If your data is really private, keep it under lock and key.* You can use all kinds of security methods to encrypt, password protect, and hide data, but if it really is that important, one obvious thing you can do is store the data on a removable storage device such as a USB flash drive or external hard drive, and, when you're not using the data, put the device in a fireproof safe. And, of course, keep at least two copies. Sounds simple, but it works. You'll learn much more about securing computers and their data in Chapter 19.

▲ *Protect your CDs, DVDs, BDs, and other storage media.* To protect discs, keep them away from direct sunlight, heat, and extreme cold. Don't allow a disc to be scratched.

▲ *Keep magnets away from your computer place.* Don't work inside the computer case with magnetized screwdrivers and or sit strong magnets on top of the computer case.

▲ *Protect electrical equipment from power surges.* Lightning and other electrical power surges can destroy computers and other electrical equipment. If the house or office building does not have surge protection equipment installed at the breaker box, be sure to install a protective device at each computer. The least expensive device is a power strip that is also a surge protector, although you might want to use a line conditioner or UPS for added protection.

▲ *Don't unpack and turn on a computer that has just come in from the cold.* If your new laptop has just arrived and sat on your doorstep in freezing weather, don't bring it in and immediately unpack it and turn it on. Wait until a computer has had time to reach room temperature to prevent damage from condensation and static electricity. In addition, when unpacking hardware or software, to help protect against static electricity, remove the packing tape and cellophane from the work area as soon as possible.

> 💡 **A+ Exam Tip** The A+ 220-701 Essentials exam expects you to know how to keep computers and monitors well ventilated and clean and to use protective covers for input devices such as the keyboard.

A+
220-701
6.1

HOW TO DISPOSE OF USED EQUIPMENT

As a PC technician, it will often be your responsibility to dispose of used equipment and consumables, including batteries, printer toner cartridges, hard drives, and monitors. Table 11-1 lists such items and how to dispose of them. Manufacturer documentation and local environmental regulators can also provide disposal instructions or guidance.

Part	How to Dispose
Alkaline batteries, including AAA, AA, A, C, D, and 9-volt	Dispose of these batteries in the regular trash. First check to see if there are recycling facilities in your area.
Button batteries used in digital cameras and other small equipment; battery packs used in notebooks	These batteries can contain silver oxide, mercury, lithium, or cadmium and are considered hazardous waste. Dispose of them by returning them to the original dealer or by taking them to a recycling center. To recycle, pack them separately from other items. If you don't have a recycling center nearby, contact your county for local regulations for disposal.
Laser printer toner cartridges	Return these to the manufacturer or dealer to be recycled.
Ink-jet printer cartridges Computer cases, power supplies, and other computer parts Monitors Chemical solvents and containers	Check with local county or environmental officials for laws and regulations in your area for proper disposal of these items. The county might have a recycling center that will receive them. Discharge a monitor before disposing of it. See the MSDS documents for chemicals to know how to dispose of them.
Storage media such as hard drives, CDs, DVDs, and BDs	Do physical damage to the device so it is not possible for sensitive data to be stolen. Then the device can be put in the trash. To meet legal requirements to destroy data, consider using a data-destruction service.

Table 11-1 Computer parts and how to dispose of them

Monitors and power supplies can contain a charge even after the devices are unplugged. Most CRT monitors today are designed to discharge after sitting unplugged for 60 minutes. To manually discharge a monitor, a high-voltage probe is used with the monitor case opened. Ask a technician trained to fix monitors to do this for you.

A+
220-701
6.1
5.1

Don't throw out a hard drive, CD, DVD, tape, or other media that might have personal or corporate data on it unless you know the data can't be stolen off the device. You need to do physical damage to the device. For example, you can assure yourself that ordinary attempts by a thief to access the data on a hard drive will fail if you take a hammer and nail and punch the drive housing, forcing the nail straight through to the other side so that all drive disks are damaged. You can also break CDs and DVDs in half and do similar physical damage to flash drives or tapes.

However, if the data is extra sensitive and *really* important, know that a skilled thief can recover some data from a hard drive or other device that has been damaged in this way. To completely destroy the data, consider a secure data-destruction service. In fact, many government and corporate organizations are required by law to completely destroy data before disposing of media. For example, a hospital is required by law to protect patient data in this way. If you work for such an organization, using a data-destruction service is your safest option. To find a service, search the Internet using the search string "secure data destruction." However, don't use a service unless you have thoroughly checked its references and guarantees of legal compliance that you need to meet.

> **A+ Exam Tip** The A+ 220-701 Essentials exam expects you to know how to follow environmental guidelines to dispose of batteries, CRTs, chemical solvents, and containers. If you're not certain how to dispose of a product, see its MSDS document.

HOW TO MOVE COMPUTER EQUIPMENT

If you are shipping a computer, be aware that rough handling can cause damage, as can exposure to water, heat, and cold. The computer can also be misplaced, lost, or stolen. If you are preparing a computer for shipping, you would also want to do the following:

- Back up all important data on the computer. How to make backups is covered in Chapter 13. Make sure that the tapes or disks holding the backup data are secured and protected during transit. Consider shipping them separately.
- Coil all external cords and secure them with plastic ties or rubber bands.
- Pack the computer, monitor, and all devices in their original shipping cartons or similar boxes with enough packing material to protect them. Each device needs to be wrapped or secured separately so devices will not bump against each other.
- Purchase insurance on the shipment. Postal insurance is not expensive, and can save you a lot of money if materials are damaged in transit.

Now let's look at your responsibility under the law to protect software copyrights.

PROTECTING SOFTWARE COPYRIGHTS

As a computer support technician, you will be faced with the legal issues and practices surrounding the distribution of software. When someone purchases software from a software vendor, that person has only purchased a license for the software, which is the right to use it. The buyer does not legally *own* the software and, therefore, does not have the right to distribute it. The right to copy the work, called a copyright, belongs to the creator of the work or others to whom the creator transfers this right. Copyrights are intended to legally protect the intellectual property rights of organizations or individuals to creative works, which include books, images, and software.

As a PC technician, you will be called upon to install, upgrade, and customize software. You need to know your responsibilities in upholding the law, especially as it applies to software copyrights.

> **Notes** While the originator of a creative work is the original owner of a copyright, the copyright can be transferred from one entity to another.

FEDERAL COPYRIGHT ACT OF 1976

The Federal Copyright Act of 1976 was designed in part to protect software copyrights by requiring that only legally obtained copies of software be used; the law also allows for one backup copy (also called an archive copy) of software to be made. Making unauthorized copies of original software violates the Federal Copyright Act of 1976 and is called software piracy or, more officially, software copyright infringement. Some software companies have taken the position that the one archive copy of the software is not allowed.

Making a copy of software and then selling it or giving it away is a violation of the law. Because it is so easy to do, and because so many people do it, many people don't realize that it's illegal. Normally, only the employee who violated the copyright law is liable for infringement; however, in some cases, an employer or supervisor is also held responsible, even when the copies were made without the employer's knowledge. The Business Software Alliance has estimated that 38 percent of software in the world is obtained illegally.

By purchasing a site license, a company can obtain the right to use multiple copies of software, which is a popular way for companies to provide software to employees. With this type of license, companies can distribute software to PCs from network servers or execute software directly off the server. Read the licensing agreement of any software to determine the terms of distribution. When you install software, this end-user licensing agreement (EULA) is usually displayed during installation and requires that you agree to it before continuing with the installation (see Figure 11-4).

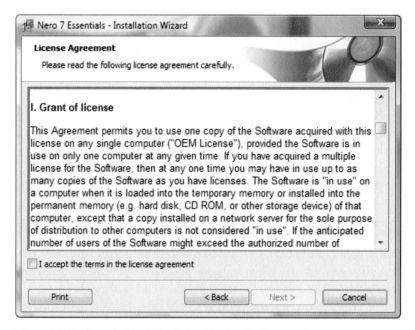

Figure 11-4 Agree to the EULA before the installation continues
Courtesy: Course Technology/Cengage Learning

INDUSTRY ASSOCIATIONS

One of two associations committed to the prevention of software piracy is the Software & Information Industry Association (*www.siia.net*), a nonprofit organization that educates the public and enforces copyright laws. The other organization, the Business Software Alliance (*www.bsa.org*), manages the BSA Anti-Piracy Hotline at 1-888-NOPIRACY. These associations are made up of hundreds of software manufacturers and publishers in North and Latin America, Europe, and Asia. They promote software raids on large and small companies; in the United States, they receive the cooperation of the U.S. government to prosecute offenders.

Vendors might sometimes sell counterfeit software by installing unauthorized software on computers for sale. This practice is called hard-disk loading. Vendors have even been known to counterfeit disk labels and Certificates of Authenticity. Warning signs that software purchased from vendors is pirated include:

- No end-user license is included.
- There is no mail-in product registration card.
- Software is installed on a new PC, but documentation and original discs are not included in the package.
- Documentation is photocopied, or discs have handwritten labels.

WHAT ARE YOUR RESPONSIBILITIES UNDER THE LAW?

Recall that according to the Federal Copyright Act of 1976, the legal users of software have the right to make one backup copy. Other rights are based on what the copyright holder allows. In 1990, the U.S. Congress passed the Software Rental Amendment Act, which prevents renting, leasing, lending, or sharing software without the express written permission of the copyright holder. In 1992, Congress instituted criminal penalties for software copyright infringement, which include imprisonment for up to five years and/or fines up to $250,000 for the unlawful reproduction or distribution of 10 or more copies of software.

As an employee of a company that has a site license to use multiple copies of the software, your responsibility is to comply with the site license agreement. It is also your responsibility to purchase only legitimate software. Purchasers of counterfeit or copied software face the risk of corrupted files, virus-infected discs, inadequate documentation, and lack of technical support and upgrades as well as the legal penalties for using pirated software.

When the software budget is very low, instead of purchasing or pirating commercial software, you might consider using open source software. Open source software is developed by volunteers, and the software is free to use, copy, and even distribute as long as you agree to the terms of the license as defined by the group making the software available. Examples of open source software are the Linux OS, Apache HTTP Server (a Web server), and Mozilla Firefox (a Web browser).

Now we're ready to look at ways to set up an effective preventive maintenance plan for personal computers.

PERSONAL COMPUTER PREVENTIVE MAINTENANCE

**A+
220-701
2.5**

Preventive maintenance can prevent certain computer problems from occurring in the first place. The more preventive maintenance work you do initially, the fewer problems you are likely to have later, and the less troubleshooting and repair you will have to do.

If you are responsible for the PCs in an organization, make and implement a preventive maintenance plan to help prevent failures and reduce repair costs and downtime. In addition, you need a disaster recovery plan to manage failures when they occur. PC failures are caused by many different environmental and human factors, including heat, dust, magnetism, power supply problems, static electricity, human error (such as spilled liquids or an accidental change of setup and software configurations), and viruses. The goals of preventive maintenance are to reduce the likelihood that the events that cause PC failures will occur and to lessen the damage if they do.

This section focuses on what to do when a computer becomes your permanent responsibility and how to create a preventive maintenance plan. This chapter contains the complete lists of tasks; some of the tasks are discussed in detail in other chapters.

SET UP A METHOD OF DOCUMENTATION

When you first set up a new computer, start a record book about this computer, using either a file on disk or a notebook dedicated to this machine. In this notebook or file, record any changes in setup data as well as any problems you experience or maintenance that you do on this computer. Be diligent in keeping this notebook up to date, because it will be invaluable in diagnosing problems and upgrading equipment. Keep a printed or handwritten record of all changes to BIOS setup data and jumpers on the motherboard, and store the record with the hardware and software documentation.

If you are not the primary user of the computer, you might want to keep the hardware documentation separate from the computer itself. Label the documentation so that you can easily identify that it belongs to this computer. Keep this hardware documentation and your notes in a safe place. Some support people tape a large envelope inside the computer case; the envelope contains important documentation and records specific to that computer. On the other hand, if you're also responsible for software reference manuals, know that these manuals need to be kept in a location that is convenient for users.

> **Notes** If you are not using call-tracking software, you might want to keep a record of all troubleshooting you do on a computer in a word-processing document that lists all the problems you have encountered and the solutions you used. This will help save time when troubleshooting problems you have encountered before. Store the document file on a CD-RW, flash drive, or floppy disk that you keep with the computer's documentation. You might want to make a new printout each time the document changes. Don't store the document on the hard drive of the computer it applies to because it will not be available if the hard drive fails.

CREATE A PREVENTIVE MAINTENANCE PLAN

It is important to develop an overall preventive maintenance plan. If your company has established written guidelines for PC preventive maintenance, read them and follow the procedures necessary to make them work. If your company has no established plan, make your own.

A preventive maintenance plan tends to evolve from a history or pattern of malfunctions within an organization. For example, dusty environments can mean more maintenance, whereas a clean environment can mean less maintenance. Table 11-2 lists some guidelines for developing a preventive maintenance plan that might work for you.

> 💡 **A+ Exam Tip** The A+ 220–701 Essentials exam expects you to know how to clean internal and external components and use appropriate cleaning materials as part of a regular preventive maintenance plan.

Component	Maintenance
Computer	**Physically inspect the computer by doing the following:** ▲ Make sure the computer is in a proper environment. Problems to look for are listed earlier in the chapter. ▲ Check that air vents on the computer case or monitor are not blocked by papers, books, drapes, or other obstructions. ▲ Make sure the inside of the computer case is free from dust. Use an antistatic vacuum, blower, or can of compressed air to blow the dust out of the case and clean vents, power supply, and fans. ▲ Verify that chips and expansion cards are firmly seated. ▲ Check cables and cords for wear and tear. Look for trip hazards and correct them if necessary.
Keyboard	▲ Clean the keyboard. Unplug the keyboard and then blow or vacuum it out. To dislodge debris, turn the keyboard upside down and bump it. Use cleaning wipes to clean the surface.
Mouse	▲ Clean the mouse. To clean a wheel mouse, remove the cover of the mouse ball from the bottom of the mouse. The cover usually comes off

Table 11-2 Guidelines for developing a PC preventive maintenance plan

Component	Maintenance
	with a simple press and shift or turn motion. Clean the rollers with a cotton swab dipped in a very small amount of liquid soap. The sticky side of duct tape works well to clean the mouse ball.
Monitor	◢ Clean the screen with a lint-free cloth. You can also use special monitor wipes that are safe for CRT and LCD monitors.
Printers	◢ Using compressed air or a vacuum, clean out the dust and bits of paper. Small pieces of paper can be removed with tweezers, preferably insulated ones. ◢ Clean the paper path with a soft, lint-free cloth. ◢ Don't re-ink ribbons or use recharged toner cartridges. ◢ If the printer uses an ozone filter, replace it as recommended by the manufacturer. ◢ Replace other components as recommended by the manufacturer. You can purchase maintenance kits from the printer manufacturer, which include a scheduled maintenance plan for the printer. How to perform these scheduled maintenances is covered in Chapter 22.
UPS or surge protector	◢ Verify the system is protected against electrical surges by using a UPS or surge protector. ◢ Run a weak battery test on the UPS. ◢ Run a diagnostic test on the UPS as appropriate.
Backup of data	◢ If the computer is used to hold important data, verify data is being backed up on a regular basis and backup media is being kept in an offsite location. How to schedule backups is covered in Chapter 13.
Hard drive	◢ Rearrange noncontiguous parts of files (called defragmenting the drive), delete unneeded files, and check the drive for errors. How to do all this is covered in Chapter 13.
Clean up the start routine	◢ To keep Windows from starting slowly, reduce Windows startup programs to a minimum (covered in Chapters 13 and 14). ◢ Delete temporary files and check the hard drive for errors (covered in Chapter 13).
Drivers and firmware updates	◢ Update firmware or device drivers only if the device is giving problems (covered in Chapter 5).
Security	◢ Verify Windows has all updates and patches installed and that Windows is set to automatically download and install updates (covered in Chapter 12). ◢ Verify that antivirus software is installed, running, and updated (covered in Chapter 20). ◢ Verify that a personal firewall is configured and running on the computer (covered in Chapter 19).
Software	◢ If directed by your employer, check that only authorized software is present.
Written records	◢ Keep a record of all software, including version numbers and the OS installed on the PC. ◢ Keep a record of all hardware components installed, including hardware settings. ◢ Record when and what preventive maintenance is performed. ◢ Record any repairs done to the PC.

11

A+ 220-701

Table 11-2 Guidelines for developing a PC preventive maintenance plan (continued)

A+
220-701
2.5

📄 **Notes** In most situations, you don't need to back up installed applications. If the application gets corrupted, you can install it again using the setup CDs. It's extremely important that you have the original setup CDs handy when a hard drive fails—without these CDs, you won't be able to reinstall the software. Users that you support also need to understand that you cannot reinstall software installed on their systems if the software has been pirated and the CDs or DVDs are no longer available.

HOW TO TROUBLESHOOT A PC PROBLEM

A+
220-701
2.1

When a computer doesn't work and you're responsible for fixing it, you should generally approach the problem first as an investigator and discoverer, always being careful not to compound the problem through your own actions. If the problem seems difficult, see it as an opportunity to learn something new. Ask questions until you understand the source of the problem. Once you understand it, you're almost done, because most likely the solution will be evident. If you take the attitude that you can understand the problem and solve it, no matter how deeply you have to dig, you probably *will* solve it.

One systematic method to solve a problem used by most expert troubleshooters is the six steps diagramed in Figure 11-5. These steps are:

1. Interview the user and back up data before you make any changes to the system.

2. Examine the system, analyze the problem, and make an initial determination of what is the source of the problem.

3. Test your theory. If the theory is not confirmed, form another theory or escalate.

4. After you know the source of the problem, plan what to do to fix the problem and then fix it.

5. Verify the problem is fixed and that the system works. Take any preventive measures to make sure the problem doesn't happen again.

6. Document activities, outcomes, and what you learned.

Now let's examine the process step by step. As you learn about these six steps, you'll also learn about 15 rules useful when troubleshooting that are interspersed among the steps. Here's the first rule.

Rule 1: Approach the Problem Systematically

When trying to solve the problem, start at the beginning and walk through the situation in a thorough, careful way. This one rule is invaluable. Remember it and apply it every time. If you don't find the explanation to the problem after one systematic walkthrough, then repeat the entire process. Check and double-check to find the step you overlooked the first time. Most problems with computers are simple, such as a loose cable or circuit board. Computers are logical through and through. Whatever the problem is, it's also very logical. Also, if you are faced with more than one problem on the same computer, work on only one problem at a time. To try to solve multiple problems at the same time can get too confusing.

💡 **A+ Exam Tip** The A+ 220–701 Essentials exam expects you to know about all the aspects of troubleshooting theory and strategy and how to apply the troubleshooting procedures and techniques described in this section. At the front of the book, read over the A+ 220–701 Objective 2.1 and compare it to Figure 11-5.

A+
220-701
2.1

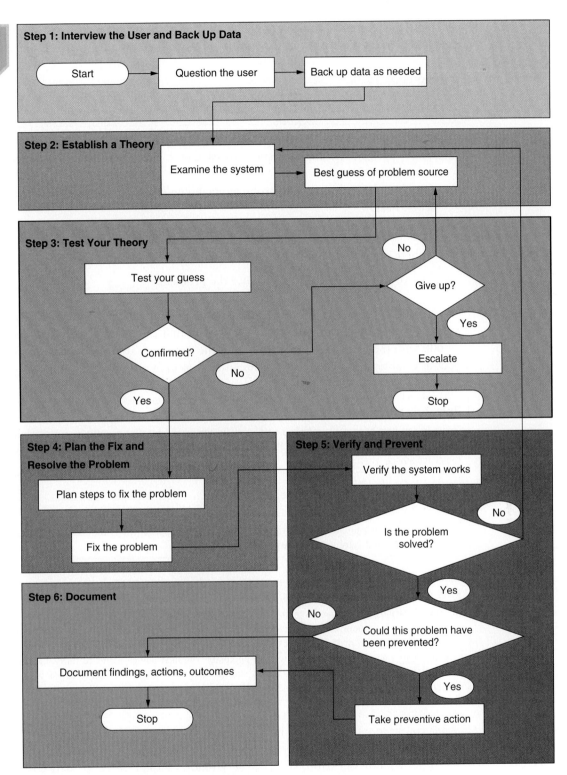

Figure 11-5 General approach to problem solving
Courtesy: Course Technology/Cengage Learning

11

A+ 220-701

STEP 1: INTERVIEW THE USER AND BACK UP DATA

Every troubleshooting situation begins with interviewing the user if he or she is available. Sometimes you might be presented with a PC to fix when all you have is a written description of the problem and you don't have the opportunity to talk with the user. However, if you can speak with the user, ask questions to help you identify the problem, how to reproduce it, and possible sources of the problem. Also ask about any data on the PC that is not backed up.

> **💡 A+ Exam Tip** The A+ 220-701 Essentials exam expects you to know how to interact with a user and know what questions to ask, given a troubleshooting scenario.

Chapter 3 lists several sample questions to ask a user. Here are the four most important ones:

1. Can you please describe the problem, including error messages, failures, and what you see or hear?

2. What changes have recently been made to the system?

3. Is there important data on the system that is not backed up?

4. Can you show me how to reproduce the problem?

Based on the answers you receive, ask more penetrating questions until you feel the user has given you all the information he or she knows that can help you solve the problem. As you talk with the user, don't forget to use all the communication skills that you learned about in Chapter 3. As you talk with the user, keep in mind rules 2, 3, and also 4.

Rule 2: Establish Your Priorities

This rule can help make for a satisfied customer. Decide what your first priority is. For example, it might be to recover lost data, or to get the PC back up and running as soon as possible. Ask the user or customer for advice when practical.

Rule 3: Beware of User Error

Remember that many problems stem from user error. If you suspect this is the case, ask the user to show you the problem and carefully watch what the user is doing.

Rule 4: Keep Your Cool and Don't Rush

In some situations, you might be tempted to act too quickly and to be drawn into the user's sense of emergency. But keep your cool and don't rush. For example, when a computer stops working, if unsaved data is still in memory or if data or software on the hard drive has not been backed up, look and think carefully before you leap! A wrong move can be costly. The best advice is not to hurry. Carefully plan your moves. Read the documentation if you're not sure what to do, and don't hesitate to ask for help. Don't simply try something, hoping it will work, unless you've run out of more intelligent alternatives!

After you have talked with the user, be sure to back up any important data that is not currently backed up before you begin work on the PC. If the PC is working well enough to boot to the Windows desktop, you can use Windows Explorer to copy data to a flash drive, another computer on the network, or other storage media.

> **💡 A+ Exam Tip** The A+ 220-701 Essentials exam expects you to know the importance of making backups before you make changes to a system.

If the computer is not healthy enough to use Windows Explorer, don't do anything to jeopardize the data. If you must take a risk with the data, let it be the user's decision to do so, not yours. Try to boot the system. If the system will not boot to the Windows desktop, recall from Chapter 8 that you can remove the hard drive from the system and use a PATA to USB converter or a SATA to USB converter to connect the drive to a USB port on another computer. You can then copy the data to the other computer. Next, return the hard drive to the original computer so you can begin troubleshooting the problem.

If possible, have the user verify that all important data is safely backed up before you continue to the next troubleshooting step. If you're new to troubleshooting and don't want the user looking over your shoulder while you work, you might want to let him or her know you'd prefer to work alone. You can say something like, "Okay, I think I have everything I need to get started. I'll let you know if I have another question."

STEP 2: EXAMINE THE SYSTEM AND MAKE YOUR BEST GUESS

You're now ready to start solving the problem. Rules 5 and 6 can help.

Rule 5: Make No Assumptions

This rule is the hardest to follow, because there is a tendency to trust anything in writing and assume that people are telling you exactly what happened. But documentation is sometimes wrong, and people don't always describe events as they occurred, so do your own investigating. For example, if the user tells you that the system boots up with no error messages, but that the software still doesn't work, boot for yourself. You never know what the user might have overlooked.

Rule 6: Try the Simple Things First

Most problems are so simple that we overlook them because we expect the problem to be difficult. Don't let the complexity of computers fool you. Most problems are easy to fix. Really, they are! To save time, check the simple things first, such as whether a power switch is not turned on or a cable is loose. Generally, it's easy to check for a hardware problem before you check for a software problem. For example, if a USB drive is not working, verify the drive works on another computer before verifying the drivers are installed correctly.

Follow these steps to form your best guess (best theory) and test it:

1. *Reproduce the problem and observe for yourself what the user has described.* For example, if the user tells you the system is totally dead, find out for yourself. Plug in the power and turn on the system. Listen for fans and look for lights and error messages. As another example, suppose the user tells you that Internet Explorer will not open. Try opening it yourself to see what error messages might appear. As you investigate the system, refrain from making changes until you've come up with your theory as to what the source of the problem is. Can you duplicate the problem? Intermittent problems are generally more difficult to solve than problems that occur consistently.

2. *Decide if the problem is hardware or software related.* Sometimes you might not be sure, but make your best guess. For example, if the system fails before Windows starts to load, chances are the problem is a hardware problem. If the user tells you the system has not worked since the lightning storm the night before, chances are the problem is electrical. If the problem is that Windows Explorer will not open even though the Windows desktop loads, you can assume the problem is software related. In another example, suppose a user complains that his Word documents are getting corrupted. Possible sources of the problem might be that the user does not know how to

A+
220-701
2.1

save documents properly, the software or the OS might be corrupted, the PC might have a virus, or the hard drive might be intermittently failing. Investigate for yourself and then decide if the problem is caused by software, hardware, or the user.

3. *Make your best guess as to the source of the problem.* Here are some practical examples of what a best guess might be, keeping in mind the rule to check the simple things first:

◢ The video does not work. Your best guess is the monitor cables are loose or the monitor is not turned on.

◢ Spreadsheets are getting corrupted. Your best guess is the user is not saving the documents correctly.

◢ The DVD drive is not reading a DVD. Your best guess is the DVD is scratched.

◢ The system refuses to boot and gives the error that the hard drive is not found. Your best guess is internal cables to the drive are loose.

If you're having a problem deciding what might be the source of the problem, try searching these resources for ideas and tips:

◢ User manuals and installation manuals for a device or software often list symptoms of problems with possible solutions and troubleshooting tips.

◢ Use a search engine to search the Internet for help. Use, in your search string, an error message, symptom, hardware device, or description of the problem. For the most reliable information about a hardware device or application, see the Web site of the manufacturer (see Figure 11-6). These sites might offer troubleshooting and support pages,

Figure 11-6   Search manufacturer Web sites for help with a hardware or software product
Courtesy: Course Technology/Cengage Learning

help forums, chat sessions, and e-mail support. For Windows problems, the best Web sites to search are *technet.microsoft.com* or *support.microsoft.com*.

▲ Training materials, technical books, reference manuals, and textbooks like this one can all be good sources of help.

> **Notes** To limit your search to a particular site when using *www.google.com*, use the site parameter in the search box. For example, to search only the Microsoft site for information about the defrag command, enter this search string: **defrag site:microsoft.com**.

APPLYING CONCEPTS

Possibly the most powerful strategy in this entire chapter for troubleshooting is to use a search engine to find insights and solutions on the Internet. The chances are always good that someone has had exactly the same problem, presented the problem on some forum on the Internet, and someone else has presented a step-by-step solution. All you have to do is find it! As you practice this type of Web research, you'll get better and better at knowing how to form a search string and which Web sites are trustworthy and present the best information. If your first searches don't work, please don't give up! It might take patient searching for 15 or 20 minutes to find the solution you need. As you search, most likely you will learn more and more about the problem. But sometimes too much information can overwhelm you. Here are a few tips to narrow down an Internet search and zero in on the solution:

1. Go to *www.google.com* and click **Advanced Search**. In the Advanced Search window, shown in Figure 11-7, click **Date, usage rights, numeric range, and more**. Under Date, select past 24 hours, past week, past month, or past year.

2. To limit your search to only one site, include the site parameter in your Google search string. For example, to limit your search to the ASUS site when searching for Vista drivers for your P5AD2 motherboard, use this search string: **asus P5AD2 Vista drivers site:asus.com**. It's best to not include the www in the site name so that addresses such as support.asus.com will be used.

3. Limit your search results by adding more detail to your search string. For example, instead of searching on "driver Asus motherboard" search on "Vista audio driver Asus P5AD2 motherboard."

4. Speaking of drivers for a motherboard, consider the audio drivers might not come from ASUS, the board manufacturer. Don't forget to check the Web site of the chipset manufacturer (Intel at *www.intel.com*) or the audio controller manufacturer (C-Media at *www.cmedia.com.tw*). If you don't know who these manufacturers are, you can find that information on the Internet. For example, a search on "audio controller Asus P5AD2" will tell you that the audio controller for this board was built by C-Media.

So now let's practice. Suppose you have used Disk Management in Windows XP to configure a hard drive as a dynamic disk. But now you need to upgrade to Windows Vista Home Premium, which does not support dynamic disks. Is there a way to convert a dynamic disk to a basic disk without losing all the data on the disk? Search the Internet for the step-by-step solution to do this. What was the search string you used that led you to the solution? On what Web site did you find the solution?

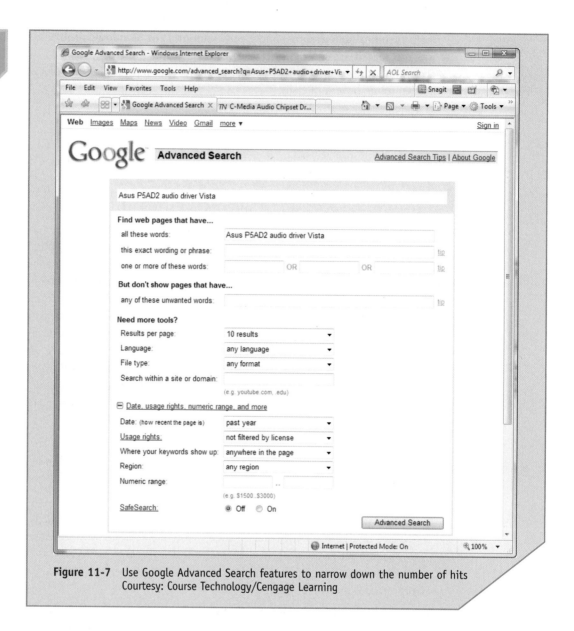

Figure 11-7   Use Google Advanced Search features to narrow down the number of hits
Courtesy: Course Technology/Cengage Learning

STEP 3: TEST YOUR THEORY

For simple problems, you can zip right through Steps 3, 4, and 5 in Figure 11-5 quickly. Here are two examples where Steps 3, 4, and 5 go very fast:

▲ The video does not work and you suspect loose cables or the monitor is not turned on. You check the video cable connection (Step 3) and discover it's loose. As you connect it (Step 4), the video display works. Problem solved. So now you take the time to screw the video cable to the connection (Step 5) so the problem won't happen again.

▲ Spreadsheets are getting corrupted. As you watch the user save a file, you discover he is saving files in a wrong format that other software in the office cannot read (Step 3). You step the user through saving the file correctly and then verify that others can open the file (Step 4). You explain to the user which format to use (Step 5). The problem then is solved, and it's not likely to happen again.

Here are two examples of Step 3 which include testing a guess that is not correct:

▲ The CD drive won't read a CD and you suspect the CD is scratched. When you check the disc, it looks fine. Your next guess is the CD drive is not recognized by Windows. You check Device Manager, and it reports errors with the drive. Your next guess is that drivers are corrupted.

▲ The system refuses to boot and gives the error message that the hard drive is not found. Internal cable connections are solid. Your next guess is the power supply is not supplying power to the drive.

Here are two examples of Step 3 where your guess is correct and then you move on toward Step 4 to plan a solution:

▲ Word files are getting corrupted. After eliminating several simple causes, you guess that the hard drive is going bad. You check Event Viewer, a Windows utility that reports errors with hardware devices, and discover Windows has recorded write errors to the drive multiple times (Step 3). Your theory is confirmed that the drive is bad and needs replacing (Step 4).

▲ Video does not work. You check cables and power and verify monitor settings controlled by buttons on the front of the monitor are all okay, but still no video. You guess the video cable might be bad and exchange it with one you know is good, but still no video. Therefore, you guess that the monitor is bad. You move the monitor to a working PC and it still does not work. You try a good monitor on the first PC and it works fine. Your guess that the monitor is bad has been confirmed (Step 3). Next, you plan how to purchase a new monitor (Step 4).

As you test your guesses, keep in mind rules 7 through 13.

Rule 7: Trade Known Good for Suspected Bad

When diagnosing hardware problems, this method works well if you can draw from a group of parts that you know work correctly. Suppose, for example, video does not work. The parts of the video subsystem are the video card, the power cord to the monitor, the cord from the monitor to the PC case, and the monitor itself. Also, don't forget that the video card is inserted into an expansion slot on the motherboard, and the monitor depends on electrical power. As you suspect each of these five components to be bad, you can try them one at a time beginning with the easiest one to replace: the monitor. Trade the monitor for one that you know works. If this theory fails, trade the power cord, trade the cord to the PC video port, move the video card to a new slot, and trade the video card.

When you're trading a good component for a suspected bad one, work methodically by eliminating one component at a time. Don't trade the video card and the monitor and then turn on the PC to determine if they work. It's possible that both the card and the monitor are bad, but assume that only one component is bad before you consider whether multiple components need trading.

In this situation, suppose you keep trading components in the video subsystem until you have no more variations. Next, take the entire subsystem—video card, cords, and monitor—to a PC that you know works, and plug each of them in. If they work, you have isolated the problem to the PC, not the video. Now turn your attention back to the PC: the motherboard, the software settings within the OS, the video driver, and other devices. Knowing that the video subsystem works on the good PC gives you a valuable tool. Compare the video driver on the good PC to the one on the bad PC. Make certain the BIOS settings, software settings, and other settings are the same.

A+
220-701
2.1

Rule 8: Trade Suspected Bad for Known Good

An alternate approach works well in certain situations. If you have a working PC that is configured similarly to the one you are troubleshooting (a common situation in many corporate or educational environments), rather than trading good for suspected bad, you can trade suspected bad for good. Take each component that you suspect is bad and install it in the working PC. If the component works on the good PC, then you have eliminated it as a suspect. If the working PC breaks down, then you have probably identified the bad component.

Rule 9: Divide and Conquer

This rule is the most powerful. Isolate the problem. In the overall system, remove one hardware or software component after another, until the problem is isolated to a small part of the whole system. As you divide a large problem into smaller components, you can analyze each component separately. You can use one or more of the following to help you divide and conquer on your own system:

◢ In Windows, stop all nonessential services running in the background to eliminate them as the problem.
◢ Boot from a bootable CD or DVD to eliminate the OS and startup files on the hard drive as the problem.

Remove any unnecessary hardware devices, such as a scanner card, internal modem, CD drive, and even the hard drive. Once down to the essentials, start exchanging components you know are good for those you suspect are bad, until the problem goes away. You don't need to physically remove the CD drive or hard drive from the bays inside the case. Simply disconnect the data cable and the power cable. Remember that the problem might be a resource conflict. If the network card worked well until the CD drive was reconnected and now neither works, try the CD drive without the network card. If the CD drive works, you most likely have a resource conflict.

Rule 10: Become a Researcher

Following this rule is the most fun. When a computer problem arises that you can't easily solve, be as tenacious as a bulldog. Search the Internet, ask questions, then read more, make some phone calls, and ask more questions. Take advantage of every available resource, including online help, the Internet, documentation, technical support, and books such as this one. Learn to perform advanced searches using a good search engine on the Web, such as *www.google.com*. What you learn will be yours to take to the next problem. This is the real joy of computer troubleshooting. If you're good at it, you're always learning something new.

Rule 11: Write Things Down

Keep good notes as you're working. They'll help you think more clearly. Draw diagrams. Make lists. Clearly and precisely write down what you're learning. If you need to leave the problem and return to it later, it's difficult to remember what you have observed and already tried. When the problem gets cold like this, your notes will be invaluable.

Rule 12: Don't Assume the Worst

When it's an emergency and your only copy of data is on a hard drive that is not working, don't assume that the data is lost. Much can be done to recover data. If you want to recover lost data on a hard drive, don't write anything to the drive; you might write on top of lost data, eliminating all chances of recovery.

Rule 13: Reboot and Start Over

This is an important rule. Fresh starts are good, and they uncover events or steps that might have been overlooked. Take a break! Get away from the problem. Begin again.

By the time you have finished Step 3, the problem will have been solved or you will know the source of the problem and will be ready to plan a solution.

STEP 4: PLAN YOUR SOLUTION AND THEN FIX THE PROBLEM

Some solutions, such as replacing a hard drive or a motherboard, are expensive and time consuming. You need to carefully consider what you will do and the order you will do it. When planning and implementing your solution, keep rules 14 and 15 in mind.

Rule 14: Use the Least Invasive Solution First

As you solve computer problems, always keep in mind that you don't want to make things worse, so you should use the least invasive solution. Keep in mind that you want to fix the problem in such a way that the system is returned to normal working condition with the least amount of effort. For example, don't format the hard drive until you've first tried to fix the problem without having to erase everything on the drive.

Rule 15: Know Your Starting Point

Find out what works and doesn't work before you take anything apart or try some possible fix. Suppose you decide the power supply is bad and exchange it. After you make the exchange, you discover the CD-ROM drive doesn't work. You don't know if you broke the drive while working on the system or it was already broken before you started. As much as possible, find out what works or what doesn't work before you attempt a fix. For example, you can reboot the computer and read a file from CD or use an application to print a file on the network.

Do the following to plan your solution and fix the problem:

1. Consider different solutions, and select the least invasive one. In other words, choose the solution that fixes the problem by making as few changes to the system as possible. Some solutions are obvious, such as replacing a bad monitor, but others might not be so obvious. For example, if Windows is corrupted and your options are to reinstall Windows or repair it, it's better to repair it so there's less work to do to restore the system to good working order and to return it to the configuration the user had before the problem occurred.

2. If hardware needs replacing, follow guidelines given in other chapters to select a replacement part that is compatible with your system.

3. Before installing the new part, as best you can, determine what works and doesn't work about the system so you know your starting point.

4. Install the new part. This might be as simple as plugging up a new monitor. Or it might be as difficult as replacing a hard drive, reinstalling Windows and applications software, and restoring data from backups.

STEP 5: VERIFY THE FIX AND TAKE PREVENTIVE ACTION

After you have implemented your solution, reboot the system and verify all is well. Can you reach the Internet, use the printer, or burn a CD? If possible, have the user check everything and verify that the job is done satisfactorily. If either of you find a problem, return to Step 2 in the troubleshooting process to reexamine the system and form a new theory as to the cause of the problem.

After you and the user have verified all is working, ask yourself the question, "Could this problem have been prevented?" If so, go the extra mile to instruct the user, install a surge protector, or whatever else is appropriate to prevent future problems.

A+
220-701
2.1
2.2

STEP 6: DOCUMENT WHAT HAPPENED

Good documentation helps you take what you learned into the next troubleshooting situation, train others, develop effective preventive maintenance plans, and satisfy any audits or customer or employer queries about your work. Be sure to write down the initial symptoms, the source of the problem, and what you did to fix it. Figure 11-8 shows a Service Call Report Form that might be used in a small computer repair center.

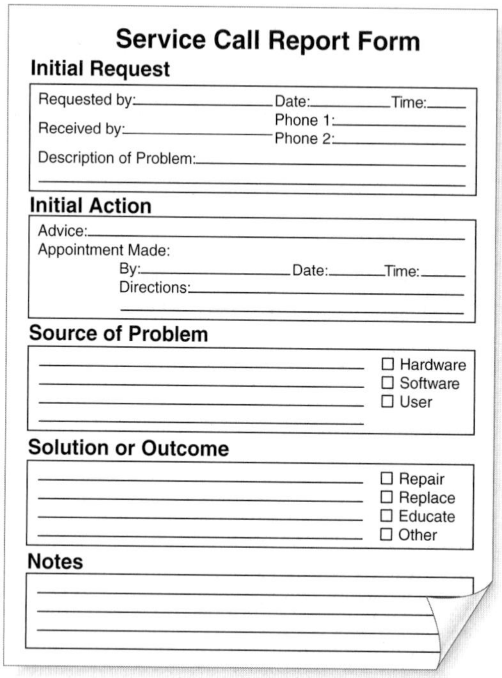

Service Call Report Form

Initial Request

Requested by:________ Date:______ Time:______
Received by:________ Phone 1:______
Phone 2:______
Description of Problem:________

Initial Action

Advice:________
Appointment Made:
By:________ Date:______ Time:______
Directions:________

Source of Problem

☐ Hardware
☐ Software
☐ User

Solution or Outcome

☐ Repair
☐ Replace
☐ Educate
☐ Other

Notes

Figure 11-8 Service call report form
Courtesy: Course Technology/Cengage Learning

APPLYING CONCEPTS

Intermittent problems can make troubleshooting challenging. The trick in diagnosing problems that come and go is to look for patterns or clues as to when the problems occur. If you or the user can't reproduce the problem at will, ask the user to keep a log of when the problems occur and exactly what messages appear. Tell the user that intermittent problems are the hardest to solve and might take some time, but that you won't give up. Show the user how to get a printed screen of the error messages when they appear. Here's one method to print a screen shot:

1. Press the **Print Screen** key to copy the displayed screen to the Windows Clipboard.
2. Launch the Paint software accessory program and paste the contents of the Clipboard into the document. You might need to use the Zoom Out command on the document first. You can then print the document with the displayed screen, using Paint. You can also paste the contents of the Clipboard into a document created by a word-processing application such as Word.

>> CHAPTER SUMMARY

▲ A Material Safety Data Sheet (MSDS) tells you how to deal with accidents that happen with chemicals.

▲ Avoid trip hazards by moving cables out of the way or installing protective covers over the cables.

▲ Dispose of used computer equipment, batteries, and printer cartridges according to guidelines in your county. Discharge a CRT monitor before disposing of it.

▲ Destroy storage devices such as hard drives or CDs before throwing them in the trash so that sensitive data cannot be stolen off the device.

▲ Never ship a PC when the only copy of important data is on its hard drive.

▲ The buyer of software does not legally own the software or have the right to distribute it. According to the Federal Copyright Act of 1976, you have the right to make one backup copy of software.

▲ When a PC is your permanent responsibility, keep good backups of data and system files, document all setup changes, problems, and solutions, and take precautions to protect the system against viruses and other attacks.

▲ The goals of preventive maintenance are to make PCs last longer and work better, protect data and software, and reduce repair costs.

▲ A PC preventive maintenance plan includes blowing dust from the inside of the computer case, keeping a record of setup data, backing up the hard drive, and cleaning the mouse, monitor, and keyboard.

▲ Protecting software and hardware documentation is an important preventive maintenance chore.

▲ The six steps in the troubleshooting process are as follows: 1. Interview the user and back up data, 2. Examine the system and form a theory of probable cause, 3. Test your theory, 4. Plan a solution and implement it, 5. Verify all works and take appropriate preventive measures, and 6. Document what happened and the outcome.

11

>> KEY TERMS

For explanations of key terms, see the Glossary near the end of the book.

copyright	license	site license
hard-disk loading	Material Safety Data Sheet (MSDS)	trip hazard

>> REVIEWING THE BASICS

1. If you spill a cleaning solution on your clothes and hands, what is the best way to find out how to deal with the spill?

2. What is the term used to describe a network cable lying loose in a high-traffic area?

3. When lifting a heavy object, should you bend your back over the object or stoop down to the object, keeping your back straight?

4. Why should a tower case not sit on thick carpet?

5. What can you do to protect a keyboard that is used in an extremely dusty area?

6. Why is it not a good practice to unpack computer parts immediately after they have been delivered on a cold day?

7. Why is it not a good idea to throw used batteries in the trash?

8. What is the best way to get rid of laser printer toner cartridges?

9. What should you do to a failed hard drive that was used in the Accounting Department before you put the drive in the trash?

10. When shipping a computer, why is it not a good idea to ship backups of the system in the same package with the computer?

11. Which law defines software copyright infringement?

12. What is the difference between a license to use software and a site license to use software?

13. Why is it not a good idea to buy software that is on CDs with handwritten labels?

14. What are the six steps used by troubleshooters to solve PC problems?

15. When solving a PC problem, why is it important to use the least obstructive solution first?

>> THINKING CRITICALLY

1. If computers in your office are your responsibility, what should you do when you visit a user's desk and discover a network cable running across the room?

   a. Ask the user to please not leave cables on the floor where someone can trip.

   b. Ask the user permission to move the cable.

   c. Move the cable so it is not a trip hazard.

   d. Put a sign up to tell people to watch for the cable.

2. As a help-desk technician, list some good detective questions to ask if the user calls to say, "My PC won't boot."

3. Someone calls saying he has attempted to install a new monitor, but the monitor does not work. List some questions you would ask.

>> HANDS-ON PROJECTS

PROJECT 11-1: Safely Clean Computer Equipment

Following guidelines in the chapter, practice some preventive maintenance tasks by following these steps to clean a computer:

1. Shut down the computer and unplug it. Press the power button to drain power.

2. Clean the keyboard, monitor, and mouse. For a wheel mouse, remove the ball and clean the wheels.

3. Clean the outside of the computer case.

4. Open the case and using a ground bracelet, clean the dust from the case. Make sure all fans move freely.

5. Verify the cables are out of the way of airflow. Use cable ties as necessary.

6. Check that each expansion card and memory module is securely seated in its slot.

7. Power up the system and make sure all is working.

8. Clean up around your work area. If you left dust on the floor as you blew it out of the computer case, be sure to clean it up.

PROJECT 11-2:   Developing Help-Desk Skills

Pair up with a second person in your class or lab environment. Then, without either of you watching, have a third person in your class or lab environment create an error on a computer so that the computer does not boot properly. Now, have your partner sit at the computer and play the role of an inexperienced user who tries to start up the system and receives an error he does not know how to handle. You will sit with your back to the partner/user and you cannot see the computer. In this setup, troubleshoot the problem and talk the user through to a solution. While doing so, abide by these rules:

1. You can't turn around to look at the screen or the computer.

2. You have to practice professional mannerisms and speech.

3. As you work, you have to keep a log of the "phone call to the help desk," recording in the log the major steps toward diagnosing and correcting the problem.

When the problem is resolved, have the third person create a different problem that causes the PC not to boot correctly, and exchange roles with your partner.

PROJECT 11-3:   Researching Disposal Rules

Research the laws and regulations in your community concerning the disposal of batteries and old computer parts. Answer these questions regarding your community:

1. How do you properly dispose of a monitor?

2. How do you properly dispose of a battery pack used by a notebook computer?

3. How do you properly dispose of a large box of assorted computer parts, including hard drives, floppy drives, computer cases, and circuit boards?

PROJECT 11-4:   Researching PC Support

The Internet is an excellent resource to use when problem solving, and it's helpful to know which Web sites are trustworthy and useful. Access each of the Web sites listed in Table 11-3, and print one Web page from each site that shows information that might be useful for a support technician. If the site offers a free e-mail newsletter, consider subscribing to it.

11

Organization	Web Site
CNET, Inc.	*www.cnet.com*
Experts Exchange (subscription site)	*www.experts-exchange.com*
F-Secure Corp	*www.f-secure.com*
How Stuff Works	*www.howstuffworks.com*
Kingston Technology (information about memory)	*www.kingston.com*
Michael Karbo	*www.karbosguide.com*
Microsoft Technical Resources	*support.microsoft.com*
PC Today Online	*www.pctoday.com*
PC World	*www.pcworld.com*
Tom's Hardware Guide	*www.tomshardware.com*
WebMediaBrands	*www.webopedia.com*
ZDNet (publishes several technical magazines)	*www.zdnet.com*

Table 11-3   Web sites of technical information

>> REAL PROBLEMS, REAL SOLUTIONS

REAL PROBLEM 11-1: Troubleshooting PC Problems for Friends and Family

You have learned much about PC troubleshooting and repair already in this book. Now it's time to try your hand at some real-life troubleshooting. Make yourself available to family and friends to help them with their computer problems. For the first three problems you tackle, keep notes that describe the initial problem, what you did to solve it or to escalate it to others, and the outcome. Then answer the following questions:

1. List what you learned about technology from these three problems.

2. List what you learned about working with people when helping them with these three problems.

3. What one thing will you do differently when faced with similar problems?

4. What is something that you recognize you need to know, that you don't yet know, about PC troubleshooting that would have helped you with these three problems?

Installing Windows

Windows Vista, XP, and 2000 all share the same basic Windows architecture, and they all have similar characteristics. Windows Vista and Windows XP are both available for purchase, but you can no longer purchase Windows 2000. However, because many individual users and corporations still rely on Windows 2000, you need to know how to support it. At the time this book went to print, Windows 7 is available in the Release Candidate version (Windows 7 RC). The Release Candidate version of an operating system is the last beta version released before retail versions become available. How to install and support Windows 7 is not covered in this book.

This chapter discusses how to plan a Windows Vista, XP, and 2000 installation and the steps to perform each installation, including what to do after the OS is installed.

> **Notes** This book does not cover DOS or Windows 9x. However, you can learn about both operating systems by studying the content on the CD that accompanies this book. See the content "Windows 9x/Me Commands and Startup Disk" and "Supporting Windows 9x/Me."

> **A+ Exam Tip** The content in this chapter applies only to the A+ 220-701 Essentials exam.

HOW TO PLAN A WINDOWS INSTALLATION

A+
220-701
3.1

As a PC support technician, you can expect to be faced with installing Windows in a variety of situations. You might need to install Windows on a new hard drive, after an existing Windows installation has become corrupted, or to upgrade from one OS to another. Many decisions need to be made before and during the installation. Which OS version do you purchase? Does the hardware qualify for this version? Which method do you use to start the installation, and what decisions will you need to make after the installation has begun? Answers to all these questions are covered in this part of the chapter.

CHOOSE THE VERSION OF WINDOWS

When deciding which operating system to buy, know that the Windows operating system can be purchased as a retail version or OEM (Original Equipment Manufacturer) version (see Figure 12-1). The OEM version costs less than the retail version, but can only be installed on a new PC for resale.

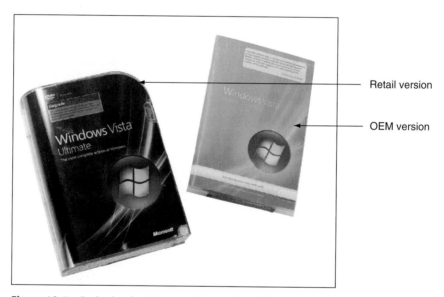

Retail version

OEM version

Figure 12-1 Packaging for Windows Vista retail and OEM versions
Courtesy: Course Technology/Cengage Learning

Now let's look at the different editions of Windows Vista and XP, the upgrade paths for each OS, and the minimum hardware requirements of each.

EDITIONS OF VISTA

Microsoft has released several editions of Vista designed to satisfy a variety of consumer needs. All the editions are included on the Windows Vista setup DVD; the edition installed depends on the product key that you enter during the installation. Therefore, upgrading to a better edition of Vista can easily be accomplished by using the Windows Anytime Upgrade feature. Here are the Vista editions:

▲ **Windows Vista Starter** has the most limited features and is intended to be used in developing nations. Microsoft reports that more than 139 nations, including Brazil, Thailand, and India, have benefited from Vista Starter.

A+
220-701
3.1

- Windows Vista Home Basic is similar to Windows XP Home Edition, and is designed for low-cost home systems that don't require full security and networking features.
- Windows Vista Home Premium is similar to Windows Vista Home Basic, but includes additional features such as the Aero user interface.
- Windows Vista Business is intended for business users. Computers can join a domain, support Group Policy, and use the Encrypted File System for better security. You can also purchase multiple site licenses (also called volume licensing) using this version. Consumer features not included in Windows Vista Business or Windows Vista Enterprise include Windows Media Center, Movie Maker, DVD Maker, and parental controls.
- Windows Vista Enterprise includes additional features over Windows Vista Business. The major additional security feature is BitLocker, which is useful to secure data stored on a hard drive if the drive is stolen. Multiple site licensing is available.
- Windows Vista Ultimate includes every Windows Vista feature. You cannot purchase multiple licensing with this edition.

The major features for all editions are listed in Table 12-1.

Feature	Starter	Home Basic	Home Premium	Business	Enterprise	Ultimate
Aero user interface			X	X	X	X
BitLocker hard drive encryption					X	X
Optional dual processors*				X	X	X
Complete PC backup				X	X	X
Encrypting File System (EFS)				X	X	X
IE parental controls	X	X	X			X
Network and Sharing Center	X	X	X	X	X	X
Scheduled and network backups			X	X	X	X
Tablet PC			X	X	X	X
Windows DVD Maker			X			X
Windows Media Center			X			X
Windows Movie Maker			X			X
Windows SideShow			X	X	X	X
Shadow Copy backup				X	X	X
Join a domain				X	X	X
Group Policy				X	X	X
Processor: 32-bit or 64-bit		X	X	X	X	X
Flip 3D display			X	X	X	X
Remote Desktop				X	X	X
Windows Meeting Space			X	X	X	X

*Multicore processors are allowed for all editions.

Table 12-1 Vista editions and their features

12

A+ 220-701

A+
220-701
3.1

WINDOWS XP EDITIONS

Windows XP comes in several editions: Windows XP Professional, Windows XP Home Edition, Windows XP Media Center Edition, Windows XP Tablet PC Edition, and Windows XP Professional x64 Edition (formally called Windows XP 64-Bit Edition), which uses 64-bit code.

Windows XP Professional offers these features (note that these features are not included with Windows XP Home Edition):

▲ A way for a user to control the computer from a remote location, called Remote Desktop
▲ A way for an administrator to manage user profiles from a server (roaming profiles)
▲ Additional security features
▲ Multilingual capabilities
▲ Support for higher-performance processors

Windows XP Media Center Edition is an enhanced edition of Windows XP Professional, and includes additional support for digital entertainment hardware such as video recording integrated with TV input. Windows XP Tablet PC Edition is designed for laptops and tablet PCs.

> **Notes** Windows XP was the first Microsoft OS to embed Windows Internet Explorer, Windows Media Player, a Windows firewall, and other Microsoft products into the OS. Some users see this as a disadvantage, and others see it as an advantage. Tight integration allows applications to interact easily with other applications and the OS, but makes it more difficult for third-party software to compete with Microsoft applications, and more difficult to remove or reinstall an integrated component that is giving problems.

32-BIT OR 64-BIT VERSIONS

Recall from Chapter 2 that an OS is built using either 32-bit or 64-bit code. Use a 64-bit OS if you need increased performance and your system has enough resources to support a 64-bit OS. For Windows Vista, you can purchase an OEM version of the OS in either a 32-bit or 64-bit version. Windows Vista Ultimate retail edition comes with two DVDs: one 32-bit DVD and one 64-bit DVD (see Figure 12-2). Microsoft does not offer 64-bit

32-bit DVD

64-bit DVD

Figure 12-2 Windows Vista Ultimate can be purchased only as a single license version and comes with two DVDs
Courtesy: Course Technology/Cengage Learning

versions for other Vista retail editions. For these editions, you must purchase the 32-bit OS and use the coupon inside the box to order the 64-bit DVD from Microsoft. Windows XP Professional x64 Edition is the only edition of XP that uses 64-bit code. One reason to use a 64-bit OS is the ability to install more RAM. Table 12-2 shows how much memory each OS can support.

Operating System	32-Bit Version	64-Bit Version
Vista Ultimate	4 GB	128 GB
Vista Enterprise	4 GB	128 GB
Vista Business	4 GB	128 GB
Vista Home Premium	4 GB	16 GB
Vista Home Basic	4 GB	8 GB
Vista Starter	1 GB	NA
XP Professional	4 GB	128 GB
XP Home Edition	4 GB	NA

Table 12-2 Maximum memory supported by Windows editions

UPGRADE PATHS FOR EACH OS

All the retail editions of Windows can be purchased as an upgrade or for a clean install. The upgrade license costs considerably less than the clean install license. However, even if you purchase an upgrade license of Windows, you still might be required to perform a clean install due to the fact that some features from the old OS might not be compatible with or carry forward to the new OS. When you purchase the upgrade version of Windows, note that regardless of the path that you use—the upgrade or the clean install—Windows setup will verify whether the system is qualified to use the upgrade license.

> **Note**   If Service Pack 2 or a later service pack is applied to Windows XP, you can use **Windows Easy Transfer** to transfer Windows XP user data and preferences to Windows Vista.

Upgrade options from old OSs to Vista are outlined in Table 12-3. To see an example of a forced "clean install," examine the Windows XP Professional to Windows Vista Home Premium path. The clean install is necessary because Windows XP Professional has features that are not offered by Windows Vista Home Premium. The upgrade path from Windows 2000 to Vista is another example. The clean install is necessary because the Vista setup program does not handle an upgrade from Windows 2000.

> **A+ Exam Tip**   The A+ 220-701 Essentials exam expects you to know the upgrade paths available to Windows Vista/XP/2000.

> **Note**   You cannot upgrade from Windows 95/98/Me or Windows NT to Windows Vista; you must purchase the more expensive for-a-new-PC version of Vista for these installations.

A+
220-701
3.1

From This OS	To Vista Home Basic, 32-Bit	To Vista Home Premium, 32-Bit	To Vista Business, 32-Bit	To Vista Ultimate, 32-Bit	To Any 64-Bit Vista Edition
Vista Home, 64-bit	N/A	Clean install	Clean install	Clean install	Upgrade
XP Professional	Clean install	Clean install	Upgrade	Upgrade	Clean install
XP Home	Upgrade	Upgrade	Upgrade	Upgrade	Clean install
XP Media Center	Clean install	Upgrade	Clean install	Upgrade	Clean install
XP Tablet PC	Clean install	Clean install	Upgrade	Upgrade	Clean install
XP x64	Clean install	Clean install	Clean install	Clean install	Clean install
Windows 2000	Clean install	Clean install	Clean install	Clean install	Clean install

Table 12-3 Upgrade paths to Windows Vista

The upgrade paths to Windows XP are listed in Table 12-4.

From This OS	To XP Home Edition	To XP Professional	To XP x64
Windows 98/Me	Upgrade	Upgrade	Clean install
Windows 95	Clean install	Clean install	Clean install
Windows 2000	Clean install	Upgrade	Clean install
Windows NT	Clean install	Upgrade	Clean install
XP Home Edition	NA	Upgrade	Clean install

Table 12-4 Upgrade paths to Windows XP

> **Note** All editions of Windows 9x/Me and Windows NT Workstation 3.51 and higher can be upgraded to Windows 2000.

A+
220-701
3.1
3.3

MINIMUM HARDWARE REQUIREMENTS

Here are the minimum hardware requirements for Windows Vista. However, as you consider this list, please note that with the limited memory and video listed in the second and third bullets, you won't be able to see the Aero user interface. Also, know that Vista comes on a single DVD. If your computer has a CD drive, you can order the multiple set of Vista CDs from Microsoft after you have purchased the Vista DVD. Also know that Microsoft occasionally changes the minimum and recommended requirements for an OS.

- ◢ A processor rated at least 800 MHz
- ◢ 512 MB of RAM
- ◢ SVGA video
- ◢ A 20 GB hard drive with at least 15 GB free space
- ◢ A CD-ROM drive

A+
220-701
3.1
3.3

> **Note** For best performance, a Vista system needs 2 GB of RAM or more. Also, Vista is most often sold in retail stores on DVD, so having a DVD drive makes your installation easier.

Recommended hardware requirements for Windows Vista Home Premium, Business, Enterprise, and Ultimate editions are:

- A processor rated at least 1 GHz, which can be a 32-bit or 64-bit processor
- 1 GB of RAM
- A video card or embedded video chip that supports DirectX 9 or higher and the Windows Display Driver Model (WDDM)
- 128 MB of graphics memory
- A 40 GB hard drive with at least 15 GB free space
- A DVD-ROM drive
- Internet access

Recommended requirements for Vista Home Basic are:

- A processor rated at least 800 MHz, which can be a 32-bit or 64-bit processor
- 512 MB of RAM
- A video card or embedded video chip that supports DirectX 9 or higher
- 32 MB of graphics memory
- A 20 GB hard drive with at least 15 GB free space
- A DVD-ROM drive
- Internet access

Table 12-5 lists the minimum and recommended requirements for Windows XP. For Windows 2000, you must have at least 650 MB of free space on your hard drive, at least 64 MB of RAM, and a 133-MHz Pentium-compatible CPU or higher.

Component or Device	Minimum Requirement	Recommended Requirement
One or two CPUs	Pentium II 233 MHz or better	Pentium II 300 MHz or better
RAM	64 MB	128 MB up to 4 GB
Hard drive partition	2 GB	More than 2 GB
Free space on the hard drive partition	1.5 GB (bare bones)	2 GB or more
CD-ROM drive or DVD-ROM drive	12x	12x or faster
Video	Super VGA (800x600)	Higher resolutions are nicer
Input devices	Keyboard and mouse or other pointing device	Keyboard and mouse or other pointing device

Table 12-5   Minimum and Recommended Requirements for Windows XP Professional

HARDWARE COMPATIBILITY

Many hardware manufacturers have chosen to not produce Vista drivers for their older devices, so it's very important to find out if your hardware will be compatible with Vista. Microsoft offers the Windows Vista Compatibility Center at *www.microsoft.com/windows/compatibility*

A+
220-701
3.1
3.3

(see Figure 12-3). From there you can search for each device to see if it's listed as having Vista drivers. If it's not listed, it still might work. Go to the Web site of the device manufacturer, and look for Vista drivers for the device. These drivers might not be certified by Vista, but will still work unless you plan to use a 64-bit version of Vista. All 64-bit drivers must be Microsoft certified. Use Device Manager to find out which devices are installed in your XP system.

Figure 12-3 Windows Vista Compatibility Center
Courtesy: Course Technology/Cengage Learning

Another way to find out if your Windows XP system qualifies for Windows Vista is to run the Vista Upgrade Advisor. Go to the *www.microsoft.com* site and search on "Vista Upgrade Advisor." Then download and run the advisor. For upgrading to Windows XP, you can run the XP Readiness Analyzer. Use the following command from the Windows XP CD, substituting the drive letter of your CD-ROM drive for D in the command line, if necessary:

```
D:\I386\Winnt32 /checkupgradeonly
```

Depending on the release of Windows XP, your path might be different. The process takes about 10 minutes to run and displays a report that you can save and later print. The default name and path of the report is C:\Windows\compat.txt. The report is important if you have software you are not sure will work under Windows XP.

If you are not sure if your devices will work under the OS to which you are upgrading, one solution is to set up a dual boot. A **dual boot** allows you to install the new OS without disturbing the old one so you can boot to either OS. After the installation, you can test your software or hardware. If they work under the new OS, you can delete the old one. If they don't work, you can still boot to the old OS and use it. How to set up a dual boot is covered later in the chapter.

Before you install a new OS, be sure you have device drivers for all your critical devices such as your network card or motherboard. To find the drivers, look on the CD that came bundled with the device or check the Web site of the device manufacturer.

CHOOSE THE METHOD OF INSTALLATION

Depending on the circumstances and the available hardware, you have options as to the method used for the installation. Choices are the boot device you will use, how you might choose to use the network, and options involving installations from a hard drive image, recovery CDs, factory recovery partitions, and repairs to the existing installation. All these options are discussed next.

BOOT MEDIA USED FOR THE INSTALLATION

If an OS is not already installed on the hard drive, you must boot using the device from which you will install the OS. The boot device most likely will be the DVD or CD drive. However, you can use any device that the PC is capable of booting from. For example, suppose you want to install Windows Vista from the Vista setup DVD, but the system has a CD drive. You can use an external DVD drive that connects to the PC by way of a USB port. Access BIOS setup and set the boot order for USB as the first boot device. You can then boot from the external DVD drive and install Vista. Recall from earlier chapters that the boot order is the order of devices that BIOS looks to for an OS. To change the boot order, enter BIOS setup and look for the appropriate screen. The BIOS screen shown in Figure 12-4 shows a removable device as the first boot device.

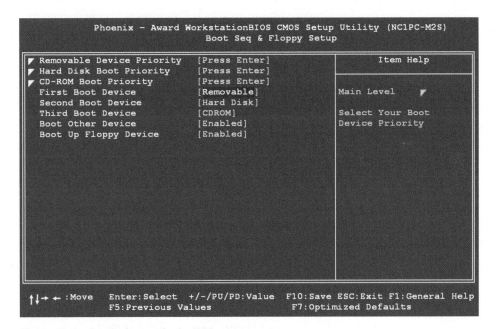

Figure 12-4 Set the boot order in BIOS setup
Courtesy: Course Technology/Cengage Learning

NETWORK INSTALLATION

You can copy the setup files on the Windows CD or DVD to a file server on the network. If you will be doing multiple installations, this method might save you some time. Copy the files from the CD or DVD to a folder on the server and share the folder. Then at each PC, you can execute the Setup program on the server. A server used in this way is called a **distribution server**. How to share folders on a network is covered in Chapter 19.

> 💡 **A+ Exam Tip** The A+ 220-701 Essentials exam expects you to know about unattended installations and about the convenience of putting the Windows setup files on a file server.

> 📄 **Notes** Before installing Windows on a single computer, you might want to copy the Windows installation files to the hard drive. You can do this if the hard drive is already formatted and you don't intend to format it during the installation.

UNATTENDED INSTALLATION

Windows offers a number of options for installations that can be automated so that you don't actually need to sit at the computer and respond to the questions that setup asks during installation. One method, called an unattended installation, is performed by storing the answers to installation questions in a text file or script that Windows calls an answer file. A sample answer file is stored on the Windows DVD or CD. System administrators who need to perform many installations might take the time to develop an answer file to perform unattended installations. Unattended installations work for both upgrades and clean installs. How to set up unattended installations is beyond the scope of this book.

INSTALL FROM AN IMAGE

Another option is drive imaging, sometimes called disk cloning or disk imaging. A drive image is a copy of the entire volume on which Windows is installed to another bootable media such as CDs or USB drives. When the image is created, all contents of the drive, including the OS, applications, and data, get duplicated to the other media. Images are created to make it easier to recover a hard drive from a catastrophic failure or to make it easier to deploy Windows and applications to many computers in a corporation. To set up a new drive from an image, you only need to copy the image to the drive rather than install Windows, applications (such as Microsoft Office), and data. Many corporations have a standard image of a hard drive that includes the OS and its settings and company-specific standard applications.

The original image is created by first installing Windows and then using the Windows utility sysprep.exe to remove configuration settings, such as the computer name that uniquely identifies the PC. Then, all applications are installed. Next, drive-imaging software is used to clone the entire hard drive to another media. Examples of drive-imaging software are True Image by Acronis (*www.acronis.com*) and Norton Ghost by Symantec Corp (*www.symantec.com*). Another example is Clonezilla managed by NCHC (*www.clonezilla.org*), which is free.

To use the image of the hard drive, you boot from the bootable media on which the image is stored and follow directions on-screen to copy the image to the hard drive. Figure 12-5 shows the opening menu for the Acronis software after you boot from a CD that holds the image. On the next screen, you can select the option to restore from backup. On the following screen (see Figure 12-6), you point to the file that holds the image, which is MyBackup2 in the figure. The software then copies the image to the drive.

> 💡 **A+ Exam Tip** The A+ 220-701 Essentials exam expects you to know about installing an OS from a drive image. You are not expected to know how to create the image.

RECOVERY CDS AND DVDS

If you have a notebook computer or a brand-name computer, such as a Dell, IBM, or Gateway, and you need to reinstall the OS, use the recovery CD or DVD provided by the manufacturer instead of a regular Windows Setup CD. This recovery CD or DVD, as shown

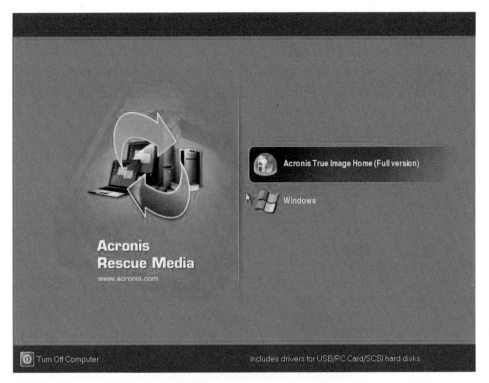

Figure 12-5 Opening menu after booting from the Acronis bootable media
Courtesy: Course Technology/Cengage Learning

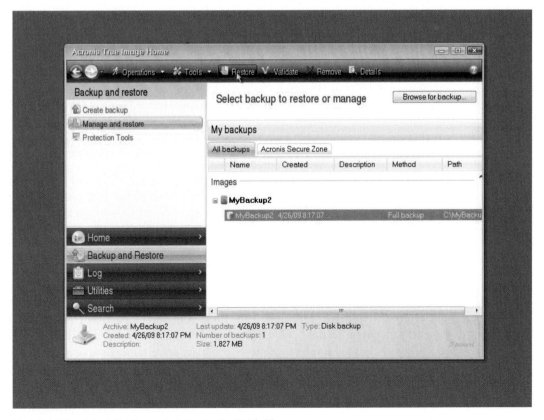

Figure 12-6 Select the image to copy to the hard drive
Courtesy: Course Technology/Cengage Learning

A+
220-701
3.3

in Figure 12-7, has drivers specific to your system. Also, the Windows build that is on the recovery disc might be different from the one provided by an off-the-shelf Windows Setup disc. For example, a Windows XP Home Edition installation on a notebook computer might have been built with all kinds of changes made to it by the notebook manufacturer. These changes will make it different from a Windows XP Home Edition bought in a retail store.

Figure 12-7 Windows Setup CD and Windows Recovery CDs for a notebook computer
Courtesy: Course Technology/Cengage Learning

When you purchase a brand-name computer, the recovery CD is sometimes included in the package. If it is not included, you can order it from the manufacturer. To order it, go to the manufacturer's Web site support section and find the recovery CD specific to your desktop or notebook computer. If you use it to reinstall the OS, be sure to also install all the service packs and updates to the OS. How to install updates and service packs is covered later in the chapter.

> **Notes** In general, it's best to not upgrade an OS on a notebook unless you want to use some feature the new OS offers. For notebooks, follow the general rule, "If it ain't broke, don't fix it." For example, if a notebook is working well with Windows 2000 installed and serving its purpose, leave it alone. The most important reason to not upgrade a notebook OS is that notebook manufacturers are not committed to publish drivers for an OS the notebook was not designed to use. Many hardware components in a notebook are proprietary, and the notebook manufacturer is the only source for these drivers.

FACTORY RECOVERY PARTITION

For some brand-name computers, the hard drive contains a hidden recovery partition that can be used to reinstall Windows. Sometimes this hidden partition contains a utility that can be used to create a recovery CD. However, the CD must have already been created if it is to be there to help you in the event the entire hard drive fails. To access the utilities on the hidden partition, press a key during startup. The key to press is displayed on the screen early in the boot before the OS is loaded. If you don't see the message, search the Web site of the computer manufacturer to find the key combination. For one Dell laptop, you press Ctrl and F11 to start the recovery. One Gateway computer displays the message "Press F11 to start recovery." When you press these keys, a menu is displayed giving you the opportunity to reinstall Windows from setup files kept in the hidden partition.

A+
220-701
3.3

REPAIR AN EXISTING INSTALLATION

For desktop computers that use off-the-shelf Windows installations, Windows offers several different ways to repair the installation. The technique to use depends on how serious the problem is. Chapter 15 covers what to do when Windows Vista startup fails and what to do when Windows XP or Windows 2000 fails to start. Before you reinstall the OS, be sure to check out this chapter to make sure there is not an easier way to repair the existing installation.

INSTALLATION IN A VIRTUAL COMPUTER

Another type of Windows installation is when you install Windows in a virtual computer. A virtual computer or virtual machine is software that simulates the hardware of a physical computer. Using this software, you can install and run multiple operating systems at the same time on a PC (see Figure 12-8). These multiple instances of operating systems can be used to train users, run legacy software, and support multiple operating systems. For example, help-desk technicians can run a virtual machine for each OS they support on a single PC and quickly and easily switch from one OS to another by clicking a window. Another reason to use a virtual machine is that you can capture screen shots of the boot process in a virtual machine, which is the way the screen shots during the boot were made for this book.

To install an OS in a virtual machine, you first install the virtual machine software. Then use it to set up a virtual machine. Then you start this virtual machine and boot from the Windows setup CD or DVD to install the OS the same as is done with a normal PC. You must have a valid Windows license and product key for the virtual machine installation the same as for a

12

A+ 220-701

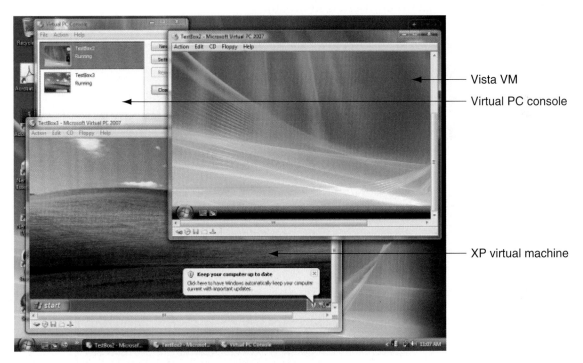

Vista VM

Virtual PC console

XP virtual machine

Figure 12-8 Two virtual machines running under Virtual PC
Courtesy: Course Technology/Cengage Learning

normal Windows installation on a physical PC. For example, in Figure 12-9, Virtual PC already has two machines set up and running. To set up a third virtual machine, click **New** in the Virtual PC Console box on the left side of the figure. A wizard launches and steps you through the process of creating a new machine. During the process, you can select the hard drive size and how much memory the machine has installed. The right side of Figure 12-9 shows one window in the wizard where you select what OS you plan to install in the machine, and the wizard recommends how much RAM the machine needs for this OS.

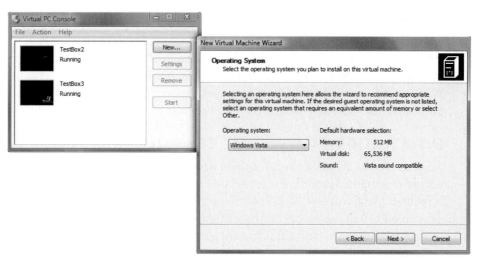

Figure 12-9 Using Virtual PC to set up a new virtual machine
Courtesy: Course Technology/Cengage Learning

After the machine is set up, you can click **Settings** in the console to change the hardware configuration of a machine. To install an OS in this machine, insert the setup CD or DVD in the optical drive, and, in the Virtual PC Console box, select the new machine and click **Start**. A window opens showing the virtual machine booting and then loading the setup program on the disc (see Figure 12-10).

Figure 12-10 The new virtual machine loading OS files from the setup DVD
Courtesy: Course Technology/Cengage Learning

The two most popular virtual machine programs for Windows are Virtual PC by Microsoft and VMware by VMware, Inc. For the Mac OS, VMware Fusion by VMware, Inc, is the most popular. Virtual PC is free for downloading from the Microsoft Web site. VMware must be purchased, but offers more features than does Virtual PC. Recall from

A+
220-701
3.3

Chapter 2 that VMware Fusion makes it possible to install Windows in a virtual machine on a Mac. You will learn to use Virtual PC in a project at the end of this chapter.

CHOOSE THE TYPE OF INSTALLATION: UPGRADE, CLEAN INSTALL, OR DUAL BOOT

If you are installing Windows on a new hard drive, then you are doing a clean install. If Windows is already installed on the hard drive and you want to install a different Windows operating system, then you have three choices:

- *Clean install.* You can perform a clean install, overwriting the existing operating system and applications.
- *Upgrade.* If the upgrade paths allow it, you can perform an upgrade installation. You can upgrade Windows XP to Vista, or you can upgrade Windows 2000 or Windows 98/Me to Windows XP.
- *Dual boot.* You can install Windows Vista or Windows XP in a second partition on the hard drive and create a dual-boot situation with the other OS.

Each of these options has advantages and disadvantages.

CLEAN INSTALL—ERASING EXISTING INSTALLATIONS

A clean install that overwrites the existing installation has some advantages; one advantage is that you get a fresh start. With an upgrade, problems with applications or the OS might follow you into the Windows Vista/XP load. If you erase everything (format the hard drive), then you are assured that the registry as well as all applications are as clean as possible. The disadvantage is that after Windows Vista/XP is installed, you must reinstall application software on the hard drive and restore the data from backups. If you do a clean install, you can choose to format the hard drive first, or simply do a clean install on top of the existing installation. If you don't format the drive, the data will still be on the drive, but the previous operating system settings and applications will be lost.

If you decide to do a clean install, verify that you have all the application software CDs or floppy disks and software documentation. Back up all the data, and verify that the backups are good. Then, and only then, format the hard drive or begin the clean install without formatting the drive. If you don't format the hard drive, be sure to run a current version of antivirus software before you begin the installation.

UPGRADE INSTALLATIONS

The advantages of upgrading are that all applications and data and most OS settings are carried forward into the new Windows environment, and the installation is faster. If you perform an upgrade, you must begin the installation while you are in the current OS (from the Windows desktop). An upgrade installation is appropriate if the system is generally healthy and does not have problems.

CREATING A DUAL BOOT

Don't create a dual boot unless you need two operating systems, such as when you need to verify that applications and hardware work under Windows Vista before you delete the old OS. Windows Vista/XP/2000 all require that they be the only operating system installed on a partition. So to set up a dual boot, you'll need at least two partitions on the hard drive or a second hard drive.

12

A+ 220-701

A+
220-701
3.3

UNDERSTAND THE CHOICES YOU'LL MAKE DURING THE INSTALLATION

While Windows is installing, you must choose which drive and partition to install Windows, which file system to use, and how Windows will connect to the network. These three choices are discussed next.

DRIVES, PARTITIONS, AND FILE SYSTEMS

Recall from Chapter 8 that a hard drive set up by Windows can have up to four partitions. The first 512-byte sector on the drive, called the master boot record (MBR), holds the partition table. The MBR keeps track of where the partitions are located on the drive, the size of each partition, and which partition is the active partition (the bootable partition). The drive can have up to three primary partitions (also called volumes) and one extended partition, which can contain one or more logical drives. The active partition is always a primary partition. Each partition is formatted with a file system that keeps track of where folders and files are stored on the partition.

Windows assigns two different functions to hard drive partitions holding the OS (see Figure 12-11). The system partition, normally drive C, is the active partition of the hard drive. This is the partition that contains the OS boot record. Remember that the MBR program looks to this OS boot record for the boot program as the first step in turning the PC over to an OS. The other partition, called the boot partition, is the partition where the Windows operating system is stored.

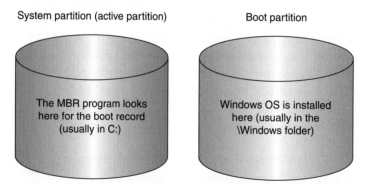

System partition (active partition)   Boot partition

The MBR program looks here for the boot record (usually in C:)

Windows OS is installed here (usually in the \Windows folder)

Figure 12-11   Two types of Windows hard drive partitions
Courtesy: Course Technology/Cengage Learning

Notes   Don't be confused by the terminology here. It is really true that, according to Windows terminology, the Windows OS is on the boot partition, and the boot record is on the system partition, although that might seem backward. The PC boots from the system partition and loads the Windows operating system from the boot partition.

For most installations, the system partition and the boot partition are the same (drive C:), and Windows is installed in C:\Windows (for Windows Vista/XP) or C:\Winnt (for Windows 2000). An example of when the system partition and the boot partition are different is when Windows Vista is installed as a dual boot with Windows XP. Figure 12-12 shows how Windows Vista is installed on drive E and Windows XP is installed on drive C. For Windows Vista, the system partition is drive C and the boot partition is drive E. (For Windows XP on this computer, the system and boot partitions are both drive C.)

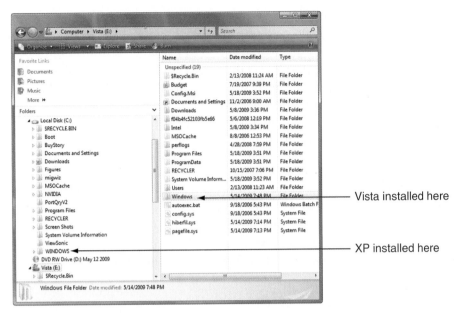

Figure 12-12 Windows Vista and Windows XP installed on the same system
Courtesy: Course Technology/Cengage Learning

When you install Windows, you must decide which drive and partition will hold the OS and the size of this partition. You can leave some space unallocated during the installation and later use the Disk Management utility to partition and format the space.

For most situations, you will have available a single hard drive and allocate all the space to drive C. However, here are reasons to use more than one volume on the drive:

▲ You plan to install more than one OS on the hard drive, creating a dual-boot system. For example, you might want to install Windows XP on one partition and Windows Vista on another, so you can test software under both operating systems. For this situation, install XP first using a partition that takes up only part of the hard drive. Later, you can install Vista on a second partition on the drive. (When setting up a dual boot, always install the older OS first.)

▲ Some people prefer to use more than one volume to organize data on their hard drives. For example, you might want to install Windows and all your applications on one volume and your data on another. Having your data on a separate volume makes backing up easier. In another situation, you might want to set up a volume on the drive that is used exclusively to hold backups of data on another computer on the network.

> ⚡ **Caution** It's convenient to back up one volume to another volume on a different hard drive. However, don't back up one volume to another volume on the same hard drive, because when a hard drive fails, quite often all volumes on the drive are damaged and you will lose both your data and your backup.

The size of the volume that will hold Vista and its applications should be at least 20 GB, with at least 15 GB free space. An XP volume that will also hold applications needs to be at least 5 GB, although you can get by with less.

The volume on which Vista is installed will automatically be formatted using the NTFS file system. In the XP installation, you can choose between FAT32 and NTFS. Choose NTFS unless

A+
220-701
3.3

the size of the volume is 2 GB or less. FAT32 does not use as much overhead as NTFS and is a better choice for these smaller volumes. Here are the advantages NTFS offers over FAT32:

▲ NTFS uses smaller cluster sizes than FAT32, which means it makes more efficient use of disk space when storing many small files. Recall that a file is stored in whole clusters, and the unused space at the end of the last cluster, called slack, is wasted free space.

▲ NTFS retains two copies of its critical file system data and can use the extra copy to automatically recover from a corrupted file system.

▲ NTFS supports encryption (encoding files so they can't be deciphered by others) and disk quotas (limiting the hard drive space available to a user).

▲ NTFS supports compression (reducing the size of files and folders). FAT32 supports compression of an entire volume but not compression of individual files or folders.

▲ NTFS offers better security. For example, if you boot the system from another boot media such as a CD, you can access a volume using a FAT file system. If the volume uses NTFS, an administrator password is required to gain access.

A+
220-701
3.3
4.1

NETWORK CONFIGURATION

A Windows computer can be configured to work as one node in a workgroup or one node on a domain. A Windows **workgroup** is a logical group of computers and users that share resources (Figure 12-13), where administration, resources, and security on a

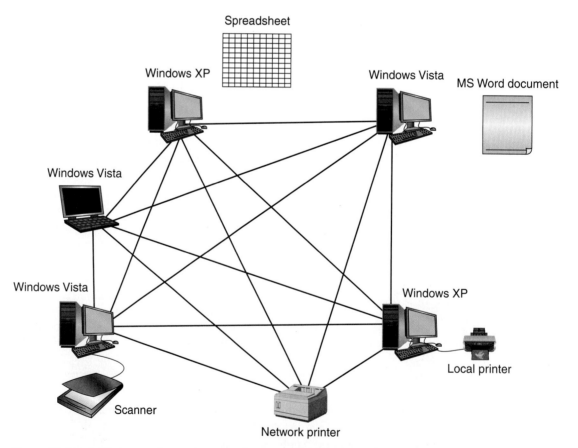

Figure 12-13   A Windows workgroup is a type of peer-to-peer network where no single computer controls the network and each computer controls its own resources
Courtesy: Course Technology/Cengage Learning

A+
220-701
3.3
4.1

workstation are controlled by that workstation. Each computer maintains a list of users and their rights on that particular PC. A workgroup is a type of peer-to-peer (P2P) network, which is a network that is managed by each computer without centralized control. A Windows domain is a group of networked computers that share a centralized directory database of user account information and security for the entire group of computers (Figure 12-14). A Windows domain is a type of client/server network, which is a network where resources are managed by a centralized computer. Using the client/server model, the directory database is controlled by a Network Operating System (NOS). Examples of network operating systems are Windows Server, Novell NetWare, UNIX, Linux, and Mac OS.

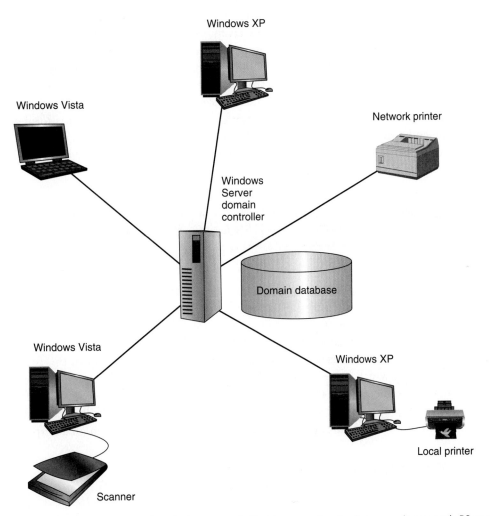

Figure 12-14 A Windows domain is a type of client/server network where security on each PC or other device is controlled by a centralized database on a domain controller
Courtesy: Course Technology/Cengage Learning

Note When looking at the diagrams in Figures 12-13 and 12-14, know that the connecting lines describe the logical connections between computers and not the physical connections. Both networks might be physically connected the same way, but logically, resources are controlled using a centralized database or controlled by each computer on the network.

A+
220-701
3.3
4.1

An example of a network operating system is Windows Server 2008, which controls a network using the directory database called Active Directory. The database of resources on the network including user accounts is managed in Active Directory by a network administrator or system administrator. Access to the network is controlled by the permissions assigned to a user account that is managed by Active Directory. If you are installing Windows on a PC that belongs to a domain, the administrator will tell you the information you need during the installation to join the domain. You'll need to know the domain name, computer name, username, and password. All users of this computer must have their own domain-level accounts (called a global account) assigned by the network or system administrator.

Regardless of whether Windows computers belong to a domain or workgroup, every Windows computer has an administrator account by default. This account is a type of local account, meaning that it is only recognized by the local computer. An administrator has rights and permissions to all computer software and hardware resources on the local computer. During the Vista installation, you are given the opportunity to enter a password to a local user account that is assigned administrator privileges. The default administrator account is disabled by default. During a Windows XP/2000 installation, you are given the opportunity to enter a password to the default administrator account and this account is enabled by default.

You can log on as an administrator after the OS is installed and create local user accounts that apply to this one computer. A user can log onto the system with a local account even if the computer belongs to a domain. However, resources managed by the domain will not be available until the user logs on with a domain-level account and password. How to set up local accounts is covered in Chapter 19.

> **Notes** Windows Vista and XP Home Editions do not support joining a domain. If you plan to join a domain on your network, install Vista Business, Enterprise, or Ultimate editions, Windows XP Professional, or Windows 2000 Professional.

When deploying Vista or XP in a large organization, the User State Migration Tool (USMT) might be used to transfer user settings and data from an old PC to a new one. The User State Migration Tool (USMT) is a command-line tool that works only when the new Windows Vista or XP system is a member of a Windows domain.

An administrator uses two commands at the command prompt of this tool: the scanstate command, which is used to copy the information from the old computer to a server or removable media, and the loadstate command, which is used to copy the information to the new computer. These two commands can be stored in batch files and executed automatically when installing Vista or XP over a large number of computers in an enterprise.

> **A+ Exam Tip** The A+ 220-701 Essentials exam expects you to know that the User State Migration Tool can be used to migrate user data to a new PC as part of the installation process.

Incidentally, when a Windows domain is not involved, Windows XP offers the Files and Settings Transfer Wizard and Windows Vista uses Windows Easy Transfer to copy user data and settings from one computer to another. How to use either utility can be found in Windows Help and Support.

> **A+ Exam Tip** When moving user data and settings from one PC to another, the best practice is to leave the user data and settings on the original PC untouched for at least two months. This practice gives the user plenty of time to make sure everything has been moved over.

A+
220-701
3.3
4.1

In summary, you need to know how to configure the computer to access the network. You should know these things before you begin the installation:

- ◢ The computer name and workgroup name for a peer-to-peer network.
- ◢ The username, user password, computer name, and domain name for a domain network.
- ◢ For TCP/IP networks, an IP address uniquely identifies the computer on the network. You need to know how this IP address is assigned. It might be assigned dynamically (IP address is assigned by a server each time it connects to the network) or statically (IP address is permanently assigned to the workstation). If the network is using static IP addressing, you need the IP address for the workstation.

FINAL CHECKLIST BEFORE BEGINNING THE INSTALLATION

Before you begin the installation, complete the final checklist shown in Table 12-6 to verify that you are ready.

Questions to Answer	Further Information
Does the PC meet the minimum or recommended hardware requirement?	CPU: RAM: Hard drive partition size: Free space on the partition:
Do you have in hand the Windows device drivers for your hardware devices and application setup CDs?	List hardware and software that need to be upgraded:
Do you have the product key available?	Product key:
How will users be recognized on the network?	Workgroup name: Domain name: Computer name:
How will the PC be recognized on the network?	Static or dynamic IP addressing: IP address (for static addressing):
Will you do an upgrade or clean install?	Current operating system: Does the old OS qualify for an upgrade?

For a clean install, will you set up a dual boot?	List reasons for a dual boot:
	 For a dual boot
	   Size of the second partition:
	   Free space on the second partition:
	   File system you plan to use:

Have you backed up important data on your hard drive?	Location of backup:

Table 12-6 Checklist to complete before installing Windows

> **Notes** The product key is written on the cover of the Windows setup CD or DVD or affixed to the back of the Windows documentation booklet, as shown in Figure 12-15. Technicians sometimes mount the product key sticker on the side of a computer. Try looking for it there (see Figure 12-16). For notebook computers, look for the product key sticker on the bottom of the notebook. If you have lost the product key and are moving this Windows XP installation from one PC to another, you can use a utility to find out the product key. On the PC that has the old Windows XP installation, download and run the key finder utility from Magical Jelly Bean Software at *www.magicaljellybean.com/keyfinder.shtml*. For Windows Vista, the product key is displayed in the System window. Click **Start**, right-click **Computer**, and select **Properties** from the shortcut window.

12

A+ 220-701

Figure 12-15 The product key is on a sticker on the back of the Windows XP documentation
Courtesy: Course Technology/Cengage Learning

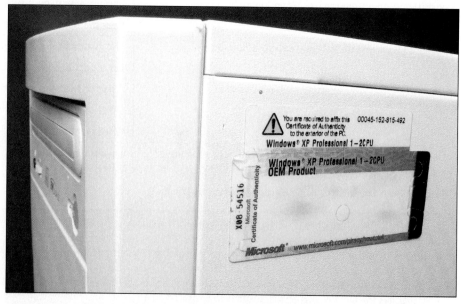

Figure 12-16 The product key is sometimes placed on the side or front of a computer case
Courtesy: Course Technology/Cengage Learning

Before we get into the step-by-step instructions of installing an OS, here are some general tips about installing Windows:

▲ If you want to begin the installation by booting from the Windows CD or DVD or other media such as a USB device, verify that the boot sequence is first the optical drive or USB device, and then the hard drive.

▲ Also, because Windows prefers to handle its own Plug and Play hardware installations without the help of BIOS, Microsoft recommends that you disable the Plug and Play feature of your motherboard BIOS.

▲ Disable any virus protection setting that prevents the boot sector from being altered.

▲ For a notebook computer, connect the AC adapter and use this power source for the complete OS installation, updates, and installation of hardware and applications. You don't want the battery to fail you in the middle of the installation process.

HOW TO INSTALL WINDOWS VISTA

A+
220-701
3.3

In this part of the chapter, you will learn how to install Vista as an upgrade, clean install, and dual boot.

PERFORMING A VISTA IN-PLACE UPGRADE

To upgrade from Windows XP to Windows Vista, follow these steps:

1. Close any open applications. Close any boot management software or antivirus software that might be running in the background.

2. From the Windows XP desktop, launch the Windows Vista CD or DVD. The opening menu shown in Figure 12-17 appears. Click **Install now**.

Figure 12-17 Windows Vista Setup opening menu
Courtesy: Course Technology/Cengage Learning

12

A+ 220-701

3. On the next screen, you can choose to allow the setup program to download updates for the installation. If you have Internet access, click **Go online to get the latest updates for installation (recommended)**. Setup will download the updates, as shown in Figure 12-18. When using this option, you'll need to stay connected to the Internet throughout the installation.

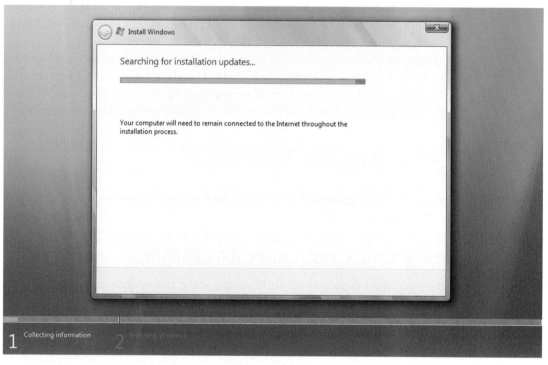

Figure 12-18 Setup uses the Internet to update the installation process
Courtesy: Course Technology/Cengage Learning

4. On the next screen, as shown in Figure 12-19, enter the Vista product key. It's printed on a sticker inside the CD or DVD case.

5. On the next screen, accept the license agreement.

6. On the next screen, shown in Figure 12-20, select the type of installation you want, either an upgrade or a clean install. Select **Upgrade**.

7. The installation is now free to move forward. The PC will reboot several times. At the end of this process, a screen appears asking for your country, time, currency, and keyboard layout. Make your selections and click **Next**.

> **Note** Notice in Figure 12-19 the checkbox "Automatically activate Windows when I'm online." Normally, you would leave this option checked so that Vista activates immediately. However, if you are practicing installing Vista and intend to install it several times using the same DVD, you might choose to uncheck this box and not enter the product key during the installation. When you do that, you will be prompted to select the edition of Vista to install. You can later decide to enter the product key and activate Vista after the installation.

8. On the following screens, you are asked to enter a user name, password, computer name, date, and time. In addition, you are asked how you want to handle Windows updates. The user name that you enter will be assigned administrative permissions.

A+
220-701
3.3

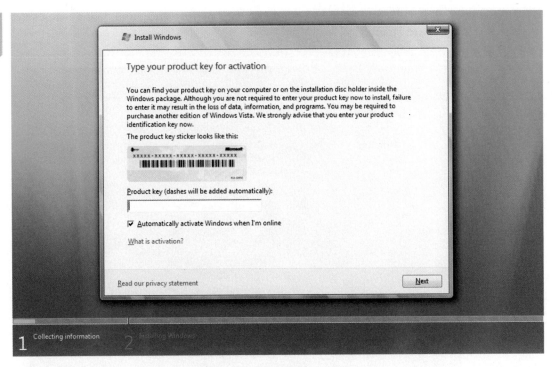

Figure 12-19   Enter the product key found inside the Vista CD or DVD case
Courtesy: Course Technology/Cengage Learning

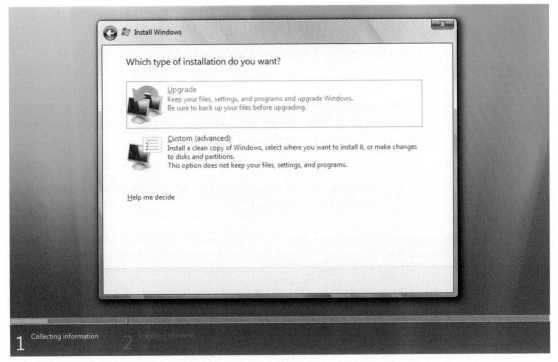

Figure 12-20   Select the type of installation you want
Courtesy: Course Technology/Cengage Learning

12

A+ 220-701

A+
220-701
3.3

9. Finally, Setup checks your computer's performance, and then a logon screen appears (see Figure 12-21).

Figure 12-21 Vista logon screen after the installation
Courtesy: Course Technology/Cengage Learning

PERFORMING A CLEAN INSTALL OR DUAL BOOT

To perform a clean install of Windows Vista or a dual boot with another OS, do the following:

1. Boot directly from the Windows Vista CD or DVD. If you have trouble booting from the disc, go into BIOS setup and verify that your first boot device is the optical drive. Select your language preference, and then the opening menu shown earlier in Figure 12-17 appears. Click **Install now**.

2. On the next screens, enter the product key and accept the license agreement.

3. On the next screen, shown earlier in Figure 12-20, select the type of installation you want. Choose **Custom (advanced)**.

> **Note** If your computer refuses to boot from the DVD, verify that your optical drive is a DVD drive. Perhaps it is only a CD drive. If this is the case, you can use another computer on your network that has a DVD drive to read the disc. This computer can act as your file server for the Vista installation on the first PC, or you can copy the installation files on the DVD across the network to a folder on the hard drive of your first PC and install the OS from this folder.

4. On the next screen, you will be shown a list of partitions on which to install the OS. For example, the computer shown in Figure 12-22 has two hard drives (Disk 0 and Disk 1), each with one partition. You can choose to install Vista on drive C: (the only partition on the first hard drive) or drive E: (the only partition on the second hard drive). For this computer, Windows XP is installed on drive C:. If you choose drive C:, then you will be

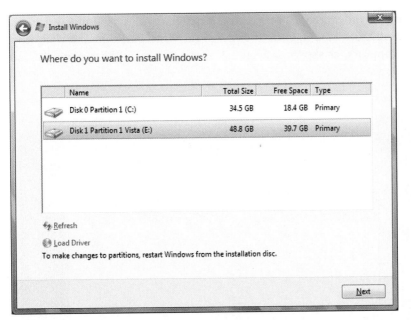

Figure 12-22 Select a partition to install Vista in a clean install or dual boot environment
Courtesy: Course Technology/Cengage Learning

performing a clean install on top of Windows XP, erasing XP. If you choose drive E:, then you will be installing Vista on the second hard drive and the system will function with a dual boot configuration. Make your selection and click **Next**.

In another example where the installation begins with a new hard drive, the setup screen in Figure 12-23 appears. Suppose you want to install Vista on this drive and later install Windows 7 as a dual boot. To allocate only part of the drive for the Vista partition, click

Figure 12-23 Installation with a single clean hard drive
Courtesy: Course Technology/Cengage Learning

A+
220-701
3.3

Drive options (advanced). Options to manage partitions appear. Click **New.** On the next screen (see Figure 12-24), enter the size of the Vista partition and click **Apply.** The new partition appears, as shown in Figure 12-25, and we still have plenty of room on the drive for Windows 7.

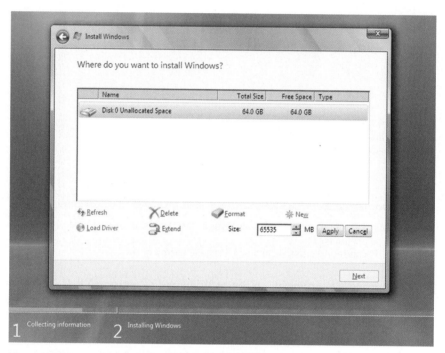

Figure 12-24   Options are available to manage partitions
Courtesy: Course Technology/Cengage Learning

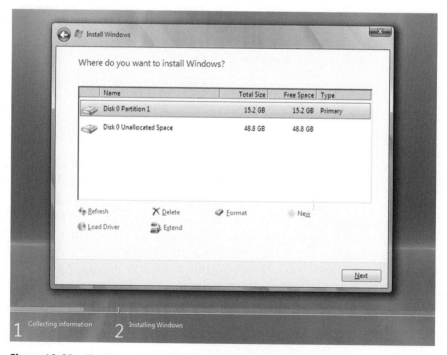

Figure 12-25   The Vista partition using part of the available space
Courtesy: Course Technology/Cengage Learning

The installation now continues the same way as an upgrade installation.

After the installation, when you boot with a dual boot, the boot loader menu automatically appears and asks you to select an operating system, as shown in Figure 12-26.

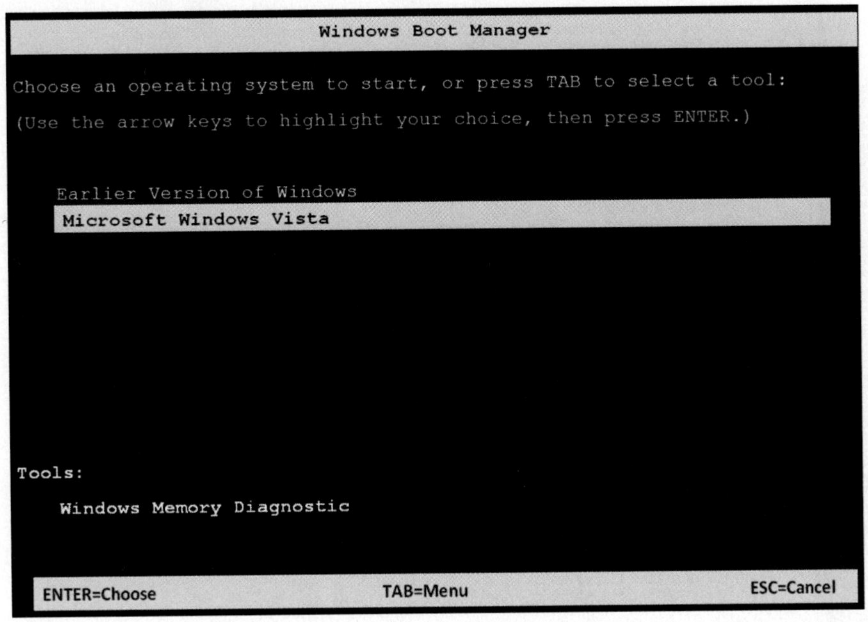

```
                        Windows Boot Manager

Choose an operating system to start, or press TAB to select a tool:
(Use the arrow keys to highlight your choice, then press ENTER.)


    Earlier Version of Windows
    Microsoft Windows Vista






Tools:

    Windows Memory Diagnostic




 ENTER=Choose              TAB=Menu                    ESC=Cancel
```

Figure 12-26 Vista boot loader menu
Courtesy: Course Technology/Cengage Learning

When using a dual boot, you can execute an application while Windows Vista or XP is loaded even if the application is installed under the other OS. If the application is not listed in the Start menu, locate the program file in Windows Explorer. Double-click the application to run it from Windows Vista or XP. You do not have to install an application twice under each OS.

PERFORMING A CLEAN INSTALL USING THE VISTA UPGRADE DVD

With Windows 2000/XP, you could use an upgrade CD to install the OS even when an OS was not installed. During the installation, you were required to provide the setup CD of an older version of Windows to prove that you had the right to use the upgrade CD. However, Vista does not make this provision. Vista setup expects that an old OS is installed if you use the upgrade DVD.

This requirement presents a problem when you cannot boot your Windows XP system to start the Vista installation from within Windows XP. You have two options in this situation. One option is to reinstall Windows XP and then install Windows Vista as an upgrade. Another option is to use the Vista upgrade DVD to perform a clean install. However, during the Vista installation, when you enter the product key, Vista verifies that the product key is for an upgrade DVD or for-a-new-PC DVD. If you are using an upgrade product key for a clean install, Setup gives you an error, and stops the installation. The error message is, "To use the product key you entered, start the installation from your existing version of Windows." Follow these steps to get around that error:

1. Boot from the Vista DVD and start the installation. When you get to the installation window that asks you to enter your product key, don't enter the key and uncheck **Automatically activate Windows when I'm online.**

A+
220-701
3.3

2. A message appears asking you to enter the key. Click **No** to continue. On the next window (see Figure 12-27), select the edition of Vista you have purchased, check **I have selected the edition of Windows that I purchased**, and click **Next**.

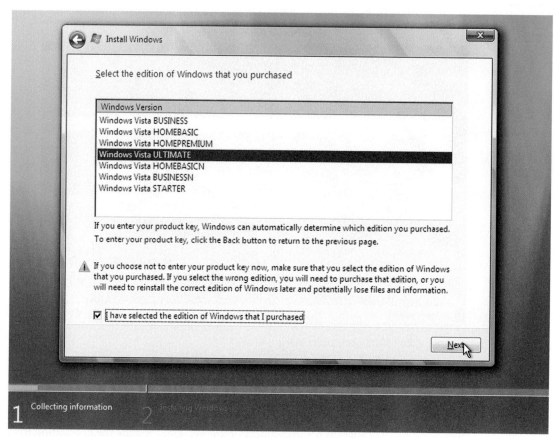

Figure 12-27 Installing Windows Vista without entering the product key
Courtesy: Course Technology/Cengage Learning

3. Complete the installation. You will not be able to activate Vista without the product key.

4. From the Vista desktop, start the installation routine again, but this time as an upgrade. If you get an error, restart the installation. Enter the product key during the installation and Vista will activate with no problems.

> **Notes** If you have problems installing Windows, search the Microsoft Web site (*support.microsoft.com*) for solutions. Vista Setup creates several log files during the installation that can help you solve a problem. To see a list of log files, visit the *support.microsoft.com* site and search on "Vista installation logs."

WHAT TO DO AFTER THE VISTA INSTALLATION

After you have installed Vista, you need to do the following:

1. Verify that you have network access.

2. Activate Windows.

3. Install updates and service packs for Windows.

4. Verify automatic updates are set as you want them.

5. Configure Vista components.

6. Install hardware.

7. Install applications.

If Windows is installed in a workgroup and not a domain, in addition to these seven steps, you need to create a local user account for each user of this PC. How to create local accounts is covered in Chapter 19. Now let's look at the details of the seven items from the preceding list.

VERIFY THAT YOU HAVE NETWORK ACCESS

When you install Windows, the setup process should connect you to the network and to the Internet, if available. To verify that you have network and Internet access, do the following:

1. For Vista, click **Start, Network** to open the Network window (see Figure 12-28). You should see other computers and resources on the network in the right pane, and you should be able to drill down to see shared resources on these computers.

Figure 12-28   Use the Network window to access resources on your network
Courtesy: Course Technology/Cengage Learning

2. If the Network window does not show other computers on your network, first try rebooting the PC. Then verify that the computer, workgroup, or domain names are correct using the System dialog box. Click **Start**, right-click **Computer**, and select **Properties** from the shortcut menu. The System window appears, as shown in Figure 12-29.

3. Under *Computer name, domain, and workgroup settings*, click **Change settings** and respond to the UAC box. The System Properties dialog box is displayed, as shown in the left side of Figure 12-30. (If you are installing a Vista Home edition, the Network ID button in the figure will be missing because these editions cannot join a domain.) If the

A+
220-701
3.3

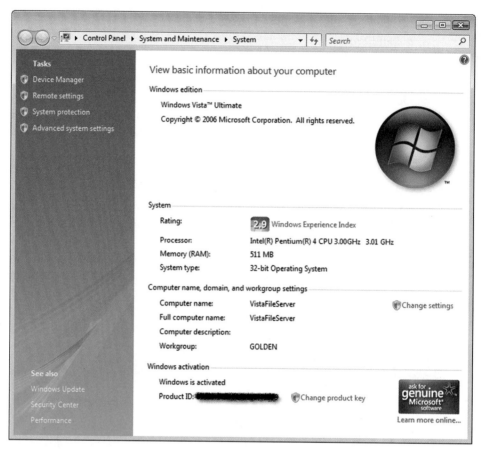

Figure 12-29 Use the System window to change computer settings
Courtesy: Course Technology/Cengage Learning

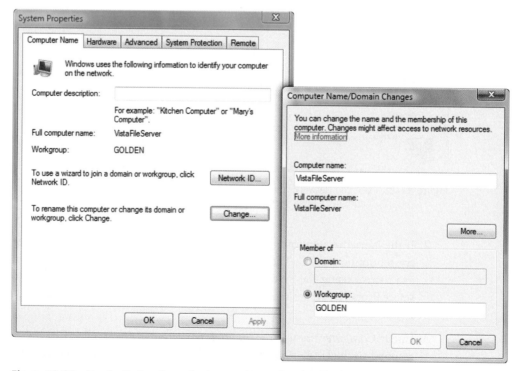

Figure 12-30 Use the System Properties box to change the workgroup name, domain name, or computer name
Courtesy: Course Technology/Cengage Learning

A+
220-701
3.3

computer name, workgroup name, or domain name is not correct, click **Change** to make your changes and respond to the UAC box. The dialog box to make your changes is shown on the right side of Figure 12-30. You will need to restart the computer before your changes will take effect.

4. To verify that you have Internet access, open **Internet Explorer** and try to navigate to a couple of Web sites.

> **Notes** If your computer is part of a Windows domain, when Windows Vista starts up, it displays a blank screen instead of a logon screen. To log onto the domain, press Ctrl+Alt+Del to display the logon screen. If you want to log onto the local machine instead of the domain, type **.*username*.** For example, to log onto the local machine using the local user account "Jean Andrews," type **.\\Jean Andrews.**

If you have problems with accessing the network or the Internet, you'll need to dig a little deeper into Windows networking, which is covered in Chapter 17.

ACTIVATE WINDOWS VISTA

Product activation is a method used by Microsoft to prevent unlicensed use of its software so that you must purchase a Windows license for each installation of Windows. After you install Windows Vista or XP, you have 30 days to activate the OS. (Windows 2000 does not require activating.) If you don't activate Vista within the given time, the screen in Figure 12-31 is displayed, forcing you to activate Vista, enter or purchase a new product key for the activation, or convert Windows to Reduced Functionality Mode (RFM), which greatly limits what you can do in Vista. After you are in RFM mode, if you activate Windows, it will return to the fully functioning mode.

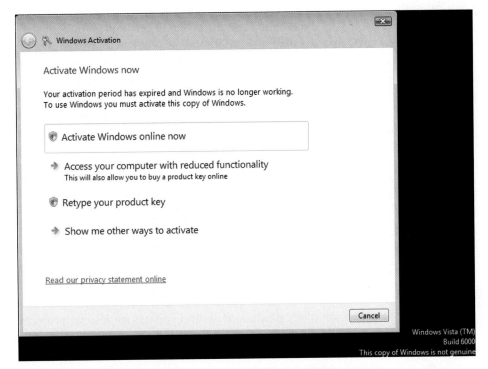

Figure 12-31 Vista informs the user that the activation period has expired
Courtesy: Course Technology/Cengage Learning

12

A+ 220-701

A+
220-701
3.3

> **Notes** If you need more than 30 days before you activate Windows, you can use this command in a command prompt window: **slmgr –rearm**. Your activation period will be extended an additional 30 days from the day you issue the command. You can use the command three times, at which time Vista will revert to RFM mode.

To view the activation status and activate Windows Vista, open the System window. For example, in Figure 12-32, to activate Vista, click **25 day(s) to activate. Activate Windows now.**

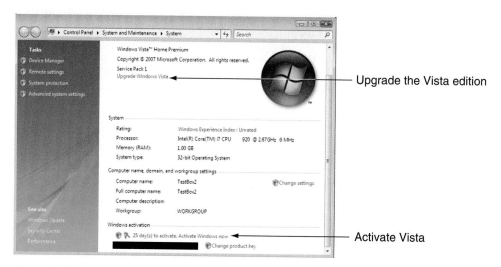

Figure 12-32 Activate or upgrade Vista or change the product key
Courtesy: Course Technology/Cengage Learning

If you install Windows from the same DVD on a different computer, and you attempt to activate Windows from the new PC, a dialog box appears telling you of the suspected violation of the license agreement. You can call a Microsoft operator and explain what caused the discrepancy. If your explanation is reasonable (for example, you uninstalled Windows Vista from one PC and installed it on another), the operator can issue you a valid certificate. You can then type the certificate value into a dialog box to complete the boot process.

Also, notice in Figure 12-32 that you can see and change the product key at any time. If you change the key after Vista is activated, you must activate Vista again, because the activation is tied to the product key and the system hardware. Incidentally, if you replace the motherboard or replace the hard drive and memory at the same time, you must also reactivate Vista.

> **Note** If you have purchased Windows Vista Home Basic, Home Premium, or Business editions, you can upgrade them to Vista Ultimate. To do that, in the System window, click **Upgrade Windows Vista** (see Figure 12-32). You are taken to the Microsoft Web site (*www.microsoft.com*) to purchase the upgrade and download an upgrade program file, which includes a new product key. You use the downloaded file and the Vista DVD to install the new edition of Windows Vista. A Vista DVD contains the setup files for Vista Home, Business, and Ultimate editions.

A+
220-701
3.3
2.5

INSTALL WINDOWS UPDATES AND SERVICE PACKS

The Microsoft Web site offers patches, fixes, and updates for known problems and has an extensive knowledge base documenting problems and their solutions. It's important to keep these updates current on your system to fix known problems and plug up security holes that might allow viruses and worms in. Be sure to install updates before you attempt to install software or hardware.

To download and apply Windows updates, click **Start, All Programs**, and **Windows Update**. The Windows Update window appears, as shown in Figure 12-33 for Vista, but the XP window is similar. Click **Install updates** and follow directions on-screen.

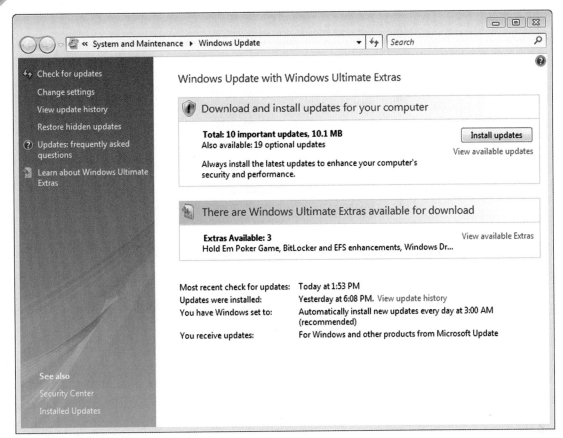

Figure 12-33 Download and install updates for your computer
Courtesy: Course Technology/Cengage Learning

If your Windows setup DVD or CD is old, or the PC hasn't been updated in a while, Windows selects the updates in the order you can receive them, and will not necessarily list all the updates you need on the first pass. After you have installed the updates listed, go back and start again until Windows Updates tells you there is nothing left to update. If Windows requests a restart after an update, do that before you install more updates. It might take two or more passes to get the PC entirely up to date.

So far, Microsoft has released two major service packs for Windows Vista. When the update process is ready to install a service pack, you'll see it listed as the only update to download and install. It will take some time and a reboot to complete the process of installing a service pack. Only the latest service pack for an OS will install because the latest service pack includes all the content from previous service packs.

CONFIGURE AUTOMATIC UPDATES

During the Vista installation, you were asked how you want to handle Vista updates. To verify or change this setting, in the left pane of the Windows Update window, click **Change settings**. From the Change settings window, shown in Figure 12-34, you can decide how often, when, and how you want Vista to install updates. The recommended setting is to allow Vista to automatically download and install updates daily. However, if you are not always connected to the Internet, your connection is very slow, or you want more control over which updates are installed, you might want to manage the updates differently.

A+
220-701
3.3
2.5

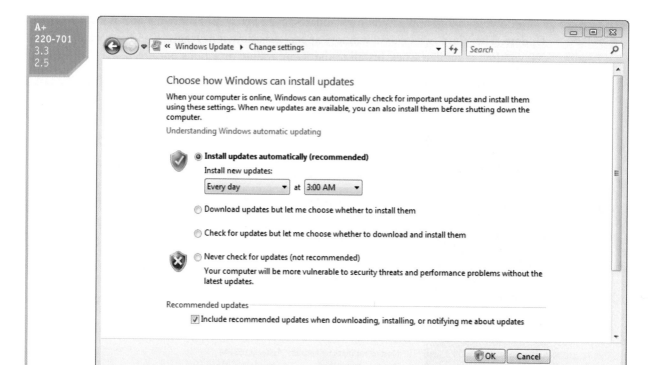

Figure 12-34 Manage how and when Vista is updated
Courtesy: Course Technology/Cengage Learning

CONFIGURE VISTA COMPONENTS

When Vista is first installed, by default, it turns certain software components on and others off. To see how these features are set and change these settings, from Control Panel, click **Programs**. The Programs window appears, as shown in Figure 12-35. Click **Turn Windows features on or off** and respond to the UAC box. The Windows Features dialog box opens. To expand groups of items, click the plus sign beside a check box. Generally, the features are set as they should be. However, to meet specific user needs, you might need to turn on Telnet client, Telnet server, FTP server, or some similar seldom-used Windows feature. To get more information about an item, search for it in Windows Help and Support. Check or uncheck a feature to turn it on or off. Click **OK** when you're done.

A+
220-701
2.5

INSTALL HARDWARE

You're now ready to install the hardware devices that were not automatically installed during the installation. As you install each device, reboot and verify that the software or device is working before you move on to the next item. Most likely, you will need to do the following:

- Use the CD that came bundled with the motherboard to install the drivers for the motherboard. If you were not able to connect to the network earlier in the installation process, it might be because the drivers for the network port are not installed. Installing the drivers on the motherboard CD can solve the problem.
- Even though Windows has embedded video drivers, install the driver CD that came bundled with the video card to use all the features the card offers.
- Install the printer. To install a local USB printer, all you have to do is plug in the USB printer, and Windows will install the printer automatically. How to install other types of printers is covered in Chapter 22.

Figure 12-35   Use the Vista Programs window to manage installed software
Courtesy: Course Technology/Cengage Learning

Recall that the primary tool for managing hardware in Windows is Device Manager. To access Device Manager, click **Start**, right-click **Computer**, and click **Properties** on the shortcut menu. In the System window that appears, in the left pane, click **Device Manager** (see Figure 12-36), and respond to the UAC box. Use Device Manager to uninstall devices, update drivers, and troubleshoot problems with devices.

To install a new hardware device, always read and follow manufacturer directions for the installation. Sometimes you are directed to install the drivers before you connect the device, and sometimes you will first need to connect the device. When you first connect a new device, the Found New Hardware Wizard launches to step you through the installation. However, you can cancel the wizard and run the installation program on the CD that came bundled with the device. If errors occur when installing the drivers, try the installation while the system is booted into Safe Mode. Recall that to boot to Safe Mode, press **F8** during startup and select **Safe Mode with Networking** from the boot options menu.

INSTALL APPLICATIONS

To install applications, insert the setup CD or DVD, and follow directions on-screen to launch the installation routine. For software downloaded from the Internet, open Windows Explorer and double-click the program filename to begin the installation. If the install process gives errors, try starting the installation by right-clicking the program filename and selecting **Run as administrator** from the shortcut menu (see Figure 12-37). You'll then need to respond to the UAC box, which might require you to enter an administrator password. (Running an application as an administrator is sometimes called a secondary logon.)

A+
220-701
2.2
3.1

A+
220-701
2.2
3.1

If an application gives errors after it is installed, try to change the environment in which it runs. To do that, use Windows Explorer to locate the executable program file. The file has an .exe file extension, and will most likely be in a subfolder of the \Program Files folder. Then, right-click the filename and select **Properties** from the shortcut menu. The program properties

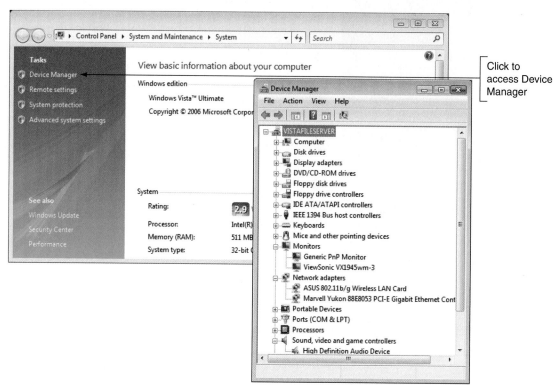

Figure 12-36 Access Device Manager from the System window
Courtesy: Course Technology/Cengage Learning

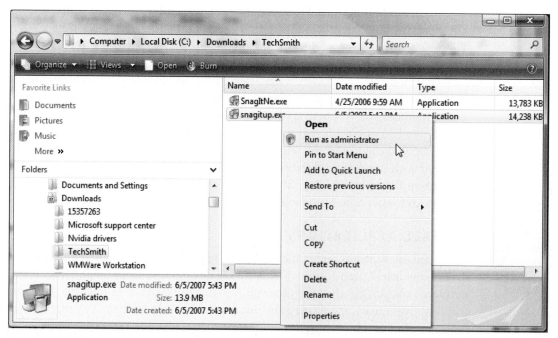

Figure 12-37 Execute a program using administrative privileges
Courtesy: Course Technology/Cengage Learning

window opens. Click the **Compatibility** tab (see Figure 12-38). If the program was written for an older OS, check **Run this program in compatibility mode for** and select the OS, as shown in the figure. You can also try checking **Run this program as an administrator**. But only try one option at a time and restart the system after each change. If you still get errors, try running the installation routine while the system is booted into Safe Mode.

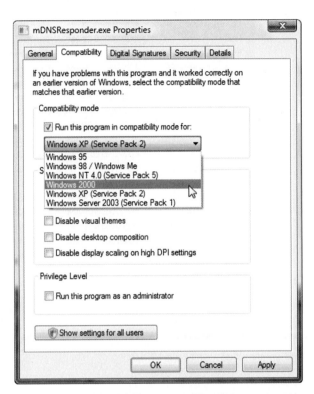

Figure 12-38 Change the environment under which a program runs
Courtesy: Course Technology/Cengage Learning

For all of the 64-bit versions of Vista, as well as the one 64-bit version of Windows XP, here's one more tip that might help when programs refuse to install or later the program runs with errors. By default, 64-bit Vista and XP install 64-bit programs in the \Program Files folder and install 32-bit programs in the \Program Files (x86) folder (see Figure 12-39). However, 32-bit programs might give errors when installed in this second folder. To correct the problem, uninstall the program and perform the installation routine again. During the installation, you are given the opportunity to select the folder to hold the program files. Change the selection to another folder that you have created. For example, some application developers suggest you create a folder named \Program Files x86 to install their 32-bit applications using 64-bit Windows Vista or XP.

If you still have problems with the program or its installation, look for solutions at the Microsoft Web site at *support.microsoft.com*. Search on the error message, application name, or symptom of the problem. Also search the Web site of the application developer for help with error messages. Be sure you have downloaded and installed all Windows patches because these sometimes resolve problems with applications.

In Windows Vista, use the Programs window to manage software, including installed applications and Windows components. From Control Panel, click **Programs**. The list of tools to manage installed programs appears in the right pane of the Programs window shown in Figure 12-40.

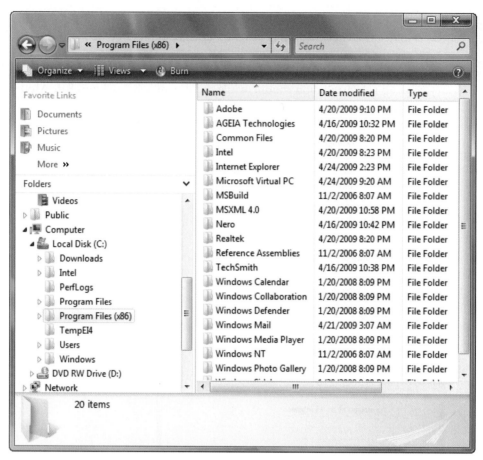

Figure 12-39   Two folders to hold program files using a 64-bit version of Vista
Courtesy: Course Technology/Cengage Learning

Figure 12-40   Manage software on your PC using the Programs window
Courtesy: Course Technology/Cengage Learning

A+
220-701
2.2
3.1

To see a list of installed programs, under Programs and Features, click **Uninstall a program**. The Programs and Features window shown in Figure 12-41 appears. Select a program from the list. Based on the software, the buttons at the top of the list will change. For example, in Figure 12-41, the SnagIt8 software offers the option to Uninstall, Change, or Repair the software.

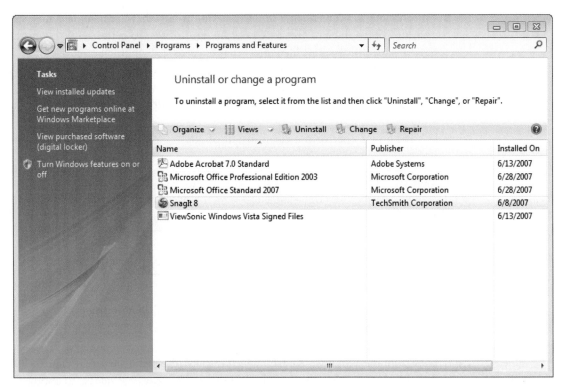

Figure 12-41 Select a program from the list to view your options to manage the software
Courtesy: Course Technology/Cengage Learning

A+
220-701
3.3

You should now have Windows Vista configured and functioning as you want it. To finish up, do one last restart and verify that everything is working and looking good. After you have verified everything, it's a good idea to back up the entire volume on which Vista is installed. How to perform a complete PC backup is covered in the next chapter.

HOW TO INSTALL WINDOWS XP

This section explains the steps to install Windows XP as a clean install (with and without another OS already installed), as an upgrade, and in a dual-boot environment. Before we get into the step-by-step instructions, here are two important tips about installing XP:

▲ You can use two programs to install Windows 2000 or 32-bit versions of Windows XP: Winnt.exe and Winnt32.exe. Winnt.exe is the 16-bit version of the setup program and Winnt32.exe is the 32-bit version. Both are located in the \i386 folder on the CD. You can use Winnt.exe for a clean install on a computer running MS-DOS, but not to perform an upgrade. Use Winnt32.exe for a clean install or an upgrade on a computer running Windows. Regardless of whether you use Winnt.exe or Winnt32.exe, the program executed is called Setup in Windows documentation. In addition, if you boot from the Windows 2000/XP CD, the Setup.exe program in the root directory of the CD is launched, which displays a setup menu.

12

A+ 220-701

A+
220-701
3.3

▲ When installing 64-bit Windows XP, the installation folder on the setup CD is named \AMD64. The \i386 folder is still present, however, and contains files used during the installation. To install 64-bit Windows XP, you must perform a clean installation (not an upgrade) by booting from the setup CD. After the installation, Windows installs 64-bit applications in the \Program Files folder and installs 32-bit applications in the \Program Files (x86) folder.

▲ An error might occur during the installation if files that are using a folder structure that exceeds 256 characters are stored on the hard drive. To get around this problem, if you have a path (folders and filenames) that exceeds 256 characters, move these folders and files to another media such as a USB drive or another computer on the network. Later, you can restore the folders and files to the hard drive. After the installation, you might find these folders and files still on the hard drive although filenames might be truncated.

Now let's see how to perform a clean install of XP.

Notes When installing Windows from across the network to a remote PC, you can only do a clean install. In this situation, run Winnt32.exe on the local Windows computer to perform a clean install on the remote PC.

WINDOWS XP CLEAN INSTALL WHEN AN OS IS NOT ALREADY INSTALLED

Follow these general directions to perform a clean install of Windows XP on a PC that does not already have an OS installed:

1. Boot from the Windows XP CD, which displays the menu shown in Figure 12-42. Note that this menu might change slightly from one Windows XP release to another. Press **Enter** to select the first option. If your PC does not boot from a CD, go to a command prompt and enter the command **D:\i386\Winnt.exe**, substituting the drive letter of your CD-ROM

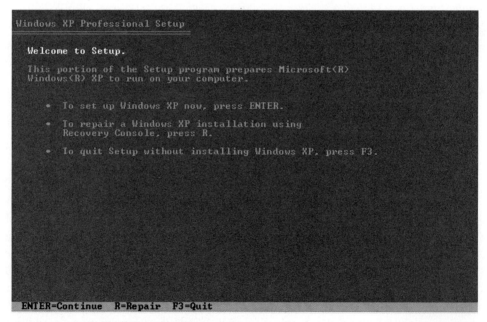

Figure 12-42 Windows XP Setup opening menu
Courtesy: Course Technology/Cengage Learning

A+
220-701
3.3

drive for D, if necessary. (The path might vary depending on the release of Windows XP.) The End-User License agreement appears. Accept the agreement by pressing **F8**.

2. Setup lists all partitions that it finds on the hard drive, the file system of each partition, and the size of the partition. It also lists any unpartitioned free space on the drive. From this screen, you can create and delete partitions and select the partition on which you want to install Windows XP. If you plan to have more than one partition on the drive, create only one partition at this time. The partition must be at least 2 GB in size and have 1.5 GB free. However, if you have the space, make it much larger so all applications can be installed on this partition—say about 10 GB. After the installation, you can use Disk Management to create the other partitions. Figure 12-43 shows an example of the list provided by Setup when the entire hard drive has not yet been partitioned.

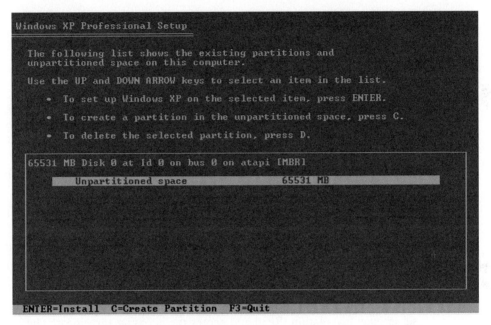

Figure 12-43 During Setup, you can create and delete partitions and select a partition on which to install Windows XP
Courtesy: Course Technology/Cengage Learning

3. If you created a partition in Step 2, Setup asks which file system you want to use to format the partition, NTFS or FAT. If the partition is at least 2 GB in size and you select FAT, Setup automatically uses the FAT32 file system. Select a file system for the partition. The Setup program formats the drive, completes the text-based portion of setup, and loads the graphical interface for the rest of the installation. The PC then restarts.

4. Select your geographical location from the list provided. Windows XP will use it to decide how to display dates, times, numbers, and currency.

5. Enter your name, the name of your organization, and your product key.

6. Enter the computer name and the password for the local Administrator account. If you are joining a domain, the computer name is the name assigned to this computer by the network administrator managing the domain controller.

Notes It is *very* important that you remember the Administrator password. You cannot log on to the system without it.

12

A+ 220-701

A+
220-701
3.3

7. Select the date, time, and time zone. The PC might reboot.

8. If you are connected to a network, you will be asked to choose how to configure your network settings. The Typical setting installs Client for Microsoft Networks, File and Printer Sharing, and TCP/IP using dynamically assigned IP addresses. The Custom setting allows you to configure the network differently. If you are not sure which to use, choose the Typical setting. You can change them later. How networks are configured is covered in Chapter 17.

9. Enter a workgroup or domain name. If you are joining a domain, the network administrator will have given you specific directions on how to configure user accounts on the domain.

> **Notes** During a normal Windows XP installation, setup causes the system to reboot three times.

WINDOWS XP CLEAN INSTALL WHEN AN OS IS ALREADY INSTALLED

For an XP clean install on a PC that already has an OS installed, follow these general directions:

> 💡 **A+ Exam Tip** The A+ 220–701 Essentials exam expects you to know how to do a Windows Vista/XP/2000 clean install and an upgrade to Windows Vista/XP/2000.

1. Close any open applications. Close any boot management software or antivirus software that might be running in the background.

2. Insert the Windows XP CD in the CD drive. Autorun launches the opening window shown in Figure 12-44. Your screen might look different depending on the release of Windows XP you are using. (If the opening window does not appear, you can start the installation by using this command in the Run dialog box: **D:\i386\winnt32.exe**, where you substitute the drive letter of your CD drive for D, if necessary.)

3. Select the option to **Install Windows XP**. On the next screen, under Installation Type, select **New Installation**. Read and accept the licensing agreement. The installation process works the same as in the preceding procedure, picking up with Step 2.

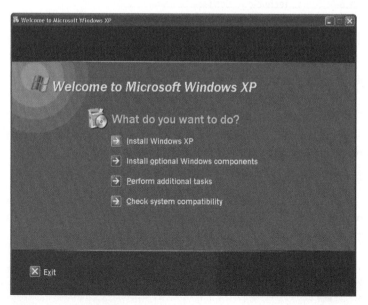

Figure 12-44 Windows XP Setup menu
Courtesy: Course Technology/Cengage Learning

A+
220-701
3.3

UPGRADE TO WINDOWS XP

When performing an upgrade to Windows XP, follow these general directions:

1. Clean up the hard drive: Erase unneeded or temporary files, empty the Recycle Bin, defragment the drive (use Windows 9x/Me or Windows 2000 Disk Defragmenter), and scan the drive for errors (use Windows 9x/Me ScanDisk or Windows 2000 Chkdsk).

2. If you do not have the latest BIOS for your motherboard, flash your BIOS.

3. Back up important files.

4. Scan the hard drive for viruses, using a current version of antivirus software.

5. If you have a compressed hard drive, decompress the drive. The only exception is that if you are using Windows NT file compression on an NTFS drive, you do not need to decompress it.

6. Uninstall any hardware or software that you know is not compatible with Windows XP, and for which you have no available upgrade. Reboot the system.

7. You're now ready to do the upgrade. Insert the Windows XP Upgrade CD in the CD drive. The Autorun feature should launch the Setup program, with the menu shown in Figure 12-44. Select the option to **Install Windows XP**.

8. If the Setup menu does not appear, you can enter the Setup command in the Run dialog box. Use the command **D:\i386\winnt32.exe**, where you substitute the drive letter of your CD-ROM drive for D, if necessary. Also, the path on your setup CD might be different, depending on the OS release you are using.

9. On the next screen, under Installation Type, select **Upgrade**. The menu gives you two options:

   ◢ *Express Upgrade*. This upgrade uses existing Windows folders and all the existing settings it can.
   ◢ *Custom Upgrade*. This upgrade allows you to change the installation folder and the language options. Using this option, you can also change the file system to NTFS.

10. Select the type of upgrade, and accept the licensing agreement.

11. Select the partition on which to install Windows XP. If the drive is configured as FAT and you want to convert to NTFS, specify that now. Note that Windows XP has an uninstall utility that allows you to revert to Windows 98 if necessary. This uninstall tool does not work if you convert FAT to NTFS.

12. Setup does an analysis of the system and reports any compatibility problems. Stop the installation if the problems indicate that you will not be able to operate the system after the installation.

13. For an upgrade from Windows 98 or Windows Me to Windows XP, the Setup program converts whatever information it can in the registry to Windows XP. At the end of the installation, you are given the opportunity to join a domain. For Windows NT and Windows 2000 upgrades, almost all registry entries are carried forward into the new OS; the information about a domain is not requested because it is copied from the old OS into Windows XP.

Notes When upgrading to Windows XP, it is best to install NTFS at the same time you install the OS from the setup CD, though you can convert a FAT file system to NTFS after Windows is installed. To convert a FAT32 volume to an NTFS volume, first back up all important data on the drive and then use this command at a command prompt: **convert D: /FS:NTFS**, where D: is the drive to be converted. Keep in mind that the program requires some free space on the drive. If it doesn't find enough free space, the program terminates.

A+
220-701
3.3

DUAL BOOT USING WINDOWS XP

You can configure Windows XP to set up a dual boot with another operating system. Start the installation as you would for a clean install on a PC with another operating system already installed. When given the opportunity, choose to install Windows XP on a different partition than the other OS. Windows XP recognizes that another OS is installed and sets up the startup menu to offer it as an option for booting.

> **Notes** When setting up a dual boot, always install the older operating system first, because the last operating system installed manages the dual boot. A newer OS will be aware of how an older operating system boots, but an older OS will not know how a newer OS boots and will not manage the boot correctly.

WHAT TO DO AFTER THE XP INSTALLATION

After you have installed XP, you need to do the following:

1. *Verify you can access the network and the Internet.* To access the network, click **Start, My Network Places**. If you don't see network resources, try rebooting the PC. Use Device Manager to verify that the network card is installed and functioning with no errors. You might need to install device drivers for the network card or for the motherboard network port.

> **A+ Exam Tip** If you don't see My Network Places on the Start menu, you can add it. Right-click **Start** and select **properties**. On the **Start Menu** tab of the Taskbar and Start Menu Properties box, click **Customize**. In the Customize Start Menu box, click the **Advanced** tab. Check **My Network Places** and click **OK** twice to close both boxes.

2. *Activate XP.* You cannot boot the PC using XP if it is not activated after the 30-day trial period is up. Using Windows XP, you cannot change or view the product key unless you are in the process of activating XP. The first time you log on to the system after the installation, the Activate Windows dialog box appears showing three options (see Figure 12-45). If you use the first option and have an Internet connection, activation takes place immediately without your further involvement.

3. *Install Windows updates and service packs.* The process works the same as it does in Vista, which is discussed earlier in the chapter.

4. *Configure automatic updates.* To control how XP automatically deals with updates, click **Start**, right-click **My Computer**, and click **Properties**. In the System Properties window, click the **Automatic Updates** tab (see Figure 12-46).

   You'll want to make these automatic update settings according to how the PC connects to the Internet and user habits. For an always-up broadband connection (such as cable modem or DSL), select **Automatic (recommended)** and choose to automatically download and install updates every day. If the PC doesn't have an always-up Internet connection (such as dial-up), you might want to select **Notify me but don't automatically download or install them**. This option works better if a user doesn't want to be bothered with a long and involved download when the PC first connects to the ISP using a slow dial-up connection. Discuss the options with the user. Make sure the user understands that if the update process is not fully automated, he or she needs to take the time to do the updates at least once a week.

A+
220-701
3.3

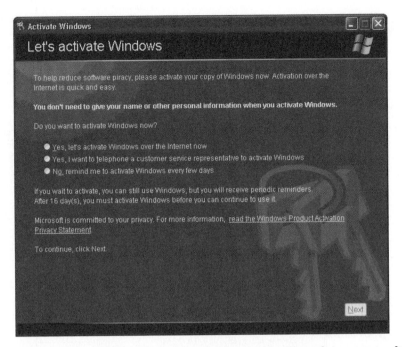

Figure 12-45   Product activation is a strategy used by Microsoft to prevent software piracy
Courtesy: Course Technology/Cengage Learning

12

A+ 220-701

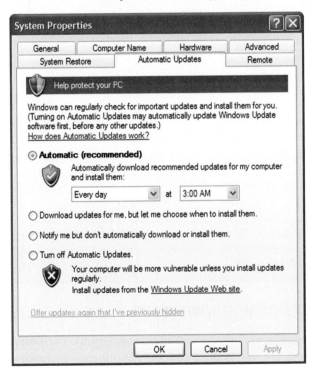

Figure 12-46   Set Automatic Updates for automatic and daily updating
Courtesy: Course Technology/Cengage Learning

5. *Install and configure XP components.* Windows XP offers additional components that are not installed during the Windows installation. To install an XP component, open the Add or Remove Programs applet in Control Panel. Click **Add/Remove Windows Components,** as shown in Figure 12-47. Then check a component you want to install and click **Next.** Follow the directions on-screen.

6. *Install hardware and applications.* Hardware and applications install as they do under Vista.

A+
220-701
3.3

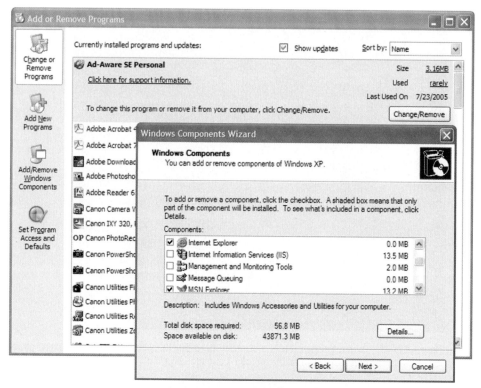

Figure 12-47 Add or remove Windows components using the Add or Remove Programs applet
Courtesy: Course Technology/Cengage Learning

HOW TO INSTALL WINDOWS 2000

Microsoft no longer supports Windows 2000, so you should never be called on to install it on a new PC. However, occasionally you might need to reinstall 2000 on a PC because the hard drive has been replaced or the Windows 2000 installation is corrupted. In these situations, you will be performing a clean installation of the OS and not an upgrade.

> **Notes** If you are having problems with Windows Setup detecting your hard drive, the problem might be out-of-date BIOS. Try flashing BIOS and then attempting the Windows installation again. Chapter 5 gives more information about flashing BIOS.

CLEAN INSTALLATION OF WINDOWS 2000

The Windows 2000 package comes with documentation and a CD. For United States distributions, the package includes a floppy disk to provide 128-bit data encryption. (This disk was not included in distributions to other countries because of laws that prohibited 128-bit data-encryption software from leaving the United States.)

If your PC is capable of booting from a CD, then insert the CD and turn on the PC. The Welcome to Setup screen appears (see Figure 12-48). Press **Enter** to begin the installation. On the next screen, press **F8** to accept the end-user license agreement (EULA). Then skip to Step 6 in the following list of steps. However, if your PC does not boot from a CD and you have a clean, empty hard drive, first create a set of Windows 2000 setup disks to boot the PC and to begin the installation. The remaining installation is done from the CD.

A+
220-701
3.3

A+ Tip The A+ 220-701 Essentials exam expects you to know how to perform a clean install of Windows 2000 Professional.

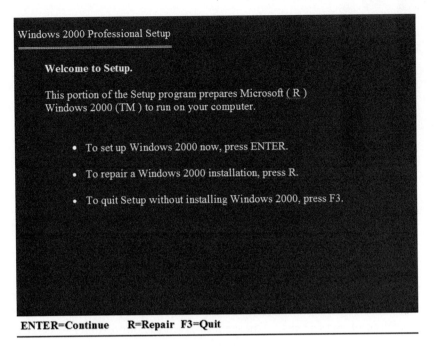

Windows 2000 Professional Setup

Welcome to Setup.

This portion of the Setup program prepares Microsoft (R) Windows 2000 (TM) to run on your computer.

- To set up Windows 2000 now, press ENTER.

- To repair a Windows 2000 installation, press R.

- To quit Setup without installing Windows 2000, press F3.

ENTER=Continue   R=Repair F3=Quit

Figure 12-48 Windows 2000 setup screen after booting from the setup CD
Courtesy: Course Technology/Cengage Learning

To make the four setup disks, follow these directions:

1. Using a working PC, format four floppy disks.

2. Place the Windows 2000 CD in the CD drive and a formatted floppy disk in the floppy disk drive. For Windows 9x/Me, click **Start,** then **Run,** and enter this command in the Run dialog box (substitute the letter of the CD-ROM drive for D: and the letter of the floppy drive for A:, if necessary):

   `D:\bootdisk\makeboot.exe A:`

3. Insert new disks in the drive as requested. Label the disks Windows 2000 Setup Disks 1, 2, 3, and 4.

4. Now begin the Windows 2000 installation. Boot the PC from the first setup disk created earlier. You will be asked to insert each of the four disks in turn and then asked to insert the Windows 2000 CD.

5. The Windows 2000 license agreement appears. Accept the agreement and the Welcome screen appears, as shown in Figure 12-49. Select **Install a new copy of Windows 2000** and click **Next.** On the next screen, accept the license agreement. The setup process is now identical to that of booting directly from the CD. Save the four setup floppy disks in case you have future problems with Windows 2000.

6. Windows 2000 searches the hard drive for partitions and asks which partition to use. If a partition needs to be created, Setup asks you which file system to use. If the partition is larger than 2 GB, and you select the FAT file system, then Windows 2000 automatically formats the drive using the FAT32 file system rather than the FAT16 file system.

12

A+ 220-701

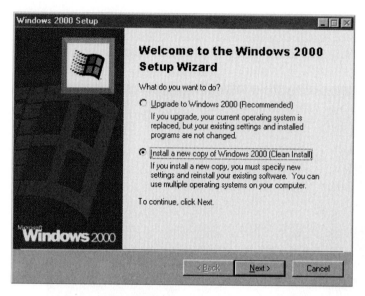

Figure 12-49 Using the Setup Wizard, you can do an upgrade, do a clean install, or create a dual boot
Courtesy: Course Technology/Cengage Learning

7. During installation, you are given the opportunity to change your keyboard settings for different languages, enter your name and company name, and enter the product key found on the CD case. You are also given the opportunity to enter date and time settings and an administrator password.

8. If Setup recognizes that you are connected to a network, it provides the Networking Settings window to configure the computer to access the network. If you select Typical settings, then Setup automatically configures the OS for your network. If you later discover the configuration is not correct, you can make changes after the installation.

9. At this point in the installation, you are asked to remove the Windows 2000 CD and click **Finish**. The computer then restarts. After Windows 2000 loads, it completes the process of connecting to the network. You are asked questions about the type of network. (For example, does the network use a domain or workgroup?)

CLEAN INSTALL OF WINDOWS 2000 WHEN AN OS IS ALREADY INSTALLED

To do a clean install of Windows 2000 when an OS is already installed, do the following:

1. Insert the Windows 2000 CD in the CD-ROM drive. If your PC detects the CD, a window opens with the message "This CD-ROM contains a newer version of Windows than the one you are presently using. Would you like to upgrade to Windows 2000?" Answer **No**. The Install Windows 2000 window appears (see Figure 12-50). If the setup routine does not launch automatically, start the installation by entering the command **D:\i386\ winnt32.exe** in the Run dialog box. Substitute the drive letter of the CD drive for D:, if necessary.

2. In the install window in Figure 12-50, click **Install Windows 2000**. The Windows Setup Wizard opens, as shown in Figure 12-49. Select **Install a new copy of Windows 2000 (Clean Install)**. Windows displays the license agreement and asks you to accept it. Enter the product key from the back of the CD case, and you will be given the opportunity to select special options. After a reboot, the installation continues as described earlier.

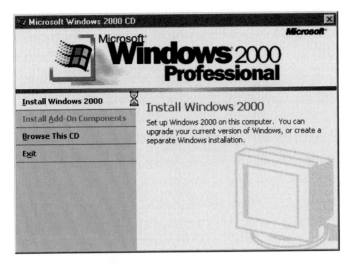

Figure 12-50 Windows 2000 Setup window
Courtesy: Course Technology/Cengage Learning

> **Notes** During installation, Windows 2000 records information about the installation to a file called Setuplog.txt. This file can be useful when troubleshooting any problems that occur during installation.

>> CHAPTER SUMMARY

- Windows can be purchased as the less expensive OEM version or the more expensive retail version. The OEM version can only be installed on a new PC for resale.

- Editions of Vista are Vista Starter, Home Basic, Home Premium, Business, Enterprise, and Ultimate.

- Editions of XP are Home Edition, XP Professional, Media Center Edition, Tablet PC Edition, and XP Professional x64 Edition.

- Windows Vista can be purchased using 32-bit or 64-bit code. The retail version of Vista Ultimate comes with two DVDs: a 32-bit DVD and a 64-bit DVD.

- A 32-bit OS cannot address as much RAM as a 64-bit OS. The ability to use more RAM is one reason to use a 64-bit OS.

- You can purchase the less expensive upgrade version of Windows if the new Windows OS has an upgrade path allowed using your older version of Windows.

- Before purchasing Windows, make sure your system meets the minimum hardware requirements and all the hardware and applications will work under the OS.

- You can start a Windows installation by booting from a CD or DVD, USB drive, or other boot media. You can also install the OS from files stored on another computer on the network.

- Windows can be installed directly from the CD or DVD, as an unattended installation, from an image, from a hidden recovery partition, or from recovery CDs. You can also repair an existing installation using processes defined by each OS.

- Windows can be installed as an upgrade, a clean installation, or in a dual boot environment with another OS.

◢ During the Windows installation, you decide which drive and partition will hold the OS. In some cases, you also decide which file system to use for the Windows volume.

◢ A Windows computer can use a workgroup or domain configuration to join a network. Using a workgroup, each computer on the network is responsible for sharing its resources with other computers on the network. In a domain, the domain controller manages network resources.

◢ Of all Windows user accounts, the administrator account has the most privileges and rights. It can create user accounts and assign them rights.

◢ Microsoft uses product activation to prevent the use of its software products, including Windows Vista and XP, on more than one computer.

◢ After the installation, verify you have network access, activate Windows, install any Windows updates or service packs, verify automatic updates is configured correctly, install and configure Windows components, install hardware and applications, create user accounts, and verify user data.

>> KEY TERMS

For explanations of key terms, see the Glossary near the end of the book.

Active Directory	loadstate	Windows Vista Business
administrator account	local account	Windows Vista Enterprise
answer file	peer-to-peer (P2P)	Windows Vista Home Basic
boot loader menu	product activation	Windows Vista Home Premium
boot partition	scanstate	Windows Vista Starter
client/server	sysprep.exe	Windows Vista Ultimate
disk cloning	system partition	Windows XP Home Edition
distribution server	unattended installation	Windows XP Media Center
domain	User State Migration Tool	Edition
drive imaging	(USMT)	Windows XP Professional
dual boot	Windows Anytime Upgrade	Windows XP Tablet PC Edition
global account	Windows Easy Transfer	workgroup

>> REVIEWING THE BASICS

1. Which is the least expensive edition of Vista that can use the Aero user interface?

2. Which three editions of Vista allow you to join a domain on a network?

3. Are there any editions of Vista that do not include the Network and Sharing Center?

4. Which edition of Windows XP supports 64-bit applications?

5. Which was the first Windows OS to come with Internet Explorer embedded in the OS?

6. What is the maximum amount of RAM that 32-bit Vista Ultimate can address?

7. What is the maximum amount of RAM that 64-bit Vista Home Premium can address?

8. Can you perform an upgrade installation of Windows XP Professional to Windows Vista Home Premium?

9. Can you use the upgrade DVD of Windows Vista Home Premium to perform a clean install on a PC that already has Windows XP Professional installed?

10. What is the minimum amount of RAM needed to install Windows Vista?

11. How much space on the hard drive does it take to install Windows Vista?

12. If you are trying to set up a dual boot between Windows XP and Windows Vista, which OS do you install first?

13. How do you start the process to reinstall an OS on a laptop computer using the backup files stored on a recovery partition?

14. What are examples of two applications that can create virtual machines?

15. If you suspect a PC is infected with a virus, why is it not a good idea to perform an upgrade installation of Windows rather than a clean install?

16. Explain the difference between the Windows boot partition and the Windows system partition.

17. What is the minimum number of partitions required in a system to set up a dual boot with Windows XP and Windows Vista?

18. What is the name of the domain controller database used by Windows Server 2008?

19. What are the two commands used by the User State Migration tool?

20. To use the User State Migration tool, how must a computer connect to the network?

21. Can you install Vista as an upgrade to Windows XP if you boot the system using the Vista DVD?

22. What file system does Vista use for the Windows volume?

23. Are you required to enter the product key during the Vista installation? During the XP installation?

24. After a Windows installation, what is the easiest way to determine that you have Internet access?

25. How many days do you normally have after a Vista or XP installation to activate the OS?

26. In which folder does Vista Home Premium, 64-bit version, install 32-bit programs?

27. In which folder does Vista Home Premium, 64-bit version, install 64-bit programs?

28. What mode of operation can be used to correct a problem with a Windows 98 application installed on a Windows Vista computer?

29. What is the difference between the two installation programs, Winnt.exe and Winnt32.exe?

30. What is the maximum character length of a path (folders and filenames) that will carry forward into a Windows XP installation?

>> THINKING CRITICALLY

1. You are planning an upgrade from Windows XP to Windows Vista. Your system uses a network card that you don't find listed on the Microsoft Windows Vista list of compatible devices. What do you do next?

   a. Abandon the upgrade and continue to use Windows XP.

   b. Check the Web site of the NIC manufacturer for a Windows Vista driver.

   c. Buy a new network card.

   d. Install a dual boot for Windows XP and Windows Vista and only use the network when you have Windows XP loaded.

2. You have just installed Windows Vista and now attempt to install your favorite game that worked fine under Windows XP. When you attempt the installation, you get an error. What is your best next step?

   a. Purchase a new version of your game, one that is compatible with Windows Vista.

   b. Download any service packs or patches to Windows Vista.

   c. Reinstall Windows XP.

3. If you find out that one of your applications is not supported by Windows Vista and you still want to use Vista, what can you do to solve this incompatibility problem?

4. Is it possible to install Windows Vista on a system that does not have a DVD drive? Explain your answer.

>> HANDS-ON PROJECTS

PROJECT 12-1:   Preparing for Windows Vista

Use the Microsoft Web site *www.microsoft.com/windows/compatibility* to research whether a home or lab PC that does not have Windows Vista installed qualifies for Vista. Fill in the following table and print the Web pages showing whether each hardware device and application installed on the PC qualify for Vista.

Hardware Device or Application	Specific Device Name or Application Name and Version	Does It Qualify for Windows Vista?
Motherboard or BIOS		
Video card		
Modem card (if present)		
Sound card (if present)		
Printer (if present)		
Network card (if present)		
CD-ROM drive (if present)		
DVD drive (if present)		
SCSI hard drive (if present)		
Other device		
Application 1		
Application 2		
Application 3		

PROJECT 12-2:   Preparing for an Upgrade

On a PC with Windows XP or an earlier version of Windows installed, access the Microsoft Web site (*www.microsoft.com*) and locate and run the Vista Upgrade Advisor to find out if the PC is ready for a Windows Vista installation. Make a list of any hardware or software components found incompatible with Vista, and draw up a plan for getting the system ready for a Vista upgrade.

PROJECT 12-3: Updating Windows

On a Windows Vista or XP system connected to the Internet, click **Start, All Programs,** and **Windows Update.** Click **Check for updates.** This takes you to the Microsoft Web site, which searches your system and recommends Windows updates. Print the Web page showing a list of recommended updates. For a lab PC, don't perform the updates unless you have your instructor's permission.

PROJECT 12-4: Install and Run Microsoft Virtual PC

Go to the Microsoft Web site (*www. microsoft.com*) and download Virtual PC. Install Virtual PC on your computer. Use it to install either Windows XP or Vista. You do not have to activate the OS and you will have 30 days to use it before it will not work. You can use the installation in the next 30 days as you work through the projects using Windows XP or Vista in the next few chapters of this book.

PROJECT 12-5: Installing Windows Components

Using Windows XP, log on with Administrator privileges and install a Windows component. What component did you install? List the steps you used to install the component.

PROJECT 12-6: Using the Internet for Problem Solving

Access the *support.microsoft.com* Web site for Windows Vista or XP support. Print one article from the Knowledge Base that addresses a problem when installing Windows Vista or XP.

PROJECT 12-7: Installing Windows Vista or XP

> ⚡ **Caution** This project will erase everything on your hard drive. Do not do it if you have important data on the hard drive.

Prepare your hard drive for a clean installation of Windows Vista or XP by formatting the hard drive. Follow the instructions in the chapter to install Windows Vista or XP. Write down each decision you had to make as you performed the installation. If you get any error messages during the installation, write them down and list the steps you took to recover from the error. How long did the installation take?

>> REAL PROBLEMS, REAL SOLUTIONS

REAL PROBLEM 12-1: A Corrupted Windows Installation

As a PC support technician for a small organization, it's your job to support the PCs, the small network, and the users. One of your coworkers, Jason, comes to you in a panic. His Windows Vista system won't boot, and he has lots of important data files in several locations on the drive. He has no idea in which folder some of the files are located. Besides the applications data he's currently working on, he's especially concerned about losing e-mail addresses, e-mail, and his Internet Explorer Favorites links.

After trying everything you know about recovering Windows Vista, you conclude the OS is corrupted beyond repair. Based on what you have learned in this and previous chapters, list the steps you would take to reinstall Windows Vista and recover all the data that Jason needs.

REAL PROBLEM 12-2: Troubleshooting an Upgrade

Your friend, Thomas, has upgraded his Windows 2000 desktop computer to Windows XP. After the installation, he made many unsuccessful attempts to connect to the Internet using his dial-up modem. The modem just refuses to work, and he has turned to you for help. He tells you the internal modem came installed on the original PC and is a Smart Link 56K modem by Uniwill Computer Corporation. Do the following to plan your troubleshooting approach:

1. List the questions you should ask Thomas to help diagnose the problem.

2. List the steps you would take if you were sitting at the computer solving the problem.

3. What do you think is the source of the problem? Explain your answer.

Maintaining Windows

In the last chapter, you learned how to install Windows Vista, XP, and 2000. This chapter takes you to the next step in learning how to support a Windows operating system: maintaining the OS after it is installed. Most Windows problems stem from poor maintenance. If you are a PC support technician responsible for the ongoing support of several computers, you can make your work easier and your users happier by setting up and executing a good maintenance plan for each computer you support. A well-maintained computer gives fewer problems and performs better than one that is not maintained. In this chapter, you will learn how to schedule regular maintenance tasks, how to prepare for disaster by setting up backup routines for user data and system files, how to manage files and folders that users and the system depend on, and how to manage a hard drive.

In this chapter, we use Windows Vista as our primary OS, but, as you read, know that we'll point out any differences between Windows Vista and Windows XP/2000 so that you can use this chapter to study all three operating systems. As you read, you might consider following the steps in the chapter first using a Windows Vista system, and then going through the chapter again using a Windows XP system. Because it is unlikely that you will support many Windows 2000 systems, steps to maintain this OS are kept to a bare minimum.

SCHEDULED PREVENTIVE MAINTENANCE

A+
220-701
2.5

One of the most common Windows problems creeps up on us over time as we install and uninstall software and use our computers for all sorts of things—Windows just gets tired and slow. Most often, the slow performance caused by all these activities could have been prevented by good maintenance. Regular preventive maintenance includes verifying Windows settings, defragmenting the hard drive, checking the drive for errors, reducing the startup process to essentials, and doing whatever else is necessary to free up enough space on the hard drive for Windows to perform well. All these tasks are discussed next.

> **Notes** When you're responsible for a computer, be sure to keep good records of all that you do to maintain, upgrade, or fix the computer. When performing preventive maintenance, take notes and include those in your documentation.

VERIFY CRITICAL WINDOWS SETTINGS

In the last chapter, you learned how to configure Windows so that updates are downloaded and installed daily. However, users sometimes change these settings without realizing their importance, and some Windows updates, such as installing a service pack, require you to manually start them.

To help out the primary user of a computer, explain to him or her the importance of automatic Windows updates. Also, if appropriate, you need to show the user how to manually check for and install updates. In addition, at least once a month, but preferably more often, verify that all updates and service packs are installed and Windows Updates is configured correctly. Do the following for Windows Vista:

1. Click **Start**, right-click **Computer**, and select **Properties** from the shortcut menu. In the System window, verify that all service packs are installed. For example, in the System window in Figure 13-1, notice that Vista Service Pack 1 is installed. As of the writing of this book, Microsoft has released one service pack for Windows Vista, but is expected to release SP2 soon. Be aware of which service packs have been released for the OS you are supporting and verify that all have been installed.

2. To see how many updates are waiting to be installed, in the System window, click the **Windows Update** link in the left pane. In Figure 13-2, notice that this system has three important updates not yet installed.

3. To view these updates, click **View available updates**. Figure 13-3 shows the three important updates and several optional ones. By default, the important updates are selected. Select the updates you want installed and click **Install**. After the installation, restart the system and check for more updates. Some updates will not show up until other updates are installed. If a service pack shows up, know that it will appear as the only available update and will require that you manually install it by following the directions on-screen. Keep installing updates until Windows reports there are no important updates to install.

4. To verify how Windows installs updates, click **Change settings** in the left pane of the Windows Update window. Note in Figure 13-4 that this system is set so that updates are not automatically installed. For sure, you'll need to manually download and install all updates on this computer, and then ask the user for permission to set updating to install automatically. Make that note in your documentation. (One reason some users

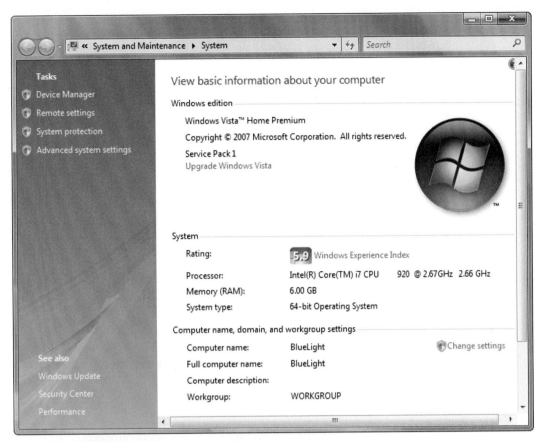

Figure 13-1 The System window gives information about hardware and the currently installed OS, including which service packs are installed
Courtesy: Course Technology/Cengage Learning

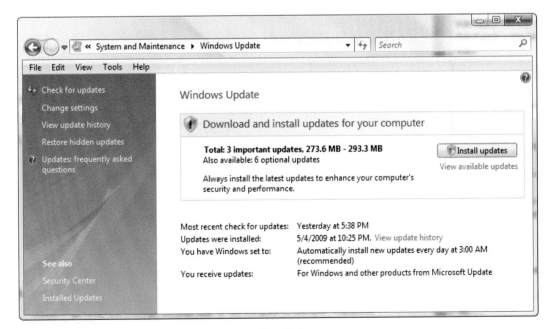

Figure 13-2 Important Windows updates are not installed
Courtesy: Course Technology/Cengage Learning

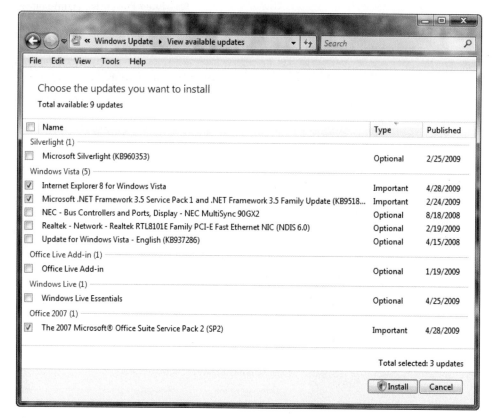

Figure 13-3 Select the updates you want to install
Courtesy: Course Technology/Cengage Learning

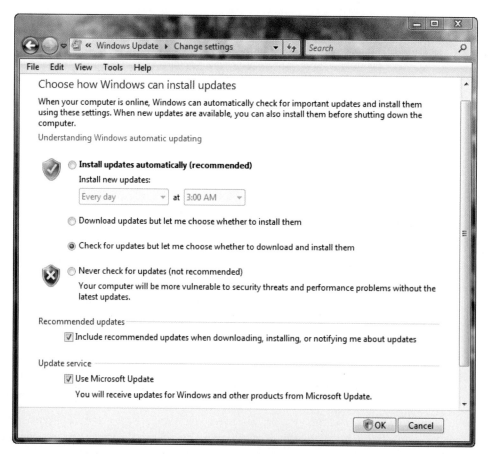

Figure 13-4 Use the Change settings link in the Windows Update window to note how Windows
updates are set to be installed
Courtesy: Course Technology/Cengage Learning

A+
220-701
2.5

would not set updating to automatic is that they have a slow Internet connection that is only connected when working on the PC, and they don't want to be bothered with downloading updates as they work. Also, some more experienced users don't trust all Vista updates and want to read up on them before they are installed, or they know that a particular update does not apply to their system.)

For Windows XP, use the System Properties box to see which service packs are installed (see Figure 13-5). Currently, Microsoft offers three service packs for Windows XP. As you can see from Figure 13-5, this XP computer has only one service pack installed. To view and manually install updates, click **Start, All Programs,** and **Windows Updates,** and then follow the directions on-screen. To see how Windows XP installs updates, click **Start,** right-click **My Computer,** and select **Properties** from the shortcut menu. In the System Properties box, click the **Automatic Updates** tab. For Windows 2000, to install updates, click **Start** and **Windows Updates.** Microsoft published four service packs for Windows 2000 before it stopped supporting the OS.

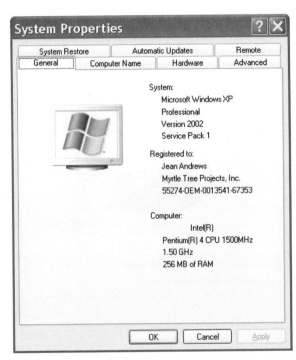

Figure 13-5 Use the System Properties window to find out what Windows XP service packs are installed
Courtesy: Course Technology/Cengage Learning

To protect a system against malicious attack, you also need to verify that antivirus software is configured to scan the system regularly and that it is up-to-date. If you discover it is not scanning regularly, take the time to do a thorough scan for viruses. Also, verify that Windows Firewall is up and configured correctly. How to do all these tasks is covered in Chapter 20.

CLEAN UP THE HARD DRIVE

Windows needs free space on the hard drive for normal operation, for defragmenting the drive, for burning CDs and DVDs, and for a variety of other tasks, so it's important to delete unneeded files occasionally. To find out how much free space is on the hard drive, open Windows Explorer and look at the volume on which Windows is installed. This volume most likely is drive C. Right-click the drive and select **Properties** from the shortcut menu. For example, free space on drive C in Figure 13-6 is only 1.59 GB. Yikes! Even for a small drive, you need at least 3 GB of free space, and you're likely to need much more. As you can see in the figure, the size of the

13

A+ 220-701

volume is 71.5 GB, which is a pretty large drive to be so full. Are there other partitions on the drive or other hard drives installed that can hold some of this data? To know for sure, turn to Disk Management. But first use Disk Cleanup to delete temporary files on the drive.

To use Disk Cleanup for Vista, follow these steps. You can also access the utility by entering cleanmgr.exe in the Start Search box. The XP Disk Cleanup utility works about the same as Vista.

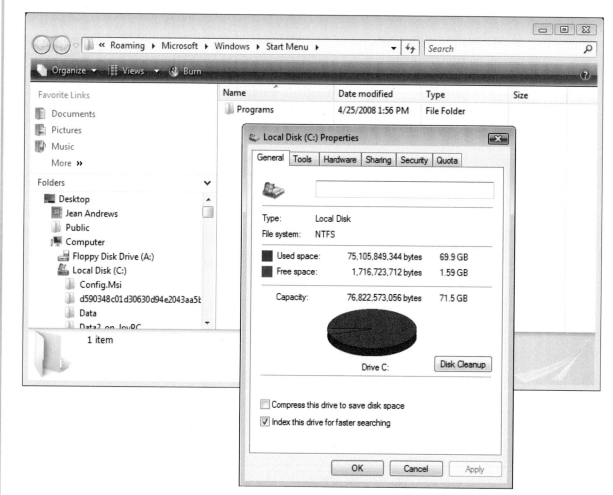

Figure 13-6   Use Windows Explorer to find out how much free space is on drive C
Courtesy: Course Technology/Cengage Learning

1. In Windows Explorer, right-click the drive and select **Properties** from the shortcut menu. The Disk Properties box appears, as shown on the left side of Figure 13-7.

2. On the General tab, click **Disk Cleanup**. A dialog box opens asking if you want to clean up only your files or files from all users on this computer. Click your choice. If you have selected to clean up the files of all users, you'll need to respond to the UAC box. Next, Disk Cleanup calculates how much space can be freed and then displays the Disk Cleanup window, also shown on the right side of Figure 13-7. From this window, you can select nonessential files to delete in order to save drive space.

Notice in Figure 13-7 the option to delete files from a Previous Windows installation(s), which can free up 10.0 GB of hard drive space. This 10 GB is used by the Windows.old folder. When Vista is installed on a system to replace or upgrade a previous Windows installation, it stores the old Windows, Program Files, and Documents and

A+
220-701
2.5

Settings folders in the Windows.old folder. If the user assures you that no information, data, or settings are needed from the old Windows installation, it's safe to delete these files to free up the 10 GB.

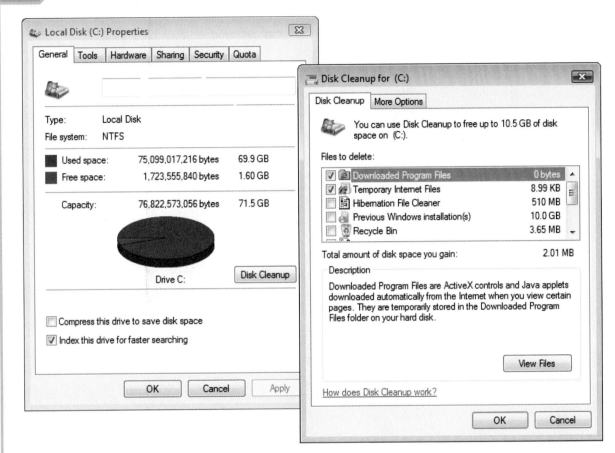

Figure 13-7 The Properties window for a drive provides Disk Cleanup, a quick and easy way to delete temporary files on a hard drive
Courtesy: Course Technology/Cengage Learning

If you still need to free up more disk space on a Windows Vista machine, click the **More Options** tab (see Figure 13-8) on the Disk Cleanup box. In the Programs and Features area, click **Clean up**. You are taken to the Vista Programs and Features window where you can uninstall unneeded software to recover that space. Also on the More Options tab of the Disk Cleanup box, when you click **Clean up** under the System Restore and Shadow Copies area, Windows will delete all but the most recent restore points that are created by System Restore. (You will learn more about System Restore later in the chapter.) In Windows XP, the More Options tab offers a third option to delete installed Windows components that you don't need.

DEFRAG THE HARD DRIVE

Another problem that might slow down a hard drive is fragmentation. Fragmentation happens over time as Windows writes files, deletes files, and writes new files to your drive. Files end up in fragmented segments all over the drive. Then, when Windows reads a fragmented file, the drive must work hard to move its read-write head all over the drive to retrieve the file. Also, if a file becomes corrupted, data-recovery utilities are less likely to be able to find all the pieces to the file if the file is fragmented rather than written on the drive in one

13

A+ 220-701

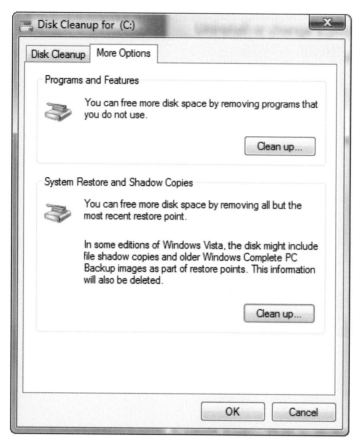

Figure 13-8 More options to free up hard drive space
Courtesy: Course Technology/Cengage Learning

location. For these reasons, you should defragment your hard drive every week as part of a good maintenance plan. Defragmenting rearranges files on the drive into as few segments as possible.

Depending on how fragmented the drive and how large the drive, defragmenting it can take less than an hour or as long as all night. Therefore, it's best to start the defrag utility when you aren't going to be using the PC for a while. By default, Vista automatically defrags a drive every Wednesday at 1:00 AM. To find out if this setting has been changed or to manually defrag the drive, close all open applications and then, using Windows Explorer, open the Properties box for the drive and click the **Tools** tab. Click **Defragment Now** and respond to the UAC box. In the Disk Defragmenter window (see Figure 13-9), verify that Vista is set to automatically defrag. You can also click **Defragment now** to defrag the drive immediately. Later in the chapter, you will learn to use the Defrag command to defrag the drive from a command prompt window.

For Windows XP, first close all open applications, and then using Windows Explorer, open the Properties box for the drive. Click the **Tools** tab and then click **Defragment Now**. In the Disk Defragment window, click **Defragment** to start the process. Figure 13-10 shows XP defragmenting a volume.

Generally, defragmenting a hard drive should be done when the hard drive is healthy; that is, it should be done as part of routine maintenance. To fully defrag the drive, 15 percent of the drive must be free. If there is less than 15 percent free space, Windows will partially defrag the drive. If you get an error message when attempting to defrag, try the utilities discussed next to repair the hard drive and then try to defrag again.

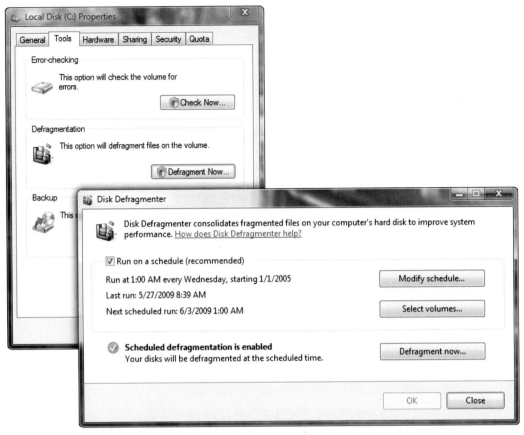

Figure 13-9 The Properties box for a drive allows you to manage the Disk Defragmenter
Courtesy: Course Technology/Cengage Learning

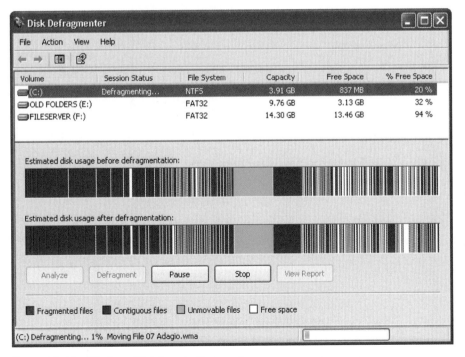

Figure 13-10 Windows XP defragmenting a volume
Courtesy: Course Technology/Cengage Learning

A+
220-701
2.5

> **Notes** Windows XP Professional offers Task Scheduler that can be used to launch a program to run at scheduled times such as weekly. Using it, you can set XP to automatically defragment the hard drive each week. How to use Task Scheduler is covered in Chapter 14.

CHECK THE HARD DRIVE FOR ERRORS

Next, to make sure the drive is healthy, you need to search for and repair file system errors using the Windows Chkdsk utility. This utility searches for bad sectors on a volume and recovers the data from them if possible. A sector can go bad over time and becomes unreliable. The Chkdsk utility tries to recover the data from these sectors and then marks the sector as bad so that data will no longer be written to it. (In Windows Explorer, the Chkdsk utility is called Error Checking.) As with defragmenting, error checking and repair can take a long time depending on the size of the drive and how many files are present.

To launch the Chkdsk utility in Vista or XP, use one of two methods:

▲ Using Windows Explorer, right-click the drive, and select **Properties** from the short-cut menu. Click the **Tools** tab, as shown in Figure 13-11, and then click **Check Now**. For Vista, respond to the UAC box. For either OS, the Check Disk dialog box

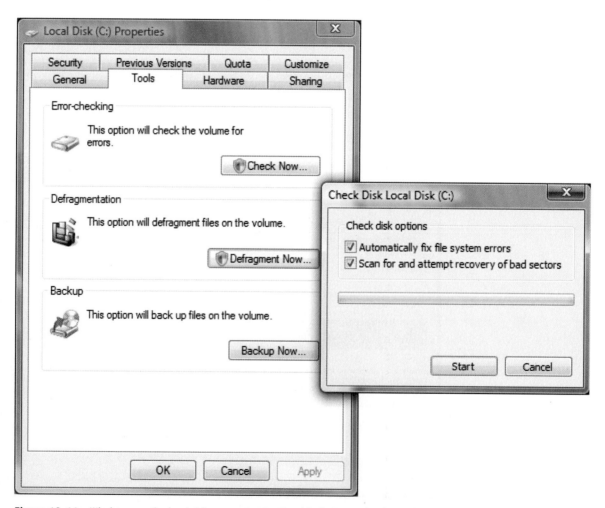

Figure 13-11 Windows repairs hard drive errors under the drive's Properties box using Windows Explorer
Courtesy: Course Technology/Cengage Learning

appears, also shown in Figure 13-11. Check the **Automatically fix file system errors** and **Scan for and attempt recovery of bad sectors** check boxes, and then click **Start**. For the utility to correct errors on the drive, it needs exclusive use of all files on the drive. When Windows has this exclusive use, the drive is called a locked drive. If files are open, a dialog box appears telling you about the problem and asking your permission to scan the drive the next time Windows starts. Reboot the system and let her rip.

▲ Use the Chkdsk command in a command prompt window. (Vista requires an elevated command prompt window.) For Vista, click **Start**, click **All Programs**, and click **Accessories**. Right-click **Command Prompt**, select **Run as administrator** from the shortcut menu, and respond to the UAC box. For XP, enter **cmd** in the Run dialog box. In the command prompt window for either OS, enter this Chkdsk command:

```
chkdsk c:/r
```

> **Notes** The Chkdsk command is also available from the Windows Vista Recovery Environment and the Windows XP Recovery Console. You will learn to use Chkdsk under both environments later in the book.

> 💡 **A+ Exam Tip** The A+ 220-701 Essentials exam expects you to know about the outdated Windows 9x/Me Scandisk command. The Windows 9x/Me command, Scandisk C, is equivalent to Chkdsk C: /R in Windows Vista/XP/2000. Both commands find bad sectors on a hard drive and attempt to recover data from these sectors. Know that neither Scandisk or Chkdsk can actually fix a bad sector.

Before you move on to the next step in cleaning up Windows, reboot the system and verify all is well. If the drive was heavily fragmented with errors and unneeded files, you should now see a marked improvement in performance.

VERIFY STARTUP PROGRAMS

When software is installed, it sometimes adds itself to the list of processes that are automatically launched at startup. Applications are launched at startup by a shortcut or program file in a startup folder, an entry in the registry, or an entry in the Scheduled Task list.

Over time, many startup programs can accumulate on a system, which can cause startup to be slow and the system to become sluggish. Each program loaded at startup uses up some memory and adds to the time needed to start Windows. As a part of good routine maintenance, you need to check the programs launched at startup, and verify that the ones there are actually needed. Examples of programs that you might want to remove from the startup list are chat programs, programs to handle multimedia that you don't use very often, programs that monitor the Internet for updates to software installed on your system, and pop-up blockers.

If you can reduce the list of startup programs, performance might dramatically improve and errors at startup can be eliminated. In this chapter, you will learn about the easy-to-use tools to view and stop startup programs. In the next chapter, you will learn about other advanced tools, such as Msconfig, that you can use to eliminate startup programs that are more difficult to reach.

Let's first look at how to view and temporarily disable startup programs in Vista and then we'll see how to do the same tasks using Windows XP.

A+
220-701
2.5

STARTUP PROGRAMS IN WINDOWS VISTA

Certain folders are designated as startup folders for all user accounts or a particular user account. Placing a program or a shortcut to a program in one of these folders causes the program to launch at startup. In addition to startup folders, entries in several keys of the registry can cause programs to be launched at startup. The startup folders that Windows Vista uses are:

- ◢ **For individual users:** C:\Users*username*\AppData\Roaming\Microsoft\Windows\Start Menu\Programs\Startup
- ◢ **For all users:** C:\ProgramData\Microsoft\Windows\Start Menu\Program\Startup

Follow these steps to use Software Explorer to view and stop startup programs in Vista:

1. In Control Panel under Programs, click **Change startup programs**. In the Windows Defender Software Explorer window, under the Category drop-down menu, select **Startup Programs** (see Figure 13-12). A list of applications and services that are launched at startup appears.

2. When you select a program on the left, notice on the right side you can see how the program is launched at startup. For example, in Figure 13-12, the selected program is launched by way of a registry entry. To temporarily disable a startup program, click **Disable** at the bottom of the window.

3. You might find startup programs that are launched by way of a program file or shortcut placed in a startup folder. For example, you can see in Figure 13-13 that the Snagit

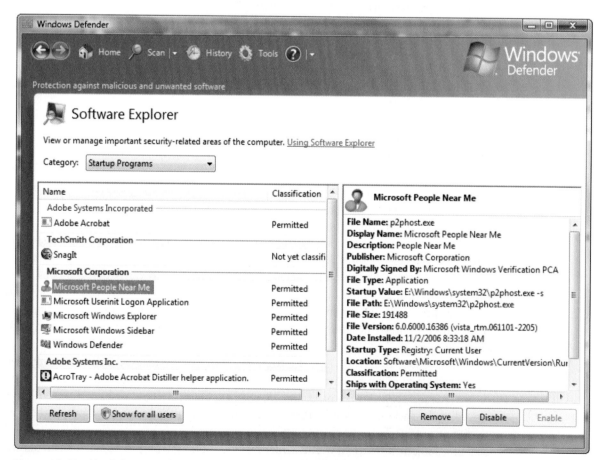

Figure 13-12 Use Software Explorer in Vista to find out what programs are launched at startup
Courtesy: Course Technology/Cengage Learning

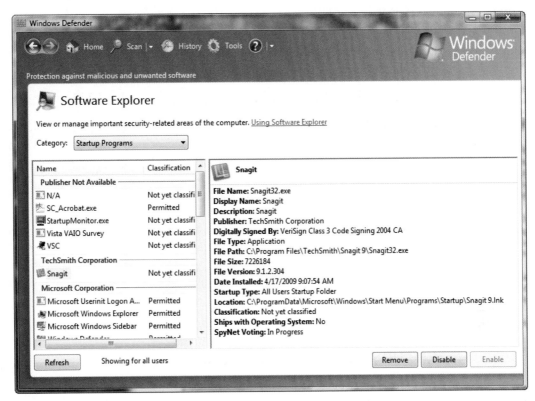

Figure 13-13 A startup program is launched by using a startup folder
Courtesy: Course Technology/Cengage Learning

program starts because of any entry in the all-users startup folder. To stop this startup program you can (a) click **Disable** to temporarily stop it; (b) click **Remove** to delete it from the all-users startup folder; or (c) use the Snagit menus to configure Snagit not to start at startup.

4. As you view startup programs, if you find one that is no longer needed on the system and can be uninstalled, open the Control Panel, and then click **Uninstall a program**. In the Programs and Features window, select the program and click **Uninstall**.

As you smoke out unnecessary or unwanted programs, it helps to know which ones you definitely want to keep. Table 13-1 lists the minimum number of programs that you would find running in a barebones Windows Vista system immediately after startup. Any other programs you find listed in Software Explorer should be considered guilty of unnecessarily using resources until you've checked them out. If you need help identifying a program,

Program	Description	Startup Programs	Currently Running Programs*
userinit.exe	**Userinit Logon Application**	X	
explorer.exe	**Windows Explorer**	X	X
MSASCui.exe	**Windows Defender**	X	X
Dwm.exe	**Desktop Window Manager**		X
taskeng.exe	**Task Scheduler Engine**		X

*Programs that continue to run after startup is completed or are launched by other startup programs

Table 13-1 Programs launched at startup on a barebones Vista system

A+
220-701
2.5

search the Internet for information about the program using a search engine, such as *www.google.com*. However, be cautious when taking advice from some sites. Many Web sites try to convince you a good program is bad so you will download and use their software to remove it.

STARTUP PROGRAMS IN WINDOWS XP

Windows XP does not offer the convenient Vista Software Explorer tool. For Windows XP, you must manually check the startup folders and delete or move the entries you don't want. (If you're not sure if you want to permanently delete an entry from a startup folder, move it to another folder. If you change your mind, you can later move it back.) The startup folders that Windows XP uses are:

- ▲ **For individual users:** C:\Documents and Settings*username*\StartMenu\Programs\Startup
- ▲ **For all users:** C:\Documents and Settings\All Users\Start Menu\Program\Startup

Next, look for any software that is no longer needed by the system and can be uninstalled. In the Control Panel, use the Add or Remove Programs applet to uninstall programs.

FREE UP ADDITIONAL HARD DRIVE SPACE

After you have cleaned up all unneeded files on the hard drive, use Windows Explorer to find out how much free space is on the drive. There is no set minimum free space for Vista, because the amount depends on how Vista and its applications are used. A good rule of thumb is to shoot for at least 15 percent of the drive to be free. If you still don't have that much, you can consider the following to get some additional space:

MOVE SOME DATA TO OTHER DRIVES OR DEVICES

Most of us enjoy our digital cameras, and we tend to keep a lot of photos on a hard drive. To free up that space, gather them all up and burn them to a few CDs or DVDs. Home videos or movies installed on a hard drive can take up tons of space. Consider an external hard drive to hold them all, or burn them to DVDs.

CONSIDER DRIVE OR FOLDER COMPRESSION

If a volume is formatted using the NTFS file system, you can compress folders on the drive to save space, even if the drive is the one on which Windows is installed. However, know that drive compression will slow down a system because every file that is opened must be decompressed before it can be used. To avoid this problem, it's better to upgrade to a larger hard drive, or move some data to another media. If you do decide to compress a folder, right-click the folder and select **Properties**. On the General tab, click **Advanced**. In the Advanced Attributes box (see Figure 13-14), click **Compress contents to save disk space** and click **OK** and then click **Apply**. If you decide to compress the entire drive, right-click the drive and click **Properties** from the shortcut menu. On the General tab, click **Compress this drive to save disk space** and click **Apply**.

REORGANIZE FOLDERS AND VOLUMES

Does the drive have more than one volume, such as drive C and drive D? If so, you can move some data or applications to another volume. To move applications from one volume or hard drive to another, you'll first have to uninstall the application. Most applications install their program files in the C:\Program Files folder, but during installation, they suggest

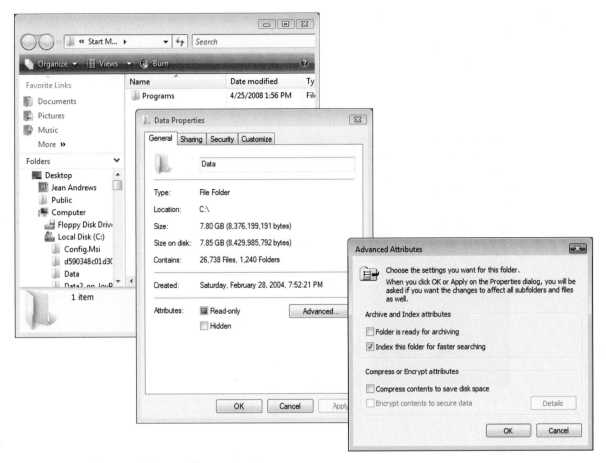

Figure 13-14 Compress folders or files to save disk space
Courtesy: Course Technology/Cengage Learning

this location and give you the opportunity to change it. You can then point to a different volume in the system to hold the application. Later in the chapter, you will learn how to use Disk Management to extend the size of a volume or to expand the usable space on a volume by mounting a drive to the volume.

> **Notes** Vista installs on an NTFS volume, but if a second volume on the drive is formatted using the FAT32 file system, you can convert the volume to NTFS. For large drives, NTFS is more efficient and converting might improve performance. NTFS also offers better security and file and folder compression. For two Microsoft Knowledge Base articles about converting from FAT to NTFS, go to *support.microsoft*.com and search for articles 314097 and 156560.

MOVE THE VIRTUAL MEMORY PAGING FILE

A+
220-701
3.3

Windows uses a file, Pagefile.sys, in the same way it uses memory. This file is called **virtual memory** and is used to enhance the amount of RAM in a system. Normally, the file, **Pagefile.sys**, is a hidden file stored in the root directory of drive C. To save space on drive C, you can move Pagefile.sys to another partition on the same hard drive or to a different hard drive, but don't move it to a different hard drive unless you know the other hard drive is at least as fast as this drive. If the drive is at least as fast as the drive on which Windows is installed, performance should improve. Also, make sure the new volume has plenty of free space to hold the file—at least three times the amount of installed RAM.

A+
220-701
3.3

To change the location of Pagefile.sys using Vista, follow these steps:

1. Click **Start**, right-click **Computer**, and click **Properties**. The System window appears.

2. Click **Advanced system settings** and respond to the UAC box. The System Properties box appears (see Figure 13-15).

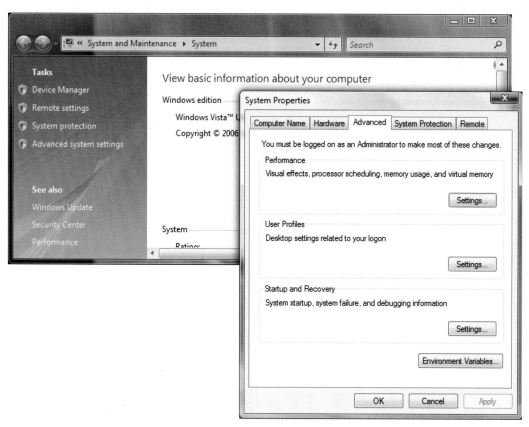

Figure 13-15 Manage virtual memory using the System Properties box
Courtesy: Course Technology/Cengage Learning

3. On the Advanced tab in the Performance section, click **Settings**. In the Performance Options box, select the **Advanced** tab and click **Change**. The Virtual Memory dialog box appears.

4. Uncheck **Automatically manage paging file size on all drives** (see Figure 13-16). Select the drive. For best performance, allow Windows to manage the size of the paging file. Select **System managed size** and click **Set**.

5. Click **OK**. Windows informs you that you must restart the system for the change to take effect. Click **OK** to close the warning box.

6. Click **Apply** and **OK** to close the Performance Options box. Click **OK** to close the System Properties box and then restart the system.

For Windows XP, click **Start**, right-click **My Computer**, select **Properties**, and then click the **Advanced** tab. In the Performance section, click **Settings**, click the **Advanced** tab, and then click **Change**. The Virtual Memory box that appears looks and works similarly to the Vista Virtual Memory box in Figure 13-16.

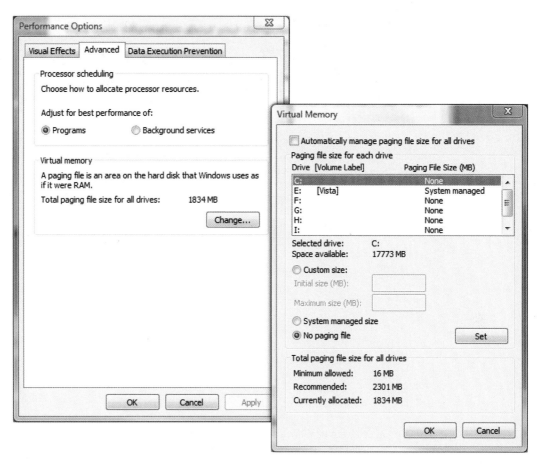

Figure 13-16 Move Pagefile.sys to a different drive
Courtesy: Course Technology/Cengage Learning

LIMIT SPACE USED BY INTERNET EXPLORER

Here are some things you can do to save space on your Windows volume that is normally used by Internet Explorer:

▲ *Suggestion 1:* Reduce the amount of space Internet Explorer is allowed to use to cache files. In Internet Explorer, click **Tools**, then **Internet Options**. The Internet Options window opens. On the General tab under Browsing history, click **Settings**. In the Temporary Internet Files and History Settings dialog box, change the amount of disk space to use (see Figure 13-17). Microsoft recommends that you not reduce the size below 50 MB.

▲ *Suggestion 2:* If you have some room on a second volume, you can move the Internet Explorer cache folder to that volume. Normally, this Vista folder is C:\Users*username*\AppData\Local\Microsoft\Windows\Temporary Internet Files. To move it somewhere else, on the General tab of the Internet Options window under Browsing history, click **Settings**. In the settings dialog box, click **Move folder**. In the Browse for Folder box, select the destination folder and click **OK** three times to close all boxes.

▲ *Suggestion 3:* You can also set IE to empty the cache folder each time you close the browser. To do that, on the Internet Options window, click the **Advanced** tab. Scroll down to the Security section, check **Empty Temporary Internet Files folder when**

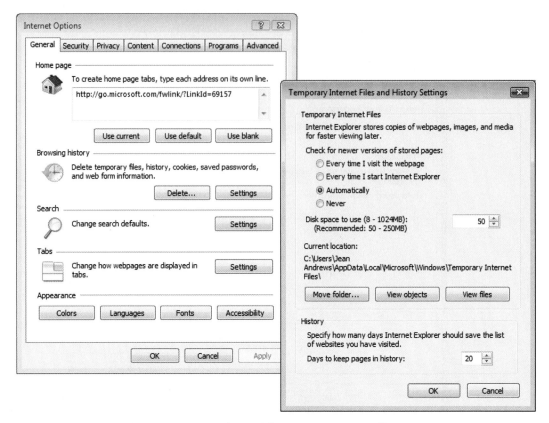

Figure 13-17 Allocate hard drive space to be used for temporary Internet files
Courtesy: Course Technology/Cengage Learning

browser is closed (see Figure 13-18) and click **Apply**. This setting is also good to use when you're using a public computer and want to make sure you don't leave tracks about your private surfing habits.

If you still don't have enough free space on the Windows volume, consider adding a second hard drive to the system. In fact, if you install a second hard drive that is faster than the Windows hard drive, know that reinstalling Windows on the faster hard drive will improve performance. You can then use the slower and older hard drive for data.

Now let's look at how to perform on-demand backups and routine scheduled backups of user data and Windows system files.

BACKUP PROCEDURES

A backup is an extra copy of a data or software file that you can use if the original file becomes damaged or destroyed. Losing data due to system failure, a virus, file corruption, or some other problem really makes you appreciate the importance of having backups.

> 📝 **Notes** With data and software, here's a good rule of thumb: If you can't get along without it, back it up.

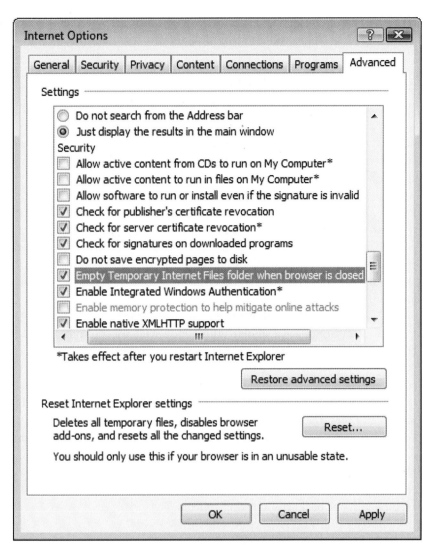

Figure 13-18 Set Internet Explorer not to keep a cache after the browser is closed
Courtesy: Course Technology/Cengage Learning

APPLYING CONCEPTS Dave was well on his way to building a successful career as a PC repair technician. His PC repair shop was doing well, and he was excited about his future. But one bad decision changed everything. He was called to repair a server at a small accounting firm. The call was on the weekend when he was normally off, so he was in a hurry to get the job done. He arrived at the accounting firm and saw that the problem was an easy one to fix, so he decided not to do a backup before working on the system. During his repairs, the hard drive crashed and all data on the drive was lost—four million dollars worth! The firm sued, Dave's business license was stripped, and he was ordered to pay the money the company lost. A little extra time to back up the system would have saved his whole future. True story!

Because most of us routinely write data to the hard drive, in this section, we focus on backing up from the hard drive to another media. However, when you store important data on any media—such as a flash drive, external hard drive, or CD—always keep a copy of the data on another media. Never trust important data to only one media.

A+
220-701
2.5

In this part of the chapter, you'll see how to make a disaster recovery plan and then learn how to back up user data, critical system files, and the entire hard drive.

PLANNING FOR DISASTER RECOVERY

The time to prepare for disaster is before it occurs. If you have not prepared, the damage from a disaster will most likely be greater than if you had made and followed disaster plans. Suppose the hard drive on your PC stopped working and you lost all its data. What would be the impact? Are you prepared for this to happen? Consider these points and tips when making your backup and recovery plans:

▲ *Point 1*. Decide on the backup media (tape, CD, DVD, flash drive, another hard drive, or other media). Even though it's easy to do, don't make the mistake of backing up your data to another partition or folder on your same hard drive. When a hard drive crashes, most likely all partitions go down together and you will have lost your data and your backup. Back up to another media and, for extra safety, store it at an off-site location.

▲ *Point 2*. Windows XP/2000 offers the Ntbackup.exe program to back up files and folders, and Vista offers a similar utility. However, you can purchase third-party backup software that might be easier to use and offer more features. For example, in Chapter 10, you saw an external hard drive by Maxtor (see Figure 13-19) that comes bundled with a backup utility. Recall that you can select folders and file types (identified by the file extension) to back up and the days and times to back up. At scheduled times, the utility copies the files and folders to the external hard drive, keeping 10 levels of backups. At any time, if you push the button on the front of the drive, a backup is created on the spot. Many backup devices have similar features. However, before you decide to use an all-in-one backup system such as this one, be certain you understand the risks of not keeping backups at an off-site location and keeping all your backups on a single media.

Figure 13-19 This external hard drive by Maxtor uses a USB port and comes bundled with backup software
Courtesy: Course Technology/Cengage Learning

A+
220-701
2.5

◢ *Point 3.* Because backing up data takes time and backup media is expensive, you can use a selective backup plan where you only back up data that changes often. For example, you might ask users to store all their data in certain folders and then you only maintain current backups of these folders rather than back up an entire hard drive. Also, note that scheduled backups that run during the night are the least disruptive for users.

◢ *Point 4.* Data should be backed up after about every four to ten hours of data entry. This might mean you back up once a day, once a week, or once a month.

◢ *Point 5.* So that you'll have the right information when you need to recover data from your backups, always record your regular backups in a log with the following information:

- Folders or drives backed up

- Date of the backup

- Type of backup

- Label identifying the tape, disk, or other media

If you discover that data has been lost days or weeks ago, you can use this backup log or table to help you recover the data. Keep the records in a notebook. You can also store the records in a log file (a file where events are logged or recorded) each time you back up. Store the file on a flash drive or another PC. Figure 13-20 shows one example of a backup log table.

Folder Backup Up	Date	Type of Backup	Tape Label
C:\Payroll	2010-06-04	Full	June, First Friday
C:\Payroll	2010-06-07	Incremental	Monday
C:\Payroll	2010-06-08	Incremental	Tuesday
C:\Payroll	2010-06-09	Incremental	Wednesday
C:\Payroll	2010-06-10	Incremental	Thursday
C:\Payroll	2010-06-11	Full	June, Second Friday
C:\Payroll	2010-06-14	Incremental	Monday

Figure 13-20 Keeping backup logs can help you when recovering data
Courtesy: Course Technology/Cengage Learning

◢ *Point 6.* When you perform a backup for the first time or set up a scheduled backup, verify that you can use the backup tape or disks to successfully recover the data. This is a very important step in preparing to recover lost data. After you create a backup, erase a file on the hard drive, and use the recovery procedures to verify that you can re-create the file from the backup. This verifies that the backup medium works, that the recovery software is effective, and that you know how to use it. After you are convinced that the recovery works, document how to perform it.

◢ *Point 7.* Keep your backups in a safe place and routinely test them. Don't leave a backup tape or drive lying around for someone to steal. Backups of important and sensitive data should be kept under lock and key. In case of fire, keep enough backups off-site so that you can recover data even when the entire building is destroyed. Routinely verify that your backups are good by performing a test recovery of a backed-up file or folder. Backups are useless if the data on the backup is corrupted.

Notes If you travel a lot and your organization doesn't provide online backup, keeping good backups of data on your notebook computer might be a problem. Several Internet companies have solved this backup-on-the-go problem by providing remote backup services over the Internet. In a hotel room or other remote location, connect to the Internet and back up your data to a Web site's file server. If data is lost, you can easily recover it by connecting to the Internet and logging into your backup service Web site. If security is a concern, be sure you understand the security guarantees of the site. Two online backup services are Norton Online Backup (*www.backup.com*) and Remote Backup Systems (*www.remote-backup.com*).

13

A+ 220-701

A+
220-701
2.5

BACK UP USER DATA

In this part of the chapter, you'll see how to back up user data using Windows Vista and Windows XP/2000.

WINDOWS VISTA BACKUP UTILITY

The Windows Vista backup utility, called the Backup and Restore Center, limits your decisions about which user files and folders on a Vista system you can back up. You are forced to back up data for all users. Follow these steps to back up files and folders:

1. Connect your backup device to your PC. If you are using an external hard drive, use Windows Explorer to verify you can access the drive.

2. From Control Panel, under System and Maintenance, click **Back up your computer**. The Backup and Restore Center window appears, as shown in Figure 13-21.

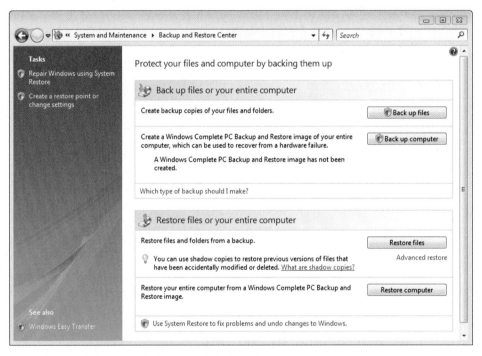

Figure 13-21 Windows Vista Backup and Restore Center
Courtesy: Course Technology/Cengage Learning

⚡ **Caution** Before starting a backup on a laptop, plug the laptop into an AC outlet so that the process will not be interrupted by a failed battery.

3. Click **Back up files** and respond to the UAC box. On the next window (see Figure 13-22) select where you want to save your backup and click **Next**.

4. On the next window, select the volumes on your computer that contain folders or files you want to back up and click **Next**.

5. On the next window, shown in Figure 13-23, select the type of files you want to back up and click **Next**.

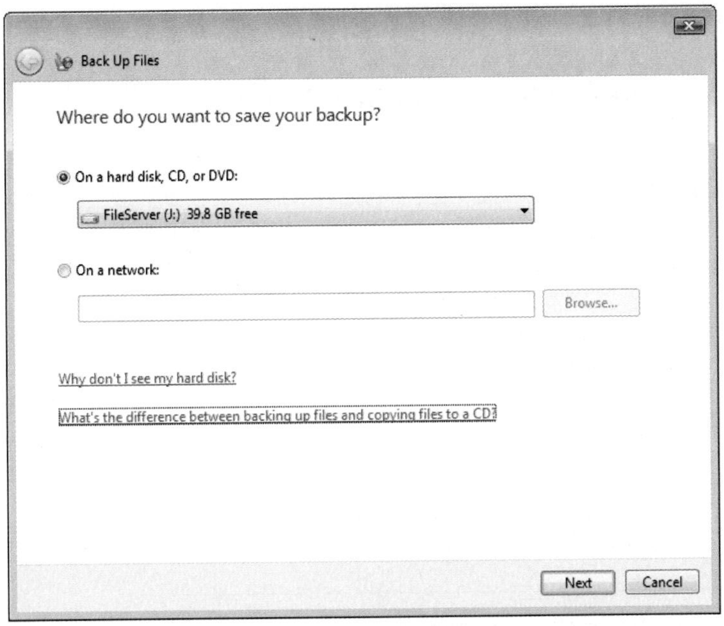

Figure 13-22 Select your backup location for files and folders
Courtesy: Course Technology/Cengage Learning

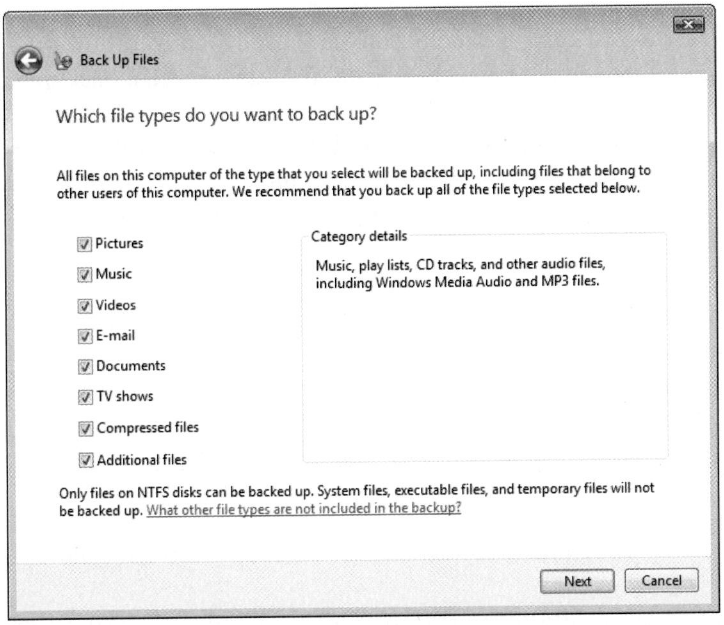

Figure 13-23 Select the type of files to back up
Courtesy: Course Technology/Cengage Learning

6. The next window lets you select how often (daily, weekly, or monthly), what day (day of week or day of month), and what time of day to schedule automatic incremental backups of today's full backup. (An incremental backup backs up only files that have changed since the last full backup or the last incremental backup.) Make your selections and click **Save settings and start backup**.

To see the status of the last backup, click **Start, All Programs, Accessories, System Tools, Backup Status and Configuration**. The Backup Status and Configuration window opens, as shown in Figure 13-24. Using this window, you can change the backup settings. When you change the settings, a new, full backup is created.

A+
220-701
2.5

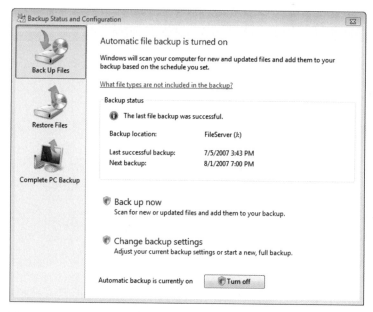

Figure 13-24   Backup Status and Configuration window
Courtesy: Course Technology/Cengage Learning

To restore files from backup, on the Backup Status and Configuration window, click **Restore Files** and follow the directions on-screen to select a specific backup and specific folders or files to restore.

Because Windows Vista backup gives you so little control over the folders you choose to back up, many people turn to third-party backup utilities. If you use one of these utilities, besides the folders that contain your documents, spreadsheets, databases, and other data files, you also might want to back up these folders:

- ▲ *Your e-mail messages and address book.* For Windows Mail, back up this folder: C:\Users*username*\AppData\Local\Microsoft\Windows Mail.
- ▲ *Your Internet Explorer favorites list.* To back up your IE favorites list, back up this folder: C:\Users*username*\Favorites.

BACK UP USER DATA WITH WINDOWS 2000/XP

To perform a backup using Ntbackup.exe under Windows 2000/XP, follow these steps:

1. Click **Start,** point to **All Programs (Programs** for Windows 2000), point to **Accessories,** point to **System Tools,** and then click **Backup.** The Backup Wizard appears (see Figure 13-25). Click **Advanced Mode.**

2. The Backup utility opens. Click the **Backup** tab. Your screen should look like Figure 13-26. If you want to perform a backup immediately, check the drive and subfolders to back up.

3. In the lower-left corner of the Backup Utility window, note the text box labeled Backup media or file name, which specifies where to back up to. To change this location, click the **Browse** button. The Save As dialog box appears. Navigate to the drive and path where you'd like to save the backup file and enter a name for the file. Click **Save.** The new path and name for the backup file appear in the text box.

A+
220-701
2.5

Figure 13-25 Backup or Restore Wizard
Courtesy: Course Technology/Cengage Learning

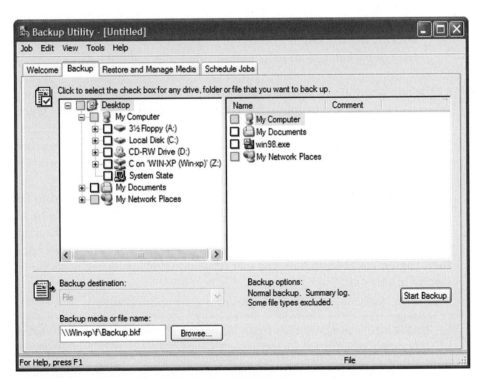

Figure 13-26 You can perform an immediate backup from the Backup tab
Courtesy: Course Technology/Cengage Learning

13

A+ 220-701

4. Click the **Start Backup** button in the lower-right corner. The Backup Job Information box appears. If you want to replace an existing backup, select **Replace the data on the media with this backup**. To append the data, select **Append the backup to the media**. Then click **Start Backup**.

A+
220-701
2.5

You can schedule a single backup to be done at a later time or repeated on a schedule until you terminate the schedule. When planning routinely scheduled backups, you have some options so that you don't have to back up everything at each backup. It's a lot less expensive and less time-consuming to only back up what's changed since the last backup. Windows 2000/XP offers these options for scheduled backups:

- *Full backup (also called a normal backup)*. All files selected for backup are copied to the backup media. Each file is marked as backed up by clearing its archive attribute. Later, if you need to recover data, this full backup is all you need. (After the backup, if a file is changed, its archive attribute is turned on to indicate the file has changed since its last backup.)

- *Copy backup*. All files selected for backup are copied to the backup media, but files are not marked as backed up (meaning file archive attributes are not cleared). A Copy backup is useful if you want to make a backup apart from your regularly scheduled backups.

- *Incremental backup*. All files that have been created or changed since the last backup are backed up, and all files are marked as backed up (meaning file archive attributes are cleared). Later, if you need to recover data, you'll need the last full backup and all the incremental backups since this last full backup.

- *Differential backup*. All files that have been created or changed since the last full or incremental backup are backed up, and files are not marked as backed up. Later, if you need to recover data, you'll need the last full backup and the last differential backup.

- *Daily backup*. All files that have been created or changed on this day are backed up. Files are not marked as backed up. Later, if you need to recover data, you'll need the last full backup and all daily backups since this last full backup.

The two best ways to schedule backups are a combination of full backups and incremental backups, or a combination of full backups and differential backups. When using incremental backups, because they are smaller than differential backups, you save time and money when backing up. On the other hand, recovering data is less time-consuming when using differential backups because you only need two backups to perform a full recovery (the last full backup and the last differential backup).

For a business with heavy data entry, suppose you decide you need to back up every night at 11:55 PM. To implement this backup plan, you might decide to schedule two backups: a full backup each Friday at 11:55 PM, and a differential backup each Monday, Tuesday, Wednesday, and Thursday at 11:55 PM. In a project at the end of this chapter, you'll learn how you can reuse tapes on a rotating basis for a backup plan similar to this one.

> **Notes** When making your backup plan, for extra protection, take into account that you might want to keep several generations of backups on hand. If you always overwrite the backup with a new backup, you only have one generation of backups. However, sometimes a file gets corrupted or accidentally deleted and you don't discover the problem for several weeks. If you don't keep several generations of backups, you will have no chance of recovering the data. On the other hand, if you back up weekly and keep the last 10 weeks of backups, you can go back and search previous backups to recover the file.

To schedule a backup, do the following:

1. Open the backup utility and click the **Schedule Jobs** tab, as shown in Figure 13-27. Select a date on which you want to schedule a backup, and then click the **Add Job** button.

A+
220-701
2.5

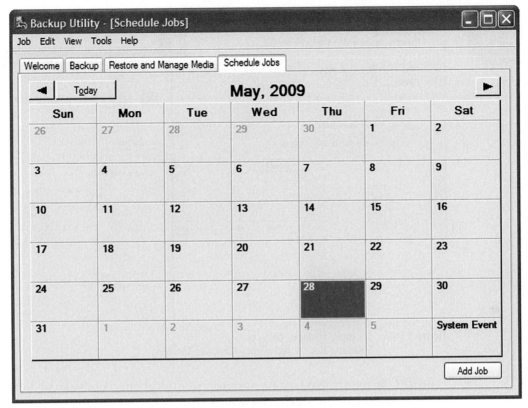

Figure 13-27 The Schedule Jobs tab of the Windows 2000/XP Backup Utility window
Courtesy: Course Technology/Cengage Learning

2. The Backup Wizard opens. On the first screen, click **Next**. Select **Back up selected files, drives, or network data**, and then click **Next**.

3. On the next screen, select the drives, folders, or files you want to back up, and then click **Next**.

4. Follow the steps through the wizard to choose where you want to save your backup, give a name to the backup, and select the type of backup (Normal, Copy, Incremental, Differential, or Daily). Note that a Normal backup is a full backup.

5. Then you are asked if you want to verify the data after backup and compress the data. Next, you must decide if you want to append the data to an existing backup or replace an existing backup. Your decision largely depends on how much space you have available for backups.

6. When asked if you want to perform the backup now or later, select **Later** and give the backup a name, as shown on the left side of Figure 13-28. Click the **Set Schedule** button.

7. The Schedule Job window appears, as shown on the right side of Figure 13-28. Schedule how often the backup is to occur, and then click **OK**. Notice in the figure that a backup is scheduled for each Monday, Tuesday, Wednesday, and Thursday at 11:55 PM.

8. Click **Next** in the wizard, and follow the remaining instructions to complete the backup. At the end of the process, the wizard gives you an on-screen report summarizing information about the backup.

13

A+ 220-701

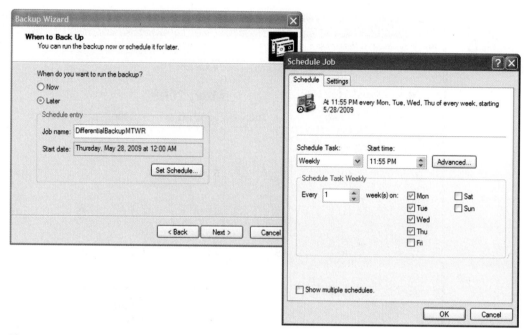

Figure 13-28   Schedule repeated backups
Courtesy: Course Technology/Cengage Learning

Besides the folders that contain documents, spreadsheets, databases, and other data files, you also might want to back up these folders:

▲ *E-mail messages and address book.* For Outlook and Outlook Express, back up this folder: C:\Documents and Settings*username*\Local Settings\Application Data\Microsoft\Outlook.

▲ *Internet Explorer favorites list.* To back up an IE favorites list, back up this folder: C:\Documents and Settings*username*\Favorites.

To recover files, folders, or the entire drive from backup using the Windows 2000/XP Backup utility, click the **Restore and Manage Media** tab on the Backup Utility window, and then select the backup job to use for the restore. The Backup utility displays the folders and files that were backed up with this job. You can select the ones that you want to restore. When you restore from backup, you'll lose all the data you've entered in restored files since the backup, so be sure to use the most recent backup and then re-enter the data that's missing.

> **Notes** By default, Windows XP Home Edition does not automatically install the Backup utility. To install it manually, go to the \VALUEADD\MSFT\NTBACKUP folder on your Windows XP setup CD and double-click **Ntbackup.msi**. The installation wizard will complete the installation.

BACK UP SYSTEM FILES

Windows Vista and XP use System Restore to keep backups of critical system files. In addition, Windows XP and Windows 2000 allow you to use the Backup utility to back up the system state data, which are the files critical to a successful operating system load. This backup includes all files necessary to boot the OS, the Windows 2000/XP registry, and all system files in the %*SystemRoot*% folder (the folder in which Windows 2000/XP is installed). Let's first see how to use Windows Vista/XP System Restore and then we'll look at how to back up the system state.

HOW TO USE VISTA AND XP SYSTEM RESTORE

System Restore restores the system to its condition at the time a snapshot was taken of the system settings and configuration. These snapshots are called **restore points**. If System Restore is turned on, Windows automatically creates a restore point before you install new software or hardware or make other changes to the system. You can also manually create a restore point at any time. In this part of the chapter, you will learn how to create a restore point, how to make sure restore points are being created automatically, and how to use these restore points.

Manually Create a Restore Point

To manually create a restore point using Windows Vista, follow these steps:

1. Click **Start**, right-click **Computer**, and select **Properties** from the shortcut menu. The System window opens.

2. Click **Advanced system settings** and respond to the UAC box. The System Properties box opens.

3. Click the **System Protection** tab (see the left side of Figure 13-29). Click **Create**.

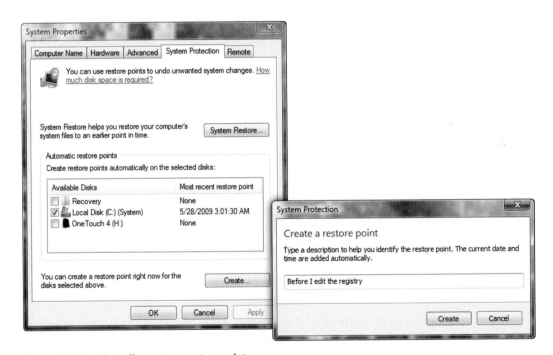

Figure 13-29   Manually create a restore point
Courtesy: Course Technology/Cengage Learning

4. In the System Protection box (right side of Figure 13-29), enter a description of the restore point and click **Create**.

5. Click **OK** twice to close both boxes. Close the System window.

To create a restore point using Windows XP, click **Start, All Programs, Accessories, System Tools**, and **System Restore**. In the System Restore dialog box, select **Create a restore point** and click **Next**. In the next box, enter a description and click **Create**.

A+
220-701
2.5

Keep System Protection Turned On

System Protection creates restore points at regular intervals and just before you install software or hardware. However, to make sure System Protection has not been turned off, click **Start**, right-click **Computer**, and select **Properties** from the shortcut menu. In the System window, click **System protection** and respond to the UAC box. The System Protection tab of the System Properties box appears (see Figure 13-30). Make sure the drive on which Windows is installed is checked, indicating that restore points are created automatically. If you make a change to this window, click **Apply** and then click **OK**.

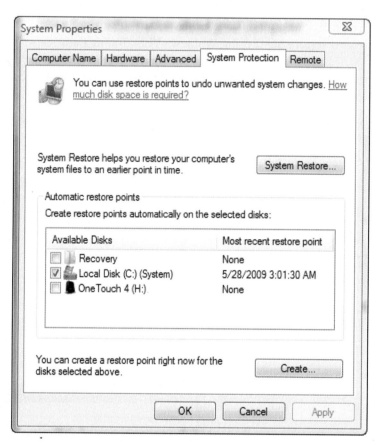

Figure 13-30   Make sure System Protection is turned on
Courtesy: Course Technology/Cengage Learning

Here is some useful information about how and when restore points are made: Restore points are normally kept in the folder C:\System Volume Information, which is not accessible to the user. Restore points are taken at least every 24 hours, and they can use up to 15 percent of disk space. If disk space gets very low, restore points are no longer made, which is one more good reason to keep about 15 percent or more of the hard drive free.

How to Apply a Restore Point

If you restore the system to a previous restore point, user data on the hard drive will not be altered, but you can affect installed software and hardware, user settings, and OS configuration settings. When you use System Restore to roll back the system to a restore point, any changes made to these settings after the restore point was created are lost; therefore, always use the most recent restore point that can fix the problem so that you make the least intrusive changes to the system.

A+
220-701
2.5

If Vista will not boot, you can launch System Restore from the Vista Recovery Environment, which you will learn to use in Chapter 15. From the Windows Vista or Windows XP desktop, to return the system to a previous restore point, do the following:

1. Click **Start, All Programs, Accessories, System Tools, System Restore** and respond to the UAC box. The System Restore box opens (see Figure 13-31).

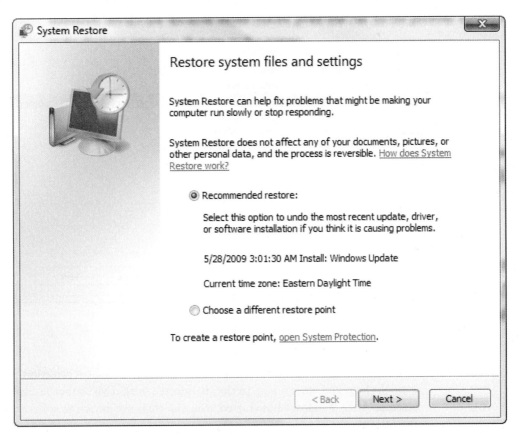

Figure 13-31 System Restore utility opening window
Courtesy: Course Technology/Cengage Learning

2. If multiple restore points exist, the box displays two options. Click **Next** to use the recommended restore point. If you don't want to use the recommended restore point, select **Choose a different restore point,** click **Next,** and select a restore point from a list (see Figure 13-32) and click **Next.** Click **Finish.** The system restarts and the restore point is applied.

Points to Remember About System Restore

System Restore is a great tool to try to fix a device that is not working, restore Windows settings that are giving problems, or solve problems with applications. Although it's a great tool in some situations, it does have its limitations. Keep these points in mind:

▲ *Point 1:* Restore points replace certain keys in the registry but cannot completely rebuild a totally corrupted registry. Therefore, System Restore can recover from errors only if the registry is somewhat intact.

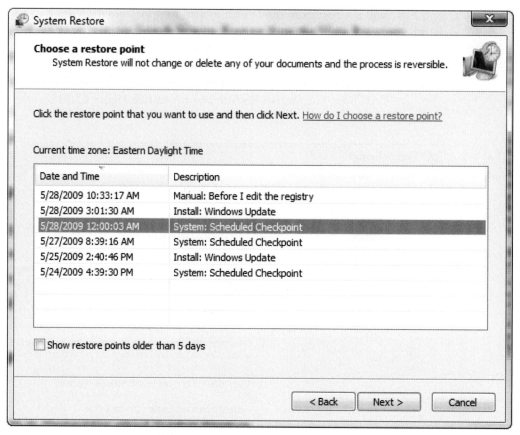

Figure 13-32   Select a restore point
Courtesy: Course Technology/Cengage Learning

> ◢ *Point 2:* The restore process cannot remove a virus or worm infection. However, it might help you start a system that is infected with a virus that launches at startup. After Windows has started, you can then use antivirus software to remove the infection.
>
> ◢ *Point 3:* System Restore might create a new problem. I've discovered that whenever I use a restore point, my antivirus software gets all out of whack and sometimes even needs reinstalling. Therefore, use restore points sparingly.
>
> ◢ *Point 4:* System Restore might make many changes to a system. If you know which change caused a problem, try to undo that particular change first. The idea is to use the least invasive solution first. For example, if updating a driver has caused a problem, first try Driver Rollback to undo that change. Driver Rollback is performed using Device Manager.
>
> ◢ *Point 5:* System Restore won't help you if you don't have restore points to use. System Protection must be turned on so that restore points are automatically created.
>
> ◢ *Point 6:* Restore points are kept in a hidden folder on the hard drive. If that area of the drive is corrupted, the restore points are lost. Also, if a user turns System Protection off, all restore points are lost.
>
> ◢ *Point 7:* Viruses and other malware sometimes hide in restore points. To completely clean an infected system, you need to delete all restore points by turning System Protection off and back on.

In Chapters 15 and 16, you will learn about other tools and methods to use when recovering from a corrupted Vista installation.

A+
220-701
2.5

HOW TO BACK UP THE SYSTEM STATE USING WINDOWS XP AND 2000

When you back up the system state data, you cannot select which files you want to back up because Windows 2000/XP always backs up all of them. A typical system state backup includes over 2,500 files and 500 MB of data. Here is the process for backing up the system state:

1. Click **Start,** point to **All Programs** (**Programs** in Windows 2000), **Accessories, System Tools,** and then click **Backup.** (Or you can enter **Ntbackup.exe** in the Run dialog box.) Depending on how the utility is configured, the Backup Utility window opens or the Backup or Restore Wizard launches (refer back to Figure 13-25). If the wizard launches, click **Advanced Mode** to see the Backup Utility window.

2. On the Backup Utility window, click the **Backup** tab (see Figure 13-33).

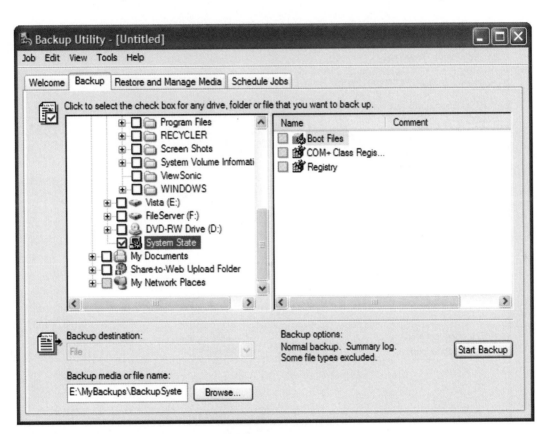

Figure 13-33 Back up the Windows XP/2000 system state
Courtesy: Course Technology/Cengage Learning

3. Check the **System State** box in the list of items you can back up. Notice in Figure 13-33 that the system state includes the boot files and the registry. It also includes the COM+(Component Object Model) Registration Database, which contains information about applications and includes files in the Windows folders.

4. Click **Browse** to point to where you want the backup saved. You can back up to any media, including a folder on the hard drive, USB drive, tape drive, or network drive. For better protection, back up to another media than your hard drive, such as another hard drive on the network. Click **Start Backup** to begin the process. A dialog box appears. Click **Start Backup** again.

A+
220-701
2.5

> **Notes** When you back up the system state, the registry is also backed up to the folder
> *%SystemRoot%*\repair\RegBack. If you later have a corrupted registry, you can copy files from this
> folder to the registry folder, which is *%SystemRoot%*\System32\Config.

If Windows gives errors or the registry gets corrupted, you can restore the system to the state it
was in when the last System State backup was made. To do that, following the instructions given
in Step 1 at the beginning of this section, open the Backup Utility window. Then click the **Restore
and Manage Media** tab (**Restore** tab in Windows 2000), which is shown in Figure 13-34.

> 💡 **A+ Exam Tip** The A+ 220-701 Essentials exam expects you to know how to use Ntbackup.exe to
> back up the system state.

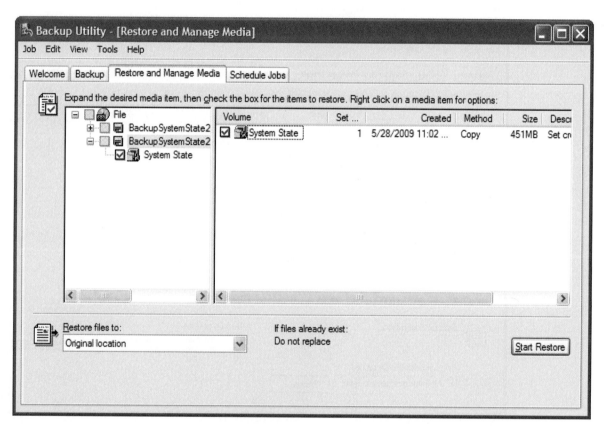

Figure 13-34   Restore the system state from the Restore and Manage Media tab of the Backup dialog box
Courtesy: Course Technology/Cengage Learning

From the Restore and Manage Media tab, first select the backup you want to restore.
Then, in the list box in the lower-left corner, select the location to which the backup is to be
restored. To restore the system state, select **Original location**. Click the **Start Restore** button
in the lower-right corner. A warning box appears stating that you will overwrite the existing
state. Click **OK** to start the process. Remember that you can restore the system state as a
way of restoring the registry.

The biggest limitation to using the Backup utility to restore the system state is that, in order
to use the utility, you must be able to boot to the Windows desktop. How to deal with
problems when you can't boot to the Windows desktop is covered in Chapters 15 and 16.

BACK UP THE ENTIRE HARD DRIVE

Besides backing up user data or system files, you can also back up the entire hard drive using Windows Vista Complete PC Backup or Windows XP Automated System Recovery. How to use both tools is covered next.

WINDOWS VISTA COMPLETE PC BACKUP

A Complete PC backup makes a backup of the entire volume on which Vista is installed and can also back up other volumes. The best practice to protect a Windows Vista system is to make a Complete PC backup after you have installed Vista, all hardware devices, and all applications. This backup works similarly to recovery CDs or DVDs that come with a brand-name computer. Recall that these recovery CDs or DVDs can be used to recover from a failed hard drive. The process returns a system to its original state at the time of purchase.

> **Notes** Complete PC backup is not available in Vista Starter or Vista Home editions.

The Complete PC backup must be saved to a local device such as an external hard drive or to DVDs. Don't back up the volume to another partition on the same hard drive. After the initial backup is made, Vista will automatically keep this backup current by making incremental backups. Vista does not keep multiple copies of backups made using the Complete PC backup method, as it does when backing up files and folders.

Follow these steps to create the initial Complete PC backup:

1. Connect your backup device to your PC. If you're using an external hard drive, use Windows Explorer to verify you can access the drive.

2. From Control Panel, under System and Maintenance, click **Back up your computer**. The Backup and Restore Center window appears as shown earlier in Figure 13-21.

3. Click **Back up computer** and respond to the UAC dialog box. Vista searches for available backup devices and then displays the list. Select the backup media and click **Next**.

4. In the next window, Vista Backup shows you the Vista volume it will back up and gives you the opportunity to select other volumes it finds to include in the backup. Make your selections and click **Next**.

5. In the next window (see Figure 13-35), the backup tells you the maximum amount of space expected for the backup, assuming no compression and room for housekeeping data about the backup. If you are backing up to DVDs, the backup tells you about how many DVDs are required. Click **Start backup** to begin the backup.

In the event your hard drive fails or Vista is so corrupted you cannot recover it, you can restore the volume or volumes from your Complete PC backup. Because the entire Vista volume will be overwritten, you must perform the operation from the Vista setup DVD using the Windows Recovery Environment (Windows RE).

Follow these steps to recover the system from backup:

1. Because this process will erase everything on the Vista volume and any other volumes included in the Complete PC backup, make every attempt to save any important data on these volumes before you continue with these steps.

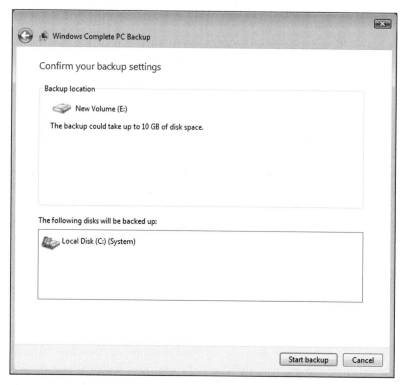

Figure 13-35 Confirm your backup settings and begin the backup
Courtesy: Course Technology/Cengage Learning

2. Connect the backup device to your computer.

3. Boot from the Vista DVD and select your language and keyboard layout preferences, as shown in Figure 13-36. Click **Next**.

4. The Install Windows screen appears. Click **Repair your computer** (see Figure 13-37).

Figure 13-36 Select language and keyboard preferences
Courtesy: Course Technology/Cengage Learning

Figure 13-37   Opening menu when you boot from the Vista DVD
Courtesy: Course Technology/Cengage Learning

5. System Recovery searches for an installed OS. If it finds one, select it and click **Next**. If it does not find an installed OS, just click **Next**.

6. If System Recovery presents a logon dialog box, log onto the system using an administrator account and password.

7. The System Recovery Options window shown in Figure 13-38 appears. Click **Windows Complete PC Restore**, and follow the directions on-screen to restore the system from backup.

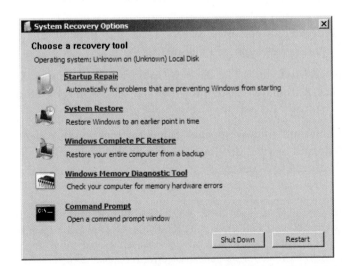

Figure 13-38   Restore the system to previous Complete PC backup
Courtesy: Course Technology/Cengage Learning

In Chapter 15, you'll learn more about the Windows Recovery Environment, including how to use all the options shown in Figure 13-38, and what you can do to recover a failed Vista system without having to revert to the last Complete PC backup.

WINDOWS XP AUTOMATED SYSTEM RECOVERY

You can use the Windows XP Automated System Recovery (ASR) tool to back up the entire volume on which Windows is installed (most likely drive C). Later, if Windows gets corrupted, you can recover the system from the last time you made an ASR backup. Keep in mind, however, that everything on the volume since the ASR backup was made is lost, including installed software and device drivers, user data, and any changes to the system configuration.

In this section, you will learn how to make the ASR backup and how to restore the system from the backup. You'll also learn about the best practices for using the ASR tool.

Creating the ASR Backup and ASR Disk

The ASR backup process creates two items: a full backup of the drive on which Windows is installed and an ASR floppy disk on which information that will help Windows use Automated System Recovery is stored. The ASR backup process places the location of the backup file on the floppy. The backup file will be just as large as the contents of the hard drive volume, so you will need a massive backup medium, such as a partition on a different hard drive, a tape drive, or a writeable CD-R or CD-RW drive.

> ⚡ **Caution** Do not back up drive C to a folder on drive C. The ASR backup process allows you to do this, but restoring later from this backup does not work. In addition, when a hard drive partition fails, most likely other partitions on the drive will also be lost, and so will your backup if you've put it on one of these other partitions. Therefore, to better protect your installation, back up to a different hard drive or other media.

Follow these directions to create the backup and the ASR floppy disk:

> 📝 **Notes** To use Automated System Recovery in Windows XP Home Edition, the Backup utility must first be installed.

1. Click **Start, All Programs, Accessories, System Tools**, and **Backup**. The Backup or Restore Wizard appears (refer back to Figure 13-25).

2. Click the **Advanced Mode** link. The Backup Utility window appears. On the Welcome tab, click **Automated System Recovery Wizard**. On the following window, click **Next**.

3. The Backup Destination window appears. Select the location of the medium to receive the backup and insert a disk into the floppy disk drive. This disk will become the ASR disk. Click **Next**.

> 📝 **Notes** The ASR process assumes you have a floppy disk drive. If your computer does not have this drive, you can use an external floppy drive. If you don't have either, it's possible to skip the step of making the ASR disk at the time you make the ASR backup. However, you must make the ASR disk later before you can perform the ASR restore. And, a floppy disk drive is required to perform an ASR restore. You will learn how to create an ASR disk in a project at the end of this chapter.

4. Click **Finish**. The backup process shows its progress, as seen in Figure 13-39.

5. When the backup is finished, label the disk with the name "ASR Disk," the date it was created, and the computer's name, and put the disk in a safe place.

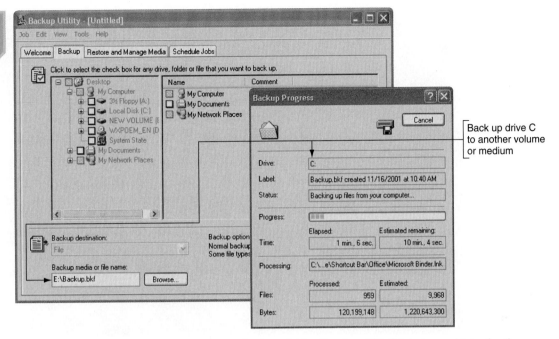

Figure 13-39 The Backup utility can create a backup of drive C and an ASR disk to be used later for the Automated System Recovery utility
Courtesy: Course Technology/Cengage Learning

Restoring the System Using an ASR Backup

To restore the Windows volume to its state when the last ASR backup was made, do the following:

1. Insert the Windows XP CD in the CD-ROM drive, and hard boot the PC.

2. You will see a message that says "Press any key to boot from CD." Press any key.

3. A blue screen appears with the message "Press F6 to load RAID or SCSI drivers." If your system uses RAID, SCSI, or some SATA drives, press **F6**. If your system does not use these drives, ignore the message.

4. At the bottom of the blue screen, a message says, "Press F2 to run the Automated System Recovery process." Press **F2**.

5. The screen shown in Figure 13-40 appears, instructing you to insert the ASR floppy disk. Insert the disk and then press **Enter**.

Windows XP Setup then does the following:

1. Loads files it needs to run

2. Repartitions and reformats the drive

3. Installs Windows from the Windows XP CD

4. Launches the Automatic System Recovery Wizard to restore the Windows system state, applications, and data to what they were at the time of the last ASR backup

As the ASR recovery process progresses, it erases everything on the volume being restored and reformats the volume just before the Windows XP installation process begins. After the process is finished, restart the system and then restore data from recent backups of user data.

A+ 220-701 2.5 3.4

13

A+ 220-701

A+
220-701
2.5
3.4

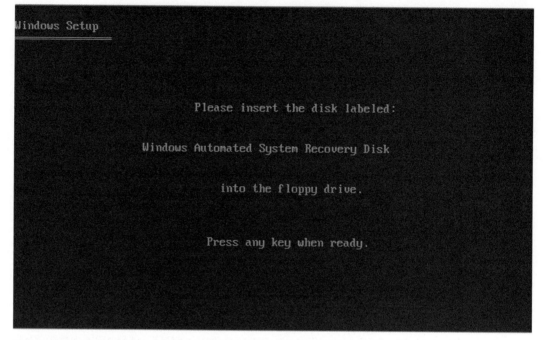

Figure 13-40 Automatic System Recovery process must have the ASR floppy disk
Courtesy: Course Technology/Cengage Learning

> 💡 **A+ Exam Tip** Content on the A+ 220-701 Essentials exam ends here and content on the A+ 220-702 Practical Application exam begins.

MANAGING FILES, FOLDERS, AND HARD DRIVES

A+
220-702
2.2

If you are a PC support technician, users are likely to ask you to help them manage their data, configure Windows, set up network resources, and help them keep the PC in good working order. All this requires that you know how to manage folders and files and understand the directory structures used by Windows Vista, XP, and 2000 so that you will know where to look on the hard drive to find the folders and files you need. In this part of the chapter, you will learn about these directory structures and to use several commands useful for managing files and folders. Then you'll learn how to manage hard drives and their partitions.

DIRECTORY STRUCTURES

Directory locations you need to be aware of include those for user files, system files, fonts, temporary files, program files, and offline files and folders. When a user first logs onto Windows Vista, a user profile is created that consists of two general items:

▲ A user folder together with its subfolders. These items are created under the %*SystemDrive*%\Users folder, for example, C:\Users\Jean Andrews.
▲ A file named Ntuser.dat in the user's folder. The file contains user settings. Each time the user logs on, the contents of this file are copied to a location in the registry.

The user folder for an account (for example, C:\Users\Jean Andrews) contains a group of subfolders organized as shown in Figure 13-41. This group of folders and subfolders is called the user profile namespace.

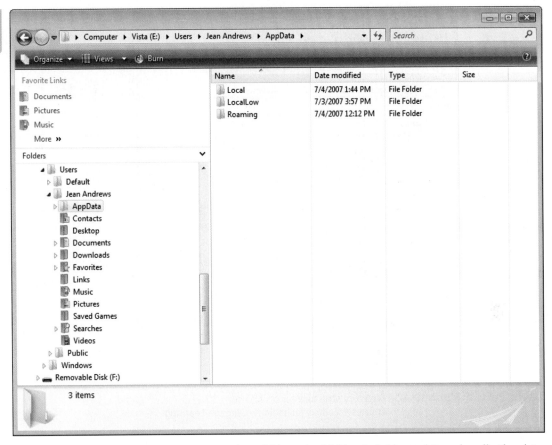

Figure 13-41 A user profile namespace contains a folder and subfolders to hold user data and application data
Courtesy: Course Technology/Cengage Learning

Also notice in Figure 13-41 the \Users\Public folder. Microsoft encourages you to put files in this Public folder that will be shared on the network so that your private user data folders are better protected.

In Windows XP, the folder for a user account is stored in the C:\Documents and Settings folder. The folders in the user accounts folder for Windows XP are organized as shown in Figure 13-42.

Windows Vista and XP are normally installed in the C:\Windows folder. Windows 2000 is installed in C:\Windows or C:\Winnt. Here are some other important folder locations:

- The Windows registry is stored in the \Windows\system32\config folder.
- A backup of the registry is stored in the \Windows\system32\config\RegBack folder.
- Fonts are stored in the \Windows\Fonts folder.
- Program files are stored in C:\Program Files for 32-bit versions of Windows.
- In 64-bit versions of Vista and XP, 64-bit programs are stored in the C:\Program Files folder and 32-bit programs are stored in C:\Program Files (x86) folder.
- Temporary files used by Windows when it is installing software and performing other maintenance tasks are stored in the \Windows\Temp folder.
- For Windows Vista, temporary files used by Internet Explorer are stored in C:\Users*username*\AppData\Local\Microsoft\Windows\Temporary Internet Files. This folder holds cookies, cached Web page content, and Internet Explorer history.
- For Windows XP, temporary files used by Internet Explorer are stored in C:\Documents and Settings*username*\Local Settings\Temporary Internet Files.

A+
220-702
2.2

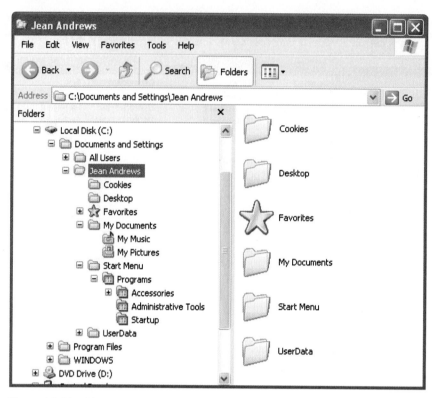

Figure 13-42 Directory structure for an XP user
Courtesy: Course Technology/Cengage Learning

▲ The client-side caching (CSC) folder used to store offline files and folders is C:\Windows\
CSC. This folder is created and managed by the Windows Offline Files utility. The utility
makes it possible for a user to work with a copy of folders and files stored on the local
network when his computer is not connected to the network. Later, when a connection
happens, Windows syncs up the offline files and folders stored in the C:\Windows\CSC
folder with those on the network.

A+
220-702
2.1

COMMANDS TO MANAGE FILES AND FOLDERS

Remember from Chapter 2 that you open a command prompt window that provides a
Command Line Interface (CLI). Using this window, you can enter command lines to perform a
variety of tasks, such as deleting a file or running the System Information Utility
(msinfo32.exe) utility. Recall from Chapter 2 that you can enter **cmd.exe** in the Vista Start
Search box or the XP Run box to open a command prompt window (see Figure 13-43).

Figure 13-43 Use the exit command to close the command prompt window
Courtesy: Course Technology/Cengage Learning

A+
220-702
2.1

This method works for both 32-bit and 64-bit versions of Windows. If you need an elevated command prompt window in Vista, click **Start**, **All Programs**, and **Accessories** and right-click **Command Prompt**. Then select **Run as administrator** from the shortcut window. When you're working in a command prompt window, type **cls** and press **Enter** to clear the window. To retrieve the last command you entered, press the up arrow. To retrieve the last command line one character at a time, press the right arrow. To close the window, type **exit** (see Figure 13-43) and press **Enter**.

Many of the commands you will learn about in this section can also be used from the Vista Recovery Environment or the Windows 2000/XP Recovery Console. These operating systems can be loaded from the Windows setup CD or DVD to troubleshoot a system when the Windows desktop refuses to load. How to use the Recovery Environment and the Recovery Console is covered in Chapters 15 and 16.

> **Notes** As you work through the commands in this part of the chapter, keep in mind that if you enter a command and want to terminate its execution before it is finished, you can press Ctrl+Break to do so.

If the command you are using applies to files or folders, the path to these files or folders is assumed to be the default drive and directory. The default drive and directory, also called the current drive and directory, shows in the command prompt. It is the drive and directory that the command will use if you don't give a drive and directory in the command line. For example, in Figure 13-43, the default drive is C: and the default path is C:\Documents and Settings\Jean Andrews. If you use a different path in the command line, the path you use overrides the default path. Also know that Windows makes no distinction between uppercase and lowercase in command lines.

Now let's look at the file naming conventions you will need to follow when creating files, wildcard characters you can use in command lines, and several commands useful for managing files and folders. Only the most common parameters are included with the commands; know that additional parameters might be available.

FILE NAMING CONVENTIONS

When using the command prompt window to create a file, keep in mind that filename and file extension characters can be the letters a through z, the numbers 0 through 9, and the following characters:

```
_ ^ $ ~ ! # % & - { } ( ) @ ' `
```

In a command prompt window, if a filename has spaces in it, it is sometimes necessary to enclose the filename in double quotation marks.

WILDCARD CHARACTERS IN COMMAND LINES

As you work at the command prompt, you can use wildcard characters in a filename to say that the command applies to a group of files or to abbreviate a filename if you do not know the entire name. The question mark (?) is a wildcard for one character, and the asterisk (*) is a wildcard for one or more characters. For example, if you want to find all files in a directory that start with A and have a three-letter file extension, you would use the following command:

```
dir a*.???
```

13

A+ 220-702

> 💡 **A+ Exam Tip**   The A+ 220-702 Practical Application exam expects you to know how to use the Dir, Edit, Copy, Xcopy, Format, MD, CD, RD, Defrag, Chkdsk, and Help commands, which are all covered in this section.

> 📝 **Notes**   Many commands can use parameters in the command line to affect how the command will work. Parameters often begin with a slash followed by a single character. In this chapter, you will learn about the basic parameters used by a command for the most common tasks. For a full listing of the parameters available for a command, use the Help command. Another way to learn about commands is to follow this link on the Microsoft Web site: *http://technet.microsoft.com/en-us/library/cc772390(WS.10).aspx*.

Help or <command name> /?

Use this command to get help about any command. You can enter help followed by the command name or enter the command name followed by /?. Table 13-2 lists some sample applications of this command:

Command	Result
help xcopy xcopy /?	Gets help about the Xcopy command
help	Lists all commands
help xcopy |more	Lists information one screen at a time

Table 13-2   Sample help commands

Dir [<filename>] [/p] [/s] [/w]

Use this command to list files and directories. In Microsoft documentation about a command (also called the command syntax), the brackets [ ] in a command line indicate the parameter is optional. In addition, the parameter included in < >, such as <filename>, indicates that you can substitute any filename in the command. This filename can include a path or file extension. Table 13-3 lists some examples of the Dir command.

Command	Result
dir /p	Lists one screen at a time
dir /w	Presents information using wide format, where details are omitted and files and folders are listed in columns on the screen
dir *.txt	Lists all files with a .txt file extension in the default path
dir d:\data*.txt	Lists all files with a .txt file extension in the D:\data folder
dir myfile.txt	Checks that a single file, such as myfile.txt, is present
dir /s	Include subdirectory entries

Table 13-3   Sample dir commands

Del or Erase <filename>

The Del or Erase command erases files or groups of files. Note that in the command lines in this section, the command prompt is not bolded, but the typed command is in bold.

To erase all files in the E:\Docs directory, use the following command:

```
C:\> erase e:\docs\*.*
```

To erase all files in the current default directory, use the following command:

```
E:\Docs> del *.*
```

To erase all files that are in the current directory and that have no file extensions, use the following command:

```
E:\Docs> del *.
```

To erase the file named Myfile.txt, use the following command:

```
E:\> del myfile.txt
```

A+
220-702
2.1

copy *<source>* [*<destination>*] [/A] [/V] [/Y]

The Copy command copies a single file or group of files. The original files are not altered. To copy a file from one drive to another, use a command similar to this one:

```
E:\> copy C:\Data\Myfile.txt E:\mydata\Newfile.txt
```

The drive, path, and filename of the source file immediately follow the Copy command. The drive, path, and filename of the destination file follow the source filename. If you do not specify the filename of the destination file, the OS assigns the file's original name to this copy. If you omit the drive or path of the source or the destination, then the OS uses the current default drive and path.

To copy the file Myfile.txt from the root directory of drive C to drive E, use the following command:

```
C:\> copy myfile.txt E:
```

Because the command does not include a drive or path before the filename Myfile.txt, the OS assumes that the file is in the default drive and path. Also, because there is no destination filename specified, the file written to drive E will be named Myfile.txt.

To copy all files in the C:\Docs directory to the USB flash drive designated drive E, use the following command:

```
C:\> copy c:\docs\*.* E:
```

To make a backup file named System.bak of the System file in the \Windows\system32\config directory of the hard drive, use the following command:

```
C:\Windows\system32\config> copy system system.bak
```

If you use the Copy command to duplicate multiple files, the files are assigned the names of the original files. When you duplicate multiple files, the destination portion of the command line cannot include a filename.

A+
220-702
2.1

Three switches or parameters that are useful with the Copy command are the following:

▲ **/A.** When the /A switch is used at the end of the command line, only files that have the archive attribute on are copied. The attribute is not changed by the copying process. Recall from earlier in the chapter that the archive attribute is used to determine if a file has changed since the last backup. When a backup is made, the attribute is turned off. Later, when the file changes, Windows turns the archive attribute on to indicate the file needs backing up again.

▲ **/V.** When the /V switch is used, the size of each new file is compared to the size of the original file. This slows down the copying, but verifies that the copy is done without errors.

▲ **/Y.** When the /Y switch is used, a confirmation message does not appear asking you to confirm before overwriting a file.

> **Notes** When trying to recover a corrupted file, you can sometimes use the Copy command to copy the file to new media, such as from the hard drive to a USB drive. During the copying process, if the Copy command reports a bad or missing sector, choose the option to ignore that sector. The copying process then continues to the next sector. The corrupted sector will be lost, but others can likely be recovered. The Recover command can be used to accomplish the same thing.

Recover <filename>

Use the Recover command to attempt to recover a file when parts of the file are corrupted. The command is best used from the Vista Recovery Environment or the XP Recovery Console (discussed in Chapters 15 and 16). To use it, you must specify the name of a single file in the command line, like so:

```
C:\Data> Recover Myfile.doc
```

A+
220-702
2.1

Xcopy <source> [<destination>] [/S] [/C] [/Y] [/D:date]

The Xcopy command is more powerful than the Copy command. It follows the same general command-source-destination format as the Copy command, but it offers several more options. Table 13-4 shows some of these options.

Command	Result
`xcopy C:\docs\*.* E:/S`	Use the /S switch to include subdirectories in the copy. This command copies all files in the directory C:\docs, as well as all subdirectories under \Docs and their files, to drive E.
`xcopy C:\docs\*.* E:/D:03/14/10`	The /D switch examines the date. This command copies all files from the directory C:\Docs created or modified on or after March 14, 2010.
`xcopy C:\docs\*.* E:/Y`	Use the /Y switch to overwrite existing files without prompting.
`xcopy C:\docs\*.* E:/C`	Use the /C switch to keep copying even when an error occurs.

Table 13-4 Xcopy commands and results

Robocopy <source> [<destination>] [*/S*] [*/E*] [*/LOG:*filename] [*/LOG+:*filename] [*/move*] [*/purge*]

The Robocopy (Robust File Copy) command is new with Windows Vista and is similar to the Xcopy command. It offers more options than Xcopy and is intended to replace Xcopy. A few options for Robocopy are listed in Table 13-5.

Command	Result
robocopy C:\docs*.* E:/S	The /S switch includes subdirectories in the copy, but does not include empty directories.
robocopy C:\docs*.* E:/E	The /E switch includes subdirectories, even the empty ones.
robocopy C:\docs*.* E:/LOG:Mylog.txt	Records activity to a log file.
robocopy C:\docs*.* E:/LOG+:Mylog.txt	Appends a record of all activity to an existing log file.
robocopy C:\docs*.* E:/move	Moves files and directories, deleting them from the source.
robocopy C:\docs*.* E:/purge	Deletes files and directories at the destination that no longer exist at the source.

Table 13-5 Robocopy commands and results

A+
220-702
2.1

MD [drive:]path

The MD command (make directory) creates a subdirectory under a directory. To create a directory named \Game on drive C, you can use this command:

```
C:\> MD C:\game
```

The backslash indicates that the directory is under the root directory. If a path is not given, the default path is assumed. This command also creates the C:\game directory:

```
C:\> MD game
```

To create a directory named chess under the \game directory, you can use this command:

```
C:\> MD C:\game\chess
```

Figure 13-44 shows the result of the Dir command on the directory \game. Note the two initial entries in the directory table: . (dot) and . . (dot, dot). The MD command creates these two entries when the OS initially sets up the directory. You cannot edit these entries with normal OS commands, and they must remain in the directory for the directory's lifetime. The . entry points to the subdirectory itself, and the .. entry points to the parent directory, which, in this case, is the root directory.

CD [drive:]path *or CD..*

The CD command (for "change directory") changes the current default directory. You enter CD followed by the drive and the entire path that you want to be current, like so:

```
D:\> CD C:\game\chess
```

13

A+ 220-702

A+
220-702
2.1

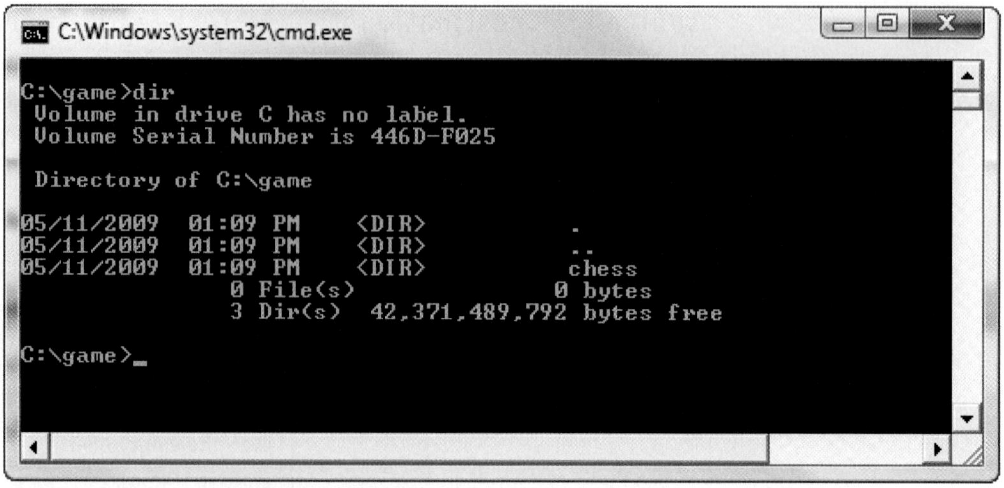

```
■ C:\Windows\system32\cmd.exe

C:\game>dir
 Volume in drive C has no label.
 Volume Serial Number is 446D-F025

 Directory of C:\game

05/11/2009  01:09 PM    <DIR>          .
05/11/2009  01:09 PM    <DIR>          ..
05/11/2009  01:09 PM    <DIR>          chess
               0 File(s)              0 bytes
               3 Dir(s)  42,371,489,792 bytes free

C:\game>_
```

Figure 13-44 Results of the Dir command on the \Game directory
Courtesy: Course Technology/Cengage Learning

The command prompt now looks like this:

```
C:\game\chess>
```

To move from a child directory to its parent directory, use the .. variation of the command:

```
C:\game\chess> CD..
```

The command prompt now looks like this:

```
C:\game>
```

Remember that .. always means the parent directory. You can move from a parent directory to one of its child directories simply by stating the name of the child directory:

```
C:\game> CD chess
```

The command prompt now looks like this:

```
C:\game\chess>
```

Remember not to put a backslash in front of the child directory name; doing so tells the OS to go to a directory named Chess that is directly under the root directory.

RD [drive:]path

The RD command (remove directory) removes a subdirectory. Before you can use the RD command, three things must be true:

▲ The directory must contain no files.
▲ The directory must contain no subdirectories.
▲ The directory must not be the current directory.

A+
220-702
2.1

A directory is ready for removal when only the . and .. entries are present. For example, to remove the \game directory when it contains the chess directory, the chess directory must first be removed, like so:

```
C:\> RD C:\game\chess
```

Or, if the \game directory is the current directory, you can use this command:

```
C:\game> RD chess
```

After you remove the chess directory, you can remove the \game directory. However, it's not good to attempt to saw off a branch while you're sitting on it; therefore, you must first leave the \game directory like so:

```
C:\game> CD..
C:\> RD \game
```

A+
220-702
2.1
2.3

chkdsk [drive:] [/f] [/r]

The Chkdsk command (check disk) fixes file system errors and recovers data from bad sectors. Earlier in the chapter, you learned to use Chkdsk from the drive properties box. Recall that a file is stored on the hard drive as a group of clusters (also called allocation units). The FAT or MFT is responsible for keeping a record of each cluster that belongs to a file. In Figure 13-45, you can see that each cell in the FAT represents one cluster and contains a pointer to the next cluster in a file.

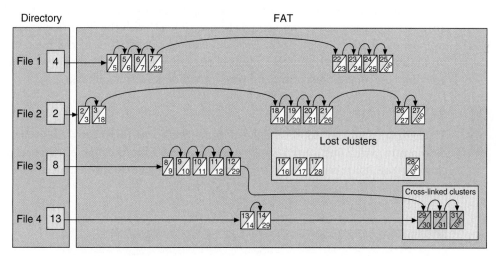

Figure 13-45 Lost and cross-linked clusters
Courtesy: Course Technology/Cengage Learning

Used with the /F parameter, Chkdsk searches for and fixes two types of file system errors made by the FAT or MFT:

- *Lost clusters (also called lost allocation units).* Lost clusters are clusters that are marked as used clusters in the FAT or MFT, but the cluster does not belong to any file. In effect, the data in these clusters is lost.
- *Cross-linked clusters.* Cross-linked clusters are clusters that are marked in the FAT or MFT as belonging to more than one file.

A+
220-702
2.1
2.3

Used with the /R parameter, Chkdsk checks for lost clusters and cross-linked clusters and also checks for bad sectors on the drive. The FAT and MFT keep a table of bad sectors that they normally do not use. However, over time, a sector might become unreliable. If Chkdsk determines that a sector is unreliable, it attempts to recover the data from the sector and also marks the sector as bad so that the FAT or MFT will not use it again.

Used without any parameters, the Chkdsk command only reports information about a drive and does not make any repairs.

In the sample commands following, we're not showing the command prompt; the default drive and directory are not important. To check the hard drive for file system errors and repair them, use this command:

```
chkdsk C:/F
```

To redirect a report of the findings of the Chkdsk command to a file that you can later print, use this command:

```
chkdsk C:>Myfile.txt
```

Use the /R parameter of the Chkdsk command to fix file system errors and also examine each sector of the drive for bad sectors, like so:

```
chkdsk C:/R
```

If Chkdsk finds data that it can recover, it asks you for permission to do so. If you give permission, it saves the recovered data in files that it stores in the root directory of the drive.

The Chkdsk command will not fix anything unless the drive is locked, which means the drive has no open files. If you attempt to use Chkdsk with the /F or /R parameter when files are open, Chkdsk tells you of the problem and asks permission to run the next time Windows is restarted. Know that the process will take plenty of time. For Windows Vista, you must use an elevated command prompt window to run Chkdsk.

A+
220-702
2.3

Defrag [drive:] [-C]

The Defrag command examines a hard drive or disk for fragmented files (files written to a disk in noncontiguous clusters) and rewrites these files to the disk or drive in contiguous clusters. You use this command to optimize a hard drive's performance. Table 13-6 shows two examples of the command.

Command	Result
defrag C:	Defrag drive C
defrag -c	Defrag all volumes on the computer including drive C

Table 13-6   Defrag commands and results

The Defrag command requires an elevated command prompt window in Windows Vista. It is not available under the Windows Vista Recovery Environment. It is not available from the Windows 2000/XP Recovery Console, and the command is not included with Windows 2000. Earlier in the chapter, you learned to defrag a drive using the Windows drive properties box.

Edit [drive:path] <filename>

The Edit program (Edit.com) is a handy, "quick and dirty" way to create and edit text files while working at a command prompt. For example, to create a file named Mybatch.bat in the C:\Data folder, use this command (a discussion of .bat files is coming up):

```
C:\> EDIT C:\Data\Mybatch.bat
```

If the file does not already exist, Edit creates an empty file. Later, when you exit the Edit editor, changes you made are saved to the newly created file. Figure 13-46 shows the Mybatch.bat file being edited.

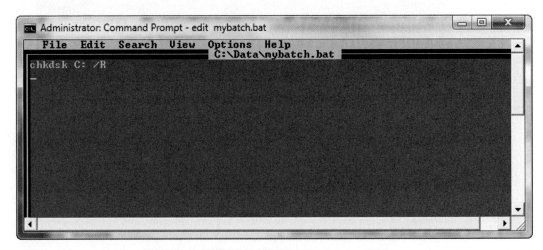

Figure 13-46 Using the Edit editor to create and edit the Mybatch.bat file
Courtesy: Course Technology/Cengage Learning

After you have made changes in this window, you can exit the Edit editor this way: Press the **Alt** key to activate the menus, select the **File** menu, and then choose **Exit**. When asked if you want to save your changes, respond **Yes** to exit the editor and save changes. (You can also use your mouse to point to menu options.)

A file with a .bat file extension is called a batch file. You can use a batch file to execute a group of commands from a command prompt. To execute the commands stored in the Mybatch.bat file, enter the command Mybatch.bat at a command prompt, as shown in Figure 13-47. Notice in the figure that the Chkdsk command could not run because the system is currently in use.

> **Notes** Do not use word-processing software, such as Word or WordPerfect, to edit a batch file, unless you save the file as a text (ASCII) file. Word-processing applications use control characters in their document files. These characters keep the OS from interpreting commands in a batch file correctly.

Format <drive:> [/v:label] [/q] [fs:<filesystem>]

You can format a floppy disk using Windows Explorer, and you can format a hard drive using Disk Management. In addition, you can use the Format command from a command prompt window and from the Vista Recovery Environment and the Windows 2000/XP Recovery Console. Table 13-7 lists various sample uses of the Format command.

A+
220-702
2.1

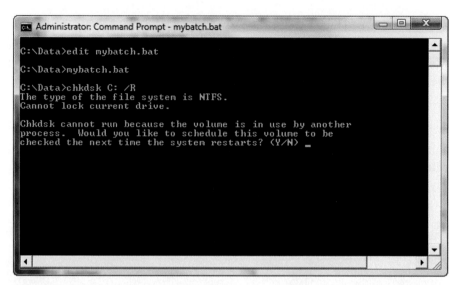

Figure 13-47 Executing the batch file
Courtesy: Course Technology/Cengage Learning

Command	Description
Format A:/V:*mylabel*	Allows you to enter a volume label only once when formatting several disks. The same volume label is used for all disks. A volume label appears at the top of the directory list to help you identify the disk.
Format A:/Q	Re-creates the root directory and FAT to quickly format a previously formatted disk that is in good condition. /Q does not read or write to any other part of the disk.
Format D:/FS:NTFS	Formats drive D using the NTFS file system.
Format D:/FS:FAT32	Formats drive D using the FAT32 file system.
Format D:/FS:EXFAT	Formats drive D using the extended FAT file system.

Table 13-7 Format commands and results

A+
220-702
2.3

USE DISK MANAGEMENT TO MANAGE HARD DRIVES

The primary tool for managing hard drives is Disk Management. You first learned to use the tool in Chapter 8 to partition and format a new hard drive after it was installed. In this chapter, you will learn to use Disk Management to manage partitions, mount a drive, and troubleshoot problems with the hard drive. Before you tackle this part of the chapter, you need to be aware of the following terms, some of which were introduced in Chapter 8.

▲ A partition is a division of a hard drive. Windows can track up to four partitions on a drive and keeps this tracking information in a partition table that is written in the first 512-byte sector of the drive.

▲ A drive can have one, two, or three primary partitions, also called volumes. One of these primary partitions can be designated the active partition, which is the partition that startup BIOS turns to for an OS to load. A hard drive can also have one extended partition which can hold one or more logical drives. For XP, this one extended partition can be the second, third, or fourth partition on the drive. For Vista, the extended partition must be the fourth partition. A logical drive is sometimes called a logical partition. Partitions are created during the Windows installation, by using the Disk

Management utility from within Windows, or by using the Diskpart command in the Vista Recovery Environment or the XP Recovery Console.

◢ A file system is used to manage files and folders on the volume or logical drive. A cluster is a group of sectors used to hold a file, and the number of sectors in a cluster is determined by the file system used and the size of the drive. A file is stored in one or more clusters. The last cluster might have sectors that go unused, and this wasted space is called slack.

◢ File systems supported by Windows include NTFS, FAT32, and exFAT. Recall from Chapter 12 that unless the drive is very small, the best file system to use is NTFS. Installing a file system on a volume or logical drive is called formatting. Formatting can be done using Disk Management, Windows Explorer, or the Format command.

> **Notes** Windows Vista allows you to resize partitions, but Windows XP does not. For XP, you can use third-party software such as PartitionMagic by Symantec (*www.symantec.com*) to create, resize, move, split, or combine partitions without erasing data. It can also convert one file system to another without losing data.

Now let's see how to manage volumes on a drive.

MANAGING HARD DRIVE VOLUMES

Recall from Chapter 8 that when a new hard drive is first installed in a system, you must first initialize the disk. Do the following:

1. To open Disk Management using Vista, click **Start**, right-click **Computer** (for Windows XP, right-click **My Computer**), and select **Manage** from the shortcut menu. Respond to the UAC box. In the Computer Management window, click **Disk Management**. (Alternately, you can enter **diskmgmt.msc** in the Start Search box.) The Disk Management window opens. Right-click the disk and select **Initialize Disk** from the shortcut menu (see Figure 13-48).

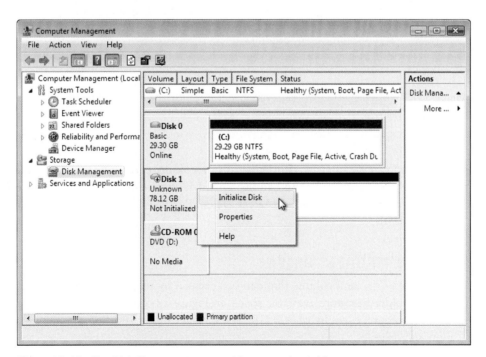

Figure 13-48 Use Disk Management to partition a new hard drive
Courtesy: Course Technology/Cengage Learning

A+
220-702
2.3

2. To create a new volume on a drive, right-click in the unallocated space, select **New Simple Volume** from the shortcut menu, and follow the directions on-screen to select the size of the volume, assign a drive letter and name to the volume, and select the file system.

In Windows Vista, you can use Disk Management to resize volumes. Right-click a partition, and the shortcut menu shown in Figure 13-49 appears. Using this menu, you can shrink a volume, delete a volume, or use unallocated space on the drive to extend the size of the volume. Also notice on the menu the ability to mark the partition as the one active partition on the drive (the one the OS will boot from). Note that any primary partition can be the active partition. You can also change the drive letter for the volume and format the volume, which erases all data on it.

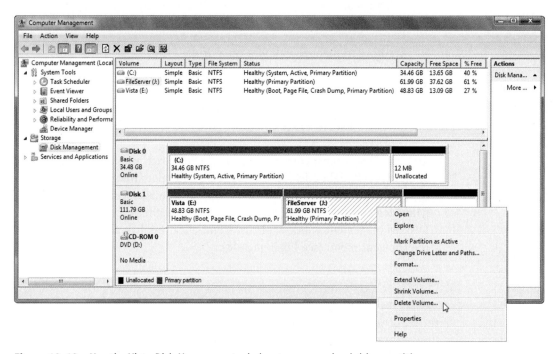

Figure 13-49   Use the Vista Disk Management window to manage hard drive partitions
Courtesy: Course Technology/Cengage Learning

In Windows XP, the size of a partition or volume cannot be changed unless you use third-party software. You can use Disk Management to delete a partition. To do so, right-click the partition and select **Delete Partition** from the shortcut menu (see Figure 13-50).

HOW TO MOUNT A DRIVE

A mounted drive is a volume that can be accessed by way of a folder on another volume so that the folder has more available space. In Figure 13-51, the mounted drive gives the C:\Data folder a capacity of 700 GB. The C:\Data folder is called the mount point for the mounted drive.

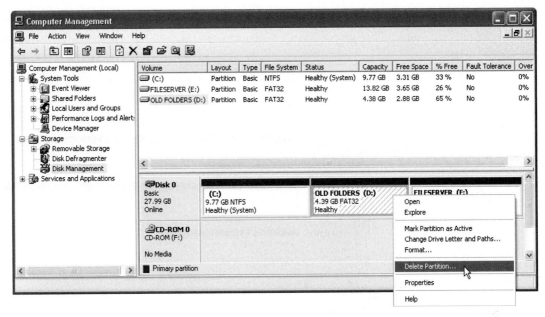

Figure 13-50 Use the Disk Management window in Windows XP to delete a partition
Courtesy: Course Technology/Cengage Learning

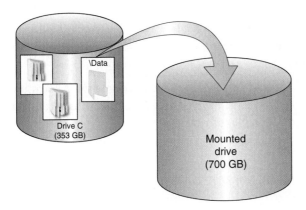

Figure 13-51 The C:\Data folder is the mount point for the mounted drive
Courtesy: Course Technology/Cengage Learning

Follow these steps to mount a drive using Windows Vista or XP:

1. Make sure the volume that is to host the mounted drive uses the NTFS file system. The folder on this volume, called the mount point, must be empty. Use Windows Explorer to create a new folder or empty an existing folder. In our example, we are mounting a drive to the C:\Data folder.

2. Open Disk Management. Right-click in the unallocated space of Disk 1 (the second hard drive) and select **New Simple Volume** from the shortcut menu (see Figure 13-52). The New Simple Volume Wizard launches. Click **Next**.

3. On the next window (see Figure 13-53), specify the amount of unallocated space you want to devote to the volume and click **Next**.

A+
220-702
2.3

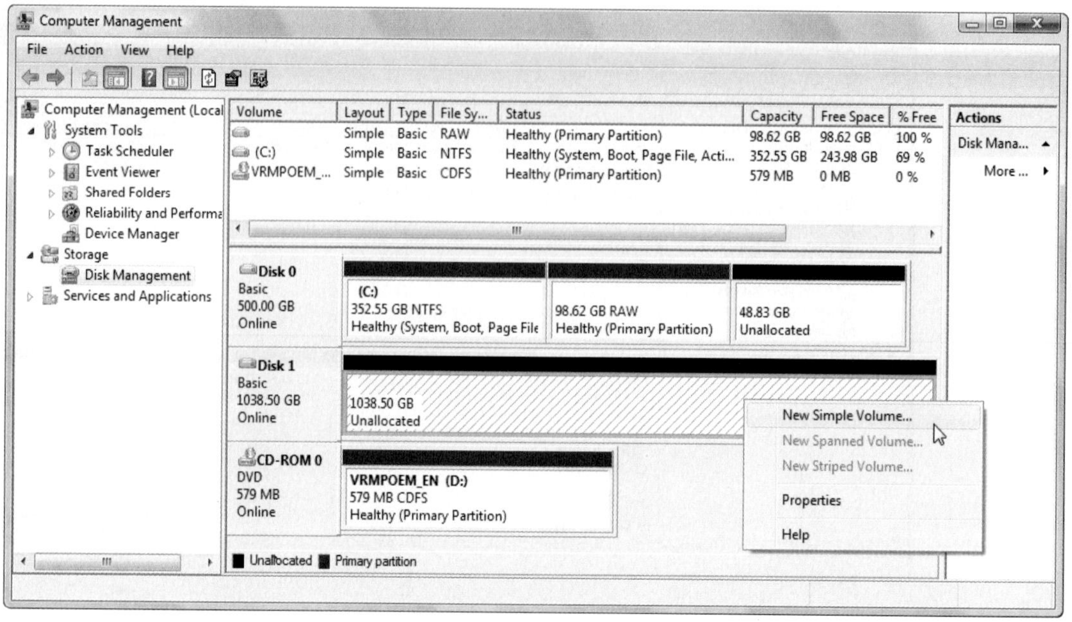

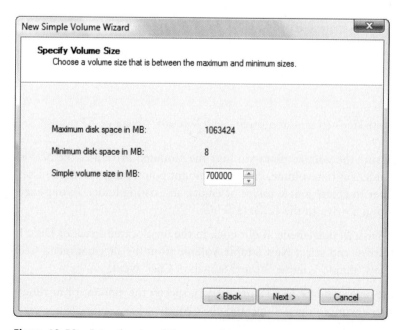

Figure 13-52   Shortcut menu for unallocated space on a drive
Courtesy: Course Technology/Cengage Learning

4. On the next window (see Figure 13-54), select **Mount in the following empty NTFS folder**. Then click **Browse** to locate the C:\Data folder or enter the path to the folder. Click **Next** to continue.

5. The next window (see Figure 13-55) gives you choices for the Allocation unit size (this is the cluster size). It's best to leave the size at the Default value. You can also enter a volume label if you like. Click **Next** to continue.

Figure 13-53   Enter the size of the new volume
Courtesy: Course Technology/Cengage Learning

A+
220-702
2.3

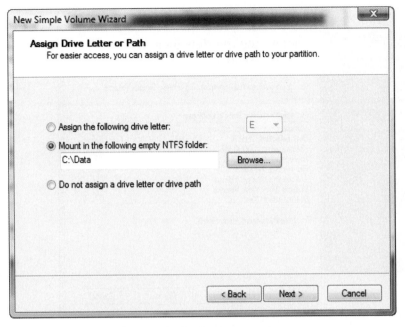

Figure 13-54 Select the mount point for the new volume
Courtesy: Course Technology/Cengage Learning

6. The wizard reports your decisions on the final window (see Figure 13-56). Click **Finish** to create the mounted drive. The status of the drive is reported as Formatting until the format is complete.

13

A+ 220-702

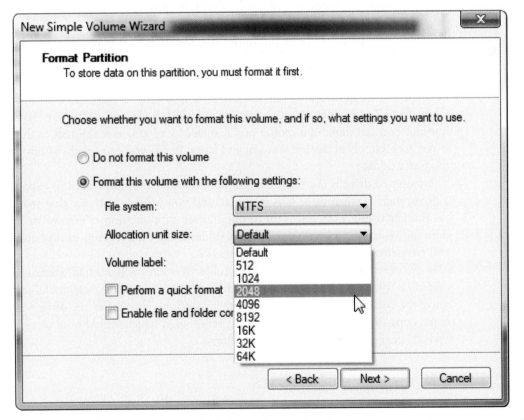

Figure 13-55 You can change the default cluster size for the volume
Courtesy: Course Technology/Cengage Learning

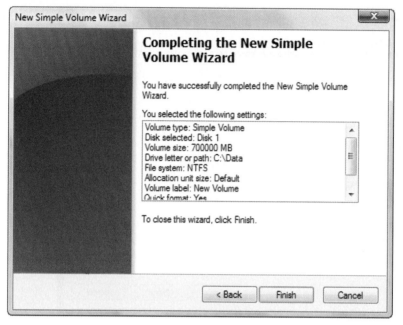

Figure 13-56   The wizard reports settings for the volume
Courtesy: Course Technology/Cengage Learning

7. Close the Disk Management window and open Windows Explorer. Right-click the C:\Data folder and select **Properties** from the shortcut menu. The Properties box opens and shows that the folder Type is a Mounted Volume (see Figure 13-57). When you click **Properties** in the properties box, you can see that the capacity of the folder is 683 GB, which is the size of the mounted volume less overhead.

In the above example, it's interesting to note that drive C still reports a capacity of 353 GB, while the C:\Data folder reports a capacity of 683 GB. The inside appears bigger than the outside! You can think of a mount point, such as C:\Data, as a shortcut to the second drive. If you look closely at the left window in Figure 13-57, you can see the shortcut icon beside the \Data folder.

A mounted drive is useful in these sample situations: (a) You need to expand the space on a drive, such as when drive C is too small and you want to enhance that space using space on another volume; (b) you want to put all user data on another volume or hard drive other than the Windows volume (the C:\Users folder is the mount point in this situation); or (c) you have run out of drive letters A through Z.

In the previous example, the C:\Data folder was empty. If we had wanted to mount the drive in a folder that had data in it, such as the C:\Users folder, we would first have had to move the contents of this folder to another location. Then, after the drive was mounted, we could copy the contents back to the C:\Users folder, which would now be greatly expanded and physically located on a different volume.

WINDOWS DYNAMIC DISKS

Recall from Chapter 8 that hard drives are normally configured as a basic disk, which uses the MBR partition table. Windows Vista Business, Enterprise, and Ultimate editions and Windows XP Professional can use a second type of organization called a dynamic disk.

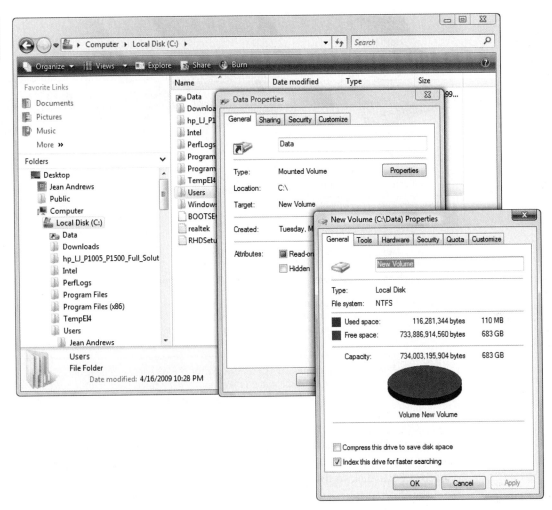

Figure 13-57 The mounted drive shows as a very large folder
Courtesy: Course Technology/Cengage Learning

(Windows Vista Home editions and Windows XP Home editions do not support dynamic disks.) Basic disks use MBR partitions, volumes, and logical drives. Dynamic disks use dynamic volumes, and these volumes can span more than one hard drive. Data to configure each hard drive is stored in a disk management database that resides in the last 1 MB of storage space at the end of a hard drive. Because of the way the database works, it is considered more reliable than the MBR method. Here are four uses of dynamic disks:

▲ For better reliability, you can configure a hard drive as a dynamic disk and allocate the space as a simple dynamic volume. This is the best reason to use dynamic disks and is a recommended best practice.

▲ You can implement dynamic disks on multiple hard drives to extend a volume across these drives (called spanning).

▲ Dynamic disks can be used to piece data across multiple hard drives (called stripping or RAID 0) to improve performance.

▲ For Windows XP, you can use dynamic disks to mirror two hard drives for fault tolerance (called mirroring or RAID 1). This feature is not available in Windows Vista.

Figure 13-58 shows the difference between basic disks and dynamic disks and how dynamic disks are used to span or stripe across multiple drives.

A+
220-702
2.3

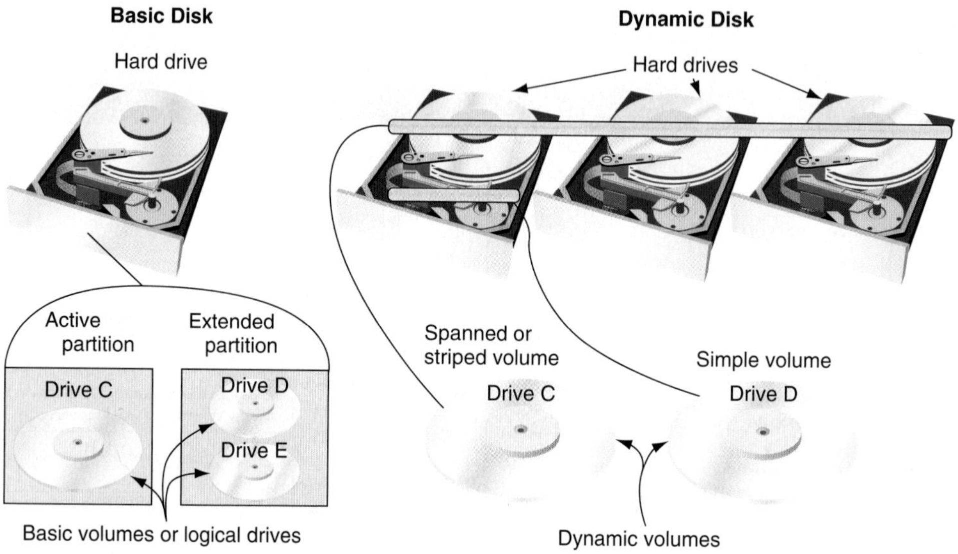

Basic Disk

Hard drive

Dynamic Disk

Hard drives

Active partition   Extended partition

Drive C   Drive D

Drive E

Basic volumes or logical drives

Spanned or striped volume

Drive C

Simple volume

Drive D

Dynamic volumes

Figure 13-58   Basic disks use partitions to organize a hard drive, and dynamic disks use dynamic
volumes to organize multiple hard drives
Courtesy: Course Technology/Cengage Learning

> **Notes**   A dynamic disk requires 1 MB of storage for the disk management database. If you are parti-
> tioning a basic disk and expect that one day you might want to convert it to a dynamic disk, leave 1 MB
> of space on the drive unpartitioned. Later, this space can be used for the disk management database.

You can use Disk Management to convert two or more basic disks to dynamic disks. Then
you can use unallocated space on these disks to create a spanned or striped volume. To
convert a basic disk to dynamic, right-click the disk and select **Convert to Dynamic Disk**
from the shortcut menu (see Figure 13-59). Then right-click free space on the disk and
select **New Spanned Volume** or **New Striped Volume** (see Figure 13-60).

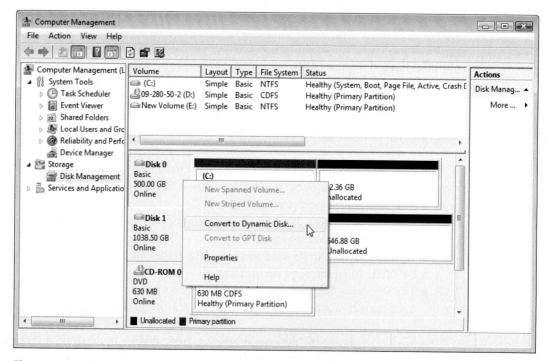

Figure 13-59   Convert a basic disk to a dynamic disk
Courtesy: Course Technology/Cengage Learning

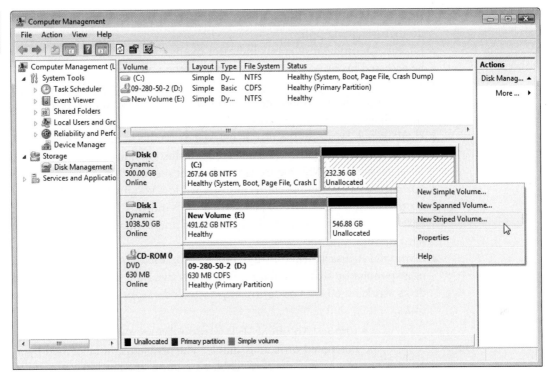

Figure 13-60 Create a spanned or striped volume
Courtesy: Course Technology/Cengage Learning

Now for some serious cautions about software RAID: Microsoft warns that when dynamic disks are used for spanning or RAID, the risk of catastrophic failure increases and can lead to data loss. Microsoft suggests you only use spanning or RAID with dynamic disks when you have no other option and recommends that RAID be implemented using hardware RAID rather than using dynamic disks. In other words, spanning and software RAID aren't very safe—use hardware RAID instead.

> **Notes** When Windows implements RAID, know that you cannot install an OS on a spanned or striped volume that uses software RAID. You can, however, install Windows on a hardware RAID drive.
> Also, after you have converted a basic disk to a dynamic disk, you cannot revert it to a basic disk without losing all data on the drive.

USING DISK MANAGEMENT TO TROUBLESHOOT HARD DRIVE PROBLEMS

Notice in Figure 13-60 that this system has two hard drives, Disk 0 and Disk 1, and information about the disk and volumes is shown in the window. When you are having a problem with a hard drive, it helps to know what the information in the Disk Management window means. Here are the drive and volume statuses you might see in this window:

- *Healthy.* The healthy volume status shown in Figure 13-60 indicates that the volume is formatted with a file system and that the file system is working without errors.
- *Failed.* A failed volume status indicates a problem with the hard drive or the file system has become corrupted. To try to fix the problem, make sure the hard drive data cable and power cable are secure. Data on a failed volume is likely to be lost. For

dynamic disks, if the disk status is Offline, try bringing the disk back online (how to do that is coming up).

◢ *Online*. An online disk status indicates the disk has been sensed by Windows and can be accessed by either reading or writing to the disk.

◢ *Active*. One volume on the system will be marked as Active. This is the volume that startup BIOS looks to in order to load an OS. The OS boot record is located at the beginning of the active partition.

◢ *Unallocated*. Space on the disk is marked as unallocated if it has not yet been partitioned. To create a partition using some of this unallocated space, right-click in it and select **New Simple Volume** from the shortcut menu.

◢ *Formatting*. This volume status appears while a volume is being formatted.

◢ *Basic*. When a hard drive is first sensed by Windows, it is assigned the Basic disk status. A basic disk can be partitioned and formatted as a stand-alone hard drive.

◢ *Dynamic*. A disk marked as dynamic can be used with other dynamic disks in a spanned or striped volume. When this dynamic volume is set up, the disks work together. The following status indicators apply only to dynamic disks:

- *Offline*. An offline disk status indicates a dynamic disk has become corrupted or is unavailable. The problem can be caused by a corrupted file system, the drive cables are loose, the hard drive has failed, or another hardware problem. If you believe the problem is corrected, right-click the disk and select **Reactivate Disk** from the shortcut menu to bring the disk back online.

- *Foreign drive*. If you move a hard drive that has been configured as a dynamic disk on another computer to this computer, this computer will report the disk as a foreign drive. To fix the problem, you need to import the foreign drive. To do that, right-click the disk and select **Import Foreign Disks** from the shortcut menu. You should then be able to see the volumes on the disk.

- *Healthy (At Risk)*. The dynamic disk can be accessed, but I/O errors have occurred. Try returning the disk to online status. If the volume status does not return to healthy, back up all data and replace the drive.

If you are still having problems with a hard drive, volume, or mounted drive, check Event Viewer for events about the drive that might have been recorded there. These events might help you understand the nature of the problem and what to do about it. How to use Event Viewer is covered in the next chapter.

REGIONAL AND LANGUAGE SETTINGS

One more task you might be called on to do as a part of maintaining a computer is to help a user configure a computer to use a different language. Suppose a user needs to see Windows messages in Spanish and wants to use a Spanish keyboard, such as the one in Figure 13-61. Configuring a computer for another language involves downloading and installing the language pack, changing the Windows display language, changing how numbers are formatted, and changing the language used for keyboard input.

A+
220-702
2.3

Figure 13-61 Spanish keyboard
Courtesy: Course Technology/Cengage Learning

13

A+ 220-702

Using Windows Vista Ultimate, follow these steps to configure the computer to use Spanish for the display and keyboard:

1. Windows Vista Ultimate offers Language Interface Packs (LIP) for many languages. You first need to download the Spanish LIP using Windows Update. Click **Start**, **All Programs**, and **Windows Update**. In the Windows Update window, click **View available updates**.

2. In the View available updates window (see Figure 13-62), under the list of Windows Vista Ultimate Language Packs, select the **Spanish Language Pack**. Make sure other updates that you don't want are not selected. Click **Install** and respond to the UAC box.

3. You are now ready to configure the computer to use the new language. Open Control Panel and click **Clock, Language, and Region**. In the Clock, Language, and Region window, click **Regional and Language Options**. The Regional and Language Options dialog box opens (see Figure 13-63).

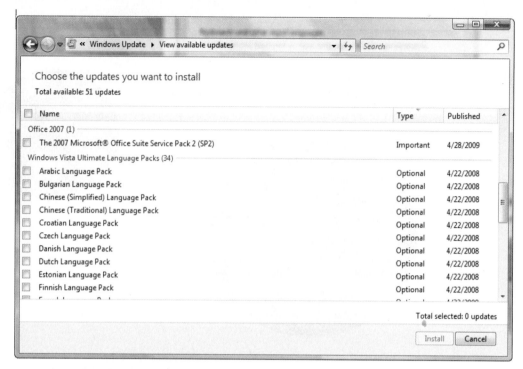

Figure 13-62 Select the language to download and install
Courtesy: Course Technology/Cengage Learning

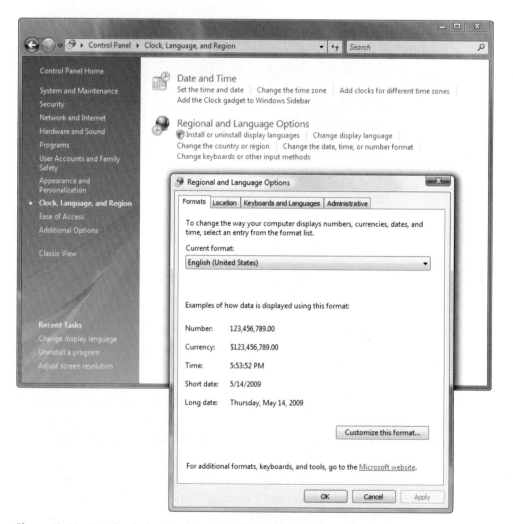

Figure 13-63 Use the Regional and Language Options box to change language settings
Courtesy: Course Technology/Cengage Learning

4. To change the format used to display numbers, currencies, dates, and time, select the language from the drop-down list under Current format (see Figure 13-64).

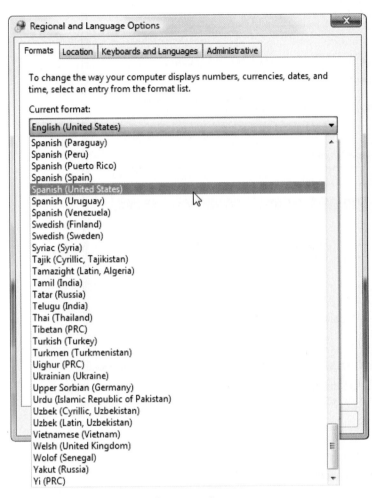

Figure 13-64 Select how to format numbers
Courtesy: Course Technology/Cengage Learning

5. To change the display language, click the Keyboards and Language tab. Select **español** from the drop-down menu (see Figure 13-65). The language appears in the list of installed languages because the Spanish language was installed in Step 2.

6. To change the keyboard layout, click **Change keyboards**. On the General tab of the Text Services and Input Languages box, click **Add** (see the left side of Figure 13-66). In the Add Input Language box, select a Spanish keyboard, as shown on the right side of Figure 13-66. Click **OK**.

7. The Spanish keyboard is now added to the list of input languages. Under Default input language, select the Spanish language and click **Apply**. Click **OK** to close the dialog box.

A+
220-702
2.3

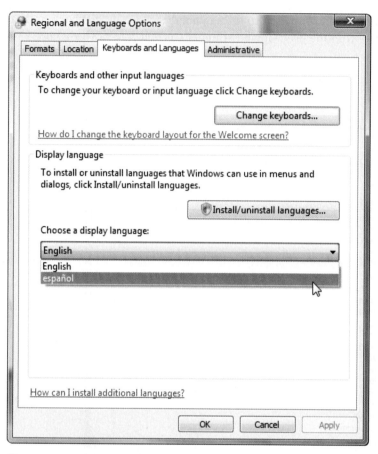

Figure 13-65 Select the display language
Courtesy: Course Technology/Cengage Learning

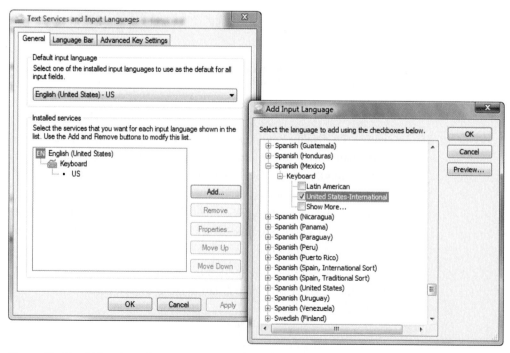

Figure 13-66 Add an input language
Courtesy: Course Technology/Cengage Learning

A+
220-702
2.3

8. On the Regional and Language Options box, click **Apply** and then click **OK** to close the box. A message appears that says you must log off before changes will take effect (see Figure 13-67). Click **Log off now**.

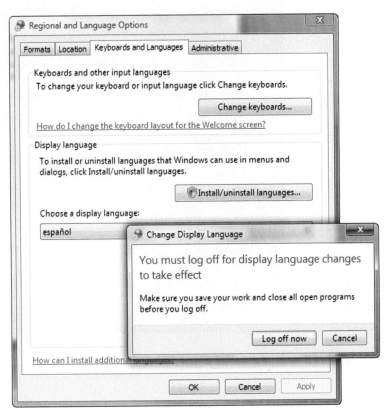

Figure 13-67 Log off before language changes will take effect
Courtesy: Course Technology/Cengage Learning

9. After logging back on the system, you will see the Start menu in Español, as shown in Figure 13-68.

Windows Vista Ultimate offers language packs through Windows Update. For other Vista editions, you can go to the Microsoft Web site (*www.microsoft.com*) and download the Language Interface Pack (LIP). Then double-click the downloaded file to install the language. After the language pack is installed, use Control Panel to change the Windows display for the installed language. You also need to change the format used for numbers, currencies, dates, and time. And, if a special keyboard is to be used, you need to change the input language.

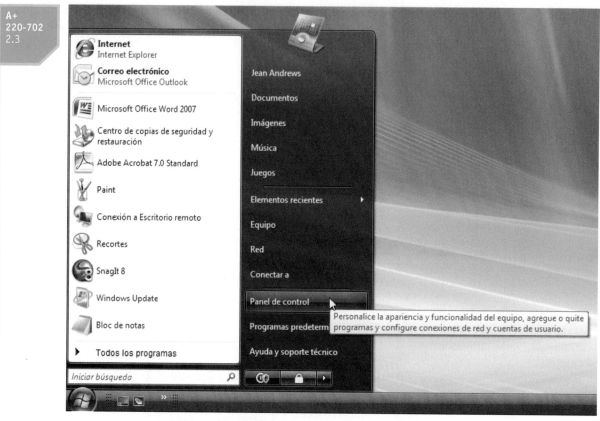

Figure 13-68 Display language in Spanish
Courtesy: Course Technology/Cengage Learning

>> CHAPTER SUMMARY

◢ Regular preventive maintenance includes verifying Windows settings, defragmenting the hard drive, checking the drive for errors, reducing the startup process to essentials, and doing whatever else is necessary to free up enough space on the hard drive for Windows to perform well.

◢ The easiest way to clean up temporary files is to use the Disk Cleanup utility on the drive properties box.

◢ By default, Vista automatically defrags weekly. With XP and Vista, you can also defrag the hard drive at any time by using the drive properties box or the Defrag command.

◢ Use the Chkdsk utility to check the drive for errors and recover data. The utility can be accessed from a command prompt or the drive properties box.

◢ Windows uses startup folders to hold shortcuts to programs or program files that are launched at startup.

◢ The Vista Defender Software Explorer window is used to control startup programs.

◢ Vista uses the Programs and Features window to uninstall software, and XP uses the Add and Remove Programs window for the same purpose.

◢ For best performance, allow at least 15 percent free space on the Windows volume. If you need more free space on this volume, you can move data to other media, compress folders, reinstall software on a different volume, move the virtual memory paging file to another volume or drive, and limit the space on the volume used by Internet Explorer.

◢ Virtual memory uses hard drive space as memory to increase the total amount of memory available. Virtual memory is stored in a paging file named Pagefile.sys.

◢ You need a plan for disaster recovery in the event the hard drive fails. This plan needs to include routine backups of data and system files.

◢ The Windows Vista Backup and Restore Center and the Windows 2000/XP Ntbackup utility can be used to schedule routine backups of user data files.

◢ Vista backup uses a full or incremental backup method. Choices for backups available under Ntbackup include full, copy, incremental, differential, and daily backups.

◢ Vista and XP back up system files using restore points created by System Protection. Later, you can use System Restore to restore the system to one of these restore points.

◢ You can back up and restore the system state using the Windows 2000/XP Ntbackup utility.

◢ Windows Vista Complete PC Backup or Windows XP Automated System Recovery can back up the entire hard drive.

◢ Commands useful to manage files, folders, and storage media include Help, Dir, Del, Copy, Recover, Xcopy, Robocopy, MD, CD, RD, Chkdsk, Defrag, Edit, and Format.

◢ Use Disk Management to manage hard drives and partitions. Use it to create, delete, and resize (Vista only) partitions, mount a drive, manage dynamic disks, and solve problems with hard drives.

◢ Change the display and input language and the format used for numbers, currencies, dates, and times using the Regional and Language Options dialog box accessed from Control Panel.

13

>> KEY TERMS

For explanations of key terms, see the Glossary near the end of the book.

Automated System Recovery	dynamic volumes	System Restore
batch file	fragmented files	system state data
Chkdsk	mount point	user profile namespace
Complete PC Backup	mounted drive	virtual memory
Defrag	Pagefile.sys	wildcard
dynamic disks	restore points	

>> REVIEWING THE BASICS

1. What is the purpose of the Windows.old folder?

2. How can you delete the Windows.old folder?

3. By default, when does Vista automatically defrag a drive?

4. Using Vista, what type of command prompt window is needed to run the Chkdsk command?

5. What is the path to the startup folder for each user in Windows Vista?

6. What is the path to the startup folder for all users in Windows Vista?

7. What utility does Vista use to manage startup programs?

8. What Vista window is used to uninstall software?

9. What is the path to the Windows XP startup folder for each user?

10. What is the path to the Windows XP startup folder for all users?

11. What is the normal path of the Windows paging file used for virtual memory?

12. What is the path to the Internet Explorer cache folder in Windows Vista?

13. Why is it important to not store a backup of drive C on another partition on the same hard drive?

14. What is the program filename of the Windows XP backup utility?

15. What program file must you execute to install the Backup utility in Windows XP Home Edition?

16. What is the %*SystemRoot*% folder as used in Microsoft documentation?

17. What Vista utility creates restore points?

18. How can you delete all restore points?

19. Where are restore points kept?

20. In what folder does Windows XP store a backup of the registry when backing up the system state?

21. Which editions of Vista don't include Complete PC backup?

22. What two components are created when you back up an XP system using the Automated System Recovery process?

23. What file in the user account folder stores user settings?

24. In what folder is the registry stored?

25. In what folder are 32-bit programs stored by a 64-bit edition of Windows Vista?

26. What is the purpose of the C:\Windows\CSC folder?

27. In a command line, what is the purpose of the ? in a filename?

28. What is the purpose of the |more parameter at the end of a command line?

29. What is the command to list all files and subdirectories in a directory?

30. What command is replacing Xcopy?

31. Which is more stable, RAID implemented by Windows or RAID implemented by hardware?

32. When you move a dynamic disk to a new computer, what status will Disk Management first assign the drive?

33. Which edition of Vista allows you to install a language pack by using Windows Update?

>> THINKING CRITICALLY

1. Write and test commands to do the following:

   (Answers can vary)

   a. Create a folder named C:\data

   b. Create a folder named C:\data\test1 and a folder named C:\data\test2

   c. Copy Notepad.exe to the Test1 folders.

   d. Move Notepad.exe from the Test1 folder to the Test2 folder.

   e. Make C:\ the default folder.

   f. Without changing the default folder, list all files in the Test2 folder.

   g. Delete the Test2 folder.

   h. Delete the C:\data folder.

2. You are trying to clean up a slow Windows Vista system and discover that the 75 GB hard drive has only 5 GB free space. The entire drive is taken up by drive C. What is the best way to free up some space?

   a. Compress the entire hard drive.

   b. Move the \Program Files folder to an external hard drive.

   c. Delete the Windows.old folder.

   d. Reduce the size of the paging file.

3. Which is the best first step to protect important data on your hard drive?

   a. Use dynamic disks to set up a striped volume so that the data has redundancy.

   b. Back the data up to another media.

   c. Compress the folder that holds the data.

   d. Put password protection on the data folder.

>> HANDS-ON PROJECTS

PROJECT 13-1: Using System Restore

Do the following to find out how System Restore works and how it can affect a system:

1. Create a restore point.

2. Make a change to the display settings.

3. Change the desktop background.

4. Restore the system using System Restore.

Are the changes still in effect? Why or why not?

PROJECT 13-2: Cleaning Up Your Hard Drive

Log onto Vista using an account with Administrator rights. Open **Windows Explorer** and right-click drive **C**. On the shortcut menu, click **Properties** and then click **Disk Cleanup** in the properties box. Clean up files for all users. In the Disk Cleanup box, select **Downloaded Program Files, Temporary Internet Files, Recycle Bin,** and **Temporary files** and click **OK**.

Next, log onto the system using an account that does not have Administrator rights. How are you limited in the way you can perform a Disk Cleanup? Why do you think this limitation exists?

PROJECT 13-3: Problem-Solving Using the Microsoft Knowledge Base

Your hard drive has been attacked by a malicious virus, and you have decided to restore your hard drive from the last backup made by the ASR backup process. You cannot find the ASR floppy disk required for the restore process. Search the Microsoft Knowledge Base for the steps to re-create the ASR floppy disk when the ASR backup is available. Print the Knowledge Base article.

PROJECT 13-4: Restoring the System State

Understanding the importance of making backups is essential to learning to support Windows. Do the following to examine the power and limitations of backing up the system state data:

1. Back up the Windows 2000/XP system state to a folder on your network or hard drive. What is the path to your backup?

2. Make several changes to the Windows environment: Using the Display Properties window, change the wallpaper background of the desktop, the screen resolution, and the Windows Theme. What are these new settings?

3. Using the Add or Remove Programs applet in Control Panel, remove and add a Windows component. Which component did you remove? Which component did you add?

4. Reboot your system and verify your changes were all implemented.

5. Now restore the system state from the backup you made. Which of your changes were undone and which (if any) were left untouched?

PROJECT 13-5: Using CCleaner to Optimize and Clean a System

CCleaner by Piriform (*www.ccleaner.com*) is freeware that can be used to optimize and clean a Windows system. It removes files that are no longer needed and can clean the registry of unused keys. Go to the *www.ccleaner.com* Web site, investigate the software, and download the latest version. Install and run it and then answer the following questions:

1. What is the version of CCleaner that you installed?

2. Will CCleaner work on a 64-bit installation of Windows?

3. Did CCleaner attempt to add a program to your startup programs?

4. How much space on the hard drive did CCleaner offer to free?

5. List up to four registry keys that CCleaner offered to remove.

6. List up to three programs CCleaner offered to uninstall.

7. Do you think you would like to keep CCleaner installed on your system? Why or why not?

>> REAL PROBLEMS, REAL SOLUTIONS

REAL PROBLEM 13-1: Using Microsoft SyncToy

You own a small computer service company and have several clients who work out of a home office. Jason is one of them. Jason uses Windows XP on his desktop and Vista on his laptop. He travels with his laptop but uses his desktop computer when he's at home. He keeps all his important data files in a folder, C:\Data, on his desktop computer. When he leaves for a business trip, he copies only the files from the \Data folder to his laptop that he expects to use on the trip. On the trip, some of these files are edited or deleted, and some new files are created. When he gets back home, he copies one file at a time from the laptop to the desktop using his home network. However, he has told you that occasionally he forgets to copy the files from the laptop to the desktop before he makes changes in the desktop files. Therefore, he's concerned that if he copied the entire \Data folder from the laptop to the desktop, he might lose an important change.

He has asked you to help him find a better method to synchronize his \Data folders on these two computers. After a little research, you find the free Microsoft SyncToy utility on the Microsoft Web site and decide you need to test it to see if it will meet Jason's needs. Set up a testing situation and then answer the following questions:

1. List the high-level steps (not the keystrokes) you used to test the utility.

2. What test files did you use to test it?

3. What problems, if any, did you encounter in the testing process?

4. Do you think the utility is a good fit for Jason? Why or why not?

REAL PROBLEM 13-2: Problems Starting Windows XP

Tim, a coworker who uses many different applications on his Windows XP system, complains to you that his system is very slow starting up and responding when he loads and unloads applications. You suspect the system is loading too many services and programs during startup that are sucking up system resources. What do you do to check for startup processes and eliminate the unnecessary ones? If you have access to a Windows system that needs this type of service, test your answers on this system. Write down at least 10 things you should do or try that were discussed in the chapter to speed up a sluggish Windows XP installation.

REAL PROBLEM 13-3: Cleaning Up a Sluggish Windows Vista System

Using all the tools and techniques presented in this chapter, clean up a sluggish Windows Vista system. Take detailed notes as you go, showing what you checked before you started to solve the problems, what you did to solve the problems, and what the results were of your efforts. What questions did you have along the way? Bring these questions to class for discussion.

CHAPTER
14

Optimizing Windows

In the last chapter, you learned about the tools and strategies to maintain Windows and its hardware resources and about the importance of keeping good backups of data and system files. This chapter takes you one step further as a PC support technician so that you can get the best performance out of Windows. We begin the chapter learning about the Windows tools you'll need to optimize Windows. As a support technician, because you might be called on to edit the Windows registry, you'll also learn about the registry and how to safely edit it manually. Then we turn our attention to the steps you can follow to cause a sluggish Windows system to perform at its best. As you read, you might consider following the steps in the chapter first using a Windows Vista system and then going through the chapter again using a Windows XP system.

WINDOWS UTILITIES AND TOOLS TO SUPPORT THE OS

A+
220-701
3.2

Windows offers some powerful tools to help you understand what is happening behind the scenes with processes that are launched during and after startup, with events that might indicate a problem with software, hardware, or security, and with performance. By knowing how and when to use these tools, you can quickly zero in on a Windows problem or a performance block. In this part of the chapter, you will learn how to use the tools and then later in the chapter, you will see how these tools can help you when following the step-by-step strategy to optimize Windows.

Tools covered in this part of the chapter include Task Manager, System Configuration Utility (commonly called MSconfig), Services console, Computer Management console, Microsoft Management Console (MMC), Event Viewer, Reliability and Performance Monitor, and the Registry Editor. So, let's get started.

> 💡 **A+ Exam Tip** The A+ 220-701 Essentials exam expects you to know how to use Task Manager, MSconfig, the Services console, Computer Management console, MMC, Event Viewer, and Performance Monitor (also called the System Monitor).

TASK MANAGER

Task Manager (Taskmgr.exe) lets you view the applications and processes running on your computer as well as information about process and memory performance, network activity, and user activity. There are several ways you can access Task Manager:

- ◢ Press **Ctrl+Alt+Delete**. Depending on your system, Task Manager appears or the Windows Security screen appears. If the security screen appears, click **Start Task Manager**.
- ◢ Right-click a blank area on the taskbar, and then select **Task Manager** on the shortcut menu.
- ◢ Press **Ctrl+Shift+Esc**.
- ◢ Enter **taskmgr.exe** in the Vista Start Search box or the XP Run dialog box and press **Enter**.

Windows Vista Task Manager has six tabs: Applications, Processes, Services, Performance, Networking, and Users (see Figure 14-1). Windows XP Task Manager does not have the Services tab (see Figure 14-2). The Windows XP Users tab shows only when a system is set for Fast User Switching and lets you monitor other users logged onto the system.

Let's see how each tab of the Task Manager window works.

APPLICATIONS TAB

On the Applications tab shown in Figure 14-1, each application loaded can have one of two states: Running or Not Responding. If an application is listed as Not Responding, you can end it by selecting it and clicking the **End Task** button at the bottom of the window. The application will attempt a normal shutdown; if data has not been saved, you are given the opportunity to save it.

PROCESSES TAB

The Processes tab of Task Manager lists system services and other processes associated with applications, together with how much CPU time and memory the process uses. This

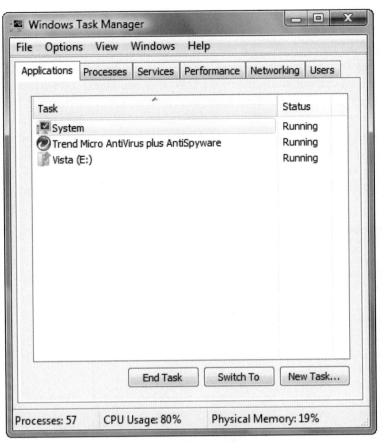

Figure 14-1 The Applications tab in Task Manager shows the status of active applications
Courtesy: Course Technology/Cengage Learning

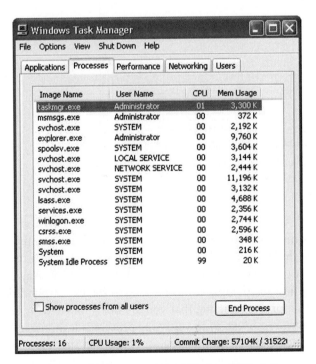

Figure 14-2 This Processes tab of Windows XP Task Manager shows Windows
processes before any applications are installed
Courtesy: Course Technology/Cengage Learning

A+
220-701
3.2

information can help you determine which applications are slowing down your system. The Processes tab for Windows Vista Task Manager (see Figure 14-3) shows the processes running under the current user. This screen shot was taken immediately after a Vista installation before any applications were installed. To see all processes running, click **Show processes from all users** and respond to the UAC box (see Figure 14-4). Task Manager now shows processes running under the current user, System, Local Service, and Network Service accounts. Services running under these last three accounts cannot display a dialog box on-screen or interact with the user. To do that, the service must be running under a user account. Also, a service running under the System account has more core privileges than does a service running under another account. Figure 14-2 shows the list of processes for a Windows XP system immediately after the installation was completed with no applications installed.

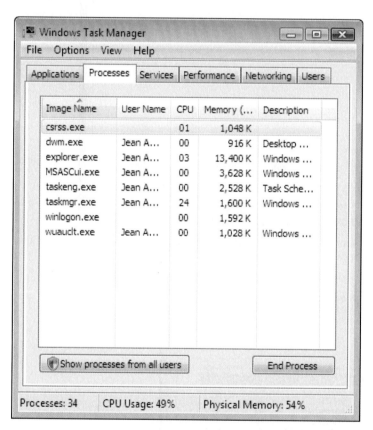

Figure 14-3 Processes running under the current user for a new Vista installation
Courtesy: Course Technology/Cengage Learning

When you have a sluggish Windows system, close all open applications and open Task Manager. Check the **Applications** tab to make sure no applications are running. Then click the **Processes** tab. Compare the list in Figure 14-2 (for Windows XP) or Figure 14-3 (for Windows Vista) with the list of processes running on the sluggish system. Any extra processes you see might be caused by unwanted applications running in the background or malicious software running. If you see a process running that you are not familiar with, search the Microsoft Web site (*support.microsoft.com*) to verify the process is legitimate. If you don't find it there, do a general Google search on the process. If you find that the process is not legitimate, stop the process and immediately run antivirus software. Chapter 20 gives more information about ridding your system of malicious software and about the processes you see listed in the Task Manager window.

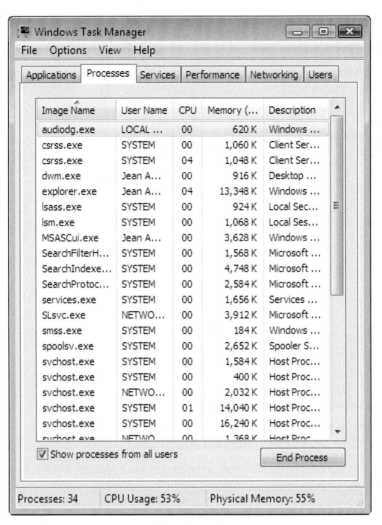

Figure 14-4 Vista processes for all users
Courtesy: Course Technology/Cengage Learning

> ⚡ **Caution** A word of caution is important here: Many Web sites will tell you a legitimate process is malicious so that you will download and use their software to get rid of the process. However, their software is likely to be adware or spyware that you don't want. Make sure you can trust a site before you download from it or take its advice.

To stop a process using Task Manager, select the process and click **End Process**. The process is ended abruptly. If the process belongs to an application, you will lose any unsaved information in the application. Therefore, if an application is hung, try using the Applications tab to end the task before turning to the Processes tab to end its underlying process.

When an application is listed on the Applications tab, you can right-click it and select **Go To Process** on the shortcut menu (see Figure 14-5). Task Manager will take you to the Processes tab and the running process for this application.

If you want to end the process and all related processes, right-click the process and select **End Process Tree** from the shortcut menu. Be careful to not end critical Windows processes; ending these might crash your system.

Each application running on your computer is assigned a priority level, which determines its position in the queue for CPU resources. You can use Task Manager to change the priority level for an application that is already loaded. If an application performs slowly, increase

A+
220-701
3.2

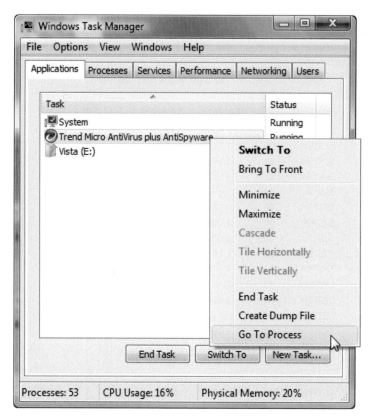

Figure 14-5 Find the running process for this running application
Courtesy: Course Technology/Cengage Learning

its priority. You should only do this with very important applications, because giving an application higher priority than certain background system processes can sometimes interfere with the operating system.

> **Notes** If your desktop locks up, you can use Task Manager to refresh it. To do so, press **Ctrl+Alt+Del** and then click **Task Manager**. Click the **Processes** tab. Select **Explorer.exe** (the process that provides the desktop) and then click **End Process**. Click **End process** in the warning box. Then click the **Applications** tab. Click **New Task**. Enter **Explorer.exe** in the Create New Task dialog box and click **OK**. Your desktop will be refreshed and any running programs will still be open.

To use Task Manger to change the priority level of an open application, do the following:

1. In Task Manager, click the **Applications** tab. Right-click the application and select **Go To Process** from the shortcut menu. The Processes tab is selected and the process that runs the application is selected.

2. Right-click the selected process. From the shortcut menu that appears, set the new priority to **AboveNormal** (see Figure 14-6). If that doesn't give satisfactory performance, then try **High**.

> **Notes** Remember: any changes you make to an application's priority level affect only the current session.

SERVICES TAB

The third Vista tab, the Services tab, is shown in Figure 14-7. This tab lists the services currently installed along with the status of each service. Recall that a service is a program that runs in the background and is called on by other programs to perform a background task.

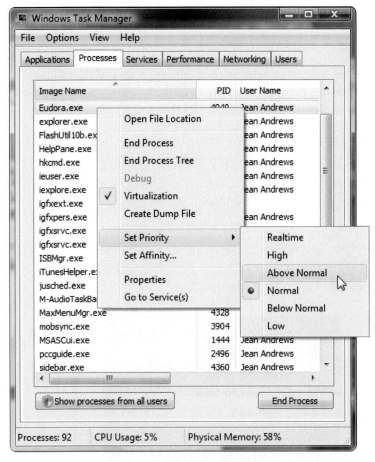

Figure 14-6 Change the priority level of a running application
Courtesy: Course Technology/Cengage Learning

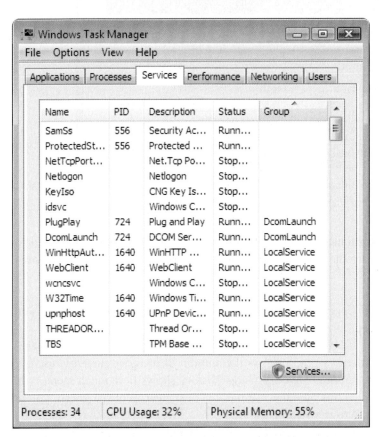

Figure 14-7 This Services tab of Windows Vista Task Manager gives the current status of all installed services
Courtesy: Course Technology/Cengage Learning

A+
220-701
3.2

Running services are sometimes listed in the notification area of the taskbar. To manage a service, click the **Services** button at the bottom of the window to go to the Services console. How to use this console is discussed later in the chapter.

PERFORMANCE TAB

The fourth Vista tab, the Performance tab, is shown in Figure 14-8. It provides details about how a program uses system resources. You can use these views to identify which applications and processes use the most CPU time.

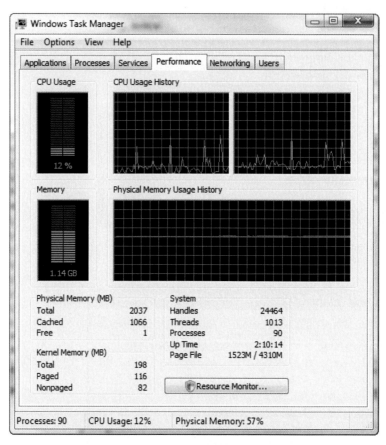

Figure 14-8 The Performance tab window shows details about how system resources are being used
Courtesy: Course Technology/Cengage Learning

On the Performance tab, you'll find five graphs near the top of the window and three frames near the bottom of the window. Here is an explanation of how they are used:

- ◢ The *CPU Usage* graph indicates the percentage of time the CPU is currently being used.
- ◢ The *CPU Usage History* graphs show this same percentage of use over recent time.
- ◢ The left *Memory* graph shows the amount of memory currently used.
- ◢ The right *Physical Memory Usage History* shows how much memory has recently been used. If this blue bar is a flat line near the top of the graph, you need to add more RAM to the system.
- ◢ The *Physical Memory (MB)* frame lists Total (amount of RAM), Cached (RAM that has recently been cached), and Free (RAM that recently has not been used).

A+
220-701
3.2

◢ The *Kernel Memory* frame indicates how much RAM and virtual memory the core kernel components of Windows are using. This frame lists Total (sum of RAM and virtual memory), Paged (how much of the paging file the kernel uses), and Nonpaged (how much RAM the kernel uses).

◢ The *System* frame gives information about the overall system status. This frame lists Handles (number of running objects used by all processes), Threads (number of subprocesses), Processes (number of running processes), Up Time (time since the computer was last restarted), and Page File (the first number is the amount of RAM and virtual memory currently in use, and the second number is total RAM and virtual memory).

To get even more detailed information about how Windows is performing, click the **Resource Monitor** button. You will be taken to the Resource Monitor window, discussed later in the chapter.

NETWORKING TAB

The Networking tab lets you monitor network activity and bandwidth used. You can use it to see how heavily the network is being used by this computer. For example, in Figure 14-9,

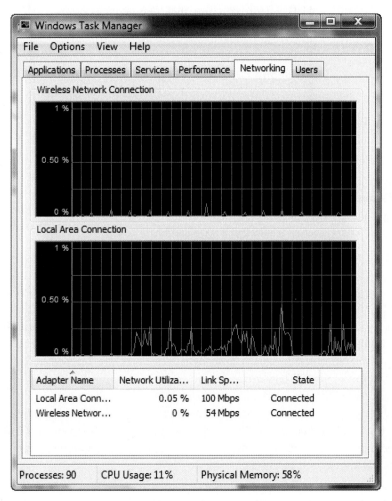

Figure 14-9 Use the Networking tab of Task Manager to monitor network activity
Courtesy: Course Technology/Cengage Learning

14

A+ 220-701

A+
220-701
3.2

you can see that the wireless connection is running at 54 Mbps, while the local (wired) connection is running at 100 Mbps. You can also see moderate network activity.

USERS TAB

The Users tab shows all users currently logged on the system. To improve Windows performance or just before you shut down the system, you can log off a user. To log off a user, first select the **Processes** tab and click **Show processes from all users** and respond to the UAC box. Then return to the Users tab, select the user, and click **Logoff**. The dialog box shown in Figure 14-10 appears, warning that unsaved data might be lost. Click **Log off user** to complete the operation.

Figure 14-10 Use Task Manager to log off a user
Courtesy: Course Technology/Cengage Learning

APPLYING CONCEPTS

Suppose a friend asks you to help her solve a problem with her Windows XP system that is moving very slowly. You open Task Manager, select the **Processes** tab, and see a window similar to that in Figure 14-11. Notice that the Ccapp.exe process is using 99 percent of CPU time. When you click the **Performance** tab, you see why the system is running so slowly (see Figure 14-12). This one process is consistently using most of the CPU resources.

When you try to lower the priority of this process, you discover the process will not relinquish priority (see Figure 14-13). The next step is to investigate the process. Is it legitimate? Is it a virus? Can it be better managed or not used? If you do a Google search on Ccapp.exe, you'll discover the process belongs to Norton AntiVirus software. The solution is to disable scanning of outgoing e-mail so the process will not lock up the CPU.

A+
220-701
3.2

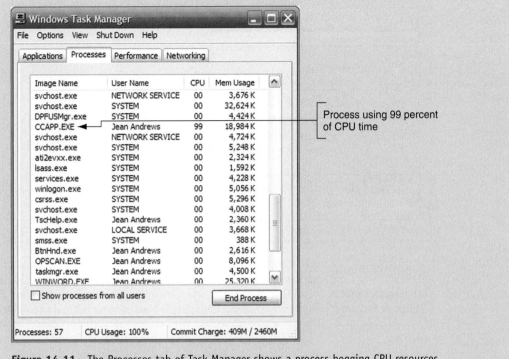

Process using 99 percent of CPU time

Figure 14-11 The Processes tab of Task Manager shows a process hogging CPU resources
Courtesy: Course Technology/Cengage Learning

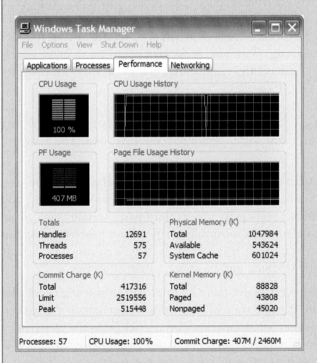

Figure 14-12 The Performance tab shows a heavily used CPU
Courtesy: Course Technology/Cengage Learning

14

A+ 220-701

A+
220-701
3.2

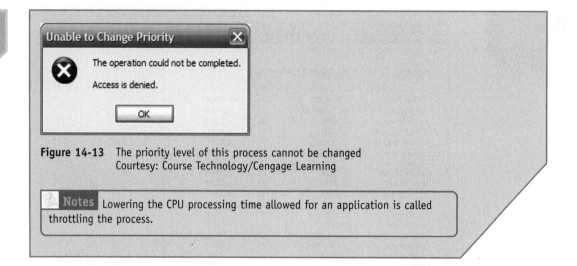

Figure 14-13 The priority level of this process cannot be changed
Courtesy: Course Technology/Cengage Learning

Notes Lowering the CPU processing time allowed for an application is called throttling the process.

A+ Exam Tip Task Manager gives good information, but doesn't always give the full picture of running processes. One tool that gives better information than Task Manager is Process Explorer by Microsoft Technet (*technet.microsoft.com*). The utility is free, and you will learn to use it in Chapter 20.

SYSTEM CONFIGURATION UTILITY (MSCONFIG)

You can use the System Configuration Utility (Msconfig.exe), which is commonly pronounced "M-S-config," to find out what processes are launched at startup and to temporarily disable a process from loading. This utility is included with Windows Vista and Windows XP, but it is not included with Windows 2000.

MSconfig is a temporary fix to disable a program or service at startup, but it should not be considered a permanent fix. Once you've decided you want to make the change permanent, use other tools to permanently remove that process from Windows startup. Follow these steps to learn to use MSconfig:

1. To start MSconfig, enter **msconfig.exe** in the Vista Start Search box or the XP Run box and press **Enter**. For Vista, respond to the UAC box. The System Configuration box opens.

2. Click the **Services** tab to see a list of all services launched at startup (see Figure 14-14). Notice that this tab has a Disable all button. If you use that button, you'll disable all nonessential Windows services as well as third-party services such as virus scan programs. Use it only for the most difficult Windows problems, because you'll disable some services that you might really want, such as Windows Task Scheduler, Print Spooler, Automatic Updates, and the System Restore service.

3. To view only those services put there by third-party software, check **Hide all Microsoft services**. If you have antivirus software running in the background (and you should), you'll see that listed as well as any service launched at startup and put there by installed software. Uncheck all services that you don't want. If you don't recognize a service, try entering its name in a search string at *www.google.com* for information about the program. If the program is a service, you can permanently stop it by using the Services console, discussed next.

4. Click the **Startup** tab to see a list of programs that launch at startup (see Figure 14-15). To disable all nonessential startup tasks, click **Disable all**. Or you can check and

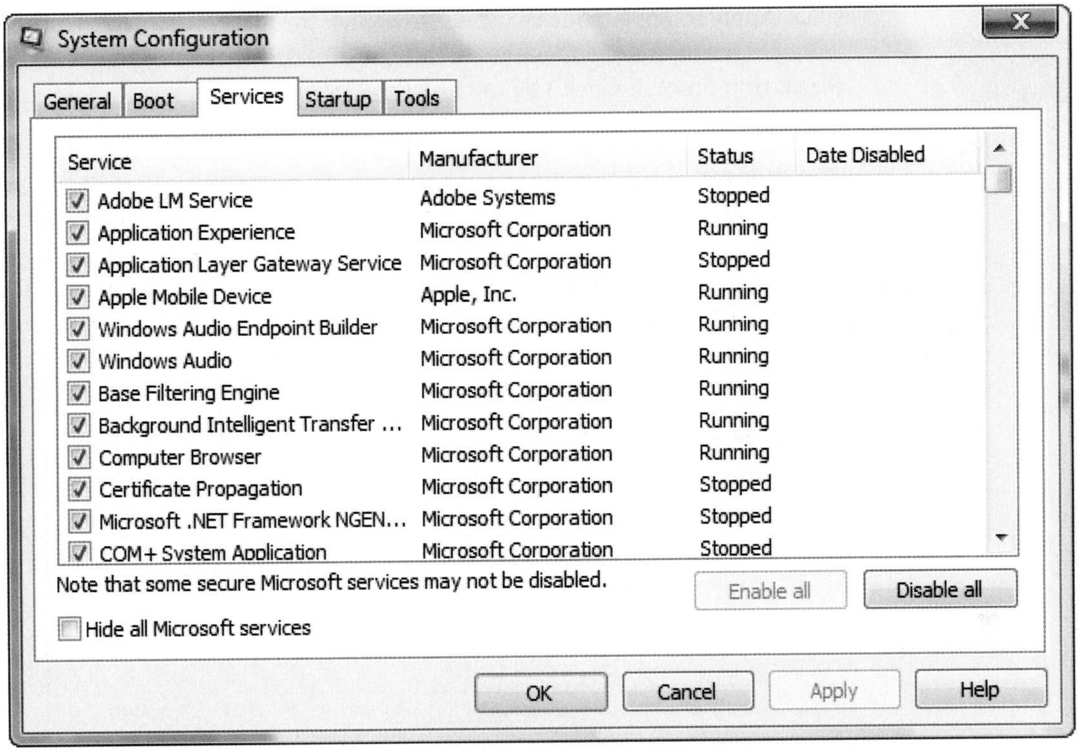

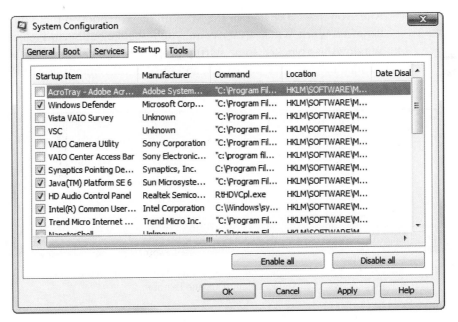

Figure 14-14 Use MSconfig to view and control services launched at startup
Courtesy: Course Technology/Cengage Learning

Figure 14-15 Select startup processes to enable or disable
Courtesy: Course Technology/Cengage Learning

uncheck an individual startup program to enable or disable it. The Startup tab can be useful when trying to understand how a program is launched at startup because it offers the Location column. This column shows the registry key or startup folder where the startup entry is made. How to find and change registry keys is covered later in the chapter.

A+
220-701
3.2

5. Click **Apply** to apply your changes. Now click the **General** tab and you should see Selective startup selected, as shown in Figure 14-16. MSconfig is now set to control the startup process. Click **OK** to close the MSconfig box.

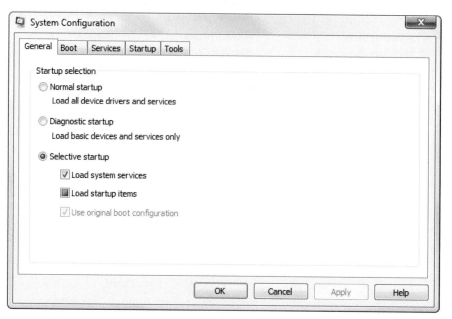

Figure 14-16 MSconfig is set to control the Windows startup programs
Courtesy: Course Technology/Cengage Learning

6. After you make a change in the MSconfig box, reboot so that you can see what happens. When Windows starts up, you'll see the bubble in Figure 14-17 that says Windows has blocked some startup programs. Remember, using MSconfig is recommended only as a temporary fix, and this bubble reminds us of that.

Figure 14-17 The System Configuration utility has blocked some startup programs
Courtesy: Course Technology/Cengage Learning

7. Watch for error messages during the boot that indicate you've created a problem with your changes. For instance, after the boot, you find out you can no longer use that nifty little utility that came with your digital camera. To fix the problem, you need to find out which service or program you stopped that you need for that utility. Go back to the MSconfig tool and enable that one service and reboot. MSconfig should only be used to temporarily disable a program. Use other tools, such as the Services console or startup folders, to permanently remove it from the

startup process. Once the program is removed from the startup process, you will no longer need MSconfig and can return it to normal startup mode.

Recall from Chapter 13 that Software Explorer in Windows Vista can also be used to monitor startup programs and to enable and disable a startup program. Software Explorer is more convenient to use than MSconfig.

> **Notes** MSconfig reports only what it is programmed to look for when listing startup programs and services. It looks only in certain registry keys and startup folders, and sometimes MSconfig does not report a startup process. Therefore, don't consider its list of startup processes to be complete.

SERVICES CONSOLE

The Services console is used to control the Windows and third-party services installed on a system. To launch the Services console, type **Services.msc** in the Vista Start Search box or the XP Run box and press **Enter**. For Vista, respond to the UAC box. If the **Extended** tab at the bottom of the window is not selected, click it (see Figure 14-18).

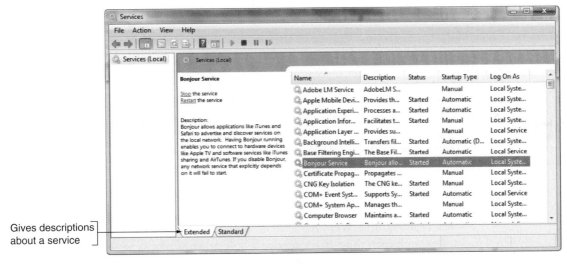

Gives descriptions about a service

Figure 14-18 The Services window is used to manage Windows services
Courtesy: Course Technology/Cengage Learning

As you select each service, the area on the left describes the service. If the description is missing, most likely the service is a third-party service put there by an installed application. To get more information about a service or to stop or start a service, right-click its name and select **Properties** from the shortcut menu. In the Properties box (see Figure 14-19), the startup types for a service are:

- ▲ *Automatic (Delayed Start)*. Starts shortly after startup, after the user logs on, so as not to slow down the startup process
- ▲ *Automatic*. Starts when Windows loads
- ▲ *Manual*. Starts as needed
- ▲ *Disabled*. Cannot be started

A+
220-701
3.2

> **Notes** If you suspect a Windows system service is causing a problem, you can use MSconfig to disable the service. If this works, then try replacing the service file with a fresh copy from the Windows setup CD or DVD.

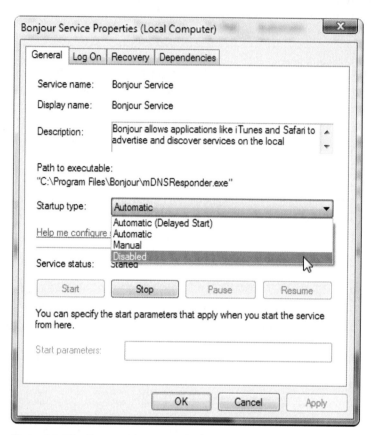

Figure 14-19 Use a service properties box to manage a service
Courtesy: Course Technology/Cengage Learning

When cleaning up a Windows system, one step is to disable or uninstall unwanted services. Research each third-party service whose Startup type is set to Automatic, and decide if you need to disable the service or uninstall the software responsible for the service. For most Windows services, you can use the Control Panel or other Windows utilities to control a particular service. For example, you can stop and start Automatic Updates from the XP System Properties box or uninstall software using the Vista Programs and Features window. Third-party services can often be stopped by using the utility that installed the service. You can access the utility from the Start menu. However, you can also use the Services console to disable a service. In the console, use its Properties box (see Figure 14-19). In the Startup type drop-down list, select **Disabled** and then click **Apply**.

COMPUTER MANAGEMENT

Computer Management (Compmgmt.msc) is a window that consolidates several Windows administrative tools that you can use to manage the local PC or other computers on the network. To use most of these tools, you must be logged on as an administrator, although you can view certain settings and configurations in Computer Management if you are logged on with lesser privileges.

A+
220-701
3.2

As with most Windows tools, there are several ways to access Computer Management:

⊿ Enter **compmgmt.msc** in the Vista Start Search box or the XP Run box and press **Enter**. For Vista, respond to the UAC box.

⊿ Click **Start**, right-click **Computer** (**My Computer** for XP) and select **Manage** from the shortcut menu. For Vista, respond to the UAC box.

⊿ In Control Panel, click **System and Maintenance** (for XP, click **Performance and Maintenance**), click **Administrative Tools**, and double-click **Computer Management**. For Vista, respond to the UAC box.

The Computer Management window opens (see Figure 14-20). Using this window, you can access Task Scheduler (Vista only), Event Viewer, Shared Folders, Reliability and Performance, Device Manager, Disk Management, Services console, Indexing Service, and manage user groups (covered in Chapter 20). You can also monitor problems with hardware, software, and security. Several tools available from the Computer Management window are covered in this chapter.

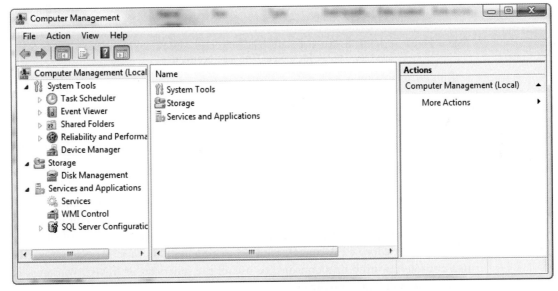

Figure 14-20 Windows Computer Management combines several administrative tools into a single easy-to-access window
Courtesy: Course Technology/Cengage Learning

> **Notes** By default, the Administrative Tools group is found in Control Panel, but you can add the group to the All Programs menu. To do that, right-click the taskbar and select **Properties** from the shortcut menu. The Taskbar and Start Menu Properties box opens. Select the **Start Menu** tab and then click **Customize** (as shown on the left side of Figure 14-21). The Customize Start Menu box opens. Scroll down through the list, select **Display on the All Programs menu**, and click **OK**. Click **Apply** and **OK** to close the Taskbar and Start Menu Properties box. Now, to use the Administrative Tools group, click **Start, All Programs**, and **Administrative Tools**. (To add the tool to the All Programs menu in Windows XP, in the Customize Start Menu box, click the **Advanced** tab.)

14

A+ 220-701

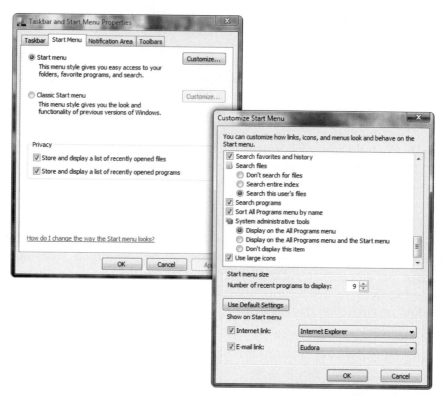

Figure 14-21 Use the Taskbar and Start Menu Properties window to change items on the Start menu
Courtesy: Course Technology/Cengage Learning

MICROSOFT MANAGEMENT CONSOLE (MMC)

Microsoft Management Console (MMC; the program file is mmc.exe) is a Windows utility that can be used to build your own customized console windows. A console is a single window that contains one or more administrative tools such as Device Manager or Disk Management. In a console, these individual tools are called snap-ins. An example of a console is Computer Management, which has a filename of Compmgmt.msc. (Event Viewer, Device Manager, Disk Management, and Task Scheduler are examples of snap-ins that appear in that console.) A console is saved in a file with an .msc file extension, and a snap-in in a console can itself be a console. To use all the functions of MMC, you must be logged on with administrator privileges.

You can use MMC to create a console that contains some popular utility tools. Follow these steps for Windows to create a console:

1. Enter **mmc.exe** in the Vista Start Search box or the XP Run box and press **Enter**. For Vista, respond to the UAC box. An empty console window appears, as shown in Figure 14-22.

2. Click **File** on the menu bar and then click **Add/Remove Snap-in**. The Add or Remove Snap-ins box opens, as shown at the top of Figure 14-23.

3. Select a snap-in from the list on the left. Notice a description of the snap-in appears at the bottom of the window. The snap-ins that appear in this list depend on the edition of Vista you have installed and what other components are installed on the system. Click **Add** to add the snap-in to the console. (For Windows XP, in the Add/Remove Snap-In box, click **Add**. A list of snap-ins appears. Select one and click **Add**.)

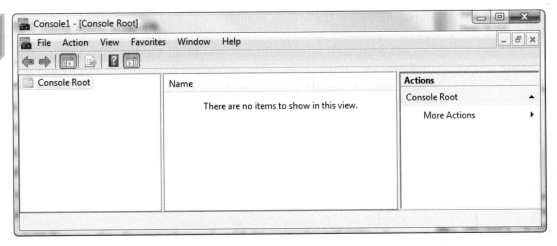

Figure 14-22 An empty console
Courtesy: Course Technology/Cengage Learning

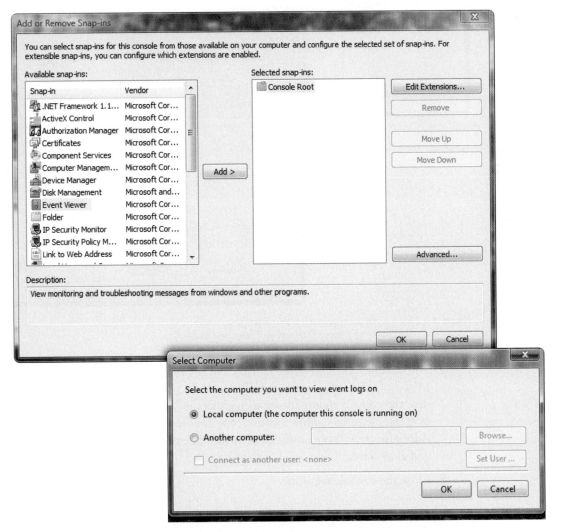

Figure 14-23 Add a snap-in to the new console
Courtesy: Course Technology/Cengage Learning

A+
220-701
3.2

4. If parameters for the snap-in need defining, a dialog box opens that allows you to set up these parameters. The dialog box offers different selections, depending on the snap-in being added. For example, when Event Viewer is selected, the Select Computer box appears, asking you to select the computer that Event Viewer will monitor (see the bottom of Figure 14-23). Select **Local computer (the computer this console is running on)** and click **OK**. (For XP, click **Finish**.) The snap-in now appears in the list of snap-ins for this console.

5. Repeat Steps 3 and 4 to add all the snap-ins that you want to the console. When you finish, click **OK** in the Add or Remove Snap-ins box shown in Figure 14-23.

6. The left side of Figure 14-24 shows a console with two snap-ins added. To save the console, click **File** on the menu bar and then click **Save As**. The Save As dialog box opens, as shown on the right side of the figure.

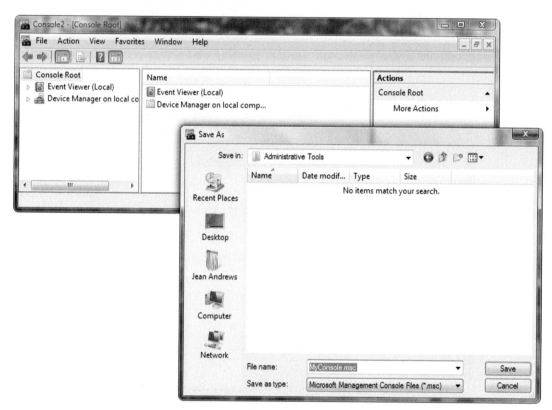

Figure 14-24 Saving a console with two snap-ins
Courtesy: Course Technology/Cengage Learning

7. The default location for the console file is C:\Users*username*\AppData\Roaming\Microsoft\Windows\Start Menu\Programs\Administrative Tools. However, you can save the console to any location, such as the Windows desktop. However, if you save the file to its default location, the console will appear as an option under Administrative Tools on the Start menu. Select the location for the file, name the file, and click **Save**.

8. Close the console window.

> **Notes** After you create a console, you can copy the .msc file to any computer or place a shortcut to it on the desktop.

A+
220-701
3.2

EVENT VIEWER

Event Viewer (Eventvwr.msc) is a Windows tool useful for troubleshooting problems with Windows, applications, and hardware. Of all these types of problems, it is most useful when troubleshooting problems with hardware. Event Viewer displays logs of significant events such as a hardware or network failure, OS error messages, a device or service that has failed to start, or General Protection Faults.

Note that Event Viewer is also a Computer Management console snap-in. You can open it by using the Computer Management window, by entering **Eventvwr.msc** in the Vista Start Search box or the XP Run box, using the Administrative Tools applet in Control Panel, or by clicking **Start, All Programs, Administrative Tools, Event Viewer**. (This last option assumes Administrative Tools has been added to the All Programs menu.) All of these methods open the window in Figure 14-25 (for Windows Vista after you respond to the UAC box) and the window in Figure 14-26 (for Windows XP).

Event Viewer manages logs of events. The logs that Event Viewer keeps partly depend on the edition of Windows you are using. For example, in Figure 14-26, the Media Center log is kept by Windows XP Media Center Edition. Event Viewer logs can be filtered and sorted in several ways. The different views of logs are listed in the left pane. You can click a triangle beside a view to see subcategories of logs within that view. Depending on the OS version and original equipment manufacturer (OEM) features, Event Viewer shows three or more views of logs. The three most important views of logs are described next:

▲ The *Application* log records events about applications and Windows utilities such as when an application was unable to open a file or when Windows created a restore point. The application events recorded depend on what the developer of the application set to trigger a log entry. All users can view this log. (In Vista, the Application log is a subcategory to the Windows Logs.)

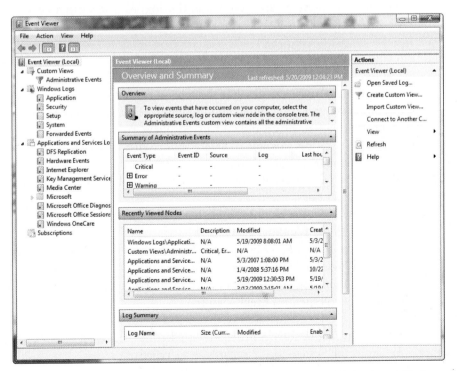

Figure 14-25 Use Event Viewer to see information about events with hardware, Windows, security, and applications
Courtesy: Course Technology/Cengage Learning

14

A+ 220-701

A+
220-701
3.2

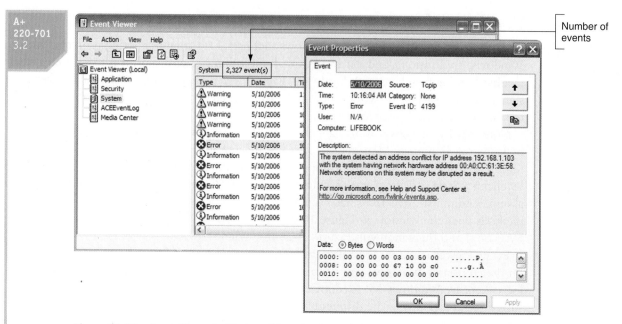

Figure 14-26   Event Viewer in Windows XP works about the same way as the Vista Event Viewer
Courtesy: Course Technology/Cengage Learning

▲ The *Security* log records events based on audit policies, which an administrator sets to monitor user activity such as successful or unsuccessful attempts to access a file or log on to the system. Only an administrator can view this log. (In Vista, the Security log is a subcategory to the Windows Logs.)

▲ The *System* log records events triggered by Windows components, such as a device driver failing to load during the boot process or a problem with hardware. Windows determines which events are recorded in this log. All users can access this log file. (In Vista, the System log is a subcategory to the Windows Logs.)

The following logs are new to Windows Vista:

▲ *Custom Views* allows you to select the type of event to appear in a view. Too much information is not a good thing, and the logs can get very long and give lots of unimportant information. By creating a Custom View, you can decide which types of events you want to see. (It is possible to create similar custom views in Windows XP, but only by using more advanced tools.)

▲ The *Setup* log records events about installing an application. The log is a subcategory to the Windows Logs.

▲ The *Forwarded Events* records events logged by remote computers. The log is a subcategory to the Windows Logs.

▲ The *Applications and Services Logs* are a group of several logs, each devoted to a particular Windows component or application.

▲ The *Subscriptions* log can be customized to collect certain events you require that are not normally collected by Event Viewer.

Unless you are trying to solve a problem with security, the most important event log for other problems is the System log. It records three types of events:

▲ *Information* events are recorded when a driver, service, or application functions successfully.

A+
220-701
3.2

▲ *Warning* events are recorded when something happens that may indicate a future problem but does not necessarily indicate that something is presently wrong with the system. For example, low disk space might trigger a warning event.

▲ *Error* events are recorded when something goes wrong with the system, such as a necessary component failing to load, data getting lost or becoming corrupted, or a system or application function ceasing to operate.

To view a log within Event Viewer, click the log that you want to view in the left pane. This generates a summary of events that appears on the right. For Windows Vista, select an event to see information about it in the lower pane of Event Viewer. Figure 14-27 shows an event in the System log about a conflict in IP addresses with another computer on the network, and gives a suggestion as to how to handle the problem. For Windows XP, double-click an event to see details about it (refer back to Figure 14-26).

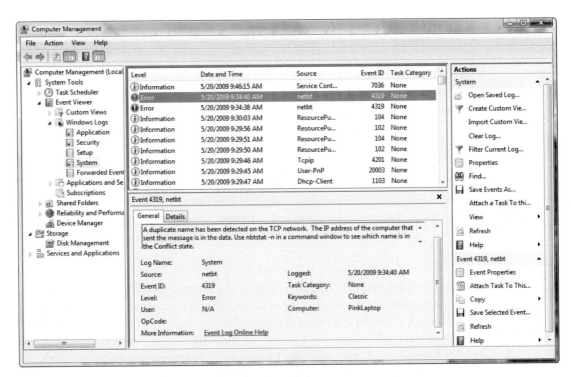

Figure 14-27 A conflicting IP address triggers an error event
Courtesy: Course Technology/Cengage Learning

When you are trying to solve a Windows, hardware, application, or security problem, Event Viewer can be your first source of information about the nature of the problem. You can find out if the problem is recent or has been going on for some time. Sometimes, you can even see what just occurred to the system when the problem started and see what other problems started at the same time. All this can be useful information to track the source of a problem.

To save time, you might want to view only certain events and not the entire list to make your search easier. Fortunately, you can filter events so only certain ones are listed. To do that, right-click a log in the left pane and select **Filter Current Log** from the shortcut menu.

14

A+ 220-701

A+
220-701
3.2

(For Windows XP, select **Properties** from the shortcut menu and then click the **Filter** tab.) The Filter Current Log box appears. See Figure 14-28 for Vista; the XP box looks and works about the same way.

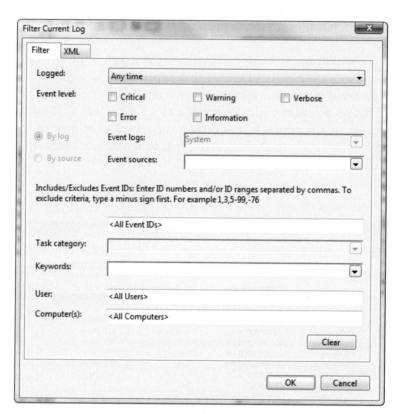

Figure 14-28 Criteria to filter events in Event Viewer
Courtesy: Course Technology/Cengage Learning

You can filter events on the time logged, the event level (critical, error, warning, information, or verbose), event source (for example, application, driver, service, or Windows component), event ID (identifies the type of event, such as a service has failed to load), keyword, user, and computer. To view the most significant events to troubleshoot a problem, check **Critical** and **Error** under the Event level. Critical events are those errors that Windows believes are affecting critical Windows processes.

Another way you can avoid a ballooning log file is to set a size limit, and specify what happens when the log reaches this limit. To control the size of a log file and see general information about the log, right-click the log, select **Properties** on the shortcut menu, and click the **General** tab (see Figure 14-29). You can set the maximum size of the log file. You can also set the log to overwrite events as needed, archive the log when full, and clear the log manually. To clear the log manually, click **Clear Log**. Before clearing the log, Event Viewer gives you a chance to save it.

Event Viewer can be useful when you suspect someone is attempting to illegally log onto a system and you want to view login attempts, or the network is giving intermittent problems. But Event Viewer is most useful in solving intermittent hardware problems. For example, on our network we have a file server and several people in the office update Microsoft Word documents stored on the server. For weeks, people complained about these Word documents

A+
220-701
3.2

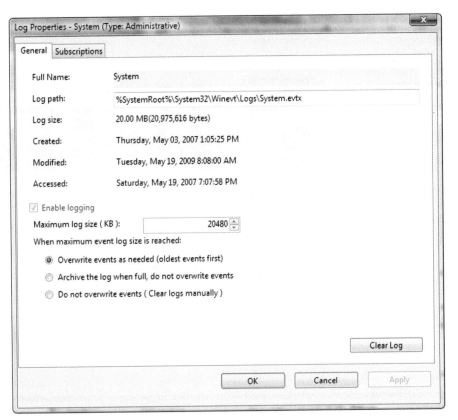

Figure 14-29 View information about a log, including maximum size of the log file in the Log Properties box
Courtesy: Course Technology/Cengage Learning

14

A+ 220-701

getting corrupted. We downloaded the latest patches for Windows and Microsoft Office and scanned for viruses, thinking that the problem might be with Windows or the application. Then we suspected a corrupted template file for building the Word documents. But nothing we did solved our problem of corrupted Word documents. Then one day someone thought to check Event Viewer on the file server. The Event Viewer had faithfully been recording errors when writing to the hard drive. What we had suspected to be a software problem was, in fact, a failing hard drive, which was full of bad sectors. We replaced the drive and the problem went away.

RELIABILITY AND PERFORMANCE MONITOR

Windows Reliability and Performance Monitor is another MMC snap-in (Perfmon.msc) that collects, records, and displays events. In Windows XP, this monitor is called the Performance Monitor or the System Monitor. These events, called Data Collector Sets, help you track the performance and reliability of Windows. To start the monitor, you can use the Administrative Tool applet in Control Panel, open the Computer Management Console, or enter **perfmon.msc** in the Vista Start Search box or the XP Run box. If Administrative Tools is added to the All Programs menu, you also can click **Start, All Programs, Administrative Tools, Reliability and Performance Monitor** (for XP, click **Performance**). The monitor window is shown in Figure 14-30 for Windows Vista after you respond to the UAC box. The XP Performance monitor is set up differently, but provides similar information, and is shown in Figure 14-31.

A+
220-701
3.2

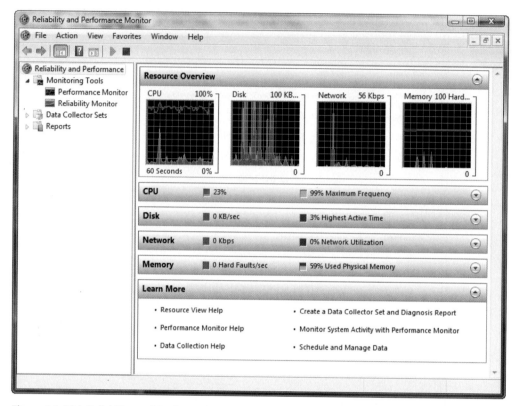

Figure 14-30 Reliability and Performance Monitor window shows the Resource Overview screen
Courtesy: Course Technology/Cengage Learning

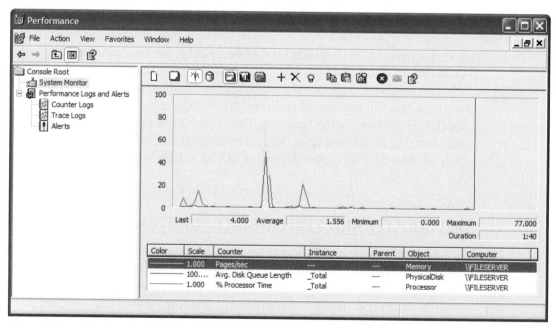

Figure 14-31 Windows XP Performance Monitor (also called the System Monitor)
Courtesy: Course Technology/Cengage Learning

The Reliability and Performance Monitor for Vista contains three monitoring tools:

◢ In the window shown in Figure 14-30, click **Performance Monitor** to see a real-time view of Windows performance counters (see Figure 14-32). You can add your own performance counters to this view by clicking the green plus sign, called the Add button, at the top of the Performance Monitor pane.

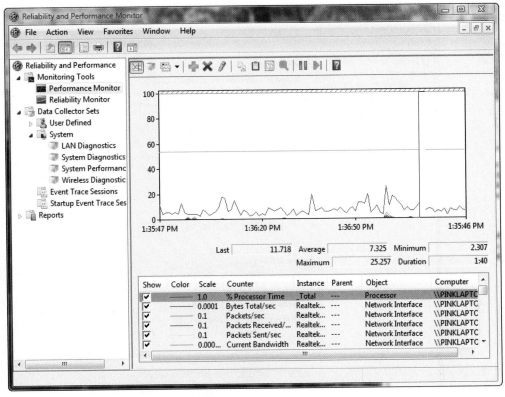

Figure 14-32 Performance monitor view shows real-time tracking of Windows performance counters
Courtesy: Course Technology/Cengage Learning

◢ Click **Reliability Monitor** to see a view of historical data that shows how stable the Windows system is. To get detailed information about a problem, click a day that shows an error and then click the plus sign beside the error's category. For example, in Figure 14-33, there was a Windows failure on May 1, 2009. When you click that date and then click the plus sign beside Windows Failures in the lower part of the pane, you can see what happened to Windows that day.

◢ The Data Collector Sets utility can be used to collect your own data about the system. Click **Data Collector Sets** and drill down to a subcategory that appears in the right pane (see Figure 14-34). Right-click a category and select **Start** from the shortcut menu shown in the figure. Wait while data is collected and then fills the middle pane. In our example, we're using System Diagnostics.

To view the system diagnostics data as a report, right-click **System Diagnostics** and select **Latest Report** from the shortcut menu. The report for one system is shown in Figure 14-35, which reports the system is experiencing excessive paging and needs more memory. (In this situation, note that the Reliability and Performance Monitor was started in the Computer Management console.)

THE REGISTRY EDITOR

Many actions, such as installing application software or hardware, can result in changes to the registry. These changes can create new keys, add new values to existing keys, and change existing values. For a few difficult problems, you might need to edit or remove a registry key. This part of the chapter looks at how the registry is organized, which keys might hold entries causing problems, and how to back up and edit the registry using the Registry Editor (regedit.exe). Let's first look at how the registry is organized, and then you'll learn how to back up and edit the registry.

A+
220-701
3.2

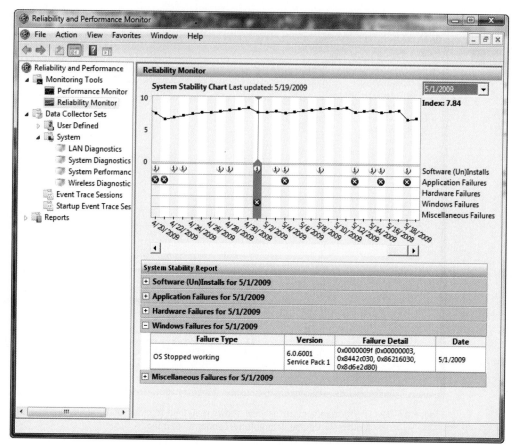

Figure 14-33   Reliability Monitor shows a history of the system that can help identify problems with
the stability of Windows
Courtesy: Course Technology/Cengage Learning

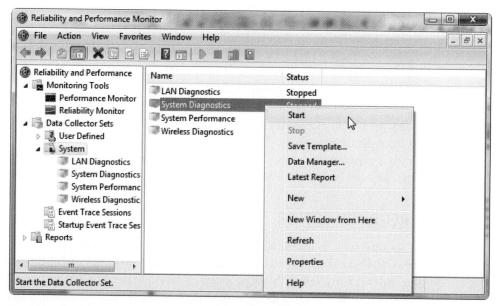

Figure 14-34   Collect data from a Data Collector Set to analyze
Courtesy: Course Technology/Cengage Learning

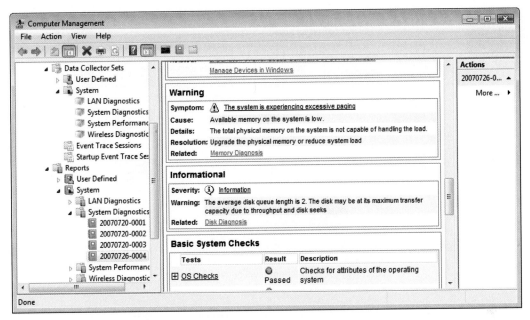

Figure 14-35 Reported results of collecting data about System Diagnostics
Courtesy: Course Technology/Cengage Learning

HOW THE REGISTRY IS ORGANIZED

The most important Windows component that holds information for Windows is the registry. The registry is a database designed with a treelike structure (called a hierarchical database) that contains configuration information for Windows, users, software applications, and installed hardware devices. During startup, Windows builds the registry in memory and keeps it there until Windows shuts down. During startup, after the registry is built, Windows reads from it to obtain information to complete the startup process. After Windows is loaded, it continually reads from many of the subkeys in the registry.

Windows builds the registry from the current hardware configuration and from information it takes from these files:

▲ Five files stored in the C:\Windows\System32\config folder; these files are called hives, and they are named the SAM (Security Accounts Manager), Security, Software, System, and Default hives. (Each hive is backed up with a log file and a backup file, which are also stored in the C:\Windows\System32\config folder.)

▲ For Windows Vista, the C:\Users*username*\Ntuser.dat file, which holds the preferences and settings of the currently logged on user.

▲ Windows XP uses information about the current user stored in two files:

- C:\Documents and Settings*username*\Ntuser.dat

- C:\Documents and Settings*username*\Local Settings\Application Data\Microsoft\Windows\Usrclass.dat

After the registry is built in memory, it is organized into five treelike structures (see Figure 14-36). Each of the five segments is called a key. Each key can have subkeys, and subkeys can have more subkeys and can be assigned one or more values. The way data is organized in the hive files is different from the way it is organized in registry keys. Figure 14-37 shows the relationship between registry keys and hives.

A+
220-701
3.2

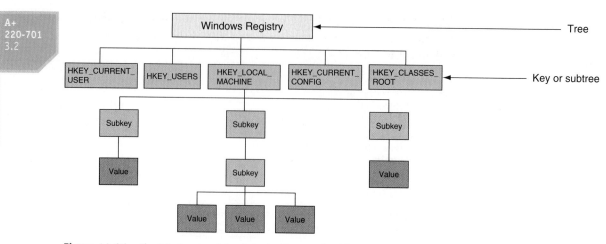

Figure 14-36 The Windows registry is logically organized in an upside-down tree structure of keys, subkeys, and values
Courtesy: Course Technology/Cengage Learning

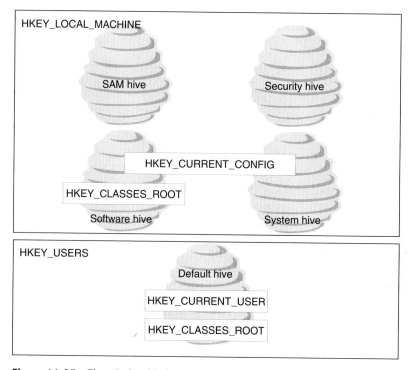

Figure 14-37 The relationship between registry subtrees (keys) and hives
Courtesy: Course Technology/Cengage Learning

Here are the five keys, including where they get their data and their purposes:

▲ *HKEY_LOCAL_MACHINE (HKLM)* is the most important key and contains hardware, software, and security data. The data is taken from four hives: the SAM hive, the Security hive, the Software hive, and the System hive. In addition, the HARDWARE subkey of HKLM is built when the registry is first loaded, based on data collected about the current hardware configuration.

▲ *HKEY_CURRENT_CONFIG (HKCC)* contains Plug and Play information about the hardware configuration that is used by the computer at startup. Information that identifies each hardware device installed on a PC is kept in this area. Some of the data

A+
220-701
3.2

is gathered from the current hardware configuration when the registry is first loaded into memory. Other data is taken from the HKLM key, which got its data primarily from the System hive.

▲ *HKEY_CLASSES_ROOT (HKCR)* stores information that determines which application is opened when the user double-clicks a file. This process relies on the file's extension to determine which program to load. For example, this registry key might hold the information to cause Microsoft Word to open when a user double-clicks a file with a .doc file extension. Data for this key is gathered from HKLM key and the HKCU key.

▲ *HKEY_USERS (HKU)* contains data about all users and is taken from the Default hive.

▲ *HKEY_CURRENT_USER (HKCU)* contains data about the current user. The key is built when a user logs on using data kept in the HKEY_USERS key and data kept in the Ntuser.dat file of the current user.

> **Notes** Device Manager reads data from the HKLM\HARDWARE key to build the information it displays about hardware configurations. You can consider Device Manager to be an easy-to-view presentation of this HARDWARE key data.

BEFORE YOU EDIT THE REGISTRY, BACK IT UP!

As you investigate startup problems and see a registry entry that needs changing, remember that it is important to use caution when editing the registry. If possible, make the change from the Windows tool that is responsible for the key—for example, by using the Vista Programs and Features window in Control Panel. If that doesn't work and you must edit the registry, always back up the registry before attempting to edit it. Changes made to the registry are implemented immediately. *There is no undo feature in the Registry Editor, and no opportunity to change your mind once the edit is made.*

Here are the ways to back up the registry:

▲ *Use System Protection to create a restore point.* A restore point keeps information about the registry. You can restore the system to a restore point to undo registry changes, as long as the registry is basically intact and not too corrupted. Also know that, if System Protection is turned on, Windows Vista automatically makes a daily backup of the registry hive files to the C:\Windows\System32\Config\RegBack folder.

▲ *Back up a single registry key just before you edit the key.* This method, called exporting a key, should always be used before you edit the registry. How to export a key is coming up in this chapter.

▲ *Make an extra copy of the C:\Windows\System32\config folder.* This is what I call the old-fashioned shotgun approach to backing up the registry. This backup will help if the registry gets totally trashed. You can boot from the Windows setup CD or DVD and use the Vista Recovery Environment or the XP Recovery Console to restore the folder from your extra copy. This method is drastic and not recommended except in severe cases. But, still, just to be on the safe side, I make an extra copy of this folder just before I start any serious digging into the registry.

▲ *For Windows XP, back up the system state.* Use Ntbackup in Windows XP or 2000 to back up the system state, which also makes an extra copy of the registry hives. Windows XP stores the backup of the registry hives in the C:\Windows\repair folder. Windows 2000 stores the backup in the C:\Windows\repair\RegBack folder.

14

A+ 220-701

A+
220-701
3.2

In some situations, such as when you're going to make some drastic changes to the registry, you'll want to play it safe and use more than one backup method. Extra registry backups are always a good thing! You learned how to create a restore point and back up the system state in Chapter 13. Now let's look at how to back up an individual key in the registry, and then you'll learn how to edit the registry.

> **Notes** Although you can edit the registry while in Safe Mode, you cannot create a restore point in Safe Mode.

Backing Up and Restoring Individual Keys in the Registry

A less time-consuming method of backing up the registry is to back up a particular key that you plan to edit. However, know that if the registry gets corrupted, having a backup of only a particular key most likely will not help you much when trying a recovery. Also, although you could use this technique to back up the entire registry or an entire tree within the registry, it is not recommended.

To back up a key along with its subkeys in the registry, follow these steps:

1. Open the Registry Editor. To do that, click **Start** and type **regedit** in the Start Search dialog box, press **Enter**, and respond to the UAC box. Figure 14-38 shows the Registry Editor with the five main keys and several subkeys listed. Click the triangles on the left to see subkeys. When you select a subkey, such as KeyboardClass in the figure, the names of the values in that subkey are displayed in the right pane along with the data assigned to each value.

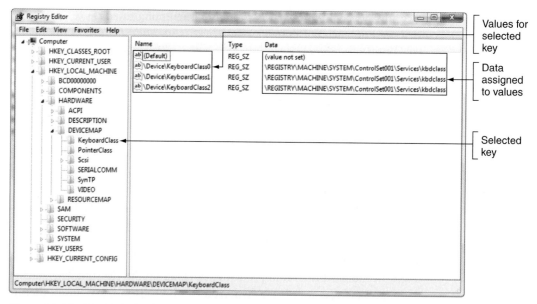

Figure 14-38   The Registry Editor showing the five main keys, subkeys, values, and data
Courtesy: Course Technology/Cengage Learning

2. Suppose we want to back up the registry key that contains a list of installed software, which is HKLM\Software\Microsoft\Windows\CurrentVersion\Uninstall. (HKLM stands for HKEY_LOCAL_MACHINE.) First click the appropriate triangles to navigate to the key. Next, right-click the key and select **Export** on the shortcut menu, as shown in Figure 14-39. The Export Registry File dialog box appears.

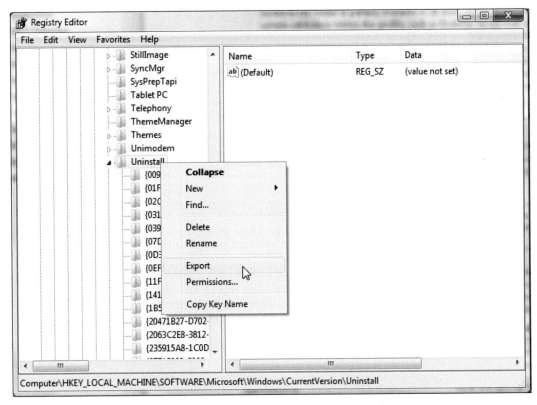

Figure 14-39 Using the Windows Registry Editor, you can back up a key and its subkeys with the Export command
Courtesy: Course Technology/Cengage Learning

3. Select the location to save the export file and name the file. A convenient place to store an export file while you edit the registry is the desktop. Click **Save** when done. The file saved will have a .reg file extension.

4. You can now edit the key. Later, if you need to undo your changes, exit the Registry Editor and double-click the saved export file. The key and its subkeys saved in the export file will be restored. After you're done with an export file, delete it.

Editing the Registry

When you make a change in Control Panel, Device Manager, or many other places in Windows, the registry is modified automatically. This is the only way most users will ever change the registry. However, on rare occasions, you might need to edit the registry manually.

Before you edit the registry, you should use one or more of the four backup methods just discussed so that you can restore it if something goes wrong. To edit the registry, open the Registry Editor (**regedit.exe**), and locate and select the key in the left pane of the Registry Editor, which will display the values stored in this key in the right pane. To edit, rename, or delete a value, right-click it and select the appropriate option from the shortcut menu. For example, in Figure 14-40, I'm ready to delete the value NapsterShell and its data. Changes are immediately applied to the registry and there is no undo feature. (However, Windows or applications might need to read the changed value before it affects their operations.) Notice in Figure 14-40 that the selected key is displayed in the status bar at the bottom of the editor window. If the status bar is missing, click **View** on the menu bar and make sure **Status Bar** is checked. To search the registry for keys, values, and data, click **Edit** on the menu bar and then click **Find**.

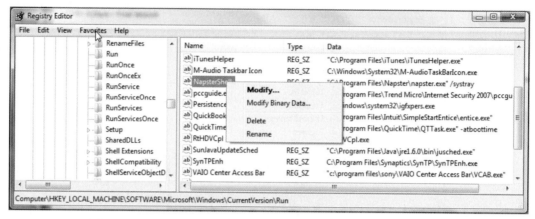

Figure 14-40   Right-click a value to modify, delete, or rename it
Courtesy: Course Technology/Cengage Learning

> ⚡ **Caution**   Changes made to the registry take effect immediately. Therefore, take extra care when editing the registry. If you make a mistake and don't know how to correct a problem you create, then double-click the exported key to recover. When you double-click an exported key, the registry is updated with the values stored in this key.

> 💡 **A+ Exam Tip**   Content on the A+ 220-701 Essentials exam ends here and content on the A+ 220-702 Practical Application exam begins.

IMPROVING WINDOWS PERFORMANCE

Sluggish Windows systems are so frustrating, and as a PC support technician, you need to know how to configure the Windows environment for optimum performance using the tools that were introduced in the first part of this chapter and in the last chapter.

In this part of the chapter, you'll learn step-by-step procedures to search for problems affecting performance and how to clean up the Windows startup process that goes beyond the routine maintenance tasks you learned about in Chapter 13. We're assuming you can start Windows with no errors. If you are having trouble loading Windows, it's best to address the error first rather than to use the tools described here to improve performance. How to handle errors that keep Windows from starting is covered in Chapters 15 and 16.

Now let's look at 11 steps you can take to improve Windows performance. After that, you'll learn how to manually remove software and how to use a monitor to alert you of changes that might affect performance.

STEP 1: PERFORM ROUTINE MAINTENANCE

It might seem pretty mundane, but the first things you need to do to improve performance are the obvious routine maintenance tasks that you learned in Chapter 13. These tasks are summarized here:

▲ *Verify critical Windows settings.* Make sure Windows updates are current and service packs are installed. Verify that antivirus software is updated and set to routinely scan for viruses. If a recent scan has not been performed or you suspect a virus is present,

A+
220-702
2.3
2.4

download the latest updates to the antivirus software and scan the system. Make sure Windows Firewall is turned on. How to use antivirus software and Windows Firewall is covered in later chapters.

▲ *Clean up the hard drive.* Make sure at least 15 percent of drive C is free.

▲ *Defrag the hard drive.* Vista automatically does that weekly, but XP does not. A seriously fragmented hard drive can significantly affect performance.

▲ *Check the hard drive for errors.* Run Chkdsk to check the hard drive for errors and recover data.

▲ *Disable or remove unwanted startup programs.* For Vista, use Software Explorer to view and disable startup programs. For XP, check the startup folders for programs that you can remove from these folders to speed up the startup process. If you find programs that are no longer needed, use the Vista Programs and Features window or the XP Add or Remove Programs window to uninstall them.

▲ *Back up data.* As always, if valuable data is not backed up, back it up before you do anything else. Recall from Chapter 13 that you can use the Vista Backup and Restore Center or the Windows XP Ntbackup utility to back up data. Don't risk the data without the user's permission.

📝 **Notes** Viruses, adware, worms, and other malicious software can use Windows resources and pull a system down. Keep antivirus software running in the background. If you see a marked decrease in Windows performance, scan the hard drive for viruses, worms, and adware.

STEP 2: CHECK IF THE HARDWARE CAN SUPPORT THE OS

The system might be slow because the OS does not have the hardware resources it needs. Use the Vista Windows Experience Index, upgrade advisors, and System Information to find out if the system can support the OS. If you find that the system does not meet the minimum requirements or hardware is not compatible, discuss the situation with the user. You might be able to upgrade the hardware or install another OS that is compatible with the hardware that is present.

WINDOWS VISTA EXPERIENCE INDEX

Windows Experience Index, under Windows Vista, is a summary index designed to measure the overall performance of a system. You can use it to compare systems and identify performance bottlenecks in a particular system. To use it, click **Start**, right-click **Computer**, and select **Properties** from the shortcut menu. In the System window, click **Windows Experience Index**. The Performance Information and Tools window appears. Figure 14-41 shows the window for a system with performance issues, and Figure 14-42 shows the window for a high-end system. Currently, index scores range from 1.0 to 5.9 for Windows Vista.

The base score is the lowest score of all components and identifies the bottleneck for the system. In the case of the computer in Figure 14-41, this bottleneck is memory. Therefore, to improve performance on this system, a memory upgrade should be considered. However, don't always assume a hardware upgrade is necessary. If the bottleneck appears to be graphics, the problem might be solved by updating the graphics drivers or by updating Windows. Try updating the graphics drivers before you consider upgrading the video card.

CHECK FOR HARDWARE OR SOFTWARE COMPATIBILITY

To make sure that all hardware or software installed on the system is compatible with Windows Vista, use the Vista Upgrade Advisor. Download the program from the Microsoft

14

A+ 220-702

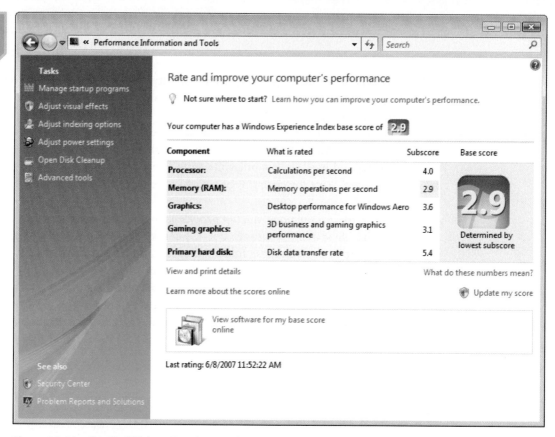

Figure 14-41   Use the Windows Experience Index to get a snapshot of a computer's performance and identify potential bottlenecks
Courtesy: Course Technology/Cengage Learning

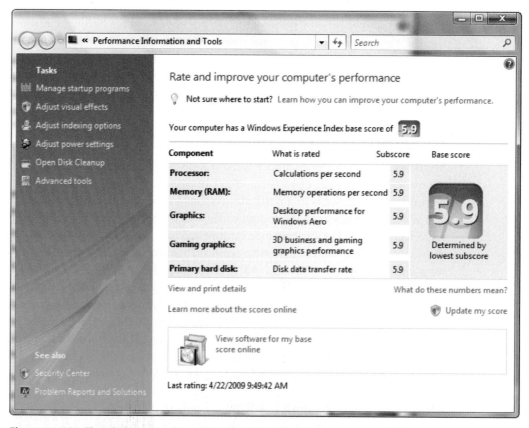

Figure 14-42   The Windows Experience Index for this system reports no potential bottlenecks
Courtesy: Course Technology/Cengage Learning

A+
220-702
2.3
2.4

Web site at *www.microsoft.com/windows/windows-vista/get/upgrade-advisor.aspx*. Be sure to connect your printer and USB devices before you use the program to scan the system. If the scan finds software or hardware that has compatibility issues with Vista, it might report an update that you can use. Follow any guidelines it gives to solve the problem.

For Windows XP, the upgrade advisor is no longer available on the Microsoft Web site, but you can find it on the XP setup CD. Run this program from a command prompt window: **D:\I386\Winnt32 /checkupgradeonly**. You might need to substitute a different drive letter for your optical drive.

You can also use the System Information Utility (msinfo32.exe) to find information about the installed processor and its speed, how much RAM is installed, and free space on the hard drive. Compare all these values to the minimum and recommended requirements for Windows listed in Chapter 12.

If you suspect the processor is not fast enough for the system, you can use Performance Monitor to see how well it's performing. Following instructions given earlier in the chapter, open the Reliability and Performance Monitor. To get more detailed information, click Performance Monitor, which is tracking CPU activity (see Figure 14-43). Leave the window open on the screen as you perform various operations and watch the percentage activity of the CPU.

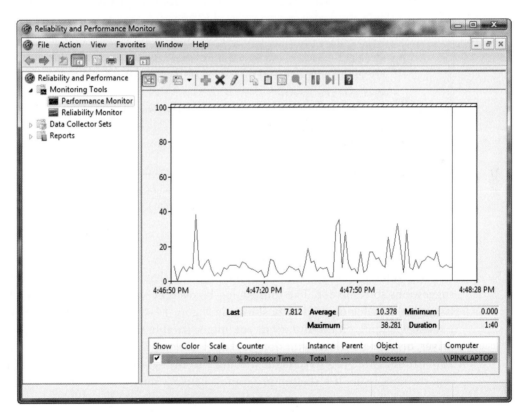

Figure 14-43 The Performance monitor tracking CPU performance
Courtesy: Course Technology/Cengage Learning

STEP 3: CHECK FOR PERFORMANCE WARNINGS

Windows Vista tracks issues that are interfering with performance. To see these warnings, click **Advanced tools** in the Windows Experience Index window shown in Figures 14-41 and 14-42. The Advanced Tools window appears, as shown in Figure 14-44. If Windows knows of performance issues, they are listed at the top of this window. For the computer in Figure 14-44, four issues are reported.

A+
220-702
2.3
2.4

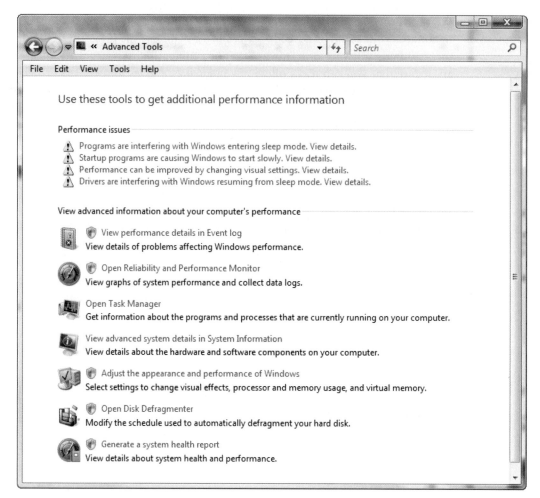

Figure 14-44　Vista provides these warnings and tools to improve Vista performance
Courtesy: Course Technology/Cengage Learning

When you click an issue, a dialog box appears that describes the issue and gives suggestions to resolve it. The four dialog boxes that will appear when you click the four issues listed in Figure 14-44 are shown in Figure 14-45. You will need to investigate each issue. Depending on the situation, you might be able to resolve an issue by updating a driver, disabling a device you don't need, or changing a setting in Windows or in an application. After you have made a change to the system, restart Windows before tackling the next issue. If a startup program is causing startup to be slow, consider removing it from the startup process and starting it manually as needed. After you have resolved an issue or have decided to live with it, you can click **Remove from list** so that it will no longer appear in the list of issues.

Tools that can help you improve Windows performance are listed in the lower part of the Advanced Tools window. When you click **View performance details in Event log**, you are taken to a log that tracks error events and warning events that are affecting performance (see Figure 14-46). Other tools that can be accessed through the Advanced Tools window are the Reliability and Performance Monitor, Task Manager, System Information, the Performance Options box, and Disk Defragmenter.

Windows XP does not offer the Advanced Tools window. For XP, open the Computer Management console and click Event Viewer. Then click the System log

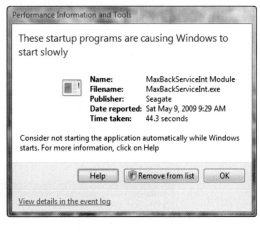

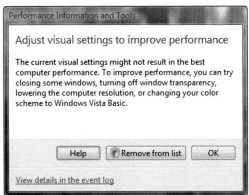

Figure 14-45 Windows reports four issues that are affecting performance
Courtesy: Course Technology/Cengage Learning

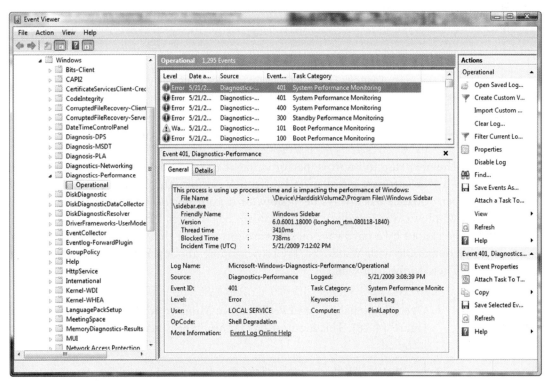

Figure 14-46 Event Viewer log reporting warning and error events affecting performance
Courtesy: Course Technology/Cengage Learning

A+
220-702
2.3
2.4

(see Figure 14-47). To sort the events by type, click the Type column. Look for events that might indicate a performance problem. To see details about an event, double-click it. The Event Properties box opens, shown on the right side of Figure 14-47. You can then scroll through the details of events by clicking the up and down arrows in the top-right side of this box.

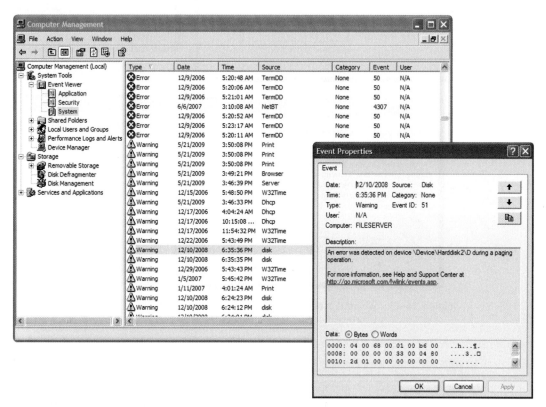

Figure 14-47 Windows XP Event Viewer shows events sorted by type
Courtesy: Course Technology/Cengage Learning

STEP 4: CHECK THE RELIABILITY MONITOR

The next step to improve performance is to try to determine if a problem with a hardware or software installation is affecting performance. You need to know if Windows performance has always been slow, or if poor performance began sometime after Windows was installed. If the problem began after Windows was installed, it might be caused by a hardware or software installation that has a problem or is not compatible with Windows. Try to determine about the time the problem started. Then do the following:

1. Open the **Reliability and Performance Monitor** and click the **Reliability Monitor** (see Figure 14-48). This monitor has faithfully been recording events since Windows was installed.

2. Scroll through the graph to find the day that the problem began. Look for failures related to software installations, applications, hardware, Windows, and other failures that happened about the time the problem occurred. To see details about

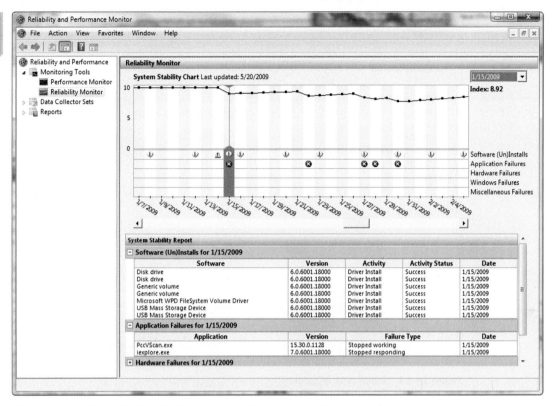

Figure 14-48 Use Reliability Monitor to search for when a problem began
Courtesy: Course Technology/Cengage Learning

the failure, click it. Also look for a dip in the line graph at the top of the Reliability Monitor graph. You can see such a dip in Figure 14-48 when drivers were installed. These drivers were installed for a Maxtor external hard drive that automatically makes backups of user data on this computer. Looking back at Figure 14-45, you can see that the Maxtor backup service is slowing down Windows startup. Options to fix the problem are to update the drivers or stop the service from launching at startup.

STEP 5: DISABLE THE INDEXER FOR WINDOWS SEARCH

The Windows indexer is responsible for maintaining an index of files and folders on a hard drive to speed up Windows searches. The indexing service has a low priority and only works when it senses that the hard drive is not being accessed by a service with a higher priority. However, it might still slow down performance. Do the following to find out if this service is causing a performance problem:

1. Find out if the indexing service is currently indexing the system. To do that, enter Index in the Vista Start Search box and select Indexing Options from the programs list. The Indexing Options box opens. If you see the indexing status is *Indexing speed is reduced due to user activity* (see Figure 14-49), know that indexing is in progress. Wait until the status changes to *Indexing complete*. You can now stop the indexing service.

2. To stop the indexing service, click **Start** and enter **services** in the Start Search box and press **Enter**. Respond to the UAC box. The Services console opens (see the left side of Figure 14-50).

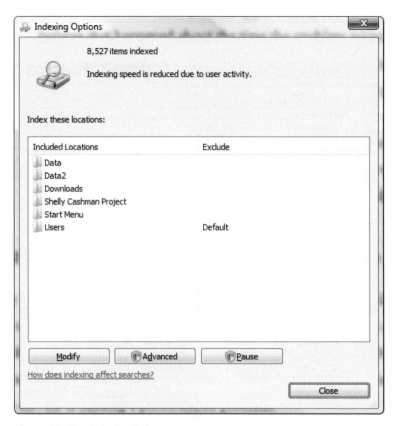

Figure 14-49 Indexing is in progress
Courtesy: Course Technology/Cengage Learning

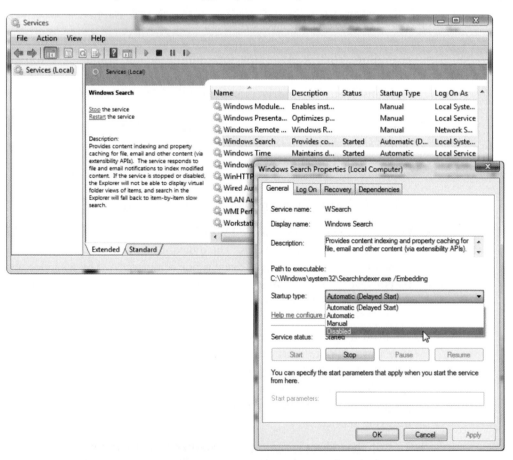

Figure 14-50 Windows Search service Startup type is Automatic (Delayed Start)
Courtesy: Course Technology/Cengage Learning

A+
220-702
2.3
2.4

3. Scroll down to and right-click the **Windows Search** service. Select **Properties** from the shortcut menu. The properties box opens. Change the Startup type to **Disabled** (see the right side of Figure 14-50). Click **Stop** to stop the service.

4. Click **Apply** and **OK** to close the properties box. Close the Services console window. Restart the computer.

5. Run the system for a while and see if performance improves.

6. If performance does not improve, restart the indexing service. To do that, use the Services console to set the status of the Windows Search service to **Automatic (Delayed Start)** and start the service. Then move on to the next section, *Step 6: Disable the Vista Aero Interface.*

7. If performance does improve, it is possible that the problem was caused by a corrupted index database. To rebuild the database, first use the Services console to set the Windows Search service status back to **Automatic (Delayed Start)** and to start the service.

8. Open the Indexing Options box, click **Advanced**, and respond to the UAC box. The Advanced Options box opens (see Figure 14-51).

9. To rebuild the indexing database, click **Rebuild**. A dialog box appears warning you that this can take some time. Click **OK**. Close the Indexing Options box.

10. After running the system for a while, if the performance problem returns, you can disable the Windows Search service and leave it disabled. However, know that searching will not be as fast without indexing.

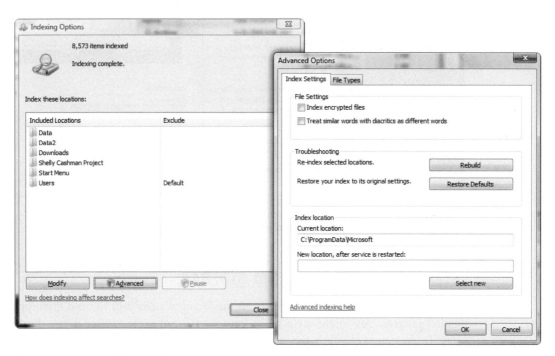

Figure 14-51 Rebuild the indexing database
Courtesy: Course Technology/Cengage Learning

A+
220-702
2.3
2.4

STEP 6: DISABLE THE VISTA AERO INTERFACE

The Vista Aero interface (also called the Aero Glass) might be slowing down the system because it uses memory and computing power. Try disabling it. If performance improves, you can conclude that the hardware is not able to support the Aero interface. At that point, you might want to upgrade memory, upgrade the video card, or leave the Aero interface disabled. To disable the Aero interface, do the following:

1. Right-click the desktop and select **Personalize** from the shortcut menu. The Personalization window opens. Click **Window Color and Appearance**. Then click **Open classic appearance properties for more color options**. The Appearance Settings box opens, shown on the right of Figure 14-52.

2. Under Color scheme, select **Windows Vista Basic** and click **Apply**. Close the dialog box and window.

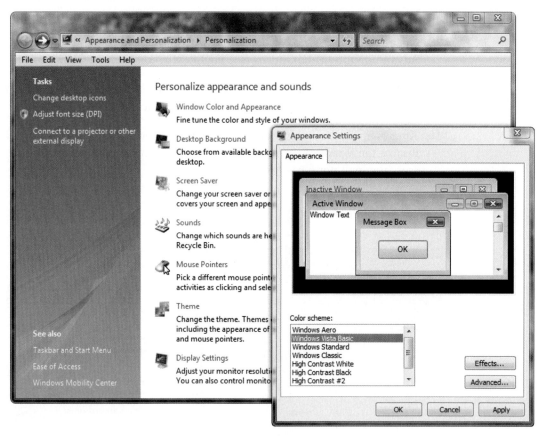

Figure 14-52 Disable Aero Glass to conserve system resources
Courtesy: Course Technology/Cengage Learning

STEP 7: DISABLE THE VISTA SIDEBAR

Recall that the Vista sidebar appears on the Windows desktop to hold miniapplications called gadgets. You might see a slight improvement in performance if you disable the sidebar. To do that, right-click the sidebar and select **Properties** from the shortcut menu. The

Windows Sidebar Properties box appears (see Figure 14-53). Uncheck **Start Sidebar when Windows starts**. Then click **Apply** and **OK** to close the box.

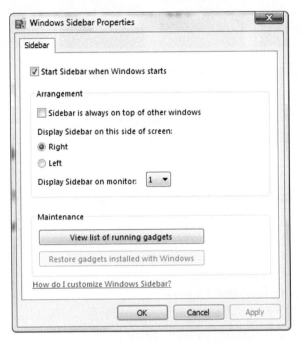

Figure 14-53 Disable the Vista sidebar to improve performance
Courtesy: Course Technology/Cengage Learning

14

A+ 220-702

STEP 8: PLUG UP ANY MEMORY LEAKS

If you notice that performance slows after a system has been up and running without a restart for some time, suspect a memory leak. A memory leak is caused when an application does not properly release memory allocated to it that it no longer needs and continually requests more memory than it needs. To see how much memory an application has allocated to it that is not available to other programs, open the Reliability and Performance Monitor. Click the down arrow on the Memory bar. For example, in Figure 14-54, you can see that the sidebar.exe program (Vista sidebar) is using a significant amount of memory compared to other running applications.

Another way to search for a memory leak is to use Task Manager. Open Task Manager and click the **Processes** tab. On the menu bar, click **View, Select Columns**. Verify that the Memory Private Working Set, Handles, and Threads columns are checked and click **OK**. If you observe that the values in these three columns increase over time for a particular program, suspect the program has a memory leak. To sort the data by one column, click the column label. For example, the Task Manager window shown in Figure 14-55 is sorted by Memory. To solve the problem of a program that has a memory leak, try to get an update or patch from the program manufacturer's Web site.

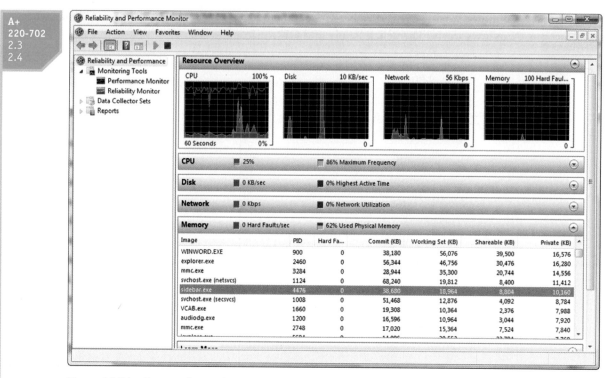

Figure 14-54 Memory allocated to the Vista sidebar program
Courtesy: Course Technology/Cengage Learning

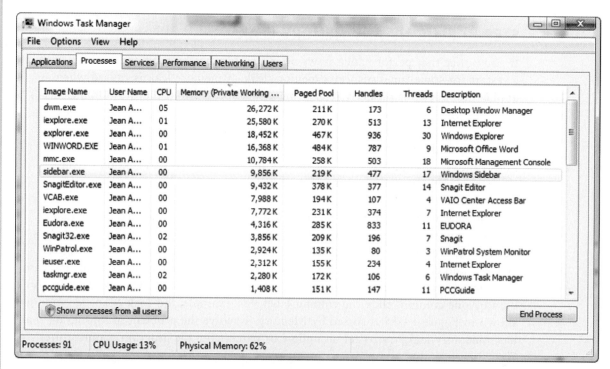

Figure 14-55 Task Manager shows how memory is allocated for an application
Courtesy: Course Technology/Cengage Learning

A+
220-702
2.3
2.4

STEP 9: CONSIDER DISABLING THE VISTA UAC BOX

One task that might slightly improve performance on a Vista system is to disable the UAC box. Even though you might see a slight performance gain, disabling it is not recommended. The UAC box can protect your system against users making unauthorized changes and against malware installing itself without your knowledge. It's best to keep it up and running. However, if you do decide to disable it, here's how:

1. Open Control Panel and click **User Accounts and Family Safety**. In the window that opens, click **User Accounts**. In the User Accounts window (see Figure 14-56), click **Turn User Account Control on or off**. Respond to the UAC box.

2. Uncheck **Use User Account Control (UAC) to help protect your computer**. Click **OK**. Close the User Accounts window.

STEP 10: CONSIDER USING VISTA READYBOOST

Windows Vista ReadyBoost uses a flash drive or secure digital (SD) memory card to boost hard drive performance. The faster flash memory is used as a buffer to speed up hard drive access time. You see the greatest performance increase using ReadyBoost when you have a slow hard drive (running at less than 7200 RPM). To find out what speed your hard drive is using, use System Information (Msinfo32.exe) and drill down to the Storage Disks (see Figure 14-57). The model of the hard drive appears in the right pane. Use Google to search on this brand and model; a quick search shows this drive runs at 5400 RPM. It's, therefore, a good candidate to benefit from ReadyBoost.

When you first connect a flash device, Windows will automatically test it to see if it qualifies for ReadyBoost. To qualify, it must have a capacity of 256 MB to 4 GB with at least 256 MB of free space, and run at about 2 MB/sec of throughput. If the device qualifies, Windows will ask you permission to use the device for ReadyBoost, which will tie up at least 256 MB

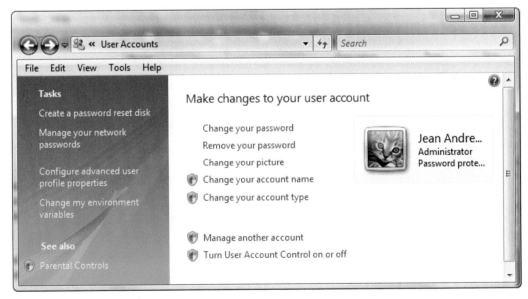

Figure 14-56 Control the User Account Control box
Courtesy: Course Technology/Cengage Learning

14

A+ 220-702

A+
220-702
2.3
2.4

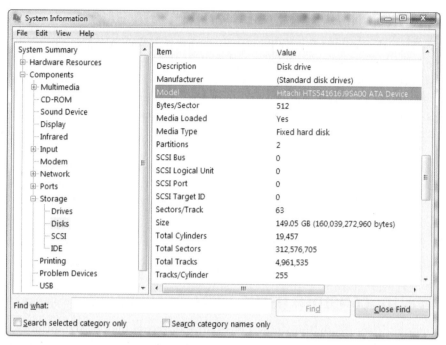

Figure 14-57 Use the System Information window to find out the brand and model of your hard drive
Courtesy: Course Technology/Cengage Learning

of free space. You can manually have Windows test a memory card or flash drive for ReadyBoost by right-clicking the device and selecting Properties from the shortcut menu. On the device properties window, click the **ReadyBoost** tab, as shown in Figure 14-58.

The best flash devices to use for ReadyBoost are the ones that use the faster buses. For example, an onboard memory card reader in a laptop will be faster than a USB 1.1 external

Figure 14-58 Offer a device for Windows to use for ReadyBoost
Courtesy: Course Technology/Cengage Learning

A+
220-702
2.3
2.4

memory card reader. When you remove the device, no data is lost because the device only holds a copy of the data.

STEP 11: CLEAN WINDOWS STARTUP

As a part of routine maintenance, you need to verify that startup programs are kept to a minimum so as to not slow down Windows startup or Windows performance. These routine chores include checking startup folders in Windows XP and Software Explorer in Windows Vista. If you still need to improve Windows performance, you can dig deeper into startup processes to make sure that unnecessary programs are not using up resources. To clean Windows startup, you can use Safe Mode and MSconfig to find out more about the problem, and then you can disable or uninstall programs causing the problem. So let's get started.

OBSERVE PERFORMANCE IN SAFE MODE

To find out if programs and services are slowing down Windows startup, boot the system in Safe Mode and watch to see if performance improves. Recall that Safe Mode loads a minimum configuration of hardware and software. If performance improves when you start the system in Safe Mode, you can assume that nonessential startup programs are slowing down the system when Windows boots normally. If you have a stopwatch or a watch with a second hand, you can time a normal Windows startup from the moment you press the power button until the wait icon on the Windows desktop disappears. Then time the system when it boots into Safe Mode. If the difference is significant, follow the steps in this part of the chapter to reduce Windows startup to essentials. To boot the system in Safe Mode, press **F8** while Windows is loading and then select Safe Mode with Networking from the boot options menu (see Figure 14-59).

14

A+ 220-702

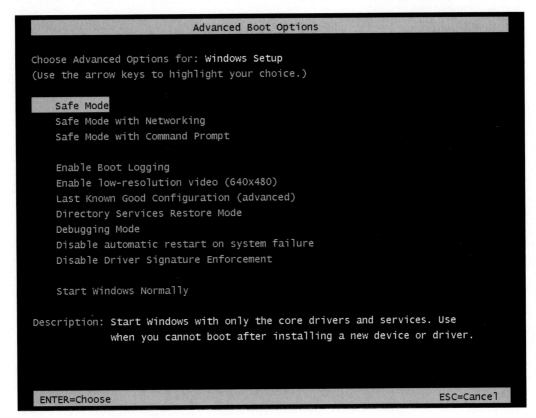

Figure 14-59 Windows Advanced Boot Options menu allows you to launch Safe Mode
Courtesy: Course Technology/Cengage Learning

A+
220-702
2.3
2.4

If the performance problem still exists in Safe Mode, then you can assume that the problem is with a hardware device, a critical driver, or a Windows component. How to solve problems with these components is covered in Chapters 15 and 16. If the problem does not occur when booting into Safe Mode, then use the tools discussed next to find the nonessential service or program causing the problem.

A+
220-702
2.3
2.4
2.1

USE MSCONFIG TO FIND A STARTUP PROGRAM AFFECTING PERFORMANCE

You can use the MSconfig utility to zero in on the service or other program that is slowing down startup. The process of using MSconfig to find the programs causing the problem is described in Figure 14-60. The recommended strategy uses a search technique called a half-again search.

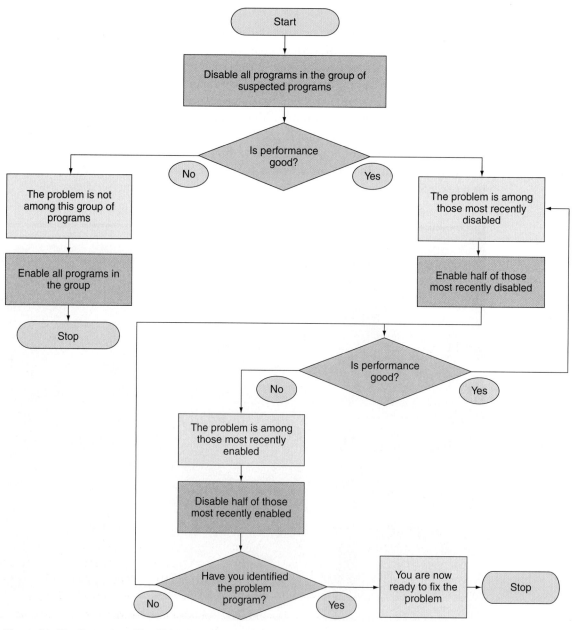

Figure 14-60   Strategy to identify the program(s) causing the problem
Courtesy: Course Technology/Cengage Learning

APPLYING CONCEPTS You can demonstrate the effectiveness of the half-again search technique (also called a binary search) by playing the number guessing game with a friend. Tell your friend to pick a number between one and 1,000,000. Tell him you can guess the number if he will answer no more than 21 questions. The first question is "Is the number between one and 500,000?" If the answer is "No," then you know the number is between 500,000 and 1,000,000. The next half-again question is, "Is the number between 500,000 and 750,000?" Using this technique, you can zero in on the answer in fewer than 21 questions.

Follow these steps using MSconfig to identify one or more programs as the source of the problem:

1. To launch the utility, enter **msconfig.exe** in the Vista Start Search box or the XP Run box and press **Enter**. For Vista, respond to the UAC box.

2. To look for the problem among the non-Microsoft services, click the **Services** tab (see Figure 14-61). Check **Hide all Microsoft services,** and then click **Disable all**. Click **Apply**. Close the System Configuration window and restart the computer.

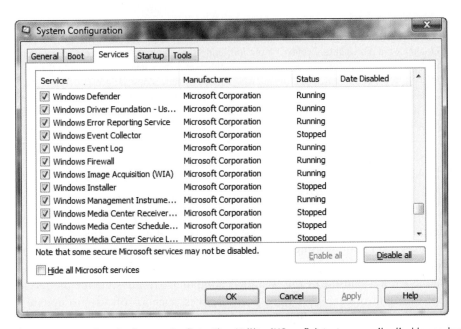

Figure 14-61 Use the System Configuration Utility (MSconfig) to temporarily disable services
Courtesy: Course Technology/Cengage Learning

3. Has performance improved? If so, you can assume that one or more services you disabled are the source of the problem. You can find out which service is causing the problem by enabling them one at a time, restarting the system each time, until the problem returns. This process can take a lot of time! A faster approach is to use the half-again technique. With this technique, use MSconfig to enable half the services you disabled and then restart the system. Did the problem return? If so, disable half of those you just enabled and restart again. If not, enable half of the disabled services. Restart the system and look for a performance improvement.

4. Keep repeating Step 3 until you have identified the service that is causing the problem. Next, try to update the service, or, if it is nonessential, consider uninstalling or permanently disabling it. To permanently disable a service, use the Services console.

5. If performance does not improve by disabling all services, you can assume the problem is not with the services. In that case, enable them all and select the Startup tab.

6. Disable all the programs listed on the Startup tab and restart the system. If performance improves, begin the process diagramed in Figure 14-60 to enable half the programs that are disabled until you zero in on the problem.

7. If no non-Microsoft service or startup program caused the problem, then you can assume the problem is caused by a Microsoft service. Disable all services, including the Microsoft services and test performance. If performance improves, use MSconfig to keep enabling services until you find the Microsoft service causing the problem. You can then update the service or replace it using tools described in Chapters 15 and 16.

8. Remember that you don't want to permanently leave MSconfig in control of startup. After you have used MSconfig to identify the problem, use other tools such as the Services console or startup folders to permanently remove them from startup. After the problem is fixed, return MSconfig to a normal startup.

> ⚡ **Caution**   Be aware that when you disable all Microsoft services, you are disabling Networking, Event Logging, Error Reporting, Windows Firewall, Windows Installer, Windows Backup, Print Spooler, Windows Update, System Protection, and other important services. These services should only be disabled when testing for performance problems and then immediately enabled when the test is finished. Also, know that if you disable the Volume Shadow Copy service, all restore points kept on the system will be lost. If you intend to use System Restore to fix a problem with the system, don't disable this service. If you are not sure what a service does, read its description in the Services console before you change its status.

DISABLE OR UNINSTALL BACKGROUND PROCESSES AND STARTUP PROGRAMS

Recall that you can stop a service or other program using Task Manager, and you can use MSconfig to stop it from starting at startup. You can also use Task Manager to view resources a program is using and change the priority level of a running program. However, all these solutions should be considered temporary fixes. To permanently manage a service, use the services console or the Windows component responsible for the service, such as an applet in Control Panel. For third-party services, such as software to update an application or software to download digital photos, the application is likely to have a management utility to control the service or background process.

When investigating a service, try using a good search engine on the Web to search for the name of the service or the name of the program file that launches the service. Either can give you information you need to snoop out unwanted services. If you're not sure you want to keep a certain service, use MSconfig to temporarily disable it at the next boot so that you can see what happens.

> 📝 **Notes**   One service you might want to disable in the Services console is the Windows Installer service that is responsible for uninstalling and installing software. You can then manually start the service if you need to install or uninstall software.

A+
220-702
2.3
2.4

When you permanently disable a service using the Services console or some other tool, don't forget to reboot to make sure everything works before moving on to the next tool to use in cleaning up startup: Task Scheduler.

CHECK FOR UNWANTED SCHEDULED TASKS

Home and business editions of Windows Vista and Windows XP Professional offer a Task Scheduler that can be set to launch a task or program at a future time, including at startup. Task Scheduler stores tasks in a file stored in the C:\Windows\System32\Tasks folder. For example, in Figure 14-62, there are four scheduled tasks showing and other tasks are stored in three folders.

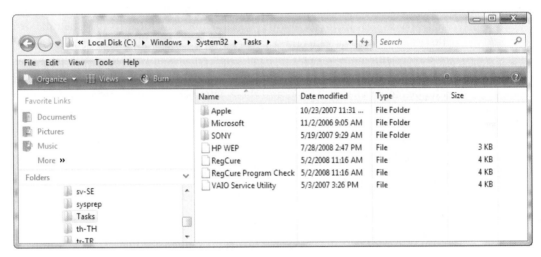

Figure 14-62 The Tasks folder can contain tasks that launch at startup
Courtesy: Course Technology/Cengage Learning

To view a list of scheduled tasks, click **Start, All Programs, Accessories, System Tools,** and **Task Scheduler**. The Task Scheduler window opens as shown in Figure 14-63 for Vista after you have responded to the UAC box. For a bare-bones Vista system, the Microsoft folder will be the only item listed in the Task Scheduler Library on the left. But for this system, other folders and tasks are present. To see details about a task,

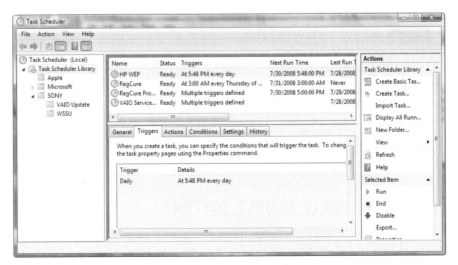

Figure 14-63 View and manage tasks from the Task Scheduler window
Courtesy: Course Technology/Cengage Learning

14

A+ 220-702

A+
220-702
2.3
2.4

including what triggers it, what actions it performs, the conditions and settings related to the task, and the history of past actions, select the task and then click the tabs in the lower-middle pane. For example, in Figure 14-63 you can see that the HP WEP task is scheduled to run at 5:48 PM daily.

> **Notes** Windows Vista automatically runs Disk Defragmenter weekly, but Windows XP does not offer this feature. For XP, you can use Task Scheduler to schedule Disk Defragmenter to run weekly.

Tasks can be scheduled to run when users log on, when Windows launches, or at a particular time of day, week, or month. Tasks can be scheduled to run one time or many times. Tasks can be applications, services, or other background processes. Tasks can be scheduled to download e-mail or open Internet Explorer and download a Web page. Tasks can also consist of batch programs or Windows scripting. Using the Task Scheduler window, you can add, delete, or change a task, and these actions can also be performed at a command prompt.

> **Notes** Tasks can be hidden in the Task Scheduler window. To be certain you're viewing all scheduled tasks, unhide them. In the menu bar, click **View**, and then **Show Hidden Tasks**.

All this information is helpful when researching scheduled tasks to unravel the mystery of processes or activities that fail or bog down a system. In cleaning up startup, be sure to check the Task Scheduler window *after* you have run antivirus software and disabled or uninstalled all startup programs you don't want. If you still find scheduled tasks present in the Task Scheduler window, research each task by searching for information about it on the Internet. (Be sure you use reliable Web sites to get your information.) If you decide you don't want a task, rather than deleting it, select the task and click **Disable** in the Actions pane so that you can undo your change if necessary. The exception to this rule is if you know the task is malware; in this case, definitely delete it!

> **Notes** When searching the Internet for information about a process, be sure to use reliable Web sites to get your information. Some sites will tell you a good process is a bad one just so you'll purchase their software to scan the system for errors.

In the process of cleaning up startup, you might run into software that you'll want to uninstall. In the next part of the chapter, you'll learn how to manually remove software when normal uninstall methods fail.

HOW TO MANUALLY REMOVE SOFTWARE

In this part of the chapter, we focus on getting rid of programs that refuse to uninstall or give errors when uninstalling. In these cases, you can manually uninstall a program. Doing so often causes problems later, so use the methods discussed in this section only as a last resort after normal uninstall methods have failed.

> **Notes** Before uninstalling software, make sure it's not running in the background. Antivirus software cannot be uninstalled if it's still running. You can use Task Manager to end all processes related to the software, and you can use the Services console to stop services related to the software. Then remove the software.

FIRST TRY THE UNINSTALL ROUTINE

Most programs written for Windows have an uninstall routine which can be accessed from the Vista Programs and Features applet in the Control Panel, the XP Add Remove Programs applet in the Control Panel, or a utility in the All Programs menu. For example, in Figure 14-64 you can see in the All Programs menu that Uninstall is an option for the RegCure software installation. Click this option and follow the directions on-screen to uninstall the software. Alternately, you can use the applet in Control Panel to remove the software.

Figure 14-64 Most applications have an uninstall utility included with the software
Courtesy: Course Technology/Cengage Learning

MANUALLY DELETE THE PROGRAM FILES

If the uninstall routine does not work or is missing, as a last resort, you can manually delete the program files and registry entries used by the software you want to uninstall. In our example, we'll use the RegCure software by ParetoLogic, Inc. as the software to be deleted. Follow these steps:

1. Most likely, the program files are stored in the C:\Program Files folder on the hard drive (see Figure 14-65). For 64-bit editions of Vista, also look for program files in the C:\Program Files (x86) folder. Using Windows Explorer, look for a folder in these folders that contains the software. In Figure 14-65, you can see the RegCure folder under the Program Files folder. Keep in mind, however, that you might not find the program files you're looking for in the C:\Program Files or C:\Program Files (x86) folder because when you install software, the software installation program normally asks you where to install the software. Therefore, the program files might be anywhere, and you might need to search a bit to find them.

2. Delete the RegCure folder and all its contents. You'll need to confirm the deletion several times as Windows really doesn't like your doing such things.

A+
220-702
2.3
2.4

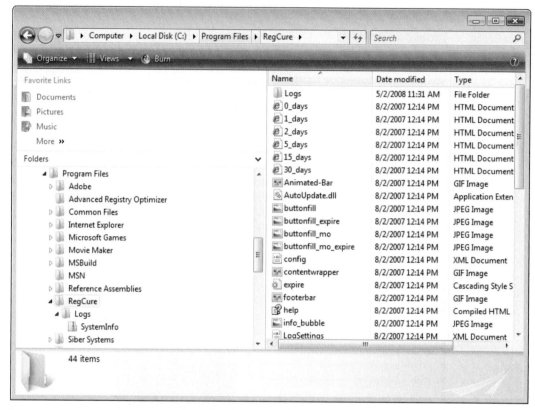

Figure 14-65   Program files are usually stored in the C:\Program Files folder
Courtesy: Course Technology/Cengage Learning

DELETE REGISTRY ENTRIES

Editing the registry can be dangerous, so do this with caution and be sure to back up first! Do the following to delete the registry entries for a program, which cause it to be listed as installed software in the Vista Programs and Features window or the XP Add or Remove Programs window of Control Panel:

1. Using one or more of the following methods, back up the registry: Use Windows XP NTbackup to back up the system state, back up the C:\Windows\System32\config folder, or create a restore point.

2. Click **Start,** type **regedit** in the Vista Start Search box or the XP Run box and press **Enter.** For Vista, respond to the UAC box.

3. Locate this key, which contains the entries that comprise the list of installed software in Control Panel: HKEY_LOCAL_MACHINE\Software\Microsoft\Windows\CurrentVersion\ Uninstall.

4. Back up the Uninstall key to the Windows desktop so that you can backtrack if necessary. To do that, right-click the Uninstall key and select **Export** from the shortcut menu (see Figure 14-39 earlier in the chapter).

5. In the Export Registry File dialog box, select the **Desktop.** Enter the filename as **Save Uninstall Key,** and click **Save.** You should see a new icon on your desktop named Save Uninstall Key.reg.

6. The Uninstall key can be a daunting list of all the programs installed on your PC. When you expand the key, you might see a long list of subkeys in the left pane, which

A+
220-702
2.3
2.4

have meaningless names that won't help you find the program you're looking for. Select the first subkey in the Uninstall key and watch as its values and data are displayed in the right pane (see Figure 14-66). Step down through each key, watching for a meaningful name of the subkey in the left pane or meaningful details in the right pane until you find the program you want to delete.

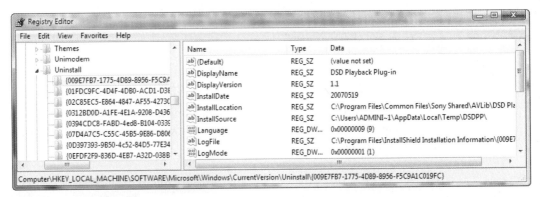

Figure 14-66   Select a subkey under the Uninstall key to display its values and data in the right pane
Courtesy: Course Technology/Cengage Learning

7. To delete the key, right-click the key and select **Delete** from the shortcut menu (see Figure 14-67). When the Confirm Key Delete dialog box appears asking you to confirm the deletion, click **Yes**. Be sure to search through all the keys in this list because the software might have more than one key. Delete them all and exit the Registry Editor.

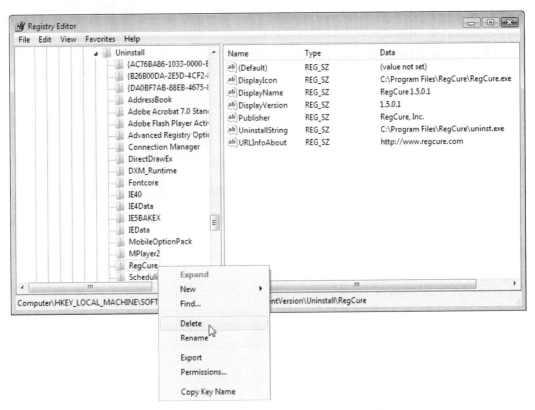

Figure 14-67   Delete the registry key that lists the software as installed software
Courtesy: Course Technology/Cengage Learning

14

A+ 220-702

A+
220-702
2.3
2.4

8. Open the Vista Programs and Features window or the XP Add or Remove Programs window and verify that the list of installed software is correct and the software you are uninstalling is no longer listed.

9. If the list of installed software is not correct, to restore the Uninstall registry key, double-click the **Save Uninstall Key.reg** icon on your desktop.

10. As a last step when editing the registry, clean up after yourself by deleting the Save Uninstall Key.reg icon and file on your desktop. Right-click the icon and select **Delete** from the shortcut menu.

REMOVE THE PROGRAM FROM THE ALL PROGRAMS MENU

To remove the program from the All Programs menu, right-click it and select **Delete** from the shortcut menu (see Figure 14-68). Click **Yes** and then **Continue** to confirm the deletion and respond to the UAC box.

Figure 14-68 Delete the program from the All Programs menu
Courtesy: Course Technology/Cengage Learning

Restart the PC and watch for any startup errors about a missing program file. The software might have stored startup entries in the registry, in startup folders, or as a service that is no longer present and causing an error. If you see an error, use MSconfig to find out how the program is set to start. This entry point is called an orphaned entry. You'll then need to delete this startup entry by editing the registry, deleting a shortcut in a startup folder, or disabling a service using the Services console.

An example of an orphaned entry that resulted in a startup error after software was removed is shown in Figure 14-69. Somewhere in the system, the command to launch OsisOijw.dll is still working even though this DLL file has been deleted.

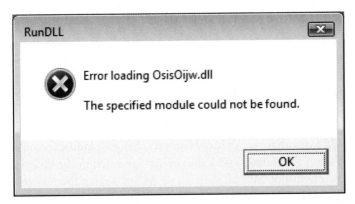

Figure 14-69 Startup error indicates an entry to launch a program has not been removed
Courtesy: Course Technology/Cengage Learning

One way to find this orphaned entry point is to use MSconfig. Figure 14-70 shows the MSconfig window, showing us that the DLL is launched from a registry key.

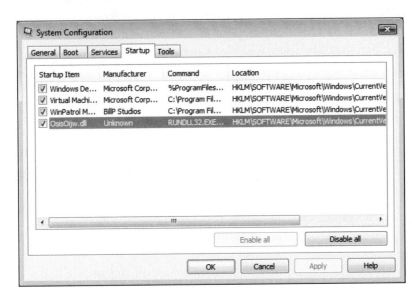

Figure 14-70 MSconfig shows how the DLL is launched during startup
Courtesy: Course Technology/Cengage Learning

The next step is to back up the registry and then use the Registry Editor to find and delete the key (see Figure 14-71).

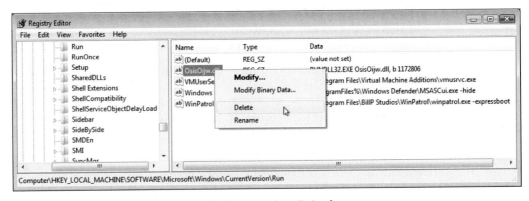

Figure 14-71 Delete the registry key left there by uninstalled software
Courtesy: Course Technology/Cengage Learning

REGISTRY KEYS THAT AFFECT STARTUP AND LOGON EVENTS

You have just seen how you can edit the registry to remove the entries left there by software that you have manually removed. Listed in this section are some registry keys where startup processes can be located. If a system is giving repeated startup errors or you have just removed several programs, you might want to search through these registry keys for processes left there by uninstalled or corrupted software that might be giving startup problems.

As you read through this list of registry keys to search, know that the list is not exhaustive. With experience, you'll learn that the registry is an everchanging landscape of keys and values.

Registry keys that affect the startup and logon events are listed in the bulleted list below. Your registry might or might not have all these keys. As you search the registry for entries in these keys, don't forget to first back up the registry. Because you'll be searching all over the registry and not just in one particular place, it's a good idea to create a restore point as well as back up the C:\Windows\System32\config folder so that the entire registry will be backed up.

These keys cause an entry to run once and only once at startup:

- ▲ HKLM\Software\Microsoft\Windows\CurrentVersion\RunOnce
- ▲ HKLM\Software\Microsoft\Windows\CurrentVersion\RunServiceOnce
- ▲ HKLM\Software\Microsoft\Windows\CurrentVersion\RunServicesOnce
- ▲ HKCU\Software\Microsoft\Windows\CurrentVersion\RunOnce

Check each key in the list above and move on to the next list.

Group Policy (an administrator's tool to control what a user can do on a system) places entries in the following keys to affect startup:

- ▲ HKCU\Software\Microsoft\Windows\CurrentVersion\Policies\Explorer\Run
- ▲ HKLM\Software\Microsoft\Windows\CurrentVersion\Policies\Explorer\Run

Windows loads many DLL programs from the following key, which is sometimes used by malicious software. Entries in this key are normal, so don't delete one unless you know it's causing a problem:

- ▲ HKLM\Software\Microsoft\Windows\CurrentVersion\ShellServiceObjectDelayLoad

Entries in the keys listed next apply to all users and hold legitimate startup entries. Don't delete an entry unless you suspect it to be bad:

- ▲ HKLM\Software\Microsoft\Windows\CurrentVersion\Run
- ▲ HKCU\Software\Microsoft\Windows NT\CurrentVersion\Windows
- ▲ HKCU\Software\Microsoft\Windows NT\CurrentVersion\Windows\Run
- ▲ HKCU\Software\Microsoft\Windows\CurrentVersion\Run

These keys and their subkeys contain entries that pertain to background services that are sometimes launched at startup:

- ▲ HKLM\Software\Microsoft\Windows\CurrentVersion\RunService
- ▲ HKLM\Software\Microsoft\Windows\CurrentVersion\RunServices

The following key contains a value named BootExecute, which is normally set to autochk. It causes the system to run a type of Chkdsk program to check for hard drive integrity when it was previously shut down improperly. Sometimes another program adds itself to this

A+
220-702
2.4

value, causing a problem. For more information about this situation, see the Microsoft Knowledge Base article 151376, "How to Disable Autochk If It Stops Responding During Reboot" at *support.microsoft.com*.

▲ HKLM\System\CurrentControlSet\Control\Session Manager

Here is an assorted list of registry keys that have all been known to cause various problems at startup. Remember, before you delete a program entry from one of these keys, research the program filename so that you won't accidentally delete something you want to keep:

▲ HKCU\Software\Microsoft\Command
▲ HKCU\Software\Microsoft\Command Processor\AutoRun
▲ HKCU\Software\Microsoft\Windows\CurrentVersion\RunOnce\Setup
▲ HKCU\Software\Microsoft\Windows NT\CurrentVersion\Windows\load
▲ HKLM\Software\Microsoft\Windows NT\CurrentVersion\Windows\AppInit_DLLs
▲ HKLM\Software\Microsoft\Windows NT\CurrentVersion\Winlogon\System
▲ HKLM\Software\Microsoft\Windows NT\CurrentVersion\Winlogon\Us
▲ HKCR\batfile\shell\open\command
▲ HKCR\comfile\shell\open\command
▲ HKCR\exefile\shell\open\command
▲ HKCR\htafile\shell\open\command
▲ HKCR\piffile\shell\open\command
▲ HKCR\scrfile\shell\open\command

MONITOR THE STARTUP PROCESS

If you keep the startup process clean, you are more likely to keep Windows performing well. You can use several third-party tools to monitor any changes to startup. A good one is WinPatrol by BillP Studios (*www.winpatrol.com*). Download and install the free program to run in the background to monitor all sorts of things, including changes to the registry, startup processes, Internet Explorer settings, and system files. In Figure 14-72, you can see how WinPatrol gave an alert when it detected that Adobe Update Manager was placing an entry in the registry to launch at startup to update the Adobe software. WinPatrol displays a little black Scotty dog in the notification area of the taskbar to indicate it's running in the background and guarding your system. Also, many antivirus programs monitor the startup process and inform you when changes are made.

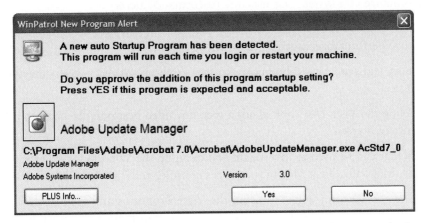

Figure 14-72 WinPatrol by BillP Studios alerts you when the startup process is about to be altered
Courtesy: Course Technology/Cengage Learning

>> CHAPTER SUMMARY

▲ Task Manager (Taskmgr.exe) lets you view services and other running programs, CPU and memory performance, network activity, and user activity. It is useful to stop a process that is hung.

▲ The MSconfig (Msconfig.exe) tool can be used to temporarily disable startup processes to test for performance improvement and find a startup program causing a problem.

▲ The Services console (Services.msc) is used to manage services. When and if a service starts can be controlled from this console.

▲ The Computer Management console (Compmgmt.msc) contains a group of Windows administrative tools useful for managing a system.

▲ The Microsoft Management Console (MMC) can be used to build your own custom consoles from available snap-ins.

▲ Event Viewer (Eventvwr.msc) is a console that displays a group of logs kept by Windows useful for troubleshooting problems with software and hardware and also audits Windows security.

▲ The Vista Reliability and Performance Monitor (Perfmon.msc) and the XP Performance Monitor (also called the System Monitor) can be useful when trying to find out the source of a performance drain on the system.

▲ The Registry Editor (Regedit.exe) is used to edit the register in real time. There is no way to undo changes you make to the registry. Therefore, you should always make a backup before editing it.

▲ The 11 high-level steps to improve Windows performance are (1) routine maintenance, (2) check if hardware can support the OS, (3) check for performance warnings, (4) check the Reliability Monitor, (5) disable indexing for Windows search, (6) disable the Vista Aero glass, (7) disable the Vista sidebar, (8) plug up memory leaks, (9) disable the Vista UAC box, although this is not a recommended best practice, and (10) use ReadyBoost to improve a slow hard drive's performance, and (11) clean up Windows startup.

▲ The Windows Vista Experience Index gives a high-level measurement of the overall performance of a system and lists any performance alerts.

▲ Disabling the Vista Aero glass and the Vista sidebar can save on system resources and improve performance, especially if memory is low.

▲ Memory leaks are caused by poorly written applications that request memory they don't need.

▲ Disabling the Vista UAC box is not a recommended best practice because it improves the security of a system.

▲ Tools that can be used to investigate and clean up the Windows start process include Safe Mode, MSconfig, Task Manager, Services console, and Task Scheduler.

▲ If software does not uninstall using the Vista Programs and Features window or the XP Add or Remove Programs window, you can manually uninstall the software.

>> KEY TERMS

For explanations of key terms, see the Glossary near the end of the book.

Computer Management
   (Compmgmt.msc)
console
Data Collector Sets
Event Viewer (Eventvwr.msc)
HKEY_CLASSES_ROOT
   (HKCR)
HKEY_CURRENT_CONFIG
   (HKCC)
HKEY_CURRENT_USER
   (HKCU)

HKEY_LOCAL_MACHINE
   (HKLM)
HKEY_USERS (HKU)
Microsoft Management
   Console (MMC)
Perfmon.msc
ReadyBoost
registry
Registry Editor (Regedit.exe)
Reliability and Performance
   Monitor

snap-ins
System Configuration Utility
   (Msconfig.exe)
Task Manager (Taskmgr.exe)
Task Scheduler
Vista Upgrade Advisor
Windows Experience Index

>> REVIEWING THE BASICS

1. List four ways to start Task Manager.

2. If a program is not responding, how can you stop it?

3. If a program is using too much of system resources and bogging down other applications, what can you do to fix the problem?

4. How can you get a list of users currently logged onto the computer?

5. What is the program filename and extension of the System Configuration utility?

6. What tool in Windows Vista, used to temporarily disable a startup program, is not available in Windows XP?

7. If a nonessential service is slowing down startup, how can you permanently disable it?

8. What should be the startup type of a service that should not load at startup but might be used later after startup? What tool can you use to set the startup type of a service?

9. List three snap-ins that can be found in both the Windows Vista and Windows XP Computer Management windows that are used to manage hardware and track problems with hardware.

10. What is the file extension of a console that is managed by Microsoft Management Console?

11. What are the program filename and extensions of the Microsoft Management Console?

12. Which log in Event Viewer would you use to find out about attempted logins to a computer?

13. Which log in Event Viewer would you use if you suspect a problem with the hard drive?

14. What is the program filename and extension of the Reliability and Performance Monitor?

15. What is the path to the Ntuser.dat file in Windows Vista?

16. How is the Ntuser.dat file used?

17. Which registry key contains information that Device Manager uses to display information about hardware?

18. What tool in Windows XP do you use to back up the system state?

14

19. What is the Vista tool that can give you a quick report of the overall performance of the system?

20. To improve Windows performance, you decide to disable the indexer used for Windows search. Will Windows search still work?

21. What three indicators in Task Manager can be used to find which program has a memory leak?

22. Why is it best to not disable the UAC box?

23. What key do you press at startup to load the system in Safe Mode?

24. If performance improves when Windows is loaded in Safe Mode, what can you conclude?

25. If performance does not improve when Windows is loaded in Safe Mode, what can you conclude?

26. When using MSconfig to stop startup services, including Microsoft services, which service should you not stop so that restore points will not be lost?

27. What is the purpose of the Windows Installer service?

28. In what folder does Task Scheduler keep scheduled tasks?

29. In what folder is most installed software likely to be found?

30. What is the name of the Control Panel applet used to uninstall software in Vista?

>> THINKING CRITICALLY

1. You need to install a customized console on 10 computers. What is the best way to do that?

   a. When installing the console on the first computer, write down each step to make it easier to do the same chore on the other nine.

   b. Create the console on one computer and copy the .mmc file to the other nine.

   c. Create the console on one computer and copy the .msc file to the other nine.

2. What is the name of the program that you can enter in the Vista Start Search box to execute Event Viewer? What is the process that is running when Event Viewer is displayed on the screen? Why do you think the running process is different from the program name?

3. When cleaning up the startup process, which of these should you do first?

   a. Run MSconfig to see what processes are started.

   b. If an error message is displayed when you start Windows, investigate the message.

   c. After you have launched several applications, use Task Manager to view a list of running tasks.

   d. Run the Defrag utility to optimize the hard drive.

4. Using the Internet, investigate each of the following startup processes. Identify the process and write a one-sentence description.

   a. Acrotray.exe

   b. Ieuser.exe

5. Using Task Manager, you discover an unwanted program that is launched at startup. Of the items listed below, which ones might lead you to the solution to the problem? Which ones would not be an appropriate solution to the problem? Explain why they are not appropriate.

   a. Look at the registry key that launched the program to help determine where in Windows the program was initiated.

   b. Use Task Manager to disable the program.

   c. Search Task Scheduler for the source of the program being launched.

   d. Use MSconfig to disable the program.

   e. Search the startup folders for the source of the program.

>> HANDS-ON PROJECTS

PROJECT 14-1: Researching Running Processes

Boot to the Windows desktop and then use Task Manager to get a list of all the running processes on your machine. Use the Vista Snipping Tool to save and print the Task Manager screens showing the list of processes. Next, boot the system into Safe Mode and use Task Manager to list running processes. Which processes that were loaded normally are not loaded when the system is running in Safe Mode?

PROJECT 14-2: Monitoring Startup Items with WinPatrol

1. Using the System Configuration Utility (MSconfig), disable all the non-Windows startup items. Restart your computer.

2. Download and install WinPatrol from *www.winpatrol.com*.

3. Using the System Configuration Utility (MSconfig), enable all of the disabled startup items and restart the computer.

4. Are the startup programs able to start? What messages are displayed on the screen?

PROJECT 14-3: Practicing Launching Programs at Startup

Do the following to practice launching programs at startup, listing the steps you took for each activity:

1. Configure Scheduled Tasks to launch Notepad each time the computer starts and any user logs on. List the steps you took.

2. Put a shortcut in a startup folder so that any user launches a command prompt window at startup.

3. Restart the system and verify that both programs are launched. Did you receive any errors?

4. Remove the two programs from the startup process.

14

PROJECT 14-4: Practicing Manually Removing Software

To practice your skills of manually removing software, install WinPatrol from *www.winpatrol.com*. (If you did Project 14-2, the software is already installed.) Then, following directions in the chapter, manually remove the software, listing the steps you used. After you have manually removed the software, reboot the system. Did you get any error messages?

PROJECT 14-5: Editing and Restoring the Registry

Practice editing and restoring the registry by doing the following to change the name of the Recycle Bin on the Windows desktop:

1. Using the Registry Editor, export the registry key HKEY_CURRENT_USER\Software\ Microsoft\Windows\CurrentVersion\Explorer to an export file stored on the desktop. The data entry for this key is set to "Value not set," which means the default name, Recycle Bin, is used.

2. To change the name of the Recycle Bin on the Windows Vista desktop for the currently logged-on user, click the following subkey, which holds the name of the Recycle Bin: HKEY_CURRENT_USER\Software\Microsoft\Windows\CurrentVersion\Explorer\CLSID\ 645FF040-5081-101B-9F08-00AA002F954E.

3. To enter a new name for the Recycle Bin, in the right pane, double-click **Default**. The Edit String box appears. The Value data text box in the dialog box should be empty. If a value is present, you selected the wrong value. Check your work and try again.

4. Enter a new name for the Recycle Bin, for example, "Trash Can." Click **OK**.

5. Move the Registry Editor window so that you can see the Recycle Bin on the desktop. Don't close the window.

6. Right-click the desktop and select **Refresh** on the shortcut menu. The name of the Recycle Bin changes.

7. To restore the name to its default value, in the Registry Editor window, again double-click the name of the value, delete your entry, and click **OK**.

8. To verify the change is made, refresh the Windows desktop. The Recycle Bin name should return to its default value.

9. Exit the Registry Editor and then delete the exported registry key stored on the desktop.

10. From these directions, you can see that changes made to the registry take effect immediately. Therefore, take extra care when editing the registry. If you make a mistake and don't know how to correct a problem you create, then you can restore the key that you exported by exiting the Registry Editor and double-clicking the exported key.

PROJECT 14-6: Using the Microsoft Management Console

Using the Microsoft Management Console, follow the step-by-step directions in the chapter to create a customized console. Put two snap-ins in the console: Device Manager and Event Viewer. Store a shortcut to your console on the Windows desktop.

PROJECT 14-7: Finding Windows Utilities

The following table lists some important Windows utilities covered in this chapter. Fill in the right side of the table with the filename and path of each utility. (*Hint*: You can use Windows Explorer or Search to locate files.)

Utility	Filename and Path in Windows Vista	Filename and Path in Windows XP
Task Manager		
System Configuration Utility		
Services Console		
Computer Management		
Microsoft Management Console		
Event Viewer		
Reliability and Performance Monitor		
Registry Editor		

>> REAL PROBLEMS, REAL SOLUTIONS

REAL PROBLEM 14-1: Problems Starting Windows XP

Tim, a coworker who uses many different applications on his Windows XP system, complains to you that his system is very slow starting up and responding when he loads and unloads applications. You suspect the system is loading too many services and programs during startup that are sucking up system resources. What do you do to check for startup processes and eliminate the unnecessary ones? If you have access to a Windows XP system that needs this type of service, test your answers on this system. Write down at least 10 things you should do or try that were discussed in the chapter to speed up a sluggish Windows XP installation.

REAL PROBLEM 14-2: Cleaning Up Startup

Using a computer that has a problem with a sluggish startup, apply the tools and procedures you learned in this chapter to clean up the startup process. Take detailed notes of each step you take and the results. (If you are having a problem finding a computer with a sluggish startup, consider offering your help to a friend, a family member, or a nonprofit organization.)

14

Tools for Solving Windows Problems

In this chapter, you will learn:

- About Windows tools useful to solve problems caused by hardware, applications, and failed Windows components
- About Windows Vista tools that can help when Vista gives problems when starting
- About Windows 2000/XP tools that can help with XP or 2000 startup problems

This chapter is about the tools that you need to know how to use when solving problems with Windows 2000/XP/Vista. We first focus on the tools that can help you when a hardware device, application, or a Windows component fails. Then you'll learn about the tools used when Windows Vista gives problems at startup. Finally, you'll learn about tools that are useful for solving Windows 2000/XP startup problems. Understanding how Vista and 2000/XP start up can help you understand why and how a particular Windows tool functions. Therefore, in the chapter, you'll also learn what happens when these operating systems are loaded.

In the next chapter, we continue our discussion of how to solve Windows problems by learning the strategies and techniques for solving problems with hardware, applications, and Windows. In that chapter, you'll learn how to diagnose a Windows problem and learn which tool is best to use for each situation you face. Consider this chapter and the next a one-two punch for learning to be an expert Windows troubleshooter.

> 💡 **A+ Exam Tip** All the content in this chapter applies to the A+ 220-701 Essentials exam, covering the tools and utilities needed to solve Windows problems. The next chapter covers the content on the A+ 220-702 Practical Application exam, where you are expected to know when and where to use Windows problem-solving tools in troubleshooting situations.

TOOLS TO HELP WITH BLUE SCREEN ERRORS, SYSTEM LOCKUPS, AND I/O DEVICE ERRORS

A+
220-701
2.2

In this part of the chapter, you will learn to use several tools and settings useful when dealing with Windows problems that occur after startup. These tools and settings include Vista Problem Reports and Solutions window, XP Error Reporting, Vista Memory Diagnostics, System File Checker, Driver Verifier, startup settings, tools to verify driver signatures, Device Manager, and diagnostic utilities that come bundled with a hardware device. Then we'll summarize when to use each tool when faced with a specific type of Windows problem.

Table 15-1 is a summary of the Windows tools covered in this and other chapters and is given to you as a quick-and-easy reference of these tools.

Tool	Available in Win Vista	Available in Win XP	Description
Add or Remove		X	▲ Accessed from Control Panel. ▲ Use it to uninstall, repair, or update software or certain device drivers that are causing a problem.
Advanced Boot Options Menu	X	X	▲ Accessed by pressing the F8 key when Windows first starts to load. ▲ Use several options on this menu to help you troubleshoot boot problems.
Automated System Recovery (ASR)		X	▲ Accessed from the Windows XP setup CD. ▲ Use ASR as a last resort because the volume on which Windows is installed is formatted and then restored from the most recent backup. All data and applications written to the drive since the last backup are lost.
Backup (Ntbackup.exe)		X	▲ Enter Ntbackup.exe in the XP Run dialog box. ▲ Use it to restore the system state, data, and software from previously made backups.
Backup and Restore Center	X		▲ Accessed from the Start menu. ▲ Use it to back up user data.
Boot logging	X	X	▲ Press F8 at startup and select from the Advanced Boot Options menu. ▲ Use events logged to the Ntbtlog.txt file to investigate the source of an unknown startup error.
Bootcfg (Bootcfg.exe)		X	▲ Enter Bootcfg at a command prompt. ▲ Use it to view the contents of the Boot.ini file.

Table 15-1 Windows Vista/XP maintenance and troubleshooting tools

A+
220-701
2.2

Tool	Available in Win Vista	Available in Win XP	Description
Cacls.exe	X	X	▲ At a command prompt, enter Cacls with parameters. ▲ Use it to gain access to a file when permissions to the file are in error or corrupted. The utility can change the access control list (ACL) assigned to a file or group of files to control which users have access to a file.
Chkdsk (Chkdsk.exe)	X	X	▲ At a command prompt, enter Chkdsk with parameters. ▲ Use it to check and repair errors on a volume or logical drive. If critical system files are affected by these errors, repairing the drive might solve a startup problem.
Cipher.exe	X	X	▲ At a command prompt, enter Cipher with parameters. ▲ Log in as an administrator and use this command to decrypt a file that is not available because the user account that encrypted the file is no longer accessible.
Compact.exe	X	X	▲ At a command prompt, enter Compact with parameters. ▲ Use it with an NTFS file system to display and change the compressions applied to files and folders.
Complete PC Backup	X		▲ Accessed from Control Panel. ▲ Use it to back up the entire Windows volume. Vista can also keep future incremental backups of the volume. ▲ When restoring the system using Complete PC Backup, all data on the Windows volume is lost.
Computer Management (Compmgmt.msc)	X	X	▲ Accessed from Control Panel or you can enter Compmgmt.msc at a command prompt. ▲ Use it to access several snap-ins to manage and troubleshoot a system.
Defrag.exe	X	X	▲ At a command prompt, enter Defrag with parameters. ▲ Use it to defragment a drive to improve drive performance and access time.
Device Driver Roll Back	X	X	▲ Accessed from Device Manager. ▲ Use it to replace a driver with the one that worked before the current driver was installed.

Table 15-1 Windows Vista/XP maintenance and troubleshooting tools (continued)

15

A+ 220-701

A+
220-701
2.2

Tool	Available in Win Vista	Available in Win XP	Description
Device Manager (Devmgmt.msc)	X	X	▲ Accessed from the Vista System window or XP System Properties window. ▲ Use it to solve problems with hardware devices, to update device drivers, and to disable and uninstall a device.
Disk Cleanup (Cleanmgr.exe)	X	X	▲ Accessed from a drive's properties window or by entering Cleanmgr at a command prompt. ▲ Use it to delete unused files to make more disk space available. Not enough free hard drive space can cause boot problems.
Disk Defragmenter (Dfrg.msc)	X	X	▲ Accessed from a drive's properties window. ▲ Use it to defragment a volume to improve performance.
Disk Management (Diskmgmt.msc)	X	X	▲ Accessed from the Computer Management console, or enter Diskmgmt.msc at a command prompt. ▲ Use it to view and change partitions on hard drives and to format drives.
Driver Signing and Digital Signatures (Sigverif.exe)	X	X	▲ At a command prompt, enter Sigverif with parameters. ▲ When a device driver or other software is giving problems, use it to verify that the software has been approved by Microsoft.
Driver Verifier (verifier.exe)	X	X	▲ Enter verifier.exe at a command prompt. ▲ Use it to identify a driver that is causing a problem. The tool puts stress on selected drivers, which causes the driver with a problem to crash.
Error Reporting	X	X	▲ This automated Windows service displays error messages when an application error occurs. ▲ Follow directions on-screen to produce an error report and send it to Microsoft. Sometimes the Microsoft Web site responds with suggestions to solve the problem. ▲ Vista keeps a history of past problems and solutions, but XP does not.

Table 15-1   Windows Vista/XP maintenance and troubleshooting tools (continued)

A+ 220-701 2.2	Tool	Available in Win Vista	Available in Win XP	Description
	Event Viewer (Eventvwr.msc)	X	X	◢ Accessed from the Computer Management console. ◢ Check the Event Viewer logs for error messages to help you investigate all kinds of hardware, security, and system problems.
	Group Policy (Gpedit.msc)	X	X	◢ At a command prompt, enter Gpedit.msc or use the Computer Management console. ◢ Use it to display and change policies controlling users and the computer.
	Last Known Good Configuration	X	X	◢ Press F8 at startup and select from the Advanced Boot Options menu. ◢ Use this tool when Windows won't start normally and you want to revert the system to before a Windows setting, driver, or application that is causing problems was changed.
	Memory Diagnostics (mdsched.exe)	X		◢ Enter mdsched.exe in a command prompt window. ◢ Use it to test memory.
	Performance Monitor (Perfmon.msc)	X	X	◢ At a command prompt, enter Perfmon.msc. ◢ Use it to view information about performance to help you identify a performance bottleneck. ◢ Vista calls the tool the Reliability and Performance Monitor.
	Program Compatibility Wizard	X	X	◢ Accessed by way of a desktop shortcut to a legacy application. ◢ Use it to resolve issues that prevent legacy software from working.
	Programs and Features window	X		◢ Accessed from Control Panel. ◢ Use it to uninstall, repair, or update software or certain device drivers that are causing a problem.
	Recovery Console		X	◢ Accessed from the Windows XP/2000 setup CD. ◢ Boot up this command-driven OS when you cannot boot from the hard drive. Use it to troubleshoot a Windows XP/2000 startup problem and recover data from the hard drive.
	Registry Editor (Regedit.exe)	X	X	◢ At a command prompt, enter Regedit. ◢ Use it to view and edit the registry.

Table 15-1 Windows Vista/XP maintenance and troubleshooting tools (continued)

15

A+ 220-701

Tool	Available in Win Vista	Available in Win XP	Description
Runas.exe	X	X	▲ At a command prompt, enter Runas with parameters. ▲ Use it to run a program using different permissions than those assigned to the currently logged-on user.
Safe Mode	X	X	▲ At startup, press F8 and select the option from the Advanced Boot Options menu. ▲ Use it when Windows does not start or starts with errors. Safe Mode loads the Windows desktop with a minimum configuration. In this minimized environment, you can solve a problem with a device driver, display setting, or corrupted or malicious applications.
SC (Sc.exe)	X	X	▲ At a command prompt, enter Sc with parameters. ▲ Use it to stop or start a service that runs in the background.
Services (Services.msc)	X	X	▲ At a command prompt, enter Services.msc. ▲ Graphical version of SC.
Software Explorer	X		▲ Accessed from the Windows Defender window. ▲ Use it to view and change programs launched at startup.
System Configuration Utility (Msconfig.exe)	X	X	▲ Enter Msconfig.exe in the Vista Start Search box or the XP Run box. ▲ Troubleshoot the startup process by temporarily disabling startup programs and services.
System File Checker (Sfc.exe)	X	X	▲ At a command prompt, enter Sfc with parameters. ▲ Use it to verify the version of all system files when Windows loads. Useful when you suspect system files are corrupted, but you can still access the Windows desktop.
System Information (Msinfo32.exe)	X	X	▲ Enter Msinfo32.exe in the Vista Start Search box or the XP Run box. ▲ Use it to display information about hardware, applications, and Windows.
System Information (Systeminfo.exe)	X	X	▲ At a command prompt, enter Systeminfo. ▲ A text-only version of the System Information window. To direct that information to a file, use the command Systeminfo.exe >Myfile.txt. Later the file can be printed and used to document information about the system.

Table 15-1   Windows Vista/XP maintenance and troubleshooting tools (continued)

A+
220-701
2.2

Tool	Available in Win Vista	Available in Win XP	Description
System Restore	X	X	▲ Accessed from the Start menu or when loading Safe Mode. ▲ Use it to restore the system to a previously working condition; it restores the registry, some system files, and some application files.
Task Killing Utility (Tskill.exe)	X	X	▲ At a command prompt, enter Tskill with parameters. ▲ Use it to stop or kill a process or program currently running. Useful when managing background services such as an e-mail server or Web server.
Task Lister (Tasklist.exe)	X	X	▲ At a command prompt, enter Tasklist. ▲ Use it to list currently running processes similar to the list provided by Task Manager.
Task Manager (Taskman.exe)	X	X	▲ Right-click the taskbar and select Task Manager. ▲ Use it to list and stop currently running processes. Useful when you need to stop a locked-up application.
Windows Defender	X		▲ Accessed from Control Panel. ▲ Monitors activity and alerts you if a running program appears to be malicious or damaging the system.
Windows File Protection	X	X	▲ Windows background service ▲ Runs in the background to protect system files and restore overwritten system files as needed.
Windows Firewall	X	X	▲ Service that runs in the background to prevent or filter uninvited communication from another computer.
Windows Recovery Environment (recenv.exe)	X		▲ Windows RE is an OS loaded from the Vista setup DVD, which provides a graphic and command-line interface. ▲ Use the tool to solve Vista startup problems.
Windows Update (Wupdmgr.exe)	X	X	▲ Accessed from the Start menu. ▲ Use it to update Windows by downloading the latest patches from the Microsoft Web site.

Table 15-1 Windows Vista/XP maintenance and troubleshooting tools (continued)

15

A+ 220-701

A+
220-701
2.2

> **💡 A+ Exam Tip**   If an often-used Windows utility can be launched from a command prompt, the
> A+ 220-701 Essentials exam expects you to know the program name of that utility.

VISTA PROBLEM REPORTS AND SOLUTIONS

Use the Windows Vista Problem Reports and Solutions tool to deal with an immediate hardware or software problem and use its history feature to help you understand the history of a specific problem or the general history of problems with the system. When a problem occurs, Vista Error Reporting displays an error screen and invites you to check for a solution. If the problem happens in the kernel mode of Windows, a STOP or blue screen error occurs, and the error screen appears on the next restart. For example, after a STOP error occurred on one system and the system was restarted, the screen in Figure 15-1 appeared. If

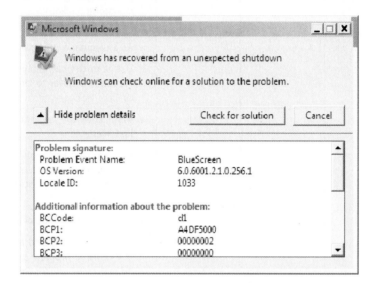

Figure 15-1   Windows reports information about an error
Courtesy: Course Technology/Cengage Learning

the user clicks **Check for solution,** Microsoft displays information about the problem and its solution. User mode errors that don't produce a STOP error can appear as a bubble in the notification area (see Figure 15-2). Click the bubble to see possible solutions for the problem. One such solution is shown in Figure 15-3.

When a problem occurs, Windows records the error and possible solutions. Some of these solutions might not have yet been tried. To see a list of solutions that have not yet been applied for known problems, click **Start,** click **All Programs,** click **Maintenance,** and click **Problem Reports and Solutions.** The Problem Reports and Solutions window in Figure 15-4 appears. Click an item in the list to get more details and possibly apply the solution. Click **Check for new solutions** to send information to Microsoft and possibly find new solutions to known problems. These new solutions to old problems appear with the red word "New" in the figure.

Figure 15-2   Vista error reporting gives an error alert
Courtesy: Course Technology/Cengage Learning

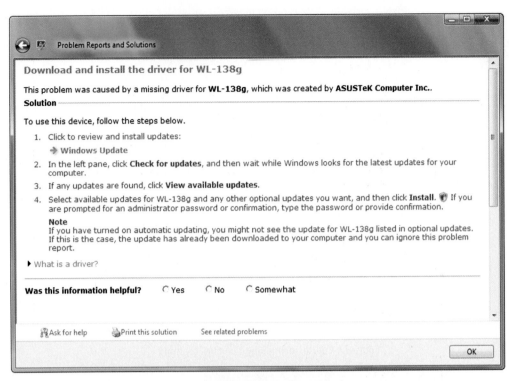

Figure 15-3 Microsoft gives suggestions for a solution to a problem
Courtesy: Course Technology/Cengage Learning

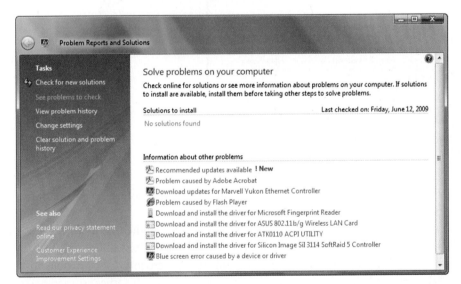

Figure 15-4 Known problems and solutions
Courtesy: Course Technology/Cengage Learning

To see a history of past problems, click **View problem history**; the window in Figure 15-5 appears. Problems are listed by category. Click a problem to see details about the problem. This window is a great tool if you need to understand the history of problems on a computer that you are troubleshooting.

XP ERROR REPORTING

Windows XP offers a similar tool, called Error Reporting. When XP encounters a problem with an application, one thing it might do is display a message about the problem similar to the one shown in Figure 15-6. If you are connected to the Internet, you can click **Send Error Report** to

A+
220-701
2.2

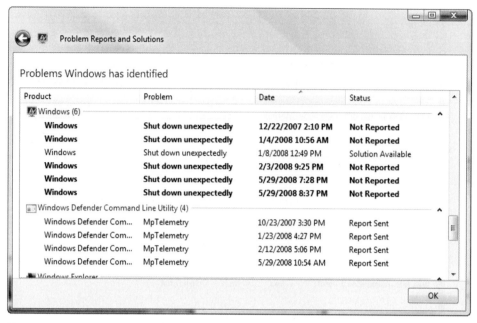

Figure 15-5 Use the Problem Reports and Solutions tool to view a history of past problems
Courtesy: Course Technology/Cengage Learning

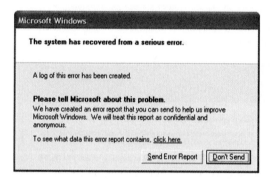

Figure 15-6 A serious Windows error sometimes generates this
Microsoft Windows error reporting box
Courtesy: Course Technology/Cengage Learning

get suggestions about the problem from Microsoft. Microsoft will also use the information you send to help with future Windows updates and patches.

After the information is sent, a dialog box similar to the one in Figure 15-7 appears. Click **More information** to see Microsoft insights and suggestions about the problem. Your browser will open and display information from Microsoft. If the problem is caused by a Microsoft product such as Internet Explorer or Microsoft Office, sometimes the Web site will point you to a patch you can download to fix the problem. An example of an available patch is also shown in Figure 15-7.

The XP Error Reporting does not keep a history of previous errors as does the Vista Problem Reports and Solutions tool.

MEMORY DIAGNOSTICS

Errors with memory are often difficult to diagnose because they can appear intermittently and might be mistaken as application errors, user errors, or other hardware component errors. Sometimes these errors cause the system to hang, a blue screen error might occur, or the system continues to function with applications giving errors or data getting corrupted. You can quickly identify a problem with memory or eliminate memory as the source of a problem by

A+
220-701
2.2

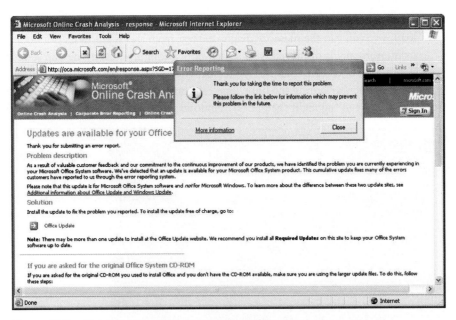

Figure 15-7 Click More information to see Microsoft insights into a problem
Courtesy: Course Technology/Cengage Learning

using the Vista **Memory Diagnostics** tool. It tests memory for errors and works before Windows Vista is loaded. The diagnostic test can be initiated using one of these four methods:

Method 1: If Vista Error Reporting detects that memory might be failing, the utility will prompt the user to test memory on the next reboot. If the user agrees by clicking **Check for problems the next time you start your computer,** then diagnostic tests are run on the next restart. After the Windows desktop loads, a bubble message appears giving the test results. If the test shows that memory is giving errors, replace the memory modules.

Method 2: You can test memory at any time using the command prompt. To do so, click **Start, All Programs, Accessories, Command Prompt.** The Command Prompt window opens. Type **mdsched.exe,** press **Enter,** and respond to the UAC box. In the dialog box that appears (see Figure 15-8), you can choose to run the test now or on the next restart.

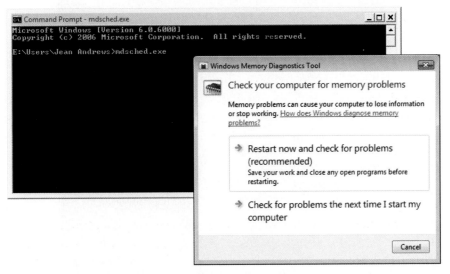

Figure 15-8 Use the mdsched.exe command to test memory
Courtesy: Course Technology/Cengage Learning

15

A+ 220-701

A+
220-701
2.2

Method 3: When troubleshooting a failed system, if the Windows Vista desktop cannot load, you can run the memory diagnostic test from the Windows Vista boot menu. This menu normally is displayed with a dual-boot configuration so you can select the OS to load. If you are not using a dual-boot machine, you can force the menu to be displayed by pressing the Spacebar during the boot. The resulting menu appears, as shown in Figure 15-9. Use the Tab key to highlight the option **Windows Memory Diagnostic** and press **Enter**.

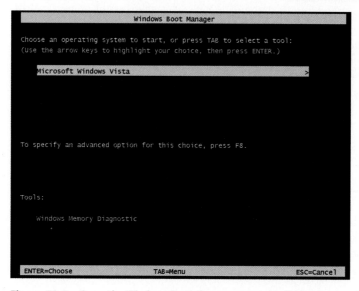

Figure 15-9   Force the Windows Boot Manager menu to display by pressing the Spacebar during the boot
Courtesy: Course Technology/Cengage Learning

Method 4: For any computer that has a DVD drive, you can run the test using the Windows Vista DVD, even if the computer is using a different OS than Vista, by doing the following:

1. Boot from the Vista DVD. On the window that appears, select your language preference and click **Next**.

2. On the opening menu of the Vista DVD, click **Repair your computer**, as shown in Figure 15-10. In the next box, select the Vista installation to repair and click **Next**.

Figure 15-10   Opening menu when you boot from the Vista DVD
Courtesy: Course Technology/Cengage Learning

3. The System Recovery Options window appears (see Figure 15-11). Click **Windows Memory Diagnostic Tool**.

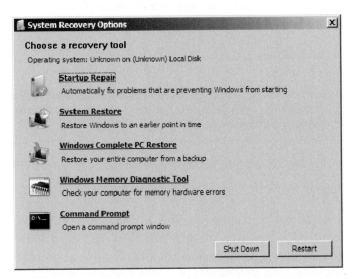

Figure 15-11 Test memory using the System Recovery Options menu
Courtesy: Course Technology/Cengage Learning

4. On the next window, click **Restart now and check for problems (recommended)**. The system will reboot and the memory test will start.

When the Vista desktop refuses to load but you can boot from the hard drive to the Vista boot menu, use Method 3. If you cannot boot from the hard drive or if Vista is not installed on the drive, use Method 4.

SYSTEM FILE CHECKER

A Windows application or hardware problem might be caused by a corrupted Windows system file. That's where System File Checker might help. System File Checker (SFC) is a Windows Vista and XP utility that protects system files and keeps a cache of current system files in case it needs to refresh a damaged file. To use the utility to scan all system files and verify them, first close all applications and then enter the command **sfc / scannow** in a command prompt window (see Figure 15-12). For Vista, use an elevated

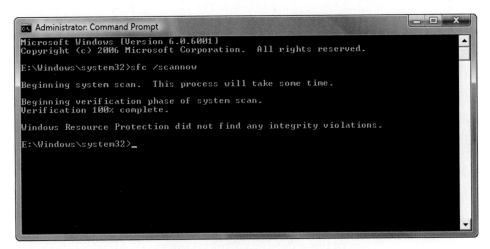

Figure 15-12 Use System File Checker to verify Windows system files
Courtesy: Course Technology/Cengage Learning

A+
220-701
2.2

command prompt window. If corrupted system files are found, you might need to provide the Windows setup CD or DVD to restore the files. If you have problems running the utility, try the command **sfc/ scanonce**, which scans files immediately after the next reboot.

> 💡 **Tip**　　Recall from Chapter 13 that you can get an elevated command prompt window in Vista by clicking **Start**, **All Programs**, and **Accessories**. Then right-click **Command Prompt** and select **Run as administrator** from the shortcut menu.

DRIVER VERIFIER

For hardware problems, **Driver Verifier (verifier.exe)** is a Windows Vista/XP/2000 utility that runs in the background to put stress on drivers as they are loaded and running. When a problem occurs, a STOP error is generated so you can identify the problem driver. The tool is useful for troubleshooting intermittent problems that are not easily detected by other means.

To use Driver Verifier to monitor drivers, follow these steps:

1. Click **Start**, enter **verifier.exe** in the Start Search box, press **Enter**, and respond to the UAC box. The Driver Verifier Manager window opens (see Figure 15-13).

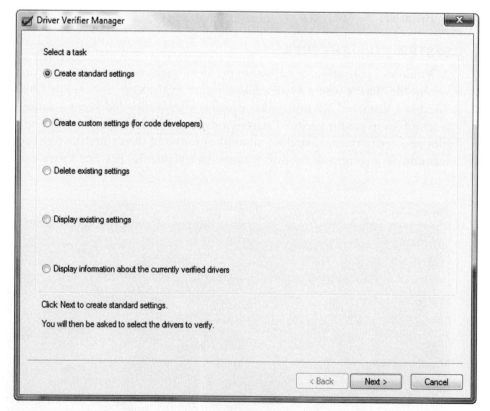

Figure 15-13　Configure Driver Verifier to test drivers
Courtesy: Course Technology/Cengage Learning

A+
220-701
2.2

2. Select **Create standard settings** and click **Next**. The window in Figure 15-14 appears.

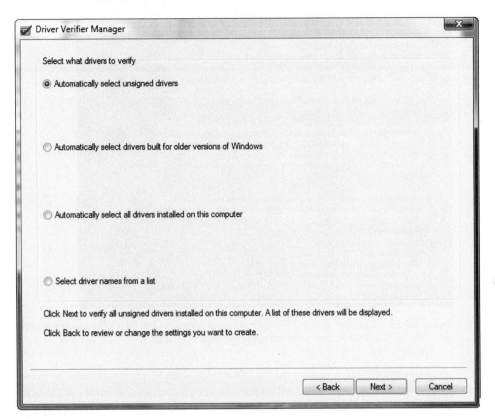

Figure 15-14 Select the type of drivers for Driver Verifier to test
Courtesy: Course Technology/Cengage Learning

3. Depending on what you suspect to be the problem with your hardware, you need to select which type of drivers to monitor (unsigned drivers, older drivers, all drivers, or specific drivers that you can select from a list that appears on the next screen). If you are not sure which ones, to be on the safe side, select **Automatically select all drivers installed on this computer**. (When you do that, the Next in the window changes to Finish.) Then click **Finish**. However, be aware that the more drivers the utility monitors, the more system performance will be affected.

4. Restart the system.

Driver Verifier attempts to overload the drivers it monitors, which can cause a STOP error. The STOP error message tells you which driver caused the error, thus identifying a driver with problems. For example, Figure 15-15 shows a STOP error screen caused during startup by the driver, mrv8ka51.sys. Which device does this driver belong to? There are several ways to get at that information; one way is to look at the file Properties box. First find the file in the C:\Windows\System32\drivers folder. Right-click the file and select **Properties** from the shortcut menu. In the file Properties box, select the **Details** tab, which shows that this driver file belongs to the wireless adapter (see Figure 15-16). The next step to fix the problem is to update the driver.

After Driver Verifier has located the problem, to turn it off, click **Start**, enter **verifier.exe** in the Start Search box, press **Enter**, and respond to the UAC box. The Driver Verifier Manager window opens (refer to Figure 15-13). Select **Delete existing settings** and click **Finish**. Click **Yes** in the warning box, and then click **OK**. Restart your computer.

15

A+ 220-701

A+
220-701
2.2

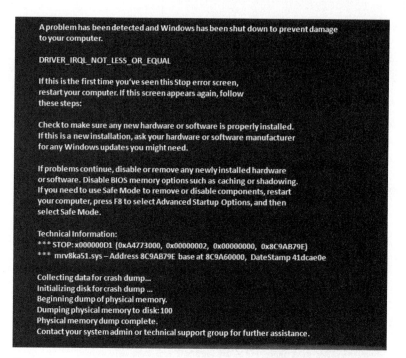

A problem has been detected and Windows has been shut down to prevent damage to your computer.

DRIVER_IRQL_NOT_LESS_OR_EQUAL

If this is the first time you've seen this Stop error screen, restart your computer. If this screen appears again, follow these steps:

Check to make sure any new hardware or software is properly installed. If this is a new installation, ask your hardware or software manufacturer for any Windows updates you might need.

If problems continue, disable or remove any newly installed hardware or software. Disable BIOS memory options such as caching or shadowing. If you need to use Safe Mode to remove or disable components, restart your computer, press F8 to select Advanced Startup Options, and then select Safe Mode.

Technical Information:
*** STOP: x000000D1 (0xA4773000, 0x00000002, 0x00000000, 0x8C9AB79E)
*** mrv8ka51.sys – Address 8C9AB79E base at 8C9A60000, DateStamp 41dcae0e

Collecting data for crash dump...
Initializing disk for crash dump ...
Beginning dump of physical memory.
Dumping physical memory to disk: 100
Physical memory dump complete.
Contact your system admin or technical support group for further assistance.

Figure 15-15 This blue screen STOP error message identifies the driver file causing a problem
Courtesy: Course Technology/Cengage Learning

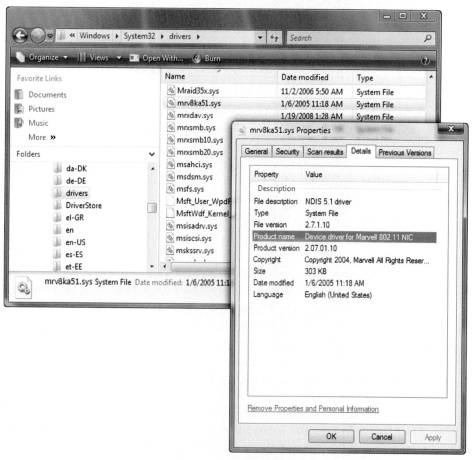

Figure 15-16 The file Properties box reports the driver product information
Courtesy: Course Technology/Cengage Learning

If Driver Verifier runs for a few days and has still not found the problem, it probably will not help you. Turn it off so that it will not continue to degrade system performance. One other caution: If the computer is a file server that many users depend on for top performance, consider the problems you might cause these users before you decide to use the Driver Verifier.

APPLYING CONCEPTS | STARTUP AND RECOVERY SETTINGS TO GET OUT OF AN ENDLESS LOOP

Remember that STOP error that happened during startup and is shown in Figure 15-15? With normal Windows settings, if a STOP error occurs during startup, the system displays the error screen for a moment and then automatically restarts the system, which can result in an endless cycle of restarts, which is exactly what happened in this example with the wireless adapter problem. The support technician got around the problem by booting the system into Safe Mode, which did not load Driver Verifier, and, therefore, allowed the Windows desktop to load. Then she changed the setting that caused Windows to automatically restart. Here's how to change that setting:

1. Click **Start**, right-click **Computer**, and select **Properties** from the shortcut menu.

2. In the System window (see the upper part of Figure 15-17), click **Advanced system settings** and respond to the UAC box. (For Windows XP, in the System Properties window, click the **Advance** tab.)

3. In the System Properties box (see the lower-left of Figure 15-17) in the Startup and Recovery section, click **Settings**.

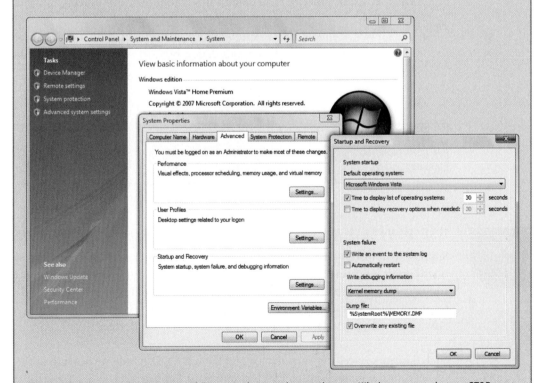

Figure 15-17 Use the Startup and Recovery box to change the way Windows responds to a STOP error during startup
Courtesy: Course Technology/Cengage Learning

15

A+ 220-701

4. In the Startup and Recovery box (see the lower-right of Figure 15-17), uncheck **Automatically restart**. Click **OK** twice to close both boxes. Then close the System window.

Next, she restarted the system normally. This time the STOP error remained frozen on-screen so that she could read it. After she wrote down the information she needed, she restarted the system again in Safe Mode and this time stopped Driver Verifier. Then she restarted Windows normally, located the driver, and updated it. The process required a lot of restarts, but it did find the driver causing the problem.

TOOLS TO VERIFY DRIVER SIGNATURES

Boot problems, an unstable Windows system, or error messages might be caused by drivers that Microsoft has not validated and are not digitally signed or by drivers that have changed since they were signed. If you suspect a problem with a driver, do one of the following to verify that it is digitally signed by Microsoft:

- *Use the File Signature Verification tool.* The File Signature Verification tool displays information about digitally signed files, including device driver files and application files, and logs information to C:\Windows\Sigverif.txt. To use the tool, type the **sigverif.exe** command in the Vista Start Search box or the XP Run box.
- *Use the Driver Query tool.* The Driver Query tool can be used to direct information about drivers to a file, including information about digital signatures. Enter this command in the Vista Start Search box or the XP Run box: **driverquery /si >myfile.txt**. The file will be stored in the default drive and directory unless you specify some other path.
- *Use Device Manager.* If you know which device is causing a problem, use Device Manager. In the device's Properties dialog box, the digital signature information is given on the Driver tab.

Notes Use the Driver Query tool to save information about your system to a file when the system is healthy. Later, if you have a problem with drivers, you can compare reports to help identify the problem driver.

USE DEVICE MANAGER TO UPDATE AND ROLL BACK DRIVERS

Suppose you install a new application on your computer and the function keys on your keyboard don't work the way the application says they should. Or suppose you read that your sound card manufacturer has just released a driver update for your card and you want to try it out. Both of these situations are good reasons to try the Update Driver process. Here's how to use Device Manager to update the drivers for a device:

1. Locate drivers for your device and have the CD handy or download the driver files from the manufacturer's Web site to your hard drive.

2. Using Device Manger, right-click the device and select **Properties** from the shortcut menu. The Properties window for that device appears. Select the **Driver** tab and click **Update Driver**. The Update Driver Software box opens (see Figure 15-18).

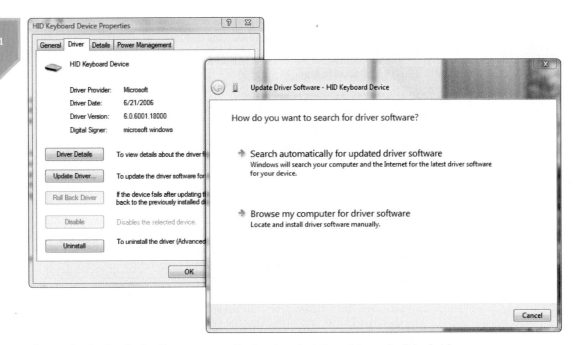

Figure 15-18 Use Device Manager properties box to uninstall, update, and roll back drivers
Courtesy: Course Technology/Cengage Learning

3. To search the Internet for drivers, click **Search automatically for updated driver software**. (Vista searches the Microsoft Web site and the manufacturer's Web site, but XP searches only the Microsoft Web site for drivers.) If you have already downloaded drivers to your PC, click **Browse my computer for driver software**, and point to the downloaded files. Remember, Windows is looking for an .inf file to identify the drivers. Continue to follow the directions on-screen to complete the installation.

> **Notes** Using Windows Vista, you cannot use Device Manager without responding correctly to the UAC box. For Windows XP, you must be logged on with administrator privileges to make changes from Device Manager.

If you update a driver and the new driver does not perform as expected, you can revert to the old driver by using the Driver Rollback feature. To revert to a previous driver, open the Properties window for the device (see the left side of Figure 15-18), and click **Roll Back Driver**. If a previous driver is available, it will be installed. In many cases, when a driver is updated, Windows saves the old driver in case you want to revert to it. Keep in mind that Windows does not save printer drivers when they are updated and also doesn't save drivers that are not functioning properly at the time of an update.

> **Notes** By default, Device Manager hides legacy devices that are not Plug and Play. To view installed legacy devices, click the **View** menu of Device Manager, and check **Show hidden devices** (see Figure 15-19).

A+
220-701
2.2
2.5

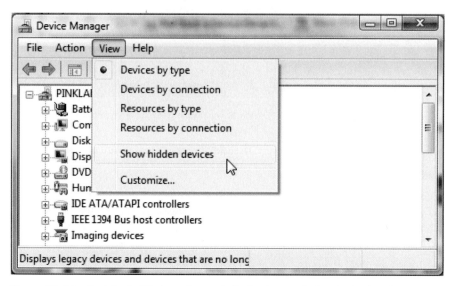

Figure 15-19 By default, Windows does not display legacy devices in Device Manager; you show these hidden devices by using the View menu
Courtesy: Course Technology/Cengage Learning

A+
220-701
2.2

UTILITIES BUNDLED WITH A HARDWARE DEVICE

Many devices come with diagnostic utilities included on the setup CD. Sometimes these utilities are installed when you install the device, and sometimes you need to launch the utility from the setup CD. When you have problems with a device, look for this utility either in the Start, All Programs menu or on the setup CD. Use it to test and diagnose problems with the device.

TYPES OF ERRORS AND TOOLS TO USE

Recall that a blue screen error happens when processes running in kernel mode encounter a problem and Windows must stop the system. In such situations, a blue screen appears with a cryptic error message such as the one in Figure 15-20. This particular blue screen appeared a few seconds

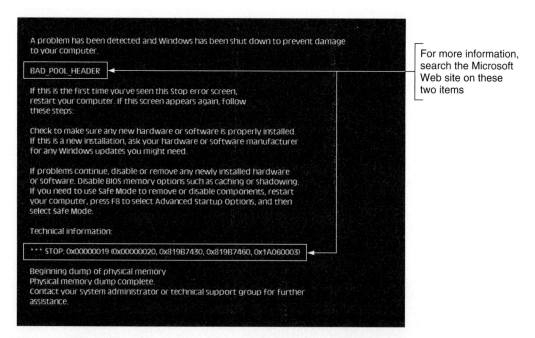

Figure 15-20 A blue screen of death (BSOD) is definitively not a good sign; time to start troubleshooting
Courtesy: Course Technology/Cengage Learning

A+
220-701
2.2

after a USB wireless adapter was plugged into a notebook computer. Look on the blue screen for the stop error at the top and the specific number of the error near the bottom of the screen, as labeled in Figure 15-20. For more information about a blue screen, search the Microsoft Web site on these two items. As for the tools useful in solving blue screen errors, put the Internet at the top of your list! (But don't forget that some sites are unreliable and others mean you harm.) Immediately after you restart the system, the Vista Problem Reports and Solutions window might appear with useful information. Event Viewer might also provide events it has logged.

A system lockup means that the computer freezes and must be restarted. These errors are most likely caused by hardware such as memory, the motherboard, CPU, video card, or the system overheating. I/O devices such as the keyboard, mouse, or monitor or application errors don't usually cause a system to lock up. When a system freezes and you must restart it, check Event Viewer to see if it has reported a hardware failure. Other tools that can help are the Reliability and Performance Monitor, Vista Problem Reports and Solutions window, and Vista Memory Diagnostics. When I/O devices give errors, be sure to check Device Manager for warnings and Event Viewer for information it has tracked.

> **A+ Exam Tip** The A+ 220-701 Essentials exam expects you to know the difference between a blue screen error and a system lockup error.

When solving problems with any kind of hardware, it's important that you check for physical damage to the device. If you feel excessive heat coming from the computer case or a peripheral device, immediately unplug the device or power down the system. Don't turn the device or system back on until the problem is solved; you don't want to start a fire! Other symptoms that indicate potential danger are strong electrical odors, unusual noises, liquid spills on a device, and visible damage such as a frayed cable, melted plastic, or smoke. In these situations, turn off the equipment immediately.

As you learn to solve computer problems, see each new problem as the potential to learn something new. Don't forget to search the Internet for information on each problem you face when you don't immediately know the solution. Installation manuals and training materials can also be good sources of information.

VISTA TOOLS FOR SOLVING STARTUP PROBLEMS

A+
220-701
2.2
3.4

Tools that can be used to troubleshoot and solve startup problems with Windows Vista are the Advanced Boot Options menu, the Vista Recovery Environment, and the command prompt window in Windows RE. The Advanced Boot Options menu is also available in Windows 2000/XP, although when using these OSs it is called the Advanced Options menu. As you learn to use each tool, keep in mind that you want to use the tool that makes as few changes to the system as possible to fix the problem.

Before we discuss the Windows tools, let's turn our attention to learning about the files that Vista needs to start successfully and the step-by-step process of loading the OS. The better you understand this process, the more likely you will be able to solve a problem when Vista cannot start.

> ⚡ **Caution** This chapter often refers to the Windows setup CD or DVD. If you have a notebook computer or a brand-name computer such as a Dell, IBM, Lenovo, or Gateway, be sure to use the manufacturer's recovery CDs or DVD instead of a regular Windows setup disc. This recovery disc has drivers specific to your system, and the Windows build might be different from that of an off-the-shelf Windows setup disc. For example, Windows Vista Home Premium installed on a notebook computer might have been built with all kinds of changes made to it by the notebook manufacturer and is, therefore, different from the Windows Vista Home Premium that you can buy in a retail store.

15

A+ 220-701

FILES NEEDED TO START WINDOWS VISTA

A Windows Vista system has successfully started when you can log onto Windows and the Windows desktop is loaded. To successfully start, a computer needs the bare-bones minimum of hardware and software. If one of these hardware or software components is missing, corrupted, or broken, the boot fails. To start, a computer needs a CPU, motherboard, memory, power supply, and boot device (hard drive, optical disc, or other boot device).

Table 15-2 lists the files necessary to start Windows Vista. The MBR sector and the OS boot sector are included in the table to complete the list of software components needed to load Vista when Vista loads from the hard drive. Vista startup is managed by two files: the Windows Boot Manager (BootMgr) and the Windows Boot Loader (WinLoad.exe). Vista configuration data is stored in the Vista Boot Configuration Data (BCD) file. Also notice in Table 15-2 that the BootMgr file and the BCD file are stored in the system partition (the active partition) and the other files are stored in the boot partition. For most installations, the system partition and the boot partition are the same (drive C).

Component or File	Path*	Description
MBR	First sector of the hard drive called the master boot record	Contains the partition table and the master boot program used to locate and start the BootMgr program.
OS boot record	First sector of the system partition (most likely drive C)	Windows XP uses this sector, but Vista does not use it.
BootMgr	Root directory of system partition (C:\)	Windows Boot Manager manages the initial startup of the OS.
BCD	Boot folder of the system partition (C:\Boot)	Boot Configuration Data file contains boot parameters.
WinLoad.exe	C:\Windows\System32	Windows Boot Loader loads and starts essential Windows processes.
Ntoskrnl.exe	C:\Windows\System32	Vista kernel.
Hal.dll	C:\Windows\System32	Dynamic link library handles low-level hardware details.
Smss.exe	C:\Windows\System32	Sessions Manager file responsible for loading user mode graphics components.
Csrss.exe	C:\Windows\System32	Win32 subsystem.
Winlogon.exe	C:\Windows\System32	Logon process.
Services.exe	C:\Windows\System32	Service Control Manager starts and stops services.
Lsass.exe	C:\Windows\System32	Authenticates users.
System registry hive	C:\Windows\System32\ Config\System	Holds data for the HKEY_LOCAL_MACHINE key of the registry.
Device drivers	C:\Windows\System32\ Drivers	Drivers for required hardware.

*It is assumed that Windows is installed in C:\Windows.

Table 15-2   Software components and files needed to start Windows Vista

Don't be confused with the terminology here. It is really true that, according to the terms used by Microsoft documentation, the Windows OS is on the boot partition, and the boot record is on the system partition, although that might seem backward. The PC boots from the system partition and loads the Windows Vista operating system from the boot partition. The system partition contains the files that tell a computer where to look to start Windows. The boot partition contains the \Windows folder where system files are located. Most of the time the boot partition and the system partition are the same partition (drive C). The only time they are different is in a dual-boot configuration. For example, if Vista has been installed in a dual-boot configuration with Windows XP, the system partition is most likely drive C (where Windows XP is installed), and Vista is installed on another drive, such as drive E, which Vista calls the boot partition. The PC boots from drive C and then loads Vista system files stored on drive E in the E:\Windows folder.

The Vista **Boot Configuration Data (BCD)** file is structured the same as a registry file and contains configuration information about how Vista is started. Here is the type of information contained in the BCD file:

- Settings that control BootMgr and WinLoad.exe
- Settings that control WinResume.exe, the program that resumes Vista from hibernation
- Settings that start and control the Windows Memory Diagnostic program (\Boot\MemTest.exe)
- Settings that launch Ntldr to load a previous OS in a dual-boot configuration
- Settings to load a non-Microsoft operating system (such as the Mac OS or Linux)

STEPS TO START A VISTA COMPUTER

Now let's look at the steps to start a Windows Vista computer. Several of these steps are diagrammed in Figures 15-21 and 15-22 to help you visually understand how the steps work.

> 💡 **A+ Exam Tip** The A+ 220-701 Essentials exam expects you to recognize symptoms of problems when Windows starts. Understanding the startup process can help you recognize at what point in startup a problem occurs.

Study these steps carefully, because the better you understand startup, the more likely you'll be able to solve startup problems.

1. Startup BIOS first checks all the essential hardware components to make sure they're working and displays its progress on-screen. (The computer is sometimes configured to show a manufacturer's logo or welcome screen instead.) If it has a problem and the video system is working, it displays an error message. If video is not working, BIOS might attempt to communicate an error with a series of beeps (called beep codes) or speech (for speech-enabled BIOS). The process of BIOS checking hardware is called POST (Power-On Self Test).

2. After POST, the BIOS turns to CMOS RAM to find out to which device it should look to find an operating system. One of the settings stored in CMOS is the boot sequence, which is a list of devices such as a DVD drive, floppy drive, USB device,

A+
220-701
2.2
3.4

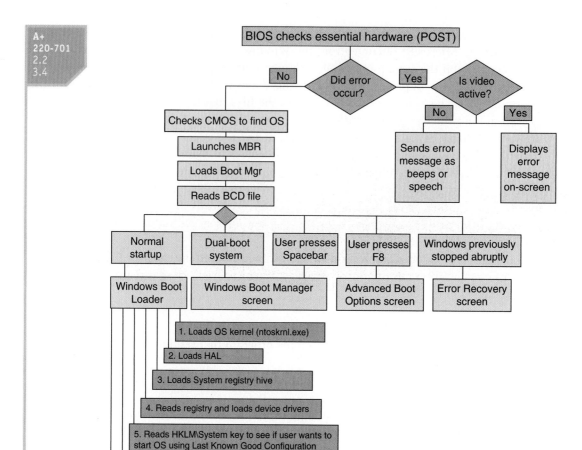

Figure 15-21   Steps to booting the computer and loading Vista
Courtesy: Course Technology/Cengage Learning

or hard drive, arranged in the order they should be searched for a bootable OS. The BIOS looks to the first item in the list for storage media that contains an OS to load. If it doesn't find a bootable OS, it moves to the next item in the list. You can change the boot sequence in BIOS setup. Usually the OS is loaded from the hard drive.

3. The BIOS finds and launches the small program in the master boot record (MBR) of the hard drive. This program points to the BootMgr program stored in the root of the system partition. BootMgr is launched.

4. BootMgr starts in 16-bit mode and switches the processor to 32-bit or 64-bit mode. (Starting in 16-bit mode is necessary because all processors start in 16-bit mode, also called real mode.)

5. BootMgr reads the BCD file. The next step, one of five, depends on these factors:

   Option 1: For normal startups that are not dual booting, no menu appears and BootMgr finds and launches Windows Boot Loader (WinLoad.exe).
   Option 2: If the computer is set up for a dual-boot environment, BootMgr displays the Windows Boot Manager screen, as shown in Figure 15-23.

A+
220-701
2.2
3.4

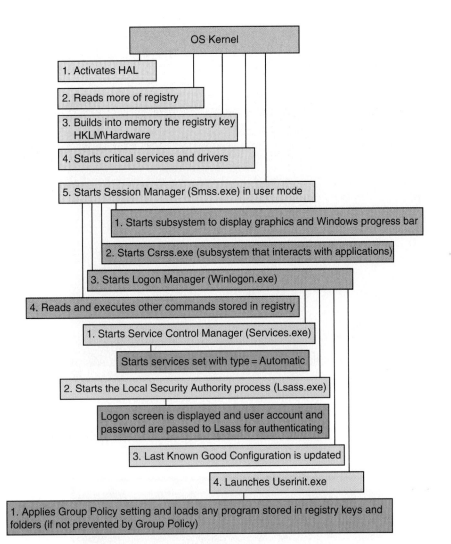

Figure 15-22 Steps to complete loading Vista
Courtesy: Course Technology/Cengage Learning

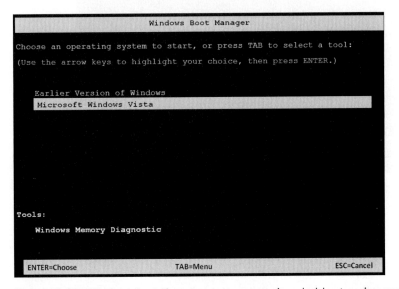

Figure 15-23 Windows Boot Manager screen appears in a dual-boot environment
Courtesy: Course Technology/Cengage Learning

15

A+ 220-701

Option 3: If the user presses the Spacebar, the Windows Boot Manager screen appears.

Option 4: If the user presses F8, BootMgr displays the Advanced Boot Options screen, as shown in Figure 15-24.

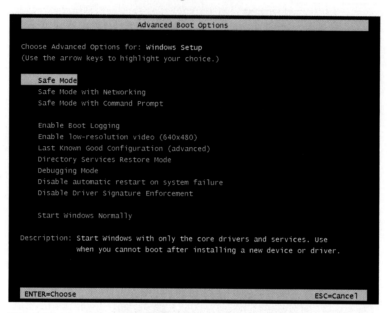

Figure 15-24   Press F8 to see the Advanced Boot Options menu
Courtesy: Course Technology/Cengage Learning

Option 5: If Windows was previously stopped abruptly, the Windows Error Recovery screen (see Figure 15-25) appears.

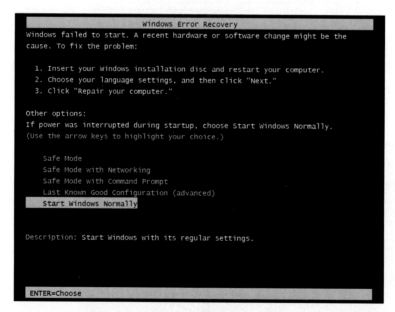

Figure 15-25   This window appears if Windows has been abruptly stopped
Courtesy: Course Technology/Cengage Learning

6. For normal startups, WinLoad loads into memory the OS kernel and Ntoskrnl.exe, but does not yet start them. WinLoad also loads into memory the Hardware Abstraction Layer (Hal.dll), which will later be used by the kernel.

7. WinLoad loads into memory the system registry hive (C:\Windows\System32\Config\ System).

8. WinLoad then reads the registry key just created, HKEY_LOCAL_ MACHINE\
SYSTEM\Services, looking for and loading into memory device drivers that must be
launched at startup. The drivers are not yet started.

9. WinLoad reads data from the HKEY_LOCAL_MACHINE\SYSTEM key
that tells the OS if the user wants to start the OS using the Last Known Good
Configuration.

10. WinLoad starts up the memory paging process and then turns over startup to the OS
kernel.

11. The kernel (Ntoskrnl.exe) activates the HAL, reads more information from the
registry, and builds into memory the registry key HKEY_LOCAL_ MACHINE\
HARDWARE, using information that has been collected about the hardware.

12. The kernel then starts critical services and drivers that are configured to be started by
the kernel during the boot. Recall that drivers interact directly with hardware and
run in kernel mode, while services interact with drivers. Most services and drivers are
stored in C:\Windows\System32 or C:\Windows\System32\Drivers and have an .exe,
.dll, or .sys file extension.

13. After all services and drivers configured to load during the boot are started, the kernel starts the Session Manager (Smss.exe), which runs in user mode.

14. Smss.exe starts the part of the Win32 subsystem that displays graphics and the
Windows **progress bar** is displayed on the screen (see Figure 15-26). When you see
the progress bar, you know the Windows kernel has loaded successfully.

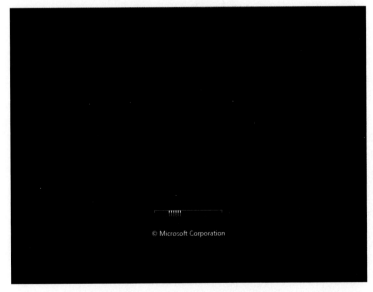

Figure 15-26   The progress bar indicates that the Windows graphics subsystem is running and the kernel has successfully loaded
Courtesy: Course Technology/Cengage Learning

15. Smss.exe then starts the client/server run-time subsystem (Csrss.exe), which also runs
in user mode. Csrss.exe is the Win32 subsystem component that interacts with
applications.

16. Smss.exe starts the Logon Manager (Winlogon.exe) and reads and executes other
commands stored in the registry, such as a command to replace system files placed
there by Windows Update.

A+
220-701
2.2
3.4

17. Winlogon.exe starts the Service Control Manager (Services.exe). Services.exe starts all services listed with the startup type of Automatic in the Services console.

18. Winlogon.exe starts the Local Security Authority process (Lsass.exe). The logon screen appears (see Figure 15-27), and the user account and password are passed to the Lsass.exe process for authenticating. The Last Known Good Configuration information in the registry is updated.

Figure 15-27   Windows Vista logon screen
Courtesy: Course Technology/Cengage Learning

19. Winlogon.exe launches Userinit.exe and the Windows desktop (Explorer.exe).

20. Userinit.exe applies Group Policy settings and any programs not trumped by Group Policy that are stored in these registry keys and folders:

- HKLM\Software\Microsoft\Windows\CurrentVersion\Runonce
- HKLM\Software\Microsoft\Windows\CurrentVersion\Policies\Explorer\Run
- HKLM\Software\Microsoft\Windows\CurrentVersion\Run
- HKCU\Software\Microsoft\Windows NT\CurrentVersion\Windows\Run
- HKCU\Software\Microsoft\Windows\CurrentVersion\Run
- HKCU\Software\Microsoft\Windows\CurrentVersion\RunOnce
- *Systemdrive*\ProgramData\Microsoft\Windows\Start Menu\Programs\Startup
- *Systemdrive*\Users*username*\AppData\Roaming\Microsoft\Windows\Start Menu\Programs\Startup

The Windows startup is officially completed when the Windows desktop appears and the wait circle disappears.

With this basic knowledge of the boot in hand, let's turn our attention to the Windows tools that can help you solve problems when Vista refuses to load.

ADVANCED BOOT OPTIONS MENU

The Vista Advanced Boot Options menu (refer back to Figure 15-24) appears when a user presses F8 as Vista is loading. You need to be familiar with each option on this menu and know how to use it.

A+
220-701
2.2
3.4

SAFE MODE ON THE ADVANCED BOOT OPTIONS MENU

Safe Mode boots the OS with a minimum configuration and can be used to solve problems with a new hardware installation or problems caused by user settings. Safe Mode boots with the mouse, monitor (with basic video), keyboard, and mass storage drivers loaded. It uses the default system services (it does not load any extra services) and does not provide network access. It uses a plain video driver (Vga.sys) instead of the video drivers specific to your video card.

When you boot in Safe Mode, you will see "Safe Mode" in all four corners of your screen. In addition, you have a GUI interface in Safe Mode. The screen resolution is 600 x 800 and the desktop wallpaper (background) is black. Figure 15-28 shows Vista in Safe Mode.

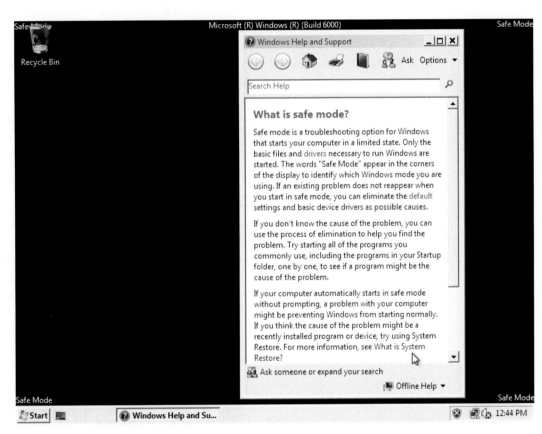

Figure 15-28 Safe Mode loads a minimum Vista configuration
Courtesy: Course Technology/Cengage Learning

Here's a list of things you can do in Safe Mode to recover the system:

1. When Safe Mode first loads, if Windows senses the problem is drastic, it gives you the opportunity to go directly to System Restore. Use System Restore unless you know exactly what it is you need to do to solve your problem.

2. If you suspect a virus, scan the system for viruses. You can also use Chkdsk to fix hard drive problems. Your hard drive might be full; if so, make some free space available.

3. Use Device Manager to uninstall or disable a device with problems or to roll back a driver.

15

A+ 220-701

A+
220-701
2.2
3.4

4. Use Msconfig to disable unneeded services or startup processes. Recall from Chapter 14 that you can use Msconfig to disable many services and startup processes, and then enable them one group at a time until you discover the one causing the problem.

5. If you suspect a software program you have just installed, use the Programs and Features window to uninstall it.

6. You can also use System Restore from within Safe Mode to restore the system to a previous restore point.

7. If you don't know the source of a problem that prevents a normal startup, but you can launch Safe Mode, you can investigate the problem while in Safe Mode. Use Event Viewer and other detective tools to find information saved during previously failed startups that can help you identify the source of a problem.

Here are some tips about loading Safe Mode that you need to be aware of:

▲ From the Advanced Boot Options menu, first try Safe Mode with Networking. If that doesn't work, try Safe Mode. And if that doesn't work, try Safe Mode with Command Prompt.

▲ Know that Safe Mode won't load if core Windows components are corrupted.

▲ When you load Windows in Safe Mode, all files used for the load are recorded in the Ntbtlog.txt file. Use this file to identify a service, device driver, or application loaded at startup that is causing a problem.

SAFE MODE WITH NETWORKING

Use this option when you are solving a problem with booting and need access to the network to solve the problem. For example, you might need to download updates to your antivirus software. Another example is when you have just attempted to install a printer, which causes the OS to hang when it boots. You can boot into Safe Mode with Networking and download new printer drivers from the network. Uninstall the printer and then install it again from the network. Also use this mode when the Windows installation files are available on the network, rather than the Windows setup CD or DVD, and you need to access those files.

SAFE MODE WITH COMMAND PROMPT

If the first Safe Mode option does not load the OS, then try Safe Mode with command prompt. This Safe Mode option does not load a GUI desktop automatically. You would use it to get a command prompt only. At the command prompt, use the SFC command to verify system files. Also use the Chkdsk command to check for file system errors. If the problem is still not solved, you can use this command to launch System Restore: **C:\Windows\system32\ restore\rstrui.exe**. Then follow the directions on-screen to select a restore point.

ENABLE BOOT LOGGING

When you boot with this option, Windows loads normally and you access the regular desktop. However, all files used during the load process are recorded in a file, C:\Windows\Ntbtlog.txt (see Figure 15-29). Thus, you can use this option to see what did and did not load during the boot. For instance, if you have a problem getting a

Notes The Ntbtlog.txt file is also generated when you boot into Safe Mode.

device to work, check Ntbtlog.txt to see what driver files loaded. Boot logging is much more effective if you have a copy of Ntbtlog.txt that was made when everything worked as it should. Then you can compare the good load to the bad load, looking for differences.

```
ntbtlog.txt - Notepad
File  Edit  Format  View  Help
Did not load driver @msports.inf,%*pnp0401.devicedesc%;ECP Printer Port
Did not load driver @msports.inf,%*pnp0501.devicedesc%;Communications Port
Did not load driver @netrasa.inf,%mp-l2tp-dispname%;WAN Miniport (L2TP)
Did not load driver @netrasa.inf,%mp-bh-dispname%;WAN Miniport (Network Monitor)
Did not load driver @netrasa.inf,%mp-ip-dispname%;WAN Miniport (IP)
Did not load driver @netrasa.inf,%mp-ipv6-dispname%;WAN Miniport (IPv6)
Did not load driver @netrasa.inf,%mp-pppoe-dispname%;WAN Miniport (PPPOE)
Did not load driver @netrasa.inf,%mp-pptp-dispname%;WAN Miniport (PPTP)
Did not load driver @netsstpa.inf,%mp-sstp-dispname%;WAN Miniport (SSTP)
Loaded driver \SystemRoot\System32\Drivers\Fs_Rec.SYS
Loaded driver \SystemRoot\System32\Drivers\Null.SYS
Loaded driver \SystemRoot\System32\Drivers\Beep.SYS
Loaded driver \SystemRoot\System32\drivers\vga.sys
Did not load driver RDPCDD.SYS
Did not load driver RDPENCDD.SYS
Loaded driver \SystemRoot\System32\Drivers\Msfs.SYS
Loaded driver \SystemRoot\System32\Drivers\Npfs.SYS
Did not load driver RasAcd.SYS
Did not load driver tdx.SYS
Did not load driver Smb.SYS
Did not load driver AFD.SYS
Did not load driver netbt.SYS
Did not load driver PSched.SYS
Did not load driver NetBIOS.SYS
```

Figure 15-29 Sample Ntbtlog.txt file
Courtesy: Course Technology/Cengage Learning

Notes If Windows hangs during the boot, try booting using the option Enable Boot Logging. Then look at the last entry in the Ntbtlog.txt file. This entry might be the name of a device driver causing the system to hang.

ENABLE LOW-RESOLUTION VIDEO (640X480)

In Windows XP, this option is called "Enable VGA Mode." Use this option when the video setting does not allow you to see the screen well enough to fix a bad setting. This can happen when a user creates a desktop with black fonts on a black background, or something similar that makes it impossible to see the desktop. Booting in this mode gives you a very plain, standard VGA video. You can then go to the Display settings, correct the problem, and reboot normally. You can also use this option if your video drivers are corrupted and you need to update, roll back, or reinstall your video drivers.

LAST KNOWN GOOD CONFIGURATION

Registry settings collectively called the Last Known Good Configuration are saved in the registry each time the user successfully logs onto the system. If your problem is caused by a bad hardware or software installation and you get an error message the first time you restart the system after the installation, using the Last Known Good can, in effect, undo your installation and solve your problem. Do the following:

1. While startup BIOS is finishing up and just before Windows begins to load, press **F8**. The Advanced Boot Options menu appears (see Figure 15-30 for the Vista menu, but the XP menu is similar). If the problem is so severe that this menu does not appear, then the next step is to boot from the Windows setup CD or DVD.

2. Select **Last Known Good Configuration** (**advanced**) and press **Enter**. The system will reboot.

Remember, the Last Known Good registry settings are saved each time a user logs on to Windows. Therefore, it's important to try the Last Known Good early in the troubleshooting

```
┌─────────────────────────────────────────────────────────────────────┐
│                          Advanced Boot Options                        │
├─────────────────────────────────────────────────────────────────────┤
│                                                                       │
│  Choose Advanced Options for: Windows Setup                           │
│  (Use the arrow keys to highlight your choice.)                       │
│                                                                       │
│      Safe Mode                                                        │
│      Safe Mode with Networking                                        │
│      Safe Mode with Command Prompt                                    │
│                                                                       │
│      Enable Boot Logging                                              │
│      Enable low-resolution video (640x480)                            │
│      Last Known Good Configuration (advanced)                         │
│      Directory Services Restore Mode                                  │
│      Debugging Mode                                                   │
│      Disable automatic restart on system failure                     │
│      Disable Driver Signature Enforcement                            │
│                                                                       │
│      Start Windows Normally                                           │
│                                                                       │
│  Description: Start Windows with only the core drivers and services. Use│
│               when you cannot boot after installing a new device or driver.│
│                                                                       │
│                                                                       │
│                                                                       │
│  ENTER=Choose                                              ESC=Cancel  │
└─────────────────────────────────────────────────────────────────────┘
```

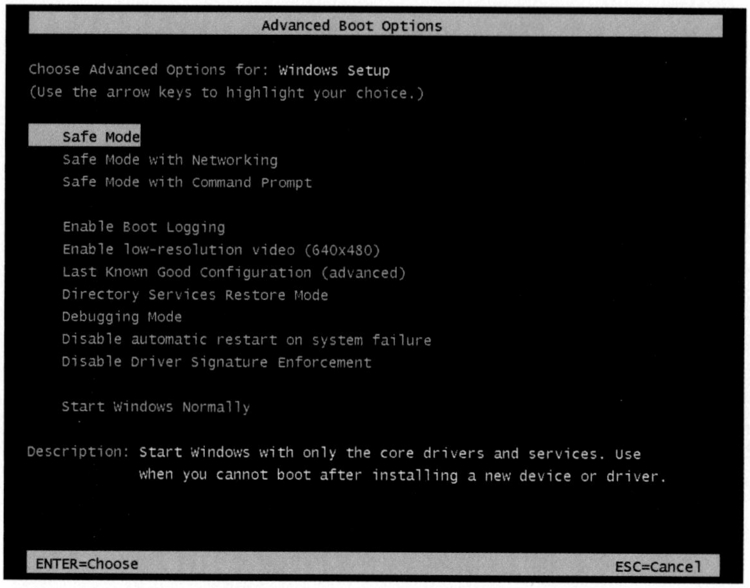

Figure 15-30   Press F8 to see the Advanced Boot Options menu
Courtesy: Course Technology/Cengage Learning

session before it's overwritten. (However, know that if you log onto the system in Safe Mode, the Last Known Good is not saved.) For Windows Vista, if the Last Known Good Configuration doesn't work, your next option is the Startup Repair process in the Windows Recovery Environment.

DIRECTORY SERVICES RESTORE MODE (WINDOWS DOMAIN CONTROLLERS ONLY)

This option applies only to domain controllers and is used as one step in the process of recovering from a corrupted Active Directory. Recall that Active Directory is the domain database managed by a domain controller that tracks users and resources on the domain.

DEBUGGING MODE

This mode gives you the opportunity to move system boot logs from the failing computer to another computer for evaluation. To use this mode, both computers must be connected to each other by way of the serial port. Then, you can reboot into this mode and Windows on the failing computer will send all the boot information through the serial port and on to the other computer. For more details, see the *Windows Vista Resource Kit,* the *Windows XP Professional Resource Kit,* or the *Windows 2000 Professional Resource Kit* (Microsoft Press).

DISABLE AUTOMATIC RESTART ON SYSTEM FAILURE

By default, Windows automatically restarts immediately after it encounters a system failure, which is also called a stop error or a blue screen error. This type of error can be especially troublesome if you're trying to shut down a system and it encounters an error. The error can cause the system to continually reboot rather than shut down. For Windows Vista or XP, choose **Disable automatic restart on system failure** to stop the rebooting. (The option is not on the Windows 2000 Advanced Options menu.)

From the Windows desktop, you can modify this same setting using the System Properties window. Click the **Advanced** tab. For Windows Vista and XP, under Startup and Recovery, click **Settings**, and, for Windows 2000, click **Startup and Recovery**. On the Startup and Recovery window, uncheck **Automatically restart**, as shown earlier in Figure 15-17. The next time the system encounters a stop error, it will shut down and not automatically restart.

THE WINDOWS RECOVERY ENVIRONMENT (WINDOWS RE)

The Windows Vista Recovery Environment (RecEnv.exe), also known as Windows RE, is an operating system launched from the Vista DVD that provides a graphical and command-line interface. Our goal in this section is to help you become familiar with Windows RE, and, in Chapter 16, you'll learn to use it to solve startup problems.

Follow these steps to start up and explore Windows RE:

1. Using a computer that has Windows Vista installed, boot from the Vista setup DVD. (To boot from a DVD, you might have to change the boot sequence in BIOS setup to put the optical drive first above the hard drive.) Select your language preference, as shown in Figure 15-31, and click **Next**.

Figure 15-31 Select your language preference
Courtesy: Course Technology/Cengage Learning

2. The Install Windows screen appears, as shown in Figure 15-32. Click **Repair your computer**. The recovery environment (RecEnv.exe) launches and displays the System Recovery Options dialog box (see Figure 15-33).

3. Select the Vista installation to repair and click **Next**.

4. The System Recovery Options window in Figure 15-34 appears, listing recovery options.

5. The first tool, Startup Repair, can automatically fix many Windows problems, including those caused by corrupted or missing system files. You can't cause any additional problems by using it and it's easy to use. Therefore, it should be your first recovery

Figure 15-32   Launch Windows RE after booting from the Vista DVD
Courtesy: Course Technology/Cengage Learning

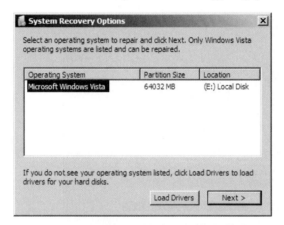

Figure 15-33   Select a Vista installation to repair
Courtesy: Course Technology/Cengage Learning

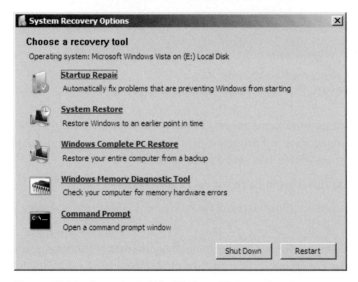

Figure 15-34   Recovery tools in Windows RE
Courtesy: Course Technology/Cengage Learning

option when Vista refuses to load. Click **Startup Repair** and the tool will examine the system for errors (see Figure 15-35).

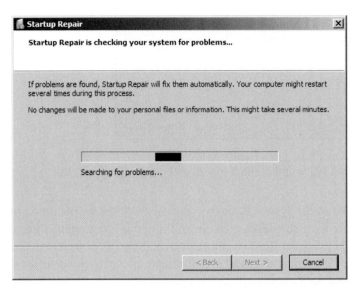

Figure 15-35 Startup Repair searches the system for problems it can fix
Courtesy: Course Technology/Cengage Learning

6. Based on what it finds, it will suggest various solutions. For example, it might suggest you use System Restore or suggest you immediately reboot the system to see if the problem has been fixed. For the system in Figure 15-36, a reboot is suggested.

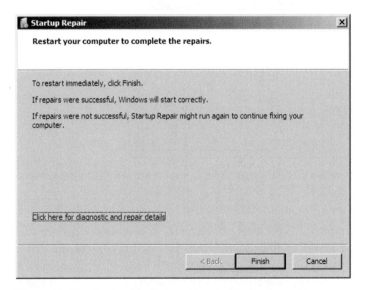

Figure 15-36 Startup Repair has attempted to fix the problem
Courtesy: Course Technology/Cengage Learning

7. To see a list of items examined and actions taken by Startup Repair, click **Click here for diagnostic and repair details**. The dialog box showing the list of repairs appears, as shown in Figure 15-37. A log file can also be found at C:\Windows\System32\LogFiles\SRT\ SRTTrail.txt.

A+
220-701
2.2
3.4

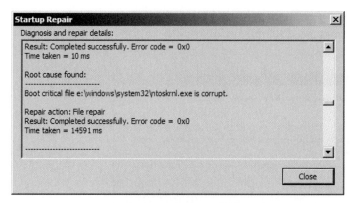

Figure 15-37 Details of actions taken by Startup Repair
Courtesy: Course Technology/Cengage Learning

8. System Restore in the System Recovery Options window works the same as Windows System Restore from the desktop to return the system to its state when a restore point was made. Click **System Restore** and then click **Next**; a list of restore points appears (see Figure 15-38). Select the most recent restore point to make the least intrusive changes to the system.

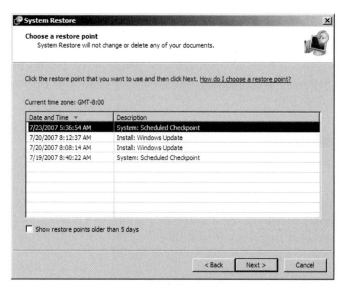

Figure 15-38 Select the most recent restore point to make fewer changes to the system
Courtesy: Course Technology/Cengage Learning

9. Windows Complete PC Restore can be used to completely restore drive C and possibly other drives to their state when the last backups of the drives were made. The backups are made using Complete PC Backup, which you learned about in Chapter 13. When you use Complete PC Restore, everything on the hard drive is lost because the restore process completely erases the drive and restores the OS, user information, applications, and data as they were captured at the time the last Complete PC Backup was made. Therefore, before using Complete PC Restore, consider how old the backup is. Perhaps you can use it to restore drive C and then boot into Windows, reinstall applications installed since the last backup, and use other backups of data more recent than the last Complete PC Backup was made to restore the data.

A+
220-701
2.2
3.4

10. Use the Windows Memory Diagnostic Tool, which you learned to use earlier in the chapter, to test memory.

11. Click **Command Prompt** to open a command prompt window. See Figure 15-39 for an example of this window where the diskpart command is being used. You can use this window to repair a corrupted Vista system or recover data. Commands to use in this window are covered later in the chapter.

Figure 15-39 The command prompt window resembles the Windows XP Recovery Console
Courtesy: Course Technology/Cengage Learning

12. As you use a tool in the System Recovery Options window, be sure to reboot after each attempt to fix the problem to make sure the problem has not been resolved before you try another tool. To exit the Recovery Environment, click **Shut Down** or **Restart**.

THE COMMAND PROMPT WINDOW IN WINDOWS RE

Use the command prompt window in Windows RE when graphical tools available in Windows RE fail to solve the Vista problem. In the following subsections, we'll look at some commands that are helpful when solving boot problems. In Chapter 13, you learned about other commands, some of which can be used in the Windows RE command prompt window.

COMMANDS TO REPAIR SYSTEM FILES, BOOT RECORDS, AND PARTITIONS

Table 15-3 lists some commands that can help you repair a system. To get helpful information about a command, enter the command followed by /?, such as **bcdedit /?**.

> **Note** For a complete list of Diskpart commands, go to the Microsoft support site (*support.microsoft.com*) and search on "DiskPart Command-Line Options."

COMMANDS TO RESTORE THE REGISTRY

If key registry files are corrupted or deleted, the system will not start. You can use the Windows RE command prompt window to restore registry files using those saved in the C:\Windows\System32\Config\RegBack folder. This RegBack folder contains partial backups of the registry files put there after a successful boot. Use the commands in Table 15-4 to restore the registry files.

15

A+ 220-701

Command Line	Description
Bootrec /scanOS	Scans the hard drive for Windows installations not stored in the BCD
Bootrec /rebuildBCD	Scans for Windows installations and rebuilds the BCD
Bcdedit	Manually edits BCD; be sure to make a copy of the file before you edit it
Bootrec /fixboot	Repairs the boot sector of the system partition
Bootrec /fixmbr	Repairs the MBR
Diskpart	Manages partitions and volumes
	Enter the command to open a DISKPART> command prompt and then use these commands:
	Clean—Removes any partition or volume information from the selected drive. Can be used to remove dynamic disk information or a corrupted partition table
	List disk—Lists installed hard drives
	List partition—Lists partitions on selected drive
	Select disk—Selects a hard drive. For example: *select disk 0*
	Select partition—Selects a partition on the selected drive
	Active—Makes the selected partition the active partition
	Inactive—Makes the selected partition inactive
Bootsect	Repairs problems with dual-booting PCs. You can also use the command to remove Vista from a dual-boot configuration so that you can delete an old operating system used in the dual boot.
Chkdsk c: /r	Repairs errors on drive C

Table 15-3 Commands used in the command prompt window of Windows RE to repair system files and the file system

Command Line	Description
1. c:	Makes drive C the current drive.
2. cd \windows\system32\config	Makes the Windows registry folder the current folder.
3. ren default default.save	Renames the five registry files.
4. ren sam sam.save	
5. ren security security.save	
6. ren software software.save	
7. ren system system.save	
8. cd regback	Makes the registry backup folder the current folder.
9. copy system c:\windows\system32\config	For hardware problems, first try copying just the System hive from the backup folder to the registry folder and then reboot.

Table 15-4 Steps to restore the registry files

A+
220-701
2.2
3.4

Command Line	Description
10. copy software c:\windows\system32\config	For software problems, first try copying just the Software hive to the registry folder, and then reboot.
11. copy system c:\windows\system32\config 12. copy software c:\windows\system32\config 13. copy default c:\windows\system32\config 14. copy sam c:\windows\system32\config 15. copy security c:\windows\system32\config	If the problem is still not solved, try copying all five hives to the registry folder and reboot.

Table 15-4 Steps to restore the registry files (continued)

After you try each fix, reboot the system to see if the problem is solved before you do the next fix.

WINDOWS 2000/XP TOOLS FOR SOLVING STARTUP PROBLEMS

To know how to support the Windows 2000/XP boot process, it's not necessary to understand every detail of this process, but it does help to have a general understanding of the more important steps. In this part of the chapter, you learn what happens during the boot process and about the Boot.ini file. Then you'll learn about tools that can help when Windows 2000/XP gives startup problems, including the Advanced Options Menu, the Windows 2000/XP Boot Disk, the Recovery Console, and the Windows 2000 Emergency Repair process.

WHAT HAPPENS WHEN WINDOWS 2000/XP STARTS UP

A Windows 2000/XP system has started up when the user has logged on, the Windows desktop is loaded, and the hourglass associated with the pointer has disappeared. Table 15-5 outlines the steps in the boot sequence for Intel-based computers up to the point that the boot loader program, Ntldr, turns control over to the Windows core component program, Ntoskrnl.exe.

Step	Step Performed By	Description
1.	Startup BIOS	Startup BIOS runs the POST (power-on self test).
2.	Startup BIOS	Startup BIOS turns to the hard drive to find an OS. It first loads the MBR (Master Boot Record) and runs the master boot program within the MBR. (Recall that the master boot program is at the very beginning of the hard drive, before the partition table information.)
3.	MBR program	The MBR program uses partition table information to find the active partition. It then loads the OS boot sector (also called the OS boot record) from the active partition and runs the program in this boot sector.
4.	Boot sector program	This boot sector program launches Ntldr (NT Loader).

Table 15-5 Steps in the Windows 2000/XP boot process for systems with Intel-based processors

15

A+ 220-701

A+
220-701
2.2
3.4

Step	Step Performed By	Description
5.	Ntldr, the Windows 2000/XP boot-strap loader program	Ntldr changes the processor from real mode to 32-bit flat memory mode, in which 32-bit code can be executed.
6.	Ntldr	Ntldr launches the minifile system drivers so that files can be read from either a FAT system or an NTFS file system on the hard drive.
7.	Ntldr	Ntldr reads the Boot.ini file, a hidden text file that contains information about installed OSs on the hard drive. Using this information, Ntldr builds the boot loader menu described in the file. The menu is displayed if Ntldr recognizes a dual-boot system or sees a serious problem with the boot (see Figure 15-40). Using the menu, a user can decide which OS to load or accept the default selection by waiting for the preset time to expire.
8.	Ntldr	If the user chooses an OS other than Windows 2000/XP, then Ntldr runs Bootsect.dos and Ntldr is terminated. Bootsect.dos is responsible for loading the other OS.
9.	Ntldr	If the user chooses Windows 2000/XP, then the loader runs Ntdetect.com, a 16-bit real mode program that queries the computer for time and date (taken from CMOS RAM) and surveys hardware (buses, drives, mouse, ports). Ntdetect passes the information back to Ntldr. This information is used later to update the Windows 2000/XP registry concerning the Last Known Good hardware profile used.
10.	Ntldr	Ntldr then loads Ntoskrnl.exe, Hal.dll, and the System hive. Recall that the System hive is a portion of the Windows 2000/XP registry that includes hardware information used to load the proper device drivers for the hardware that's present. Ntldr then loads these device drivers.
11.	Ntldr	Ntldr passes control to Ntoskrnl.exe; Ntoskrnl.exe continues to load the Windows desktop and the supporting Windows environment.

Table 15-5　Steps in The Windows 2000/XP boot process for systems with Intel-based processors (continued)

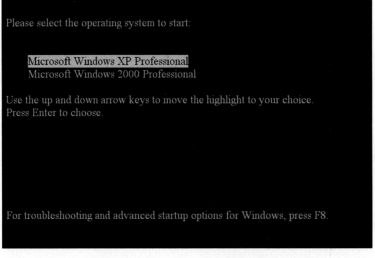

Figure 15-40　The Windows 2000/XP boot loader menu allows the user to choose which OS to load
Courtesy: Course Technology/Cengage Learning

FILES NEEDED TO START WINDOWS 2000/XP

The files needed to boot Windows 2000/XP successfully are listed in Table 15-6. Several of these system files form the core components of Windows 2000/XP.

File	Location and Description
Ntldr	▲ Located in the root folder of the system partition (usually C:\) ▲ Boot-strap loader program
Boot.ini	▲ Located in the root folder of the system partition (usually C:\) ▲ Text file contains boot parameters
Bootsect.dos	▲ Located in the root folder of the system partition (usually C:\) ▲ Used to load another OS in a dual-boot environment
Ntdetect.com	▲ Located in the root folder of the system partition (usually C:\) ▲ Real-mode program detects hardware present
Ntbootdd.sys	▲ Located in the root folder of the system partition (usually C:\) ▲ Required only if a SCSI boot device is used
Ntoskrnl.exe	▲ Located in \%SystemRoot%\system32 folder of the boot partition (usually C:\Windows\system32) ▲ Core component of the OS executive and kernel services
Hal.dll	▲ Located in \%SystemRoot%\system32 folder of the boot partition (usually C:\Windows\system32) ▲ Hardware abstraction layer
Ntdll.dll	▲ Located in \%SystemRoot%\system32 folder of the boot partition (usually C:\Windows\system32) ▲ Intermediating service to executive services; provides many support functions
Win32k.sys Kernel32.dll Advapi32.dll User32.dll Gdi32.dll	▲ Located in \%SystemRoot%\system32 folder of the boot partition (usually C:\Windows\system32) ▲ Core components of the Win32 subsystem
System	▲ Located in \%SystemRoot%\system32\config folder of the boot partition (usually C:\Windows\system32\config) ▲ Registry hive that holds hardware configuration data, including which device drivers need loading at startup
Device drivers	▲ Located in \%SystemRoot%\system32\drivers folder of the boot partition (usually C:\Windows\system32\drivers) ▲ Windows and third-party drivers needed for startup
Pagefile.sys	▲ Located in the root folder of the system partition (usually C:\) ▲ Virtual memory swap file

Table 15-6 Files needed to boot Windows 2000/XP successfully

Notes When repairing a corrupted hard drive, a support person often copies files from one PC to another. However, the Bootsect.dos file contains information from the partition table for a particular hard drive and cannot be successfully copied from another PC.

A+
220-701
2.2
3.4

THE BOOT.INI FILE

One key file used by Windows 2000/XP startup is Boot.ini. Recall that the Boot.ini file is a hidden text file stored in the root directory of the active partition that Ntldr reads to see what operating systems are available and how to set up the boot. You can view and edit the Boot.ini file, which might be necessary when you are trying to solve a difficult boot problem. Figure 15-41 shows an example of a Boot.ini file for Windows XP. Figure 15-42 shows a similar file for a system that uses a Windows 2000 and Windows XP dual boot.

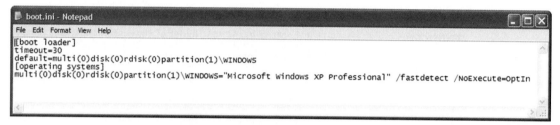

Figure 15-41   A sample Windows XP Boot.ini file
Courtesy: Course Technology/Cengage Learning

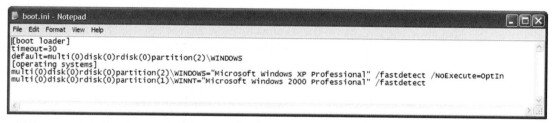

Figure 15-42   A sample Boot.ini file on a dual-boot system
Courtesy: Course Technology/Cengage Learning

Before you can view or edit the Boot.ini file using a text editor such as Notepad, you must first change the folder options to view hidden system files. To do so, open **Windows Explorer**, select the root directory, click **Tools** on the menu bar, click **Folder Options**, and then select the **View** tab. Uncheck the option to **Hide protected operating system files**.

There are two main sections in Boot.ini: the [boot loader] section and the [operating systems] section. The [boot loader] section contains the number of seconds the system gives the user to select an operating system before it loads the default operating system; this is called a timeout. In Figure 15-41, the timeout is set to 30 seconds, the default value. If the system is set for a dual boot, the path to the default operating system is also listed in the [boot loader] section. In Figure 15-42, you can see the default OS is loaded from the \Windows folder in the second partition.

The [operating systems] section of the Boot.ini file provides a list of operating systems that can be loaded, including the path to the boot partition of each operating system. Here is the meaning of each entry in Figure 15-42:

- *Multi(0).* Use the first hard drive controller.
- *Disk(0).* Use only when booting from a SCSI hard drive.
- *Rdisk(0).* Use the first hard drive.
- *Partition(1).* Use the first partition on the drive.

A+
220-701
2.2
3.4

Switches are sometimes used in the [operating systems] section. In Figure 15-41, the first switch used in this Boot.ini file is /fastdetect, which causes the OS not to attempt to inspect any peripherals connected to a COM port (serial port) at startup.

The second switch is /NoExecute=OptIn. This switch is new with Windows XP Service Pack 2 and is used to configure Data Execution Prevention (DEP). DEP stops a program if it tries to use a protected area of memory, which some viruses attempt to do.

Although you can change the Boot.ini file by editing it, a better way to make changes is by using the System Properties box. To access it, right-click My Computer and select Properties from the shortcut menu. Several of the startup and recovery options that you can change in this box are recorded as changes to Boot.ini.

> **Notes** Many technical people use the terms "boot" and "startup" interchangeably. However, in general, the term "boot" refers to the hardware phase of starting up a computer. Microsoft consistently uses the term "startup" to refer to how its operating systems are booted, well, started, I mean.

ADVANCED OPTIONS MENU

As a PC boots and the "Starting Windows" message appears at the bottom of the screen, press the F8 key to display the Windows XP **Advanced Options menu,** which is shown in Figure 15-43, or the Windows 2000 Advanced Options menu, which is shown in Figure 15-44. This menu can be used to diagnose and fix problems when booting Windows 2000/XP. The purpose of each menu option is outlined earlier in the chapter.

WINDOWS 2000/XP BOOT DISK

A Windows 2000/XP boot disk can be used to boot the system bypassing the boot files stored in the root directory of drive C. If you boot from the disk and the Windows 2000/XP desktop loads successfully, then the problem is associated with damaged sectors or missing or damaged files in the root directory of drive C that are required to boot the OS. These sectors

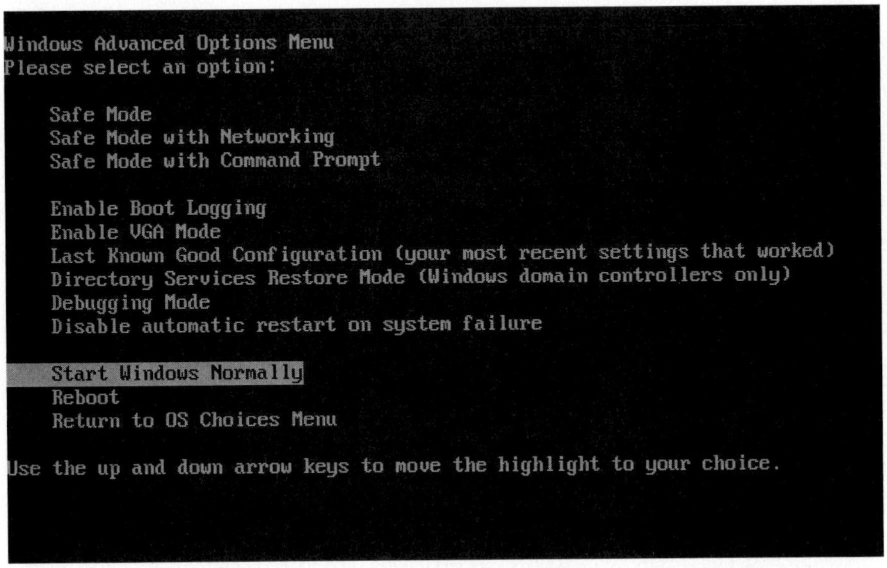

15

A+ 220-701

```
Windows Advanced Options Menu
Please select an option:

    Safe Mode
    Safe Mode with Networking
    Safe Mode with Command Prompt

    Enable Boot Logging
    Enable VGA Mode
    Last Known Good Configuration (your most recent settings that worked)
    Directory Services Restore Mode (Windows domain controllers only)
    Debugging Mode
    Disable automatic restart on system failure

    Start Windows Normally
    Reboot
    Return to OS Choices Menu

Use the up and down arrow keys to move the highlight to your choice.
```

Figure 15-43 Press the F8 key at startup to display the Windows XP Advanced Options menu
Courtesy: Course Technology/Cengage Learning

```
Windows 2000 Advanced Options Menu
Please select an option:

        Safe Mode
        Safe Mode with Networking
        Safe Mode with Command Prompt

        Enable Boot Logging
        Enable VGA Mode
        Last Known Good Configuration
        Directory Services Restore Mode (Windows 2000 domain controllers only)
        Debugging Mode

        Boot Normally

Use ↑ and ↓ to move the highlight to your choice.
Press Enter to choose.
```

Figure 15-44   The Windows 2000 Advanced Options menu
Courtesy: Course Technology/Cengage Learning

and files include the master boot program; the partition table; the OS boot record; the boot files Ntldr file, Ntdetect.com file, and Ntbootdd.sys (if it exists); and the Boot.ini file. In addition, the problem can be caused by a boot sector virus. However, a boot disk cannot be used to troubleshoot problems associated with unstable device drivers or any other system files stored in the \Windows folder or its subfolders.

You first create the boot disk by formatting the disk using a working Windows 2000/XP computer and then copying files to the disk. These files can be copied from a Windows 2000/XP setup CD, or a Windows 2000/XP computer that is using the same version of Windows XP or Windows 2000 as the problem PC. Do the following to create the disk:

1. Obtain a floppy disk and format it on a Windows 2000/XP computer.

2. Using Explorer, copy Ntldr and Ntdetect.com from the \i386 folder on the Windows 2000/XP setup CD or a Windows 2000/XP computer to the root of the floppy disk.

3. If your computer boots from a SCSI hard drive, then obtain a device driver (*.sys) for your SCSI hard drive, rename it **Ntbootdd.sys,** and copy it to the root of the floppy disk. (If you used an incorrect device driver, then you will receive an error after booting from the floppy disk. The error will mention a "computer disk hardware configuration problem" and that it "could not read from the selected boot disk." If this occurs, contact your computer manufacturer or hard drive manufacturer for the correct version of the SCSI hard drive device driver for your computer.)

4. Look at Boot.ini on the problem computer, and then obtain an identical copy from another known good computer (or create your own) and copy it to the root of the floppy disk.

5. If you can't find a good Boot.ini file to copy, you can use the lines listed below to create a Boot.ini file. These lines work for a Boot.ini file if the problem computer is booting from an IDE hard drive:

```
[boot loader]

timeout=30

default=multi(0)disk(0)rdisk(0)partition(1)\WINDOWS

[operating systems]

multi(0)disk(0)rdisk(0)partition(1)\WINDOWS="Microsoft Windows
XP Professional" /fastdetect
```

A+
220-701
2.2
3.4

6. Write-protect the floppy disk so that it cannot become infected with a virus.

7. You have now created the Windows 2000/XP boot disk. Check BIOS setup to make sure the first boot device is set to the floppy disk, and then insert the boot disk and reboot your computer.

> **♥ Tip**   If you are creating your own Boot.ini file, be sure to enter a hard return after the /fastdetect switch in the last line of the file.

> **Notes** To learn more about the Windows XP boot disk, see the Microsoft Knowledge Base Articles 305595 and 314503 at the Microsoft Web site *support.microsoft.com*. To learn more about the Windows 2000 boot disk, see the Microsoft Knowledge Base Article 301680.

If the Windows 2000/XP desktop loads successfully, then do the following to attempt to repair the Windows 2000/XP installation:

1. Load the Recovery Console and use the Fixmbr and Fixboot commands to repair the MBR and the OS boot sector.

2. Run antivirus software.

3. Use Disk Management to verify that the hard drive partition table is correct.

4. Defragment your hard drive.

5. Copy Ntldr, Ntdetect.com, and Boot.ini from your floppy disk to the root of the hard drive.

6. If you're using a SCSI hard drive, copy Ntbootdd.sys from your floppy disk to the root of the hard drive.

If the Windows 2000/XP desktop did not load by booting from the boot disk, then the next tool to try is the Recovery Console.

RECOVERY CONSOLE

The Advanced Options Menu can help if the problem is a faulty device driver or system service. However, if the problem goes deeper than that, the next tool to use is the Recovery Console. Use it when Windows 2000/XP does not start properly or hangs during the load. It works even when core Windows system files are corrupted. The Recovery Console is a command-driven operating system that does not use a GUI. With it, you can access the FAT16, FAT32, and NTFS file systems.

Using the Recovery Console, you can:

▲ Repair a damaged registry, system files, or file system on the hard drive.

▲ Enable or disable a service or device driver.

▲ Repair the master boot program on the hard drive or the boot sector on the system partition.

15

A+ 220-701

◢ Repair a damaged Boot.ini file.

◢ Recover data when the Windows installation is beyond repair.

The Recovery Console is designed so that someone can't maliciously use it to gain unauthorized access. You must enter the Administrator password in order to use the Recovery Console and access an NTFS volume. Unless you first set certain parameters, you are not allowed into all folders, and you cannot copy files from the hard drive to a removable media. If the registry is so corrupted that the Recovery Console cannot read the password in order to validate it, you are not asked for the password, but you are limited in what you can do at the Recovery Console.

Now let's look at a list of Recovery Console commands, how to access the Recovery Console, how to use it to perform several troubleshooting tasks, and how to install the Recovery Console on the boot loader menu.

LIST OF RECOVERY CONSOLE COMMANDS

As a summary reference, Table 15-7 lists Recovery Console commands and their descriptions.

Command	Description	Examples
Attrib	Changes the attributes of a file or folder.	To remove the read-only, hidden, and system attributes from the file: `C:\> Attrib -r -h -s filename`

Batch	Carries out commands stored in a batch file.	To execute the commands in File1:
		
		`C:\> Batch File1.bat`
		
		To execute the commands in File1 and store the results of the commands to File2:
		
		`C:\> Batch File1.bat File2.txt`

Cd	Displays or changes the current folder. It cannot be used to change drives.	To change folders to the C:\Windows\system folder:
		
		`C:\> Cd C:\windows\system`
		
		`C:\windows\system>`

Chkdsk	Checks a disk and repairs or recovers the data.	To check drive C: and repair it: `C:\> Chkdsk C: /r`
Cls	Clears the screen.	`C:\> Cls`
Copy	Copies a single file. Use the command to replace corrupted system files or save data files to another media when the hard drive is failing.	To copy the file File1 on the CD to the hard drive's Winnt folder, naming the file File2: `C:\> Copy D:\File1 C:\Winnt\File2`
Del	Deletes a file.	To delete File2: `C:\Winnt> Del File2`
Dir	Lists files and folders. Wildcard characters are allowed.	To list all files with an .exe file extension: `C:\> Dir *.exe`

Table 15-7 Commands available from the Recovery Console

A+
220-701
2.2
3.4

Command	Description	Examples
Disable	Disables a service or driver. Use it to disable a service or driver that starts and prevents the system from booting properly. After you disable the service, restart the system to see if your problem is solved.	To disable the Event Log service: `C:\> Disable eventlog`
Diskpart	Creates and deletes partitions on the hard drive.	Enter the command with no arguments to display a user interface: `C:\> Diskpart`
Enable	Displays the status and enables a Windows system service or driver.	To display the status of the Event Log service: `C:\> Enable eventlog`
Exit	Quits the Recovery Console and restarts the computer.	`C:\> Exit`

Expand	Expands compressed files and extracts files from cabinet files and copies the files to the destination folder.	To extract File1 from the Drivers.cab file:
		`C:\> Expand D:\i386\Drivers.cab -f:File1`
		To expand the compressed file, File1.cp_:
		`C:\> Expand File1.cp_`

Fixboot	Rewrites the OS boot sector on the hard drive. If a drive letter is not specified, the system drive is assumed.	To repair the OS boot sector of drive C: `C:\> Fixboot C:`
Fixmbr	Rewrites the Master Boot Record boot program.	To repair the Master Boot Record boot program: `C:\> Fixmbr`

Format	Formats a logical drive. If no file system is specified, NTFS is assumed.	To format using the NTFS file system:
		`C:\> Format D:`
		To format using the FAT32 file system:
		`C:\> Format D:/fs:FAT32`

Help	Help utility appears for the given command.	To get help with the Fixboot command: `C:\> Help fixboot`
Listsvc	Lists all available services. This command has no parameters.	`C:\> Listsvc`
Logon	Allows you to log onto an installation with the Administrator password. Use it to log onto a second installation of Windows in a dual-boot environment.	When logged onto the first Windows installation, use this command to log onto the second installation: `C:\> logon 2` If you don't enter the password correctly after three tries, the system automatically reboots.
Map	Lists all drive letters and file system types.	`C:\> Map`

Table 15-7 Commands available from the Recovery Console (continued)

15

A+ 220-701

Command	Description	Examples
Md or Mkdir	Creates a folder.	`C:\> MD C:\TEMP`
More or Type	Displays a text file on-screen.	`C:\> Type filename.txt`
Rd or Rmdir	Deletes a directory.	`C:\> RD C:\TEMP`
Rename or Ren	Renames a file.	`C:\> Rename File1.txt File2.txt`
Set	Displays or sets Recovery Console environmental variables.	**To turn off the prompt when you are overwriting files:** `C:\> Set nocopyprompt=true`
Systemroot	Sets the current directory to the directory where Windows 2000/XP is installed.	`C:\> Systemroot` `C:\WINDOWS>`

Table 15-7   Commands available from the Recovery Console (continued)

APPLYING CONCEPTS   HOW TO ACCESS THE RECOVERY CONSOLE

The Recovery Console software is on the Windows 2000/XP setup CD and the four Windows 2000 setup disks. You can launch the Recovery Console from the CD or four disks, or manually install the Recovery Console on the hard drive and launch it from there.

How to access the Recovery Console using Windows XP. For Windows XP, to use the Recovery Console, insert the Windows XP setup CD in the CD drive and restart the system. When the Windows XP Setup opening menu appears (see Figure 15-45), press **R** to load the Recovery Console.

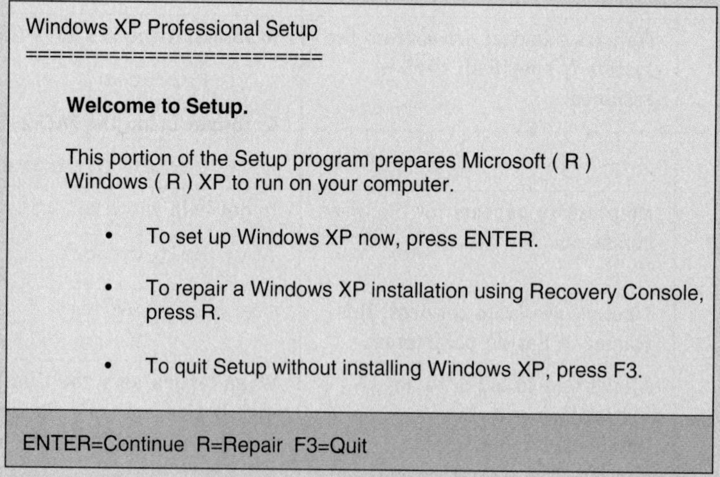

```
Windows XP Professional Setup
=============================

    Welcome to Setup.

    This portion of the Setup program prepares Microsoft ( R )
    Windows ( R ) XP to run on your computer.

        •   To set up Windows XP now, press ENTER.

        •   To repair a Windows XP installation using Recovery Console,
            press R.

        •   To quit Setup without installing Windows XP, press F3.

ENTER=Continue  R=Repair  F3=Quit
```

Figure 15-45   Windows XP Setup opening menu
Courtesy: Course Technology/Cengage Learning

Access the Recovery Console using Windows 2000. For Windows 2000, you can boot from the Windows 2000 setup CD or you can boot from the four setup disks. Use the four setup disks if the computer will not boot from a CD drive. If you have not already created the Windows 2000 setup

A+
220-701
2.2
3.4

disks, you can go to a working Windows 2000 PC and create the disks by following the directions given in Chapter 12. Follow these steps to load Windows 2000 from the disks or from the setup CD and access the Recovery Console:

1. Insert the first of the four setup disks, and restart the PC. You are directed to insert each of the four disks in turn, and then the Setup screen appears, as shown in Figure 15-46. If you boot from the Windows 2000 setup CD, the same screen appears.

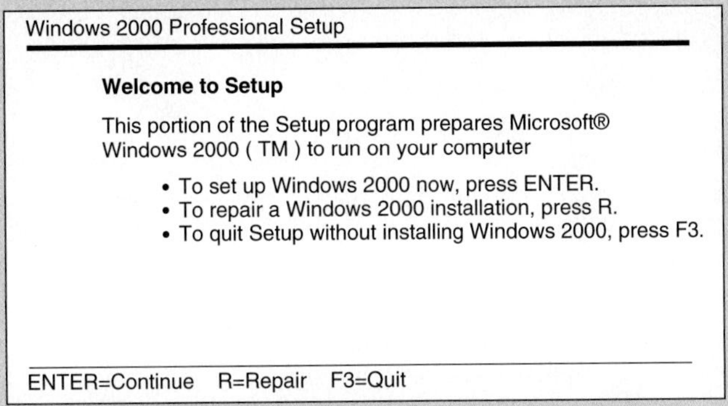

```
Windows 2000 Professional Setup
─────────────────────────────────────

   Welcome to Setup

   This portion of the Setup program prepares Microsoft®
   Windows 2000 ( TM ) to run on your computer

        • To set up Windows 2000 now, press ENTER.
        • To repair a Windows 2000 installation, press R.
        • To quit Setup without installing Windows 2000, press F3.




─────────────────────────────────────
ENTER=Continue    R=Repair    F3=Quit
```

Figure 15-46 Use this Windows 2000 Setup screen to access the Recovery Console
Courtesy: Course Technology/Cengage Learning

2. Type **R** to select the "To repair a Windows 2000 installation" option. The Windows 2000 Repair Options window opens (see Figure 15-47). Type **C** to select the Recovery Console.

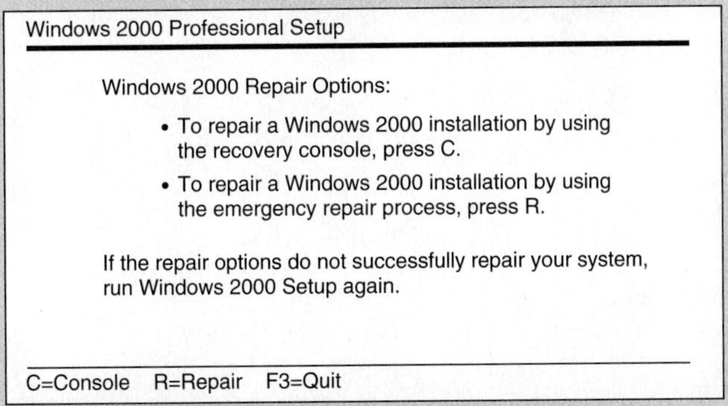

```
Windows 2000 Professional Setup
─────────────────────────────────────

   Windows 2000 Repair Options:

        • To repair a Windows 2000 installation by using
          the recovery console, press C.
        • To repair a Windows 2000 installation by using
          the emergency repair process, press R.

   If the repair options do not successfully repair your system,
   run Windows 2000 Setup again.


─────────────────────────────────────
C=Console    R=Repair    F3=Quit
```

Figure 15-47 Windows 2000 offers two repair options
Courtesy: Course Technology/Cengage Learning

3. Note that as the Recovery Console attempts to load and give you access to the hard drive, it will display one of the following screens depending on the severity of the problem with the drive:

   ◢ If the Recovery Console cannot find the drive, the window in Figure 15-48 appears. Consider the problem hardware related. You might have a totally dead drive.

15

A+ 220-701

A+
220-701
2.2
3.4

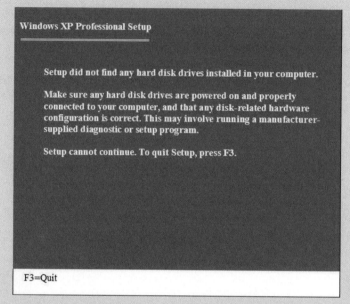

Figure 15-48 Windows setup cannot find a hard drive
Courtesy: Course Technology/Cengage Learning

⬛ If the Console can find the hard drive, but cannot read from it, the window in Figure 15-49 appears. Notice in the window the C prompt (C:\>), which seems to indicate that the Recovery Console can access the hard drive, but the message above the C prompt says otherwise. When you try the DIR command, as shown in Figure 15-49, you find out that drive C: is not available. The Diskpart, Fixmbr, and Fixboot commands might help.

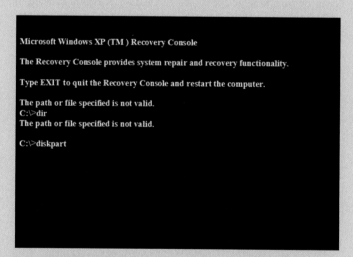

Figure 15-49 The Recovery Console cannot read from the hard drive
Courtesy: Course Technology/Cengage Learning

⬛ If the Console is able to read drive C, but Windows is seriously corrupted, the window in Figure 15-50 appears. Use the DIR command to see what files or folders are still on the drive. Is the \Windows folder present? If not, then you might need to reformat the drive and reinstall Windows. But first try to find any important data that is not backed up.

A+
220-701
2.2
3.4

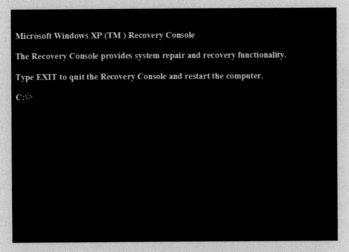

Figure 15-50 The Recovery Console can read drive C, but cannot find a Windows installation
Courtesy: Course Technology/Cengage Learning

◢ If the Console is able to determine that one or more Windows installations is on the drive, it gives you a choice of with which installation you want to work. If only one installation is showing, as in Figure 15-51, type **1** and press **Enter**. Next, you will be asked for the Administrator password. Enter the password and press **Enter**. The command prompt shows the Windows folder is the current working directory. You can now use the Recovery Console to try to find the problem and fix it. How to do that is coming up next.

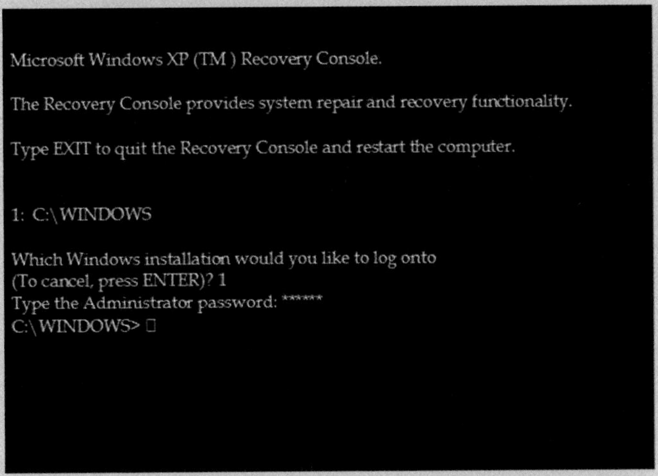

Microsoft Windows XP (TM) Recovery Console.

The Recovery Console provides system repair and recovery functionality.

Type EXIT to quit the Recovery Console and restart the computer.

1: C:\WINDOWS

Which Windows installation would you like to log onto
(To cancel, press ENTER)? 1
Type the Administrator password: ******
C:\WINDOWS>

Figure 15-51 The Recovery Console has found a Windows installation
Courtesy: Course Technology/Cengage Learning

4. To exit the Recovery Console, type **Exit** and press **Enter**. The system will attempt to boot to the Windows desktop.

15

A+ 220-701

A+
220-701
2.2
3.4

USE THE RECOVERY CONSOLE TO FIX HARD DRIVE PROBLEMS

Here are the commands you can use to examine the hard drive structure for errors and possibly fix them:

> **Notes** Here are two useful tips to help you when using the Recovery Console: To retrieve the last command entered, press **F3** at the command prompt. To retrieve the command one character at a time, press the **F1** key.

▲ *Fixmbr and Fixboot.* The Fixmbr command restores the master boot program in the MBR, and the Fixboot command repairs the OS boot record. As you enter each command, you're looking for clues that might indicate at what point the drive has failed. For example, Figure 15-52 shows the results of using the Fixmbr command, which appears to have worked without errors, but the Fixboot command has actually failed. This tells us that most likely the master boot program is healthy, but drive C is not accessible. After using these commands, if you don't see any errors, exit the Recovery Console and try to boot from the hard drive.

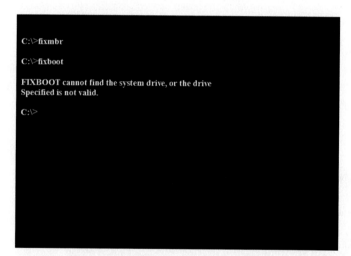

```
C:\>fixmbr

C:\>fixboot

FIXBOOT cannot find the system drive, or the drive
Specified is not valid.

C:\>
```

Figure 15-52 Results of using the Fixmbr and Fixboot commands in the Recovery Console
Courtesy: Course Technology/Cengage Learning

▲ *Diskpart.* Use the Diskpart command to view, create, and delete partitions on the drive. Type **Diskpart** and press **Enter** and a full screen appears, listing the partitions the Console sees on the drive. See Figure 15-53.
▲ *Chkdsk.* Use this command to repair the file system and recover data from bad sectors: **chkdsk C: /r**.

USE THE RECOVERY CONSOLE TO RESTORE THE REGISTRY

Earlier in the chapter, you learned how to use commands in the command prompt window of the Vista Recovery Environment to restore the registry files from backup. These backup hive files are located in the C:\Windows\System32\config\regback folder. You can use a similar group of commands to restore the Windows XP or Windows 2000 registry hive files

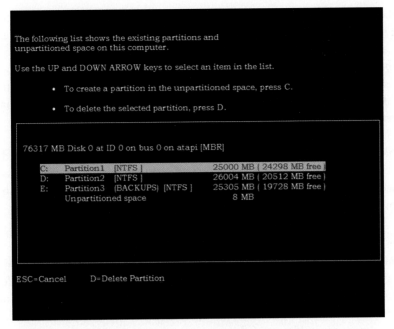

The following list shows the existing partitions and
unpartitioned space on this computer.

Use the UP and DOWN ARROW keys to select an item in the list.

- To create a partition in the unpartitioned space, press C.

- To delete the selected partition, press D.

76317 MB Disk 0 at ID 0 on bus 0 on atapi [MBR]

C:	Partition1	[NTFS]	25000 MB (24298 MB free)
D:	Partition2	[NTFS]	26004 MB (20512 MB free)
E:	Partition3	(BACKUPS) [NTFS]	25305 MB (19728 MB free)
	Unpartitioned space		8 MB

ESC=Cancel   D=Delete Partition

Figure 15-53 Using the Diskpart screen, you can view, delete, and create
partitions
Courtesy: Course Technology/Cengage Learning

from backups. The Windows XP backup files are stored in C:\Windows\System32\
config\repair, and the Windows 2000 backup files are stored in C:\Windows\System32\con-
fig\repair\regback. See Table 15-3 for the commands to use.

USE THE RECOVERY CONSOLE TO DISABLE A SERVICE OR DEVICE DRIVER

Sometimes when Windows fails, it first displays a stop error (blue screen error). The stop
error might give the name of a service or device driver that caused the problem. If the service or driver is critical to Windows operation, booting into Safe Mode won't help because
the service or driver will be attempted in Safe Mode. The solution is to boot the system
using the Recovery Console and copy a replacement program file from the Windows
2000/XP setup CD to the hard drive.

In order to know what program file to replace, you'll need to know the name or description of the service or driver causing the problem. If an error message doesn't give you the
clue you need, you might try to boot to the Advanced Options Menu (press **F8** while booting) and then select **Enable Boot Logging**. Then compare the Ntbtlog.txt file to one generated on a healthy system. You might be able to find the driver or service that caused the
boot to halt.

If you know the service causing the problem, use these commands to list services and disable and enable a service:

- ◢ *Listsvc.* Enter the command Listsvc to see a list of all services currently installed,
  which includes device drivers. The list scrolls on and on, showing the name of each
  service, a brief one-line description, and its status (disabled, manual, or auto). To find
  the service giving the problem, you'll have to have more information than what this
  list shows.
- ◢ *Disable.* Use the Disable command to disable a service. For example, to disable the
  service SharedAccess, which is the Windows Firewall service, use this command: **disable**

A+
220-701
2.2
3.4

sharedaccess. Before you enter the command, be sure to write down the current startup type that is displayed so that you'll know how to enable the service later. For services that are auto-started like this one, the startup type is service_auto_start.

▲ *Enable.* Use the Enable command followed by the name of the service to show the current status of a service. To enable the service, use the startup type in the command line. For example, to reinstate the Firewall service, use this command: **enable sharedaccess service_auto-start.**

If you think you've found the service that is causing the problem, disable it and reboot the system. If the problem disappears or the error message changes, you might have found the right service to replace. The next step is to replace the program file with a fresh copy from the Windows setup CD.

USE THE RECOVERY CONSOLE TO RESTORE SYSTEM FILES

Based on error messages and your research about them, if you think you know which Windows system file is corrupted or missing, you can use the Recovery Console to copy a new set of system files from the Windows setup CD to the hard drive. For example, suppose you get an error message that Ntldr is corrupted or missing. To replace the file, you could execute the commands in Figure 15-54.

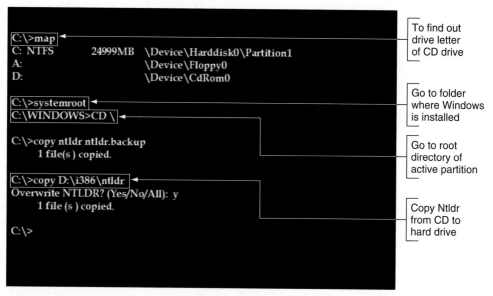

Figure 15-54 Recovery Console command to repair Ntldr
Courtesy: Course Technology/Cengage Learning

Here are other commands to use to restore system files:

▲ *Map.* Displays the current drive letters. This command is useful to find your way around the system, such as when you need to know the drive letter for the CD drive.

▲ *Systemroot.* Use this command to make the Windows directory the default directory (refer to Figure 15-54 for an example of its use).

▲ *CD.* Change directory. For example, to move to the root directory, use **CD \.**

▲ *Delete.* Deletes a file. For example, to delete Ntldr in the Temp directory, use this command: **Delete C:\temp\ntldr.**

▲ *Copy.* To make a backup of the current Ntldr file, use this command:

```
copy ntldr ntldr.backup
```

To copy the Ntldr file from the Windows setup CD to the root directory of the hard drive, use this command:

```
copy D:\i386\ntldr C:\
```

Substitute the drive letter for the CD drive in the command line.

A compressed file uses an underscore as the last character in the file extension; for example, Netapi32.dl_. When you use the Copy command, the file will automatically uncompress. For example, use this command to copy Netapi32.dl_ from the setup CD:

```
copy D:\i386\netapi32.dl_ netapi32.dll
```

▲ *Bootcfg.* This command lets you view and edit the Boot.ini file. Here are useful parameters:

- **bootcfg /list**   Lists entries in Boot.ini
- **bootcfg /copy**   Makes a copy of Boot.ini before you rebuild it
- **bootcfg /rebuild**   Rebuilds the Boot.ini file

▲ *Expand.* When you're looking for a certain file on the Windows 2000/XP setup CD, you'll find cabinet files that hold groups of compressed files (cabinet files have a .cab file extension). Use the Expand command to extract these files. Here are some useful parameters of the Expand command:

To list all files in the driver.cab cabinet file:

```
expand D:\i386\driver.cab -f:* /d
```

To extract a file, first use the Cd command to change the default folder to the location where you want the extracted file to go. Then use the Expand command to extract the file. For example, to extract the Splitter.sys file from the Driver.cab file and copy it from the setup CD to the hard drive, use these two commands:

```
cd C:\windows\system32\drivers
expand D:\i386\driver.cab /f:splitter.sys
```

You can also use the Expand command to uncompress a compressed file. For example, to expand a file and copy it to the current folder, use this command:

```
expand D:\i386\netapi32.dl_
```

USE THE RECOVERY CONSOLE TO RECOVER DATA

If your hard drive is corrupted, you still might be able to recover data. The problem with using the Recovery Console to do the job is that, by default, it will not allow you to go into folders other than the system folders or to copy data onto removable media. To do these tasks, you first need to change some Recovery Console settings. Then you can use the Copy command to copy data from the hard drive to other media.

15

A+ 220-701

Here are the commands you'll need to change the settings:

◢ To allow access to all files and folders on all drives:

```
set allowallpaths=true
```

◢ To allow you to copy any file to another media such as a USB drive or floppy disk:

```
set allowremovablemedia=true
```

◢ To allow the use of wildcard characters * and ?:

```
set allowwildcards=true
```

OPTIONAL INSTALLATION OF THE RECOVERY CONSOLE

Although the Recovery Console can be launched from the Windows setup CD to recover from system failure, you can also install it on your working system so that it appears on the OS boot loader menu. You can then use it to address less drastic problems that occur when you can boot from the hard drive.

To install the Recovery Console:

1. Open a command window.
2. Change from the current directory to the \i386 folder on the Windows 2000/XP CD.
3. Enter the command **winnt32 /cmdcons**. The Recovery Console is installed.
4. Restart your computer. Recovery Console should now be shown with the list of available operating systems on the OS boot loader menu.

WINDOWS 2000 EMERGENCY REPAIR PROCESS

The Windows 2000 Emergency Repair Process should be used only as a last resort because it restores the system to the state it was in immediately after the Windows 2000 installation. All changes made since the installation are lost. The process uses an Emergency Repair Disk (ERD), which contains information about your current installation. The Windows 2000 ERD points to a folder on the hard drive where the registry was backed up when Windows 2000 was installed. This folder is *%SystemRoot%*\repair, which, in most systems, is C:\Winnt\repair.

APPLYING CONCEPTS Using the Windows 2000 ERD to recover from a corrupted registry returns you to the installation version of the registry, and you lose all changes to the registry since that time. Because of the way the ERD works, you do not need to update the disk once you've created it. Before a problem occurs, follow these directions to create the disk:

1. Click **Start**, point to **Programs**, **Accessories**, and **System Tools**, and then click **Backup**. The Backup window appears with the Welcome tab selected (see Figure 15-55). Select **Emergency Repair Disk**.

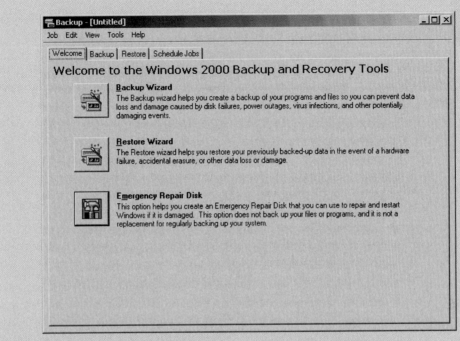

Figure 15-55 Use the Backup window to back up the registry and create an emergency repair disk
Courtesy: Course Technology/Cengage Learning

2. The Backup tab and the Emergency Repair Diskette dialog box open. If you check the box shown in Figure 15-56, the system backs up your registry to a folder under the Repair folder, *%SystemRoot%*\repair\RegBack.

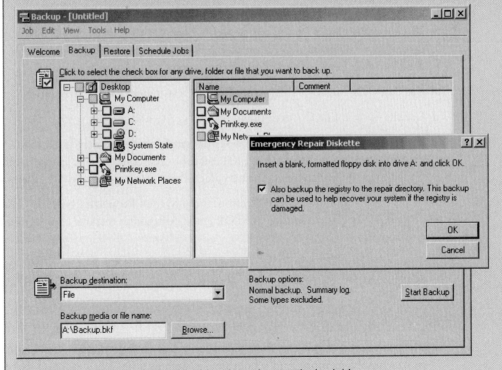

Figure 15-56 Create an ERD and back up the registry to the hard drive
Courtesy: Course Technology/Cengage Learning

3. Click **OK** to create the disk. Label the disk "Windows 2000 Emergency Repair Disk," and keep it in a safe place.

If your hard drive fails, you can use the ERD to restore the system, including system files, boot files, and the registry, to its state at the end of the Windows 2000 installation. Follow these steps:

1. Check BIOS setup to make sure the floppy drive appears before the hard drive in the OS boot order.

2. Boot the PC from the four Windows 2000 setup disks. The Setup menu appears (refer back to Figure 15-46). Select option **R**.

3. When the Windows 2000 Repair Options window opens (refer back to Figure 15-47), select option **R**.

4. You are instructed to insert the Emergency Repair Disk. Follow the instructions on the screen to repair the installation.

5. If this process does not work, then your next option is to reinstall Windows 2000. If you don't plan to reformat the drive, you need to scan the drive for errors before you reinstall Windows. To do that, you can boot to the Recovery Console and use the Chkdsk command to scan the drive for errors. If you suspect that a virus damaged the file system, also use the Fixmbr command to replace the master boot program in case it has been corrupted by the virus.

>> CHAPTER SUMMARY

▲ The Vista Problem Reports and Solution tool and the XP Error Reporting tool can report errors about hardware, applications, and Windows and suggest a solution. In addition, the Vista tool keeps a history of past problems and solutions.

▲ Use the Vista Memory Diagnostics tool to test memory during the boot.

▲ Use the System File Checker (SFC) tool to verify and restore system files.

▲ The Driver Verifier (verifier.exe) tool puts stress on device drivers so that a driver with a problem can be identified. Don't use the tool on a computer unless you understand the potential problems it might cause by degraded performance and STOP errors.

▲ Use the Startup and Recovery section in the System Properties box to keep Windows from automatically restarting after a STOP error. Automatic restarts can put the boot into an endless loop.

▲ Tools to verify that drivers are digitally signed are the File Signature Verification tool (sigverif.exe), the Driver Query tool (driverquery), and the driver Properties box of Device Manager.

▲ Use Device Manager to enable and disable devices and to update and roll back drivers.

▲ The hardware components required for a successful boot are the CPU, motherboard, power supply, memory, and a boot device such as a hard drive or CD drive.

▲ When you first turn on a system, startup BIOS on the motherboard takes control to examine hardware components and find an operating system to load.

▲ Vista startup is managed by the Windows Boot Manager (BootMgr) and the Windows Boot Loader (WinLoad.exe).

▲ The Vista Boot Configuration Data (BCD) file contains information about settings that control BootMgr, WinLoad.exe, WinResume.exe, and the Windows Memory Diagnostic program, settings that launch Ntldr for loading a previous OS in a dual-boot configuration, and settings to load a non-Microsoft operating system.

▲ The Advanced Boot Options menu offers Safe Mode, Safe Mode with networking, Safe Mode with command prompt, enable boot logging, enable low-resolution video (enable VGA mode in Windows XP/2000), Last Known Good Configuration, directory services restore mode, debugging mode, and disable automatic restart on system failure. This last option is not available in Windows 2000.

▲ Windows Vista Recovery Environment can be started from the Vista setup DVD.

▲ The boot process for Windows 2000/XP uses files stored in the root directory of the hard drive and the C:\Windows\system32 folder.

▲ The boot process can be customized with entries in Boot.ini. The Boot.ini file can be edited with a text editor, but it is best to change the file using the System Properties dialog box.

▲ Tools to use to troubleshoot problems with loading Windows 2000/XP are the Advanced Options menu, the boot disk, and the Recovery Console.

▲ The Recovery Console is a command interface with a limited number of commands available to troubleshoot a failing Windows 2000/XP load. The console requires that you enter the Administrator password.

>> KEY TERMS

15

Advanced Options menu
Boot Configuration Data (BCD) file
Boot.ini
Driver Query
Driver Verifier (verifier.exe)
Emergency Repair Disk (ERD)

Emergency Repair Process
File Signature Verification
Last Known Good Configuration
Memory Diagnostics
progress bar
Recovery Console
System File Checker (SFC)

Windows Boot Loader (WinLoad.exe)
Windows Boot Manager (BootMgr)
Windows RE
Windows Vista Recovery Environment (RecEnv.exe)

>> REVIEWING THE BASICS

1. Blue screen errors happen when which type of processes encounter an error?

2. Which Vista tool keeps a record of STOP errors and allows you to view a history of these errors?

3. When you allow Windows XP Error Reporting to send a report to Microsoft of an error, what does Microsoft give in return?

4. What is the command to use the Vista Memory Diagnostics tool?

5. What method can you use to test memory on a Windows XP system by using the Vista Memory Diagnostics tool without having to install Vista on the system?

6. What is the command to use the System File Checker to immediately verify system files? To verify system files on the next restart?

7. Why might it not be wise to use the Driver Verifier tool on a computer that serves up files to an office of 10 people?

8. A blue screen error halts the system while it is booting, and the booting starts over in an endless loop of restarts. How can you solve this problem?

9. What three Windows tools can be used to verify that a driver is digitally signed?

10. What does Windows call the process of undoing a driver update?

11. Is the BootMgr file stored in the boot partition or the system partition?

12. Where is the master boot record (MBR) located?

13. What is the name of the Windows Vista boot loader program? Where is the program located?

14. What is the name of the Vista kernel program?

15. What is the name of the program that manages Windows logon?

16. Which registry hive is loaded first during Windows startup?

17. Where does Windows store device driver files?

18. What is the first thing that BIOS checks?

19. Which key do you press to launch the Advanced Boot Options window during Windows startup?

20. What can you assume about the Vista startup when you see the progress bar on-screen?

21. When is the Windows startup process completed?

22. At what point in Windows startup are the settings that are called the Last Known Good Configuration saved?

23. What command in Windows RE can you use to rebuild the BCD file?

24. What command in Windows RE gives you an opportunity to manage partitions and volumes installed on the system?

25. What is the name and path of the log file created by Vista Startup Repair?

26. If you are having a problem with a driver, which of the following is the least invasive solution: update the driver or use System Restore?

27. What tool can you use to stop a program that is hung?

28. If an application works when the system is loaded in Safe Mode, but does not work when Windows is loaded normally, what can you assume?

29. What are the three stages of the Vista startup process?

30. What is the name of the log file and its location that is created when you enabled boot logging from the Advanced Boot Options startup menu?

31. In the Windows 2000/XP boot process, what is the name of the program file that reads and loads the boot menu?

32. Where is the Boot.ini file stored?

33. What two subfolders in the C:\Windows\system32 folder contain files needed for Windows startup?

>> THINKING CRITICALLY

1. When the Windows Vista registry is corrupted and you cannot boot from the hard drive, what tool or method is the best option to fix the problem?.

   a. Boot into Safe Mode and use System Restore to repair the registry.

   b. Use the Last Known Good Configuration on the Advanced Boot Options menu.

   c. Use commands from the Windows Recovery Environment to recover the registry from backup.

   d. Reinstall Windows Vista using the Complete PC Restore process.

2. Your Windows XP system boots to a blue screen and no desktop. What do you do first?

   a. Reinstall Windows XP.

   b. Attempt to boot into the Advanced Options menu.

   c. Attempt to boot into the Recovery Console.

   d. Attempt to use the Automated System Recovery.

3. You have important data on your hard drive that is not backed up and your Windows installation is so corrupted you know that you must repair the entire installation. What do you do first? Why?

   a. Use System Restore.

   b. Make every attempt to recover the data.

   c. Perform an in-place upgrade of Windows Vista.

   d. Reformat the hard drive and reinstall Windows Vista.

4. As a helpdesk technician, list four good detective questions to ask if a user calls to say, "My PC won't boot."

5. Reword the following questions that might be asked when interviewing a user over the telephone. Your new questions should reflect a more positive attitude toward the user.

   a. Did you drop your laptop?

   b. Did you forget to recharge the laptop battery?

   c. You say the problem is that Microsoft Word is giving an error, but do you really know how to use that application?

>> HANDS-ON PROJECTS

PROJECT 15-1: Support for Your Installed Hardware and Software

Do the following to find out what kind of support and replacement parts are available for your computer:

1. Make a list of all the installed hardware components on your computer that are considered field replaceable components needed to boot the system, including the motherboard, processor, power supply, optical drive, hard drive, and memory.

2. Search the Web for the device manufacturer Web pages that show what support is available for the devices, including any diagnostic software, technical support, and device driver updates.

3. Print a Web page showing a replacement part for each device that fits your system. If possible, show the exact match for a replacement part.

4. Make a list of all installed applications on your computer.

5. For each application, print a Web page showing the support available on the software manufacturer's Web site for the application.

PROJECT 15-2: Practicing Solving Boot Problems

This project is best done on a lab computer rather than your personal computer. Unplug the computer, open the case, and disconnect the data cable to your hard drive. Turn the computer back on and boot the system. What error message did you see? Now reboot using your Windows Vista setup DVD. Try to load the Recovery Environment. What error messages did you receive, if any? Power down your computer, unplug it, and reconnect your hard drive. Reboot and verify that Windows Vista loads successfully.

PROJECT 15-3: Practicing Using the Recovery Environment

Boot from the Vista DVD and launch the Recovery Environment. Then do the following:

1. Execute the Startup Repair Process. What were the results?

2. Execute System Restore. What is the most recent restore point? (Do not apply the restore point.)

3. Using the command prompt window, open the Registry Editor. What command did you use? Close the editor.

4. Using the command prompt window, copy a file from your Documents folder to a flash drive. Were you able to copy the file successfully? If not, what error message(s) did you receive?

PROJECT 15-4: Using Ntbtlog.txt

Compare an Ntbtlog.txt file created during a normal boot to one created when booting into Safe Mode. Note any differences you find.

PROJECT 15-5: More Practice with Windows RE

Using Windows Explorer, rename the BootMgr file in the root directory of drive C. Reboot the system. What error message do you see? Now use Windows RE to restore the BootMgr file. List the steps taken to complete the repair.

PROJECT 15-6: Problem-Solving Using the Microsoft Knowledge Base

You are trying to clean up a hard drive to free some disk space. You notice the hard drive has a C:\Windows.Old folder that uses 10 GB. However, in the Disk Cleanup dialog box, you don't see the option to delete Previous Windows Installations. Using the Microsoft support site (*support.microsoft.com*), find the Knowledge Base Article that allows you to manually delete the folder. Answer these questions:

1. What is the Article ID for this article?

2. What are the three command lines needed to delete the folder?

3. Explain the purpose of each of the three commands, and explain the purpose of each parameter in the command line.

PROJECT 15-7: Using Boot Logs and System Information to Research Startup

Boot logs can be used to generate a list of drivers that were loaded during a normal startup and during the Safe Mode startup. By comparing the two lists, you can determine which drivers are not essential to startup. Also, the System Information utility (msinfo32.exe) can help you find out information about a driver or service. Do the following to research startup:

1. To turn on boot logging, boot to the Advanced Boot Options menu and choose Enable Boot Logging. Then boot to the normal Windows desktop. Print the file C:\Windows\ntbtlog.txt and save the file to a different location on the hard drive.

2. Reboot the system in Safe Mode. Print the file C:\Windows\ntbtlog.txt and save the file to a different location on the hard drive. Using the two lists, identify the drivers that were loaded normally but not loaded during Safe Mode.

3. The next step is to identify each hardware component that uses the device drivers you identified in Step 2. These are the drivers that were loaded normally, but not loaded during Safe Mode. Use the System Information utility (msinfo32.exe) to drill down to each hardware component or use the search feature at the bottom of the System Information window. When you find the hardware component, look for the device drivers that are associated with the component.

As you identify the drivers not loaded during Safe Mode, it might be helpful to know that these registry keys list the drivers and services that are loaded during Safe Mode:

▴ Lists drivers and services loaded during Safe Mode:
   HKLM\System\CurrentControlSet\Control\SafeBoot\Minimal

▴ Lists drivers and services loaded during Safe Mode with Networking:
   HKLM\System\CurrentControlSet\Control\SafeBoot\Network

PROJECT 15-8: Researching Software to Compare Text Files

Comparing boot log files manually can be tedious work, and a utility that compares text files looking for differences can be a great help. Finding the best utility can, however, be a challenge. Vista offers the Comp command, and Windows XP support tools include Windiff.exe. Alternately, you can find and download another file comparison program from the Internet. Do the following to research file comparison programs:

1. In a command prompt window, use the Vista Comp command to compare the two log files you saved in Project 15-7.

2. Locate a file comparison program on the Internet, copy it to your Vista computer, and install it. Be sure to verify that the site you are using is reliable before you download a file from it—you don't want to download malware to your PC. Use the program to compare the two log files.

3. If you have access to a Windows XP computer that has the system tools installed, copy the Windiff.exe program to your Vista computer and use it to compare the two log files.

4. Which file comparison program do you like best? Why?

>> REAL PROBLEMS, REAL SOLUTIONS

REAL PROBLEM 15-1: Finding an Unknown Device (Challenging Real Problem)

Someone has come to you for help with their computer. They are unable to connect to the Internet and are not sure why. After some investigation, you realize that they have just replaced the network adapter, but have lost the driver CD for the adapter and its documentation. Windows does not recognize the device type and there is no model information on the device itself. To find the correct drivers, you need to know the exact brand and model of the device. Use the following steps to retrieve this information. By following these steps, you'll learn to use the Ultimate Boot CD, which can be a valuable utility to add to your PC repair kit.

1. Go to the Ultimate Boot CD download page at *www.ultimatebootcd.com/download.html* and read the directions about creating the Ultimate Boot CD. The CD is created using an ISO image. An ISO image is a file that contains all the files that were burned to an original CD or DVD. This ISO image is then used to create copies of the original CD or DVD. The process has three steps: (1) Download the ISO image as a compressed, self-extracting .exe file, (2) Decompress the compressed file to extract the ISO file having an .iso file extension, (3) Use CD burning software to burn the CD from the ISO image.

2. Now that you understand the process, follow directions to download to your hard drive a compressed and self-extracting executable (.exe) file containing the ISO image. The current version of the Ultimate Boot CD as of the printing of this book is Version 4.1.1 and the file to download is ubcd411.exe.

3. Double-click the downloaded file to execute it and extract the ISO image. (For Version 4.1.1, the new file will be named ubcd411.iso.)

4. You'll need software to burn the ISO image to the CD. (Do not just burn the .iso file to the CD. The software extracts the files inside the ISO image and burns these files to the CD to create a bootable CD holding many files.) The Ultimate Boot CD Web site suggests some free CD burning software that supports ISO images. Download and execute one of these products to burn the ISO image to the CD. Using a permanent marker, label the CD "Ultimate Boot CD" and include the version number that you downloaded.

5. Boot the computer from the CD and find a tool that will retrieve the brand and model number of the NIC (network adapter). What software on the CD did you decide to use?

6. Use the program to find the make and model number of the NIC installed in your system and write down this information.

7. Using the acquired information, search the Internet for the correct driver.

8. Does this driver match the driver installed on your system?

9. Answer the following questions about other programs on the Ultimate Boot CD:

   a. Some antivirus software reports that some programs on the Ultimate Boot CD are viruses. Search the Ultimate Boot CD Web site for the name of one of these programs. What is its name and what is the purpose of the program? Is the program truly a virus?

   b. Name one other program on the Ultimate Boot CD that you believe will be useful when troubleshooting. Describe what the program does.

15

Fixing Windows Problems

In the last chapter, you learned about the several Windows Vista and XP tools that can help you solve Windows problems. Those tools can help when problems arise with a hardware device, application, or Windows components. In addition, some Windows tools are specifically designed to help you solve startup problems with Windows Vista, XP, or 2000. In this chapter, we focus on the techniques and methods to use when all these types of problems occur. You will learn how to put to good use the tools you learned about in Chapter 15. In short, this chapter is the practical application of the tools in Chapter 15.

When a computer gives problems, refuses to boot, or the Windows desktop refuses to load, it takes a cool head to handle the situation gracefully. What helps more than anything else is to have a good plan so you don't feel so helpless. This chapter is designed to give you just that—a plan with all the necessary details so that you can determine just what has gone wrong and what to do about it. Knowledge is power. When you know what to do, the situation doesn't seem nearly as hopeless.

In the chapter, you'll first learn what to do when problems occur after the boot with hardware or software. Then we'll turn to how to solve problems that occur during the boot. Because solving boot problems with Windows Vista is done differently than when solving boot problems with Windows XP/2000, we'll cover Vista boot problems separately from XP/2000 boot problems.

> 💡 **A+ Exam Tip** All the content in this chapter applies to the A+ 220-702 Practical Application exam objectives that focus on solving Windows problems.

FIXING PROBLEMS CAUSED BY HARDWARE

A+
220-702
2.1
2.3
2.4

Now let's look at some general steps to use when solving a problem caused by a hardware device or its drivers. These general steps assume you know how to use the tools discussed in Chapter 15. As you read, you can refer back to Chapter 15 to see the details of how to use a tool mentioned here.

If you don't know which device is causing a problem, follow these steps to find out:

▲ *Research an error message.* If you see an error message that appears during or after the boot, investigate the message. The Internet is a great source. Enter the message in a Google.com search string. Recall that an error message might appear during the boot if a missing program file is referenced in the registry. Also, if you get an error message about a service or driver that has failed to start, search on the filename of the service or driver to find out which component, application, or device uses the service or driver. The System Information utility (msinfo32.exe) can help.

▲ *Use the Vista Problem Reports and Solutions window or the XP Error Reporting window.* These tools can help identify and resolve blue screen errors, errors that cause the system to lock up, and errors caused by device drivers, and services and applications that fail to start. The description of the problem should include clues that can help you identify the device, Windows component, or application causing the problem. For example, Figure 16-1 shows a message that appeared after a Vista system encountered a blue screen error. When you click **Check for solution**, a solution window (see Figure 16-2) appears. For Vista, even if time has passed since the error occurred or the error caused the system to hang resulting in a restart, you can open the Vista Problem Reports and Solutions window to see past problems listed with suggestions for a solution. To open the window, click **Start, All Programs, Maintenance**, and **Problem Reports and Solutions**.

▲ *Check logs in Event Viewer.* In Event Viewer, the Administrative Events log under Custom Views shows only warnings and error events (see Figure 16-3). Click the label at the top of a column to sort the events to help you search through them as you look

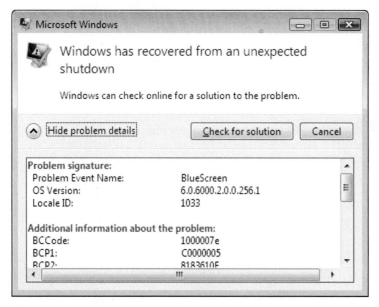

Figure 16-1 Message that appeared after a Vista blue screen error
Courtesy: Course Technology/Cengage Learning

A+
220-702
2.1
2.3
2.4

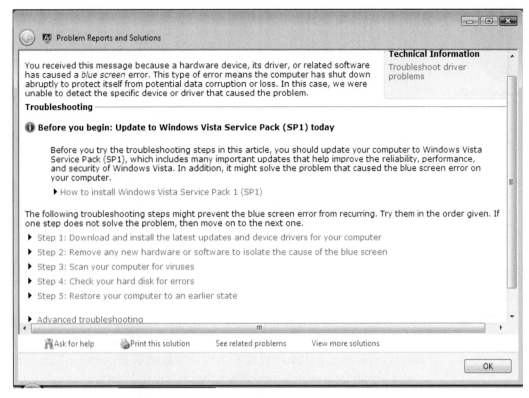

Figure 16-2 Windows suggests Windows update might solve a blue screen problem
Courtesy: Course Technology/Cengage Learning

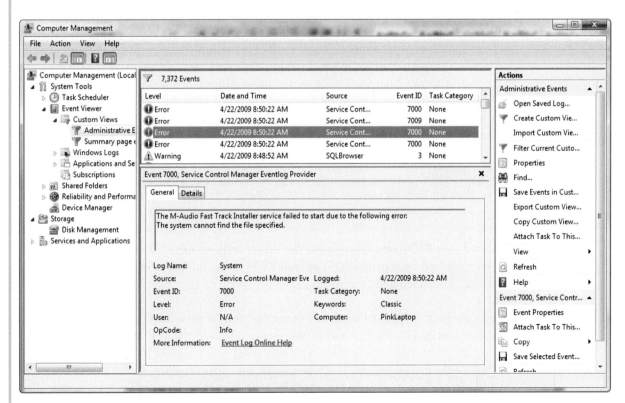

Figure 16-3 Administrative Events log shows error and warning events
Courtesy: Course Technology/Cengage Learning

16

A+ 220-702

A+
220-702
2.1
2.3
2.4

for useful information. Notice in Figure 16-3, a service used by audio failed to start. The problem happened when Windows could not find the specified file. Updating or reinstalling the audio drivers would fix this problem of no audio. Errors that cause the system to lock up might also be recorded here.

▲ *Check the Reliability and Performance Monitor.* In this window, click the Reliability Monitor. Look for error events that occurred about the time the problem started. How to use the Reliability and Performance Monitor is covered in Chapter 14.

▲ *Consider recent changes.* What hardware or software changes have you or someone else recently made? Maybe the change affected something that you have not yet considered. Once I installed a hard drive, turned on the system, and got beep code errors during the power-on self test (POST). I opened the case and checked the drive and connections. It all looked fine, so I tried to boot again with the same results. The second time I opened the case I discovered that I had bumped a memory module while closing the case. Reseating the module solved my problem.

When you know which device is causing a problem, do the following to investigate the device and its drivers to discover the source of the problem:

1. *Check the simple things first.* Most computer problems are simple and easy to solve. Check the simple things: Is the external device plugged in and turned on? Are the data cable connections solid at both ends? For sound, is the volume knob turned up? Is there a wall light switch controlling the power, and is it turned on? Is the power strip you're using plugged in and turned on? For expansion cards and memory modules, are they seated solidly in their slots?

2. *Check that Device Manager recognizes the device with no errors or warnings.* Check Device Manager to verify that the device is enabled and Windows thinks the device should be working. If you see errors or warnings in Device Manager (displayed as a yellow triangle or question mark, as shown in Figure 16-4), these issues must be resolved before you continue. If you're not sure which device is giving the problem, disable a suspected device to see if the problem goes away. For devices that don't appear in Device Manager—such as a scanner, printer, or some USB or FireWire devices—use the utility program that came bundled with the device to check for errors. You should find the program on the **Start, All Programs** menus. For printers, also use the Printers window to check for problems.

> 💡 **A+ Exam Tip** The A+ 220-702 Practical Application exam expects you to know how to use Device Manager to solve a hardware problem.

3. *Check that BIOS setup recognizes the device with no errors.* For a device that should be recognized by startup BIOS, go into BIOS setup and make sure the device is correctly detected and is enabled.

To solve a problem with a device driver or service, follow these steps. Be sure to reboot the system after you make a change and before you move on to the next step:

1. *Update the device drivers.* For best results, first download the driver files to your hard drive from the device manufacturer's Web site. Then, in Device Manager, update the drivers using these downloaded files. If you don't like the results of the update, you can roll back the driver to undo the update.

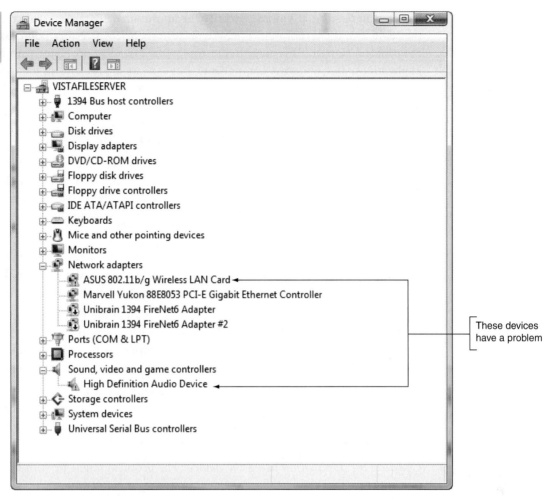

A+
220-702
2.1
2.3
2.4

Figure 16-4 Device Manager indicates a problem with a yellow triangle
Courtesy: Course Technology/Cengage Learning

2. *Update Windows.* Sometimes a Windows update solves a problem with a hardware device. On the other hand, Windows might be the problem. If the device was working and now does not, consider whether a Windows update might have caused the problem. Check the Microsoft support site (*support.microsoft.com*) for information and a fix.

3. *Try moving the device to a different port or connector.* For external USB devices, try a different USB port. For internal devices, try moving the device to a different expansion slot or connecting it to a different connector on the motherboard. Perhaps the current connector or port is bad, disabled, or not configured correctly.

4. *Try reinstalling the device.* To get a clean start with a device, you can uninstall it and start over. In Device Manager, right-click the device and select **Uninstall**. Then reboot the PC. When Windows starts, it should detect a new hardware device and launch the Found New Hardware Wizard. Then you can install the device drivers again. Did the Found New Hardware Wizard launch? If not, the device might be bad or the port it is using might be bad or disabled.

5. *Try moving the device to a different computer.* If the device works on another computer, move it back to the original computer. If it still does not work on the original computer, the problem might be with the port or expansion slot the device is using.

16

A+ 220-702

A+
220-702
2.1
2.3
2.4

6. *Use System Restore.* If you can identify the approximate date the error started and that date is in the recent past, use System Restore. Select a restore point just before the problem started. Reverting to a restore point can solve problems with hardware, applications, and Windows components, but can cause problems of its own, so use it with caution.

7. *Check the manufacturer's documentation.* When installing a device, sometimes the device will not work unless you run the setup CD for the device *before* you physically install the device. (This is sometimes true of internal modem cards, network adapters, and USB devices.) To know the right order, read the manufacturer's documentation. You should also find troubleshooting guidelines there for the device and how to use any diagnostic software the manufacturer offers. Also, the manufacturer's Web site should have a support section, including FAQs about the device. When all else fails, I've often found my solution there.

8. *Search the Internet for help.* Look for forums where others have posted the same problem with the same device. Someone else has likely posted a solution. However, be careful and don't take the advice unless you trust the Web site.

9. *Boot into Safe Mode.* If the system is caught in an endless loop of restarts, boot into Safe Mode. Then, using the instructions given in Chapter 15, use the Startup and Recovery section of the System Properties box to uncheck **Automatically restart**.

10. *Use the System File Checker.* For essential hardware devices, use the System File Checker (SFC) to verify and replace system files. Use the command sfc /scannow or sfc /scanonce. Later in the chapter, you will learn other steps to take if Windows Vista or Windows 2000/XP give startup errors.

11. *Consider the application using the device.* The problem might be with the application software that is controlling the device. For example, if you are having problems trying to use a USB scanner, try scanning using a different application.

12. *Replace the device.* After you've tried all this and the problem is still not solved, it's time to assume the device is just not working. Replace it with a new one.

> 📝 **Notes** There's a lot of detail about troubleshooting in this section. Here's a shortcut that might help: When you are faced with a hardware problem, do two things: Check the cable connections and check the log files. Just remembering these two steps can serve you well.

FIXING PROBLEMS CAUSED BY APPLICATIONS

A+
220-702
2.3
2.4

Problems with applications might be caused by the application, the hardware, the operating system, the data, other applications in conflict with this one, or the user. Follow these steps to get to the source of the problem. After you have made a change, be sure to restart and check to see if the problem is resolved before you move on to the next step:

Do the following to find the source of the problem and fix it:

1. *Interview the user and back up data.* Find out as much information as you can from the user about the problem, when it started, and what happened to the system about the time the problem started. Also ask if valuable data is on the system. If so, back it up.

2. *Ask the user to reproduce the problem while you watch.* Many problems with applications are caused by user error. Watch carefully as the user shows you the problem. If you see him making a mistake, be tactful and don't accuse. Just explain the problem and its solution. It's better to explain and teach rather than fix the problem yourself; that way, the user learns from the experience.

3. *Use Task Manager to end a process that is not responding.* If an application is locked up, use Task Manager to end it.

4. *Try a reboot.* Reboot the system and see if that solves the problem.

5. *Suspect a virus is causing a problem.* Scan for viruses and check Task Manager to make sure some strange process is not interfering with your applications.

6. *Allow Windows to provide a solution.* For Vista, use the Problem Reports and Solutions tool to search for the problem and suggested solutions. For XP, if Error Reporting displays a window (see Figure 16-5), click **Send Error Report** in the window and follow through by applying any recommended solutions.

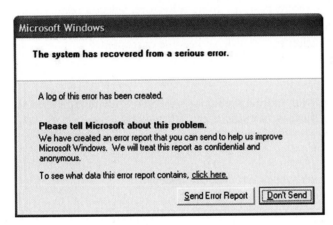

Figure 16-5 A serious Windows error sometimes generates this
Microsoft Windows error-reporting box
Courtesy: Course Technology/Cengage Learning

7. *Windows update might solve the problem.* When Microsoft is aware of application problems caused by Windows, it sometimes releases a patch to solve the problem. Make sure Windows updates are current. Know that these updates include updates for other Microsoft products such as Microsoft Office.

8. *Download updates or patches for the application.* Software manufacturers often publish updates or patches for their software to address known problems. You can go to the software manufacturer's Web site to download these updates and get information about known problems.

9. *Use the application setup to repair the installation.* The application setup might have this option to repair the installation. Look for it in the Vista Programs and Features window, the XP Add or Remove Programs window, or on the setup CD for the application.

10. *Consider data corruption.* It might appear that the application has a problem when the problem is really a corrupted data file. Try creating an entirely new data file. If

A+
220-702
2.3
2.4

that works, then suspect that previous errors might be caused by corrupted data. You might be able to recover part of a corrupted file by changing its file extension to .txt and importing it into the application as a text file.

11. *Try restoring default settings.* Maybe a user has made one too many changes to the application settings, which can cause a problem with missing toolbars and other functions. Write down each setting the user has changed and then restore all settings back to their default values. If the problem is solved, restore each setting to the way the user had it until you find the one causing the problem. The process will take some time, but users can get upset if you change their application settings without justification.

12. *Uninstall and reinstall the application.* Sometimes an application gives problems because the installation gets corrupted. You can try uninstalling and reinstalling the application. However, in doing so you might lose any customized settings, macros, or scripts. Also know this still might not solve a problem with a corrupted application because registry entries might not be properly reset during the uninstall process.

13. *Use System Restore.* If you can identify the approximate date the error started and that date is in the recent past, use System Restore. Select a restore point just before the problem started. Reverting to a restore point can solve problems with registry entries the application uses that have become corrupted.

> 💡 **A+ Exam Tip** A+ 220-702 Practical Application exam expects you to know when and how to use System Restore to solve a Windows, hardware, or application problem.

If the application has never worked, follow these steps:

1. *Run the application as an administrator.* The application might require that the user have privileges not assigned to the current account. Try running the application with administrator privileges, which Windows calls a secondary logon. To do that, right-click the application icon on the desktop or the application name in the **All Programs** menu, and select **Run as administrator** from the shortcut menu (see Figure 16-6). If this fixes the problem, you can make this setting permanent. To do that, use Windows Explorer: Locate the program filename (most likely in a subfolder of the Program Files folder), right-click it, and select **Properties** from the shortcut menu. Then click the **Compatibility** tab and check **Run this program as an administrator** (see Figure 16-7). Click **Apply** and then close the Properties box.

2. *Install the application as an administrator.* By default, Windows does not allow standard or limited accounts to install applications. To install software, first log onto the system as an administrator.

3. *Consider whether an older application is having compatibility problems with Vista.* Some older applications cannot run under Vista or run with errors. Here are some steps you can take to fix the problem:

   a. Go to the Windows Vista Compatibility Center site at *www.microsoft.com/ windows/compatibility* and search for the application. The site reports problems and solutions for known legacy software. For example, when you search on the

A+
220-702
2.3
2.4

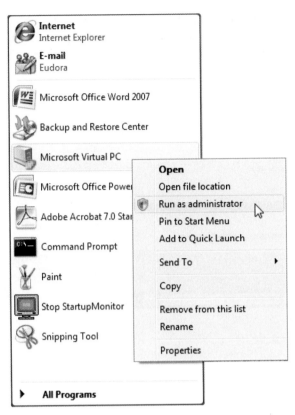

Figure 16-6 To elevate an application's privileges, run the application as an administrator
Courtesy: Course Technology/Cengage Learning

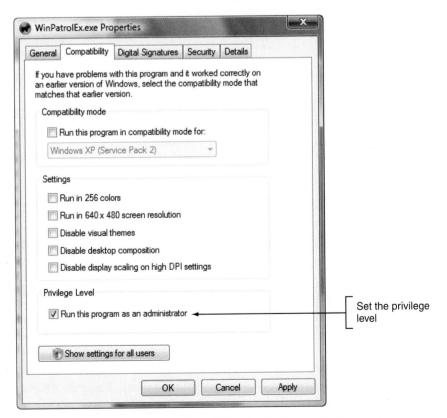

Figure 16-7 Permanently change the privilege level of an application
Courtesy: Course Technology/Cengage Learning

16

A+ 220-702

A+
220-702
2.3
2.4

application WinPatrol, you find that Version 11 is not compatible with Vista, but Version 14 is compatible (see Figure 16-8). If the application is known to not be compatible with the OS you are using, try to replace or upgrade the software.

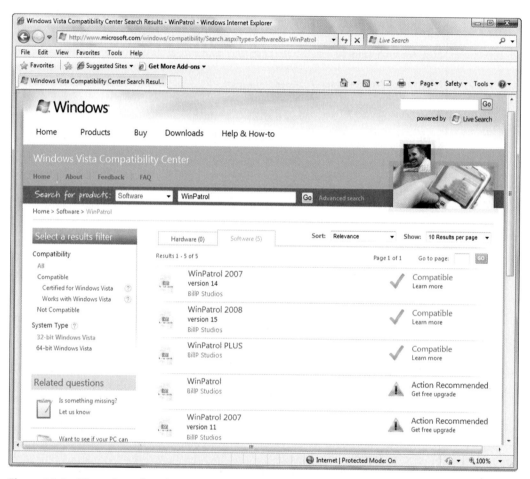

Figure 16-8   Microsoft tracks software and hardware compatible with Vista
Courtesy: Course Technology/Cengage Learning

   b. Try running the application in compatibility mode. To do that, on the Compatibility tab of the program file Properties box shown earlier in Figure 16-7, check **Run this program in compatibility mode for:**. Then, in the drop-down menu, select the operating system that the application was written to run under. Click **Apply** and close the **Properties** box.

4. *Verify that the application is digitally signed.* Although applications that are not digitally signed can still run on Windows, a digital signature does verify that the application is not a rogue application and that it is certified as Windows-compatible by Microsoft. To view the digital signature, in Windows Explorer, find the program filename (most likely in a subfolder of the Program Files folder), right-click the filename, and select **Properties** from the shortcut menu. Select the **Digital Signatures** tab and click **Advanced** (see Figure 16-9). If the Digital Signatures tab is missing, the program is not digitally signed.

A+
220-702
2.3
2.4

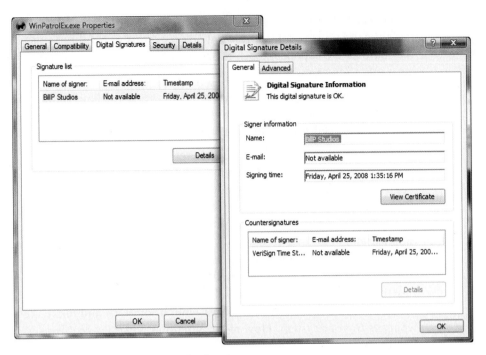

Figure 16-9 This program is digitally signed
Courtesy: Course Technology/Cengage Learning

The problem might be caused by other applications, services the application uses, Windows, or hardware. Do the following to check these possibilities:

1. *Another application might be interfering.* Close all other applications. Another application might be corrupted or have a data file open that this application needs.

2. *Use the Services console.* Check this console to make sure a service the application uses has started. If the service has failed to start, make sure it has an Automatic or Manual setting.

3. *You might be low on system resources.* Close all other applications. Check Task Manager to make sure that unnecessary processes are closed. If you must run more than one application at a time, you can increase the priority level for an application that is not getting its fair share of resources. To do that, on the **Processes** tab of Task Manager, right-click the application and select **Set Priority**. Then increase the priority level. This setting applies to the current session only. Also, consider that your system might be running low on memory. For good performance, Windows Vista needs at least 2 GB of RAM, and XP needs at least 1 GB of RAM. For great performance, use more than that. See Chapter 14 for more suggestions to optimize Windows.

4. *Verify Windows system files.* Corrupted Windows system files can cause application errors. To have Windows verify system files and replace a bad one with a good one, use the System File Checker (sfc.exe) utility. You learned how to use the utility in Chapter 15.

5. *The problem might be bad memory.* Following the directions given in Chapter 15, use the Memory Diagnostics tool (mdsched.exe) to test memory. If it finds errors, replace the memory modules.

6. *Use Event Viewer to look for clues.* The Event Viewer logs might give clues about applications and the system.

16

A+
220-702
2.3
2.4

7. *Use the Reliability Monitor to look for clues.* The Reliability Monitor might help you discover the source of the problem. Look for errors with other applications or with key hardware components such as the hard drive. Hard drive errors often appear as an application error.

8. *Use the Chkdsk command to check the hard drive.* To eliminate the hard drive as the source of an application error, use the Chkdsk command to check the drive. Recall the command is **chkdsk C: /r** and, for Vista, must be executed from an elevated command prompt.

9. *Run the application in Safe Mode with Networking.* Press **F8** at startup to display the Advanced Boot Options menu and select **Safe Mode with Networking** from the menu. If the application works in Safe Mode, then you can assume the problem is not with the application, but with the operating system, device drivers, or other applications that load at startup which are conflicting with the application. In this situation, approach the problem as a Windows problem rather than an application problem. There are several methods and tools to troubleshoot Windows Vista, all discussed in the next part of the chapter. As you read, look for ways to repair Windows Vista that require the least amount of work and make the fewest drastic changes to your system. How to fix Windows XP/2000 problems is covered later in the chapter.

TROUBLESHOOTING VISTA STARTUP

A+
220-702
2.4

This section is written as step-by-step instructions for problem-solving, so that you can use it to solve a boot problem with Windows Vista by following the steps. Each step takes you sequentially through the boot process and shows you what to do when the boot fails at that point in the process. Therefore, your first decision in troubleshooting a failed boot is to decide at what point in the boot the failure occurred. Next, you have to decide which tool will be the least invasive to use, yet still will fix the problem. The idea is to make as few changes to your system as possible in order to solve the problem without having to do a lot of work to return the system to normal (such as having to reinstall all your applications). And, as with every computer problem, if user data is at risk, you need to take steps to back up the data as soon as possible in the troubleshooting process.

To determine where in the boot process the failure occurred, we'll focus on these three startup stages of the boot:

▲ *Stage 1: Before the progress bar.* When you see the Microsoft progress bar appear, you know the Windows kernel, including all critical services and drivers, has loaded. Any problems that occur before the progress bar appears are most likely related to corrupt or missing system files or hardware. Your best Vista tools to use for these problems are Startup Repair and System Restore.

▲ *Stage 2: After the progress bar and before logon.* After the progress bar appears, user mode services and drivers are loaded and then the logon screen appears. Problems with these components can best be solved using Startup Repair, the Last Known Good Configuration, System Restore, Safe Mode, Device Manager, and MSconfig.

▲ *Stage 3: After logon.* After the logon screen appears, problems can be caused by startup scripts, applications set to launch at startup, and desktop settings. Use MSconfig to temporarily disable startup programs. Other useful tools to solve the problem are Software Explorer and Safe Mode.

Recall that all three stages of the Vista boot are described in detail in Chapter 15. Also in Chapter 15, you'll find detailed descriptions of the Windows troubleshooting tools used here. Now let's take a closer look at how to address problems at each of the three stages of Vista startup.

PROBLEMS AT STAGE 1: BEFORE THE PROGRESS BAR APPEARS

As always, first check with the user to find out if important data is on the hard drive and not backed up. Make every effort to copy the data to a safe location before you start troubleshooting the original problem. How to recover data from a system that refuses to boot is covered later in the chapter in the section "How to Recover Lost Data."

Remember, if the progress bar has not yet appeared, some portions of the Vista kernel and critical drivers and services to be started by the kernel have not yet started. Therefore, the problem is with hardware or these startup files. Hardware that might be failing includes the power supply, motherboard, CPU, memory, hard drive, video, or keyboard. If any one of these devices is not working, the error is communicated using beep codes, or using on-screen or voice error messages—and then the computer halts.

As you perform each troubleshooting step, be sure to restart the system to see if the problem is solved before you apply the next step.

IS THE SCREEN BLANK?

If you see absolutely nothing on the screen, check that the system is getting power and the monitor is plugged in and turned on. Can you hear the spinning fan or hard drive inside the computer case? Are lights on the front of the case lit? If not, suspect that power is not getting to the system. Check that the system is not in standby mode or hibernation: Try waking up the system by pressing any key or a special standby key on laptops, or by pressing the power-on button. Is the monitor totally without lights, or is the screen blank but the LED light on front of the monitor is lit? If the LED light is lit, try rebooting the system. If the LED light is not lit, check that power is getting to the monitor. Is it turned on?

Try trading the monitor for one you know is good. If you can hear a spinning drive and see lights on the front of the computer case and know the monitor works, the video card might be bad or not seated properly in its slot, the memory might be bad, the video cable might be bad, or a component on the motherboard might have failed.

DOES THE COMPUTER APPEAR TO HAVE POWER?

If you can't hear the spinning drive or see lights on the front of the case, suspect the electrical system. Check power connections and switches. The power supply might be bad or connections inside the case might be loose.

DOES AN ERROR MESSAGE APPEAR BEFORE VISTA STARTS?

Recall that when you first turn on a system, startup BIOS takes control, checks essential hardware devices, and searches for an OS to load. If it has a problem while doing all that and the video system is working, it displays an error message on-screen. If video is not working, it might attempt to communicate an error with a series of beeps (called beep codes) or speech (for speech-enabled BIOS).

For messages displayed on-screen that apply to nonessential hardware devices such as DVD drives or floppy drives, you might be able to bypass the error by pressing a key and moving forward in the boot. However, for errors with essential hardware devices such as the one shown in Figure 16-10, focus your attention on the error message, beep code, or voice message describing the problem. For example, notice in Figure 16-10 that the system is

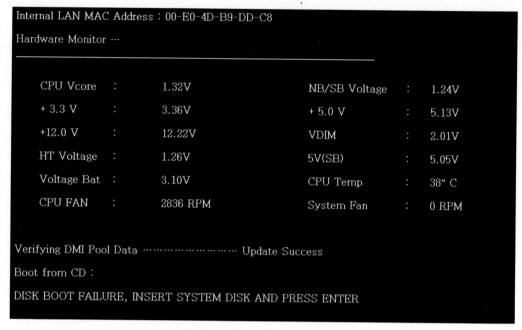

Internal LAN MAC Address : 00-E0-4D-B9-DD-C8

Hardware Monitor ···

CPU Vcore	:	1.32V	NB/SB Voltage	:	1.24V
+ 3.3 V	:	3.36V	+ 5.0 V	:	5.13V
+12.0 V	:	12.22V	VDIM	:	2.01V
HT Voltage	:	1.26V	5V(SB)	:	5.05V
Voltage Bat	:	3.10V	CPU Temp	:	38° C
CPU FAN	:	2836 RPM	System Fan	:	0 RPM

Verifying DMI Pool Data ·························· Update Success

Boot from CD :

DISK BOOT FAILURE, INSERT SYSTEM DISK AND PRESS ENTER

Figure 16-10   This error message at POST indicates a hardware problem
Courtesy: Course Technology/Cengage Learning

attempting to boot from the CD. It should be booting from the hard drive, but moved on to the CD when it did not find a hard drive present. If you don't know what the error message or beep codes mean, you can search the Web site of the motherboard manufacturer or do a general search of the Web using a search engine such as Google.

CAN STARTUP BIOS ACCESS THE HARD DRIVE?

Error messages generated by startup BIOS that pertain to the hard drive can be caused by a variety of things. Here is a list of text error messages that indicate that BIOS could not find a hard drive:

- ◢ Hard drive not found
- ◢ Fixed disk error
- ◢ Disk boot failure, insert system disk and press enter
- ◢ No boot device available

The problem might be a physical problem with the drive, the data cable, power, or the motherboard. Start with checking BIOS setup to verify that BIOS detected the drive correctly. If the drive was not detected, check the autodetection setting. (Chapter 8 shows sample BIOS setup screens for these hard drive settings.) If autodetection is turned off, turn it on and reboot. Your problem might be solved. If startup BIOS still doesn't find the drive, power down the system, unplug it, and open the case. Physically check the hard drive power and data cable connections at both ends. Sometimes cables work their way loose. Be careful not to touch circuit boards or the processor as you work, and to protect the system against static electricity, wear an antistatic bracelet that is clipped to the computer case.

Here is a list of error messages that indicate the BIOS was able to find the hard drive but couldn't read what was written on the drive or could not find what it was looking for:

- ◢ Invalid boot disk
- ◢ Inaccessible boot device

▲ Invalid drive specification
▲ Invalid partition table
▲ No operating system found, Missing operating system, Error loading operating system
▲ Couldn't find bootmgr or bootmgr is missing

💡 **A+ Exam Tip** The A+ 220-702 Practical Application exam expects you to be able to resolve a problem that gives the error messages "Invalid boot disk" or "Inaccessible boot drive."

For these error messages, you need to boot from the Windows Vista setup DVD, but first check BIOS setup to make sure the boot sequence lists the DVD drive before the hard drive.

USE BIOS SETUP TO SET THE BOOT SEQUENCE

To access BIOS setup, reboot the PC and look on-screen for a message such as "Press DEL for setup" or "Press F2 for BIOS settings" or something similar. Press that key and the BIOS setup utility loads. Find the screen, such as the one in Figure 16-11, that lets you set the boot sequence. The boot sequence is the order of devices to which BIOS looks to find an OS to load. Make sure that the DVD drive is listed before the hard drive so that you can force the system to boot from the Windows Vista setup DVD. Save your settings and exit BIOS setup.

The next step is to try to boot from the Windows Vista setup DVD.

CAN YOU BOOT FROM THE VISTA SETUP DVD?

Now that you have made sure that BIOS setup is configured to boot first from the DVD drive before it turns to the hard drive, you can try to boot from the Windows Vista setup DVD. If you cannot boot from this disc, the problem is not just the hard drive. Study the

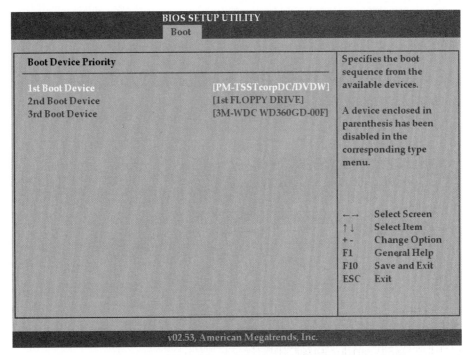

Figure 16-11 Verify that the boot sequence looks to the DVD drive before it checks the hard drive for an operating system
Courtesy: Course Technology/Cengage Learning

A+
220-702
2.4

error message and solve the immediate hardware problem. It's possible the hard drive and the optical drive have failed, but the floppy drive might still work. If you have a DOS or Windows 9x startup floppy disk, you can try booting from the floppy. If you can boot from the floppy, then you have proven the problem is with both the hard drive and the DVD drive.

If you are able to boot from the Vista DVD, the window shown in Figure 16-12 appears. If you see this window, you have proven that the problem is isolated to the hard drive. Now the trick is to find out exactly what is wrong with the drive and fix it.

Figure 16-12 Select your language preference
Courtesy: Course Technology/Cengage Learning

CAN WINDOWS RE FIND THE VISTA INSTALLATION?

At this point, click **Next** in Figure 16-12 and then click **Repair your computer** to attempt to launch Windows RE. The first thing Windows RE does is attempt to locate a Vista installation on the hard drive (see Figure 16-13). If it cannot locate the installation, but BIOS setup

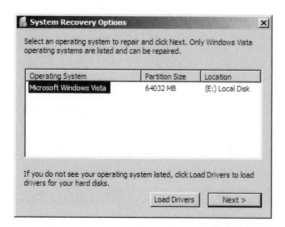

Figure 16-13 Select a Vista installation to repair
Courtesy: Course Technology/Cengage Learning

A+
220-702
2.4

recognizes the drive, then the drive partitions and file systems might be corrupted. If Windows RE does locate the installation, the problem is more likely to be limited to corrupted or missing system files or drivers.

As you attempt each fix in the following list, be sure to restart the system after each step to find out if the problem still exists or has changed:

1. Run Startup Repair. This process can sometimes fix drastic problems with system files and boot records.

2. Run System Restore. The process won't help if the file system is corrupted.

3. Restart the system and press **F8** during the boot to launch the Advanced Boot Options menu, as shown in Figure 16-14. If the boot menu does not appear, chances are the problem is a corrupted boot sector. If the boot menu appears, chances are the BCD file or other startup files are the problem. If you do see the menu, enable boot logging and reboot. Then check the boot log (\Windows\ntbtlog.txt) for the last entry, which might indicate which system file is missing or corrupt. (If the hard drive is at all accessible, your best chance of viewing the boot log file is to use the command prompt window and the Type command.)

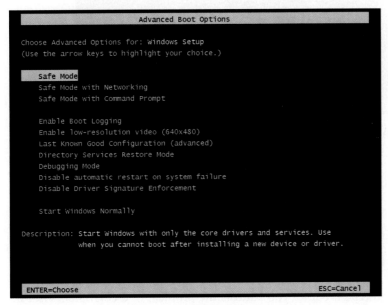

Figure 16-14   Press F8 to see the Advanced Boot Options menu
Courtesy: Course Technology/Cengage Learning

4. If the boot menu does not appear, return to Windows RE, launch the command prompt window, and attempt to repair the boot sector. Try these commands: **bootrec /fixmbr** and **bootrec /fixboot**. Also try the **Diskpart** command followed by the command **list volume**. Does the OS find the system volume? If not, the entire partition might be lost.

5. If the boot menu does appear, return to Windows RE, launch the command prompt window, and attempt to repair the BCD file. Try this command: **bootrec /rebuildbcd**.

6. Try to repair a corrupted file system by using the command prompt window and the **chkdsk c: /r** command.

16

A+ 220-702

A+
220-702
2.4

7. When startup files are missing or corrupt, sometimes Vista displays an error message similar to the one shown in Figure 16-15, which names the file giving the problem. You can replace the file by going to a healthy Vista computer and copying the file to a removable media. Then, on the problem computer, boot to Windows RE, open the command prompt window, and rename the original file so you will not overwrite it with the replacement and you can backtrack if necessary. Then copy the replacement file to the hard drive.

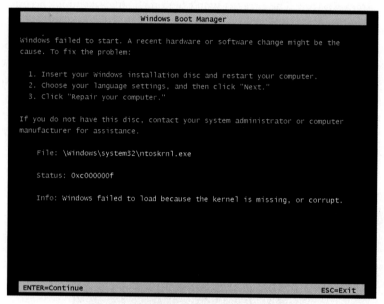

Figure 16-15 Windows Vista might display a screen similar to this one when a critical startup file is missing or corrupt
Courtesy: Course Technology/Cengage Learning

8. Try using the command prompt window to access drive C. If you can get to a C prompt, use the **DIR** command to list folders and files. If you see a good list, check the log file, C:\Windows\System32\LogFiles\SRT\SRTTrail.txt, for clues. (Recall this log file is kept by the Startup Repair process of Windows RE.) If you cannot get a good list of contents of drive C, most likely the Vista installation is destroyed beyond repair. Before you address the problem of a corrupted Vista installation, make every effort to copy data to another media. You can use copy commands in the Windows RE command prompt window or move the drive to a working computer to copy files.

OPTIONS TO RECOVER FROM A CORRUPTED VISTA INSTALLATION

If you are not able to repair the corrupted installation using the techniques in the previous list, your next step is to consider what options are available to restore the system. Your options depend on backups available. Here are your choices to restore a corrupted installation:

▲ *Option 1:* If you have a Complete PC backup, use it to restore the system to the last backup. If data is on the hard drive that has not been backed up, make every effort to copy this data to a safe place before you restore the system.

◢ *Option 2:* If you don't have a Complete PC backup but you do have backups of the data on the hard drive, install Windows Vista on the partition, formatting the hard drive during the installation. You'll need to install all applications again and then restore the data.

◢ *Option 3:* If you don't have a Complete PC backup and you also don't have backups of the data on the drive (worst case scenario), try to copy the data and then perform a reinstallation of Windows Vista. Even if you cannot copy the data, you might be able to recover it after the reinstallation. If you have data on the same partition as Vista, don't format during the Vista installation.

STEPS TO REINSTALL WINDOWS VISTA

Follow these steps to reinstall Vista when the OS refuses to boot and there is important data on the drive:

1. Boot from the Vista DVD, select the language, and then select **Install now** from the opening menu. Follow the directions on-screen to install the OS.

2. When given the opportunities, enter the product key and accept the license agreement. For the type of installation, select **Custom** (**advanced**).

3. When asked where you want to install the OS, select the partition on which Vista is installed.

Vista setup will move all folders of the old installation into the \Windows.Old folder, including the \Windows, \Users, and \Program Files folders. A fresh, clean installation of Vista will then be installed in the \Windows folder. If you suspect the hard drive might be failing or need reformatting, immediately save all important data to a removable media and reinstall Windows Vista a second time, this time reformatting the hard drive. If you believe the hard drive is healthy, then follow these steps to get things back to their original order:

1. Run Chkdsk to fix errors on the drive.

2. Install all applications and device drivers.

3. Create all user accounts and customize Vista settings. Then copy all user data and other folders from the \Windows.Old folder to the new installation. How to create user accounts is covered in Chapter 17.

4. To free up disk space, delete the \Windows.Old folder. To do that, using the Disk Cleanup utility in the Properties box for drive C, select **Previous Windows installation(s)** (see Figure 16-16). Note that this option will not be available if the \Windows.Old folder does not exist.

REINSTALL VISTA ON A LAPTOP OR BRAND-NAME COMPUTER

If you have a laptop or a brand-name computer such as a Gateway, Dell, or IBM, most likely the manufacturer has set up a hidden partition on the hard drive that can be used to recover the Windows installation. During startup, you'll see a message on-screen such as "Press F2 to recover the system" or "Press F11 to start recovery." When you press the appropriate key, a menu should appear that gives you two options: one repairs the Windows installation, saving user data, while the other reformats drive C and restores your system to the way it was when purchased. First, try to save user data before you attempt the destructive recovery. If neither method works, the hidden partition might be corrupted or the hard drive might be physically damaged.

A+
220-702
2.4

If the recovery process stored on the hard drive doesn't work, try to use the recovery CD or DVD that came bundled with your computer to repair the installation. If you don't have the recovery disc, you might be able to buy one from the computer manufacturer. For notebook computers, you absolutely must have this recovery disc to reinstall Windows because the device drivers on the disc are specific to your notebook. If you cannot buy a recovery disc, you might be able to download the drivers from the notebook manufacturer's Web site. Download them to another computer and burn them to a DVD or CD that you can use on the notebook to install drivers.

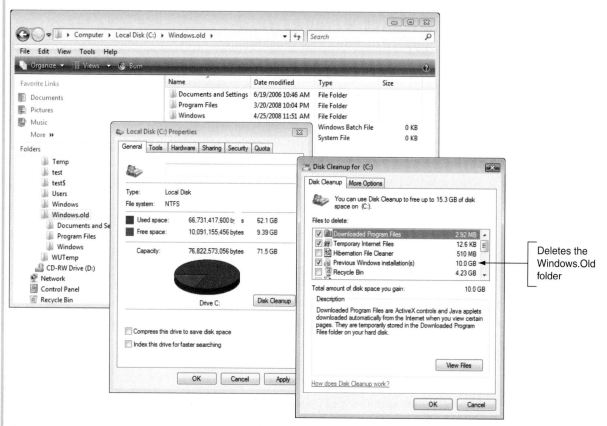

Figure 16-16 Free up disk space by deleting the Windows.Old folder
Courtesy: Course Technology/Cengage Learning

> **⚡ Caution** When you first become responsible for a laptop computer, it's extremely important that you create or obtain the recovery DVD or CDs that you will need in case the hard drive crashes. Without this recovery media, it's almost impossible to recover the system using a new hard drive. And, laptop manufacturers don't make these media available to customers after the laptop is a few years old. Get the recovery media in hand while it is still available! You might be able to create the media from the hard drive while the system is still healthy. See the laptop documentation for instructions.

PROBLEMS AT STAGE 2: AFTER THE PROGRESS BAR APPEARS AND BEFORE LOGON

When you see the Microsoft progress bar appear during the boot, you know the Windows kernel has loaded successfully and critical drivers and services configured to be started by the kernel are running. You also know the Session Manager (Smss.exe) running in user mode has started the Win32 subsystem necessary to provide the graphics of the progress bar. If the progress bar has appeared and the logon screen has not yet been displayed, most likely the problem is caused by a corrupted driver or service that is started after the kernel has finished its part of the boot. Your general attack plan to fix the problem is to isolate and disable the Windows component, service, or application causing trouble. However, if user data on the hard drive is not backed up, do what you can to copy that data to another media before you focus on the problem at hand.

Follow these steps:

1. Launch Windows RE from the Vista setup DVD and run **Startup Repair** from the Recovery Environment menu (see Figure 16-17). It can't do any harm, it's easy to use, and it might fix the problem.

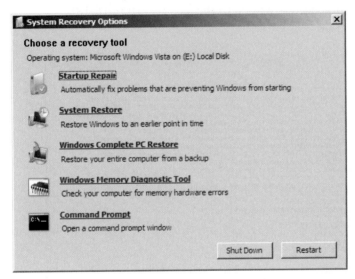

Figure 16-17   Recovery tools in Windows RE
Courtesy: Course Technology/Cengage Learning

2. Reboot and press **F8** to launch the Advanced Boot Options menu. Then select the **Last Known Good Configuration**. It's important to try this option early in the troubleshooting process, because you might accidentally overwrite a good Last Known Good with a bad one as you attempt to log on with the problem still there.

3. In Windows RE, run **System Restore**. Select the latest restore point. If that doesn't fix the problem, try an earlier one.

4. Try booting into **Safe Mode**. If you don't know the source of the problem, here are some things you can try to discover the source and hopefully solve the problem:

   a. Immediately run antivirus software to eliminate a virus as the problem.

   b. Run Chkdsk c: /r to check and repair the hard drive.

   c. Examine all the logs in Event Viewer for errors that might point to the problem.

> **Notes**   The Last Known Good Configuration is updated after you log on normally to Vista. However, logging onto a computer when booting into Safe Mode does not update the Last Known Good.

A+
220-702
2.4

d. Use Software Explorer and MSconfig to stop any applications just installed. Then uninstall and reinstall the application.

e. Use Device Manager to check for hardware errors and disable any devices just installed. If you have just updated a driver, roll back the driver.

f. Open an elevated command prompt window and use the System File Checker (SFC) tool to search for and replace corrupted system files. The command **sfc /scannow** searches for and replaces corrupted system files. Be sure to restart the system after this command is finished.

g. Rename the \Windows\Ntbtlog.txt file to keep it from being overwritten so you can view it later.

5. Boot to the Advanced Boot Options menu and select **Enable Boot Logging**. Windows starts logging information to the log file \Windows\Ntbtlog.txt. Every driver that is loaded or not loaded is written to the file (see Figure 16-18).

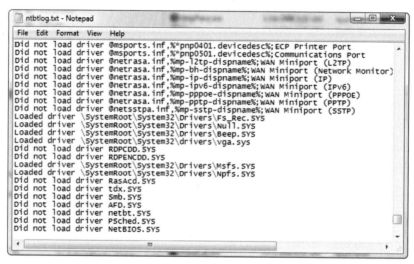

Figure 16-18 Sample Ntbtlog.txt file
Courtesy: Course Technology/Cengage Learning

6. Compare the Ntbtlog.txt file to the one that was created in Safe Mode. If the boot failed, look at the last entry in the Ntbtlog.txt file that was generated. Find that entry in the one created while booting into Safe Mode. The next driver listed in the Safe Mode Ntbtlog.txt file is likely the one giving problems.

7. The easiest way to view the logs is to boot into Safe Mode and view the files with Notepad. If you can't boot into Safe Mode, you can still view the file using the Windows RE command prompt window. Try replacing the program file listed last in the log or disabling the device or service. If that doesn't work, then you'll need to dig a little deeper to identify the culprit. Here are some tips for identifying a device or service causing the problem:

   ◢ *Tip 1:* Try to boot into Safe Mode. Then use MSconfig to disable all nonessential services and programs. Reboot normally. If the problem goes away, you can enable services and programs until you find the one causing the problem.

   ◢ *Tip 2:* In Safe Mode, examine Event Viewer logs for errors.

   ◢ *Tip 3:* In Safe Mode, use System Information (msinfo32.exe) to find the program filenames of drivers and services. Useful information can be found at these locations: Services in the Software Environment group and Problem Devices in the Components group.

◢ *Tip 4:* Compare the entries in the Ntbtlog.txt file when booting in Safe Mode to the entries when booting normally. Consider that the culprit might be any item that is loaded for a normal boot but not loaded for Safe Mode. Disable each driver one at a time until the problem goes away.

◢ *Tip 5:* If the computer will not boot into Safe Mode, compare the Ntbtlog.txt file to one created on a similar computer booted into Safe Mode. Look for a service or driver listed as loaded on the good computer that is not loaded or is missing on the bad computer.

> **♥ A+ Exam Tip** The A+ 220-702 Practical Application exam expects you to know how to use System Information to help you resolve a Windows startup problem.

8. After you believe you've identified the problem service or device, if you can boot into Safe Mode, first use Device Manager to disable the device or use the Services console to disable the service. Then reboot, and, if the problem goes away, restore the program file and enable the driver or service.

9. If you cannot boot into Safe Mode, open the command prompt window of the Recovery Environment. Then back up the registry and open the Registry Editor using the regedit command. Drill down to the service or device key. The key that loads services and drivers can be found in this location:

HKEY_LOCAL_MACHINE\System\CurrentControlSet\Services

10. Disable the service or driver by changing the Start value to 0x4. Close the Registry Editor and reboot. If the problem goes away, use the Copy command to replace the program file, and restart the service or driver.

PROBLEMS AT STAGE 3: AFTER WINDOWS LOGON

Problems that occur after the user logs onto Windows are caused by applications or services configured to launch at startup. Programs can be set to launch at startup by placing their shortcuts in startup folders, by Scheduled Tasks, or by software installation processes that affect registry entries. If you see an error message at startup that gives you a clue as to which service or program is at fault, test your theory by using MSconfig to disable that program. Recall from Chapter 14 that you can also use MSconfig to temporarily disable groups of startup services and startup programs and then enable a few services and programs until you find the one causing the problem.

Table 16-1 summarizes some error messages including blue screen or STOP errors you might encounter during the boot and what to do about them. STOP errors occur when the Windows kernel encounters an error in a kernel mode process, which most likely points to a hardware or driver problem.

HOW TO RECOVER LOST DATA

When data is lost or corrupted, you might be able to recover it using Windows tools, third-party software, or commercial data recovery services. This section discusses your options to recover lost data.

A+
220-702
2.4

Error or Error Message	Description and What to Do
Non-system disk or disk error Replace and press any key when ready	Startup BIOS could not find a boot device. Check BIOS setup for the boot sequence and try to boot from another device.
Invalid partition table Error loading operating system Missing operating system	MBR record is damaged or the active partition is corrupt or missing. Use the repair commands from the Windows RE command prompt window.
An application launched at startup that gives errors or takes up resources	Use Software Explorer to remove it from the list of startup programs.
Stop 0xc0000034 or The Windows Boot Configuration Data file is missing required information	The C:\Boot\BCD file is corrupted or missing. Use the Startup Repair tool in Windows RE or the Bootrec command.
Stop 0x0A or IRQL_NOT_LESS_OR_EQUAL	Caused by a driver or service making an illegal access to memory. Try the Last Known Good Configuration. Then look for an incompatible driver or service.
Stop 0x1E or KMODE_EXCEPTION_NOT-HANDLED	A bad driver or service has performed an illegal action. Look for corrupted or bad drivers or services. Try updating firmware.
Stop 0x24 or NTFS_FILE_SYSTEM	Suspect a failing hard drive or bad third-party disk utility tools.
Stop 0x2E or DATA_BUS_ERROR	A hardware problem most likely caused by failing memory or a corrupted hard drive.
Stop 0x50 or PAGE_FAULT_IN_NONPAGED_AREA	Caused by failing memory or bad software. Test memory using the Memory Diagnostic tool.
Stop 0x7B or INACCESSIBLE_BOOT_DEVICE	Windows cannot access the hard drive. This is probably caused by installing bad or incorrect hard drive drivers.
Stop 0xFE or BUGCODE_USB_DRIVER	Caused by corrupted USB drivers. Update the motherboard drivers for the USB ports.
Any other Stop error that occurs during startup	Other Stop errors are most likely caused by a corrupted registry, a system file that is missing or damaged, or a device driver that is missing or damaged. Use the Startup Repair tool and then examine the log file it creates at C:\Windows\System32\LogFiles\Srt\Srttail.txt.
Any Stop error that occurs during a Vista installation	See the Microsoft Knowledge Base article 935806 for a list of Stop errors during installation and what to do about them.

Table 16-1 Error messages during the Vista startup and what to do about them

RECOVER A DELETED OR CORRUPTED DATA FILE

Here are some things to try to recover a deleted or corrupted data file:

▲ If you have accidentally deleted a data file, to get it back, look in the Recycle Bin. Drag and drop the file back to where it belongs, or right-click the file and click **Restore** on the shortcut menu.

A+
220-702
2.4

◢ If a data file is corrupted, you can try to use the Recover command. To use the command, the volume on which the file is located cannot be in use. The easiest way to do that is to boot into Windows RE and open a command prompt window. For example, Figure 16-19 shows the command **recover C:\Data\Mydata.txt**. Notice in the figure that the C drive is not the current drive. The drive is not used when you load Windows RE and drive C is not the current or default drive.

Figure 16-19 Use the Recover command to recover a corrupted file while the volume on which it is stored is not in use
Courtesy: Course Technology/Cengage Learning

◢ If an application's data file gets corrupted, go to the Web site of the application manufacturer and search the support section for what to do to recover the file. For example, if an Excel spreadsheet gets corrupted, search the Knowledge Base at *support.microsoft.com* for solutions.

◢ Third-party software can help recover deleted and corrupted files. On the Internet, do a search on "data recovery" for lots of examples. One good product is GetDataBack by Runtime Software (*www.runtime.org*), which can recover data and program files even when Windows cannot recognize the drive. It can read FAT and NTFS file systems and can solve problems with a corrupted partition table, boot record, or root directory.

RECOVER DATA FROM A COMPUTER THAT WILL NOT BOOT

If Windows is corrupted and the system will not boot, recovering your data might be your first priority. One way to get to the data is to remove your hard drive from your computer and install it as a second nonbooting hard drive in another system. After you boot up the system, you should be able to use Windows Explorer to copy the data to another medium. If the data is corrupted, try to use data recovery software.

Recall from Chapter 8 that for less than $30 you can purchase an IDE to USB converter kit or a SATA to USB converter kit that includes a data cable and power adapter. (For notebook hard drives, the IDE to USB kit needs to include an adapter for these smaller drives. This extra adapter is not needed for SATA notebook hard drives because these SATA connectors are the same size as those used for desktop drives.) You can use one of these kits to temporarily connect a desktop or notebook hard drive to a USB port on a working computer. Set the drive beside your computer

16

A+ 220-702

A+
220-702
2.4

and plug one end of the data cable into the drive and the other into the USB port. (For an IDE drive, a jumper on the drive must be set to the master setting.) The AC adapter supplies power to the drive. While power is getting to the drive, be careful to not touch the circuit board on the drive.

Using Windows Explorer, you can browse the drive and copy data to other media. After you have saved the data, use Disk Management to try to repartition and reformat the drive. You can also use diagnostic software from the hard drive manufacturer to examine the drive and possibly repair it.

USE A DATA RECOVERY SERVICE

If your data is extremely valuable and other methods have failed, you might want to consider a professional data recovery service. They're expensive, but getting the data back might be worth it. To find a service, use Google.com and search on "data recovery." Before selecting a service, be sure to read up on reviews, understand the warranty and guarantees, and perhaps get a recommendation from a satisfied customer.

TROUBLESHOOTING WINDOWS 2000/XP STARTUP

In Chapter 15, you learned how the Windows 2000/XP boot process works and about the different tools you can use to solve boot problems. These tools include the Advanced Options menu, the boot disk, the Recovery Console, the Windows XP Automated System Recovery process, and the Windows 2000 Emergency Repair process. Before you read this part of the chapter, you might want to take a few moments to review the steps to loading Windows 2000/XP outlined in Chapter 15 and also the tools to solve Windows 2000/XP startup problems. With this knowledge in hand, you're ready to face Windows 2000/XP startup problems. Follow these steps:

1. As with every PC problem, begin by interviewing the user to find out what has recently changed, what happened just before the problem started, and how to reproduce the problem. Ask what has recently happened. Has new hardware or software been installed? Don't forget to ask about any important data that is not backed up.

2. If important data is not backed up, make every effort to copy the data to another media before you try to solve the Windows problem. Don't risk the data without the user's permission. If the system is giving so many errors that you cannot copy data, try booting into Safe Mode (see Figure 16-20). If Safe Mode doesn't load, you can use the Recovery Console to access the data. If Recovery Console cannot access the hard drive, you can move the hard drive to another computer and access it as a second drive in that computer. An IDE to USB or SATA to USB converter kit works well to make the connection so that you don't have to install the drive in the other computer case.

3. Next, determine at what point in the boot the system fails. Decide if you think the problem is hardware or software related.

4. If you think the problem is related to hardware, check the simple things first. Turn off the power and restart the system. Check for loose cables, switches that are not on, stuck keys on the keyboard, a wall outlet switch that has been turned off, and similar easy-to-solve problems.

A+
220-702
2.4

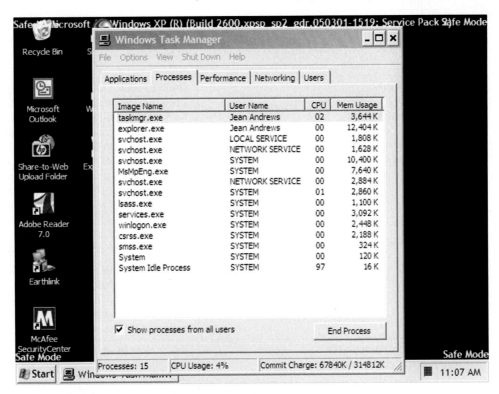

Figure 16-20 Windows XP Safe Mode with Task Manager
Courtesy: Course Technology/Cengage Learning

5. If an error message is displayed on-screen, start by addressing it. Table 16-2 lists several startup errors and what to do about them. As you work to correct the problem and restore the system, always keep in mind to use the least drastic solution that will change as little of the system as possible.

6. If you think the problem is software related and you cannot boot to the Windows desktop, try booting to the Advanced Options menu (hold down **F8** while Windows loads) and select the **Last Known Good Configuration**. If you want to use this option, it's important to use it early in the troubleshooting process before you accidentally overwrite the Last Known Good Configuration.

> **A+ Exam Tip** The A+ 220-702 Practical Application exam expects you to be able to select the appropriate next step in troubleshooting a failed boot when given a specific scenario. As you study the tools and methods in this part of the chapter, pay attention to how a technique affects the installed OS, applications, and data. The idea is to fix the problem by using the tool that least affects the OS, applications, and data.

7. If you can load the Windows desktop, but the system is giving many errors or is extremely slow, suspect a virus is present. Run antivirus software to scan the entire hard drive for malicious software. If the antivirus software won't work or is not installed, boot into Safe Mode and install and run the software there. You will learn more about using antivirus software in Chapter 20.

8. If the system has recently been changed, such as installing software or hardware, assume the installation is the guilty party until it's proven innocent. Use Device Manager to disable or uninstall the device. If this solves the problem, then try to find updated device drivers for the device. Search the Microsoft Web site for known problems with the device or search the device manufacturer Web site. Try updating or rolling back the device drivers.

16

A+ 220-702

Error Message	What It Means and What to Do About It
Errors that occur before the Windows load begins:	
Hard drive not found Fixed disk error Disk boot failure, insert system disk and press enter No boot device available	Startup BIOS cannot find the hard drive. Problems with the hard drive and its subsystem are covered in Chapter 8.
Invalid boot disk Inaccessible boot device Invalid partition table Error loading operating system Missing operating system No operating system found Error loading operating system	The program in the MBR displays these messages when it cannot find the active partition on the hard drive or the boot sector on that partition. Use the Diskpart command from the Recovery Console to check the hard drive partition table for errors. Sometimes Fixmbr solves the problem. Third-party recovery software such as PartitionMagic might help. If a setup program came bundled with the hard drive (such as Data Lifeguard from Western Digital or MaxBlast from Maxtor), use it to examine the drive. Check the hard drive manufacturer's Web site for other diagnostic software.
Black screen with no error messages	This is likely to be a corrupted MBR, partition table, boot sector, or Ntldr file. Boot the PC using a Windows 2000/XP boot disk and then try the fixmbr and fixboot commands from the Recovery Console. You might have to reinstall Windows.
When you first turn on the computer, it continually reboots.	This is most likely a hardware problem. Could be the CPU, motherboard, or RAM. First disconnect or remove all nonessential devices such as USB or FireWire devices. Inside the case, check all connections using safety precautions to protect the system against static electricity as you work. Try reseating RAM. Check for fans that are not working, causing the CPU to quickly overheat.
Windows gives an error and then automatically restarts in an endless loop.	To stop the automatic restarts, press F8 to load the Advanced Options Menu. Then select Disable Automatic Restart on System Failure. You will then be able to read the error message and can turn your attention to addressing this error.
A disk read error occurred Missing NTLDR NTLDR is missing NTLDR is compressed	A disk is probably in the floppy disk drive. Remove the disk and reboot. When booting from the hard drive, these errors occur if Ntldr has been moved, renamed, or deleted, or is corrupted, if the boot sector on the active partition is corrupted, or you have just tried to install an older version of Windows, such as Windows 98, on the hard drive. First try replacing Ntldr. Then check Boot.ini settings.
When you first turn on a system, it begins the boot process, but then powers down.	The CPU might be quickly overheating. Check for fans not running. Is this a new CPU installation? If so, make sure the cooler assembly on top of the CPU is correctly installed.
STOP errors that cause Windows to lock up:	
A text error message appears on a blue screen and then the system halts.	Stop errors are usually caused by viruses, errors in the file system, a corrupted hard drive, or a hardware problem. Search the Microsoft Web site for information about an unidentified stop error. Several stop errors and their solutions can be found in Table 16-1 earlier in the chapter.

Table 16-2 Error messages during Windows 2000/XP startup and what to do about them

A+
220-702
2.4

Error Message	What It Means and What to Do About It
Startup errors that occur because a program is corrupted or not found:	
A device has failed to start Service failed to start Program not found	A registry entry or startup folder is referencing a startup program it cannot find. Use MSconfig or the Services Console to find the entry and then replace the missing program. These errors are sometimes caused by uninstall routines that left behind these orphan entries. Depending on the error, the system might or might not halt.

Table 16-2   Error messages during Windows 2000/XP startup and what to do about them (continued)

9. If a new application or utility program has just been installed, go to the Add or Remove Programs applet in Control Panel and uninstall the software. Reboot the system. If the problem goes away, then try reinstalling the software. If the problem comes back, go to the software manufacturer's Web site and download and install any updates or fixes.

10. If the system will not start normally, try to boot into Safe Mode. If you boot into Safe Mode and Windows XP recognizes System Restore has previously been used to create restore points, Windows XP gives you the opportunity to launch the System Restore Wizard (see Figure 16-21). The wizard gives you the opportunity to choose a restore point from those previously saved. Recall that when Windows is restored to a restore point, all Windows settings are returned to the way they were when the restore point was created.

11. After you boot into Safe Mode, you can use the SFC, Chkdsk, and Defrag commands to verify system files and clean the hard drive. How to do these tasks is covered in Chapter 13. Use antivirus software to scan for viruses. Restart the system. If the problem is not solved, then use System Restore to restore previous settings. The idea is to fix the problem while making as few changes to the system as necessary.

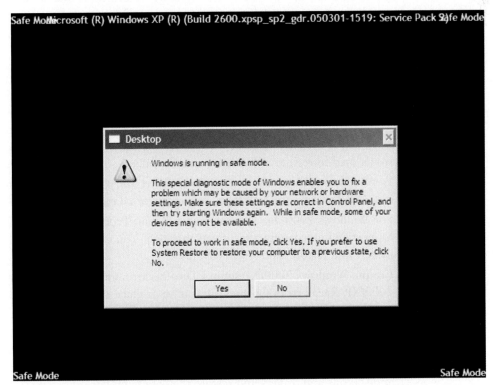

Figure 16-21   Windows XP gives you the opportunity to launch System Restore before it loads Safe Mode
Courtesy: Course Technology/Cengage Learning

16

A+ 220-702

12. If you cannot boot into Safe Mode, try Safe Mode with Command Prompt. Then try these commands, rebooting between commands: **Sfc.exe**, **Chkdsk C: /r**, and **C:\Windows\system32\restore\rstrui.exe**.

13. If you cannot boot from the hard drive, try creating and using a Windows 2000/XP boot disk. If you can boot to the Windows desktop when using this boot disk, you can assume that the boot files in the root directory of drive C are missing or corrupted. If necessary, you can restore these files using the Recovery Console. Also use Fixmbr and Fixboot to repair the MBR and boot sector.

14. If you cannot boot from the Windows 2000/XP boot disk, load the Recovery Console and do the following to restore system files. After you have made a change, restart the system to find out if the problem is fixed or has changed before you attempt the next fix:

    a. Get a directory listing of files in the root directory. If you see garbage on the screen instead of a clean directory list, most likely the hard drive file system is corrupted or the hard drive is physically damaged.

    b. Use the Chkdsk command to scan the hard drive for errors.

    c. Try copying the backup copies of the registry files from the \Windows\repair folder to the \Windows\system32\config folder. Directions are given in Chapter 15. Reboot to see if the problem is solved.

    d. If you have previously identified a key Windows service that is causing the problem, you can locate the file in the \Windows folder and replace it with a fresh copy from the Windows 2000/XP setup CD.

    e. To see a list of all services you can disable, use the Listsvc command. Use the Disable and Enable commands to try disabling each service one by one until you find the one causing the problem.

    f. For Windows XP, try using System Restore to return the system to a previously saved restore point.

    g. If you have a backup of the system state, use Ntbackup to restore the system state using this backup.

15. If the problem is still not solved, it's time to assume that the Windows installation is corrupted and you need to restore the Windows installation. However, if there is data on the hard drive that is not backed up, first look over the section "How to Recover Lost Data" earlier in the chapter. There might be a way to recover the data before you use one of the following methods to restore the Windows installation. Here are the tools used to restore a Windows installation:

    a. For Windows XP, use Automated System Recovery to restore the system to the last ASR backup. You will then need to restore data from backups.

    b. For Windows 2000, use the Emergency Repair Process to restore Windows 2000 to its state immediately after it was installed. You can then install applications and drivers and restore data from backups.

    c. Use the Windows 2000/XP setup CD to perform an in-place upgrade of Windows 2000/XP. Recall from Chapter 12 that an in-place upgrade installs Windows on top of the existing installation so that applications and drivers don't have to be reinstalled. The data might not be disturbed.

    d. If the in-place upgrade does not work, use the Windows 2000/XP setup CD to perform a clean install of Windows 2000/XP. You will then need to reinstall applications and drivers and restore the data from backups.

> **Notes** For a laptop or other brand-name computer, don't forget to reinstall Windows using recovery CDs provided by the computer manufacturer. Alternately, it might be possible to reinstall Windows from a recovery partition on the hard drive.

As you work to solve a Windows problem, keep in mind that many tools are at your disposal. As you decide which tool to use to correct a problem, always use the least drastic solution to make the fewest possible changes to the system. For example, if you know a driver is giving a problem, even though you can use System Restore to restore the system before the driver was installed, doing so is more drastic than simply rolling back the driver. Always choose the method that makes as few changes to the system as possible and still solves the problem.

> **Notes** When using System Restore and system state backups, you run the risk of undoing *desired* changes to the Windows environment and software installations. Before using one of these fixes, consider what desired changes will be lost when you apply the fix.

When you think the problem is solved, be sure to restart the system one last time to make sure all is well. Verify that everything is working and then ask the user to also verify that the problem is solved and all is working. And don't forget the paperwork. As you work, keep notes about the original symptoms, what you're doing, and the outcome. This paperwork will be a great help the next time you're faced with a similar problem.

>> CHAPTER SUMMARY

- When solving a problem caused by hardware, first identify the device causing the problem. Tools that can help are error messages that are displayed on the screen, the Vista Problem Reports and Solutions tool, the XP Error Reporting tool, Event Viewer, and Reliability and Performance Monitor.

- To fix a problem with a device or its drivers, use Device Manager, Windows update, System Restore, Safe Mode, System File Checker, and possibly use BIOS setup.

- To fix a problem with an application, use Task Manager, antivirus software, Vista Problem Reports and Solutions, XP Error Reporting, Windows updates, System Restore, and the Web site of the application developer.

- Windows Vista tools and techniques used to troubleshoot a failed boot include Last Known Good Configuration, Startup Repair, System Restore, Safe Mode, Command Prompt, in-place upgrade of Windows Vista, Complete PC Restore, and reformatting the hard drive and reinstalling Windows.

- Startup Repair in the Windows Recovery Environment can automatically fix many Windows problems, including those caused by a corrupted BCD file and missing system files. You can't cause any additional problems by using it and it's easy to use. Therefore, it should be your first recovery option when Vista refuses to load.

- Last Known Good Configuration can solve problems caused by a bad hardware or software installation by undoing the install.

- Use the command prompt window in Windows RE when the other RE tools fail to solve the problem.

16

◢ Your first decision in troubleshooting a failed Vista boot is to decide at what point in the boot the failure occurred. Determine if the failure occurred before the progress bar, after the progress bar and before logon, or after logon.

◢ If a hard drive contains valuable data but will not boot, you might be able to recover the data by installing the drive in another system as the second, nonbooting hard drive in the system.

◢ If you can boot from the Windows 2000/XP boot disk and load the Windows desktop, you have proven the problem is with the boot files in the root directory of the hard drive.

◢ Access the Recovery Console by first booting from the Windows 2000/XP CD, or the four Windows 2000 setup disks, or install the console under the boot loader menu and access it from there.

◢ The Windows 2000 Emergency Repair Process lets you restore the system to its state at the end of the Windows 2000 installation. Don't use it unless all other methods fail, because you will lose all changes made to the system since the installation. The Emergency Repair Process requires the emergency repair disk.

◢ You can use the Windows 2000/XP setup CD to perform an in-place upgrade or clean installation of Windows.

>> KEY TERMS

For explanations of key terms, see the Glossary near the end of the book.

secondary logon

>> REVIEWING THE BASICS

1. When you have a problem with a USB device, what is the simplest way to determine that the USB port is good?

2. When you have a problem with a USB device, what is the simplest way to determine that the USB device is not causing the problem?

3. How can you determine that device drivers loaded at startup are not interfering with an application that is having problems?

4. What is the command used for testing memory?

5. If you are not sure which device is causing a video problem—the monitor or the video card—which one should you exchange first? Why?

6. What type of device, when installed, is not listed in BIOS setup, Device Manager, or the Printers window?

7. What is the term used to describe undoing a driver update?

8. What Windows Vista tool can you use to uninstall a USB device?

9. What Windows XP tool can you use to uninstall a FireWire device?

10. What Windows tool can you use to uninstall a network card?

11. What Windows tool can you use to restore the Windows system to a previous point in time before a device was installed?

12. What Windows tool can you use to update your video drivers?

13. What symbols might Device Manager use to indicate a device is not working?

14. What level of permission must a user account have to install software?

15. If a computer won't boot, to figure out if the problem is related to the hard drive or other vital hardware component, what would be the first step?

16. What is another name for a Windows Stop error?

17. What is the name of the folder that is created when files from an old installation are moved during a reinstall of Vista?

18. What is the purpose of the hidden partition used by many of the brand-name computer companies?

19. What information is contained in the C:\Windows\System32\LogFiles\SRT\SRTTrail.txt file?

20. What is the name of the log file that Windows uses when booting in Safe Mode?

>> THINKING CRITICALLY

1. Windows Vista refused to start and the error message says something about the WinLoad program file being missing. Which action is the best way to fix the problem? Why?

   a. Boot from the Vista DVD and use the command prompt window to copy the WinLoad file from a working PC to this PC.

   b. Boot from the Vista DVD and use the Startup Repair tool.

   c. Use the latest Complete PC backup to restore the system.

   d. Boot into Safe Mode and restore the program from backup.

2. An error message is displayed during Vista startup before the progress bar appeared about missing services program files. You try to boot into Safe Mode, but get the same error message. Next, you use the Vista DVD to boot into the Recovery Environment. Select the best two tasks to fix the problem and order them correctly.

   a. Use System Restore to restore the system to a previous restore point.

   b. Use the command prompt to disable and then replace the service.

   c. Use Startup Repair.

   d. Use Complete PC Restore.

3. You tried to use the Automated System Recovery to restore a failed Windows XP system. The process failed with errors, but there is an extremely important data file on the hard drive that you need to recover. The hard drive is using the NTFS file system. What do you do?

   a. Most likely the file is toast. The ASR process probably destroyed the file if it were not already destroyed.

   b. Boot to the Recovery Console using the Windows XP setup CD and attempt to recover the file.

   c. Reinstall Windows XP and then recover the file.

   d. Boot to the Advanced Options menu and use Safe Mode to recover the file.

16

4. When you start Windows XP, you see an error message about a service that has failed to start and then the system locks up. You think this service is related to a critical Windows process. What do you try first? Second?

   a. Boot into Safe Mode and run System Restore.

   b. Select the Last Known Good Configuration on the Advanced Options menu.

   c. Perform an in-place upgrade of Windows XP.

   d. Use the Recovery Console to restore the system file.

5. Which statement(s) are true about the Windows 2000/XP boot disk?

   a. The boot disk can be used to boot the system to the Windows 2000/XP desktop when Ntldr is missing from the hard drive.

   b. The boot disk can be used to boot to the desktop even when the C:\Windows folder is corrupted.

   c. The boot disk can be used in place of the boot files in the root directory of the active partition.

   d. The boot disk can be used to boot to the desktop even when the partition table is corrupted.

>> HANDS-ON PROJECTS

PROJECT 16-1: Digging Deeper into System File Checker

The System File Checker tool can be used to find and replace corrupted Vista system files. The tool keeps a log of its actions, and, if it cannot replace a corrupted file, you can find that information in the log file. Then you can manually replace the file. Locate the Microsoft Knowledge Base Article 929833 at the *support.microsoft.com* site. Do whatever research is necessary to understand the steps in the article to manually replace a corrupted file and answer these questions:

1. What are other parameters for the sfc command besides /scannow?

2. Explain the purpose of the findstr command when finding the log file.

3. Can a filename other than sfcdetails.txt be used in the findstr command line? Explain your answer.

4. What is the purpose of the edit command?

5. Explain the purpose of the takeown command when replacing a system file.

6. Explain why the icacls command is needed in the process.

7. List some ways that you can locate a known good copy of the corrupted system file.

PROJECT 16-2: Practice Using the Recovery Console

To get some practice using the Recovery Console, first boot from your Windows 2000/XP setup CD and load the Recovery Console. Then do the following:

1. Get a directory listing of C:\. Are files normally hidden in Windows Explorer displayed in the list?

2. Create a folder on your hard drive named C:\Temp.

3. List the files contained in the Drivers.cab cabinet file.

4. Expand one of these files and put it in the C:\Temp folder.

5. Exit the Recovery Console and reboot.

PROJECT 16-3:   More Practice with Recovery Console

Using Windows Explorer, rename the Ntldr file in the root directory of drive C. Reboot the system. What error message do you see? Now use Recovery Console to restore Ntldr without using the renamed Ntldr file on drive C. Copy the file from the Windows setup CD to drive C. List the commands you used to do the job.

PROJECT 16-4:   Sabotage a Windows XP System

In a lab environment, follow these steps to find out if you can corrupt a Windows XP system so that it will not boot, and then repair the system.

1. Looking at Figure 16-22, make a list of the user-mode processes critical to Windows XP.

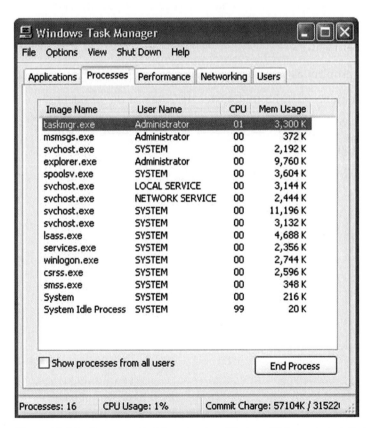

Figure 16-22   Processes that launch when Windows XP is newly installed
Courtesy: Course Technology/Cengage Learning

2. Rename or move one of the program files shown in Figure 16-22. Which program file did you select? In what Windows folder did you find it?

3. Restart your system. Did an error occur? Check in Explorer. Is the file restored? What Windows feature repaired the problem?

4. Try other methods of sabotaging the Windows XP system, but carefully record exactly what you did to sabotage the boot. Can you make the boot fail?

5. Now recover the Windows XP system. List the steps you took to get the system back to good working order.

PROJECT 16-5: Using a Windows 2000/XP Boot Disk

Create a Windows 2000/XP boot disk and use it to boot your computer. Describe how the boot worked differently from booting entirely from the hard drive.

>> REAL PROBLEMS, REAL SOLUTIONS

REAL PROBLEM 16-1: Fixing a PC Problem

This project should be fun, extremely useful, and give you an opportunity to find out just how much you have learned so far from this book. Make yourself available to family and friends who have problems with their computers. For each problem, don't forget to follow the procedures for troubleshooting you have learned in this book, especially the one about backing up user data before you make any changes to a system. For the first three problems you face, keep a record that includes this information:

1. Describe the problem as the user described it to you.

2. Briefly list the things you did to discover the cause of the problem.

3. What was the final solution?

4. How long did it take you to fix the problem?

5. What would you do differently the next time you encounter this same problem?

Networking Essentials

In this chapter, you'll learn about the technologies and hardware used to build networks, and how Windows supports and manages a network connection, including how computers are identified and addressed on a network. You'll also learn to connect a computer to a network and what to do when that connection gives problems. In the next chapter, you'll learn how to set up, configure, and support a small network.

The focus in this and the next chapter is to prepare you so that you can assume total responsibility for supporting both wired and wireless networks in a small-office-home-office (SOHO) environment. Consider this chapter the introductory chapter toward that end.

> **♀ A+ Exam Tip** All the content in this chapter applies toward the networking objectives of the A+ 220-701 Essentials exam. The A+ 220-702 Practical Application exam networking objectives are covered in the next chapter. The A+ 220-701 Essentials exam expects you to know about networking terms, concepts, protocols, and hardware, and to know how to connect a computer to an existing network.

NETWORKING TECHNOLOGIES

A+
220-701
4.1
4.3

A computer network is created when two or more computers can communicate with each other. Networks can be categorized by several methods, including the technology used and the size of the network. When networks are categorized by size or physical area they cover, these are the categories used:

- ▲ *PAN.* A PAN (personal area network) consists of personal devices at close range such as a cell phone, PDA, and notebook computer in communication. PANs can use wired connections (such as USB or FireWire) or wireless connections (such as Bluetooth or infrared).
- ▲ *LAN.* A LAN (local area network) covers a small local area such as a home, office, other building, or small group of buildings. LANs can use wired (most likely Ethernet) or wireless (most likely 802.11, also called Wi-Fi) technologies. A LAN is used for workstations, servers, printers, and other devices to communicate and share resources.
- ▲ *Wireless LAN.* A wireless LAN (WLAN) covers a limited geographical area, and is popular in places where networking cables are difficult to install, such as outdoors, in public places, and in homes that are not wired for networks. They are also useful in hotel rooms.
- ▲ *MAN.* A MAN (metropolitan area network) covers a large campus or city. (A small MAN is sometimes called a CAN or campus area network.) Newer technologies used are wireless and Ethernet with fiber-optic cabling. Older technologies used are ATM and FDDI.
- ▲ *WAN.* A WAN (wide area network) covers a large geographical area and is made up of many smaller networks. The best-known WAN is the Internet. Some technologies used to connect a single computer or LAN to the Internet include DSL, cable modem, satellite, cellular WAN, and fiber optic.

> 💡 **A+ Exam Tip** The A+ 220-701 Essentials exam expects you to know about a LAN and a WAN.

Networks are built using one or more technologies that provide varying degrees of bandwidth. Bandwidth (the width of the band) is the theoretical number of bits that can be transmitted over a network at one time, similar to the number of lanes on a highway. In practice, however, the networking industry refers to bandwidth as a measure of the maximum rate of data transmission in bits per second (bps), thousands of bits per second (Kbps), millions of bits per second (Mbps), or billions of bits per second (Gpbs). Bandwidth is the theoretical or potential speed of a network, whereas data throughput is the actual speed. In practice, network transmissions experience delays that result in slower network performance. These delays in network transmissions are called latency. Latency is measured by the round-trip time it takes for a data packet to travel from source to destination and back to source.

In this chapter, we focus on network technologies used for a local network (LAN) and those used to connect to the Internet. To connect to the Internet, a network first connects to an Internet Service Provider (ISP), such as Earthlink or Comcast (see Figure 17-1). When connecting to an ISP, know that upload speeds are generally slower than download speeds. These rates differ because users generally download more data than they upload. Therefore, an ISP devotes more of the available bandwidth to downloading and less of it to uploading.

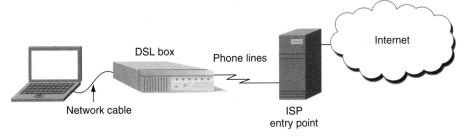

Figure 17-1 Use an ISP to connect to the Internet
Courtesy: Course Technology/Cengage Learning

Table 17-1 lists network technologies, their speeds, and their uses. Older technologies no longer widely used and not listed in the table include X.25, Frame Relay, ISDN, Token Ring, FDDI, and ATM. The table is more or less ordered from slowest to fastest maximum bandwidth, although latency can affect the actual bandwidth of a particular network.

Technology	Maximum Speeds	Common Uses
Wireless Networks		
Bluetooth 2.0 (BT2)	Up to 2 Mbps	Short-range wireless technology used for a PAN (personal area network).
GSM mobile phone service	Up to 3 Mbps	Cellular wireless technology used for voice and data transmissions over mobile phones; first became popular in Europe.
CDMA mobile phone service	Up to 3 Mbps	Cellular wireless technology used for mobile phones; losing popularity.
G3 mobile phone service	Up to 2.4 Mbps	Cellular mobile phone technology allows for transmitting data, video, and text.
Wi-Fi 802.11b wireless	Up to 11 Mbps	First 802.11 standard that was widely used, but is being replaced by 802.11g and n.
Bluetooth 3.0 (BT3)	Up to 24 Mbps	Latest Bluetooth standard just released that is not yet available in devices.
Wi-Fi 802.11a wireless	Up to 54 Mbps	Shorter range than 802.11b, but faster.
Wi-Fi 802.11g wireless	Up to 54 Mbps	Compatible with and replacing 802.11b.
802.16 wireless (WiMAX)	Up to 75 Mbps	Offers ranges up to 6 miles.
802.11n wireless	Up to 160 Mbps	Latest Wi-Fi technology.
Wired Networks		
Dial-up or regular telephone (POTS, for plain old telephone service)	Up to 56 Kbps	Slow access to an ISP using a modem and dial-up connection.
SDSL (Symmetric Digital Subscriber Line)	Up to 2.3 Mbps	Equal bandwidths in both directions. SDSL is a type of broadband technology. (Broadband refers to a networking technology that carries more than one type of signal, such as DSL and telephone.)

Table 17-1 Networking technologies (continued)

A+
220-701
4.1
4.3

Technology	Maximum Speeds	Common Uses
ADSL (Asymmetric DSL)	640 Kbps upstream and up to 8 Mbps downstream	Most bandwidth is from ISP to user. Slower versions of ADSL are called ADSL Lite or DSL Lite. ISP customers pay according to a bandwidth scale.
Ethernet	10 Mbps	Slowest Ethernet network, replaced by Fast Ethernet. Variations of Ethernet are used for almost all local networks.
Cable modem	4 to 16 Mbps, depends on the type of cable used	Connects a home or small business to an ISP; is usually purchased with a cable television subscription. Cable modem is a type of broadband technology that is used in conjunction with television on the same cable. Fiber-optic cable gives highest speeds.
Dedicated line using fiber optic	Up to 20 Mbps upstream and 50 Mbps downstream	Dedicated line from ISP to business or home. Speeds vary with price.
T3	45 Mbps	Dedicated lines used by large companies that require a lot of bandwidth and transmit extensive amounts of data.
VDSL (very-high-bit-rate DSL)	Up to 52 Mbps	This latest version of DSL is asymmetric DSL that works only a short distance.
Fast Ethernet	100 Mbps	Used for local networks.
Gigabit Ethernet	1 Gbps	Fastest Ethernet standard for a local network.
10-gigabit Ethernet	10 Gbps	Newest Ethernet standard expected to largely replace SONET, OC, and ATM because of its speed, simplicity, and lower cost.
OC-1, OC-3, OC-24, up to OC-3072	52 Mbps, 155 Mbps, 1.23 Gbps, 160 Gbps	Optical Carrier levels (OCx) used for Internet backbones; they use fiber-optic cabling.
SONET (Synchronous Optical Network)	Up to 160 Gbps	Major backbones built using fiber-optic cabling make use of different OC levels.

Table 17-1 Networking technologies

A+ Exam Tip The A+ 220-701 Essentials exam expect you to be able to compare and contrast these network types: Dial-up, DSL, cable, satellite, fiber, 802.11, Bluetooth, and cellular.

Notes The Institute of Electrical and Electronics Engineers (IEEE) creates standards for computer and electronics industries. Of those standards, IEEE 802 applies to networking. For example, IEEE 802.2 describes the standard for Logical Link Control, which defines how networks that use different protocols communicate with each other. (Remember that protocols are rules for communication.) For more information on the IEEE 802 standards, see the IEEE Web site, *www.ieee.org*.

A+
220-701
4.1
4.3

When two devices on a network communicate, they must use the same protocols, so that the communication makes sense. For almost all networks today, including the Internet, the protocol used is called **TCP/IP (Transmission Control Protocol/Internet Protocol)**. TCP/IP is actually a group of protocols that control many different aspects of communication. Before data is transmitted on a network, it is first broken up into segments. Each data segment is put into a **packet** with information about the packet put at the beginning and the end of the data. This information identifies the type of data, where it came from, and where it's going. Information at the beginning of the data is called a header, and information at the end of the data is called a trailer. If the data to be sent is large, it is first divided into several packets, each small enough to travel on the network.

> **A+ Tip** The A+ 220-701 Essentials exam expects you to be familiar with many networking terms. This chapter is full of key terms you need to know for the exam.

You can connect a computer or LAN to the Internet using a broadband, wireless, or dial-up connection. Now let's look at some of the important details of each type of connection.

BROADBAND TECHNOLOGIES

Broadband technologies used to connect to the Internet are cable modem, DSL, fiber-optic, satellite and ISDN. **ISDN (Integrated Services Digital Network)** is an outdated broadband technology developed in the 1980s that uses regular phone lines, and is accessed by a dial-up connection. In most areas of the country, cable modem and DSL compete as the two most popular ways to connect to the Internet. Let's first compare these two technologies and then we'll look at satellite and fiber-optic dedicated lines.

COMPARE CABLE MODEM AND DSL

Cable modem and DSL are the two most popular ways to connect to the Internet.

▲ **Cable modem** communication uses cable lines that already exist in millions of households. Just as with cable TV, cable modems are always connected (always up). With a cable modem, the TV signal to your television and the data signals to your PC share the same coax cable. Just like a dial-up modem, a cable modem converts a PC's digital signals to analog when sending them and converts incoming analog data to digital.

▲ **DSL (Digital Subscriber Line)** is a group of broadband technologies that covers a wide range of speeds. DSL uses ordinary copper phone lines and a range of frequencies on the copper wire that are not used by voice, making it possible for you to use the same phone line for voice and DSL at the same time. When you make a regular phone call, you dial in as usual. However, the DSL part of the line is always connected (always up) for most DSL services. A few DSL services offer the option to connect on demand. For these services, a username and passcode are sent to the ISP when making a connection. Asymmetric DSL (ADSL) uses one upload speed from the consumer to an ISP and a faster download speed. Symmetric DSL (SDSL) uses equal bandwidths in both directions.

17

A+ 220-701

A+
220-701
4.1
4.3

Here are some important similarities and differences between cable modem and DSL:

◢ Both cable modem and DSL can sometimes be purchased on a sliding scale, depending on the bandwidth you want to buy. Subscriptions offer residential and the more-expensive business plans. Business plans are likely to have increased bandwidth and better support when problems arise.

◢ With cable modem, you share the TV cable infrastructure with your neighbors, which can result in service becoming degraded if many people in your neighborhood are using cable modem at the same time. I once used cable modem in a neighborhood where I found I needed to avoid Web surfing between 5:00 and 7:00 p.m. when folks were just coming in from work and using the Internet. With DSL, you're using a dedicated phone line, so your neighbors' surfing habits are not important.

◢ With DSL, static over phone lines in your house can be a problem. The DSL company provides filters to install at each phone jack (see Figure 17-2), but still the problem might not be fully solved. Also, your phone line must qualify for DSL; some lines are too dirty (too much static or noise) to support DSL.

Figure 17-2   When DSL is used in your home, filters are needed on every
phone jack except the one used by the DSL modem
Courtesy: Course Technology/Cengage Learning

◢ Setup of cable modem and DSL works about the same way, using either a cable modem box or a DSL box for the interface between the broadband jack (TV jack or phone jack) and the PC. Figure 17-3 shows the setup for a cable modem connection using a network cable between the cable modem and the PC.

◢ With either installation, in most cases, you can have the cable modem or DSL provider do the entire installation for you at an additional cost. A service technician comes to your home, installs all equipment, including a network card if necessary, and configures your PC to use the service.

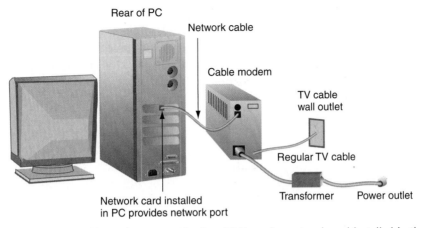

Figure 17-3 Cable modem connecting to a PC through a network card installed in the PC
Courtesy: Course Technology/Cengage Learning

▲ In most cases, cable modem and DSL use a network port or a USB port on the PC to connect to the cable modem or DSL box. A DSL box is shown in Figure 17-4.

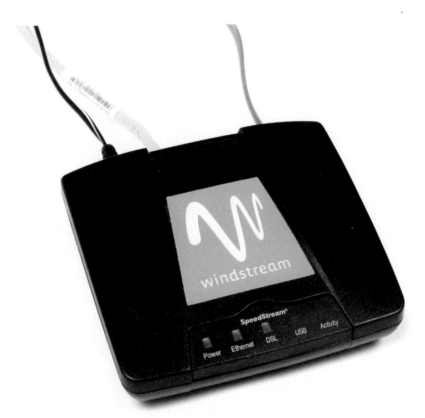

Figure 17-4 This DSL box connects to a phone jack and a PC to provide a broadband connection to an ISP
Courtesy: Course Technology/Cengage Learning

SATELLITE

People who live in remote areas and want high-speed Internet connections often are limited in their choices. DSL and cable modem options might not be available where they live, but satellite access is available from pretty much anywhere. Internet access by

A+
220-701
4.1
4.3

satellite is available even on airplanes. Passengers can connect to the Internet using a wireless hotspot and satellite dish on the plane. A satellite dish mounted on top of your house or office building communicates with a satellite used by an ISP offering the satellite service (see Figure 17-5). One disadvantage of using satellite for an Internet connection is that it experiences delays in transmission (called latency), especially when uploading, more so than DSL or cable modem.

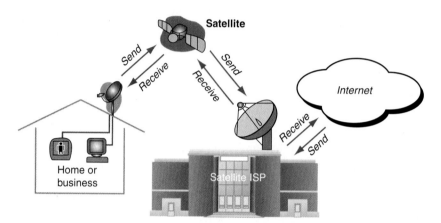

Figure 17-5   Communication by satellite can include television and Internet access
Courtesy: Course Technology/Cengage Learning

DEDICATED LINE USING FIBER OPTIC

Another broadband technology used for Internet access is fiber optic. The technology uses a dedicated line from your ISP to your place of business or residence. This dedicated line is called a point-to-point (PTP) connection because no other business or residence shares the line with you. Many types of cabling can be used for dedicated lines, but fiber-optic cabling is becoming popular. Television, Internet data, and voice communication all share the broadband fiber-optic cable. Verizon calls the technology FiOS (Fiber Optic Service), and the fiber-optic cabling is used all the way from the ISP to your home. Other providers might provide fiber-optic cabling up to your neighborhood and then use coaxial cable (similar to that used in cable modem connections) for the last leg of the connection to your business or residence. Upstream and downstream speeds and prices vary.

WIRELESS TECHNOLOGIES

Wireless networks, as the name implies, use radio waves or infrared light instead of cables or wires to connect computers or other devices. Although wireless networks have some obvious advantages in places where running cables would be difficult or overly expensive, wireless networks tend to be slower than wired networks, especially when they are busy. Another problem with wireless networks is security.

Now let's look at some details of several wireless technologies used to connect two devices or connect to a local network or to the Internet, including Wi-Fi, WiMAX, cellular, and Bluetooth. One other wireless technology that you need to be aware of is infrared, which is discussed in Chapter 9.

A+
220-701
4.1
4.3
5.2

WI-FI OR 802.11 WIRELESS

By far, the most popular technology for wireless local networks is IEEE 802.11, first published in 1990. These standards are also called **Wi-Fi (Wireless Fidelity)**. Most wireless devices today support three IEEE standards; look for **802.11b/g/n** on the packages. Several IEEE 802.11 standards are listed below:

▲ *802.11g and 802.11b.* These two standards use a frequency range of 2.4 GHz in the radio band and have a distance range of about 100 meters. 802.11b/g has the disadvantage that many cordless phones use the 2.4-GHz frequency range and cause network interference. 802.11g runs at 54 Mbps and 802.11b runs at 11 Mbps. Apple Computer calls 802.11b **AirPort**, and it calls 802.11g AirPort Extreme.

▲ *802.11n.* This latest Wi-Fi standard uses **multiple input/multiple output (MIMO)** technology whereby two or more antennas are used at both ends of transmission. 802.11n can use the 2.4 GHz range and be compatible with 802.11b/g, or it can use the 5.0 GHz range and be compatible with the older 802.11a standard. Figure 17-6 shows an 802.11b/g/n network adapter. Speeds of up to 600 Mbps are possible with 802.11n.

▲ *802.11a.* This standard is no longer widely used. It works in the 5.0-GHz frequency range and is, therefore, not compatible with 802.11b/g. It has a shorter range from a wireless device to an access point (50 meters compared with 100 meters for 802.11b/g), supports 54 Mbps, and does not encounter interference from cordless phones, microwave ovens, and Bluetooth devices, as does 802.11b/g.

Figure 17-6 Wireless network adapter supports 802.11g/b/n
Courtesy: Course Technology/Cengage Learning

▲ *802.11k and 802.11r.* These two standards were designed to help manage connections between wireless devices and access points. Normally, if a wireless device senses more than one access point, by default, it connects to the access point with the strongest signal, which can cause an overload on some access points while other access points are idle. The 802.11k standard defines how wireless network traffic can better be distributed over multiple access points covering a wide area so that the access point with the strongest signal is not overloaded. The 802.11r standard defines how a mobile wireless device can easily and quickly transition as it moves out of range of one access point and into the range of another.

17

A+ 220-701

A+
220-701
4.1
4.3
5.2

▲ *802.11d.* This standard is designed to run in countries outside the United States where other 802.11 versions do not meet the legal requirements for radio band technologies.

Wireless LANs are so convenient for us at work and at home, but the downside of having a wireless network is that if we don't have the proper security in place, anyone with a wireless computer within range of our access point can use the network—and, if they know how, can intercept and read all the data sent across the network. They might even be able to hack into our computers by using our own wireless network against us. For all these reasons, it's terribly important to secure a wireless network.

> **A+ Exam Tip**   The A+ 220-701 Essentials exam expects you to be familiar with wireless encryption, including WEPx, WPAx, and client configuration (SSID).

Securing a wireless network is generally done in three ways:

▲ *Method 1: Data encryption*—Data sent over a wireless connection can be encrypted. The three main protocols for encryption for 802.11 wireless networks are WEP (Wired Equivalent Privacy), WPA (Wi-Fi Protected Access), and WPA2 (Wi-Fi Protected Access 2). With any of these protocols, data is encrypted using a firmware program on the wireless device and is only encrypted while the data is wireless; the data is decrypted before placing it on the wired network. With WEP encryption, data is encrypted using either 64-bit or 128-bit encryption keys. (Because the user can configure only 40 bits of the 64 bits, 64-bit WEP encryption is sometimes called 40-bit WEP encryption.) WEP was first defined by 802.11b. Because the key used for encryption is static (it doesn't change), a hacker can easily decrypt the code and read WEP-encrypted data. Therefore, WEP encryption is no longer considered secure. WPA encryption, also called TKIP (Temporal Key Integrity Protocol) encryption, is stronger than WEP and was designed to replace it. With WPA encryption, encryption keys are changed at set intervals. The latest and best wireless encryption standard is WPA2, also called the 802.11i standard or AES (Advanced Encryption Standard). When buying wireless devices, be sure the encryption methods used are compatible! When connecting to a wireless network that is using WEP or WPA encryption, you must enter the passphrase or key that is used to encrypt the data.

▲ *Method 2: Disable SSID broadcasting*—The name of the wireless access point is called the Service Set Identifier (SSID). Normally, the SSID is broadcast so that anyone with a wireless computer can see the name and use the network. If you hide the SSID, a computer can see the wireless network, but can't use it unless the SSID is known. Best practice when hiding the SSID is to also change the default name so that it cannot easily be guessed. Disabling SSID broadcasting is normally not used when data encryption is used. When you attempt to connect to a network that declares itself an "Unnamed Network," you are given the opportunity to enter the SSID to complete the connection.

▲ *Method 3: Filter MAC addresses*—A wireless access point can filter the MAC addresses of wireless NICs that are allowed to use the access point. A MAC (Media Access Control) address is a 6-byte number that uniquely identifies a network adapter on a computer. This type of security prevents uninvited guests from using the wireless LAN, but does not prevent others from receiving data in the air. Also, knowledgeable users can hack through MAC address filtering, and it is, therefore, considered a weak security measure. To connect to a wireless network that is set to filter MAC addresses, the administrator of the network must enter the MAC address of your wireless network adapter in the table of MAC addresses that are allowed to use the network.

A+
220-701
4.1
4.3

WIMAX OR 802.16 WIRELESS

A newer IEEE wireless standard is WiMAX, which is defined under IEEE 802.16d and 802.16e. WiMAX supports up to 75 Mbps with a range up to several miles and uses 2- to 11-GHz frequency. The WiMAX range in miles depends on many factors. For a wide-area network, WiMAX cellular towers are generally placed 1.5 miles apart to assure complete coverage. WiMAX is used in wide-area public hot spots and as a wireless broadband solution for business and residential use. It is often used as a last-mile solution for DSL and cable modem technologies, which means that the DSL or cable connection goes into a central point in an area, and WiMAX is used for the final leg to the consumer.

> **Notes** For more information on Wi-Fi, see *www.wi-fi.org*, and for more information on AirPort, see *www.apple.com*. For information on Bluetooth, see *www.bluetooth.com*. For information on WiMAX, see *www.wimaxforum.org*.

CELLULAR WAN

A cellular network or cellular WAN can be used when a wireless network must cover a wide area. The network consists of cells and each cell is controlled by a base station (see Figure 17-7). The base station is a fixed transceiver and antenna. WiMAX is sometimes used to build a cellular network, but the most common type of cellular networks are cell phone networks. Cell phones are called that because they use a cellular network.

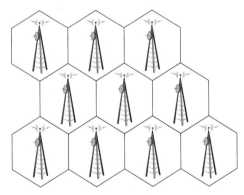

Figure 17-7 A cellular WAN is made up of many cells that provide coverage over a wide area
Courtesy: Course Technology/Cengage Learning

Cell phone networks use one of the following competing technologies:

▲ **GSM (Global System for Mobile Communications)** is an open standard that uses digital communication of data, and is accepted and used worldwide.
▲ **CDMA (Code Division Multiple Access)** is used by most cell phone service providers in the United States for domestic calls. If your cell phone supports the technology, you might be able to purchase a GSM plan for international calling at a higher rate.
▲ **TDMA (Time Division Multiple Access)** is an older, outdated technology used in the United States.

The ability to use your cell phone to browse the Web, stream music and video, play online games, use instant messaging and video conferencing is called **3G (Third Generation)** technology.

17

A+ 220-701

A+
220-701
4.1
4.3

All wireless phone systems, including cellular, use **full-duplex** transmission, which means both people in a conversation can talk or transmit at the same time. This is possible because the cell phones are using one frequency to transmit data and another to receive data. In contrast, walkie-talkies use **half-duplex** transmission, which means transmission works in only one direction at a time because the walkie-talkies are using the same frequency to both send and receive data. Full-duplex and half-duplex transmissions are illustrated in Figure 17-8.

(a) Mobile phone   (b) Walkie-talkie

Figure 17-8   Full-duplex and half-duplex transmission
Courtesy: Course Technology/Cengage Learning

BLUETOOTH

Bluetooth is a standard for short-range wireless communication and data synchronization between devices. Bluetooth, which has a range of only 10 meters, works in the 2.4-GHz frequency range, transfers data at up to 3 Mbps, is easy to configure, and is used for short-range personal network connections. For example, wireless headsets, mice, keyboards, and printers might use Bluetooth to communicate with a laptop that serves as the Bluetooth base station. For security, Bluetooth transmissions are encrypted. Cellular phones sometimes use Bluetooth wireless technology to make the short wireless hop between the phone and a wireless headset (see Figure 17-9). In this case, the phone serves as the base station for the headset.

Also, a cellular phone might use Bluetooth to communicate with a notebook computer, as shown in Figure 17-10. The notebook communicates with the nearby cellular phone, which communicates with the cellular WAN to provide Internet access for the notebook.

DIAL-UP TECHNOLOGY

Of all the types of networking connections, dial-up or POTS (Plain Old Telephone Service) is the least expensive and slowest connection to the Internet. Dial-up connections are painfully slow, but many times we still need them when traveling, and they're good at home when our broadband connection is down or when we just plain want to save money. Connecting to a network, such as the Internet, using a modem and regular phone line is

A+
220-701
4.1
4.3

Figure 17-9 This wireless headset accessory for a mobile phone uses Bluetooth wireless between the headset and the phone
Courtesy of Tekkeon, Inc.

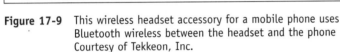

Figure 17-10 Bluetooth can be used for short transmissions between personal devices such as a cell phone and notebook computer
Courtesy: Course Technology/Cengage Learning

called **dial-up networking**. Dial-up networking works by using **PPP (Point-to-Point Protocol)** to send data packets over phone lines. PPP is, therefore, called a line protocol.

Modem cards in desktop computers provide two phone jacks (called **RJ-11 jacks**) so that one can be used for dial-up networking and the other jack can be used to plug in an extension telephone (see Figure 17-11). Laptop computers that have embedded modem capability generally have only a single phone jack. The most recent standard used by modems is the V.92 standard. Modem standards haven't changed in several years, because dial-up networking has reached its maximum bandwidth and is being outdated by other technologies to connect to the Internet.

> **Notes** Because of the sampling rate (8,000 samples every second) used by phone companies when converting an analog signal to digital, and taking into account the overhead of data transmission (bits and bytes sent with the data that are used to control and define transmissions), the maximum transmission rate that a modem can attain over a regular phone line is about 56,000 bps, or 56 Kbps. Although theoretically possible, most modem connections don't actually attain this speed. When connecting to an ISP using a dial-up connection, to achieve 56 Kbps, the ISP must use a digital connection to the phone company.

17

A+ 220-701

A+
220-701
4.1
4.3

Figure 17-11 This 56K V.92 PCI modem card comes bundled with a phone cord and setup CD
Courtesy: Course Technology/Cengage Learning

INTERNET ACCESS WHEN YOU TRAVEL

When traveling in the past, the only way to connect to the Internet was to find a telephone line and use your laptop computer to dial in to your ISP. Today, we have many options:

▲ A cellular Internet card, also called an air card, works like a cell phone to connect to a cellular WAN to give your computer Internet access. The device can be a USB device or can be a card that inserts into a PC Card slot or ExpressCard slot on a laptop. The AirCard 402 shown in Figure 17-12 is a combo device that includes an adapter so that it can fit either a PC Card slot or an ExpressCard slot. Use an Internet card wherever you have a cell phone signal to connect your PC to the Internet. You pay for the service through your cell phone provider.

Figure 17-12 AirCard 402 Modem by Sierra Wireless fits a PC Card or ExpressCard slot on a laptop to provide GPS and Internet through a cellular network
Courtesy of Sierra Wireless

▲ Find a public Wi-Fi hot spot and connect your laptop wirelessly. You'll sometimes pay a fee to use the hotspot.
▲ Mobile satellite broadband can be used by travelers who want to tote about a portable satellite dish. Figure 17-13 shows a dish by Ground Control (*www.groundcontrol.com*) mounted on top of a truck. Dishes can also be purchased to mount on top of an RV or that are small enough to pack with a laptop. Some satellite dish systems can automatically point the dish to the southern sky to make a high-speed connection.

A+
220-701
4.1
4.3

Figure 17-13 This satellite Internet system by Ground Control gives high-speed Internet access anywhere
Courtesy of Ground Control

HARDWARE USED BY LOCAL NETWORKS

A+
220-701
1.2
1.9
4.1

In this part of the chapter, you will learn about the hardware devices that create and connect to networks. Hardware discussed includes desktop and laptop devices, cables and their connectors, hubs, switches, wireless access devices, and routers.

NETWORKING ADAPTERS AND PORTS

A desktop to laptop computer connects to a local network using an Ethernet wired network or wireless networking.

A+
220-701
1.2
1.9
4.1
2.2

ETHERNET NETWORK ADAPTERS AND PORTS

A PC makes a direct connection to a network by way of a network adapter, which might be a network port embedded on the motherboard or a network interface card (NIC), using an expansion slot, such as the one shown in Figure 17-14. In addition, the adapter might also be an external device connecting to the PC using a USB port. The adapter provides an RJ-45 port (RJ stands for registered jack) that looks like a large phone jack. Laptops can make connections to a network through a PC Card NIC, a built-in network port, or an external device that connects to the laptop by way of a USB port. (You will learn about PC Cards in Chapter 21.)

17

A+ 220-701

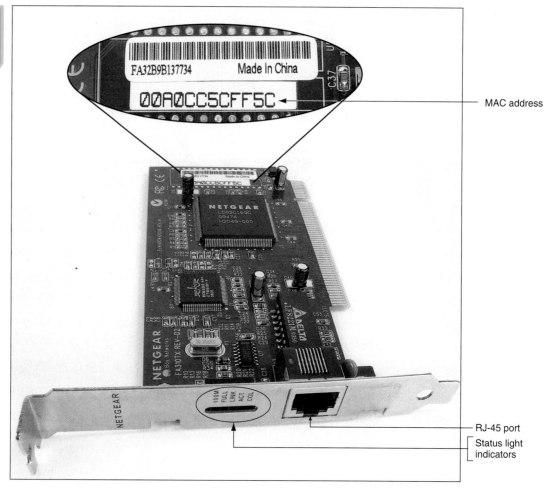

MAC address

RJ-45 port

Status light
indicators

Figure 17-14   Ethernet network card showing its MAC address
Courtesy: Course Technology/Cengage Learning

> **A+ Exam Tip**   The A+ 220-701 Essentials exam expects you to know the purpose of an RJ-45 port
> and an RJ-11 port.

Most network cards also provide status light indicators near the RJ-45 port. You can see
a bank of these indicators on the card in Figure 17-14. Depending on the card, the lights
might indicate the speed of transmission being used among those the card supports,
connectivity, and activity. For a network port on the motherboard, a solid light indicates
connectivity and a blinking light indicates activity. For example, in Figure 17-15, the
yellow light blinks to indicate activity and the green light is steady or solid to indicate
connectivity. When you first discover you have a problem with a PC not connecting to a
network, be sure to check the status light indicators to verify you have connectivity and
activity. If not, then the problem is related to hardware. Check the cable connections at
both ends. If the connections are solid, then the problem is with the NIC, the cable, or
other networking hardware.

Every network adapter (including a network card, onboard wireless, or wireless NIC) has
a 48-bit (6-byte) number hard-coded on the card by its manufacturer that is unique for that

Figure 17-15 Status indicator lights for the embedded network port
Courtesy: Course Technology/Cengage Learning

Yellow light blinks
with activity

Steady green light
indicates connectivity

adapter, and this number is used to identify the adapter on the network. The number is
written in hex and is called the **MAC (Media Access Control) address**, **hardware address**,
physical address, **adapter address**, or **Ethernet address**. An example of a MAC address is
00-0C-6E-4E-AB-A5. Part of the MAC address refers to the manufacturer, and the second
part of the address is a serial number assigned by the manufacturer. Therefore, no two
adapters should have the same MAC address. Most likely the MAC address is printed on
the card, as shown in Figure 17-14. Every NIC used today for a wired network follows the
Ethernet standards. Recall that the four speeds for Ethernet are 10 Mbps, 100 Mbps
(Fast Ethernet), 1 Gbps (Gigabit Ethernet), and 10 Gbps (10-gigabit Ethernet). Most network cards sold today use Gigabit Ethernet and also support the two slower speeds.

WI-FI WIRELESS ADAPTERS

Wi-Fi wireless connections using 802.11b/g/n standards can
be made with a variety of devices, four of which are shown in
Figure 17-16. In addition, most laptops sold today have a
wireless antenna embedded inside the laptop.

▶ **Video**
Wireless Network Cards

CABLES AND CONNECTORS

Several variations of Ethernet cables and connectors have evolved over the years, and are
primarily identified by their speeds and the types of connectors used to wire these networks.
Table 17-2 compares cable types and Ethernet versions.

💡 **A+ Exam Tip** The A+ 220-701 Essentials exam expects you to know the details shown in
Table 17-2.

17

A+ 220-701

A+
220-701
4.2

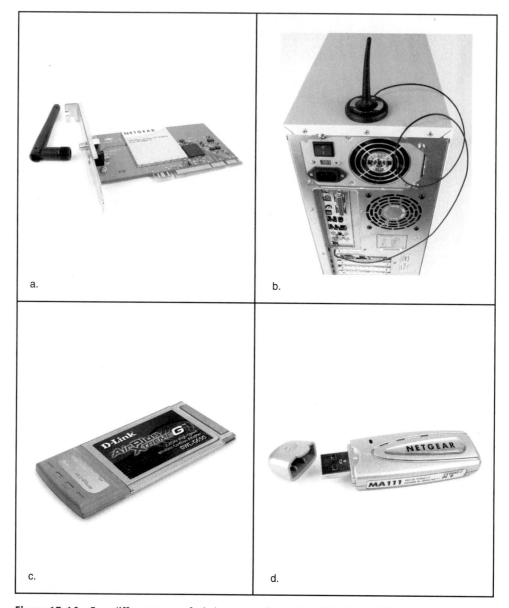

Figure 17-16 Four different types of wireless network adapters: (a) wireless NIC that fits in a PCI slot; (b) onboard wireless with an antenna that can be moved; (c) PC Card wireless NIC with embedded antenna; and (d) wireless NIC that uses a USB port on a desktop or notebook computer
Courtesy: Course Technology/Cengage Learning

As you can see from Table 17-2, the three main types of cabling used by Ethernet are twisted-pair, coaxial, and fiber optic. Coaxial cable is older and almost never used today. Within each category, there are several variations:

▲ *Twisted-pair cable.* Twisted-pair cable is the most popular cabling method for local networks. It comes in two varieties: unshielded twisted pair (UTP) cable and shielded twisted pair (STP) cable. UTP cable is the most common and least expensive. UTP is rated by category: CAT-3 (Category 3) is less expensive than the more popular CAT-5 cable or enhanced CAT-5 (CAT-5e). CAT-6 has less crosstalk than CAT-5 or CAT-5e. STP uses a covering around the pairs of wires inside the cable that protects it from electromagnetic interference caused by electrical motors, transmitters, or high-tension lines. It costs more than unshielded cable, so it's used only when the situation

A+
220-701
4.2

Cable System	Speed	Cables and Connectors	Example of Connectors	Maximum Cable Length
10Base2 (ThinNet)	10 Mbps	Coaxial uses a BNC connector.	Courtesy of Cables4Computer.com	185 meters or 607 feet
10Base5 (ThickNet)	10 Mbps	Coaxial uses an AUI 15-pin D-shaped connector.	Courtesy of Black Box Corporation	500 meters or 1,640 feet
10BaseT, 100BaseT (Twisted-pair), Gigabit Ethernet, and 10-Gigabit Ethernet	10 Mbps, 100 Mbps, 1 Gbps, or 10 Gbps	Twisted pair (UTP or STP) uses an RJ-45 connector.	Courtesy of Tyco Electronics	100 meters or 328 feet
10BaseF, 10BaseFL, 100BaseFL, 100BaseFX, 1000BaseFX, or 1000BaseX (fiber optic)	10 Mbps, 100 Mbps, 1 Gbps, or 10 Gbps	Fiber-optic cable uses ST or SC connectors (shown to the right) or LC and MT-RJ connectors (not shown).	Courtesy of Black Box Corporation	Up to 2 kilometers (6,562 feet)

Table 17-2 Variations of Ethernet and Ethernet cabling

demands it. Twisted-pair cable has four pairs of twisted wires for a total of eight wires and uses a connector called an RJ-45 connector. Figure 17-17 shows unshielded twisted-pair cables and the RJ-45 connector.

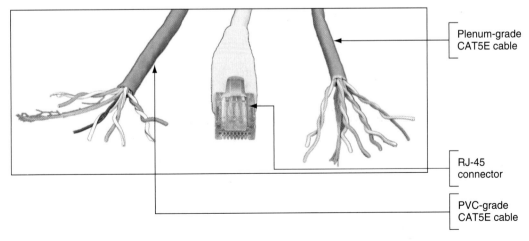

Figure 17-17 The most common networking cable for a local network is UTP cable using an RJ-45 connector
Courtesy: Course Technology/Cengage Learning

17

A+ 220-701

A+
220-701
4.2

> 📝 **Notes** Normally, the plastic covering of a cable is made of PVC (polyvinyl chloride), which is not safe when used inside plenums (areas between the floors of buildings). In these situations, plenum cable covered with Teflon is used because it does not give off toxic fumes when burned. Plenum cable is two or three times more expensive than PVC cable. Figure 17-17 shows plenum cable and PVC cable, both of which are unshielded twisted pair CAT5e cables.

▲ *Coaxial cable.* Coaxial cable has a single copper wire down the middle and a braided shield around it (see Figure 17-18). The cable is stiff and difficult to manage, and is no longer used for networking. RG6 coaxial cable is used for cable TV, having replaced the older and thinner RJ59 coaxial cable once used for cable TV.

Figure 17-18 Coaxial cable and a BNC connector are used with ThinNet Ethernet
Courtesy: Course Technology/Cengage Learning

▲ *Fiber optic.* **Fiber-optic cables** transmit signals as pulses of light over glass strands inside protected tubing, as illustrated in Figure 17-19. Fiber-optic cable comes in two types: single-mode (thin, difficult to connect, expensive, and best performing) and multimode (most popular). A single-mode cable uses a single path for light to travel in the cable and multimode cable uses multiple paths for light. Both single-mode and multimode fiber-optic cables can be constructed as loose-tube cables for outdoor use or tight-buffered cable for indoor or outdoor use. Loose-tube cables are filled with gel to prevent water from soaking into the cable, and tight-buffered cables are filled with yarn to protect the fiber-optic strands, as shown in Figure 17-19.

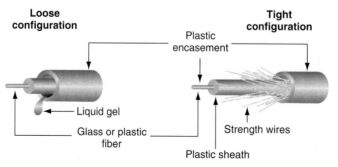

Figure 17-19 Fiber-optic cables contain a glass core for transmitting light
Courtesy: Course Technology/Cengage Learning

A+
220-701
4.2

Fiber-optic cables can use one of four connectors, all shown in Figure 17-20. The two older types are ST (straight tip) and SC (subscriber connector or standard connector). Two newer types are LC (local connector) and MT-RJ (mechanical transfer registered jack) connectors. Any one of the four connectors can be used with either single-mode or multimode fiber-optic cable.

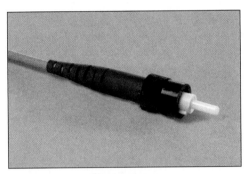

(a) ST (straight tip)

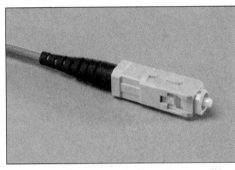

(b) SC (standard connector)

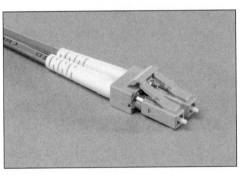

(c) LC (local connector)

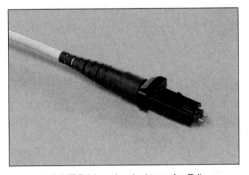

(d) MT-RJ (mechanical transfer RJ)

Figure 17-20   Four types of fiber-optic connectors: (a) ST, (b) SC, (c) LC, and (d) MT-RJ
Courtesy of Fiber Communications, Inc. (*www.fiberc.com*)

17

A+ 220-701

💡 **A+ Exam Tip**   The A+ 220-701 Essentials exam expects you to know about these cable types: Plenum, PVC, UTP, CAT3, CAT5, CAT5e, CAT6, STP, fiber, and coaxial cable.

Each version of Ethernet can use more than one cabling method. Here is a brief description of the types of Ethernet identified by the cabling methods they use:

▲ *10-Mbps Ethernet.* This first Ethernet specification was invented by Xerox Corporation in the 1970s, and later became known as Ethernet.

▲ *100-Mbps Ethernet or Fast Ethernet.* This improved version of Ethernet (sometimes called **100BaseT** or **Fast Ethernet**) operates at 100 Mbps and uses STP or UTP cabling rated CAT-5 or higher. 100BaseT networks can support slower

A+
220-701
4.2

speeds of 10 Mbps so that devices that run at either 10 Mbps or 100 Mbps can coexist on the same LAN. Two variations of 100BaseT are 100BaseTX and 100BaseFX. The most popular variation is 100BaseTX. 100BaseFX uses fiber-optic cable.

▲ *1000-Mbps Ethernet or Gigabit Ethernet.* This version of Ethernet operates at 1000 Mbps and uses twisted-pair cable and fiber-optic cable. Gigabit Ethernet is currently replacing 100BaseT Ethernet as the choice for LAN technology. Because it can use the same cabling and connectors as 100BaseT, a company can upgrade from 100BaseT to Gigabit without great expense.

▲ *10-Gigabit Ethernet.* This version of Ethernet operates at 10 billion bits per second (10Gbps) and uses fiber cable. It can be used on LANs, MANs, and WANs, and is also a good choice for backbone networks. (A backbone network is a channel whereby local networks can connect to wide area networks or to each other.)

HUBS AND SWITCHES

A+
220-701
4.1

Older Ethernet networks that used coaxial cable connected all the devices (called nodes) on the network in a logical bus formation, which means that nodes were all strung together in a daisy chain with terminators at each end, similar to how SCSI devices are chained together. Today's Ethernet networks use a star formation (called a star topology) whereby nodes are connected to a centralized hub or switch (see Figure 17-21). PCs on the LAN are like points of a star around the hub or switch in the middle, which connects the nodes on the LAN. An Ethernet hub transmits the data packet to every device, except the device that sent the transmission, as shown in Figure 17-21.

You can think of a hub (see Figure 17-22) as just a pass-through and distribution point for every device connected to it, without regard for what kind of data is passing through

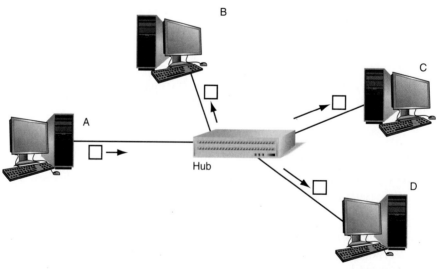

Figure 17-21 Any data received by a hub is replicated and passed on to all other devices connected to it
Courtesy: Course Technology/Cengage Learning

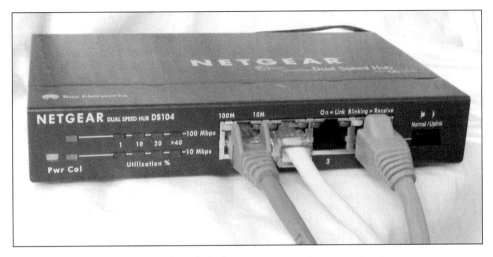

Figure 17-22   A hub is a pass-through device to connect nodes on a network
Courtesy: Course Technology/Cengage Learning

and where the data might be going. Hubs are outdated technology, having been replaced by switches.

A **switch** (see Figure 17-23) is smarter and more efficient than a hub, as it keeps a table of all the devices connected to it. It uses this table to determine which path to use when sending packets. The switch only passes data to the device to which the data is addressed.

Figure 17-23   A five-port Gigabit Ethernet switch by Linksys
Courtesy: Course Technology/Cengage Learning

As network needs grow, you can add a switch so that you can connect more devices to the network. Figure 17-24 shows an example of a network that uses three switches in

A+
220-701
4.1

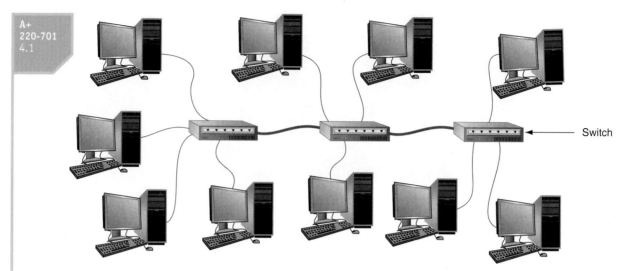

Figure 17-24 An Ethernet network with three switches
Courtesy: Course Technology/Cengage Learning

sequence. Physically, the network cables that run between two switches or a switch and a computer might be inside a building's walls with a network jack on the wall providing an RJ-45 connector. You plug a network cable into the jack to make the connection. In practice, a small network might begin as one switch and three or four computers. As the need for more computers grows, new switches are added to provide these extra connections.

Another reason to add a switch to a network is to regenerate the network signal. STP and UTP Ethernet cables should not exceed 100 meters (about 328 feet) in length. If you need to reach distances greater than that, you can add a switch in the line, which regenerates the signal.

Two types of network cables can be used when building a network: a patch cable and a crossover cable. A patch cable (also called a straight-through cable) is used to connect a computer to a hub or switch. A crossover cable is used to connect two like devices such as a switch to a switch or a PC to a PC (to make the simplest network of all).

The difference in a patch cable and a crossover cable is the way the transmit and receive lines are wired in the connectors at each end of the cables. A crossover cable has the transmit and receive lines reversed so that one device receives off the line to which the other device transmits. You can use a crossover cable to connect a switch to a switch. However, some switches have an uplink port so that you can use a patch cable to connect it to another switch. Other switches use auto-uplinking, which means you can connect a switch to a switch using a patch cable on any port.

A patch cable and a crossover cable look identical and have identical connectors. One way to tell them apart is to look for the labeling imprinted on the cables, as shown in Figure 17-25. If you don't see labeling, know that you can use a cable tester to find out what type of cable you have.

WIRELESS ACCESS POINTS

Wireless devices can communicate directly (such as a PC to a PC, which is called Ad Hoc mode), or they can connect to a LAN by way of a wireless access point (AP), as shown in

A+
220-701
4.1

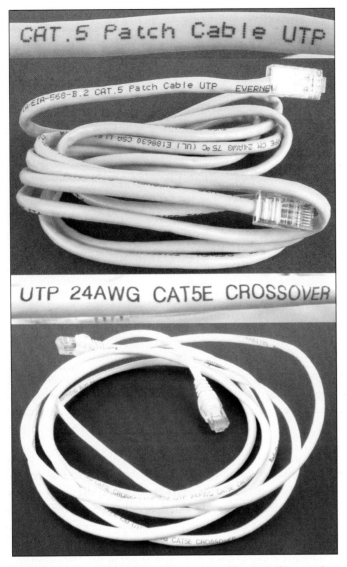

Figure 17-25 Patch cables and crossover cables look the same but
are labeled differently
Courtesy: Course Technology/Cengage Learning

Figure 17-26. Multiple access points can be positioned so that nodes can access at least one
access point from anywhere in the covered area. When devices use an access point, they
communicate through the access point instead of communi-
cating directly. Often a wireless access point is doing double
duty as a router, a device that connects one network to
another.

▶ Video
Using a Multifunction Router

💡 **A+ Exam Tip** The A+ 220-701 Essentials exam expects you to know the differences among a hub,
switch, and router.

17

A+ 220-701

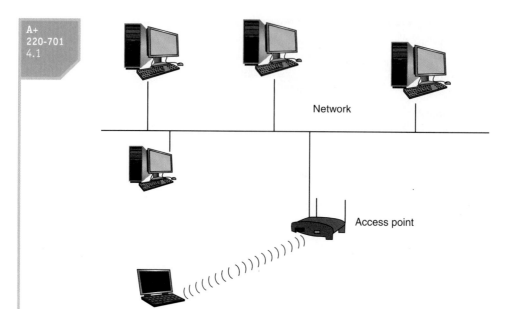

Figure 17-26   Nodes on a wireless LAN connect to a wired network by way of an
access point
Courtesy: Course Technology/Cengage Learning

> **Notes**   The wired network in Figure 17-26 shows connectivity but does not indicate the details of that connectivity. Know that, in practice, this network might involve switches and hubs.

ROUTERS

A **router** is a device that manages traffic between two networks. In Figure 17-27, you can see that a router stands between the ISP network and the local network. The router is the gateway to the Internet. Note in the figure that computers can connect to the router directly or by way of one or more switches. Routers can range from small ones designed to manage a small network connecting to an ISP (costing less than $100) to those that manage multiple networks and extensive traffic (costing several thousand dollars).

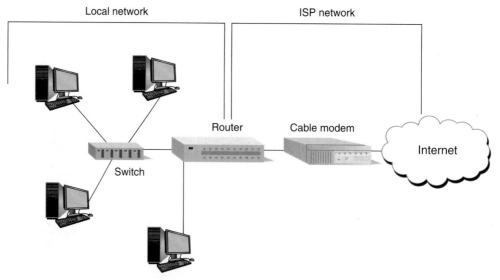

Figure 17-27   A router stands between a local network and the Internet and manages traffic between them
Courtesy: Course Technology/Cengage Learning

A+
220-701
4.1

Four companies that make routers suitable for small networks are D-Link (*www.dlink.com*), Linksys (*www.linksys.com*), NetGear (*www.netgear.com*), and Belkin (*www.belkin.com*). An example of a multifunction router is the Wireless-N Gigabit Router by Linksys shown in Figures 17-28 and 17-29. It has one port for the broadband modem and four ports for computers on the network. The router is also an 802.11b/g/n wireless access point having multiple antennas to increase speed and range using Multiple In, Multiple Out (MIMO) technology. The antennas are built in.

Figure 17-28 The Wireless-N Gigabit router by Linksys has built-in wireless antennas and can be used with a DSL or cable modem Internet connection
Courtesy: Course Technology/Cengage Learning

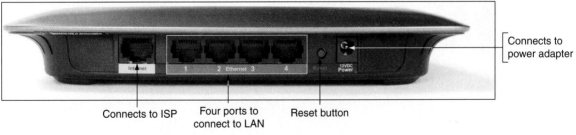

Connects to power adapter

Connects to ISP   Four ports to connect to LAN   Reset button

Figure 17-29 Connectors and ports on the back of the Linksys router
Courtesy: Course Technology/Cengage Learning

A **DHCP (dynamic host configuration protocol)** server gives IP addresses to computers on the network when they attempt to initiate a connection to the network and request an IP address. With a DHCP server on the network, computers can use dynamic IP addressing, so that you don't have to assign and keep up with unique IP addresses for each computer.

The router shown in Figure 17-28 is typical of many brands and models of routers used in a small office or small home network to manage the Internet connection. This router is several devices in one:

▲ *Function 1:* As a router, it stands between the ISP network and the local network, routing traffic between the two networks.

17

A+ 220-701

▲ *Function 2:* As a switch, it manages four network ports that can be connected to four computers or to a switch or hub that connects to more than one computer.

▲ *Function 3:* As a DHCP server, all computers can receive their IP address from this server. With a DHCP server on the network, computers can use dynamic IP addressing so that you don't have to assign and keep up with unique IP addresses for each computer.

▲ *Function 4:* As a wireless access point, a computer can connect to the network using a wireless device. This wireless connection can be secured using four different wireless security features.

▲ *Function 5:* As a firewall, unwanted traffic initiated from the Internet can be blocked. These firewall functions include a security feature called NAT redirection. NAT (Network Address Translation) is a protocol that substitutes the IP address of the router for the IP address of other computers inside the network when these computers need to communicate on the Internet. You will learn more about NAT in Chapter 18. Another firewall feature is to restrict Internet access for computers behind the firewall. Restrictions can apply to days of the week, time of day, keywords used, or certain Web sites.

In the small office setting pictured in Figure 17-30, a router connects four network jacks that are wired in the walls to four other jacks in the building. Two of these remote jacks have switches connected that accommodate two or more computers.

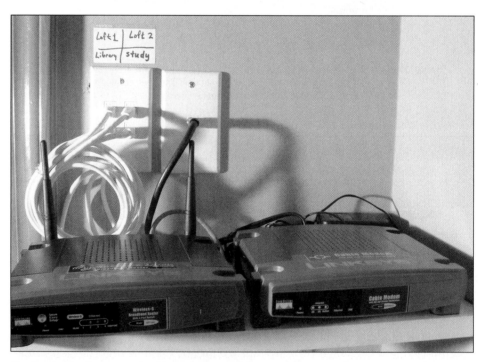

Figure 17-30   A router and cable modem are used to provide Internet access for a small network
Courtesy: Course Technology/Cengage Learning

> **Notes** The speed of a network depends on the speed of each device on the network. Routers, switches, and network adapters currently run at three speeds: Gigabit Ethernet (1,000 Mbps or 1 Gbps), Fast Ethernet (100 Mbps), or Ethernet (10 Mbps). If you want your entire network to run at the fastest speed, make sure all your devices are rated for Gigabit Ethernet. Very few networks today use 10 Mbps Ethernet, and Gigabit Ethernet is slowly replacing Fast Ethernet as the most popular standard.

A+
220-701
4.1

So far in this chapter, we've looked at all the different hardware devices and hardware technologies to build networks. Each hardware device on a network, such as a NIC, switch, router, or wireless access point, uses a hardware protocol to communicate on the network. For most wired LANs, that protocol is Ethernet. However, in addition to the hardware protocol, there is a layer of network communication at the operating system level. The next section looks at the different OS networking protocols and how they work.

WINDOWS ON A NETWORK

Most applications that use the Internet are **client/server applications**, which means that two computers and two applications are involved. The client application (for example, a Web browser) on one computer makes a request for data from the server application (for example, a Web server) on another computer (see Figure 17-31). In this client/server environment, the application serving up data is called the server and the computer on which this server application is installed can also be referred to as the server. In other words, a server is any computer or application serving up data when that data is requested.

Communication between a client application and a server application happens at three levels (hardware, operating system, and application) and is dependent on one computer addressing the other computer is such a way that they find one another. Now let's see how these three levels for communication on a network work and how computers find each other on a network.

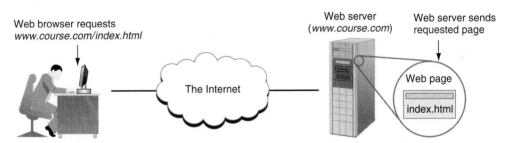

Figure 17-31 A Web browser (client software) requests a Web page from a Web server (server software); the Web server returns the requested data to the client
Courtesy: Course Technology/Cengage Learning

17

A+ 220-701

LAYERS OF NETWORK COMMUNICATION

When your computer at home is connected to your ISP off somewhere in the distance, your computer and a computer on the Internet are communicating at the application, operating system, and hardware levels. The computers need a way to address each other at each level. These three levels and the addresses used at each level are diagrammed in Figure 17-32. Listed next is a description of each level of communication:

▲ *Level 1: Hardware level.* At the root level of communication is hardware. The hardware or physical connection might be wireless or might use network cables, phone lines (for DSL or dial-up), or TV cable lines (for cable modem). For local wired or wireless networks, a network adapter inside your computer is part of this physical network. The rules for communication are predetermined and these rules are called protocols. Recall that each network adapter is assigned a MAC address, and this address is used to uniquely identify a computer on a local network.

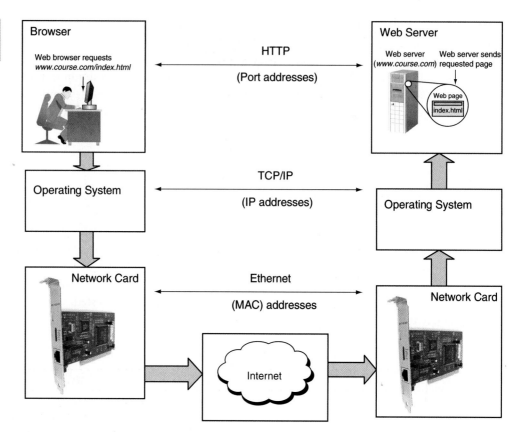

Figure 17-32 Network communication happens in layers
Courtesy: Course Technology/Cengage Learning

▲ *Level 2: Operating system level.* An OS is responsible for managing communication between itself and another computer, using rules for communication that both operating systems understand. This group, or suite, of communication protocols is collectively called TCP/IP. One OS addresses the other OS using addresses called IP addresses. An **IP address** is a 32-bit string used to identify a computer on a network. These 32 bits are organized into four groups of eight bits each, which are presented as four decimal numbers separated by periods, such as 72.56.105.12. Because the largest possible 8-bit number is 255, each of the four numbers can be no larger than 255. A network can use static IP addressing, in which each computer is assigned an IP address that never changes, or dynamic IP addressing, in which each time the computer connects to the network, it gets a new IP address from the DHCP server (called leasing the IP address). IP addresses are used to identify a computer both inside and outside its local network. Consider a MAC address a local address and an IP address a long-distance address, as shown in Figure 17-33.

▲ *Level 3: Application level.* When you use the Internet to surf the Web or download your e-mail, you are using an application on your computer called an Internet client. For Web surfing, that client, such as Internet Explorer or Firefox, is called a browser. The client communicates with another application somewhere on the Internet, called a server. Examples of server applications are your e-mail server at your ISP or a Web server anywhere on the Web. The client and server applications are each assigned a number that uniquely identifies the application on the computer. This number is called a **port number**, **port**, or **port address**. Table 17-3 lists common port assignments for some well-known applications. For example, you can address a Web server by entering

A+
220-701
4.1

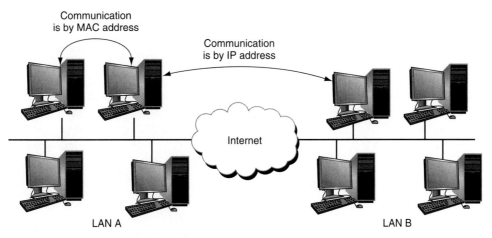

Figure 17-33 Computers on the same LAN use MAC addresses to communicate, but computers on different LANs use IP addresses to communicate over the Internet
Courtesy: Course Technology/Cengage Learning

Port	Protocol	Service	Description
20	FTP	FTP	File transfer data.
21	FTP	FTP	File transfer control information.
22	SSH	Secure Shell	Remote control to a networked computer that includes encrypting transmitted login information and data.
23	Telnet	Telnet	Remote control to a networked computer from a command prompt that does not use encryption.
25	SMTP	Email	Simple Mail Transfer Protocol; used by a client to send e-mail.
53	DNS	DNS server	Domain Name Service; used to find an IP address when a computer's character-based name is known.
80	HTTP	Web server	World Wide Web protocol.
110	POP3	Email	Post Office Protocol, version 3; used by a client to receive e-mail.
143	IMAP	Email	Internet Message Access Protocol, a newer protocol used by clients to receive e-mail.
443	HTTPS	Web server	HTTP with added security that includes authentication and encryption.
3389	RDP	Remote Desktop	Remote Desktop Protocol used to connect to a computer. Transmissions are encrypted. Remote Desktop and Remote Assistance both use RDP.

Table 17-3 Common TCP/IP port assignments for client/server applications

into a browser address box an IP address followed by a colon and then the port number. These values are known as a socket. For example, suppose a computer with an IP address of 136.60.30.5 is running an e-mail server application as well as a Web server application. If a client computer sends a request to 136.60.30.5:25, the e-mail server that is listening at that port responds. On the other hand, if a request is sent to 136.60.30.5:80, the Web server listening at port 80 responds (see Figure 17-34).

17

A+ 220-701

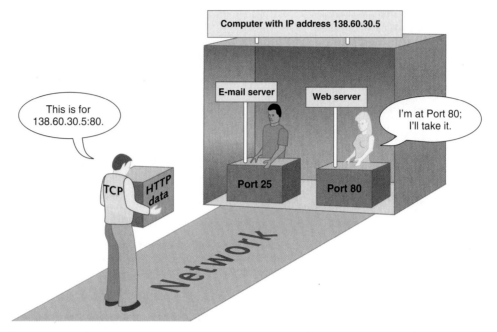

Figure 17-34 Each server running on a computer is addressed by a unique port number
Courtesy: Course Technology/Cengage Learning

💡 **A+ Exam Tip** The A+ 220-701 Essentials exam expects you to know the common port assignments of the HTTP, FTP, POP, SMTP, Telnet, and HTTPS protocols.

Figure 17-35 shows how communication moves from a browser to the OS to the hardware on one computer and on to the hardware, OS, and Web server on a remote computer. As you connect a computer to a network, keep in mind that the connection must work at all three levels. And when things don't work right, it helps to understand that you must solve the problem at one or more levels. In other words, the problem might be with the physical equipment, with the OS, or with the application.

Now let's turn our attention to the details of understanding how IP addresses are used on a network.

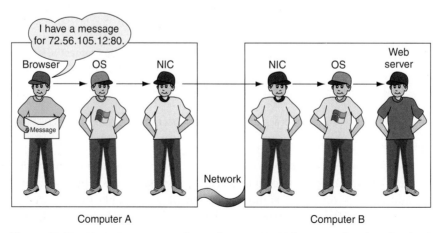

Figure 17-35 How a message gets from a browser to a Web server using three levels of communication
Courtesy: Course Technology/Cengage Learning

A+
220-701
4.1

UNDERSTANDING IP ADDRESSES AND HOW THEY ARE USED

All protocols of the TCP/IP suite identify a device on the Internet or an intranet by its IP address. (An intranet is a private network that uses the TCP/IP protocols.) An IP address is 32 bits long, made up of 4 bytes, each 8 bits long. When displayed, an IP address is expressed as four decimal numbers separated by periods, as in this address: 190.180.40.120. The largest possible 8-bit number is 11111111, which is equal to 255 in decimal, so the largest possible IP address in decimal is 255.255.255.255, which in binary is 11111111.11111111.11111111.11111111. Each of the four numbers separated by periods is called an octet (for 8 bits) and can be any number from 0 to 255, making a total of 4.3 billion potential IP addresses (256x256x256x256). Because of the allocation scheme used to assign these addresses, not all of them are available for use.

> **Notes** The standard that determines an IP address has 32 bits is called the IPv4 (IP version 4) standard. Partly because of a potential shortage of IP addresses, the IPv6 (IP version 6) standard has been developed, which uses 128 bits for an IP address. Windows Vista and Windows XP with Service Pack 2 support IPv6, although 128-bit IP addresses are seldom used.

The first part of an IP address identifies the network, and the last part identifies the host. It's important to understand how the bits of an IP address are used, in order to understand how routing happens over interconnected networks such as the Internet, and how TCP/IP can locate an IP address anywhere on the globe. When data is routed over interconnected networks, the network portion of the IP address is used to locate the right network. After the data arrives at the local network, the host portion of the IP address is used to identify the one computer on the network that is to receive the data. Finally, the IP address of the host must be used to identify its MAC address so the data can travel on the host's LAN to that host. The next section explains this in detail.

CLASSES OF IP ADDRESSES

The Internet Corporation for Assigned Names and Numbers (ICANN) is responsible for keeping track of assigned IP addresses and domain names. IP addresses that are leased by companies and individuals through ICANN are divided into three classes: Class A, Class B, and Class C, based on the number of possible IP addresses in each network within each class. IP addresses are assigned to these classes according to the scheme outlined in Table 17-4.

Class	Network Octets*	Total Number of Possible Networks or Licenses	Total Number of Possible IP Addresses in Each Network
A	1.x.y.z to 126.x.y.z	127	16 million
B	128.0.x.y to 191.255.x.y	16,000	65,000
C	192.0.0.x to 223.255.255.x	2 million	254

*An x, y, or z in the IP address stands for an octet used to identify hosts.

Table 17-4 Classes of IP addresses

17

A+ 220-701

A+
220-701
4.1

You can determine the class of an IP address and the size or type of company to which an address is licensed by looking at the address. More important, you also can determine what portion of an IP address is dedicated to identifying the network and what portion is used to identify the host on that network.

> **♥ A+ Exam Tip** The A+ 220-701 Essentials exam expects you to know how to identify the class of any given IP address.

Figure 17-36 shows how each class of IP address is divided into the network and host portions. A Class A address uses the first (leftmost) octet for the network address and the remaining octets for host addresses. A Class A license assigns a single number that is used in the first octet of the address, which is the network address. The remaining three octets of the IP address can be used for host addresses that uniquely identify each host on this network. The first octet of a Class A license is a number between 0 and 126. For example, if a company is assigned 87 as its Class A network address, then 87 is used as the first octet for every host on this one network. Examples of IP addresses for hosts on this network are 87.0.0.1, 87.0.0.2, and 87.0.0.3. (The last octet does not use 0 or 255 as a value, so 87.0.0.0 is not valid.) In the example address 87.0.0.1, the 87 is the network portion of the IP address, and 0.0.1 is the host portion. Because three octets can be used for Class A host addresses, one Class A license can have approximately 256x256x254 host addresses, or about 16 million IP addresses. Only very large corporations with heavy communication needs have been able to obtain a Class A license.

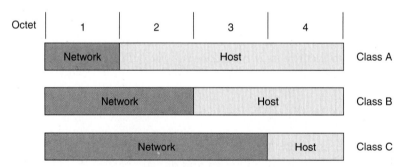

Figure 17-36 The network portion and host portion for each class of IP addresses
Courtesy: Course Technology/Cengage Learning

A Class B address uses the first two octets for the network portion and the last two for the host portion. A Class B license assigns a number for each of the two leftmost octets, leaving the third and fourth octets for host addresses. How many host addresses are there in one Class B license? The number of possible values for two octets is about 256x254, or about 65,000 host addresses in a single Class B license. (Some IP addresses are reserved, so these numbers are approximations.) The first octet of a Class B license is a number between 128 and 191, which gives about 63 different values for a Class B first octet. The second number can be between 0 and 255, so there are approximately 63x256, or about 16,000, Class B networks. For example, suppose a company is assigned 135.18 as the network address for its Class B license. The first two octets for all hosts on this network are 135.18, and the company uses the last two octets for host addresses. Examples of IP addresses on this company's Class B network are 135.18.0.1, 135.18.0.2, and 135.18.0.3. In the first example listed, 135.18 is the network portion of the IP address, and 0.1 is the host portion.

A+
220-701
4.1

A Class C license assigns three octets as the network address. With only one octet used for the host addresses, there can be only 254 host addresses on a Class C network. The first number of a Class C license is between 192 and 223. For example, if a company is assigned a Class C license for its network with a network address of 200.80.15, some IP addresses on the network would be 200.80.15.1, 200.80.15.2, and 200.80.15.3.

Class D and Class E IP addresses are not available for general use. Class D addresses begin with octets 224 through 239 and are used for multicasting, in which one host sends messages to multiple hosts, such as when the host transmits a video conference over the Internet. Class E addresses begin with 240 through 254 and are reserved for research.

SUBNET MASKS

The subnet mask used in the TCP/IP configuration for a network tells the OS which part of an IP address is the network portion and which part identifies the host. Using a subnet mask, a computer or other device can know if an IP address of another computer is on its network or another network (see Figure 17-37).

Figure 17-37 A host (router, in this case) can always determine if an IP address is on its network
Courtesy: Course Technology/Cengage Learning

A subnet mask is a group of ones followed by a group of zeros. The ones in a subnet mask say, "On our network, this part of an IP address is the network part," and the group of zeros says, "On our network, this part of an IP address is the host part." For example, Table 17-5 shows the subnet masks that might be used for three IP addresses.

17

A+ 220-701

Class	Subnet Mask	Address	Network ID	Host ID
Class A	11111111.00000000.00000000.00000000	89.100.13.78	89	100.13.78
Class B	11111111.11111111.00000000.00000000	190.78.13.250	190.78	13.250
Class C	11111111.11111111.11111111.00000000	201.18.20.208	201.18.20	208

Table 17-5   Default subnet masks for classes of IP addresses

These three subnet masks would be displayed in a TCP/IP configuration window like this:

◢ Subnet mask of 11111111.00000000.00000000.00000000 is displayed as 255.0.0.0
◢ Subnet mask of 11111111.11111111.00000000.00000000 is displayed as 255.255.0.0
◢ Subnet mask of 11111111.11111111.11111111.00000000 is displayed as 255.255.255.0

Subnet masks that contain all ones or all zeros in an octet are called classful subnet masks, and the three subnet masks shown above are classful subnet masks. A classless subnet mask can have a mix of zeros and ones in one octet such as 11111111.11111111.11110000.00000000, which can be written as 255.255.240.0. These types of classless subnet masks are used to segment large corporate networks into subnetworks, or subnets, using a system called Classless Interdomain Routing (CIDR).

APPLYING | CONCEPTS   Larry is setting up a new computer on a network. He creates TCP/IP settings to use static IP addressing. He assigns a subnet mask of 255.255.240.0 and an IP address of 15.50.212.59 to this computer. Suppose this computer wants to communicate with a computer assigned an IP address of 15.50.235.80. When the communication reaches the router controlling the network, the router must decide if these two computers are in the same subnet so that it will know how to route the request. The router compares the binary values of the first two octets and determines they match. It then compares the binary values of the third octet, like this:

```
212 = 11010100

235 = 11101011
```

To be in the same subnet, the first four bits must match, which they don't. Therefore, these two computers are not in the same subnet. The router then knows to route the data to another subnet. However, an IP address that is in the same subnet as 15.50.212.59 is 15.50.220.100, because the first two octets match and the first four bits of the third octet match (comparing 11010100 to 11011100).

Notes   Sometimes using CIDR notation, an IP address and subnet mask are written using a shorthand notation like this: 15.50.212.59/20, where the /20 means that the subnet mask is written as 20 ones followed by enough zeros to complete the full 32 bits.

DIFFERENT WAYS OF ASSIGNING IP ADDRESSES

When a small company is assigned a Class C license, it obtains 254 IP addresses for its use. If it has only a few hosts (for example, fewer than 25 on a network), many IP addresses go unused, which is one reason there is a shortage of IP addresses. But suppose that the company grew and now has 300 workstations on the network and is running out of IP addresses. There are two approaches to solving this problem: Use private IP addresses or use dynamic IP addressing. Many companies combine both methods. An explanation of each of these solutions follows.

Public, Private, and Reserved IP Addresses

When a company applies for a Class A, B, or C license, it is assigned a group of IP addresses that are different from all other IP addresses and are available for use on the Internet. The IP addresses available to the Internet are called public IP addresses.

One thing to consider, however, is that not all of a company's workstations need to have Internet access, even though they might be on the network. So, although each workstation might need an IP address to be part of the TCP/IP network, those not connected to the Internet don't need addresses that are unique and available to the Internet; these workstations can use private IP addresses. Private IP addresses are IP addresses used on private intranets that are not allowed on the Internet. A computer using a private IP address on a private network can still access the Internet if a router or other device that stands between the network and the Internet is using NAT redirection. Recall that when using NAT redirection, the device substitutes its own public IP address for the private IP address of a computer behind the firewall.

Because of NAT redirection, a small company can rely solely on private IP addresses for its internal network and use only the s one public IP address assigned to it by its ISP for Internet communication. IEEE recommends that the following IP addresses be used for private networks :

- 10.0.0.0 through 10.255.255.255
- 172.16.0.0 through 172.31.255.255
- 192.168.0.0 through 192.168.255.255

> **Notes** IEEE, a nonprofit organization, is responsible for many Internet standards. Standards are proposed to the networking community in the form of an RFC (Request for Comment). RFC 1918 outlines recommendations for private IP addresses. To view an RFC, visit the Web site *www.rfc-editor.org*.

When assigning isolated IP addresses, also keep in mind that a few IP addresses are reserved for special use by TCP/IP and should not be assigned to a device on a network. Table 17-6 lists these reserved IP addresses.

IP Address	How It Is Used
255.255.255.255	Broadcast messages
0.0.0.0	Currently unassigned IP address
127.0.0.1	Indicates your own workstation and is called the loopback address

Table 17-6 Reserved IP addresses

A+
220-701
4.1

All IP addresses on a network must be unique for that network. (Figure 17-38 shows the Windows XP error that appears when two computers on the network have been assigned the same IP address.) A network administrator might assign an IP address to a stand-alone computer (for example, if someone is testing networking software on a PC that is not connected to the network). As long as the network is a private network, the administrator can assign any IP address, although a good administrator avoids using the reserved addresses.

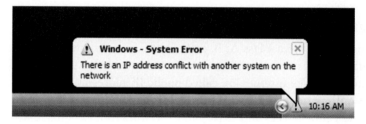

Figure 17-38 An error occurs when two networked computers use the same IP address
Courtesy: Course Technology/Cengage Learning

Dynamically Assigned IP Addresses

If an administrator must configure each host on a network manually, assigning it a unique IP address, the task of going from PC to PC to make these assignments and keeping up with which address is assigned to which PC can be an administrative nightmare. The solution is to have a server automatically assign an IP address to a workstation each time it comes onto the network. Instead of permanently assigning a **static IP address** to a workstation, a dynamic IP address is assigned for the current connection only. When the connection terminates, the IP address is returned to the list of available addresses.

When a workstation has an IP address assigned to it, it is said that the workstation is leasing the IP address. An ISP customarily uses dynamic IP addressing for its individual subscribers and static IP addresses for its business subscribers.

Recall that a DHCP server manages dynamically assigned IP addresses on a network. Workstations that work with DHCP servers are called DHCP clients. DHCP software resides on both the client and the server to manage the dynamic assignments of IP addresses. DHCP client software is built into Windows.

> 💡 **A+ Exam Tip** The A+ 220-701 Essentials exam expects you to know what a DHCP server is and understand how to use static and dynamic IP addressing.

When you configure a DHCP server, you specify the range of IP addresses that can be assigned to clients on the network. Figure 17-39 shows the configuration window for a DHCP server embedded as firmware on a router. In the figure, you can see that the router's IP address is 192.168.1.1, and the starting IP address to be assigned to clients is 192.168.1.100. Because the administrator specified that the server can have up to 50 clients, the range of IP addresses is, therefore, 192.168.1.100 to 192.168.1.149. Also shown in the figure is a list of currently assigned IP addresses and the MAC address of the computer that currently leases that IP address.

When a PC first connects to the network, it attempts to lease an address from the DHCP server. If the attempt fails, it uses an **Automatic Private IP Address (APIPA)** in the address range 169.254.*x.y*. How to configure a Windows workstation to use dynamic or static IP addressing is covered later in the chapter.

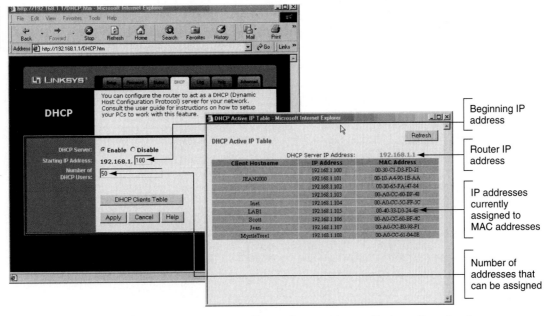

Figure 17-39 A DHCP server has a range of IP addresses it can assign to clients on the network
Courtesy: Course Technology/Cengage Learning

Now let's see how character-based names can be used in place of IP addresses to identify computers and networks.

CHARACTER-BASED NAMES IDENTIFY COMPUTERS AND NETWORKS

Remembering an IP address is not always easy, so character-based names are used to substitute for IP addresses. Here are the possibilities:

▲ A host name, also called a computer name, is the name of a computer and can be used in place of its IP address. Examples of host names are www, ftp, Jean's Computer, TestBox3, and PinkLaptop. You assign a host name to a computer when you first configure it for a network connection. The name can have up to 63 characters, including letters, numbers, and special characters. On a local network, you can use the computer name in the place of an IP address to identify a computer. To find out and change the computer name in Vista, click **Start**, right-click **Computer** and select **Properties** from the shortcut menu. In the System window, click **Advanced system settings** and respond to the UAC box. In the System Properties box, click the **Computer Name** tab (see Figure 17-40). For XP, click **Start**, right-click **My Computer**, and select **Properties** from the shortcut menu. Then click the **Computer Name** tab.

▲ A NetBIOS name can be up to 15 characters. NetBIOS (Network Basic Input/Output System) is a protocol that applications use to communicate with each other. NetBIOS was used by a Windows networking protocol called NetBEUI (NetBIOS Extended User Interface, pronounced *net-BOO-ee*). NetBEUI has been replaced by TCP/IP, and NetBIOS names are only used when the network is supporting a legacy application that requires a computer name no longer than 15 characters.

▲ A workgroup name identifies a workgroup. The workgroup name is only recognized within the local network.

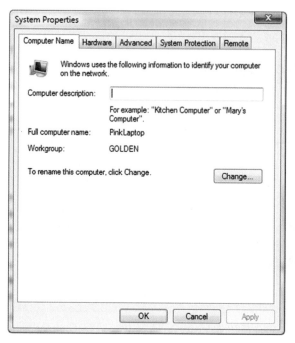

Figure 17-40 View and change the computer name
Courtesy: Course Technology/Cengage Learning

▲ A domain name identifies a network. Examples of domain names are the names that appear before the period in microsoft.com, course.com, and mycompany.com. The letters after the period are called the top-level domain and tell you something about the domain. Examples are .com (commercial), .org (nonprofit), .gov (government), and .info (general use).

▲ A fully qualified domain name (FQDN) identifies a computer and the network to which it belongs. An example of an FQDN is www.course.com. The host name is *www* (a Web server), *course* is the domain name, and *com* is the top-level domain name of the Course Technology network. Another FQDN is *joesmith.mycompany.com*.

On the Internet, a fully qualified domain name must be associated with an IP address before this computer can be found. This process of associating a character-based name with an IP address is called name resolution. The protocol and service used to track these names are called DNS (Domain Name System, also called Domain Name Service). A DNS server can find an IP address for a computer when the fully qualified domain name is known. (An older proprietary Microsoft service used to track NetBIOS names is WINS (Windows Internet Naming Service). Your ISP is responsible for providing you access to one or more DNS servers as part of the service it provides for Internet access. When a Web hosting site first sets up your Web site, IP address, and domain name, it is responsible for entering the name resolution information into its primary DNS server. This server can present the information to other DNS servers on the Web and is called the authoritative name server for your site.

> **Notes** When you enter a fully qualified domain name such as www.microsoft.com in a browser address bar, that name is translated into an IP address followed by a port number. It's interesting to know that you can skip the translation step and enter the IP address and port number in the address box. See Figure 17-41.

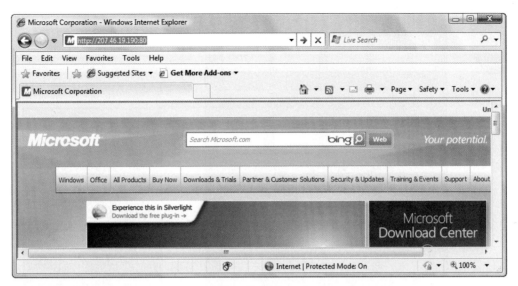

Figure 17-41 A Web site can be accessed by its IP address and port number
Courtesy: Course Technology/Cengage Learning

💡 **A+ Exam Tip** The A+ 220-701 Essentials exam expects you to be familiar with a DNS service.

When Windows is trying to resolve a computer name to an IP address, it first looks in the **Hosts file** in the C:\Windows\System32\drivers\etc folder. This file, which has no file extension, contains computer names and their associated IP addresses on the local network. An administrator is responsible for manually editing the hosts file when the association is needed on the local network. If the computer name is not found in the hosts file, Windows then turns to a DNS server if it has the IP address of the server. For NetBIOS names, Windows first looks for entries in the LMHosts file in the C:\Windows\System32\drivers\etc folder before it turns to a WINS server to resolve the NetBIOS name.

Notes For an entry in the Hosts file to work, the remote computer must always use the same IP address. One way to accomplish this is to assign a static IP address to the computer. Alternately, if your DHCP server supports this feature, you can configure it to assign the same IP address to this computer each time if you tell the DHCP server the computer's MAC address. This method of computer name resolution is often used for intranet Web servers, Telnet servers, and other servers.

TCP/IP PROTOCOL LAYERS

Recall that a protocol is an agreed-to set of rules for communication between two parties. Operating systems and client/server applications on the Internet all use protocols that are supported by TCP/IP. The left side of Figure 17-42 shows these different layers of protocols and how they relate to one another. As you read this section, this figure can serve as your road map to the different protocols.

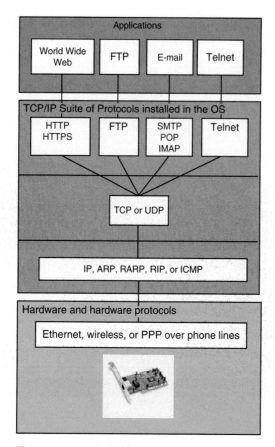

Figure 17-42   How software, protocols, and technology on a TCP/IP network relate to each other
Courtesy: Course Technology/Cengage Learning

> **Notes** When studying networking theory, the OSI Model is used, which divides network communication into seven layers. In the OSI Model, protocols used by hardware are divided into two layers (data link and physical), and TCP/IP protocols used by the OS are divided into five layers (network, transport, session, presentation, and application). These seven layers are shown on the right side of Figure 17-42.

In the following sections, the more significant applications and operating system protocols are introduced. However, you should know that the TCP/IP protocol suite includes more protocols than just those mentioned in this chapter; some of them are shown in Figure 17-42.

TCP/IP PROTOCOLS USED BY APPLICATIONS

Some common applications that use the Internet are Web browsers, e-mail, chat, FTP, Telnet, Remote Desktop, and Remote Assistance. When one of these applications wants to send data to a counterpart application on another host, it makes an API (application programming interface) call to the operating system, which handles the request. (An API call is a common way for an application to ask an operating system to do something.) The API call causes the OS to generate a request. Here is a bit of information about several of these application protocols:

▲ *HTTP.* HTTP (Hypertext Transfer Protocol) is the protocol used for the World Wide Web and used by Web browsers and Web servers to communicate. You can see when a

A+
220-701
4.1

browser is using this protocol by looking for http at the beginning of a URL in the address bar of a browser, such as *http://www.microsoft.com*.

▲ *HTTPS*. The **HTTPS (HTTP secure)** protocol is used by Web browsers and servers to encrypt the data before it is sent and then decrypt it before the data is processed. To know this secure protocol is being used, look for https in the URL, as in *https://www.wachovia.com*.

▲ *FTP*. **FTP (File Transfer Protocol)** is used to transfer files between two computers. Web browsers can use the protocol. Also, special FTP client software such as CuteFTP by GlobalSCAPE (*www.cuteftp.com*) can be used, as the software offers more features for file transfer than does a browser. To use FTP from your browser, enter the address of an FTP site in the address box. When the browser recognizes the site is using the FTP protocol, you will see ftp in the URL, as in *ftp://ftp.cengage.com*. Sometimes it's easier to use Windows Explorer to transfer files rather than Internet Explorer. To use Windows Explorer for file transfers in Windows Vista, on the menu bar of Internet Explorer, click **Page, Open FTP site in Windows Explorer**. Then click **Allow** in the Internet Explorer Security box (see Figure 17-43). Windows Explorer opens, showing files and folders on the FTP site. Using Windows XP, Internet Explorer works similar to Windows Explorer when you navigate to an FTP site.

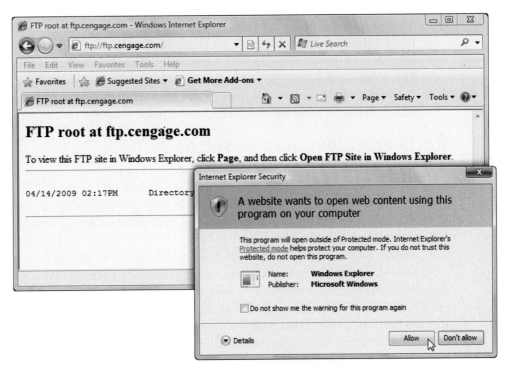

Figure 17-43   Open Windows Explorer to transfer files using FTP
Courtesy: Course Technology/Cengage Learning

▲ *SMTP*. **SMTP (Simple Mail Transfer Protocol)** is used to send an e-mail message to its destination (see Figure 17-44). An improved version of SMTP is **SMTP AUTH (SMTP Authentication)**. This protocol is used to authenticate a user to an e-mail server when the e-mail client first tries to connect to the e-mail server to send e-mail. Using SMTP AUTH, an extra dialogue between the client and server happens before the client can fully connect that proves the client is authorized to use the service. After authentication, the client can then send e-mail to the e-mail server. The e-mail server that takes care of sending e-mail messages (using the SMTP protocol) is often referred to as the SMTP server.

17

A+ 220-701

A+
220-701
4.1

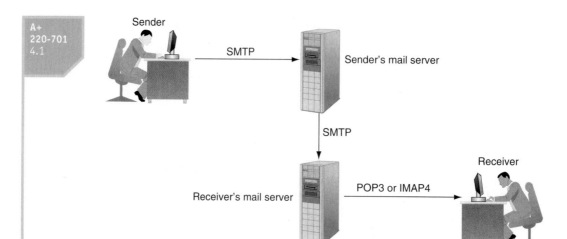

Figure 17-44 The SMTP protocol is used to send e-mail to a recipient's mail server, and the POP3 or IMAP4 protocol is used to download e-mail to the client
Courtesy: Course Technology/Cengage Learning

▲ *POP and IMAP.* After an e-mail message arrives at the destination e-mail server, it remains there until the recipient requests delivery. The recipient's e-mail server uses one of two protocols to deliver the message: POP3 (Post Office Protocol, version 3) or IMAP4 (Internet Message Access Protocol, version 4), which is a newer e-mail protocol. IMAP is slowly replacing POP for receiving e-mail. IMAP gives more control over how e-mail is stored on the server and client machines.

▲ *Telnet.* The Telnet protocol is used by the Telnet client/server applications to allow an administrator or other user to control a computer remotely.

TCP/IP PROTOCOLS USED BY THE OS

Looking back at Figure 17-42, you can see three layers of protocols between the applications and the hardware protocols. These three layers make up the heart of TCP/IP communication. In the figure, TCP or UDP manages communication with the applications protocols above them as well as the protocols shown underneath TCP and UDP, which control communication on the network.

Remember that all communication on a network happens by way of packets delivered from one location on the network to another. When a Web browser makes a request for data from a Web server, a packet is created and an attempt is made to deliver that packet to the server. In TCP/IP, the protocol that guarantees packet delivery is TCP (Transmission Control Protocol). TCP makes a connection, checks whether the data is received, and resends it if it is not. TCP is, therefore, called a **connection-oriented** protocol. TCP is used by applications such as Web browsers and e-mail. Guaranteed delivery takes longer and is used when it is important to know that the data reached its destination.

On the other hand, UDP (User Datagram Protocol) does not guarantee delivery by first connecting and checking whether data is received; thus, UDP is called a **connectionless protocol** or a **best-effort protocol**. UDP is primarily used for broadcasting and other types of transmissions, such as streaming video or sound over the Web, where guaranteed delivery is not as important as fast transmission.

For TCP to guarantee delivery, it uses IP to establish a session between client and server to verify that communication has taken place. When a TCP packet reaches its destination, an acknowledgment is sent back to the source (see Figure 17-45). If the source TCP does not receive the acknowledgment, it resends the data or passes an error message back to the higher-level application protocol.

A+
220-701
4.1

Figure 17-45 TCP guarantees delivery by requesting an acknowledgment
Courtesy: Course Technology/Cengage Learning

A+
220-701
4.1
3.2

PING, IPCONFIG, AND TELNET

Three TCP/IP utilities used to solve problems with TCP/IP and communicate on a TCP/IP network are Ping, Ipconfig, and Telnet. In this part of the chapter, you will learn to use all three. In the next chapter, you will learn about other TCP/IP utilities and how to use them when troubleshooting a network or Internet connection.

USE PING TO TEST FOR CONNECTIVITY

The Ping (Packet InterNet Groper) command tests connectivity by sending an echo request to a remote computer. If the remote computer is online and detects the signal, it responds to the ping. When testing for connectivity or problems with name resolution, Ping should be the first tool you use. A few examples are shown in Table 17-7. The first two examples are shown in Figure 17-46.

Ping Command	Description
Ping 69.32.142.109	To test for connectivity using an IP address. If the remote computer responds, the round-trip times are displayed.
Ping –a 69.32.142.109	The –a parameter tests for name resolution. Use it to display the host name and verify DNS is working.
Ping –t 69.32.142.109	The –t parameter causes pinging to continue until interrupted. To display statistics, press Ctrl-Break. To stop pinging, press Ctrl-C.
Ping –l 6500 69.32.142.109	The –l parameter changes the size of the data packet sent with the ping. Default size is 32 bytes, and the size can be up to 65,527 bytes.
Ping 127.0.0.1	A loopback address test. The IP address 127.0.0.1 always refers to the local computer. If the local computer does not respond, you can assume there is a problem with the TCP/IP configuration.
Ping www.course.com	Use a host name to find out the IP address of a remote computer. If the computer does not respond, assume there is a problem with DNS. On the other hand, some computers are not configured to respond to pings.

Table 17-7 Examples of the Ping command

17

A+ 220-701

```
C:\Windows\system32\cmd.exe

Microsoft Windows [Version 6.0.6001]
Copyright (c) 2006 Microsoft Corporation.  All rights reserved.

C:\Users\Jean Andrews>ping 69.32.142.109

Pinging 69.32.142.109 with 32 bytes of data:
Reply from 69.32.142.109: bytes=32 time=70ms TTL=111
Reply from 69.32.142.109: bytes=32 time=69ms TTL=111
Reply from 69.32.142.109: bytes=32 time=86ms TTL=111
Reply from 69.32.142.109: bytes=32 time=69ms TTL=111

Ping statistics for 69.32.142.109:
    Packets: Sent = 4, Received = 4, Lost = 0 (0% loss),
Approximate round trip times in milli-seconds:
    Minimum = 69ms, Maximum = 86ms, Average = 73ms

C:\Users\Jean Andrews>ping -a 69.32.142.109

Pinging tluser.thomsonlearning.com [69.32.142.109] with 32 bytes of data:
Reply from 69.32.142.109: bytes=32 time=87ms TTL=111
Reply from 69.32.142.109: bytes=32 time=69ms TTL=111
Reply from 69.32.142.109: bytes=32 time=86ms TTL=111
Reply from 69.32.142.109: bytes=32 time=87ms TTL=111

Ping statistics for 69.32.142.109:
    Packets: Sent = 4, Received = 4, Lost = 0 (0% loss),
Approximate round trip times in milli-seconds:
    Minimum = 69ms, Maximum = 87ms, Average = 82ms

C:\Users\Jean Andrews>_
```

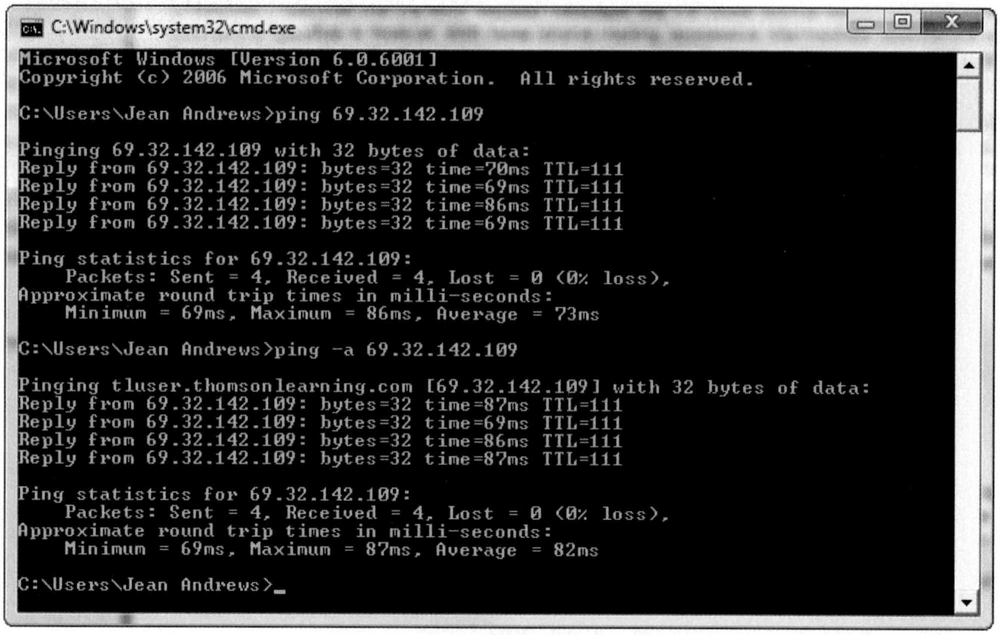

Figure 17-46 Use the Ping command to test for connectivity and name resolution
Courtesy: Course Technology/Cengage Learning

USE IPCONFIG TO TROUBLESHOOT TCP/IP CONFIGURATION

The Ipconfig command can display TCP/IP configuration information and refresh the IP address. When using the Ipconfig command in Vista, use an elevated command prompt window. Some examples of the command are listed in Table 17-8.

Ipconfig Command	Description
Ipconfig /all	Displays TCP/IP information (see Figure 17-47).
Ipconfig /release	Release the IP address when dynamic IP addressing is being used.
Ipconfig /renew	Lease a new IP address from a DHCP server.
Ipconfig /displaydns	Displays information about name resolutions that Windows currently holds in the DNS resolver cache.
Ipconfig /flushdns	Flushes the name resolver cache, which might solve a problem when the browser cannot find a host on the Internet.

Table 17-8 Examples of the Ipconfig command

USE TELNET TO COMMUNICATE WITH A REMOTE COMPUTER

Using Telnet, a user connects to a remote computer and controls it through the command prompt window provided by Telnet. Telnet was once a popular method for an administrator to connect to a server to troubleshoot a problem on the server. However, because Telnet only provides a command-line interface and is not secure, other methods such as Remote Assistance and Remote Desktop are becoming more popular than Telnet. You will learn to use these tools in the next chapter.

💡 **A+ Exam Tip** The A+ 220-701 Essentials exam expects you to be able to use a Telnet interface as well as the Ping and Ipconfig utilities.

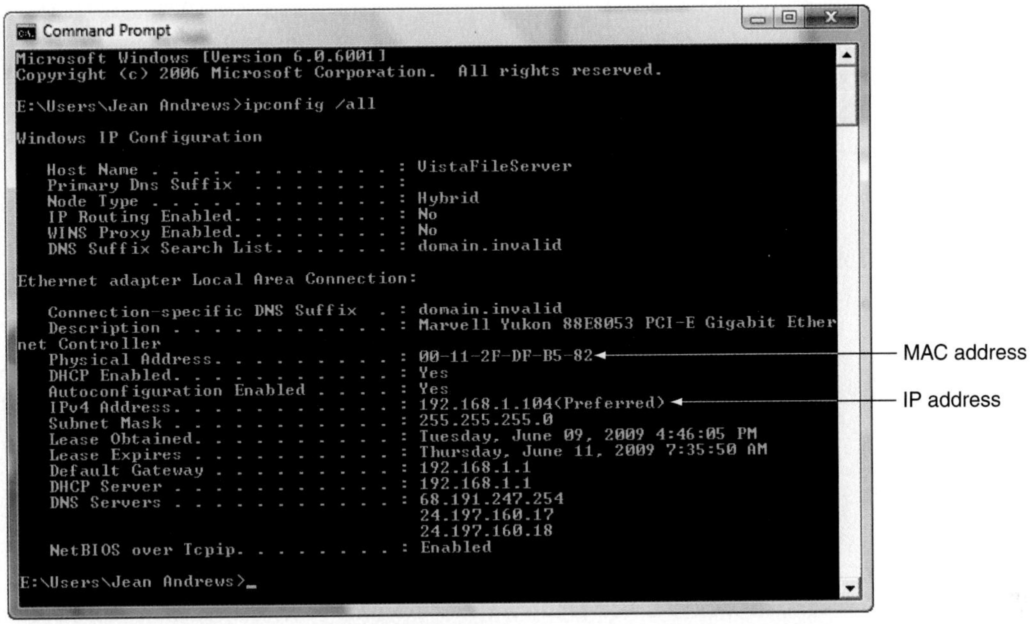

Figure 17-47 Results of the ipconfig /all command
Courtesy: Course Technology/Cengage Learning

Here are some tips about using Telnet:

▲ Telnet is a client/server application. That means one computer (the remote computer) is running the Telnet server and another computer (the local computer) runs the Telnet client. The Telnet server must be configured on Windows Vista Business or Ultimate editions or Windows XP Professional. Any Windows computer can run the Telnet client.

▲ For a user to log into a remote computer using Telnet, the user account must belong to the TelnetClients group. This user account and password must match the account and password used on the local computer.

▲ The Telnet server application must be running on the remote computer before you use Telnet. The service can be started from the Services console and set to start automatically or manually.

▲ By default, the Telnet client and server applications are installed on Windows XP, but not on Vista. For Vista, you must manually install the server and/or client.

Some Telnet commands are listed in Table 17-9.

Telnet Command	Explanation
Set localecho	Displays command responses that are given by the remote computer.
Set ntlm	Uses NTLM to authenticate login account and password. NTLM is a Windows authentication protocol for user IDs and passwords.
Open *<host name>* *[port]*	Connect to the remote computer. Use either the IP address or computer name to identify the computer. If you don't specify a port, port 23 will be used.
Close	Closes the current connection to a remote computer.
Quit	Closes the Telnet window.

Table 17-9 Telnet commands (continued)

A+
220-701
4.1
3.2

Telnet Command	Explanation
Ctrl+]	Switch from the remote computer session mode window to the Telnet command mode window.
Press the Enter key	Switch from the Telnet command mode window to the remote computer session mode window.

Table 17-9   Telnet commands

APPLYING CONCEPTS

To use Telnet, you need a user account and password that match on both computers. User accounts can be created using the Control Panel for all versions of Windows or using Computer Management for Vista Ultimate and Business editions or for XP Professional. If you need to create a new user account on either computer, follow these steps using Control Panel:

1. For Vista, click **Add or remove user accounts** in Control Panel and respond to the UAC box. In the Manage Accounts window, click **Create a new account** (see Figure 17-48).

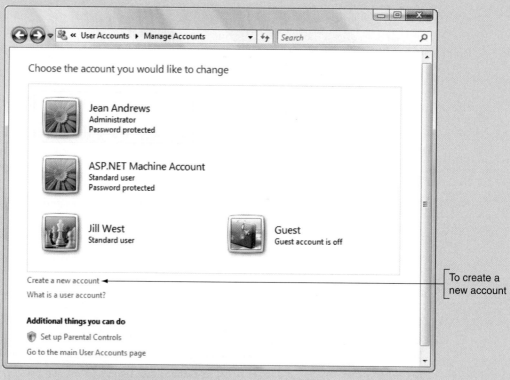

Figure 17-48   Create a new user account
Courtesy: Course Technology/Cengage Learning

2. In the next window, enter the user name (see Figure 17-49). Select if the account will be a Standard or Administrator account. A standard account has fewer privileges than an administrator account, but either account type can use Telnet. Click **Create Account**.

3. To create a password for the account, in the Manage Account box, click the account icon and click **Create a password** on the next box. Enter the new password and click **Create password**.

A+
220-701
4.1
3.2

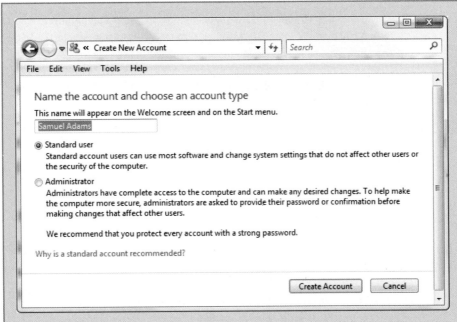

Figure 17-49 Decide the privilege level for the new account
Courtesy: Course Technology/Cengage Learning

To create a new account in Windows XP, open the **User Accounts** applet in Control Panel and click **Create a new account**. Enter an account name and click **Next**. For the privilege level of the account, select either Computer administrator or Limited. Click **Create Account**.

Using two computers that are networked together, you can use the following steps to practice using Telnet. The remote computer must use Windows XP Professional or Windows Vista Ultimate or Business. On the remote computer, follow these steps to configure and start the Telnet server application:

1. If you are using Vista, you need to install the Telnet server application. To do that, open the Control Panel and click **Programs**. Then click **Turn Windows features on or off** and respond to the UAC box.

2. In the Windows Features box, check **Telnet Server** (see Figure 17-50). Click **OK**. (For XP, the Telnet server and client are installed by default.)

Figure 17-50 Turn on the Telnet client and server applications
Courtesy: Course Technology/Cengage Learning

17

A+ 220-701

A+
220-701
4.1
3.2

3. To add the user account to the TelnetClients group, enter **Compmgmt.msc** in the Vista Start Search box or the XP Run box and press **Enter**. For Vista, respond to the UAC box. The Computer Management console opens (see the left side of Figure 17-51).

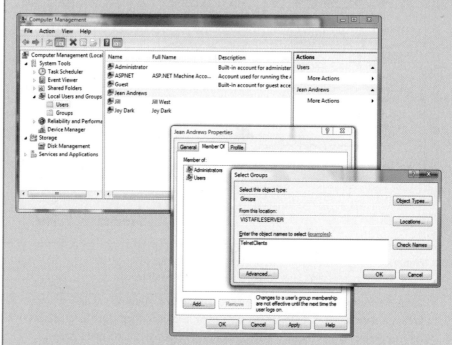

Figure 17-51 Add the user to the TelnetClients group
Courtesy: Course Technology/Cengage Learning

4. Drill down to the user account under **System Tools**, **Local Users and Groups**, and **Users**. Right-click the user and select **Properties** from the shortcut menu. The user Properties box opens. Click the **Member Of** tab.

5. Click **Add**. In the Select Groups box (the right side of Figure 17-51), type **TelnetClients** in the objects area (be sure to type it exactly as shown). Click **OK**. In the user Properties box, click **Apply** and click **OK** to close the box. Close the **Computer Management** console.

6. The next step is to start the Telnet server: To open the Services console, type **Services.msc** in the Vista Start Search box or XP Run box and press **Enter**. For Vista, respond to the UAC box. Scroll down to the Telnet service. Right-click it and select **Properties** from the shortcut menu. In the properties box, change the Startup type of Telnet to **Manual**. Click **Apply**. Click **Start** to start the Telnet service. Close the Telnet Properties box and the Services console.

7. To find out the IP address of this computer, open a command prompt window and enter the command **ipconfig /all**. Look for the IP address in the output, as shown in Figure 17-47 earlier in the chapter. In our example, the IP address is 109.168.1.104.

On the second or local computer, do the following to "telnet in" to the remote computer:

1. Log onto Windows with a user account and password that is the same as that on the remote computer.

2. Recall that Vista does not automatically install Telnet. For Vista, open **Control Panel** and turn on the **Telnet Client** application, following the steps given earlier (refer back to Figure 17-50).

3. You are now ready to open the Telnet client application. In the Vista Start Search box or the XP Run box, enter **Telnet** and press **Enter**. The Telnet command prompt window opens (see Figure 17-52). To see the results of commands executed by the remote computer, enter the command **set localecho** and press **Enter**.

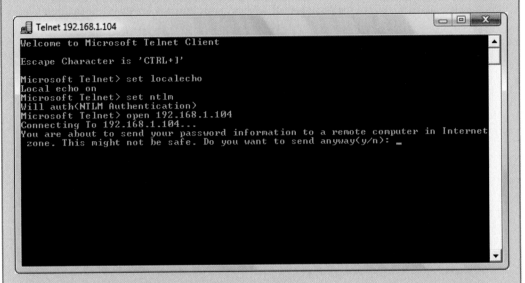

Figure 17-52 Telnet command prompt window
Courtesy: Course Technology/Cengage Learning

4. To use the NTLM authentication protocol for user accounts and passwords, enter the command **set ntlm** and press **Enter**.

5. To open the connection to the remote computer, enter the command **open 192.168.1.104**, substituting the IP address of your Telnet server in the command line. Press **Enter** after the command. You should now see the message that appears near the bottom of Figure 17-52.

6. Enter **y** to complete the connection. The window changes from the Telnet command mode to the remote computer session mode (see Figure 17-53). The prompt in this window is that provided by the remote computer. Commands you enter in this window are Windows commands (not Telnet commands) that are executed by the remote computer. At this point, you would enter whatever Windows commands you needed to do your work on the remote computer.

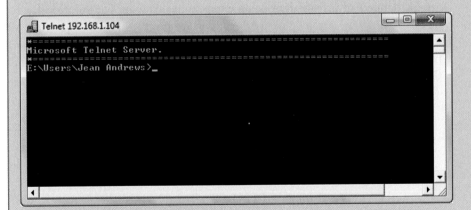

Figure 17-53 Telnet window in session mode with the remote computer
Courtesy: Course Technology/Cengage Learning

A+
220-701
4.1
3.2

Because localecho is on, each letter you enter appears twice in the command line, and you will be able to see the results of the command as displayed by the remote computer. To see how a command works in this window, enter the **dir** command and press **Enter**.

7. To return to the Telnet command mode window, enter **Ctrl+]**. To switch from the Telnet window to the session mode window, press **Enter**. Press **Ctrl+]** to return one more time to the Telnet command mode window.

8. Enter **close** and press **Enter** to close the connection. Enter **quit** and press **Enter** to close the Telnet window.

> **Notes** You can use the computer name rather than the IP address to connect to a remote computer. If the computer name is not recognized, add it to the bottom of the C:\Windows\System32\drivers\etc\hosts file on the local computer. For example, if the computer name of the remote computer is FileServer, add this line to the bottom of the file: 192.168.1.104 FileServer. To edit the hosts file, first remove the read-only attribute from the \etc folder.
>
> If you plan to use this same computer name to initiate Telnet sessions in the future, the Telnet server needs to use static IP addressing. This way, the Hosts file will always be accurate.

The major disadvantage of using Telnet to connect to a remote computer is the lack of security. The Telnet protocol does not encrypt transmitted data, which can therefore be read by others on the network. A better protocol to use is Secure Shell (SSH). The protocol is supported by Windows, but Windows does not provide SSH applications. Therefore, you must use third-party SSH applications such as SecureCRT by Van Dyke (*www.vandyke.com*). Two versions of SSH exist; be sure to select an application that uses SSH Version 2 to get the best security.

VIRTUAL PRIVATE NETWORKS

A+
220-701
4.1

Many people travel on their jobs or work from home, and the need is constantly growing for people to access private corporate data from somewhere on the Internet. Also growing are the dangers of private data being exposed in this way. The solution for securing private data traveling over a public network is a **virtual private network (VPN)**. A VPN works by using encrypted data packets between a private network and a computer somewhere on the Internet, as shown in Figure 17-54. The VPN is managed by client/server software such as Citrix Access Gateway by Citrix Systems (*www.citrix.com*).

With a VPN, security is attained using both of these methods:

◢ User accounts and passwords are required for connection to the corporate network. When the remote user sends this information to the authentication server, the data is encrypted. The encryption protocols supported by Windows for the user account and password data are EAP (Extensible Authentication Protocol), SPAP (Shiva Password Authentication Protocol), CHAP (Challenge Handshake Authentication Protocol), and MS-CHAP (Microsoft CHAP).

◢ After the user is authenticated, a tunnel is created so that all data sent between the user and the company is strongly encrypted. One of these four tunneling protocols is used: Point-to-Point Tunneling Protocol (PPTP), Layer Two Tunneling Protocol

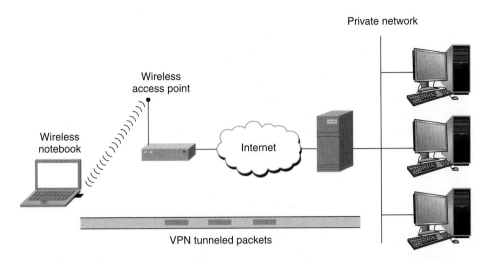

Figure 17-54 With a VPN, tunneling is used to send encrypted data over wired and wireless networks and the Internet
Courtesy: Course Technology/Cengage Learning

(L2TP), SSL (Secure Sockets Layer), or IPsec (IP security). Of the four, PPTP is the weakest protocol. The strongest protocol is a combination of L2TP and IPSec, which is called L2TP over IPSec. The two most popular protocols are SSL and IPsec.

When you first configure a computer to connect to a corporate network by way of the Internet, follow links on the corporate Web site to download the VPN client software. Then install the software on the computer and configure it to use the VPN. The user authorized to use the VPN will need to enter the user account and password authorized on the VPN to test the connection and make sure he or she can access resources on the corporate network. The resources the user can access depend on the permissions assigned the account.

Now that you know about networking hardware and the operating system methods and protocols used on a network, let's turn our attention to how to connect a computer to a network.

HOW TO CONNECT A COMPUTER TO A NETWORK

Connecting a computer to a network is quick and easy in most situations. In this part of the chapter, you'll learn to connect a computer to a network using both wired and wireless connections. Then we'll look at what can go wrong and how to fix problems when the connection doesn't work.

CONNECT TO A NETWORK USING AN ETHERNET CONNECTION

To connect a computer to a network using a wired connection, follow these steps:

1. If the network adapter is not yet installed, install it now following the steps given in Chapter 9 to install an expansion card. These steps include physically installing the card, installing drivers, and using Device Manager to verify that Windows recognizes the adapter without errors.

2. Connect a network cable to the Ethernet RJ-45 port and to the network wall jack or directly to a switch or router. (Connecting a PC directly to a switch or router might require a crossover cable.) Indicator lights near the network port should light up to

A+
220-701
4.1
1.10
3.2

indicate connectivity and activity. If you connected the cable directly to a switch or router, verify the light at that port is also lit.

3. By default, Windows assumes dynamic IP addressing and automatically configures the network connection. To find out if the connection is working, click **Start, Network** to open the Network window (see Figure 17-55). For Windows XP, click **Start, My Network Places** to open the My Network Places window. You should see icons that represent other computers on the network. Double-click a computer and drill down to shared folders and files to verify you can access these resources.

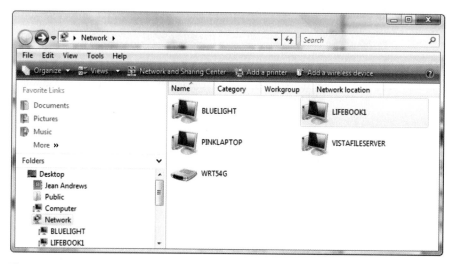

Figure 17-55   The Vista Network window shows resources on the network
Courtesy: Course Technology/Cengage Learning

4. To verify you have Internet connectivity, open Internet Explorer and browse to a few Web sites.

If the connection does not work, it's time to verify that network settings are configured correctly. Follow these steps using Windows Vista:

1. Verify that Device Manager recognizes the network adapter without errors. If you find an error, try updating the network adapter drivers. If that doesn't work, then try uninstalling and reinstalling the drivers. Make sure Device Manager recognizes the network adapter without errors before you move on to the next step.

2. If Network is not listed in the Start menu, open **Control Panel**. Click **Network and Internet** and then click **Network and Sharing Center**. In the Network and Sharing Center window (see the top part of Figure 17-56), click **Connect to a network**.

3. When Vista recognizes available networks, they are listed in the Connect to a network box shown in the lower part of Figure 17-56. If none are shown, click **Diagnose why Windows can't find any networks**. Then follow the recommendations that appear.

For Windows XP, to connect to a network or repair a connection, click **Start**, right-click **My Network Places**, and select **Properties** from the shortcut menu. The **Network Connections** window opens. Right-click the **Local Area Connection** icon, and then select **Repair** from the shortcut menu. See Figure 17-57. To connect to a network, in the Network Connections window, click **Create a new connection**.

A+
220-701
4.1
1.10
3.2

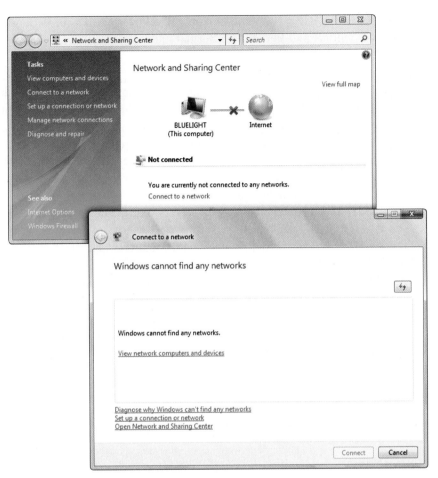

Figure 17-56 Vista Network and Sharing Center manages network connections
Courtesy: Course Technology/Cengage Learning

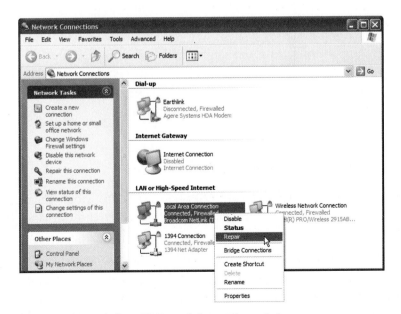

Figure 17-57 Windows XP Network Connections window
Courtesy: Course Technology/Cengage Learning

17

A+ 220-701

A+
220-701
4.1
1.10
3.2

Most networks use DHCP servers and dynamic IP addressing. If your network uses static IP addressing, you will need to know this information:

◢ The IP address for this computer.
◢ The subnet mask. A **subnet mask** is a group of four dotted decimal numbers such as 255.255.0.0 that tells TCP/IP if a computer's IP address is on the same or a different network.
◢ The default gateway. A **gateway** is a computer or other device, such as a router, that allows a computer on one network to communicate with a computer on another network. A **default gateway** is the gateway a computer uses to access another network if it does not have a better option.
◢ The IP addresses of one or more DNS servers that the network uses.

Follow these steps to verify and change TCP/IP settings:

1. Click **Start**, right-click **Network**, and select **Properties** from the shortcut menu. The Network and Sharing Center opens. In the left pane, click **Manage network connections**. In the Network Connections window, right-click **Local Area Connection** and select **Properties** from the shortcut menu. Respond to the UAC box. The properties box appears (see the left side of Figure 17-58).

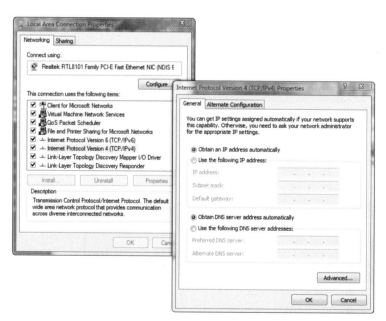

Figure 17-58 Verify and change TCP/IP settings
Courtesy: Course Technology/Cengage Learning

2. Select **Internet Protocol Version 4 (TCP/IPv4)** and click **Properties**. The properties box on the right side of Figure 17-58 appears. Settings are correct for dynamic IP addressing.

3. To change the settings to static IP addressing, select **Use the following IP address**. Then enter the IP address, subnet mask, and default gateway.

4. If you have been given the IP addresses of DNS servers, check **Use the following DNS server addresses** and enter up to two IP addresses. If you have other DNS IP addresses, click **Advanced** and enter them on the **DNS** tab of the Advanced TCP/IP Settings box.

A+
220-701
4.1
1.10
3.2

5. By the way, if the computer you are using is a laptop that moves from one network to another, you can click the **Alternate Configuration** tab and configure static IP address settings for a second network (see Figure 17-59). One way to use this configuration is to configure the General tab to use dynamic IP addressing and configure the Alternate Configuration tab to use static IP addressing. Using this method, the computer will first try to use dynamic IP addressing. If that is not available on the network, it then applies the static IP address settings. If static IP address settings are not available on this tab, the computer uses an automatic private IP address (APIPA).

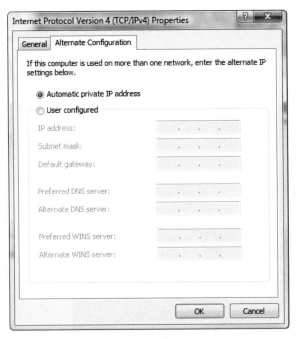

Figure 17-59   Alternate configuration that applies if the first
TCP/IP settings do not work
Courtesy: Course Technology/Cengage Learning

17

A+ 220-701

> 💡 **A+ Exam Tip**   The A+ 220-701 Essentials exam expects you to know the basics of configuring static and dynamic IP addressing and DNS server IP addresses.

To verify and change the TCP/IP setting for Windows XP, click **Start**, right-click **My Network Places**, and select **Properties** from the shortcut menu. The **Network Connections** window opens. Right-click the **Local Area Connection** icon, and then select **Properties** from the shortcut menu. Refer back to Figure 17-57. The properties box opens. Select **Internet Protocol (TCP/IP)** and click **Properties**. Configure the TCP/IP properties the same as with Windows Vista.

> 📹 Video
> Setting up a Network with Hub and Patch Cables

CONNECT TO A NETWORK USING A WIRELESS CONNECTION

A+
220-701
1.10
3.2

Wireless networks are either public, unsecured hotspots or private, secured hotspots. In this part of the chapter, you learn how to connect to each.

A+
220-701
1.10
3.2

HOW TO CONNECT TO A PUBLIC WIRELESS HOTSPOT

When using a public wireless hotspot, know that whatever you send over the network might be read by others. Also, unless you protect your computer by using strong firewall settings, your computer might get hacked. Here are the steps to connect to a public hotspot for a laptop using Windows Vista and how to protect your computer on that network:

1. Install the wireless adapter. For external adapters such as the one shown in Figure 17-60, be sure to follow the manufacturer's instructions for the installation. Most likely you'll be asked to first install the software before installing the device. During the installation process, you will be given the opportunity to use the manufacturer's configuration utility to manage the wireless adapter or to use Windows to do the job. For best results, use the utility provided by the manufacturer. In the following steps, we're using the Windows utility.

Figure 17-60 Plug the wireless USB adapter into the USB port
Courtesy: Course Technology/Cengage Learning

2. For embedded wireless, turn on your wireless device. For some laptops, that's done by a switch on the keyboard (see Figure 17-61) or on the side of the laptop. The wireless antenna is usually in the lid of a notebook and gives best performance when the lid is fully raised. For a desktop computer, make sure the antenna is in an upright position (see Figure 17-62).

3. Using your mouse, hover over or double-click the network icon in your notification area. Vista reports that wireless networks are available (see Figure 17-63).

4. Click **Connect to a network**. A list of available networks appears (see Figure 17-64).

5. If you select an unsecured network, Vista warns you about sending information over it. Click **Connect Anyway**.

Figure 17-61   Turn on the wireless switch on your laptop
Courtesy: Course Technology/Cengage Learning

Figure 17-62   Raise the antenna on a NIC to an upright position
Courtesy: Course Technology/Cengage Learning

Figure 17-63   Windows reports that wireless networks are available
Courtesy: Course Technology/Cengage Learning

17

A+ 220-701

A+
220-701
1.10
3.2

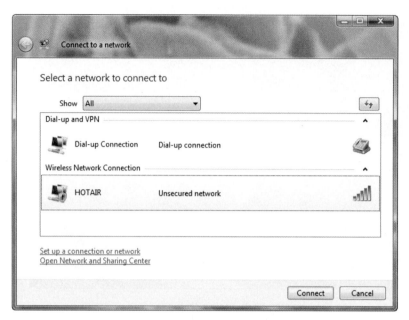

Figure 17-64   Select a wireless network
Courtesy: Course Technology/Cengage Learning

6. Vista reports the connection is made using the window in Figure 17-65. If you are comfortable with Vista automatically connecting to this network in the future, check **Save this network**. Close the window. If you hover your mouse pointer over the network icon in the notification area or double-click it, you can see the network to which you are connected (see Figure 17-66).

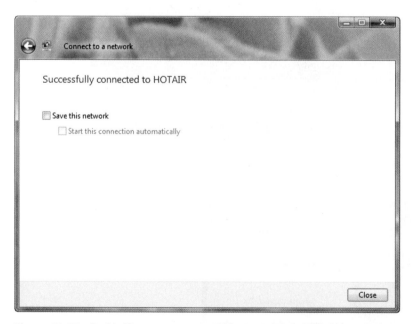

Figure 17-65   Decide if you want to save this network connection
Courtesy: Course Technology/Cengage Learning

A+
220-701
1.10
3.2

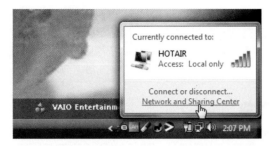

Figure 17-66 Find out to which network you are connected
Courtesy: Course Technology/Cengage Learning

7. To verify firewall settings and check for errors, open the Network and Sharing Center window (see Figure 17-67). Verify that Vista has configured the network as a public network and that Sharing and Discovery settings are all turned off. If Vista reports it has configured the network as a Private network, click **Customize** and change the setting to Public. In the figure, you can see there is a problem with the Internet connection from the HOTAIR network to the Internet.

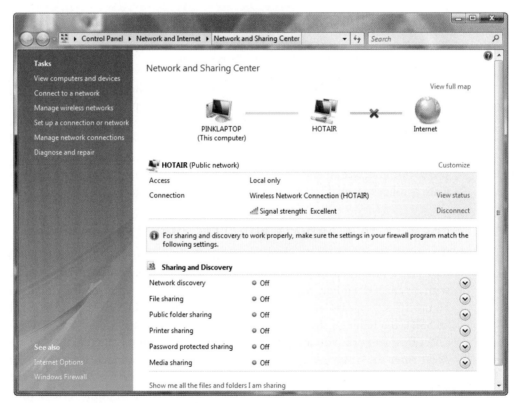

Figure 17-67 Verify that your connection is secure
Courtesy: Course Technology/Cengage Learning

8. Open your browser to test the connection. For some hotspots, a home page appears and you must enter a code or agree to the terms of use (see Figure 17-68).

17

A+ 220-701

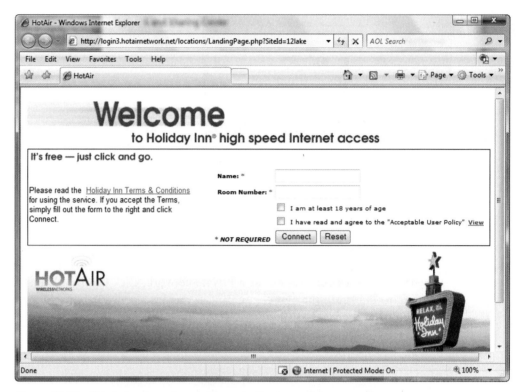

Figure 17-68 This hotspot requires you agree to the terms of use
Courtesy: Course Technology/Cengage Learning

When selecting a public hotspot, watch out for rogue hotspots trying to trick you into using them. For example, suppose you sit down at a coffee shop with your laptop to surf the Web. When you try to connect to the free hotspot provided by the coffee shop, you see two unsecured hotspots available. One is named JoesCoffeeShop and the other is named FreeInternet. Most likely the first one is provided by the coffee shop and is the one to choose. However, if you're not sure, ask an employee. The danger in connecting to unknown hotspots is that malware and hackers might be waiting for unsecured computers to connect.

CONNECT TO A PRIVATE WIRELESS NETWORK

When connecting to a private and secured wireless access point, you must provide the information that proves you have the right to use the network. If the network is protected with an encryption key, when you first attempt to connect, a screen similar to that in Figure 17-69 appears so that you can enter the key. If the access point is not broadcasting its SSID, the name of the wireless network will appear as "Unnamed Network." When you select this network, you are given the opportunity to enter the name of the network. If you don't enter the name correctly, you will not be able to connect. It is also possible that a private and secured wireless access point has been configured for MAC address filtering in order to control which wireless adapters can use the access point. Check with the network administrator to determine if this is the case; if necessary, give the administrator the adapter's MAC address to be entered into a table of acceptable MAC addresses.

To know the MAC address of your wireless adapter, for an external adapter, you can look on the back of the adapter itself (see Figure 17-70) or in the adapter documentation. Also, if the adapter is installed on your computer, you can open a command prompt window and enter the command **ipconfig/all**, which displays your TCP/IP configuration for all network connections. The MAC address is called the Physical Address in the display (see Figure 17-71).

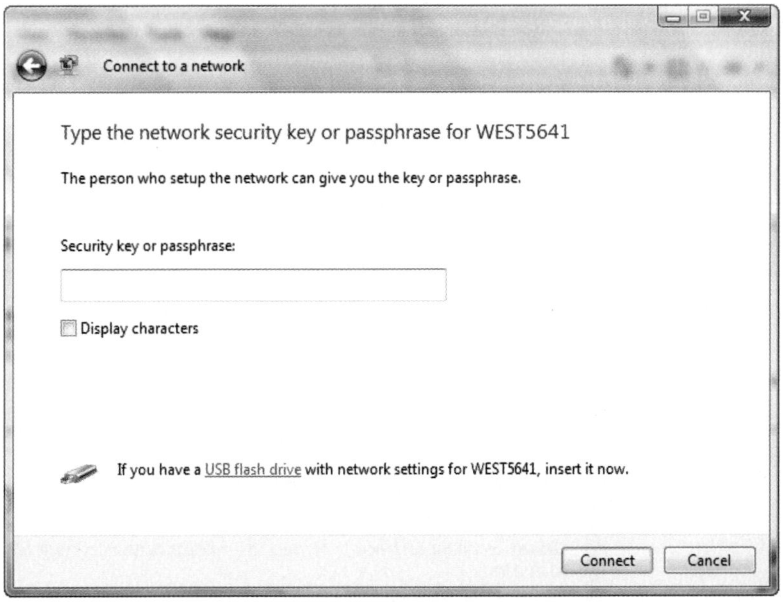

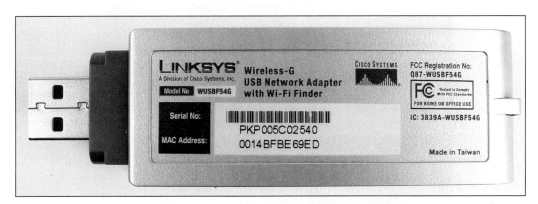

Figure 17-69 To use a secured wireless network, you must know the encryption key
Courtesy: Course Technology/Cengage Learning

Figure 17-70 The MAC address is printed on the back of this USB wireless adapter
Courtesy: Course Technology/Cengage Learning

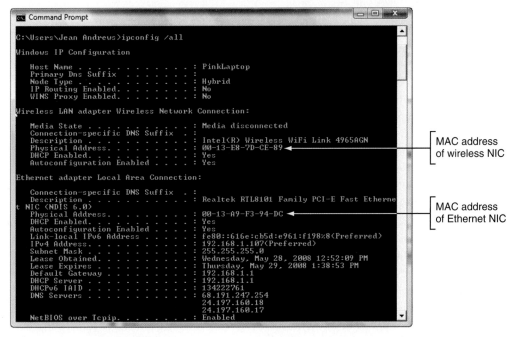

Figure 17-71 Use the ipconfig /all command to display TCP/IP configuration data
Courtesy: Course Technology/Cengage Learning

17

A+ 220-701

909

A+
220-701
1.10
3.2

Here are the steps to connect to a public or private hot spot when using Windows XP:

1. Right-click **My Network Places** and select **Properties**. The Network Connections window opens. Right-click the **Wireless Network Connection** icon and select **View Available Wireless Networks** from the shortcut menu. The Wireless Network Connection window opens (see Figure 17-72). Select an unsecured network from those listed and click **Connect**.

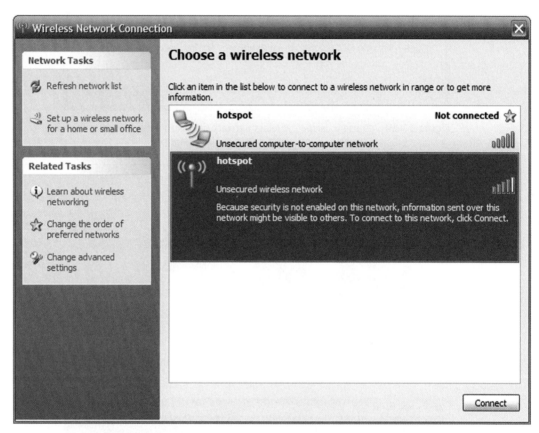

Figure 17-72   Available wireless hot spots
Courtesy: Course Technology/Cengage Learning

2. When you select a secured network from the list, you must enter the key in a dialog box, as shown in Figure 17-73.

If you're having a problem making the connection and you know the SSID of the hot spot, you can enter the SSID. Click **Change advanced settings** in the Network Connections window. The Wireless Network Connection Properties dialog box opens. Click the **Wireless Networks** tab (see Figure 17-74). Click **Add**.

The Wireless network properties window opens (see Figure 17-75). Enter the SSID of the network and make sure that Network Authentication is set to **Open** and Data encryption is set to **Disabled**. Click **OK**. When a dialog box opens to warn you of the dangers of disabling encryption, click **Continue Anyway**. Click **OK** to close the Wireless Network Connection Properties dialog box. Try again to connect to the hot spot.

Video
Installing a Wireless NIC

A+
220-701
1.10
3.2

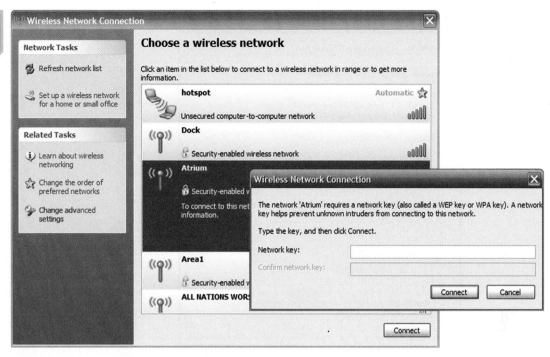

Figure 17-73   To use a secured wireless network, you must know the encryption key
Courtesy: Course Technology/Cengage Learning

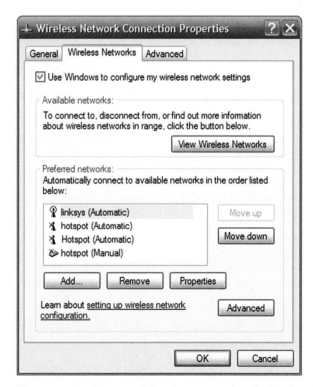

Figure 17-74   Manage wireless hot spots using the Wireless Network Connection Properties box
Courtesy: Course Technology/Cengage Learning

17

A+ 220-701

A+
220-701
1.10
3.2

Figure 17-75 Enter the SSID of a hot spot to which you want to connect
Courtesy: Course Technology/Cengage Learning

>> CHAPTER SUMMARY

▲ Networks are categorized in size as a PAN, LAN, Wireless LAN, MAN, or WAN.

▲ Performance of a network technology is measured in bandwidth and latency.

▲ The two most popular ways to connect to the Internet are cable modem and DSL. Other methods used include satellite, dedicated fiber optic, dial-up, and wireless technologies such as WiMAX and a cellular WAN.

▲ Security is a major issue for wireless networks. Security measures used include encryption, disabling SSID broadcasting, and filtering MAC addresses. Encryption standards used include WEP, WPA, and WPA2.

▲ Technology used by cell phones that allows us to browse the Web, stream music and video, play online games, and use chat and video conferencing is called 3G.

▲ Bluetooth is a wireless standard used for personal networks such as connecting a PDA to a laptop.

▲ An Internet card or air card makes it possible to connect a laptop to the Internet using a cellular WAN normally used by cell phones.

▲ Networking hardware used on local networks includes a network adapter, cables and connectors, wireless access points, routers, switches, and hubs.

▲ Most wired local networks use twisted-pair cabling which can be unshielded twisted pair (UTP) cable or shielded twisted pair (STP) cable. UTP is rated by category: CAT-3, CAT-5, CAT-5e, and CAT-6.

▲ A multifunction router can also be a switch, proxy server, DHCP server, wireless access point, firewall, or Internet access restriction device.

▲ Networking communication happens at three levels: hardware, operating system, and application levels.

▲ Ways of addressing networks, computers, and applications include domain names, IP addresses, ports, computer names, and NetBIOS names.

▲ TCP/IP uses protocols at the application level (such as FTP, HTTPS, HTTP, and Telnet), at the TCP level (using TCP or UPD), and at the IP level.

▲ Classes of IP addresses that can be used by the public include Class A, Class B, and Class C. Some IP addresses are private IP addresses that can be used only on intranets.

▲ A computer is configured to use dynamic or static IP addresses.

▲ A PC support person needs to know how to make a wired or wireless connection to an existing network and troubleshoot a connection that is giving problems.

>> KEY TERMS

For explanations of key terms, see the Glossary near the end of the book.

100BaseT
10Base2
10Base5
10BaseT
3G (Third Generation)
802.11b/g/n
access point (AP)
adapter address
AirPort
Automatic Private IP Address (APIPA)
bandwidth
base station
best-effort protocol
Bluetooth
BNC connector
broadband
cable modem
CAT-3 (Category 3)
CAT-5
CAT-6
CDMA (Code Division Multiple Access)
cellular network
cellular WAN
classful subnet masks
classless subnet masks
client/server applications
coaxial cable
computer name
connectionless protocol
connection-oriented protocol
crossover cable
data throughput
default gateway
DHCP (Dynamic Host Configuration Protocol)

dial-up networking
DNS (Domain Name System or Domain Name Service)
DNS server
domain name
DSL (Digital Subscriber Line)
dynamic IP address
enhanced CAT-5 (CAT-5e)
Fast Ethernet
fiber optic
fiber-optic cable
firewall
FTP (File Transfer Protocol)
full-duplex
fully qualified domain name (FQDN)
gateway
Gigabit Ethernet
GSM (Global System for Mobile Communications)
half-duplex
hardware address
host name
Hosts file
HTTP (Hypertext Transfer Protocol)
HTTPS (HTTP secure)
hub
IMAP4 (Internet Message Access Protocol, version 4)
Institute of Electrical and Electronics Engineers (IEEE)
Internet card
Internet Service Provider (ISP)
intranet
IP address

ISDN (Integrated Services Digital Network)
LAN (local area network)
latency
MAC (Media Access Control) address
MAN (metropolitan area network)
multicasting
multiple input/multiple output (MIMO)
name resolution
NAT (Network Address Translation)
NetBIOS (Network Basic Input/Output System)
NetBIOS name
network adapter
Network Address Translation (NAT)
network interface card (NIC)
octet
packet
PAN (personal area network)
patch cable
physical address
Ping (packet internet groper)
POP3 (Post Office Protocol, version 3)
port
port address
port number
PPP (Point-to-Point Protocol)
private IP addresses
public IP addresses
RJ-11
RJ-45

17

router
Service Set Identifier (SSID)
shielded twisted pair
  (STP) cable
SMTP (Simple Mail Transfer
  Protocol)
SMTP AUTH (SMTP
  Authentication)
status light indicators
subnet mask

switch
TCP (Transmission Control
  Protocol)
TCP/IP (Transmission Control
  Protocol/Internet Protocol)
TDMA (Time Division Multiple
  Access)
Telnet
ThickNet
ThinNet

UDP (User Datagram Protocol)
unshielded twisted pair (UTP)
  cable
virtual private network (VPN)
WAN (wide area network)
WEP (Wired Equivalent Privacy)
Wi-Fi (Wireless Fidelity)
wireless LAN (WLAN)
WPA (Wi-Fi Protected Access)
WPA2 (Wi-Fi Protected Access 2)

>> REVIEWING THE BASICS

1. Place the following networking technologies in the order of their highest speed, from slowest to fastest: fiber optic, dial-up networking, cable modem, Fast Ethernet

2. What is the difference between ADSL and SDSL?

3. Among satellite, cable modem, and DSL, which technology experiences more latency?

4. When using DSL to connect to the Internet, the data transmission shares the cabling with what other technology?

5. When using a cable modem to connect to the Internet, the data transmission shares the cabling with what other technology?

6. Which version of 802.11 technologies can use two antennas at both the access point and the network adapter?

7. Which wireless encryption standard is stronger, WEP or WPA?

8. What is the name of the port used by an Ethernet cable? What is the name of the port used by a dial-up modem?

9. If you want to upgrade your 100BaseT Ethernet network so that it will run about 10 times the current speed, what technology would you use?

10. What is the maximum length of a cable on a 100BaseT network?

11. What does the 100 in the name 100BaseT indicate?

12. Which type of networking cable is more reliable, STP or UTP?

13. Which is more expensive, UTP CAT5e cabling or STP CAT5e cabling?

14. How can you tell the difference between a patch cable and a crossover cable by examining the cable?

15. What type of server serves up IP addresses to computers on a network?

16. What type of protocol is used to present a public IP address to computers outside the LAN to handle requests to use the Internet from computers inside the LAN?

17. How many bits are in an IPv4 IP address?

18. What port does the SMTP protocol use by default?

19. Which protocol does a Web server use when transmissions are encrypted for security?

20. What type of server resolves fully qualified domain names to IP addresses?

21. What is the maximum length of a NetBIOS name?

22. What is the name of the file that keeps associations between computer names and IP addresses on the local computer?

23. What protocol is replacing the POP protocol used to receive e-mail?

24. Approximately how many IP addresses are available for a single Class A IP license? Class B? Class C?

25. What are IP addresses called that begin with 10, 172.16, or 192.168?

26. In what class is the IP address 185.75.255.10?

27. In what class is the IP address 193.200.30.5?

28. Describe the difference between public and private IP addresses. If a network is using private IP addresses, how can the computers on that network access the Internet?

29. Why is it unlikely that you will find the IP address 192.168.250.10 on the Internet?

30. If no DHCP server is available on a network, what type of configuration must computers on the network use for assignments of IP addresses?

31. If a computer is found to have an IP address of 169.254.1.1, what can you assume about how it received that IP address?

32. What command can be used to cause Windows to release its IP address?

33. What is the purpose of the command, ping 127.0.0.1?

>> THINKING CRITICALLY

1. You have just installed a network adapter and have booted up the system, installing the drivers. You open My Network Places on a remote computer and don't see the computer on which you just installed the NIC. What is the first thing you check?

   a. Is File and Printer Sharing installed?

   b. Is the NetBEUI protocol installed?

   c. Are the lights on the adapter functioning correctly?

   d. Has the computer been assigned a computer name?

2. Your job is to support the desktop computers in a small company of 32 employees. A consulting firm is setting up a private Web server to be used internally by company employees. The static IP address of the server is 192.168.45.200. Employees will open their Web browser and enter *personnel.mycompany.com* in the URL address box to browse this Web site. What steps do you take so that each computer in the company can browse the site using this URL?

3. Linda has been assigned the job of connecting five computers to a network. The room holding the five computers has three network jacks that connect to a switch in an electrical closet down the hallway. Linda decides to install a second switch in the room. The new switch has four network ports. She uses one port to connect the switch to a wall jack. Now she has five ports available (two wall jacks and three switch ports). While installing and configuring the NICs in the five computers, she discovers that the PCs connected to the two wall jacks work fine, but the three connected to the switch refuse to communicate with the network. What could be wrong and what should she try next?

17

>> HANDS-ON PROJECTS

PROJECT 17-1: Investigating Your PC

If you are connected to the Internet or a network, answer these questions:

1. What is the hardware device used to make this connection (network card, onboard port, wireless)? List the device's name as Windows sees it.

2. If you are connected to a LAN, what is the MAC address of the NIC? Print the screen that shows the address.

3. What is the IP address of your PC?

4. What Windows utilities did you use to answer the first three questions?

PROJECT 17-2: Researching IP Address Classes

Use the Web site *www.flumps.org/ip/* by Paul Rogers to answer these questions:

1. List three companies that have a Class A IP address license.

2. List three companies that have a Class B IP address license.

3. Who owns IP address class license 9.x.y.z?

4. Find another Web site on the Internet that gives similar information. How does the information on the new site compare with the information on the *www.flumps.org/ip/* site?

PROJECT 17-3: Researching Switches

A PC support technician is often called on to research equipment to maintain or improve a PC or network and make recommendations for purchase. You have been asked to upgrade a small network that consists of one switch and four computers from 100BaseT to Gigabit Ethernet. The switch connects to a router that already supports Gigabit Ethernet. Do the following to price the hardware needed for this upgrade:

1. Find three switches by different manufacturers that support Gigabit Ethernet and have at least five ports. Print the Web pages describing each switch.

2. Compare the features and prices of the two switches. Which switch would you recommend for a small business network? What information might you want to know before you make your recommendation?

3. Find three network adapters by different manufacturers to install in the desktop computers that support Gigabit Ethernet. Print Web pages for each NIC.

4. Compare features of the three network adapters. Which one would you recommend and why?

5. What is the total price of the upgrade, including one switch and four network adapters?

PROJECT 17-4: Researching a Wireless LAN

Suppose you want to connect two computers to your company LAN using a wireless connection. Use the Internet to research the equipment needed to create the wireless LAN, and answer the following:

1. Print a Web page showing an access point device that can connect to an Ethernet LAN.

2. How much does the device cost? How many wireless devices can the access point support at one time? How is the device powered?

3. Print three Web pages showing three different network adapters a computer can use to connect to the access point. Include one external device that uses a USB port and one internal device. Verify the devices use the same technology standards as the access point. How much does each device cost?

4. Which technology standards did you match to make sure the adapters and access point are compatible?

5. What is the total cost of implementing a wireless LAN with two computers using the wireless access point?

>> REAL PROBLEMS, REAL SOLUTIONS

REAL PROBLEM 17:1 Setting Up a Small Network

You've been using a Windows 2000 desktop computer for several years, but finally the day has come! You purchase a wonderful and new Windows Vista notebook computer complete with all the bells and whistles. Now you are faced with the task of transferring all your e-mail addresses, favorite Web site links, and files to your notebook.

Your old desktop doesn't have a CD burner, so burning a CD is out of the question. You considered the possibility of e-mailing everything from one computer to another or using floppy disks, but both solutions are not good options. Then the thought dawns on you to purchase a crossover cable and connect the two computers in the simplest possible network. Practice this solution by using a crossover cable to connect two computers and share files between them.

17

Networking Practices

In the last chapter, you learned about hardware used to build a network and how to connect a computer to an existing network. This chapter takes the next logical step in learning about networking by discussing connections to the Internet using Windows and how to set up a Small Office Home Office (SOHO) network. You will then learn about several tools and utilities that you will need when supporting a small wired or wireless network. Finally, you will learn how to troubleshoot problems when network and Internet connections fail.

Security is always a huge concern when dealing with networks. In this chapter, you will learn how to use a software and hardware firewall to protect a network. In the next chapter, we take security to a higher level and discuss all the many tools and techniques you can use to protect a single computer or a SOHO network.

> 💡 **A+ Exam Tip** All the content in this chapter applies to networking objectives on the A+ 220-702 Practical Application exam.

CONNECTING TO THE INTERNET

A+
220-702
3.2

In this part of the chapter, you'll learn how to connect a single PC to the Internet and then how to use Windows Firewall to protect that connection. Later in the chapter, you'll learn how to use a router to create a more sophisticated and secure Internet connection that can support multiple computers all accessing the Internet.

You need to know how to connect to the Internet when using cable modem, DSL, satellite, dial-up, and ISDN connections. All these types of connections are covered in the following sections.

> 💡 **A+ Exam Tip** The A+ 220-702 Practical Application exam expects you to know how to connect to the Internet when using a DSL, cable modem, satellite, ISDN, or dial-up connection.

Generally, when setting up a cable modem or DSL connection to the Internet, the installation goes like this:

1. Connect the PC to the cable modem or DSL box. Connect the cable modem to the TV jack or the DSL box to the phone jack. Plug in the power and turn on the broadband device.

2. Configure the TCP/IP settings for the connection to the ISP.

3. Test the connection by using a browser to surf the Web.

Now let's look at the specific details of making a cable modem connection or DSL connection to the Internet.

CONNECT TO THE INTERNET USING CABLE MODEM

To set up a cable modem installation to the Internet, you'll need the following:

- ◢ Internet service provided by your cable modem company.
- ◢ A computer with an available network or USB port.
- ◢ A cable modem and a network or USB cable to connect to the PC.
- ◢ The TCP/IP settings to use to configure TCP/IP provided by the cable modem company. For most installations, you can assume dynamic IP addressing is used. If static IP addressing is used, you'll need to know the IP address, the IP address of one or two DNS servers, the subnet mask, and the IP address of the default gateway (the IP address of a server at the ISP).

The setup for a cable modem connection using a network cable is shown in Figure 18-1. Follow these instructions to connect a computer to the Internet using a cable modem connection, an Ethernet cable to connect the PC to the modem, and dynamic IP addressing:

1. Select the TV wall jack that will be used to connect your cable modem. You want to use the jack that connects directly to the point where the TV cable comes into your home, with no splitters between this jack and the entrance point. Otherwise, in-line splitters can degrade the signal quality and make your connection erratic. The cable company can test each jack and tell you which jack is best to use for the cable modem—one good reason to have a technician come and hook you up for the first time. Later, if your cable modem connection is constantly going down, you might consider that you've chosen the wrong jack for the connection.

A+
220-702
3.2

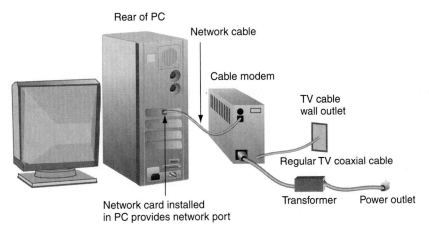

Figure 18-1 Cable modem connecting to a PC through a network card installed in the PC
Courtesy: Course Technology/Cengage Learning

2. Using coaxial cable, connect the cable modem to the TV wall jack. Plug in the power cord to the cable modem.

3. When using a network port on your PC, connect one end of the network cable to the network port on the PC, and the other end to the network port on the cable modem.

> 💡 **Tip**   A network cable is sometimes called an Ethernet cable or a patch cable. A network port can also be called an Ethernet port. You need to be familiar with all these terms, and they are all used in this chapter.

4. Vista automatically creates a new always-up network connection and displays the Set Network Location window shown in Figure 18-2. Select the location, most likely **Home**.

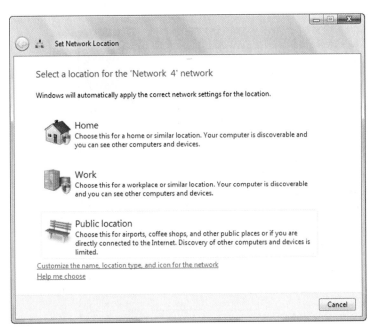

Figure 18-2 Vista asks for the location of the new connection so that it can configure the firewall
Courtesy: Course Technology/Cengage Learning

A+
220-702
3.2

5. For Windows XP, right-click **My Network Places** and select **Properties** from the shortcut menu. The Network Connections window opens. See Figure 18-3. Click **Create a new connection.**

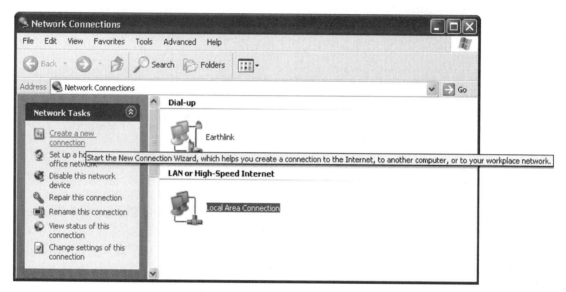

Figure 18-3   Using Windows XP, launch the New Connection Wizard
Courtesy: Course Technology/Cengage Learning

6. The New Connection Wizard opens. Click **Next** to skip the welcome screen. On the next screen, select **Connect to the Internet** and click **Next.**

7. On the next screen, select **Set up my connection manually** and click **Next.** On the following screen (see Figure 18-4), select **Connect using a broadband connection that is always on** and then click **Next.** The wizard creates the connection. Click **Finish** to close the wizard.

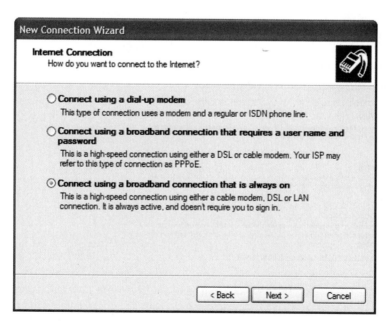

Figure 18-4   Choose the type of Internet connection
Courtesy: Course Technology/Cengage Learning

Notes When setting up a cable modem, you might want to connect your TV to the same jack that the cable modem is using. In this situation, connect a splitter to the jack and then connect the cable modem and TV cables to the splitter. If the connection gives problems, try removing the splitter.

Follow these directions if you are using a USB cable to connect your cable modem to your computer:

1. When using a USB port on your PC, first read the directions that came with your cable modem to find out if you should install the software before or after you connect the cable modem. For most installations, you begin by connecting the cable modem.

2. Connect the USB cable to your PC and to the cable modem. Plug in and turn on the cable modem and Windows will automatically detect it as a new USB device. When the Found New Hardware Wizard launches (see Figure 18-5), click **Locate and install driver software**, respond to the UAC box, and insert the USB driver CD that came with your cable modem. The wizard searches for and installs these drivers.

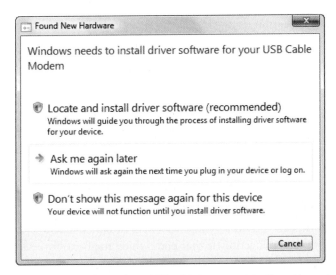

Figure 18-5 When using a USB cable to connect to the cable modem, the Found New Hardware Wizard will install the cable modem drivers
Courtesy: Course Technology/Cengage Learning

3. You can now pick up with Step 4 above to configure the Vista or XP connection.

After the connection is configured in Windows, you are ready to activate your service and test the connection. Do the following:

1. The cable company must know the MAC address of the cable modem you have installed. If you have received the cable modem from your cable company, the company already has the MAC address listed as belonging to you and you can skip this step. If you purchased the cable modem from another source, look for the MAC address somewhere on the back or bottom of the cable modem. See Figure 18-6. Contact the cable company and tell them the new MAC address.

Figure 18-6 Look for the MAC address of the cable modem printed on the modem
Courtesy: Course Technology/Cengage Learning

2. Test the Internet connection using your Web browser. If you are not connected, try the following:

   a. For Vista, open the Network and Sharing Center window and select **Diagnose and repair** under Tasks. This will walk you through a few basic steps to try to resolve the issue. For XP, in the Network Connections window, select the network connection and then click **Repair this connection**.

   b. If this doesn't work, turn off the PC and the cable modem. Wait a full five minutes until all connections have timed out at the cable company. Turn on the cable modem and wait for the lights on the front of the modem to settle in. Then turn on the PC. After the PC boots up, again check for connectivity.

   c. Try another cable TV jack in your home.

3. If this doesn't work, call the cable company's help desk. The technician there can release and restore the connection at that end, which might restore service. If this doesn't work, there might be a problem with the cable company's equipment, which the company will need to repair.

CONNECT TO THE INTERNET USING DSL

DSL service and an older technology, ISDN, are provided by the local telephone company. (An up-and-coming, second-generation DSL, called DSL over Fiber in the Loop [DFITL], uses dedicated fiber-optic cable to bring DSL to your neighborhood.) A DSL installation works pretty much the same way as a cable modem installation.

Here are the steps that are different:

1. Read the directions that came with the DSL modem and follow them. If your DSL modem came with a setup CD, you can run that setup to step you through the installation, including installing the drivers for a modem that uses a USB connection. You might be instructed to run a setup CD on your PC before you connect the modem, or you might need to install the modem first.

A+
220-702
3.2

2. To prevent static on the line, install a telephone filter on every phone jack in your house that is being used by a telephone, fax machine, or dial-up modem. See Figure 18-7.

Figure 18-7 A DSL filter is required to eliminate static on regular telephones
Courtesy: Course Technology/Cengage Learning

3. Connect the DSL modem as shown in Figure 18-8. If necessary, you can use a Y-splitter on the wall jack (as shown in Figure 18-8) so that a telephone can use the same jack. Be sure to add a filter between the splitter and the telephone; the filter also appears in the diagram. On the other hand, you can use a filter such as that shown in Figure 18-7 that can plug directly into the wall jack and serve both a telephone and the DSL modem. Plug the DSL modem into the DSL port on a filter or directly into a wall jack. (Don't connect the DSL modem to a telephone port on the filter; this setup would prevent DSL from working.) Plug in the power to the DSL modem. Connect a network cable or USB cable between the DSL modem and the PC.

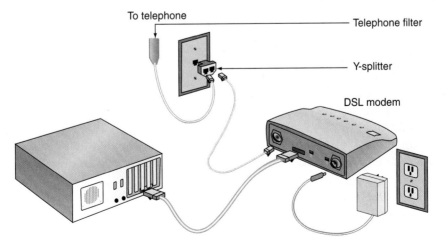

Figure 18-8 Sample setup for DSL
Courtesy: Course Technology/Cengage Learning

18

A+ 220-702

A+
220-702
3.2

4. Follow the steps given earlier to use Vista or XP to configure the DSL connection, which works the same way as with cable modem.

5. Open your browser and surf the Web to test the connection.

6. If you did not receive the DSL modem from the telephone company, you might need to call the DSL help desk and give them the MAC address of the modem and have them reset the connection on their end.

If your DSL connection requires a user name and password or static IP addressing, see the next section on how to configure these connections.

CONNECT TO THE INTERNET USING AN ON-DEMAND BROADBAND CONNECTION OR STATIC IP ADDRESSING

Most broadband connections today are always up and use dynamic IP addressing, which are the assumptions that Vista and XP make when they create and configure a new network connection. But some business services for cable modem or DSL use static IP addressing, and a less expensive DSL service might use an on-demand connection.

Follow these steps to create an on-demand broadband connection to the Internet:

1. Follow directions given in this chapter to connect the cable modem or DSL modem to the PC and to connect the modem to the wall jack. Vista will automatically create a new connection configured with dynamic IP addressing and an always-up connection.

2. Click **Start**, right-click **Network,** and select **Properties** from the shortcut menu. The Network and Sharing Center window opens. See Figure 18-9.

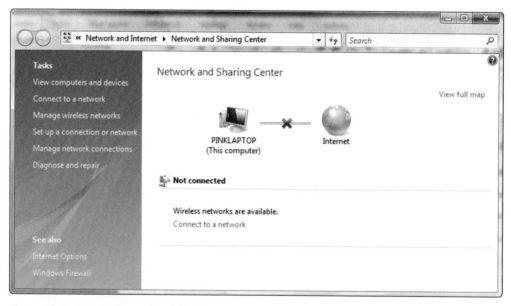

Figure 18-9   Use the Network and Sharing Center to create and manage network connections
Courtesy: Course Technology/Cengage Learning

3. Click **Set up a connection or network.** On the next screen (see Figure 18-10), select **Connect to the Internet** and click **Next.**

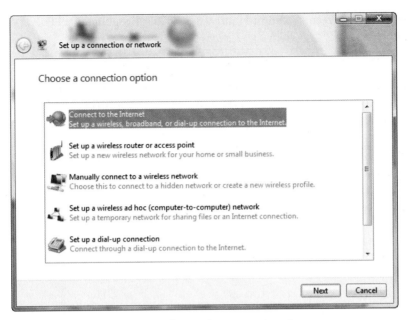

Figure 18-10 Select the type of network you want to set up
Courtesy: Course Technology/Cengage Learning

> **Notes** An on-demand broadband connection that is not always up requires that a user name and password be authenticated at the ISP each time you make the connection. The logon is managed by a protocol called PPPoE (Point-to-Point-Protocol over Ethernet), which is why the connection is sometimes called a PPPoE connection.

4. If the computer has other network connections that are not currently active, the screen in Figure 18-11 appears. Select **No, create a new connection** and click **Next**.

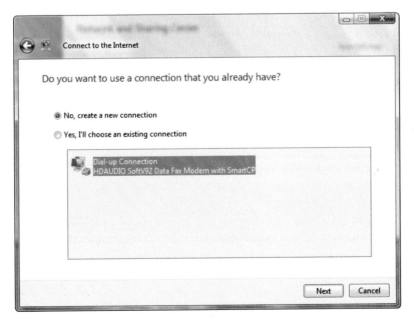

Figure 18-11 Choose the option to create a new network connection
Courtesy: Course Technology/Cengage Learning

5. On the next screen shown in Figure 18-12, click **Broadband (PPPoE)**.

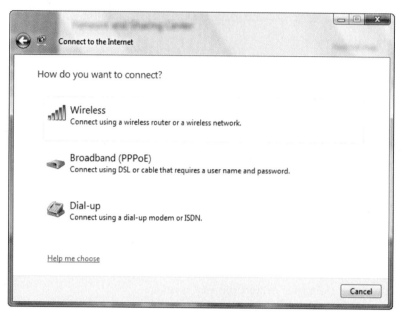

Figure 18-12   Choose to create a broadband connection
Courtesy: Course Technology/Cengage Learning

6. On the next screen (see Figure 18-13), fill in the information for the User name and Password given to you by your ISP. The Connection name can be any name you like. At the bottom of the screen there is also a check box that will allow other users on this computer to use the connection. Click **Connect**.

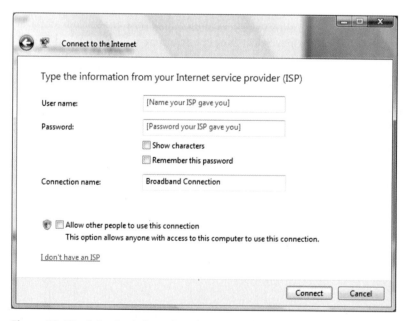

Figure 18-13   Enter the information given to you by your ISP
Courtesy: Course Technology/Cengage Learning

7. Vista assumes the connection will use dynamic IP addressing and attempts to make the connection. If you are using static IP addressing, the connection will fail and you will see the screen in Figure 18-14. For that situation, click **Set up the connection anyway**. On the next screen, click **Close**.

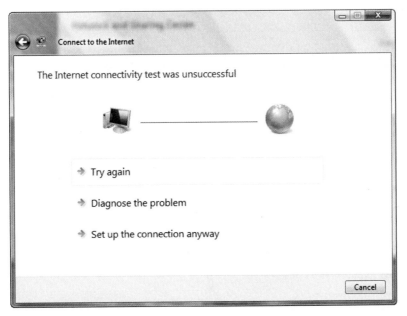

Figure 18-14 The connection failed
Courtesy: Course Technology/Cengage Learning

8. For Windows XP, you can configure an on-demand connection when first configuring the network connection using the New Connection Wizard. The window on the wizard that you use is shown earlier in Figure 18-4. Click **Connect using a broadband connection that requires a user name and password.** Follow the wizard through to complete the on-demand setup.

> **Notes** If your broadband subscription is not always up and requires you to enter your username and password each time you connect, using a router with auto-connecting ability can be a great help. It can automatically pass the username and password to your broadband provider without your involvement. The router can also be set to auto-refresh a connection before it expires.

Follow these steps to configure a network connection for static IP addressing:

1. In the Vista Network and Sharing Center window, click **Manage network connections.** The Network Connections window appears, showing each network the computer has set up (see Figure 18-15). The broadband connection icon will have whatever name you gave it; the default name is Broadband Connection, as shown in the figure. Right-click **Broadband Connection,** select **Properties** from the shortcut menu, and respond to the UAC box. The Broadband Connection Properties box appears.

2. Select the **Networking** tab, which is shown in the left side of Figure 18-16. On this tab, select **Internet Protocol Version 4 (TCP/IPv4)** and click **Properties.** The properties box appears, as shown on the right side of Figure 18-16.

3. For static IP addressing, select **Use the following IP address** and enter the IP address, subnet mask, and default gateway given to you by your ISP. Then enter the IP addresses given to you by your ISP for the first two DNS servers. If your ISP gave you IP addresses for a third or fourth DNS server, click **Advanced** and enter those IP addresses on the DNS tab in the Advanced TCP/IP Settings box and click **OK.**

4. Click **OK** twice to close the two dialog boxes. Then close the Network Connections window.

Figure 18-15   Use the Network Connections window to manage these connections
Courtesy: Course Technology/Cengage Learning

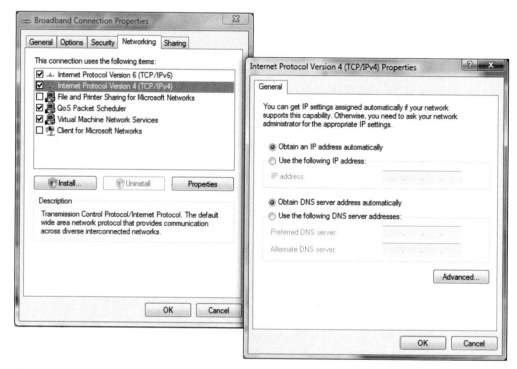

Figure 18-16   Use the Connection Properties box to configure IP addressing
Courtesy: Course Technology/Cengage Learning

5. To configure a Windows XP network connection for static IP addressing, right-click the **Local Area Connection** icon in the Network Connections window, and then select **Properties** from the shortcut menu. (Local Area Connection is the default name for this icon; it might have been given a different name.) The properties box opens. Select **Internet Protocol (TCP/IP)** and click **Properties**. Configure the TCP/IP properties the same as with Windows Vista.

CONNECT TO THE INTERNET USING SATELLITE

The Federal Communications Commission (FCC) requires that a trained technician install a satellite Internet service. The technician that does the installation will generally follow these steps:

1. The technician installs the satellite dish. For North America, the dish faces south with an unobstructed view of the southern sky.

2. Double coaxial cables are installed from the dish to the room in your building where the satellite modem will sit. The modem should sit near your computer or router.

3. Coaxial cables are plugged into two ports on the modem, most likely labeled Sat In and Sat Out. An Ethernet cable is connected to the RJ-45 port on the modem and the RJ-45 port on your PC.

4. The connection is configured in Windows. A satellite service is an always-up service that most likely uses dynamic IP addressing.

CONNECT TO THE INTERNET USING A DIAL-UP CONNECTION

You never know when you might be called on to support an older dial-up connection. Here are the bare-bones steps you need to set up and support this type connection:

1. Install an internal or external dial-up modem. How to install a modem card is covered in Chapter 9. Make sure Device Manager recognizes the card without errors.

2. Plug the phone line into the modem port on your computer and into the wall jack.

3. For Vista, open the Network and Sharing Center window and click **Set up a connection or network**.

4. On the next window, select **Set up a dial-up connection** and click **Next**.

5. On the next window (see Figure 18-17), enter the phone number to your ISP, your ISP username and password, and the name you decide to give the dial-up connection, such as the name and city of your ISP. Then click **Connect**.

6. For Windows XP, click **Create a new connection** in the Network Connections window. Follow the steps of the wizard, which are similar to those of Vista.

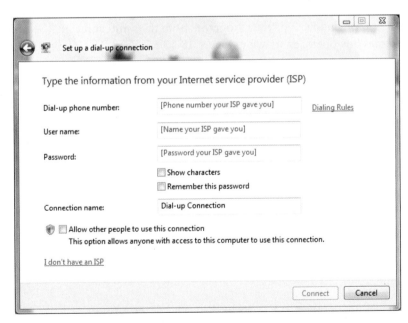

Figure 18-17 Configure a dial-up connection
Courtesy: Course Technology/Cengage Learning

To use the connection, go to the Vista Network and Sharing Center and click **Connect to a network**. Select the dial-up connection, and click **Connect**. The Connect dialog box appears (see Figure 18-18). Click **Dial**. You will hear the modem dial up the ISP and make the connection. For XP, double-click the connection icon in the Network Connections window, and then click **Dial**.

A+
220-702
3.2

Figure 18-18 Make a dial-up connection to your ISP
Courtesy: Course Technology/Cengage Learning

To view or change the configuration for the dial-up connection, do the following:

1. In the Vista Network and Sharing Center, click **Manage network connections**, and then right-click **Dial-up Connection** (or other name assigned the connection) and select **Properties** from the shortcut menu. For XP, right-click the connection icon in the Network Connections window and select **Properties** from the shortcut menu. The connection Properties box opens, as shown in Figure 18-19 for Vista. The XP box is similar.

Figure 18-19 Configure an Internet connection using the Properties window of the connection icon
Courtesy: Course Technology/Cengage Learning

2. Use the tabs on this window to configure TCP/IP (Networking tab), control the way Windows attempts to dial the ISP when the first try fails (Options tab), and change other dialing features.

If the dial-up connection won't work, here are some things you can try:

- Is the phone line working? Plug in a regular phone and check for a dial tone. Is the phone cord securely connected to the computer and the wall jack?
- Does the modem work? Check Device Manager for reported errors about the modem. Does the modem work when making a call to another phone number (not your ISP)?
- Check the Dial-up Connection Properties box for errors. Is the phone number correct? Does the number need to include a 9 to get an outside line? Has a 1 been added in front of the number by mistake? If you need to add a 9, you can put a comma in the field like this "9,4045661200", which causes a slight pause after the 9 is dialed.
- Try dialing the number manually from a phone. Do you hear beeps on the other end?
- Try another phone number.
- When you try to connect, do you hear the number being dialed? If so, the problem is most likely with the phone number, the phone line, or the username and password.
- Is TCP/IP configured correctly? Most likely you need to set it to obtain an IP address automatically.
- Reboot your PC and try again.
- If the computer has two RJ-11 ports, try the other port.
- Try removing and reinstalling the dial-up connection.

> **Notes** If you want to disable call waiting while you're connected to the Internet, enter *70 in front of the phone number.

CONNECT TO THE INTERNET USING ISDN

ISDN is an older, outdated technology and it's unlikely you'll ever be called on to set up an ISDN connection. But, just in case, here are a few essential tips that will make your work easier:

- The phone line that is handling the ISDN connection can support one or two ISDN connections or an ISDN connection and a regular telephone call.
- The ISDN equipment consists of an ISDN modem. The modem might also be able to serve double duty as a router for a small LAN.
- Logically, the ISDN modem contains two pieces of equipment. An NT1 (Network Terminator 1) device interfaces between the phone company and the home or business telephone network. A TA (terminal adapter) device interfaces with the local network. In most cases, both devices are contained in the modem box that uses an RJ-11 jack to connect to the telephone line and an RJ-45 jack to connect to the network.
- Charges for the ISDN line might be based on per-minute use. If that's the case, make sure your e-mail software or browser is not set to make the connection automatically when you don't want to incur a charge.
- When you first set up ISDN, connect the modem box and then configure the ISDN connection in the same way you would configure a dial-up connection using a regular phone line.

A+
220-702
3.2

IMPLEMENT WINDOWS FIREWALL AND VISTA NETWORK SECURITY

The Internet is a nasty and dangerous place infested with hackers, viruses, worms, and thieves. Knowing how to protect a single PC or a LAN is an essential skill of a PC support technician. The three most important things you can do to protect a single computer or network are to:

- ◢ Keep Windows updates current so that security patches are installed as soon as they are available.
- ◢ Use a software and/or hardware firewall.
- ◢ Run antivirus software and keep it current.

In earlier chapters, you learned how to keep Windows updates current. In the next chapter, you'll learn all about using antivirus software. In this section, you'll learn to use a software firewall and a hardware firewall. Software firewalls are appropriate when you're protecting a single personal computer that is connected directly to the Internet or is part of a local network. A hardware firewall, such as a multipurpose router, is used to protect all computers on the network from malicious activity coming from the Internet. In this part of the chapter, you'll learn to use a software firewall. Later in the chapter, you'll learn how to set up a hardware firewall.

A hardware or software firewall can function in several ways:

- ◢ Firewalls can filter data packets, examining the destination IP address or source IP address or the type of protocol used (for example, TCP or UDP).
- ◢ Firewalls can filter ports so that outside client applications or programs cannot communicate with inside services listening at these ports. Certain ports can be opened, for example, when your network has a Web server and you want Internet users to be able to access it.
- ◢ Firewalls can block certain activity that is initiated from inside the network—such as preventing users behind the firewall from using applications like FTP over the Internet. When evaluating firewall software, look for its ability to control traffic coming from both outside and inside the network.
- ◢ Some firewalls can filter information such as inappropriate Web content for children or employees, and can limit the use of the Internet to certain days or times of the day.

Some examples of firewall software are ZoneAlarm (see Figure 18-20) by Check Point Software (*www.zonealarm.com*), Firewall Software Blade by Check Point Software (*www.checkpoint.com*), and Windows Firewall. In addition, Norton 360 by Symantec (*www.symantec.com*) and McAfee VirusScan Plus by McAfee (*www.mcafee.com*) include antivirus software as well as a software firewall.

Windows Vista automatically configures Windows Firewall based on the type of network it believes you are connected to. Vista can assign you a public profile, a private profile, or a domain profile. A **public profile** offers the highest level of protection when you are connected to a public network. A **private profile** offers moderate protection when you are connected to a private network, and the least protection is used for a **domain profile**, when your PC is on a domain and security is managed by the domain's operating system, such as Windows Server 2008. When a PC first connects to a new network that is not part of a domain, Vista asks you if the network is a public or private network (refer back to Figure 18-2). It saves this response and applies it each time you reconnect to this network. Windows XP automatically sets the firewall for a moderate level of protection.

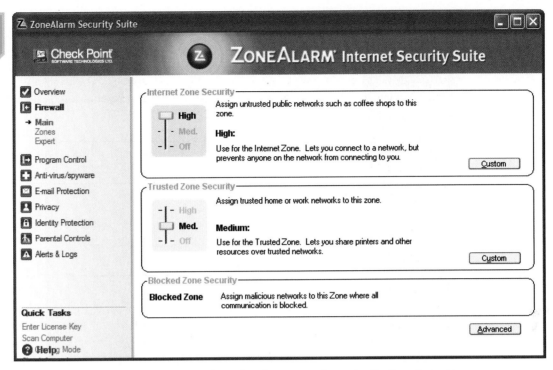

Figure 18-20 ZoneAlarm allows you to determine the amount of security the firewall provides
Courtesy: Course Technology/Cengage Learning

For Windows Vista, to see how firewall protection is set for a public or private network, use the Network and Sharing Center window by following these steps:

1. Click **Start**, right-click **Network**, and select **Properties** from the shortcut menu. The Network and Sharing Center window opens.

2. For the window showing in Figure 18-21, the PC is connected to a wired and wireless network. The wired network is set to Private and the wireless network is set to Public. Because the PC is connected to a public network, the Sharing and Discovery settings at the bottom of the window are turned off. To change the security setting for the Public network, click **Customize**.

3. The Set Network Location box appears (see Figure 18-22). To allow for less security and more communication on the network, click **Private** and then click **Next**.

4. Sharing and Discovery settings are now less secure, allowing the PC to be seen on the network (Network discovery), files on the PC to be shared with others on the network (File sharing), and printers installed on this PC to be shared (Printer sharing). These are the standard settings for a private network. To change a setting under the Sharing and Discovery group, click the down arrow to the right of the item and turn the item on or off (see Figure 18-23). In Chapter 19, you will learn to use Windows Explorer to share files and folders on the network.

To see how Windows Firewall is configured for Vista, follow these steps:

1. For Vista, in the left pane of the Network and Sharing Center window, click **Windows Firewall**. The Windows Firewall dialog box opens (see Figure 18-24). No matter what type of network you are connected to, Windows Firewall should always be turned on unless you are using a third-party software firewall instead of Windows Firewall.

18

A+ 220-702

A+
220-702
3.2

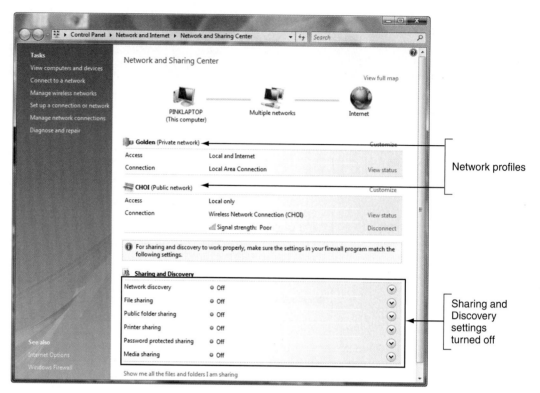

Figure 18-21 Security is high when connected to a public network
Courtesy: Course Technology/Cengage Learning

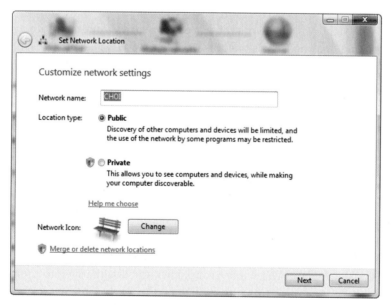

Figure 18-22 Change the security settings for a network
Courtesy: Course Technology/Cengage Learning

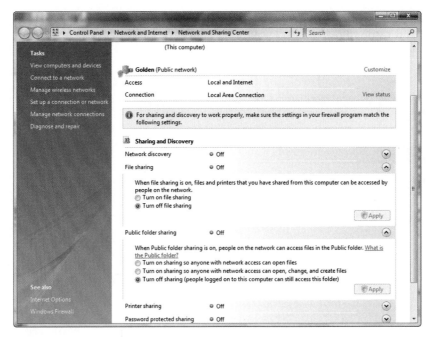

Figure 18-23 Change the setting of an item under the Sharing and Discovery group
Courtesy: Course Technology/Cengage Learning

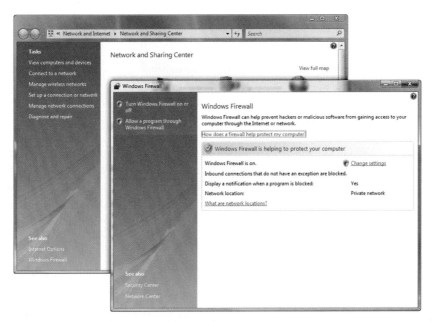

Figure 18-24 Windows Firewall is turned on
Courtesy: Course Technology/Cengage Learning

18

A+ 220-702

A+
220-702
3.2

2. To see the details of how Windows Firewall is working, click **Change settings** and respond to the UAC box. The Windows Firewall Settings box opens (see Figure 18-25).

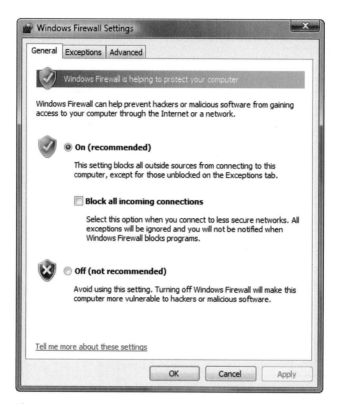

Figure 18-25 Windows Firewall is on but not working at its highest security level
Courtesy: Course Technology/Cengage Learning

3. Notice the check box for *Block all incoming connections*, which controls communication initiated from another computer. For a private network, Vista does not check this box. When connected to a public network, the box is checked. To see what incoming connections are allowed, click the **Exceptions** tab (see Figure 18-26).

4. Notice in Figure 18-26 that File and Printer Sharing is checked. This means that another computer can initiate communication with this computer to access a shared file or printer. You can change individual settings on this Exceptions tab by checking or unchecking items. Recall from Chapter 17 that a computer uses a port number to control incoming activity from client applications or programs on the network. This Exceptions box controls these ports. Each item in the list is associated with one or more ports, which are opened or closed based on the settings on this tab.

After you have Windows Firewall configured the way you want it, click **Apply** and click **OK** to close the Windows Firewall Settings window.

To view and change the Windows Firewall settings for Windows XP, use the Network Connections window. In the left pane, click **Change Windows Firewall settings**. The Windows Firewall window opens, as shown in Figure 18-27. Verify that **On (recommended)** is selected.

A+
220-702
3.2

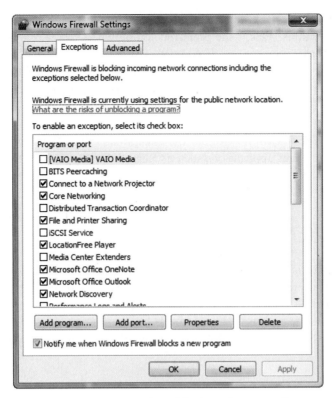

Figure 18-26   Exceptions allowed for incoming connections
Courtesy: Course Technology/Cengage Learning

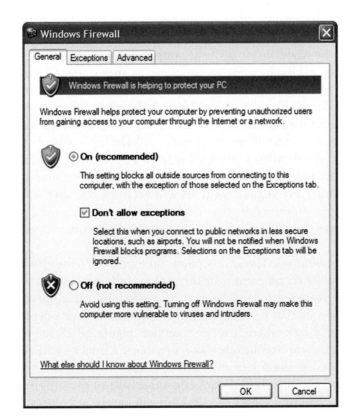

Figure 18-27   Windows Firewall for Windows XP is set for maximum protection
Courtesy: Course Technology/Cengage Learning

18

A+ 220-702

A+
220-702
3.2

If you don't want to allow any communication to be initiated from remote computers, check **Don't allow exceptions**. This is the preferred setting when you're traveling or using public networks or Internet connections. If you are on a local network and need to allow others on the network to access your computer, uncheck **Don't allow exceptions**. Then click the **Exceptions** tab to select the exceptions to allow. For example, if you want to share files and folders on your local network, use the Exceptions tab to allow File and Printer Sharing activity.

Later in the chapter, you'll learn how to use the Exceptions tab of Windows Firewall to allow certain client applications such as Remote Desktop access to your computer.

SETTING UP A SOHO NETWORK

A PC support technician is likely to be called on to set up a small office or home office network. To set up this network, you need to know how to physically connect computers to a network and how to install and configure a multipurpose router to stand between the network and the Internet. And, finally, you need to know how to set up and secure a wireless access point. All these skills are covered in this part of the chapter.

PHYSICALLY CONFIGURE A SMALL NETWORK

To set up a small network, you'll need computers, switches, network cables, a router, and whatever device (for example, a DSL or cable modem) that provides Internet access. Recall from the last chapter that a switch is used to connect two or more computers by way of Ethernet patch cables (also called network cables). Some network cables might be wired inside walls of your building with wall jacks that use RJ-45 ports. If network cables are lying on the floor, be sure to install them against the wall so they won't be a trip hazard. Take care that cables don't exceed the recommended length. Recall from Chapter 17 that 10BaseT, 100BaseT, and 1000BaseT Ethernet networks (also called Ethernet, Fast Ethernet, and Gigabit Ethernet) can use UTP or STP cables no longer than 100 meters (328 feet). For Fast Ethernet or Gigabit Ethernet, always use twisted-pair cables rated at CAT5e or higher. To connect multiple computers, use switches rated at the same speed as your router and network adapters. For best results, buy Gigabit switches and network adapters, a Gigabit router, and CAT6 cables. However, if some devices run at slower speeds, most likely a switch or router can still support the higher speeds for other devices on the network.

If your router is also your wireless access point, take care in planning where to place it. Place the wireless access point near the center of the area where you want your wireless network. The router also needs to have access to your cable modem, DSL modem, or whatever device that provides Internet access. That device needs access to the cable TV or phone jack where it receives service. Figure 18-28 shows a possible inexpensive wiring job where two switches and a router are used to wire two rooms for five workstations and a network printer. The only inside-wall wiring that is required is two back-to-back RJ-45 wall jacks on either side of the wall between the two rooms. The plan allows for all five desktop computers and a network

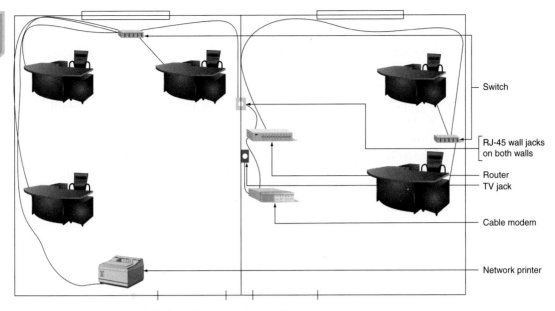

Figure 18-28 Plan the physical configuration of a small network
Courtesy: Course Technology/Cengage Learning

printer to be wired with cabling neatly attached to the baseboards of the office without being a trip hazard.

INSTALL AND CONFIGURE A ROUTER FOR A SMALL NETWORK

To install a router that comes with a setup CD, run the setup program on one of your computers on the network (doesn't matter which one). Follow the instructions on the setup screen to disconnect the cable modem or DSL modem from your host computer and connect it to the router. Next, connect the computers on your network to your router. A computer can connect directly to a network port on the router, or you can connect a switch or hub to one port on the router. The switch or hub can then provide multiple ports for computers to connect. Plug in the router and power it on.

You'll be required to sign in to the utility using a default password. The first thing you want to do is reset this password so that others cannot change your router setup.

> ⚡ **Caution** Changing the router password is especially important if the router is a wireless router. Unless you have disabled or secured the wireless access point, anyone outside your building can use your wireless network. If they guess the default password to the router, they can change the password to hijack your router. Also, your wireless network can be used for criminal activity. When you first install a router, before you do anything else, change your router password and disable the wireless network until you have time to set up and test the wireless security. And, to give even more security, change the default name to another name if the router utility allows that option.

A+
220-702
3.2

The setup program will then step you through the process of configuring the router. After you've configured the router, you might have to turn the cable modem or DSL modem off and back on so that it correctly syncs up with the router. If you don't get immediate connectivity to the Internet on all PCs, try refreshing the IP address or rebooting each PC.

Now let's look at how a Linksys router, such as the one shown in Figure 18-29, is configured. The methods are typical of what you might see for several brands and models of small office or home office routers. Firmware on the router (which can be flashed for updates) contains a configuration program that you access using a Web browser from anywhere on the network. In your browser address box, enter the IP address of the router (for our router, it's 192.168.1.1) and press **Enter**. A logon box appears (see Figure 18-30). Use the account name and password given in the router documentation to sign in.

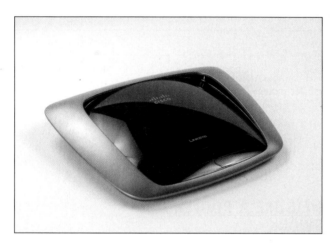

Figure 18-29 This router by Linksys allows computers on a LAN to share a broadband Internet connection and is an access point for computers with wireless adapters
Courtesy: Course Technology/Cengage Learning

Figure 18-30 Log in to the router configuration utility
Courtesy: Course Technology/Cengage Learning

A+
220-702
3.2

The main Setup window appears, as shown in Figure 18-31. For most situations, the default settings on this and other screens should work to provide network access without any changes.

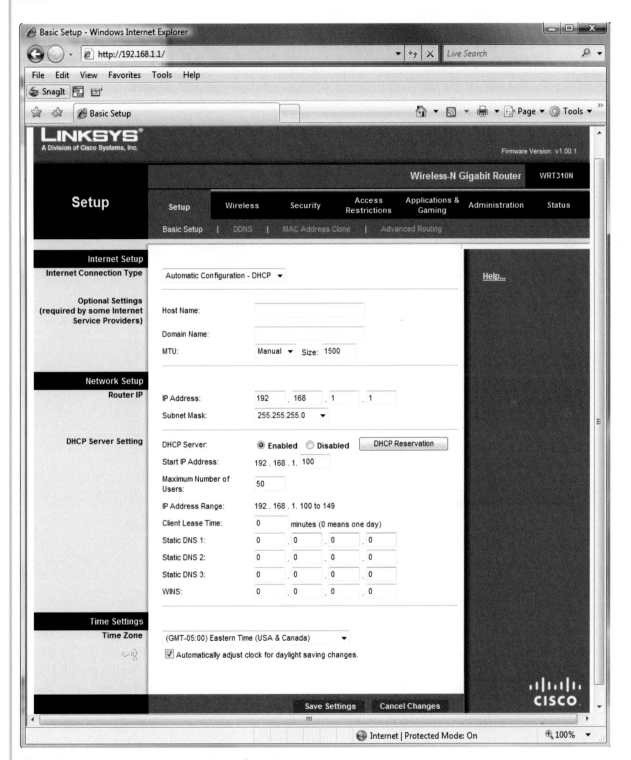

Figure 18-31   Basic Setup screen used to configure the router
Courtesy: Course Technology/Cengage Learning

A+
220-702
3.2

Following are some changes that you might need to make to the router's configuration. The first one should always be done:

◢ It's extremely important to protect access to your network and prevent others from hijacking your router. Do that by changing the password to the router firmware. If the firmware offers the option, disable the ability to configure the router from over the wireless network (see Figure 18-32).

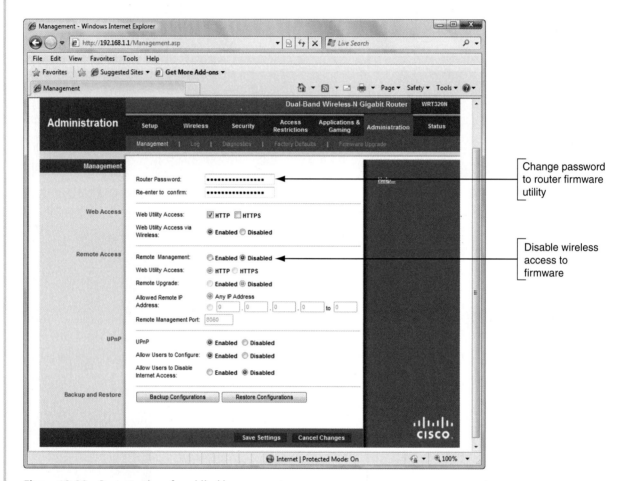

Figure 18-32   Prevent others from hijacking your router
Courtesy: Course Technology/Cengage Learning

◢ In the Internet Setup area, dynamic IP addressing is called Automatic Configuration — DHCP. If a host name and domain name have been given to you by your ISP, enter them here. Most likely, you'll leave them blank.

◢ If your ISP has assigned you a static IP address, click the drop-down box near the top of the Internet Settings area and change this setting to Static IP (see Figure 18-33). You can then enter the IP address assigned to you by your ISP as well as the subnet mask and IP addresses of the default gateway and DNS servers.

◢ You can configure the DHCP server under Network Setup in Figure 18-31. Notice in the figure that the router is configured to serve up to 50 leased IP addresses beginning with IP address 192.168.1.100. You can also disable the DHCP server if you want to use static IP addressing on your network or you already have another DHCP server on the network.

◢ One or more computers on your network might require a static IP address. For example, in the last chapter, you learned how to set up and use a Telnet server. Recall that you could access the server from another computer by using the host name of the

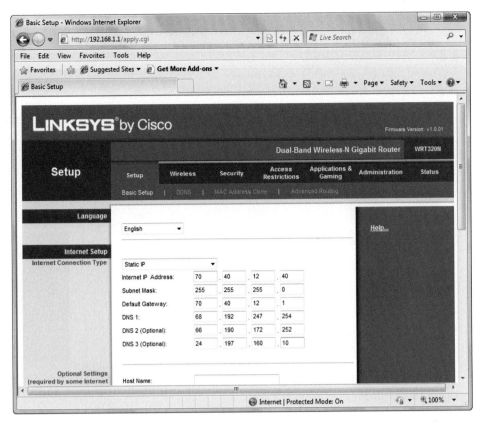

Figure 18-33 Configure the router for static IP addressing
Courtesy: Course Technology/Cengage Learning

server. The host name was associated to the server's IP address by making an entry in the Hosts file on the local computer. To make this entry always work, the Telnet server needs a static IP address. To set the router to serve up this same IP address to the Telnet server each time it connects to the network, click **DHCP Reservation** in Figure 18-31. You will then be able to enter a reserved IP address and the MAC address of the computer (Telnet server in our example) that is to receive this reserved IP address.

▲ If you have problems with the router or decide to keep firmware updates current, these updates can be downloaded and installed. First download the upgrade file from the Web site of the router manufacturer. Be sure to download the correct file for your router model and verify the firmware version is higher than the version already installed. If the router offers the option, back up the current firmware before you start the update. Next, to update the router firmware using the downloaded file, click the **Administration** tab and then click **Firmware Upgrade**. On the Firmware Upgrade window (see Figure 18-34), click **Browse** and point to the downloaded file. Then click **Upgrade** to begin the update. Don't disturb the router until the update has completed.

CONFIGURE THE HARDWARE FIREWALL

To configure the hardware firewall router feature, you need to do the following:

▲ In the window shown in Figure 18-31, click the **Security** link. The window shown in Figure 18-35 appears. The most important setting on this window is to enable SPI Firewall Protection. SPI (stateful packet inspection) examines each data packet and rejects those unsolicited by the local network. Enabling this feature prevents your network from being detected or accessed (without an invitation) by others on the Internet.

A+
220-702
3.2

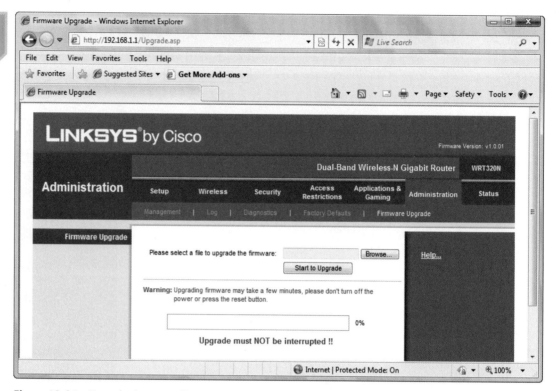

Figure 18-34 Upgrade the router firmware
Courtesy: Course Technology/Cengage Learning

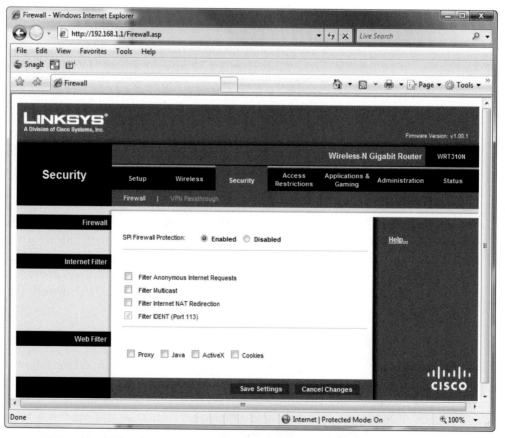

Figure 18-35 Configure the router's firewall to prevent others on the Internet from seeing or accessing your network
Courtesy: Course Technology/Cengage Learning

A+
220-702
3.2

◢ You can set policies to determine how and when users on your network can access the Internet. To do that, click **Access Restrictions**. The window shown in Figure 18-36 appears, allowing you to set policies about the day and time of Internet access, the services on the Internet that can be used, and the URLs and keywords that are not allowed.

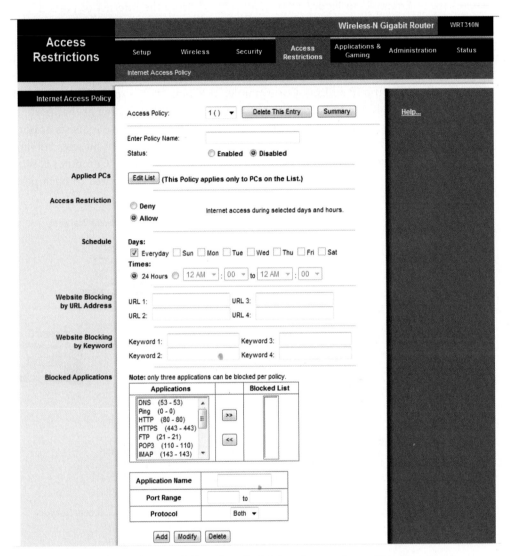

Figure 18-36 Configure the router's firewall to limit Internet access from within the network
Courtesy: Course Technology/Cengage Learning

PORT FORWARDING AND PORT TRIGGERING

Too much security is not always a good thing. There are legitimate times you want to be able to access computers on your network from somewhere on the Internet or allow others to do so, such as when you're hosting an Internet game or when you're traveling and want to use Remote Desktop to access your home computer. In this section, we'll look at how to drop your shields low enough so that the good guys can get in but the bad guys can't. However, know that when you drop your shields the least bit, you're compromising the security of your network, so be sure to use these methods sparingly.

Recall from Chapter 17 that a router can use NAT redirection to present its own IP address to the Internet in place of IP addresses of computers on the local network. The NAT protocol is also responsible for passing communication to the correct port on the correct local computer.

18

A+ 220-702

A+
220-702
3.2

Here are the ways a device using NAT can protect your network using ports:

▲ **Port filtering** is used to open or close certain ports so they can or cannot be used. Remember that applications are assigned these ports. Therefore, in effect, you are filtering or controlling what applications can or cannot be used across the firewall. For example, in Figure 18-37a, all requests from the Internet to ports 20, 443, 450, and 3389 are filtered. These ports are closed.

▲ **Port forwarding** means that when the firewall receives a request for communication from the Internet to a specific computer and port, the request will be allowed and forwarded to that computer on the network. The computer is defined to the router by its static IP address. For example, in Figure 18-37a, port 80 is open and requests to port 80 are forwarded to the Web server that is listening at that port. This one computer on the network is the only one allowed to receive requests at port 80.

▲ **Port triggering** opens a port when a PC on the network initiates communication through another port. For example, in Figure 18-37b, Computer C sends data to port 50 to a computer on the Internet. The router is configured to open port 80 for

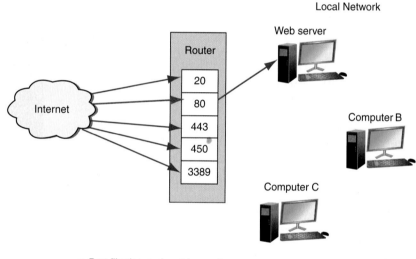

a. Port filtering and port forwarding

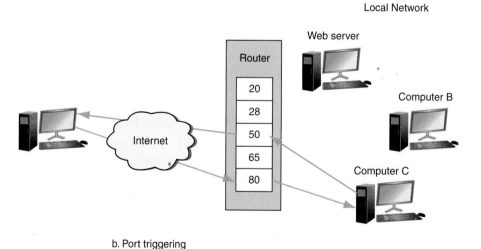

b. Port triggering

Figure 18-37   Port filtering, port forwarding, and port triggering
Courtesy: Course Technology/Cengage Learning

A+
220-702
3.2

communication from this remote computer. Port 80 is closed until this trigger occurs. Port triggering does not require a static IP address for the computer inside the network and any computer can initiate port triggering. The router will leave port 80 open for a time. If no more data is received from port 50, then it closes port 80.

> 💡 **A+ Tip** The A+ 220-702 Practical Application exam expects you to know how to implement port forwarding and port triggering.

To configure port forwarding or port triggering, use the Applications & Gaming tab shown in Figure 18-38. In the figure, the Remote Desktop application outside the network can use port forwarding to communicate with the computer whose IP address is 192.168.1.90 using port 3389. The situation is illustrated in Figure 18-39. This computer is set to support the Remote Desktop server application. Later in the chapter, you will learn to use Remote Desktop.

To configure port triggering, click the **Port Triggering** tab and enter the two ranges of ports. For example, in Figure 18-40, the Triggered Range of ports will trigger the event to open the ports listed under Forwarded Range.

Here are some tips to keep in mind when using port forwarding or port triggering:

▲ You must lease a static IP address from your ISP so that people on the Internet can find you. Most ISPs will provide you a static IP address for an additional monthly fee.
▲ For port forwarding to work, the computer on your network must have a static IP address so that the router knows where to send the communication.

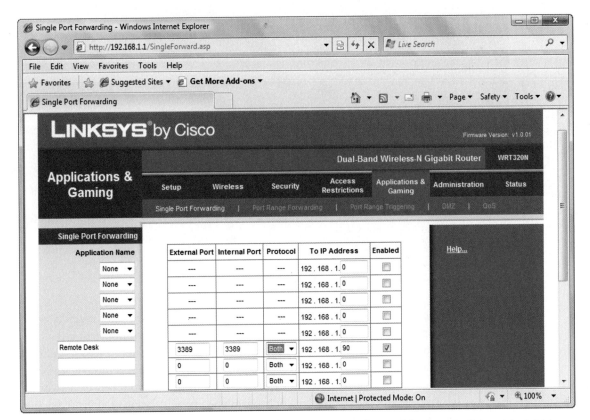

Figure 18-38 Using port forwarding, you can program your router to allow activity from the Internet to initiate a session with a computer inside the network on a certain port using a static IP address
Courtesy: Course Technology/Cengage Learning

18

A+ 220-702

A+
220-702
3.2

Figure 18-39   With port forwarding, a router allows requests initiated outside the network
Courtesy: Course Technology/Cengage Learning

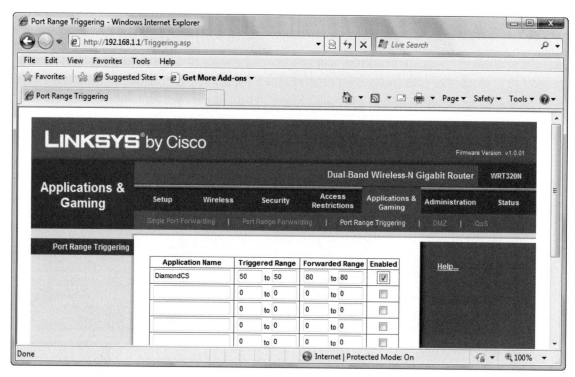

Figure 18-40   Port triggering opens a range of ports when data is sent from inside the network
Courtesy: Course Technology/Cengage Learning

▲ If the computer using port triggering stops sending data, the router might close the triggered port before communication is complete. Also, if two computers on the network attempt to trigger the same port, the router will not allow data to pass to either computer.

▲ Be aware that when you use port forwarding or port triggering, your network is more vulnerable because you are allowing external users directly into your private network. For better security, turn on port forwarding only when you know it's being used. In addition, make sure the computer that is receiving outside communication is using a software firewall (for example, Windows Firewall) and antivirus software. In fact, to be on the safe side, recognize that every computer on your network is more vulnerable and be careful to secure each one.

A+
220-702
3.2

> **💡 Tip**   By the way, if you want to use a domain name rather than an IP address to access a
> computer on your network from the Internet, you'll need to purchase the domain name and register it in the
> Internet name space to associate it with your static IP address assigned by your ISP. Several Web sites on
> the Internet let you do both; one site is by Network Solutions at *www.networksolutions.com*.

HOW TO SET UP A WIRELESS NETWORK

Some desktop computers come equipped with a wireless adapter, such as the one in Chapter 17
in Figure 17-16b, that can be configured as a client on a wireless network or as the access point
of a wireless network. A wireless access point can also be a stand-alone device such as the one
in Figure 18-41 by D-Link. The device supports 802.11g/n and contains a four-port Gigabit
switch to connect up to four devices to your wired network. An access point can also serve other
purposes, such as the Linksys multifunctional router shown earlier in Figure 18-29. When selecting a wireless access point, consider the 802.11 standards it supports and the security standards
it uses. Recall from Chapter 17 that security standards include disabling SSID broadcasting, WPA
or WPA2 encryption (or perhaps the outdated WEP encryption), and MAC address filtering.

Figure 18-41   Xtreme N Duo Wireless Bridge/Access Point by D-Link
                Photo Courtesy of D-Link Systems, Inc.

> **💡 A+ Tip**   The A+ 220-702 Practical Application exam expects you to know how to install and
> configure a wireless network, including how to implement wireless security. You need to know how to
> configure WEP, WPA, SSID, MAC filtering, and DHCP settings.

To install a stand-alone access point, position it in the center of where you want your
hotspot, and plug it in. It will have a network port to connect to a wired network or a USB
port to connect to a computer. Using one of these ports, connect the access point to a
computer so that you can configure the access point. If the access point is bundled with a
setup CD, run the setup program to step you though the installation. To configure the access
point, open a browser and enter the IP address of the access point. Firmware on the device
displays the configuration utility. Using this utility, look for ways to change these settings:

1. Look for a way to select the channel the access point will use, the ability to change the
   SSID of the access point, and the ability to disable SSID broadcasting. Figure 18-42
   shows these three settings for a multipurpose Linksys access point. Figure 18-43 shows
   how a wireless computer sees a wireless access point that is not broadcasting its SSID.
   This computer would not be able to use this access point until you entered the SSID in
   the configuration window shown in Figure 18-44.

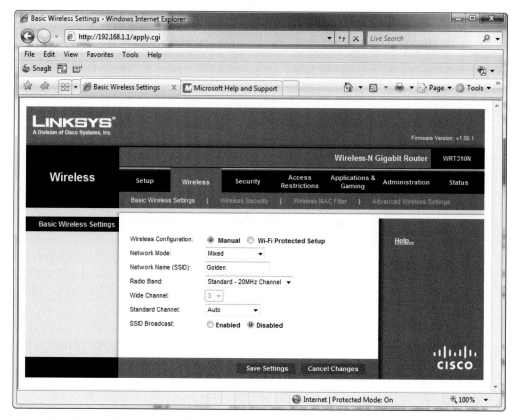

Figure 18-42 Look for the ability of the access point to disable SSID broadcasting
Courtesy: Course Technology/Cengage Learning

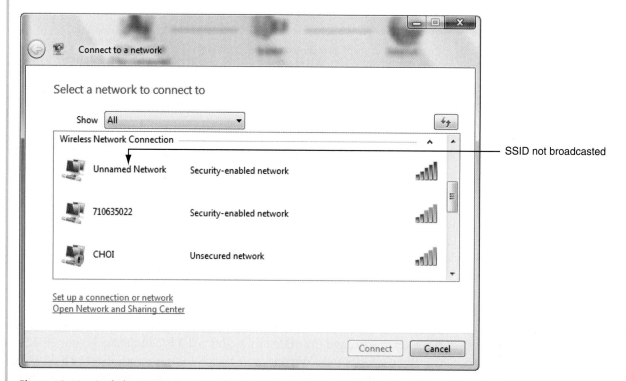

Figure 18-43 A wireless computer shows it has located three access points, but the first one listed is not broadcasting its SSID
Courtesy: Course Technology/Cengage Learning

A+
220-702
3.2

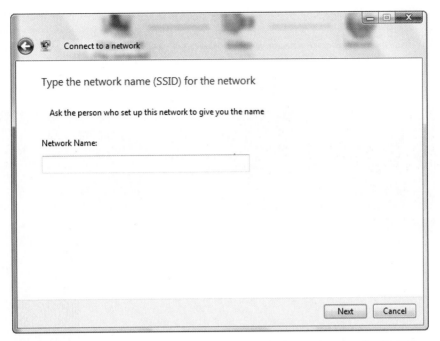

Figure 18-44 Enter the SSID of a wireless network that is not broadcasting its SSID
Courtesy: Course Technology/Cengage Learning

2. To configure data encryption on your access point, look for a wireless security screen similar to the one in Figure 18-45 where you can choose between several WEP, WPA, or RADIUS encryption methods. (RADIUS stands for Remote Authentication Dial-In User Service and uses an authentication server to control access.) WPA2 Personal is the one to choose unless one of your wireless adapters doesn't support it. Enter the passphrase for encryption on this same access point screen. When you connect a PC to this network, you'll need to enter the same passphrase.

> **Notes** To make the strongest password or passphrase, use a random group of numbers, uppercase and lowercase letters, and, if allowed, at least one symbol. Also use at least eight characters in the password.

3. Look for MAC filtering on your access point, similar to the screen in Figure 18-46. On this access point, you can enter a table of MAC addresses and decide if this list of MAC addresses is to be used to prevent or permit use of the access point.

4. Decide if your access point will serve up IP addresses (dynamic IP addressing) or if computers that connect to the access point will use static IP addresses. Dynamic IP addressing is the likely choice. To set that up, enable DHCP and set the number of IP addresses that can be used at any one time (which limits the number of computers that can use the wireless network). Also set the beginning IP address. The best choice is to begin with an IP address in the range of 192.168.x.x, so that your network will use private IP addresses. If you want to use static IP addressing on the wireless network, then disable DHCP.

5. Save all your settings for the access point and test the connection. To test it, on one of your wireless computers, follow directions given in Chapter 17 to connect to a hotspot, entering the passphrase when requested. If you don't see the network in the list of wireless networks, try moving your access point or the computer. If you still can't get a connection, remove all security measures and try again. Then restore the security features one at a time until you discover the one causing the problem.

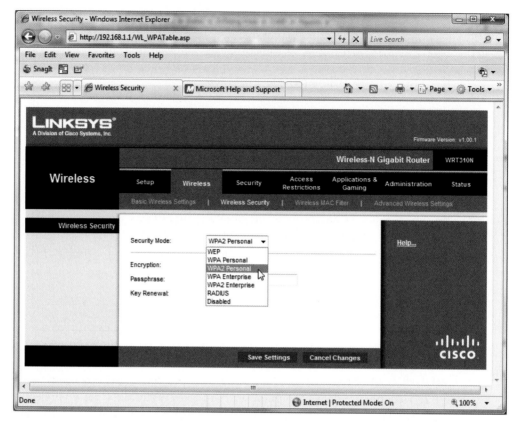

Figure 18-45 This wireless access point supports several encryption methods
Courtesy: Course Technology/Cengage Learning

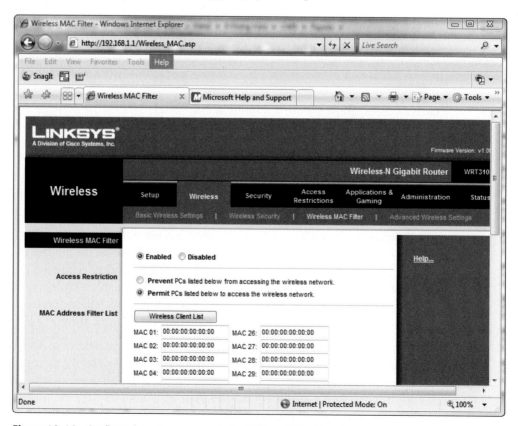

Figure 18-46 Configure how the access point will filter MAC addresses
Courtesy: Course Technology/Cengage Learning

A+
220-702
3.2

We've just configured your wireless access point to use several security features. Is it really necessary to use them all? Well, not really. Encryption is essential to keep others from hacking into your wireless data and to prevent unauthorized use of your wireless LAN. For most situations, that's all you need. For added protection, you can disable SSID broadcasting or filter MAC addresses.

TOOLS AND UTILITIES FOR SUPPORTING AND TROUBLESHOOTING NETWORKS

When supporting and troubleshooting small networks, you'll need to use cable testers to test the physical connections of the network and several TCP/IP utilities to test TCP/IP connectivity. In addition, Remote Desktop and Remote Assistance can be a great help when supporting networks and their users. In this part of the chapter, you'll learn how to use all these tools.

A+
220-702
1.4

CABLE TESTERS

A cable tester can be used to test a cable to find out if it is good or to find out what type of cable it is if the cable is not labeled. You can also use a cable tester to trace a network cable through a building. A cable tester has two components, as shown in Figure 18-47.

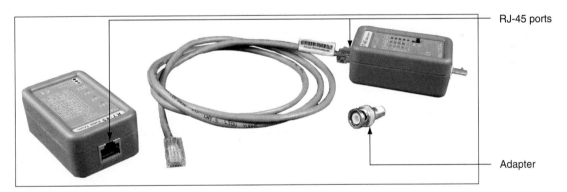

RJ-45 ports

Adapter

Figure 18-47   Use a cable tester pair to determine the type of cable and if the cable is good
Courtesy: Course Technology/Cengage Learning

18

A+ 220-702

To test a cable, connect each component to the ends of the cable and turn on the tester. Lights on the tester will show you if the cable is good and what type of cable you have. You'll need to read the user manual that comes with the cable tester to know how to interpret the lights.

You can also use cable testers to trace a network cable through a building. Suppose you see several network jacks on walls in a building, but you don't know which jacks connect. Install a short cable in each of two jacks and then use the cable tester to test the continuity, as shown in Figure 18-48. You might damage a cable tester if you connect it to a live circuit, so before you start connecting the cable tester to wall jacks, be sure that you turn off all devices on the network.

A+
220-702
1.4

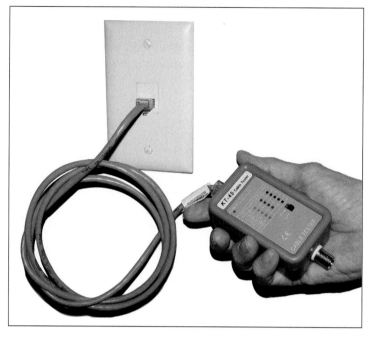

Figure 18-48 Use cable testers to trace network cables through a building
Courtesy: Course Technology/Cengage Learning

A+
220-702
2.1

TCP/IP UTILITIES

The TCP/IP component of Windows includes several utilities that can be used to troubleshoot problems with TCP/IP. The most commonly used TCP/IP utilities are Ping and Ipconfig, which you learned about in the last chapter. Table 18-1 lists these and other TCP/IP utilities, and lists the purpose for each. Most of these program files are found in the \Windows\System32 folder.

> **A+ Exam Tip** The A+ 220-702 Practical Application exam expects you to know about the following TCP/IP utilities listed in Table 18-2: Ipconfig, Ping, Net, Netstat, Tracert, Nslookup, and Telnet. You need to know when and how to use each utility, and you must be able to interpret results.

Now let's see how to use the Nslookup, Tracert, and Net utilities.

THE NSLOOKUP COMMAND

Nslookup lets you read information from the Internet name space by requesting information about domain name resolutions from the DNS server's zone data. Zone data is information about domain names and their corresponding IP addresses kept by a DNS server. For example, to find out what your DNS server knows about the domain name www.microsoft.com, use this command:

```
nslookup www.microsoft.com
```

A+
220-702
2.1

Utility	Description
Getmac	Displays the NIC's MAC address (not available in Windows 2000).

Ipconfig	Displays the IP address of the host and other configuration information. (A command used by UNIX similar to Ipconfig is ifconfig.)
	
	▲ To display all information about connections:
	
	`ipconfig /all`
	
	▲ To release the current IP address:
	
	`ipconfig /release`
	
	▲ To request a new IP address:
	
	`ipconfig /renew`
	
	▲ To display information about Ipconfig:
	
	`ipconfig /?`

Net /?	Get information about the Net command.
Net use	Displays a list of network connections.
Netstat	Displays information about current TCP/IP connections.
Nslookup	Displays information about domain names and their IP addresses.

Ping	Verifies that there is a connection on a network between two hosts. Here are variations of Ping:
	
	▲ To test for name resolution:
	
	`ping -a 69.32.142.109`
	
	▲ To continue testing until interrupted:
	
	`ping -t 69.32.142.109`
	
	▲ To test with a data packet that is 1000 bytes in size:
	
	`ping -l 1000 69.32.142.109`

Telnet	Allows you to communicate with another computer on the network remotely, entering commands to control the remote computer. The connection is not secured.
Tracert	Traces and displays the route taken from the host to a remote destination; Tracert is one example of a trace-routing utility.

Table 18-1 TCP/IP utilities available with Windows

Figure 18-49 shows the results. Notice in the figure that the DNS server knows about two IP addresses assigned to www.microsoft.com. It also reports that this information is nonauthoritative, meaning that it is not the authoritative, or final, name server for the *www.microsoft.com* computer name.

A reverse lookup is when you use the Nslookup command to find the host name when you know a computer's IP address, such as:

```
nslookup 192.168.1.102
```

18

A+ 220-702

A+
220-702
2.1

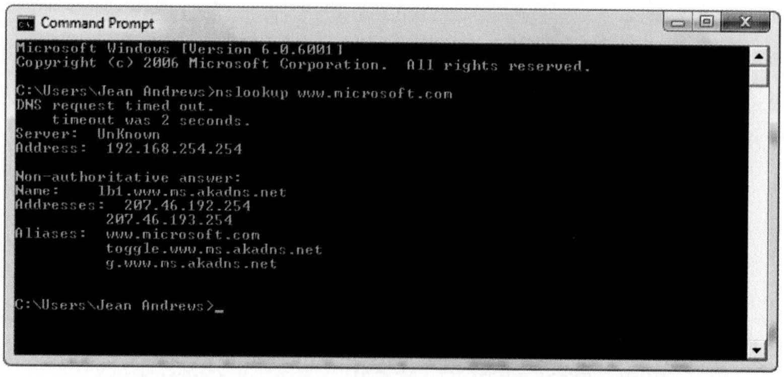

Figure 18-49 The Nslookup command reports information about the Internet name space
Courtesy: Course Technology/Cengage Learning

THE TRACERT COMMAND

The Tracert (trace route) command can be useful when you're trying to resolve a problem reaching a destination host such as an FTP site or Web site. The command sends a series of requests to the destination computer and displays each hop to the destination. For example, to trace the route to the *www.course.com* site, enter this command in a command prompt window:

```
tracert www.course.com
```

The results of this command are shown in Figure 18-50. By default, the command makes 30 requests for up to 30 hops. The final 15 requests in the figure were not needed to show the complete path to the site, causing a "Request timed out" message to appear. Also, the Tracert command depends on ICMP information sent by routers when a packet's hop count has been exceeded (see Figure 18-51). Some routers don't send this information. If a router doesn't respond, the "Request timed out" message appears.

THE NET COMMAND

The Net command is several commands in one. These options are Net accounts, Net computer, Net config, Net continue, Net file, Net group, Net help, Net helpmsg, Net localgroup,

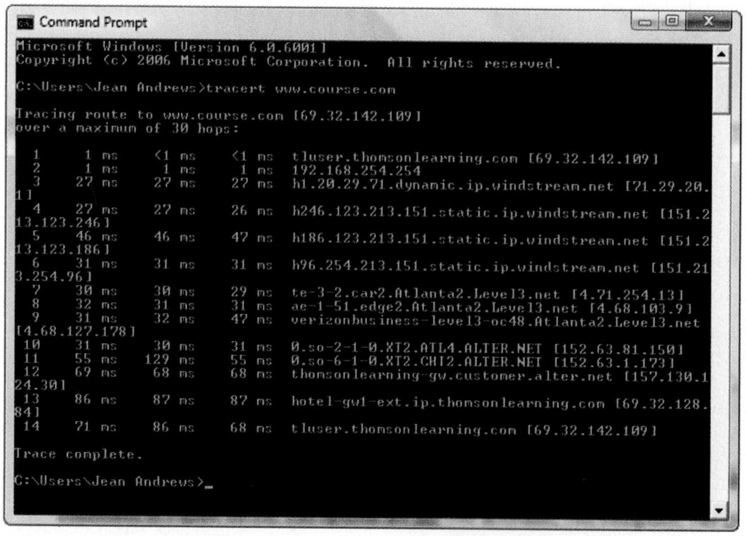

Figure 18-50 The Tracert command traces a path to a destination computer
Courtesy: Course Technology/Cengage Learning

A+
220-702
2.1

Figure 18-51 A router eliminates a packet that has exceeded its TTL
Courtesy: Course Technology/Cengage Learning

Net pause, Net print, Net session, Net share, Net start, Net statistics, Net stop, Net time, Net use, Net user, and Net view.

For example, the Net use command can make a connection to a remote computer, break a connection, or display information about all network connections. Figure 18-52 shows three Net use commands. Here is an explanation of how these commands work:

1. The first command (net use) displays current network connections. You can see that a connection to \\Vistafileserver\Data2 was attempted in order to create a network drive map to drive J:. (A network drive map makes a folder or volume on a remote computer appear as a local drive, such as J:.) The command to map the drive completed, but the server was not available.

2. The second command (net use \\Vistafileserver\Data2) made an attempt to connect to the same resource.

3. The third command (net use) shows the connection to \\Vistafileserver\Data2 is good.

You'll learn to use other variations of the Net command later in the chapter under "Problems with TCP/IP, the OS, and ISP Connectivity."

18

A+ 220-702

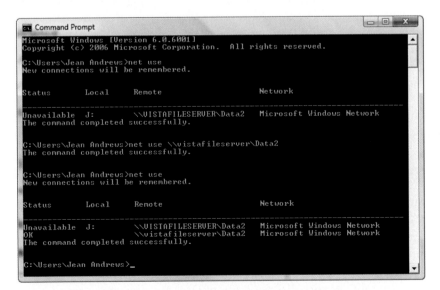

Figure 18-52 The Net use commands view and make network connections
Courtesy: Course Technology/Cengage Learning

A+
220-702
3.1

THE NETSTAT COMMAND

The Netstat command gives statistics about network activity (see Figure 18-53) and includes several parameters. One of the most useful is the –b parameter that displays the program making the connection. When you use the –b parameter, an elevated command prompt is required for Vista. Use the parameter to find malware that might be using your PC for communication on the network or Internet.

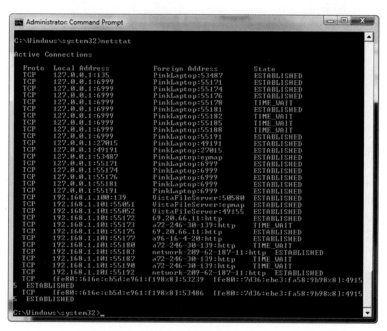

Figure 18-53   Results of a netstat command
Courtesy: Course Technology/Cengage Learning

To get the best information with the –b parameter, include a number, which tells the command to continue until manually interrupted and also send the output to a text file. For example, to collect information every five seconds and log output to the C:\netstatlog.txt file, use this command:

```
netstat -b 5 >> C:\netstatlog.txt
```

To stop the netstat command, press Ctrl-Break and then check the C:\netstatlog.txt file for suspicious activity. The use of the command can also help when trying to find programs that are not malware, but are simply using up networking resources (see Figure 18-54).

A+
220-702
3.1
2.3

REMOTE DESKTOP

Remote Desktop gives a user access to his or her Windows desktop from anywhere on the Internet. As a software developer, I find Remote Desktop extremely useful when I work from a remote location (my home office) and need to access a corporate network to support software on that network. Using the Internet, I can access a file server on these secured networks to make my software changes. It's easy to use and relatively safe for the corporate network. To use Remote Desktop, the computer you want to remotely

A+
220-702
3.1
2.3

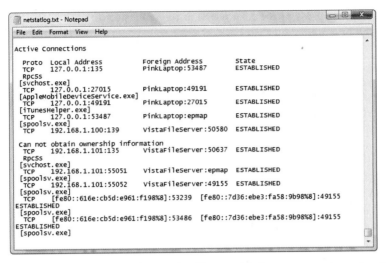

Figure 18-54 Record results to a log file to watch for programs using networking resources
Courtesy: Course Technology/Cengage Learning

access (the server) must be running Vista Business or Ultimate editions or Windows XP Professional, but the computer you're using to access it (the client) can be running any version of Windows.

> **A+ Tip** The A+ 220-702 Practical Application exam expects you to know how to use Remote Desktop.

In this section, you'll first see how Remote Desktop can be used, and then you'll see how to set it up for first use.

HOW REMOTE DESKTOP WORKS

Follow these steps to use Remote Desktop:

1. For Vista, click **Start, All Programs, Accessories** and **Remote Desktop Connection**. For XP, click **Start, All Programs, Accessories, Communications,** and **Remote Desktop Connection**. (After Service Pack 3 is applied to Windows XP, the location of Remote Desktop on the Start menu might change to **Start, All Programs, Accessories**.) The Remote Desktop Connection window opens (see Figure 18-55).

Figure 18-55 Enter the IP address of the remote computer to which you want to connect
Courtesy: Course Technology/Cengage Learning

2. Enter the IP address or the host name of the computer to which you want to connect. Begin the host name with two backslashes as in \\VistaFileServer.

> **💡 Tip** To use the host name when making a Remote Desktop connection on a local network, the host name and IP address of the remote computer must be entered in the Hosts file of the local computer.

3. If you plan to transfer files from one computer to the other, click **Options** and then click the **Local Resources** tab shown in the left side of Figure 18-56. Click **More**. The box on the right side of Figure 18-56 appears. Check **Drives**. Click **OK**. Click **Connect** to make the connection. Click **Connect** again when a warning box appears. If another warning box appears, click **Yes**.

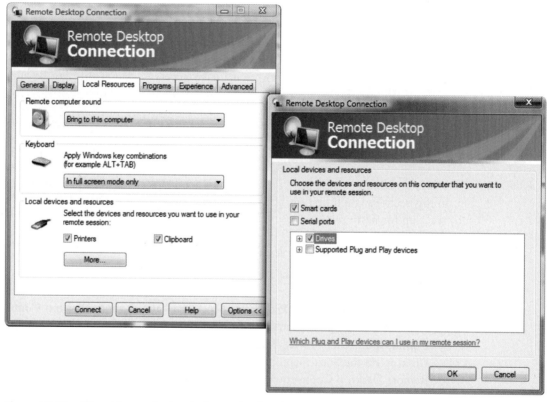

Figure 18-56 Allow drives and other devices to be shared using the Remote Desktop connection
Courtesy: Course Technology/Cengage Learning

4. A Windows security box appears that is displayed by the remote computer (see Figure 18-57). Log on using a user name and password for the remote computer.

5. The desktop of the remote computer appears, as shown in Figure 18-58. When you click the desktop, you can work with the remote computer just as if you were sitting in front of it, except response time will be slower. To move files back and forth between computers, use Windows Explorer on the remote computer. Files on your local computer will appear under Network or My Network Places in Windows Explorer on the remote computer. To close the connection to the remote computer, simply close the desktop window.

Figure 18-57 Enter your user name and password on the remote computer
Courtesy: Course Technology/Cengage Learning

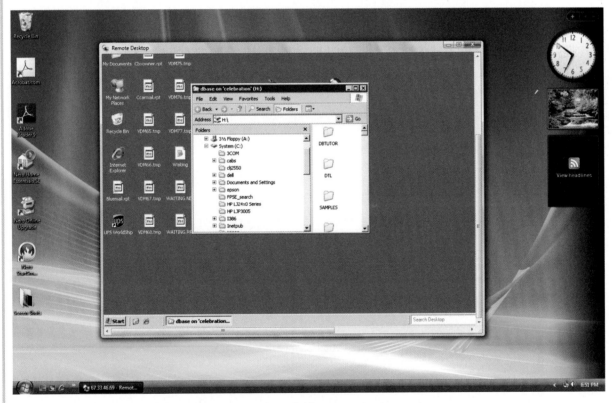

Figure 18-58 The desktop of the remote computer is available on your local computer
Courtesy: Course Technology/Cengage Learning

HOW TO SET UP REMOTE DESKTOP FOR FIRST USE

To prepare a computer to serve up Remote Desktop, you need to configure the computer for static IP addressing and also configure Remote Desktop for service. Here are the steps needed:

1. As described earlier in the chapter, you'll need a static IP address assigned to you by your ISP. Configure your computer for static IP addressing. If your computer is connected directly to your ISP, assign the IP address given you by your ISP to your computer. If you are using a router on your network, assign your computer a private IP address (for example, 192.168.1.90).

A+
220-702
3.1
2.3

2. If you are using a router on your network, configure the router for port forwarding and allow incoming traffic on port 3389. Forward that traffic to the IP address of your desktop computer. Figure 18-38 shown earlier in the chapter shows one router configured for these settings.

3. Use your browser to verify you have Internet access before you continue to the next steps. If you have a problem, first try repairing your connection and then try rebooting your PC.

You are now ready to configure Remote Desktop. In the following steps, we are using Windows Vista, but know that the steps in Windows XP work about the same way. Do the following:

1. Click **Start**, right-click **Computer** and select **Properties** from the shortcut menu. Click **Advanced system settings** and respond to the UAC box. The System Properties box appears (see the left side of Figure 18-59). Click the **Remote** tab and check **Allow connections from computers running any version of Remote Desktop (less secure)**. A dialog box might appear warning that the computer is set to go into sleep mode when not in use (see the right side of Figure 18-59). Click **OK** to close the box.

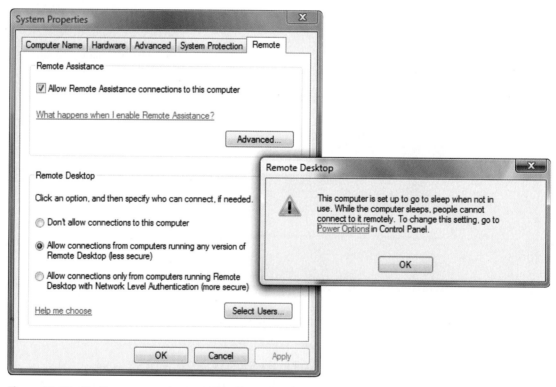

Figure 18-59   Configure a computer to run the Remote Desktop service
Courtesy: Course Technology/Cengage Learning

2. Click **Select Users**. In the dialog box that opens (see Figure 18-60), add the users of this computer who will be using Remote Desktop. Users who have administrative privileges will be allowed to use Remote Desktop by default, but other users need to be added. Click **OK** twice to exit both windows.

A+
220-702
3.1
2.3

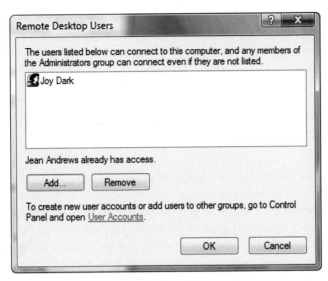

Figure 18-60 Add local users who are allowed access by way of Remote Desktop
Courtesy: Course Technology/Cengage Learning

3. Verify that Windows Firewall is set to allow Remote Desktop activity to this computer. To do that, open the **Network and Sharing Center** and click **Windows Firewall**. Then click **Change settings** and respond to the UAC box. The Windows Firewall Settings box opens. On the **General** tab, verify that Windows Firewall is turned on and that **Block all incoming connections** is *not* selected. Then click the **Exceptions** tab and verify that **Remote Desktop** is checked so that Remote Desktop incoming activity is allowed. Close all windows.

4. You are now ready to test Remote Desktop using your local network. Try to use Remote Desktop from another computer somewhere on your local network. Verify you have Remote Desktop working on your local network before you move on to the next step of testing the Remote Desktop connection from the Internet.

5. If you want Remote Desktop available at all times, use the Power Options window in Control Panel to allow the computer to wake up when it has network activity. How to manage power options is covered in Chapter 21.

18

A+ 220-702

> **Notes** Even though Windows normally allows more than one user to be logged on at the same time, this is not the case with Remote Desktop. When a Remote Desktop session is opened, all local users are logged off.

Is your computer as safe as it was before you set it to serve up Remote Desktop and enabled port forwarding to it? Actually, no, so take this into account when you decide to use Remote Desktop. In a project at the end of this chapter, you'll learn how you can take further steps to protect the security of your computer when using Remote Desktop.

REMOTE ASSISTANCE

Remote Assistance can help you support users and their computers from a distance. The user who needs your help sends you an invitation by e-mail or chat to connect to her computer using Remote Assistance. When you respond to the invitation, you can see the user's desktop just as she sees it. And, if the user gives you permission, you can take control of her computer

A+
220-702
3.1
2.3

to change settings or do whatever else is needed to fix her problem or show her how to perform a task. Think of Remote Assistance as a way to provide virtual desk-side support.

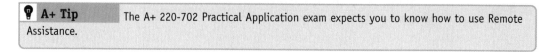

💡 **A+ Tip**   The A+ 220-702 Practical Application exam expects you to know how to use Remote Assistance.

There are several ways to initiate a Remote Assistance session:

◢ The user saves an invitation file and then sends that file to the technician. The file can be sent by any method, including e-mail, chat, or posting to a shared folder on the network. This is the easiest method to start a Remote Assistance session.

◢ The user can initiate a session by way of Windows Messenger. This method works well when the user is behind a hardware firewall that the technician must get past.

◢ The user can send an e-mail message to a corporate help desk. The e-mail contains an attached file that the technician uses to respond to the invitation. This method works well when both people belong to the same domain and no hardware firewalls are between them.

◢ The technician can initiate a session. This method is the most difficult to use, requiring that Group Policies be applied on the technician's computer.

Use the following steps to initiate a Remote Assistance session when the user sends you an invitation. First, ask the user to send you the invitation. When she does so, her computer is set up to respond to Remote Assistance communication. She must do the following:

1. Click **Start, Help and Support**. In the Help and Support window, click **Windows Remote Assistance**. The window in Figure 18-61 appears.

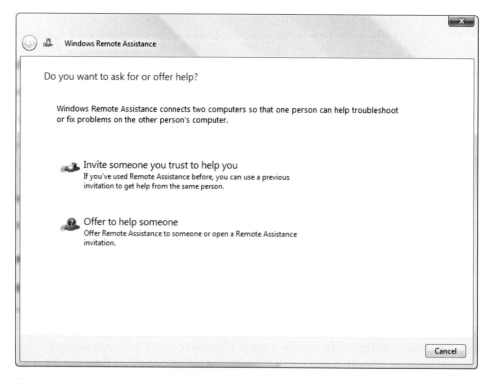

Figure 18-61   The user can invite someone to help
Courtesy: Course Technology/Cengage Learning

A+
220-702
3.1
2.3

2. Click **Invite someone you trust to help you.** On the next window, click **Save this invitation as a file.**

3. On the next window (see Figure 18-62), the user verifies the location of the file (the Windows desktop), enters a password, confirms the password, and then clicks **Finish.** The file is created and the Windows Remote Assistance window appears (see Figure 18-63).

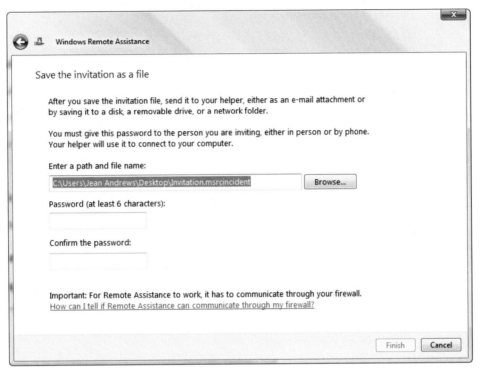

Figure 18-62 The user creates a password for you to use
Courtesy: Course Technology/Cengage Learning

Figure 18-63 Remote Assistance waiting for incoming connection
Courtesy: Course Technology/Cengage Learning

The user must send you the invitation file and tell you the password. She can attach it to an e-mail message or chat session or hand it to you on a jump drive. When you have the invitation file and password, follow these steps to accept the invitation:

1. Click **Start, Help and Support,** and click **Windows Remote Assistance.** (Alternately, you can enter **Windows Remote Assistance** in the Vista Start Search box.) On the first box (refer back to Figure 18-61), click **Offer to help someone.** On the second box (see Figure 18-64), click **Browse** and point to the location of the invitation file. Click **Finish.**

18

A+ 220-702

A+
220-702
3.1
2.3

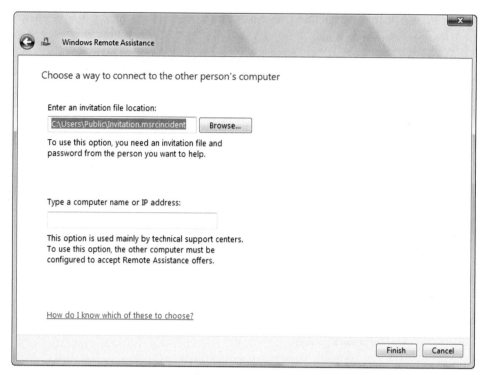

Figure 18-64   Point to the location of the invitation file
Courtesy: Course Technology/Cengage Learning

2. On the next box, enter the password given you by the user. Click **OK**.

3. The user sees the box in Figure 18-65 appear on her desktop. She must click **Yes** to allow you to connect.

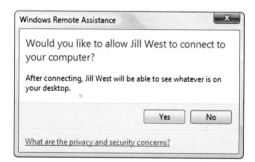

Figure 18-65   The user gives Jill West permission to connect
Courtesy: Course Technology/Cengage Learning

4. The background of the user's desktop turns black. A window on your desktop opens where you can see the user's desktop (see Figure 18-66). Here are some things you and the user can do so that you can assist the user:

▲ To open a chat session with the user, click the **Chat** icon. A chat pane appears in the Remote Assistance window on both desktops.

▲ To ask the user if you can take control of her desktop, click **Request control** in the Remote Assistance control window. When the user accepts the request, you can control her computer.

▲ The user can hide her desktop from you at any time by clicking **Pause** in the control window.

Figure 18-66 The user's desktop can be viewed by the support technician
Courtesy: Course Technology/Cengage Learning

⊿ Either of you can disconnect the session by clicking **Disconnect** in the control window.

⊿ A log file is kept of every Remote Assistance session in the C:\Users*username*\Documents\Remote Assistance Logs folder. The file includes the chat session. If you type instructions during the chat session that will later help the user, she can use the log file to remind her of what was said and done.

⊿ If an invitation created by a user is not used within six hours, the invitation expires.

If you have problems making the connection, do the following:

1. Windows Firewall on the user's computer might be blocking Remote Assistance. Verify that Remote Assistance is checked as an exception to blocked programs in the Windows Firewall window.

2. If you are outside the user's local network, the hardware firewall protecting her network might be blocking Remote Assistance. Verify that port forwarding on that hardware firewall is enabled for Remote Assistance. Remote Assistance uses port 3389, the same port used by Remote Desktop.

TROUBLESHOOTING NETWORK AND INTERNET CONNECTIONS

If you have problems connecting to the network, you can follow the flowchart in Figure 18-67 to eliminate hardware, device drivers, the Windows configuration, and applications when troubleshooting network connections. Recall that networking happens in layers. This flowchart reminds us troubleshooting problems with networking starts at the bottom layer (hardware) and proceeds to the top layer (applications).

Video
Troubleshooting a Network

A+ 220-702 3.1

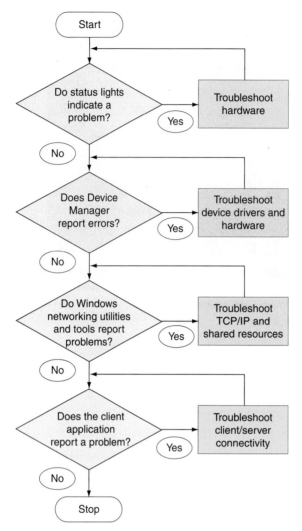

Figure 18-67 Flowchart to troubleshoot network connections
Courtesy: Course Technology/Cengage Learning

> 💡 **A+ Exam Tip** The A+ 220-702 Practical Application exam expects you to know how to troubleshoot network problems by using cable testers and, checking TCP/IP settings, firewall settings, proxy settings, and protocol settings used within client applications. All these skills are covered in this part of the chapter.

Now let's look at the strategies you can use to troubleshoot network problems, starting first with hardware and then proceeding to TCP/IP settings within Windows, and finally by checking protocol settings used with the client application that is not working.

PROBLEMS WITH HARDWARE AND DEVICE DRIVERS

A+
220-702
1.2
1.4

When a PC cannot communicate on a network, begin by checking hardware. To verify network hardware and solve problems with hardware, follow these steps:

1. Check the status indicator lights on the NIC or the motherboard Ethernet port. A steady light indicates connectivity and a blinking light indicates activity. If you don't see either light, this problem must be resolved before you consider OS or application problems.

2. Check the network cable connection at both ends. Is the cable connected to a port on the motherboard that is disabled? It might need to be connected to the network port provided by a network card. Check the indicator lights on the router or switch at the other end. Try a different port on the device.

3. For wireless networking, make sure the wireless switch on a laptop is turned on. Move the laptop to a new position in the hotspot. Rebooting a laptop often solves the problem of not receiving a signal.

4. Determine whether other computers on the network are having trouble with their connections. If the entire network is down, the problem is not isolated to the PC you are working on. Check the switch, hub, or router controlling the network.

5. Check the network cable to make sure it is not damaged. If the cable is frayed, twisted, or damaged, replace it. You can also use cable testers to verify the cable is good.

6. When using an Ethernet wall jack to connect the PC to a router or switch in another location in the building, consider that the network cabling in the walls might be bad or not connected to the router or switch at the other end. Disconnect the cable at the wall jack near your PC, and disconnect the cable at the router or switch. Next, use cable testers at both these ends to verify connectivity between the wall jack and the cable near the router or switch.

> **A+ Tip** The A+ 220-702 Practical Application exam expects you to know how and when to use cable testers.

7. Open the computer case and make sure the NIC is securely seated in the expansion slot. Try reseating the card. Reboot and check for activity lights. If you still don't see activity, replace the NIC, and then install new drivers.

To solve problems with device drivers, which might also be related to a problem with the NIC, follow these steps:

1. Make sure the network adapter and its drivers are installed by checking for the adapter in Device Manager. Device Manager should report the device is working with no problems.

2. Try updating the device drivers.

3. Try uninstalling and reinstalling the network adapter drivers. If the drivers still install with errors, try downloading new drivers from the Web site of the network card manufacturer. Also, look on the installation CD that came bundled with the adapter for a setup program. If you find one, uninstall the adapter and run this setup program.

4. Some network adapters have diagnostic programs on the installation CD. Try running the program from the CD. Look in the documentation that came with the adapter for instructions on how to install and run the program.

5. For an onboard network port, update or reinstall drivers provided by the motherboard driver CD or the motherboard Web site manufacturer.

6. If Device Manager still reports errors, try running antivirus software and updating Windows. Then try installing a known-good network adapter. If that does not work, the problem might be a corrupted Windows installation.

After you have verified the status indicator lights on the NIC and Device Manager recognizes the NIC with no errors, move on to the next step of checking TCP/IP settings.

A+
220-702
2.1
3.1

PROBLEMS WITH TCP/IP, THE OS, AND ISP CONNECTIVITY

To solve problems with Windows TCP/IP configuration and connectivity, follow these steps to verify that the local computer is communicating over the network:

1. Try to release the current IP address and lease a new address. To do this using Vista, open the Network and Sharing Center window and click **Diagnose and repair**. For XP, in the Network Connections window, right-click the network icon and select **Repair** from the shortcut window. Alternately, you can open a command prompt window and use these two commands: **ipconfig /release** followed by **ipconfig /renew**. (Vista requires an elevated command prompt window.)

2. Look for problems with the TCP/IP configuration. Enter **ipconfig /all** at the command prompt. If the TCP/IP configuration is correct and an IP address is assigned, then the IP address, subnet mask, and default gateway appear along with the MAC address. For dynamic IP addressing, if the PC cannot reach the DHCP server, then it assigns itself an Automatic Private IP Address (APIPA). The ipconfig command shows the IP address as the Autoconfiguration IPv4 Address, and the address begins with 169.254 (see Figure 18-68). In this case, suspect that the PC is not able to reach the network or the DHCP server is down.

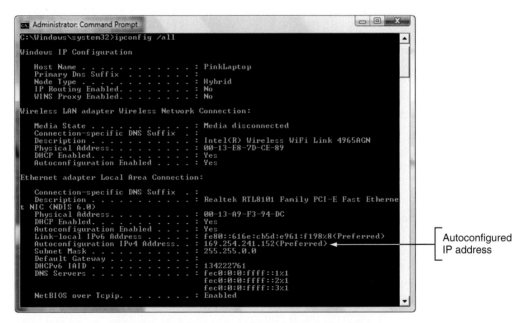

Autoconfigured
IP address

Figure 18-68 The network connection was not able to lease an IP address
Courtesy: Course Technology/Cengage Learning

3. Next, try the loopback address test. At a command prompt, enter the command **ping 127.0.0.1** (with no period after the final 1). This IP address always refers to your local computer. It should respond with a reply message from your computer. If this works, TCP/IP is likely to be configured correctly. If you get an error, then assume that the problem is on your PC. Recheck the installation and configuration of each component, such as the network card and the TCP/IP settings. Remove and reinstall each component, and watch for error messages, writing them down so that you can recognize or research them later as necessary. You might need to uninstall and reinstall the TCP/IP component. Compare the configuration to that of a working PC on the same network.

4. If you're having a problem with slow network performance, suspect a process is hogging network resources. Use the netstat command with the –b parameter described earlier in the chapter to help you find this program. Netstat can also help you find out if the program you want to use to access the network is actually running.

5. Verify that the software firewall on the PC is not the source of the problem. Is Windows Firewall set correctly? Is a third-party personal firewall blocking communication? ZoneAlarm sometimes gives problems by blocking communication that you want. Try disabling ZoneAlarm. If the connection now works, carefully check all ZoneAlarm settings.

If you are having problems reaching another computer on your network, follow these steps:

1. Open the Vista Network window or the XP My Network Places window. Normally, a computer on the network shows up in these places as an icon. Try to drill down to the shared resources on this computer. Press the F5 key to refresh the window.

2. Now try to ping the host computer you are trying to reach. If it does not respond, then the problem might be with the host computer or with the network to the computer.

3. When trying to reach a computer on your local network, try the Ping command with the IP address of the remote computer. Next, try the Ping command using the computer name of the remote computer. If the Ping command works when using an IP address, but does not work when using a host name on the local network, check the Hosts file on the local computer. Make sure the IP address and host name entry line in the file are correct. The problem might also be with wrong entries in DNS servers that are used on the corporate network. One or more DNS servers might hold an entry that relates the IP address to the wrong host name.

4. These commands can help solve problems with host names on the local network:

   a. Use the nslookup command to find the computer's IP address.

   b. Try this command: **net view \\computername**. If two computers on the network have the same computer name, the command reports this error. Then change the name of one computer.

5. If you can ping or Net view a computer, but cannot access it in the Network window or My Network Places, verify the computer is in the same domain or workgroup that the local computer is in. Also make sure the remote computer has File and Printer Sharing turned on. Also verify that the user account and password are the same on both computers.

6. Use this command to verify that resources on a remote computer are shared:

```
net view \\computername
```

The command should list the shared resources. If the command gives an error about access being denied, the problem is with permissions. Make sure the account you are using is an account recognized by the remote computer. Try this command to pass a new account to the remote computer:

```
net use \\computername /user:username
```

A+
220-702
2.1
3.1

In the above command, if there is a space in the username, enclose the username in double quotation marks, as in:

```
net use \\computername /user:"Jean Andrews"
```

7. If the net view command using a computer name does not work, try the command using the remote computer's IP address, as in:

```
net view 192.168.1.102
```

If this command works, the problem is likely with name resolution. Make sure the computer name you are using is correct and the computer is in your workgroup or domain.

8. If you're having problems getting a network drive map to work, try making the connection with the net use command like this:

```
net use z: \\computername\folder
```

To disconnect a mapped network drive, use this command:

```
net use z: /delete
```

If you can see resources on the local network, but cannot access the Internet, do the following:

1. Try to ping your default gateway using its IP address. If that doesn't work, move on to Step 5.

2. To eliminate DNS as the problem, follow these steps:

   a. Try substituting a domain name for the IP address in a ping command:

   ```
   ping www.course.com
   ```

   If this ping works, then you can conclude that DNS works. If an IP address works, but the domain name does not work, the problem lies with DNS.

   b. If DNS is being provided by your ISP and you are using dynamic IP addressing with your ISP, try rebooting the cable modem or DSL modem. Also try this command to flush the DNS cache kept on the computer:

   ```
   ipconfig /flushdns
   ```

   c. Try pinging your DNS server. To find out the IP address of your DNS server, open the firmware utility of your router and look on a status screen.

   d. If your ISP is providing you with a static IP address and with IP addresses for DNS servers, you must manually enter these values into your router firmware utility. Contact the ISP and verify the DNS IP addresses you are using are correct. You can find this information in the support section of the ISP Web site.

A+
220-702
2.1
3.1

3. If you're having a problem accessing a particular computer on the Internet, try using the tracert command, for example:

```
tracert www.course.com
```

The results show computers along the route that might be giving delays.

4. If one computer on the network cannot access the Internet but other computers can, check the MAC address filtering on the router. Make sure this computer is allowed access. To find out a PC's MAC address, use the Getmac or Ipconfig command.

5. Perhaps the problem is with your firewall. Verify your firewall settings. Zone Alarm sometimes gives this type of problem. Try disabling Zone Alarm to eliminate it as the problem. To completely disable it, make sure all Zone Alarm services and processes are stopped.

6. If you are not able to access the Internet at all, do the following to recycle the connection to your ISP:

   a. Turn off the cable modem, DSL modem, or other device that you use to connect to your ISP. Turn off the router.

   b. Turn back on the cable modem, DSL modem, or other ISP device. Wait until the lights settle. Then turn on your router.

   c. On any PC on your network, release and renew the IP address. Open your browser and try to browse some Web sites.

7. For a cable modem, check to make sure your television works. The service might be down.

8. Perhaps the problem is with your router or one of its features. Try accessing the Internet without using the router. First configure Windows Firewall on one PC for maximum protection, blocking all uninvited communication. Configure TCP/IP on your PC to match up with what your ISP is using (dynamic or static IP addressing). Then use a network cable to connect this PC directly to your cable modem, DSL modem, or other Internet device. If you can access the Internet, you have proven the problem is with the router or cables going to it. To eliminate the cables as a problem, replace them. Connect the router back up to the PC and check all the router settings. The problem might be with DHCP, the firewall settings, or port forwarding. Try updating the firmware on the router. If you are convinced all settings on the router are correct, but the connection to your ISP works without the router and does not work with the router, it's time to replace the router.

9. If you still cannot access the Internet, contact your ISP.

PROBLEMS WITH CLIENT-SIDE APPLICATIONS

Problems with client-side applications might be caused by router or firewall settings, secured connections not working, e-mail protocol settings, FTP problems, and VoIP connections. All these concerns are covered next.

ROUTER AND FIREWALL SETTINGS

When trying to use client/server applications on the Internet, your software and hardware firewalls and other security settings on the router must allow the communication.

18

A+ 220-702

A+
220-702
3.1

Open Windows Firewall on the local computer and verify these settings:

1. Following instructions given earlier in the chapter, verify Windows Firewall settings. Make sure Vista Windows Firewall is on and that **Block all incoming connections** is not checked. For XP, verify that **Don't allow exceptions** is not checked.

2. Click the **Exceptions** tab, and make sure the service or program you are trying to use is checked. If you don't see your service or program listed, click **Add program** (refer back to Figure 18-26), select the program from the list of installed programs, and click **OK**. If you know the specific port you want to open, click **Add port** (refer back to Figure 18-26) and enter any name to help you remember the purpose of this port, the port, and protocol (TPC or UDP) on the Add a Port box. Click **OK** to close the box.

If the problem is still not solved, follow these steps to make sure your router is not blocking communication:

1. Verify that NAT redirection settings are correct. Is port forwarding enabled for the specified ports? Is the range of ports correct for this client application? Check the program documentation to find out what range it uses. There might be more than one port or a range of ports. If you can't find the information in the documentation, search the Internet.

2. Is port forwarding set to the correct IP address on the network? Verify the computer is using this IP address. Set the computer for static IP addressing or set the router to always serve up this IP address to this computer.

3. Check the access restrictions screen of the router and make sure restriction policies are not applied. For example, is the router configured to deny service for a certain day of the week or time of day? Is the MAC address or the IP address of the PC in the list of addresses that are denied Internet access? Verify that a service is not blocked. For example, the IMAP and POP3 services are listed under Blocked Services in Figure 18-69. These services are needed to receive e-mail on the network.

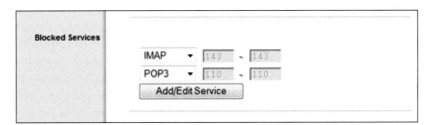

Figure 18-69 Blocked services prevent communication across the firewall
Courtesy: Course Technology/Cengage Learning

4. The access restriction feature of the router can also block certain Web sites (by URL) or block Web site content by keywords. Verify the content or site is not being blocked.

5. To verify that the router is not the problem with communication, you can connect a PC directly to the cable modem, DSL box, or other device so that the router is not involved. However, realize you're partially dropping your shields when you do so. First make sure that Windows Firewall and antivirus software is set for maximum protection, and don't leave the hardware firewall (router) out of the loop any longer than you need in order to solve the problem.

Sometimes security settings at your ISP might be a problem. For example, if you're trying to play an Internet game, you might need to contact your ISP and ask them to open a port that you need to play the game.

A+
220-702
3.1

PROXY SERVER CONNECTIONS

Many large corporations and ISPs use proxy servers to speed up Internet access. A **proxy server** is a computer that intercepts requests that a client makes of a server. It caches the Web pages and files that are requested. If another client requests the same content, the proxy server can provide the content that it has cached. When the proxy server needs to request content from a server, it substitutes its own IP address for the request in the same way that NAT works. In addition, proxy servers sometimes act as a gateway to the Internet, a firewall to protect the network, and to restrict Internet access by employees to force employees to follow company policies.

A Web browser does not have to be aware that a proxy server is in use; this type of proxy server, called a transparent proxy server, is the most common type. However, you can configure a Web browser to use a proxy server. To do that using Internet Explorer, click the **Connections** tab on the **Internet Options** box. Then click **LAN settings**. In the settings box, check **Use a proxy server for your LAN** and enter the IP address of the proxy server (see the left side of Figure 18-70). If your organization uses more than one proxy server, click **Advanced** and enter IP addresses for each type of proxy server on your network (see the right side of Figure 18-70). Click **OK** twice to close both boxes.

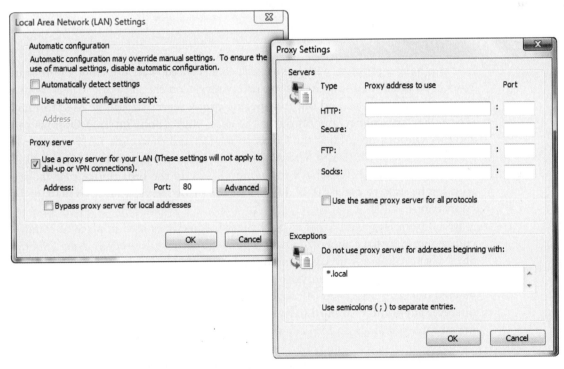

Figure 18-70 Configure Internet Explorer to use one or more proxy servers
Courtesy: Course Technology/Cengage Learning

18

A+ 220-702

SECURED CONNECTIONS

Recall that two secure protocols that encrypt all transmissions are HTTPS and SSH. The purpose of these security protocols is to prevent others on the Internet from eavesdropping on data in transit or from changing that data. (This last type of intrusion is called a man-in-the-middle attack.)

To know if a connection to a Web site is secured using Internet Explorer version 7 or higher, look for https in the browser address box and a lock icon to the right of the address box (see Figure 18-71) or, in the case of earlier versions of IE, at the bottom of the window.

A+
220-702
3.1

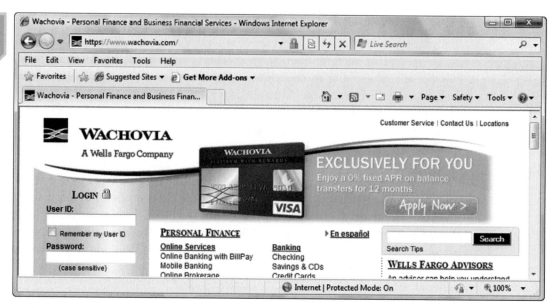

Figure 18-71 A secured connection from browser to Web server
Courtesy: Course Technology/Cengage Learning

If you have a problem with connecting to a secured Web site from a corporate network, you might be using the wrong proxy server on the network. Check with your network administrator to find out if a specific proxy server should be used to manage secure Web site connections. If this is the case, click **Tools, Internet Options** to open the Internet Options box. Click the **Connections** tab and then click **LAN settings**. In the Local Area Network (LAN) Settings box, check **Use a proxy server for your LAN** and then click **Advanced** (refer back to Figure 18-70). In the box, notice that the second row can be used to enter the IP address of the proxy server that is to manage HTTPS connections.

Recall from Chapter 17 that an SSH client is sometimes used in place of Telnet to communicate with a remote computer when high security is needed. Using SSH (Secure Shell) client software, you can communicate with a remote computer and transfer files using a secure tunneling connection. Also, an SSH version of FTP (called Secure FTP or SFTP) can be used to make these types of connections secure. Windows does not contain an SSH client or server application, so third-party software must be used. Do the following if you are having a problem making an SSH connection:

- Verify that port forwarding is enabled on your router. SSH uses port 22.
- Using Windows Firewall, add port 22 to your exceptions list and allow exceptions.
- Using the IP address of the SSH server, ping the server to verify connectivity.
- Verify that you have the correct permissions on the remote SSH server.
- Check the Web site of the SSH software for other troubleshooting tips.

E-MAIL CONNECTIONS

Problems with e-mail connections are likely caused by wrong client settings. Follow these steps to verify these critical settings:

- Check the Web site of the ISP or other group that is managing the e-mail and find out the names of the outgoing and incoming e-mail servers and the protocols being used.

A+
220-702
3.1

▲ In the e-mail client software, look for a way to view and change the incoming and outgoing mail servers. For example, in Figure 18-72, the incoming (receive e-mail) server is *pop.windstream.net* and the outgoing (send e-mail) server is *smtpauth.windstream.net*. The outgoing server is using the SMTP AUTH protocol.

▲ Verify the correct protocol is being used for incoming mail. Options are POP and IMAP (see Figure 18-73).

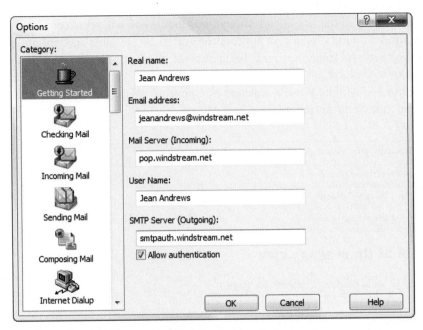

Figure 18-72 Verify the correct e-mail servers are being used
Courtesy: Course Technology/Cengage Learning

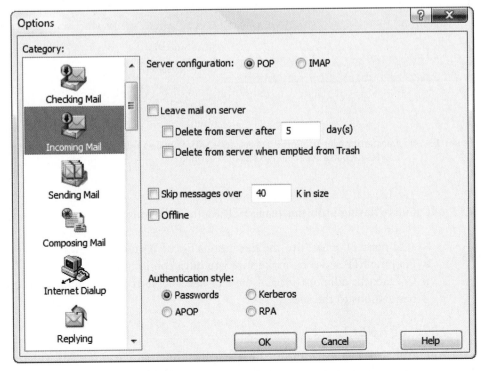

Figure 18-73 Verify the incoming e-mail protocol
Courtesy: Course Technology/Cengage Learning

18

A+ 220-702

A+
220-702
3.1

FTP CONNECTIONS

The most popular way to transfer files over the Internet is to use the File Transfer Protocol (FTP), which can transfer files between two computers using the same or different operating systems. Many software vendors use FTP sites for downloading software to their customers. When you click a link on a Web site to download a file, if the protocol in your browser address box changes from http to ftp, then you are using FTP for the download.

You can also access an FTP site directly by entering a URL that begins with ftp, such as ftp.cengage.com. If the site allows anonymous login, you will see a root level folder. If the site requires a login, a login box appears for you to enter a user account and password. Then the root level folder appears. To change the client application from Internet Explorer to Windows Explorer, on the **Page** menu, click **Open FTP Site in Windows Explorer** (see Figure 18-74). For Vista, a warning box appears asking permission to allow Internet Explorer to leave protected mode. Click **Allow**.

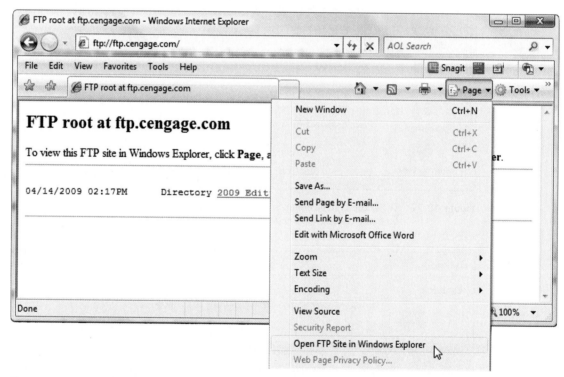

Figure 18-74 Transferring files using FTP is best done with Windows Explorer
Courtesy: Course Technology/Cengage Learning

If you are having problems using FTP, do the following:

- ◢ Add ports 20 and 21 to the Exceptions list of Windows Firewall.
- ◢ Ping the FTP server to make sure you have connectivity.
- ◢ Contact the administrator of the FTP site and verify that you have the correct permissions to the site.

VOIP CONNECTIONS

VoIP (Voice over Internet Protocol), also called Internet telephone, provides voice communication over a network and uses the VoIP protocol. Using VoIP, voice is converted to digital data for transmission over the Internet and connects to the POTS (Plain Old Telephone Service) so that people without VoIP can make and receive calls from VoIP subscribers.

A+
220-702
3.1

When setting up a VoIP service, you plug a digital telephone, such as the one shown in Figure 18-75, into a network port on a local network that is connected to the Internet and use that phone to make a phone call to anywhere on the planet. Notice in the figure, the power cord and network cable share a common cable and connector to the phone. You can also use a regular analog phone as an Internet phone if you use an Analog Telephone Adapter (ATA), such as the one shown in Figure 18-76. Plug the phone into the ATA, which uses a network cable to connect to the network. Just as with mobile phones, the digital phone or ATA is programmed for a particular phone number.

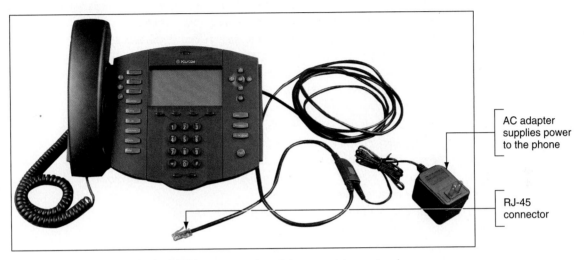

AC adapter
supplies power
to the phone

RJ-45
connector

Figure 18-75 This digital telephone has a network port to connect to a network
Courtesy: Course Technology/Cengage Learning

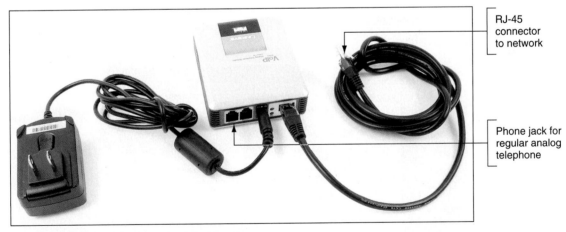

RJ-45
connector
to network

Phone jack for
regular analog
telephone

Figure 18-76 Use this ATA to turn an analog telephone into an Internet phone
Courtesy: Course Technology/Cengage Learning

18

A+ 220-702

APPLYING CONCEPTS

Quality of Service (QoS) refers to the success of communication over the Internet. Communication is degraded on the Internet when packets are dropped, delayed, delivered out of order, or corrupted. In order for VoIP to have the high quality it needs to compete with regular POTS voice communication, QoS on the Internet must be high. VoIP gave problems for many years with dropped lines, echos, delays, static, and jittered communication. ("Jitter" is the term used to describe a voice conversation that is mingled with varying degrees of delays.) However, more recently, many of these problems are for the most part solved to make VoIP a viable option for personal and business use. Recently, my daughter, Jill West, was responsible for selecting a telephone system for a small business. I asked her to describe the successes and woes of having chosen a VoIP solution. Here is her story:

We planned our company so that we all can work from our home offices and live in several regions of the country, yet we compete in a market where we must present a unified front. More and more businesses are built this way these days, and, thankfully, technology is adapting.

When we first began investigating phone systems, we tried to patchwork together various telco (local telephone company) services, but with dismal results. Then we began researching several VoIP providers, from the industry flagship Vonage (www.vonage.com), to smaller and lesser-known companies. With a little searching, we found a company that provides the services important to us. Here are a few features:

- ◢ *We were able to buy the digital phones and ATA adapters from this company that configured and tested them for us before shipping and then taught us how to use them.*
- ◢ *We were able to port our existing toll-free number to our new VoIP account.*
- ◢ *We are able to transfer live calls from one team member to another with three- or four-digit dialing and no long-distance charges for the transferred calls, even with our team spread over several states.*
- ◢ *We have an integrated voice-mail system using a Web portal. One window of our portal is shown in Figure 18-77.*
- ◢ *We can easily set up conference calls with the entire team.*
- ◢ *A single auto-attendant handles all incoming calls, or we can direct incoming calls to any number and still use the auto-attendant as a convenient backup.*
- ◢ *The company provided professional voice talent to record our auto-attendant message and other call-tree menu options.*
- ◢ *We have unlimited long distance, even for our high-volume salespeople.*

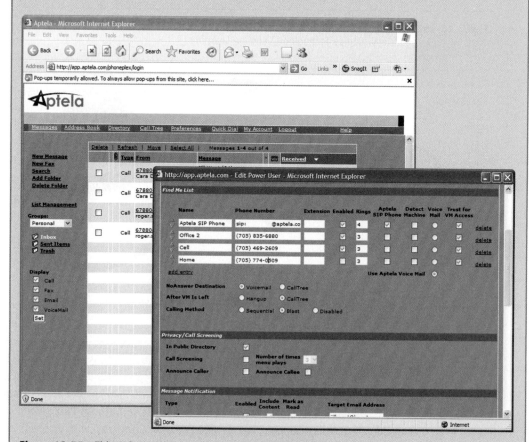

Figure 18-77 This Web portal is used to manage a VoIP service
Courtesy: Course Technology/Cengage Learning

▲ We can add or remove users as our company's payroll changes with no extensive implementation charges or technical difficulties.

▲ Each of our users can program various phone numbers into their account, such as cell phone, home phone, or home-office phone numbers. They can then tell the system at which phone to direct their individual incoming calls. Each call can be sent sequentially through the list of numbers, or "blast" all numbers simultaneously.

▲ Voice-mail messages and faxes can all be forwarded to our various e-mail accounts, and even the message itself is attached for immediate review.

▲ When we travel, we can take the service with us. I can pack my IP phone or ATA and plug it up wherever I am if I have high-speed Internet access. Even without the phone or adapter, I can still use a computer to access my Web portal and make calls from the portal Web site.

With all this, it seems there would be no drawbacks. But all is not well in paradise. We've had a few issues with dropped calls or annoying delays while talking. Sometimes we have to hang up and call the person back. Occasionally, the signal will phase out briefly, where one party can hear the other, but not vice versa. And, if your ISP drops your service for any reason, even just a temporary outage, you're pretty much without a phone. However, incoming calls are still directed through the auto-attendant, and messages are saved there until you again have access.

Overall, even with these drawbacks, VoIP was the right choice for our company. We're pleased with the features and are willing to tolerate the growing pains as technology catches up with our needs.

When setting up a VoIP system, know that each digital phone or ATA must be programmed with a phone number from the VoIP provider. Each device is also programmed to use dynamic IP addressing and must be assigned an IP address just like any other device on the network, which means your network must be using a DHCP server, such as one provided by a multipurpose router. Plug up the devices to the network and then configure the VoIP service using the Web site of the VoIP provider.

Because electrical interference can be a problem with VoIP phones, each network cable connected to a VoIP phone needs a **ferrite clamp** (see Figure 18-78) attached. Attach the

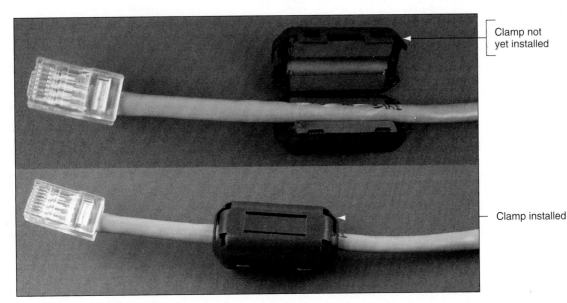

Clamp not yet installed

Clamp installed

Figure 18-78 Install a ferrite clamp on a network cable to protect against electrical interference
Courtesy: Course Technology/Cengage Learning

18

A+ 220-702

clamp on the cable near the phone port. This clamp helps to eliminate electromagnetic interference (EMI). Some cables come with preinstalled clamps, and you can also buy ferrite clamps to attach to other cables.

>> CHAPTER SUMMARY

▲ Cable modem and DSL boxes connect to a PC by way of a USB or network cable. They connect to a router using a network cable. The router provides additional firewall security to a network.

▲ If static IP addressing is used to connect to the Internet, you'll need to know the IP address assigned to you by your ISP, the IP address of one or two DNS servers, the subnet mask, and the IP address of the default gateway (the IP address of a server at the ISP). Static IP addressing is used for business accounts so that others on the Internet can initiate communication with services they provide.

▲ Satellite Internet access in North America uses a satellite dish that faces the southern sky.

▲ Vista can assign a public, private, or domain profile to a network connection. The assigned profile determines the degree of security applied. The profile with the highest security is a public profile.

▲ Vista manages network connections using the Network and Sharing Center, and XP manages connections using the Network Connections window.

▲ Windows Firewall is a software firewall that can provide varying degrees of security on a single computer.

▲ A wired network can use 10BaseT, 100BaseT, and 1000BaseT Ethernet. For fastest speeds, make sure all devices on the network use 1000BaseT.

▲ Local Ethernet networks use twisted pair (UTP or STP) cables rated at CAT5e or higher.

▲ Use a firewall on the host computer or router to protect the network from unsolicited activity from the network or Internet.

▲ It's extremely important to change the password to configure your router as soon as you install it, especially if the router is also a wireless access point.

▲ A router on a small network is most likely able to be configured to use DHCP, access restrictions, port filtering, port forwarding, and port triggering.

▲ Security for a wireless access point includes MAC address filtering, disabling SSID broadcasting, and encryption (WPA2, WPA, or WEP). The access point can also be a DHCP server.

▲ Use cable testers to test cables and trace network cables through a building.

▲ Useful Windows TCP/IP utilities are Getmac, Ipconfig, Net, Netstat, Nslookup, Ping, Telnet, and Tracert. Use third-party SSH client and server software to replace Telnet when a secured connection is needed.

▲ Remote Desktop and Remote Assistance can be used to connect remotely to a computer and manage the Windows desktop. Remote Desktop is better used to connect to your own computer, and Remote Assistance is designed to assist other users with their computers. Both use the RDP protocol.

▲ When troubleshooting network problems, check hardware, device drivers, Windows, and the client or server application, in that order.

>> KEY TERMS

For explanations of key terms, see the Glossary near the end of the book.

domain profile
ferrite clamp
File Transfer Protocol (FTP)
port filtering
port forwarding

port triggering
private profile
public profile
Quality of Service (QoS)
Remote Assistance

Remote Desktop
reverse lookup
VoIP (Voice over Internet
   Protocol)

>> REVIEWING THE BASICS

1. Give two popular examples of broadband technology.

2. Which type of broadband connection does Windows assume, on-demand or always-up?

3. What is the purpose of DSL filters on phone jacks in your home?

4. Which type profile that Vista assigns to a network connection offers the least security?

5. What is the speed in bits per second of a 1000BaseT Ethernet network?

6. What is the maximum length of an Ethernet cable on a 100BaseT network?

7. What is the first configuration change you should make when you first install a router?

8. How is a DHCP reservation on a router used?

9. Which command is used to find the DNS server's information about a domain name?

10. Which command is used to find the host name of a computer when you know its IP address?

11. Which command can give you the hop count from your computer to another?

12. What parameter can be added to the Netstat command so that you can see what program is responsible for a network connection?

13. Which editions of Windows can be used to serve up Remote Desktop?

14. Which is the easiest way to initiate a Remote Assistance session?

15. What is the listening port for Windows XP Remote Desktop?

16. Which tool, Remote Desktop or Remote Assistance, allows you to set up a chat session with the user?

17. In what folder is a log of a Remote Assistance session kept?

18. How can you physically tell if a network card is not working?

19. To know if Windows recognizes a NIC without errors, which tool do you use?

20. What is the full command line to use Ipconfig to release the current IP address?

21. What is the full command line for the loopback address test?

22. What key do you press to refresh the Network window?

23. What command can tell you if two computers on the same network have the same computer name?

24. What command lists the shared resources on a remote computer on the network?

18

25. Which type of Net command can be used to map a network drive?

26. Which command tests for connectivity between two computers?

27. List the steps to recycle the connection to an ISP when using a cable modem and router.

28. If you want to allow an exception in Windows Firewall through a certain port, but the port or program is not listed under the Exceptions tab, what can you do?

29. When an ISP gives a user the two mail server addresses, smtp.myISP.net and pop.myISP.net, which address should be used for incoming mail and which should be used for outgoing mail?

30. What device is required so that you can connect a regular telephone to a VoIP network?

>> THINKING CRITICALLY

1. You are trying to connect to the Internet using a Windows XP dial-up connection. You installed a modem card and tested it, so you know it works. Next, you create a dial-up connection icon in the Network Connections window. Then, you double-click the icon and the Connect dialog box opens. You click Dial to make the connection. An error message appears saying, "There was no dial tone." What is the first thing you do?

   a. Check Device Manager for errors with the modem.

   b. Check with the ISP to verify that you have the correct phone number, username, and password.

   c. Check the phone line to see if it's connected.

   d. Check the properties of the dial-up connection icon for errors.

2. You have set up a small LAN in your home with two Windows XP PCs connected to the Internet using a DSL connection. You have a DSL router box connected to the DSL and to a small switch. Your two PCs connect to the switch. You can browse the Internet from either PC. However, you discover that each PC cannot use the resources on the other PC. What is the problem and what do you do?

   a. The network switch is not working. Try replacing the switch.

   b. The NICs in each PC are not working. Try replacing one NIC and then the next.

   c. The Local Area Connections in the Network Connections window are not working. Delete the connections and re-create them.

   d. Files and folders are not shared on either PC. Use Windows Explorer to correct the problem.

3. You connect to the Internet using a cable modem. When you open your browser and try to access a Web site, you get the error: "The Web page you requested is not available offline. To view this page, click Connect." Select two explanations and their solutions that are reasonable and might work. Select two explanations and solutions that are not reasonable and explain why they won't work.

   a. The browser has been set to work offline. On the File menu, verify that Work Offline is not checked.

   b. The connection to the cable modem is down. In the Network and Sharing Center, click view status for the LAN connection and select Diagnose.

c. Windows Firewall is enabled on your PC. Disable it.

d. The cable modem is not working. Go to Device Manager and check for errors with the cable modem.

>> HANDS-ON PROJECTS

PROJECT 18-1: Practicing TCP/IP Networking Skills

While connected to the Internet or another TCP/IP network, answer these questions:

1. What is your current IP address?

2. Release and renew your IP address. Now what is your IP address?

3. Are you using dynamic or static IP addressing? How do you know?

4. What is your adapter address for this connection?

5. What is your default gateway IP address?

6. What response do you get when you ping the default gateway?

PROJECT 18-2: Researching Remote Assistance

A technician needs to know how to find information he needs to help users and troubleshoot problems. Using sources you can trust, answer the following. List your source of information for each question.

1. What are the steps to cancel a Remote Assistance invitation before it expires?

2. What are the steps to extend a Remote Assistance invitation from six to 12 hours?

3. What are the steps to start a Remote Assistance session when using Windows Messenger?

4. What is the time until expiration for an invitation when using Windows Vista? When using Windows XP?

PROJECT 18-3: Investigating Verizon FiOS

Verizon (*www.verizon.com*) is currently offering an alternative to DSL and cable modem for broadband Internet access. FiOS is a fiber-optic Internet service that uses fiber-optic cable all the way to your house for both your residential telephone service and Internet access. Search the Web for answers to these questions about FiOS:

1. Give a brief description of FiOS and how it is used for Internet access.

2. What downstream and upstream speeds can FiOS support?

3. When using FiOS, does your telephone voice communication share the fiber-optic cable with Internet data?

4. What does Verizon say about FiOS cabling used for television?

5. Is FiOS available in your area?

18

PROJECT 18-4: Practicing Using FTP

Practice using FTP by downloading the latest version of Firefox, a Web browser, using three different methods. Do the following:

1. Using your current browser, go to the Mozilla Web site at *www.mozilla.org* and download the latest version of Firefox. What is the version number? What is the name of the downloaded file? In what folder on your hard drive did you put the file?

2. Using your current browser as an FTP client, locate the same version of Firefox and the same file at the Mozilla FTP site (*ftp.mozilla.org*) and download it to your PC. What is the path to the Firefox file on the FTP site? In what folder on your hard drive did you put the file?

PROJECT 18-5: Teaching Yourself About Windows Meeting Space

Using the Windows Help and Support window, search for information on Windows Meeting Space. Describe the tool. When would you want to use it? What can you do with Windows Meeting Space? Set up and test the tool with a friend on a network connection.

>> REAL PROBLEMS, REAL SOLUTIONS

REAL PROBLEM 18-1: Firewalling Your Home Network

At first, Santiago had only a single desktop computer, an ink-jet printer, and a dial-up phone line to connect to the Internet. Then, his wife, Maria, decided she wanted her own computer. Later they both decided it was time for a broadband connection to the Internet and chose cable. So now, their home network looks like that shown in Figure 18-79. Santiago chose to use a crossover cable to connect the two computers, and the cable modem connects to Santiago's computer using a USB cable. The computer connected to the Internet uses Internet Connection Sharing to serve up Internet access to the other computer.

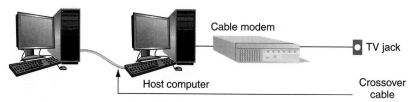

Figure 18-79 Two networked computers sharing an Internet connection
Courtesy: Course Technology/Cengage Learning

Both computers are constantly plagued with pop-up ads and worms, so Santiago has come to you for some advice. He's heard he needs to use a firewall, but he doesn't know what a firewall is or how to buy one. You immediately show him how to turn on Windows Firewall on both Vista PCs, but you know he really needs a better hardware solution. What equipment (including cables) do you recommend he buy to implement a hardware firewall? Also consider that his daughter, Sophia, has been begging for a notebook computer for her birthday, so plan for this expansion. By the way, Sophia has made it perfectly clear there's no way she'll settle for having to sit down in the same room with her parents to surf the Web, so you need to plan for a wireless connection to Sophia's bedroom.

REAL PROBLEM 18-2: More Security for Remote Desktop

When Jacob travels on company business, he finds it's a great help to be able to access his office computer from anywhere on the road using Remote Desktop. However, he wants to make sure his office computer as well as the entire corporate network is as safe as possible. One way you can help Jacob add more security is to change the port that Remote Desktop uses. Knowledgeable hackers know that Remote Desktop uses port 3389, but if you change this port to a secret port, hackers are less likely to find the open port. Search the Microsoft Knowledge Base articles (*support.microsoft.com*) for a way to change the port that Remote Desktop uses. Practice implementing this change by doing the following:

1. Set up Remote Desktop on a computer to be the host computer. Use another computer (the client computer) to create a Remote Desktop session to the host computer. Verify the session works by transferring files in both directions.

2. Next, change the port that Remote Desktop uses on the host computer to a secret port. Print a screen shot showing how you made the change. Use the client computer to create a Remote Desktop session to the host computer using the secret port. Print a screen shot showing how you made the connection using the secret port. Verify the session works by transferring files in both directions.

3. What secret port did you use? What two Microsoft Knowledge Base Articles gave you the information you needed?

18

Security Essentials

In today's computing environment, we all need to know how to keep our shields up. Security is an important concern for PC support technicians, and many of the chapters of this book have addressed security concerns as appropriate within the content of each chapter. This chapter focuses on the concepts, technologies, and best practices you need to know to protect a computer and a small network. In the next chapter, we will focus on how to apply these security measures.

In this chapter, you will learn about compliance measures you might be required by law to use in your organization or profession. You will also learn many ways to protect computing resources, including authenticating and authorizing users, locking down systems, encryption, protecting against malware, and educating your users to not compromise the system unintentionally. Finally, you will learn about the importance of maintaining the security measures you have implemented.

> 🔋 **A+ Exam Tip** All the content in this chapter applies to security objectives on the A+ 220-701 Essentials exam. Chapter 20 covers security objectives on the A+ 220-702 Practical Applications exam.

COMPLY WITH SECURITY POLICIES

A+
220-701
5.1

Sometimes an individual or company is free to decide what security measures they want to use. On the other hand, many corporations and individuals are required by law to implement one or more security standards or guidelines in order to be qualified to do business. In addition, some individuals and corporations freely decide to implement these standards and guidelines because they see value in doing so. Here are just three security standards, but many more exist:

▲ The International Organization for Standardization (ISO, *www.iso.org*) has developed two documents (ISO 17799 and ISO 27002), which describe, in detail, the recommended standards to secure computer resources. Many organizations use these standards, which are considered security benchmarks in the IT industry.

▲ In the United States, the National Institute of Standards and Technology (*www.nist.gov*) has published information technology standards for security to be followed by the U.S. government and its contractors. Other government agencies might have their own security standards.

▲ For the health care industry, the Health Insurance Portability and Accountability Act (HIPAA, pronounced "*hip*-ah") includes regulations to secure patient data that apply to all health care companies and professionals.

> 💡 **A+ Exam Tip** The A+ 220-701 Essentials exam expects you to know the importance of compliance when it comes to securing sensitive data.

Where you have a choice in the security that you use, keep in mind two goals, which are sometimes in conflict. One goal is to protect resources, and the other goal is to not interfere with the functions of the system. A computer or network can be so protected that no one can use it, or so accessible that anyone can do whatever they want with it. The trick is to provide enough security to protect your resources while still allowing users to work unhindered. Also, too much security can sometimes force workers to find nonsecure alternatives. For example, if you require users to change their passwords weekly, some of them might start writing their passwords down to help remember them.

When implementing a security plan, many organizations follow a four-step cyclic process shown in Figure 19-2. The four steps are sometimes called the Plan-Do-Study-Act (PDSA) cycle:

1. *Plan.* Your first steps to making a security plan are to find out what standards, if any, your employer or company must follow. Obtain these standards in writing, and carefully read them. Full compliance is required. If you don't implement the entire standard, your company might be at risk of a lawsuit or losing its license to do business. If you are not required to comply with security standards, use your best judgment as to which security measures mentioned in this chapter and the next will serve your purposes. Then get the approval of others in your organization. Know that many security consulting firms are available to help. However, check them out carefully before using one.

2. *Do.* Implement each security method you decide to use. The plan might need to be implemented in stages.

Figure 19-1 Security measures should protect resources without hindering how users work
© Phil Marden/Getty Images

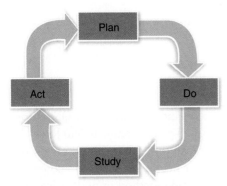

Figure 19-2 A four-step plan to develop a system for an organization
Courtesy: Course Technology/Cengage Learning

3. *Study.* A security plan needs to include methods to monitor the security of a system. You need to know when security has been compromised or when attempts have been made to hack a system. It's also important to monitor the system to make sure that users are following any security policies you have set in place.

4. *Act.* Maintain and improve your security plan as needed. As the organization changes, so do its security needs. Also, as you monitor and review the security measures you are using, you'll find better ways to implement security. Then you need to go back to the Plan stage to decide what to do to improve your security.

CONTROLLING ACCESS TO SECURED RESOURCES

Controlling access to a computer, file, folder, or network is done in Windows by using a combination of authentication and authorization techniques. First, let's look at a definition of these two key words:

▲ **Authentication** proves that an individual is who he says he is and is accomplished by a variety of techniques, including a username, password, personal identification number (PIN), smart card, or biometric data (for example, a fingerprint or iris scan). Using

A+
220-701
5.1

A+
220-701
5.1

19

A+ 220-701

Windows, this authentication is normally done when a user enters a password for his user account. After an individual is authenticated, the individual is allowed access. (In practice, even though an individual is most often a person, sometimes an individual is a computer program or process.)

▲ Authorization determines what an individual can do in the system after he or she is authenticated. The rights or privileges assigned to an individual depend on how the individual is classified. Classifications are based on job needs. A user should be allowed the rights he needs to do his job. Other rights should not be available to him. For Windows, these classifications are generally implemented in two ways: Assigning rights to user accounts or user groups and assigning permissions to data folders and files.

Keep in mind as you learn how Windows authenticates and authorizes access to computer resources, that physical security also needs to be in place. For example, not only do you need to set up a Windows file server to use password-protected user accounts, but also you might need to place the server in a room that is locked from unauthorized people. If a thief gets physical access to a computer, many of the software security measures you have used won't protect the system. These types of physical security techniques and devices are discussed later in the chapter.

Now let's see how Windows authenticates users and then we'll learn how to classify users and authorize their access to resources.

AUTHENTICATE USERS

Users of a local computer and network can be authenticated by BIOS settings that control who can use the computer and by a local user account login to Windows. After the user has logged onto Windows using a workgroup, recall that other computers on the network control who can use their resources. On larger networks, a domain controller manages authentication to the network. The most common method of authentication is to require a password, although other methods such as biometric data and smart cards can be used for authentication.

Let's first look at how Windows, BIOS, and larger networks authenticate users, and then we'll look at how to create strong passwords.

AUTHENTICATE USERS IN WINDOWS

Using Windows, controlling access to a computer or the resources on that computer is accomplished by assigning a password to each user account. As an administrator, when you first create an account, be sure to assign a password to that account. It is best to give the user the ability to change the password at any time. Recall that in Windows an administrator can create a user account by using the User Accounts window accessed from Control Panel or by using the Computer Management console. You can also control how a user logs on. And, as an administrator, you can reset a password if a user forgets it. Now let's see how to control user logon and how to deal with a forgotten password.

Controlling How a User Logs On

Normally, Windows Vista/XP provides a Welcome screen (see Figure 19-3) that appears when the PC is first booted or comes back from a sleep state. All users are listed on the Welcome screen along with a picture (which can be the user's photograph); a user clicks his or her user name and enters the password. Using this logon method, it is possible for malware to intercept the user account and password information.

Figure 19-3 Windows Vista Welcome screen
Courtesy: Course Technology/Cengage Learning

A more secure method of logon is to require that the user press **Ctrl+Alt+Del** to get to a logon window. Use this method to change the way Windows logon works:

▴ Using Vista, enter **netplwiz** in the Start Search box and press **Enter**. Respond to the UAC box. The User Accounts box appears. Click the **Advanced** tab. Check **Require users to press Ctrl+Alt+Delete** (see Figure 19-4). Click **Apply** and close the box.

Figure 19-4 Change the way users log onto Vista
Courtesy: Course Technology/Cengage Learning

▲ Using Windows XP, open **Control Panel** and then open the **User Accounts** applet. Click **Change the way users log on or off**. The User Accounts window opens, as shown in Figure 19-5. If you want to require users to press Ctrl-Alt-Delete to get a logon window, then uncheck **Use the Welcome screen**. If you want to allow only one user logged on at a time, then uncheck **Use Fast User Switching**. When you're done with your changes, click **Apply Options** to close the window.

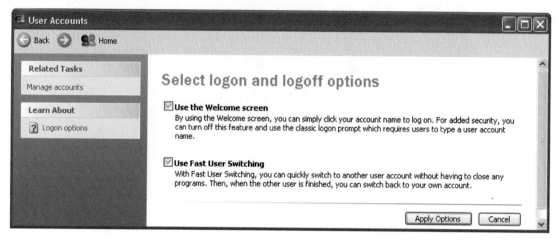

Figure 19-5 Options to change the way Windows XP users log on or off
Courtesy: Course Technology/Cengage Learning

When Crtl-Alt-Delete is required, the Windows screen looks like that in Figure 19-6. When a user presses Ctrl-Alt-Delete, the Windows Welcome screen appears that cannot be intercepted by malware.

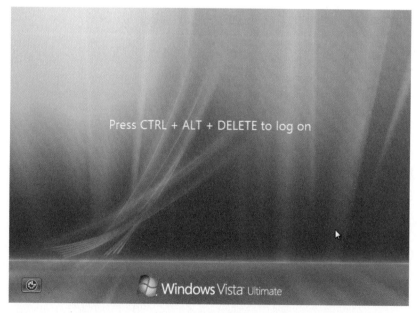

Figure 19-6 Windows Vista screen after the boot or returning from sleep state
Courtesy: Course Technology/Cengage Learning

Forgotten Password

Sometimes a user forgets his or her password or the password is compromised. If this happens and you have Administrator privileges, you can reset the password.

A+
220-701
5.1

Keep in mind, however, that resetting a password causes the OS to lock the user out from using encrypted e-mail or files and from using Internet passwords stored on the computer. For Vista Business or Ultimate editions or for XP Professional, you can reset a password using the Computer Management console. For all versions of Vista or XP, you can use a Control Panel applet to reset a password for another user. Follow these steps:

▲ For Vista, click **User Accounts and Family Safety** in the Control Panel. Then click **User Accounts** and click **Manage another account**. Respond to the UAC box. Click the account you want to change. The Change an Account window opens. Click **Change a password**. The Change Password window opens (see Figure 19-7). Enter the new password twice and a password hint. Click **Change password**. Close the window.

Figure 19-7   Reset a user's password
Courtesy: Course Technology/Cengage Learning

▲ For Windows XP, open the User Accounts applet in Control Panel. Click **Change an account** and select the account. Then click **Change the password** and enter the new password twice and a password hint. Click **Change Password** and close the window.

Because of the problem of losing encrypted data and Internet passwords when a user password is reset, each new user should create a password reset disk for use in the event the user forgets the password. Vista allows you to use a flash memory device, and XP expects you to use a floppy disk. To create the disk, open the **User Accounts** window in Control Panel, and click **Create a password reset disk** (in XP, click **Prevent a forgotten password**) in the left pane of the window shown in Figure 19-8. Follow the wizard to create the disk. Explain to the user the importance of keeping the device or disk in a safe place in case it's needed later. If a user enters a wrong password at logon, he or she will be given the opportunity to use the disk.

> **Notes** The password reset disk should be kept in a protected place so that others cannot use it to gain unauthorized access to the computer.

19

A+ 220-701

A+
220-701
5.1

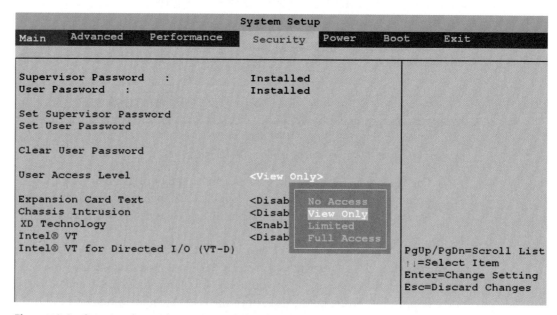

Figure 19-8 Create a password reset disk
Courtesy: Course Technology/Cengage Learning

AUTHENTICATE USERS WITH BIOS SETTINGS

Power-on passwords are assigned in BIOS setup and kept in CMOS RAM to prevent unauthorized access to the computer and/or to the BIOS setup utility. Most likely, you'll find the security screen to set the passwords under the boot menu or security menu options. For one BIOS, this security screen looks like that in Figure 19-9, where you can set a supervisor password and a user password. In addition, you can configure how the user password works.

```
                          System Setup
 Main     Advanced     Performance     Security   Power    Boot      Exit

 Supervisor Password   :              Installed
 User Password    :                   Installed

 Set Supervisor Password
 Set User Password

 Clear User Password

 User Access Level                    <View Only>

 Expansion Card Text         <Disab    No Access
 Chassis Intrusion           <Disab    View Only
 XD Technology               <Enabl    Limited
 Intel® VT                   <Disab    Full Access
 Intel® VT for Directed I/O (VT-D)                PgUp/PgDn=Scroll List
                                                  ↑↓=Select Item
                                                  Enter=Change Setting
                                                  Esc=Discard Changes
```

Figure 19-9 Set supervisor and user passwords in BIOS setup to lock down a computer
Courtesy: Course Technology/Cengage Learning

The choices under User Access Level are **No Access** (the user cannot access the BIOS setup utility), **View Only** (the user can access BIOS setup, but cannot make changes), **Limited** (the user can access BIOS setup and make a few changes such as date and time), and **Full Access** (the user can access the BIOS setup utility and make any changes). When

A+
220-701
5.1

supervisor and user passwords are both set and you boot the system, a box to enter a password is displayed. What access you have depends on which password you enter. Also, if both passwords are set, you must enter a valid password to boot the system. By setting both passwords, you can totally lock down the computer from unauthorized access.

For another computer, BIOS setup controls how to lock down a computer on the Advanced BIOS screen shown in Figure 19-10. Under the Security Option, choices are Setup and System. If you choose Setup, the power-on passwords control access only to BIOS setup. If you choose

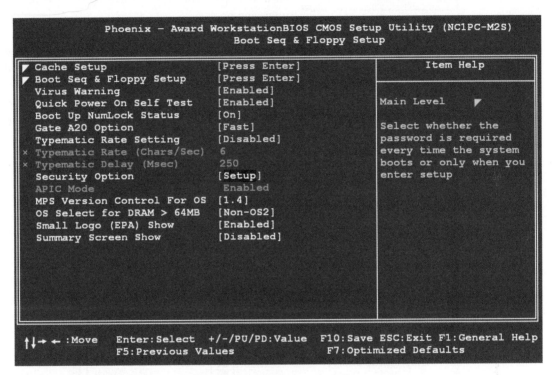

Figure 19-10 Change the way a user password functions to protect the computer
Courtesy: Course Technology/Cengage Learning

System, a power-on password is required every time you boot the system. (The supervisor and user power-on passwords for this BIOS are set on another screen.) Also notice on the setup screen in Figure 19-10, the Virus Warning option, which is enabled. If an attempt to write to the boot sectors happens, a warning message appears on-screen and an alarm beeps.

> **A+ Tip** The A+ 220-701 Essentials exam expects you to know how to use BIOS setup to secure a workstation from unauthorized use.

> **Notes** For added protection, configure the BIOS setup utility so that a user cannot boot from a removable device such as a CD, USB device, or floppy disk.

> **Caution** Recall from Chapter 5 that these supervisor and user passwords to the computer can be reset by setting a jumper on the motherboard to clear all BIOS customized settings and return BIOS setup to its default settings. To keep someone from using this technique to access the computer, you can use a computer case with a lockable side panel and install a lock on the case.

A+
220-701
5.1

In addition to power-on passwords, some notebooks give you the option of setting a hard drive password, which is set in BIOS setup and written on the hard drive. This password is sometimes called a drive lock password. Data on the hard drive cannot be changed without entering this password. The advantage of using a drive lock password over a power-on password or a Windows password is that if the hard drive is removed and installed in another notebook, it still protects the hard drive's data. Just as with the power-on password, the hard drive password is requested by the system when it is powering up.

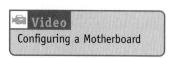

To know if your notebook supports these three types of power-on passwords, look on the BIOS setup screens. Figure 19-11 shows one notebook BIOS screen that shows the options to set four passwords (supervisor password, user password, and a hard drive password for each of two hard drives in the system). To set a hard drive password or the user password, you must first set a supervisor password. After that is set, to set a hard drive password, on the **Security** menu, select **Hard Disk Security**. The submenu in Figure 19-12 shows where you can choose to set a password for either or both hard drives.

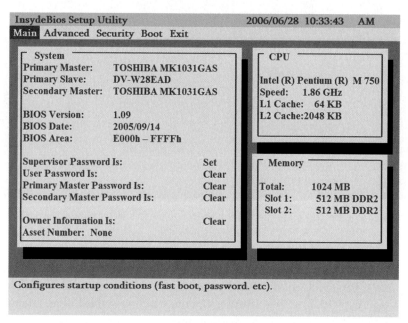

Figure 19-11 BIOS setup main menu shows support for four power-on passwords
Courtesy: Course Technology/Cengage Learning

AUTHENTICATE USERS FOR LARGER NETWORKS

How to secure a large network is beyond the scope of this book. However, as a PC support technician, you might be called on to support the devices and techniques that are used to authenticate users when they first try to connect to a large network. In this part of the chapter, you'll learn how user accounts and passwords are encrypted as this information is sent over the network when authenticating the user. You'll also learn how smart cards and biometric data can be used to authenticate users.

Encrypted User Accounts and Passwords

When logging on to a network, such as that managed by Windows Server 2008, the user account and password must be passed over the network in order to be authenticated by the

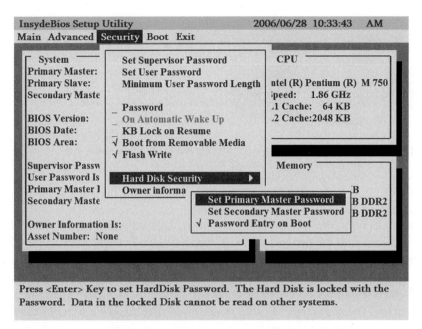

A+
220-701
5.1

Figure 19-12 Submenu shows how to set a hard drive password that will be written on the drive
Courtesy: Course Technology/Cengage Learning

domain controller. If someone intercepts that information, the network security can be compromised. For this reason, user accounts and passwords are encrypted before they are sent over the network to the computer that is the domain controller and decrypted just before they are validated. The protocols used to encrypt account names and passwords are called authentication protocols. The two most popular protocols are CHAP (Challenge Handshake Authentication Protocol) and Kerberos. Kerberos is the default protocol used by Windows Vista/XP.

Smart Cards

Besides a user account and strong password, a network might require more security to control access. Generally, the best validation to prove you are who you say you are requires a two-factor authentication: You prove you have something in your possession and you prove you know something. For example, a user can enter a user ID and password and also prove he has a token in hand. This token can take on many forms. The most popular type of token is a smart card, which is any small device that contains authentication information that can be keyed into a logon window by a user or can be read by a smart card reader, when the device is inserted in the reader. (You also need to know that some people don't consider a card to be a smart card unless it has an embedded microprocessor.)

> **A+ Tip** The A+ 220-701 Essentials exam expects you to know about using smart cards and biometric devices for hardware and software security.

Here are some variations of smart cards:

▲ One type of smart card is a key fob, so called because it fits conveniently on a keychain. RSA Security (*www.rsasecurity.com*), a leader in authentication technologies, makes several types of smart cards, called SecurIDs. One SecurID key fob by RSA Security is shown in Figure 19-13. The number on the key fob changes every 60 seconds. When a

19

A+ 220-701

Figure 19-13 A smart card such as this SecurID key fob is used to authenticate a user gaining access to a secured network
Courtesy of RSA Security

user logs on to the network, she must enter the number on the key fob, which is synchronized with the network authentication service. Entering the number proves that the user has the smart card in hand.

▲ Other smart cards that look like a credit card also have an embedded microchip that displays a number every few seconds for a user to enter during the authentication process. The advantage of using smart cards that display a number to key in is that no special equipment needs to be installed on the computer. The disadvantage is that the smart card can only validate that the person has the token in hand but can provide no additional data about the user.

▲ Other smart cards have magnetic stripes that can be read by a smart card reader that has a slot for the card (see Figure 19-14). Because these cards don't contain a

Figure 19-14 A smart card with a magnetic strip can be used inside or outside a computer network
Courtesy of IDenticard Systems

microchip, they are sometimes called memory cards, and are sometimes used to gain entrance into a building. They can also be read by a smart card reader, such as the one shown in Figure 19-15, that connects to a PC using a USB port. Used in this way, they are part of the authentication process into a network. The magnetic stripe can contain information about the user to indicate their rights on the system. Not only does the smart card validate that the person has a token, but it can also be used to control other functions on the network. The major disadvantage of this type of smart card is that each computer used for authentication must have one of these smart card reader machines installed. Also, in the industry, because a card with a magnetic stripe does not contain a microchip, some in the industry don't consider it to fit into the category of a smart card, but rather simply call it a magnetic stripe card.

Figure 19-15 This smart card reader by Athena Smartcard Solutions (*www.athena-scs.com*) uses a USB connection
Courtesy of Athena Smartcard Solutions Ltd.

◢ Another type of smart card plugs directly into a USB port, such as the one in Figure 19-16 by Aladdin (*www.aladdin.com*). The device displays a number that changes every 60 seconds, which a user can enter when logging onto the system. The device can also be read by software installed on the computer and most likely contains one or more digital certificates that a user needs to authenticate into the private network and do business on the network. A **digital certificate** is assigned by a Certification Authority (for example, VeriSign—*www.verisign. com*), and is used to prove you are who you say you are. These smart cards are designed to help encrypt any data sent over the Internet to the corporate network, such as that used by a VPN. In fact, many VPN solutions are based on a VPN router at the corporate office and a smart card token at the user end of the VPN tunnel. The advantage of this type of smart card is that it can contain sensitive data that can be read by a remote computer, but the computer does not need any special equipment to read the card. Remember that it's best to use two-factor authentication. Even though a user's password could be stored on this type of smart card, for added security, the user should still be expected to enter a password to gain access to the system.

Figure 19-16 This eToken by Aladdin can contain digital certificates so that a user can do business over a VPN
Courtesy of Aladdin

19

A+ 220-701

A+
220-701
5.1
5.2

Using Biometric Data

As part of the authentication process, rather than proving a person is in possession of a token, some systems are set to use biometric data to validate the person's physical body. A biometric device is an input device that inputs biological data about a person, which can be input data to identify a person's fingerprints, handprints, face, voice, eye, and handwritten signatures. Figure 19-17 shows one biometric input device, an iris reader, that scans your iris. Iris scanning is one of the most accurate ways to identify a person using biological data. The biometric data collected is then used to authenticate that person using some type of access control system.

Figure 19-17 The BM-ET200 iris reader by Panasonic
Courtesy of Panasonic Corporation

Using a biometric device, a person presses his finger against a fingerprint reader or puts his face in front of a Web cam that has been programmed to scan facial features, and be authenticated into a computer or network using data that has previously been recorded about this person. For desktop and notebook computer users, the most common biometric device is a fingerprint reader.

Although using biometric devices is gaining in popularity, the disadvantages of using these devices still outweigh the advantages. The most important disadvantage to using biometric devices is the danger of false negatives or false positives. For organizations with high security needs, security personnel must decide the fault tolerance limit of the input data. If you set the fault tolerance limit too low (to make sure only the person's data is the only data authenticated) then you run the risk that the person will not be authenticated (false negative). If you set the fault tolerance level too high (to make sure this person gets authenticated), you run the risk that someone with similar biometric data can get access (false positive). Biometric devices are still to be considered in the pioneering stage of development. For best security, use a combination of two authentication techniques such as a smart card and a password.

CREATE STRONG PASSWORDS

You can lock down a computer by using power-on passwords and Windows passwords. In addition, you need passwords to protect your online accounts that you access through Web sites. Also, many applications give you the option to set a password on the data files

A+
220-701
5.1
5.2

associated with the application. A password needs to be a strong password, which means it is not easy to guess by both humans and computer programs designed to hack passwords.

A strong password, such as @y&kK1ff, meets all of the following criteria:

▲ Use eight or more characters (14 characters or longer is better).
▲ If your system allows it, a passphrase rather than a password is easier to remember and harder to guess. A passphrase is made of several words with spaces allowed.
▲ Combine uppercase and lowercase letters, numbers, and symbols.
▲ Use at least one symbol in the second through sixth position of your password.
▲ Don't use consecutive letters or numbers, such as "abcdefg" or "12345."
▲ Don't use adjacent keys on your keyboard, such as "qwerty."
▲ Don't use your logon name in the password.
▲ Don't use words in any language. Don't even use numbers for letters (as in "p@ssw0rd", as programs can now guess those as well.
▲ Don't use the same password for more than one system.

> **Notes** Microsoft offers a password checker at *www.microsoft.com/protect/yourself/password/ checker.mspx*. Go to this link and enter your password in the window shown in Figure 19-18. Microsoft will then rate the strength of your password.

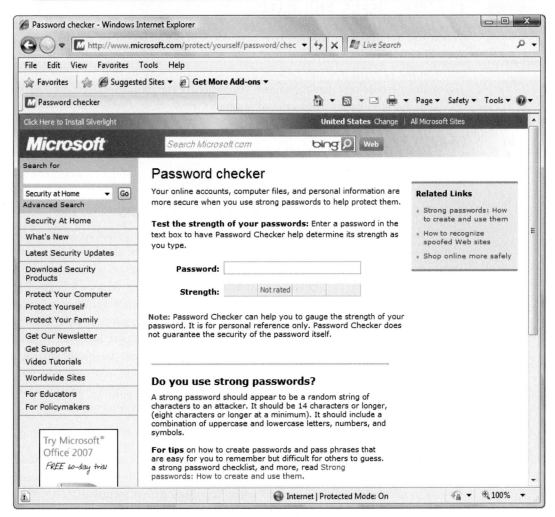

Figure 19-18 Microsoft password checker window
Courtesy: Course Technology/Cengage Learning

19

A+ 220-701

A+
220-701
5.1
5.2

In some situations, a blank Windows password might be more secure than an easy-to-guess password such as "1234." That's because you cannot log on to a Windows Vista/XP computer from a remote computer unless the user account has a password. A criminal might be able to guess an easy password and log on remotely. For this reason, if your computer is always sitting in a protected room such as your home office and you don't intend to access it remotely, you might choose to use no password. However, for notebook computers that are not always protected in public places, always use a strong password. It's too easy for a criminal to log on to your Windows notebook if you use no password. You can use Group Policy to require that every account has a password.

If you write your password down, keep it in as safe a place as you would the data you are protecting. Don't send your passwords over e-mail or chat. Change your passwords regularly, and don't type your passwords on a public computer. For example, computers in hotel lobbies or Internet cafes should only be used for Web browsing—not for logging on to your e-mail account or online banking account. These computers might be running keystroke-logging software put there by criminals to record each keystroke. Several years ago, while on vacation, I entered credit card information on a computer in a hotel lobby in a foreign country. Months later, I was still protesting $2 or $3 charges to my credit card from that country. Trust me. Don't do it—I speak from experience.

A+
220-701
5.1
3.3

CLASSIFY USERS AND DATA

When you are asked to set up a new user account on a computer, you need to classify the user. Find out the minimum set of resources the user needs on the computer and network to perform her job. All users should be classified in this way so that you give to users only the rights and permissions that they need. Also classify the data so that you know who owns the data and who needs what type of access to it.

> 💡 **A+ Exam Tip** The A+ 220-701 Essentials exam expects you to know the basics of data classifications.

CLASSIFY USER ACCOUNTS AND USER GROUPS

Computer users should be classified to determine the rights they need to do their jobs. To classify a user is to assign certain rights to that user. For example, some users need the right to log onto a system remotely and others do not. Other rights granted to users might include the right to install software or hardware, change the system date and time, change Windows Firewall settings, and so forth. Generally, when a new employee begins work, that employee's supervisor determines what rights the employee needs to perform his job. You, as the support technician, will be responsible to make sure the user account assigned to the employee has these rights and no more.

In Windows, the rights or privileges assigned to an account are established when you first create a user account and decide the account type. Recall that accounts are created from the Control Panel (using any edition of Vista or XP) or by using the Computer Management console (using Vista Business or Ultimate editions or XP Professional).

Vista offers these types of user accounts:

- ◢ An **administrator account** has complete access to the system and can make changes that affect the security of the system and other users. Recall that one account with administrative rights is created when Windows is first installed.
- ◢ A **standard account** can use software and hardware and make some system changes, but cannot make changes that affect the security of the system or other users.
- ◢ A **guest account** is normally not activated and has very limited rights.

A+
220-701
5.1
3.3

Windows XP also has an administrator account and guest account. In addition to these two accounts, XP also uses these account types:

- ◢ A limited account has read-write access only on its own folders, read-only access to most system folders, and no access to other users' data. Using a Limited account, a user cannot install applications or carry out any administrative responsibilities.
- ◢ A power user account can read from and write to parts of the system other than his own local drive, install applications, and perform limited administrative tasks.
- ◢ A backup operator account can back up and restore any files on the system regardless of its access permissions to these files.

When an account is created, it is assigned one of the account types listed above. This account type determines the rights assigned to the account. After an account is created, an administrator can use the Computer Management console in Vista Business or Ultimate editions or XP Professional to change the groups an account belongs to. By adding an account to a group, the rights and permissions assigned to that group are assigned to the account. Recall from Chapter 17 that before an account could use the Telnet service, it had to belong to the TelnetClients group. Figure 19-19 shows the Computer Management console and the Jean Andrews account being added to the TelnetClients group.

In Windows, the two terms, rights and permissions, have very different meanings when classifying user accounts and data. Rights (also called privileges) refer to the tasks

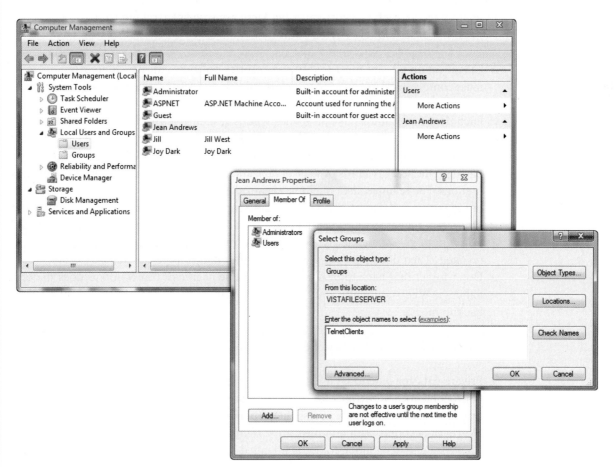

Figure 19-19 To enhance the permissions assigned to an account, add the account to a new member group
Courtesy: Course Technology/Cengage Learning

19

A+ 220-701

an account is allowed to do in the system (for example, installing software or changing the system date and time). Permissions refer to which user accounts or groups are allowed to access data. *Rights are assigned to an account, and permissions are assigned to data.*

> **Notes** If a Windows computer is configured to belong to a domain instead of a workgroup, all security is managed by the network administrator for the entire network.

One way to manage data permissions is by creating new user groups. For example, you can create an Accounting group and a Medical Records group. It's easier to give permission to use a certain data folder to the Accounting group than it is to give individual permission to each user in that group. User groups are created by using the Computer Management console, and the details of how to do that are covered in Chapter 20. After the group is created, you need to assign the correct data permissions to the group and add the users to that group who need those permissions to do their jobs.

CLASSIFY DATA

Folders and files stored on a workstation or server that contain user data need to be classified as to the permissions assigned to the data. These permissions include the user accounts or account groups that are authorized to read and/or change the data.

Data classification as it applies to security involves putting data into categories and then deciding how secure each category must be. Here are some general guidelines to help you understand the process of classifying data:

- Classification of data must follow any security policies with which your organization must comply. Find out who in your organization is responsible for compliance, and make sure your classification plan gets that person's approval.
- Each data folder must have an owner who is responsible for that data and decides who else in the organization gets access. For example, the owner of the C:\Payroll folder might be the director of the Payroll Department or someone she designates.
- Based on the security needs of your organization, you might decide on categories of classifications. For example, data might be classified as public, for official use only, confidential, or top secret. Each category demands a different level of protection and security measure.
- To protect the integrity of the data, always document when the owner of a data folder asks you to give someone else access or informs you that access to a user must be revoked. Then document when you made the change in permissions.
- Don't forget that backup media needs the same degree of protection as does the original data. When you make your backup plans, include in them how you will secure the backup media.

Here are general guidelines as to how to implement classifications of data using Windows:

- Private data for individual users is best kept in the Vista C:\Users folder or the XP C:\Documents and Settings folder for that user. User accounts with limited or standard privileges cannot normally access these folders belonging to another user account. However, accounts with administrative rights do have access.
- The Vista C:\Users\Public folder is intended to be used for folders and files that all users share.
- You can create a folder on a drive and assign share permissions to that folder and its subfolders and files. You can allow all users access or only certain users or user groups. When

A+
220-701
5.1
3.3

you assign permissions to a folder or file, you decide who can view the contents and who has the right to change the contents. For example, you might set up folders like this:

- The C:\Accounting folder contains several folders and files. Some employees in the Accounting Department need full access to these folders. Other employees need read-only access to certain subfolders in the C:\Accounting folder.

- The C:\Payroll folder contains sensitive data and only two employees need full access. One other person needs read-only access.

▲ A folder can be hidden on the network so that users cannot see the folder unless they know its name.

▲ A folder or file can also be encrypted, and a digital certificate is required for access.

▲ Passwords can be required to access shared resources.

▲ A computer can be locked down so that no files or folders are shared on the network. This is the desired setting when you use public networks such as a public wireless hotspot.

A+
220-701
3.3

SHARING FILES AND FOLDERS

Shared folders and files might be stored on a user's PC or on a file server that is dedicated to storing and serving up data files and folders. If the network is not being managed by a domain controller, each computer in the workgroup must share its folders, files, and printers before others on the network can access them.

In this chapter, you will learn how to share a folder or file without applying strict security measures. In Chapter 20, you will learn how to apply higher security to shared files and folders. Let's first see how to share a file or folder and how to solve problems with sharing. Then you'll learn how to map a network drive to make shared resources easier to access for remote users.

HOW TO SHARE A FILE OR FOLDER

Follow these steps to share a file or folder using Windows Vista:

1. Using Windows Explorer, right-click the folder or file you want to share and select **Share** from the shortcut menu. The File Sharing box opens (see Figure 19-20).

2. Click the down arrow to see a list of users of this computer. To allow everyone access, select **Everyone (All users in this list)** and click **Add**. (Alternately, you can select an individual user.) Whomever you add is assigned the permission level of Reader, as shown in Figure 19-21.

3. To allow the users the right to make changes to the folder, click the down arrow beside Reader. Notice the three choices of permission levels and the opportunity to remove the user from the list of users. Table 19-1 explains the meaning of the three permission levels. Select **Co-owner** from the shortcut menu, as shown in Figure 19-21.

4. To close the box, click **Share** and respond to the UAC box. Then click **Done**. Vista places a two-friends icon under shared folders (see Figure 19-22).

To share a folder in Windows XP, follow these steps:

1. In Windows Explorer, right-click a folder and select **Sharing and Security** from the shortcut menu. The Properties box opens with the Sharing tab active. Click **If you understand the security risks but want to share files without running the wizard, click here**. The Enable File Sharing dialog box appears. Select **Just share the folder** and click **OK**. The Sharing tab on the Properties box now has the *Share this folder on the network* check box available (see Figure 19-23). You only need to enable file sharing once. After that, the check box is always available.

19

A+ 220-701

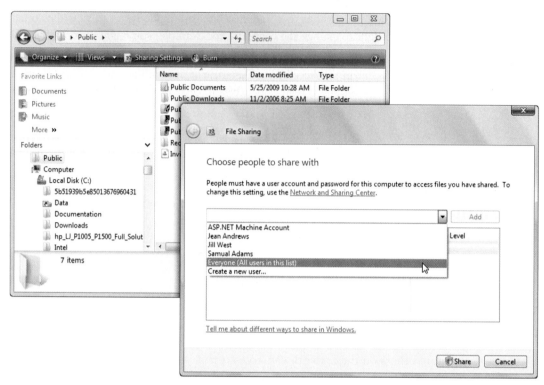

Figure 19-20   Choose people to share the folder
Courtesy: Course Technology/Cengage Learning

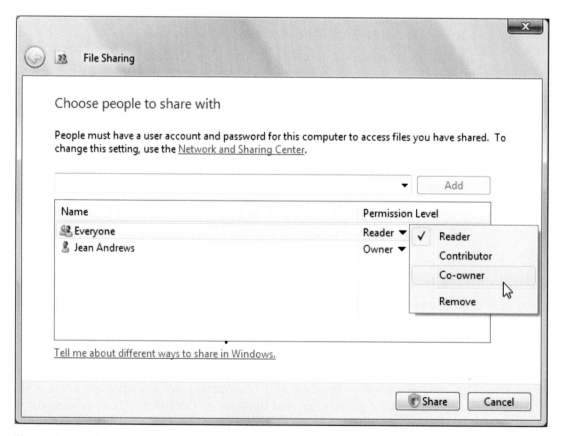

Figure 19-21   Change the permission level of a user
Courtesy: Course Technology/Cengage Learning

A+
220-701
3.3

Permission Level	Description
Reader	Can read, but not write, to the contents of the folder and its subfolders.
Contributor	Can write files and read existing files, but cannot change existing files put there by others. Applies only to folder sharing.
Co-owner	Has full control over the folder in the same way the owner does, but is not identified as the folder owner.

Table 19-1 Permission levels for files and folders in Windows Vista

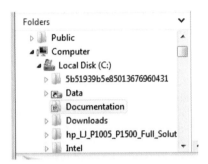

Figure 19-22 The two-friends icon indicates a shared folder
Courtesy: Course Technology/ Cengage Learning

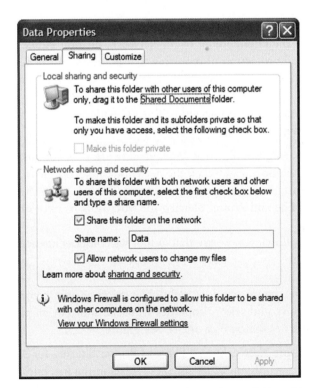

Figure 19-23 A user on a network can share a folder with others on the network
Courtesy: Course Technology/Cengage Learning

19

A+ 220-701

2. Check **Share this folder on the network**. If you want to allow others to change the contents of the folder, check **Allow network users to change my files**. Click **Apply**, and close the window.

After a folder or file is shared, other users on the network can see the folder when they open the Vista Network window or XP My Network Places.

> 📝 **Notes** When a window is open, you can press the **F5** key to refresh the contents of that window.

Some applications can also be shared with others on the network. If you share a folder that has a program file in it, a user on another PC can double-click the program file and execute it remotely on his or her desktop. This is a handy way for several users to share an application that is installed on a single PC. However, know that not all applications are designed to work this way.

> 📝 **Notes** If you are responsible for protecting shared files and folders on the network, be sure you put in place a method to back up this data on a regular basis. How to perform backups is covered in Chapter 13. Also, see Chapter 20 to find out how to set up the right security measures so that shared resources are only available to the specific users who are authorized to access these resources.

TROUBLESHOOT PROBLEMS WITH SHARED FILES AND FOLDERS

If you have problems accessing a shared resource in Vista, follow these steps:

1. Open the Network and Sharing Center (see Figure 19-24) and verify the following:

   ▲ **File sharing** is turned on.
   ▲ If you want to share the Public folder to the network, turn on **Public folder sharing**.
   ▲ If you want the added protection of requiring that all users on the network must have a valid user account and password on this computer, turn on **Password protected sharing**.
   ▲ If you want to share a printer connected to this PC with others on the network, turn on **Printer sharing**.

2. In the Network and Sharing Center, click **Manage network connections**. In the Network Connections window, right-click the network connection icon, select **Properties** from the shortcut menu, and respond to the UAC box. In the Properties dialog box, verify that **File and Printer Sharing for Microsoft Networks** is checked.

For Windows XP, do the following to verify that Windows components needed for sharing are installed and enabled:

1. Open the **Network Connections** window, right-click the connection icon (default name is **Local Area Connection**), and select **Properties** from the shortcut menu. The Local Area Connection Properties dialog box opens. See Figure 19-25.

2. Verify **Client for Microsoft Networks** and **File and Printer Sharing for Microsoft Networks** are both checked. If you don't see these items in the list, click **Install** to install them. The Select Network Component Type box appears (see the left side of Figure 19-25). Select **Client**, click **Add**, and follow the directions on-screen. When you're done, close all windows.

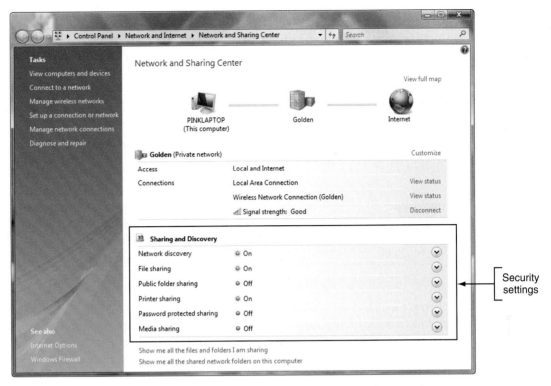

Figure 19-24 Use the Network and Sharing Center to verify the computer is set to share resources
Courtesy: Course Technology/Cengage Learning

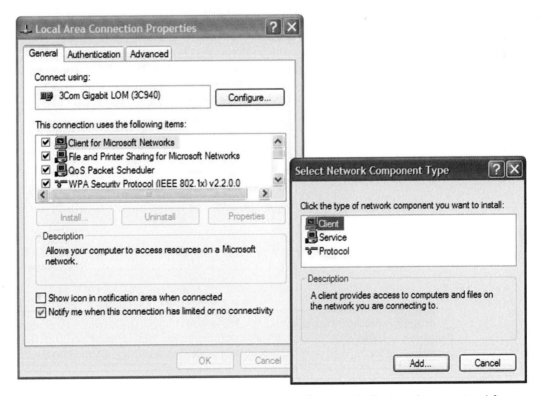

Figure 19-25 Use the Network Connections applet to install a network client, service, or protocol for Windows XP
Courtesy: Course Technology/Cengage Learning

A+
220-701
3.3

HOW TO MAP A NETWORK DRIVE

A network drive map is one of the most powerful and versatile methods of communicating over a network. A network drive map makes one PC (the client) appear to have a new hard drive, such as drive E, that is really hard drive space on another host computer (the server). This client/server arrangement is managed by a Windows component called the Network File System (NFS), which makes it possible for files on the network to be accessed as easily as if they are stored on the local computer. NFS is a type of distributed file system (DFS), which is a system that shares files on a network. Even if the host computer uses a different OS, such as UNIX, the drive map still functions.

> **Notes** A computer that does nothing but provide hard drive storage on a network for other computers is called a file server or a network attached storage (NAS) device. Other computers on the network can access this storage using a mapped network drive.

Using a mapped network drive, files and folders on a host computer are available even to network-unaware DOS applications. The path to a file simply uses the remote drive letter, such as drive K or drive Z, instead of a local drive, such as drive A or drive C. Also, mapped network drives are more reliable than using the Vista Network or XP My Network Places tool to access folders on the network.

> **Notes** You might be asking why mapped network drives are more reliable than the Vista Network and XP My Network Places windows. The answer is because these windows rely on the Windows browser subsystem. These browser services (not to be confused with Web browsers, such as Internet Explorer) periodically poll the network for resources. To avoid excessive network traffic, one computer in a workgroup is designated as the master browser. (This designation happens behind the scenes without user involvement.) If this computer is down or the network resources change after the master browser polls, the other computers on the network might report wrong resources in the Network or My Network Places windows. We see the results of this problem when we know a computer is on the network, but other Network or My Network Places windows don't report it. Mapped network drives don't rely on browser services, and are therefore, more reliable.

To set up a network drive, follow these steps:

1. On the host computer, share the folder or entire volume to which you want others to have access.

2. On the remote computer that will use the network drive, connect to the network and access **Windows Explorer**. Click the **Tools** menu and select **Map Network Drive**.

> **Notes** By default, Vista does not show the menu bar in Windows Explorer. To display the menu, click **Organize** and then click **Folder and Search Options**. In the Folder Options box, click the **View** tab. Under Advanced settings, check **Always show menus**. Click **Apply** and **OK** to close the box.

3. The Map Network Drive dialog box opens, as shown in Figure 19-26. Select a drive letter from the drop-down list.

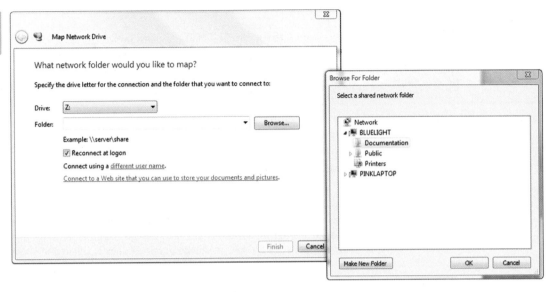

Figure 19-26 Mapping a network drive to a host computer
Courtesy: Course Technology/Cengage Learning

4. Click the **Browse** button and locate the shared folder or drive on the host computer (see the left side of Figure 19-26). Click **OK** to close the Browse For Folder dialog box, and click **Finish** to map the drive. The folder on the host computer now appears as one more drive in Explorer on your computer (see Figure 19-27).

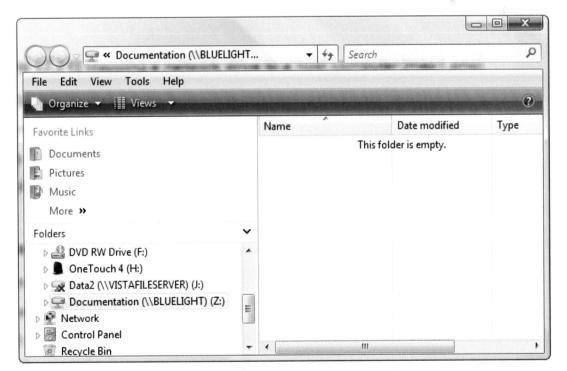

Figure 19-27 The Documentation folder on the \\Bluelight host computer is known as Drive Z on the local computer
Courtesy: Course Technology/Cengage Learning

A+
220-701
3.3

> **Notes** When mapping a network drive, you can type the path to the host computer rather than clicking the Browse button to navigate to the host. To enter the path, in the Map Network Drive dialog box, use two backslashes, followed by the name of the host computer, followed by a backslash and the drive or folder to access on the host computer. For example, to access the Public folder on the computer named Scott, enter **\\Scott\Public** and then click **Finish**.

5. If a network drive does not work, go to the Vista Network window or XP My Network Places, and verify that the network connection is good. You can also use the net use command discussed in Chapter 18 to solve problems with network connections.

> **Tip** A host computer might be in sleep mode when a remote computer attempts to make a mapped drive connection at startup. To solve this problem, change the power settings on the host computer to wake up for network activity. How to change power settings is covered in Chapter 21.

How to encrypt and hide folders and files is covered in Chapter 20. Other methods of securing the data and other resources are covered next.

ADDITIONAL METHODS TO PROTECT RESOURCES

A+
220-701
5.1

Securing data and other computer resources might seem like a never-ending task. Come to think of it, that's probably true. In this part of the chapter, you'll learn even more ways to secure a computer or small network, including hardware security devices, encryption techniques, BIOS security features, locking a workstation, protecting against malicious software, and educating users to not unintentionally compromise the security measures you've put in place.

SECURITY DEVICES TO PROTECT DATA AND COMPUTERS

Physically protecting your computer and data might be one of the security measures you implement. Here are some suggestions:

▲ *If your data is really private, keep it under lock and key.* You can use all kinds of security methods to encrypt, password protect, and hide data, but if it really is that important, one obvious thing you can do is store the data on a removable storage device such as a flash drive and, when you're not using the data, put the flash drive in a fireproof safe. And, of course, keep two copies. Sounds simple, but it works.

▲ *Lock down the computer case.* Some computer cases allow you to add a lock so that you can physically prevent others from opening the case (see Figure 19-28). Later in the chapter, you'll learn that some motherboards have a BIOS feature that alerts you when an intrusion has been detected.

▲ *Lock and chain.* You can also use a lock and chain to physically tie a computer to a desk or other permanent fixture so someone can't walk away with it. Figure 19-29 shows a cable lock system for a laptop. Most laptops have a security slot on the case to connect the cable lock.

▲ *Theft-prevention plate.* As an added precaution, physically mark a computer case or laptop so it can be identified if it is later stolen. You embed a theft-prevention plate into the case or engrave your ID information into it. The identifying numbers or bar

Figure 19-28 This computer case allows you to use a lock and key to keep intruders from opening the case
Courtesy of wesecure.com

Figure 19-29 Use a cable lock system to secure a notebook computer to a desk to help prevent it from being stolen
Courtesy of Kensington Technology Group

19

A+ 220-701

code identify you, the owner, and can also clearly establish to police that the notebook has been stolen. Two sources of theft-prevention plates and cable locks are Computer Security Products, Inc. (*www.computersecurity.com*) and Flexguard Security System (*www.flexguard.com*). To further help you identify stolen equipment, record serial numbers and model numbers in a safe place separate from the equipment.

Notebook computers are especially susceptible to thieves. Dell recently commissioned a study that showed that 12,000 laptops are stolen each year from United States airports. They also discovered that 65 percent of business travelers have not secured the corporate data on their hard drives, and 42 percent don't back up that data. Here are some common-sense rules to help protect your notebook:

◢ Use one or more Windows techniques in this chapter to protect the data on your laptop hard drive. Back up that data and don't keep the backup media in your laptop carrying case. If the case and laptop get stolen, at least you know the thief will not have easy access to your data and you have backups.

◢ When traveling, always know where your notebook is. If you're standing at an airport counter, tuck your notebook case securely between your ankles. At security checkpoints, pay attention to your belongings; tell yourself to stay focused. When flying, never check in your notebook as baggage, and don't store it in airplane overhead bins; keep it at your feet.

◢ Never leave a notebook in an unlocked car. If you leave your notebook in a hotel room, use a notebook cable lock to secure it to a table. When you're using your notebook, always lock down Windows before you walk away from it.

◢ Consider using laptop tracking software such as Computrace LoJack by Absolute Software (*www.absolute.com*). Install the software on your laptop. If the laptop is ever stolen and you report it to Absolute, the company accepts responsibility to track down the laptop. The laptop will report to Absolute the next time it connects to the Internet. Absolute then uses the information to locate the laptop and work with the police to return it to you. One feature of the software is to delete personal data on the laptop that might be used to steal your identity.

◢ When at work, lock your notebook in a secure place or use a notebook cable lock to secure it to your desk.

ENCRYPTION TECHNIQUES

Encryption puts data into code that must be translated before it can be accessed, and can be applied in several ways. Here are some of these encryption techniques:

◢ *Encrypt folders and files in Windows.* In Windows, files and folders can be encrypted using the Windows Encrypted File System (EFS). This encryption works only when using the Windows NTFS file system and the Windows Vista Ultimate and Business editions and Windows XP Professional. (Windows Vista and XP Home editions do not provide encryption.) If a folder is marked for encryption, every file created in the folder or copied to the folder will be encrypted. Encryption can apply only to this top-level folder, or it can apply to all subfolders in a folder (called inherited encryption). You can also encrypt individual files. Encrypting at the folder level in Windows is considered a best practice because it provides greater security: Any file placed in an encrypted folder is automatically encrypted so you don't have to remember to encrypt it. An encrypted file remains encrypted if you move it from an encrypted folder to an unencrypted folder on the same or another NTFS logical drive. A user does not have to go through a complex process of encryption to use EFS; from a user's perspective, it's just a matter of placing a file into a folder marked for encryption. In Windows Explorer, encrypted file and folder names are displayed in green.

◢ *Encrypt an entire hard drive.* BitLocker Encryption in Windows Vista Ultimate and Enterprise editions locks down a hard drive by encrypting the entire Vista volume and any other volume on the drive. It's a bit complicated to set up and has some restrictions that you need to be aware of before you decide to use it. It is intended to work in partnership with file and folder encryption to provide data security.

◢ *Encrypt wireless networks.* In Chapter 18, you learned how to set up a wireless network to use security. Recall from that chapter that wireless networks use WEP, WPA, or WPA2 encryption technologies. Also recall from Chapter 18 that another

A+
220-701
5.1

popular method to secure a wireless network is to change the name of the SSID and disable broadcasting that name.

▲ *Encryption used by a VPN.* Recall that a virtual private network (VPN) encrypts all transmissions to and from the client and the VPN server inside a corporate network. A VPN is considered a best practice to secure data and other network resources for those employees who travel or work from home or for trusted contractors.

▲ *Embedded encryption in devices.* Some devices such as laptops, USB flash drives, and external hard drives have built-in encryption features.

▲ *Other secured connections used for data transmissions.* Besides a VPN with a corporate network, many Web sites use secure connections to transmit sensitive data. Recall from Chapter 17 that one secure protocol used is HTTPS. You can use a similar encryption technique to encrypt your e-mail transmissions. To do that, you can download encryption software and install it into your e-mail client software. Most encryption software products use a method called Public Key Encryption, which is explained in Figure 19-30. Before you can send an encrypted message to someone, that person must first make available to you her public key. Note, however, that only she has the private key that is used to decrypt the message. Encryption software must be installed on both the sender's and receiver's e-mail client. One popular encryption software product is PGP (which stands for Pretty Good Privacy) by PGP Corporation (*na.store.pgp.com/desktop_email.html*). Encrypting Web site and e-mail transmissions usually involves using a digital certificate. Using a digital certificate ensures that you are who you say you are, and that someone else has not intercepted your transmission and is spoofing you (pretending to be you). Digital certificates are transported over the Internet and verified using PKI (Public-key Infrastructure) standards.

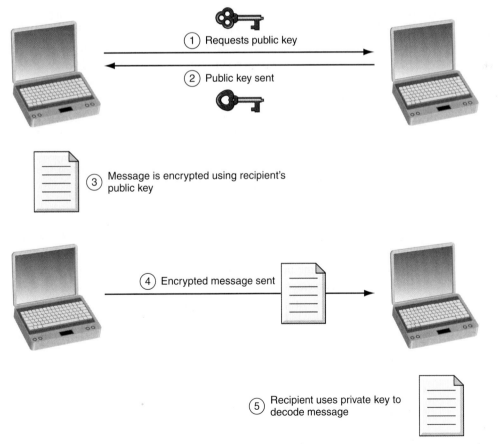

Figure 19-30 Public key encryption uses two keys: the recipient's public key to encrypt the message and her private key to decrypt it
Courtesy: Course Technology/Cengage Learning

19

A+ 220-701

A+
220-701
5.2

USE BIOS FEATURES TO PROTECT THE SYSTEM

Many motherboards for desktop and laptop computers offer several BIOS features designed to secure the system. Here is a quick summary of these methods:

▲ *Power-on passwords.* Earlier in the chapter, you learned about these passwords kept in CMOS RAM. They are set in BIOS setup and used to limit who can use the system or access BIOS setup.

▲ *Drive lock password protection.* Recall that some motherboards and hard drives allow you to set a password that must be entered before someone can access the hard drive. This password is kept on the drive and works even if the drive is moved to another computer. Some manufacturers of storage media offer similar products. For example, Seagate (*www.seagate.com*) offers Maxtor BlackArmor, a technology that encrypts an entire external storage media that is password protected.

> **Notes** Drive lock password protection might be too secure at times. I know of a situation where a hard drive with password protection became corrupted. Normally, you might be able to move the drive to another computer and recover some data. However, this drive asked for the password, but then could not confirm it. Therefore, the entire drive was inaccessible and all data was lost.

▲ *TPM (Trusted Platform Module) chip.* Many high-end computers have a chip on the motherboard called the **TPM (Trusted Platform Module) chip.** BitLocker is designed to work with this chip; the chip holds the BitLocker encryption key (also called the startup key). A notebook might be secured to a table or other fixture with a lock and chain. Even though a thief cannot steal the notebook, it's still possible to quickly remove the hard drive. If the hard drive is stolen from the notebook and installed in another computer, the data would be safe because BitLocker would not allow access without the startup key stored on the TPM chip. Therefore, this method assures that the drive cannot be used in another computer. However, if the motherboard fails and is replaced, you'll need a backup copy of the startup key to access data on the hard drive.

> **💡 A+ Exam Tip** The A+ 220-701 Essentials exam expects you to know about these BIOS security features: passwords, drive lock, TPM, and intrusion detection.

▲ *Intrusion detection.* A motherboard BIOS feature used primarily with servers is intrusion detection. A sensor device is installed inside the computer case and connected to a header (group of pins) on the motherboard. When the case cover is removed, the device sends an alert (called an interrupt), and BIOS records the event. If the power is turned off when the event occurs, the event is still recorded in BIOS. The sensor device can work by a switch or magnet that detects the cover is removed or a light sensor that detects light inside the case when the case is opened. Take a look at Figure 19-9, shown earlier in the chapter, where you can see the option to disable or enable Chassis Intrusion in BIOS setup. To use the intrusion detection feature on this system, Chassis Intrusion must be enabled.

▲ *Boot sector protection for the hard drive.* When you enable this protection, a boot sector virus cannot write to this sector. Figure 19-10, shown earlier in the chapter, shows the option enabled. Recall that the boot sector must be healthy if the hard drive is bootable. However, before you upgrade your OS, such as when you upgrade Windows Vista to Windows 7, be sure to enable writing to the boot sector, which the OS setup will want to do.

A+
220-701
5.2

LOCK A WORKSTATION

To keep a system secure, users need to practice the habit of locking down their workstation each time they step away from their desks. The quickest way to do this is to press the **Windows key** and L. Another method is to press **Ctrl-Alt-Del**. If the user is already logged on when she presses these keys, the login screen in Figure 19-31 appears for Vista. When the user clicks **Lock this computer**, Windows locks down. To unlock Windows, the user must enter her password. For this method to be effective, all user accounts need a password. You can use Group Policy to make passwords a requirement.

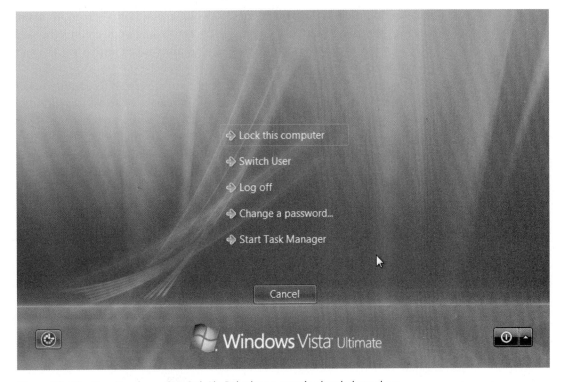

Figure 19-31 Results of pressing Crtl-Alt-Del when a user is already logged on
Courtesy: Course Technology/Cengage Learning

Also recall that when the system is powered down, power-on BIOS passwords can be required before the system can be used. For best security, use both hardware and software methods to lock a workstation.

PROTECT AGAINST MALICIOUS SOFTWARE

Malicious software, also called malware, or a computer infestation, is any unwanted program that means you harm and is transmitted to your computer without your knowledge. Grayware is any annoying and unwanted program that might or might not mean you harm. Many types of malware and grayware have evolved over the past few years, such as adware, spyware, and worms, and there is considerable overlap in what they do, how they spread, and how to get rid of them. In this part of the chapter, you'll learn about the different types of malware and grayware and how to protect a system from infection. In the next chapter, you'll learn how to clean up an infected system.

> **Notes** Malicious software is designed to do varying degrees of damage to data and software, although it does not damage PC hardware. However, when boot sector information is destroyed on a hard drive, the hard drive can appear to be physically damaged.

19

A+ 220-701

A+
220-701
5.2

WHAT ARE WE UP AGAINST?

You need to know your enemy! Different categories of malicious software and scamming techniques are listed next:

◢ A **virus** is a program that replicates by attaching itself to other programs. The infected program must be executed for a virus to run. The program might be an application, a macro in a document, a Windows system file, or one of the small programs at the beginning of the hard drive needed to boot the OS. (These programs are called the boot sector program and the master boot program.) The damage a virus does ranges from minor, such as displaying bugs crawling around on a screen, to major, such as erasing everything written on a hard drive or stealing your credit card information. The best way to protect against viruses is to always run antivirus (AV) software in the background.

◢ **Adware** produces all those unwanted pop-up ads. Adware is secretly installed on your computer when you download and install shareware or freeware, including screen savers, desktop wallpaper, music, cartoons, news, and weather alerts. Then it displays pop-up ads which might be based on your browsing habits (see Figure 19-32). Sometimes when you try to uninstall adware, it deletes whatever it was you downloaded that you really wanted to keep. And sometimes adware is also spying on you and collecting private information.

Figure 19-32   This pop-up window is luring the user to take the bait
Courtesy: Course Technology/Cengage Learning

◢ **Spyware** is software that installs itself on your computer to spy on you and to collect personal information about you that it transmits over the Internet to Web-hosting sites. These sites might use your personal data in harmless or harmful ways such as tailoring marketing information to suit your shopping habits, tracking marketing trends, or stealing your identity for harm. Spyware comes to you by way of e-mail attachments, downloaded freeware or shareware, instant messaging programs, or when you click a link on a malicious Web site.

> 💡 **A+ Exam Tip**   The A+ 220-701 Essentials exam expects you to know about viruses, Trojans, worms, spam, spyware, adware, and grayware and summarize security features to protect against them.

A+
220-701
5.2

◢ A **keylogger** tracks all your keystrokes, including passwords, chat room sessions, e-mail messages, documents, online purchases, and anything else you type on your PC. All this text is logged to a text file and transmitted over the Internet without your knowledge. A keylogger is a type of spyware that can be used to steal a person's identity, credit card numbers, Social Security number, bank information, passwords, e-mail addresses, and so forth.

◢ A **worm** is a program that copies itself throughout a network or the Internet without a host program. A worm creates problems by overloading the network as it replicates. Worms cause damage by their presence rather than by performing a specific damaging act, as a virus does. A worm overloads memory or hard drive space by replicating repeatedly. When a worm (for example, Sasser or W32.Sobig.F@mm) is loose on the Internet, it can cause damage such as sending mass e-mailings. The best way to protect against worms is to use a firewall. Antivirus software also offers protection.

◢ A **browser hijacker**, also called a home page hijacker, does mischief by changing your home page and other browser settings. Figure 19-33 shows Internet Explorer after a user tried to install a free game downloaded from the Internet. The program installed two new toolbars in his browser and changed his home page. Browser hijackers can set unwanted bookmarks, redirect your browser to a shopping site when you type in a wrong URL, produce pop-up ads, and direct your browser to Web sites that offer pay-per-view pornography.

Figure 19-33   Internet Explorer with toolbars installed and home page changed
Courtesy: Course Technology/Cengage Learning

◢ **Spam** is junk e-mail that you don't want, you didn't ask for, and that gets in your way.
◢ A **virus hoax** or e-mail hoax is e-mail that does damage by tempting you to forward it to everyone in your e-mail address book, with the intent of clogging up e-mail systems or tempting you to delete a critical Windows system file by convincing you the file is malicious. Also, some e-mail scam artists promise to send you money if you'll circulate their e-mail messages to thousands of people. I recently received one that was supposedly promising money from Microsoft for "testing" the strength of the Internet e-mail

system. Beware! Always check Web sites that track virus hoaxes before pressing that Send button! Your AV software Web site most likely keeps a database of virus hoaxes. Here are some other good sites to help you debunk a virus hoax:

- *www.hoaxkill.com* by Oxcart Software
- *www.snopes.com* by Barbara and David Mikkelson
- *www.viruslist.com* by Kaspersky Lab
- *www.vmyths.com* by Rhode Island Soft Systems, Inc.

When you get a hoax, if you know the person who sent it to you, do us all a favor and send that person some of these links!

⬛ Phishing (pronounced "fishing") is a type of identity theft where the sender of an e-mail message scams you into responding with personal data about yourself. The scam artist baits you by asking you to verify personal data on your bank account, ISP account, credit card account, or something of that nature. Often you are tricked into clicking a link in the e-mail message, which takes you to an official-looking site complete with corporate or bank logos where you are asked to enter your user ID and password to enter the site.

⬛ Scam artists use scam e-mail to lure you into their scheme. One scam e-mail I recently received was supposedly from the secretary of a Russian oil tycoon who was being held in jail with his millions of dollars of assets frozen. If I would respond to the e-mail and get involved, I was promised a 12 percent commission to help recover the funds.

⬛ A logic bomb is dormant code added to software and triggered at a predetermined time or by a predetermined event. For instance, an employee might put code in a program to destroy important files if his or her name is ever removed from the payroll file.

⬛ A Trojan horse does not need a host program to work; rather, it substitutes itself for a legitimate program. In most cases, a user launches it thinking she is launching a legitimate program. Figure 19-34 shows a pop-up that appears when you're surfing the Web. Click OK and you might introduce a Trojan into your system. A Trojan is likely to introduce one or more viruses into the system. These Trojans are called downloaders. A Trojan sometimes installs a backdoor in the system, which is a hidden way to allow malware to reach the system in secret even after the Trojan has been removed.

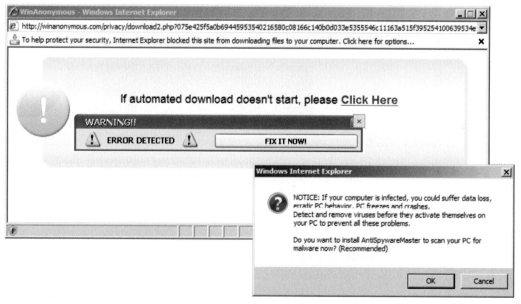

Figure 19-34 Clicking an action button on a pop-up window might invite a Trojan into your system
Courtesy: Course Technology/Cengage Learning

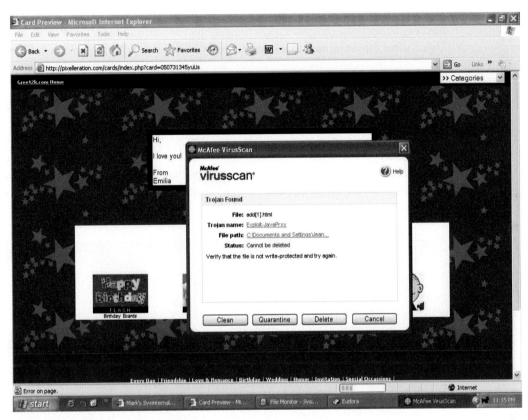

Last year, I got fooled with a Trojan when I got an e-mail message near the actual date of my birthday from someone named Emilia, whom I thought I knew. Without thinking, I clicked the link in the e-mail message to "View my birthday card to you." Figure 19-35 shows what happened when I clicked.

Figure 19-35 A Trojan can get in when you click a link in an e-mail message
Courtesy: Course Technology/Cengage Learning

A virus attacks your computer system and hides in several different ways. A **boot sector virus** can hide in either of two boot sectors of a hard drive. It can hide in the master boot program, which is the boot program in the very first 512-byte sector of a hard drive called the master boot record (MBR). A boot sector virus can also hide in the OS boot program of a hard drive, floppy disk, or other boot media. Recall that the OS boot program is stored in the first sector of the volume on which Windows is installed, called the active partition. For most hard drives, this OS boot sector is the second sector on the drive, following the MBR.

A **file virus** hides in an executable program having an .exe, .com, .sys, .vbs, or other executable file extension, or in a word-processing document that contains a macro. A **multipartite virus** is a combination of a boot sector virus and a file virus and can hide in either. A **macro** is a small program contained in a document that can be automatically executed either when the document is first loaded or later by pressing a key combination. For example, a word-processing macro might automatically read the system date and copy it into a document when you open the document. Viruses that hide in macros of document files are called macro viruses. **Macro viruses** are the most common viruses spread by e-mail, hiding in macros of attached document files. A **script virus** is a virus that hides in a script, which might execute when you click a link on a Web page or in an HTML e-mail message or when you attempt to open an e-mail attachment.

A+
220-701
5.2

One type of malware, called a rootkit, loads itself before the OS boot is complete. Because it is already loaded when the AV software loads, it is sometimes overlooked by AV software. In addition, a rootkit hijacks internal Windows components so that it masks information Windows provides to user mode utilities such as Task Manager, Windows Explorer, the registry editor, and AV software. This helps it remain undetected. Rootkits can also install a backdoor (called a backdoor rootkit) that can be used by malware or hackers to secretly gain access even after the rootkit has been cleaned from the system. Using a backdoor, a hacker can sometimes hijack the system, gaining full control of it.

HOW TO PROTECT AGAINST MALICIOUS SOFTWARE

The best practices you need to follow to protect a system against malicious software and other grayware are listed next. The first three methods are the most important ones:

▲ *Always use a software firewall.* Never, ever connect your computer to an unprotected network without using a firewall. Recall that Windows Firewall can be configured to allow no uninvited communication in or to allow in the exceptions that you specify (see Figure 19-36).

Figure 19-36 A software firewall protecting a computer
Courtesy: Course Technology/Cengage Learning

> **Notes** Even with Windows Firewall, Microsoft still recommends that you use a hardware firewall to protect your system from attack. Software firewalls are better than no firewall at all, but a hardware firewall offers greater protection.

▲ *Use antivirus (AV) software.* As a defensive and offensive measure to protect against malicious software, install and run antivirus (AV) software and keep it current. Configure the AV software so that it automatically downloads updates to the software and runs in the background. To be effective, AV software must be kept current and must be turned on. Set the AV software to automatically scan incoming e-mail attachments.

▲ *Use the Vista UAC box.* The UAC box is one of your best defenses against malware installing itself. When software attempts to install in Vista, the UAC box appears. If you don't respond to the box, Windows aborts the installation.

A+
220-701
5.2

▲ *Limit the use of administrator accounts.* If malware installs itself while you're logged on as an administrator, it will most likely be running under this account with more privileges and the ability to do more damage than if you had been logged on under a less powerful account. Use an account with lesser privileges for your everyday normal computer activities.

▲ *Set Internet Explorer for optimum security.* Internet Explorer includes the pop-up blocker, the ability to manage add-ons, the ability to block scripts and disable scripts embedded in Web pages, and the ability to set the general security level. Figure 19-37 shows the Internet Options window where many of these options are configured. For most Web browsing, set the security level to Medium-high, as shown in the figure. Also consider updating IE to the latest version because later versions are likely to have enhanced security features.

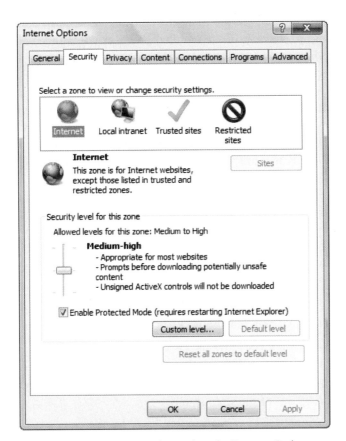

Figure 19-37 Control security settings for Internet Explorer
Courtesy: Course Technology/Cengage Learning

▲ *Use alternate client software.* Using alternate client software, including browsers and e-mail clients, can give you an added layer of protection from malicious software that targets Microsoft products. Firefox by Mozilla (*www.mozilla.org*) is an excellent browser, and Thunderbird, also by Mozilla, is a popular e-mail client. Some people even use a different OS than Windows because of security issues.

> **Notes** You might want to also consider using an alternate e-mail address. When you have to give an e-mail address to companies that you suspect might sell your address to spammers, use a second e-mail address that you don't use for normal e-mailing.

19

A+ 220-701

A+
220-701
5.2

▲ *Keep good backups.* One of the more important chores of securing a computer is to prepare in advance for disaster to strike. One of the most important things you can do to prepare for disaster is to make good backups of user data.

A+
220-701
5.1

EDUCATE USERS

Generally speaking, the weakest link in setting up security in a computer environment is people. That's because people can often be tricked into giving out private information. Even with all the news and hype about identify theft and criminal Web sites, it's amazing how well these techniques still work. Many users naively download a funny screen saver, open an e-mail attachment, or enter credit card information into a Web site, without regard to security. In the computer arena, social engineering is the practice of tricking people into giving out private information or allowing unsafe programs into the network or computer.

A good support technician is aware of the criminal practices used, and is able to teach users how to recognize this mischief and avoid it. Here is a list of important security measures that users need to follow:

▲ Never give out your passwords to anyone, not even a supervisor or tech support person who calls and asks for it. These people should know how to access the system without passwords that belong to someone else. Also, don't give out your account names. These account names are usually easy to guess, but, still, you shouldn't compromise them by giving them to others.

▲ Don't store your passwords on a computer. Some organizations even forbid employees from writing down their passwords.

▲ Don't use the same password on more than one system (computer, network, or application).

▲ Lock down your workstation each time you step away from your desk. Here are some ways to do that:

- Press the **Windows key** and L (the quickest method).
- Press **Ctrl-Alt-Del** and choose **Lock this computer** from the menu.
- For Vista, click **Start** and the lock icon (see Figure 19-38).
- For Vista, put the system into a sleep state. One way to do that is to use the sleep button shown in Figure 19-38. (You must enter a password to take Vista out of the sleep state.)
- Power down the system when you leave for the day.

Figure 19-38 Use the Vista Start menu to lock a computer
Courtesy: Course Technology/Cengage Learning

▲ Beware of social engineering techniques. Don't be fooled by phishing techniques such as the e-mail shown in Figure 19-39. When the user who received this e-mail scanned the attached file using antivirus software, the software reported the file contained a Trojan program (see Figure 19-40).

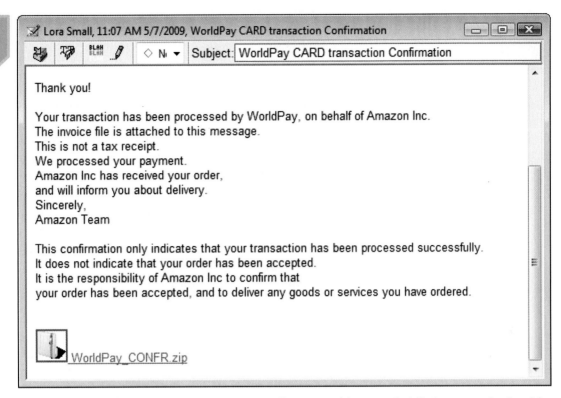

Figure 19-39   This phishing technique using an e-mail message with an attached file is an example of social engineering
Courtesy: Course Technology/Cengage Learning

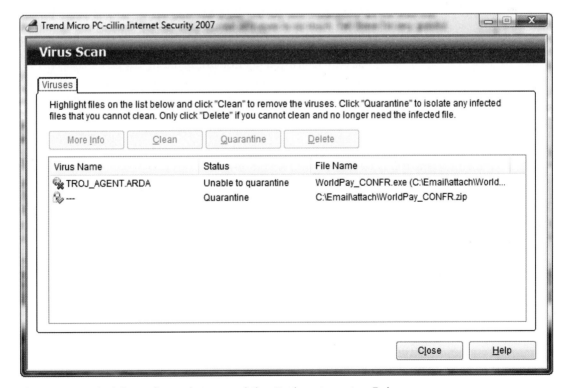

Figure 19-40   Antivirus software that scanned the attachment reports a Trojan
Courtesy: Course Technology/Cengage Learning

A+
220-701
5.1
5.2

A+ Tip The A+ 220-701 Essentials exam expects you to be aware of social engineering situations that might compromise security.

◢ Exercise good judgment when using the Internet, so that you don't compromise security. Here are six rules that can help you use the Internet responsibly:

- *Don't open e-mail attachments without scanning them for viruses first.* In fact, if you don't know the person who sent you the attachment, save yourself a lot of trouble and just delete it without opening it.

- *Don't click links inside e-mail messages.* These links might contain a malicious script. For example, you receive spam in your e-mail, open it, and click the link "Remove me" to supposedly get removed from the spam list. However, by doing so, you spread a virus or worm, or install adware onto your PC. Also, a link that appears to contain a URL might actually contain a script. For example, the e-mail text, "Click *www.symantec.com* to read about the latest virus attack," appears to have a link to the Symantec Web site, but rather points to *www.symantec.com.vbs*, which is a script embedded in the e-mail message. To keep the script from running, copy and paste the link to your browser address bar instead.

- *Don't forward an e-mail message without first checking to see if that warning is a hoax.* Save us all the time of having to delete the thing from our Inbox.

- *Always check out a Web site before you download anything from it.* Freeware isn't so free if you end up with an infected computer. Only download from trusted sites. Free music and video sites are notorious for distributing malware.

- *Never give your private information to just any ole Web site.* Use a search engine and search for information about a site before you trust it with your identity.

- *Never trust an e-mail message asking you to verify your private data on a Web site with which you do business.* If you receive an e-mail that looks like it came from your bank, your PayPal account, or your utility company, don't click those links in that message. If you think it might be legitimate, open your browser, type in the link to the business's Web site, and check out the request.

PERFORM ROUTINE SECURITY MAINTENANCE

A+
220-701
5.1
2.5

When you are responsible for the security of a computer or small network, make it a habit to check every computer for which you are responsible each month. You can use the following checklist. However, know that routine maintenance tends to evolve over time based on an organization's past problems that might need special attention. Start with this list and then add to it as the need arises:

1. Change the administrator password. (Use a strong password.)

2. Check that Windows Automatic Updates is turned on and working. For applications that users routinely rely on, you might also download and install any critical or optional updates.

3. Check that AV software is installed and current. If you are running antiadware software, also verify that it is running and current.

4. Verify that Windows Firewall is turned on. Also, verify that port security is set so that only the exceptions made to open ports are those the users of this computer need to do their jobs.

5. If you are the only user with administrative privileges of this computer, verify that Windows settings are as you intend. For example, check that important folders are shared and encrypted as you set them and that only authorized software is installed.

6. Visually check the equipment to make sure the case has not been tampered with. Is the lock secure?

7. Check Event Viewer. Take a look at the Security list, looking for failed attempts to access the system.

8. Verify that user backups of data are being done and current backups of data exist. Also verify that System Protection is set to automatically create restore points.

9. If you find you must replace storage media, don't forget to destroy all data on the media before you throw it away. If a computer is changing users or you are moving a hard drive from one computer to another, be sure to wipe clean all data on the drive. Most hard drive manufactures offer a zero-fill utility for this purpose. The utility overwrites every sector of the drive with zeros. Recall from Chapter 11 that this method works for normal security within an organization. However, if you need to destroy data so that expert criminals can't recover destroyed, deleted, or overwritten data, you'll need to use stronger methods like those discussed in Chapter 11.

10. Document your monthly maintenance and note anything unusual that you see or must change.

As a part of managing the security of a computer or network, your organization might make you accountable to fill out an incident report of unusual or atypical events. Incidents that you might be expected to report can include an attempt at breaking in to a secured computer or network, the security has been broken, an accident has occurred, property has been lost or damaged, a hazard has been reported, an alarm has been activated, unauthorized changes to a system or its data were made, or other such events. Reasons for incident reporting include the need for others to respond to an incident, the need to know about a weak security loophole that can be plugged, the need to be aware of trends in problems over the entire organization, and legal concerns.

For large networks, a computerized incident reporting tool is most likely already in place and your responsibility might be to learn how to use it, to know your user account and password to the system, and to make sure you report all incidents in a timely manner. On the other hand, old-fashioned paper reporting might be used. Either way, the incident-reporting forms will most likely include your name, job title, contact information, and full description of the incident. The description might include the system or systems affected, the people involved, the resulting damage, and if the problem is resolved or still active. Also included might be your recommendations or actions to resolve the problem.

>> CHAPTER SUMMARY

▲ Compliance with de facto or legal security policies might be required for a company or professional to do business. Ignorance of legal security requirements is not an excuse that will justify noncompliance.

▲ Implemented security measures must balance between protection (keeping resources safe) and functionality (not hindering workers doing their jobs).

▲ Controlling access to secured resources uses two techniques: authentication and authorization. Authentication proves a person or program is who they say they are. Authorization includes classifying users and data and deciding which users have access to which data resources.

▲ BIOS on the motherboard can be used to set power-on passwords and drive lock passwords to authenticate users.

▲ Other methods to authenticate users include Windows logon passwords, smart cards, and biometric data. Biometric data is not considered as secure as passwords and smart cards.

▲ Strong passwords are passwords that are not easy to guess.

▲ Windows Vista classifies user accounts as administrative accounts, standard accounts, and guest accounts. Windows XP uses these classifications: administrative accounts, limited accounts, power user accounts, backup operator accounts, and guest accounts. The account type determines the rights assigned to the user. These rights can be increased by adding the account to a new user group.

▲ When classifying data, consider the security policies with which your organization must comply, who owns each data folder, and categories of classifications. Don't forget to classify and protect backup media just as you would the original data.

▲ Security devices used to protect data and computers include fireproof safes, locks and chains, and theft-prevention plates.

▲ Encryption is putting data into code that cannot be read without a key to that code. Encryption techniques are encrypting files and folders in Windows, BitLocker Encryption to encrypt a hard drive, wireless network encryption (WEP, WAP, and WAP2), VPNs, and encrypting e-mail and Web site transmissions. This last type of encryption usually involves a digital certificate. The digital certificate proves that someone is who they say they are.

▲ Security features used by BIOS include power-on passwords, drive lock passwords, TPM chips, intrusion detection, and boot sector protection. The TPM chip is used to hold the encryption key for Windows Vista BitLocker Encryption.

▲ You can lock down a workstation using Windows. Press the Windows key and L, and then a password is required to continue using Windows. When you first turn on a computer, BIOS power-on passwords can also be used to lock down the system.

▲ Malicious software or grayware can include viruses, adware, spyware, keyloggers, worms, browser hijackers, spam e-mail, virus hoax e-mail, scam e-mail, logic bombs, and Trojans. Phishing techniques can be used to lure you into downloading or opening a malicious program.

▲ Techniques to protect against malware or grayware include firewalls, antivirus software, the Vista UAC box, limiting the use of the administrator account, Internet Explorer security settings, using alternate e-mail and browser software, and keeping good backups.

▲ Users need to know how to protect passwords, lock a workstation, and avoid social engineering attempts.

▲ When you are responsible for the security of a system, check security settings and software monthly and know how to report an incident if security is threatened.

>> KEY TERMS

For explanations of key terms, see the Glossary near the end of the book.

administrator account	guest account	power user account
adware	incident report	Public Key Encryption
antivirus (AV) software	infestation	rootkit
authentication	Kerberos	scam e-mail
authorization	key fob	script virus
backdoor	keylogger	smart card
backup operator	limited account	smart card reader
BitLocker Encryption	logic bomb	social engineering
boot sector virus	macro	spam
browser hijacker	macro viruses	spyware
CHAP (Challenge Handshake	malicious software	standard account
Authentication Protocol)	malware	strong password
data classifications	multipartite virus	TPM (Trusted Platform Module)
digital certificate	network drive map	chip
drive lock password	passphrase	Trojan horse
Encrypted File System (EFS)	password reset disk	virus
encryption	permissions	virus hoax
file virus	phishing	worm
grayware	PKI (Public-key Infrastructure)	zero-fill utility

>> REVIEWING THE BASICS

1. What industry is required by law to use the HIPAA security standards?

2. Classifying the rights assigned to a computer user depends on what one factor?

3. What applet in the XP Control Panel is used to reset a password?

4. What must a user do in order to use his password reset disk to log onto Windows?

5. Name three types of passwords that can be set in BIOS setup.

6. What is the default encryption protocol that Windows uses when sending an account name and password to a domain controller for validation?

7. What is the name for a small device that contains authentication information keyed into a logon window to gain access to a network?

8. What is the purpose of a digital certificate?

9. Who assigns a digital certificate?

10. Why is the name of your pet not a strong password?

11. In what situation might a blank password be better than an easy-to-guess password?

12. Which has more rights, a standard account or a guest account?

13. What folder in Vista is intended to be used for folders and files that all users share?

14. What file system must be used in order to encrypt folders and files in Windows Vista or XP?

15. What Vista tool can be used to encrypt an entire hard drive?

16. What is the purpose of the TPM chip on a motherboard?

17. What is the quickest way to lock down a Windows workstation?

18. Which type of malware can copy itself over a network without involving a host program?

19

19. Which type of malware substitutes itself for a legitimate program?

20. Why is it important to not click a link in an e-mail message from someone you don't know?

>> THINKING CRITICALLY

1. If you have Windows Firewall set not to allow any exceptions and keep all ports closed, which of the following activities will be allowed, and which will not be allowed? Explain your answer.

   a. You receive e-mail.

   b. You receive an MSN Messenger notice that a friend wants to have a chat session with you.

   c. Your antivirus software informs you a new update has just been downloaded and installed.

   d. You log into the computer from a remote location on the Internet using Remote Desktop.

2. Your organization has set up three levels of data classification accessed by users on a small network:

   ▲ Low security: Data in the C:\Public folder.
   ▲ Medium security: Data in a shared folder that some, but not all, user groups can access.
   ▲ High security: Data in a shared and encrypted folder that requires a password to access. The folder is shared only to one user group.

   Classify each of the sets of data:

   a. Directions to the company Fourth of July party

   b. Details of an invention made by the company president that has not yet been patented

   c. Resumes presented by several people applying for a job with the company

   d. Payroll spreadsheets

   e. Job openings at the company

3. You work in the Accounting Department and have been using a network drive to post Excel spreadsheets to your workgroup file server as you complete them. When you attempt to save a spreadsheet to the drive, you see the error message: "You do not have access to the folder 'J:\'. See your administrator for access to this folder." What should you do first? Second? Explain the reasoning behind your choices.

   a. Ask your network administrator to give you permission to access the folder.

   b. Check the Network window to verify that you can connect to the network.

   c. Save the spreadsheet to your hard drive.

   d. Using Windows Explorer, remap the network drive.

   e. Reboot your PC.

>> HANDS-ON PROJECTS

PROJECT 19-1:   E-Mail Hoax

Search through your spam and junk mail for an e-mail you think might be a hoax. (Please don't click any links or open any attachments as you search.) Using the Web sites listed earlier in the chapter for debunking virus hoaxes, search for information about this potential hoax. You might need to enter the subject line in the e-mail message into a search box on the Web site.

PROJECT 19-2:   Using Firefox

Go to the Mozilla Web site (*www.mozilla.org*) and download and install Firefox. Use it to browse the Web. How does it compare to Internet Explorer? What do you like better about it? What do you not like as well? When might you recommend to someone that they use Firefox rather than Internet Explorer? Also, download the FoxFilter plug-in from *www.mozilla.org* and install it. What are the differences between FoxFilter and the IE content filter?

PROJECT 19-3:   Using a Port Scanner

Port scanning software can be used to find out how vulnerable a computer is with open ports. This project will require the use of two computers on the same network to practice using port scanning software. Do the following:

1. Download and install Advanced Port Scanner by Famatech at *www.radmin.com* on Computer 1.

2. On Computer 2, make sure that Windows Firewall is turned on and that the **Block all incoming connections** box is checked. Also, disable any third-party personal firewalls.

3. On Computer 1, start Advanced Port Scanner and make sure that the range of IP addresses includes the IP address of Computer 2. Then click **Scan**.

4. Browse the list and find Computer 2. List the number and purpose of all open ports found on your Computer 2.

5. On Computer 2, turn Windows Firewall off.

6. On Computer 1, rescan and list the number and purpose of each port now open on Computer 2.

If Computer 2 has another personal firewall installed, turn on that firewall. On Computer 1, rescan and list the number and purpose of each port now open on Computer 2 when the personal firewall is running.

PROJECT 19-4:   Managing User Accounts

Do the following to experiment with managing user accounts:

1. Using Windows Vista, create a Standard user account and log on using that account. Can you view the contents of the Documents folder for an account with Administrator privileges?

2. Using the Standard account, try to install a program. What message do you receive?

3. What happens if you try to create a new account while logged on under the Standard account?

PROJECT 19-5:   Using Password Checker

Microsoft offers a password checker for users to know the strength of their passwords. To use the utility, go to the Microsoft Web site at *www.microsoft.com* and search for

19

"Password Checker." Use this free Microsoft utility to verify that a password you have made up is a strong password. Based on the measure of the strength of several of your passwords, what do you think the password checker is looking for?

>> REAL PROBLEMS, REAL SOLUTIONS

REAL PROBLEM 19-1: Require Passwords for User Accounts

To better secure Windows and shared resources, all user accounts on a system need a password. Using Windows Vista Ultimate or Business editions, follow these steps to use Group Policy to require that each user account on a PC have a password:

1. In the Start Search box, enter **gpedit.msc**, press **Enter** and respond to the UAC box.

2. Drill down to the **Computer Configuration, Windows Settings, Security Settings, Account Policies,** and **Password Policy** (see the left side of Figure 19-41).

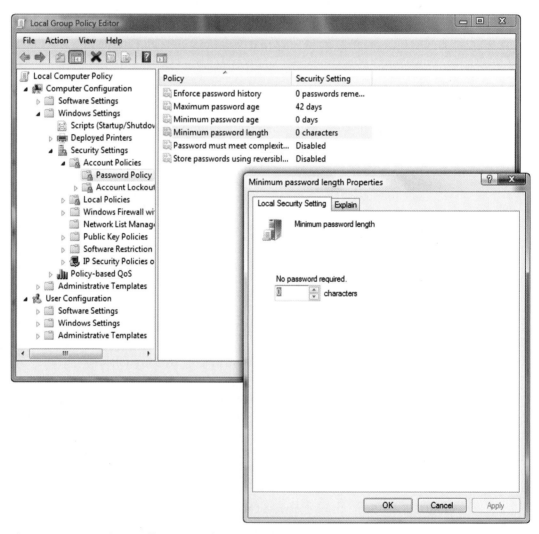

Figure 19-41   Use Group Policy to control user account passwords
Courtesy: Course Technology/Cengage Learning

3. Double-click the **Minimum password length** policy. The Properties box for the policy appears (see the right side of Figure 19-41). Enter the value of 8 for the minimum password length. Click **Apply** and **OK** to close the box.

4. List the other policies that can be set to control Windows passwords and a one-sentence description of that policy. The Explain tab in the policy's Properties box can help.

5. Close the Group Policy window.

6. Try to reset your Windows password to all blanks. What error message do you receive?

REAL PROBLEM 19-2: Recovering From a Forgotten Windows Password

Forgotten passwords can be a messy problem if you have not made a password reset disk. If you have forgotten the password for a Windows user account and you know the password for an administrator account, you can log on as an administrator and reset the forgotten password. If you don't know a password for any Windows account, here are some password recovery utilities that can help. Research each utility and describe its approach to helping with forgotten passwords and how much the utility costs. Which of the three utilities would you select for purchase and why?

▲ Ophcrack by phpBB Group at *ophcrack.sourceforge.net*

▲ Active Password Changer at *www.password-changer.com*

▲ Windows Password Reset at *ResetWindowsPassword.com*

19

Security Practices

I n Chapter 19, you learned *what* you need to do to secure a computer and its resources. In this chapter, you learn *how* to do it. In
Chapter 19, you learned the concepts and principles of classifying
users and data and protecting that data by encrypting it and applying
appropriate permissions to the data so only the authorized users can
access it. You also learned about the dangers of malicious software
and the methods to protect against it.

In this chapter, you'll learn how to apply strict sharing permissions
to data and how to encrypt data. You'll also learn how to use BIOS
features to secure a workstation. You'll also learn how to recognize
that a system is infected with malware and how to clean an infected
system.

> 💡 **A+ Exam Tip** All the content in this chapter applies to the security objectives
> of the A+ 220–702 Practical Application exam.

CONTROLLING ACCESS TO COMPUTER RESOURCES

A+
220-702
4.2

When you're responsible for controlling access to computer resources, you need to know how to control access to data folders and files, how to hide network resources, and how to use encryption technologies such as the Windows Encrypted File System (EFS) and BitLocker Encryption. You also need to know how to use BIOS features to control security. All these types of access control are covered in this part of the chapter.

CONTROLLING ACCESS TO DATA FOLDERS AND FILES

When controlling access to data folders or files, permissions to these resources are assigned to individual user accounts or user groups. Vista and XP offer several user account groups to help classify users and manage their rights on the system. Recall that Vista offers the administrator, standard user, and guest accounts, and Windows XP offers the administrator, power user, limited user (also called the users group), and guest accounts. In addition, other user groups exist, and you can create your own user groups. Recall from Chapter 19 that access control based on job descriptions is best done by creating a user group for each job class and then assigning data permissions to these groups.

Before we get into the details of how to control access with user groups, you need to be aware of these types of default user groups, which Windows might use when assigning permissions to a file or folder:

▲ The Authenticated Users group includes all user accounts that can access the system except the Guest account. These accounts include domain accounts (the user has logged onto the domain) and local accounts (the user has logged onto the local computer). The accounts might or might not require a password. When you create a folder or file that is not part of your user profile, by default, Windows gives access to all Authenticated Users.

▲ The Everyone group includes the Authenticated Users group as well as the Guest account. When you share a file or folder on the network, by default, Windows gives access to the Everyone group.

▲ Anonymous users are those users who have not been authenticated on a remote computer. If you log onto a computer using a local account and then attempt to access a remote computer, you must be authenticated on the remote computer. You will be authenticated if your user account and password on both computers match. If you logged onto your local computer with an account and password that do not match one on the remote computer, you are considered an anonymous user on the remote computer. As an anonymous user, you might be allowed to view shared resources on the remote computer in your Network or My Network Places window, but you cannot access them.

Now let's look at the details of how to control access to files and folders.

APPLYING | CONCEPTS   Nicole is responsible for a peer-to-peer network for a medical doctor's office. Four computers are connected to the small company network; one of these computers acts as the file server for the network. Nicole has created two classifications of data, Financial and Medical. Two workers (Nancy and Adam) require access to the Medical data, and two workers (Linda and Jose) require access to the

A+
220-702
4.2

Financial folder. In addition, the doctor, John, requires access to both categories of data. Here is what Nicole must do to set up the users and data:

1. Create folders named Financial and Medical on the file server. Create five user accounts, one for John, Nancy, Adam, Linda, and Jose. All the accounts belong to the Vista standard user group or the XP limited user group. Create two user groups, Financial and Medical.

2. Set the permissions on the Financial and Medical folders for local users so that only the members of the appropriate group can access each folder.

3. Share the folders on the network so that users in the Financial and Medical groups can access them from remote computers.

4. Test the access to both folders using test data and then copy all real data into the two folders and subfolders. Set up a backup plan for the two folders as you learned to do in Chapter 13.

Let's look at how each of these four steps is done.

STEP 1: CREATE FOLDERS, USER ACCOUNTS, AND USER GROUPS

Follow these steps to create the folders, user accounts, and user groups on the file server computer that is using Windows Vista Ultimate or Business editions or Windows XP Professional:

1. Log onto the system as an administrator.

2. Create the two folders C:\Financial and C:\Medical.

3. Open the Computer Management console and create user accounts for John, Nancy, Adam, Linda, and Jose. To create a new user, right-click **Users** under **Local Users and Groups** and select **New User** from the shortcut menu. (Vista and XP Home editions don't include the Local Users and Groups option in the Computer Management console.) Enter information for the new user and click **Create** (see Figure 20-1). The user will automatically be added to the Vista standard or XP limited user group.

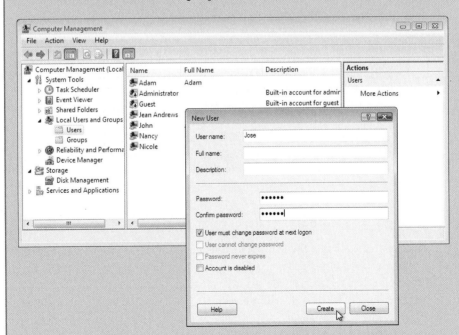

Figure 20-1 Create a new user
Courtesy: Course Technology/Cengage Learning

20

A+ 220-702

4. To create the Financial user group, right-click **Groups** under Local Users and Groups and select **New Group** from the shortcut menu. The New Group box appears. Enter the name of the group and its description (see the left side of Figure 20-2).

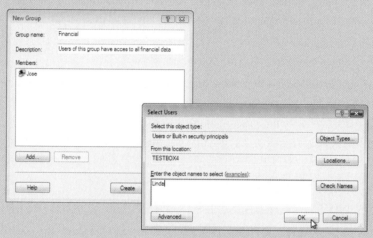

Figure 20-2 Set up a new user group
Courtesy: Course Technology/Cengage Learning

5. To add members to the Financial group, click **Add**. The Select Users box open, as shown on the right side of Figure 20-2. Under *Enter the object names to select*, enter the name of a user and click **OK**. Add all the users that need access to financial data (Jose, Linda, and John). To create the group, click **Create** in the New Group box.

6. In the same way, create the Medical group and add John, Nancy, and Adam to the group. Later, you can use the Computer Management console to add or remove users from either group.

7. Close the Computer Management console.

> **Note** If you need to change the rights of a user account to the administrator's level, use the Computer Management console and add the user to the administrators group.

> **A+ Exam Tip** The A+ 220–702 Practical Application exam expects you to be able to set up a user account or group and know how to change the group to which an account is assigned.

STEP 2: SET PERMISSIONS FOR LOCAL USERS

Windows XP uses **simple file sharing** by default, which means you have no control over who has access to a shared folder or file. (By default, Windows Vista does not use simple file sharing.) For Windows XP, to disable simple file sharing so that you have more control over access and can monitor that access, open the **Folder Options** applet in Control Panel and click the **View** tab of the Folder Options box (see Figure 20-3). Scroll down to the bottom of the **Advanced settings** list, uncheck **Use simple file sharing (Recommended)** and click **Apply**. Close the window.

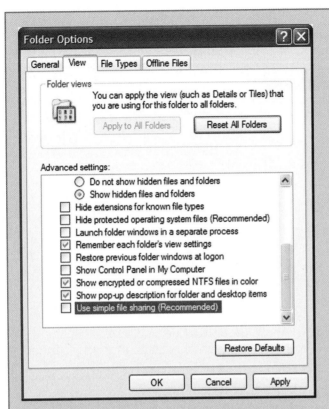

Figure 20-3 Turn off Windows XP simple file sharing so that you have
more control over access to files and folders
Courtesy: Course Technology/Cengage Learning

Follow these steps to set the permissions for the two folders and share the folders using Vista.
However, know that the XP steps work about the same way:

1. Open Windows Explorer, right-click the **Financial** folder, and select **Properties** from the
shortcut menu. The Properties box for the folder appears. Click the **Security** tab (see the
right side of Figure 20-4). (In Windows XP, the Security tab is missing until simple file
sharing is disabled.) Notice in the box, that Authenticated Users, SYSTEM, Administrators,
and Users all have access to the C:\Financial folder. When you select a user group, the
type of permissions assigned to that group appear in the Permissions for Users area. Note
that the Administrators group has full control of the folder. Also notice the checks under
Allow are dimmed. These permissions are dimmed because they have been inherited from
the parent object. **Inherited permissions** are permissions that are attained from a parent
object. In this case, the parent object is Vista default settings. However, if a folder has a
subfolder, the folder is the parent of the subfolder, and the subfolder inherits the permissions of its parent folder. **Permission propagation** is when permissions are passed from
parent to child.

2. To remove the inherited status from these permissions so we can change them, click
Advanced. The Advanced Security Settings box appears. Click **Edit**. You
can now uncheck **Include inheritable permissions from this object's parent** (see
Figure 20-5). A Windows Security warning box appears, also shown in
Figure 20-5. To keep the current permissions, but remove the inherited status placed on
them, click **Copy**.

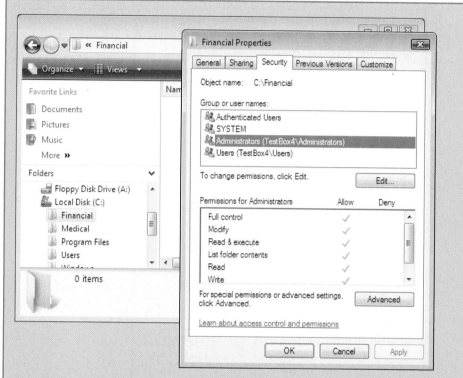

Figure 20-4 Permissions assigned to the Financial folder
Courtesy: Course Technology/Cengage Learning

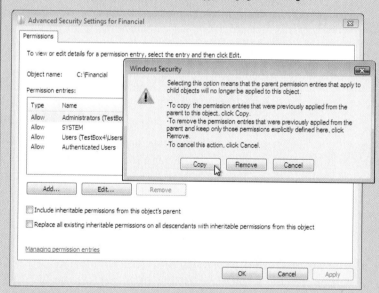

Figure 20-5 Remove the inherited status from the current permissions
Courtesy: Course Technology/Cengage Learning

3. Click **Apply** and click **OK** twice to close the Advanced Security Settings box.

4. In the Financial Properties box, notice the permissions are now checked in black, indicating they are no longer inherited permissions and can be changed. Click **Edit** to change these permissions.

5. The Permissions box opens (see Figure 20-6). Select the **Users** group and click **Remove**. Also remove the **Authenticated Users** group. Don't remove the SYSTEM group. Also, don't remove the Administrators group so that an administrator can access the data.

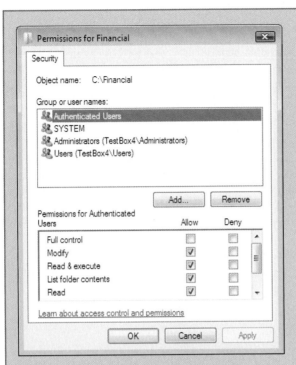

Figure 20-6 Change the permissions to a folder
Courtesy: Course Technology/Cengage Learning

6. To add a new group, click **Add**. The Select Users or Groups box opens (see Figure 20-7). Under *Enter the object names to select*, type **Financial** and click **OK**. The Financial group is added to the list of groups and users for this folder.

Figure 20-7 Add a user or group to shared permissions
Courtesy: Course Technology/Cengage Learning

7. Using the check box under Permissions for Financial, check **Allow** under **Full control** to give that permission to this user group. Click **Apply** and click **OK** twice to close the Properties box.

8. Change the permissions of the C:\Medical folder so that Authenticated Users and Users are not allowed access and the Medical group is allowed full control.

💡 **A+ Exam Tip** The A+ 220–702 Practical Application exam expects you to be able to set up share permissions and understand these terms: allow, deny, file attributes, permission propagation, and inheritance, as they apply to sharing files and folders.

A+
220-702
4.2

STEP 3: SHARE THE FOLDERS ON THE NETWORK

So far, the folders have been assigned permissions so that local users can access them. The next step is to share the two folders so that others on the network can access the folders in their Network window or My Network Places. When you share folders on the network, the permissions for remote users need to be set. These permissions, called share permissions, are different from the permissions that we created for local users.

> **Note** If a computer belongs to a domain, sharing of network resources is done at the domain level by a network administrator. In this chapter, you're learning to share resources in a workgroup on the network.

Follow these steps to share the folders on the network and set permissions for remote users:

1. Open the Medical folder's Properties box and click the **Sharing** tab (see the left side of Figure 20-8).

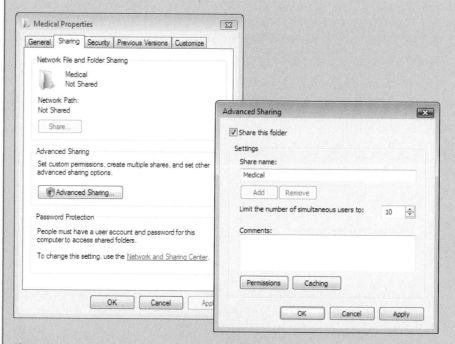

Figure 20-8 Share the folder with others on the network
Courtesy: Course Technology/Cengage Learning

2. Click **Advanced Sharing** and respond to the UAC box. In the Advanced Sharing box (see the right side of Figure 20-8), check **Share this folder.**

3. Click **Permissions.** The Permissions box appears (see Figure 20-9). By default, Windows shared a folder on the network with everyone. Select **Everyone** and click **Remove.**

4. Click **Add.** The Select User or Groups box appears (refer back to Figure 20-7), where you can add user accounts or groups that can access the folder. For the C:\Medical folder, we want to give access to the Medical user group. In the *Enter the object names to* select text box, type **Medical** and click **OK.**

A+
220-702
4.2

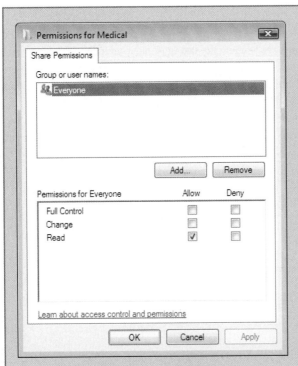

Figure 20-9 The folder is shared with Everyone
Courtesy: Course Technology/Cengage Learning

5. In Figure 20-10, notice that the permission assigned the Medical group is Read. Check **Full Control** under the Allow column and click **Apply**. Click **OK** twice and then close the Properties window.

6. Now share the Financial folder and remove share permissions to Everyone. Add share permissions for the Financial user group, giving the group full control of the folder.

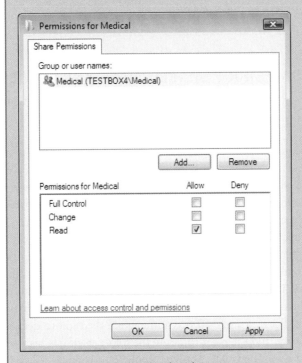

Figure 20-10 Permissions assigned to remote users
Courtesy: Course Technology/Cengage Learning

STEP 4: TEST AND GO LIVE

Do the following to test the share permissions and implement your shared folders.

1. It's now time to test your security measures. Test a user account in each user group to make sure the user can read and write to the folder he needs but cannot access the other folder. Put some test data in each folder. Then log onto the system using an account you want to test and try to access each folder. Figure 20-11 shows the box that appears when an unauthorized user attempts to access a folder. When you click **Continue**, entering an administrator's password in the resulting UAC box gives you access.

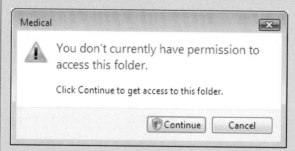

Figure 20-11 Access to a folder is controlled
Courtesy: Course Technology/Cengage Learning

2. Now that you have the security working on the one computer, go to each computer on the network and create the user accounts that will be using this computer. Then test the security and make sure each user can access or cannot access the \Financial and \Medical folders as you intend.

3. After you are convinced the security works as you want it to, move all the company data to subfolders in these folders. Check a few subfolders and files to verify that each has the permissions that you expect. And don't forget to put in place on the file server the backup procedures you learned about in Chapter 13.

SUPPORT AND TROUBLESHOOT SHARED FILES AND FOLDERS

You have just seen how to set up user groups and folder permissions assigned to these groups. Here are some tips in using these shared folders:

- Allowing users full control of a folder might be extending permissions beyond job requirements. If some users require just read-only access, you can create a new group of read-only users or you can assign read-only permission to these individual user accounts. Make certain users understand that data files shared by others on the network should not be copied to their local PC.

- If you need further control of the permissions assigned a user or group, click **Advanced** on the Security tab of a folder's Properties box. The Advanced Security Settings box appears. Click the **Permissions** tab. Select the user or group you want to edit and click **Edit**. Select a user group and click **Edit**. The Permission Entry box opens (see the right side of Figure 20-12). Originally, the Financial user group was given full control. However, using this box, you can change detailed permissions. Notice in the figure the right to delete subfolders and files has been set to Deny, and the right to delete the folder itself has been set to Deny. Click **OK** to close the box. Then click **Apply** to apply your changes. Click **OK** twice and then close the Properties box. The resulting change means that users of the Financial group cannot delete or move a file or folder. (They can, however, copy the file or folder.)

A+
220-702
4.2

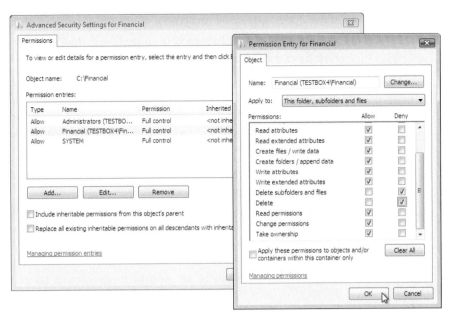

Figure 20-12 Advanced permissions settings
Courtesy: Course Technology/Cengage Learning

> 💡 **A+ Exam Tip** The A+ 220-702 Practical Application exam expects you to be able to implement share permissions so that a user can copy but not move a file or folder.

- When a subfolder is created, it is assigned certain permissions of the parent folder. These inherited permissions assigned to the child folder appear dimmed, indicating they are inherited permissions. The best way to change inherited permissions is to change the permissions of the parent object. In other words, to change the permissions of the C:\Financial\QuickBooks folder, change the permission of the C:\Financial folder. Changing permissions of a parent folder affects all subfolders in that folder.

- Permissions manually set for a subfolder or file can override inherited permissions. Permissions that are manually set are called explicit permissions. When a folder or file has inherited and explicit permissions set, it might be confusing as to exactly which permissions are in effect. To know for sure exactly which permissions for a file or folder are in effect, see the Effective Permissions tab of the Advanced Security Settings box.

- Don't forget that for best security, each user account needs a password. How to use Group Policy to require that all accounts have passwords was covered in a project at the end of Chapter 19.

- When a user accesses shared folders on a remote computer on the network that is not part of a domain, the user must have the same user account and password on the remote computer and the local computer. If these accounts and passwords don't match, the user is considered an anonymous user and is denied access to resources shared on the remote computer.

When you have a problem with a shared folder, use these tips to troubleshoot the problem:

- For Windows Vista to serve up shared folders, recall from Chapter 19 that the Network and Sharing Center must use these settings:
  - File and Printer Sharing for Microsoft Networks is turned on for the network connection.
  - File sharing is turned on.

20

A+ 220-702

A+
220-702
4.2

- Public folder sharing is turned on.

- If you want the added protection of requiring that all users on the network have a valid user account and password on this computer, turn on Password protected sharing.

- If you want shared folders on a computer to be available to anyone on the network, turn off Password protected sharing and share the folders with the Everyone group. These two settings are equivalent to simple file sharing in Windows XP.

- If you want to share a printer connected to this PC with others on the network, Printer sharing must be turned on.

▲ For Windows XP to share resources, two services, Client for Microsoft Networks and File and Printer Sharing for Microsoft Networks, must be installed and enabled for the network connection. These settings can be verified in the Network Connections window.

▲ The owner of a folder always has full permissions for the folder. If you are having a problem changing permissions and you are not the folder owner, try taking ownership of the folder. To do that, click **Advanced** on the Security tab of the folder's properties box. The Advanced Security Settings box appears. Click the **Owner** tab. Click **Edit**. The owner can then be edited (see Figure 20-13). The current owner is displayed near the top of the box. Select a user from the *Change owner to* list and click **Apply** to make that user the new owner. If a user is not listed, click **Other users or groups** and add the user. Close the Advanced Security Settings box and the Properties box, and reopen the Properties box for the change to take effect.

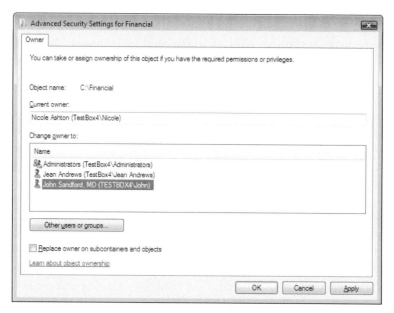

Figure 20-13   Change the owner of a folder
Courtesy: Course Technology/Cengage Learning

▲ If a remote user cannot access a shared file or folder, verify that the local user accounts and passwords match on both computers and the user has been assigned share permissions to access the file or folder.

▲ It is not necessary that all computers belong to the same workgroup in order to share resources. However, performance improves when they are all in the same workgroup.

▲ For the convenience of remote users, map network drives for shared folders that are heavily used.

HIDDEN NETWORK RESOURCES AND ADMINISTRATIVE SHARES

If you need to enhance security for a computer, you can do the following to further secure a computer and its resources:

- ◢ *Disable File and Printer Sharing.* If no resources on the computer are shared, use the Vista Network and Sharing Center or the XP Network Connections window to disable File and Printer Sharing for Microsoft Networks.
- ◢ *Hide a shared folder.* If you want to share a folder, but don't want others to see the shared folder in their Network or My Network Places window, add a $ to the end of the folder name. This shared and hidden folder is called a hidden share. Others on the network can access the folder only when they know its name. For example, if you name a shared folder Financial$, in order to access the folder, a user must enter \\*computername***Financial**$ in the Vista Start Search box (see Figure 20-14) or the XP Run box on the remote computer and press **Enter**.

Figure 20-14 Accessing a hidden, shared folder on the network
Courtesy: Course Technology/Cengage Learning

- ◢ *Make your Windows XP personal folders private.* If you are using the NTFS file system with Windows XP, folders associated with your user account can be made private so that only you can access them. To make a user folder and all its subfolders private, in Windows Explorer, drill down to a folder that is part of your user profile under the Documents and Settings folder. Right-click the folder and select **Sharing and Security** from the shortcut menu. The folder properties dialog box opens (see Figure 20-15).

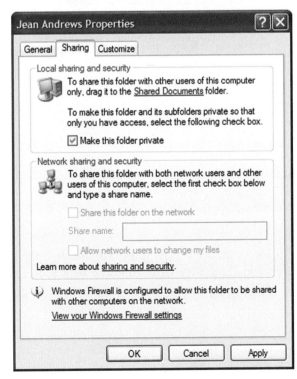

Figure 20-15 A folder that belongs to a user profile in Windows XP can be made private
Courtesy: Course Technology/Cengage Learning

20

A+ 220-702

A+
220-702
4.2

Check **Make this folder private** and click **Apply**. (If a folder is not part of a user profile in the Documents and Settings folder, this check box is dimmed.) When you make a personal folder private, be sure you have a password associated with your user account. If you don't have a password, anyone can log on as you and gain access to your private folders.

Folders on a computer that are shared with others on the network using a folder's Properties box are called local shares. For computers that belong to a domain, you need to be aware of another way folders are shared, called administrative shares. Administrative shares are the folders that are shared by default on a network that administrator accounts can access. You don't need to manually share these folders because Windows automatically does so by default. There are two types of administrative shares:

▲ *The %systemroot% folder.* Enter the path **\\computername\admin$** to access the **%systemroot%** folder (most likely the C:\Windows folder) on a remote computer. For example, in Figure 20-16, the entry in the Explorer address bar is \\BlueLight\admin$. Windows requests that the user authenticate with an administrator account to access this administrative share.

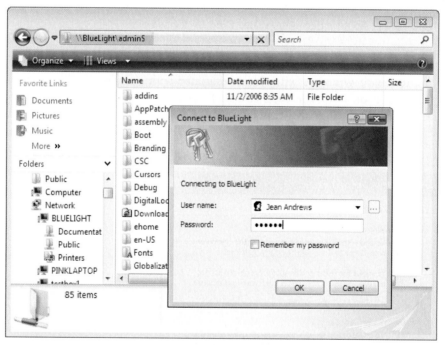

Figure 20-16   Access an administrative share on a domain
Courtesy: Course Technology/Cengage Learning

▲ *Any volume or drive.* To access the root level of any volume or drive on the network, enter the computer name and drive letter followed by a $, for example: \\BlueLight\C$.

💡 **A+ Exam Tip**   The A+ 220–702 Practical Application exam expects you to understand the difference between administrative shares and local shares.

When supporting a workgroup, you might be tempted to share all the drives on all computers so that you can have easy access remotely. However, to use local shares in this way is not a good security practice. Don't share the \Windows folder or an entire drive or volume on the network by using the folder or drive Properties box. These local shares appear in everyone's Network window or My Network Places window. You don't want your system files and folders exposed like this. Administrative shares don't appear in these places, and are therefore more secure. Also, keep in mind that administrative shares only work on a domain and are default settings.

ENCRYPTING FILES AND FOLDERS

Recall from Chapter 19 that you can encrypt a file or folder using Vista Ultimate or Business editions or Windows XP Professional. The process uses an Encrypting File System (EFS) certificate, and this certificate is required to decrypt the files. The drive holding the encrypted file or folder must use the NTFS file system. EFS encryption creates a public key and private key for the user when he first encrypts a file or folder. A recovery key is also created that can be used by an administrator to unlock an encrypted file or folder if the user's keys are not available.

> **Note** Two limitations of EFS encryption are that Windows system files cannot be encrypted (making it possible for a thief to boot the system) and the recovery key is stored on the local computer (making it possible for a thief to access it). These two security weaknesses can be solved by moving the recovery key to another media, and by using Vista BitLocker Encryption to encrypt the Windows volume.

In this part of the chapter, you will learn to encrypt and decrypt a file or folder, how to export and import EFS digital certificates, how to share an encrypted file or folder with another local user, and what to do when you have problems with encrypted files and folders.

> **A+ Exam Tip** The A+ 220–702 Practical Application exam expects you to know how to use EFS encryption and troubleshoot problems with it.

HOW TO ENCRYPT OR DECRYPT A FILE OR FOLDER

To encrypt a file or folder, do the following:

1. Right-click the folder or file you want to encrypt and select **Properties** from the shortcut menu. The Properties box for that file or folder opens, as shown on the left side of Figure 20-17.

2. On the General tab, click the **Advanced** button. The Advanced Attributes dialog box opens, as shown on the right side of Figure 20-17.

3. To encrypt the folder or file, check **Encrypt contents to secure data** and click **OK**. On the Properties window, click **Apply**. The dialog box shown in Figure 20-18 opens, asking you if you want the encryption to apply to subfolders. Make your choice and click **OK**. Then close the Properties box. Encrypted files or folders are displayed in Explorer

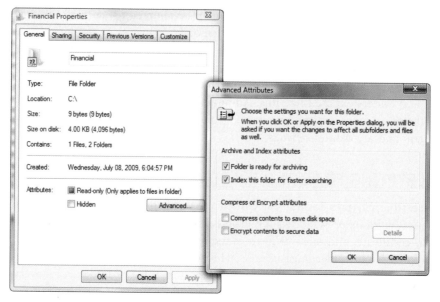

Figure 20-17 Encrypt a file or folder using the Properties box
Courtesy: Course Technology/Cengage Learning

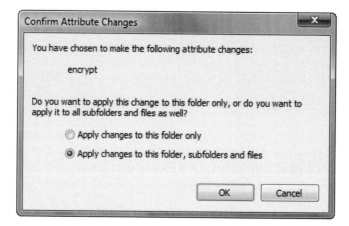

Figure 20-18 Encryption can apply to subfolders or just to the one folder
Courtesy: Course Technology/Cengage Learning

in green (see Figure 20-19). If some other user on this same computer who is not an administrator or any user on the network attempts to access the encrypted file or folder, an "Access is denied" message (also shown in Figure 20-19) or a similar error message appears.

A file or folder can be decrypted using one of these methods:

◢ On the General tab of the file's Properties box, click **Advanced**. In the Advanced Attributes dialog box, uncheck **Encrypt contents to secure data**.

◢ Encryption is removed automatically when you move a file or folder to another computer on the network or to a flash drive or FAT volume (FAT does not support encryption). Figure 20-20 shows the message you see when an encrypted file is about to be moved to a flash drive.

◢ Use the Cipher command in a command prompt window. The Cipher command can be used to encrypt, decrypt, or recover an encrypted file when the certificates are lost. For example, the command to decrypt a file is **cipher /d C:\filename.ext**.

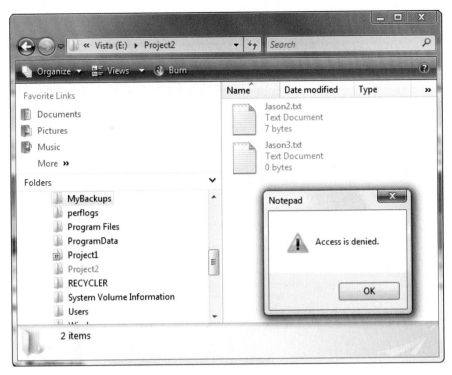

Figure 20-19 Encrypted files and folders appear in green
Courtesy: Course Technology/Cengage Learning

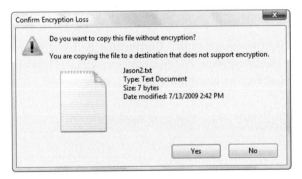

Figure 20-20 Encryption is removed when the file is copied
Courtesy: Course Technology/Cengage Learning

> **Note** Volumes formatted using the FAT file system cannot use file or folder encryption. You can, however, convert a FAT volume to NTFS so that you can use encryption.

BACK UP YOUR EFS CERTIFICATES

For a stand-alone computer that is not part of a Windows domain, the EFS encrypting process generates a self-signed digital certificate to be used for the encryption. This certificate contains the public key needed to decrypt the file or folder. When you first encrypt a file or folder, you need to create a backup copy of the certificate and the private key. If the original certificate gets corrupted, you can use these backups to access the encrypted files. You can also use the backup certificate (also called an exported certificate) on another computer where you need to access encrypted files.

20

A+ 220-702

A+
220-702
4.2

Certificates are managed using the Certificate Manager (certmgr.msc) console. Follow these steps to back up your EFS certificate:

1. Enter **certmgr.msc** in the Vista Start Search box or the XP Run box and press **Enter**. For Vista, respond to the UAC box. The Certificate Manager window opens (see Figure 20-21).

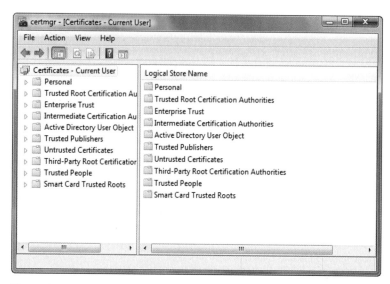

Figure 20-21 Use the Certificate Manager console to manage installed digital certificates
Courtesy: Course Technology/Cengage Learning

2. Double-click **Personal** and then double-click **Certificates**. A list of your installed certificates appears. Select all the Encrypting File System certificates. Then on the Action menu, select **All Tasks** and **Export** (see Figure 20-22).

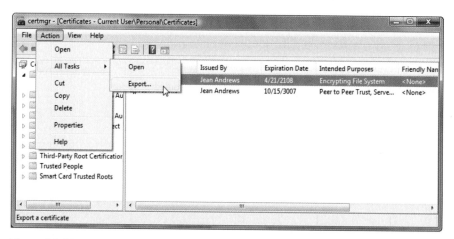

Figure 20-22 Export the selected certificates
Courtesy: Course Technology/Cengage Learning

3. The Certificate Export Wizard appears. Click **Next**.

4. On the next screen (see Figure 20-23), click **Yes, export the private key** and click **Next**. Later, in the wizard, you will be given the opportunity to enter a password to encrypt and protect the private key.

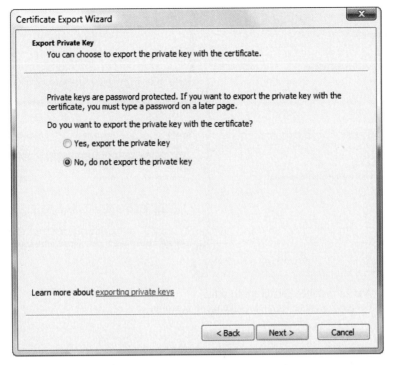

Figure 20-23 Decide if you want to export the private key
Courtesy: Course Technology/Cengage Learning

5. Follow directions on-screen to point to a backup media such as a USB flash drive to store the file and name the file. This one file holds the certificate and keys, and the default file extension will be .pfx. Be sure to store the flash drive in a secure place such as a locked safe or desk drawer.

If you want to later use the exported certificate to access encrypted files on this or another computer, you must first install the certificate and then add it to a file or folder. How to do that is discussed next.

GIVE OTHER LOCAL USERS ACCESS TO YOUR ENCRYPTED FILES

You can allow other local users of a computer to access your encrypted files. However, you cannot share an encrypted file on the network unless the computer belongs to a Windows domain. To allow other local users access to your encrypted files, you need to add another user's certificate to your encrypted file. (If a user does not have an EFS certificate, one will be created the first time he encrypts a file or folder.)

To add a certificate to an encrypted file, follow these steps:

1. Right-click the file and select **Properties** from the shortcut menu. On the General tab of the Properties box, click **Advanced**. The Advanced Attributes box opens.

2. Click **Details**. (If the Details button is dimmed, you need to select a file and not a folder.) The User Access box opens (see the left side of Figure 20-24).

3. Click **Add**. A list of installed certificates appears (see the right side of Figure 20-24). Select the certificate and click **OK**. Click **OK** two more times. Then click **Apply** in the Properties box and close the box. The other user should now be able to access the file.

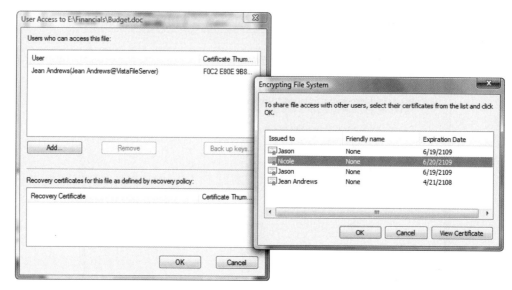

Figure 20-24 Add an installed certificate to a file
Courtesy: Course Technology/Cengage Learning

If another user wants to export his EFS certificate on his computer so that you can install this certificate on your computer, know that the user should not export his private key and give it to you. Have the user export only the certificate (which contains his public key) and not export his private key (refer back to Figure 20–23). By default, the certificate file without the private key will have a .cer file extension and the file is not password protected. He can then give you the .cer file. (For example, he can e-mail it to you.) You can then install (import) his certificate on your computer and add the certificate to each of your encrypted files to which you want to give him access.

Do the following to import the certificate on your computer:

1. Open the Certificate Manager and select the **Trusted People** folder.

2. On the Action menu, select **All Tasks** and click **Import**. The Certificate Import wizard opens. Click **Next**. Click **Browse** and point to the certificate file. Look for a file with a .cer file extension. Click **Open** and click **Next**. (If the certificate file had included the private key, the password to this key would be requested at this point.)

3. On the next screen, verify the certificate will be stored in the Trusted People store. Your screen should look like the one in Figure 20-25. Click **Next, Finish,** and **OK** to complete the wizard. The certificate is now installed on this computer. The next step will be to add the certificate to the encrypted file.

SOLVE PROBLEMS WITH ENCRYPTED FILES

Here are some tips to keep in mind when problems arise with encrypted files:

◢ If you cannot access an encrypted file after you have installed a new version of Windows and you have a backup copy of your certificate, install (import) the certificate in Windows. Then add it to the encrypted file.

◢ If you cannot access an encrypted file that was encrypted by someone else, that person must add your certificate to the encrypted file.

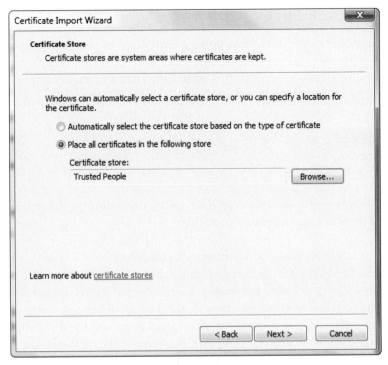

Figure 20-25 Place another person's certificate in your Trusted People store
Courtesy: Course Technology/Cengage Learning

◢ The Windows Easy Transfer process moves encrypted files and folders from one computer to another. The EFS certificates are included in these files. If you have problems accessing these encrypted files, try exporting your certificate from the original computer, installing it on the new computer, and then adding the certificate to the files.

◢ If the *Encrypt contents to secure data* check box is dimmed on the Advanced Attributes box, know that this version of Windows does not support encryption.

◢ If the Advanced button is missing on the General tab of a file or folder properties box, know that the volume is not using the NTFS file system.

◢ If you cannot access an encrypted file because the certificate is corrupted and there are no backup certificates, you might be able to recover the file using a recovery certificate. You must be logged on as an administrator. The process includes using the Cipher command to create a recovery certificate, using Group Policy to install the recovery certificate, and then using another Cipher command to add the recovery certificate to the encrypted file. The details of how to do all this are beyond the scope of this chapter. You can find the detailed instructions at *windowshelp.microsoft.com* when you search on "recovery certificate for encrypted files."

Notes When you open an encrypted file with an application, Windows decrypts the file for the application to use. While the application is working on the file, data written to the virtual memory file, Pagefile.sys, might contain decrypted data from your file. If your computer goes into hibernation while the file is open, a criminal might later be able to read the data in the Pagefile.sys file by booting the system from another OS. For this reason, disable hibernation while working on encrypted files. Also, for added protection, you can use Group Policy to configure Windows to clean out Pagefile.sys at shutdown. And, for added protection, find out where the application writes temporary data. For example, many applications write to the Windows \Temp folder, and this folder should also be encrypted.

USING BITLOCKER ENCRYPTION

Recall that BitLocker Encryption locks down a hard drive by encrypting the entire Vista volume and any other volume on the drive. BitLocker Encryption is available with Windows Vista Enterprise or Ultimate editions. It is intended to work in partnership with file and folder encryption to provide data security.

> **💡 A+ Exam Tip** The A+ 220–702 Practical Application exam expects you to know how to support BitLocker Encryption.

There are three ways to use BitLocker Encryption, depending on the type of protection you need and the computer hardware available:

▲ *Computer authentication.* Many notebook computers have a chip on the motherboard called the TPM (Trusted Platform Module) chip. The TPM chip holds the BitLocker encryption key (also called the startup key). If the hard drive is stolen from the notebook and installed in another computer, the data would be safe because BitLocker would not allow access without the startup key stored on the TPM chip. Therefore, this method authenticates the computer. However, if the motherboard fails and is replaced, you'll need a backup copy of the startup key to access data on the hard drive. (You cannot move the TPM chip from one motherboard to another.)

▲ *User authentication.* For computers that don't have TPM, the startup key can be stored on a USB flash drive (or other storage device the computer reads before the OS is loaded), and the flash drive must be installed before the computer boots. This method authenticates the user. For this method to be the most secure, the user must never leave the flash drive stored with the computer. (Instead, the user might keep the USB startup key on his or her key ring.)

▲ *Computer and user authentication.* For *best* security, a PIN or password can be required at every startup in addition to TPM. Using this method, both the computer and the user are authenticated.

BitLocker Encryption provides great security, but security comes with a price. For instance, you risk the chance your TPM will fail or you will lose all copies of the startup key. In these events, recovering the data can be messy. Therefore, use BitLocker only if the risks of BitLocker giving problems outweigh the risks of stolen data. And, if you decide to use BitLocker, be sure to make extra copies of the startup key and/or password and keep them in a safe location.

For detailed instructions on how to set up BitLocker Encryption, see the Microsoft Knowledge Base article 933246 at *support.microsoft.com*.

SUPPORTING BIOS SECURITY FEATURES THAT AFFECT ACCESS CONTROL

BIOS on a motherboard offers security features including power-on passwords, support for intrusion-detection devices, and support for a TPM chip. Power-on passwords include a supervisor password (required to change BIOS setup), user password (required to use the system or view BIOS setup), and a drive lock password (required to access the hard drive). The drive lock password is stored on the hard drive so that it will still control access to the drive in the event the drive is removed from the computer and installed in another system.

A+
220-702
4.2

💡 **A+ Exam Tip** The A+ 220-702 Practical Application exam expects you to be able to use BIOS security features including passwords, drive lock, intrusion detection, and TPM.

Recall from Chapter 19 that these three types of passwords can be set in the BIOS setup utility. If the supervisor password is set and forgotten, you cannot enter BIOS setup to change any of these passwords. To get around the problem, use the BIOS reset jumpers on the motherboard. The motherboard documentation will tell you how to set these jumpers so that all BIOS settings are returned to default values. Figure 20-26 shows the jumper group on one motherboard. To reset BIOS, the brown jumper cap is moved to a new position on this set of three jumpers.

Jumper group to reset BIOS

Figure 20-26 Use jumpers on the motherboard to reset BIOS settings
Courtesy: Course Technology/Cengage Learning

An intrusion-detection device can be installed inside the computer case and connected to pins on the motherboard. Then the intrusion-detection feature in BIOS setup must be enabled. After the security measure is in place and the case is opened, BIOS displays an alert the next time the system is powered up. For example, the alert message at startup might be "Chassis Intruded! System has halted." If you see the message, know that the case has been opened. Reboot the system and the system should start up as usual. To make sure the alert was not tripped by accident, verify that the case cover is securely in place. Also, sometimes a failed CMOS battery can trip the alert. Intrusion-detection devices are not a recommended best practice for security. False alerts are annoying, and criminals generally know how to get inside a case without tripping the alert.

When you use Windows Vista to install BitLocker Encryption, the initialization process also initializes the TPM chip. Initializing the TPM chip configures it and turns it on. After BitLocker is installed, you can temporarily turn off BitLocker, which also turns off the TPM chip. For example, you might want to turn off BitLocker to test the BitLocker recovery process. Normally, BitLocker will manage the TPM chip for you, and there is no need for you to manually change TPM chip settings. However, if you are having problems installing BitLocker, one thing you can do is clear the TPM chip. *Be careful!* If the TPM chip is being used to hold an encryption key to protect data on the hard drive and you clear the chip, the encryption key will be lost. That means all the data will be lost, too. Therefore, don't clear the TPM chip unless you are certain it is not being used to encrypt data. To initialize or clear the TPM chip, follow these steps:

1. Log onto the system with an administrator account.

2. In the Vista Start Search box, enter **tpm.msc** and press **Enter**. Respond to the UAC box.

A+
220-702
4.2

3. The TPM Management console opens. If there is no TPM chip present, the console displays a message that no TPM chip can be found. If your system has a TPM chip, the screen looks similar to the one in Figure 20-27.

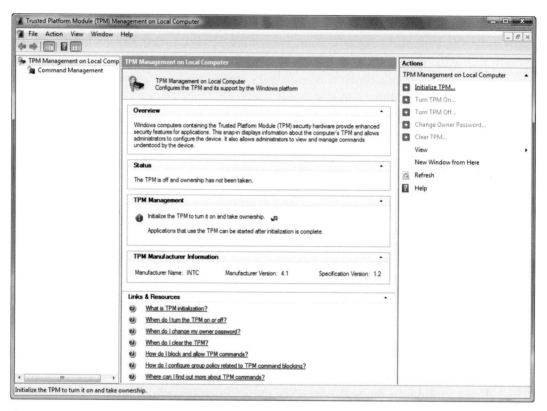

Figure 20-27 Use the TPM Management console to manage the TPM chip
Courtesy: Course Technology/Cengage Learning

4. Notice in the right pane that Initialize TPM is not dimmed, which means that the TPM chip has not yet been initialized. To initialize it, click **Initialize TPM**. A dialog box (see Figure 20-28) appears listing the steps to initialize the TPM chip, which include shutting down and restarting the system.

5. After the restart, you are given the opportunity to create the TPM owner password, save the password to a removable media, and print the password (see Figure 20-29). These steps initialize the TPM chip and assign ownership. You can then use encryption software such as BitLocker Encryption or other software embedded on the hard drive to encrypt data on the drive.

6. To clear the TPM chip after it has been initialized, under Action, click **Clear TPM** (see Figure 20-30) and follow directions on-screen. You will be asked to enter the owner password or provide the media where the password is stored. Clearing the TPM chip causes all encrypted data protected by the chip to be lost.

Also notice in Figure 20-30 that you can turn the TPM chip on or off using the Action menu.

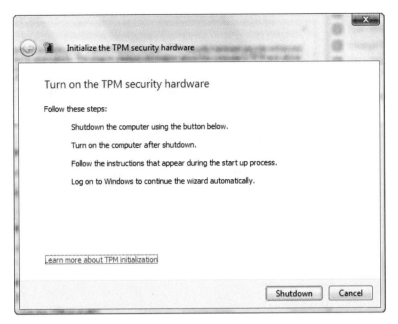

A+
220-702
4.2

Figure 20-28 Steps to initialize the TPM chip
Courtesy: Course Technology/Cengage Learning

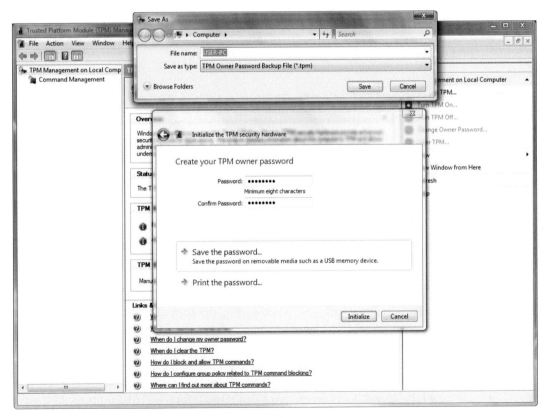

Figure 20-29 Create and save the TPM owner password
Courtesy: Course Technology/Cengage Learning

20

A+ 220-702

A+
220-702
4.2

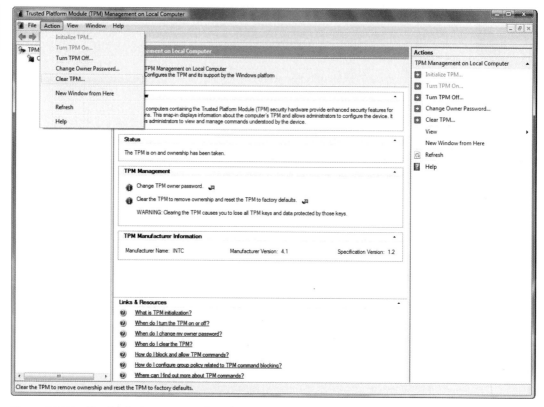

Figure 20-30 Use the Action menu to clear the TPM chip
Courtesy: Course Technology/Cengage Learning

DEALING WITH MALICIOUS SOFTWARE

A+
220-702
4.1

In this part of the chapter, you will learn how to recognize symptoms that indicate a system has been infected with malicious software, about the strategies used to deal with malware, the step-by-step plan to clean up an infected system, and how to protect a system from getting malware.

MALWARE SYMPTOMS

A PC support technician needs to know how to recognize that a system is infected with malware and how to clean an infected system. Here are some warnings that suggest malicious software is at work:

- Pop-up ads plague you when surfing the Web.
- Generally, the system works much slower than it used to. Programs take longer than normal to load.
- The number and length of disk accesses seem excessive for simple tasks. The number of bad sectors on the hard drive continues to increase.
- The access lights on the hard drive and floppy drive turn on when there should be no activity on the devices. (However, sometimes Windows performs routine maintenance on the drive when the system has been inactive for a while.)
- Strange or bizarre error messages appear. Programs that once worked now give errors.
- Less memory than usual is available, or there is a noticeable reduction in disk space.
- Strange graphics appear on your computer monitor, or the computer makes strange noises.
- The system cannot recognize the CD or DVD drive, although it worked earlier.

A+
220-702
4.1

- In Windows Explorer, filenames now have weird characters or their file sizes seem excessively large. Executable files have changed size or file extensions change without reason. Files mysteriously disappear or appear.
- Files constantly become corrupted.
- The OS begins to boot, but hangs before getting a Windows desktop.
- Your antivirus software displays one or more messages.
- You receive e-mail messages telling you that you have sent someone an infected message.
- Task Manager shows unfamiliar processes running.
- When you try to use your browser to access the Internet, strange things happen and you can't surf the Web. Your Internet Explorer home page has changed and you see new toolbars you didn't ask for.
- Even though you can browse to other Web sites, you cannot access AV software sites such as *www.symantec.com* or *www.mcafee.com*, and you cannot update your AV software.
- A message appears that a downloaded document contains macros, or an application asks whether it should run macros in a document. (It is best to disable macros if you cannot verify that they are from a trusted source and that they are free of viruses or worms.)

> **Notes** Malicious software is designed to do varying degrees of damage to data and software, although it does not damage PC hardware. However, when boot sector information is destroyed on a hard drive, the hard drive can appear to be physically damaged.

STRATEGIES FOR DEALING WITH MALWARE

Large corporations generally have a plan in place so that malware is quickly detected and does not take down the entire network. Here is what a plan might look like:

- Each computer has antivirus software installed and set to download updates regularly. The software scans all incoming e-mail. If the antivirus software (AV software) detects suspicious e-mail, the user is alerted to the quarantined file. A quarantined file is placed in a special directory and cannot be opened. The user must decide to delete the file, leave it quarantined, or release it from quarantined status.
- Each computer on the network is built using a hard drive image. If a system gets infected, a technician simply reinstalls the image. The image contains the operating system and all authorized applications that the user needs to do his job. Reinstalling from a hard drive image is much faster than going through the detailed process of removing malware from a system.
- Company policy says that all data must be installed on network drives and not on the local hard drive. The purpose of this policy is so that (1) an infected system can be restored from an image without having to deal with data on the hard drive, and (2) data on network drives are backed up on a regular basis and, therefore, safer than when stored on a local hard drive. Recall that reinstalling a hard drive image erases everything on the drive. Because all user data is stored on network drives, no user data is lost when the image is used.
- Network-monitoring software (for example, Big Brother Professional at *www.bb4.com*) is constantly monitoring the network for unusual activity. If the software discovers a computer on the network is acting suspiciously, the computer will be quarantined. A quarantined computer is not allowed to use the network, is put on a different network dedicated to quarantined computers, or is only allowed to access certain network resources. The monitoring software alerts a technician about the problem. If the technician believes the system is infected, she will reimage the hard drive. All this can take place within an hour of malware becoming active on a computer.

A+
220-702
4.1

Small businesses and individuals are unlikely to be able to put into place all the measures that large corporations use. Therefore, as a PC technician, you do need to know how to clean up an infected system (the technical term is to remediate an infected system) without having to rebuild the entire hard drive.

> **A+ Exam Tip**   The A+ 220-702 Practical Application exam expects you to be able to identify malware symptoms, quarantine infected systems, remediate an infected system, and prevent malware from infecting a system.

STEP-BY-STEP ATTACK PLAN

This section is a step-by-step attack plan to clean up an infected system. We'll first use antivirus software and antiadware software to do a general cleanup. Then we'll use some Windows tools to check out the system to make sure all remnants of malware have been removed and the system is in tip-top order.

> ⚡ **Caution**   If a system is highly infected and will later hold sensitive data, consider backing up the data, reformatting the hard drive, and reinstalling the OS and applications. In fact, Microsoft recommends this to be the safest way to deal with highly infected systems.

STEP 1: QUARANTINE AN INFECTED SYSTEM

If an infected computer is connected to a network (wired or wireless), immediately disconnect the network cable or turn off the wireless adapter. You don't want to spread a virus or worm to other computers on your network. If you need to use the Internet to download AV software or its updates, take some precautions first. Consider your options. Can you disconnect other computers from the network while this one computer is connected? Can you isolate the computer from your local network, connecting it directly to the ISP? If neither option is possible, try downloading the AV software updates while the computer is booted into Safe Mode with Networking. Malware might still be running in Safe Mode, but is less likely to do so than when the system is started normally.

Always keep in mind that data might be on the hard drive that is not backed up. Before you begin cleaning up the system, back up data to another media.

STEP 2: RUN AV SOFTWARE

A virus is often programmed to attempt to hide from antivirus (AV) software. It's also sometimes programmed to block downloading and installing the AV software if the software is not already installed. AV software can only detect viruses identical or similar to those it has been programmed to search for and recognize. Most AV software scans for unknown viruses by looking for suspicious activity typical of what viruses generally do. (This type of hit-or-miss, inaccurate scanning is called heuristic scanning.) AV software detects a known virus by looking for distinguishing characteristics called virus signatures, which is why AV software cannot always detect a virus it does not know to look for. For all these reasons, it's important to have AV software installed, have it running in the background, and regularly download updates to it.

> 📝 **Note**   If you ever encounter a virus that your updated AV software did not find, be sure to let the manufacturer of the software know so they can research the problem.

Table 20-1 lists popular antivirus software and Web sites that also provide information about viruses. Some of these products can come bundled with a software firewall and identity protection software.

Antivirus Software	Web Site
AntiVirus + AntiSpyware by Trend Micro (for home use)	www.trendmicro.com
Avast by ALWIL Software (home edition is free)	www.avast.com
AVG Anti-Virus by AVG Technologies	www.avg.com
BitDefender Antivirus	www.bitdefender.com
ClamWin Free Antivirus by ClamWin (open source and free)	www.clamwin.com
F-Secure Anti-Virus by F-Secure Corp.	www.f-secure.com
Kaspersky Anti-Virus	www.kaspersky.com
Malwarebytes (free version available)	www.malwarebytes.org
McAfee VirusScan Plus by McAfee Associates, Inc.	www.mcafee.com
Norton AntiVirus by Symantec, Inc.	www.symantec.com
Panda Antivirus Pro	www.pandasecurity.com
Windows Live OneCare by Microsoft	onecare.live.com
Worry-Free Business Security by Trend Micro (for networks)	www.trendmicro.com

Table 20-1 Antivirus software and Web sites

When selecting AV software, find out if it can:

- ◢ Automatically download new software upgrades (engine updates) and virus definitions (virus signatures) from the Internet so that your software is continually aware of new viruses.
- ◢ Allow for manually downloading updates.
- ◢ Automatically execute at startup before the system connects to a network.
- ◢ Detect macros in a word-processing document as it is loaded by the word processor.
- ◢ Automatically monitor files being downloaded from the Internet, including e-mail attachments and attachments sent during a chat session, such as when using AOL Instant Messenger.
- ◢ Schedule scans to occur automatically and allow for manual scans for viruses. It should also allow for manual scanning while the system is booted into Safe Mode.
- ◢ Scan for other types of malware, including adware, spyware, and rootkits.
- ◢ Allow you to install the software while the system is booted into Safe Mode and without Internet access. These options are important when you are trying to install the software on an infected system. However, few AV software products are available that offer this option without an extra-heavy price attached.

Note It's handy to have AV software on CD so that you don't need Internet access to download the software, but recognize that this AV software won't have the latest updates. You'll need these updates downloaded from the Internet before the software will catch newer viruses.

A+
220-702
4.1

When AV software is not already installed on an infected computer, the most effective way to clean the computer is to run AV software from another computer. Follow these steps:

1. Make sure the remote computer has its software firewall set for maximum protection and its installed AV is software is up to date and running.

2. Network the two computers and share drive C on the infected computer. (Don't connect the infected computer to the entire network.)

3. To make your work easier, you can map a network drive from the remote computer to drive C of the infected computer.

4. Perform a virus scan on the remote computer, pointing the scan to drive C on the infected computer.

If you don't have another computer available to scan the infected computer, here are steps to use AV software on the infected system that does not already have AV software installed:

1. Purchase the AV software on CD (see Figure 20-31), or use another computer to download the AV software from its Web site and then burn the downloaded files to a CD. Don't make the mistake of using the infected PC to purchase and download AV software because keyloggers might be spying and collecting credit card information.

Figure 20-31 Having AV software on CD means you don't need Internet access to install the software
Courtesy: Course Technology/Cengage Learning

2. Insert the AV software CD. Most likely the AV main menu will be displayed automatically. If it is not, use Windows Explorer to locate and execute the setup program on the CD (see Figure 20-32).

A+
220-702
4.1

Figure 20-32 Execute the setup program on the AV software CD
Courtesy: Course Technology/Cengage Learning

3. When given the opportunity, choose to scan for infections before installing the software (see Figure 20-33). The software will ask for Internet access to download the latest updates.

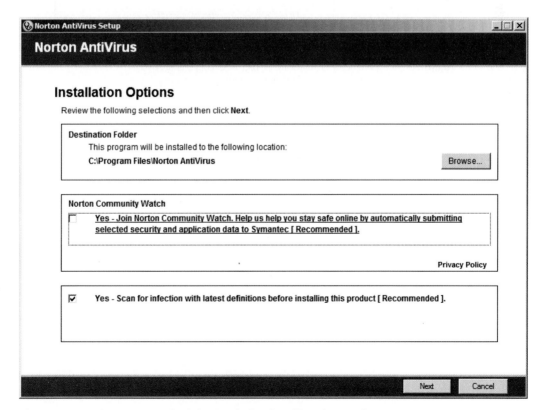

Figure 20-33 Choose to scan for infections before installing the AV software
Courtesy: Course Technology/Cengage Learning

4. The AV software gives you the chance to decide what to do with any problems it finds. Sometimes AV software detects a program that you know you have downloaded and want to keep, but the AV software recognizes it as potentially harmful. This type of software is sometimes called grayware or a PUP (potentially unwanted program). When the AV software displays the list of detected files, unless you recognize something you want to keep, I suggest you tell the AV software to delete them all.

5. The software might require a restart after the scan and before the installation completes.

6. After the reboot, allow the software to update itself again and then scan the system again. Most likely, some new malware will be discovered. For example, after AV software declared it had removed all malware it had found, on the next restart the window in Figure 20-34 appeared after Internet Explorer was launched. It's a bait window put there by malware, thus proving the system is far from clean. Keep repeating the scan until you get a clean scan. Reboot between scans and take notes of any program files the software is not able to delete.

Figure 20-34 Evidence that malware is still infecting the system
Courtesy: Course Technology/Cengage Learning

7. After the AV software performs a scan and finds no problems, it's time to see where you stand. Reboot the system and look for any error messages or problems. If you still believe the system might be infected, reboot the PC in Safe Mode and scan again. (Recall that to boot into Safe Mode, press F8 while Windows starts and then choose Safe Mode with Networking from the Advanced Boot Options menu.)

> **Note** If viruses are launched even after you boot in Safe Mode and you cannot get the AV software to work, try searching for suspicious entries in the subkeys under HKLM\System\CurrentControlSet\ Control\SafeBoot. Subkeys under this key control what is launched when you boot into Safe Mode. How to edit the registry is covered in Chapter 14.

It might be more fun to begin manually removing each program yourself, but it's probably quicker and more thorough to use antiadware software next. I suggest you resist the temptation to poke around looking for the malware and move on to the next step.

A+
220-702
4.1

STEP 3: RUN ADWARE OR SPYWARE REMOVAL SOFTWARE

Almost all AV software products today also search for adware and spyware. However, software specifically dedicated to removing this type of malware generally does a better job of it than does AV software. The next step in the removal process is to use antiadware or antispyware software.

The distinction between adware and spyware is slight, and sometimes a malicious software program is displaying pop-up ads and also spying on you. There are tons of removal software products available on the Web, but I recommend those listed in Table 20-2. They all can catch adware, spyware, cookies, browser hijackers, dialers, keyloggers, and Trojans.

Adware and Spyware Removal Software	Description
Ad-Aware by Lavasoft (*www.lavasoft.com*)	One of the most popular and successful adware and spyware removal products. It can be downloaded without support for free.
Spybot Search & Destroy by PepiMK Software (*www.safer-networking.org*)	Does an excellent job of removing malicious software and it's free.
Spy Sweeper by Webroot Software, Inc. (*www.webroot.com*)	Very good product but does require you pay a yearly subscription.
Windows Vista includes Windows Defender (*www.microsoft.com/windows/products/winfamily/defender*)	Antispyware software embedded in the OS.

Table 20-2 Removal software

Figure 20-35 shows what Search & Destroy discovered on one computer after AV software declared the system clean. Notice in the window that the software lists the exact registry keys that are infected.

To completely clean your system, you might have to run a removal product more than once or use more than one product. For example, what Ad-Aware doesn't find, Search & Destroy might, but what Search & Destroy doesn't find, Ad-Aware might find. To be sure, run two products.

STEP 4: CLEAN UP WHAT'S LEFT OVER

Next, you'll need to clean up anything the AV or antiadware software left behind. Sometimes AV software tells you it is not able to delete a file or it deletes an infected file, but leaves behind an orphaned entry in the registry or startup folders. If the AV software tells you it was not able to delete or clean a file, first check the AV software Web site for any instructions you might find to manually clean things up. In this section, you'll learn about general things you can do to clean up what might be left behind.

Respond to Any Startup Errors

On the first boot after AV software and antiadware software have declared a system is malware free, you might still find some startup errors caused by incomplete removal of the malware. Recall from Chapter 14 that you can use MSconfig.exe to find out how a startup program is launched. If the program is launched from the registry, you can back up and

A+
220-702
4.1

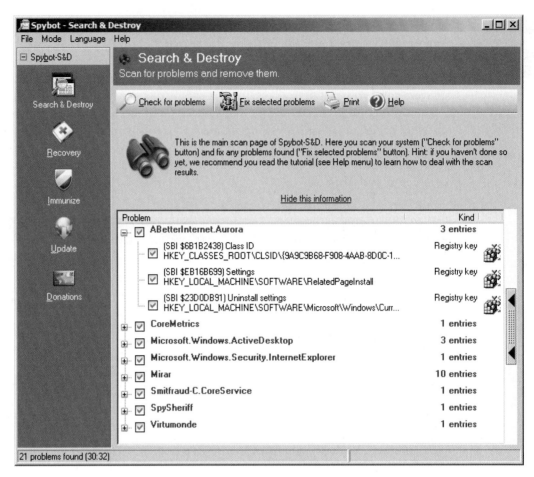

Figure 20-35 Search & Destroy showing details as it finds adware
Courtesy: Course Technology/Cengage Learning

delete the registry key. If the program is launched from a startup folder, you can move or delete the shortcut or program in the folder. See Chapter 14 for the details of how to remove unwanted startup programs.

Research Malware Types and Program Files

Your AV software might alert you to a suspicious program file that it quarantines and then asks you to decide if you want to delete it. Also, as you use Task Manager and other tools to see what programs are running in the background, you might find those that you suspect are malware. The Internet is your best tool to use when making your decision about a program. Here are some Web sites that offer virus encyclopedias that are reliable and give you symptoms and solutions for malware:

- ◢ Jim Foley, The Elder Geek at *www.theeldergeekvista.com*
- ◢ Process Library by Uniblue Systems Limited at *www.processlibrary.com*
- ◢ DLL Library by Uniblue Systems Limited at *www.liutilities.com*
- ◢ All the antivirus software sites listed earlier in the chapter in Table 20-1

Beware of using other sites! Much information on the Web is written by people who are just guessing about what they are saying, and some of the information is put there to purposefully deceive. Check things out carefully, and learn which sites you can rely on.

A+
220-702
4.1

Delete Files

For each program file the AV software told you it could not delete, try to delete the program file yourself using Windows Explorer. For peace of mind, don't forget to empty the Recycle Bin when you're done. You might need to open an elevated command prompt window and remove the hidden or system attributes on a file so that you can delete it. Recall that to open an elevated command prompt window, click **Start**, click **All Programs**, click **Accessories**, and right-click **Command Prompt**. Then select **Run as administrator** from the shortcut menu and respond to the UAC box. Figure 20-36 shows how to delete the file C:\INT0094.exe. Table 20-3 explains each command used.

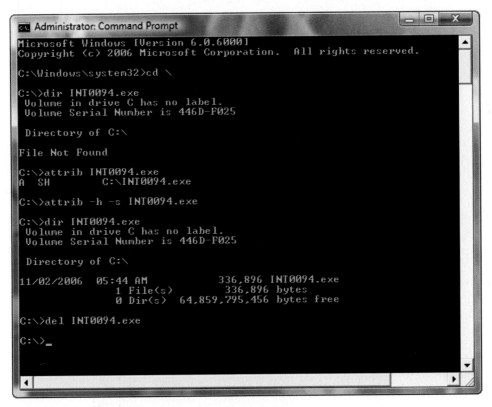

Figure 20-36 Commands to delete a hidden system file
Courtesy: Course Technology/Cengage Learning

Command	Explanation
cd \	Make the root directory of drive C the current directory.
dir INT0094.exe	The file does not appear to be in the directory.
attrib INT0094.exe	The file is actually present but hidden.
attrib –h –s INT0094.exe	Remove the hidden and system attributes of the file.
dir INT0094.exe	The dir command now displays the file.
del INT0094.exe	Delete the file.

Table 20-3 Commands to delete a hidden system file

If you are still not able to delete a file, open Task Manager and make sure the process is not running. A program file cannot be deleted if it is currently running. If you cannot end the process using Task Manager, try using the stronger Taskkill command. Follow these steps:

1. In Task Manager, select the **Processes** tab. Click **View, Select Columns**. In the Select Process Page Columns box, check **PID (Process Identifier)** and click **OK**.

2. Note the PID of the process you want to kill. For example, in Figure 20-37, to kill the process TeaTimer.exe, use the PID 2212.

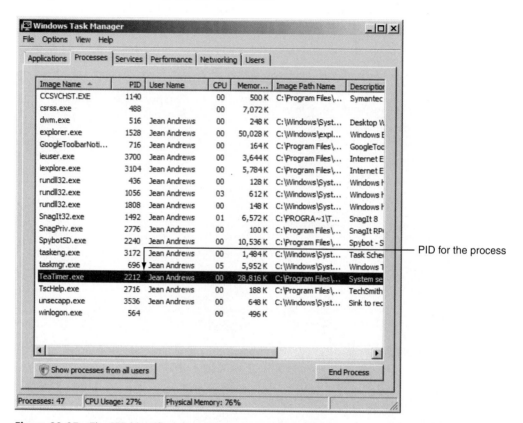

Figure 20-37   The PID identifies a process
Courtesy: Course Technology/Cengage Learning

3. In a command prompt window, enter the command **taskkill /f /pid:2212**, using the PID as seen in the Task Manager window. The /f parameter forcefully kills the process. Be careful using this command; it is so powerful that you can end critical system processes that will cause the system to shut down.

To get rid of other malware files, you might need to delete all Internet Explorer temporary Internet files. Use one of these two methods:

▲ *Method 1:* Using Windows Explorer, open the Drive C: properties window and on the General tab window, click **Disk Cleanup**. Then choose to delete files for all users and respond to the UAC box. Next, from the Disk Cleanup window shown in Figure 20-38, make sure **Temporary Internet Files** is checked and click **OK**.

▲ *Method 2:* Using Internet Explorer, click **Tools, Internet Options**. The Internet Options box opens, as shown on the left side of Figure 20-39. Under Browsing history, click **Delete**. From the Delete Browsing History box shown on the right side of Figure 20-39, not only can you delete Temporary Internet Files, but also you can delete Cookies,

A+
220-702
4.1

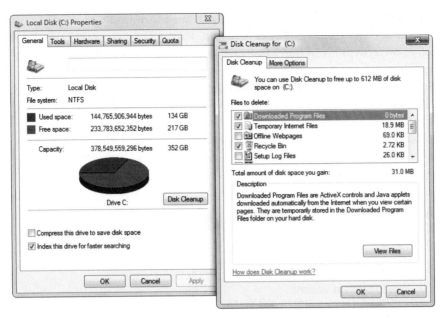

Figure 20-38 Delete all temporary Internet files
Courtesy: Course Technology/Cengage Learning

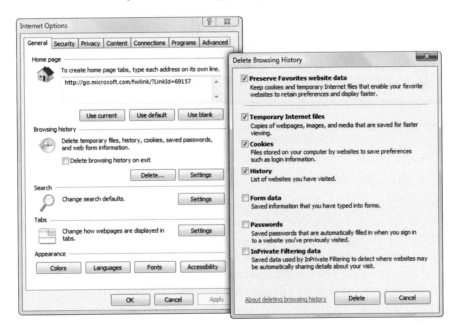

Figure 20-39 Use the Internet Properties box to delete the browsing history
Courtesy: Course Technology/Cengage Learning

History, Form data, Passwords, and InPrivate Filtering data. Make your selections and follow directions on-screen to complete the deletions. However, be aware that if you delete Cookies and Passwords, you will lose personal information saved by reputable sites such as your banking site. To keep this data from being lost, add the site to your Favorites list and check **Preserve Favorites website data**. (The check box is only available for Internet Explorer version 8 and higher.)

Purge Restore Points

Some malware hides its program files in the data storage area of the System Restore utility. Windows does not always allow AV software to look in this storage area when it is scanning

20

A+ 220-702

A+
220-702
4.1

for malware. To get rid of that malware, you must turn off System Protection, reboot your system, and turn System Protection back on. How to do that was covered in Chapter 13. Turning off System Protection causes the data storage area to be purged. You'll get rid of any malware there, but you'll also lose all your restore points.

Suppose your AV software has scanned the system and reports it has found a virus in the C:\System Volume Information_restore folder. This message means malware is in a System Restore point (see Figure 20-40). Unless you desperately need to keep a restore point you've previously made, if you see a message similar to the one in Figure 20-40 or your AV software scan feature found lots of malware in other places on the drive, the best idea is to purge all restore points.

Figure 20-40   Malware found in a restore point
Courtesy: Course Technology/Cengage Learning

Clean the Registry

Check in Chapter 14 to see a list of registry keys that can affect startup. You can search these keys and delete entries you don't want. You can also use a registry cleaning utility such as RegClean (*www.regclean.com*), RegCure (*www.regcure.com*), or RegSweep (*www.regsweep.com*) to remove orphaned entries in the registry left there by AV software. Don't forget to back up the registry before you run the product so that you can backtrack if necessary.

If you prefer to have more control over how the registry is changed, you can use Autoruns at Microsoft TechNet (*technet.microsoft.com*) to help you search for these orphaned registry entries. Figure 20-41 shows a screen shot where Autoruns is displaying an orphaned entry in the HKLM\Software\Microsoft\Windows\CurrentVersion\Run registry key used to launch the OsisOijw.dll malware program. AV software had already found and deleted this DLL file, but it left the registry key untouched.

Scan through the Autoruns window looking for suspicious entries. Research any entries that you think might be used by malware. To get rid of these entries, back up the registry and then use Regedit to delete unwanted keys or values.

After you have finished cleaning the registry, don't forget to restart the system to make sure all is well before you move on.

Clean Up Internet Explorer

Adware and spyware might install add-ons to Internet Explorer (including toolbars you didn't ask for), install cookie trackers, and change your IE security settings. Antiadware and

A+
220-702
4.1

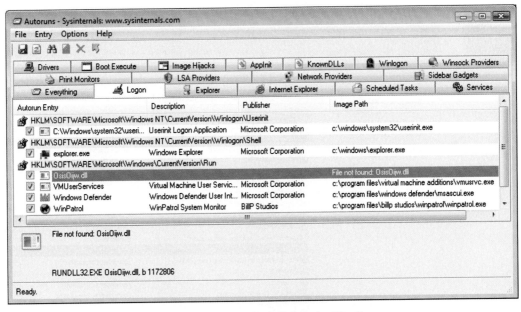

Figure 20-41 Autoruns finds orphan registry entries left there by AV software
Courtesy: Course Technology/Cengage Learning

antivirus software might have found all these items, but as a good defense, take a few minutes to find out for yourself. Follow these directions to make sure Internet Explorer is error free:

1. Open Internet Explorer and look for unwanted toolbars and home pages. For example, Figure 20-42 shows the browser has two toolbars the user doesn't want: one by Mirar and one by Google.

2. To remove these toolbars, use the Programs and Features window in Vista or the Add or Remove Programs applet in XP. Figure 20-43 shows the Vista Programs and Features window. To uninstall the toolbar program, select it, click **Uninstall/Change**, and respond to the UAC box.

Figure 20-42 Internet Explorer with toolbars installed and home page changed
Courtesy: Course Technology/Cengage Learning

20

A+ 220-702

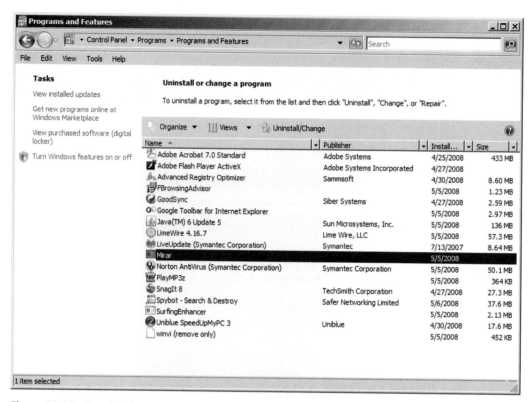

Figure 20-43   Use the Vista Programs and Features window to uninstall an IE toolbar
Courtesy: Course Technology/Cengage Learning

3. You might be in for a few surprises. When I tried to uninstall the Mirar toolbar shown in Figure 20-43, I got the window shown in Figure 20-44. I decided to go ahead and take the risk of downloading and running the uninstaller program, which did uninstall the toolbar.

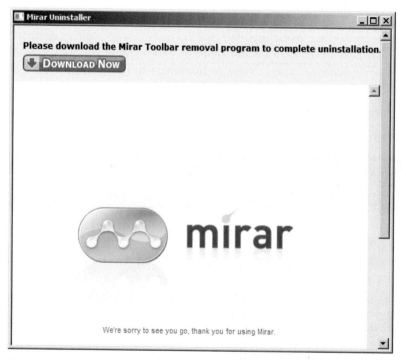

Figure 20-44   This software used a suspicious method to uninstall itself
Courtesy: Course Technology/Cengage Learning

A+
220-702
4.1

4. Continue to uninstall any other software related to the browser that is listed in the Programs and Features window or the Add or Remove Programs window.

5. Restart Vista and open Internet Explorer. On the menu bar for IE Version 7, click **Tools, Manage Add-ons,** and **Enable or Disable Add-ons.** The Manage Add-ons box appears (see Figure 20-45). (For IE Version 8, click **Tools** and **Manage Add-ons** to see a similar box.)

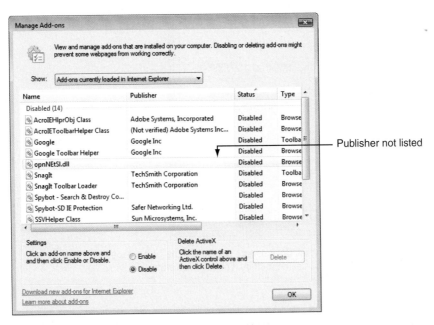

Figure 20-45 Disable add-ons that might be malware
Courtesy: Course Technology/Cengage Learning

6. Suspect any item that lists a publisher you don't trust or lists no publisher at all. To disable the add-on, select it and click **Disable.** ActiveX add-ons can be deleted from this window, but other add-ons can only be disabled. If you find a suspicious add-on, such as the one in Figure 20-45 named opnNEtSl.dll that does not declare its publisher, run the antiadware product again.

7. Close Internet Explorer and reopen it. Verify that all is working as it should.

8. To change your home page, in Internet Explorer, click **Tools** and click **Internet Options.** On the General tab under Home page, enter the new home page URL, beginning with http://. If you want IE to open two tabs with two different sites, use a second line for the second URL, as shown in Figure 20-46.

STEP 5: DIG DEEPER TO FIND MALWARE PROCESSES

It is my hope you won't need this section! Hopefully, by now your system is malware free. However, occasionally you'll need to deal with a really nasty infection that won't be found or deleted by conventional means. In this section, you'll learn to look under the hood of Windows Vista to find processes that have eluded detection by other means. You'll first see how Task Manager can be used to examine processes. Then we'll look at a third-party tool, Process Explorer by Sysinternals and Microsoft TechNet, that can be used to smoke out any lurking processes that elude normal methods of remediating an infected system.

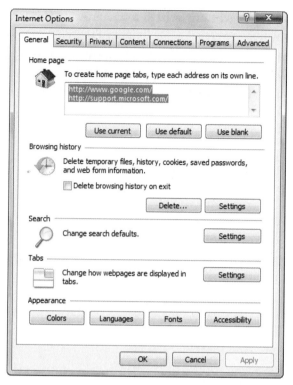

Figure 20-46   Use the Internet Options box to change the home page
Courtesy: Course Technology/Cengage Learning

Looking Under the Hood with Task Manager

Use Task Manager to search for malware processes, especially those that mask themselves as core Windows processes and elude AV software. In Figure 20-47, you can see most processes are registered as running under a user name or user account. Core Windows processes don't list the account under which they are running and not all processes are listed. To get the full picture, right-click an item that does not list a user name and select **Perform Administrative Tasks**, as shown in the figure, and respond to the UAC box.

The Task Manager window changes to show the accounts all processes are using as well as all processes currently running, including kernel mode processes (see Figure 20-48). Recall from Chapter 14 that accounts under which a process can run include the current user (in this case, Jean Andrews), System, Local Service, or Network Service account.

Sometimes a virus will disguise itself as a legitimate Windows core process such as Svchost.exe. You can recognize a program as a counterfeit process if it's not running under System, Local Service, or Network Service. If you spot an Svchost.exe process running under a user name, suspect a rat. Also, if you notice the Svchost.exe program file is located somewhere other than C:\Windows\system32, this most likely means it's a counterfeit version put there to make trouble. And how do you know the path to a program file? Click **View** on the Task Manager menu and select **Select Columns**. In the Select Process Page Columns dialog box, check **Image Path Name** and click **OK** (see Figure 20-49).

The most reliable site to use when researching processes is the Microsoft support site (*support.microsoft.com*). A search on a process name, an error message, a description of a process or problem with a process, or other related information can turn up a Knowledge Base article with the information you need.

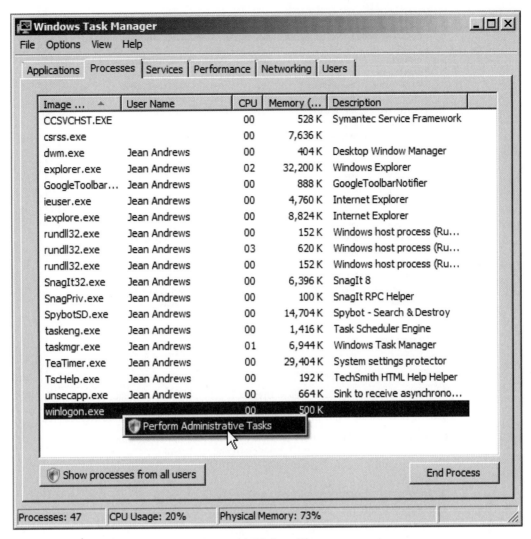

Figure 20-47 Processes currently running under Windows Vista
Courtesy: Course Technology/Cengage Learning

> **Notes** In this book, we use the most likely path to the Windows System Root folder: C:\Windows. However, your system might have a different System Root folder, such as E:\Windows. In this case, you'll need to substitute your specific System Root folder in the command line or path.

To help you with your research of core Windows processes, here is a list of processes, including their purposes and paths, that can be automatically launched depending on Windows settings:

▲ *Taskmgr.exe*. This is the Task Manager utility itself. The program file is stored in C:\Windows\system32.

▲ *Msmsgs.exe*. MSN Messenger, a chat application located in C:\Program Files\MSN Messenger. This process is not a core Windows process and can be easily removed if you don't use MSN Messenger.

▲ *Svchost.exe*. This process manages each process that is executed by a DLL. One instance of Svchost runs for each process it manages. The program file is stored in C:\Windows\system32. To see a list of services managed by Svchost, enter this command in a command-prompt window: **tasklist /SVC**.

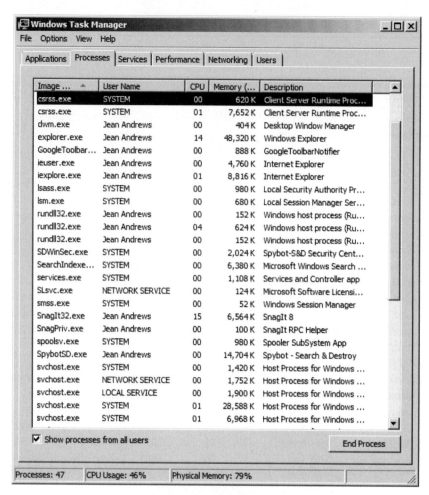

Figure 20-48 Task Manager set to show more information about processes
Courtesy: Course Technology/Cengage Learning

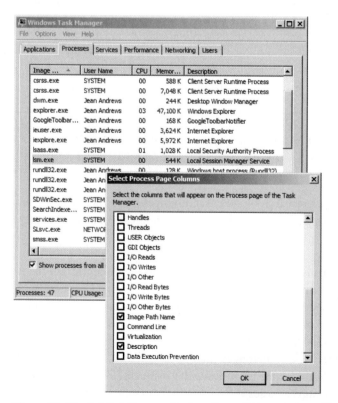

Figure 20-49 Set Task Manager to show the path to a program file
Courtesy: Course Technology/Cengage Learning

- ▲ *Explorer.exe*. The Windows graphical shell that manages the desktop, Start menu, taskbar, and file system. The program file is stored in C:\Windows.
- ▲ *Spoolsv.exe*. Handles Windows print spooling and is stored in C:\Windows\system32. Stopping and starting this process can sometimes solve a print spooling problem.
- ▲ *Lsass.exe*. Manages local security and logon policies. The program file is stored in C:\Windows\system32.
- ▲ *Services.exe*. Starts and stops services. This program file is stored in C:\Windows\system32.
- ▲ *Winlogon.exe*. Manages logon and logoff events. The program file is stored in C:\Windows\system32.
- ▲ *Csrss.exe*. Client/server run-time server subsystem; manages many commands in Windows that use graphics. The program file is stored in C:\Windows\system32.
- ▲ *Smss.exe*. Windows sessions manager; essential Windows process and is stored in C:\Windows\system32.
- ▲ *Internat.exe*. Displays an icon in the notification area of the taskbar that can be used to switch from English to another language when supplemental language support is enabled using the Regional and Language Options applet in Control Panel.
- ▲ *Mstask.exe*. The task scheduler that runs tasks at scheduled times.
- ▲ *Winmgmt.exe*. A core Windows component that starts the first time a client process requests to connect to the system.
- ▲ *System*. Windows system counter that shows up as a process, but has no program file associated with it.
- ▲ *System Idle Process*. Appears in the Task Manager to show how CPU usage is allotted. It is not associated with a program file.

Use Process Explorer at Microsoft TechNet

Process Explorer by Mark Russinovich, which is available at Microsoft TechNet, works like Task Manager, but takes us to another level of information. When you look at all the processes and services running in Task Manager, it's difficult, if not impossible, to know how these processes are related to each other. Understanding these relationships can help you identify a process that is launching other processes, which is called a process tree. By identifying the original process, the one handling other processes, you can lay the ax to the root of the tree rather than swinging at branches.

If you go to the Web site *technet.microsoft.com*, search for and download Process Explorer, and run it, the window in Figure 20-50 appears.

On this system monitored by Process Explorer, a browser hijacker is at work changing Web pages and producing pop-ups. As I watched the browser jump from one Web page to another without my involvement, Process Explorer showed me what was happening with the related processes. From the information in Figure 20-50, we see that the process, SearchIndexer.exe, has called two other processes shown in the figure. As the browser jumped from one Web page to another, these two processes completed and started up again. I was watching live malware in action!

As you can see, Process Explorer gives much information about a process and is a useful tool for software developers when writing and troubleshooting problems with their software, installation routines, and software conflicts. You can use the tool to smoke out processes, DLLs, and registry keys that elude Task Manager.

STEP 6: REMOVE ROOTKITS

A rootkit is a program that uses unusually complex methods to hide itself on a system, and many spyware and adware programs are also rootkits. The term rootkit applies to a kit or set of tools used originally on UNIX computers. In UNIX, the lowest and most powerful level of UNIX accounts is called the root account; therefore, this kit of tools was intended to keep a program working at this root level without detection.

A+
220-702
4.1

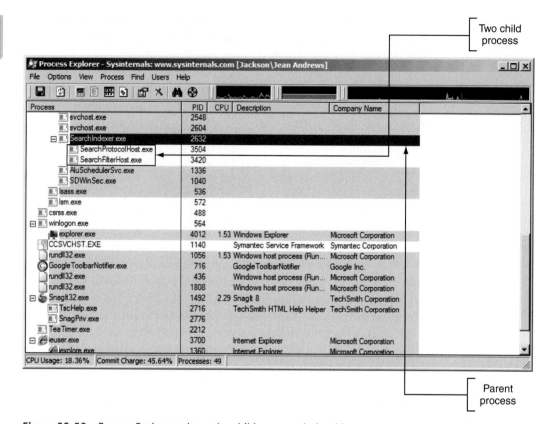

Figure 20-50 Process Explorer color codes child-parent relationships among processes and gives
information about processes
Courtesy: Course Technology/Cengage Learning

Rootkits can prevent Task Manager from displaying the running rootkit process, or may cause Task Manager to display a different name for this process. The program filename might not be displayed in Windows Explorer, the rootkit's registry keys might be hidden from the registry editor, or the registry editor might display wrong information. All this hiding is accomplished in one of two ways, depending on whether the rootkit is running in user mode or kernel mode (see Figure 20-51). A rootkit running in user mode intercepts the API calls between

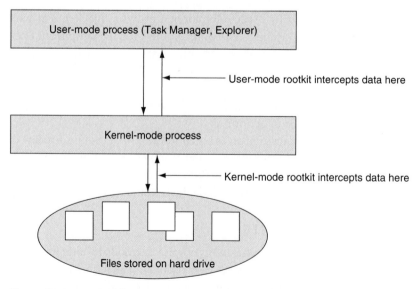

Figure 20-51 A rootkit can run in user mode or kernel mode
Courtesy: Course Technology/Cengage Learning

A+
220-702
4.1

the time when the API retrieves the data and when it is displayed in a window. A rootkit running in kernel mode actually interferes with the Windows kernel and substitutes its own information in place of the raw data read by the Windows kernel.

Because most AV software to one degree or another relies on Windows tools and components to work, the rootkit is not detected if the Windows tools themselves are infected. Rootkits are also programmed to hide from specific programs designed to find and remove them.

> **Notes** Even though the UAC box in Vista has not been all that popular with users and administrators, this box has been known to catch a rootkit before it installs itself. This makes the danger of rootkits less when using Windows Vista.

Generally, antirootkit software works to remove rootkits after they are installed by using these two methods:

- The software looks for running processes that don't match up with the underlying program filename.
- The software compares files, registry entries, and processes provided by the OS to the lists it generates from the raw data. If the two lists differ, a rootkit is suspected.

Two good antirootkit programs are:

- RootkitRevealer by Bryce Cogswell and Mark Russinovich and available at TechNet (*technet.microsoft.com*)
- BackLight by F-Secure (*www.f-secure.com*)

After you have used other available methods to remove malware and you still believe you're not clean, you might want to download and run one of these products. Close all open applications, including your AV software, and launch the product. Figure 20-52 shows the Vista desktop while Rootkit Revealer scans for rootkits. While it works, it takes complete control of the system so that you cannot use your computer while it is running.

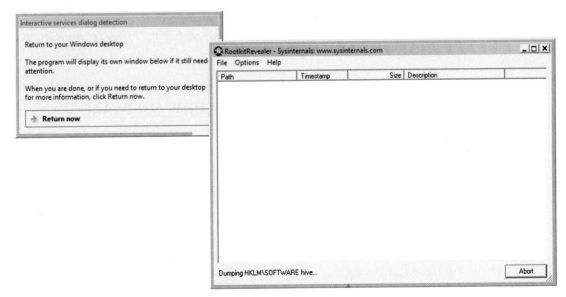

Figure 20-52 Rootkit Revealer scanning for rootkits
Courtesy: Course Technology/Cengage Learning

20

A+ 220-702

For best results when scanning for rootkits, run the antirootkit software from another networked computer so that the software is not dependent on the OS that might be infected. For example, you can share drive C on the network and then, from another computer on the network, run the antirootkit software and instruct it to scan drive C on the remote computer.

If the software detects a discrepancy that might indicate a rootkit is installed, you'll need to go to the TechNet or F-Secure Web site or do a general Web search to find information about the potential rootkit and instructions for removing it. Follow the instructions to manually remove the program and all its remnants. Sometimes the removal is so complicated, you might decide it makes more sense to just start over and reinstall Windows. If you decide to do that, be sure to format the hard drive as part of the installation process to make sure malware doesn't follow you into the new installation.

STEP 7: REPAIR BOOT BLOCKS

If an infected computer will not boot, it might be that the boot sectors of the hard drive are infected or damaged or the BIOS code might be corrupted. Here are the methods to deal with these problems:

▲ Recall that the first sector on a hard drive is called the master boot record (MBR), and is sometimes called the boot block. This sector contains the MBR program required to boot from the hard drive. The second sector on a hard drive, which is the first sector in the active partition, is the OS boot record. To repair either sector, boot from the Vista setup DVD, launch the Recovery Environment, and access the command prompt. The command **bootrec /fixmbr** repairs the MBR. The command **bootrec /fixboot** repairs the OS boot record. For Windows XP, launch the Recovery Console and use these two commands: **fixmbr** and **fixboot**. Chapter 16 gives more information about solving boot problems.

▲ A virus is rarely able to attack startup BIOS code stored on the motherboard. BIOS contains a boot block, which is a small program stored on the BIOS firmware chip that attempts to recover the BIOS when flashing BIOS has failed. If you see an error at POST, such as "Award BootBlock BIOS ROM checksum error" or a similar error, you can suspect that BIOS has become corrupted. The solution is to treat the problem as you would if flashing BIOS has failed. How to recover from errors when flashing BIOS is covered in Chapter 5. Again, however, know that viruses are unlikely to be able to gain access to BIOS programs.

PROTECT A SYSTEM AGAINST MALICIOUS SOFTWARE

Once your system is clean, you'll certainly want to keep it that way. Here is a quick recap of a few methods for protecting a system, which is covered in more detail in Chapter 19:

1. Install and run AV software. Set the software to schedule automatic scans of the system.

2. Set Windows to install updates automatically.

3. Keep a software firewall up and running.

4. For Windows Vista, keep the UAC box turned on.

5. Educate end users so they recognize social engineering situations and know how to lock down their workstations and use other security measures.

>> CHAPTER SUMMARY

▲ When setting up local shares for multiple users who have similar job needs, it is easier to assign permissions to user groups than to individual users.

▲ Windows XP uses simple file sharing, which does not give you control over who can access a shared resource.

▲ Permission propagation happens when a subfolder (child folder) inherits the permissions assigned to the parent folder. Explicit permissions can override inherited permissions.

▲ Regular permissions apply to local users of a folder or file. Share permissions apply to remote users of a folder or file.

▲ A hidden share is a shared folder or file that has a $ at the end of the file name. The folder or file does not appear in the Network window or My Network Places.

▲ Administrative shares are used on a domain so that administrators can easily access the \Windows folder and all drives and volumes on the network. Administrative shares do not work when using a workgroup.

▲ The Encrypting File System (EFS) is used with an NTFS volume for Windows Vista Ultimate and Business editions and Windows XP Professional.

▲ You can allow other local users to access your encrypted file by adding their EFS certificates to the file. You cannot share encrypted files over a network unless the computer belongs to a domain.

▲ Always back up your EFS certificate. If the original certificate gets corrupted, you might not be able to access encrypted files without a backup certificate.

▲ If you need to use the backup certificate, you must first import it into Windows and then add it to an encrypted file.

▲ Using BitLocker Encryption with Vista, you can set it to authenticate the computer, authenticate the user, or authenticate both the computer and the user. The last option is the best choice for the best security.

▲ To use BitLocker to authenticate the computer, the computer will need a TPM chip to hold the encryption key.

▲ BIOS security features include passwords, drive lock passwords, and support for a TPM chip and an intrusion-detection device.

▲ The first defense against malicious software is antivirus software. If you cannot access the Internet, install the AV software from CD onto the infected computer. Alternately, you can scan the infected computer using AV software installed on another computer.

▲ Keep AV software up to date with the latest engine updates and virus signature updates.

▲ If AV software will not run on a PC because the PC is so badly infected, try running the software while in Safe Mode or run the software from another computer.

▲ Adware and spyware removal software sometimes finds malware that AV software does not find.

▲ AV software sometimes cannot delete a malware program and you must manually delete it.

▲ Some systems become so highly infected, the only solution is to reinstall Windows.

20

>> KEY TERMS

For explanations of key terms, see the Glossary near the end of the book.

administrative shares
anonymous users
Authenticated Users group
Certificate Manager
    (certmgr.msc) console
Everyone group

hidden share
inherited permissions
local shares
permission propagation
quarantined computer
quarantined file

share permissions
simple file sharing
virus encyclopedias
virus signatures

>> REVIEWING THE BASICS

1. List the three types of user accounts used by Windows Vista.

2. List the four types of user accounts used by Windows XP.

3. Which Windows console is used to create a new user group?

4. What is the term Windows XP uses to describe sharing files when no control is allowed over who has access to a shared file?

5. What type of permission does a folder receive from its parent folder?

6. What type of permissions must be given so that a folder can be shared on the network?

7. If a folder has 10 subfolders, what is the easiest way to change the permissions for all 10 folders?

8. What two services must be running under Windows XP to share folders on the network?

9. If you are having a problem changing the permissions of a folder that was created by another user, what can you do to help solve the problem?

10. A shared folder whose name ends with a $ is called a(n)_____.

11. When is it possible to use administrative shares?

12. What can you do so that you can use file and folder encryption with a volume using the FAT file system and Windows Vista Business edition?

13. What is the command to decrypt the file myfile.doc?

14. What is the command to launch the Certificate Manager console?

15. What is the file extension used by default for a certificate file that contains the private key? That does not contain the private key?

16. If you upgrade from Windows XP to Windows Vista Ultimate and cannot access your encrypted files, what is the first thing to do?

17. What hardware component is needed to set up BitLocker Encryption so that you can authenticate the computer?

18. What is the first thing you should do when you discover a computer is infected with malware?

19. What is the best tool to use to find out the purpose of a program that is running on your system?

20. What command can be used to stop a process that is more powerful than Task Manager?

>> THINKING CRITICALLY

1. You open a folder Properties box to encrypt the folder, click Advanced, and discover *Encrypt contents to secure data* is dimmed. What is the problem?

   a. Encryption has not been enabled. Use the Computer Management console to enable it.

   b. You are not using a version of Windows that supports encryption.

   c. Most likely a virus has attacked the system and is disabling encryption.

   d. Encryption applies only to files, not folders.

2. A virus has attacked your hard drive and now when you start up Windows, instead of seeing a Windows desktop, the system freezes and you see a "blue screen of death" (an error message on a blue background). You have extremely important document files on the drive that you cannot afford to lose. What do you do first?

   a. Try a data-recovery service even though it is very expensive.

   b. Remove the hard drive from the computer case and install it in another computer.

   c. Try GetDataBack by Runtime Software (*www.runtime.org*) to recover the data.

   d. Use Windows utilities to attempt to fix the Windows boot problem.

   e. Run antivirus software to remove the virus.

3. AV software has removed malware from a highly infected system. After the first reboot, an error message is displayed that contains a reference to a strange DLL file that is missing. Which two options should you use to begin troubleshooting?

   a. Run the AV software again.

   b. Run Msconfig and look for startup entries that are launching the DLL.

   c. Run Regedit and look for keys that refer to the DLL.

   d. Search the Internet for information about the DLL.

>> HANDS-ON PROJECTS

20

PROJECT 20-1:   Sharing and Securing Folders

Using two computers, networked together, do the following to practice sharing and securing folders using Windows XP:

1. Create a user account on Computer 1 named User1. In the My Documents folder for that account, create a folder named Folder1.

2. On Computer 2, create a user account named User2. Try to access Folder1 on Computer 1. What is the result? What must you do so that the folder can be accessed?

3. Now make the folder private so that others cannot see or access it on the network. Describe how you did that.

PROJECT 20-2: Download and Use AV Software

A free trial of AVG Anti-Virus software is available on the AVG site at *www.avg.com*. Do the following to download, install, and run the software:

1. Download the free trial version of AVG Anti-Virus software from the *www.avg.com* site and install the software.

2. Perform a complete scan of the system. Were any suspicious programs found?

3. Update the software with the latest virus signatures.

4. Set the AV software to scan the system daily.

5. Set the software to scan incoming e-mail.

PROJECT 20-3: Researching Running Processes

Boot to the Windows desktop and then use Task Manager to get a list of all the running processes on your machine. Get a print screen of this list. Make a written list of each process running and write a one-sentence explanation of the process. Note that you most likely will need to use the Internet to research some of these processes.

Next, boot the system into Safe Mode and use Task Manager to list running processes. Which processes that were loaded normally are not loaded when the system is running in Safe Mode?

PROJECT 20-4: Learning to Use Autoruns

Autoruns by TechNet and Sysinternals (*technet.microsoft.com*) is similar to, but gives more information than does MSconfig. Download Autoruns and run it on your PC. How many registry keys does Autoruns list that contain startup items on your PC? Use Msconfig to get a similar list. Compare the list of startup items to that generated by Msconfig. Describe any differences between the two lists.

PROJECT 20-5: Using the Internet to Learn About Viruses

One source of information about viruses on the Web is F-Secure Corporation. Go to the Web site *www.f-secure.com*, for information about viruses. Information about viruses includes complete descriptions, symptoms, and solutions. Print a description of three viruses from this Web site, with these characteristics:

◢ One virus that destroys data on a hard drive

◢ One harmless virus that only displays garbage on the screen

◢ One virus that hides in a boot sector

The site also lists information about the most recent viruses. Search the Web site at *www.f-secure.com*, list three recent viruses, and describe their payloads.

>> REAL PROBLEMS, REAL SOLUTIONS

REAL PROBLEM 20-1: Cleaning Your System of Malware

Using the tools and techniques presented in this chapter, thoroughly clean your system of any malware. Take notes as you work and list any malware detected.

REAL PROBLEM 20-2: Researching a Laptop with a TPM Chip

Many laptops sold today have a TPM chip, and some have encryption-enabled hard drives that don't require encryption software such as BitLocker. Research the Web for a laptop that offers a TPM chip and answer these questions:

1. What is the brand and model laptop that has the TPM chip? Print the Web page listing the laptop specifications showing the chip.

2. Is the chip optional? If so, what is the cost of including the chip?

3. Does the laptop have an encryption-enabled hard drive?

4. Does the laptop come bundled with encryption software? If so, what is the name of the software?

5. Does the laptop offer a drive lock password?

6. What is the cost of the laptop, including the TPM chip?

Supporting Notebooks

So far in this book, you've learned how computers work, explored some of the devices used to work with them, examined operating systems, and discovered how to connect a PC to a network and how to secure computers from attack. Most devices and software you've learned about relate to desktop computers, which are stationary and cannot be moved easily. However, recent statistics show that more than half of personal computers purchased today are notebook computers, and almost 30 percent of personal computers currently in use are notebooks. As notebooks become more and more popular, PC service technicians will need to know how to support them. In this chapter, you'll learn about supporting, upgrading, and troubleshooting notebooks.

There was a time that a notebook was considered a "black box" to PC support technicians. If it needed servicing inside, the notebook was taken to an authorized service center supported by the notebook manufacturer. These technicians were all trained by the manufacturer to service its products. However, taking apart and servicing a notebook computer are now seen as tasks that every A+ certified technician needs to know how to do. As part of your preparation to be A+ certified, try to find an old notebook computer you can take apart. If you can locate the service manual, you should be able to take it apart, repair it (assuming the parts are still available and don't cost more than the notebook is worth), and get it up and running again. Have fun with this chapter and enjoy tinkering with that old notebook!

SPECIAL CONSIDERATIONS WHEN SUPPORTING NOTEBOOKS

A+
220-701
2.4

A notebook or laptop computer is a computer designed to be portable (see Figure 21-1). Notebooks use the same technology as PCs, but with modifications to use less power, take up less space, and operate on the move. Notebooks come in several varieties, including tablet PCs and netbooks. A tablet PC has more features than a notebook, including a touch screen that also allows you to handwrite on it with a stylus. Another variation of a notebook is a netbook that is smaller and less expensive than a notebook and has fewer features.

Figure 21-1   A notebook is a computer designed for portability
Comstock Images

In many situations, the task of troubleshooting, upgrading, and maintaining a notebook requires the same skills, knowledge, and procedures as when servicing a desktop computer. However, you should take some special considerations into account when caring for, supporting, upgrading, and troubleshooting notebooks. When you think of all the new notebooks sold this past year or so, learning about notebooks and how to support them can position you for some great career opportunities supporting notebooks!

Notebooks and their replacement parts cost more than desktop PCs with similar features because their components are designed to be more compact and stand up to travel. They use compact hard drives, small memory modules, and CPUs that require less power than regular components. Whereas a desktop computer is often assembled from parts made by a variety of manufacturers, notebook computers are almost always sold by a vendor that either manufactured the notebook or had it manufactured as a consolidated system. Factors to consider that generally apply more to notebook computers than desktop computers are the original equipment manufacturer's warranty, the service manuals and diagnostic software provided by the manufacturer, the customized installation of the OS that is unique to notebooks, and the advantage of ordering replacement parts directly from the notebook manufacturer or other source authorized by the manufacturer.

WARRANTY CONCERNS

Most manufacturers or retailers of notebooks offer at least a one-year warranty and the option to purchase an extended warranty. Therefore, when problems arise while the notebook is under warranty, you are dealing with a single manufacturer or retailer to get support or parts. After the notebook is out of warranty, this manufacturer or retailer can still be your one-stop shop for support and parts.

A+
220-701
2.4

The warranty often applies to all components in the system, but it can be voided if someone other than an authorized service center services the notebook. Therefore, you, as a service technician, must be very careful not to void a warranty that the customer has purchased. Warranties can be voided by opening the case, removing part labels, installing other-vendor parts, upgrading the OS, or disassembling the system unless directly instructed to do so by the service center help desk personnel.

Before you begin servicing a notebook, to avoid problems with a warranty, always ask the customer, "Is the notebook under warranty?" If the notebook is under warranty, look at the documentation to find out how to get technical support. Options are phone numbers, chat sessions on the Web, and e-mail. Use the most appropriate option. Before you contact technical support, have the notebook model and serial number ready (see Figure 21-2). You'll also need the name, phone number, and address of the person or company that made the purchase. Consider asking the customer for a copy of the receipt and warranty so that you'll have the information you need to talk with support personnel.

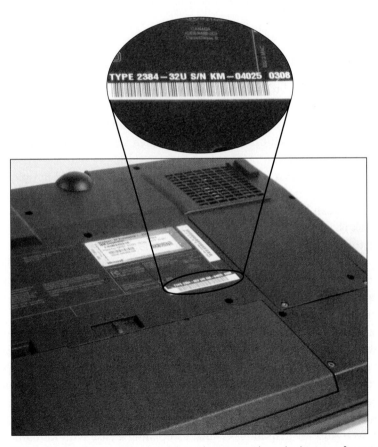

Figure 21-2 The model and serial number stamped on the bottom of a notebook are used to identify the notebook to service desk personnel
Courtesy: Course Technology/Cengage Learning

Based on the type of warranty purchased by the notebook's owner, the manufacturer might send an on-site service technician, ask you to ship or take the notebook to an authorized service center, or help you solve the problem over the phone. Table 21-1 lists some popular manufacturers of notebooks, netbooks, and tablet PCs.

Manufacturer	Web Site
Apple Computer	*www.apple.com*
ASUS	*usa.asus.com*
Compaq and HP	*www.hp.com*
Dell Computer	*www.dell.com*
Fujitsu/Fuji	*www.fujitsu.com*
Gateway	*www.gateway.com*
Lenovo (formally IBM ThinkPads)	*www.lenovo.com*
MSI Computers	*www.msicomputer.com*
Samsung	*www.samsung.com*
Sony (VAIO)	*www.sonystyle.com*
Toshiba America	*www.csd.toshiba.com*

Table 21-1   Notebook, netbook, and tablet PC manufacturers

SERVICE MANUALS AND OTHER SOURCES OF INFORMATION

Desktop computer cases tend to be similar to one another, and components in desktop systems tend to be interchangeable among manufacturers. Not so with notebooks. Notebook manufacturers tend to take great liberty in creating their own unique computer cases, buses, cables, connectors, drives, circuit boards, fans, and even screws, all of which are likely to be proprietary in design.

Every notebook model has a unique case. Components are installed in unique ways and opening the case for each notebook model is done differently. Because of these differences, servicing notebooks can be very complicated and time consuming. For example, a hard drive on one notebook is accessed by popping open a side panel and sliding the drive out of its bay. However, to access the hard drive on another model notebook, you must remove the keyboard. If you are not familiar with a particular notebook model, you can damage the case as you pry and push trying to open it. Trial and error is likely to damage a case. Even though you might successfully replace a broken component, the damaged case will result in an unhappy customer.

Fortunately, a notebook service manual can save you much time and effort—if you can locate one (see Figure 21-3). Two notebook manufacturers, Lenovo (formally IBM) and Dell, provide their service manuals online free of charge. In addition, Compaq offers detailed information on its Web site to help you service its notebooks. For example, in Figure 21-4, you can see a video in progress showing you the steps to replace the Bluetooth module in an HP or Compaq notebook. For all notebook manufacturers, check the FAQ pages of their Web sites for help in tasks such as opening a case without damaging it and locating and replacing a component.

Sometimes, you can find service manuals on the Web. To find your manual, do an Internet search on the model notebook, for example, search on "Compaq PC X1000 notebook service manual." Several Web sites offer notebook service manuals for download, including *www.eserviceinfo.com, www.tim.id.au/blog/tims-laptop-service-manuals, www.notebookrepairguide.com, www.notebook-manuals.com, www.ebooksquad.com,* and *www.laptoprepair101.com.*

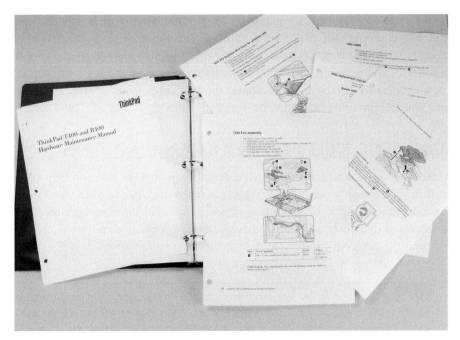

Figure 21-3 A notebook service manual tells you how to use diagnostic tools, troubleshoot a notebook, and replace components
Courtesy: Course Technology/Cengage Learning

Figure 21-4 The Compaq Web site *(www.hp.com)* provides detailed instructions for troubleshooting and replacing components
Courtesy: Course Technology/Cengage Learning

21

A+ 220-701

Don't forget about the user manuals. They might contain directions for upgrading and replacing components that do not require disassembling the case, such as how to upgrade memory or replace a new hard drive. User manuals also include troubleshooting tips and procedures and possibly descriptions of BIOS settings. In addition, you can use a Web search engine to search on the computer model, component, or error message, which might give you information about the problem and solution.

DIAGNOSTIC TOOLS PROVIDED BY MANUFACTURERS

Most notebook manufacturers provide diagnostic software that can help you test components to determine which component needs replacing. As one of the first steps when servicing a notebook, check the user manual, service manual, or manufacturer Web site to determine if diagnostic software exists and how to obtain it and use it. Use the software to pinpoint the problem component, which can then be replaced.

> **Notes** When you purchase a replacement part for a notebook from the notebook's manufacturer, most often the manufacturer also sends you detailed instructions for exchanging the part.

Check the manufacturer Web site for test software that can be downloaded for a particular model notebook. For newer notebooks, the software is stored on CDs bundled with the notebook or on the hard drive and accessed by pressing certain keys during the boot process. For older notebooks, the software is usually contained on a floppy disk and run from the disk. This test disk might come with the notebook or can be purchased from the manufacturer as a separate item.

One example of diagnostic software is PC-Doctor, which is used by several manufacturers, including Lenovo, IBM ThinkPad, Fujitsu, and HP notebooks. The test software is stored on a floppy disk, CD, or hard drive. If stored on a floppy disk or CD, you can boot from the device to run the tests. If the software is stored on the hard drive, you can run it from the Windows Start menu or by pressing a function key at startup before Windows loads. Either way, PC-Doctor can run tests on the keyboard, video, speakers, mouse, joystick, floppy disk drive, CD drive, DVD drive, wireless LAN, motherboard, processor, serial and parallel ports, hard drive, and memory. To learn how to use the software, see the notebook's service manual or user manual. You can also find a stand-alone version of PC-Doctor at *www.pc-doctor.com*. You can purchase it at this site; it's expensive, but might be worth it if you plan to service many notebooks.

THE OEM OPERATING SYSTEM BUILD

Notebook computers are sold with an operating system preinstalled at the factory. The OS installation is tailored by the manufacturer to satisfy the specific needs of the notebook. In this situation, the manufacturer is called the OEM (original equipment manufacturer) and the customized installation of the OS is called the operating system build or OS build. Drivers installed are also specific to proprietary devices installed in the notebook. Diagnostic software is often written specifically for a notebook and its installed OS. For all these reasons, use caution when deciding to upgrade to a new OS and know that, if you have problems with a device, in most circumstances, you must turn to the OEM for solutions and updates for device drivers. Now let's look at some considerations to be aware of when upgrading notebook operating systems.

THE RECOVERY CDS AND RECOVERY PARTITIONS

A+
220-701
2.4

Most notebook computers come with one or more support CDs provided by the manufacturer. This CD might or might not contain an installable version of the OS preinstalled on the notebook. If you need to install the OS again, such as when you are replacing a faulty hard drive, you might have to request that the notebook manufacturer provide you with a recovery CD for the OS installation (see Figure 21-5).

Figure 21-5 The Recovery CDs are important tools needed to recover from a failed notebook hard drive
Courtesy: Course Technology/Cengage Learning

Some notebooks come with the utilities and system files needed to install a new copy of the OS stored on the hard drive in a separate partition. This partition might or might not be hidden. Figure 21-6 shows the Disk Management information for a hard drive on one notebook that has a 3.95-GB recovery partition that is not hidden. The files stored on this partition are protected from access when using Windows Explorer, as shown in Figure 21-7.

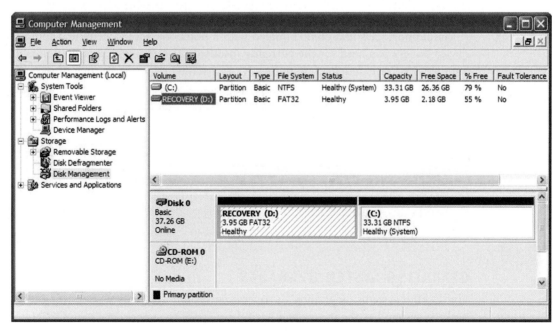

Figure 21-6 This notebook hard drive has a recovery partition that can be used to recover the system
Courtesy: Course Technology/Cengage Learning

21

A+ 220-701

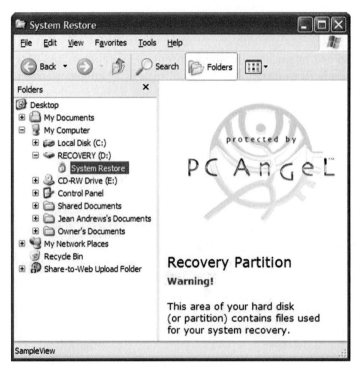

Figure 21-7 A recovery partition cannot be accessed using Windows Explorer
Courtesy: Course Technology/Cengage Learning

To know how to access the recovery tools stored on a recovery partition, see the user reference manual. Most likely, you'll see a message at the beginning of the boot, such as "Press ESC for diagnostics," or "Press F12 to recover the system." When you press the key, a menu appears giving you options to diagnose the problem, to repair the current OS installation, or to completely rebuild the entire hard drive to its state when the notebook was first purchased. Of course, this won't work if your hard drive is broken and/or the recovery partition is damaged. In this situation, you're dependent on the OS recovery CDs and other support CDs to build the new hard drive after it is installed.

The support CDs that come bundled with a notebook should definitely contain all the device drivers you need for the currently installed OS and might contain device drivers for another OS. For example, if Windows XP is installed on a system, one of the support CDs might contain device drivers for Windows Vista. The CDs might also include setup programs for the applications that come preinstalled on the notebook.

> **Notes** When you first purchase a notebook, make sure you have a recovery CD containing the installed OS so you can recover from a failed hard drive. If one doesn't come bundled with the notebook, purchase it from the notebook manufacturer. (The price should be less than $30.) Do this before problems arise. If the notebook is more than three years old, the manufacturer might no longer provide the CD.
>
> You can also download all the device drivers for the notebook from the manufacturer's Web site and burn them to CD.

OPERATING SYSTEM UPGRADES

For desktop systems, upgrading the operating system is usually a good thing to do if the desktop system has the power and hard drive space to support the new OS. Not so with notebooks. Unless a specific need to upgrade arises, the operating system preinstalled on the notebook should last the life of the notebook.

A+
220-701
2.4

As an example of a specific reason to upgrade, consider a situation in which a notebook holds private data, and you need to provide the best possible security on the notebook. In this situation, it might be appropriate to upgrade from Windows XP to Windows Vista so that you can use BitLocker Encryption.

If at all possible, always upgrade the OS using an OS build purchased from the notebook manufacturer. This set of CDs or DVDs purchased from the manufacturer should include the OS and device drivers specific to your notebook. In addition, carefully follow their specific instructions for the installation.

If you decide to upgrade the OS using an off-the-shelf version of Windows XP or Windows Vista, first determine that all components in the system are compatible with the upgrade. Be certain to have available all the device drivers you need for the new OS before you upgrade. Download the drivers from the notebook manufacturer's Web site and store them in a folder on the hard drive. After you upgrade the OS, install the drivers from this folder. The notebook manufacturer might also suggest you first flash the BIOS before you perform the upgrade. And, if applications came preinstalled on the notebook, find out if you have the applications' setup CDs, and if they will install under the new OS.

CARING FOR NOTEBOOKS

Notebook computers tend to not last as long as desktop computers because they are portable and, therefore, subjected to more wear and tear. Also, notebooks are more susceptible to worms and viruses than desktop systems, because you are more likely to use them on a public network, such as when you sit down at a coffee shop hot spot to work. A notebook's user manual gives specific instructions on how to care for the notebook. Those instructions follow these general guidelines:

- ◢ LCD panels on notebooks are fragile and can be damaged fairly easily. Take precautions against damaging a notebook's LCD panel. Don't touch it with sharp objects like ballpoint pens.
- ◢ Don't connect the notebook to a phone line during an electrical storm.
- ◢ Only use battery packs recommended by the notebook manufacturer. Keep the battery pack away from moisture or heat, and don't attempt to take the pack apart. When it no longer works, dispose of it correctly. Chapter 11 covers how to dispose of batteries. Best practices to prolong the life of your battery are discussed later in the chapter.
- ◢ Always use passwords with each Windows user account so that the laptop is better protected when connected to a public network.
- ◢ Don't tightly pack the notebook in a suitcase because the LCD panel might get damaged. Use a good-quality carrying case and make it a habit of always transporting the notebook in the carrying case. Don't place heavy objects on top of the notebook case.
- ◢ Don't pick up or hold the notebook by the display panel. Pick it up and hold it by the bottom. Keep the lid closed when the notebook is not in use.
- ◢ Don't move the notebook while the hard drive is being accessed (the drive indicator light is on). Wait until the light goes off.
- ◢ Don't put the notebook close to an appliance such as a TV, large audio speakers, or refrigerator that generates a strong magnetic field, and don't place your cell phone on a notebook while the phone is in use.
- ◢ As with any computer, keep the OS current with the latest Windows updates and use AV software.

- ▲ Never, ever connect to the Internet using a public wireless connection or ISP without first turning on a software firewall.
- ▲ Keep your notebook at a controlled temperature. For example, never leave it in a car overnight when it is cold, and don't leave it in a car during the day when it's hot. Don't expose your notebook to direct sunlight for an extended time.
- ▲ Don't leave the notebook in a dusty or smoke-filled area. Don't use it in a wet area such as near a swimming pool or in the bathtub. Don't use it at the beach where sand can get in it.
- ▲ Don't power it up and down unnecessarily.
- ▲ Protect the notebook from overheating by not running it when it's still inside the case, resting on a pillow, or partially covered with a blanket or anything else that would prevent proper air circulation around it.
- ▲ If a notebook has just come indoors from the cold, don't turn it on until it reaches room temperature. In some cases, condensation on the hard drive platters can cause problems. Some manufacturers recommend that when you receive a new notebook shipped to you during the winter, you should leave it in its shipping carton for several hours before you open the carton to prevent subjecting the notebook to a temperature shock.
- ▲ Protect a notebook against ESD. If you have just come in from the cold on a low-humidity day when there is the possibility that you are carrying ESD, don't touch the notebook until you have grounded yourself.
- ▲ Before placing a notebook in a carrying case for travel, remove any CDs, DVDs, or PC Cards, and put them in protective covers. Verify that the system is powered down and not in suspend or standby mode.
- ▲ If a notebook gets wet, you can follow steps given later in the chapter to partially disassemble it to allow internal components to dry. Give the notebook several days to dry before attempting to turn it on. Don't use heat to speed up the drying time.

A well-used notebook, especially one that is used in dusty or dirty areas, needs cleaning occasionally. Here are some cleaning tips:

- ▲ It is not necessary to disassemble a notebook for routine cleaning. In fact, you can clean the LCD panel, battery connections, keyboard, touch pad, or even memory contacts as needed without opening the notebook case.
- ▲ Clean the LCD panel with a soft dry cloth. If the panel is very dirty, you can dampen the cloth with water. Even though some books advise using a mixture of isopropyl alcohol and water to clean an LCD panel, notebook manufacturers say not to.
- ▲ Use a can of compressed air meant to be used around computer equipment to blow dust and small particles out of the keyboard, track ball, and touch pad. Turn the notebook at an angle and direct the air into the sides of the keyboard. Then use a soft, damp cloth to clean key caps and touch pad.
- ▲ Use compressed air to blow out all air vents on the notebook to make sure they are clean and unobstructed.
- ▲ If keys are sticking, remove the keyboard so you can better spray under the key with compressed air. If you can remove the key cap, remove it and clean the key contact area with contact cleaner. One example of a contact cleaner you can use for this purpose is Stabilant 22 (*www.stabilant.com*). Reinstall the keyboard and test it. If the key still sticks, replace the keyboard.
- ▲ Remove the battery and clean the battery connections with a contact cleaner.

SUPPORTING NOTEBOOK PERIPHERAL DEVICES

A notebook provides ports on its back or sides for connecting peripherals (see Figure 21-8). Here is a list of some slots, switches, and ports a notebook might have:

- ExpressCard slot with slot protective cover or older and outdated PC Card or CardBus slots with an eject button
- USB and FireWire ports
- Network port (RJ-45) and modem port (RJ-11)
- Headphone jack and microphone jack
- Volume control
- Secure Digital (SD) and other slots for flash memory cards
- For security, a Smart Card slot, fingerprint scanner, and security lock slot for installing a chain and lock
- Wireless antenna on/off switch (for onboard wireless, the antenna is inside the notebook case)
- 15-pin VGA video port
- Audio input and video input jacks if the notebook has an embedded TV tuner
- Airflow vents
- Power jack for DC or AC power adapter
- Some notebooks have an internal Bluetooth adapter to support these wireless connections
- Older notebooks might have a parallel port, serial port, PS/2 port, or infrared port

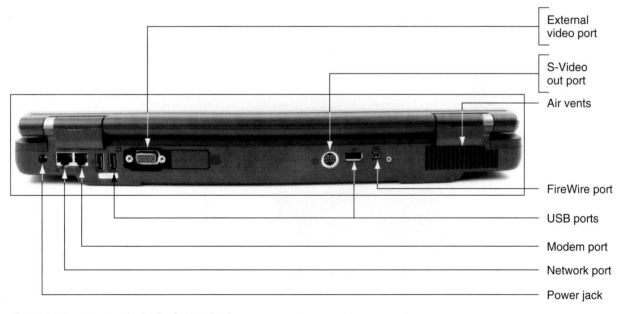

Figure 21-8   Ports on the back of a notebook
Courtesy: Course Technology/Cengage Learning

Before we get into the discussion of ports used primarily on notebooks, keep in mind that USB ports have become a popular way of adding devices to all types of computers, including notebooks. For example, Figure 21-9 shows a wireless mouse and keypad that use a receiver connected to a USB port. Installing this mouse and keypad on a notebook is very simple: You plug the receiver into the port; Windows displays a message that it has located the device, and the mouse and keypad are ready to use.

21

A+ 220-701

Figure 21-9 This wireless mouse and keypad use a receiver that connects to a USB port
Courtesy: Course Technology/Cengage Learning

PORT REPLICATORS AND DOCKING STATIONS

A+
220-701
1.10

Some notebooks have a connector on the bottom of the notebook (called a docking port) to connect to a port replicator (see Figure 21-10) or to a docking station (see Figure 21-11). A **port replicator** provides ports to allow a notebook to easily connect to a full-sized monitor, keyboard, AC power adapter, and other peripheral devices. A **docking station** provides the same functions as a port replicator, but provides additional slots for adding secondary storage devices and expansion cards. Laptop manufacturers usually offer a port replicator or docking station as additional options. If a laptop doesn't have a docking port, you can purchase a port replicator that plugs into an ExpressCard slot. To use a port replicator or docking station, plug all the peripherals into the port replicator or docking station. Then connect your notebook to the device. No software needs installing. When you need to

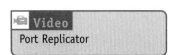
Video
Port Replicator

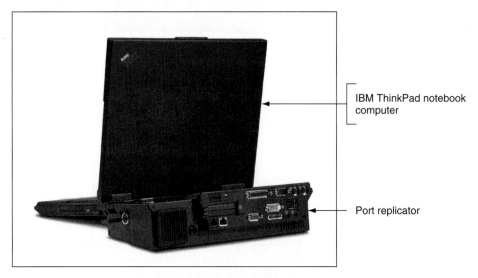

IBM ThinkPad notebook computer

Port replicator

Figure 21-10 A port replicator makes it convenient to connect a notebook computer to resources and peripherals at your office
Courtesy of IBM Corporation

A+
220-701
1.10

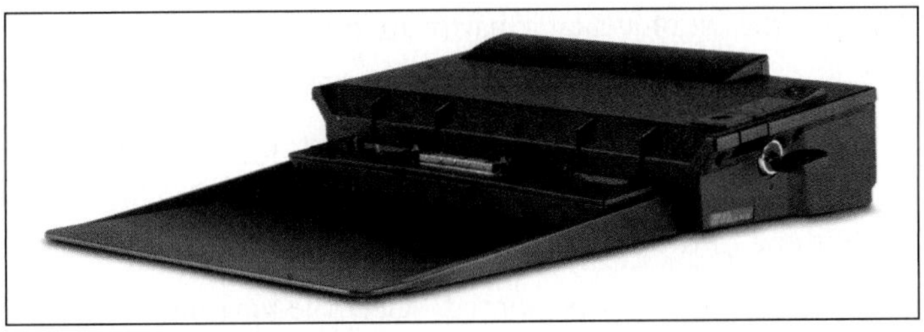

Figure 21-11   A docking station can provide extra secondary storage for a laptop
Courtesy of IBM Corporation

travel with your notebook, rather than having to unplug all the peripherals, all you have to do
is disconnect the notebook from the port replicator or docking station.

> 💡 **A+ Exam Tip**   The A+ 220-701 Essentials exam expects you to know how to use a docking station.

If a notebook using Windows XP has a docking station, you can set up one hardware
profile to use the docking station and another when you are on the road and don't have
access to the docking station. Windows Vista doesn't require you to set up hardware profiles, because it automatically senses when a docking station is present. To create a hardware
profile in Windows XP, do the following:

1. Open the **System Properties** window and click the **Hardware** tab.

2. Click the **Hardware Profiles** button at the bottom of the Hardware tab. The Hardware
   Profiles dialog box opens (Figure 21-12).

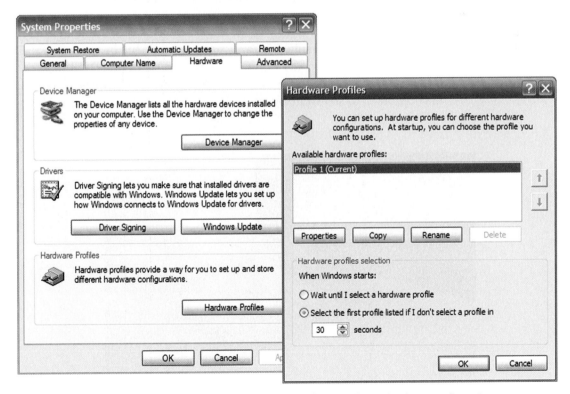

Figure 21-12   Windows XP allows you to set a hardware profile for different hardware configurations
Courtesy: Course Technology/Cengage Learning

21

A+ 220-701

A+
220-701
1.10

3. Select a profile from the list of available hardware profiles and then click the **Copy** button.

4. Type a new name for the profile, and then click **OK**.

5. Under *When Windows starts*, select either the option for Windows to wait for you to select a hardware profile or the option for Windows to start with the first profile listed if you don't select one in the specified number of seconds. Close all open windows.

6. Restart the computer and, when prompted, select the new hardware profile.

7. Open the **System Properties** dialog box. Click the **Hardware** tab, click **Device Manager**, and then double-click the icon for a device that you want enabled or disabled in the new profile. For example, you might set one profile to access a second hard drive that is installed on the docking station, which is not available when traveling.

8. Click the **General** tab in the Properties dialog box for the device. In the area for Device usage, select the option to enable or disable the device for the current profile or for all hardware profiles. Close all open dialog boxes.

A+
220-701
1.10
1.2

PC CARD, CARDBUS, AND EXPRESSCARD SLOTS

PC Card, CardBus, and ExpressCard slots can be used to connect peripheral devices to notebooks. These slot and card standards have evolved over the years and have been designed and supported by the PCMCIA (Personal Computer Memory Card International Association). PCMCIA cards include one or more variations of PC Card, CardBus, and ExpressCard. The cards are used by many devices, including modems, network cards for wired or wireless networks, sound cards, SCSI host adapters, IEEE 1394 controllers, USB controllers, flash memory adapters, TV tuners, and hard disks.

You need to be aware of the different standards for PCMCIA cards, which are summarized here, listed in the order they were introduced into the market:

1. PC Card slots originally used a 16-bit ISA bus. A PC Card is about the size of a credit card, but thicker. Originally, PC Cards were called PCMCIA Cards and the first of these cards were used to add memory to a notebook. Figure 21-13 shows a PC Card being inserted into a PC Card slot. Some PC Cards have a dongle or pigtail, such as the network card shown in Figure 21-14.

Figure 21-13 Many peripheral devices are added to a notebook using a PC Card slot; here, a Microdrive adapter PC Card is inserted in a PC Card slot
Courtesy: Course Technology/Cengage Learning

A+
220-701
1.10
1.2

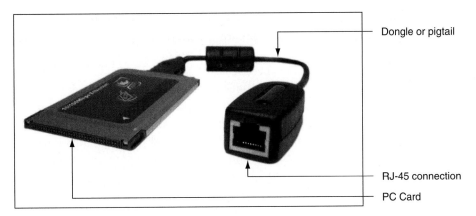

Dongle or pigtail

RJ-45 connection

PC Card

Figure 21-14 This PC Card serves as a NIC for an Ethernet network
Courtesy: Course Technology/Cengage Learning

2. Because of increasing demands for more technology packed into a PCMCIA card, three standards pertaining to size were developed and named Type I, Type II, and Type III. Generally, the thicker the PC Card, the higher the standard. A thick hard drive card might need a Type III slot, but a thin modem card might only need a Type II slot. Because they differ only in thickness, a thinner card can fit into a thicker slot:

- Type I cards can be up to 3.3mm thick and were primarily used for adding RAM to a notebook PC.
- Type II cards can be up to 5.5mm thick and are often used as modem cards. Figure 21-15 shows a Type II PC Card that is an adapter for a Microdrive device.
- Type III cards can be up to 10.5mm thick, large enough to accommodate a portable disk drive. Two Type I or Type II cards can fit into a single Type III slot and both cards can work at the same time.

Figure 21-15 A Type II PC Card adapter for a Microdrive device
Courtesy: Course Technology/Cengage Learning

21

A+ 220-701

3. **CardBus** slots improved PC Card slots by increasing the bus width to 32 bits, while maintaining backward compatibility with earlier standards. The slot uses the 32-bit PCI bus standards. CardBus slots can support the older 16-bit PC Card devices. You

A+
220-701
1.10
1.2

cannot, however, insert a CardBus card into an older 16-bit PC Card slot. A bumpy strip on the edge of a CardBus card is designed to prevent a CardBus card from being inserted into the 16-bit PC Card slots. CardBus slots come as either Type II or Type III slots and are sometimes called PC Card slots or 32-bit PC Card slots.

Figure 21-16 shows a TV tuner CardBus card. If you look closely at the edge, you can see the gold, bumpy strip that prevents a CardBus card from being inserted into a legacy PC Card slot. Compare this edge to the smooth edge of a PC Card shown in Figure 21-15. PC Card and CardBus slots look alike on a notebook computer, and you can recognize these slots by the eject button on the side of the slot (see Figure 21-17). One way to know which type slot you have is to look in Device Manager. If Device Manager shows a controller with "CardBus" in the controller title, then the slot is a 32-bit CardBus slot (see Figure 21-18).

> **A+ Exam Tip**   The A+ 220-701 Essentials exam expects you to know about PCMCIA Type I, II, and III, PC Card, CardBus, and ExpressCard slots and cards, including which bus each slot uses.

Gold, bumpy
strip identifies
a CardBus card

Figure 21-16   This TV tuner card connects to a notebook by way of a PCMCIA CardBus slot
Courtesy of AVerMedia Technologies, Inc. USA

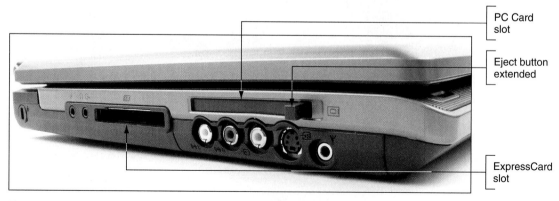

PC Card
slot

Eject button
extended

ExpressCard
slot

Figure 21-17   This notebook has one CardBus slot and one ExpressCard slot
Courtesy: Course Technology/Cengage Learning

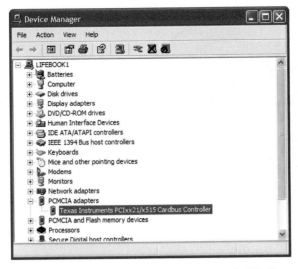

Figure 21-18 Device Manager recognizes a PCMCIA slot as a CardBus slot
Courtesy: Course Technology/Cengage Learning

4. The latest PCMCIA standard is **ExpressCard**, which uses the PCI Express bus standard or the USB 2.0 standard. Two sizes of ExpressCards exist: ExpressCard/34 is 34mm wide and ExpressCard/54 is 54mm wide. Both of these types of cards are 75mm long and 5mm high. Figure 21-19 compares a CardBus card to each of the two ExpressCard cards. An ExpressCard/34 card can fit into an ExpressCard/54 slot, but not vice versa. ExpressCard slots are not backward compatible with PC Card or CardBus cards. An ExpressCard slot is fully hot-pluggable (add a card while the system is on), hot-swappable (exchange or add a card while the system is on), and supports autoconfiguration, just as does a USB port. Figure 21-20 shows an ExpressCard/54 card that provides two eSATA ports for external SATA drives.

Windows must provide two services for a PC Card or ExpressCard: a socket service and a card service. The socket service establishes communication between the card and the

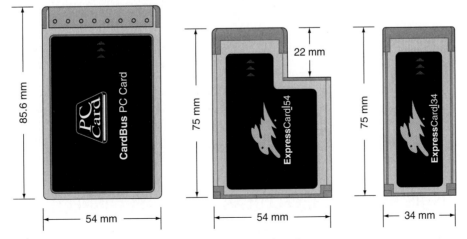

Figure 21-19 Dimensions of CardBus and ExpressCard cards
Courtesy: Course Technology/Cengage Learning

Figure 21-20   This ExpressCard/54 card supports two eSATA drives
Courtesy of SIIG, Inc.

notebook when the card is first inserted. The card service provides the device driver to interface with the card after the socket is created.

The first time you insert a PCMCIA card in a notebook, the Found New Hardware Wizard starts and guides you through the installation steps in which you can use the drivers provided by the hardware manufacturer or use Windows drivers. The next time you insert the card in the notebook, the card is detected and starts without help.

ExpressCards and PC Cards can be hot-swapped (inserted or removed while the system is on), but you must stop one card before inserting another. To stop the card, use the Safely Remove Hardware icon in the notification area, which you learned to use in Chapter 9.

After you have stopped the card, press the eject button beside the PC Card slot, which causes the button to pop out. You can then press the button again to eject the card. For an ExpressCard, push on the card, which causes it to pop out of the slot. Then, you can remove the card.

> ⚡ **Caution**   Inserting a card in a PCMCIA slot while the notebook is shutting down or booting up can cause damage to the card and/or to the notebook. Also, a card might give problems when you insert or remove the card while the system is in hibernation or sleep mode.

The trend for newer and lighter notebooks is to not include ExpressCard or PC Card slots. Instead of these slots, multiple USB ports are provided for peripherals.

> 📝 **Notes**   Recall that the PC Card uses PCI bus standards and the ExpressCard uses the PCIe or USB 2.0 bus standards. Later in the chapter, you will learn how the PCI and PCIe buses are also used inside notebooks to support a Mini PCI adapter (using the PCI bus) or a Mini PCIe adapter (using the PCIe bus).

USING BLUETOOTH, CELLULAR, AND WI-FI CONNECTIONS

A notebook might have an embedded wireless network adapter to connect to a Wi-Fi network or use a Bluetooth or infrared adapter to support a personal area network (PAN). In addition, you can install an Internet card to connect to a cellular mobile phone network. In Chapter 17, you learned how to set up and secure a Wi-Fi connection, while

A+
220-701
1.10
2.4

infrared connections were covered in Chapter 9. Let's now look at a few extra tips for supporting Wi-Fi with notebooks and then see how to set up a Bluetooth and cellular WAN connection.

SUPPORTING WI-FI CONNECTIONS

The details of connecting a computer to a Wi-Fi network are covered in Chapter 17 and will not be repeated here. In addition to the steps described in that chapter, consider these tips when connecting a notebook computer to Wi-Fi:

- In a notebook, an internal wireless adapter uses an internal antenna, and the notebook has a switch to turn on the internal wireless adapter. Look for the switch near the keyboard or on the side of the notebook (see Figure 21-21). Make sure the switch is set to the on position.
- The internal antenna might be embedded in the lid of the notebook. Raising the lid to a vertical position can sometimes improve the signal.
- For external wireless adapters, consider the possibility that an external antenna might need connecting to the device and put in a raised position, and a switch on the device must be turned on.

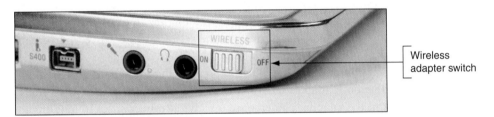

Wireless adapter switch

Figure 21-21 This switch controls an internal wireless adapter
Courtesy: Course Technology/Cengage Learning

SUPPORTING BLUETOOTH CONNECTIONS

If your notebook supports a Bluetooth connection used to connect to a printer, mouse, headset, camera, cell phone, or connect a PDA to the notebook, you need to read the documentation for configuring the Bluetooth connection that came with the notebook. If you don't have that documentation, download it from the notebook manufacturer's Web site. You'll need it, because Bluetooth setups differ from one notebook to another. Following the directions for your notebook, turn on Bluetooth. After Bluetooth is turned on, you should be able to make a connection with your Bluetooth device when it is set close to the notebook.

If you are having problems getting the Bluetooth connection to work, try the following:

- Make sure the wireless switch is turned on (for some notebooks, this switch turns on and off both the Wi-Fi and Bluetooth signal).
- Verify that Windows sees Bluetooth enabled. You might do this by using an applet in Control Panel or by using a program on the Start menu. For example, one Toshiba notebook has a Radio Control applet in Control Panel and another notebook uses Bluetooth Manager software in the Start menu. For many notebooks, you should see an icon in the notification area (system tray) showing the status of Bluetooth.

21

A+ 220-701

A+
220-701
1.10
2.4

▲ Be sure you have downloaded all Windows updates. (Windows XP Service Pack 2 is required for Bluetooth.)

▲ Look in Device Manager to make sure the Bluetooth component is recognized with no errors. For some notebooks, even though the component is an internal device, it is seen in Device Manager as a USB device.

▲ Make sure the other device has Bluetooth turned on. For example, when trying to communicate with a cell phone, you must use the menu on the phone to activate Bluetooth connections.

▲ The Bluetooth software on the notebook might have a high level of security enabled. If so, you can lower the security mode or follow directions in the documentation to pair up the two devices. Pairing up is the term used to allow the other device to use your secured Bluetooth connection and involves entering a password before the connection is established.

▲ You can also try uninstalling and reinstalling the Bluetooth drivers that come bundled on CD with your notebook.

▲ You can also try uninstalling and reinstalling the drivers for your Bluetooth device. For example, if you are trying to connect to a printer using a Bluetooth wireless connection, try first turning on Bluetooth and then uninstalling and reinstalling the printer. During the printer installation, select the Bluetooth connection for the printer port, which might be called Bluetooth COM or something similar.

For more ideas for solving a Bluetooth problem, try the Web site of the notebook manufacturer or the Web site of the device you are trying to connect to your notebook using Bluetooth.

If your notebook doesn't have Bluetooth capability and you'd like to add it, you can buy a USB Bluetooth adapter like the one shown in Figure 21-22. After you have installed the drivers and the adapter, you can use it to wirelessly connect to any Bluetooth-enabled device.

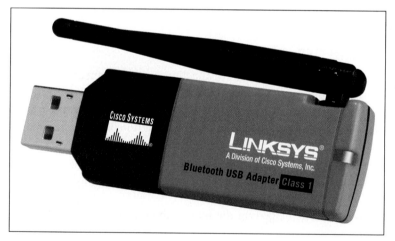

Figure 21-22   Use a USB Bluetooth adapter to add Bluetooth capability to a notebook
Courtesy of Linksys

SUPPORTING CELLULAR WAN CONNECTIONS

Recall that WiMAX (802.16 wireless) or mobile phone (GSM or CDMA) technologies can be used to build cellular WANs. You can purchase devices to connect a laptop to either type wireless network. A WiMAX device might use an ExpressCard or PC Card slot or USB port.

A device to connect to a cell phone network is called an Internet card (also called an air card). An Internet card and mobile service provide mobile broadband Internet access on a 3G network. The card is also most likely to use an ExpressCard or PC Card slot or USB port. Figure 21-23 shows the Sierra Wireless AirCard 402 modem card. The card uses an ExpressCard slot and comes with a PC Card adapter. When you insert the card into the adapter, it can be used in a 32-bit PC Card (CardBus) slot.

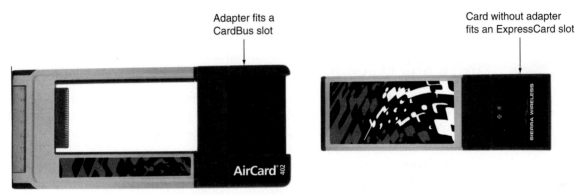

Adapter fits a
CardBus slot

Card without adapter
fits an ExpressCard slot

Figure 21-23 Sierra Wireless AirCard 402 modem card fits a PC Card or ExpressCard slot
Courtesy of Sierra Wireless

When you first install the card and its software, the best idea is to carefully follow the instructions provided by the card manufacturer. To help you get familiar with the process, here are the general steps to install an Internet card purchased from a cellular WAN provider such as Verizon or Sprint:

1. Insert the CD that came with the card and install the software on the CD.

2. Open the utility the software installed and configure the Internet card. Part of the process will be to tell the utility what type port or slot the card will use (for example, USB, PC Card, or ExpressCard).

3. Insert the card in your computer. The software should automatically detect the card and install device drivers for it.

4. You might be requested to enter the 10-digit phone number your cellular WAN provider assigned to the card and gave to you when you purchased the card. Save your settings.

5. An access manager window opens so that you can make a connection. This window should open each time you insert the card. Depending on the type of service you have purchased for the card, your browser window might open and direct you to the provider's site, where you can activate a service plan or change plans. Some plans allow for an always-up connection and others charge by bandwidth used or minutes connected. Be sure you understand the type plan you are paying for.

If you have problems making a cellular WAN connection, do the usual troubleshooting such as checking Device Manager and Event Viewer, installing Windows updates, and reinstalling the software. Be sure to check the Web site of the cellular WAN provider as well as the Web sites of the notebook or Internet card manufacturer. A very good example of what information might pop up is one on the HP Web site (*www.hp.com*) for a particular model notebook and particular Internet card that appear to not work together. The site reports that after installing this card, you must power down the notebook, remove the battery and AC adapter, wait a few minutes, reinstall the battery or AC adapter, and power up the notebook. Doing so causes the Internet card to work fine. Here are some more troubleshooting tips:

▲ When you first install an Internet card, you cannot activate the card unless you are in the coverage area of your service provider. After the service is activated, it will then work in an extended coverage area (called roaming). To activate the card, you might need to call the customer help desk for the service.

▲ As with any network connection, your software firewall must allow access to applications you might be using, such as chat, e-mail, or Remote Desktop.

POWER AND ELECTRICAL DEVICES

A notebook can be powered in several ways, including an AC adapter (which uses regular house current to power the notebook), a DC adapter (which uses DC power such as that provided by automobile cigarette lighters), and a battery pack. Some AC adapters are capable of auto-switching from 110 V to 220 V AC power, in contrast to fixed-input AC adapters that can handle only one type of AC voltage. Figure 21-24 shows an AC adapter that has a green light that indicates the adapter is receiving power.

Types of batteries include the older and mostly outdated Ni-Cad (nickel-cadmium) battery, the longer-life NiMH (nickel-metal-hydride) battery, and the current Lithium Ion (sometimes abbreviated Li-Ion) battery, which is more efficient than earlier batteries. A future battery solution is a fuel cell battery, technically called a Direct Methanol Fuel Cell (DMFC) battery. A DMFC initially provides up to five hours of battery life, and future versions will provide up to ten hours of battery life.

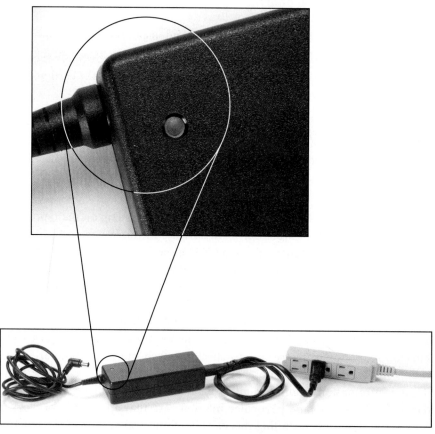

Figure 21-24 AC adapter for a notebook uses a green light to indicate power
Courtesy: Course Technology/Cengage Learning

A+
220-701
1.10
2.4
1.3
6.1

A notebook user might need one or more batteries and a DC adapter for travel and an AC adapter at home and for recharging the batteries. Figure 21-25 shows an inexpensive device that plugs into a cigarette lighter in a vehicle to provide AC power. The device is a type of inverter. (An **inverter** is an electrical device that changes DC to AC.) You can plug your AC adapter into the inverter to power a laptop in your car.

Figure 21-25 An inverter changes DC to AC and provides an outlet for your laptop's AC adapter
Courtesy: Course Technology/Cengage Learning

Here are some general dos and don'ts for switching power sources and protecting the battery, the notebook, and other electrical devices. See a user manual for specific instructions for a device.

> **Notes** If you're using the AC adapter to power your notebook when the power goes out, the installed battery serves as a built-in UPS. The battery immediately takes over as your uninterruptible power supply.

- If you need to use the notebook for extended periods away from an electrical outlet, you can use extra battery packs. When the notebook signals that power is low, shut down the system, remove the old battery and replace it with a charged one. To remove a battery, generally, you release a latch and then remove the battery, as shown in Figure 21-26.
- For some notebook batteries, don't recharge the battery pack until all the power is used. Recharging too soon can shorten the battery life. For other batteries, it doesn't matter how often you recharge them. And, for other batteries, if the battery charge does not last very long, allow the battery to fully drain all power and then recharge again. Check your user manual to learn how and when to recharge your battery.

> **Video**
> Troubleshooting Notebooks

- For some older batteries, when you're recharging the battery, don't use it until it's fully recharged. Also, some manufacturers of older batteries recommend that you don't leave the battery in the notebook while the notebook is turned on and connected to an electrical outlet. Other batteries can stay installed with no problems.

21

A+ 220-701

A+
220-701
1.10
2.4
1.3
6.1

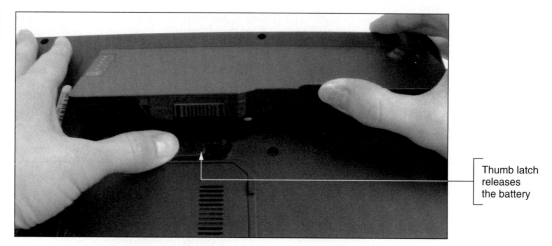

Thumb latch
releases
the battery

Figure 21-26 Release a latch to remove the battery from a notebook
Courtesy: Course Technology/Cengage Learning

▲ If you're not using the notebook for a long time (more than a month), charge the battery and remove it from the notebook. Store the notebook and battery in a cool, dry place. Leaving a battery in a notebook for extended periods when it is not used can damage the battery. And allowing the battery to remain totally drained for an extended period can shorten its lifespan.

▲ Use power-management features of your OS, which are covered later in this section. Also, to make a battery charge last longer while working with your notebook, you can dim the LCD panel and remove any unneeded peripherals such as a PC Card or ExpressCard card.

▲ CD and DVD drives use a lot of power. Therefore, whenever possible, connect the notebook to an electrical outlet to play a movie on DVD or burn a CD.

▲ Use standby or hibernate mode whenever you are not using the notebook.

▲ While working with your notebook and using the battery, if you get a message that the battery is low, you can immediately plug in the AC or DC adapter without first powering down your notebook.

▲ To conserve power when the battery is running, a notebook sometimes reduces LCD panel brightness. For example, when you unplug the AC adapter on one notebook, a message appears (see Figure 21-27) telling you brightness has been reduced. To save even more power, lower the brightness even more.

▲ A notebook has an internal surge protector. However, for extra protection, you might want to use a power strip that provides surge protection.

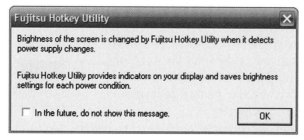

Figure 21-27 Reduce LCD panel brightness to conserve power when running the battery
Courtesy: Course Technology/Cengage Learning

▲ To verify that power is getting to a notebook, look for LED indicator lights on the notebook. Depending on the notebook, these lights indicate:

- The power indicator light says that power is getting to the system.
- The battery indicator light says that the battery, rather than the AC adapter, is powering the system.
- The HDD indicator light says that the hard drive is being accessed.

▲ If power is not getting to the system or the battery indicator light is lit when the AC adapter should be supplying power, verify the AC adapter is plugged into a live electrical outlet. Is the light on the AC adapter lit? Check if the AC adapter's plug is secure in the electrical outlet. Check the connections on both sides of the AC adapter transformer. Check the connection at the notebook. Try exchanging the AC adapter for one you know is good.

▲ If you are using an inverter to convert DC in a vehicle to AC, be sure to purchase an inverter that supplies enough power (measured in watts) to meet the needs of your notebook. Know that you should not use the inverter if it is damp or wet, and you should not allow the inverter to overheat. Keep the inverter out of direct sunlight. Don't place the inverter near inflammable materials, and make sure there's good ventilation around it when it is in use. Don't run multiple devices off the inverter at the same time or for long periods of time because drawing too much power from your cigarette lighter can burn out your car's alternator.

💡 **A+ Exam Tip** The A+ 220–701 Essentials exam expects you to know how notebooks get their power and how to troubleshoot minor problems with power.

APPLYING | CONCEPTS

If the system fails only when the AC adapter is connected, it might be defective. Try a new AC adapter, or, if you have a multimeter, use it to verify the voltage output of the adapter. Do the following for an adapter with a single center pin connector:

1. Unplug the AC adapter from the computer, but leave it plugged into the electrical outlet.

2. Using a multimeter set to measure voltage in the 1 to 20 V DC range, place the red probe of the multimeter in the center of the DC connector that would normally plug into the DC outlet on the notebook. Place the black probe on the outside cylinder of the DC connector (see Figure 21-28).

Figure 21-28 To use a multimeter to test this AC adapter, place the red probe (which, in the photo, is in the person's left hand) in the center connector and the black probe on the outside
Courtesy: Course Technology/Cengage Learning

3. The voltage range should be plus or minus five percent of the accepted voltage. For example, if a notebook is designed to use 16 V, the voltage should measure somewhere between 15.2 and 16.8 V DC.

POWER MANAGEMENT

A notebook ACPI-compliant BIOS supports features to help manage power, which were discussed in Chapter 6. The goal is to minimize power consumption to increase the time before a battery pack needs recharging. Power is managed by putting the computer into varying degrees of suspend or sleep modes. If BIOS setup has ACPI functions enabled, you can use Windows to control these power-saving features. Vista and XP manage power differently.

📷 **Video**
Troubleshooting a Boot Problem 1

Here is how Vista uses power-saving states:

◢ Sleep mode corresponds to ACPI S3 mode. It saves some work to the hard drive, saves all your work to memory, and puts the computer into a power-saving mode. In this mode, it uses a small trickle of electricity to preserve memory and the power light on the notebook might blink from time to time. (A notebook generally uses about one to two percent of battery power for each hour in sleep mode.) To wake up the computer, press the power button or, for some computers, press a key or move the mouse. Vista wakes up quickly from sleep mode (in about two seconds). When Vista is in sleep mode, it can still perform Windows updates and scheduled tasks. Vista can be configured to go to sleep after a period of inactivity, or you can manually put it to sleep. To put the system to sleep manually, click **Start** and then click the sleep button or point to the right arrow and select **Sleep** from the menu (see Figure 21-29). Notebooks are usually configured to go to sleep when you close the lid.

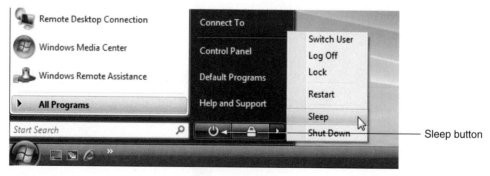

Figure 21-29 Put Vista to sleep using the Start menu
Courtesy: Course Technology/Cengage Learning

◢ Hibernation saves all work to the hard drive and powers down the system. When you press the power button, Windows reloads its state, including all open applications and documents. When Windows is in sleep mode on a notebook and senses the battery is critically low, it will put the system into hibernation.

A+
220-701
3.3

▲ In hybrid sleep, all work is saved to the hard drive, but the system still maintains a trickle of power. The advantage of hybrid sleep is if the power goes out, the system can fully reload its state when it is turned back on. Hybrid sleep is intended to be used on desktop computers as a way to protect data from being lost in a power failure. Because notebooks don't immediately lose power when the electricity goes out, hybrid sleep is usually disabled on notebooks.

> 💡 **A+ Exam Tip** The A+ 220-701 Essentials exam expects you to know how to manage power, including using suspend, hibernate, and standby modes, and to know what is a sleep timer.

In Windows XP, standby mode is similar to Vista sleep mode and corresponds to ACPI S3 mode. Work is saved to memory and a trickle of power preserves that memory. In hibernation, all work in memory is saved to the hard drive and then the power is turned off.

Follow these steps to manage power using Windows Vista:

1. In BIOS setup, make sure that ACPI power management is enabled. How to do that is covered in Chapter 6.

2. In Windows, open **Control Panel**. Click **Hardware and Sound** and then click **Power Options**. The Power Options window opens. Figure 21-30 shows the window for one brand of laptop. The labels will be different for other laptop brands. For a desktop computer, the first power plan will be labeled Balanced instead of the current label for this Sony laptop, which is VAIO Optimized. The second plan, the Power saver plan, is the one to use if you are most concerned about extending battery life.

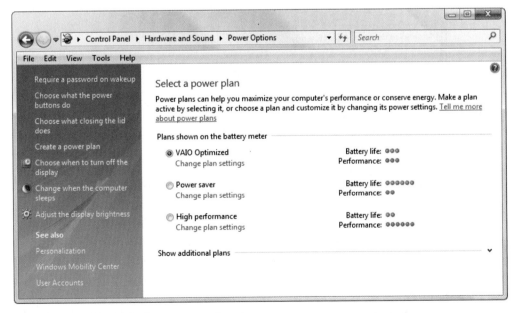

Figure 21-30 Vista uses three power-saving plans
Courtesy: Course Technology/Cengage Learning

21

A+ 220-701

3. You can customize each plan. For example, under VAIO Optimized, click **Change plan settings**. The Edit Plan Settings window appears (see Figure 21-31). Notice in the figure the various times of inactivity before the computer goes into sleep mode, which are called sleep timers.

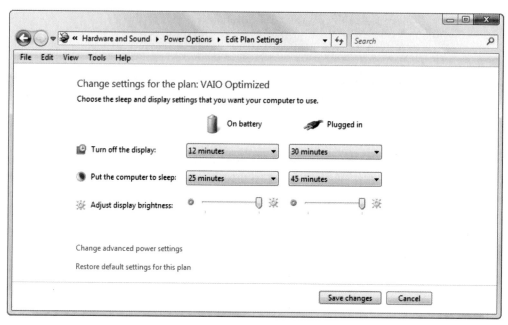

Figure 21-31   Sleep times for one power plan on a notebook
Courtesy: Course Technology/Cengage Learning

4. To see other changes you can make, click **Change advanced power settings**. Using this Power Options box (see Figure 21-32), you can do such things as turn on and off hybrid sleep, control the minutes before the hard drive turns off, control what happens when you close the lid, press the sleep button, press the power button, or set

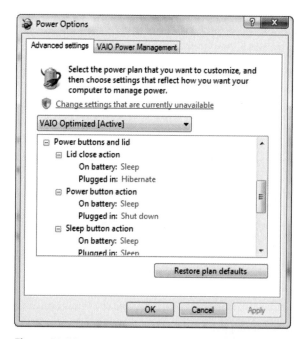

Figure 21-32   Advanced power options in Vista
Courtesy: Course Technology/Cengage Learning

A+
220-701
3.3

the brightness level of the LCD panel to conserve power. You can also use this box to set what happens when the battery gets low or critically low. Make your changes and click **OK** to close the box.

5. Click **Save changes** in the Edit Plan Settings window, and then close the window.

To manage power in Windows XP, open **Control Panel** and double-click the **Power Options** applet. Figure 21-33 shows the Power Options Properties dialog box for one Windows XP notebook. (A different brand of notebook might have different tabs in its Properties dialog box.) Use this dialog box to create, delete, and modify multiple power-management schemes to customize how Windows XP manages power consumption.

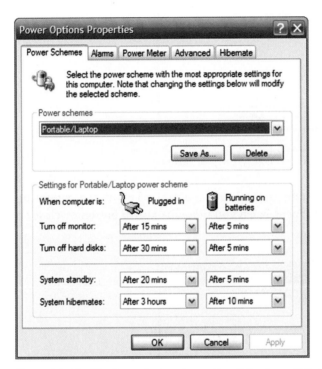

Figure 21-33   The Power Options Properties dialog box of Windows 2000/XP allows you to create and manage multiple power schemes
Courtesy: Course Technology/Cengage Learning

For example, you can configure Windows XP to cause the notebook to hibernate after a set period of time, when you press the power button, or when you close the lid of the notebook. Do the following:

> **Notes** The disadvantage of using hibernation is that it takes longer for the computer to go into suspend mode and resume from suspend mode. This extra time is required because, if hibernation is enabled, XP saves everything in memory to the hard drive before suspending.

1. In the Power Options Properties dialog box, click the **Hibernate** tab (see Figure 21-34), and verify that hibernate support is enabled. If there is no Hibernate tab, your notebook does not support hibernating.

21

A+ 220-701

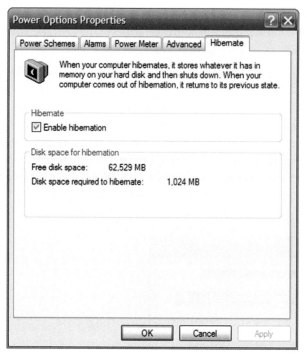

Figure 21-34   Verify that hibernate support is enabled
Courtesy: Course Technology/Cengage Learning

2. Click the **Advanced** tab, as shown in Figure 21-35. With the options on this tab, you can control what happens when you press the power button or close the lid of the notebook.

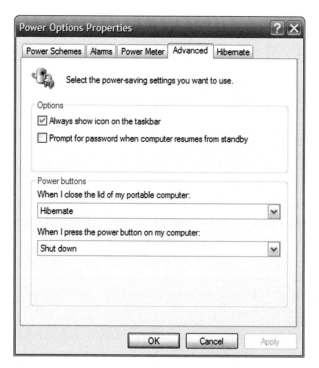

Figure 21-35   The Advanced tab of the Power Options Properties dialog box allows you to control the behavior of the power button and what happens when you close the lid of your notebook
Courtesy: Course Technology/Cengage Learning

A+
220-701
3.3

3. Click the **When I close the lid of my portable computer** list arrow and select **Hibernate**. (Other choices are Stand by, Power Off, and Do nothing. Choices vary according to notebook manufacturers.)

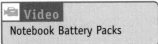
Video
Notebook Battery Packs

4. When you're done, click **Apply** and then click **OK** to close the Power Options Properties dialog box and save your changes.

When a computer is in sleep mode, hibernate mode, or shut down, you might want to wake it up remotely. For example, you might want to perform maintenance tasks on a computer without having to physically sit in front of it. Or the computer might be serving up shared folders or a mapped network drive. Users will need to be able to access the resources remotely without having to go to the computer to turn it on or wake it up. The solution is to use a power-management feature called wake on LAN. Wake on LAN allows wired or wireless network activity to power up a computer or wake it up. To use the feature, it must be enabled in BIOS setup. You also need to configure the network adapter or wireless network adapter to wake the computer. Do the following:

1. In BIOS setup, look on the Power menu for the option to wake on LAN and enable it.

2. In Device Manager, open the **Properties** box of the network adapter and click the **Power Management** tab (see Figure 21-36).

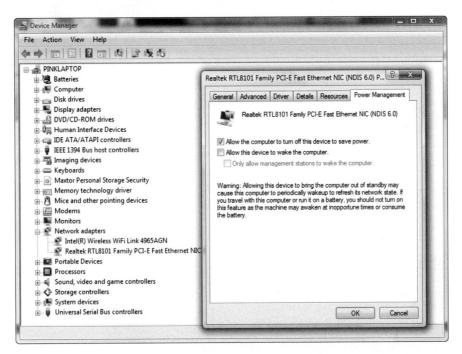

Figure 21-36 Use Device Manager to enable the wake on LAN feature for a network adapter
Courtesy: Course Technology/Cengage Learning

3. Check **Allow this device to wake the computer** and click **OK**. Depending on the situation, you might want to enable the wake on LAN feature for the wired connection but not enable it for the wireless connection. For laptops, consider not enabling wake on LAN so that it will not wake up at the wrong times and use up the battery power.

💡 **A+ Exam Tip** The A+ 220–701 Essentials exam expects you to know how to configure wake on LAN.

21

A+ 220-701

A+
220-701
1.10
2.4

INPUT DEVICES

The keyboard is the primary input device for a laptop. Sometimes crumbs, dirt, and dust get inside the keyboard and cause problems. Use compressed air or a small vacuum designed for cleaning electrical devices to blow out the keyboard. Try turning the laptop upside down and gently shaking out particles. If some keys don't work, you can try removing the keyboard from the laptop to clean it better. You might need to exchange the keyboard for a new one. How to exchange a laptop keyboard is covered later in the chapter. If you're not able to exchange the keyboard immediately, know that you can plug in an external keyboard to a USB port to use in the meantime.

A pointing device allows you to move a pointer on the screen and perform tasks such as executing (clicking) a command button. The most common pointing device on a notebook is a touch pad (see Figure 21-37). IBM and Lenovo ThinkPad notebooks use a unique and popular pointing device embedded in the keyboard (see Figure 21-38) called a TrackPoint or point stick. Some people prefer to use a USB wired or wireless mouse instead of a touch pad or TrackPoint. For notebooks, a wireless USB mouse like the one shown earlier in Figure 21-9 is handy.

Figure 21-37 The touch pad is the most common pointing device on a notebook
Courtesy: Course Technology/Cengage Learning

Figure 21-38 An IBM ThinkPad TrackPoint
Courtesy: Course Technology/Cengage Learning

A+
220-701
1.10
2.4

Another input device that can be used to hand draw is a graphics tablet, also called a digitizing tablet or digitizer, that uses a USB port (see Figure 21-39). It comes with a stylus that works like a pencil on the tablet. The graphics tablet and stylus can be a replacement to a mouse, touch pad, or TrackPoint, and some graphics tablets come with a mouse that is used on the tablet for those people who are not comfortable with using the stylus to point and click. Graphics tablets are popular with graphics artists and others who use desktop publishing applications.

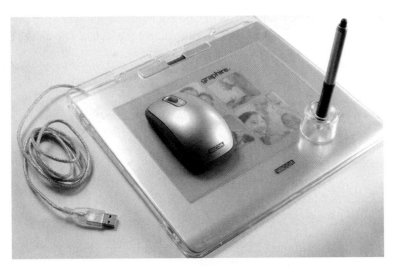

Figure 21-39 A graphics tablet and stylus are used to digitize a hand drawing
Courtesy: Course Technology/Cengage Learning

A mouse, graphics tablet, or other input device is likely to use a USB port. Most likely, the right order for installation is to first install the software that came with the device and then plug in the device. For a graphics tablet, additional software might be available to enhance the functions of the tablet, such as inputting handwritten signatures into MS Word documents.

You can adjust the way the touch pad or TrackPoint works on a laptop using the Mouse Properties box. In Control Panel, click **Mouse** to open the box shown in Figure 21-40.

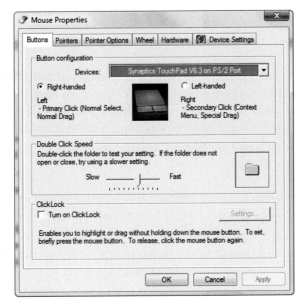

Figure 21-40 Use the Mouse Properties box to control a mouse, touch pad, or other pointing device
Courtesy: Course Technology/Cengage Learning

21

A+ 220-701

The tabs on this box vary depending on the pointing devices installed. Use the Mouse Properties box to adjust pointer speed, mouse trails, pointer size, how the touch pad buttons work, and other settings for pointing devices.

For tablet PCs, the stylus can be controlled from the Pen and Input Devices box. The box can be accessed from the Vista or XP Control Panel, and allows you to control stylus clicks and motion. Also, when a pointing device is installed, the software provides a utility to manage the device. For example, for the graphics tablet, mouse, and stylus shown in Figure 21-39, the utility shows up as the Pen Tablet icon in Control Panel. When you open the utility, Figure 21-41 appears. Using the Pen tab, you can control the stylus. The Tablet tab allows you to control some of the functions of the graphics tablets.

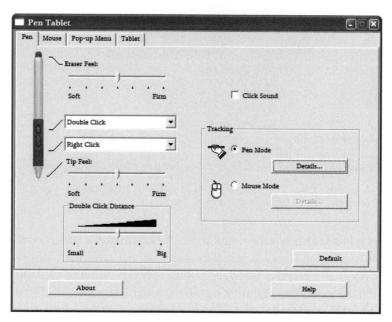

Figure 21-41 Use the Pen Tablet utility to control a stylus, mouse, and graphics tablet
Courtesy: Course Technology/Cengage Learning

VIDEO

The video system on a laptop includes the LCD panel and a video controller. The video controller might be embedded on the motherboard or be on a video card installed as an internal component. Most laptops also provide an analog 15-pin VGA port for an external monitor and perhaps an S-Video Out port to use a television as an external display device. In Chapter 9, you learned how to install and use a secondary monitor.

Use this list to help you solve problems with video:

◢ If the LCD panel shows a black screen, but the power light indicates that power is getting to the system, the video subsystem might be the source of the problem. Do the following:

• Look for an LCD cutoff switch or button on the laptop (see Figure 21-42). The switch must be on for the LCD panel to work.

• Try using an external monitor. Plug the monitor into the VGA port. Recall from Chapter 9 that you might need to use a toggle switch to activate the monitor. Most laptops use a function key for this purpose. For

A+
220-701
2.4

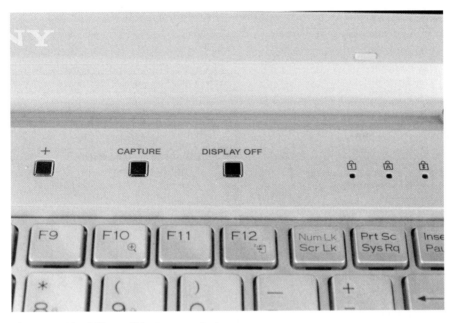

Figure 21-42 LCD cutoff button on a laptop
Courtesy: Course Technology/Cengage Learning

example, for one laptop, the combination of the Fn key and the F7 key (see Figure 21-43) toggles between using only the LCD panel, both the LCD panel and the external monitor, and only the external monitor. Try all settings.

Figure 21-43 Use the Fn key and the F7 key to toggle between display devices
Courtesy: Course Technology/Cengage Learning

- Using the external monitor for video, check Device Manager for warnings about the video controller. See Figure 21-44 for an example on the embedded video controller for one laptop.
- Check Event Viewer for reported problems with the video subsystem.
- Try updating video drivers. Download these drivers from the laptop manufacturer's Web site.
- If you still can't get the LCD panel to work, but the external monitor does work, you have proven the problem is with the LCD panel assembly. How to troubleshoot problems with this assembly is covered later in the chapter.

21

A+ 220-701

A+
220-701
2.4

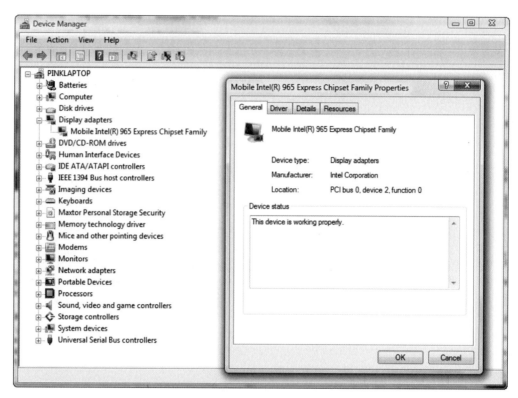

Figure 21-44 Device Manager reports no problem with the laptop's video controller
Courtesy: Course Technology/Cengage Learning

▲ To verify display settings for the LCD panel, follow directions given in Chapter 9 to change display settings. Try using the native resolution for the LCD panel. This resolution will be the highest resolution available unless you have the wrong video drivers installed.

▲ Try updating the video drivers. Download the latest drivers from the notebook manufacturer's Web site.

▲ Try adjusting the brightness, which is a function of the backlight component of the LCD panel. To adjust brightness, open the **Power Options** window and click **Adjust the display brightness**. The Edit Plan Settings window for the current power plan appears (refer to Figure 21-31 shown earlier in the chapter).

> 💡 **A+ Exam Tip** Content on the A+ 220–701 Essentials exam ends here, and content on the A+ 220–702 Practical Application exam begins.

TROUBLESHOOTING, REPLACING, AND UPGRADING INTERNAL PARTS

A+
220-702
1.3

Sometimes it is necessary to open a notebook case so that you can upgrade memory, exchange a hard drive, or replace a broken component such as the LCD panel, keyboard, processor, pointing device, fan, motherboard, CMOS battery, video card, heat sink, wireless card, or speaker. Most notebooks sold today are designed so that you can easily purchase and exchange memory modules or hard drives. However, replacing a broken LCD panel or motherboard can be a complex process, taking several hours. In this section, we'll first look at the alternatives you need to consider before you decide to take on

A+
220-702
1.3

complex repair projects, and then we'll look at how to upgrade memory, exchange a drive, and perform other complex repair projects, such as exchanging an LCD panel or motherboard.

THREE APPROACHES TO DEALING WITH A BROKEN INTERNAL DEVICE

When a component on a notebook needs replacing or upgrading, first you need to consider the warranty and how much time the repair will take. Before you decide to upgrade or repair an internal component, take into consideration these three alternatives:

▲ *Return the notebook to the manufacturer or another service center for repair.* If the notebook is under warranty, you need to return it to the manufacturer to do any serious repair work such as fixing a broken LCD panel. However, for simple repair and upgrade tasks, such as upgrading memory or exchanging a hard drive, most likely you can do these simple jobs by yourself without concern for voiding a warranty. If you're not sure about the possibility of voiding the warranty, check with the manufacturer before you begin working on the notebook. If the notebook is not under warranty and you don't have the experience or time to fix a broken component, find out how much the manufacturer will charge to do the job. Also, consider using a generic notebook repair service. Know that some notebook manufacturers refuse to sell internal components for their notebooks except to authorized service centers. In this case, you have no option but to use the service center for repairs.

▲ *Substitute an external component for an internal component.* As you'll see later in the chapter, replacing components on notebooks can be time consuming and require a lot of patience. If the notebook is not under warranty, sometimes it's wiser to simply avoid opening the case and working inside it. Instead, you could simply use BIOS setup to disable an internal component and then use an external device in its place. For example, if a keyboard fails, you can use a wireless keyboard with an access point connected to the USB port. Also, if the Ethernet port fails, the simplest solution might be to disable the port and use a PC Card network card to provide the Ethernet port.

▲ *Replace the internal device.* Before deciding to replace an internal device that is not easy to get to, such as an LCD panel, first find out if you can get the manufacturer documentation necessary to know how to open the notebook case and exchange the component. How to find this documentation was discussed earlier in the chapter. Without the instructions or a lot of experience servicing notebooks, the project could be very frustrating and result in a notebook useful only as a paperweight.

> **Notes** Before making the decision to replace an internal part, ask the question, "Can an external device or PC Card substitute?" Many customers appreciate these solutions, because most often they are much less labor-intensive and less costly.

Now let's turn our attention to how to substitute an external device for an internal one and then how to prepare to work inside a notebook computer case.

SUBSTITUTE AN INTERNAL DEVICE WITH AN EXTERNAL DEVICE

To substitute an internal device with an external device, first go into BIOS setup and disable the internal device. Press a key, such as F2 or Del to enter BIOS setup when the notebook is booting. Look for a message on-screen at the beginning of the boot telling

21

A+ 220-702

A+
220-702
1.3

which key to press. After you have disabled the internal device, install the external peripheral device as described earlier in the chapter.

PREPARATION FOR SERVICING A NOTEBOOK

Before attempting to replace or upgrade a component installed in a notebook, always do the following:

- If the computer is working, have the user back up any important data stored on the notebook.
- Ground yourself by using an antistatic ground strap. If no ground strap is available, periodically touch a metal part of the case or a port to discharge any static electricity on your body.
- Remove any PC Cards, CDs, or DVDs.
- Turn off any attached devices such as a printer and then shut down the notebook.
- Disconnect the AC adapter from the computer and from the electrical outlet.
- If the notebook is attached to a port replicator or docking station, release it to undock the computer.
- Remove the battery pack.

> **⚡ Caution** It is very important to unplug the AC adapter and remove the battery pack before working inside a notebook case. If the battery is still in the notebook, power provided by the battery could damage components as you work on them.

You are now ready to follow specific instructions for your particular notebook model to replace or upgrade an internal component. Some components can easily be accessed by either removing a panel to expose the component or by removing a screw or two and then sliding the component out the side of the case. When a component can be accessed this easily, most users can do the job if given detailed instructions. However, some components, such as the LCD panel or motherboard, are not so easily accessed. To get to these components requires opening the case and disassembling the notebook.

UPGRADING MEMORY

In this section, you'll learn about the different types of memory modules used with notebook computers and how to upgrade memory.

TYPES OF MEMORY USED IN NOTEBOOKS

Today's notebooks all use SO-DIMM (small outline DIMM) memory. You might encounter older notebooks that use SO-RIMM (small outline RIMM) memory. Table 21-2 lists SO-DIMMs and SO-RIMMs. All of these memory modules are smaller than regular DIMMs or RIMMs.

Just as with memory modules used in desktop computers, you can only use the type of memory the notebook is designed to support. The number of pins and the position of the notches on a SO-DIMM keep you from inserting the wrong module in a memory slot.

Subnotebooks sometimes use MicroDIMMs that are smaller than SO-DIMMs and have a 64-bit data path. A MicroDIMM that contains SDRAM has 144 pins. A MicroDIMM that contains DDR SDRAM has 172 pins and uses 2.5 volts of power, and a MicroDIMM

Memory Module Description	Sample Memory Module
2.66" 204-pin SO-DIMM contains DDR3 memory. The one notch on the module is offset from the center of the module.	Courtesy of Kingston Technology Corporation
2.66" 200-pin SO-DIMM contains DDR2 SDRAM. One notch is near the side of the module.	Courtesy of Kingston Technology
2.66" 200-pin SO-DIMM contains DDR SDRAM. One notch near the side of the module is slightly offset from the notch on a DDR2 SDRAM module.	Courtesy of Crucial Technology
2.66" 144-pin SO-DIMM contains SDRAM and is outdated. One notch is slightly offset from the center of the module.	Courtesy of Crucial Technology
2.35" 72-pin SO-DIMMs are outdated. They contain FPM or EDO memory and have no notch on the edge connector.	Courtesy: Course Technology/Cengage Learning
160-pin SO-RIMM contains Rambus memory and has two notches.	Courtesy of High Connection Density, Inc.

Table 21-2   Memory modules used in notebook computers

that contains DDR2 SDRAM has 214 pins and uses 1.8 volts. Figure 21-45 shows a 214-pin MicroDIMM being installed in a memory socket on a subnotebook computer.

HOW TO UPGRADE MEMORY ON A NOTEBOOK

Before upgrading memory, make sure you are not voiding your warranty. Search for the best buy, but make sure you use memory modules made by or authorized by your notebook's manufacturer and designed for the exact model of your notebook. Installing generic memory might save money, but might also void the notebook's warranty.

Video
Upgrading Memory on a Notebook

21

A+ 220-702

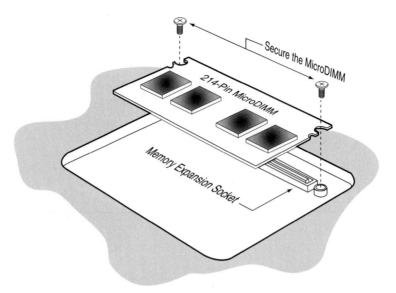

Figure 21-45 Installing a MicroDIMM in a subnotebook computer
Courtesy: Course Technology/Cengage Learning

Upgrading memory on a notebook works about the same way as with upgrading memory on a desktop: Decide how much memory you can upgrade, purchase the memory, and install it. As with a desktop computer, be sure to match the type of memory to the type the notebook supports.

APPLYING CONCEPTS Most notebooks are designed for easy access to memory. Follow these steps to exchange or upgrade memory for one notebook.

1. Back up data and shut down the system. Remove peripherals, including the AC adapter. Remove the battery. Be sure to use a ground bracelet as you work.

2. Turn the notebook over and loosen the two screws on the DIMM door. (It is not necessary to remove the screws.)

3. Raise the DIMM door (see Figure 21-46) and remove the door from its hinges. The two memory slots are exposed.

Figure 21-46 Raise the DIMM door on the bottom of the notebook
Courtesy: Course Technology/Cengage Learning

A+
220-702
1.3

1. Notice in Figure 21-47 that one slot is filled and one is available for a memory upgrade. Also notice in the figure that when you remove the DIMM door, the CMOS battery is exposed. This easy access to the battery makes exchanging it very easy. To remove a SO-DIMM, pull the clips on the side of the memory slot apart slightly (see Figure 21-48). The SO-DIMM will pop up out of the slot and can then be removed. If it does not pop up, you can hold the clips apart as you pull the module up and out of the slot.

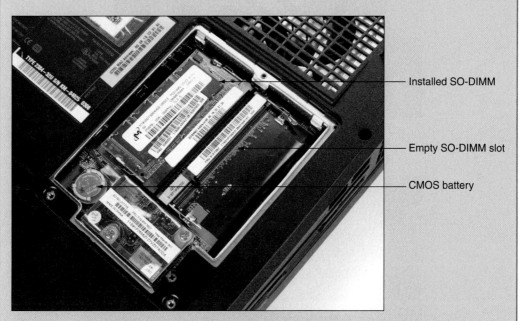

Installed SO-DIMM

Empty SO-DIMM slot

CMOS battery

Figure 21-47 SO-DIMM slots, one installed SO-DIMM, and the CMOS battery are exposed
Courtesy: Course Technology/Cengage Learning

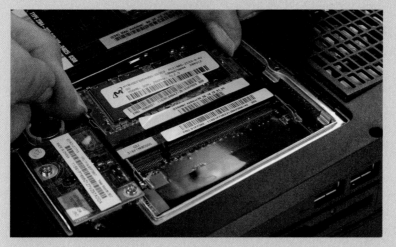

Figure 21-48 Pull apart the clips on the memory slot to release the SO-DIMM
Courtesy: Course Technology/Cengage Learning

2. To install a new SO-DIMM, insert the module into the slot (see Figure 21-49) and gently push it down until it snaps into the clips (see Figure 21-50). Replace the DIMM door.

21

A+ 220-702

Figure 21-49 Insert a new SO-DIMM into a memory slot
Courtesy: Course Technology/Cengage Learning

Figure 21-50 Push down on the SO-DIMM until it pops into the clips
Courtesy: Course Technology/Cengage Learning

REPLACING A HARD DRIVE

When purchasing and installing an internal hard drive, floppy drive, CD drive, DVD drive, or removable drive, see the notebook manufacturer's documentation about specific sizes and connectors that will fit the notebook. Also be aware of voiding a warranty if you don't follow the notebook manufacturer's directions. When purchasing a hard drive, know that hard drives for notebooks often use proprietary form factors and connectors, which means you must purchase a drive from the notebook manufacturer or at least buy one that uses the same connector and form factor. Here is what you need to know when shopping for a notebook hard drive:

▲ A desktop hard drive is 3.5 inches wide and a notebook drive is 2.5 inches wide. Figure 21-51 shows a comparison of the two sizes. Because the form factor of a notebook drive is more compact, it costs more than a desktop drive holding the same

A+
220-702
1.3

amount of data. Some notebook hard drives use SSD (solid state device) technology. Recall that these drives use memory chips to hold data, have no moving parts, cost more, use less power, are more rugged, and last longer than magnetic hard drives.

Hard drive for a
desktop computer

Hard drive for a notebook

Figure 21-51 Hard drives for notebooks are smaller than hard drives for desktop computers
Courtesy: Course Technology/Cengage Learning

▲ Notebook hard drives use either a SATA connector for a SATA drive or a 44-pin IDE connector for an IDE drive. A SATA connector on a notebook looks the same as that on a desktop. IDE connectors on a desktop motherboard use 40 pins, but notebook IDE connectors use 44 pins. Figure 21-52 shows a 44-pin IDE connector on a notebook. Check your notebook manual to know which type hard drive to buy.

Figure 21-52 A 44-pin IDE connector on a notebook motherboard
Courtesy: Course Technology/Cengage Learning

▲ For IDE drives, some notebooks use an adapter to interface between a proprietary connector on their hard drives and the 44-pin IDE connector on the notebook motherboards. You'll need to remove the old drive and see how it's connected to know if an adapter is used. If you find an adapter, most likely you can then connect the adapter to the new drive.

Before deciding to replace a hard drive, consider these issues:

▲ If the old drive has crashed, you'll need the recovery CD and notebook drivers CDs to reinstall Windows and the drivers. Make sure you have all these CDs before you start.

21

A+ 220-702

A+
220-702
1.3

◢ If you are upgrading from a low-capacity drive to a higher-capacity drive, you need to consider how you will transfer data from the old drive to the new one. One way to do that is to use a USB to IDE or USB to SATA converter that you first learned about in Chapter 8 (refer back to Figures 8-60 and 8-61). Using this converter, both drives can be up and working on the notebook at the same time, so you can copy files.

> ▣ **Video**
> Recovering Data on a Laptop

To replace a hard drive, older notebook computers required that you disassemble the notebook. With newer notebooks, you can easily replace a drive. For example, for one notebook, first power down the system, remove peripherals, including the AC adapter, and remove the battery pack. Then remove a screw that holds the drive in place (see Figure 21-53). Open the lid of the notebook slightly. Turn the notebook on its side and push the drive out of its bay (see Figure 21-54). Then remove the plastic cover from the drive. Move the cover to the new drive, and insert the new drive in the bay. Next, replace the screw and power up the system.

Figure 21-53 This one screw holds the hard drive in position
Courtesy: Course Technology/Cengage Learning

Figure 21-54 Push the drive out of its bay
Courtesy: Course Technology/Cengage Learning

When the system boots up, if BIOS setup is set to autodetect hard drives, BIOS recognizes the new drive and searches for an operating system. If the drive is new, boot from the Windows recovery CD that came from the notebook manufacturer and install the OS.

A+
220-702
1.3

> **Notes** In other chapters, it is possible to give general directions on PC repair that apply to all kinds of brands, models, and systems. Not so with notebooks. Learning to repair notebooks involves learning unique ways to assemble, disassemble, and repair notebook components for specific brands and models of notebooks.

DISASSEMBLING AND REASSEMBLING A NOTEBOOK COMPUTER

Working on notebooks requires special tools and extra patience. Just as when you are working with desktop systems, before opening the case of a notebook or touching sensitive components, you should always use a ground strap to protect the system against ESD. You can attach the alligator clip end of the ground strap to an unpainted metallic surface on the notebook. This surface could be, for instance, a port on the back of the notebook (see Figure 21-55). If a ground strap is not available, first dissipate any ESD between you and the notebook by touching a metallic unpainted part of the notebook, such as a port on the back, before you touch a component inside the case.

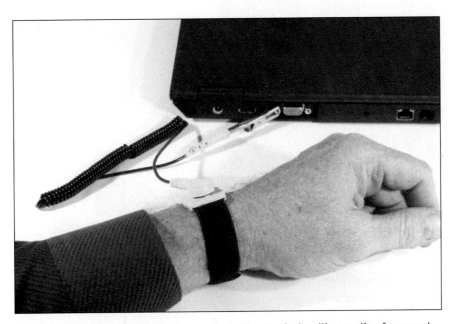

Figure 21-55   To protect the system against ESD, attach the alligator clip of a ground strap to an I/O port on the back of the notebook
Courtesy: Course Technology/Cengage Learning

Screws and nuts on a notebook are smaller than a desktop system and therefore require smaller tools. You will need the following tools to disassemble a notebook, although you can get by without several of them. See Figure 21-56 for a display of some of these tools:

- Antistatic ground strap
- Small flat-head screwdriver
- Number 1 Phillips-head screwdriver
- Dental pick (useful for prying without damaging plastic cases, connectors, and screw covers such as the one in Figure 21-57)

21

A+ 220-702

A+
220-702
1.3

Figure 21-56   Tools for disassembling a notebook computer
Courtesy: Course Technology/Cengage Learning

Figure 21-57   Use a small screwdriver or dental pick to pry up the plastic cover hiding a screw
Courtesy: Course Technology/Cengage Learning

▲ Torx screwdriver set, particularly size T5
▲ Something such as a pillbox to keep screws and small parts organized
▲ Notepad for note taking or digital camera (optional)
▲ Flashlight (optional)
▲ Three-prong extractor to pick up tiny screws (optional)

Notebooks contain many small screws of various sizes and lengths. When reassembling, put screws back where they came from so that when you reassemble the system, you won't use screws that are too long and that can protrude into a sensitive component and damage it. As you remove a screw, store or label it so you know where it goes when reassembling. One way to do that is to place screws in a pillbox with each compartment labeled. Another way is to place screws on a soft padded work surface and use white labeling tape to label each set of screws. A third way to organize screws is to put them on notebook paper and write beside them where the screw belongs (see Figure 21-58). My favorite method of keeping up with all those screws is to tape the screw beside the manufacturer documentation that I'm following to disassemble the notebook (see Figure 21-59). Whatever method you use, work methodically to keep screws and components organized so you know what goes where when reassembling.

Figure 21-58 Using a notepad can help you organize screws so you know which screw goes where when reassembling
Courtesy: Course Technology/Cengage Learning

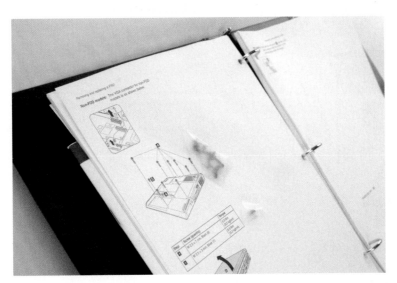

Figure 21-59 Tape screws beside the step in the manufacturer documentation that told you to remove the screw
Courtesy: Course Technology/Cengage Learning

💡 **A+ Exam Tip** The A+ 220-702 Practical Application exam expects you to know the importance of keeping parts organized when disassembling a notebook as well as the importance of having manufacturer documentation to know the steps to disassembly.

As you disassemble the computer, if you are not following directions from a service manual, keep notes as you work to help you reassemble later. Draw diagrams and label things carefully. Include in your drawings cable orientations and screw locations. You might consider using a digital camera. Photos that you take at each step in the disassemble process will be a great help when it's time to put the notebook back together.

When disassembling a notebook, consider the following tips:

▲ Make your best effort to find the hardware service manual for the particular notebook model you are servicing. The manual should include all the detailed steps to disassemble the notebook and a parts list of components that can be ordered from the notebook manufacturer. If you don't have this manual, your chances of successfully replacing an internal component are greatly reduced! And, if you don't have much experience disassembling a notebook, it is not wise to attempt to do so without this manual.

▲ Consider the warranty that might still apply to the notebook. Remember that opening the case of a notebook under warranty most likely will void the warranty. Make certain that any component you have purchased to replace an internal component will work in the model notebook you are servicing.

▲ Take your time. Patience is needed to keep from scratching or marring plastic screw covers, hinges, and the case.

▲ As you work, don't force anything. If you find yourself forcing something, you're likely to break it.

▲ Always wear a ground strap or use other protection against ESD.

▲ When removing cables, know that sometimes cable connectors are ZIF connectors. To disconnect a cable from a ZIF connector, first pull up on the connector and then remove the cable, as shown in Figure 21-60. Figure 21-61 shows a notebook using three ZIF connectors that hold the three keyboard cables in place.

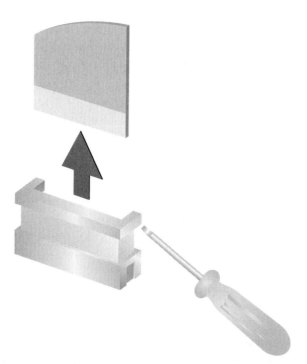

Figure 21-60 To disconnect a ZIF connector, first push up on the connector
to release the latch, and then remove the cable
Courtesy: Course Technology/Cengage Learning

▲ Again, use a dental pick or very small screwdriver to pry up the plastic cover hiding a screw.

▲ Some notebooks use plastic screws that are intended to be used only once. The service manual will tell you to be careful to not overtighten these screws and to always use new screws when reassembling a notebook.

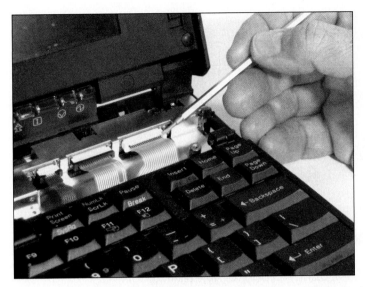

Figure 21-61 Three ZIF connectors hold the three keyboard cables in place
Courtesy: Course Technology/Cengage Learning

◢ Disassemble the notebook by removing each field replaceable unit in the order given by the service manual for your notebook. For example, one manufacturer says that to replace the motherboard for a notebook, remove components in this order: battery pack, DIMM door, keyboard, middle cover, hinge cover, DVD drive and bracket, mini PCI adapter, keyboard bezel assembly, fan assembly, CPU, CPU fixture, DVD drive bracket, floppy drive assembly, and floppy drive bracket. After all these components are removed, you can then remove the motherboard. Follow the steps to remove each component in the right order.

When reassembling a notebook, consider these general tips:

◢ Reassemble the notebook in the reverse order of the way you disassembled it. Follow each step carefully.

◢ Be sure to tighten, but not overtighten, all screws. Loose screws or metal fragments in a notebook can be dangerous; they might cause a short as they shift about inside the notebook.

◢ Before you install the battery or AC adapter, verify there are no loose parts inside the notebook. Pick it up and shake it. If you hear anything loose, open the case and find the loose component, screw, spring, or metal flake, and fix the problem.

Now let's look at the specific situations where you are disassembling a notebook to replace an LCD panel, mini PCI card, and other internal components.

REPLACING THE KEYBOARD

Replacing the keyboard is pretty easy to do. Here are typical steps that are similar to many models of notebooks:

1. Power down the notebook and remove the AC adapter and the battery pack.

2. Remove two or more screws on the bottom of the notebook (see Figure 21-62). (Only the documentation can tell you which ones, as there are probably several of them used to hold various components in place.)

3. Turn the notebook over and open the lid. Gently push the keyboard toward the lid while pulling it up to release it from the case (see Figure 21-63).

A+
220-702
1.3

Figure 21-62　Remove screws on the bottom of the notebook
Courtesy: Course Technology/Cengage Learning

Figure 21-63　Pry up and lift the keyboard out of the notebook case
Courtesy: Course Technology/Cengage Learning

4. Bring the keyboard out of the case and forward to expose the keyboard ribbon cable attached underneath the board. Use a screwdriver to lift the cable connector up and out of its socket (see Figure 21-64).

5. Replace the keyboard following the steps in reverse order.

REPLACING OPTICAL DRIVES

Most likely you'll need to first remove the keyboard to expose an optical drive. Follow along as we remove the DVD drive from one system:

1. Remove the keyboard.

2. Remove the screw that holds the DVD drive to the notebook (see Figure 21-65).

3. Slide the drive out of the bay (see Figure 21-66).

4. When you slide the new drive into the bay, make sure you push it far enough into the bay that it solidly connects with the drive connector at the back of the bay. Replace the screw.

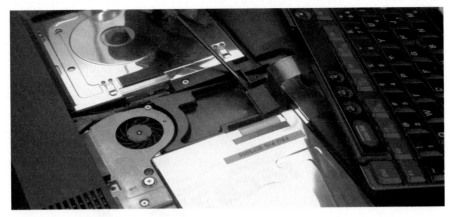

Figure 21-64 Disconnect the keyboard cable from the motherboard
Courtesy: Course Technology/Cengage Learning

Figure 21-65 Remove the screw that holds the DVD drive
Courtesy: Course Technology/Cengage Learning

Figure 21-66 Slide the drive out of the bay
Courtesy: Course Technology/Cengage Learning

REPLACING EXPANSION CARDS

A notebook does not contain the normal PCI Express or PCI slots found in desktop systems. Newer notebooks are likely to use the Mini PCI Express slots (also called Mini PCIe slots) that use the PCI Express standards applied to notebooks. These slots can be used by many kinds of Mini PCIe cards, including Wi-Fi wireless, cellular WAN, and Bluetooth Mini PCI cards. Figure 21-67 shows a Mini PCI Express Sierra Wireless mobile broadband Internet card that comes installed in several HP, Asus, and Dialogue laptops.

Figure 21-67   MC8775 PCI Express Mini card by Sierra Wireless used for voice and data transmissions on 3G networks
Courtesy of Sierra Wireless

Older notebooks use a Mini PCI slot (see Figure 21-68) which uses PCI standards. Mini PCI cards are about twice the size of Mini PCI Express cards.

Figure 21-68   A Mini PCI slot follows PCI standards applied to notebooks
Courtesy: Course Technology/Cengage Learning

A+
220-702
1.3
3.2

Mini PCI Express slots have 52 pins on the edge connector. Mini PCI slots come in three types: Type I and II Mini PCI slots use a 100-pin stacking connector, while Type III slots use a 124-pin stacking connector. Type III Mini PCI cards are smaller than Type I and II cards and are the most popular. Figure 21-69 shows an example of a Mini PCI card that you install inside a notebook to provide wireless Wi-Fi connectivity.

Figure 21-69 This Cisco wireless internal adapter is a Type III Mini PCI card made by IBM
Courtesy of IBM Corporation

Figure 21-70 shows the three steps to remove a Mini PCI Express card. The first step is to disconnect the antenna from this Wi-Fi card. Then remove the one screw at the top of the card, and pull the card forward and out of the slot.

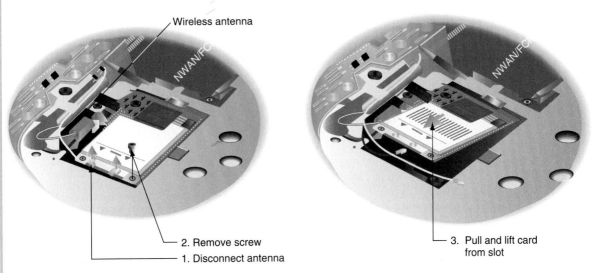

Wireless antenna

2. Remove screw
1. Disconnect antenna

3. Pull and lift card
from slot

Figure 21-70 How to remove a Mini PCI Express card
Courtesy: Course Technology/Cengage Learning

Figure 21-71 shows how to remove a Mini PCI wireless network card in a Dell notebook. First, you must remove the hinged cover and the keyboard. Then disconnect the cable to the wireless antenna from the card. Next, pull outward on the securing tabs that hold the card in place. The card will pop up slightly. Lift it out of the cavity.

21

A+ 220-702

A+
220-702
1.3
3.2

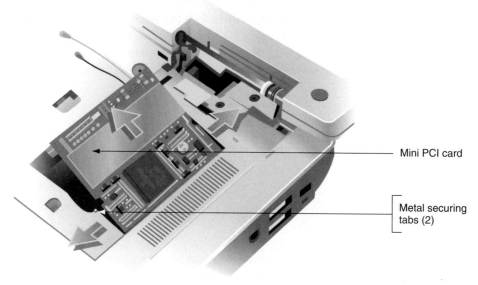

Figure 21-71 Remove a Mini PCI Card
Courtesy: Course Technology/Cengage Learning

To replace the card, align the card in the cavity and press it down until it pops in place between the two securing tabs on each side of the card. Then reconnect the wireless antenna cable, as shown in Figure 21-72. Replace the keyboard and hinged cover.

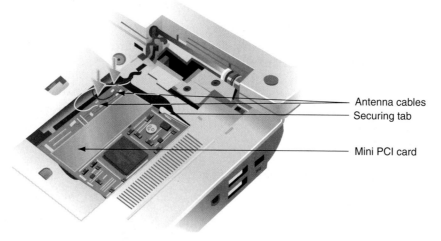

Figure 21-72 Install a Mini PCI card
© 2005 Dell Inc. All rights reserved

To tell the difference between a Mini PCIe slot and a Mini PCI slot, look for the clips on the side of the Mini PCI slot that are not present on a Mini PCIe slot. Also, the Mini PCIe slot is smaller than a Mini PCI slot. To tell the difference between a mini PCI card and a mini PCIe card, look for notches on the sides of a mini PCI card and a long, unbroken edge connector on the card. A mini PCIe card has screw holes at the top of the card and a break near the center of the edge connector.

> 💡 **A+ Exam Tip** The A+ 220-702 Practical Application exam expects you to be able to recognize Mini PCI and Mini PCIe slots.

Mini PCI and Mini PCI Express cards are often used to enhance communications options for a notebook. You have just seen how the cards can be used to provide connectivity to a

A+
220-702
1.3
3.2

cellular WAN or Wi-Fi network. In addition, the cards are used to provide a Bluetooth personal network. Keep in mind these features when selecting a Mini PCI or Mini PCIe card:

▲ Bluetooth comes in three versions. The latest version, Version 3.0, uses less power and is faster than the earlier versions. Version 2.0 is faster and uses less power than Version 1.x. For best results, use a later version of Bluetooth.

▲ Some Mini PCI and Mini PCIe cards are combo cards providing both Wi-Fi and Bluetooth ability.

▲ Mini PCI Express slots are not backward compatible with Mini PCI slots. Use the type card to match the slot your notebook provides.

> 💡 **A+ Exam Tip** The A+ 220-702 Practical Application exam expects you to know the difference between Bluetooth 1.0 and 2.0.

After you have installed a Bluetooth, cellular WAN, or other wireless adapter, follow directions given earlier in the chapter to connect the notebook to the wireless network. If you have problems making a connection, verify that Device Manager reports the device is working properly and that Event Viewer has not reported error events about the device.

REPLACING THE MOTHERBOARD AND CPU

A+
220-702
1.3

If a port or component on the motherboard fails, consider installing an external device rather than replacing the motherboard (also called the system board). Also, before you decide to replace the motherboard, check if the notebook manufacturer has diagnostic software you can download and use to verify the problem is the motherboard. Search the site for information about the error message or symptom.

You might also be called on to upgrade the CPU in a notebook. Be sure to use only a CPU supported by the notebook manufacturer for this particular notebook. Current and old CPU sockets for Intel processors include socket PPGA478, LGA775, PPGA370, SEPP242, SEPP540, PBGA479, and H-PBGA495. The first two sockets listed are the most popular. AMD sockets for notebook processors include sockets S1 and ASB1. The S1 socket is the most popular and has 638 pins.

Replacing the motherboard probably means you'll need to fully disassemble the entire notebook except the LCD assembly. Here is the general procedure for one notebook:

1. Remove the keyboard, optical drive, and mini PCI card.

2. The next step is to remove the LCD panel and keyboard bezel assembly. To do this, first remove two screws on the back of the notebook (see Figure 21-73) and the screws

Figure 21-73 Remove two screws on the back of the notebook
Courtesy: Course Technology/Cengage Learning

on the bottom of the notebook. You can then crack the case by lifting the notebook lid and keyboard bezel from the case (see Figure 21-74).

Figure 21-74 Cracking the notebook case
Courtesy: Course Technology/Cengage Learning

3. Lift up the assembly and look underneath to see two cables connecting the assembly to the motherboard (see Figure 21-75). Disconnect these two cables and set the assembly aside.

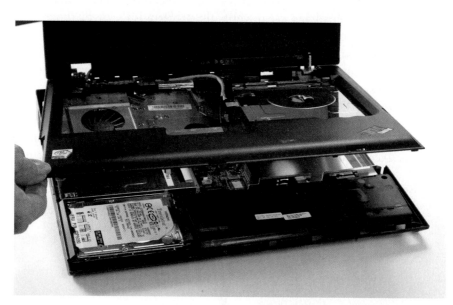

Figure 21-75 Lift the assembly to locate the two cable connections
Courtesy: Course Technology/Cengage Learning

4. Figure 21-76 shows the open case. To remove the CPU fan assembly, remove screws (see Figure 21-77) and then lift the fan assembly up.

5. Figure 21-78 shows the fan assembly lifted exposing the CPU. Notice the thermal compound on the CPU and heat sink. Disconnect the two cables connecting the fan assembly to the motherboard (see Figure 21-79).

6. To remove the CPU, turn the CPU socket screw 90 degrees to open the socket (see Figure 21-80). This notebook uses an Intel socket. All current Intel sockets, as well as

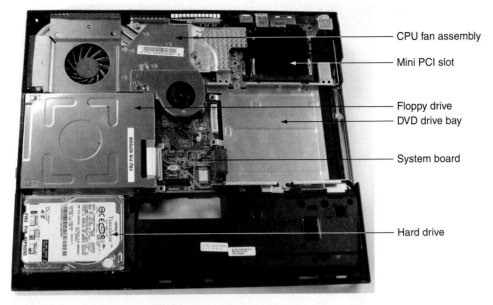

CPU fan assembly

Mini PCI slot

Floppy drive
DVD drive bay

System board

Hard drive

Figure 21-76 Components inside the open case
Courtesy: Course Technology/Cengage Learning

Figure 21-77 Remove the screws holding the CPU fan assembly in place
Courtesy: Course Technology/Cengage Learning

AMD sockets, use a screw to open and close the socket. Intel calls this screw the socket actuator. Some sockets have this screw on the side of the socket, as shown in Figure 21-80, and other sockets have the screw on the corner of the socket.

7. Lift the CPU from the socket. Be careful to lift straight up without bending the CPU pins. Figure 21-81 shows the processor out of the socket. If you look carefully, you can see the missing pins on one corner of the processor and socket. This corner is used to correctly orient the processor in the socket, which is socket 478B.

8. The DVD drive bay can now be removed as well as the floppy drive and bay. Each bay and the floppy drive are held in place with a single screw. After the drive and bays are removed, the motherboard is fully exposed.

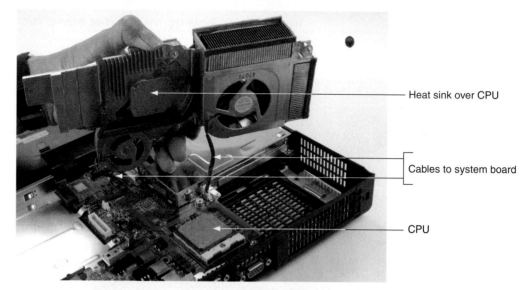

Heat sink over CPU

Cables to system board

CPU

Figure 21-78 Lifting the CPU fan assembly exposes the CPU
Courtesy: Course Technology/Cengage Learning

Figure 21-79 Disconnect the cables connecting the fan assembly to the motherboard
Courtesy: Course Technology/Cengage Learning

Figure 21-80 Open the CPU socket
Courtesy: Course Technology/Cengage Learning

Figure 21-81 The processor removed from socket 478B
Courtesy: Course Technology/Cengage Learning

9. Remove a single screw that holds the motherboard in place (see Figure 21-82) and lift the board out of the case. Figure 21-83 shows the top of the board, and Figure 21-84 shows the bottom. Both top and bottom are packed with components.

Figure 21-82 Remove the single screw attaching the motherboard to the case
Courtesy: Course Technology/Cengage Learning

10. When reassembling the system, all steps are done in reverse. If you are installing the same CPU in the new motherboard, be sure to clean the old thermal compound off the CPU and heat sink. Then apply new thermal compound to the heat sink. Don't use so much that the compound will slide off the CPU and damage it. Before you drop the CPU into the socket, be sure the socket screw is in the open position. Then delicately drop the CPU into its socket. If it does not drop completely, consider that the screw might not be in the full open position.

REPLACING THE LCD PANEL

Because the LCD panel is so fragile, it is one component that is likely to be broken when a notebook is not handled properly. If the LCD panel is dim or black when the notebook is running, first try to use the video port on the notebook to connect it to an external

A+
220-702
1.3

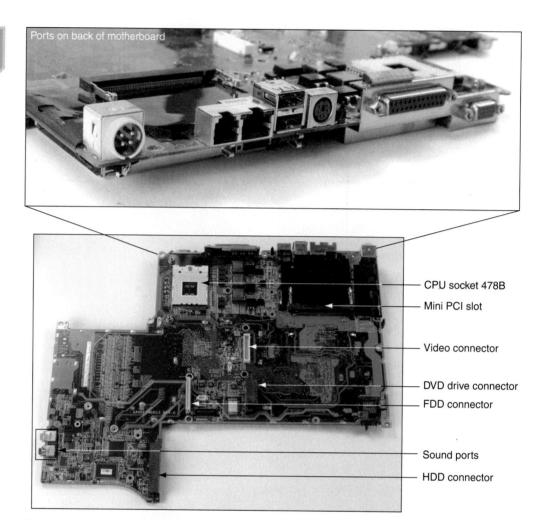

Figure 21-83 Top of the motherboard
Courtesy: Course Technology/Cengage Learning

Figure 21-84 Bottom of the motherboard
Courtesy: Course Technology/Cengage Learning

monitor. After you connect the monitor, use a function key to toggle between the LCD panel, the external monitor, and both the panel and monitor. If the external monitor works, but the LCD panel does not work, then most likely the problem is with the LCD panel assembly.

If the LCD display is entirely black, most likely you'll have to replace the entire LCD assembly. However, if the screen is dim, but you can make out that some display is present, the problem might be the video inverter, which interfaces between the LCD panel and the motherboard (see Figure 21-85). Check with the notebook manufacturer to confirm that it makes sense to first try replacing just the relatively inexpensive inverter board before you replace the more expensive entire LCD panel assembly. If the entire assembly needs replacing, the cost of the assembly might exceed the value of the notebook.

Figure 21-85   A ThinkPad video inverter card
Courtesy: Course Technology/Cengage Learning

Sometimes, a notebook LCD panel, including the entire cover and hinges, is considered a single field replaceable unit, and sometimes components within the LCD assembly are considered an FRU. For example, the field replaceable units for the display panel in Figure 21-86 are the LCD front bezel, the hinges, the LCD panel, the inverter card, the LCD interface cables, the LCD USB cover, and the rear cover. Also know that an LCD assembly might include a microphone or speakers that are embedded in the laptop lid. For other laptops, the microphone and speakers are inside the case.

Some high-end notebooks contain a video card that has embedded video memory. This video card might also need replacing. In most cases, you would replace only the LCD panel and perhaps the inverter card.

The following are some general directions to replace an LCD panel:

1. Remove the AC adapter and the battery pack.

2. Remove the keyboard.

3. Remove the screws holding the hinge in place and remove the hinge cover. Figure 21-87 shows a notebook with a metal hinge cover, but some notebooks use plastic covers that you can easily break as you remove them. Be careful with the plastic ones.

4. Remove the screws holding the LCD panel to the notebook.

5. You're now ready to remove the LCD panel from the notebook. Be aware there might be wires running through the hinge assembly, cables, or a pin connector. Cables might be connected to the motherboard using ZIF connectors. As you remove the LCD top cover, be careful to watch for how the panel is connected. Don't pull on wires or cables as you remove the cover, but first carefully disconnect them.

6. Next, remove screws that hold the top cover and LCD panel together. Sometimes, these screws are covered with black plastic circles. First use a dental pick or small screwdriver to pick off these covers. You should then be able to remove the front bezel and separate the rear cover from the LCD panel. For one LCD panel, when you separate the LCD assembly from the lid cover, you can see the inverter card. Figure 21-88 shows the inverter card being compared to the new one to make sure they match. The match is not identical, but should work.

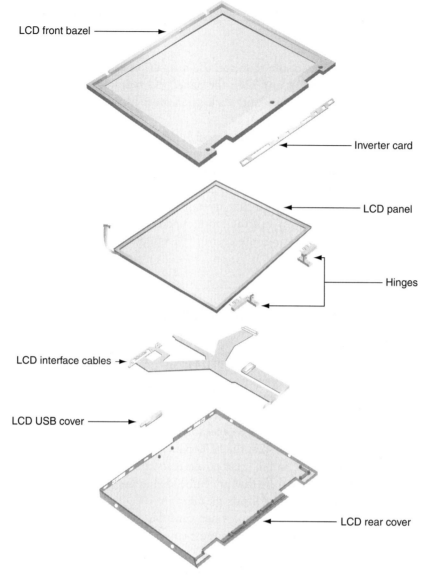

LCD front bazel

Inverter card

LCD panel

Hinges

LCD interface cables

LCD USB cover

LCD rear cover

Figure 21-86 Components in an LCD assembly
Courtesy: Course Technology/Cengage Learning

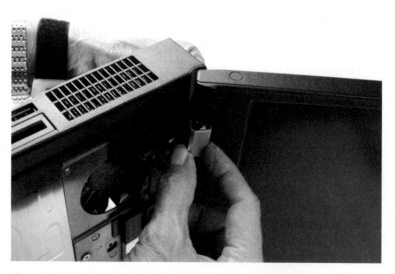

Figure 21-87 Remove the hinge cover from the notebook hinge
Courtesy: Course Technology/Cengage Learning

A+
220-702
1.3

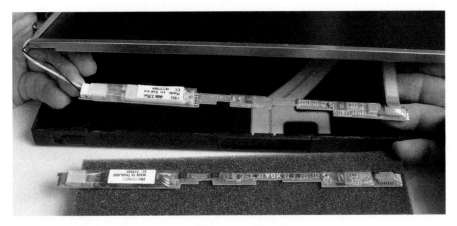

Figure 21-88 The inverter is exposed and is compared to the new one
Courtesy: Course Technology/Cengage Learning

7. Disconnect the old inverter and install the new one. When disconnecting the ribbon cable from the old inverter, notice you must first lift up on the lock holding the ZIF connector in place, as shown in Figure 21-89.

Figure 21-89 Lift up on the ZIF connector locking mechanism before removing the ribbon cable
Courtesy: Course Technology/Cengage Learning

8. Install the new inverter. Reassemble the LCD panel assembly. Make sure the assembly is put together with a tight fit so that all screws line up well.

9. Reattach the LCD panel assembly to the notebook.

21

>> **CHAPTER SUMMARY**

◢ Notebook computers are designed for travel. They use the same technology as desktop computers, with modifications for space, portability, and power conservation. A notebook generally costs more than a desktop with comparable power and features.

◢ When supporting notebooks, pay careful attention to what the warranty allows you to change on the computer.

◢ The notebook manufacturer documentation, including the service manual, diagnostic software, and Windows Recovery CD, are useful when disassembling, troubleshooting, and repairing a notebook.

◢ A notebook uses a customized installation of the Windows OS, customized by the notebook manufacturer. For most situations, the OS does not need upgrading for the life of the notebook unless you need to use features of a new OS. To perform an upgrade, obtain a customized version of the new OS from the notebook manufacturer.

◢ Port replicators and docking stations can make it easier to connect a notebook to peripherals. Docking stations can provide additional slots and bays for components.

◢ PC Cards, CardBus, and ExpressCard slots are a popular way to add peripheral devices to notebooks. Types of PC Cards that vary in thickness are Types I, II, and III. PC Cards can be used in CardBus slots. The latest I/O cards are ExpressCard/34 and ExpressCard/54, which are not backward compatible with the PC Card slots.

◢ Wireless technologies popular with notebooks include Wi-Fi, cellular WAN, and Bluetooth.

◢ A notebook can be powered by its battery pack or by an AC or DC adapter connected to a power source.

◢ Vista uses sleep mode, hybrid sleep, and hibernation to conserve power. Windows XP uses standby mode and hibernation.

◢ Input devices on a notebook can include the keyboard, mouse, touch pad, TrackPoint (point stick), graphics tablet (digitizer), and stylus.

◢ Use an external monitor to verify that a video problem is with the LCD panel rather than the internal video card or motherboard.

◢ When an internal component needs replacing, consider the possibility of disabling the component and using an external peripheral device in its place.

◢ When disassembling a notebook, the manufacturer documentation is essential.

◢ Current notebooks use SO-DIMMs and SO-RIMMs for memory. SO-DIMMs can have DDR, DDR2, or DDR3 memory.

◢ When upgrading components on a notebook, including memory, use components that are the same brand as the notebook, or use only components recommended by the notebook's manufacturer.

◢ Hard drives use a SATA or 44-pin IDE connection on a notebook.

>> KEY TERMS

For explanations of key terms, see the Glossary near the end of the book.

AC adapter	laptop computer	PCMCIA cards
auto-switching	Lithium Ion	point stick
CardBus	MicroDIMMs	port replicator
digitizer	Mini PCI	sleep timers
digitizing tablet	Mini PCI Express	stylus
docking station	Mini PCIe	touch pad
ExpressCard	notebook	TrackPoint
graphics tablet	PC Card	Wake on LAN
inverter	PC Card slots	

>> REVIEWING THE BASICS

1. Why are notebooks usually more expensive than PCs with comparable power and features?

2. What type of manual is important to have before you disassemble a notebook?

3. Why is it important to reinstall the OS on a notebook from the recovery CDs rather than using a retail version of the OS?

4. Which is likely to have more features, a port replicator or a docking station?

5. What was the first bus used by PC Card slots?

6. What bus is used by a CardBus slot?

7. What bus is used by ExpressCard slots?

8. Can you use an ExpressCard card in a CardBus slot? In a PC Card slot?

9. Can you install and use two Type I PC Card cards in a single Type III CardBus slot?

10. What prevents a CardBus card from being inserted in a 16-bit PC Card slot?

11. Name three types of wireless technologies that are used with notebooks.

12. What type of battery is currently used with notebooks?

13. What type of device changes DC to AC?

14. To what ACPI mode does Vista sleep mode correspond?

15. What Windows utility is used to enable Wake on LAN?

16. What type of pointing device is used on ThinkPad notebooks?

17. When a notebook internal device fails, what three options can you use to deal with the problem?

18. How many pins does a notebook IDE connector have? A desktop IDE connector?

19. When an LCD panel is very dim and brightness adjustments don't help, what component is likely to be the problem?

20. After you have removed the AC adapter and all peripherals, what is the next component you should always remove before servicing any internal notebook components?

>> THINKING CRITICALLY

1. Your friend has a Windows 2000 notebook computer and has purchased Windows XP and installed it as an upgrade on his notebook. He calls to tell you about the upgrade and says that he cannot connect to the Internet. His notebook has an embedded Ethernet port that he uses for communication. What do you tell him to do?

   a. Reinstall Windows 2000.

   b. Using another computer, download and install the Windows XP Ethernet drivers from the notebook manufacturer's Web site.

   c. Search the CDs that came with the notebook for Windows XP Ethernet drivers and install them.

   d. Perform a clean install of Windows XP.

21

2. A friend asks you for help in determining the best product to buy: a notebook, tablet PC, or PDA. She is a paralegal and spends a lot of time at the courthouse researching real estate titles. She wants a device to take notes with as she works. List three questions you would ask her to help her make her decision.

3. Looking back at Figure 21-83, what are the eight ports shown in the callout photo, listed from left to right?

>> HANDS-ON PROJECTS

PROJECT 21-1:   Observing Notebook Features

Examine a notebook, its documentation, and the manufacturer's Web site, and then answer these questions:

1. How do you exchange the battery pack on the notebook?

2. What type of SO-DIMM or SO-RIMM does the notebook use?

3. How much memory is currently installed?

4. What is the capacity of the hard drive?

5. What OS is installed?

6. What processor is installed?

7. What ports are on the notebook?

8. How many PC Card or ExpressCard slots does the notebook have?

9. How much does the notebook weigh?

10. What is the cost of a new battery pack?

11. Can you buy memory from the Web site? How much does it cost to upgrade the notebook's memory to full capacity?

PROJECT 21-2:   Researching Wireless Notebook Systems

Use the Web for the following research:

1. Find a notebook that has integrated wireless technology. Print the Web page advertising the notebook.

2. Drill down to the detailed specifications for the notebook, and answer these questions:

   a. What type of wireless technology does the notebook support?

   b. Does the notebook use a wireless component integrated on the motherboard or an internal adapter card?

   c. Does the notebook have a wireless switch? If so, where is the switch located?

3. Suppose you have a PC with a USB port. Find a USB wireless adapter so that your PC and notebook can connect wirelessly. Make sure that the device is compatible with the notebook's wireless technology. Print a Web page about this device.

PROJECT 21-3: Researching Notebook Service Manuals

Do the following to find a service manual for a notebook that you or a friend own:

1. What is the brand, model, and serial number of the notebook?

2. What is the Web site of the notebook manufacturer? Print a Web page on that site that shows the documentation and/or drivers available for this notebook.

3. If the Web site provides a service manual for disassembling the notebook, download the manual. Print two or three pages from the manual showing the title page and Table of Contents for the manual.

4. If the Web site does not provide a service manual, search the Internet for the manual. If you find it, download it and print the title page and Table of Contents.

PROJECT 21-4: Diagnosing Notebook Computer Problems

Suppose you spend much of your day diagnosing problems with notebook computers. Notebooks have a mini PCI or mini PCIe slot that works in a similar way to PCI and PCIe slots on desktop systems. Search the Internet for diagnostic cards that you can use in a mini PCI or mini PCIe slot that can help you diagnose hardware problems with notebooks. Print the Web pages showing your findings. Which diagnostic card would you choose to buy and why?

PROJECT 21-5: Setting Up a Service Center for Notebooks

As notebooks get more and more popular, people will be looking for ways to get them serviced without returning them to the manufacturer. If you ever intend to set up your own PC Repair Shop, you might want to consider becoming a service center for a few brands of the more popular notebooks. Reasons to become an authorized service center are that you have access to service manuals, parts lists, and wholesale parts for notebooks. Do the following to research becoming an authorized service center:

1. Select a brand of notebooks that you think you would like to service.

2. Research the Web site of this manufacturer and answer these questions:

   a. Where is the closest authorized service center for this brand notebook?

   b. What are the requirements to become an authorized service center? Print the Web page showing the requirements.

   c. Is A+ certification one of those requirements?

   d. Some notebook manufacturers offer a program that falls short of becoming an authorized service center but does provide support for IT professionals so that repair technicians can order notebook parts. Does the manufacturer offer this service? If so, what must you do to qualify?

21

If you try one brand of notebook and can't find the information you need, try another brand. Sometimes this information can only be obtained by contacting the manufacturer directly. And one more hint: to use *www.google.com* to search a particular site, begin the search string with *site:hostname.com*.

>> REAL PROBLEMS, REAL SOLUTIONS

REAL PROBLEM 21-1: Upgrading Notebook Memory

You've had your Sony VGN-CR12E VAIO notebook for a couple of years and are looking for ways to improve its performance. You've cleaned up the hard drive and defragged it, and now you're considering the possibility of upgrading memory. Windows Vista reports the system has 2 GB of RAM. You open the cover on the bottom of the case and discover that both SO-DIMM slots are filled. How much will the upgrade cost to bring total RAM in the system to 4 GB? Print the Web page to support your answer.

REAL PROBLEM 21-2: Notebook Power Problems

Julie's Windows XP Dell Inspiron 17 notebook provided Wi-Fi that no longer works, and the notebook is not under warranty. The Ethernet port does work, but Julie travels a lot and often needs to access wireless networks. Download the service manual for her notebook from *www.dell.com* and print the page that shows the location of the Wi-Fi card in the notebook. Do you think it is best to replace the internal Wi-Fi card or use an ExpressCard card or USB wireless device instead? What is the cost of purchasing the internal Wi-Fi card and about how much time do you think it will take to exchange the card? On the other hand, how much will an external wireless device cost that you could recommend to Julie as an option? Print Web pages documenting your answers.

REAL PROBLEM 21-3: Taking Apart a Notebook

If you enjoy putting together a thousand-piece jigsaw puzzle, you'll probably enjoy working on notebook computers. With desktop systems, replacing a component is not a time-consuming task, but with notebooks, the job could take half a day. If you take the time to carefully examine the notebook's case before attempting to open it, you will probably find markings provided by the manufacturer to assist you in locating components that are commonly upgraded. If you have a service manual, your work will be much easier than without one. The best way to learn to disassemble a notebook is to practice on an old one that you can afford to break. Find an old Dell or Lenovo or IBM ThinkPad for which you can download the service manual from the Dell or Lenovo Web site. Then carefully and patiently follow the disassembly instructions and then reassemble it. When done, you can congratulate yourself and move on to newer notebooks.

Supporting Printers

This chapter discusses the most popular types of printers and how to support them. As you work through the chapter, you'll learn about printer types and features, how to install a local or network printer, and how to share a printer with others on a network. You'll learn how to manage print jobs, how to protect yourself when working with printers, and how to install printer consumables. Then, you'll learn about maintaining and troubleshooting printers.

PRINTER TYPES AND FEATURES

A+
220-701
1.11

You need to be aware of the types of printers and know about other features a printer might have that you might be called on to configure, repair, or maintain. We begin with a discussion of each type of printer, so you will know the basics of how each type works. Understanding how a printer works will help you fix printer problems when they arise.

TYPES OF PRINTERS

The major categories of printer types include laser, inkjet (ink dispersion), solid ink, dye sublimation, thermal printers, and impact printers. In the following sections, we'll look at the different types of printers for desktop computing.

> **Notes** If you can afford it, the best practice is to purchase one machine for one purpose, instead of bundling many functions into a single machine. For example, if you need a scanner and a printer, purchase a good printer and a good scanner rather than a combo machine. Routine maintenance and troubleshooting are easier and less expensive on single-purpose machines, although the initial cost is higher.

LASER PRINTERS

A laser printer is a type of electrophotographic printer that can range from a small, personal desktop model to a large, network printer capable of handling and printing large volumes continuously. Figure 22-1 shows an example of a typical laser printer for a small office.

Figure 22-1   Okidata C3200n color laser printer
Courtesy: Course Technology/Cengage Learning

> **💡 A+ Exam Tip**   The A+ 220-701 Essentials exam expects you to be familiar with these types of printers: laser, inkjet, thermal, and impact.

Laser printers require the interaction of mechanical, electrical, and optical technologies to work. Laser printers work by placing toner on an electrically charged rotating drum (sometimes called the image drum) and then depositing the toner on paper as the paper moves through the system at the same speed the drum is turning. Figure 22-2 shows the six steps of laser printing.

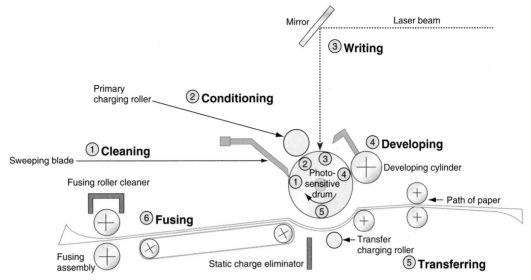

Figure 22-2   The six progressive steps of laser printing
Courtesy: Course Technology/Cengage Learning

Note that Figure 22-2 shows only a cross-section of the drum, mechanisms, and paper. Remember that the drum is as wide as a sheet of paper. The mirror, blades, and rollers in the drawing are also as wide as paper. Also know that toner responds to a charge and moves from one surface to another if the second surface has a more positive charge than the first.

> 💡 **A+ Exam Tip**   The A+ 220-701 Essentials exam expects you to know the six stages of laser printing.

The six steps of laser printing are listed next:

1. *Cleaning.* A sweeper strip cleans the drum of any residual toner, which is swept away by a sweeping blade. Erase lamps light the surface of the drum to neutralize any electrical charge left on it. These erase lamps are usually in the top cover of the printer.

2. *Conditioning.* The drum is conditioned by a roller that places a high uniform electrical charge of –600V on the surface of the drum. The roller is called the primary charging roller or primary corona, which is charged by a high-voltage power supply assembly.

3. *Writing.* A laser beam discharges a lower charge only to places where toner should go. The uniform charge applied in Step 2 is discharged only where you want the printer to print. This is done by controlling motors and mirrors that direct the laser beam to scan across the drum until it completes the correct number of passes for each inch of the drum circumference. For example, for a 1200 dots per inch (dpi) printer, the beam makes 1200 passes for every one inch of the drum circumference. The laser beam is turned on and off continually as it makes a single pass down the length of the drum, so that dots are written along the drum on every pass. For a 1200-dpi printer, 1200 dots are written along the drum for every inch of linear pass. The 1200 dots per inch down this single pass, combined with 1200 passes per inch of drum circumference, accomplish the resolution of 1200 x 1200 dots per square inch of many desktop laser printers. The laser beam has written an image to the drum surface as a –100V charge. The –100V charge on this image area will be used in the developing stage to transmit toner to the drum surface.

> 📝 **Notes** A laser printer can produce better-quality printouts than a dot matrix printer, even when printing at the same dpi, because it can vary the size of the dots it prints, creating a sharp, clear image. Hewlett-Packard (HP) calls this technology of varying the size of dots **REt (Resolution Enhancement technology)**.

4. *Developing.* The developing cylinder applies toner to the surface of the drum. The toner is charged and sticks to the developing cylinder because of a magnet inside the cylinder. A control blade prevents too much toner from sticking to the cylinder surface. As the cylinder rotates very close to the drum, the toner is attracted to the part of the surface of the drum that has a –100V charge and repelled from the –600V part of the drum surface. The result is that toner sticks to the drum where the laser beam has hit and is repelled from the area where the laser beam has not hit.

5. *Transferring.* In the transferring step (shown in Figure 22-2), a strong electrical charge draws the toner off the drum onto the paper. This is the first step that takes place outside the cartridge and the first step that involves the paper. The transfer charging roller puts a positive charge on the paper to pull the toner from the drum onto the paper. Then the static charge eliminator (refer again to Figure 22-2) weakens the charges on both the paper and the drum so that the paper does not stick to the drum. The stiffness of the paper and the small radius of the drum also help the paper move away from the drum and toward the fusing assembly. Very thin paper can wrap around the drum, which is why printer manuals usually instruct you to use only paper designated for laser printers.

6. *Fusing.* The fusing step uses heat and pressure to fuse the toner to the paper. Up to this point, the toner is merely sitting on the paper. The fusing rollers apply heat to the paper, which causes the toner to melt, and the rollers apply pressure to bond the melted toner into the paper. The temperature of the rollers is monitored by the printer. If the temperature exceeds an allowed maximum value (410 degrees F for some printers), the printer shuts down.

The first four steps use the printer components that undergo the most wear. To make the printer last longer, these steps are done inside removable cartridges that can be replaced. For older printers, all four steps were done inside one cartridge. For newer printers, the cleaning, conditioning, and writing stages are done inside the image drum cartridge. The developing cylinder is located inside the toner cartridge. The transferring is done using a transfer belt that can be replaced, and the fusing is done inside a fuser cartridge. By using these multiple cartridges inside laser printers, the cost of maintaining a printer is reduced. You can replace one cartridge without having to replace them all. The toner cartridge needs replacing the most often, followed by the image drum, the fuser cartridge, and the transfer assembly, in that order.

The previous steps describe how a black-and-white printer works. Color laser printers work in a similar way, but the writing process repeats four times, one for each toner color of cyan, magenta, yellow, and black. Each color requires a separate image drum. Then, the paper passes to the fusing stage, when the fuser bonds all toner to the paper and aids in blending the four tones to form specific colors.

INKJET PRINTERS

Inkjet printers use a type of ink-dispersion printing and don't normally provide the high-quality resolution of laser printers, but are popular because they are small and can print color inexpensively. Most inkjet printers today give photo-quality results, especially when used with photo-quality paper.

Notes Photos printed on an inkjet printer tend to fade over time, more so than photos produced professionally. To make your photos last longer, use high-quality paper (rated at high gloss or studio gloss) and use fade-resistant ink (such as Vivera ink by HP). Then protect these photos from exposure to light, heat, humidity, and polluted air. To best protect photos made by an inkjet printer, keep them in a photo album rather than displayed and exposed to light.

Earlier inkjet printers used 300 x 300 dpi, but inkjet printers today can use up to 5760 x 1440 dpi. Increasing the dpi has drawbacks. It increases the amount of data sent to the printer for a single page, and all those dots of ink can produce a wet page. An improved technology that gives photo-quality results mixes different colors of ink to produce a new color that then makes a single dot. Hewlett-Packard calls this PhotoREt II color technology. HP mixes as many as 16 drops of ink to produce a single dot of color on the page.

Inkjet printers tend to smudge on inexpensive paper, and they are slower than laser printers. If a printed page later gets damp, the ink can run and get quite messy. The quality of the paper used with inkjet printers significantly affects the quality of printed output. You should use only paper that is designed for an inkjet printer, and you should use a high-grade paper to get the best results. Figure 22-3 shows one example of an inkjet printer.

Figure 22-3 An example of an inkjet printer
Courtesy of Hewlett-Packard Company

An inkjet printer uses a print head that moves across the paper, creating one line of the image with each pass. The printer puts ink on the paper using a matrix of small dots. Different types of inkjet printers form their droplets of ink in different ways. Printer manufacturers use several technologies, but the most popular is the bubble-jet. Bubble-jet printers use tubes of ink that have tiny resistors near the end of each tube. These resistors heat up and cause the ink to boil. Then, a tiny air bubble of ionized ink (ink with an electrical charge) is ejected onto the paper. A typical bubble-jet print head has 64 or 128 tiny nozzles, all of which can fire a droplet simultaneously. (High-end printers can have as many as 3,000 nozzles.) Plates carrying a magnetic charge direct the path of ink onto the paper to form shapes.

Inkjet printers include one or more ink cartridges. When purchasing an inkjet printer, look for the kind that uses two or four separate cartridges. One cartridge is used for black ink. In addition, some color printers use one cartridge for three-color printing (colors are yellow, blue, and red, better known as yellow, cyan, and magenta, sometimes written as CcMmY). Other more expensive printers use three separate color cartridges. Some low-end inkjet printers use a single three-color cartridge and don't have a black ink cartridge. These printers must combine all colors of ink to produce a dull black. Having a separate cartridge for black ink means that it prints true black and, more important, does not use the more expensive colored ink. To save money, you should be able to replace an empty cartridge without having to replace all cartridges.

> **Notes** To save money, you can refill an ink cartridge, and many companies will sell you the tools and ink you need as well as show you how to do it. You can also purchase refilled cartridges at reduced prices. When you purchase ink cartridges, make sure you know if they are new or refilled. Also, know that, for best results, don't refill a cartridge more than three times.

Figure 22-4 shows two ink cartridges. The black cartridge is on the left and the three-color cartridge is on the right. The print head assemblage moves across the page as it prints. When not in use, the assemblage sits in the far-right position shown in the figure, which is called the home position. This position helps protect the ink in the cartridges from drying out.

Figure 22-4 The ink cartridges of an inkjet printer
Courtesy: Course Technology/Cengage Learning

IMPACT PRINTERS

An impact printer creates a printed page by using some mechanism that touches or hits the paper. The best-known impact printer is a dot matrix printer. It has a print head that moves across the width of the paper, using pins to print a matrix of dots on the page. The pins shoot against a cloth ribbon, which hits the paper, depositing the ink. The ribbon provides both the ink for printing and the lubrication for the pinheads. The quality of the print is poor

A+
220-701
1.11

compared to other printer types. However, three reasons you see impact printers still in use are: (1) they use continuous tractor feeds and fanfold paper rather than individual sheets of paper, making then useful for logging events or data; (2) they can use carbon paper to print multiple copies at the same time; and (3) they are extremely durable, give little trouble, and seem to last forever.

Occasionally, you should replace the ribbon of a dot matrix printer. If the print head fails, check on the cost of replacing the head versus the cost of buying a new printer. Sometimes, the cost of the head is so high it's best to just buy a new printer. Overheating can damage a print head (see Figure 22-5), so keep it as cool as possible to make it last longer. Keep the printer in a cool, well-ventilated area, and don't use it to print more than 50 to 75 pages without allowing the head to cool down.

Print head

Figure 22-5 Keep the print head of a dot matrix printer as cool as possible so that it will last longer
Courtesy: Course Technology/Cengage Learning

THERMAL PRINTERS AND SOLID INK PRINTERS

Two similar technologies are thermal printers and solid ink printers. Both use heat to produce printed output. **Thermal printers** use wax-based ink that is heated by heat pins that melt the ink onto paper. The print head containing these heat pins is as wide as the paper. The internal logic of the printer determines which pins get heated to produce the printed image. Thermal printers are popular in retail applications for printing receipts, bar codes, and price tags. A thermal printer can burn dots onto special paper, as done by older fax machines (called direct thermal printing), or the printer can use a ribbon that contains the wax-based ink (called thermal wax transfer printing).

One variation of thermal printing uses thermal dye sublimation technology to print identification cards and access cards (see Figure 22-6). A **dye-sublimation printer** uses solid dyes embedded on different transparent films. As the print head passes over each color film, it heats up, causing the dye to vaporize onto the glossy surface of the paper. Because the dye is vaporized onto the paper rather than jetted at it, the results are more photo-lab quality than with inkjet printing.

22

A+ 220-701

Figure 22-6 This dye sublimation printer is used to make ID cards
Courtesy of Sony Electronics, Inc.

Solid ink printers use ink stored in solid blocks, which Xerox calls color sticks. The sticks or blocks are easy to handle and several can be inserted in the printer to be used as needed, avoiding the problem of running out of ink in the middle of a large print job. The solid ink is melted into the print head, which spans the width of the paper. The head jets the liquid ink onto the paper as it passes by on a drum. The design is simple, print quality is excellent, and solid ink printers are easy to set up and maintain. The greatest disadvantage to solid ink printing is the time it takes for the print head to heat up to begin a print job, which is about 15 minutes. For this reason, some solid ink printers are programmed to anticipate that a print job might be coming based on previous use of the printer, and automatically heat up.

Table 22-1 lists some printer manufacturers.

Printer Manufacturer	Web Site
Brother	www.brother-usa.com
Canon	usa.canon.com
Dell	www.dell.com
Hewlett-Packard	www.hp.com
Konica Minolta	kmbs.konicaminolta.us
Lexmark	www.lexmark.com
Oki Data	www.okidata.com
Samsung	www.samsung.com
Seiko Epson	www.epson.com
Xerox	www.xerox.com

Table 22-1 Printer manufacturers

A+
220-701
1.11

PRINTER FEATURES

Printers can have a variety of options, including extra paper trays to hold different sizes of paper, special paper feeders or transparency feeders, staplers, collators, and sorters. Printers can print in color or black and white, and printers can print on one side of the page or automatically print on both sides (called duplex printing). (Some low-end printers offer manual duplexing, which makes it possible for you to print on both sides by putting the paper through again.) Besides these features, printers are rated by the time it takes for the first page to print (warm-up time), the resolution (for example, 1200 x 1200 dpi), the maximum pages printed per month so as not to void the warranty (called the maximum duty cycle), the printing speed (for example, 35 PPM, pages per minute), the number of sheets of paper the input bin can hold, the paper sizes supported (letter, legal, statement, or envelope), and the technology the printer uses to format a page before it is printed (PCL, PostScript, GDI, or XPS).

Printers can also be combined with fax machines, copiers, and scanners in the same machine. Most often, printers and scanners are powered by AC power or by using an AC adapter that converts power to DC. In addition, some printers are battery powered.

You also need to consider how the printer will connect to the computer or network. A local printer connects directly to a computer by way of a USB port, parallel port, serial port, wireless connection (Bluetooth, infrared, or Wi-Fi), IEEE 1394 (FireWire) port, SCSI port, PC Card, or ExpressCard connection. Many printers support more than one method. A network printer has an Ethernet port to connect directly to the network. This connection can be made to a switch, hub, or extra port on a router, or a network printer can use a Wi-Fi connection. Some printers have both an Ethernet port and a USB port (see Figure 22-7). These printers can be installed as either a network printer (connecting directly to the network) or a local printer (connecting directly to a PC) depending on which port you use.

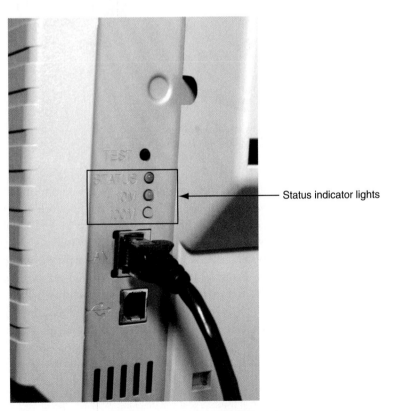

Status indicator lights

Figure 22-7 This printer has an Ethernet and USB port
Courtesy: Course Technology/Cengage Learning

22

A+ 220-701

INSTALLING AND SHARING PRINTERS

A+
220-701
1.11

The three ways to install a printer and make it available on a network are listed here:

▲ A local printer can be attached to a PC using a port (for example, USB, parallel, or wireless) on the PC (see Computer A in Figure 22-8). The printer can be dedicated to only this one PC, or you can share the printer for network users. For a shared local printer to be available to other computers on the network, the host computer must be turned on and not in sleep or standby mode. For another computer on the network to use the shared printer, the printer drivers must be installed on the remote computer.

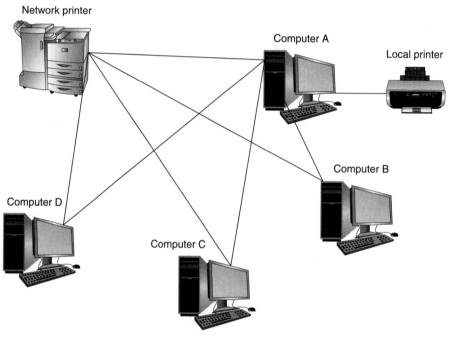

Figure 22-8   A shared local printer and a network printer
Courtesy: Course Technology/Cengage Learning

▲ A network printer with embedded logic to manage network communication can be connected directly to a network with its own NIC (see the network printer in Figure 22-8). A network printer is identified on the network by its IP address. To use the printer, any computer on the network can install drivers for this printer.

▲ A dedicated device or computer called a print server can control several printers connected to a network. For example, HP has software called HP JetDirect, designed to support HP printers in this manner. This method works best in a large enterprise network where printers are best managed from a centralized location. For more information, see the HP Web site, *www.hp.com*. How to manage a print server is not covered in this chapter.

> **Notes**   A computer can have several printers installed. Of these, Windows designates one printer to be the **default printer**, which is the one Windows prints to unless another is selected.

A+
220-701
1.11

When you install a printer, printer drivers are required that are compatible with the installed operating system. The drivers come on a CD bundled with the printer. If you are installing a printer under an operating system whose drivers are not included on the CD, you can download the drivers for the OS you are using from the printer manufacturer's Web site. When downloading drivers from a Web site, make sure you have the correct printer and OS selected. In addition, Windows provides many printer drivers that are embedded in Vista and XP.

In this part of the chapter, you will learn to install local and network printers using both Windows Vista and Windows XP. Then you'll learn how to configure printer add-ons and features. Finally, you will learn to share a printer on a network and use a shared printer. We begin with learning how to install a printer under Vista.

HOW TO INSTALL A PRINTER USING VISTA

To install a local USB printer, all you have to do is plug in the USB printer and Vista installs the printer automatically. Also, for some types of printers, you can launch the installation program that came bundled on CD with the printer or downloaded from the printer manufacturer's Web site. On the other hand, you can follow these steps to install a non-USB local printer or a network printer:

1. For a network printer, make sure the printer is connected to the network and turned on. For a wireless printer, turn on the printer and set the printer within range of the PC. For a parallel port or serial port printer, connect the printer to the PC and turn it on.

2. For Windows Vista, in Control Panel, under Hardware and Sound, click **Printer**. The Printers window opens, as shown in Figure 22-9.

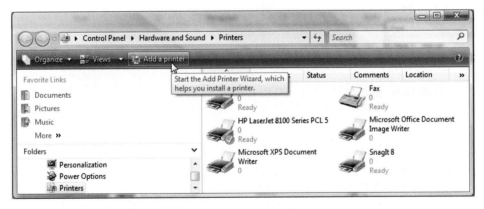

Figure 22-9 Use the Printers window to install a new printer
Courtesy: Course Technology/Cengage Learning

> **Notes** Notice in Figure 22-9 that Vista includes the Microsoft XPS Document Writer as an installed printer. When you print to this printer, the **XPS Document Writer** creates an .xps file. The file is similar to a .pdf file and can be viewed, edited, printed, faxed, e-mailed, or posted on Web sites. In Windows, the file is viewed in Internet Explorer.

3. Click **Add a printer**. In the Add Printer window that appears (see Figure 22-10), select the type of printer.

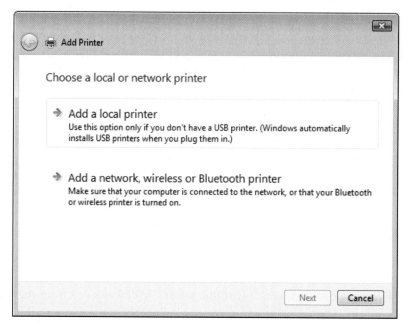

Figure 22-10   Select the type of printer to install
Courtesy: Course Technology/Cengage Learning

4. Vista searches for available printers. The next steps depend on what it found. If Vista found printers not yet installed, it lists them. Select the printer from the list and click **Next**. If your printer is not listed, click **The printer that I want isn't listed**. You will then be able to point to the port or IP address of the printer. In Figure 22-11, we are installing a network printer identified by its IP address, which is 192.168.1.109.

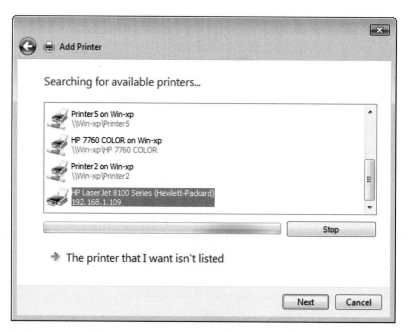

Figure 22-11   Select the printer from the list of available printers
Courtesy: Course Technology/Cengage Learning

Notes To know the IP address of a network printer, direct the printer to print a configuration page, which should include its IP address. To print the page, use buttons, keys, or other controls on the front of the printer. The printer documentation shows you how to use these controls. Some printers have a control panel on the front of the printer. For these printers, scroll through the menu to display the IP address in the panel window.

5. In the next window, shown in Figure 22-12, you can change the name of the printer, such as "John's Office Printer," or leave the printer name as is. If this printer will be your default printer, check **Set as the default printer**. Click **Next** to continue.

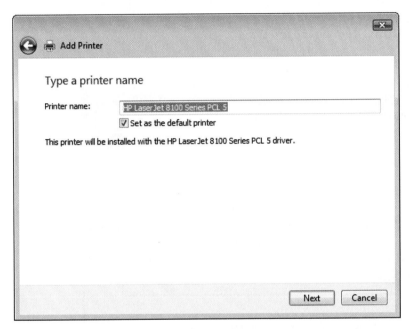

Figure 22-12 Name the printer and decide if it will be your default printer
Courtesy: Course Technology/Cengage Learning

6. To test the printer, in the next window, click **Print a test page**. Click **Finish** to complete the installation. Note that it's always a good idea to print a test page when you install a printer to verify the installation works.

HOW TO INSTALL A LOCAL PRINTER USING WINDOWS XP

Installing a local printer using Windows XP begins differently depending on the type of port you are using. For local printers that use a FireWire, USB, PC Card, ExpressCard, or wireless connection, you might need to first install the software before connecting the printer or connect the printer before installing the software. See the documentation to know which order to use.

A+ Exam Tip The A+ 220-701 Essentials exam expects you to know how to install a local and network printer.

A+
220-701
1.11

Follow these steps to install a local printer using one of these type ports:

1. Log onto the system as an administrator. Begin the installation by running the setup program that came on the CD bundled with the printer before you install the printer. If you don't have the CD, download the printer drivers from the printer manufacturer's Web site and then execute that downloaded program. The setup program installs the drivers.

2. At one point in the setup, you will be told to connect the printer. Figure 22-13 shows this step for one HP printer installation routine. Connect the printer to the port. For this printer, a USB port is used. For wireless printers, verify that the software for the wireless connection on your PC is installed and the wireless connection is enabled. For infrared wireless printers, place the printer in line of sight of the infrared port on the PC. (Most wireless printers have a status light that stays lit when a wireless connection is active.) Turn on the printer.

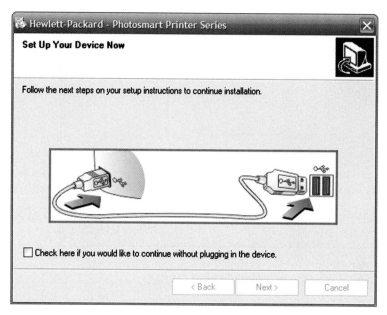

Figure 22-13 The printer setup program tells you when to connect the printer
Courtesy: Course Technology/Cengage Learning

3. The setup program detects the printer. If Windows launches the Found New Hardware Wizard, it should close quickly. If not, cancel the wizard.

4. The setup program asks if you want this printer to be the default printer. Click Yes or No to make your selection. The setup program finishes the installation.

5. You can now test the printer. Open the Printers and Faxes window by clicking **Start**, **Control Panel**, and **Printers and Faxes** (in Classic view). For Category view, click **Printers and Other Hardware** and then click **Printers and Faxes**. Either way, the Printers and Faxes window opens (see the top of Figure 22-14). Right-click the printer and select **Properties** from the shortcut menu. Click the **General** tab and then click the **Print Test Page** button, as shown in Figure 22-14.

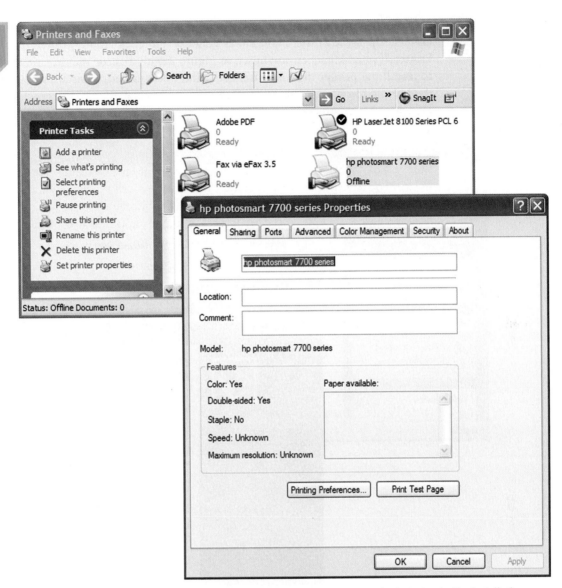

Figure 22-14 To verify a printer installation, always print a test page as the last step in the installation
Courtesy: Course Technology/Cengage Learning

Here are the directions to install a local printer using an older port, such as a SCSI, serial, or parallel port, that is not hot-pluggable:

1. Plug in the printer to the port and turn on the printer. Now, you must decide how you want to install the drivers. You can use the setup program from the printer manufacturer or use the Windows installation process. First try using the setup program that came on the printer's setup CD or downloaded from the manufacturer's Web site. If you have problems with the installation, you can then try the Windows approach.

2. To use the manufacturer's installation program, launch the printer setup program from the printer setup CD or downloaded from the manufacturer's Web site and follow the directions on-screen to install the printer.

A+
220-701
1.11

3. Alternately, you can use the Windows installation process to install the printer drivers. Open the Printers and Faxes window and click **Add a printer**. The Add Printer Wizard launches, as shown in Figure 22-15. Follow the directions on-screen to install the printer drivers. After the printer is installed, print a test page to verify the installation works.

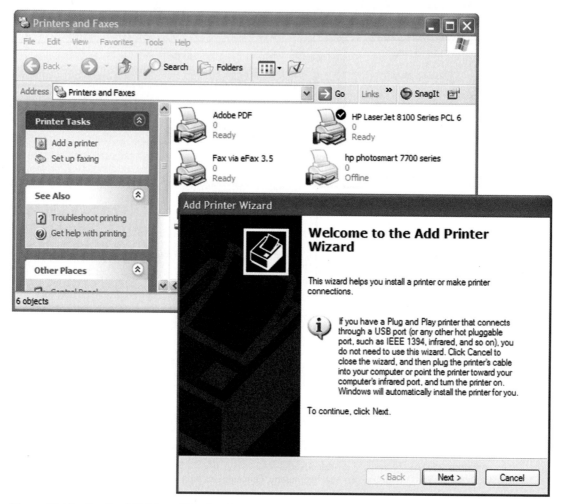

Figure 22-15　Use the Add Printer Wizard to install a printer
Courtesy: Course Technology/Cengage Learning

STEPS TO INSTALL A NETWORK PRINTER USING WINDOWS XP

Always follow manufacturer directions when installing a printer. If you don't have these instructions, here are the general steps to install a network printer using Windows XP:

1. Open the XP Printers and Faxes window and start the wizard to add a new printer. Select the option to install a local printer but do not ask Windows to automatically detect the printer.

2. On the next window shown in Figure 22-16, choose **Create a new port**. From the list of port types, select **Standard TCP/IP Port**. Click **Next** twice.

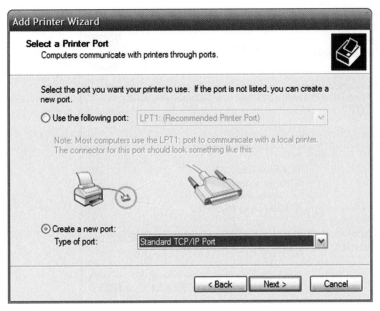

Figure 22-16 Configure a local printer to use a standard TCP/IP port
Courtesy: Course Technology/Cengage Learning

3. On the next window shown in Figure 22-17, you need to identify the printer on the network. If you know the IP address of the printer, enter it in the first box on this window and click **Next**. Some network printers have assigned printer names or the printer might have an assigned port name. To know how your network printer is configured, see the network printer's configuration window. How to access this window was discussed earlier in the chapter.

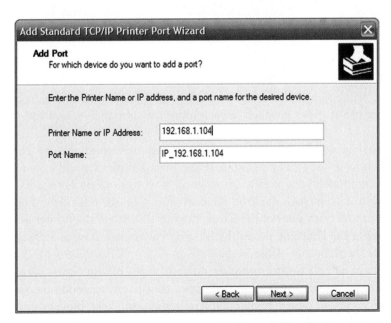

Figure 22-17 Enter the printer name or IP address to identify the printer on the network
Courtesy: Course Technology/Cengage Learning

4. On the next window (see Figure 22-18), click **Have Disk** so you can point to and use the downloaded driver files that will then be used to complete the printer installation.

22

A+ 220-701

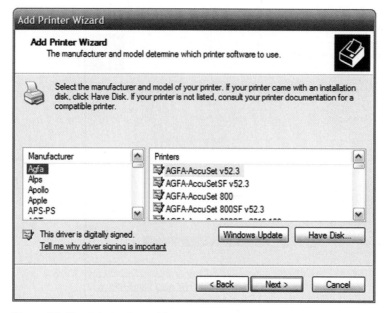

Figure 22-18 Select printer drivers
Courtesy: Course Technology/Cengage Learning

MANAGE PRINTER FEATURES AND SETTINGS

After the printer is installed, use the printer Properties box to configure add-on devices for the printer and to set printer preferences. To access the box, open the Vista Printers window or the XP Printers and Faxes window, right-click the printer, and select **Properties** from the shortcut menu. The printer Properties box appears, which is shown in Figure 22-19 for Vista. One useful option is to print a test page. To do that, click **Print Test Page** on the General tab. Use this option when you need to verify the computer can communicate with the printer.

To manage printer features and hardware devices installed on the printer, click the **Device Settings** tab (see Figure 22-20). The options on this tab depend on the installed printer. For this particular printer, duplex printing is installed, as shown in the figure. You can also control the size of the paper installed in each input tray bin and various add-on devices for this printer.

After you have installed a new printer add-on device or feature, the users of this printer need to know how to use it. For example, if you install duplexing and a user attempts to print from an application, the user needs to know how to print on both sides of the paper. When printing from Notepad, the Print window shown on the left side of Figure 22-21 appears. To print on both sides of the paper, the user can select the printer and click **Preferences**, select the **Finishing** tab in the Printing Preferences box, and check **Print On Both Sides** (see the right side of Figure 22-21).

A printer might be able to accommodate different types of input trays and feeders for various envelopes, oversized paper, colored paper, transparencies, and other media. In addition, you can install on the printer staplers, sorters, stackers, binders, and output trays so that the printer can sort output by user (called mailboxes). After you have physically installed one of these devices, use the printer properties window to enable it. For example, suppose you have installed a 3,000-sheet stapler and stacker unit on the printer whose properties window is shown in Figure 22-22. To enable this equipment, in the drop-down list of Accessory Output Bin, select **HP 3000-Sheet Stapler/Stacker** and click **Apply**. After the equipment is enabled, when a user prints, the equipment is listed as an option in the Printing Preferences window.

Figure 22-19 Use the printer Properties box to manage a printer
Courtesy: Course Technology/Cengage Learning

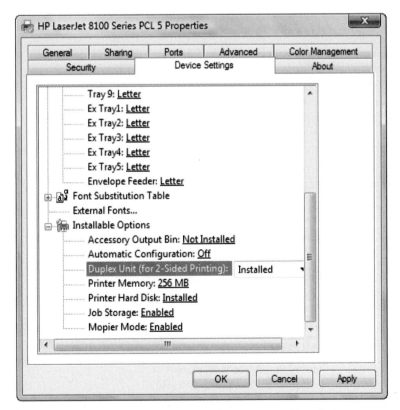

Figure 22-20 Use the Device Settings tab to manage add-on devices
Courtesy: Course Technology/Cengage Learning

A+
220-701
1.11

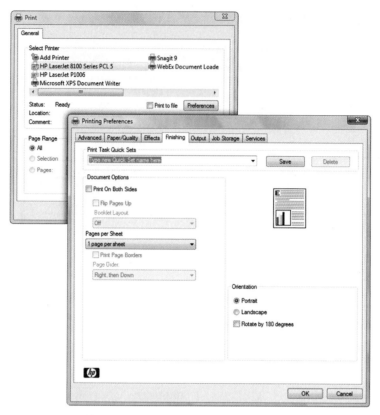

Figure 22-21 Printing on both sides of the paper
Courtesy: Course Technology/Cengage Learning

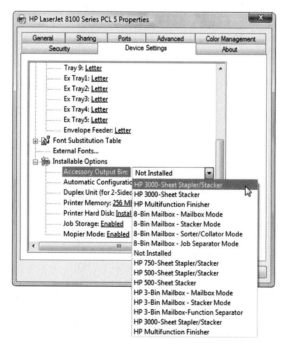

Figure 22-22 Install a printer add-on device in Windows
Courtesy: Course Technology/Cengage Learning

To access the printer Properties box using Windows XP, right-click the printer in the Printers and Faxes window and select **Properties** from the shortcut menu. On the printer's Properties box, click the **Configure** tab, as shown in Figure 22-23. Using this tab, you can enable duplexing and install add-on devices. (Also notice the Mopier Enabled option on this window, which is the ability to print and collate multiple copies of a single print job.) To apply your changes, click **Apply** and then click **OK** to close the window.

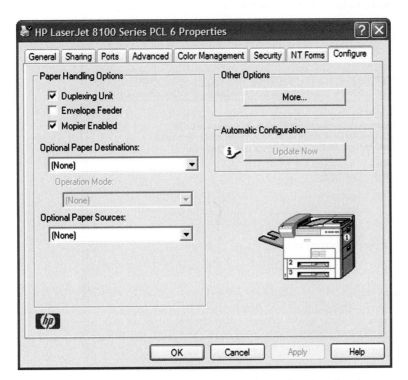

Figure 22-23 Configure printer options and settings using the printer's
Properties box
Courtesy: Course Technology/Cengage Learning

After you have installed a printer and configured all its features, show the user how to use the printer and any add-ons. These add-ons include feeders, sorters, and staplers. In addition, show the user how to install paper and envelopes in the various paper trays. Let the user know whom to contact if printer problems arise. You might also consider providing a means for the user to record problems with the printer that don't require immediate attention. For example, you can hang a clipboard and paper close to the printer for the user to write questions and comments that you can address at a later time.

SHARE AN INSTALLED PRINTER

To share an installed local or network printer using Vista, Printer sharing must be turned on in the Network and Sharing Center. To share an installed printer using XP, File and Printer Sharing must be installed, and to use a shared printer on a remote PC, Client for Microsoft Networks must be installed. In most cases, it is easiest to simply install both XP components on all computers on the network. How to install the components under Windows XP was covered in Chapter 18.

A+
220-701
1.11

Also, remote users will not be able to use the shared printer if the computer is asleep. Following instructions given in Chapter 21, make sure the computer is set to wake on LAN so that network activity will wake up the sleeping computer.

To share an installed local or network printer using Vista or XP with others on the network, follow these steps:

1. In the printer Properties box, click the **Sharing** tab (see Figure 22-24). Click **Change sharing options**. For Vista, respond to the UAC box.

Figure 22-24   Change sharing options
Courtesy: Course Technology/Cengage Learning

2. Check **Share this printer** (see Figure 22-25). You can then change the share name of the printer. Notice in Figure 22-25 the option to control where print jobs are rendered. A print job can be prepared (rendered) on the remote computer (client computer) or this computer (print server). Your choice depends on which computer you think should carry this burden. You can test several print jobs on remote computers with rendering done at either location and see which method best uses computing resources on the network.

> **Notes** Group Policy under Windows Vista can be used to limit and control all kinds of printer-related tasks, including the number of printers that can be installed using the Add Printer Wizard, how print jobs are sent to print servers (rendered or not rendered), which print servers the computer can use, and which printers on a network the computer can use.

3. If you want to make drivers for the printer available to remote users who are using an operating system other than Vista, click **Additional Drivers**.

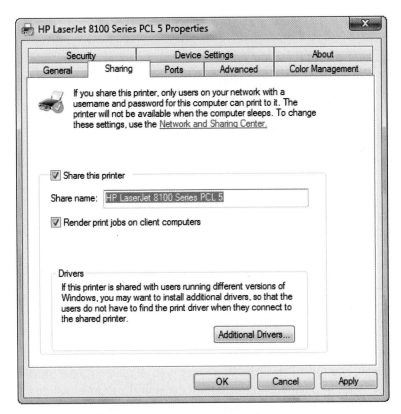

Figure 22-25 Share the printer on the network
Courtesy: Course Technology/Cengage Learning

4. The Additional Drivers box opens, as shown in Figure 22-26 for Vista. For 32-bit operating systems, select **x86**. For 64-bit operating systems, select **x64**. Click **OK** to close the box. You might be asked for the Vista setup DVD or other access to the installation files. For Windows XP, the Additional Drivers box lists specific operating systems for drivers to be made available to remote computers (see Figure 22-27).

Figure 22-26 Select additional drivers you want available for other operating systems that will use the Vista shared printer
Courtesy: Course Technology/Cengage Learning

22

A+ 220-701

Figure 22-27 Make drivers for other operating systems available
for the Windows XP shared printer
Courtesy: Course Technology/Cengage Learning

5. Click **Apply** and **OK** to close the Properties box. A shared printer shows a two-friends icon (for Vista) or a hand icon (for XP) under it in the Printers window, and the printer is listed in the Network or My Network Places windows of other PCs on the network.

HOW TO USE A SHARED PRINTER

Recall that for a remote PC to use a shared printer, the drivers for that printer must be installed on the remote PC. Here are the different ways printer drivers can be provided for the installation on a remote computer:

◢ Use printer drivers on the printer driver CD or downloaded from the printer manufacturer's Web site, or use Windows printer drivers.
◢ Use the printer drivers made available by the host PC.

You can install a shared printer on a remote computer using one of two methods: (1) Use the Vista Printer window or the XP Printers and Faxes window; or (2) use the Network or My Network Places window. Here are the steps to follow when using the first method:

1. For Vista, open the Printers window and click **Add a printer**. In the Add Printer box, select **Add a network, wireless or Bluetooth printer** (refer back to Figure 22-10). Select the shared printer from the list of available printers. Vista attempts to use printer drivers found on the host computer. If it doesn't find the drivers, you will be given the opportunity to provide them on CD or another media. Follow directions on-screen to complete the installation wizard.

2. For XP, open the Printers and Faxes window and click **Add a printer**. The Add Printer Wizard opens. Click **Next**.

3. In response to the question, "Select the option that describes the printer you want to use:" select **A network printer, or a printer attached to another computer**. Click **Next**. The Specify a Printer page of the Add Printer Wizard opens, as shown in Figure 22-28.

A+
220-701
1.11

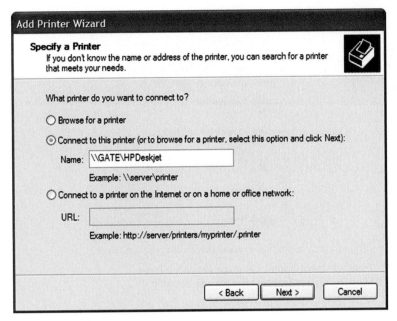

Figure 22-28 To use a network printer under Windows XP, enter the host computer name followed by the printer name, or have Windows XP browse the network for shared printers
Courtesy: Course Technology/Cengage Learning

4. Enter the host computer name and printer name. Begin with two backslashes and separate the computer name from the printer name with a backslash. Or, you can click **Browse for a printer**, click **Next**, search the list of shared printers on the network, and select the printer to install. (If your network is using static IP addressing and you know the IP address of the host PC, you can enter the IP address instead of the host name in this step.) Click **Next**.

5. Windows XP searches for Windows XP drivers on the host computer for this printer. If it finds them, they are installed. If it doesn't find the drivers, a message asks if you want to search for the proper driver. Click **OK**.

6. Click **Have Disk** to use the manufacturer's drivers, or to use Windows drivers, select the printer manufacturer and then the printer model from the list of supported printers. Follow directions on-screen to complete the installation wizard. Don't forget to print a test page to verify the installation works.

Another way to install a shared printer is to first use the Network window or My Network Places to locate the printer on the network. Do the following:

1. On a remote PC, open the **Network** window or the **My Network Places** window and find the printer. Right-click the printer and select **Connect** from the shortcut menu. See Figure 22-29.

2. If the host computer is using the same OS as you are, or if additional drivers for your OS have been installed, you can use those drivers for the installation. If Windows cannot find the right drivers, it sends you an error message and gives you the opportunity to install the drivers on the printer manufacturer's CD or downloaded from the Internet.

22

A+ 220-701

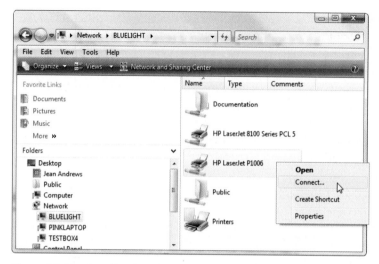

A+
220-701
1.11

Figure 22-29   Install a shared printer using the Network window
Courtesy: Course Technology/Cengage Learning

SUPPORTING PRINTERS

A+
220-701
2.2
2.3

Printers generally last for years if they are properly used and maintained. To get the most out of a printer, it's important to follow the manufacturer's directions when using the device and to perform the necessary routine maintenance. For example, the life of a printer can be shortened if you allow the printer to overheat, don't use approved paper, or don't install consumable maintenance kits when they are required.

When supporting printers using Windows, it is helpful to know about the protocols used by printers for communication between Windows and the printer, so we will begin our discussion of supporting printers here. Then, we'll turn our attention to managing printers. Later in the chapter, you'll learn how to perform the routine tasks needed to maintain a printer.

PRINTER LANGUAGES

Years ago, all printers were dot matrix printers that could only print simple text using only a single font. Communication between the OS and the printer was simple. Today's printers can produce beautiful colored graphics and text using a variety of fonts and symbols, and communication between the OS and a printer can get pretty complicated.

The languages or methods the OS and printer use for communication and building a page before it prints are in the following list. The method used depends on what the printer is designed to support and the printer drivers installed. If the printer has sophisticated firmware, it might be able to support more than one method. In this case, the installed printer drivers determine which methods can be used:

◢ *The printer uses PostScript commands to build the page.* Windows can send the commands and data needed to build a page to the printer using the PostScript language. The printer firmware then interprets these commands and draws and formats the page in the printer memory before it is printed. PostScript is a language used to communicate how a page is to print and was developed by Adobe Systems. PostScript is popular with desktop publishing, the typesetting industry, and the Macintosh OS.

A+
220-701
1.11
2.2
2.3

◢ *The printer uses PCL commands to build the page.* A printer language that competes with PostScript is PCL (Printer Control Language). PCL was developed by Hewlett-Packard but is considered a de facto standard in the printing industry. Many printer manufacturers use PCL.

◢ *The Windows GDI builds the page and then sends it to the printer.* A less-sophisticated method of communicating to a printer is to use the GDI (Graphics Device Interface) component of Windows. GDI draws and formats the page and then sends the almost-ready-to-print page to the printer in bitmap form. Because Windows, rather than the printer, does most of the work of building the page, a GDI printer needs less firmware and memory, and, therefore, generally costs less than a PCL or PostScript printer. The downside of using the GDI method is that Windows performance can suffer when printing a lot of complicated pages. Most low-end inkjet and laser printers are GDI printers. If the printer specifications don't say PCL or PostScript, you can assume it's a GDI printer. Many high-end printers support more than one protocol and can handle GDI, PCL, or PostScript printing.

◢ *Windows Vista uses XML Paper Specification (XPS) to build the page and then sends it to the printer.* XPS (XML Paper Specification) was introduced with Windows Vista and was designed to ultimately replace GDI as the method Windows uses to render the page before sending it to the printer. Vista uses either GDI or XPS for rendering based on the type of printer driver installed. Generally, PostScript and PCL are used with high-end printers, and GDI and XPS are used with low-end printers.

◢ *Raw data is printed with little-to-no formatting.* Text data that contains no embedded control characters is sent to the printer as is, and the printer can print it without any processing. The data is called raw data. Dot matrix printers that can only print simple text receive and print raw data.

USING WINDOWS TO MANAGE PRINTERS

Normally, when Windows receives a print job from an application, it places the job in a queue and prints from the queue, so that the application is released from the printing process as soon as possible. Several print jobs can accumulate in the queue, which you can view in the Vista Printers window or the XP Printers and Faxes window. This process is called spooling. (The word spool is an acronym for *si*multaneous *p*eripheral *o*perations *onl*ine.) The print queue is also called the print spool. Most printing from Windows uses spooling.

To manage the printer queue and other printer activities, use the Vista Printers window or the XP Printers and Faxes window. Using these windows, you can delete printers, change the Windows default printer, empty the printer queue to troubleshoot failed printing, and perform other printer maintenance tasks.

For example, in Figure 22-30, double-click a printer icon to open the printer status window. From this window, you can see the status and order of the print jobs. If the printer reports a problem with printing, it will be displayed as the status for the first job in the print queue. To cancel a single print job, right-click the job and select **Cancel** from the shortcut menu. To cancel all print jobs, click **Printer** on the menu and select **Cancel All Documents** (see Figure 22-30). If you still can't get the printer moving again, try pressing a cancel button on the printer or turning the printer off and on. To verify the problem with printing is solved, print a test page using the printer properties box.

When you first install a printer, Windows default settings for user accounts are applied. Using these settings, user accounts in the Everyone group are assigned the Print permission level, which means users can send documents to a printer. They cannot manage the print queue or change printer settings. Users in the administrator group (or the XP Power User group) are assigned the Manage printers permission level, which means they have complete

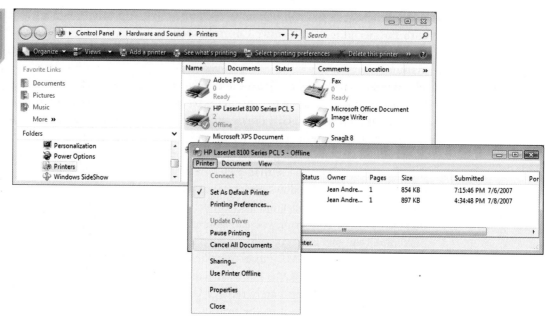

Figure 22-30 Clean the printer's queue
Courtesy: Course Technology/Cengage Learning

control over a printer, including printer settings and the print queue. A third permission level, Manage documents, can be assigned to a user so that the user can manage the print queue while not being allowed to change printer settings.

If you need to change these default permissions for a printer, in the Vista Printers window or the XP Printers and Faxes window, open the printer Properties box. Then click the **Security** tab (see Figure 22-31). Select the group or user name and change the permissions

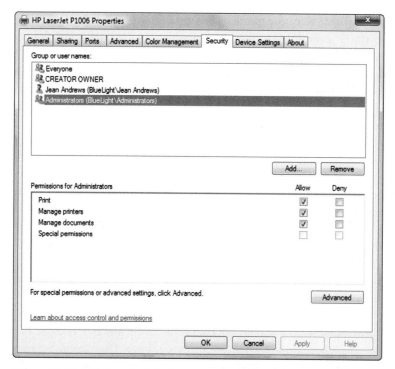

Figure 22-31 Change the default permissions for a printer
Courtesy: Course Technology/Cengage Learning

A+
220-701
1.11
2.2
2.3

for that group or user. Notice in the figure the Special permissions. These permissions are assigned to system administrators on a domain.

If you are having a problem with a printer refusing to print or you cannot use certain printer features, consider that the printer drivers might be incompatible or out of date. Search the printer manufacturer's Web site for the latest drivers, and download to your PC. Then delete the printer. To do that, right-click the printer icon in the Vista Printers or XP Printers and Faxes window, and select **Delete** from the shortcut menu. Then install the printer again, using the latest drivers.

A+
220-701
1.11
6.1

PRINTER CONSUMABLES

As an A+ certified technician, you are expected to know how to service printers, including exchanging consumables and field replaceable units. Printer manufacturers define the consumables for a specific printer in the user manual. For example, for one Okidata color laser printer, the consumables are four color toner cartridges (yellow, magenta, cyan, and black), four image drums, the transfer belt, and fuser. The user manual gives step-by-step procedures for exchanging these components, and you will learn about these later in the chapter.

For now, let's focus on how to protect yourself when working inside a printer. Some laser printer parts can get hot enough to burn you while in operation. So before you work inside a laser printer, turn it off, unplug it, and wait about 30 minutes for it to cool down. Printer parts that get hot might have one of the symbols in Figure 22-32

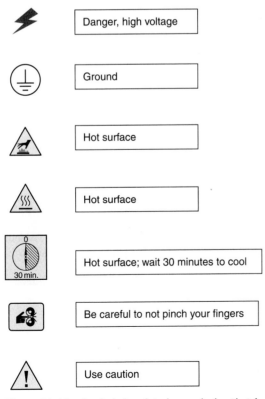

Figure 22-32 Symbols imprinted on a device that indicate danger
Courtesy: Course Technology/Cengage Learning

22

A+ 220-701

imprinted on or near them. Also notice in the figure other symbols that indicate danger. If you see these symbols on parts or in documentation, pay attention to them and stay safe.

Also know that a printer might still keep power even when the printer on/off switch is turned to off. To assure the printer has no power, unplug it. And even when a laser printer is unplugged, internal components might still hold a dangerous electrical charge for some time. Later, after you have serviced the printer, keep the power cord accessible to you. In case of an emergency, you can quickly pull the plug.

For your protection, laser printers use a laser beam that is always enclosed inside a protective case inside the printer. Therefore, when servicing a laser printer, you should never have to look at the laser beam, which can damage your eyes.

To protect memory modules and hard drives inside printers, be sure to use an antistatic ground bracelet to protect these sensitive components when installing them. It is not necessary or recommended that you wear the ground bracelet when exchanging consumables such as toner cartridges, fuser assembles, or image drums.

Here's one more tip to stay safe, but I don't want it to frighten you: When you work inside high-voltage equipment such as a laser printer, don't do it when no one else is around. If you have an emergency, someone needs to be close by to help you.

> **♥ A+ Exam Tip** The A+ 220-701 Essentials exam expects you to know about the dangers of high voltage when working inside a power supply, CRT monitor, or laser printer.

When you're responsible for a printer, make sure consumables for the printer are on hand. These consumables can include paper, ink ribbons, color sticks, toner cartridges, and ink cartridges. Know how to exchange these consumables and also know how to recognize when they need exchanging. Each printer's requirements are different, so you'll need to study the printer documentation to find out what your printer requires. Buy the products in advance of when you think you'll need them. Nothing is more frustrating to a user than to have a printer not working because the support technician responsible for the printer forgot to order extra toner cartridges.

> **Notes** When working with laser printer toner cartridges, if you get toner dust on your clothes or hands while exchanging the cartridge, don't use hot water to clean it up. Remember that heat sets the toner. Go outdoors and use a can of compressed air to blow off the toner. Then use cold water to clean your hands and clothes. It's a good idea to wear a smock or apron when working on printers.

Figure 22-33 shows an ink cartridge being installed in one inkjet printer. To replace a cartridge, turn on the printer and open the front cover. The printer releases the cartridges. You can then open the latch on top of the cartridge and remove it. Install the new cartridge as shown in the figure. To keep the old toner from making a mess, store it in a plastic bag before disposing of it.

When a cartridge is not in use, put it in the cradle on the left side of the printer to protect it from drying out, as shown in Figure 22-34.

A+
220-701
1.11
6.1

Figure 22-33 Installing an ink cartridge in an inkjet printer
Courtesy: Course Technology/Cengage Learning

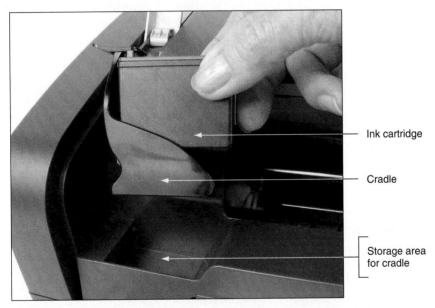

Ink cartridge

Cradle

Storage area
for cradle

Figure 22-34 Use the protective cradle to keep an ink cartridge from drying out
when it is not installed in a printer
Courtesy: Course Technology/Cengage Learning

> 💡 **A+ Exam Tip** Content on the A+ 220-701 Essentials exam ends here, and content on the A+ 220-702 Practical Application exam begins.

MAINTAINING PRINTERS

A+
220-702
1.5

Routine printer maintenance procedures vary widely from manufacturer to manufacturer and printer to printer. For each printer you support, research the printer documentation or the manufacturer's Web site for specific maintenance procedures and how often you should perform them for each printer you support. In the following sections, you'll learn about printer maintenance kits, cleaning printers, online help for printers, and updating printer firmware.

22

A+ 220-702

PRINTER MAINTENANCE KITS

Manufacturers of high-end printers provide printer maintenance kits, which include specific printer components, step-by-step instructions for performing maintenance, and any special tools or equipment you need to do maintenance. For example, the maintenance plan for the HP Color LaserJet 4600 printer says to replace the transfer roller assembly after printing 120,000 pages and replace the fusing assembly after 150,000 pages. The plan also says the black ink cartridge should last for about 9,000 pages and the color ink cartridge for about 8,000 pages. HP sells the image transfer kit, the image fuser kit, and the ink cartridges designed for this printer.

> **💡 A+ Tip**   The A+ 220-702 Practical Application exam expects you to know about the importance of resetting the page count after installing a printer maintenance kit.

To find out how many pages a printer has printed so that you know if you need to do the maintenance, you need to have the printer give you the page count since the last maintenance. You can tell the printer to display the information or print a status report by using buttons on the front of the printer (see Figure 22-35) or you can use utility software from a computer connected to the printer. See the printer documentation to know how to get this report. After you have performed the maintenance, be sure to reset the page count so it will be accurate to tell you when you need to do the next routine maintenance. Keep a written record of the maintenance and other service done. If a printer gives problems, one of the first things you can do is check this service documentation to find out if maintenance is due. You can also check for a history of prior problems and how they were resolved.

Figure 22-35   Use buttons on the front of the printer to display information, including the page count
Courtesy: Course Technology/Cengage Learning

As examples of replacing printer consumables, let's look at how to replace a toner cartridge, image drum, and fuser for the Okidata color laser printer shown earlier in Figure 22-1.

> **💡 A+ Exam Tip**   The A+ 220-702 Practical Application exam expects you to know how to exchange an image drum and a fuser assembly.

A+
220-702
1.5

A toner cartridge for this printer generally lasts for about 1500 pages. Here are the steps to replace a color toner cartridge:

1. Turn off and unplug the printer. Press the cover release button on the top-left corner of the printer and open the printer cover (see Figure 22-36).

Figure 22-36 Open the printer cover
Courtesy: Course Technology/Cengage Learning

2. Figure 22-37 shows the cover up. Notice the four erase lamps on the inside of the cover. As you work with a printer, be careful not to damage these delicate LCD stripes. Look inside the printer for the four toner cartridges and the fuser assembly labeled in Figure 22-38. Pull the blue toner cartridge release button forward to release the cartridge from the image drum below it that it is connected to (see Figure 22-39).

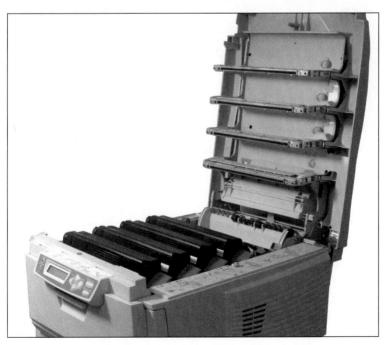

Figure 22-37 Cover lifted
Courtesy: Course Technology/Cengage Learning

22

A+ 220-702

A+
220-702
1.5

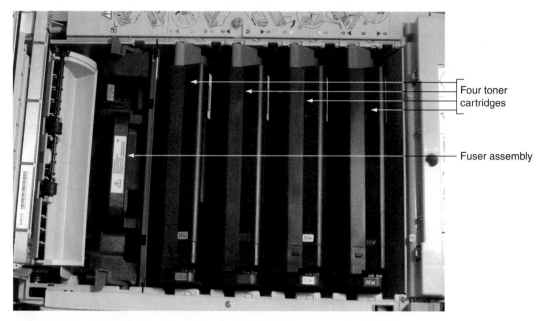

Figure 22-38 Inside the Okidata printer
Courtesy: Course Technology/Cengage Learning

Figure 22-39 Push the blue lever forward to release the toner cartridge
Courtesy: Course Technology/Cengage Learning

3. Lift the cartridge out of the printer, lifting up on the right side first and then removing the left side (see Figure 22-40). Be careful not to spill loose toner.

4. Unpack the new cartridge. Gently shake it from side to side to loosen the toner. Remove the tape from underneath the cartridge, and place the cartridge in the printer by inserting the left side first and then the right side. Push the cartridge level back into position to lock the cartridge in place. Close the printer cover.

The printer has four image drums, one for each color. The drums are expected to last for about 15,000 pages. When you purchase a new drum, the kit comes with a new color toner

Figure 22-40 Remove the toner cartridge
Courtesy: Course Technology/Cengage Learning

cartridge. Follow these steps to replace the cartridge and image drum. In these steps, we are using the yellow drum and cartridge:

1. Turn off and unplug the printer. Wait about 30 minutes after you have turned off the printer for it to cool down. Then open the printer cover. The toner cartridge is inserted into the image drum. Lift the drum together with the toner cartridge out of the printer (see Figure 22-41). Be sure to dispose of the drum and cartridge according to local regulations.

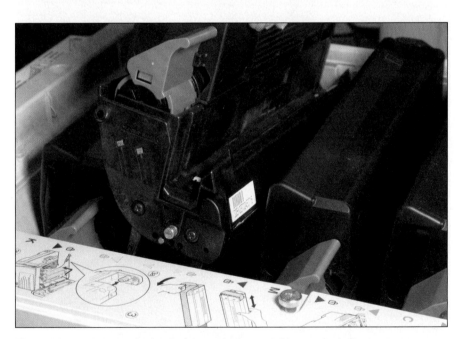

Figure 22-41 Remove the image drum and toner cartridge as one unit
Courtesy: Course Technology/Cengage Learning

2. Unpack the new image drum. Peal the tape off the drum and remove the plastic film round it. As you work, be careful to keep the drum upright so as not to spill the toner. Because the drum is sensitive to light, don't allow the drum to be exposed to bright light or direct sunlight. Don't expose it to normal room lighting for longer than five minutes.

A+
220-702
1.5

3. Place the drum in the printer. Install the new toner cartridge in the printer. Close the printer cover.

The fuser should last for about 45,000 pages. To replace the fuser, follow these steps:

1. Turn off and unplug the printer. Allow the printer to cool and open the cover.

2. Pull the two blue fuser levers forward to unlock the fuser (see Figure 22-42).

3. Lift the fuser out of the printer using the handle on the fuser, as shown in Figure 22-43.

4. Unpack the new fuser and place it in the printer. Push the two blue levers toward the back of the printer to lock the fuser in place.

Whenever you service the inside of this printer, as a last step always carefully clean the LED erase lamps on the inside of the top cover (see Figure 22-44). The printer maintenance kits you've just learned to use all include a wipe to clean these strips.

Figure 22-42 Pull the two fuser levers forward to release the fuser
Courtesy: Course Technology/Cengage Learning

Figure 22-43 Remove the fuser
Courtesy: Course Technology/Cengage Learning

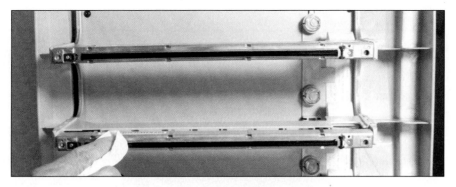

Figure 22-44 Clean the LED strips on the inside top cover
Courtesy: Course Technology/Cengage Learning

UPGRADE THE PRINTER MEMORY OR HARD DRIVE

Some printers have internal hard drives to hold print jobs and fonts, and printers might also give you the option to install additional memory in the printer. Extra memory can speed up memory performance, reduce print errors, and prevent Out of Memory errors. Check the user guide to determine how much memory the printer can support and what kind of memory to buy or what kind of internal hard drive the printer might support.

As you work with printer hardware, be sure you turn off the printer and disconnect it from the power source. Also, use an antistatic ground bracelet to protect memory modules from static electricity. Most likely, you will use a screwdriver to remove a cover plate on the printer to expose a cavity where memory or a drive can be installed. To access memory on one printer, you remove thumb screws on the back of the printer and then pull out the formatter board shown in Figure 22-45. Memory modules are installed on this board (see Figure 22-46). You can also install a hard drive in one of the two empty bays on the board. The hard drive comes embedded on a proprietary board that fits in the bay.

Figure 22-45 Remove the formatter board from the printer
Courtesy: Course Technology/Cengage Learning

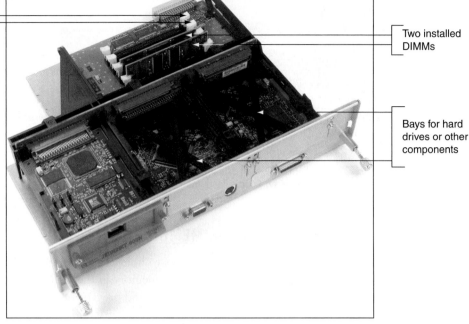

Two empty DIMM slots

Two installed DIMMs

Bays for hard drives or other components

Figure 22-46   Memory is installed on the formatter board
Courtesy: Course Technology/Cengage Learning

After this equipment is installed, you must enable and configure it using the printer properties window. For example, for the HP 8100 printer, use the Device Settings tab of the printer Properties box (see Figure 22-47). You can then set the hard drive as Installed or change the amount of Printer Memory that is installed. Some printers also give you the option to set the size of the hard drive.

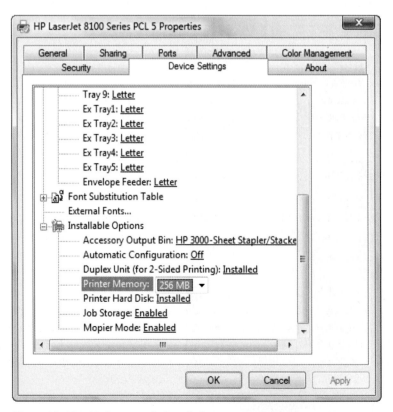

Figure 22-47   Configure newly installed memory or hard drive
Courtesy: Course Technology/Cengage Learning

A+
220-702
1.5
1.4

CLEANING A PRINTER

A printer gets dirty inside and outside as stray toner, ink, dust, and bits of paper accumulate. As part of routine printer maintenance, you need to regularly clean the printer. How often depends on how much the printer is used and the work environment. Some manufacturers suggest a heavily used printer be cleaned weekly, and others suggest you clean it whenever you exchange the toner or ink cartridges.

Clean the outside of the printer with a damp cloth. Don't use ammonia-based cleaners. Clean the inside of the printer with a dry cloth and remove dust, bits of paper, and stray toner. Picking up stray toner can be a problem. Don't try to blow it out with compressed air because you don't want the toner in the air. Also, don't use an antistatic vacuum cleaner. You can, however, use a vacuum cleaner designed to pick up toner, called a toner-certified vacuum cleaner. This type of vacuum does not allow the toner that it picks up to touch any conductive surface. Some printer manufacturers also suggest you use an extension magnet brush. The long-handled brush is made of nylon fibers that are charged with static electricity and easily attract the toner like a magnet. For a laser printer, wipe the rollers from side to side with a dry cloth to remove loose dirt and toner. Don't touch the soft black roller (the transfer roller), or you might affect the print quality. You can find specific instructions for cleaning a printer on the printer manufacturer's Web site.

For some inkjet printers, you can use software to clean the inkjet nozzles or align the cartridges, which can help improve print quality when colors appear streaked or out of alignment. How to access these tools differs from one printer to another. For some printers, a Services tab is added to the printer properties window. Other printer installations might put utility programs in the Start menu. Here is one example of how to clean and calibrate an inkjet printer installed under Windows XP that adds a tab to the Printing Preferences window:

1. On the General tab of the printer Properties box, click **Printing Preferences**. The Printing Preferences box opens. Click the **Services** tab and then click **Service this device**, as shown on the left side of Figure 22-48. The Toolbox window for the printer is displayed, as shown on the right side of the figure.

2. To calibrate the printer, click **Calibrate the Device**. In the next window, click **Calibrate**. As the printer calibrates itself, a page prints. The page contains a test pattern. If the test pattern does not look straight and smooth, first try to calibrate the printer a second time. If it still does not produce a smooth test pattern, you might have to replace the ink cartridges.

3. To have the printer automatically clean the ink nozzles, click **Clean the Print Cartridges** in the Toolbox window shown in Figure 22-48.

4. A test page prints. If the page prints sharply with no missing dots or lines, you are finished. If the page does not print correctly, perform the auto-clean again.

5. You might need to perform the auto-clean procedure six or seven times to clean the nozzles completely.

If the printer still does not print with the quality printing you expect, you can try to manually clean the cartridge nozzles. Check the printer manufacturer's Web site for directions. For most inkjet printers, you are directed to use clean, distilled water and cotton swabs to clean the face of the ink cartridge, being careful not to touch the nozzle plate. To prevent the inkjet nozzles from drying out, don't leave the ink cartridges out of their cradle for longer than 30 minutes. Here are some general directions:

1. Following manufacturer directions, remove the inkjet cartridges from the printer and lay them on their sides on a paper towel.

22

A+ 220-702

A+
220-702
1.5
1.4

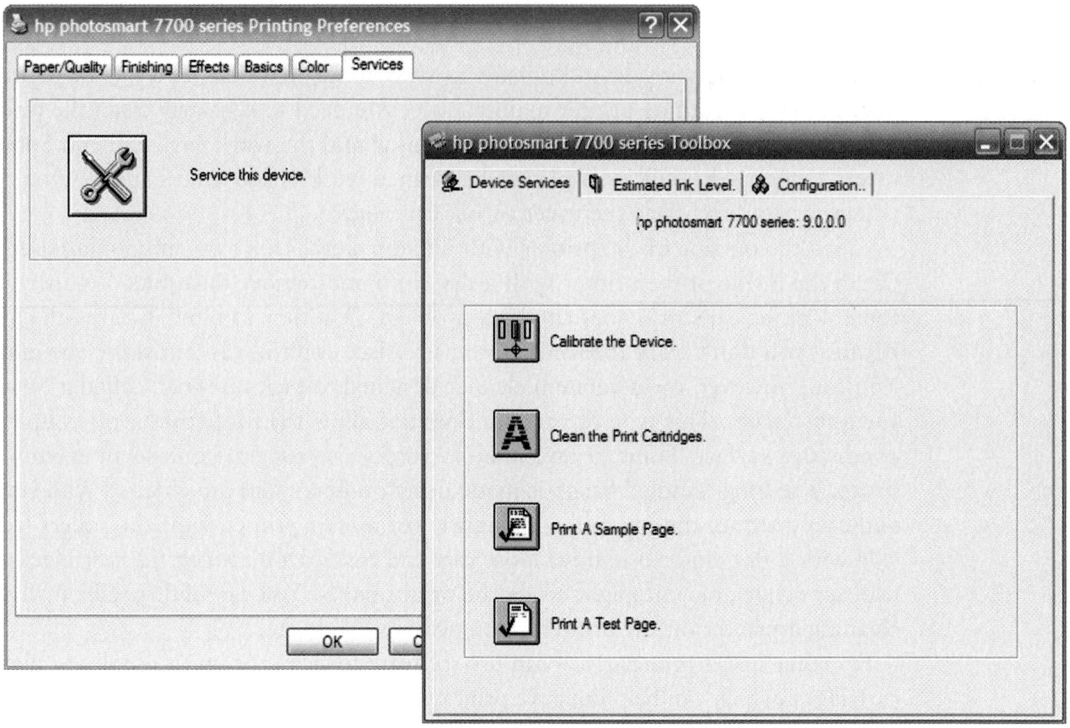

Figure 22-48 Use the Services tab in the Printing Preferences box to service this inkjet printer
Courtesy: Course Technology/Cengage Learning

2. Dip a cotton swab in distilled water (not tap water) and squeeze out any excess water.
3. Hold an ink cartridge so that the nozzle plate faces up and use the swab to wipe clean the area around the nozzle plate, as shown in Figure 22-49. Do not clean the plate itself.

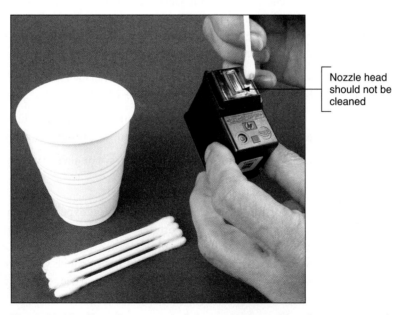

Figure 22-49 Clean the area around the nozzle plate with a damp cotton swab
Courtesy: Course Technology/Cengage Learning

A+
220-702
1.5
1.4

4. Hold the cartridge up to the light and make sure that no dust, dirt, ink, or cotton fibers are left around the face of the nozzle plate. Make sure the area is clean.

5. Clean all the ink cartridges the same way and replace the cartridges in the printer.

6. Print a test page. If print quality is still poor, try repeating the automatic nozzle cleaning process using the printer Properties window described earlier.

7. If you still have problems, you need to replace the ink cartridges.

A+
220-702
1.5

ONLINE SUPPORT FOR PRINTERS

The printer manufacturer's Web site is an important resource when supporting printers. Here are some things to look for:

- ◢ *Online documentation.* Expect the printer manufacturer's Web site to include documentation on installing, configuring, troubleshooting, using, upgrading, and maintaining the printer. Also look for information on printer parts and warranty, compatibility information, specifications and features of your printer, a way to register your printer, and how to recycle or dispose of a printer. You might also be able to download your printer manual in PDF format.

- ◢ *A knowledge base of common problems and what to do about them.* Some Web sites also offer a newsgroup service or discussion group where you can communicate with others responsible for supporting a particular printer. Also look for a way to e-mail for technical support.

- ◢ *Updated device drivers.* Sometimes, you can solve printer problems by downloading and installing the latest drivers. Also, a manufacturer makes new features and options available through these drivers. Be sure you download files for the correct printer and OS.

- ◢ *Catalog of options and upgrades for purchase.* Look for memory upgrades, optional trays, feeders, sorters, staplers, printer stands, and other equipment to upgrade your printer. Expect to find the parts as well as how to install and maintain them.

- ◢ *Replacement parts.* When a printer part breaks, buy only parts made by or approved by the printer manufacturer. Manufacturers also sell consumable supplies such as toner and ink cartridges.

- ◢ *Printer maintenance kits.* The best practice is to buy everything you need for routine maintenance either from the printer manufacturer or an approved vendor. If you buy from a nonapproved vendor, you risk damaging the printer or shortening its lifespan.

- ◢ *Additional software.* Look for software to use with your printer, such as software to produce greeting cards or edit photographs.

- ◢ *Firmware updates.* Some high-end printers have firmware that can be flashed to solve problems and add features. Be careful to verify that you download the correct update for your printer.

UPDATING PRINTER FIRMWARE

Printer firmware is updated by replacing the printer's DIMM that contains the firmware or by downloading the update from the manufacturer's Web site. Now, let's look at one example

A+
220-702
1.5

of how to upgrade the firmware on one network printer. The printer we are using is an HP 8100 DN printer. Follow these directions:

1. To know how to access the firmware utility on the printer, see the printer documentation. For this network printer, you enter its IP address in a browser address box from any computer on the network. Recall that this is the same method used to access the firmware utility for a router, which is the method typically used for any network device. The opening window of the utility opens, as shown in Figure 22-50. On this window, you can see the MAC address of the printer, the firmware version installed, the IP address, and other basic information.

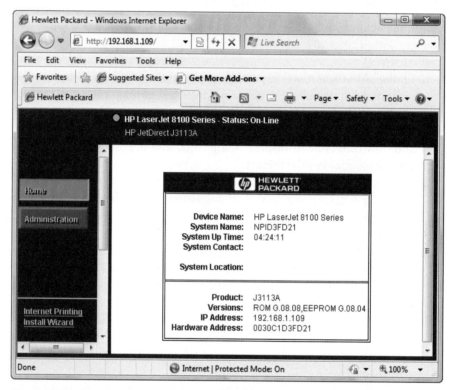

Figure 22-50   The network printer firmware is accessed on the network using a browser
Courtesy: Course Technology/Cengage Learning

2. Click **Administration** and then click the **Configuration** tab, as shown in Figure 22-51. Notice in this window you can configure the printer for static or dynamic IP addressing, which is labeled in the figure as TCP Configuration Type. If you are addressing the printer by its IP address, choose **Manual** so that the IP address doesn't change. For some printers, you can also use the control panel on the front of the printer to change how the IP address is set and to manually assign a new IP address. Some printers also give you the option to assign the IP address using the control panel on the front of the printer.

💡 **A+ Exam Tip**   The A+ 220-702 Practical Application exam expects you to know how to set the IP address of a printer.

3. To check for firmware upgrades, click the **Support** tab, which provides a connection to the HP Web site. Search the site for the printer downloads. Figure 22-52 shows the correct page for this printer. At the bottom of this page, click **Cross operating system (BIOS, Firmware, Diagnostics, etc.)**.

4. Follow the on-screen directions to download and install any available updates you select.

A+
220-702
1.5

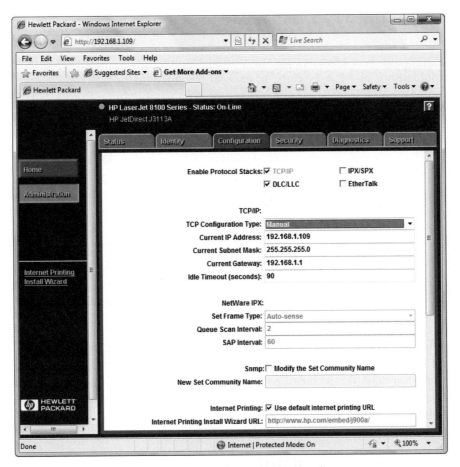

Figure 22-51 Configure a network printer for static IP addressing
Courtesy: Course Technology/Cengage Learning

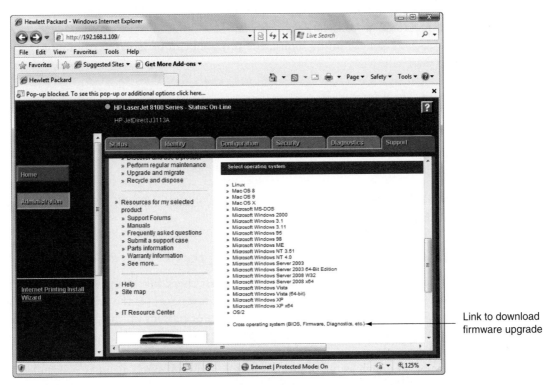

Link to download
firmware upgrade

Figure 22-52 Locate any firmware updates for the printer on the HP Web site
Courtesy: Course Technology/Cengage Learning

22

A+ 220-702

TROUBLESHOOTING PRINTERS

This section first discusses general printer troubleshooting and then explains how to troubleshoot problems specific to each of the three major types of printers. In these sections, you'll learn some general and specific troubleshooting tips. If you exhaust this list and still have a problem, turn to the manufacturer's Web site for additional information and support.

APPLYING CONCEPTS Jill is the PC support technician responsible for supporting 10 users, their peer-to-peer network, printers, and computers. Everything was working fine when Jill left work one evening, but the next morning three users meet her at the door, complaining that they cannot print to the network printer and that important work must be printed by noon. What do you think are the first three things Jill should check?

As with all computer problems, begin troubleshooting by interviewing the user, finding out what works and doesn't work, and making an initial determination of the problem. When you think the problem is solved, ask the user to check things out to make sure he is satisfied with your work. And, after the problem is solved, be sure to document the symptoms of the problem and what you did to solve it.

PRINTER DOES NOT PRINT

When a printer does not print, the problem can be caused by the printer, the PC hardware or OS, the application using the printer, the printer cable, or the network. Follow the steps in Figure 22-53 to isolate the problem.

As you can see in the figure, the problem can be isolated to one of the following areas:

- ◢ The printer itself
- ◢ Connectivity between the PC and its local printer
- ◢ Connectivity between the PC and a network printer
- ◢ The OS and printer drivers
- ◢ The application attempting to use the printer

The following sections address printer problems caused by all of these categories, starting with hardware.

PROBLEMS WITH THE PRINTER ITSELF

To eliminate the printer as the problem, first check that the printer is on, and then print a self-test page. For directions to print a self-test page, see the printer's user guide. For example, you might need to hold down a button or buttons on the printer's front panel. If this test page prints correctly, then the printer is working.

A printer test page generally prints some text, some graphics, and some information about the printer, such as the printer resolution and how much memory is installed. Verify that the information on the test page is correct. For example, if you know that the printer should

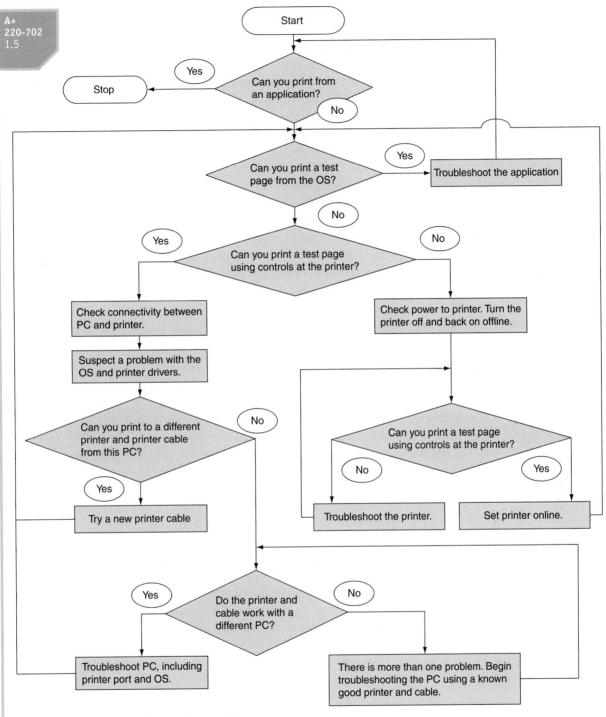

Figure 22-53 How to isolate a printer problem
Courtesy: Course Technology/Cengage Learning

have 2 MB of on-board printer memory, but the test only reports 1 MB, then there is a problem with memory. If the information reported is not correct and the printer allows you to upgrade firmware on the printer, try doing that next.

> **A+ Exam Tip** The A+ 220-702 Practical Application exam expects you to know how to determine if connectivity between the printer and the PC is the problem when troubleshooting printer issues.

22

A+ 220-702

If the self-test page does not print or prints incorrectly (for example, it has missing dots or smudged streaks through the page), then troubleshoot the printer until it prints correctly. Does the printer have paper? Is the paper installed correctly? Is there a paper jam? Is the paper damp or wrinkled, causing it to refuse to feed? Are the printer cover and rear access doors properly closed and locked? Try resetting the printer. For a laser printer, check that a toner cartridge is installed. For an inkjet printer, check that ink cartridges are installed. Has the protective tape been removed from the print cartridge? Check that power is getting to the printer. Try another power source. Check the user guide for the printer and the printer Web site for troubleshooting suggestions. For a laser printer, replace the toner cartridge. For inkjet printers, replace the ink cartridge. Check the service documentation and printer page count to find out if routine maintenance is due or if the printer has a history of similar problems. Other things to try to troubleshoot problems with laser, inkjet, and dot matrix printers are covered later in the chapter.

If none of these steps works, you might need to take the printer to a certified repair shop. Before you do, though, try contacting the manufacturer. The printer documentation can be very helpful and most often contains a phone number for technical support. You might also be able to open a chat session on the printer Web site.

PROBLEMS WITH A LOCAL PRINTER CABLE OR PORT

If the printer self-test worked, but the OS printer test did not work, check for connectivity problems between the printer and the PC. For a local printer connected directly to a PC, the problem might be with the printer cable or the port the printer is using. Do the following:

▲ Check that the cable is firmly connected at both ends. For a USB port, try a different port. For some parallel ports, you can use a screwdriver to securely anchor the cable to the parallel port with two screws on each side of the port. If you suspect the cable is bad, you can use a multimeter to check the cable.

▲ Try a different cable. For older parallel cables, make sure the cable is no longer than 10 feet and verify that the cable is IEEE 1284-compliant.

▲ Try printing using the same printer and printer cable but a different PC.

▲ Use Device Manager to verify the port the printer is using is enabled and working properly. Try another device on the same port to verify the problem is not with the port.

▲ Use BIOS setup to check how the port is configured. Is it enabled? For a parallel port, is the port set to ECP or bidirectional? Recall that an ECP parallel port requires the use of a DMA channel. Try setting the port to bidirectional.

▲ If you have access to a port tester device, test the port.

PROBLEMS WITH CONNECTIVITY FOR A NETWORK PRINTER OR SHARED PRINTER

If the self-test page prints but the OS test page does not print and the printer is a network printer or shared printer, the problem might be with connectivity between the PC and the network printer or with the host computer that is sharing the printer.

Follow these steps to solve problems with network printers:

▲ Is the printer online?

▲ Turn the printer off and back on. Try rebooting the PC.

▲ Verify that the correct default printer is selected.

▲ Using the Vista Printers or XP Printers and Faxes window, delete the printer, and then install the printer again.

- Can you print to another network printer? If so, there might be a problem with the printer. Look at the printer's configuration.
- Try pinging the printer. Try using another network cable for the printer. Check status indicator lights on the printer network port and on the switch or router the printer connects to.
- Run diagnostic software provided by the printer manufacturer.
- Are error codes displayed on the printer LCD window? If so, search the printer Web site for an explanation of the error code and how to deal with it. For example, error codes that begin with 79 for many HP printers indicate bad memory.
- Try flashing the network printer's firmware.

Follow these steps to solve problems with shared printers:

- If the printer is installed directly to one computer and shared with other computers on the network, check that you can print a test page from the computer that has the printer attached to it locally. Right-click the printer you want to test, and choose **Properties** from the shortcut menu. Click the **Print Test Page** button to send a test page to the printer.
- If you cannot print from the local printer, solve the problem there before attempting to print over the network.
- Verify that the correct default printer is selected.
- Return to the remote computer, and verify that you can access the computer to which the printer is attached. Go to the Network or My Network Places window, and attempt to open shared folders on the printer's computer. Perhaps you have not entered a correct user ID and password to access this computer; if so, you will be unable to use the computer's resources.
- Using the Vista Printers or XP Printers and Faxes window, delete the printer, and then install the printer again.
- Can you print to another shared printer? If so, there might be a problem with the printer. Look at the printer's configuration.
- Is enough hard drive space available on the client or host PC?

A network printer has a network port and connects directly to the network and not to an individual PC. However, you need to be aware of a problem that can happen when one computer shares a network printer with others on the network. When a network printer is shared by a computer, the printer appears in the Network or My Network Places windows of other computers on the network. A user of one of these computers can right-click the shared printer and select **Connect** from the shortcut menu. If the first computer has the OS drivers the second computer needs, the connection happens quickly, and the printer is ready to use. Look back at Figure 22-8; the installation would be like Computer D communicating with the network printer by way of Computer A. Installing a network printer this way can cause problems later.

Let's look at an example of this situation. Figure 22-54 shows a Printers window with several installed printers. Notice the two installations of the HP LaserJet 8100 printer. The first installation was done installing the LaserJet 8100 as a network printer addressed by its IP address. The second installation was done by using a shared printer that was shared by another computer on the network named Bluelight. When you print using the first installation of the LaserJet 8100, you print directly over the network to the printer. But when you print to the second installation of the LaserJet 8100, you print by way of the Bluelight computer.

A+
220-702
1.5

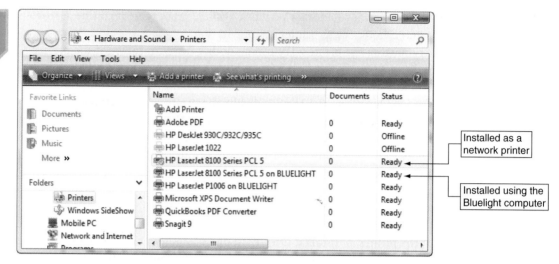

Figure 22-54 A network printer installed using two methods
Courtesy: Course Technology/Cengage Learning

The disadvantage of using the second method is that the computer sharing the printer must be turned on when other computers on the network want to use the network printer. Suppose you are troubleshooting a network printer problem. One troubleshooting step is to make certain that the printer is not installed as a printer shared by another computer and the other computer is turned off or asleep. The best solution to this problem is to reinstall the printer as a network printer and not as a shared printer dependent on another computer to work. Then, to prevent the problem from happening again, remove the shared status from the network printer on the first computer. Doing so removes it from the Network or My Network Places window of other computers on the network.

A+
220-702
1.5
2.4

PROBLEMS PRINTING FROM WINDOWS

If a self-test page works and you have already stepped through checking the printer connectivity, but you still cannot print a test page from Windows, try the following:

◢ The print spool might be stalled. Try deleting all print jobs in the printer's queue. Double-click the printer icon in the Vista Printers or XP Printers and Faxes window. Select **Printer** on the menu bar, and then select **Cancel All Documents**. (It might take a moment for the print jobs to disappear.) If the printer is still hung, try using buttons on the front of the printer to cancel print jobs. You can also power cycle the printer (turn it off and back on).

> 💡 **A+ Exam Tip** The A+ 220-702 Practical Application exam expects you to know how to solve problems with the print spool.

◢ Verify that the correct default printer is selected.
◢ Verify that the printer is online. See the printer documentation for information on how to determine the status from the control panel of the printer.
◢ If you still cannot print, reboot the PC. Verify that the printer cable or cable connections are solid.

A+
220-702
1.5
2.4

▲ Try deleting the printer and then reinstalling it.

▲ Check the printer manufacturer's Web site for an updated printer driver. Download and install the correct driver.

▲ Check Event Viewer for recorded events that have to do with the printer or the port it is using. For example, Figure 22-55 shows a recorded event about a print job. To make it easier to find events about printers, click the **Source** column title to sort the events by source.

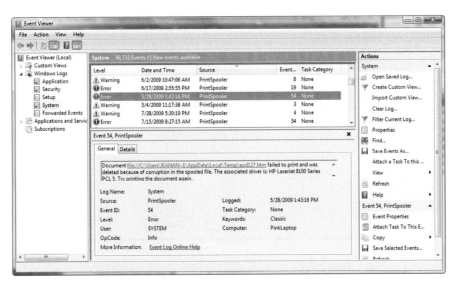

Figure 22-55 Check Event Viewer for recorded errors about the printer or its port
Courtesy: Course Technology/Cengage Learning

▲ For printers that use a parallel port, in the printer's Properties dialog box, select the **Ports** tab and uncheck **Enable bidirectional support** for this printer. See Figure 22-56 for an example in XP. An older PC and printer might have a problem with bidirectional communication.

▲ Verify printer properties. Try lowering the resolution.

▲ Try disabling printer spooling. On the printer's Properties dialog box, select the **Advanced** tab and then select **Print directly to the printer** (see Figure 22-57 for an XP example). Click **Apply**. Spooling holds print jobs in a queue for printing, so if spooling is disabled, printing from an application can be slower.

▲ If you have trouble printing from an application, you can also bypass spooling in the application by selecting the option to print to a file. Then drag that file to the icon representing your printer in the Vista Printers or XP Printers and Faxes window.

▲ Verify that enough hard drive space is available for the OS to create temporary print files.

▲ Use Chkdsk to verify that the hard drive does not have errors. Use Defragmenter to optimize the hard drive.

▲ Boot Windows into Safe Mode and attempt to print. If this step works, there might be a conflict between the printer driver and another driver or application.

▲ Check the printer documentation for troubleshooting steps to solve printer problems. Look for diagnostic software that you can download from the printer manufacturer's Web site or diagnostic routines you can run from the printer menu.

22
A+ 220-702

A+
220-702
1.5
2.4

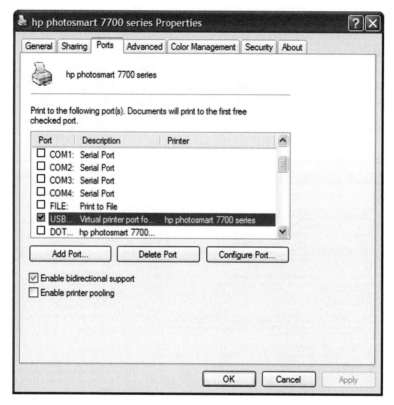

Figure 22-56 On this tab, you can enable and disable bidirectional support for a printer
Courtesy: Course Technology/Cengage Learning

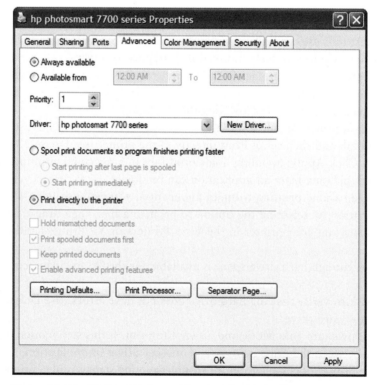

Figure 22-57 Disable printer spooling
Courtesy: Course Technology/Cengage Learning

A+
220-702
1.5
2.4

PROBLEMS PRINTING FROM APPLICATIONS

If you can print a Windows test page, but you cannot print from an application, try the following:

- Verify that the correct printer is selected in the Print Setup dialog box.
- Try printing a different file within the same application.
- Using the Vista Printers or XP Printers and Faxes window, delete any files in the print spool. Try canceling print jobs using controls at the printer. If the printer is still hung, power cycle the printer (turn it off and back on).
- Reboot the PC. Immediately enter Notepad or WordPad, type some text, and print.
- Reopen the application giving the print error and attempt to print again.
- Try creating data in a new file and printing it. Keep the data simple.
- Try printing from another application.
- If you can print from other applications, consider reinstalling the problem application.
- Close any applications that are not being used.
- Add more memory to the printer.
- Remove and reinstall the printer drivers.
- For legacy DOS applications installed in Windows, you might need to exit the application before printing will work. Verify that the printer is configured to handle DOS printing.

A+
220-702
1.5

PROBLEMS WITH LASER PRINTERS

This section covers some problems that can occur with laser printers. For more specific guidelines for your printer model, refer to the printer documentation or the manufacturer's Web site.

> **A+ Exam Tip** The A+ 220-702 Practical Application exam expects you to know how to resolve problems with paper jams, blank paper, error codes, out of memory errors, lines and smearing, garbage printout, ghosted images, and no connectivity. All these problems are covered in this part of the chapter.

POOR PRINT QUALITY OR A TONER LOW MESSAGE IS DISPLAYED

Poor print quality, including faded, smeared, wavy, speckled, or streaked printouts, often indicates that the toner is low. All major mechanical printer components that normally create problems are conveniently contained within the replaceable toner cartridge. In most cases, the solution to poor-quality printing is to replace this cartridge. Follow these general guidelines:

- If you suspect the printer is overheated, unplug it and allow it to cool for 30 minutes.
- The toner cartridge might be low on toner or might not be installed correctly. Remove the toner cartridge and gently rock it from side to side to redistribute the toner. Replace the cartridge. To avoid flying toner, don't shake the cartridge too hard.
- If this doesn't solve the problem, try replacing the toner cartridge immediately.
- EconoMode (a mode that uses less toner) might be on; turn it off.
- The printer might need cleaning. Some printers have a cleaning utility program that you can run from the printer menu or from software downloaded to the PC. On some laser printers, you can clean the mirror. Check the user guide for directions.

◢ A single sheet of paper might be defective. Try new paper.

◢ The paper quality might not be high enough. Try a different brand of paper. Only use paper recommended for use with a laser printer. Also, some types of paper can receive print only on one side.

◢ Clean the inside of the printer with a dry, lint-free cloth. Don't touch the transfer roller, which is the soft, spongy black roller.

◢ If the transfer roller is dirty, the problem will probably correct itself after several sheets print. If not, take the printer to an authorized service center.

◢ Does the printer require routine maintenance? Check the Web site of the printer manufacturer for how often to perform the maintenance and to purchase the required printer maintenance kit.

> **Notes** Extreme humidity can cause the toner to clump in the cartridge and give a Toner Low message. If this is a consistent problem in your location, you might want to invest in a dehumidifier for the room where your printer is located.

PRINTER STAYS IN WARM-UP MODE

The "warming up" message on the front panel of the printer (refer back to Figure 22-35) should turn off as soon as the printer establishes communication with the PC. If this doesn't happen, try the following:

1. Turn off the printer and disconnect the cable to the computer.

2. Turn on the printer. If it now displays a Ready message, the problem is communication between the printer and computer.

3. Verify that the cable is connected to the correct port.

4. Verify that data to the installed printer is being sent to the correct port. For example, open the Properties dialog box of the installed printer and click the Ports tab, as shown earlier in Figure 22-56.

5. Try rebooting the PC.

6. Try printing from another PC.

7. Consider that the network connecting the printer and PC is down.

A PAPER JAM OCCURS OR PAPER OUT MESSAGE APPEARS

If paper is jammed inside the printer, follow the directions in the printer documentation to remove the paper. Don't jerk the paper from the printer mechanism, but pull evenly on the paper, with care. Here are some guidelines:

◢ Check for jammed paper from both the input tray and the output bin. Check both sides.

◢ If there is no jammed paper, then remove the tray and check the metal plate at the bottom of the tray. Can it move up and down freely? If not, replace the tray.

◢ When you insert the tray in the printer, does the printer lift the plate as the tray is inserted? If not, the lift mechanism might need repair.

◢ Damp paper can cause paper jams. Be sure to only use dry paper in a printer.

ONE OR MORE WHITE STREAKS APPEAR IN THE PRINT

Do the following:

◢ Remove the toner cartridge, shake it from side to side to redistribute the toner supply. If this solves the problem, know that the cartridge is low on toner and will need replacing soon.

◢ Streaking is usually caused by a dirty developer unit or corona wire. The developer unit is contained in the toner cartridge. Replace the cartridge or check the printer documentation for directions on how to remove and clean the developer unit. Allow the corona wire to cool and clean it with a lint-free swab.

PRINT APPEARS SPECKLED

For this problem, do the following:

◢ Try replacing the cartridge. If the problem persists, the power supply assembly might be damaged.

◢ Replace the laser drum.

> **Notes** If loose toner comes out with your printout, the fuser is not reaching the proper temperature. Professional service is required.

PRINTED IMAGES ARE DISTORTED

If printed images are distorted and there is no paper jam, foreign material inside the printer might be interfering with the mechanical components. Check for debris that might be interfering with the printer operation. If the page has a gray background or gray print, the image drum is worn out and needs to be replaced.

GHOSTED IMAGES PRINT

A ghosted image appears a few inches below the actual darker image on the page. Ghosted images are usually caused by a problem with the image drum or toner cartridge. The drum is not fully cleaned in the cleaning stage, and toner left on it causes the ghost image. If the printer utility installed with the printer offers the option to clean the drum, try that first. The next solution is to replace the less expensive toner cartridge. If the problem is still not solved, replace the image drum.

GARBAGE PRINTOUTS

If symbols or other special characters don't print correctly, try using binary (bitmap) printing rather than asking the printer to interpret the characters. To make the change when printing a document, open the printer Properties box. For example, follow these steps to print in binary using Microsoft Word:

1. When you execute the print command for a Microsoft Word document, the Print box shown in Figure 22-58 appears. Click **Properties**.

2. The printer Properties box appears. The steps to print in binary might differ depending on the printer you are using. For one printer, click the **Advanced** tab. If necessary, drill down to Document Options, Printer Features, Send True Type as Bitmap (see Figure 22-59). Set the option to **Enabled** and click **OK**. Click **OK** in the Print box to print the document.

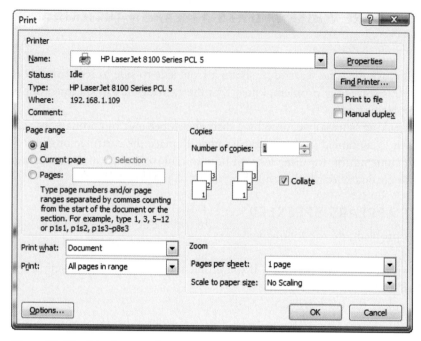

Figure 22-58 Print box to print a document
Courtesy: Course Technology/Cengage Learning

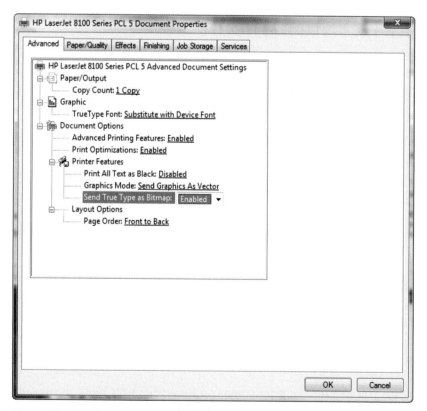

Figure 22-59 Print a document as binary
Courtesy: Course Technology/Cengage Learning

A+
220-702
1.5

If the problem is not solved, search the Web site of the printer manufacturer for other solutions.

PRINTING IS SLOW

Laser printers are rated by two speed properties: the time it takes to print the first page (measured in seconds) and the print speed (measured in pages per minute). Try the following if the printer is slow:

- Space is needed on the hard drive to manage print jobs. Verify that the hard drive has enough space and clean up the drive. Install a larger drive if necessary.
- Add more memory to the printer. See the printer manual for directions.
- Lower the printer resolution and the print quality (which lowers the REt settings).
- Upgrade the computer's memory or the CPU.

THE PRINTER MAKES A STRANGE NOISE

The printer might not be sitting level or stable. Check inside the printer for jammed paper or loose or broken parts. The cover or paper trays on the printer might not be fully closed.

ERROR CODES APPEAR IN THE PRINTER CONTROL PANEL WINDOW

If a high-end printer has a control panel on the front, it might display an error message or error code. Most likely the code will not explain the problem. You'll need to search the printer documentation or Web site to find out the meaning of the code. For example, error codes in the 79.xx range for HP printers can indicate a variety of problems from a print job with characters it does not understand to a failed memory module in the printer. To isolate the problem, HP suggests you first cancel all print jobs and disconnect the printer from the network. If the control panel reports "Ready," then you can assume the problem is with the network, computers, or print jobs, and not with the printer. If the error code is still displayed, the problem is with the printer. To isolate the problem that exists with the printer, HP suggests you remove any third-party memory modules installed in the printer. If the problem still exists, then you are instructed to remove the hard drive to eliminate it as the problem. If you still see the error code displayed, HP requests you contact them for further help.

A PORTION OF THE PAGE DOES NOT PRINT

For some laser printers, an error occurs if the printer does not have enough memory to hold the entire page. For other printers, only a part of the page prints. Some might signal this problem by flashing a light or displaying an error message on their display panels. (Some HP LaserJet printers have a control panel and send an error message for low memory, "20 Mem Overflow." Other printers might say "Out of memory".) The solution is to install more memory or to print only simple pages with few graphics. Print a self-test page to verify how much memory is installed. Some printers give you the option to install a hard drive in the printer to give additional printer storage space.

22

A+ 220-702

A+
220-702
1.5

PROBLEMS WITH INKJET PRINTERS

This section covers some problems that can occur with inkjet printers. For more specific guidelines for your printer, refer to the printer documentation or the manufacturer's Web site.

PRINT QUALITY IS POOR

Is the correct paper for inkjet printers being used? The quality of paper determines the final print quality, especially with inkjet printers. In general, the better the quality of the paper used with an inkjet printer, the better the print quality. Do not use less than 20-LB paper in any type of printer, unless the printer documentation specifically says that a lower weight is satisfactory. Here are some more things to check:

- Is the ink supply low, or is there a partially clogged nozzle?
- Remove and reinstall the cartridge.
- Follow the printer's documentation to clean each nozzle.
- In the Printer Setup dialog box, click the Media/Quality tab, and then change the Print Quality selection. Try different settings with sample prints.
- Is the print head too close to or too far from the paper?
- There is a little sponge in some printers near the carriage rest that can become clogged with ink. It should be removed and cleaned.
- If you are printing transparencies, try changing the fill pattern in your application.

PRINTING IS INTERMITTENT OR ABSENT

For these problems, do the following:

- Make sure the correct printer driver is installed.
- Is the ink supply low?
- Are nozzles clogged?
- Replace the ink cartridges or replenish the ink supply.
- Sometimes, leaving the printer on for a while will heat up the ink nozzles and unclog them.

Video
Replacing Ink Cartridges

LINES OR DOTS ARE MISSING FROM THE PRINTED PAGE

The ink nozzles on an inkjet cartridge occasionally dry out, especially when the printer sits unused for a long time. Symptoms are missing lines or dots on the printed page. Follow directions given earlier in the chapter for cleaning inkjet nozzles.

INK STREAKS APPEAR ON THE PRINTED PAGE

Sometimes, dust or dirt gets down into the print head assemblage, causing streaks or lines on the printed page. Follow the manufacturer's directions to clean the inkjet nozzles.

PAPER IS JAMMED

Inkjet printers have a door in the back of the printer that you can open to gently remove jammed paper, as shown in Figure 22-60. Don't try to pull the paper out from the front of the printer because doing so can tear the paper, leaving pieces inside the printer.

A+
220-702
1.5

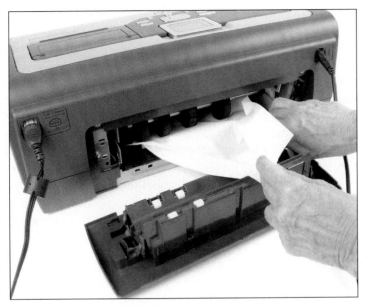

Figure 22-60 Open the door on the back of an inkjet printer to remove jammed paper
Courtesy: Course Technology/Cengage Learning

PROBLEMS WITH IMPACT PRINTERS

This section covers some problems that can occur with dot matrix printers. Again, for more specific guidelines for your printer, see the printer documentation or the manufacturer's Web site.

PRINT QUALITY IS POOR

For poor print quality, do the following:

- Begin with the ribbon. Does it advance normally while the carriage moves back and forth? If not, replace the ribbon.
- If the new ribbon still does not advance properly, check the printer's advance mechanism.
- Adjust the print head spacing. Look for a lever adjustment you can use to change the distance between the print head and plate.
- Check the print head for dirt. Make sure it's not hot before you touch it. If debris has built up, wipe each wire with a cotton swab dipped in alcohol or contact cleaner.

PRINT HEAD MOVES BACK AND FORTH BUT NOTHING PRINTS

Do the following:

- Check the ribbon. Is it installed correctly between the plate and print head?
- Does the ribbon advance properly? Is it jammed? If the ribbon is dried out, it needs to be replaced.

A+
220-702
1.5

APPLYING | CONCEPTS

Now back to Jill and her company's network printer problem. Generally, Jill should focus on finding out what works and what doesn't work, always remembering to check the simple things first. Jill should first go to the printer and check that the printer is online and has no error messages, such as a Paper Out message. Then, Jill should ask, "Can anyone print to this printer?" To find out, she should go to the closest PC and try to print a Windows test page. If the test page prints, she should next go to one of the three PCs that do not print and begin troubleshooting that PC's connection to the network. If the test page did not print at the closest PC, the problem is still not necessarily the printer. To eliminate the printer as the problem, the next step is to print a self-test page at the printer. If that self-test page prints, then Jill should check other PCs on the network. Is the entire network down? Can one PC see another PC on the network? Perhaps part of the network is down (maybe because of a switch or hub serving one part of the network).

>> CHAPTER SUMMARY

- ▲ The two most popular types of printers are laser and inkjet. Other types of printers are solid ink, dye sublimation, thermal printers, and impact printers (dot matrix). Laser printers produce the highest quality, followed by inkjet printers. Dot matrix printers have the advantage of being able to print multicopy documents.

- ▲ The six steps that a laser printer performs to print are cleaning, conditioning, writing, developing, transferring, and fusing. These stages (except for transferring) take place inside removable cartridges, which makes the printer easier to maintain.

- ▲ Inkjet printers print by shooting ionized ink at a sheet of paper. The quality of the printout largely depends on the quality of paper used with the printer.

- ▲ Dot matrix printers are a type of impact printer. They print by projecting pins from the print head against an inked ribbon that deposits ink on the paper.

- ▲ Thermal printers use heat to melt the ink during printing. Dye-sublimation printers are a type of thermal printer used to print ID cards. Solid ink printers are thermal printers that use blocks of solid ink.

- ▲ Printer features include duplex printing, extra paper trays to hold different sizes of paper, special paper feeders or transparency feeders, staplers, collators, and sorters. Printers can be combined with fax machines and copiers.

- ▲ A printer is installed as a local printer connected directly to a computer, a network printer that works as a device on the network, or a network printer connected to a print server. A local printer can be shared so that others can use it as a resource on the network.

- ▲ A local printer can connect directly to a computer by way of a USB port, parallel port, serial port, wireless connection (Bluetooth, infrared, or Wi-Fi), IEEE 1394 (FireWire) port, SCSI port, PC Card, or ExpressCard connection.

- ▲ Vista generally installs printers using the Printers window, and XP uses the Printers and Faxes window. USB printers are installed automatically with Vista and by using the printer setup CD in XP. The last step to install a printer is to print a printer test page.

▲ You can share an installed printer on the network so that other users can access the printer through the computer it connects to. The host computer must be on and awake to serve up the printer.

▲ Network printers are usually indentified on the network by their IP address.

▲ Printers can process print jobs using PostScript, PCL (Printer Control Language), GDI, or XPS (Vista only) input. In addition, printers can receive raw data that can be printed with no processing.

▲ The Windows print spool is managed from the Vista Printers window or the XP Printers and Faxes window.

▲ Printer consumables include paper, ink ribbons, ink cartridges, toner cartridges, image drum cartridge, fuser cartridge, and transfer belt. Keep consumables on hand so they will be available before they are needed. For longer lasting consumables, such as a fuser cartridge, check the page count of the printer to know when service is due and you need to order the part.

▲ Memory and a hard drive can be added to a printer to improve performance and prevent errors.

▲ The nozzles of an inkjet printer tend to clog or dry out, especially when the printer remains unused. The nozzles can be cleaned automatically by means of printer software or buttons on the front panel of the printer.

▲ Printer firmware can be upgraded to solve printing errors.

▲ When troubleshooting printers, first isolate the problem. Narrow the source to the printer, cable, PC hardware, operating system (including the device driver), application software, or network. Test pages printed directly at the printer or within Windows can help narrow down the source of the problem.

>> KEY TERMS

For explanations of key terms, see the Glossary near the end of the book.

default printer	network printer	REt (Resolution Enhancement
duplex printing	PCL (Printer Control	technology)
dye-sublimation printer	Language)	solid ink printers
extension magnet brush	PostScript	spooling
GDI (Graphics Device Interface)	power cycle	thermal printers
inkjet printers	print spool	XPS Document Writer
laser printer	printer maintenance kits	XPS (XML Paper Specification)
local printer	raw data	

22

>> REVIEWING THE BASICS

1. List the six steps used by a laser printer to print a page.

2. Which document exhibits better quality, one printed with 600 dpi or one printed with 1200 dpi? Why?

3. During the laser printing process, what determines when the toner sticks to the drum and when it does not stick to the drum?

4. What type printer is most dependent on the quality paper it uses to get the best printing results?

5. Why is it less expensive to maintain an inkjet printer that has a black ink cartridge than one that does not?

6. What should you do if an inkjet printer prints with missing dots or lines on the page?

7. What can you do to help a dot-matrix printer last longer?

8. What feature on a printer must be enabled so that a printer can automatically print on both sides of the paper?

9. What two Windows XP components are used to share resources on a network and access those shared resources?

10. How do you share a local printer with others in the workgroup?

11. What kind of printer is assigned an IP address?

12. What company developed PostScript? PCL?

13. Which printer language is new to Windows Vista?

14. What tool can you use to remove loose toner from inside a printer?

15. Where is the best place to look for a firmware upgrade for a printer?

16. How can you prove a printer problem is not with the printer itself, but lies with the network, computer, OS, or application?

17. When you get a toner-low message, what can you do to extend the life of the toner cartridge before you replace the cartridge?

18. What causes a ghosted image on a printout?

19. List two possible ways to improve printing speed.

20. What is likely the problem when a portion of a complicated page does not print?

>> THINKING CRITICALLY

1. A Windows XP computer has a locally installed printer that you must make available to eight other Windows XP computers on the network. What is the best way to do this?

   a. Use the Add Printer icon in the Printers window for each of the eight PCs.

   b. Use My Network Places to install the printer on each of the eight PCs.

   c. Use the printer manufacturer's setup program from the printer's CD on each of the eight PCs.

   d. Install the printer on each of the eight PCs while sitting at the host PC. Use My Network Places on the host PC.

2. You are not able to print a Word document on a Windows Vista computer to a network printer. The network printer is connected directly to the network, but when you look at the Printers window, you see the name of the printer as \\SMITH\HP LaserJet 8100. In the following list, select the possible sources of the problem.

   a. The SMITH computer is not turned on.

   b. The HP LaserJet 8100 printer is not online.

c. The SMITH printer is not online.

d. The Windows Vista computer has a stalled print spool.

e. The HP LaserJet 8100 computer is not logged on to the workgroup.

3. You are not able to print a test page from your Windows Vista PC to your local HP DeskJet printer. Which of the following are possible causes of the problem?

a. The network is down.

b. The printer cable is not connected properly.

c. The Windows print spool is stalled.

d. You have the wrong printer drivers installed.

e. File and Printer Sharing is not enabled.

>> HANDS-ON PROJECTS

PROJECT 22-1:   Practicing Printer Maintenance

For an inkjet printer, follow the procedures in the printer's user guide to clean the printer nozzles and ink cartridges. For a laser printer, follow the procedures in its user guide to clean the inside of the printer where the toner cartridge is installed.

PROJECT 22-2:   Sharing a Local Printer

Practice networking skills using Windows Vista or XP:

1. Share a local printer with others on the network.

2. Install a shared printer on a remote PC. Verify that you can print to the printer.

PROJECT 22-3:   Researching Printer Web Sites

Your company plans to purchase a new printer, and you want to evaluate the printer manufacturers' Web sites to determine which site offers the best support. Research three Web sites listed in Table 22-1 and answer these questions, supporting your answers with printed pages from the Web site:

1. Which Web site made it easiest for you to select a new printer, based on your criteria for its use?

2. Which Web site made it easiest for you to find help for troubleshooting printer problems?

3. Which Web site gave you the best information about routine maintenance for its printers?

4. Which Web site gave you the best information about how to clean its printers?

PROJECT 22-4:   Researching a Printer Maintenance Plan

You have been asked to recommend a maintenance plan for a laser printer. Search the manufacturer's Web site for information, and then write a maintenance plan. Include in the plan

22

the tasks that need to be done, how often they need doing, and what tools and components are needed to perform the tasks. Use the Hewlett-Packard LaserJet CP2025dn printer unless your instructor tells you to use a different printer, perhaps one that is available in your lab.

>> REAL PROBLEMS, REAL SOLUTIONS

REAL PROBLEM 22-1: Selecting a Color Printer for a Small Business

Jack owns a small real estate firm and has come to you asking for help with his printing needs. Currently, he has a color inkjet printer that he is using to print flyers, business cards, brochures, and other marketing materials. However, he is not satisfied with the print quality and wants to invest in a printer that produces more professional-looking hard copy. He expects to print no more than 8,000 sheets per month and needs the ability to print envelopes, letter-size and legal-size pages, and business cards. He wants to be able to automatically print on both sides of a legal-size page to produce a three-column brochure. Research printer solutions and do the following:

1. Print Web pages showing three printers to present to Jack that satisfy his needs. Include at least one laser printer and at least one printer technology other than laser in your selections.

2. Print Web pages showing the routine maintenance requirements of these printers.

3. Print Web pages showing all the consumable products (other than paper) that Jack should expect to have to purchase in the first year of use.

4. Calculate the initial cost of the equipment and the total cost of consumables for one year (other than paper) for each printer solution.

5. Prepare a list of advantages and disadvantages for each solution.

6. Based on your research, which of the three solutions do you recommend? Why?

CompTIA A+ Acronyms

CompTIA provides a list of acronyms which you need to know before you sit for the A+ exams. You can download the list from the CompTIA Web site at *www.comptia.org*. The list is included here for your convenience. However, CompTIA occasionally updates the list, so be sure to check the CompTIA Web site for the latest version.

Acronym	Spelled Out
AC	alternating current
ACPI	advanced configuration and power interface
ACT	activity
ADSL	asymmetrical digital subscriber line
AGP	accelerated graphics port
AMD	advanced micro devices
AMR	audio modem riser
APIPA	automatic private Internet protocol addressing
APM	advanced power management
ARP	address resolution protocol
ASR	automated system recovery
AT	advanced technology
ATA	advanced technology attachment
ATAPI	advanced technology attachment packet interface
ATM	asynchronous transfer mode
ATX	advanced technology extended
BIOS	basic input/output system
BNC	Bayonet-Neill-Concelman or British Naval Connector
BTX	balanced technology extended
CD	compact disc
CDFS	compact disc file system
CD-ROM	compact disc-read-only memory
CD-RW	compact disc-rewriteable
CFS	Central File System, Common File System, Command File System
CMOS	complementary metal-oxide semiconductor
COMx	communication port (x = port number)
CPU	central processing unit
CRT	cathode-ray tube
DAC	discretionary access control
DB-9	9-pin D shell connector
DB-25	serial communications D-shell connector, 25 pins
DC	direct current
DDOS	distributed denial of service
DDR	double data-rate
DDR RAM	double data-rate random access memory
DDR SDRAM	double data-rate symmetric dynamic random access memory
DFS	distributed file system
DHCP	dynamic host configuration protocol
DIMM	dual inline memory module

Acronym	Spelled Out
DIN	Deutsche Industrie Norm
DIP	dual inline package
DLP	digital light processing
DLT	digital linear tape
DMA	direct memory access
DMZ	demilitarized zone
DNS	domain name service or domain name server
DOS	denial of service
DPMS	display power management signaling
DRAM	dynamic random access memory
DSL	digital subscriber line
DVD	digital video disc or digital versatile disc
DVD-R	digital video disc-recordable
DVD-RAM	digital versatile disc-random access memory
DVD-ROM	digital video disc-read only memory
DVD-RW	digital video disc-rewriteable
DVI	digital visual interface
ECC	error correction code
ECP	extended capabilities port
EEPROM	electrically erasable programmable read-only memory
EFS	encrypting file system
EIDE	enhanced integrated drive electronics
EMI	electromagnetic interference
EMP	electromagnetic pulse
EPP	enhanced parallel port
EPROM	erasable programmable read-only memory
ERD	emergency repair disk
ESD	electrostatic discharge
EVDO	evolution data optimized or evolution data only
EVGA	extended video graphics adapter/array
FAT	file allocation table
FAT12	12-bit file allocation table
FAT16	16-bit file allocation table
FAT32	32-bit file allocation table
FDD	floppy disk drive
Fn	Function (referring to the function key on a laptop)
FPM	fast page-mode
FQDN	fully qualified domain name
FRU	field replaceable unit
FTP	file transfer protocol

A

Acronym	Spelled Out
Gb	gigabit
GB	gigabyte
GDI	graphics device interface
GHz	gigahertz
GPS	global positioning system
GSM	global system for mobile communication
GUI	graphical user interface
HAL	hardware abstraction layer
HCL	hardware compatibility list
HDD	hard disk drive
HDMi	high definition media interface
HPFS	high performance file system
HTML	hypertext markup language
HTTP	hypertext transfer protocol
HTTPS	hypertext transfer protocol over secure sockets layer
ICMP	Internet control message protocol
ICR	intelligent character recognition
IDE	integrated drive electronics
IEEE	Institute of Electrical and Electronics Engineers
IIS	Internet information server
IMAP	Internet mail access protocol
I/O	input/output
IP	Internet protocol
IPCONFIG	Internet protocol configuration
IPP	Internet printing protocol
IPSEC	Internet protocol security
IPX	internetwork packet exchange
IPX/SPX	internetwork packet exchange/sequenced packet exchange
IR	infrared
IrDA	Infrared Data Association
IRQ	interrupt request
ISA	industry standard architecture
ISDN	integrated services digital network
ISO	Industry Standards Organization
ISP	Internet service provider
JBOD	just a bunch of disks
Kb	kilobit
KB	Kilobyte or knowledge base
LAN	local area network

Acronym	Spelled Out
LBA	logical block addressing
LC	Lucent connector
LCD	liquid crystal display
LDAP	lightweight directory access protocol
LED	light emitting diode
Li-on	lithium-ion
LPD/LPR	line printer daemon / line printer remote
LPT	line printer terminal
LPT1	line printer terminal 1
LVD	low voltage differential
MAC	media access control / mandatory access control
MAPI	messaging application programming interface
MAU	media access unit, media attachment unit
Mb	megabit
MB	megabyte
MBR	master boot record
MBSA	Microsoft Baseline Security Analyzer
MFD	multifunction device
MFP	multifunction product
MHz	megahertz
MicroDIMM	micro dual inline memory module
MIDI	musical instrument digital interface
MIME	multipurpose Internet mail extension
MLI	multiple link interface
MMC	Microsoft management console
MMX	multimedia extensions
MP3	Moving Picture Experts Group Layer 3 Audio
MP4	Moving Picture Experts Group Layer 4
MPEG	Moving Picture Experts Group
MSCONFIG	Microsoft configuration
MSDS	material safety data sheet
MUI	multilingual user interface
NAC	network access control
NAS	Network-attached storage
NAT	network address translation
NetBIOS	networked basic input/output system
NetBEUI	networked basic input/output system extended user interface
NIC	network interface card
NiCd	nickel cadmium

A

Acronym	Spelled Out
NiMH	nickel metal hydride
NLX	new low-profile extended
NNTP	network news transfer protocol
NTFS	new technology file system
NTLDR	new technology loader
OCR	optical character recognition
OEM	original equipment manufacturer
OS	operating system
PAN	personal area network
PATA	parallel advanced technology attachment
PC	personal computer
PCI	peripheral component interconnect
PCIe	peripheral component interconnect express
PCIX	peripheral component interconnect extended
PCL	printer control language
PCMCIA	Personal Computer Memory Card International Association
PDA	personal digital assistant
PGA	pin grid array
PGA2	pin grid array 2
PIN	personal identification number
PKI	public key infrastructure
PnP	plug and play
POP3	post office protocol 3
POST	power-on self test
POTS	plain old telephone service
PPP	point-to-point protocol
PPTP	point-to-point tunneling protocol
PRI	primary rate interface
PROM	programmable read-only memory
PS/2	personal system/2 connector
PSTN	public switched telephone network
PSU	power supply unit
PVC	permanent virtual circuit
PXE	preboot execution environment
QoS	quality of service
RAID	redundant array of independent (or inexpensive) disks
RAM	random access memory
RAS	remote access service
RDRAM	RAMBUS dynamic random access memory

Acronym	Spelled Out
RF	radio frequency
RFI	radio frequency interference
RGB	red green blue
RIMM	RAMBUS inline memory module
RIP	routing information protocol
RIS	remote installation service
RISC	reduced instruction set computer
RJ	registered jack
RJ-11	registered jack function 11
RJ-45	registered jack function 45
RMA	returned materials authorization
ROM	read only memory
RS-232	recommended standard 232
RTC	real-time clock
SAN	storage area network
SATA	serial advanced technology attachment
SC	subscription channel
SCP	secure copy protection
SCSI	small computer system interface
SCSI ID	small computer system interface identifier
SD card	secure digital card
SDRAM	symmetric dynamic random access memory
SEC	single edge connector
SFC	system file checker
SGRAM	synchronous graphics random access memory
SIMM	single inline memory module
SLI	scalable link interface or system level integration or scanline interleave mode
S.M.A.R.T.	self-monitoring, analysis, and reporting technology
SMB	server message block or small to midsize business
SMTP	simple mail transport protocol
SNMP	simple network management protocol
SoDIMM	small outline dual inline memory module
SOHO	small office/home office
SP	service pack
SP1	service pack 1
SP2	service pack 2
SP3	service pack 3
SP4	service pack 4
SPDIF	Sony-Philips digital interface format

A

Acronym	Spelled Out
SPGA	staggered pin grid array
SPX	sequenced package exchange
SRAM	static random access memory
SSH	secure shell
SSID	service set identifier
SSL	secure sockets layer
ST	straight tip
STP	shielded twisted pair
SVGA	super video graphics array
SXGA	super extended graphics array
TB	terabyte
TCP	transmission control protocol
TCP/IP	transmission control protocol/Internet protocol
TDR	time domain reflectometer
TFTP	trivial file transfer protocol
UAC	User Access Control
UART	universal asynchronous receiver transmitter
UDF	user-defined functions or universal disk format or universal data format
UDMA	ultra direct memory access
UDP	user datagram protocol
UNC	universal naming convention
UPS	uninterruptible power supply
URL	uniform resource locator
USB	universal serial bus
USMT	user state migration tool
UTP	unshielded twisted pair
UXGA	ultra extended graphics array
VESA	Video Electronics Standards Association
VFAT	virtual file allocation table
VGA	video graphics array
VoIP	voice over Internet protocol
VPN	virtual private network
VRAM	video random access memory
WAN	wide area network
WAP	wireless application protocol
WEP	wired equivalent privacy
WIFI	wireless fidelity
WINS	Windows Internet name service

Acronym	Spelled Out
WLAN	wireless local area network
WPA	wireless protected access
WUXGA	wide ultra extended graphics array
XGA	extended graphics array
ZIF	zero-insertion-force
ZIP	zigzag inline package

A

Keystroke Shortcuts in Windows

This appendix lists a few handy keystrokes to use when working with Windows, including the function keys you can use during startup. You can also use the mouse to do some of these same things, but keystrokes are sometimes faster. Also, in some troubleshooting situations, the mouse is not usable. At those times, knowing these keystrokes can get you out of a jam.

General Action	Keystrokes	Description
While loading Windows	F8	To display the Advanced Boot Options menu.
	Spacebar	To display the Windows boot menu.
Managing Windows and applications	F1	To display Help.
	Alt+Tab	To move from one loaded application to another.
	Ctrl+Tab and Ctrl+Shift+Tab	To move through tabbed pages in a dialog box.
	Alt+ESC	To cycle through items in the order they were opened.
	F6	To cycle through screen elements in a window or on the desktop.
	Win or Ctrl+Esc	Display Start menu. Use arrow keys to move over the menu. (The Win key is the one labeled with the Windows flag icon.)
	Win+E	Start Windows Explorer.
	Win+M	Minimize all windows.
	Win+Tab	Move through items on the taskbar.
	Win+R	Display the Run dialog box.
	Win+Break	Display the Vista System window or the XP System Properties window.
	F5	Refresh the contents of a window.
	Alt+F4	Close the active application window, or, if no window is open, shut down Windows.
	Ctrl+F4	Close the active document window.
	Alt+Spacebar	To display the System menu for the active window. To close this window, you can then use the arrow key to step down to Close.
	Alt+M	First put the focus on the Start menu (use Win or Ctrl+Esc) and then press Alt+M to minimize all windows and move the focus to the desktop.
	F10 or Alt	Activate the menu bar in the active program.
	Ctrl+Alt+Del	Display the Task List, which you can use to switch to another application, end a task, or shut down Windows.
	Application	When an item is selected, display its shortcut menu. (The Application key is labeled with a box and an arrow.)
Working with text anywhere in Windows	Ctrl+C	Shortcut for Copy.
	Ctrl+V	Shortcut for Paste.
	Ctrl+A	Shortcut for selecting all text.
	Ctrl+X	Shortcut for Cut.
	Ctrl+Z	Shortcut for Undo.
	Ctrl+Y	Shortcut for Repeat/Redo.
	Shift+arrow keys	To select text, character by character.
Managing files, folders, icons, and shortcuts	Ctrl+Shift while dragging a file	Create a shortcut.
	Ctrl while dragging a file	Copy a file.

General Action	Keystrokes	Description
	Shift+Delete	Delete a file without placing it in the Recycle Bin.
	F2	Rename an item.
	Alt+Enter	Display an item's Properties window.
Selecting items	Shift+click	To select multiple entries in a list (such as filenames in Explorer), click the first item, hold down the Shift key, and click the last item you want to select in the list. All items between the first and last are selected.
	Ctrl+click	To select several nonsequential items in a list, click the first item to select it. Hold down the Ctrl key and click other items anywhere in the list. All items you click are selected.
Using menus	Alt	Press the Alt key to activate the menu bar.
	Alt, letter	After the menu bar is activated, press a letter to select a menu option. The letter must be underlined in the menu.
	Alt, arrow keys, Enter	In a window, use the Alt key to make the menu bar active. Then use the arrow keys to move over the menu tree and highlight the correct option. Use the Enter key to select that option.
	Esc	Press Esc to exit a menu without making a selection.
Copying to the Clipboard	Print Screen	Copy the desktop to the Clipboard.
	Alt+Print Screen	Copy the active window to the Clipboard.

B

GLOSSARY

This glossary defines the key terms listed at the end of each chapter and other terms related to managing and maintaining a personal computer.

100BaseT An Ethernet standard that operates at 100Mbps and uses twisted-pair cabling up to 100 meters (328 feet). *Also called* Fast Ethernet. Variations of 100BaseT are 100BaseTX and 100BaseFX.

10Base2 An outdated Ethernet standard that operates at 10 Mbps and uses small coaxial cable up to 500 meters long. *Also called* ThinNet.

10Base5 An outdated Ethernet standard that operates at 10 Mbps and uses thick coaxial cable up to 500 meters long. *Also called* ThickNet.

10BaseT An Ethernet standard that operates at 10 Mbps and uses twisted-pair cables up to 100 meters (328 feet).

3DNow! A processor instruction set by AMD designed to improve performance with 3D graphics and other multimedia data.

3G (Third Generation) The ability to use your cell phone to browse the Web, stream music and video, play online games, and use instant messaging and video conferencing.

80 conductor IDE cable An IDE cable that has 40 pins but uses 80 wires, 40 of which are ground wires designed to reduce crosstalk on the cable. The cable is used by ATA/66 and higher IDE drives.

802.11b/g/n *See* IEEE 802.11a/b/g/n.

A+ Certification A certification awarded by CompTIA (The Computer Technology Industry Association) that measures a PC technician's knowledge and skills.

AC adapter A device that converts AC to DC and uses regular house current to power a notebook computer.

Accelerated Graphics Port (AGP) A 32-bit wide bus standard developed specifically for video cards that includes AGP 1x, 2x, 3x, 4x, and 8x standards. AGP has been replaced by the PCI Express standards.

access point (AP) A device connected to a LAN that provides wireless communication so that computers, printers, and other wireless devices can communicate with devices on the LAN.

ACPI (Advanced Configuration and Power Interface) Specification developed by Intel, Compaq, Phoenix, Microsoft, and Toshiba to control power on computers and other devices.

Active Directory A Windows server directory database and service that is used in managing a domain to allow for a single point of administration for all shared resources on a network, including files, peripheral devices, databases, Web sites, users, and services.

active partition The primary partition on the hard drive that boots the OS. Windows 2000/XP/Vista calls the active partition the system partition.

adapter address *See* MAC address.

adapter card A small circuit board inserted in an expansion slot and used to communicate between the system bus and a peripheral device. *Also called* an interface card.

administrative shares The folders that are shared by default on a network domain that administrator accounts can access.

administrative tools Tools that you can use to manage the local PC or other computers on the network.

administrator account In Windows 2000/XP/Vista, an account that grants to the administrator(s) rights and permissions to all hardware and software resources, such as the right to add, delete, and change accounts and to change hardware configurations.

Advanced Configuration and Power Interface (ACPI) *See* ACPI (Advanced Configuration and Power Interface).

Advanced Options menu A Windows 2000/XP/Vista menu that appears when you press F8 when Windows starts. The menu can be used to troubleshoot problems when loading Windows 2000/XP/Vista. In Vista, the menu is called the Advanced Boot Options menu.

adware Software installed on a computer that produces pop-up ads using your browser; the ads are often based on your browsing habits.

Aero user interface The Vista 3D user interface. *Also called* Aero glass.

AirPort   The term Apple computers use to describe the IEEE 802.11b standard.

alternating current (AC)   Current that cycles back and forth rather than traveling in only one direction. In the United States, the AC voltage from a standard wall outlet is normally between 110 and 115V. In Europe, the standard AC voltage from a wall outlet is 220V.

ammeter   A meter that measures electrical current in amps.

ampere or amp (A)   A unit of measurement for electrical current. One volt across a resistance of one ohm will produce a flow of one amp.

anonymous users   User accounts that have not been authenticated on a computer.

ANSI (American National Standards Institute)   A nonprofit organization dedicated to creating trade and communications standards.

answer file   A text file that contains information that Windows requires in order to do an unattended installation.

antistatic wrist strap   *See* ground bracelet.

antivirus (AV) software   Utility programs that prevent infection or scan a system to detect and remove viruses. McAfee Associates' VirusScan and Norton AntiVirus are two popular AV packages.

application program interface (API) call   A request from software to the OS to access hardware or other software using a previously defined procedure that both the software and the OS understand.

ATAPI (Advanced Technology Attachment Packet Interface)   An interface standard, part of the IDE/ATA standards, that allows tape drives, optical drives, and other drives to be treated like an IDE hard drive by the system.

ATX   The most common form factor for PC systems presently in use, originally introduced by Intel in 1995. ATX motherboards and cases make better use of space and resources than did the earlier AT form factor.

ATX12V power supply   A power supply that provides a 12V power cord with a 4-pin connector to be used by the auxiliary 4-pin power connector on motherboards used to provide extra power for processors.

audio/modem riser (AMR)   A specification for a small slot on a motherboard to accommodate an audio or modem riser card. A controller on the motherboard contains some of the logic for the audio or modem functionality.

Authenticated Users group   All user accounts that have been authenticated to access the system except the Guest account. *Compare to* anonymous users.

authentication   The process of proving an individual is who they say they are before they are allowed access to a computer, file, folder, or network. The process might use a password, PIN, smart card, or biometric data.

authorization   Controlling what an individual can or cannot do with resources on a computer network. Using Windows, authorization is granted by the rights assigned to user accounts and permissions assigned to computer resources.

autodetection   A feature of system BIOS and hard drives that automatically identifies and configures a new drive in BIOS setup.

Automated System Recovery (ASR)   The Windows XP process that allows you to restore an entire hard drive volume or logical drive to its state at the time the backup of the volume was made.

Automatic Private IP Address (APIPA)   An IP address in the address range 169.254.x.y, used by a computer when it cannot successfully lease an IP address from a DHCP server.

auto-switching   A feature of an AC adapter whereby the device can automatically switch from 110 V to 220 V AC power, in contrast to fixed-input AC adapters that can handle only one type of AC voltage.

backdoor   A hidden way to allow malware to reach the system in secret even after the malware has been removed.

back-side bus (BSB)   The portion of a processor's internal bus that connects the processor to the internal memory cache. The bus operates at a much higher frequency than the front side bus.

backup   An extra copy of a file, used in the event that the original becomes damaged or destroyed.

backup operator   A Windows user account that can back up and restore any files on the system regardless of its having access to these files.

backward-compatible   A technology, software, or device that works with older or legacy technologies, software, or devices.

bandwidth   In relation to analog communication, the range of frequencies that a communications channel or cable can carry. In general use, the term refers to the volume of data that can travel on a bus or over a cable stated in bits per second (bps), kilobits per second (Kbps), or megabits per second (Mbps). *Also called* data throughput or line speed.

base station   A fixed transceiver and antenna used to create one cell within a cellular network.

basic disk   A way to partition a hard drive, used by all versions of Windows, that stores information about the drive in a partition table at the beginning of the drive. *Compare to* dynamic disk.

batch file   A text file containing a series of OS commands. Autoexec.bat is a batch file.

best-effort protocol   *See* connectionless protocol.

binary number system   The number system used by computers; it has only two numbers, 0 and 1, called binary digits, or bits.

biometric device   An input device that inputs biological data about a person; the data can identify a person's fingerprints, handprints, face, voice, eye, and handwriting.

BIOS (basic input/output system)   Firmware that can control much of a computer's input/output functions, such as communication with the floppy drive and the monitor.

BIOS setup   The program in system BIOS that can change the values in CMOS RAM. *Also called* CMOS setup.

bit (binary digit)   A 0 or 1 used by the binary number system.

BitLocker Encryption   A utility in Windows Vista Ultimate and Enterprise editions that is used to lock down a hard drive by encrypting the entire Vista volume and any other volume on the drive.

block mode   A method of data transfer between hard drive and memory that allows multiple data transfers on a single software interrupt.

blue screen errors   A Windows error that displays against a blue screen and causes the system to halt. *Also called* a stop error.

Bluetooth   A standard for wireless communication and data synchronization between devices, developed by a group of electronics manufacturers and overseen by the Bluetooth Special Interest Group. Bluetooth uses the same frequency range as 802.11b, but does not have as wide a range.

Blu-ray Disc (BD)   An optical disc technology that uses the UDF version 2.5 file system and a blue laser beam, which is shorter than any red beam used by DVD or CD discs. The shorter blue laser beam allows Blu-ray discs to store more data than a DVD.

BNC connector   A connector used with thin coaxial cable. Some BNC connectors are T-shaped and called T-connectors. One end of the T connects to the NIC, and the two other ends can connect to cables or end a bus formation with a terminator.

Boot Configuration Data (BCD)   A Vista file structured the same as a registry file and contains configuration information about how Vista is started. The BCD file replaces the Boot.ini file used in Windows 2000/XP.

boot loader   An operating system program responsible for managing the process of loading the OS during the boot.

boot loader menu   A startup menu that gives the user the choice of which operating system to load such as Windows XP or Windows Vista which are both installed on the same system, creating a dual boot.

boot partition   The hard drive partition where the Windows 2000/XP/Vista OS is stored. The system partition and the boot partition may be different partitions.

boot record   The first sector of a floppy disk or hard drive volume; it contains information about the disk or volume. On a hard drive, if the boot record is in the active partition, then it can be used to boot the OS. *Also called* boot sector.

boot sector   *See* boot record.

boot sector virus   An infectious program that can replace the boot program with a modified, infected version, often causing boot and data retrieval problems.

boot.ini   A Windows 2000/XP hidden text file that contains information needed to start the boot and build the boot loader menu.

booting   The process of starting up a computer and loading an operating system.

BootMgr   The Vista program file responsible for beginning the process of loading and starting Vista. The program file has no file extension and is stored in the root directory of the system partition (which, most likely, is drive C:).

Briefcase   A system folder in Windows 9x/Me that is used to synchronize files between two computers.

broadband   A transmission technique that carries more than one type of transmission on the same medium, such as voice and DSL on a regular telephone line.

brownouts   Temporary reductions in voltage, which can sometimes cause data loss. *Also called* sags.

browser hijacker   A malicious program that infects your Web browser and can change your home page or browser settings. It can also redirect your browser to unwanted sites, produce pop-up ads, and set unwanted bookmarks. *Also called* a home page hijacker.

BTX (Balanced Technology Extended)   A form factor used by motherboards and computer cases that was expected to replace ATX. It has higher quality fans, is designed for better air flow, and has improved structural support for the motherboard. The BTX form factor has not gained full acceptance by the computer manufacturer community.

Burst EDO (BEDO) A refined version of EDO memory that significantly improved access time over EDO. BEDO was not widely used because Intel chose not to support it. BEDO memory is stored on 168-pin DIMM modules.

bus The paths, or lines, on the motherboard on which data, instructions, and electrical power move from component to component.

bus riser *See* riser card.

byte A collection of eight bits that can represent a single character.

C states Defined by ACPI and used by a processor to stop its internal operations to conserve power. Using C0 though C6 states, the processor shuts down various internal components (for example, the core clock, buffers, cache, and core voltage).

cabinet file A file with a .cab extension that contains one or more compressed files and is often used to distribute software on disk. The Extract command is used to extract files from the cabinet file.

cable modem A technology that uses cable TV lines for data transmission requiring a modem at each end. From the modem, a network cable connects to a NIC in the user's PC, or a USB cable connects to a USB port.

call tracking A system that tracks the dates, times, and transactions of help-desk or on-site PC support calls, including the problem presented, the issues addressed, who did what, and when and how each call was resolved.

capacitor An electronic device that can maintain an electrical charge for a period of time and is used to smooth out the flow of electrical current. Capacitors are often found in computer power supplies.

card reader *See* media reader.

CardBus A PCMCIA specification that improved on the earlier PC Card standards. It improves I/O speed, increases the bus width to 32 bits, and supports lower-voltage PC Cards, while maintaining backward compatibility with earlier standards.

cards Adapter boards or interface cards placed into expansion slots to expand the functions of a computer, allowing it to communicate with external devices such as monitors or speakers.

CAS Latency (CL) A method of measuring access timing to memory, which is the number of clock cycles required to write or read a column of data off a memory module. CAS stands for Column Access Strobe. *Compare to* RAS Latency.

case fan A fan inside a computer case used to draw air out of or into the case.

CAT-3 (Category 3) A rating used for UTP cable that is less expensive than the more popular CAT-5 cable.

CAT-5 A rating used for UTP cable. CAT-5 or higher cabling is required for Fast Ethernet.

CAT-6 A rating used for UTP cables that has less crosstalk than CAT-5 or CAT-5e cables.

CD (compact disc) An optical disc technology that uses a red laser beam and can hold up to 700 MB of data.

CDFS (Compact Disc File System) The 32-bit file system for CD discs and some CD-R and CD-RW discs. *See also* Universal Disk Format (UDF).

CDMA (Code Division Multiple Access) A protocol standard used by cellular WANs and cell phones.

CD-R (CD-recordable) A CD drive that can record or write data to a CD. The drive may or may not be multisession, but the data cannot be erased once it is written.

CD-RW (CD-rewritable) A CD drive that can record or write data to a CD. The data can be erased and overwritten. The drive may or may not be multisession.

cellular network A network that can be used when a wireless network must cover a wide area. The network is made up of cells, each controlled by a base station. *Also called* a cellular WAN.

cellular WAN *See* cellular network.

central processing unit (CPU) *Also called* a microprocessor or processor. The heart and brain of the computer, which receives data input, processes information, and executes instructions.

Centrino A technology used by Intel whereby the processor, chipset, and wireless network adapter are all interconnected as a unit which improves laptop performance.

Certificate Manager (certmgr.msc) console A Windows console used to manage digital certificates including EFS certificates. Using the console, you can install or back up a certificate.

CHAP (Challenge Handshake Authentication Protocol) A protocol used to encrypt account names and passwords that are sent to a network controller for validation.

chassis air guide (CAG) A round air duct that helps to pull and direct fresh air from outside a computer case to the cooler and processor.

child directory *See* subdirectory.

chip creep A condition in which chips loosen because of thermal changes.

chipset A group of chips on the motherboard that controls the timing and flow of data and instructions to and from the CPU.

chkdsk A Windows utility that searches for bad sectors on a volume and recovers data from them if possible.

clamping voltage The maximum voltage allowed through a surge suppressor, such as 175 or 330 volts.

classful subnet mask A subnet mask that contain all ones or all zeroes in an octet. For example, 11111111.11111111.11111111.00000000 or 255.255.255.0.

classless subnet mask A subnet mask that can have a mix of zeroes and ones in one octet. For example, 11111111.11111111.11110000.00000000 or 255.255.240.0.

client/server A computer concept whereby one computer (the client) requests information from another computer (the server).

client/server applications An application that has two components. The client software requests data from the server software on the same or another computer.

clock speed The speed, or frequency, expressed in MHz, that controls activity on the motherboard and is generated by a crystal or oscillator located somewhere on the motherboard.

cluster One or more sectors that constitute the smallest unit of space on a disk for storing data (also referred to as a file allocation unit). Files are written to a disk as groups of whole clusters.

CMOS (complementary metal-oxide semiconductor) The technology used to manufacture microchips. CMOS chips require less electricity, hold data longer after the electricity is turned off, and produce less heat than earlier technologies. The configuration or setup chip is a CMOS chip.

CMOS battery The battery on the motherboard used to power the CMOS chip when the computer is unplugged.

CMOS configuration chip A chip on the motherboard that contains a very small amount of memory, or RAM, enough to hold configuration, or setup, information about the computer. The chip is powered by a battery when the PC is turned off. *Also called* CMOS setup chip or CMOS RAM chip.

CMOS RAM Memory contained on the CMOS configuration chip.

CMOS setup The program in system BIOS that can change the values in CMOS RAM. *Also called* BIOS setup.

CMOS setup chip *See* CMOS configuration chip.

coaxial cable Networking cable used with 10-Mbps Ethernet ThinNet or ThickNet.

cold boot *See* hard boot.

COM1 (Communications port 1) The number assigned a serial port that determines the system resources used by the port. A port might be called a COM1 port or a COM2 port.

command prompt window A Windows utility that is used to enter multiple commands to perform a variety of tasks.

communication and networking riser (CNR) A specification for a small expansion slot on a motherboard that accommodates a small audio, modem, or network riser card.

compact case A type of case used in low-end desktop systems. Compact cases, *Also called* low-profile or slimline cases, follow either the NLX, LPX, or Mini LPX form factor. They are likely to have fewer drive bays, but they generally still provide for some expansion.

Complete PC Backup A Vista utility that can make a backup of the entire volume on which Vista is installed and can also back up other volumes.

compressed (zipped) folder A folder with a .zip extension that contains compressed files. When files are put in the folder, they are compressed. When files are moved to a regular folder, the files are decompressed.

Computer Management (Compmgmt.msc) A window that consolidates several Windows utilities called snap-ins.

computer name Character-based host name or NetBIOS name assigned to a computer.

connectionless protocol A protocol such as UDP that does not require a connection before sending a packet and does not guarantee delivery. An example of a UDP transmission is streaming video over the Web. *Also called* a best-effort protocol.

connection-oriented protocol In networking, a protocol that confirms that a good connection has been made before transmitting data to the other end. An example of a connection-oriented protocol is TCP.

console A window in which one or more Windows utility programs have been installed. The window is created using Microsoft Management Console, and installed utilities are called snap-ins.

constant angular velocity (CAV) A technology used by hard drives and newer CD-ROM drives whereby the disk rotates at a constant speed.

constant linear velocity (CLV) A CD-ROM format in which the spacing of data is consistent on the CD, but the speed of the disc varies depending on whether the data being read is near the center or the edge of the disc.

Cool'n'Quiet A feature of AMD processors that lowers power requirements and helps keep a system quiet.

cooler A combination cooling fan and heat sink mounted on the top or side of a processor to keep it cool.

copyright An individual's right to copy his/her own work. No one else, other than the copyright owner, is legally allowed to do so without permission.

C-RIMM (Continuity RIMM) A placeholder RIMM module that provides continuity so that every RIMM slot is filled.

CrossFire A technology by ATI Technologies that allows for multiple video cards to be installed in the same system. *Compare to* SLI (Scalable Link Interface).

crossover cable A cable used to connect two PCs into the simplest network possible. Also used to connect two hubs to two switches.

CRT (Cathode-Ray Tube) An older technology used by monitors in which the filaments at the back of a cathode tube shoot a beam of electrons to the screen at the front of the tube.

data bus The lines on the system bus that the CPU uses to send and receive data.

data cartridge A type of tape medium typically used for backups. Full-sized data cartridges are $4 \times 6 \times \frac{1}{2}$ inches in size. A minicartridge is only $3\frac{1}{4} \times 2\frac{1}{2} \times \frac{3}{3}$ inches.

data classifications Categories of data used to determine who owns the data and who needs what type of access to it.

Data Collector Sets A utility within the Reliability and Performance Monitor that is used to collect your own data about a system.

data line protector A surge protector designed to work with the telephone line to a modem.

data migration Moving data from one application to another application or from one storage media to another, and most often involves a change in the way the data is formatted.

data path size The number of lines on a bus that can hold data, for example, 8, 16, 32, and 64 lines, which can accommodate 8, 16, 32, and 64 bits at a time.

data throughput *See* bandwidth.

daughter card *See* riser card.

DDR *See* Double Data Rate SDRAM.

DDR SDRAM *See* Double Data Rate SDRAM.

DDR2 *See* DDR2 SDRAM.

DDR2 SDRAM A version of SDRAM that is faster than DDR and uses less power. *Also called* DDR2.

DDR3 A version of SDRAM that is faster than DDR2 memory and that can use triple channels.

default gateway The gateway a computer on a network will use to access another network unless it knows to specifically use another gateway for quicker access to that network.

default printer The printer Windows prints to unless another printer is selected.

Defrag (Defrag.exe) Windows program and command to defragment a volume.

defragment To rewrite a file to a disk in one contiguous chain of clusters, thus speeding up data retrieval.

degauss button A button on a CRT monitor that can be pressed to eliminate accumulated or stray magnetic fields around the monitor which can cause a CRT monitor to flicker or have wavy lines.

desktop The initial screen that is displayed when an OS has a GUI interface loaded.

desktop case A computer case that sits flat on a desktop doing double duty as a monitor stand.

device driver A program stored on the hard drive that tells the computer how to communicate with a hardware device such as a printer or modem.

DHCP (Dynamic Host Configuration Protocol) A protocol used by a server to assign dynamic IP addresses to computers on a network when they first access the network.

diagnostic card Adapter cards designed to discover and report computer errors and conflicts at POST time (before the computer boots up), often by displaying a number on the card.

dial-up networking A Windows utility that uses a modem and telephone line to connect to a network.

digital certificate A code used to authenticate the source of a file or document or to identify and authenticate a person or organization sending data over a network. The code is assigned by a certificate authority such as VeriSign and includes a public key for encryption. *Also called* digital ID or digital signature.

digitizer   *See* graphics tablet.

digitizing tablet   *See* graphics tablet.

DIMM (dual inline memory module)   A miniature circuit board installed on a motherboard to hold memory. DIMMs can hold up to 4 GB of RAM on a single module.

diode   An electronic device that allows electricity to flow in only one direction. Used in a rectifier circuit.

DIP (dual inline package) switch   A switch on a circuit board or other device that can be set to on or off to hold configuration or setup information.

direct current (DC)   Current that travels in only one direction (the type of electricity provided by batteries). Computer power supplies transform AC to low DC.

Direct Rambus DRAM   A memory technology by Rambus and Intel that uses a narrow network-type system bus. Memory is stored on a RIMM module. *Also called* RDRAM, Rambus, or Direct RDRAM.

Direct RDRAM   *See* Direct Rambus DRAM.

disk cloning   *See* drive imaging.

disk imaging   *See* drive imaging.

Disk Management   A Windows utility used to display, create, and format partitions on basic disks and dynamic volumes on dynamic disks.

disk quota   A limit placed on the amount of disk space that is available to users. Requires a Windows NTFS volume.

disk thrashing   A condition that results when the hard drive is excessively used for virtual memory because RAM is full. It dramatically slows down processing and can cause premature hard drive failure.

distribution   Any version of Linux.

distribution server   A file server holding Windows setup files used to install Windows on computers networked to the server.

DMA (direct memory access) channel   A number identifying a channel whereby a device can pass data to memory without involving the CPU. Think of a DMA channel as a shortcut for data moving to/from the device and memory.

DMA (direct memory access) transfer mode   A transfer mode used by devices, including the hard drive, to transfer data to memory without involving the CPU.

DNS (Domain Name System or Domain Name Service)   A distributed pool of information (called the name space) that keeps track of assigned host names and

domain names and their corresponding IP addresses, and the system that allows a host to locate information in the pool.

DNS server   A computer that can find an IP address for another computer when only the fully qualified domain name is known.

docking station   A device that receives a notebook computer and provides additional secondary storage and easy connection to peripheral devices.

domain   In Windows, a logical group of networked computers, such as those on a college campus, that share a centralized directory database of user account information and security for the entire domain.

domain name   A unique, text-based name that identifies a network. A fully qualified domain name is sometimes loosely called a domain name. *Also see* fully qualified domain name.

domain profile   The level of protection that Vista uses for Windows Firewall when it recognizes the computer is connected to a domain. The protection level is low because Vista expects network security is being managed by the domain's operating system. *Compare to* private profile and public profile.

Double Data Rate SDRAM (DDR SDRAM)   A type of memory technology used on DIMMs that runs at twice the speed of the system clock. *Also called* DDR SDRAM, SDRAM II, and DDR.

double-sided   A DIMM feature whereby memory chips are installed on both sides of a DIMM.

DRAM   *See* dynamic RAM (DRAM).

drive image   An exact duplicate of a hard drive stored on another media such as a group of CDs or DVDs. *Also see* drive imaging.

drive imaging   Making an exact image of a hard drive, including partition information, boot sectors, operating system installation, and application software to replicate the hard drive on another system or recover from a hard drive crash. *Also called* disk cloning or disk imaging.

drive lock password   A password stored on a hard drive. You must enter the password at startup before you can access data on the drive. The password is set using BIOS setup screens.

Driver Query   A Windows tool that can be used to direct information about drivers to a file, including information about digital signatures.

Driver Verifier (verifier.exe)   A Windows utility that runs in the background to put stress on drivers as they are loaded and running and that is used to troubleshoot intermittent driver problems that are not easily detected by other means.

DSL (Digital Subscriber Line) A telephone line that carries digital data from end to end, and is used as a type of broadband Internet access.

dual boot The ability to boot using either of two different OSs, such as Windows XP and Windows Vista.

dual channels A motherboard feature that improves memory performance by providing two 64-bit channels between memory and the chipset. DDR, DDR2, and DDR3 DIMMs can use dual channels.

dual core A processor package that contains two core processors, thus supporting four instructions at once.

dual inline package (DIP) switch *See* DIP (dual inline package) switch.

dual ranked Double-sided DIMMs that provide two 64-bit banks. The memory controller accesses first one bank and then the other. Dual-ranked DIMMs do not perform as well as single-ranked DIMMs.

duplex printing Printing on both sides of the paper.

DVD (Digital Versatile Disc or Digital Video Disc) A technology used by optical discs that uses a red laser beam and can hold up to 17 GB of data.

DVI-D A DVI (Digital Visual Interface) video port that works only with digital monitors.

DVI-I A DVI (Digital Visual Interface) video port that supports both analog and digital monitors.

dxdiag.exe A Windows command to display information about hardware and diagnose problems with DirectX.

dye-sublimation printer A type of printer with photo-lab-quality results that uses transparent dyed film. The film is heated, which causes the dye to vaporize onto glossy paper.

dynamic disks A way to partition one or more hard drives, in which information about the drive is stored in a database at the end of the drive. *Compare to* basic disk.

dynamic IP address An assigned IP address that is used for the current session only. When the session is terminated, the IP address is returned to the list of available addresses.

dynamic RAM (DRAM) The most common type of system memory, it requires refreshing every few milliseconds.

dynamic volume A volume type used with dynamic disks by which you can create a single volume that uses space on multiple hard drives.

ECC (error-correcting code) A chipset feature on a motherboard that checks the integrity of data stored on DIMMs or RIMMs and can correct single-bit errors in a byte. More advanced ECC schemas can detect, but not correct, double-bit errors in a byte.

ECP (Extended Capabilities Port) A bidirectional parallel port mode that uses a DMA channel to speed up data flow.

EDO (extended data out) A type of outdated RAM that was faster than conventional RAM because it eliminated the delay before it issued the next memory address.

EIDE (Enhanced IDE) A standard for managing the interface between secondary storage devices and a computer system. A system can support up to four parallel ATA IDE devices such as hard drives, CD-ROM drives, and DVD drives.

electromagnetic interference (EMI) A magnetic field produced as a side effect from the flow of electricity. EMI can cause corrupted data in data lines that are not properly shielded.

electrostatic discharge (ESD) Another name for static electricity, which can damage chips and destroy motherboards, even though it might not be felt or seen with the naked eye.

elevated command prompt window A Vista command prompt window that allows commands that require administrative privileges.

Emergency Repair Disk (ERD) A Windows 2000 record of critical information about your system that can be used to fix a problem with the OS. The ERD enables restoration of the Windows 2000 registry on your hard drive.

Emergency Repair Process A Windows 2000 process that restores the OS to its state at the completion of a successful installation.

Encrypted File System (EFS) A way to use a key to encode a file or folder on an NTFS volume to protect sensitive data. Because it is an integrated system service, EFS is transparent to users and applications.

encryption The process of putting readable data into an encoded form that can only be decoded (or decrypted) through use of a key.

Energy Star "Green" systems that satisfy the EPA requirements to decrease the overall consumption of electricity. *See also* Green Standards.

enhanced CAT-5 (CAT-5e) A improved version of CAT-5 cable that reduces crosstalk.

Enhanced Intel SpeedStep Technology (EIST) A processor feature used by Intel that steps down processor frequency when the processor is idle to conserve power and lower heat.

EPP (Enhanced Parallel Port) A parallel port that allows data to flow in both directions (bidirectional port) and is faster than original parallel ports on PCs that allowed communication only in one direction.

escalate When a technician passes a customer's problem to higher organizational levels because he or she cannot solve the problem.

Event Viewer (Eventvwr.msc) A Windows tool useful for troubleshooting problems with Windows, applications, and hardware. It displays logs of significant events such as a hardware or network failure, OS failure, OS error messages, a device or service that has failed to start, or General Protection Faults.

Everyone group In Windows, the Authenticated Users group as well as the Guest account. When you share a file or folder on the network, Windows, by default, gives access to the Everyone group.

Execute Disable Bit A processor security feature by Intel that prevents software from executing or reproducing itself if it appears to be malicious.

executive services In Windows 2000/XP/Vista, a group of components running in kernel mode that interfaces between the subsystems in user mode and the HAL.

expansion card A circuit board inserted into a slot on the motherboard to enhance the capability of the computer.

expansion slot A narrow slot on the motherboard where an expansion card can be inserted. Expansion slots connect to a bus on the motherboard.

expert system Software that uses a database of known facts and rules to simulate a human expert's reasoning and decision-making processes.

ExpressCard The latest PCMCIA standard for notebook I/O cards that uses the PCI Express and USB 2.0 data transfer standards. Two types of Express-Cards are ExpressCard/34 (34mm wide) and ExpressCard/54 (54mm wide).

extended partition The only partition on a hard drive that can contain more than one logical drive. In Windows, a hard drive can have only a single extended partition. *Compare to* primary partition.

extension magnet brush A long-handled brush made of nylon fibers that are charged with static electricity to pick up stray toner inside a printer.

external SATA (eSATA) A standard for external drives based on SATA that uses a special external shielded SATA cable up to 2 meters long. eSATA is up to six times faster than USB or FireWire.

faceplate A metal or plastic plate that comes with the computer case and fits over the empty drive bays or slots for expansion cards to create a well-fitted enclosure around them.

Fast Ethernet *See* 100BaseT.

FAT (file allocation table) A table on a hard drive or floppy disk used by the FAT file system that tracks the clusters used to contain a file.

FAT12 The 12-bit wide, one-column file allocation table for a floppy disk, containing information about how each cluster or file allocation unit on the disk is currently used.

fault tolerance The degree to which a system can tolerate failures. Adding redundant components, such as disk mirroring or disk duplexing, is a way to build in fault tolerance.

ferrite clamp A clamp installed on a network cable to protect against electrical interference.

fiber optic A dedicated, leased line used for Internet access that uses fiber-optic cable from the ISP to residence or place of business.

fiber-optic cable Cable that transmits signals as pulses of light over glass strands inside protected tubing.

field replaceable unit (FRU) A component in a computer or device that can be replaced with a new component without sending the computer or device back to the manufacturer. Examples: power supply, DIMM, motherboard, floppy disk drive.

file allocation table (FAT) *See* FAT (file allocation table).

file allocation unit *See* cluster.

file attribute The properties assigned to a file. Examples of file attributes are read-only and hidden status.

file extension A portion of the name of a file that is used to identify the file type. In command lines, the file extension follows the filename and is separated from it by a period. For example, Msd.exe, where exe is the file extension.

File Signature Verification A Windows tool that displays information about digitally signed files, including device driver files and application files, and logs information to C:\Windows\Sigverif.txt.

file system The overall structure that an OS uses to name, store, and organize files on a disk. Examples of file systems are NTFS and FAT32.

File Transfer Protocol (FTP) *See* FTP (File Transfer Protocol).

file virus A virus that inserts virus code into an executable program file and can spread whenever that program is executed.

filename The first part of the name assigned to a file. In DOS, the filename can be no more than eight characters long and is followed by the file extension. In Windows, a filename can be up to 255 characters.

firewall Hardware or software that protects a computer or network from unauthorized access.

FireWire *See* IEEE 1394.

firmware Software that is permanently stored in a chip. The BIOS on a motherboard is an example of firmware.

flash ROM ROM that can be reprogrammed or changed without replacing chips.

flat panel monitors *See* LCD (Liquid Crystal Display) monitor.

FlexATX A version of the ATX form factor that allows for maximum flexibility in the size and shape of cases and motherboards. FlexATX is ideal for small, custom systems.

floppy disk drive (FDD) A drive that can hold either a $5\frac{1}{2}$ inch or $3\frac{1}{4}$ inch floppy disk. *Also called* floppy drive.

floppy drive *See* floppy disk drive (FDD).

folder *See* subdirectory.

form factor A set of specifications on the size, shape, and configuration of a computer hardware component such as a case, power supply, or motherboard.

formatting Preparing a hard drive volume, logical drive, or floppy disk for use by placing tracks and sectors on its surface to store information (for example, FORMAT A:).

FPM (fast page memory) An outdated memory mode used before the introduction of EDO memory. FPM improved on earlier memory types by sending the row address just once for many accesses to memory near that row.

fragmented file A file that has been written to different portions of the disk so that it is not in contiguous clusters.

front panel header A group of pins on a motherboard that connect to wires that are connected to the front panel of the computer case.

front-side bus (FSB) *See* system bus.

FTP (File Transfer Protocol) The protocol used to transfer files over a TCP/IP network.

full-duplex Communication that happens in two directions at the same time.

fully qualified domain name (FQDN) A host name and a domain name such as *jsmith.amazon.com*. Sometimes loosely referred to as a domain name.

gateway A computer or other device that connects networks.

GDI (Graphics Device Interface) A core Windows component responsible for building graphics data

to display or print. A GDI printer relies on Windows to construct a page to print and then receives the constructed page as bitmap data. *Also see* XPS (XML Paper Specification).

General Protection Fault (GPF) A Windows error that occurs when a program attempts to access a memory address that is not available or is no longer assigned to it.

Gigabit Ethernet A version of Ethernet that supports rates of data transfer up to 1 gigabit per second.

gigahertz (GHz) One thousand MHz, or one billion cycles per second.

global account Sometimes called a domain user account, the account is used at the domain level, created by an administrator, and stored in the SAM (security accounts manager) database on a Windows domain controller.

graphical user interface (GUI) An interface that uses graphics as compared to a command-driven interface.

graphics card *See* video card.

graphics tablet An input device that can use a stylus to hand draw. It works like a pencil on the tablet and uses a USB port.

grayware A program that AV software recognizes to be potentially harmful or potentially unwanted.

Green Standards A computer or device that conforms to these standards can go into sleep or doze mode when not in use, thus saving energy and helping the environment. Devices that carry the Green Star or Energy Star comply with these standards.

ground bracelet A strap you wear around your wrist that is attached to the computer case, ground mat, or another ground so that ESD is discharged from your body before you touch sensitive components inside a computer. *Also called* static strap, ground strap, ESD bracelet.

GSM (Global System for Mobile Communications) An open standard for cellular WANs and cell phones that uses digital communication of data and is accepted and used worldwide.

guest account A user account that has limited permissions on a system and cannot make changes to it. Guest user accounts are intended for one-time or infrequent users of a workstation.

HAL (hardware abstraction layer) The low-level part of Windows 2000/XP/Vista, written specifically for each CPU technology, so that only the HAL must change when platform components change.

half-duplex Communication between two devices whereby transmission takes place in only one direction at a time.

half-life   The time it takes for the strength of a storage media to weaken by half. *Also called* life expectancy or shelf life.

hard boot   Restart the computer by turning off the power or by pressing the Reset button. *Also called* a cold boot.

hard copy   Output from a printer to paper.

hard disk drive (HDD)   *See* hard drive.

hard drive   The main secondary storage device of a PC. Two technologies are currently used by hard drives: magnetic and solid state. *Also called* a hard disk drive (HDD).

hard drive dock   A device used to house and protect a hard drive outside the computer case and connect it to an eSATA, USB, or other type port on the computer. *Also called* a toaster.

hard-disk loading   The illegal practice of installing unauthorized software on computers for sale. Hard-disk loading can typically be identified by the absence of original software disks in the original system's shipment.

hardware   The physical components that constitute the computer system, such as the monitor, the keyboard, the motherboard, and the printer.

hardware address   *See* MAC address.

HDMI (High-Definition Multimedia Interface)   A digital audio and video interface standard currently used on televisions and other home theater equipment and expected to ultimately replace DVI.

head   The top or bottom surface of one platter on a hard drive. Each platter has two heads.

heat sink   A piece of metal, with cooling fins, that can be attached to or mounted on an integrated chip (such as the CPU) to dissipate heat.

hertz (Hz)   Unit of measurement for frequency, calculated in terms of vibrations, or cycles per second. For example, for 16-bit stereo sound, a frequency of 44,000Hz is used. *See also* megahertz.

hidden share   A folder whose folder name ends with a $ symbol. When you share the folder, it does not appear in the Network window or My Network Places window.

high-level formatting   Formatting performed by the Windows Format program (for example, FORMAT C:/S), the Windows installation program, or the Disk Management utility. The process creates the boot record, file system, and root directory on the volume or logical drive and makes the volume or drive bootable). *Also called* OS formatting or operating system formatting.

HKEY_CLASSES_ROOT (HKCR)   A Windows registry key that stores information to determine which application is opened when the user double-clicks a file.

HKEY_CURRENT_CONFIG (HKCC)   A Windows registry key that contains Plug and Play information about the hardware configuration that is used by the computer at startup.

HKEY_CURRENT_USER (HKCU)   A Windows registry key that contains data about the current user. The key is built when a user logs on using data kept in the HKEY_USERS key and data kept in the Ntuser.dat file of the current user.

HKEY_LOCAL_MACHINE (HKLM)   An important Windows registry key that contains hardware, software, and security data. The key is built using data taken from the SAM hive, the Security hive, the Software hive, and the System hive and from data collected at startup about the hardware.

HKEY_USERS (HKU)   A Windows registry key that contains data about all users and is taken from the Default hive.

hop count   *See* time to live (TTL).

host   Any computer or other device on a network that has been assigned an IP address. *Also called* node.

host adapter   The circuit board that controls a SCSI bus supporting as many as seven or fifteen separate devices. The host adapter controls communication between the SCSI bus and the PC.

host bus   *See* memory bus or system bus.

host name   A name that identifies a computer, printer, or other device on a network. The host name together with the domain name is called the fully qualified domain name.

hosts file   A file in the C:\Windows\System32\ drivers\etc folder that contains computer names and their associated IP addresses on the local network. The file has no file extension.

hot-plugging   Plugging in a device while the computer is turned on. The computer will sense the device and configure it without rebooting. In addition, the device can be unplugged without an OS error. *Also called* hot-swapping.

hot-swapping   *See* hot-plugging.

HTML (HyperText Markup Language)   A markup language used for hypertext documents on the World Wide Web. This language uses tags to format the document, create hyperlinks, and mark locations for graphics.

HTTP (Hypertext Transfer Protocol)   The communications protocol used by the World Wide Web.

HTTPS (HTTP secure)   A version of the HTTP protocol that includes data encryption for security.

hub   A network device or box that provides a central location to connect cables and distributes incoming data packets to all other devices connected to it. *Compare to* switch.

hybrid hard drive   A hard drive that uses both magnetic and SSD technologies. The bulk of storage uses the magnetic component, and a storage buffer on the drive is made of an SSD component. Vista ReadyDrive supports hybrid hard drives.

hypertext   Text that contains links to remote points in the document or to other files, documents, or graphics. Hypertext is created using HTML and is commonly distributed from Web sites.

Hyper-Threading   The Intel technology that allows each logical processor within the processor package to handle an individual thread in parallel with other threads being handled by other processors within the package.

HyperTransport   The AMD technology that allows each logical processor within the processor package to handle an individual thread in parallel with other threads being handled by other processors within the package.

i.Link   *See* IEEE 1394.

I/O address   Numbers that are used by devices and the CPU to manage communication between them.

I/O controller card   An older card that can contain serial, parallel, and game ports and floppy drive and IDE connectors.

I/O shield   A plate installed on the rear of a computer case that provides holes for I/O ports coming off the motherboard.

IDE (Integrated Drive Electronics or Integrated Device Electronics)   A hard drive whose disk controller is integrated into the drive, eliminating the need for a controller cable and thus increasing speed, as well as reducing price. *See also* EIDE.

IEEE 1284   A standard for parallel ports and cables developed by the Institute for Electrical and Electronics Engineers and supported by hardware manufacturers.

IEEE 1394   Standards for an expansion bus that can also be configured to work as a local bus. It is expected to replace the SCSI bus, providing an easy method to install and configure fast I/O devices. *Also called* FireWire and i.Link.

IEEE 1394.3   A standard, developed by the 1394 Trade Association, that is designed for peer-to-peer data transmission and allows imaging devices to

send images and photos directly to printers without involving a computer.

IEEE 802.11a/b/g/n   IEEE specifications for wireless communication and data synchronization. Also known as Wi-Fi. IEEE b/g/n standards are current, and IEEE 802.11a is outdated. Apple Computer's versions of 802.11 standards are called AirPort and AirPort Extreme.

IMAP4 (Internet Message Access Protocol version 4)   Version 4 of the IMAP protocol, which is an e-mail protocol used to download incoming email and has more functionality than its predecessor, POP. IMAP can archive messages in folders on the e-mail server and can allow the user to choose not to download attachments. *Compare to* POP (Post Office Protocol).

incident report   A report your organization might require to report unusual or atypical events.

infestation   Any unwanted program that is transmitted to a computer without the user's knowledge and that is designed to do varying degrees of damage to data and software. There are a number of different types of infestations, including viruses, Trojan horses, worms, and logic bombs. *See* malicious software.

infrared transceiver   A wireless transceiver that uses infrared technology to support some wireless devices such as keyboards, mice, and printers. A motherboard might have an embedded infrared transceiver, or the transceiver might plug into a USB or serial port. The technology is defined by the Infrared Data Association (IrDA). *Also called* an IrDA transceiver, IR transceriver, or infrared port.

inherited permissions   Permissions assigned by Windows that are attained from a parent object.

inkjet printer   A type of ink dispersion printer that uses cartridges of ink. The ink is heated to a boiling point and then ejected onto the paper through tiny nozzles.

Institute of Electrical and Electronics Engineers (IEEE)   A nonprofit organization that develops standards for the computer and electronics industries.

intelligent UPS   A UPS connected to a computer by way of a USB or serial cable so that software on the computer can monitor and control the UPS. *Also called* smart UPS.

interlaced   A type of display in which the electronic beam of a monitor draws every other line with each pass, which lessens the overall effect of a lower refresh rate.

internal bus The bus inside the CPU that is used for communication between the CPU's internal components.

Internet card A device that plugs into a computer and works like a cell phone to connect to a cellular WAN to give your computer Internet access. *Also called* an air card.

Internet Service Provider (ISP) A commercial group that provides Internet access for a monthly fee; AOL, Earthlink, and Comcast are large ISPs.

intranet A private network that uses the TCP/IP protocols.

inverter A device that converts DC to AC.

IP (Internet Protocol) The rules of communication in the TCP/IP stack that control segmenting data into packets, routing those packets across networks, and then reassembling the packets once they reach their destination.

IP address A 32-bit address consisting of four numbers separated by periods, used to uniquely identify a device on a network that uses TCP/IP protocols. The first numbers identify the network; the last numbers identify a host. An example of an IP address is 206.96.103.114.

IR transceiver *See* infrared transceiver.

IrDA (Infrared Data Association) transceiver *See* infrared transceiver.

IRQ (Interrupt ReQuest) line A line on a bus that is assigned to a device and is used to signal the CPU for servicing. These lines are assigned a reference number (for example, the normal IRQ for a printer is IRQ 7).

ISA (Industry Standard Architecture) slot An older slot on the motherboard used for slower I/O devices, which can support an 8-bit or a 16-bit data path. ISA slots have been replaced by PCI slots.

ISDN (Integrated Services Digital Network) A broadband telephone line that can carry data at about five times the speed of regular telephone lines. Two channels (telephone numbers) share a single pair of wires.

isochronous data transfer A method used by IEEE 1394 and other technologies to transfer data continuously without breaks.

joule A measure of work or energy. One joule of energy produces one watt of power for one second.

JPEG (Joint Photographic Experts Group) A graphical compression scheme that allows the user to control the amount of data that is averaged and sacrificed as file size is reduced. It is a common Internet file format. Most JPEG files have a .jpg extension.

jumper Two wires that stick up side by side on the motherboard or other device and are used to hold configuration information. The jumper is considered closed if a cover is over the wires, and open if the cover is missing.

Kerberos A protocol used to encrypt account names and passwords that are sent to a network controller for validation. Kerberos is the default protocol used by Windows 2000/XP/Vista.

kernel The portion of an OS that is responsible for interacting with the hardware.

kernel mode A Windows 2000/XP/Vista "privileged" processing mode that has access to hardware components.

key (1) In encryption, a secret number or code used to encode and decode data. (2) In Windows, a section name of the Windows registry.

key fob A device, such as a type of smart card, that can fit conveniently on a key chain.

keyboard A common input device through which data and instructions may be typed into computer memory.

keylogger A type of spyware that tracks your keystrokes, including passwords, chat room sessions, e-mail messages, documents, online purchases, and anything else you type on your PC. Text is logged to a text file and transmitted over the Internet without your knowledge.

KVM (Keyboard, Video, and Mouse) switch A switch allows you to use one keyboard, mouse, and monitor for multiple computers. Some KVM switches also include sound ports so that speakers and a microphone can be shared among multiple computers.

LAN (local area network) A computer network that covers only a small area, usually within one building.

land grid array (LGA) A feature of a CPU socket whereby pads, called lands, are used to make contact in uniform rows over the socket. *Compare to* pin grid array (PGA).

lands Microscopic flat areas on the surface of a CD or DVD that separate pits. Lands and pits are used to represent data on the disk.

laptop computer *See* notebook.

laser printer A type of printer that uses a laser beam to control how toner is placed on the page and then uses heat to fuse the toner to the page.

Last Known Good Configuration In Windows 2000/XP/Vista, registry settings and device drivers that were in effect when the computer last booted successfully. These settings can be restored during the startup process to recover from errors during the last boot.

latency   Delays in network transmissions resulting in slower network performance. Latency is measured by the round-trip time it takes for a data packet to travel from source to destination and back to source.

LBA (logical block addressing) mode   A mode of addressing information on hard drives in which the BIOS and operating system view the drive as one long linear list of LBAs or addressable sectors.

LCD (Liquid Crystal Display) monitor   A monitor that uses LCD technology. LCD produces an image using a liquid crystal material made of large, easily polarized molecules. LCD monitors are flatter than CRT monitors and take up less desk space. *Also called* a flat-panel monitor.

Level 1 (L1) cache   Memory on the processor die used as a cache to improve processor performance.

Level 2 (L2) cache   Memory in the processor package, but not on the processor die. The memory is used as a cache or buffer to improve processor performance. *Also see* Level 1 (L1) cache.

Level 3 (L3) cache   Cache memory further from the processor core than Level 2 cache, but still in the processor package.

license   Permission for an individual to use a product or service. A manufacturer's method of maintaining ownership, while granting permission for use to others.

limited account   Windows XP user accounts known as Users in Windows 2000, which have read-write access only on their own folders, read-only access to most system folders, and no access to other users' data. In Windows Vista, a standard account is a limited account.

line conditioners   A device that regulates, or conditions power, providing continuous voltage during brownouts and spikes.

line protocol   A protocol such as PPP used to send data packets destined for a network over telephone lines.

liquid cooling system   A method to cool overclocked processors that uses a small pump inside the computer case and tubes that move water or other liquid around components and then away from them to a place where fans can cool the liquid.

Lithium Ion   Currently the most popular type of battery popular with notebook computers that is more efficient than earlier types. Sometimes abbreviated as "Li-Ion" battery.

loadstate   A command used by the User State Migration Tool (USMT) to copy user settings and data temporarily stored on a server or removable media to a new computer. *Also see* scanstate.

local account   A user account that applies only to the local computer and cannot be used to access resources from other computers on the network. *Compare to* global account.

local bus   A bus that operates at a speed synchronized with the CPU frequency. The system bus is a local bus.

local printer   A printer connected to a computer by way of a port on the computer. *Compare to* network printer.

local profile   User profile that is stored on a local computer and cannot be accessed from another computer on the network.

local shares   Folders on a computer that are shared with others on the network by using a folder's Properties box. Local shares are used with a workgroup and not with a domain.

logic bomb   A type of malicious software that is dormant code added to software and triggered at a predetermined time or by a predetermined event.

logical drive   A portion or all of a hard drive extended partition that is treated by the operating system as though it were a physical drive. Each logical drive is assigned a drive letter, such as drive F, and contains a file system. *Compare to* volume.

Logical Unit Number (LUN)   A number assigned to a logical device (such as a tray in a CD changer) that is part of a physical SCSI device, which is assigned a SCSI ID.

low-level formatting   A process (usually performed at the factory) that electronically creates the hard drive tracks and sectors and tests for bad spots on the disk surface.

low-profile cases   *See* compact case.

LPT (Line Printer Terminal)   Assignments of system resources that are made to a parallel port and that are used to manage a print job. Two possible LPT configurations are referred to as LPT1: and LPT2:.

MAC (Media Access Control) address   A 48-bit hardware address unique to each NIC card or onboard network controller and assigned by the manufacturer. The address is often printed on the adapter as hexadecimal numbers. An example is 00 00 0C 08 2F 35. *Also called* a physical address, an adapter address, or a hardware address.

macro   A small sequence of commands, contained within a document, that can be automatically executed when the document is loaded, or executed later by using a predetermined keystroke.

macro viruses A virus that can hide in the macros of a document file.

magnetic hard drive One of two technologies used by hard drives where data is stored as magnetic spots on disks that rotate at a high speed. The other technology is solid state drive (SSD).

main board *See* motherboard.

malicious software Any unwanted program that is transmitted to a computer without the user's knowledge and that is designed to do varying degrees of damage to data and software. Types of infestations include viruses, Trojan horses, worms, adware, spyware, keyloggers, browser hijackers, dialers, and downloaders. *Also called* malware or an infestation.

malware *See* malicious software.

MAN (metropolitan area network) A network that covers a large campus or city. A small MAN is sometimes called a CAN or campus area network.

Master Boot Record (MBR) The first sector on a hard drive, which contains the partition table and a program the BIOS uses to boot an OS from the drive.

master file table (MFT) The database used by the NTFS file system to track the contents of a volume or logical drive.

Material Safety Data Sheet (MSDS) A document that explains how to properly handle substances such as chemical solvents; it includes information such as physical data, toxicity, health effects, first aid, storage, disposal, and spill procedures.

media reader A device that provides slots for memory cards and can be an internal or external device. *Also called* a card reader or memory card reader/writer.

megahertz (MHz) One million Hz, or one million cycles per second. *See* hertz (Hz).

memory Physical microchips that can hold data and programming, located on the motherboard or expansion cards.

memory bank The memory a processor addresses at one time. Today's desktop and notebook processors use a memory bank that is 64 bits wide.

memory cache A small amount of faster RAM that stores recently retrieved data, in anticipation of what the CPU will request next, thus speeding up access.

memory card reader/writer *See* media reader.

Memory Diagnostics (mdsched.exe) A Vista utility used to test memory.

memory dump The contents of memory saved to a file at the time an event halted the system. Support technicians can analyze the dump file to help understand the source of the problem.

memory paging In Windows, swapping blocks of RAM memory to an area of the hard drive to serve as virtual memory when RAM is low.

MicroATX A version of the ATX form factor. MicroATX addresses some new technologies that were developed after the original introduction of ATX.

microcode A programming instruction that can be executed by a CPU without breaking the instruction down into simpler instructions. Typically, a single command line in a Visual Basic or C++ program must be broken down into numerous microcode commands.

MicroDIMM A type of memory module used on sub-notebooks that has 144 pins and uses a 64-bit data path.

microprocessor *See* central processing unit (CPU).

Microsoft Management Console (MMC) A Windows utility to build customized consoles. These consoles can be saved to a file with an .msc file extension.

MIDI (Musical Instrument Digital Interface) A set of standards that are used to represent music in digital form. A MIDI port is a 5-pin DIN port that looks like a keyboard port, only larger.

mid-tower The most versatile and popular computer case, which is midrange in size and generally has around six expansion slots and four drive bays; provides moderate potential for expansion.

Mini PCI The PCI industry standard for desktop computer expansion cards, applied to a much smaller form factor for notebook expansion cards.

Mini PCI Express A standard used for notebook internal expansion slots that follows the PCI Express standards applied to notebooks. *Also called* Mini PCIe.

Mini PCIe *See* Mini PCI Express.

minicartridge A tape drive cartridge that is only $3\frac{1}{4}$ x $2\frac{1}{2}$ x $\frac{3}{5}$ inches. It is small enough to allow two drives to fit into a standard $5\frac{1}{2}$-inch drive bay of a PC case.

mirrored volume The term used by Windows for the RAID 1 level that duplicates data on one drive to another drive and is used for fault tolerance.

MMX (Multimedia Extensions)   Multimedia instructions built into Intel processors to add functionality such as better processing of multimedia, SIMD support, and increased cache.

modem riser card   A small modem card that uses an AMR or CNR slot. Part of the modem logic is contained in a controller on the motherboard.

monitor   The most commonly used output device for displaying text and graphics on a computer.

motherboard   The main board in the computer, *Also called* the system board. The CPU, ROM chips, DIMMs, RIMMs, and interface cards are plugged into the motherboard.

motherboard bus   *See* system bus.

mount point   A folder that is used as a shortcut to space on another volume which effectively increases the size of the folder to the size of the other volume. *Also see* mounted drive.

mounted drive   A volume that can be accessed by way of a folder on another volume so that the folder has more available space. *Also see* mount point.

mouse   A pointing and input device that allows the user to move a cursor around a screen and select items with the click of a button.

MP3   A method to compress audio files that uses MPEG level 1. It can reduce sound files as low as a 1:24 ratio without losing much sound quality.

MPEG (Moving Pictures Experts Group)   A processing-intensive standard for data compression for motion pictures that tracks movement from one frame to the next and only stores the data that has changed.

multicasting   A process in which a message is sent by one host to multiple hosts, such as when a video conference is broadcast to several hosts on the Internet.

multi-core processing   A processor technology whereby the processor housing contains two or more processor cores that operate at the same frequency, but independently of each other.

multimeter   A device used to measure the various components of an electrical circuit. The most common measurements are voltage, current, and resistance.

multipartite virus   A combination of a boot sector virus and a file virus. It can hide in either type of program.

multiple input/multiple output (MIMO)   A feature of the IEEE 802.11n standard for wireless networking whereby two or more antennas are used at both ends of transmissions to improve performance.

multiplier   The factor by which the bus speed or frequency is multiplied to get the CPU clock speed.

multiprocessor platform   A system that contains more than one processor. The motherboard has more than one processor socket and the processors must be rated to work in this multi-processor environment.

multisession   A feature that allows data to be read from or written to a CD during more than one session. This is important if the disk was only partially filled during the first write.

name resolution   The process of associating a character-based computer name to an IP address.

NAT (Network Address Translation)   A protocol used to convert private IP addresses on a LAN to a public IP address before a data packet is sent over the Internet.

native resolution   The actual (and fixed) number of pixels built into an LCD monitor. For the clearest display, always set the resolution to the native resolution.

NetBEUI (NetBIOS Extended User Interface)   A fast, proprietary, and outdated Microsoft networking protocol used only by Windows-based systems, and limited to LANs because it does not support routing.

NetBIOS (Network Basic Input/Output System)   An API protocol used by some applications to communicate over a NetBEUI network. NetBIOS has been replaced by Windows Sockets over a TCP/IP network.

NetBIOS name   A computer name with a maximum of 15 characters that is suitable for use by the NetBIOS protocol.

netbook   A low-end, inexpensive laptop with a small 9 or 10 inch screen and no optical drive that is generally used for Web browsing, email, and word processing by users on the go.

network adapter   *See* network interface card.

Network Address Translation (NAT)   *See* NAT (Network Address Translation).

network drive map   Mounting a drive to a computer, such as drive E, that is actually hard drive space on another host computer on the network.

network interface card (NIC)   An expansion card that plugs into a computer's motherboard and provides a port on the back of the card to connect a PC to a network. *Also called* a network adapter.

network printer   A printer that any user on the network can access, through its own network card and connection to the network, through a connection to a standalone print server, or through a connection to a computer as a local printer, which is shared on the network.

New Technology file system (NTFS)   *See* NTFS (NT file system).

NLX   A low-end form factor that is similar to LPX but provides greater support for current and emerging processor technologies. NLX was designed for flexibility and efficiency of space.

node   *See* host.

noise   An extraneous, unwanted signal, often over an analog phone line, that can cause communication interference or transmission errors. Possible sources are fluorescent lighting, radios, TVs, lightning, or bad wiring.

noninterlaced   A type of display in which the electronic beam of a CRT monitor draws every line on the screen with each pass.

nonvolatile   Refers to a kind of RAM that is stable and can hold data as long as electricity is powering the memory.

North Bridge   That portion of the chipset hub that connects faster I/O buses (for example, AGP buses) to the system bus. *Compare to* South Bridge.

notebook   A portable computer that is designed for travel and mobility. Notebooks use the same technology as desktop PCs, with modifications for conserving voltage, taking up less space, and operating while on the move. *Also called* a laptop computer.

notebook cases   Cases used for notebook computers, which are proprietary in design, leave almost no room for expansion, and include a thermometer that controls the case fan.

notification area   An area to the right of the taskbar that holds the icons for running services; these services include the volume control and network connectivity. *Also called* the system tray or systray.

NTFS (NT file system)   The file system for the Windows 2000/XP/Vista operating system. NTFS cannot be accessed by other operating systems such as DOS or Windows Me. It provides increased reliability and security in comparison to other methods of organizing and accessing files. Vista requires that NTFS be used for the volume on which Vista is installed.

Ntldr (NT Loader)   In Windows 2000/XP, the OS loader used on Intel systems.

octet   Term for each of the four 8-bit numbers that make up an IP address. For example, the IP address 206.96.103.114 has four octets.

octo core   A processor package that contains eight cores and supports 16 instructions at once.

ohm (Ω)   The standard unit of measurement for electrical resistance. Resistors are rated in ohms.

on-board ports   Ports that are directly on the motherboard, such as a built-in keyboard port or on-board network port.

operating system (OS)   Software that controls a computer. An OS controls how system resources are used and provides a user interface, a way of managing hardware and software, and ways to work with files.

operating system formatting   *See* high-level formatting.

original equipment manufacturer (OEM) license   A software license that only manufacturers or builders of personal computers can purchase to be installed only on a computer intended for sale.

overclocking   Running a processor at a higher frequency than is recommended by the manufacturer, which can result in an unstable system, but is a popular thing to do when a computer is used for gaming.

P states   Standards for processors established by ACPI that define how processor frequency and voltage can be lowered to conserve power when the processor is not in use.

P1 connector   Power connection on an ATX or BTX motherboard, which can have 20 or 24 pins.

packet   Segment of network data that also includes header, destination address, and trailer information that is sent as a unit. *Also called* data packet or datagram.

page fault   An OS interrupt that occurs when the OS is forced to access the hard drive to satisfy the demands for virtual memory.

page file   *See* swap file.

pagefile.sys   The Windows 2000/XP/Vista swap file.

PAN (personal area network)   A small network consisting of personal devices at close range; the devices can include cell phones, PDAs, and notebook computers.

parallel ATA (PATA)   An older IDE cabling method that uses a 40-pin flat or round data cable or an 80-conductor cable and a 40-pin IDE connector. *See also* serial ATA.

parallel port   A female 25-pin port on a computer that can transmit data in parallel, 8 bits at a time, and is usually used with a printer. The names for parallel ports are LPT1 and LPT2.

parity   An error-checking scheme in which a ninth, or "parity," bit is added. The value of the parity bit is set to either 0 or 1 to provide an even number of ones for even parity and an odd number of ones for odd parity.

parity error   An error that occurs when the number of 1s in the byte is not in agreement with the expected number.

partition   A division of a hard drive that can hold volumes. Windows can support up to four partitions on one hard drive.

partition table   A table at the beginning of the hard drive that contains information about each partition on the drive. The partition table is contained in the Master Boot Record.

passphrase   A type of password that can contain a phrase where spaces are allowed. A passphrase is stronger than a one-word password.

password reset disk   A device that holds a copy of the Windows password. Vista allows the device to be a flash media, but XP expects the device to be a floppy disk.

patch   An update to software that corrects an error, adds a feature, or addresses security issues. *Also called* an update or service pack.

patch cable   A network cable that is used to connect a PC to a hub, switch, or router.

path   A drive and list of directories pointing to a file such as C:\Windows\System32.

PC Card   A credit-card-sized adapter card that can be slid into a slot in the side of many notebook computers and is used by modems, network cards, and other devices. The card can use either a 16-bit or 32-bit data path. *Also called* PCMCIA Card.

PC Card slot   An expansion slot on a notebook computer, into which a PC Card is inserted. Older PC Card slots used a 16-bit data path, but newer slots use a 32-bit data path. *Also called* a PCMCIA Card slot.

PCI (Peripheral Component Interconnect) bus   A bus common to desktop computers that uses a 32-bit-wide or a 64-bit data path. Several variations of PCI exist. One or more notches on a PCI slot keep the wrong PCI cards from being inserted in the PCI slot.

PCI Express (PCIe)   The latest evolution of PCI, which is not backward-compatible with earlier PCI slots and cards. PCIe slots come in several sizes including PCIe x1, PCIe x4, PCIe x8, and PCIe x16.

PCL (Printer Control Language)   A printer language developed by Hewlett-Packard that communicates to a printer how to print a page.

PCMCIA (Personal Computer Memory Card International Association) Card   *See* PC Card.

peer-to-peer (P2P)   As applied to networking, a network of computers that are all equals, or peers. Each computer has the same amount of authority, and each can act as a server to the other computers.

perfmon.msc   The program file for the Windows Reliability and Performance Monitor console.

peripheral device   Devices that communicate with the CPU but are not located directly on the motherboard, such as the monitor, floppy drive, printer, and mouse.

permission propagation   When Windows passes permissions from parent objects to child objects.

permissions   Refer to the user accounts or user groups allowed to access data. Varying degrees of access can be assigned to a folder or file including full control, write, delete, or read-only.

phishing   (1) A type of identity theft where a person is baited into giving personal data to a Web site that appears to be the Web site of a reputable company with which the person has an account. (2) Sending an e-mail message with the intent of getting the user to reveal private information that can be used for identify theft.

physical address   *See* MAC address.

pin grid array (PGA)   A feature of a CPU socket whereby the pins are aligned in uniform rows around the socket.

Ping (packet internet groper)   A Windows and Unix command used to troubleshoot network connections. It verifies that the host can communicate with another host on the network.

pinout   A description of how each pin on a bus, connection, plug, slot, or socket is used.

PIO (Programmed I/O) transfer mode   A transfer mode that uses the CPU to transfer data from the hard drive to memory. PIO mode is slower than DMA mode.

pits   Recessed areas on the surface of a CD or DVD, separating lands, or flat areas. Lands and pits are used to represent data on a disc.

pixel   A small spot on a fine horizontal scan line. Pixels are illuminated to create an image on the monitor.

PKI (public key infrastructure)   The standards used to encrypt, transport, and validate digital certificates over the Internet.

point stick   A unique and popular pointing device embedded in the keyboard of IBM and Lenovo ThinkPad notebooks. *Also called* TrackPoint.

POP (Post Office Protocol) The protocol that an e-mail server and client use when the client requests the downloading of e-mail messages. The most recent version is POP3. POP is being replaced by IMAP.

port (1) As applied to services running on a computer, a number assigned to a process on a computer so that the process can be found by TCP/IP. *Also called* a port address or port number. (2) Another name for an I/O address. *See also* I/O address. (3) A physical connector, usually at the back of a computer, that allows a cable from a peripheral device, such as a printer, mouse, or modem, to be attached.

port address *See* I/O address.

port filtering To open or close certain ports so they can or cannot be used. A firewall uses port filtering to protect a network from unwanted communication.

port forwarding A technique that allows a computer on the Internet to reach a computer on a private network using a certain port when the private network is protected by a firewall device using NAT. Port forwarding is *Also called* tunneling.

port number *See* port.

port replicator A device designed to connect to a notebook computer in order to make it easy to connect the notebook to peripheral devices.

port triggering When a firewall opens a port because a computer behind the firewall initiates communication on another port.

POST (power-on self test) A self-diagnostic program used to perform a simple test of the CPU, RAM, and various I/O devices. The POST is performed by startup BIOS when the computer is first turned on, and is stored in ROM-BIOS.

PostScript A printer language developed by Adobe Systems which tells a printer how to print a page.

power conditioner A line conditioner that regulates, or conditions, power, providing continuous voltage during brownouts.

power cycle To turn a device off and back on.

power scheme A feature of Windows XP support for notebooks that allows the user to create groups of power settings for specific sets of conditions.

power supply A box inside the computer case that supplies power to the motherboard and other installed devices. Power supplies provide 3.3, 5, and 12 volts DC. *Also called* a power supply unit (PSU).

power supply tester A device that can test the output of each power cord coming from a power supply.

power supply unit (PSU) *See* power supply.

power user account A Windows XP account type that can read from and write to parts of the system other than the user's own folders, install applications, and perform limited administrative tasks.

PowerNow! An AMD technology that increases performance and lowers power requirements for processors.

power-on password A password that a computer uses to control access during the boot process.

PPP (Point-to-Point Protocol) A protocol that governs the methods for communicating via modems and dial-up telephone lines. The Windows Dial-up Networking utility uses PPP.

PPPoE (Point-to-Point Protocol over Ethernet) The protocol that describes how a PC is to interact with a broadband converter box, such as a cable modem, when the two are connected by an Ethernet cable, connected to a NIC in a PC.

primary partition A hard disk partition that can contain only one volume. The primary partition or volume contains a file system. In Windows, a hard drive can have up to three primary partitions. *Compare to* extended partition.

primary storage Temporary storage on the motherboard used by the CPU to process data and instructions. Memory is considered primary storage.

print spool A queue for print jobs.

printer A peripheral output device that produces printed output to paper. Different types include dot matrix, ink-jet, and laser printers.

printer maintenance kit A kit purchased from a printer manufacturer that contains the parts, tools, and instructions needed to perform routine printer maintenance.

private IP address An IP address that is used on a private TCP/IP network that is isolated from the Internet.

private profile The level of protection that Vista uses for Windows Firewall when it recognizes the computer is connected to a private network that is not part of a domain. This level offers moderate protection. *Compare to* public profile and domain profile.

processor *See* central processing unit (CPU).

processor frequency The frequency at which the CPU operates. Usually expressed in GHz.

product activation The process that Microsoft uses to prevent software piracy. For example, once Windows Vista is activated for a particular computer, it cannot be legally installed on another computer.

program A set of step-by-step instructions to a computer. Some are burned directly into chips, while others are stored as program files. Programs are written in languages such as Visual Basic and C++.

program file A file that contains instructions designed to be executed by the CPU.

progress bar A bar that displays when Vista is starting that indicates the kernel has loaded successfully and the user mode components of Vista are currently loading.

protocol A set of rules and standards that two entities use for communication.

public IP address An IP address available to the Internet.

Public Key Encryption An encryption technology that uses a public key and private key. The public key must be shared with others so they can use it to encrypt data that you can later decrypt by using your private key.

public profile The level of protection that Vista uses for Windows Firewall when it recognizes the computer is connected to an unsecured network. This level of protection is higher than that offered by the private profile and domain profile.

quad core A processor package that contains four cores and supports eight instructions at once.

Quality of Service (QoS) A measure of the success of communication over the Internet. Communication is degraded on the Internet when packets are dropped, delayed, delivered out of order, or corrupted. VoIP requires a high QoS.

quarantined computer A computer that is suspected of infection and is not allowed to use the network, is put on a different network dedicated to quarantined computers, or is allowed to access only certain network resources.

quarantined file A file that is suspected of infection and is placed in a special directory and cannot be opened. The user must decide to delete the file, leave it quarantined, or release it from quarantine status.

radio frequency interference (RFI) Interference produced by a magnetic field that is a side effect of electricity and is in the radio frequency range.

RAID (redundant array of inexpensive disks or redundant array of independent disks) Several methods of configuring multiple hard drives to store data to increase logical volume size and improve performance, or to ensure that if one hard drive fails, the data is still available from another hard drive.

RAID 0 Using space from two or more physical disks to increase the disk space available for a single volume. Performance improves because data is written evenly across all disks. Windows calls RAID 0 a striped volume.

RAID 1 A type of drive imaging that duplicates data on one drive to another drive and is used for fault tolerance. Windows calls RAID 1 a mirrored volume.

RAID 5 A technique that stripes data across three or more drives and uses parity checking, so that if one drive fails, the other drives can re-create the data stored on the failed drive. RAID 5 drives increase performance and provide fault tolerance. Windows calls these drives RAID-5 volumes.

RAID-5 volumes *See* RAID 5.

RAM (random access memory) Memory modules on the motherboard containing microchips used to temporarily hold data and programs while the CPU processes both. Information in RAM is lost when the PC is turned off.

RAM drive An area of memory that is treated as though it were a hard drive, but works much faster than a hard drive. The Windows 9x/Me startup disk uses a RAM drive. *Compare to* virtual memory.

Rambus *See* Direct Rambus DRAM.

RAS Latency (RL) A method of measuring access timing to memory, which is the number of clock cycles required to write or read a row of data off a memory module. RAS stands for Row Access Strobe. *Compare to* CAS Latency.

raw data Data sent to a printer without any formatting or processing.

RDRAM *See* Direct Rambus DRAM.

read/write head A sealed, magnetic coil device that moves across the surface of a disk either reading data from or writing data to the disk.

ReadyBoost A Vista utility that uses a flash drive or secure digital (SD) memory card to boost hard drive performance.

ReadyDrive The Vista technology that supports a hybrid hard drive.

Recovery Console A Windows 2000/XP command interface utility and OS that can be used to solve problems when Windows cannot load from the hard drive.

rectifier An electrical device that converts AC to DC. A PC power supply contains a rectifier.

refresh rate As applied to monitors, the number of times in one second an electronic beam can fill the screen with lines from top to bottom. *Also called* vertical scan rate.

Regedit.exe The program file used to edit the Windows registry.

registry A database that Windows uses to store hardware and software configuration information, user preferences, and setup information.

Registry Editor (Regedit.exe) The Windows utility used to edit the Windows registry.

Reliability and Performance Monitor A MMC snap-in (Perfmon.msc) that collects, records, and displays events, called Data Collector Sets, that can help track the performance and reliability of Windows. In Windows XP, this monitor is called the Performance Monitor or the System Monitor.

re-marked chips Chips that have been used and returned to the factory, marked again, and resold. The surface of the chips may be dull or scratched.

Remote Assistance A Windows XP/Vista feature that allows a support technician at a remote location to have full access to the Windows desktop.

Remote Desktop A Windows tool that gives a user access to his or her Windows desktop from anywhere on the Internet.

resistor An electronic device that resists or opposes the flow of electricity. A resistor can be used to reduce the amount of electricity being supplied to an electronic component.

resolution The number of pixels on a monitor screen that are addressable by software (example: 1024x768 pixels).

restore point A snapshot of the Windows XP/Vista system, usually made before installation of new hardware or applications.

REt (Resolution Enhancement technology) The term used by Hewlett-Packard to describe the way a laser printer varies the size of the dots used to create an image. This technology partly accounts for the sharp, clear image created by a laser printer.

reverse lookup To find the host name when you know a computer's IP address. The Nslookup command can perform a reverse lookup.

RGB (red, green, and blue) The three colors used to create a color space that consists of three dots, one for each color; *Also called* a triad.

RIMM A type of memory module developed by Rambus, Inc.

riser card A card that plugs into a motherboard and allows for expansion cards to be mounted parallel to the motherboard. Expansion cards are plugged into slots on the riser card.

RJ-11 A phone line connection found on modems, telephones, and house phone outlets.

RJ-45 connector A connector used with twisted-pair cable that connects the cable to the NIC.

ROM (read-only memory) Chips that contain programming code and cannot be erased.

root directory The main directory created when a hard drive or disk is first formatted. In Linux, it's indicated by a forward slash. In DOS and Windows, it's indicated by a backward slash.

rootkit A type of malicious software that loads itself before the OS boot is complete and can hijack internal Windows components so that it masks information Windows provides to user-mode utilities such as Windows Explorer or Task Manager.

router A device that connects networks and makes decisions as to the best routes to use when forwarding packets.

RS-232c (Reference Standard 232 revision c or Recommended Standard 232 revision c) The interface standard used by a serial port, which is sometimes called an RS-232 port.

S.M.A.R.T. (Self-Monitoring Analysis and Reporting Technology) A system BIOS and hard drive feature that monitors hard drive performance, disk spin up time, temperature, distance between the head and the disk, and other mechanical activities of the drive in order to predict when the drive is likely to fail.

S/PDIF (Sony-Philips Digital Interface) sound port A sound port that connects to an external home theater audio system, providing digital output and the best signal quality.

S1 state The ACPI power saving mode where the hard drive and monitor are turned off and everything else runs normally.

S2 state The ACPI power saving mode where the hard drive, monitor, and processor are turned off.

S3 state The ACPI power saving mode where everything is shut down except RAM and enough of the system to respond to a wake-up call such as pressing the keyboard. *Also called* sleep mode or standby mode.

S4 state The ACPI power saving mode where everything in RAM is copied to a file on the hard drive and the system is shut down. When the system is turned on, the file is used to restore the system to its state before shut down. *Also called* hibernation.

sags *See* brownouts.

scam e-mail   E-mail sent by a scam artist intended to lure you into a scheme.

scanstate   A command used by the User State Migration Tool (USMT) to copy user settings and data from an old computer to a server or removable media. *Also see* loadstate.

script virus   A type of virus that hides in a script which might execute when you click a link on a Web page or in an HTML e-mail message, or when you attempt to open an e-mail attachment.

SCSI (Small Computer System Interface)   A fast interface between a host adapter and the CPU that can daisy chain as many as 7 or 15 devices on a single bus.

SCSI host adapter card   A card that manages the SCSI bus and serves as the gateway to the system bus. *Also called* the host adapter.

SCSI ID   A number from 0 to 15 assigned to each SCSI device attached to the daisy chain.

secondary logon   Using administrative privileges to perform an operation when you are not logged on with an account that has these privileges.

secondary storage   Storage that is remote to the CPU and permanently holds data, even when the PC is turned off, such as a hard drive.

sector   On a disk surface one segment of a track, which almost always contains 512 bytes of data.

sequential access   A method of data access used by tape drives, whereby data is written or read sequentially from the beginning to the end of the tape or until the desired data is found.

serial ATA (SATA)   An ATAPI cabling method that uses a narrower and more reliable cable than the 80-conductor cable. *See also* parallel ATA.

serial ATA cable   An IDE cable that is narrower and has fewer pins than the parallel IDE 80-conductor cable.

serial attached SCSI (SAS)   A SCSI standard that allows for more than 15 devices on a single SCSI chain, uses smaller, longer, round cables, and uses smaller hard drive form factors that can support larger capacities than earlier versions of SCSI.

serial port   A male 9-pin or 25-pin port on a computer system used by slower I/O devices such as a mouse or modem. Data travels serially, one bit at a time, through the port. Serial ports are sometimes configured as COM1, COM2, COM3, or COM4.

service   A program that runs in the background to support or serve Windows or an application.

service pack   *See* patch.

Service Set Identifier (SSID)   The name of the access point for a wireless network.

session   An established communication link between two software programs. On the Internet, a session is created by TCP.

SFC (System File Checker)   A Windows tool that checks to make sure Windows is using the correct versions of system files.

shadow RAM or shadowing ROM   ROM programming code copied into RAM to speed up the system operation, because of the faster access speed of RAM.

share permissions   Allowing access to folders to remote users on the network, including assigning varying degrees of access to specific user accounts and user groups.

shell   The portion of an OS that relates to the user and to applications.

shielded twisted pair (STP) cable   A cable that is made of one or more twisted pairs of wires and is surrounded by a metal shield.

shortcut   An icon on the desktop that points to a program that can be executed or to a file or folder.

sigverif.exe   A Windows utility that allows you to search for digital signatures.

SIMD (single instruction, multiple data)   A process that allows the CPU to execute a single instruction simultaneously on multiple pieces of data, rather than by repetitive looping.

SIMM (single inline memory module)   A miniature circuit board used in older computers to hold RAM. SIMMs holds 8, 16, 32, or 64 MB on a single module.

simple file sharing   Sharing folders or files with remote network users where you have no control over who has access to the shared folder or file.

simple volume   A type of dynamic volume used on a single hard drive that corresponds to a primary partition on a basic disk.

single channel   The memory controller on a motherboard that can access only one DIMM at a time. *Compare to* dual channel and triple channel.

single ranked   DIMMs that provide only one 64-bit bank. All memory chips on the DIMM are accessed at the same time. *Compare to* dual ranked.

single-sided   Memory chips embedded on only a single side of a DIMM.

site license   A license that allows a company to install multiple copies of software, or to allow multiple employees to execute the software from a file server.

slack   Wasted space on a hard drive caused by not using all available space at the end of clusters.

sleep timers   The various times of inactivity before the computer goes into sleep mode.

SLI (Scalable Link Interface)   A technology by NVIDIA that allows for multiple video cards to be installed in the same system. *Compare to* CrossFire.

slimline cases   *See* compact case.

smart card   Any small device that contains authentication information that can be keyed into a logon window or read by a reader to authenticate a user on a network.

smart card reader   A device that can read a smart card used to authenticate a person onto a network.

smart UPS   *See* intelligent UPS.

SMTP (Simple Mail Transfer Protocol)   The protocol used by e-mail clients and servers to send e-mail messages over the Internet. *Also see* POP and IMAP.

SMTP AUTH (SMTP Authentication)   A protocol that is used to authenticate or prove that a client who attempts to use an email server to send email is authorized to use the server. The protocol is based on the Simple Authentication and Security Layer (SASL) protocol.

snap-in   A Windows utility that can be installed in a console window by Microsoft Management Console.

social engineering   The practice of tricking people into giving out private information or allowing unsafe programs into the network or computer.

socket   *See* session.

SO-DIMM (small outline DIMM)   A type of memory module used in notebook computers that uses DIMM technology. A DDR3 SO-DIMM has 204 pins. A DDR2 or DDR SO-DIMM has 200 pins. Older, outdated SO-DIMMs can have 72 pins or 144 pins.

soft boot   To restart a PC without turning off the power, for example, in Windows XP, by clicking Start, Turn Off Computer, and Restart. *Also called* warm boot.

soft power   *See* soft switch.

soft switch   A button or switch on an ATX or BTX system that allows an OS to power down the system and a feature that allows for activity such as a keystroke or network activity to power up the system. *Also called* soft power.

software   Computer programs, or instructions to perform a specific task. Software may be BIOS, OSs, or applications software such as a word-processing or spreadsheet program.

solid ink printer   A type of printer that uses sticks or blocks of solid ink. The ink is melted and then jetted onto the paper as the paper passes by on a drum.

solid state device (SSD)   An electronic device with no moving parts. A storage device that uses memory chips to store data instead of spinning disks (such as those used by magnetic hard drives and CD drives). Examples of solid state devices are jump drives (*Also called* key drives or thumb drives), flash memory cards, and solid state disks used as hard drives in notebook computers designed for the most rugged uses. *Also called* solid state disk (SSD) or solid state drive (SSD).

solid state disk (SSD)   *See* solid state device (SSD).

solid state drive (SSD)   A hard drive that has no moving parts. *Also see* solid state device (SSD).

SO-RIMM (small outline RIMM)   A 160-pin memory module used in notebooks that uses Rambus technology.

South Bridge   That portion of the chipset hub that connects slower I/O buses (for example, a PCI bus) to the system bus. *Compare to* North Bridge.

spacers   *See* standoffs.

spam   Junk e-mail you don't ask for, don't want, and that gets in your way.

spanned volume   A type of dynamic volume used on two or more hard drives that fills up the space allotted on one physical disk before moving to the next.

spanning   Using a spanned volume to increase the size of a volume.

spikes   Temporary surges in voltage, which can damage electrical components. *Also called* swells.

spooling   Placing print jobs in a print queue so that an application can be released from the printing process before printing is completed. Spooling is an acronym for simultaneous peripheral operations online.

spyware   Malicious software that installs itself on your computer to spy on you. It collects personal information about you that it transmits over the Internet to Web-hosting sites that intend to use your personal data for harm.

SRAM   *See* static RAM.

SSE (Streaming SIMD Extension)   A CPU technology that allows the CPU to receive a single instruction and then execute it on multiple pieces of data. SSE also improves on 3D graphics.

SSE2   An improved version of SSE that has a larger instruction set.

SSE3   A CPU instruction set that improved on the earlier SSE2 instruction set.

SSE4 A CPU instruction set that improved 3D imaging for gaming and improved performance with data mining applications over the earlier SSE3 instruction set.

SSL (secure socket layer) A secure protocol developed by Netscape that uses a digital certificate including a public key to encrypt and decrypt data.

staggered pin grid array (SPGA) A feature of a CPU socket whereby the pins are staggered over the socket in order to squeeze more pins into a small space.

standard account The Vista user account type that can use software and hardware and make some system changes, but cannot make changes that affect the security of the system or other users.

Standard Parallel Port (SPP) An outdated parallel port that allows data to flow in only one direction and is the slowest of the three types of parallel ports. *Also called* a Centronics port. *Compare to* EPP (Enhanced Parallel Port) and ECP (Extended Capabilities Port).

standoffs Round plastic or metal pegs that separate the motherboard from the case, so that components on the back of the motherboard do not touch the case.

startup BIOS Part of system BIOS that is responsible for controlling the PC when it is first turned on. Startup BIOS gives control over to the OS once it is loaded.

startup password *See* power-on password.

stateless Term for a device or process that manages data or some activity without regard to all the details of the data or activity.

static electricity *See* ESD.

static IP address An IP address permanently assigned to a workstation.

static RAM (SRAM) RAM chips that retain information without the need for refreshing, as long as the computer's power is on. They are more expensive than traditional DRAM.

status light indicators Lights on the back of a NIC that indicate connectivity and network activity.

stop error An error at the kernel level that is severe enough to cause the operating system to stop all processes.

striped volume A type of dynamic volume used for two or more hard drives that writes to the disks evenly rather than filling up allotted space on one and then moving on to the next. *Compare to* spanned volume.

strong password A password that is not easy to guess.

stylus A device that is included with a graphics tablet that works like a pencil on the tablet.

subdirectory A directory or folder contained in another directory or folder. *Also called* a child directory or folder.

subnet mask A group of four numbers (dotted decimal numbers) that tell TCP/IP if a remote computer is on the same or a different network.

Super VGA (SVGA) A standard set by the Video Electronics Standards Association (VESA) for a CRT monitor that includes a minimum refresh rate of 70 Hz and a minimum resolution of 800 x 600.

Super VGA (SVGA) monitor A CRT monitor that meets the VESA standard for Super VGA, which includes a resolution of 800 x 600 and a refresh rate of 70 Hz.

surge protector *See* surge suppressor.

surge suppressor A device or power strip designed to protect electronic equipment from power surges and spikes. *Also called* a surge protector.

Surround Sound A sound compression standard that supports up to 10 different speakers, each producing a different sound. Also known Dolby AC-3, Dolby Digital Surround, or Dolby Surround Sound.

S-Video port A 4-pin round video port that sends two signals over the cable, one for color and the other for brightness, and is used by some high-end TVs and video equipment.

swap file A file on the hard drive that is used by the OS for virtual memory. *Also called* a page file.

swells *See* spikes.

switch A device used to segment a network. It can decide which network segment is to receive a packet, on the basis of the packet's destination MAC address.

synchronous DRAM (SDRAM) A type of memory stored on DIMMs that runs in sync with the system clock, running at the same speed as the motherboard.

sysprep.exe A Windows utility that is used to remove configuration settings, such as the computer name, that uniquely identifies the PC from the Windows installation. The installation can then be used to create a drive image for cloning to multiple computers.

system BIOS BIOS located on the motherboard.

system board *See* motherboard.

system bus   The bus between the CPU and memory on the motherboard. The bus frequency in documentation is called the system speed, such as 400 MHz. *Also called* the memory bus, front-side bus, local bus, or host bus.

system clock   A line on a bus that is dedicated to timing the activities of components connected to it. The system clock provides a continuous pulse that other devices use to time themselves.

System Configuration Utility (Msconfig.exe)   A Windows utility that can identify what processes are launched at startup and can temporarily disable a process from loading.

System File Checker (SFC)   *See* SFC (System File Checker).

system partition   The active partition of the hard drive containing the boot record and the specific files required to load Windows 2000/XP/Vista.

System Restore   A Windows XP/Vista utility used to restore the system to a restore point.

system state data   In Windows 2000/XP, files that are necessary for a successful load of the operating system.

system tray   *See* notification area.

systray   *See* notification area.

Task Manager (Taskmgr.exe)   A Windows utility that lets you view the applications and processes running on your computer as well as information about process and memory performance, network activity, and user activity.

Task Scheduler   A Windows tool that can set a task or program to launch at a future time, including at startup.

taskbar   A bar normally located at the bottom of the Windows desktop, displaying information about open programs and providing quick access to others.

TCP (Transmission Control Protocol)   Part of the TCP/IP protocol suite. TCP guarantees delivery of data for application protocols and establishes a session before it begins transmitting data.

TCP/IP (Transmission Control Protocol/Internet Protocol)   The suite of protocols that supports communication on the Internet. TCP is responsible for error checking, and IP is responsible for routing.

TDMA (Time Division Multiple Access)   A protocol standard used by cellular WANs and cell phones.

technical documentation   The technical reference manuals, included with software packages and hardware, that provide directions for installation, usage, and troubleshooting. The information extends beyond that given in user manuals.

telephony   A term describing the technology of converting sound to signals that can travel over telephone lines.

Telnet   A Windows command-line client/server application that allows an administrator or other user to control a computer remotely.

terminating resistor   The resistor added at the end of a SCSI chain to dampen the voltage at the end of the chain.

thermal compound   A creamlike substance that is placed between the bottom of the cooler heatsink and the top of the processor to eliminate air pockets and to help to draw heat off the processor.

thermal printer   A type of line printer that uses wax-based ink, which is heated by heat pins that melt the ink onto paper.

ThickNet   *See* 10Base5.

ThinNet   *See* 10Base2.

thread   Each process that the CPU is aware of; a single task that is part of a longer task or program.

ticket   An entry in a call-tracking system made by whoever receives a call for help and used to track and document actions taken. The ticket stays open until the issue is resolved.

TIFF (Tagged Image File Format)   A bitmapped file format used to hold photographs, graphics, and screen captures. TIFF files can be rather large, and have a .tif file extension.

time to live (TTL)   Number of routers a network packet can pass through on its way to its destination before it is dropped. *Also called* hop count.

TLS (Transport Layer Security)   A protocol used to secure data sent over the Internet. It is an improved version of SSL.

top-level domain   The highest level of domain names, indicated by a suffix that tells something about the host or network. For example, .com is for commercial use and .edu is for educational institutions.

touch pad   The most common pointing device on a notebook; a pad near the keyboard that controls the Windows cursor.

touch screen   An input device that uses a monitor or LCD panel as a backdrop for user options. Touch screens can be embedded in a monitor or LCD panel or installed as an add-on device over the monitor screen.

tower case   The largest type of personal computer case. Tower cases stand vertically and can be as high as two feet tall. They have more drive bays and are a good choice for computer users who anticipate making significant upgrades.

TPM (Trusted Platform Module) chip   A chip on a motherboard that holds an encryption key required at startup to access encrypted data on the hard drive. Vista BitLocker Encryption can use the TPM chip.

trace   A wire on a circuit board that connects two components or devices.

track   One of many concentric circles on the surface of a hard drive or floppy disk.

TrackPoint   *See* point stick.

transformer   A device that changes the ratio of current to voltage. A computer power supply is basically a transformer and a rectifier.

transistor   An electronic device that can regulate electricity and act as a logical gate or switch for an electrical signal.

trip hazard   Loose cables or cords in a traffic area where people can trip over them.

triple channels   When the memory controller accesses three DIMMs at the same time. DDR3 DIMMs support triple channeling.

triple core   A processor package that contains three core processors, thus supporting six instructions at once.

Trojan horse   A type of infestation that hides or disguises itself as a useful program, yet is designed to cause damage when executed.

TV tuner card   An adapter card that receives a TV signal and displays TV on the computer screen.

UART (universal asynchronous receiver-transmitter)   A chip that controls serial ports. It sets protocol and converts parallel data bits received from the system bus into serial bits.

UDF (Universal Disk Format) file system   *See* Universal Disk Format (UDF) file system.

UDP (User Datagram Protocol)   A connectionless protocol that does not require a connection to send a packet and does not guarantee that the packet arrives at its destination. UDP is faster than TCP because TCP takes the time to make a connection and guarantee delivery.

unattended installation   A Windows installation that is done by storing the answers to installation questions in a text file or script that Windows calls an answer file so that the answers do not have to be typed in during the installation.

uninterruptible power supply (UPS)   *See* UPS (uninterruptible power supply).

Universal Disk Format (UDF) file system   A file system for optical media used by all DVD discs and some CD-R and CD-RW discs.

universal serial bus (USB) port   *See* USB (universal serial bus) port.

unshielded twisted pair (UTP) cable   A cable that is made of one or more twisted pairs of wires and is not surrounded by shielding.

UPS (uninterruptible power supply)   A device designed to provide a backup power supply during a power failure. Basically, a UPS is a battery backup system with an ultrafast sensing device.

URL (Uniform Resource Locator)   An address for a resource on the Internet. A URL can contain the protocol used by the resource, the name of the computer and its network, and the path and name of a file on the computer.

USB (universal serial bus) port   A type of port designed to make installation and configuration of I/O devices easy, providing room for as many as 127 devices daisy-chained together.

USB host controller   Manages the USB bus. If the motherboard contains on-board USB ports, the USB host controller is part of the chipset. The USB controller uses only a single set of resources for all devices on the bus.

User Account Control (UAC) dialog box   A Vista security feature that displays a dialog box each time a user attempts to perform an action that can be done only with administrative privileges.

user mode   In Windows 2000/XP/Vista, a mode that provides an interface between an application and the OS, and only has access to hardware resources through the code running in kernel mode.

user password   A power-on password required to view or edit BIOS setup or use the computer. The password is set on a BIOS setup screen.

user profile   A personal profile about a user that enables the user's desktop settings and other operating parameters to be retained from one session to another.

user profile namespace   The group of folders and subfolders in the C:\Users folder that belong to a specific user account.

User State Migration Tool (USMT)   A Windows XP/Vista utility that helps you migrate user files and preferences from one computer to another in order to help a user make a smooth transition from one computer to another.

VGA (Video Graphics Adapter)   An outdated VESA standard for CRT monitors.

video capture card   An adapter card that captures video input and saves it to a file on the hard drive.

video card   An interface card installed in the computer to control visual output on a monitor. *Also called* display adapter or graphics card.

video memory   Memory used by the video controller. The memory might be contained on a video card or be part of system memory. When part of system memory, the memory is dedicated by Windows to video.

virtual machine (VM)   One or more logical machines created within one physical machine.

virtual memory   A method whereby the OS uses the hard drive as though it were RAM. *Compare to* RAM drive.

virtual private network (VPN)   A security technique that uses encrypted data packets between a private network and a computer somewhere on the Internet.

virus   A program that often has an incubation period, is infectious, and is intended to cause damage. A virus program might destroy data and programs or damage a disk drive's boot sector.

virus encyclopedias   Databases about viruses that are kept on the Internet.

virus hoax   E-mail that does damage by tempting you to forward it to everyone in your e-mail address book with the intent of clogging up e-mail systems or by persuading you to delete a critical Windows system file by convincing you the file is malicious.

virus signature   A set of distinguishing characteristics of a virus used by antivirus software to identify the virus.

Vista Upgrade Advisor   An Internet tool that can be run on a PC to determine if an XP system qualifies for Vista.

VoIP (Voice over Internet Protocol)   An application that provides voice communication over a network and uses the VoIP protocol. *Also called* Internet telephone.

volatile   Refers to a kind of RAM that is temporary, cannot hold data very long, and must be frequently refreshed.

volt (V)   A measure of potential difference in an electrical circuit. A computer ATX power supply usually provides five separate voltages: +12V, –12V, +5V, –5V, and +3.3V.

voltage   Electrical differential that causes current to flow, measured in volts. *See* volt.

voltage selector switch   A switch on a computer power supply used to set voltage to 115 V or 230 V.

voltmeter   A device for measuring electrical AC or DC voltage.

volume   A primary partition that has been assigned a drive letter and can be formatted with a file system such as NTFS. *Compare to* logical drive.

wait state   A clock tick in which nothing happens, used to ensure that the microprocessor isn't getting ahead of slower components. A 0-wait state is preferable to a 1-wait state. Too many wait states can slow down a system.

Wake on LAN   Configuring a computer so that it will respond to network activity when the computer is in a sleep state.

WAN (wide area network)   A network or group of networks that span a large geographical area.

warm boot   *See* soft boot.

watt (W)   The unit used to measure power. A typical computer may use a power supply that provides 500W.

wattage   Electrical power measured in watts.

WEP (Wired Equivalent Privacy)   A data encryption method used on wireless networks that uses either 64-bit or 128-bit encryption keys that are static keys, meaning the key does not change while the wireless network is in use.

Wi-Fi (Wireless Fidelity)   *See* IEEE 802.11.

wildcard   A *or ? character used in a command line that represents a character or group of characters in a filename or extension.

Windows Anytime Upgrade   Upgrading to a better edition of Vista without having to redo the installation.

Windows Boot Loader (WinLoad.exe)   One of two programs that manage the loading of Vista. The program file is stored in C:\Windows\System32, and it loads and starts essential Vista processes.

Windows Boot Manager (BootMgr)   The Vista program that manages the initial startup of Vista. The BootMgr program file is stored in the C:\ root directory and has no file extension.

Windows Easy Transfer   A Windows tool used to transfer Windows XP/Vista user data and preferences to the Windows XP/Vista installation on another computer.

Windows Experience Index   A Vista feature that gives a summary index designed to measure the overall performance of a system.

Windows RE   *See* Windows Vista Recovery Environment (RecEnv.exe).

Windows Vista Business   The Vista edition designed for business users and includes support for a domain, Group Policy, and Encrypted File System, and does not include consumer features such as Movie Maker.

Windows Vista Enterprise   The Vista edition that expands on Windows Vista Business, adding security features such as BitLocker Encryption.

Windows Vista Home Basic   The Vista edition that is designed for low-cost home systems that don't require full security and networking features. It does not include the Aero glass interface.

Windows Vista Home Premium   The Vista edition that includes more features than Windows Vista Home Basic, including the Aero user interface, DVD Maker, Media Center, SideShow, and backups.

Windows Vista Recovery Environment (RecEnv.exe)   An operating system launched from the Vista DVD that provides a graphical and command line interface and used to solve problems when Vista will not boot from the hard drive. *Also called* Windows RE.

Windows Vista Starter   The Vista edition with the most limited features and intended to be used in developing nations.

Windows Vista Ultimate   The Vista edition that includes every Windows Vista feature. Multiple licensing is not available.

Windows XP Home Edition   The XP edition that does not include Remote Desktop, multilingual capabilities, roaming profiles, and support for high-end processors.

Windows XP Media Center Edition   The XP edition is an enhanced version of XP Professional that includes support for digital entertainment hardware.

Windows XP Professional   The XP edition that includes Remote Desktop, roaming profiles, multilingual capabilities and enhanced security features.

Windows XP Tablet PC Edition   The XP edition designed for notebooks and tablet PCs.

WINS (Windows Internet Naming Service)   A Microsoft resolution service with a distributed database that tracks relationships between NetBIOS names and IP addresses. *Compare to* DNS.

WinSock (Windows Sockets)   A part of the TCP/IP utility software that manages API calls from applications to other computers on a TCP/IP network.

wireless LAN (WLAN)   A type of LAN that does not use wires or cables to create connections, but instead transmits data over radio or infrared waves.

workgroup   In Windows, a logical group of computers and users in which administration, resources, and security are distributed throughout the network, without centralized management or security.

worm   An infestation designed to copy itself repeatedly to memory, on drive space or on a network, until little memory, disk space, or network bandwidth remains.

WPA (WiFi Protected Access)   A data encryption method for wireless networks that use the TKIP (Temporal Key Integrity Protocol) encryption method and the encryption keys are changed at set intervals while the wireless LAN is in use.

WPA2 (WiFi Protected Access 2)   A data encryption standard compliant with the IEEE802.11i standard that uses the AES (Advanced Encryption Standard) protocol. WPA2 is currently the strongest wireless encryption standard.

XPS (XML Paper Specification)   A standard introduced with Windows Vista and designed to ultimately replace GDI as the method Windows uses to render a printed page before sending it to the printer.

XPS Document Writer   A Vista feature that creates a file with a .xps file extension. The file is similar to a .pdf file and can be viewed, edited, printed, faxed, emailed, or posted on Web sites.

zero insertion force (ZIF) socket   A socket that uses a small lever to apply even force when you install the microchip into the socket.

zero-fill utility   A utility provided by a hard drive manufacturer that fills every sector on the drive with zeroes.

INDEX